Index to Plays in Periodicals

Revised and expanded edition

by
Dean H. Keller

The Scarecrow Press, Inc.
Metuchen, N.J., & London
1979

Library of Congress Cataloging in Publication Data

Keller, Dean H
    Index to plays in periodicals.

    1. Drama--Bibliography.   2. Periodicals--Indexes.
I. Title.
Z5781.K43   1979   [PN1721]   016.80882   79-962
ISBN 0-8108-1208-8

Copyright © 1979 by Dean H. Keller

Manufactured in the United States of America

For
Pat, Jonathon and Jennifer
with love and thanks

CONTENTS

Introduction					vii

Periodicals Indexed				viii

Author Index					1

Title Index					677

INTRODUCTION

This revised and expanded edition of the Index to Plays in Periodicals and its Supplement, published by The Scarecrow Press, Inc. in 1971 and 1973, combines the 7,417 entries in those volumes and adds 2,145 new citations. The number of periodicals now indexed, usually for their entire runs, through 1976, now totals 267.

The features of the previous indexes have been retained in this edition. The book is arranged in two parts: the Author Index containing the main entry with all the information necessary to locate the play, and the Title Index. Each entry in the Author Index is numbered and entries in the Title Index are keyed to the Author Index by the author's name and number. There are cross references for joint authors, translators, adapters, editors, and pseudonyms.

A typical author entry contains the author's full name, his or her dates when these have been determined, the title of the play, the number of acts in the play, a brief description of the play (comedy, tragedy, satire, etc.) when such a description is provided by the periodical publishing the play, the name of the periodical in which the play appears, the volume and date of the periodical, the pages on which the play will be found, the names of translators, editors, adapters, etc., and the language in which the play is printed if it is other than English. On occasion, the same play will appear in the same periodical more than once. In that case, all references are combined in one entry. If the same play appears in separate periodicals, separate entries are provided.

One of the pleasurable aspects of working on an index such as this is the contact one has with teachers, librarians, publishers, playwrights, and others who use the index and take time to comment upon it. We considered all of their suggestions and used many of them in this new edition. I am especially grateful to librarians in several public and university libraries who went out of their way to make their collections easily available to me. The debt I owe to my wife, who helped with every phase of this work, as she did with the previous indexes, is immeasurable.

Dean H. Keller

Kent State University Libraries

PERIODICALS INDEXED

Accent
Akros
Allegorica
American Magazine
American Mercury
American Prefaces
Americas
Anglo-Saxon Review
Arena
Arion (Austin)
Arion, new series (Boston)
Art and Literature
Asia
Atlantic Monthly
Avant Scène
Baltimore Repertory
Bermondsey Book
Better Homes and Gardens
Bibelot
Blackwood's Magazine
Blast
Bookman (London)
Bookman (New York)
Botteghe Oscure
Broom
Butterfly, new series
Calendar of Modern Letters
Canadian Forum

Canadian Theatre Review
Carolina Quarterly
Catholic World
Century
Chap Book (Chicago)
Chapbook (London)
Chelsea
Chicago Review
Chimera
Chinese Literature
Christian Century
Cimmarron Review
City Lights Journal
Claremont Quarterly
Classical Journal
Clipper
Colliers
Commentary
Confrontation
Contact
Contemporary Review
Corno Emplumado
Cosmopolitan
Coterie
Criterion
Current Literature
Dance Perspectives
December

Decision
DeKalb Literary Arts Journal
Delineator
Dial
Discovery
Dome
Dome, new series
Double Dealer
Drama (New York)
Drama and Theatre
Drama at Calgary
Drama Review
Dramatics
Dramatika
Dramatist
Dramma
Dublin Magazine
Dublin Magazine, new series
Dust
Edge
Educational Theater Journal
Egoist
Elementary School Teacher
Encounter
English Review
Eros
Esquire
Evergreen Review
Everybody's Magazine
Falcon
Fantasy
Fiction
First Person
First Stage
Floating Bear
Fortnightly

Fortnightly, new series
Forum
Freelance
Furioso
Gambit
Glebe
Golden Book
Golden Hind
Harper's Bazaar
Harper's Magazine
Harper's Weekly
Hearst's Magazine
Hispanic Review
Horizon
Horn Book
House and Garden
Hudson Review
Independent
Industrial Arts and Vocational Education
Industrial Arts Magazine
Industrial Education Magazine
Interim
International
Intrepid
Irish Review
Irish Writing
Journal of Home Economics
Journal of Irish Literature
Journal of the National Education Association
Kansas Quarterly
Kenyon Review
Ladies' Home Journal
Landfall
Laughing Horse

Learning With....
Library Journal
Life and Letters
Literary Review
Little Magazine
Little Review
Living Age
Locus Solus
London Aphrodite
London Magazine
London Magazine, new series
London Mercury
Longman's Magazine
McClure's Magazine
Mademoiselle
Mainstream
Mask
Massachusetts Review
Masses and Mainstream
Mésures
Midland
Midway
Minnesota Review
Mirror of Taste
Modern International Drama
Modern Language Journal
Music and Letters
Nassau Review
Nature Magazine
Negro History Bulletin
Negro Story
New Coterie
New Directions in Prose and Poetry
New Editions
New England Magazine

New Mexico Quarterly
New Numbers
New Renaissance
New Republic
New World Writing
New Writers
New Yorker
Nimbus
19th Century
North American Review
North American Review, new series
Ohio Review
One-Act Play Magazine
Open Window
Opportunity
Origin, second series
Others
Outlook
Overland, new series
PMLA
Palms
Partisan Review
Penguin New Writing
Performance
Performing Arts in Canada
Perspectives, U.S.A.
Petite Illustration, vols. 86-198.
Pharos
Philological Quarterly
Pictorial Review
Players Magazine
Playground
Plays
Plays and Players, 1966-1977
Poet Lore

Poetry	Southwest Review
Poetry and Drama	Spectaculum
Poetry Journal	Sturm
Prairie Schooner	Sunset
Prism International	Survey Graphic
Publishers Weekly	Survey Midmonthly
Putnam's Magazine	Texas Quarterly
Quarterly Journal of Speech	Texas Review
Quarterly Review of Literature	Theater Arts
Queen's Quarterly	Theatre
Quest	This Quarter
Quixote	Toucan
Resource	Touchstone
Reveille	Trace
Review of English Literature	Transatlantic Review (London)
Review of Reviews	Transatlantic Review (Paris)
St. Nicholas	Transition
Salmagundi	Tri-Quarterly
Samhain	Tulane Drama Review
San Francisco Review	Twentieth Century
Saturday Evening Post	Twice a Year
Saturday Review of Literature	Two Worlds
Savoy	Vers et Prose
Scene	Virginia Quarterly Review
Scholastic	Wake
Scribner's	Western Review
Scripts	Wilson Library Bulletin
Senior Scholastic	Windmill
Seven Arts	Woman's Home Companion
Sewanee Review	Works
Shenandoah	World Outlook
Show	Wort
Sipario	Writer
Smart Set	Yale Review
Smoke	Yellow Book
South Dakota Review	

AUTHOR INDEX

A

Abba, Marta, 1906- , translator see Turgenev, I. 8951

1. Abbe, George. Shatter the Day. 3 acts. Poet Lore, 63 (Winter, 1968), 447-495.

2. Abbensetts, Michael. Sweet Talk. 1 act. Plays & Players, 20 (August, 1973), i-xv.

3. Abbott, Avery. Mr. Enright Entertains; A Possibility in One Act. Poet Lore, 34 (September, 1923), 127-144.

Abbott, Elisabeth, translator see Pirandello, L. 7203

4. Abbott, George, 1887- and Richard Pike Bissell, 1913- . The Pajama Game. 2 acts. Theatre Arts, 39 (September, 1955), 36-61.

5. ———— and Douglass Wallop, 1920- . Damn Yankees. 2 acts. Theatre Arts, 40 (November, 1956), 34-59.

———— see also Weidman, J. 9263

6. Abel, Barbara. The Clean Up. 1 act. Survey Midmonthly, 74 (September, 1938), 275-277.

7. Abel, Lionel, 1910- . Ajax. 1 act. Salmagundi, 2 (Winter, 1968), 75-103.

8. ————. John the Bastard. 1 act. Salmagundi, 18 (Winter, 1972), 31-63.

9. ————. The Poetry Recital. 1 act. Transatlantic Review (London), 2 (Winter, 1959-60), 138-142.

10. Abercrombie, Lascelles, 1881-1938. The Adder. 1 act. Poetry and Drama, 1 (March, 1913), 100-119.

11. ————. The Deserter. 1 act, comedy. Theatre Arts, 6 (July, 1922), 237-254.

12. ————. The End of the World. 2 acts. New Numbers, 1 (April, 1914), 61-96.

3

Abony 4

13. Abony, Arpad. Tattica sbagliata. 1 act. Il Dramma, 33 (January 1, 1928), 42-44. Taulero Zulberti, translator. In Italian.

Absalom, R. N. L., translator see Mazzucco, R. 5718

14. Abse, Dannie, 1923- . Gone. 1 act. Gambit, 1 [1963], 69-83.

15. _____. Gone. 1 act. Transatlantic Review (London), 12 (Spring, 1963), 124-140.

Abzac, Guy d' see Lery, M. 4935

Acampora, Giovanna, translator see Moliere 6113

16. Aceto, Gennaro, 1928- . Uno dopo l'altro. Il Dramma, 48 (September-October, 1972), 130-146. In Italian.

17. Achard, Marcel, 1899- . Adam. 3 acts. Il Dramma, n. s., 29 (January 15, 1947), 9-36. Carlo Lari, translator. In Italian.

18. _____. Auprès de ma Blonde. 5 acts. Il Dramma, n. s., 31/32 (February 15/March 1, 1947), 14-48. Olga Aillaud, translator. In Italian.

19. _____. La Bagatelle. 3 acts. L'Avant Scène, 196 (May 1, 1959), 7-33. In French.

20. _____. La Belle Marinière. 3 acts. Petite Illustration, 88 (January 11, 1930), 1-26. In French.

21. _____. Colui che viveva la sua morte. 1 act. Il Dramma, n. s., 139/140 (August 15/September 1, 1951), 101-108. Suzanne Rochat, translator. In Italian.

22. _____. Les Compagnons de la Marjolaine. 3 acts. Il Dramma, n. s., 176 (March 1, 1953), 23-53. Gianni Nicoletti, translator. In Italian.

23. _____. Il Corsaro. 2 acts. Il Dramma, 321 (January 1, 1940), 4-23. Alberto Casella, translator. In Italian.

24. _____. La demoiselle de petite vertu. 3 acts, comedy. Sipario, 5, 52 (August, 1950), 41066. Luciana Cane and Gigi Cane, translators. In Italian.

25. _____. Domino. 3 acts, comedy. L'Avant Scène, 172 (April 15, 1958), 5-34. In French.

26. _____. Domino. 3 acts, comedy. Petite Illustration, 182 (June 25, 1932), 1-34. In French.

5   Achard

27. _____. La Femme en Blanc. 3 acts. Petite Illustration, 185 (July 1, 1933), 1-30. In French.

28. _____. L'Idiote. 3 acts, comedy. L'Avant Scène, 244 (June 1, 1961), 9-41. In French.

29. _____. L'Idiote. 3 acts. Il Dramma, n. s., 302 (November, 1961), Silvana d'Arborio, translator. In Italian.

30. _____. Jean de la Lune. 3 acts, comedy. L'Avant Scène, 247 (July 15, 1961), 6-34. In French.

31. _____. Jean de la Lune. 3 acts, comedy. Petite Illustration, 87 (August 10, 1929), 1-30. In French.

32. _____. Le Moulin de la Galette. 3 acts. L'Avant Scène (ROST), 63 (June, 1952), 1-38. In French.

33. _____. Le Moulin de la Galette. 3 acts, comedy. Sipario, 9, 98 (June, 1954), 31-54. Olga de Vellis Aillaud, translator. In Italian.

34. _____. Nous Irons à Valparaiso. 4 acts. Il Dramma, n. s., 79 (February 15, 1949), 5-37. Carlo Lari, translator. In Italian.

35. _____. Patate. 3 acts. L'Avant Scène, 178 (July 15, 1958), 7-36. In French.

36. _____. Patate. 3 acts, comedy. Sipario, 13, 141 (January, 1958), 37-58. Diego Fabbri, translator. In Italian.

37. _____. Petrus. 3 acts, comedy. Petite Illustration, 187 (March 31, 1934), 1-42. In French.

38. _____. La signora vestita di bianco. 3 acts. Il Dramma, 177 (January 1, 1934), 4-34. Evelina Levi, translator. In Italian.

39. _____. Les Sourires Inutiles. 1 act. Il Dramma, n. s., 190 (October 1, 1953), 26-34. Sergio Cenalino, translator. In Italian.

40. _____. Turlututu. 3 acts, comedy. L'Avant Scène, 290 (June 15, 1963), 8-37. In French.

41. Achard, Paul. Amicizie periclose. 8 parts. Il Dramma, n. s., 211/212 (August 15/September 1, 1954), 5-44. In Italian.

42. _____. Les Misérables. 2 parts. L'Avant Scène, 146, 1-31. In French.

43. Acheson, Sam. We Are Besieged. 3 acts. Southwest Review, 27 (Autumn, 1941), 1-95.

44. Achille, Giuseppe, 1902- . Ambizione. 3 acts. Il Dramma, 383 (August 1, 1942), 7-27. In Italian.

45. _____. . . . E dev'essere un maschio. 4 parts. Il Dramma, 335 (August 1, 1940), 4-28. In Italian.

_____, translator see Dumas, A. 2687

_____ see also Corradini, B. 2029, 2030, 2031, 2032

Acord, Jan, adaptor see Hearn, L. 4007

46. Acquabona, Plinio. Daccapo. 3 parts. Il Dramma, n.s., 334/335 (July/August, 1964), 12-39. In Italian.

47. Acting Charade, An. Living Age, 104 (February, 1870), 428-434.

48. Adam, Alfred Roger, 1908- . Many. 3 acts. Il Dramma, n.s., 230 (November, 1955), 4-35. Guilio Pacuvio, translator. In Italian.

49. _____. La Terre Est Basse. 3 acts, comedy. L'Avant Scène, 161, 4-35. In French.

50. Adam, Paul. Dialogue Pathetique. Vers et Prose, 15 (September-November, 1908), 1-35. In French.

51. Adam, Villiers de L'Isle. La Revolte. 1 act. Fortnightly, 68 (December, 1897), 862-874. Theresa Barclay, translator.

52. Adami, Giuseppe, 1887-1946. Il brigante e la diva. 1 act. Il Dramma, 334 (July 15, 1940), 35-39. In Italian.

53. _____. Felicita Colombo. 3 acts. Il Dramma, 225 (January 1, 1936), 2-23. In Italian.

54. _____. Paola Travasa. 3 acts. Il Dramma, 313 (September 1, 1939), 4-21. In Italian.

55. _____. La piccola felicità. 3 acts. Il Dramma, 196 (October 15, 1934), 4-30. In Italian.

56. _____. Provincia. 3 acts. Il Dramma, 237 (July 1, 1936), 6-26. In Italian.

57. Adamov, Arthur, 1908- . As We Were. 1 act. Evergreen Review, 1 (No. 4), 113-126. Richard Howard, translator.

58. _____. The Big and the Little Maneuver. Modern International Drama, 5 (Fall, 1971), 7-26. Myron Ernst, translator.

59. _____. Comme Nous Avons Eté. 1 act. Il Dramma, n.s., 191 (October 15, 1953), 10-14. Gian Renzo Moreto, translator. In Italian.

60. _____. En Fiacre. 1 act. L'Avant Scène, 294 (September 1, 1963), 39-46. In French.

61. _____. En Fiacre. 1 act. Il Dramma, 51 (August-September, 1975), 41-51. Romeo De Baggis, translator. In Italian.

62. _____. Finita la Commedia. 1 act. Sipario, 228 (April, 1965), 54-64. Masolino D'Amico, translator. In Italian.

63. _____. La Grande et la Petite Manoeuvre. 4 acts. L'Avant Scène (OST), 35 (December, 1950), 3-20. In French.

64. _____. The Invasion. 4 acts. Modern Drama, 2 (September, 1968), 59-75. Robert J. Doan, translator.

65. _____. Le Ping-Pong. 2 parts. L'Avant Scène, 104, 1-27. In French.

66. _____. Professor Taranne. 1 act. New World Writing, 13 (1958), 193-211. Richard Howard, translator.

67. _____. Tous Contre Tous. 2 parts. L'Avant Scène, 78 (May 25, 1953), 5-31. In French.

68. _____. Una donna dolce. 1 act. Il Dramma, 46 (April, 1970), 46-51. Piero Sanavio, translator. In Italian.

_____, adapter see Gorky, M. 3646

_____, translator see Frisch, M. 3316

_____, translator see Gogol, N. V. 3603

_____, translator see Gorky, M. 3649

69. Adams, E. C. L. Congaree Sketches. six 1-act sketches. Dublin Magazine, n.s., 2 (January-March, 1927), 26-33.

70. Adams, Phoebe-Lon. The Argument. 1 act. Plays, 4 (April, 1945), 49-50.

71. _____. The Helpful Cats. 1 act. Plays, 3 (April, 1944), 60-62.

72. _____. The Incompetent Godmother. 1 act. Plays, 2 (March, 1943), 37-41.

73. _____. The Toys on Strike. 1 act. Plays, 3 (January, 1944), 52-54.

74. Adcock, Irma Fitz. The Royal Cloth of China. 1 act. Plays, 20 (February, 1961), 49-55.

75. Adimari, Alessandro. L'Adorazione de'Re Magi. 3 acts. Il Dramma, n.s., 338/339 (November/December, 1964), 23-40. In Italian.

76. Adler, Jack. The Bed. 1 act. First Stage, 2 (Fall, 1963), 390-396.

77. Adoum, Jorge Enrique. The Sun Trampled Beneath the Horses' Hooves. 1 act. Massachusetts Review, 15 (Spring/Summer, 1974), 285-324. David Arthur McMurray and Robert Marquez, translators.

78. Aeschylus, 525-456 B.C. Prometheus Bound. 1 act, tragedy. Review of English Literature, 8 (January, 1967), 10-38. Edmund Blunden, translator.

79. _____. Prometheus Bound. 1 act, tragedy. Theatre Arts, 11 (July, 1927), 545-562. Edith Hamilton, translator.

80. Aguila, Carlos d'. Leonard de Vinci. 1 act. L'Avant Scène, 363 (September 1, 1966), 33-37. In French.

_____ see also Marais, C. 5525

81. Aguirre, Isidora, 1919- . The Pascualas. 3 acts. Poet Lore, 59 (No. 4), 291-336. Willis Knapp Jones, translator.

Aguirre, Maria Luisa, translator see Sastre, A. 7972

Ah Chia see Wong Ou-hung 9540

82. Ah Chien. Boulder Bay. Chinese Literature, 4 (1976), 55-122.

83. _____. Investigation of a Chair. Chinese Literature, 9 (1976), 3-16.

Ahnfelt, Astrid, translator see Bergman, H. 813

84. Aichinger, Ilse, 1921- . At a Lost Outpost. 1 act. Literary Review, 17 (Summer, 1974), 508-510. Frederick Garber, translator.

85. Aide, Charles Hamilton, 1826-1906. Colour-Blind: A Comedy of Twenty Minutes. 1 act. Anglo-Saxon Review, 5 (June,

1900), 130-140.

86. _____. A Gleam in the Darkness. 1 act. Fortnightly, 72 (December, 1899), 905-913.

87. _____. A Lesson in Acting. 1 act. 19th Century, 44 (November, 1898), 760-768.

Aillaud, Olga de Vellis, translator see Achard, M. 18, 33

_____, translator see Ayme, M. 476

_____, translator see Saint-Granier 7860

Ajmerito, Lella, translator see Mavor, O. H. 5695

88. Akins, Zoë, 1886-1958. Daddy's Gone A-Hunting. 1 act. Everybody's Magazine, 45 (December, 1921), 93-100.

89. _____. Did It Really Happen? 1 act. Smart Set, 52 (May, 1917), 343-352.

90. _____. The Little Miracle. 1 act. Ladies' Home Journal, 53 (April, 1936), 20-31, 148-150, 152-154, 156.

91. _____. The Magical City (Broadway Legend). 1 act. Forum, 55 (May, 1916), 507-550.

92. _____. The Portrait of Tiero. 1 act, tragedy. Theatre Arts, 4 (October, 1920), 316-337.

93. _____. Such a Charming Young Man. 1 act, comedy. Smart Set, 48 (April, 1916), 67-78.

94. Aksjonov, Vasilij. Vsegda v Prodaze. 2 acts, fantasy. Sipario, 254 (June, 1967), 74-95. Giovanni Buttafava, translator. In Italian.

Al-Hakim, Tawfiq see Hakim, Tawfiq Al- 3830

95. Aladar, Laszlo. Mancia competente. 3 acts. Il Dramma, 174 (November 15, 1933), 4-33. Mario Blanco, translator. In Italian.

96. Alarcón y Mendoza, Juan Ruiz de, 1580?-1639. The Truth Suspected. 3 acts. Poet Lore, 38 (1927), 475-530. Julio del Toro and Robert V. Finney, translators.

97. Albee, Edward, 1928- . An American Dream. Mademoiselle, 52 (November, 1960), 86-89.

98. _____. A Delicate Balance. 2 acts. L'Avant Scène, 400 (April 1, 1968), 9-34. Matthieu Galey, adapter. In French.

Albee 10

99. _____. Everything in the Garden. 2 acts. Sipario, 24, 284 (December, 1969), 103-126. Paola Ojetti, translator. In Italian.

100. _____. Who's Afraid of Virginia Woolf? 3 acts. L'Avant Scène, 339 (August, 1965), 10-51. Jean Can, adapter. In French.

101. _____. Who's Afraid of Virginia Woolf? 3 acts. Spectaculum, 7 (1964), 9-101. Pinkas Braun, translator. In German.

102. _____. The Zoo Story. 1 act. L'Avant Scène, 334 (May 15, 1965), 8-16. Matthieu Galey, translator. In French.

103. _____. The Zoo Story. 1 act. Evergreen Review, 4 (March-April, 1960), 28-52.

104. Albert, Laura. The Flower That Grew Overnight. 1 act. Plays, 35 (May, 1976), 59-62.

105. Albert, Rollin'. Hero Here at Heorot. 1 act. Plays, 35 (February, 1976), 49-54.

106. _____. Hounded by Basketballs. 1 act. Plays, 35 (April, 1976), 1-13.

107. _____. A New Angle on Christmas. 1 act. Plays, 36 (December, 1976), 37-42.

108. _____. A New Cinderella. 1 act. Plays, 35 (November, 1975), 1-13.

Albini, Ettore see Bettini, P. 900

109. Alcott, Louisa May, 1832-1888. The Adventures of Jo March. 1 act. Plays, 33 (February, 1974), 63-71. Adele Thane, adapter.

110. _____. Little Women. 1 act. Plays, 14 (December, 1954), 13-23. AND Plays, 28 (December, 1968), 85-95. AND Plays, 35 (December, 1975), 85-95. Olive J. Morley, adapter.

111. _____. Little Women. 1 act. Plays, 17 (October, 1957) 87-96. AND Plays, 21 (April, 1962), 85-96. Lewy Olfson, adapter.

112. _____. A Merry Christmas from Little Women. 1 act. Plays, 26 (December, 1966), 88-96. Walter Hackett, adapter.

113. _____. Romance for Jo March. 1 act. Plays, 32 (Octo-

ber, 1972), 81-91. Olive J. Morley, adapter.

114. Alderman, Elinor R. Anyone for the Moon? 1 act. Plays, 19 (March, 1960), 1-10.

115. _____. Bad Day at Bleak Creek. 1 act. Plays, 17 (October, 1957), 23-35.

116. _____. Hamelot. 1 act. Plays, 29 (January, 1970), 11-19.

117. _____. The Wonderful Witchware Store. 1 act. Plays, 16 (October, 1956), 63-67. AND Plays, 34 (October, 1974), 69-73.

118. Aldington, Richard, 1892-1962, translator see Gourmont, R. de 3671, 3673

119. Aldis, Mary Reynolds, 1872-1949. Extreme Unction. 1 act. Little Review, 2 (April, 1915), 31-37.

120. _____. Ten P. M., A Problem Play. 1 act. Drama, 11 (March, 1921), 187-188.

121. Aldrich, Thomas Bailey, 1936-1907. Marjorie Daw. 1 act. Plays, 21 (February, 1962), 67-78. Lewy Olfson, adapter.

122. _____. Mercedes. 2 acts. Harper's, 57 (September, 1878), 524-531.

123. _____. Pauline Pavlovna. 1 act. Harper's, 76 (December, 1887), 50-56.

124. Alencar, José Martiniano de, 1829-1877. The Jesuit. 4 acts. Poet Lore, 30 (Winter, 1919), 475-547. Edgardo R. De Britto, translator.

125. Alessi, Rino, 1885- . Il colore dell'anima. 3 acts. Il Dramma, 156 (February 15, 1933), 4-32. In Italian.

126. Alessio, Giovanni. L'uomo amore. 4 episodes. Il Dramma, 106 (January 15, 1931), 33-37. In Italian.

Alexander, Archibald, translator see Sudermann, H. 8605

127. Alexander, Hartley Burr, 1873-1939. The Annunciation. 1 act. Midland, 1 (June, 1915), 177-185.

128. _____. Kills-with-Her-Man. 1 act. Theatre Arts, 12 (June, 1928), 439-446.

129. _____. The Singing Girl of Copan, A Ballet in the Maya Mode. 1 act. Theatre Arts, 17 (August, 1933), 595-597.

Alexander 12

_____, editor see Three Chinese Folk-Dramas . . .
8855

130. Alexander, I. J. Enemy, A Monologue. 1 act. Theatre Arts, 28 (September, 1944), 529-533.

131. Alexander, Louise E. Mr. Jay Does Some Thinking. 1 act. Plays, 3 (January, 1944), 48-50.

132. Alexander, Ronald, 1917- . Time Out for Ginger. 3 acts, comedy. Theatre Arts, 38 (February, 1954), 36-64.

Alexis, Alex, translator see Guitry, S. 3781

_____, translator see Moineaux, G. 6105

_____, translator see Provins, M. 7315

133. Alfred, William, 1922- . Agamemnon. 4 acts, tragedy. Botteghe Oscure, 11 (1953), 249-353.

134. Alger, Esther Marion. In'ependence. 1 act. Poet Lore, 41 (Spring, 1930), 140-149.

135. Alice-Heidi's Secrets. 1 act. Horn Book, 2 (June, 1926), 40-42.

Alkinson, Clinton J., translator see Goll, Y. 3616

136. Allais, Alphonse. Le Pauvre Bougre et le Bon Génie. 1 act. L'Avant Scène, 98, 35-38. In French.

Allan, Ted see MacDougall, R. 5173

Allemandi, Umberto, translator see Mouloudji, M. 6276

137. Allen, Caroline K. Futility. 1 act. One-Act Play Magazine, 3 (May-June, 1940), 336-341.

Allen, Donald, 1912- , translator see Ionesco, E. 4382, 4387

138. Allen, Hayward F. The "Revolutionary/Birth" Play. Intrepid, 11-12 (March, 1969), 1-16.

139. _____. The "U.S. #6" Play. Intrepid, 9 (December, 1967), n. p.

140. Allen, James Lane, 1849-1925. Heaven's Little Ironies. 1 act. Bookman [New York], 51 (August, 1920), 616-619.

141. Allen, James M. The Wind Blows, A Play in One Act for the Negro Theatre. One-Act Play Magazine, 2 (March, 1939),

794-814.

142. Allen, John. Busmen (Living Newspaper from England). 1 act. One-Act Play Magazine, 2 (August-September, 1938), 211-252.

143. Allen, Lewis. The After-Dinner Speaker. 1 act. Smart Set, 42 (April, 1914), 99-101.

Allen, Margaret F., adapter see Wilde, O. 9366

144. Allen, R. A. Gentlemen All. 1 act. Smart Set, 63 (December, 1920), 73-79.

Allen, Ruth C., translator see Messager, C. 5790

145. Allen, Woody. Death Knocks. 1 act. The New Yorker, 44 (July 27, 1968), 31-33.

146. Allensworth, Carl. Ring Once for Central. 1 act, comedy. One-Act Play Magazine, 3 (November-December, 1940), 491-513.

147. Allioux, Alain. L'Homme et la Perruche. 1 act. L'Avant Scène, 303 (January 15, 1964), 33-38. In French.

148. Allred, Joan. All This and Alan, Too. 1 act. Plays, 5 (October, 1945), 9-15. AND Plays, 12 (May, 1953), 74-80. AND Plays, 23 (April, 1964), 37-43.

149. _____ and Pearl Allred. Society Page. 1 act. Plays, 11 (March, 1952), 1-17.

150. _____ and Thatcher Allred. Orchids for Margaret. 1 act. Plays, 4 (April, 1945), 1-17. AND Plays, 14 (January, 1955), 1-17. AND Plays, 27 (March, 1968), 23-39.

Allred, Pearl see Allred, J. 149

Allred, Thatcher see Allred, J. 150

151. Alma-Tadema, Sir Lawrence, 1836-1912. Love and Death. 1 act. Harper's, 90 (December, 1894), 151-152.

152. _____. Merciful Soul. 1 act. Anglo-Saxon Review, 3 (December, 1899), 107-128.

153. _____. The Silent Voice. 1 act. Harper's, 93 (August, 1896), 400-409.

Alpern, H., translator see Unamuno, M. de 8968

154. Alston, Tyrone, et al. Tyrone and the Robbers. 1 act.

Scripts, 1 (October, 1972), 76-80.

155. Altendorf, Wolfgang, 1921- . Der Arme Mensch. 1 act. Il Dramma, n.s., 176 (March 1, 1953), 11-21. Italo Alighiero Chiusano, translator. In Italian.

156. _____. Schlagwetter. 1 act. Il Dramma, n.s., 218/219 (December 1/15, 1954), 110-118. Italo Alighiero Chiusano, translator. In Italian.

Alvarez Quintero, Joaquin, 1873-1944 see Alvarez Quintero, S. 157-174

157. Alvarez Quintero, Serafin, 1871-1938, and Joaquin Alvarez Quintero, 1873-1944. La bella Lucerito. 1 act. Il Dramma, 154 (January 15, 1933), 35-37. Gilberto Beccari, translator. In Italian.

158. _____. A Bright Morning. 1 act, comedy. Poet Lore, 27 (Winter, 1916), 669-679. Carlos C. Castillo and E. L. Overman, translators.

159. _____. By the Light of the Moon. 1 act. Poet Lore, 48 (Summer, 1942), 99-110. William Dyer Moore, translator.

160. _____. By Their Words Ye Shall Know Them. 1 act, comedy. Drama, 25 (February, 1917), 26-39.

161. _____. Il centenario. 3 acts. Il Dramma, 121 (September 1, 1931), 4-30. Gilberto Beccari, translator. In Italian.

162. _____. Cuore alla mano. 1 act. Il Dramma, 170 (September 15, 1933), 40-43. Gilberto Beccari, translator. In Italian.

163. _____. Fiammellina. 1 act. Il Dramma, 115 (June 1, 1931), 34-37. Gilberto Beccari, translator. In Italian.

164. _____. Il fiore nel libro. 1 act. Il Dramma, 177 (January 1, 1934), 37-41. In Italian.

165. _____. Matinée de Soleil. 1 act. L'Avant Scène, 114, 33-38. Jean Camp, adapter. In French.

166. _____. Mattina di sole. 1 act. Il Dramma, 64 (April 15, 1929), 41-44. Gilberto Beccari, translator. In Italian.

167. _____. Le nozze di Quinita. 3 acts. Il Dramma, 28 (October 15, 1927), 7-34. In Italian.

168. _____. Papa Juan or the Centenarian. 3 acts, comedy.

Poet Lore, 29 (Spring, 1918), 253-318. Thomas Walsh, translator.

169. _____. Il pittore di ventagli. 1 act. Il Dramma, 172 (October 15, 1933), 38-41. Gilberto Beccari, translator. In Italian.

170. _____. Quando l'amore brucia. 1 act. Il Dramma, 89 (May 1, 1930), 30-35. Gilberto Beccari and C. Vicesvinci, translators. In Italian.

171. _____. Rosa e Rosina. 1 act. Il Dramma, 157 (March 1, 1933), 42-44. In Italian.

172. _____. Senza parole. 1 act. Il Dramma, 63 (April 1, 1929), 30-38. Gilberto Beccari, translator. In Italian.

173. _____. Tamburo e sonaglio. 3 acts. Il Dramma, 117 (July 1, 1931), 4-29. Angelo Norsa, translator. In Italian.

174. _____. Widows' Eyes. 1 act, comedy. Poet Lore, 40 (1929), 552-566. Ana Lee Utt, translator.

175. Alvaro, Corrado. Lunga notte di Medea. 2 parts, tragedy. Sipario, 4, 40-41 (August-September, 1949), 45-58. In Italian.

_____, translator see Shakespeare, W. 8178

176. Aman-Jean, François. Le Gardien des Oiseaux. 1 act. L'Avant Scène, 104, 29-35. In French.

177. Ambition, a Farce. 1 act. Blackwood's Magazine, 50 (October, 1841), 432-448.

178. Ames, Thomas. Are You Perfect? 1 act. Dramatika, 2 (October, 1968), 36.

179. Amiel, Denys, 1884- . L'Age du Fer. 3 parts. Petite Illustration, 183 (November 26, 1932), 1-30. In French.

180. _____. Confession. 1 act. L'Avant Scène, 252 (November 1, 1961), 43-44. In French.

181. _____. Confidences. 1 act. L'Avant Scène, 193 (March 15, 1959), 29-33. In French.

182. _____. Décalage. 3 acts. Petite Illustration, 179 (June 6, 1931), 1-29. In French.

183. _____. Il desiderio. 3 acts. Il Dramma, 57 (January 1, 1929), 7-38. In Italian.

184. _____. La Femme en Fleur. 3 acts. Petite Illustration, 193 (April 11, 1936), 1-30. In French.

185. _____. La Jeunesse. 3 acts. Il Dramma, n.s., 41 (July 1, 1947), 9-29. Carlo Lari, translator. In Italian.

186. _____. Ma Liberté! 3 acts, comedy. Petite Illustration, 196 (February 13, 1937), 1-34. In French.

187. _____. Maison Monestier. 3 acts. Il Dramma, n.s., 33 (March 15, 1947), 8-34. Lida Ferro, translator. In Italian.

188. _____. Il primo amante. 3 acts. Il Dramma, 62 (March 15, 1929), 4-38. Lucio d'Ambra, translator. In Italian.

189. _____. Tre, rosso, dispari. 3 acts. Il Dramma, 144 (August 15, 1932), 4-42. Alessandro de Stefani, translator. In Italian.

190. _____. Trois et Une . . . 3 acts. Petite Illustration, 186 (October 28, 1933), 1-30. In French.

_____, adapter see Zilahy, L. 9650

191. _____, and M. Amiel Petry. Famiglia. 3 acts. Il Dramma, 325 (March 1, 1940), 7-27. Guglielmo Forzi, translator. In Italian.

192. Anagnostaki, Loula, 1925- . The Town. 1 act. Chicago Review, 21 (August, 1969), 88-105. Aliki Halls, translator.

193. Andersen, Hans Christian, 1805-1875. The Emperor and the Nightingale. 1 act. Plays, 26 (April, 1967), 49-54. Michael T. Leech, adapter.

194. _____. The Emperor's New Clothes. 1 act. Plays, 12 (April, 1953), 61-65. Deborah Newman, adapter.

195. _____. The Emperor's Nightingale. 1 act. Plays, 22 (November, 1962), 41-50. AND Plays, 34 (October, 1974), 59-68. Adele Thane, adapter.

196. _____. The Emperor's Nightingale. 1 act. Plays, 28 (May, 1969), 82-87. Barbara Winther, adapter.

197. _____. Once Upon a Tinderbox. 1 act. Plays, 33 (November, 1973), 48-54. Frances Mapp, adapter.

198. _____. The Princess and the Pea. 1 act. Plays, 18 (January, 1959), 45-50. Helen Louise Miller, adapter.

199. _____. The Princess and the Pea. 1 act. <u>Plays</u>, 32 (May, 1973), 73-78. Lewis Mahlmann, and David Cadwalader Jones, adapters.

200. _____. The Real Princess. 1 act. <u>Plays</u>, 14 (April, 1955), 71-76. Deborah Newman, adapter.

201. _____. The Snow Queen. 1 act. <u>Plays</u>, 26 (February, 1967), 69-74. Michael T. Leech, adapter.

202. _____. The Swineherd. 1 act. <u>Plays</u>, 26 (March, 1967), 75-81. Adele Thane, adapter.

203. _____. The Tinderbox. 1 act. <u>Plays</u>, 30 (December, 1970), 61-65.

Anderson, Farris, translator see Vallejo, A. B. 9004

204. Anderson, Harold L. It's Really Quite Simple. 1 act. <u>One-Act Play Magazine</u>, 2 (October, 1938), 394-404.

205. Anderson, Lee, 1896- . Wet Saturday. 1 act. <u>One-Act Play Magazine</u>, 3 (November-December, 1940), 523-537. John Collier, adapter.

206. Anderson, Mary E. Hurray for Families. 1 act. <u>Learning With...</u>, 4 (January, 1976), 19-20.

207. Anderson, Maxwell, 1888-1959. Anne of the Thousand Days. <u>Theatre Arts</u>, 33 (June, 1949), 57-92.

208. _____. The Bad Seed. 2 acts. <u>Theatre Arts</u>, 39 (December, 1955), 35-59.

209. _____. Barefoot in Athens. 2 acts. <u>Theatre Arts</u>, 36 (October, 1952), 36-63.

210. _____. Joan of Lorraine. 2 acts. <u>Il Dramma</u>, n.s., 95 (October 15, 1949), 7-38. Gigi Cane, translator. In Italian.

211. _____. Joan of Lorraine. 2 acts. <u>Theatre Arts</u>, 32 (Spring, 1948), 61-92.

212. _____. Winterset. 3 acts. <u>Il Dramma</u>, n.s., 5 (January 15, 1946), 9-29. Vinicio Marinucci, translator. In Italian.

213. _____ and Kurt Weill, 1900-1950. Lost in the Stars. 2 acts, tragedy. <u>Theatre Arts</u>, 34 (December, 1950), 57-88.

214. Anderson, Robert, 1926- . All Summer Long. 2 acts.

Theatre Arts, 39 (August, 1955), 35-63.

215. _____. Silent Night, Lonely Night. 2 acts. Theatre Arts, 45 (December, 1961), 25-56.

216. _____. Tea and Sympathy. 3 acts. L'Avant Scène, 152, 1-27. Roger-Ferdinand, adapter. In French.

217. _____. Tea and Sympathy. 3 acts. Sipario, 11, 118 Supplement (February, 1956), 3-20. Luigi Squarzina, translator. In Italian.

218. _____. Tea and Sympathy. 3 acts. Theatre Arts, 38 (September, 1954), 34-61.

219. _____. You Know I Can't Hear You When the Water's Running. 4 parts. Sipario, 24, 273 (January, 1969), 60-72. Garineri and J. Giovannini, translators. In Italian.

220. Anderson, Robert A. The Gold Mine at Jeremiah Flats. 1 act. Plays, 23 (October, 1963), 17-30.

221. _____. Trouble in Outer Space. 1 act. Plays, 26 (December, 1966), 1-9.

222. Andersson, Donald and Sid Dimond. The Cross of Gold. 1 act. Plays, 11 (October, 1951), 69-74.

223. _____. The Mayflower Compact. 1 act. Plays, 11 (November, 1951), 71-77.

224. André, Michel. La Bonne Planque. 3 acts, comedy. L'Avant Scène, 293 (August 1, 1963), 9-37. In French.

225. _____. Virginie. 3 acts, comedy. L'Avant Scène, 144, 1-39. In French.

Andreucci, Costanza, translator see Marivaux, P. 5556

226. Andrews, John William. Four Antarctica. 1 act. Poet Lore, 52 (Summer, 1946), 99-116.

227. _____. He Is Something! 1 act. Poet Lore, 58 (Autumn, 1963), 258-270.

228. Andrews, Mary Raymond Shipman, d. 1936. The Ditch. 5 acts. Scribner's, 63 (April, 1918), 405-414.

229. _____. A West Point Regulation. 1 act, comedy. McClure's, 23 (August, 1904), 385-394.

230. Andreyev, Leonid Nikolaevich, 1871-1919. He Who Gets Slapped. 4 acts. Dial, 70 (March, 1921), 247-300.

Gregory Zilboarg, translator.

231. _____. He Who Gets Slapped. Everybody's Magazine, 47 (December, 1922), 112-118.

232. _____. An Incident. 1 act. Poet Lore, 27 (Spring, 1916), 171-179. Leo Pasvolsky, translator.

233. _____. King-Hunger. 1 act. Poet Lore, 22 (Winter, 1911), 401-459. Eugene M. Kayden, translator

234. _____. Love of One's Neighbor. 1 act. Glebe, 1 (No. 4, 1914), 5-40. Thomas Seltzer, translator.

235. _____. Love of One's Neighbour. 1 act, comedy. Golden Book, 4 (August, 1926), 181-190. Thomas Seltzer, translator.

236. _____. La Pensée. 1 act. L'Avant Scène, 257 (January 15, 1962), 8-26. Carlos Semprun, adapter. In French.

237. _____. The Pretty Sabine Women. 3 acts. Drama, 4 (February, 1914), 34-71. Thomas Seltzer, translator.

238. _____. A Steed in the Senate. 1 act, satire. Living Age, 322 (September 6, 1924), 498-507.

239. _____. To the Stars. 4 acts. Poet Lore, 18 (No. 4, 1907), 417-467. A. Goudiss, translator.

Angeli, M., translator see Bernard, T. 840

Angioletti, Paola, translator see Vulpescu, R. 9176

_____, translator see Worms, J. 9565

240. Anglund, Bob. The Christmas Cat. 1 act. Better Homes and Gardens, 39 (December, 1961), 44-45, 87-88.

241. Angoff, Charles, 1902- . Benefit for the Seamen. 1 act. North American Review, 248 (Winter, 1939-40), 234-243.

242. _____. Editorial Conference. 1 act. North American Review, 248 (Autumn, 1939), 33-40.

243. Aniante, Antonio, 1900- . Gelsomino d'Arabia. 3 acts. Il Dramma, 11 (October, 1926), 7-31. In Italian.

244. _____. La rosa di zolfo. 8 parts. Il Dramma, n.s., 262 (July, 1958), 9-34. In Italian.

245. Anouilh, Jean, 1910- . L'Alouette. 4 acts. L'Avant Scène, 320 (October 15, 1964), 11-38. In French.

246. _____. L'Alouette. 4 acts, comedy. Sipario, 8, 92 (December, 1953), 38-58. Silvio Giovaninetti, translator. In Italian.

247. _____. Antigone. tragedy. Il Dramma, n. s., 8 (March 1, 1946), 11-27. Adolfo Franci, translator. In Italian.

248. _____. Ardèle, ou la Marguerite. 1 act. L'Avant Scène, 181 (September 15, 1958), 6-20. In French.

249. _____. Ardele, ou la Marguerite. 3 acts. Sipario, 4, 38 (June, 1949), 41-59. Edoardo Anton, translator. In Italian.

250. _____. Le bal des voleurs. Sipario, 2, 19 (November, 1947), 33-48. Luciano Salce, translator. In Italian.

251. _____. Becket. 4 acts. L'Avant Scène, 282-283 (February 15-March 1, 1963), 11-53. In French.

252. _____. Boulanger, la Boulangère et le Petit Mitron. 1 act. L'Avant Scène, 433 (September 15, 1969), 7-31. In French.

253. _____. Cécile, ou L'Ecole des Pères. 1 act, comedy. L'Avant Scène, 101, 27-36. In French.

254. _____. Cecile, ou L'Ecole des Pères. 1 act, comedy. Sipario, 12, 135-136 (July-August, 1957), 54-62. Enzo Ferrieri, translator. In Italian.

255. _____. Cher Antoine, ou L'Amour Raté. 4 acts, comedy. L'Avant Scène, 455 (September 1, 1970), 7-37. In French.

256. _____. Colombe. 4 acts, comedy. Sipario, 9, 97 (May, 1954), 33-56. In Italian.

257. _____. Episode from an Author's Life. 1 act. Educational Theatre Journal, 16 (March, 1964), 1-15. John Harvey, translator.

258. _____. Eurydice. 4 acts. Il Dramma, n. s., 50/51 (December 1/15, 1947), 13-38. Adolfo Franci, translator. In Italian.

259. _____. The Fighting Cock. 2 acts. Plays and Players, 13 (July, 1966), 31-46, 71-72. Lucienne Hill, translator.

260. _____. La Foire D'Empoigne. 1 act, farce. L'Avant Scène, 282-283 (February 15-March 1, 1963), 57-70. In French.

261. _____. La Foire d'Empoigne. 1 act. Sipario, 19, 215

(March, 1964), 51-62. Sandro Bajini, translator. In Italian.

262. _____. La grotte. 2 acts. Sipario, 18, 211 (November, 1963), 47-68. Silvana Ottieri Mauri, translator. In Italian.

263. _____. L'Hurluberlu. 4 acts. L'Avant Scène, 246 (July 1, 1961), 9-39. In French.

264. _____. L'Hurluberlu. 4 acts, comedy. Sipario, 15, 166 (February, 1960), 45-68. Luigi Squarzina, translator. In Italian.

265. _____. L'Invitation au chateau. 5 acts. Sipario, 4, 42 (October, 1949), 49-69. Edoardo Anton, translator. In Italian.

266. _____. The Lark. 2 acts. Theatre Arts, 41 (March, 1957), 33-56. Lillian Hellman, adapter.

267. _____. Leocadia. 5 acts, comedy. Sipario, 8, 81 (January, 1953), 37-54. Giulio Cesare Castello, translator. In Italian.

268. _____. Monsieur Barnett. 1 act. L'Avant Scène, 559 (March 1, 1975), 3-19. In French.

269. _____. Ne Reveillez Pas Madame! 3 acts. L'Avant Scène, 508 (December 15, 1972), 7-40. In French.

270. _____. L'Orchestre. 1 act. L'Avant Scène, 276 (November 15, 1962), 30-38. In French.

271. _____. Ornifle, ou Le Courant d'Air. 4 acts, comedy. Sipario, 12, 131 (March, 1957), 34-64. Vittorio Gassman, translator. In Italian.

272. _____. Les Poissons Rouges, ou Mon Père ce Héros. 4 acts. comedy. L'Avant Scène, 478 (September 1, 1971), 7-28, 37-47. In French.

273. _____. La Repetition, ou, L'Amour Puni. 5 acts, comedy. Sipario, 6, 58 (February, 1951), 41-64. Edoardo Anton, translator. In Italian.

274. _____. Le Songe du Critique. 1 act. L'Avant Scène, 243 (May 15, 1961), 31-35. In French.

275. _____. Time Remembered. 2 acts. Theatre Arts, 43 (February, 1959), 25-46. Patricia Moyes, translator.

276. _____. Tu Etais si Gentil Quand tu Etais Petit! L'Avant

Scène, 499 (July 15, 1972), 7-31. In French.

277. _____. La Valse des Toreadors. 5 acts, comedy. L'Avant Scene, 541 (May 15, 1974), 7-33. In French.

278. _____. Le Voyageur sans Bagages . . . 1 act. Petite Illustration, 196 (April 10, 1937), 1-23. In French.

279. _____. Le Voyageur sans Bagages. 1 act. Sipario, 2, 16-17 (August-September, 1947), 25-42. Cesare Vico Lodovici, translator. In Italian.

280. _____. The Waltz of the Toreadors. 3 acts, comedy. Theatre Arts, 41 (September, 1957), 34-54. Lucienne Hill, translator.

281. _____. Y'avait un Prisonnier. 3 acts, comedy. Petite Illustration, 191 (May 18, 1935), 1-34. In French.

_____, adapter see Shakespeare, W. 8192

_____, adapter see Wilde, O. 9368

282. _____ and Roland Laudenbach, 1921- . La Petite Molière. L'Avant Scène, 210 (December 15, 1959), 10-42. In French.

Anouilh, Nichole, adapter see Shakespeare, W. 8192

283. Anshutz, H. L. This Moment. 3 acts. Interim, 3 (No. 2, 1948), 24-36.

284. Anstruther, Eva. Bon Secours, A Little Miracle Play. 1 act. Forthnightly, 79 (February, 1903), 358-364.

285. Antoine, Andre-Paul, 1892- . Le Condamné de Pichwickton. 1 act. L'Avant Scène, 265 (May 15, 1962), 31-38. In French.

286. _____. L'Ennemie. 3 acts, comedy. Petite Illustration, 87 (June 29, 1929), 1-30. In French.

287. _____. Je Suis Seule ce Soir. 1 act. L'Avant Scène, 129, 37-43. In French.

288. Antòn, Edoardo. La faccia del mostro. 1 act. Il Dramma, n.s., 291 (May, 1962), 33-48. In Italian.

289. _____. La fidanzata del bersagliere. 1 act. Il Dramma, n.s., 291 (December, 1960), 47-63. In Italian.

290. _____. Libertà provisoria. 1 act. Il Dramma, n.s., 338/339 (November/December, 1964), 65-73. In Italian.

291. _____. Morte di un bengalino. 1 act. Il Dramma, n. s., 325 (October, 1963), 45-56. In Italian.

292. _____. Mulini a vento. 3 acts. Il Dramma, 290 (September 15, 1938), 4-21. In Italian.

293. _____. La ragazza al balcone. 1 act. Il Dramma, n. s., 303 (December, 1961), 17-31. In Italian.

294. _____. Il serpente a sonagli. 3 acts. Il Dramma, 220 (October 15, 1935), 2-26. In Italian.

_____, translator see Anouilh, J. 249, 265, 273

295. Antona-Traversi, Giannino. L'unica scusa. 1 act. Il Dramma, 42 (May 15, 1928), 41-45. In Italian.

296. Antonelli, Luigi. L'amore deve nascere. 3 acts. Il Dramma, 402/403 (May 15/June 1, 1943), 9-29. In Italian.

297. _____. Avventura sulla spiaggia. 3 acts. Il Dramma, 166 (July 15, 1933), 5-33. In Italian.

298. _____. Bisogna non perdere il treno. 1 act. Il Dramma, 122 (September 15, 1931), 39-42. In Italian.

299. _____. Il cenno. 1 act. Il Dramma, 13 (December, 1926), 39-43. In Italian.

300. _____. Il dramma, la commedia, la farsa. 3 acts. Il Dramma, 1 (December, 1925), 9-28. In Italian.

301. _____. Incontro sentimentale. 1 act. Il Dramma, 114 (May 15, 1931), 31-36. In Italian.

302. _____. Il maestro. 3 acts. Il Dramma, 183 (April 1, 1934), 4-30. In Italian.

303. _____. Mio figlio, ecco il guaio. 3 acts. Il Dramma, 221 (November 1, 1935), 2-26. In Italian.

304. _____. La rosa dei venti. 3 acts. Il Dramma, 42 (May 15, 1928), 4-38. In Italian.

305. _____. L'uomo che incontrò se stesso. 3 acts. Il Dramma, 176 (December 15, 1933), 4-31. In Italian.

306. Antrobus, John. You'll Come to Love Your Sperm Test. 3 acts. New Writers, 4 (1967), 107-166.

307. Apel, Paolo. Giovanni l'idealista. 3 acts. Il Dramma, 99 (October 1, 1930), 4-34. Goffredo Pautassi, translator. In Italian.

308. Apollonio, Mario, 1901- . Inno d'avvento. 1 act. Il Dramma, n.s., 44 (December, 1968), 15-22. In Italian.

309. Applegate, Allita E. The Choice of Giannetta. 1 act. Poet Lore, 36 (Autumn, 1925), 405-414.

310. Apples: A Comedy. 1 act. Living Age, 138 (August 24, 1878), 502-509.

Aragno, Riccardo, translator see Wilde, O. 9367

_____, translator see Wilder, T. 2265, 9396, 9400

311. Aragon, Louis. Au Pied du Mur. 2 acts. Drama Review, 18 (December, 1974), 89-107. Nancy Nes, translator.

312. Arauz, Alvardo. Castilla Vuelve à Castilla. 1 act. L'Avant Scène, 236 (January 15, 1965), 33-35. Andre Camp, translator. In French.

313. _____. La Reine sans Repos. 1 act. L'Avant Scène, 277 (December 1, 1962), 33-35. Mireille Pezzani, translator. In French.

314. Arbusov, Alexey Nikolayevitch, 1908- . Irkutskaja Istorija. 2 parts. Sipario, 16, 180 (April, 1961), 57-73. Milly di Monticelli and Tatiana Isanz, translators. In Italian.

315. _____. Moj bednyk Marat. 3 acts, comedy. Sipario, 254 (June, 1967), 59-73. Milly di Montinelli, translator. In Italian.

316. _____. The Promise. 3 acts. Plays and Players, 14 (March, 1967), 31-46, 71-73. Ariadne Nicolaeff, translator.

Arcangeli, Bruno, translator see Giraudoux, J. 3562

_____, translator see Harris, E. 3920

_____, translator see Luc, J. B. 5074

_____, translator see Mouloudji, M. 6275

_____, translator see Odets, C. 6773

_____, translator see Saroyan, W. 7946, 7952

317. Archer, Leonard C. Frederick Douglass, A Testament of Freedom. 1 act. Negro History Bulletin, 13 (March, 1950), 134-139.

318. Archibald, William, 1924- . The Innocents. 2 acts. Si-

pario, 6, 66 (October, 1951), 33-53. Giulio Cesare Castello, translator. In Italian.

319. _____. The Innocents. 2 acts, tragedy. Theatre Arts, 35 (January, 1951), 57-88.

320. Arden, John, 1930- . The Armstrong's Last Goodnight. 3 acts. Sipario, 21, 244-245 (August-September, 1966), 49-70. Ettore Capriolo, translator. In Italian.

321. _____. The Bagman; or, The Impromptu of Muswell Hill; An Autobiographical Play. Scripts, 1 (June, 1972), 85-110.

322. _____. Serjeant Musgrave's Dance. 3 acts. L'Avant Scène, 309 (April 15, 1964), Maurice Pons, translator. In French.

323. _____. Serjeant Musgrave's Dance. 3 acts. Sipario, 17, 196-197 (August-September, 1962), 78-99. Ettore Capriolo, translator. In Italian.

324. _____. The True History of Squire Jonathan and His Unfortunate Treasure. 1 act. Plays and Players, 15 (August, 1968), 60-64.

325. _____ and Margaretta D'Arcy. The Ballygombeen Bequest. 1 act. Scripts, 1 (September, 1972), 4-50.

326. _____. The Island of the Mighty. 3 parts. Performance, 7 (Fall, 1973), 47-140.

327. _____. The Island of the Mighty. 3 parts. Plays and Players, 20 (February, 1973), I-XXXII; (March, 1973), I-XIV.

328. Ardrey, Robert, 1908- . God and Texas. 1 act. Theatre Arts, 27 (August, 1943), 524-532.

329. _____. La Tour d'Ivoire. 3 acts. L'Avant Scène, 183 (October 15, 1958), 9-33. Jean Mercure, adapter. In French.

Arene, Emmanuel see Caillavet, G.-A. de 1490

330. Arent, Arthur, 1904- . Ethiopia. 1 act. Educational Theatre Journal, 20 (March, 1968), 19-31.

Arest, Georges see Balachova, T. 527

_____, adapter see Merimee, P. 5773

331. Arial, Rebecca. How Many Dark Ships in the Forest? 1 act. DeKalb Literary Arts Journal, 5 (No. 4, 1972), 17-32.

332. Aristophanes, c. 450-c. 385 B.C. The Congresswomen. Arion, 6 (Spring, 1967), 23-37. Douglass Parker, translator.

333. _____. Knights Prologue. Arion, 1 (Spring, 1962), 79-94. William Arrowsmith, translator.

334. _____. Lysistrata, in a Free Adaptation by Ivan Grazni. 3 acts. Eros, 1 (Winter, 1962), 81-96.

335. _____. Lysistrata Takes Command. 1 act. Plays, 32 (January, 1973), 23-29. E. M. Nightingale, adapter.

336. _____. Thesmophoriazusae. Arion, 2 (Autumn, 1963), 78-85. Ian Fletcher, translator.

Arlen, Michael, pseud. see Kuyumjian, D. 4740

337. Arlett, Vera Isabel, 1896- . The Gardener. 1 act. Poet Lore, 41 (Summer, 1930), 305-313.

338. _____. The Last Man. 1 act. Poet Lore, 41 (Autumn, 1930), 410-418.

339. Arley, Catherine. La Femme de Paille. 2 acts, comedy. L'Avant Scène, 591 (July 15, 1976), 35-56. In French.

340. Armont, Paul. Ces Messieurs de la Santé. 3 acts, comedy. Petite Illustration, 179 (July 25, 1931), 1-38. In French.

341. _____ and Marcel Gerbidon. L'Amoureuse Aventure. 3 acts, comedy. Petite Illustration, 87 (March 9, 1929), 1-30. In French.

342. _____. Audace avventura. 3 acts. Il Dramma, 70 (July 15, 1929), 4-36. In Italian.

343. _____. Una donnina senza importanza. 3 acts. Il Dramma, 76 (October 15, 1929), 4-42. In Italian.

344. Armstrong, Louise Van Voorhis. Dolls. A Christmas Nonsense Play. 1 act. Drama, 11 (November, 1920), 52-57.

345. _____. The Old History Book. 1 act. Drama, 12 (January, 1922), 125-129, 137.

346. Armstrong, Paul, 1869-1915. Mr. Lorelei, A Folk Comedy. 1 act. Smart Set, 48 (January, 1916), 233-242.

347. Arnaud, Georges. Sweet Confessions. 1 act. Evergreen Review, 1 (No. 3), 135-159. David Noakes, translator.

348. Arnaud, Michel, 1907- . Minuit en Plein Jour, ou Vessies

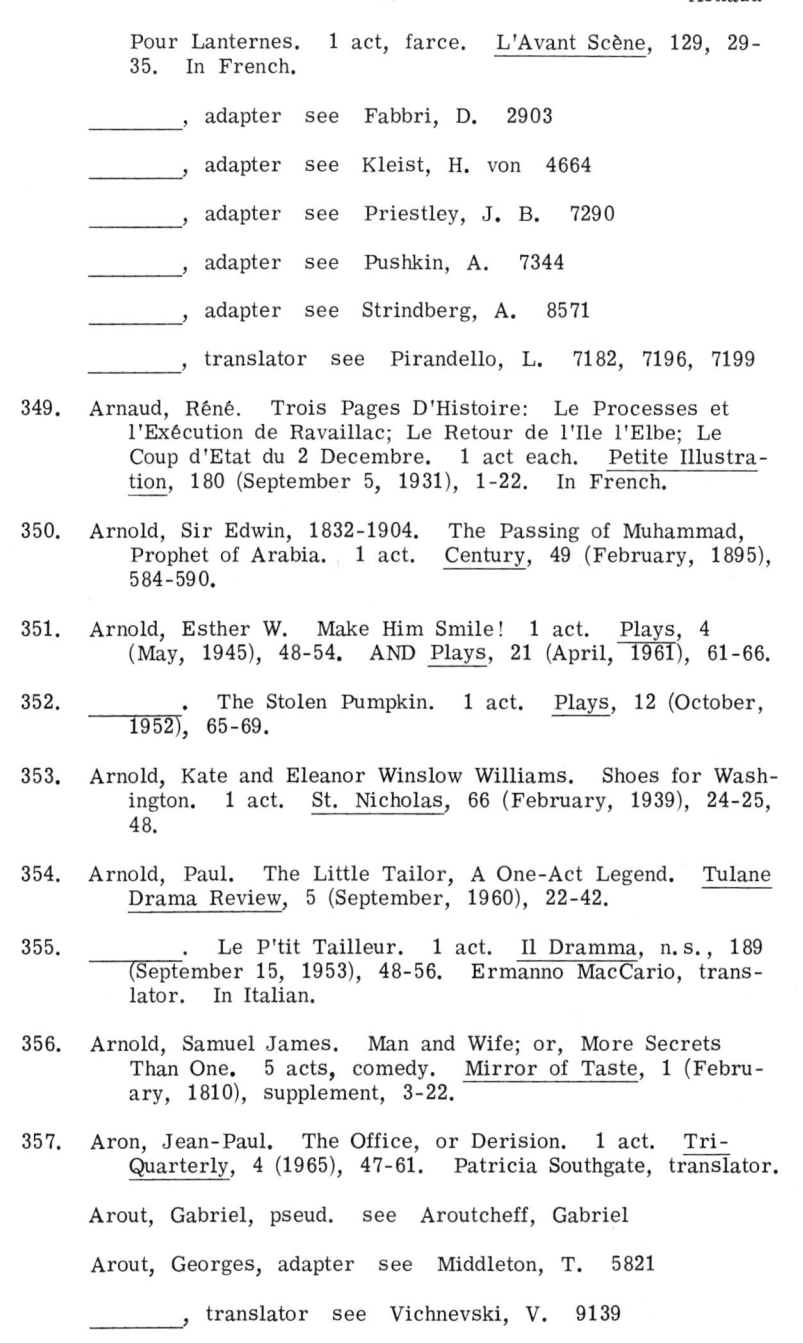

Pour Lanternes. 1 act, farce. L'Avant Scène, 129, 29-35. In French.

_____, adapter see Fabbri, D. 2903

_____, adapter see Kleist, H. von 4664

_____, adapter see Priestley, J. B. 7290

_____, adapter see Pushkin, A. 7344

_____, adapter see Strindberg, A. 8571

_____, translator see Pirandello, L. 7182, 7196, 7199

349. Arnaud, Réné. Trois Pages D'Histoire: Le Processes et l'Exécution de Ravaillac; Le Retour de l'Ile l'Elbe; Le Coup d'Etat du 2 Decembre. 1 act each. Petite Illustration, 180 (September 5, 1931), 1-22. In French.

350. Arnold, Sir Edwin, 1832-1904. The Passing of Muhammad, Prophet of Arabia. 1 act. Century, 49 (February, 1895), 584-590.

351. Arnold, Esther W. Make Him Smile! 1 act. Plays, 4 (May, 1945), 48-54. AND Plays, 21 (April, 1961), 61-66.

352. _____. The Stolen Pumpkin. 1 act. Plays, 12 (October, 1952), 65-69.

353. Arnold, Kate and Eleanor Winslow Williams. Shoes for Washington. 1 act. St. Nicholas, 66 (February, 1939), 24-25, 48.

354. Arnold, Paul. The Little Tailor, A One-Act Legend. Tulane Drama Review, 5 (September, 1960), 22-42.

355. _____. Le P'tit Tailleur. 1 act. Il Dramma, n.s., 189 (September 15, 1953), 48-56. Ermanno MacCario, translator. In Italian.

356. Arnold, Samuel James. Man and Wife; or, More Secrets Than One. 5 acts, comedy. Mirror of Taste, 1 (February, 1810), supplement, 3-22.

357. Aron, Jean-Paul. The Office, or Derision. 1 act. Tri-Quarterly, 4 (1965), 47-61. Patricia Southgate, translator.

Arout, Gabriel, pseud. see Aroutcheff, Gabriel

Arout, Georges, adapter see Middleton, T. 5821

_____, translator see Vichnevski, V. 9139

358. Aroutcheff, Gabriel, 1930- . Les Alpinistes. 1 act. L'-
Avant Scène, 287 (May 1, 1963), 45-46. In French.

359. _____. Il ballo del tenente Helt. 3 acts. Il Dramma,
n.s., 139/140 (August 15/September 1, 1951), 65-84.
Giuseppina Rosi, translator. In Italian.

360. _____. Cet Animal Etrange. 2 acts. L'Avant Scène
236 (January 15, 1954), 9-31. In French.

361. _____. Cet Animal Etrange. 2 acts. Sipario, 250 (February, 1967), 49-64. Pier Benedetto Bertoli, translator.
In Italian

362. _____. Crime et Châtiment. 2 parts. L'Avant Scène,
287 (May 1, 1963), 9-43. In French.

363. _____. La Dame de Trèfle. 3 acts. Il Dramma, n.s.,
206 (June 1, 1954), 5-26. Nicoletta Neri, translator.
In Italian.

364. _____. Entre Chien et Loup. 3 acts. L'Avant Scène,
129, 1-28. In French.

365. _____. Gog e magog. 3 acts. Sipario, 174 (October,
1960), 53-74. Maria Pia D'Arborio, translator. In Italian.

366. _____. Laure et les Jacques. 4 acts, comedy. L'Avant
Scène, 308 (April 1, 1964), 9-29. In French.

367. _____. La Passion d'Anna Karenine. 5 acts. L'Avant
Scène, 592 (August, 1976), 3-34. In French.

368. _____. Des Pommes Pour Eve. 9 parts. L'Avant Scène,
437 (November 15, 1969), 7-35. In French.

_____, translator see Delaney, S. 2290

_____, translator see MacDougall, R. and T. Allan 5173

_____, translator see Vichnevski, V. 9139

369. _____ and Jean Locher. Guillaume le Confident. 3 acts,
comedy. L'Avant Scène (OST), 44 (June, 1951), 1-38.
In French.

Aroutcheff, Georges, translator see Vichevski, V. 9139

370. Arpino, Giovanni. La riabilitazione. 1 act. Il Dramma, 45,
no. 13 (October, 1969), 48-57. In Italian.

371. Arrabal, Fernando, 1932- . L'Architecte et L'Empereur
d'Assyrie. 2 acts. L'Avant Scène, 443 (February 15,
1970), 7-33. In French.

372. _____. The Cages. 1 act. Drama and Theatre, 7 (November 3, 1969), 193-195. Bettina L. Knapp, translator.

373. _____. Impossible Lover. 1 act. Drama Review (TDR), 13 (Fall, 1968), 82-86. Bettina L. Knapp, translator.

374. _____. Picnic on the Battlefield. 1 act. Evergreen Review, 4 (November-December, 1960), 76-90. James Hewitt, translator.

375. _____. Prima Communion. 1 act. El Corno Emplumado, 29 (1969), 112-117. In Spanish.

376. _____. Solemn Communion: Panic Ceremony. 1 act. Drama Review (TDR), 13 (Fall, 1968), 77-80. Bettina L. Knapp, translator.

377. _____. The Solemn Communion. 1 act. Gambit, 3 (No. 2), 5-13. John Calder, translator.

378. _____. Strip-Tease of Jealousy, Ballet in One Act. Drama Review (TDR), 13 (Fall, 1968), 80-82. Bettina L. Knapp, translator.

379. _____. The Tricycle. 2 acts. Modern International Drama, 9 (Spring, 1976), 67-91. David Herzberger, translator.

380. Arrault, Albert. Eugénie Grandet. 4 acts. Petite Illustration, 196 (March 13, 1937), 1-30. In French.

Arrowsmith, William, 1924- , translator see Aristophanes 333

_____, translator see Euripides 2879

_____, translator see Pavese, C. 7018

381. Arrufat, Anton. Carnival Saturday. 1 act. Americas, 10 (October, 1958), 20-25.

382. Artaud, Antonin, d. 1948. The Philosopher's Stone, A Mime Play. 1 act. Tulane Drama Review, 9 (Spring, 1965), 89-94.

383. _____. Spurt of Blood. 1 act. Evergreen Review, 7 (January-February, 1963), 62-66. Lawrence Ferlinghetti, translator.

384. Arthur, Katherine. Pot Luck. 1 act. Plays, 21 (April, 1962), 1-17.

385. Arthur, Kay. Moonlight Is When. 1 act. Plays, 24 (March,

1965), 3-16.

386. _____. Mother Goes Modern. 2 acts. Plays, 25 (May, 1966), 1-14.

387. _____. A Thing of Beauty. 1 act. Plays, 22 (November, 1962), 1-12.

388. Arthur, Richard. Odysseus and Calypso. 1 act. North American Review, 177 (July, 1903), 123-137.

Artini, Anamaria, translator see Behan, B. 728

389. Artsybashev, Mikhail Petrovich, 1878-1927. War. 4 acts. Drama, 21 (February, 1921), 12-86. Thomas Seltzer, translator.

390. Artu', Galar E. Un po' di bufera.... 1 act. Il Dramma, 183 (April 1, 1934), 34-42. In Italian.

391. _____. Il trattato scomparso. 3 acts. Il Dramma, 168 (August 15, 1933), 4-41. In Italian.

392. _____. Uguale ma diverso. 1 act. Il Dramma, 188 (June 15, 1934), 33-41. In Italian.

393. Asbrand, Karin. And Sew On. 1 act. Plays, 4 (November, 1944), 47-48.

394. _____. Anders Paints a Picture. 1 act. Plays, 25 (January, 1966), 55-60.

395. _____. Bright Comes. 1 act. Plays, 5 (March, 1946), 43-46.

396. _____. China Comes to You. 1 act. Plays, 3 (April, 1944), 41-46.

397. _____. Colors Mean So Much. 1 act. Plays, 5 (May, 1946), 63-65.

398. _____. Crystal Flask. 1 act. Plays, 5 (October, 1945), 43-47.

399. _____. Gold in Your Garden. 1 act. Plays, 22 (March, 1963), 77-80.

400. _____. Hi, Neighbor. 1 act. Plays, 3 (May, 1944), 58-60.

401. _____. I Can Get Along. 1 act. Plays, 9 (May, 1950), 58-63.

402. _____. Little Christmas Guest. 1 act. <u>Plays</u>, 5 (December, 1945), 53-54.

403. _____. Little Hero of Holland. 1 act. <u>Plays</u>, 2 (February, 1943), 37-43.

404. _____. Little Polka Dot. 1 act. <u>Plays</u>, 10 (May, 1951), 30-34.

405. _____. The Magic of Flowers. 1 act. <u>Plays</u>, 21 (March, 1962), 73-76.

406. _____. Pandora's Box. 1 act. <u>Plays</u>, 15 (January, 1956), 79-82.

407. _____. Pot of Gold for Mother. 1 act. <u>Plays</u>, 21 (May, 1962), 65-68.

408. _____. Pottery Lane. 1 act. <u>Plays</u>, 11 (January, 1952), 42-48. AND <u>Plays</u>, 20 (April, 1961), 75-81.

409. _____. The Secret of the Church Mouse. 1 act. <u>Plays</u>, 18 (April, 1959), 81-85.

410. _____. Skin Deep. 1 act. <u>Plays</u>, 4 (April, 1945), 40-44.

411. _____. So This Is China. 1 act. <u>Plays</u>, 9 (March, 1950), 52-61.

412. _____. Star Dust. 1 act. <u>Plays</u>, 2 (April, 1943), 56-58.

413. _____. Thankful's Pumpkin. 1 act. <u>Plays</u>, 3 (November, 1943), 63-65.

414. _____. Tick Tock. 1 act. <u>Plays</u>, 12 (December, 1952), 57-60.

415. _____. Valerie's Valentine. 1 act. <u>Plays</u>, 5 (February, 1946), 46-49.

416. _____. When the Sandman Went to Sleep. 1 act. <u>Plays</u>, 2 (December, 1942), 56-60.

_____, adapter see Spyri, J. 8458

Asckenary, Ysidor, translator see Hervieu, P. 4085, 4086

417. Ashbery, John, 1927- . The Philosopher. <u>Art and Literature</u>, 2 (Summer, 1964), 171-194.

_____, translator see Jarry, A. 4448

418. Ashburn, W. David, 1922- . The Salesman Ruptured by a

Streetcar. A One-Act Burlesque. Carolina Quarterly, 7 (Winter, 1955), 9-20.

419. Ashman, A., 1894- . Michal, the Daughter of Saul. 3 acts. Literary Review, 1 (Spring, 1958), 337-384.

420. Ashman, Jane. Birthdays of Frances Willard. 1 act. Scholastic, 35 (September 25, 1939), 29-31.

421. Asimov, Isaac, 1920- . The Story Machine. 1 act. Plays, 17 (February, 1958), 13-23. AND Plays, 29 (May, 1970), 25-34.

422. Askew, Claude. Marquise and Woman. An Incident During the Reign of Terror. 1 act. Smart Set, 7 (July, 1902), 83-86.

423. Aspenstrom, Werner. The Apes Shall Inherit the Earth. 1 act, satire. Tulane Drama Review, 6 (November, 1961), 92-97. Leif Sjoberg and Randolph Goodman, translators.

424. _____. The Poet and the Emperor, a Radio Comedy. 1 act. Tulane Drama Review, 6 (November, 1961), 98-116. Paul Britten Austin, translator.

Assur, Jane see Thompson, D. K. 8840

425. Asturias, Miguel Angel, 1899- . Soluna. 2 acts. Il Dramma, n.s., 380/381 (May/June, 1968), 57-78. Piero Raimondi, translator. In Italian.

426. _____. Torotumbo. 2 acts. Il Dramma, 45, no. 7 (April, 1969), 33-47. Amos Segala, translator. In Italian.

427. Athayde, Roberto, 1949- . Madame Marquerite; Monologue tragicomique. L'Avant Scène, 561 (April 1, 1975), 3-25. Jean-Loup Dabadie, adapter.

428. Atherton, Camille Skrivanek. Chit-Chat on a Rat. 1 act. First Stage, 2 (Winter, 1962-63), 37-41.

429. Atherton, Marguerite. Old King Cole's Christmas. 1 act. Plays, 17 (December, 1957), 70-74.

430. Atkins, Charles L. Prisoners. 1 act. Christian Century, 53 (October 21, 1936), 1388-1390.

431. Atkins, Russell. The Abortionist. 1 act. Free Lance, 2 (No. 1, 1954), 19-25.

432. _____. The Corpse. 1 act. Western Review, 18 (Winter, 1954), 149-158.

433. Aub, Max. Les Hommes de Haute Vertu. 1 act. L'Avant Scène, 351 (February 15, 1966), 38-42. Robert Marrast, translator. In French.

434. _____. Les Morts. 1 act. L'Avant Scène, 288 (May 15, 1963), 38-43. Andre Ricard, translator. In French.

435. _____ and Andre Camp. La Cachette d'Harpagon. 1 act. L'Avant Scène, 319 (October 1, 1964), 32-36. In French.

436. Aubert, Réné, 1899- . La Cirque aux Illusions. 2 acts. L'Avant Scène, 116, 25-40. In French.

437. _____. Les Poissons D'Or. 2 acts. L'Avant Scène, 116, 1-23. In French.

438. Auden, Wystan Hugh, 1907-1973. Paid on Both Sides, A Charade. 1 act. Criterion, 9 (January, 1930), 268-290.

_____, translator see Brecht, B. 690, 1309

_____, translator see Loki's Flyting 5021

439. _____ and Christopher Isherwood, 1904- . Le Chien Sous la Peau. 1 act. Mesures, 3 (April 15, 1937), 13-42. Armand Petitjean, translator. In French.

440. _____ and Chester Kallman, 1921- . Delia, or A Masque of Night. 1 act. Botteghe Oscure, 12 (1953), 164-210.

441. Audiberti, Jacques, 1899-1965. L'Ampelour. 1 act. Mesures, 3 (July 15, 1937), 5-36. In French.

442. _____. L'Armoire Classique. 1 act. L'Avant Scène, 205 (October 1, 1959), 38-41. In French.

443. _____. Le Cavalier Seul. 3 acts. L'Avant Scène, 533 (January 15, 1974), 7-39. In French.

444. _____. L'Effet Glapion. 2 acts, comedy. L'Avant Scène, 205 (October 1, 1959), 10-35. In French.

445. _____. La Logense. 3 acts, comedy. L'Avant Scène, 473 (June 1, 1971), 7-36. In French.

446. _____. La Mal Court. 3 acts, comedy. L'Avant Scène, 137, 3-25. In French.

447. _____. La Megere Apprivoisee. 3 acts, comedy. L'Avant Scène, 166, 6-42. In French.

448. _____. Pucelle. 3 acts. L'Avant Scène, (OST), 32 (November, 1950), 3-34. In French.

449. _____. Quoat-Quoat. 1 act. L'Avant Scène, 419 (February 1, 1969), 7-27. In French.

450. _____. Quoat-Quoat. Sipario, 2, 16-17 (August-September, 1947), 61-76. Ivo Chiesa, translator. In Italian.

451. _____. Quoat-Quoat. Spectaculum, 3 (1960), 7-55. In German.

_____, translator see Filippo, E. de 3018

452. Audouard, Yvan, 1914- . La Bonne Compagnie. 3 acts, comedy. L'Avant Scène (OST), 23 (April, 1950), 3-27. In French.

453. Augias, Corrado. Direzione Memorie. 1 act. Sipario, 21 (November, 1966), 55-62. In Italian.

454. _____. Riflessi di conoscenza. 2 acts. Sipario, 263 (March, 1968), 53-64. In Italian.

455. Augier, Emile, 1820-1889. Giboyer's Son. 5 acts, comedy. Drama, 1 (November, 1911), 31-137. Benedict Papot, translator.

456. _____. Marriage of Olympe. 3 acts. Drama, 5 (August, 1915), 358-439. Barrett H. Clark, translator.

Aumont, Jean-Pierre see Shaw, I. 8227

457. Aurio, Alberto. Natale. 1 act. Il Dramma, 178 (January 15, 1934), 20-33. In Italian.

Auslander, Joseph, 1897- see Davidson, G. 2197

458. Austen, Jane, 1775-1817. Pride and Prejudice. 1 act. Plays, 16 (January, 1957), 37-48. AND Plays, 35 (February, 1976), 85-96. Olive J. Morley, adapter.

459. _____. Pride and Prejudice. 1 act. Plays, 10 (March, 1951), 66-79. AND Plays, 26 (April, 1967), 83-96. Deborah Newman, adapter.

460. Austin, Helen H. Almost Everyman. 1 act. Quarterly Journal of Speech, 5 (January, 1919), 45-53.

461. Austin, Mary Hunter, 1868-1934. The Man Who Didn't Believe in Christmas. 1 act. St. Nicholas, 45 (December, 1917), 156-162.

462. _____. Sekala Ka'ajma. 1 act, dance-drama. Theatre Arts, 13 (April, 1929), 267-278.

Austin, Paul Britten, translator see Aspenstrom, W. 424

463. Auto de los Reyes Magos. 1 act. Poet Lore, 39 (Summer, 1928), 306-309. Willis Knapp Jones, translator.

Autrusseau, Jacqueline, translator see Frisch, M. 3316

464. Averchenko, Arkadi, 1881-1925. Man with the Green Necktie; A Russian Comedy. 1 act. Golden Book, 17 (May, 1933), 449-453. Bernard Guilbert Guerney, translator.

465. Avermaete, Roger, 1893- . Les Papiers. 1 act. L'Avant Scène, 473 (June 1, 1971), 39-42. In French.

466. Axelrod, George, 1922- . The Seven Year Itch. 3 acts, comedy. Theatre Arts, 38 (January, 1954), 34-61.

467. Ayckbourn, Alan. Relatively Speaking. 2 acts, comedy. L'Avant Scène, 462 (December 15, 1970), 7-35. Eric Kahane, adapter. In French.

468. Ayme, Marcel, 1902- . Clerambard. 4 acts, comedy. L'Avant Scène (OST), 24 (May, 1950), 3-38. In French.

469. _____. Clerambard. 4 acts, comedy. Sipario, 5, 54 (October, 1950), 45-68. Flaminio Bollin, translator. In Italian.

470. _____. Clerambard. 2 acts, comedy. Theatre Arts, 42 (June, 1958), 26-51. Norman Denny and Alvin Sapinsley, adapters.

471. _____. Lucienne et le Boucher. 4 acts. Sipario, 4, 34 (February, 1949), 41-67. Giulio Cesare Castello, translator. In Italian.

472. _____. Les Oiseaux de Lune. 4 acts. L'Avant Scène, 135, 1-35. In French.

473. _____. Les Quatre Verites. 4 acts, comedy. L'Avant Scène, 91, 1-32. In French.

474. _____. Les Quatre Verites. 4 acts, comedy. Sipario, 11, 125 (September, 1956), 34-56. Cesare Vico Lodovici, translator. In Italian.

475. _____. La Tête des Autres. 3 acts, comedy. L'Avant Scène, 203 (September 1, 1959), 7-34. In French.

476. _____. La Tête des Autres. 4 acts. Sipario, 7, 79 (November, 1952), 32-55. Olga de Vellis Aillaud, translator. In Italian.

_____, adapter see Miller, A. 5849

Aza, Vital see Carrion, M. R. 1617

B

477. Babel, Isaac, 1894-1941. Marie. L'Avant Scène, 576 (December 1, 1975), 3-24. Lily Denis, adapter. In French.

478. _____. Maria. 1 act. Tri-Quarterly, 5 (1966), 10-36. Denis Caslon, translator

479. Bacchelli, Riccardo, 1891- . Il figlio di ettore. 3 acts, tragedy. Sipario, 13, 143 (March, 1958), 35-51. In Italian.

480. _____. Nostos. 2 parts. Sipario, 13, 143 (March, 1958), 52-59. In Italian.

481. _____. La Notte di un nevrastenico. 1 act. Il Dramma, n.s., 251/252 (August/September, 1957), 92-95. In Italian.

Baccolo, Luigi, translator see Sade, D.-A. F. de 7845

482. Bach, Marcus. Flag Stop. 1 act. Senior Scholastic, 52 (April 5, 1948), 18-21. AND Senior Scholastic, 60 (March 19, 1952), 36-37, 40-41, 43, 45.

Bachem, Michael, translator see Lenz, S. 4920

483. Bachmann, Ingeborg. Die Zikaden. 1 act. Sipario, 20, 229 (May, 1965), 55-64. Annamaria Carpi, translator. In Italian.

484. Bacon, Jean. La Colombe a Deux Têtes. 1 act. L'Avant Scène, 482 (November 1, 1971), 43-49. In French.

485. _____. Si Madame Me Permet. 1 act, comedy. L'Avant Scène, 189 (January 15, 1959), 33-39. In French.

486. Bacon, Josephine Dodge Daskam, 1876-1961. The First of October. 1 act, comedy. Harper's, 109 (October, 1904), 721-733.

487. _____. The Twilight of the Gods. 1 act. Forum, 53 (January, 1915), 7-20.

488. _____. The Wanderers. 1 act. Century, 62 (August, 1901), 583-589.

Bacon, Lucille, translator see Pshibishvsky, S. 7322

489. Badessi, Giancarlo and Giancarlo Cobelli. La caserma della fate. Sipario, 226 (February, 1965), 50-62. In Italian.

Badet, Andre de, 1891- , translator see Benavente, J. 749

Badia, Gilbert, translator see Brecht, B. 1287

_____, translator see Walser, M. 9195

490. Bagg, Robert. The Pope's Right Knee. 1 act. Massachusetts Review, 10 (Summer, 1969), 570-582.

491. Bagnara, Mario, 1935- . Attacco alla coscienza. 1 act. Il Dramma, 46, no. 3 (March, 1970), 101-115. In Italian.

492. _____. Cosma Perduto. 3 acts, comedy. Il Dramma, (April, 1975), 25-49. In Italian.

Bagstad, Anna Emilia, translator see Fulda, L. 3339

_____, translator see Moratin, J. 6214

_____, translator see Rostand, E. 7719

493. Baher, Constance Whitman. Cinder-Rabbit. 1 act. Plays, 26 (March, 1967), 61-69.

494. _____. The Enchanted Princess. 1 act. Plays, 24 (May, 1965), 55-65.

495. _____. Robin Hood Outwits the Sheriff. 1 act. Plays, 25 (February, 1966), 51-60.

496. _____. The Trial of Manfred the Magician. 1 act. Plays, 26 (December, 1966), 59-68.

497. _____. Vanessa and the Blue Dragon. 1 act. Plays, 28 (November, 1968), 53-60.

498. Bahr, Hermann, 1863-1934. The Mongrel. 1 act. Living Age, 324 (January 3, 1925), 70-76.

499. _____. The Poor Fool. 1 act. One-Act Play Magazine, 2 (May, 1938), 3-33. Mrs. Frank E. Washburn-Freund, translator.

500. _____. Substitute Government, A Satire on Post-War Ethics. 1 act. Living Age, 316 (February 17, 1923), 402-406.

501. Bailac, Généviève. Montemor, ou La Couronne et le Sang. 5 acts. L'Avant Scène, 154, 1-19. In French.

502. Bailly, André. La commedia nella commedia. 1 act. Il Dramma, 96 (August 15, 1930), 44-45. In Italian.

503. Bailey, Anne Howard. The Christmas Visitor. 1 act. Plays, 28 (December, 1968), 1-10.

504. ———. The Narrow Man. 2 acts. The Writer, 70 (April, 1957), 22-28.

505. Bailey, Carolyn Sherwin. The Foolish Mouse. 1 act. Delineator, 75 (June, 1910), 557.

506. Bailey, Frederick. Set It Down with Gold on Lasting Pillars. 1 act. The Scene, 1 (1972), 79-85.

507. Bailey, Helen Cheyney. The Demigod. 1 act. Drama, 32 (November, 1918), 505-514.

508. Bailey, Paul. A Worthy Guest. 2 acts. Plays and Players, 21 (July, 1974), 55-65.

509. Baird, George M. P. The Waiting Room. 1 act. Drama, 15 (October, 1924), 6-9.

510. Bajard and Vailler. La tredicesima sedia. 3 acts. Il Dramma, 96 (August 15, 1930), 4-29. In Italian.

511. Bajini, Sandro. Eugenio, o Il trionfo della salute. 3 acts. Sipario, 220-221 (August-September, 1964), 81-96. In Italian.

———, translator see Anouilh, J. 261

512. Bakeless, John. Mrs. Malvolio. 1 act. Scholastic, 23 (October 28, 1933), 4-6, 30-31.

513. Bakeless, Katherine Little, 1895- . Good Words for a Stirring Tune. 1 act. Plays, 4 (May, 1945), 74-79.

514. ———. Most Memorable Voyage. 1 act. Plays, 15 (October, 1955), 32-42.

515. ———. My Patriot Mother. 1 act. Plays, 18 (February, 1959), 21-34.

516. ———. A Nation's Song Is Born. 1 act. Plays, 3 (December, 1943), 70-77.

517. Baker, Gretta. Guaranteed Forever. 1 act. Senior Scholastic, 45 (December 11, 1944), 17-18.

518. Baker, Jane L. A Challenge to Young America. 1 act. Plays, 3 (October, 1943), 65-69.

519. Baker, Jessie M. The Crowning of the Queen. 1 act. St. Nicholas, 42 (May, 1915), 634-637.

520. Baker, Nina Brown. A Dish for the Colonel. 1 act. Plays, 3 (November, 1943), 18-25.

521. ———. Juarez the Just. 1 act. Plays, 2 (December, 1942), 7-17.

522. Baker, Virgil L. When the Sap's a-Runnin'. 1 act. One-Act Play Magazine, 3 (February, 1940), 112-143.

523. Baker, William M. Circe's Auction. 1 act. St. Nicholas, 12 (February, 1885), 308-311.

524. Bal, Claude. Si la Foule Nous Voit Ensemble . . . 5 acts. L'Avant Scène, 216, 8-29. In French.

525. Balachova, Tania, 1902- . Lady Macbeth. 1 act. L'Avant Scène, 408 (August, 1968), 37-42. In French.

526. ———. La Matinée d'un Homme de Lettres. 1 act. L'Avant Scène, 89, 39-44. In French.

527. ——— and Georges Arest. Nausicaa du Mackensie. 2 acts. L'Avant Scène (OST), 53 (December, 1951), 1-30. In French.

Balchin, Nigel see Millar, R. 5833

528. Balderston, John Lloyd, 1889- . A Morality Play for the Leisure Class. 1 act. Golden Book, 10 (September, 1929), 87-90.

529. ———. A Morality Play for the Leisure Class. 1 act. Harper's, 141 (September, 1920), 491-497.

Baldick, Robert, translator see Schehade, G. 8022

530. Baldini, Gabriele, 1919- . Le muse. 1 act. Il Dramma, 45, no. 10 (July, 1969), 65-70. In Italian.

531. Balducci, Alfredo, 1920- . I dadi e l'archibugio. 3 acts. Sipario, 172-173 (August-September, 1960), 57-79. In Italian.

532. ———. Don Giovanni al rogo. 2 parts. Il Dramma, n.s., 374/375 (November/December, 1967), 111-131. In Italian.

533. ———. La Nuova isola. Sipario, 337 (June, 1974), 62-80. In Italian.

Balf, Miriam see Rubio, E. 7780

534. Balk, Theo. Zwischenspiel Im Himmel. 1 act. Das Wort, 2 (August, 1936), 58-64. In German.

535. Balla, Giacomo, 1871-1958. Per comprendere il pianto. Sipario, 260 (December, 1967), 94. In Italian.

Balla, Ignazio, translator see Fodor, L. 3178, 3180, 3182

_____, translator see Herczeg, F. 4066

_____, translator see Molnar, F. 6135, 6140, 6151, 6166

_____, translator see Szecsen, S. 8679

536. Ballesteros, Antonio Martinez. The Best of All Possible Worlds. 3 acts. First Stage, 5 (Fall, 1966), 172-193. Sevilla Gross and Henry F. Salerno, translators.

537. _____. The Position. 1 act. Modern International Drama, 4 (Spring, 1971), 7-12. Robert Lima, translator.

538. _____. The Straw Men. 1 act. Modern International Drama, 3 (September, 1969), 41-49. Leon F. Lyday, translator.

539. Balzac, Honore de, 1799-1850. Le Faiseur. 2 parts. L'Avant Scène, 524 (September 1, 1973), 7-39. In French.

540. Bangs, John Kendrick, 1862-1922. The Bicyclers. 1 act, farce. Harper's, 91 (November, 1895), 961-968.

541. _____. A Chafing-Dish Party. 1 act. Harper's, 94 (December, 1896), 159-166.

542. _____. A Dramatic Evening. 1 act, farce. Harper's, 90 (December, 1894), 158-164.

543. _____. The Fatal Message. 1 act, farce. Harper's, 92 (February, 1896), 479-485.

544. _____. The Golfiacs. 1 act, farce. Harper's, 95 (June, 1897), 151-159.

545. _____. The Minister's First "At Home." 1 act, farce. Ladies' Home Journal, 26 (March, 1909), 16, 90-91.

546. _____. A Proposal Under Difficulties. 1 act, farce. Harper's, 91 (June, 1895), 151-160.

547. _____. The Real Thing. 1 act, farce. Harper's Bazaar,

43 (February, 1909), 134-143.

548. Banti, Anna. Artemisia. 3 acts. Botteghe Oscure, 24 (Autumn, 1959), 297-361. In Italian.

549. Banville, Theodore de, 1823-1891. Gringoire, the Ballad Monger. 1 act, comedy. Poet Lore, 27 (Spring, 1916), 129-163. Arthur B. Myrick, translator.

550. Barabas, Paul. E facile per gli uomini. 3 acts. Il Dramma, 241 (September 1, 1936), 2-22. In Italian.

551. Baraldi, Ita. Dopo la recita. 1 act. Il Dramma, 428/429/430 (June 15, July 1, July 15, 1944), 55-57. In Italian.

552. Barasch, Norman, 1922- , and Carroll Moore, 1913- . Make a Million. 3 acts. Theatre Arts, 43 (June, 1959), 25-48.

553. _____. Send Me No Flowers. 3 acts. Theatre Arts, 45 (June, 1961), 33-57.

Barbaro, Elena, translator see Witkiewicz, S. I. 5914

Barbaro, Umberto, 1902- , translator see Schnitzler, A. 8060, 8061, 8062, 8071

554. Barbeau, Jean. Goglu. 1 act. Canadian Theatre Review, 11 (Summer, 1976), 102-117.

555. _____. Solange. 1 act. Canadian Theatre Review, 11 (Summer, 1976), 93-101.

556. Barbee, Lindsey. The Boston Tea Party. 1 act. Plays, 5 (May, 1946), 42-47.

557. _____. Columbus Sails the Sea. 1 act. Plays, 4 (October, 1944), 44-51.

558. _____. Dolly Saves the Picture. 1 act. Plays, 5 (February, 1946), 49-57.

559. _____. The Dream Comes True. 1 act. Plays, 3 (May, 1944), 56-57.

560. _____. First! 1 act. Plays, 4 (April, 1945), 72-76.

561. _____. The First Day of April. 1 act. Plays, 27 (April, 1968), 45-50.

562. _____. The Flag of the United States. 1 act. Plays, 4 (February, 1945), 42-46.

563. _____. The Four Extra Valentines. 1 act. Plays, 5 (February, 1946), 42-46.

564. _____. Happy New Year. 1 act. Plays, 4 (January, 1945), 60-63.

565. _____. The Holly Hangs High. 1 act. Plays, 5 (December, 1945), 34-40.

566. _____. Hunt for the Violet. 1 act. Plays, 4 (May, 1945), 36-40.

567. _____. It's a Magic Time. 1 act. Plays, 5 (October, 1945), 53-55.

568. _____. A Letter to Lincoln. 1 act. Plays, 5 (January, 1946), 45-50.

569. _____. Martha Has a Vision. 1 act. Plays, 3 (February, 1944), 43-46.

570. _____. Melissa's Muffins. 1 act. Plays, 10 (January, 1951), 48-52.

571. _____. So Proud to Serve. 1 act. Plays, 5 (December, 1945), 65-69.

572. _____. Sword in Hand. 1 act. Plays, 5 (February, 1946), 23-32.

573. _____. Thirteen and Hallowe'en. 1 act. Plays, 4 (October, 1944), 52-53.

574. _____. A Valentine's Dance. 1 act. Plays, 4 (February, 1945), 39-42.

575. Barbour, Ralph Henry. The Conspirators, A Christmas Play. 1 act. New England Magazine, 37 (December, 1907), 425-432.

Barclay, Theresa, translator see Adam, V. 51

576. Barclay, Sir Thomas, 1853-1941. Gambetta and Bismark: A Dialogue. 1 act. Fortnightly, 120 (June, 1923), 909-919.

577. _____. Gambetta and Dr. Stresemann. 1 act. Fortnightly, 120 (November, 1923), 765-773.

578. _____. Gambetta and Monsieur Poincaré. 1 act. Fortnightly, 120 (July, 1923), 1-7.

579. _____. Gambetta Calls on Signor Mussolini. 1 act. Fortnightly, 120 (December, 1923), 872-878.

580. _____. Gambetta's Love Story. 3 acts. Fortnightly, 120 (July, 1923), 215-232.

581. _____. Gambetta's Shade and M. Poincaré Again. 1 act. Fortnightly, 120 (October, 1923), 600-605.

582. _____. In Gremio Decorum: A Super-Historical Phantasy. 1 act. 19th Century, 79 (March, 1916), 554-568.

583. _____. The Sands of Fate: Berlin, July 24 to 31, 1914, A Historical Phantasy. 3 acts. 19th Century, 78 (August, 1915), 444-476.

Bardi, Gino, translator see Miller, A. 5843

Barer, Marshall see Thompson, J. 8847

584. Barillet, Pierre, 1923- , and Jean-Pierre Grédy, 1920- . Ami-Ami. 3 acts. Il Dramma, n.s., 174 (February 1, 1953), 9-40. Paola Ojetti, translator. In Italian.

585. _____. Le Chinois. 3 acts, comedy. L'Avant Scène, 322 (November 15, 1964), 47-76. In French.

586. _____. Les Choutes. 4 acts, comedy. L'Avant Scène, 274 (October 15, 1962), 43-72. In French.

587. _____. Le Don D'Adele. 4 acts. L'Avant Scène (OST), 19 (February, 1950), 3-38. In French.

588. _____. Fleur de Cactus. 2 acts, comedy. L'Avant Scène, 322 (November 15, 1964), 11-46. In French.

589. _____. Folle Amanda. 2 acts, comedy. L'Avant Scène, 482 (November 1, 1971), 7-39. In French.

590. _____. L'Or et la Paille. 3 acts, comedy. L'Avant Scène, 142, 1-38. In French.

591. _____. Peau de Vache. L'Avant Scène, 577 (December 15, 1975), 3-40. In French.

592. _____. 4 Pièces sur Jardin: La Lampe de Gallé Betty de la Ponche. Toréador. Joyeux Noël. 1 act each. L'Avant Scène, 425 (May 1, 1969), 7-36. In French.

593. _____. La Reine Blanche. 3 acts, comedy. L'Avant Scène, 87, 1-33. In French.

594. _____. Une Rose au Petit Dejeuner. 3 acts, comedy. L'Avant Scène, 532 (January 1, 1974), 7-39. In French.

_____, adapter see Shaffer, P. 8165, 8170

_____, adapter see Sheridan, R. B. 8247

_____, translator see Slade, B. 8310

595. Baring, Maurice, 1874-1945. After Euripides's Electra. 1 act, comedy. Golden Book, 17 (March, 1933), 257-261.

596. _____. Calypso. 1 act, comedy. London Mercury, 18 (July, 1928), 245-248.

597. _____. Don Juan's Failure. 1 act. Golden Book, 13 (April, 1931), 69-71.

598. _____. The Double Game. 3 acts, tragedy. English Review, 9 (September, 1911), 252-289.

599. _____. The Rehearsal. 1 act. Golden Book, 9 (March, 1929), 104-106.

Barini, Tilde, translator see Boal, A. and G. Guarnieri 1029

600. Barker, Colleen and Johnnie Medina. Nursery Tale Trio: The Little Red Hen. Three Billy Goats Gruff. Chicken-Little. 1 act each. Plays, 30 (January, 1971), 69-72.

601. Barker, George, 1913- . In the Shade of the Old Apple Tree. 1 act. New World Writing, 14 (1958), 286-317.

602. Barker, Howard. Heroes of Labour. 1 act. Gambit, 8 (No. 29, 1976), 49-76.

603. _____. Stripwell. 2 acts. Plays and Players, 23 (November-December, 1975), 39-50; 41-50.

604. Barlach, Ernest. The Poor Relation. 5 acts. Prisim International, 7 (Spring, 1968), 9-80. Marketa Goetz Stankiewicz, translator.

605. Barnes, Djuna, 1892- . A Passion Play. 1 act. Others, 4 (February, 1918), 5-17.

606. _____. She Tells Her Daughter. 1 act. Smart Set, 72 (November, 1923), 77-80.

607. _____. Three from the Earth. 1 act. Little Review, 6 (November, 1919), 3-15.

608. Barnes, Eleanor. Close to the Wind. 1 act. Poet Lore, 40 (Winter, 1929), 588-596.

609. Barnes, Peter, 1931- . The Ruling Class. 2 acts. L'Avant Scène, 517 (May 1, 1973), 7-42. Claude Roy, translator. In French.

610. ———. The Ruling Class. 2 acts. Sipario, 26, 305 (October, 1971), 50-80. Maria Silvia Codecasa, translator. In Italian.

611. Barnett, Grace T. Treasure in the Smith House. 1 act. Plays, 9 (May, 1950), 43-52. AND Plays, 20 (February, 1961), 63-72. AND Plays, 32 (January, 1973), 31-39.

Barnstone, Willis, translator see Neruda, P. 6464

———, translator see Vega, L. de 9056

612. Baroja, Pio, 1872-1956. L'Orrendo delitto di Penaranda del Campo. 1 act, comedy. Il Dramma, 48 (November-December, 1972), 125-137. Elena Clementelli, translator. In Italian.

613. Barr, Betty and Gould Stevens. The Good and Obedient Young Man, A Play in the Japanese Manner. 1 act. Theatre Arts, 15 (February, 1931), 134-139.

614. Barr, June. An April Fool Surprise. 1 act. Plays, 11 (April, 1952), 59-62.

615. ———. Buried Treasure. 1 act. Plays, 12 (February, 1953), 58-61. AND Plays, 24 (March, 1965), 77-80.

616. ———. The Lazy Little Raindrop. 1 act. Plays, 9 (March, 1950), 68-71.

617. ———. Roddy's Candy Bar. 1 act. Plays, 11 (May, 1952), 63-66.

618. ———. A Winter Thaw. 1 act. Plays, 10 (January, 1951), 64-68.

619. ———, adapter. The Lion and the Mouse. 1 act. Plays, 10 (October, 1950), 64-66.

620. ———, adapter. Old Mother Hubbard. 1 act. Plays, 9 (January, 1950), 57-62.

621. ———, adapter. Rapunzel. 1 act. Plays, 9 (October, 1949), 49-53.

622. Barr, Mark. The Man and the Turtle. 1 act. Century, 120 (Winter, 1930), 18-28.

Barrault, Jean-Louis see Gide, A. 3506

623. Barrett, Wilton Agnew. Evangel. 1 act. Poetry, 29 (February, 1927), 259-265.

624. Barrie, Sir James Matthew, 1860-1937. Barbara's Wedding; An Echo of the War. 1 act. Reveille, 1 (August, 1918), 20-33.

625. ———. The Little Minister. 1 act. Plays, 29 (February, 1970), 83-95. Adele Thane, adapter.

626. ———. Mary Rose. 3 acts. Il Dramma, n.s., 147/148 (December 15, 1951/January 1, 1952), 68-99. Ada Salvatore, translator. In Italian.

627. ———. Quality Street. 1 act. Plays, 18 (March, 1959), 87-96. Lewy Olfson, adapter.

628. ———. Rosalind. 1 act. Il Dramma, 59 (February 1, 1929), 33-42. In Italian.

629. ———. Shall We Join the Ladies? 1 act. Il Dramma, n.s., 161 (July 15, 1952), 55-61. Alessandro Benni, translator. In Italian.

630. ———. The Truth About the Russian Dancers. 1 act. Dance Perspectives, 14 (Spring, 1962), 11-30.

631. ———. The Wedding Guest. 4 acts. Fortnightly, 74 Supplement (December, 1900), 1-42.

632. Barrier, Maurice. L'Examinatoire. 1 act. L'Avant Scène, 415 (December 1, 1968), 33-38. In French.

633. ———. L'Explication. 1 act. L'Avant Scène, 441 (January 15, 1970), 33-35. In French.

634. ———. Au Restaurant. 1 act. L'Avant Scène, 438 (December 1, 1969), 38-43. In French.

635. Barrington, Margaret. The Bear. 1 act. Dublin Magazine, 1 (March, 1924), 731-735.

636. Barrios, Eduardo. Papa and Mama. 1 act, satire. Poet Lore, 33 (Summer, 1922), 286-290. Willis Knapp Jones, translator.

637. Barrows, Marjorie. The Valentine Tree. 1 act. Plays, 17 (February, 1958), 67-71.

Barry, Christiane, adapter see Ford, J. 3217

638. Barry, Philip, 1896-1949. Holiday. 3 acts. Il Dramma, 387 (October 1, 1942), 5-32. Vinicio Marinucci, transla-

tor. In Italian.

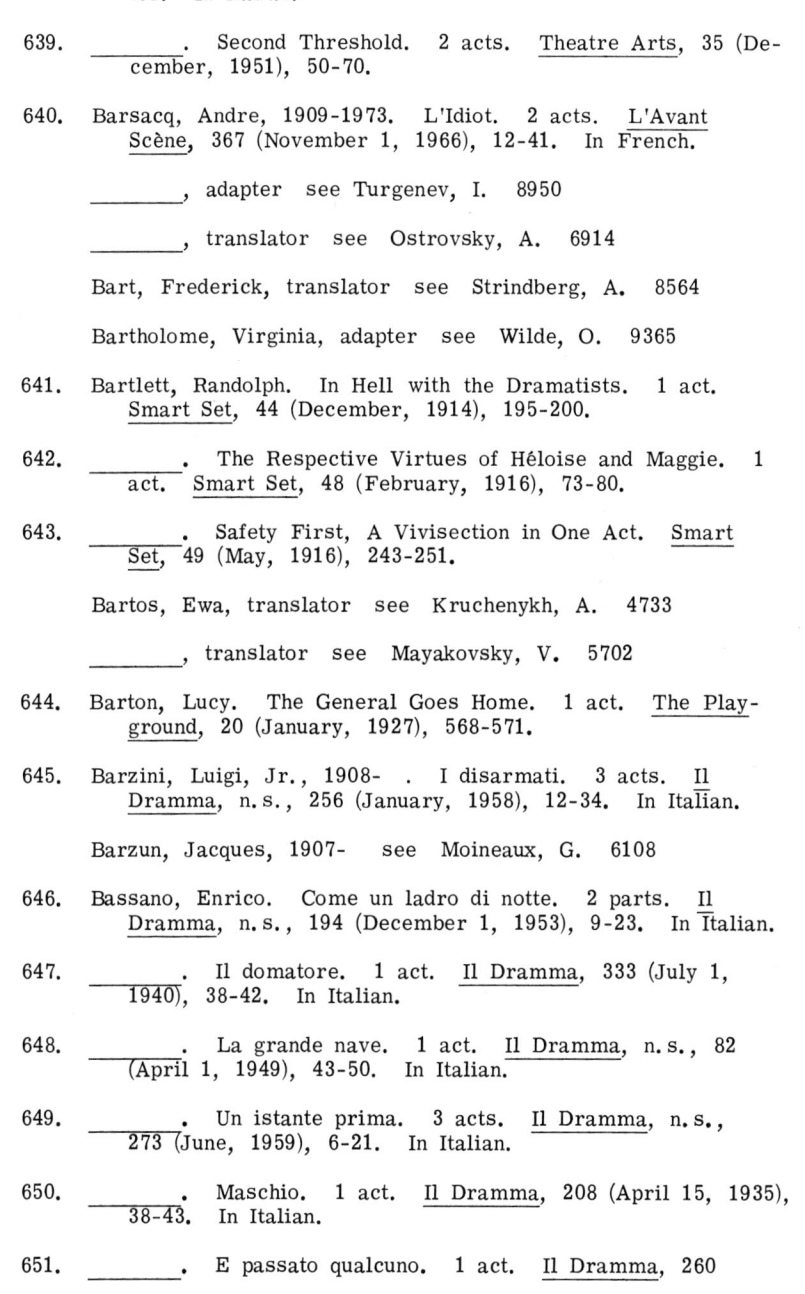

639. _____. Second Threshold. 2 acts. Theatre Arts, 35 (December, 1951), 50-70.

640. Barsacq, Andre, 1909-1973. L'Idiot. 2 acts. L'Avant Scène, 367 (November 1, 1966), 12-41. In French.

_____, adapter see Turgenev, I. 8950

_____, translator see Ostrovsky, A. 6914

Bart, Frederick, translator see Strindberg, A. 8564

Bartholome, Virginia, adapter see Wilde, O. 9365

641. Bartlett, Randolph. In Hell with the Dramatists. 1 act. Smart Set, 44 (December, 1914), 195-200.

642. _____. The Respective Virtues of Héloise and Maggie. 1 act. Smart Set, 48 (February, 1916), 73-80.

643. _____. Safety First, A Vivisection in One Act. Smart Set, 49 (May, 1916), 243-251.

Bartos, Ewa, translator see Kruchenykh, A. 4733

_____, translator see Mayakovsky, V. 5702

644. Barton, Lucy. The General Goes Home. 1 act. The Playground, 20 (January, 1927), 568-571.

645. Barzini, Luigi, Jr., 1908- . I disarmati. 3 acts. Il Dramma, n.s., 256 (January, 1958), 12-34. In Italian.

Barzun, Jacques, 1907- see Moineaux, G. 6108

646. Bassano, Enrico. Come un ladro di notte. 2 parts. Il Dramma, n.s., 194 (December 1, 1953), 9-23. In Italian.

647. _____. Il domatore. 1 act. Il Dramma, 333 (July 1, 1940), 38-42. In Italian.

648. _____. La grande nave. 1 act. Il Dramma, n.s., 82 (April 1, 1949), 43-50. In Italian.

649. _____. Un istante prima. 3 acts. Il Dramma, n.s., 273 (June, 1959), 6-21. In Italian.

650. _____. Maschio. 1 act. Il Dramma, 208 (April 15, 1935), 38-43. In Italian.

651. _____. E passato qualcuno. 1 act. Il Dramma, 260

(June 15, 1937), 25-29. In Italian.

652. _____. Il pellicano ribelle. 2 acts. Il Dramma, n.s., 205 (May 15, 1954), 9-21. In Italian.

653. _____. I ragazzi mangiano i fiori. 3 acts. Il Dramma, 363 (October 1, 1941), 7-24. In Italian.

654. _____. Sole per due. 3 acts. Il Dramma, 308 (June 15, 1939), 4-23. In Italian.

655. _____. La tua carne. 3 acts. Il Dramma, n.s., 345/346 (June/July, 1965), 14-35. In Italian.

656. _____. Uno cantava per tutti. 3 acts. Il Dramma, n.s., 67/68/69 (August 15, September 1/15, 1948), 41-59. In Italian.

657. _____, and Dario G. Martini. Vento d'Agosto. 1 act. Il Dramma, n.s., 292 (January, 1961), 32-41. In Italian.

658. Basshe, Emjo. Snickering Horses (Log of a Journey). 1 act. One-Act Play Magazine, 2 (November, 1938), 435-452.

659. Basudeb, Sree. Aunt Lasmi. 1 act, tragedy. Poet Lore, 35 (Spring, 1924), 101-113.

660. _____. "Still It Is Spring". 1 act, tragedy. Poet Lore, 42 (Spring, 1935), 364-381.

661. Bataille, Henry, 1872-1922. La dichiarazione. 1 act. Il Dramma, 70 (July 15, 1929), 40-45. In Italian.

662. _____. Maman Colibri'. 4 acts. Il Dramma, n.s., 169 (November 15, 1952), 9-38. Olga De Vellis Aillaud, translator. In Italian.

663. _____. Le Songe d'un Sois D'Amour. Vers et Prose, 21 (April-June, 1910), 87-122. In French.

664. Batchelder, Frank Roe. We Choose a Name. 1 act. Smart Set, 10 (June, 1903), 73-75.

665. Bate, Lucy. The Great Silkie of Sule Skerry. Scripts, 1 (June, 1972), 111-127.

666. Bates, Arlo. A Business Meeting. 1 act. Ladies' Home Journal, 20 (March, 1903), 15.

667. _____. The Interrupted Proposal. 1 act. Ladies' Home Journal, 23 (February, 1906), 10.

668. Bates, Joshua. The Decree Nisi. 1 act. Smart Set, 28

(July, 1909), 117-124.

669. Bates, William Oscar, 1852-1924. Asaph. 1 act, comedy. Drama, 10 (March-April, 1920), 227-235.

670. _____. Dryad and the Deacon. 1 act. Drama, 10 (March-April, 1920), 217-219.

671. _____. In the Light of the Manger; A Prophetic Fantasy. 1 act. Drama, 11 (December, 1920), 102-103.

672. _____. Merry Mount; A Comedy of New England Beginnings. 3 acts. Drama, 10 (July, August, September, 1920), 335-347.

Batistich, John J., translator see Vojnovich, I. 9169

Batlle, Carlos de, adapter see Feliu y Condina, J. 2980

673. Baty, Gaston. Crime et Châtiment. 3 parts. Petite Illustration, 186 (September 2, 1933), 1-30. In French.

674. _____. Madame Bovary. 3 parts. Petite Illustration, 195 (November 28, 1936), 1-36. In French.

Baudrillard, Jean, translator see Brecht, B. 1287

675. Bauer, Josef Martin, 1901- . Parla Kellermann. 1 act, monologue. Il Dramma, n.s., 130 (April 1, 1951), 53-57. Dante Raiteri, translator. In Italian.

Baukage, Hilmar, translator see Chekhov, A. 1765

676. Baum, Lyman Frank, 1856-1919. The Wizard of Oz. 1 act. Plays, 22 (April, 1963), 83-96. AND Plays, 32 (April, 1973), 29-42. AND Plays, 36 (November, 1976), 59-72. Lynne Sharon Schwartz, adapter.

677. _____. The Wonderful Wizard of Oz. 6 acts. Plays, 25 (March, 1966), 49-58. Frances Mapp, adapter.

678. _____. The Wizard of Oz. 1 act. Plays, 35 (February, 1976), 55-63. Lewis Mahlmann and David Cadwalader Jones, adapters.

679. Baumer, Marie. For Lack of a Nail. 1 act. Plays, 2 (October, 1942), 63-68.

Baxandall, Lee, translator see Brecht, B. 1283

680. Baxter, David. Will Somebody Please Say Something? 2 acts. Plays and Players, 14 (April, 1967), 27-42, 61-64.

681. Baxter, James K., 1926- . The Band Rotunda. 2 acts. Landfall, 22 (March, 1968), 27-55.

682. _____. Jack Winter's Dream. 1 act. Landfall, 10 (September, 1956), 180-194.

683. Bayley, Jefferson. Olympus Farewell. 3 acts. First Stage, 2 (Fall, 1963), 336-362.

684. Beach, Marcia Moray. Mayday! 1 act. Plays, 31 (May, 1972), 17-26.

685. _____. On the Fence. 1 act. Plays, 10 (March, 1951), 33-41. AND Plays, 21 (May, 1962), 45-53.

686. Bealmear, J. H. Dr. Leviticus and the Wicked Imp. 1 act. Plays, 26 (January, 1967), 57-64.

687. _____, adapter. The Covetous Councilman. 1 act. Plays, 27 (May, 1968), 53-58.

688. Beatty, Jerome, Jr. Yes, Virginia, There Is a South Pole Santa Claus. 1 act. Collier's, 136 (December 23, 1955), 70, 72-74.

689. Beatty, Jessica. Everyday Fairies. 1 act. Woman's Home Companion, 42 (May, 1915), 38, 56-57.

690. Beaumarchais, Pierre Augustin Caron de, 1732-1799. Le Barbier de Seville, ou La Précaution Inutile. 4 acts, comedy. L'Avant Scène, 457 (October 1, 1970), 7-37. In French.

691. Beaumont, Arthur. The Seven Little Dwarfs. 1 act. Everybody's Magazine, 1 (September, 1899), 47-55.

Beaumont, Paule de, adapter see Christie, A. 1825

692. Bebnone, Palou. Kaltouma. 1 act. L'Avant Scène, 327 (February 1, 1965), 33-39. In French.

Beccari, Gilberto, translator see Alvarez Quintero, S. and J. Alvarez Quintero 157, 161, 162, 163, 166, 169, 170, 172

_____, translator see Benavente y Martinez, J. 742, 748

_____, translator see Garcia-Alvarez, E., and P. Munoz-Seca 3372, 3373

_____, translator see Martinez Sierra, G. 5627, 5633

_____, translator see Munoz-Seca, P. 6297

_____, translator see Sevilla, L. F. de and R. Sepulveda 8159

693. Beck, Julian and Judith Malina. The Legacy of Cain: Favela. Scripts, 1 (November, 1971), 5-16.

694. Beckett, Samuel, 1906- . Breath. 1 act. Gambit, 4 (No. 16), 5-9.

695. _____. Cascando. 1 act. Evergreen Review, 7 (May-June, 1963), 47-57.

696. _____. Ceneri. 1 act. Il Dramma, n.s., 282 (March, 1960), 33-40. Amleto Micozzi, translator. In Italian.

697. _____. La Dernière Bande. 1 act. L'Avant Scène, 222, 25-28. In French.

698. _____. Eh Joe, A Television Play. Evergreen Review, 13 (January, 1969), 43-46.

699. _____. Embers. 1 act. L'Avant Scène, 313 (June 15, 1964), 21-25. In French.

700. _____. Embers. 1 act. Evergreen Review, 3 (November-December, 1959), 28-41.

701. _____. Endgame. 1 act. Spectaculum, 2 (1959), 7-42. In German.

702. _____. Fin de Partie. 1 act. L'Avant Scène, 156, 7-22. In French.

703. _____. Happy Days. 2 acts. L'Avant Scène, 313 (June 15, 1964), 10-19. In French.

704. _____. Happy Days. 2 acts. Spectaculum, 5 (1963), 7-31. Erika Tophoven and Elmar Tophoven, translators. In German.

705. _____. Kommen und Gehen. 1 act. Spectaculum, 9 (1966), 9-11. Erika Tophoven and Elmar Tophoven, translators. In German.

706. _____. Krapp's Last Tape. 1 act. Evergreen Review, 2 (Summer, 1958), 13-24.

707. _____. Krapp's Last Tape. 1 act. Spectaculum, 3 (1960), 57-65. In German.

708. _____. Play. 1 act. Evergreen Review, 8 (December,

1964), 43-47.

709. _____. Play. 1 act. Spectaculum, 6 (1963), 9-19. Erika Tophoven and Elmar Tophoven, translators. In German.

710. _____. Waiting for Godot. 2 acts. Theatre Arts, 40 (August, 1956), 36-61.

711. _____. Words and Music. 1 act. Evergreen Review, 6 (November-December, 1962), 34-43.

_____, translator see Pinget, R. 7168, 7169

712. Becque, Henri, 1837-1899. The Crows. 4 acts, comedy. Drama, 2 (February, 1912), 14-126. Benedict Papot, translator.

713. _____. La Navette. 1 act, comedy. L'Avant Scène, 133, 27-35. In French.

714. Becquer, Gustavo Adolfo, 1836-1870. Jealousy. 1 act. Poet Lore, 45 (Nos. 3-4, 1939), 326-333. George H. Daugherty, Jr., translator.

715. Bedos, Guy, Jean-Loup Dabadie, 1938- , and Christopher Frank, 1942- . Guy Bedos/Sophie Daumier; 29 Sketches. L'Avant Scène, 538 (April 1, 1974), 7-31. In French.

Beebe, Beatrice B., translator see Kotzebue, A. F. F. von 4693-4697

716. Beer, Jean de, 1911- . Daniele, Fille de Dieu. 3 parts. L'Avant Scène, 76 (April 10, 1953), 11-33. In French.

717. Beer, Thomas, 1889-1940. Bud on Nantucket Island. 1 act. Scribner's, 91 (January, 1932), 43-47.

718. Beerbohm, Max, 1872-1956. Savonarola. 4 acts, tragedy. English Review, 28 (March, 1919), 188-201.

719. _____. Savonarola. 4 acts, tragedy. Living Age, 301 (April 12, 1919), 98-112.

720. _____. A Social Success. 1 act, satire. Golden Book, 20 (July, 1934), 112-122.

721. Begovic, Milan. L'avventuriero davanti alla porta. 3 acts. Il Dramma, 379 (June 1, 1942), 7-35. Gian Capo, translator. In Italian.

722. Behan, Brendan, 1923-1964. The Big House. 1 act. Evergreen Review, 5 (September-October, 1961), 40-63.

723. _____. The Big House. 1 act. Irish Writing, 37 (Autumn, 1957), 17-34.

724. _____. The Big House. 1 act. Sipario, 337 (June, 1974), 52-61. Romeo de Baggis, translator. In Italian.

725. _____. The Hostage. 3 acts. L'Avant Scène, 266 (June 1, 1962), 10-31. Jean Paris and Jacqueline Sundstrom, adapters. In French.

726. _____. The Hostage. 3 acts. Theatre Arts, 46 (November, 1962), 25-56.

727. _____. The Quare Fellow. 1 act. Esquire, 48 (August, 1957), 24-33.

728. _____. Richard's Cork Leg. Sipario, 323 (April, 1973), 60-80. Annamaria Artini and Romeo de Baggis, translators. In Italian.

729. Behrman, Samuel Nathaniel, 1893- . Never Stretch Your Legs in a Taxi. 1 act. Smart Set, 62 (August, 1920), 71-76.

730. Beith, John Hay, 1876-1952. Cuor di leone. 3 acts. Il Dramma, 205 (March 1, 1935), 4-28. Geoffredo Pautassi, translator. In Italian.

Belamich, Andre, adapter see Garcia Lorca, F. 3376

Belitt, Ben, 1911- , translator see Lorca, F. G. 5043

731. Bell, Robert. Minor Characters. 1 act. The Butterfly, 2, n.s. (No. 4, 1899), 168-172.

732. Bellah, Melanie. The Blue Toadstool. 1 act. Plays, 9 (March, 1950), 65-68.

Bellak, Georges see Quentin, P. 7363

733. Bellido, José Maria. Fantastic Suite: Tremor No. 3: Sol-Fa for Butterflies. Modern International Drama, 6 (Spring, 1973), 41-56. Marcia C. Wellworth, translator.

734. _____. The Interrogation. 1 act. Drama and Theatre, 9 (Spring, 1971), 177-178. Calvin C. Smith, translator.

735. _____. Madam Takes a Bath. 5 acts. First Stage, 5 (Winter, 1966-67), 244-265. Adrienne S. Mandel, translator.

736. _____. The Scorpion. 1 act. Drama and Theatre, 11 (Spring, 1973), 171-188. Calvin C. Smith, translator.

737. Bellow, Saul, 1915- . Orange Soufflé. 1 act. Esquire, 64 (October, 1965), 131, 134, 136.

738. _____. A Wen. 1 act. Esquire, 62 (January, 1965), 72-74, 111.

739. _____. The Wrecker. 1 act. New World Writing, 6 (1954), 271-287.

740. Bellussi, Germano. Una lady per la morte. 1 act. Il Dramma, n.s., 334/335 (July/August, 1964), 110-115. In Italian.

Beltramo, Mario, translator see Coward, N. 2065, 2066, 2068

_____, translator see Priestley, J. B. 7299

741. Benavente y Martinez, Jacinto, 1866-1954. Bonds of Interest. 3 acts, comedy. Drama, 20 (November, 1915), 568-643. John Garrett Underhill, translator.

742. _____. Il cameriere di Don Giovanni. 1 act. Il Dramma, 63 (April 1, 1929), 41-43. Gilberto Beccari, translator. In Italian.

743. _____. The Governor's Wife. 3 acts, comedy. Poet Lore, 29 (Spring, 1918), 1-72. John Garrett Underhill, translator.

744. _____. His Widow's Husband. 1 act, comedy. Golden Book, 3 (March, 1926), 342-354. John Garrett Underhill, translator.

745. _____. No Smoking. 1 act, comedy. Drama, 7 (February, 1917), 78-88. John Garrett Underhill, translator.

746. _____. The Prince Who Learned Everything Out of Books. 3 acts. Poet Lore, 29 (Winter, 1918), 505-530. John Garrett Underhill, translator.

747. _____. Saturday Night, a Novel for the Stage. 1 act. Poet Lore, 29 (Summer, 1918), 127-193. John Garrett Underhill, translator.

748. _____. La senora ama. 3 acts. Il Dramma, 137 (May 1, 1932), 6-34. Gilberto Beccari, translator. In Italian.

749. _____. Le Sourire de la Joconde. 1 act. L'Avant Scène, 75 (March 20, 1953), 19-23. André de Badet, translator. In French.

750. Bence, Barry. Where's the Baby? 1 act. Learning With...,

3 (December, 1975), 27-28.

751. Benchley, Robert Charles, 1889-1945. Do I Hear Twenty Thousand? 1 act. Bookman [New York], 69 (March, 1929), 14-17.

752. Benco, Silvio, 1874- . L'uomo malato. 3 acts. Sipario, 333 (February, 1974), 60-80. In Italian.

753. Bene, Carmelo. Il rosa e il nero. 2 parts. Sipario, 21 (October, 1966), 27-41. In Italian.

754. Benedetti, Benedetto. Sospiro no. 3. 2 acts. Il Dramma, 48 (February-March, 1972), 61-85. In Italian.

755. Benedikt, Michael, 1935- . Finding Arthur's Organ, or No Man Is an Island. 1 act. Art and Literature, 7 (Winter, 1965), 180-184.

756. _____. The Orgy Bureau. 1 act. Chelsea, 22/23 (June, 1968), 94-110.

757. Benesch, Walter. Three Eschatologists and a Bassoon; a Five Act Play for Four Minutes. Trace, 62/63 (1967), 454-455.

758. Benet, Stephen Vincent, 1898-1943. A Child Is Born. 1 act. Saturday Review of Literature, 25 (December 26, 1942), 7-9.

759. _____. Listen to the People. 1 act. Scholastic, 40 (February 2-7, 1942), 17-19, 24.

760. _____. They Burned the Books. 1 act. Scholastic, 41 (September 14-19, 1942), 25-28.

761. _____. A Time to Reap. 1 act. Scholastic, 42 (May 3-8, 1943), 15-18.

762. Bengel, Ben. "All Aboard!" 1 act. Senior Scholastic, 45 (December 4, 1944), 11-13, 18.

763. _____. "All Aboard!" 1 act. Theatre Arts, 28 (September, 1944), 500-504.

764. _____. Plant in the Sun. 1 act. One-Act Play Magazine, 1 (December, 1937), 713-741.

765. Benjamin, Jerry. Nothing. 1 act. Works, 2 (Summer, 1970), 74-83.

766. Benn, Gottfried, 1886-1956. The Voice Behind the Curtain. New Directions, 22 (1970), 88-108. David Harris, translator.

767. Benner, Richard V. The Last of the Order. 2 acts. Drama at Calgary, 4 (April, 1969), 61-93.

768. _____. The Love Feast. 1 act. Drama at Calgary, 3 (No. 1, 1969), 71-84.

769. Bennett, Alan. Getting On. Plays and Players, 19 (January, 1972), 65-84.

770. Bennett, Arnold, 1867-1931. The Honeymoon. 3 acts, comedy. McClure's, 36 (March, April, 1911), 501-513; 688-706.

771. _____. What the Public Wants. 4 acts. English Review, 1 (Supplement (July, 1909), 1-63.

772. _____. What the Public Wants. 4 acts. Living Age, 262, 263 (September 25, October 2, 9, 16, 1909), 801-820; 32-44; 104-117; 172-180.

773. _____. What the Public Wants. 4 acts. McClure's, 34 (January, February, March, 1910), 301-315; 419-429; 499-517.

774. Bennett, Helen Cotts. Rumpelstiltsken. 1 act. Plays, 5 (November, 1945), 47-52.

775. _____. Sleeping Beauty. 1 act. Plays, 4 (November, 1944), 35-41. AND Plays, 20 (April, 1961), 59-64.

776. Bennett, Rowena. The Cat and the Queen. 1 act. Plays, 22 (February, 1963), 72-74.

777. _____. The First Easter Eggs. 1 act. Plays, 11 (April, 1952), 55-58.

778. _____. The French Doll's Surprise. 1 act. Plays, 25 (May, 1966), 85-86.

779. _____. Good Morning, Mr. Rabbit. 1 act. Plays, 17 (April, 1958), 72-74.

780. _____. Granny Goodman's Christmas. 1 act. Plays, 15 (December, 1955), 63-66.

781. _____. The Hare and the Tortoise. 1 act. Plays, 5 (January, 1946), 60-63.

782. _____. In the Witch's House. 1 act. Plays, 4 (March, 1945), 47-50.

783. _____. The King's Holiday. 1 act. Plays, 21 (October, 1961), 71-74.

784. _____. The Lion and the Mouse. 1 act. Plays, 5 (November, 1945), 53-55.

785. _____. The Littlest Artist. 1 act. Plays, 4 (February, 1945), 47-49.

786. _____. The Magic Weaver. 1 act. Plays, 20 (April, 1961), 71-74.

787. _____. The Man and the Satyr. 1 act. Plays, 5 (April, 1946), 67-69.

788. _____. The Mouse and the Country Mouse. 1 act. Plays, 5 (December, 1945), 56-59.

789. _____. Out of the Clock. 1 act. Plays, 4 (January, 1945), 54-56.

790. _____. Pixie in a Trap. 1 act. Plays, 22 (October, 1962), 72-74.

791. _____. The Prince and the Peddlers. 1 act. Plays, 22 (November, 1962), 75-78.

792. _____. The Runaway Pirate. 1 act. Plays, 10 (November, 1950), 54-56.

793. _____. Santa Claus and the Three Polar Bears. 1 act. Plays, 23 (December, 1963), 81-85.

794. _____. The Scarecrow and the Witch. 1 act. Plays, 20 (October, 1960), 57-62.

795. _____. School for Scamperers. 1 act. Plays, 20 (May, 1961), 69-72.

796. _____. The Shoemaker and the Elves. 1 act. Plays, 22 (December, 1962), 77-81.

797. _____. A Valentine for Mary. 1 act. Plays, 27 (February, 1968), 69-71.

798. _____. Visitors for Nancy Hanks. 1 act. Plays, 4 (January, 1945), 18-27.

799. _____. Waking the Daffodil. 1 act. Plays, 26 (April, 1967), 73-74.

800. _____. What Will the Toys Say? 1 act. Plays, 21 (December, 1961), 76-79.

801. _____. The Winter Hazards. 1 act. Plays, 22 (January, 1963), 69-72.

802. _____, adapter. The Child Who Was Made of Snow. 1 act. Plays, 26 (December, 1966), 72-74.

803. _____, adapter. Piccola. 1 act. Plays, 28 (December, 1968), 68-73.

804. _____, adapter. Snow-White and Rose-Red. 1 act. Plays, 24 (October, 1964), 53-64.

Benni, Alessandro, translator see Barrie, Sir J. M. 629

805. Benson, Edward Frederic, 1867-1940. The Gospel of the Gourmet: A Dialogue. 1 act. Fortnightly, 96 (July, 1911), 160-174.

806. Benson, Islay. Long Live Christmas. 1 act. Plays, 21 (December, 1961), 57-66.

807. Benson, Stuart and Mercedes De Acosta. For France: A War Episode in One Act. Outlook, 116 (July 25, 1917), 482-483.

808. Bentley, Eric, 1916- . Larry Parks' Day in Court. Scripts, 1 (March, 1972), 4-22.

809. _____. Roaring All Day Long: An Epilogue. New Directions, 16 (1956), 81-90.

_____, translator see Brecht, B. 1288, 1289

_____, translator see Chekhov, A. P. 1778

_____, translator see Gogol, N. 3600

_____, translator see Pirandello, L. 7195

810. Bentley, Leverett D. G. At Whitsuntide. 1 act. New England Magazine, n.s., 42 (May, 1910), 331-339.

811. Beolco, Angelo, 1502-1542. Fiorina. 3 parts. Il Dramma, 380 (June 15, 1942), 37-41. Cesco Cocco, translator. In Italian.

812. Bercovici, Eric. The Heart of Age. 1 act. New World Writing, 4 (1953), 105-118.

Beresford, J. D. see Craven, A. 2096

Bergerot, Henry, translator see Frisch, M. 3315, 3316

Bergil, Rene see Franck, P. 3256

813. Bergman, Hjalmar, 1883-1931. The Nobel Prize. 3 acts. Il Dramma, 401 (May 1, 1943), 7-30. Astrid Ahnfelt, translator. In Italian.

814. _____. Une Saga. 4 acts. L'Avant Scène, 199 (June 15, 1959), 11-34. Carl-Gustaf Bjurstrom and Roger Richard, adapters. In French.

815. _____. Saga. 4 acts. Il Dramma, n.s., 287/288 (August/September, 1960), 22-42. Giacomo Oreglia and Maripiera de Vecchis, translators. In Italian.

816. Bergman, Ingmar, 1918- . Peinture sur Bois. 1 act. L'Avant Scène, 199 (June 15, 1959), 36-41. Catherine Ekeram and Ulf Ekeram, adapters. In French.

817. _____. Pittura su legno. 1 act. Il Dramma, n.s., 283 (April, 1960), 49-58. Maripiera de Vecchis, translator. In Italian.

818. _____. Wood Painting, A Morality Play. 1 act. Tulane Drama Review, 6 (November, 1961), 140-152. Randoph Goodman and Leif Sjoberg, translators.

Beria, Giancarlo Galassi, translators see Clott, J. J. 1906

_____, translator see Gilroy, F. D. 3546

819. Berkeley, Reginald Cheyne, 1890- . Eight O'Clock. 1 act, tragedy. London Mercury, 6 (October, 1922), 591-601.

Berkey, Ralph, 1912- , see Denker, H. 2332

820. Berkman, Alexander. The Great Game. 1 act. The Blast, 1 (January 29, 1916), 8.

821. Bermel, Albert. One Leg Over the Wrong Wall. 3 acts. Drama and Theatre, 8 (Spring, 1970), 198-220.

822. _____. The Work-Out. 1 act. Gambit, 3 (1963), 5-17.

_____, translator see Jarry, A. 4450

_____, translator see Languirand, J. 4801

_____, translator see Molière 6118

823. Bernanos, Georges, 1888-1948. Dialogues des Carmelites. 2 parts, tragedy. L'Avant Scène, 337 (July 1, 1965), 10-36. In French.

Bernard, Edmond, translator see Caragiale, I. L. 1592

824. Bernard, Jean-Jacques, 1888- . Chic e moche. 1 act. Il Dramma, n.s., 253 (October, 1957), 29-33. Lucio Scialpi, translator. In Italian.

825. ———. La Leçon de Français. 1 act. L'Avant Scène, 155, 45-47. In French.

826. ———. Nationale 6. 5 acts. Petite Illustration, 192 (November 23, 1935), 1-26. In French.

827. ———. Notre-Dame d'En Haut. 5 parts. Il Dramma, n.s., 160 (July 1, 1952), 7-32. Sergio Cenalino, translator. In Italian.

828. ———. Il segreto d'Arvers. 1 act. Il Dramma, 148 (October 15, 1932), 38-44. Enzo Gariffo, translator. In Italian.

829. ———. Les Soeurs Guedonec. 1 act. Petite Illustration, 180 (December 26, 1931), 1-11. In French.

830. ———. Two Men. 1 act. One-Act Play Magazine, 1 (July, 1937), 237-249. Bryna E. Mason, translator.

———, translator see Zorzi, G. 9657

831. Bernard, Kenneth. Goodbye, Dan Bailey. 2 acts. Drama and Theatre, 9 (Spring, 1971), 179-198.

832. ———. The Lovers. 1 act. Trace, 69 (1968), 521-527.

833. ———. Marko's: A Vegetarian Fantasy. 1 act. Massachusetts Review, 10 (Summer, 1969), 557-569.

834. ———. Mary Jane. 1 act. Confrontation, 4 (Winter, 1970/71), 45-50.

835. Bernard, O. and H. Fremont. L'attaché d'ambasciata. 3 acts. Il Dramma, 27 (October 1, 1927), 6-39. In Italian.

836. Bernard, Roger. La Hauteur de la Nuit. 3 acts. Botteghe Oscure, 8 (1951), 31-104. In French.

837. Bernard, Tristan, 1866-1947. La Crise Ministerielle. 1 act, comedy. Petite Illustration, 181 (March 5, 1932), 1-8. In French.

838. ———. L'Ecole du Piston. 1 act. Petite Illustration, 184 (February 4, 1933), 1-8. In French.

839. ———. English As She Is Spoke. 1 act, comedy. Golden Book, 7 (May, 1928), 677-683. J. Harris Gable, translator.

840. _____. L'incidente del 7 Aprile. 1 act. Il Dramma, 77 (November 1, 1929), 32-39. M. Angeli, translator. In Italian.

841. _____. Jules, Juliette et Julien, ou L'Ecole du Sentiment. 3 acts, comedy. Petite Illustration, 87 (October 12, 1929), 1-22. In French.

842. _____. Langrevin Père et Fils. 5 acts, comedy. Petite Illustration, 88 (November 29, 1930), 1-30. In French.

843. _____. Il nodo nel fazzoletto. Il Dramma, 110 (March 15, 1931), 38-41. Lucio Ridenti and Vittorio Guerriero, translators. In Italian.

844. _____. Pagare i debiti. 1 act. Il Dramma, 54 (November 15, 1928), 37-44. In Italian.

845. _____. La Partie de bridge. 1 act. Petite Illustration, 198 (September 25, 1937), 1-4. In French.

846. _____. Il pittore esigente. 1 act. Il Dramma, 38 (March 15, 1928), 36-44. Vittorio Guerriero, translator. In Italian.

847. _____. Il pretendento. 1 act. Il Dramma, 121 (September 1, 1931), 42-44. In Italian.

848. _____. Le Prince Charmant. 3 acts, comedy. Petite Illustration, 184 (February 4, 1933), 1-22. In French.

849. _____. Quella che attendevo. 3 acts. Il Dramma, 103 (December 1, 1930), 32-42. In Italian.

850. _____. La rivelazione AND La casa del delitto. Il Dramma, 109 (March 1, 1931), 34-37. Lucio Ridenti and Vittorio Guerriero, translators. In Italian.

851. _____. Le Sauvage. 4 acts. Petite Illustration, 181 (January 9, 1932), 1-22. In French.

852. _____. Le Sexe Fort. 3 acts, comedy. Petite Illustration, 183 (October 22, 1932), 1-21. In French.

853. _____. Sketches Radiophoniques: Le Narcotique; La Morale et le Hasard; Révélation; Expedition Nocturne; La Maison du crime; Une Operation Magistrale; Le Triomphe de la Science; Le Coup de Cyrano; Un Mystère sans importance. 1 act each. Petite Illustration, 88 (October 11, 1930), 1-32. In French.

854. _____. Il vero coraggio. 1 act. Il Dramma, 46 (July 15, 1928), 42-44. Giuseppe Faraci, translator. In Italian.

855. _____ and Albert Centurier. L'Ecole des charlatans. 4 acts. Petite Illustration, 88 (August 2, 1930), 1-22. In French.

856. _____ and André Godfernaux. Triplepatte. 5 acts. Il Dramma, 6 (May, 1926), 5-35. P. F. Zappa, translator. In Italian.

857. _____ and Max Maurey. Un Ami D'Argentine. 4 acts. Petite Illustration, 178 (February 14, 1931), 1-34. In French.

Bernard-Luc, Jean, pseud. see Boudousse, Jean 1207

858. Bernède, Arthur. La Dame de Coeur. 1 act. Smart Set, 26 (October, 1908), 131-134. In French.

Berney, William see Richardson, H. 7530

859. Bernhardt, Lysiane Sarah. L'Aven. 1 act. L'Avant Scène, 539 (April 15, 1974), 43-50. In French.

860. Bernstein, Elsa Porges, 1866- . John Herkner. 5 acts. Poet Lore, 22 (Autumn, 1911), 321-397. Mary Harned, translator.

861. _____. Twilight. 5 acts. Poet Lore, 23 (Winter, 1912), 369-443. Paul H. Grummann, translator.

862. Bernstein, Henry, 1876-1953. Le Coeur. 5 acts. Petite Illustration, 196 (April 3, 1937), 1-34. In French.

863. _____. Espoir. 5 acts. Petite Illustration, 193 (April 4, 1936), 1-38. In French.

864. _____. La Soif. 3 acts. L'Avant Scène (OST), 17 (January, 1950), 3-34. In French.

Bernstein, J. S., translator see Ruibal, J. 7788

865. Berquier-Marinier, Marcelle. Amour, Délices et Or. 1 act, comedy. L'Avant Scène, 203 (September 1, 1959), 36-44. In French.

866. Berr, Georges and Louis Verneuil. Les Fontaines Lumineuses. 3 acts, comedy. Petite Illustration, 193 (February 15, 1936), 1-38. In French.

867. _____. Miss France. 4 acts, comedy. Petite Illustration, 88 (July 26, 1930), 1-42. In French.

868. _____. Mon Crime! 2 acts, comedy. Petite Illustration, 188 (May 19, 1934), 1-38. In French.

_____ see also Verneuil, L. 9102

869. Berri, Gino. Un incendente al caffè Minerva. 1 act. Il Dramma, 19 (June 1, 1927), 36-44. In Italian.

870. Berridge, W. Lloyd. Thrift. 1 act. Ladies' Home Journal, 35 (November, 1918), 57.

871. Bertolazzi, Carlo. L'Egoista. 4 acts. Il Dramma, n.s., 291 (December, 1960), 76-98. In Italian.

872. ———. La Gibigianna. 3 acts. Il Dramma, 396 (February 15, 1943), 7-25. In Italian.

873. ———. In verziere. 1 act. Il Dramma, 441/442/443 (January 1, February 1, 15, 1945), 53-57. In Italian.

874. Bertoli, Pier Benedetto. L'Andirivieni. 2 parts. Sipario, 21 (April, 1966), 40-52. In Italian.

875. ———. Le cose più grandi di loro. 1 act. Il Dramma, 44, no. 2 (November, 1968), 75-79. In Italian.

876. ———. I diari. 3 acts. Sipario, 14 (July-August, 1959), 65-80. In Italian.

———, translator see Aroutcheff, G. 361

877. Bertolini, Alberto. Borinage. 5 parts. Il Dramma, n.s., 157 (May 15, 1952), 6-32. In Italian.

878. ———. Notturni. 2 parts. Il Dramma, n.s., 274 (July, 1959), 36-57. In Italian.

879. Berton, Réné. La Lumière Dans le Tombeau. 2 acts. Petite Illustration, 87 (August 17, 1929), 1-14. In French.

880. Bertuetti, Eugenio, 1895- , and Sergio Pugliese. Il velo bianco. 3 acts. Il Dramma, 305 (May 1, 1939), 4-18. In Italian.

881. Besant, Sir Walter, 1836-1901 and Walter Harries Pollock, 1850-1926. The Charm. 2 acts. Cosmopolitan, 20 (February, 1896), 374-388.

882. Besier, Rudolf, 1878-1942. The Barretts of Wimpole Street. 5 acts. Il Dramma, n.s., 227/228 (August/September, 1955), 24-56. Ada Salvatore, translator. In Italian.

———, translator see Neven, C. 6473

883. Besnard, Lucien. Un uomo onesto. 1 act. Il Dramma, 129 (January 1, 1932), 39-45. In Italian.

———, translator see Sherriff, R. C. 8252

884. Besoyan, Rick, 1924- . Little Mary Sunshine. 2 acts. Theatre Arts, 44 (December, 1960), 27-56.

885. Bessey, Rafael M. Saavedray. La Chinita. 1 act. Poet Lore, 37 (Spring, 1926), 107-119. Lilian Saunders, translator.

Besson, Benno, adapter see Moliere 6113

Best, Sasha, translator see Duhamel, G. 2679, 2680, 2681

886. Betrayed. A Scenario of the Commedia dell'Arte. 3 acts. The Mask, 7 (July, 1914), 53-57.

887. Betti, Ugo, 1892-1953. Un albergo sul porto. 3 acts. Il Dramma, 406/407 (July 15/August 1, 1943), 13-30. In Italian.

888. _____. Un Beau Dimanche de Septembre. 3 acts, comedy. L'Avant Scène, 214, 8-28. Huguette Hatem, adapter. In French.

889. _____. Il cacciatore d'anitre. 6 parts. Il Dramma, 329 (May 1, 1940), 6-22. In Italian.

890. _____. La casa sull'acqua. 3 acts. Il Dramma, 366 (November 15, 1941), 7-21. In Italian.

891. _____. Corruzione al palazzo di giustizia. 3 acts. Sipario, 4 (March, 1949), 41-56. In Italian.

892. _____. Delitto all' isola della Capre. 3 acts. L'Avant Scène, 424 (April 15, 1969), 7-27. Maurice Clavel, translator. In French.

893. _____. Il diluvio. 3 acts. Il Dramma, 397/398 (March 1/15, 1943), 11-29. In Italian.

894. _____. Ispezione. 3 acts. Sipario, 2 (March-April, 1947), 37-56. In Italian.

895. _____. Lotta fino all'alba. 3 acts. Sipario, 4 (August-September, 1949), 77-91. In Italian.

896. _____. La padrona. 3 acts. Sipario, 3 (August-September, 1953), 34-44. In Italian.

897. _____. La regina e gli insorti. 4 acts. Sipario, 6 (May, 1951), 41-59. In Italian.

898. _____. Spiritismo nell'antica casa. 3 acts. Sipario, 5 (July, 1950), 45-62. In Italian.

899. _____. Il vento notturno. 3 acts. Il Dramma, n.s., 19/20 (August 15/September 1, 1946), 57-81. In Italian.

900. Bettini, Pompeo and Ettore Albini. I vincitori. 4 acts. Sipario, 16 (August-September, 1961), 51-64. In Italian.

901. Beven, Donald, 1920- , and Edmund Trzcinski, 1921- . Stalag 17, A Comedy Melodrama. 3 acts. Theatre Arts, 37 (February, 1953), 34-63.

902. Bevilacqua, Giuseppe. La farfalle dalle ali di fuoco. 2 acts. Il Dramma, 67 (June 1, 1929), 28-45. In Italian.

903. _____. Ghibli. 3 acts. Il Dramma, 277 (March 1, 1938), 4-25. In Italian.

904. _____. Girandola. 3 acts. Il Dramma, 315 (October 1, 1939), 4-19. In Italian.

905. _____. In campagna è un' altra cosa. 1 act. Il Dramma, 187 (June 1, 1934), 28-37. In Italian.

906. _____. Io fui, sono e sarò. 3 acts. Il Dramma, 265 (September 1, 1937), 2-24. In Italian.

907. _____. La note è bella. 1 act. Il Dramma, 52 (October 15, 1928), 35-39.

908. _____. Notturno del tempo nostro. 3 acts. Il Dramma, 169 (September 1, 1933), 4-31. In Italian.

909. _____. La via lattea. 1 act. Il Dramma, 44 (June 15, 1928), 21-30. In Italian.

910. Beye, Holly. It's All (Y)ours! 1 act. Quarterly Review of Literature, 11 (No. 1, 1961), 1-35.

911. _____. Th(us). 1 act. Quarterly Review of Literature, 11 (No. 1, 1961), 36-66.

912. Biagi, Enzo, 1920- . Giulia viene da lontano. 3 acts. Il Dramma, n.s., 190 (October 1, 1953), 5-17. In Italian.

Biancoli, Maria Pia, translator see Philips, F. C. 7119

913. Biancoli, Oreste, 1897- . Noi due. 3 acts. Il Dramma, 227 (February 1, 1936), 2-26. In Italian.

914. _____. Il secondo tempo. 1 act. Il Dramma, 218 (September 15, 1935), 31-38. In Italian.

915. _____. Il signore dalle gardenie. 1 act. Il Dramma, 84 (February 15, 1930), 36-43. In Italian.

_____ see also Falconi, D. 2919

_____, translator see Hatvany, L. 3962

Bibesco, Antoine, 1878-1951, adapter see Coward, N. 2079

916. Biel, Nicholas. Gone for a Soldier. 2 acts. Gambit, 3 (No. 10), 3-66.

917. _____. Sound on the Goose. 3 acts. First Stage, 3 (Winter, 1963-64), 13-41.

918. Bier, Richard. Fire and Ice. 1 act. DeKalb Literary Arts Journal, 8 (Winter, 1975), 6-13.

919. Bierce, Ambrose, 1942-1914? A Strained Relation. 2 acts. Cosmopolitan, 42 (March, 1907), 583-584.

920. Bierling, J. C. Eleanor. No Brave Soldier. 1 act. Plays, 2 (April, 1943), 31-37.

921. Bierstadt, Edward Hale, 1891- . The Fifth Commandment. 1 act. Drama, 10 (June, 1920), 317-321.

922. Bigelow, Julie Helene. The Fascinating Mrs. Osborne. 1 act. Smart Set, 35 (December, 1911), 129-134.

923. Biggs, Louise. The Key to Understanding. 1 act. Plays, 21 (November, 1961), 48-52.

924. Bigiaretti, Libero, 1906- . Licenza di matrimonio. 1 act. Il Dramma, 44, no. 2 (November, 1968), 62-64. In Italian.

925. Bihan, Michel le. L'Ere Quaternaire. L'Avant Scène, 488 (February 1, 1972), 31-40. In French.

926. _____. Square X. L'Avant Scène, 488 (February 1, 1972), 11-18. In French.

927. Bille, S. Corinna. Il diavolo e la sposa. 1 act. Il Dramma, 45, no. 6 (March, 1969), 84-85. In Italian.

928. Billetdoux, François, 1927- . Bien Amicalement. 1 act, dramatic comedy. L'Avant Scène, 193 (March 15, 1959), 25-28. In French.

929. _____. Comment Va le Monde, Monsieur? 4 acts, comedy. L'Avant Scène, 311 (May 15, 1964), 11-39. In French.

930. _____. Le comportement des epoux Bredburry. 4 acts, comedy. Sipario, 18 (April, 1963), 37-55. Ettore Capri-

931. ———. Il Faut Passer Par Les Nuages. 5 acts. L'Avant Scène, 332 (April 15, 1965), 10-41. In French.

932. ———. Femmes Parallèles. 1 act. L'Avant Scène, 469/470 (April 1/15, 1971), 35-42. In French.

933. ———. Pour Finale. 1 act, comedy. L'Avant Scène, 284 (March 15, 1963), 46-54. In French.

934. ———. Tchin-Tchin. 4 acts, comedy. L'Avant Scène, 193 (March 15, 1959), 7-23. In French.

935. ———. Va Donc Chez Torpe. 4 acts, comedy. L'Avant Scène, 273 (October 1, 1962), 9-27. In French.

936. ———. Les Veuves; tapisserie lyrique. L'Avant Scène, 571 (September 15, 1975), 19-40. In French.

937. Binazzi, Massimo. L'eletto. 1 act. Sipario, 20 (August-September, 1965), 23-37. In Italian.

938. ———. Le furie. 2 parts. Sipario, 18 (March, 1963), 25-47. In Italian.

939. ———. Gli estranei. 3 acts. Il Dramma, n.s., 241 (October, 1956), 10-33. In Italian.

940. ———. La paura. Sipario, 31 (May, 1976), 62-80. In Italian.

941. Bindamin, Madeline. Laughter. 1 act. One-Act Play Magazine, 3 (May-June, 1940), 342-354.

Binder, Judity see Serrano, N. 8155

Bingham, Gabrielle, translator see Weisenborn, G. 9272

942. Bingham, June, 1919- . Trial by Fury. 1 act. Plays, 4 (November, 1944), 51-57.

Binham, Philip, translator see Haavikko, P. 3795

943. Binkley, Frances W. Masque of Tomes: or, Boy Gets Book. 1 act. Wilson Library Bulletin, 23 (September, 1948), 66-67.

944. Binyon, Laurence, 1869-1943. Paris and Oenone. 1 act, tragedy. Fortnightly, o.s., 83 (June, 1905), 1137-1147.

945. Birabeau, André, 1890- . Bagi perduti. 3 acts. Il Dramma, 165 (July 1, 1933), 4-34. In Italian.

946. _____. Baisers Perdus. 3 acts, comedy. Petite Illustration, 182 (July 2, 1932), 1-26. In French.

947. _____. Calore del seno. 4 acts. Il Dramma, 331 (June 1, 1940), 6-35. In Italian.

948. _____. Il contratto. 1 act. Il Dramma, 113 (May 1, 1931), 36-41. In Italian.

949. _____. Un Dejeuner d'amoureux. 1 act, comedy. Petite Illustration, 87 (November 16, 1929), 1-7. In French.

950. _____. Fiston. 4 acts, comedy. Petite Illustration, 193 (April 18, 1936), 1-34. In French.

951. _____. Un grande amore sta per incominciare. 1 act. Il Dramma, 428/429/430 (June 15/July 1/15, 1944), 59-63. Claudina Casassa, translator. In Italian.

952. _____. Ma Soeur de luxe. 3 acts, comedy. Petite Illustration, 186 (September 30, 1933), 1-30. In French.

953. _____. Madre natura. 3 acts. Il Dramma, n.s., 22 (October 1, 1946), 7-33. Silvano D'Arborio, translator. In Italian.

954. _____. Pamplemousse. 3 acts, comedy. Petite Illustration, 197 (July 31, 1937), 1-34. In French.

955. _____. Peccatuccio. 3 acts. Il Dramma, 51 (October 1, 1928), 7-44. In Italian.

956. _____. La provetta. 1 act. Il Dramma, 83 (February 1, 1930), 39-41. Vittorio Zorelli, translator. In Italian.

957. _____. Il sentiero degli scolari. 3 acts. Il Dramma, 64 (April 15, 1929), 4-37. In Italian.

958. _____. La signora è servita. 1 act. Il Dramma, 132 (February 15, 1932), 34-41. Vittorio Guerriero, translator. In Italian.

959. _____. Souviens Toi Mon Amour. 3 acts. Il Dramma, n.s., 222 (March, 1955), 6-38. Alessandro de Stefani, translator. In Italian.

960. _____ and Georges Dolley. Cote D'Azur. 3 acts. comedy. Petite Illustration, 178 (March 28, 1931), 1-34. In French.

961. Biraghi, Guglielmo, 1927- . Il sole e la luna. 2 parts. Il Dramma, n.s., 354 (March, 1966), 6-22. In Italian.

962. Birimisa, George. Daddy Violet. 1 act. Prism International, 7 (Spring, 1968), 83-102.

963. Birnbaum, Perry. American Answer. 1 act. Scholastic, 36 (February 12, 1940), 23-24, 28.

964. Birnkrant, Samuel. A Whisper in God's Ear. 3 acts. Drama and Theatre, 8 (Spring, 1970), 168-188.

965. Biro, Lajos, 1880-1950. The Bridegroom. 1 act, comedy. Drama, 30 (May, 1918), 154-175. Charles Recht, translator.

966. _____. The Bridegroom. 1 act, comedy. Two Worlds, 1 (No. 1, 1926), 66-77.

967. _____. The Grandmother. 1 act, tragi-comedy. Drama, 30 (May, 1918), 176-196. Charles Recht, translator.

968. Birth of the Christ, The. 1 act. Resource, 3 (November, 1961), 5-11.

Bissell, Richard Pike, 1913- see Abbott, G. 4

969. Bissell, Walter L. The Great Lexicographer. 1 act. Scholastic, 23 (January 20, 1934), 4-6, 29.

970. Bisson, André. La Chatelaine de Shenstone. 4 acts, comedy. Petite Illustration, 88 (May 31, 1930), 1-29. In French.

971. _____. La Rosa di Gerico. 1 act. Il Dramma, 152 (December 15, 1932), 35-42. Enzo Gariffo, translator. In Italian.

972. _____. La Rose de Jericho. 1 act, comedy. Petite Illustration, 88 (September 6, 1930), 1-9. In French.

973. _____ and Meg Villars. Le Jour de Gloire. 3 acts. Petite Illustration, 196 (February 27, 1937), 1-39. In French.

Björkman, Edwin, translator see Strindberg, A. 8576

974. Bjørnson, Bjørnstjerne, 1932-1910. Between the Acts. 1 act. Poet Lore, 47 (Winter, 1941), 291-314. Joseph A. Weingarten, translator.

975. _____. A Glove. 3 acts, comedy. Poet Lore, 4 (Nos. 1-7, 1892), 7-13; 70-81; 128-135; 204-212; 254-261; 332-360. Thyge Sogard, translator.

976. _____. Laboremus. 3 acts. Fortnightly, 75 Supplement (May, 1901), 1-32.

977. _____. Leonarda. 4 acts, comedy. Drama, 1 (August, 1911), 16-76. Daniel L. Hanson, translator.

978. _____. When the New Wine Blooms. 3 acts, comedy. Poet Lore, 22 (No. 1, 1911), 1-69. Lee M. Hollander, translator.

Bjurstrom, Carl-Gustaf, adapter see Bergman, H. 814

_____, translator see Strindberg, A. 8567

979. Black, Campbell, 1944- . And They Used to Star in Movies. Transatlantic Review, 45 (Spring, 1973), 17-33.

Blackman, Carree Horton, translator see Dumas, A. 2691

980. Blackmore, Peter, 1909- . La Duchesse D'Algues. 2 acts, comedy. L'Avant Scène (ROST), 72 (January, 1953), 1-35. Constance Coline, translator. In French.

981. _____. Miranda. 3 acts. Il Dramma, n.s., 175 (February 15, 1953), 9-39. Paola Ojetti, translator. In Italian.

982. Blackmore, Richard Doddridge, 1825-1900. Lorna Doone. 1 act. Plays, 12 (October, 1952), 82-93. Jane McGowan, adapter.

983. Blackwood, Tom. The Mayfiles. 1 act. Dramatics, 45 (December, 1973), 7-11.

984. Blaine, Betty Gray. The Courtroom of Terror. 1 act. Plays, 18 (October, 1958), 74-78.

985. _____. The Gift Horse. 1 act. Plays, 20 (April, 1961), 31-44.

986. _____. Let It Snow. 1 act. Plays, 16 (January, 1957), 69-73.

987. _____. Mother Goose's Magic Cookies. 1 act. Plays, 22 (January, 1963), 77-83.

988. _____. Peter's Easter Basket Company. 1 act. Plays, 16 (April, 1957), 35-40.

989. _____. The Rosy-Cheeked Ghosts. 1 act. Plays, 17 (October, 1957), 45-49. AND Plays, 31 (October, 1971), 52-56.

989a. Blake, Gary. Preservatives. 1 act. Dramatika, 9 (Spring, 1972), n.p.

990. Blake, Robert. The Law Takes Its Toll. 1 act. American

Mercury, 17 (July, 1929), 263-270.

991. _____. The Law Takes Its Toll. 1 act. The Review of Reviews, 80 (August, 1929), 88-90.

992. Blanc-Peridier, Adrienne. La Marraine de Musset. 1 act. L'Avant Scène, 264 (May 1, 1962), 41-43. In French.

993. Blanchard, Edwin H. The Girl That God Made. 1 act. Smart Set, 64 (April, 1921), 127-128.

Blanche, Francis, adapter see Murray, J. and A. Boretz 6407

994. Blanchon, Jean. Il borghese romantico. 3 acts. Il Dramma, 34 (January 15, 1928), 7-36. Flavia Steno, translator. In Italian.

Blanco, Mario, 1914- , translator see Aladar, L. 95

995. Bland, Edith Nesbit, 1858- . Cinderella. 1 act. Delineator, 74 (December, 1909), 504-505.

Bland, Joellen, adapter see Clemens, S. L. 1884, 1885, 1889

_____, adapter see Dickens, C. 2472, 2478

_____, adapter see Moliere 6120

996. Bland, Peter. Father's Day. 3 acts. Landfall, 21 (September, 1967), 258-292.

997. _____. Shsh! He's Becoming a Republic. 1 act. Landfall, 24 (September, 1970), 261-279.

998. Blank, Franklin. Struggle for an Unknown Cause. 1 act, tragedy. Journal of Irish Literature, 5 (May, 1976), 123-130.

999. Blankfort, Michael, 1907- . The Brave and the Blind. 1 act. One-Act Play Magazine, 1 (May, 1937), 54-88.

1000. Blanton, Catherine. The Dulce Man. 1 act. Plays, 22 (January, 1963), 55-60.

1001. Bledsoe, Thomas. A (W)hor(e)s Opera. 1 act. Trace, 66 (1967), 402-407.

1002. Bloch, Bertram, 1892- . Humpty Dumpty, A Fantasy. 1 act. Poet Lore, 32 (Spring, 1921), 76-97.

1003. _____. Maiden Over the Wall. 1 act, fantasy. Drama,

31 (August, 1918), 436-453.

1004. _____. Morals and Circumstances. 1 act. Smart Set, 58 (April, 1919), 87-95.

1005. Bloch, Jean-Richard, 1884- . The Two Temptations. 2 acts. Living Age, 342 (July, 1932), 431-436.

_____, translator see Frank, L. 3264

1006. Block, Bette. Land of the Free. 1 act. Plays, 29 (January, 1970), 21-32.

1007. _____. Mother's Day--2005 A.D. 1 act. Plays, 31 (May, 1972), 35-42.

Blodgett, Anne K., translator see Lorca, F. G. 5045

1008. Blok, Alexander, 1880-1921. Dialogue About Love, Poetry and Government Service. 1 act. Dublin Magazine, n.s., 22 (April-June, 1947), 18-27. Blainaid Salkeld, translator.

1009. _____. Love, Poetry and Civic Service. 1 act. Poet Lore, 57 (Spring, 1953), 99-110. F. O'Dempsey, translator.

1010. _____. The Show Booth. 1 act. Dublin Magazine, 1 (June, 1924), 929-937. Padraic Colum and Vadim Uraneff, translators.

1011. _____. The Song of Fate. 1 act. Poet Lore, 44 (No. 1, 1938), 1-41. Oleta Joan O'Connor and George Rapall Noyes, translators.

1012. _____. The Unknown Woman. 1 act. Transition (Nos. 2, 3, 4, May, June, July, 1927), 52-63; 96-109; 90-100. Olive Frances Murphy, translator.

1013. Blondel, Jean. Nous N'Avons Plus de Souvenirs. 3 acts. Il Dramma, n.s., 40 (July 1, 1947), 9-40. Claudina Casassa, translator. In Italian.

1014. Blondin, Antoine, 1922- , and Paul Guimard, 1921- . Un Garçon D'Honneur. 4 acts. L'Avant Scène, 227, 9-33. In French.

Bloom, Phillip, 1918- see Dalrymple, J. 2165

Bloomfield, Leonard, 1887- , translator see Hauptmann, G. 3972

1015. Blossom, Roberts. Two Ears. 1 act. Chelsea, 10 (Sep-

Blossom

tember, 1961), 83-86.

1016. _____. White-Negro. 1 act. Chelsea, 16 (March, 1965), 31-38.

1017. Blouet, Paul, 1848-1903. The Pleasures of Poverty. 1 act. North American Review, 169 (August, 1899), 285-288.

1018. Blue Jackets, or His Majesty's Service. 1 act, farce. The Mask, 5 (July, 1912), 60-71.

1019. Blum, Rene and Georges Delaquis. Les Amours du Poete. 5 acts, comedy. Petite Illustration, 181 (February 27, 1932), 1-30. In French.

1020. Blumenfeld, Lenore. Another Way to Weigh an Elephant. 1 act. Plays, 32 (October, 1972), 55-58.

1021. _____. Encapsulated; A Multi-Media One Act. Dramatics, 44 (December, 1972), 4-9.

1022. _____. The King's Dreams. 1 act. Plays, 36 (November, 1976), 39-46.

1023. _____. The Mirror of Matsuyama. 1 act. Plays, 32 (January, 1973), 41-46.

1024. _____. Thrift, Chinese Style. 1 act. Plays, 32 (May, 1973), 63-68.

1025. _____, adapter. Martina the Ant. 1 act. Plays, 32 (May, 1973), 41-44.

1026. _____, adapter. Poor Wives, Lazy Husbands. 1 act. Plays, 32 (April, 1973), 24-28.

Blunden, Edmund, 1896- , translator see Aeschylus 78

1027. Bly, Robert. The Satisfaction of Vietnam. 1 act. Chelsea, 24/25 (October, 1968), 32-46.

1028. Boal, Augusto, 1930- . Zio Paperone. 2 acts. Sipario, 315-316 (August-September, 1972), 99-112. Marga Feriani Vidusso, translator. In Italian.

1029. _____ and Gianfrancesco Guarnieri, 1936- . Arena raconta Zambi. 2 acts. Sipario, 26 (August-September, 1971), 101-112. Tilde Barini and Daniela Ferioli, translators. In Italian.

1030. Boatright, Mody Coggin, 1896- . The Age of Accountability. 1 act, tragedy. Poet Lore, 40 (Summer, 1929), 295-302.

1031. _____. C. C. 1 act, tragedy. Poet Lore, 41 (Spring, 1930), 124-131.

1032. Bobb, Ralph. A Hundred Fires. 1 act. Drama and Theatre, 10 (Winter, 1971/72), 113-119.

1033. _____. A Late Spring. 4 acts. First Stage, 2 (Summer, 1963), 202-231.

Bobich, Gica, translator see Yu T'Ang Ch'un 9624

1034. Boccioni, Umberto, 1882-1916. Il corpo che sale. Sipario, 260 (December, 1967), 95. In Italian.

1035. _____. Genio e colura. Sipario, 260 (December, 1967), 95. In Italian.

Bocquet-Roudy, Anne, adapter see Rosselson, L. 7711

1036. Bodenheim, Maxwell, 1895-1954. The Cloud Descends. 1 act. Poetry, 14 (September, 1919), 295-300.

1037. _____. The Gentle Furniture Shop. 1 act. Drama, 10 (January, 1920), 132-133.

1038. _____. Poet's Heart. 1 act. Little Review, 4 (July, 1917), 21-24.

1039. _____. The Unimagined Heaven. 1 act. Seven Arts, 2 (June, 1917), 193-198.

1040. _____. The Wanderer. 1 act. Seven Arts, 2 (September, 1917), 603-607.

1041. _____ and Ben Hecht, 1894-1964. Mrs. Margaret Calhoun. 1 act. Smart Set, 52 (August, 1917), 73-77.

_____ see also Saphier, W. 7923

1042. Bodet, Robert. La comparsa. 1 act. Il Dramma, 128 (December 15, 1931), 38-39. In Italian.

1043. _____. S. M. la Primattrice. 1 act. Il Dramma, 124 (October 15, 1931), 40-44. In Italian.

Bodini, Vittorio, 1914- , translator see Cervantes Saavedra, M. de 1693

1044. Boiko, Claire. Ah See and the Six-Colored Heaven. 1 act. Plays, 30 (March, 1971), 65-70.

1045. _____. Al Adams and the Wonderful Lamp. 1 act. Plays, 35 (February, 1976), 1-10.

1046. _____. All About Mothers. 1 act. Plays, 24 (May, 1965), 71-74.

1047. _____. All Hands on Deck. 1 act. Plays, 26 (January, 1967), 35-43.

1048. _____. All Points West. 1 act. Plays, 26 (November, 1966), 41-46.

1049. _____. Anywhere and Everywhere. 1 act. Plays, 22 (January, 1963), 73-76.

1050. _____. The Arabian Knight. 1 act. Plays, 31 (March, 1972), 1-12.

1051. _____. Before Your Very Eyes. 1 act. Plays, 30 (April, 1971), 1-8.

1052. _____. La Belle Telephone. 1 act. Plays, 30 (February, 1971), 13-19.

1053. _____. Beware the Genies! 1 act. Plays, 28 (January, 1969), 81-86.

1054. _____. The Big Shoo. 1 act. Plays, 24 (October, 1964), 41-46.

1055. _____. The Book That Saved the Earth. 1 act, comedy. Plays, 27 (January, 1968), 37-42.

1056. _____. The Boy from Next Tuesday. 1 act. Plays, 33 (October, 1973), 81-86.

1057. _____. Brave Trudy and the Dragon. 1 act. Plays, 32 (December, 1972), 61-66.

1058. _____. Buttons, Pirates and Pearls! 1 act. Plays, 33 (January, 1974), 46-55.

1059. _____. Captain Scrimshaw's Treasure. 1 act. Plays, 35 (January, 1976), 33-40.

1060. _____. The Care and Feeding of Mothers. 1 act. Plays, 31 (May, 1972), 69-72.

1061. _____. Carry On, Cupid! 1 act. Plays, 32 (February, 1973), 35-41.

1062. _____. The Christmas Revel. 1 act. Plays, 24 (December, 1964), 39-50.

1063. _____. Cinder-Riley. 1 act. Plays, 20 (March, 1961), 51-56.

1064. _____. A Clean Sweep. 1 act. Plays, 25 (January, 1966), 73-77.

1065. _____. Corinna Goes A-Maying. 1 act. Plays, 27 (May, 1968), 85-92.

1066. _____. The Crocus Who Couldn't Bloom. 1 act. Plays, 20 (May, 1961), 77-82.

1067. _____. Cupivac. 1 act. Plays, 26 (May, 1967), 59-63.

1068. _____. Cybernella, or, The Triumph of Technological True Love. 1 act. Plays, 35 (May, 1976), 17-26.

1069. _____. Destination: Christmas! 1 act. Plays, 30 (December, 1970), 43-52.

1070. _____. The Exterior Decoration. 1 act. Plays, 23 (March, 1964), 60-64.

1071. _____. The Fastest Thimble in the West. 1 act. Plays, 33 (April, 1974), 1-15.

1072. _____. The Franklin Reversal. 1 act. Plays, 24 (November, 1964), 47-53.

1073. _____. Ghost Wanted. 1 act. Plays, 31 (October, 1971), 17-27.

1074. _____. Halloween Hullabaloo. 1 act. Plays, 34 (October, 1974), 47-51.

1075. _____. Honorable Cat's Decision. 1 act. Plays, 31 (May, 1972), 57-62.

1076. _____. Hotel Oak. 1 act. Plays, 29 (April, 1970), 47-52.

1077. _____. How Mothers Came to Be. 1 act. Plays, 30 (May, 1971), 73-76.

1078. _____. How to Choose a Boy. 1 act. Plays, 27 (January, 1968), 67-70.

1079. _____. The Insatiable Dragon, A Chinese Folktale. 1 act. Plays, 25 (April, 1966), 63-68.

1080. _____. Jack Jonette's Ride. 1 act. Plays, 31 (April, 1972), 43-49.

1081. _____. Joe White and the Seven Lizards. 1 act. Plays, 29 (May, 1970), 1-12.

Boiko

1082. _____. Johnny Question-Mark. 1 act. Plays, 29 (November, 1969), 1-16.

1083. _____. Just Visiting? 1 act. Plays, (November, 1974) 66-70.

1084. _____. Kitten Capers. 1 act. Plays, 22 (October, 1962), 81-84.

1085. _____. Lady Moon and the Thief, a Chinese Fantasy. 1 act. Plays, 27 (October, 1967), 77-82.

1086. _____. A Likely Lad. 1 act. Plays, 31 (February, 1972), 55-61.

1087. _____. Lion the Lamb. 1 act. Plays, 24 (March, 1965), 81-84.

1088. _____. The Little Red Hen. 1 act. Plays, 28 (March, 1969), 69-75.

1089. _____. The Long Table. 1 act. Plays, 29 (November, 1969), 89-95.

1090. _____. The Marmalade Overture. 1 act. Plays, 24 (November, 1964), 79-81.

1091. _____. The Marvelous Time Machine. 1 act. Plays, 18 (May, 1959), 35-41.

1092. _____. May Basket Fantasia. 1 act. Plays, 28 (May, 1969), 36-40.

1093. _____. Meet the Pilgrims. 1 act. Plays, 25 (November, 1965), 74-78.

1094. _____. Melinda's Incredible Birthday. 1 act. Plays, 28 (January, 1969), 45-51.

1095. _____. The Mobius Strip. 1 act. Plays, 30 (October, 1970), 13-22.

1096. _____. Monkey Business. 1 act. Plays, 31 (October, 1971), 73-76.

1097. _____. Mother Goose's Christmas Surprise. 1 act. Plays, 25 (December, 1965), 77-82.

1098. _____. My Cousin from Tycho. 1 act. Plays, 31 (November, 1971), 37-46.

1099. _____. Next Stop--Spring! 1 act. Plays, 28 (March, 1969), 53-58.

1100. _____. Number One Apple Tree Lane. 1 act. Plays, 27 (May, 1968), 69-73.

1101. _____. On Camera, Noah Webster! 1 act. Plays, 31 (November, 1971), 57-62.

1102. _____. One Hundred Words. 1 act. Plays, 29 (May, 1970), 45-48.

1103. _____. Operation Litterbug. 1 act. Plays, 20 (April, 1961), 65-68.

1104. _____. Pandora's Perilous Predicament. 1 act. Plays, 31 (February, 1972), 37-44.

1105. _____. Penny Wise. 1 act. Plays, 24 (January, 1965), 78-82.

1106. _____. Pepe and the Cornfield Bandit. 1 act. Plays, 30 (October, 1970), 47-52.

1107. _____. Peter, Peter, Peter! 1 act. Plays, 23 (February, 1964), 45-53.

1108. _____. The Petticoat Revolution. 1 act. Plays, 29 (April, 1970), 21-29. AND Plays, 35 (April, 1976), 65-73.

1109. _____. Presidents on Parade. 1 act. Plays, 32 (November, 1972), 63-73.

1110. _____. The Princess and the Heard Boy. 1 act. Plays, 33 (May, 1974), 53-57.

1111. _____. The Punctuation Proclamation. 1 act. Plays, 23 (April, 1964), 65-68.

1112. _____. A Real Old English Christmas. 1 act. Plays, 33 (December, 1973), 1-12.

1113. _____. Reel Life, Inc. 1 act. Plays, 34 (January, 1975), 45-51.

1114. _____. Rhubarb. 1 act. Plays, 32 (March, 1973), 31-41.

1115. _____. Roamin' Jo and Juli, or, How the West Was Lost. 1 act. Plays, 26 (April, 1967), 1-13.

1116. _____. The Roaring Twenties in Whippoorwill Falls. 1 act. Plays, 34 (February, 1975), 1-13.

1117. _____. A Roman Romance. 1 act. Plays, 31 (March,

1972), 49-54.

1118. _____. Rowdy Kate. 1 act. Plays, 31 (May, 1972), 1-16.

1119. _____. The Runaway Bookmobile. 1 act. Plays, 25 (November, 1965), 60-66.

1120. _____. Scaredy Cat. 1 act. Plays, 26 (October, 1966), 41-46.

1121. _____. The Search for the Sky-Blue Princess. 1 act. Plays, 31 (April, 1972), 61-69.

1122. _____. The Shakespeares. 1 act. Plays, 35 (April, 1976), 79-84.

1123. _____. Small Crimson Parasol. 1 act. Plays, 25 (January, 1966), 67-72.

1124. _____. The Snowman Who Overstayed. 1 act. Plays, 26 (March, 1967), 70-74.

1125. _____. A Song Goes Forth. 1 act. Plays, 28 (October, 1968), 83-86.

1126. _____. Spaceship Santa Maria. 1 act. Plays, 25 (October, 1965), 61-67.

1127. _____. Star Bright. 1 act. Plays, 25 (December, 1965), 63-67.

1128. _____. Star Fever. 1 act. Plays, 30 (March, 1971), 15-24.

1129. _____. The Star Spangled Time Machine. 1 act. Plays, 36 (October, 1976), 76-84.

1130. _____. Sun Up! 1 act. Plays, 23 (April, 1964), 73-76.

1131. _____. The "T" Party. 1 act. Plays, 23 (November, 1963), 78-82.

1132. _____. Take Me to Your Marshall. 1 act. Plays, 29 (January, 1970), 45-51.

1133. _____. A Tale of Two Drummers. 1 act. Plays, 27 (February, 1968), 39-45.

1134. _____. The Tall Silk Hat. 1 act. Plays, 33 (November, 1973), 39-47.

1135. _____. The Tall Tale Tournament. 1 act. Plays, 31 (December, 1971), 67-72.

1136. _____. Terrible Terry's Surprise. 1 act. Plays, 22 (April, 1963), 65-70.

1137. _____. Trick or Treat for UNICEF. 1 act. Plays, 31 (October, 1971), 57-62.

1138. _____. Trouble in Tree-Land. 1 act. Plays, 23 (May, 1964), 83-86.

1139. _____. The Wayward Witch. 1 act. Plays, 21 (October, 1961), 49-52.

1140. _____. We Interrupt This Program.... 1 act. Plays, 34 (December, 1974), 45-51.

1141. _____. Whatever Happened to Mother Nature? 1 act. Plays, 31 (January, 1972), 77-80.

1142. _____. Wheels! A Ballad of the Highway. 1 act. Plays, 35 (January, 1976), 62-68.

1143. _____. Who Will Bell the Cat? 1 act. Plays, 31 (January, 1972), 67-72.

1144. _____. Who's Afraid of the Big, Bad Pumpkin? 1 act. Plays, 33 (October, 1973), 61-66.

1145. _____. The Wild Indian and the Gentleman's Gentleman. 1 act. Plays, 34 (May, 1975), 39-48.

1146. _____. The Wild Rabbit Chase. 1 act. Plays, 28 (April, 1969), 35-43.

1147. _____. The Wonderful Circus of Words. 1 act. Plays, 21 (November, 1961), 53-58. AND Plays, 36 (November, 1976), 47-51.

1148. _____. Yankees vs. Redcoats. 1 act. Plays, 35 (May, 1976), 63-66.

1149. _____. Yes, Yes, a Thousand Times Yes! or The Hero Still Pursues Her. 1 act. Plays, 28 (November, 1968), 35-44.

1150. _____. Young Abe's Destiny. 1 act. Plays, 26 (February, 1967), 43-48.

1151. _____, adapter. Snowflake. 1 act. Plays, 31 (February, 1972), 77-83.

1152. Boleslawsky, Richard. The First Lesson in Acting; A Pseudo-Morality. 1 act. Theatre Arts, 7 (October, 1923),

Boll, Annemarie, translator see Synge, J. 8673

1153. Böll, Heinrich, 1917- . Lebbra. 1 act. Il Dramma, (October, 1971), 23-40. Alighiero Chiusano, translator. In Italian.

_____, translator see Synge, J. 8673

Boll, Ilka, translator see Rozewicz, T. 7777

1154. Bolla, Nino, 1896- . Il chiromante. 1 act. Il Dramma, 198 (November 15, 1934), 28-29. In Italian.

Bollin, Flamino, translator see Ayme, M. 469

1155. Bolotowsky, Ilya. A Neurotic Lion. 1 act. The Quest, 3 (Summer/Fall, 1968), 59-71.

1156. Bolt, Carol. Maurice. 1 act. Performing Arts in Canada, 11 (Winter, 1974), 42-50.

1157. Bolt, Robert, 1924- . A Man for All Seasons. 2 acts. Theatre Arts, 47 (May, 1963), 33-66.

1158. _____. Thomas More. 2 acts. L'Avant Scène, 294 (September 1, 1963), 10-37. Pol Quentin, translator. In French.

Bolton, Guy, 1884- , translator see Marcelle-Maurette 5532

1159. Bommart, Jean, 1894- . Blanc et Rouge. 3 acts. Petite Illustration, 193 (January 4, 1936), 1-34. In French.

1160. Bompiani, Valentino, 1898- . Anche i grassi hanno l'onore. 3 acts. Sipario, 5 (June, 1950), 53-69. In Italian.

1161. _____. La conchiglia all'orecchio. 3 acts. Il Dramma, 354 (May 15, 1941), 9-26. In Italian.

1162. _____. La conchiglia all'orecchio. 3 acts. Sipario, 13 (July, 1958), 37-51. In Italian.

1163. _____. La domenica ci si riposa. 2 parts, comedy. Sipario, 11 (June, 1956), 36-47. In Italian.

1164. _____. Terese-Angelica. 3 acts. Il Dramma, n.s., 208 (July 1, 1954), 5-27. In Italian.

1165. Bona, Giampiero, 1926- . L'accoppiamento. Sipario, 326 (July, 1973), 65-80. In Italian.

1166. Bonacci, Anna. La casa delle nubili. 3 acts. Il Dramma, 239 (August 1, 1936), 6-26. In Italian.

1167. _____. Sulle soglie della storia. 3 acts. Il Dramma, n.s., 131 (April 15, 1951), 7-28. In Italian.

1168. _____ and Elaine Charles. Le Confiseur. 1 act. L'Avant Scène, 207 (November 1, 1959), 36-38. In French.

Bonacelli, Paolo, translator see Panizza, O. 6951

Bonanni, Camillo, adapter see Della Porta, G. B. 2304

1169. Bond, Edward, 1935- . Early Morning. Sipario, 301 (June, 1971), 52-80.

1170. _____. Lear. 3 acts. Sipario, 317 (October, 1972), 57-80. Alvise Sapori, translator. In Italian.

1171. _____. Narrow Road to the Deep North. 2 parts. Plays and Players, 15 (September, 1968), 27-42.

1172. _____. The Narrow Road to the Deep North. 2 acts. Sipario, 25 (December, 1970), 115-127. Silvia Codecasa, translator. In Italian.

1173. _____. Passion. 1 act. Plays and Players, 18 (June, 1971), 66-69.

1174. _____. Saved. Plays and Players, 13 (January, 1966), 29-44, 67-69.

1175. _____. Saved. Sipario, 252 (April, 1967), 42-64. Gigi Lunari, translator. In Italian.

1176. _____. The Sea. Sipario, 335 (April, 1974), 58-80. Alvise Sapori, translator. In Italian.

1177. Bond, Nelson, 1908- , and David Kent. Mr. Mergenthwirker's Lobblies. 3 acts, comedy-fantasy. Theatre Arts, 35 (July, 1951), 62-79.

1178. Bond, Virginia. The Treasure Chest. 1 act. Plays, 16 (March, 1957), 79-81.

Bondi, Juriz see Mejerchol'd, V. 5737

1179. Bonea, Sharron. God's Love Has Made It So. 1 act. Learning With..., 3 (December, 1975), 21-22.

1180. Bonelli, Luigi. Cicero. 3 acts. Il Dramma, 206 (March 15, 1935), 4-29. In Italian.

1181. _____. Dramma di sogni. 1 act. Il Dramma, 124 (October 15, 1931), 34-39. In Italian.

1182. _____. Il medico della signora malata. 3 acts. Il Dramma, 18 (May, 1927), 9-26. In Italian.

1183. _____. Non voglio sposare Minnie. 1 act. Il Dramma, 275 (February 1, 1938), 11-20. In Italian.

1184. _____. La quarta parete. 1 act. Il Dramma, 292 (October 15, 1938), 27-34. In Italian.

1185. _____. Storienko. 3 acts. Il Dramma, 30 (November 15, 1927), 7-18. In Italian.

1186. _____. Il Topo. 2 parts. Il Dramma, 46 (July 15, 1928), 4-16. In Italian.

1187. _____ and Aldo de Benedetti. L'uomo che sorride. 3 acts. Il Dramma, 214 (July 15, 1935), 5-35. In Italian.

Bonfante, Lariss, translator see Hrotsitha 4262

1188. Bonn, John E. 15-Minute Red Revue; An Agit-Prop Play. Drama Review, 17 (December, 1973), 102-109.

1189. Bonner, Marita. The Pot Maker. 1 act. Opportunity, 5 (February, 1927), 43-46.

Bonnieres, Philippe see Saint-Granier 7860

1190. Bonora, Anton Luca. Ritorno di Solitudine. 1 act, comedy. Sipario, 10 (June, 1955), 53-56. In Italian.

1191. Bontempelli, Massimo. Innocenza di Camilla. 3 acts, comedy. Sipario, 4 (August-September, 1949), 59-75. In Italian.

_____, translator see Crommelynck, F. 2117

_____, translator see Montherlant, H. de 6193

1192. Book Play for High Schools. 1 act. Wilson Library Bulletin, 4 (March, 1930), 323-327.

1193. Books in the Woods. 1 act. Wilson Library Bulletin, 10 (October, 1935), 114-117.

1194. Boothman, Marion L. Four Keys to the Library. 1 act. Wilson Library Bulletin, 7 (October, 1932), 106-113.

Booty, Jill, translator see Vicente, G. 9138

1195. Borel, Jacques. Tata, ou de l'education. 2 acts. L'Avant Scène, 491 (March 15, 1972), 7-32. In French.

Boretz, Allen, 1900- see Murray, J. 6407

1196. Borg, Washington. In collaborazione. 1 act. Il Dramma, 98 (September 15, 1930), 39-45. In Italian.

1197. ———. Nuda. 3 acts. Il Dramma, 45 (July 1, 1928), 7-39. In Italian.

1198. Borgese, Elisabeth Mann. Soltanto il orgo. 3 acts. Sipario, 18 (March, 1963), 48-58. Alfredo Rizzardi, translator. In Italian.

Borghesio see Mor, E. 6209, 6210

Borgomaneri, translator see Molnar, F. 6135, 6140, 6166

1199. Borie, Gilbert. Korane. 1 act. L'Avant Scène, 196 (May 1, 1959), 35-40. In French.

Bost, Pierre, 1901- , adapter see Greene, G. 3716

——— see Puget, C. 7328, 7329

1200. Botrel, Theodore Jean Marie, 1868- . Du Guesclin. 3 acts. Poet Lore, 30 (Summer, 1919), 159-207. Elizabeth S. Dickerman, translator.

1201. Bottomley, Gordon, 1874-1948. The Crier by Night. 1 act. Bibelot, 15 (1909), 299-333.

1202. ———. Laodice and Danaë. 1 act. The Poetry Journal, 4 (September, 1915), 1-13; (October, 1915), 47-67.

1203. ———. Maids of Athens. 1 act. Dublin Magazine, n.s., 20 (October-December, 1945), 3-21.

1204. ———. The Riding to Lithend. 1 act, tragedy. Bibelot, 16 (1910), 3-62.

1205. Boucherit, S. Le Commissionnaire. 1 act. Smart Set, 4 (August, 1901), 139-142. In French.

1206. Bouchet, Pierre. Tout un dimanche ensemble. 1 act. L'Avant Scène, 511 (February 1, 1973), 31-37. In French.

1207. Boudousse, Jean, 1909- . Le Complexe de Philemon. 3 acts, comedy. L'Avant Scène (OST), 40 (March, 1951), 1-44. In French.

1208. _____. La Feuille de Vigne. 3 acts, comedy. L'Avant Scène (ROST), 66 (September, 1952), 1-38. In French.

1209. _____. Hibernatus. 4 acts, comedy. L'Avant Scène, 151, 1-32. In French.

1210. _____. Je T'enleve. 1 act. L'Avant Scène, 151, 35-39. In French.

1211. _____. Notte degli uomini. 1 act. Il Dramma, n.s., 144 (November 1, 1951), 8-20. Connie Ricono, translator. In Italian.

1212. Bouhelier, Saint-Georges de, 1876- . Jeanne d'Arc, La Pucelle de France. 4 acts. Petite Illustration, 189 (December 8, 1934), 1-48. In French.

1213. _____. Napoleon. 4 acts. Petite Illustration, 184 (April 8, 1933), 1-46. In French.

1214. _____. Le Roi sans couronne. 5 acts. Vers et Prose, 29 (July-September, 1912), 5-44; 31 (October-December, 1912), 93-103; 32 (January-March, 1913), 79-86.

1215. _____. Le Sang de Danton. 3 acts. Petite Illustration, 180 (October 10, 1931), 1-40. In French.

1216. Boularan, Jacques, 1895- . L'Age du Juliette. 3 acts, comedy. Petite Illustration, 190 (March 9, 1935), 1-34. In French.

1217. _____. La cara ombra. 3 acts, comedy. Sipario, 10 (March, 1955), 27-55. Ada Salvatore, translator. In Italian.

1218. _____. ". . . Ce Soir, A Samarcande". 3 acts. L'Avant Scène (OST), 36 (January, 1951), 3-44. In French.

1219. _____. Charmante Soirée. 3 acts, comedy. L'Avant Scène, 125, 1-31. In French.

1220. _____. Débouche. 3 acts. Il Dramma, 81 (January 1, 1930), 4-36. Yorickson, translator. In Italian.

1221. _____. Etienne. 3 acts. Petite Illustration, 88 (October 18, 1930), 1-34. In French.

1222. _____. Mademoiselle. 3 acts, comedy. L'Avant Scène, 158, 1-38. In French.

1223. _____. Mademoiselle. 3 acts, comedy. Petite Illustration, 183 (September 24, 1932), 1-38. In French.

1224. _____. La Manière Forte. 3 acts, comedy. L'Avant Scène, 114, 1-31. In French.

1225. _____. Signor Bracoli. 4 acts. Petite Illustration, 183 (December 10, 1932), 1-38. In French.

1226. _____. La signorina. 3 acts. Il Dramma, 195 (October 1, 1934), 4-42. Alessandro de Stefani, translator. In Italian.

1227. _____. Une Tant Belle Fille. 3 acts. Petite Illustration, 87 (January 12, 1929), 1-38. In French.

1228. _____. Tovaritch. 4 acts, comedy. Petite Illustration, 189 (December 19, 1934), 1-38. In French.

1229. _____. Ventose. 3 acts, comedy. Petite Illustration, 86 (January 21, 1928), 1-34. In French.

1230. _____. Venus de Milo. 2 acts, comedy. L'Avant Scène, 286 (April 15, 1963), 9-37. In French.

_____, adapter see Kaufman, G. S. and E. Ferber 4560

_____, translator see Hecht, B. and C. MacArthur 4019, 4020

1231. Boulle, Pierre, 1912- . William Conrad. 4 acts. L'Avant Scène, 258 (February 1, 1962), 8-36. In French.

1232. Bourbon, Antoine. Un Extraordinaire Bonhomme de Neige. 1 act. L'Avant Scène, 126, 43-47. In French.

1233. Bourdet, Edouard, 1887-1945. La Fleur des Pois. 4 acts, comedy. L'Avant Scène, 220, 8-44. In French.

1234. _____. Fric-Frac. 5 acts, comedy. Petite Illustration 197 (June 12, 1937), 1-38. In French.

1235. _____. Margot. 2 acts. Petite Illustration, 193 (January 11, 1936), 1-39. In French.

1236. _____. La prigioniera. 3 acts. Il Dramma, n. s., 9 (March 15, 1946), 10-35. In Italian.

1237. _____. Les Temps Difficiles. 4 acts. Petite Illustration, 189 (November 10, 1934), 1-46. In French.

1238. _____. "Vient de Paraitre". 4 acts, comedy. Petite Illustration, 86 (June 2, 1928), 1-46. In French.

1239. Bourjaily, Vance, 1922- . $4000. An Opera in Five Scenes.

North American Review, n. s., 6 (Winter, 1969), 17-26.

1240. Bouteille, Romain, 1937- . Le soir des diplomates. 3 acts. L'Avant Scène, 511 (February 1, 1973), 7-27. In French.

1241. Bouvelet, Jehan and Ed J. Bradby. Au Clair de la Lune. 4 acts. Petite Illustration, 87 (November 30, 1929), 1-30. In French.

1242. Bowering, George, 1935- . The Home for Heroes. 1 act. Prism International, 3 (Winter, 1962), 6-15.

1243. Bowhay, B. L. The State Supreme. 3 acts. Drama, 6 (January-February, 1915), 17-80.

1244. Bowles, Jane, 1917-1973. A Quarreling Pair. 1 act. Art and Literature, 2 (Summer, 1964), 65-69.

1245. Bowman, Louise Morey. And Forbid Them Not. 1 act. Poetry, 13 (March, 1919), 306-307.

1246. Boyajian, Aram. Beauty Sleeping Black. 1 act. Dramatika, 4 (Fall, 1969), n. p.

1247. _____. Susby Berkeley at Dachau. 1 act. Dramatika, 8 (Fall, 1971), n. p.

1248. _____. Cinema-Verite. 1 act. Dramatika, 3 (March, 1969), 21-22.

1249. _____. Habits. 1 act. Dramatika, 8 (Fall, 1971), n. p.

1250. _____. Lick. 1 act. Dramatika, 3 (March, 1969), 20.

1251. _____. 3, A Play. 1 act. Dramatika, 2 (October, 1968), 9-11.

1252. Boyer, Francois, 1920- . Dieu aboie-t-il? 2 parts. L'Avant Scène, 498 (July 1, 1972), 7-25. In French.

1253. Boyesen, Algernon. Don Juan Duped. 1 act. Smart Set, 33 (April, 1911), 131-140.

Boysson, Pascale de, adapter see Schisgal, M. 8029, 8030, 8031

1254. Bracco, Roberto, 1862-1943. The Hidden Spring. 4 acts. Poet Lore, 18 (No. 2, 1907), 143-186. Dirce St. Cyr, translator.

1255. _____. The Little Saint. 2 acts. Gambit, 6, 33-78. Victor Rietti, translator.

1256. _____. La luce di Santa Agnese. 1 act. Il Dramma, n.s., 236 (May, 1956), 52-55. In Italian.

1257. _____. Phantasms. 4 acts. Poet Lore, 19 (Autumn, 1908), 241-292. Dirce St. Cyr, translator.

Brackley, Lady Elizabeth see Cavendish, Lady J. 1676

1258. Bradbury, Ray, 1920- . The Veldt. 1 act. Il Dramma, (October, 1974), 25-42. Liana C. Ferri, translator. In Italian.

Bradby, Ed J. see Bouvelet, J. 1241

Braddel, M. see Hart, A. 3936

1259. Bradford, Benjamin. Concentric Circles. 1 act. The Scene, 1 (1972), 106-139.

1260. _____. Geometric Progression. 1 act, comedy. DeKalb Literary Arts Journal, 3 (No. 2, 1969), 61-84.

1261. Bradford, Gamaliel, 1863-1932. Little Glimpses of Great People. 1 act. Southwest Review, 10 (October, 1924), 40-48.

1262. Bradford, Roark, 1896- . How Come Christmas, a Modern Morality. 1 act. Harper's, 162 (December, 1930), 45-49.

1263. _____. How Come Christmas? 1 act. Scholastic, 19 (December 12, 1931), 15-16.

1264. Bradley, Polly Lewis. Professor Countdown Takes Off. 1 act. Plays, 20 (April, 1961), 83-87.

Brady, Jack see Williams, O. 9416

1265. Bragaglia, Anton Giulio, 1890- . Don Chisciotte. 3 acts. Il Dramma, 29 (November 1, 1927), 8-36. In Italian.

_____, translator see Ghelderode, M. de 3459

1266. Braibanti, Aldo. Ododrama. Sipario, 24 (February, 1969), 37.

1267. Braid, Angus, 1945- . Outport. 1 act. Performing Arts in Canada, 8 (Winter, 1971), 13-21.

1268. Brainville, Yves. L'Obstacle, ou Alexandre le Petit. 5 acts. L'Avant Scène (OST), 41 (April, 1951), 1-36. In French.

1269. Braley, Berton, 1882- . It All Depends, A Versatile Drama. 2 acts. Cosmopolitan, 74 (June, 1923), 62-64.

1270. Brancati, Vitaliano. Don Giovanni Involontario. 3 acts, comedy. Sipario, 9 (November, 1954), 38-55. In Italian.

1271. _____. Raffaele. 3 acts, comedy. Botteghe Oscure, 2 (1948), 122-190. In Italian.

Brandon, James R., translator see Kanjincho 4545

Brandt, W. R., translator see Heijermans, H. 4032

Brantzell, Aura Woodin see Pollock, A. L. 7231

1272. Brasillach, Robert. La Reine de Cesaree. 5 acts, tragedy. L'Avant Scène, 523 (August 1, 1973), 7-28. In French.

1273. Brasseur, Pierre, 1905- . L'Enfant du Dimanche. 2 acts, comedy. L'Avant Scène, 195 (April 15, 1959), 7-35. In French.

1274. Bratt, Harald. Vita privata di un uomo celebre. 4 acts. Il Dramma, 369 (January 1, 1942), 7-31. In Italian.

Braun, Pinkas, translator see Albee, E. 101

Braun, Richard, translator see Herondas 4079

1275. Breal, Pierre Aristide, 1905- . Edmée. 3 acts, comedy. L'Avant Scène (OST), 43 (June, 1951), 1-30. In French.

1276. _____. La Grande Oreille. 2 parts, comedy. L'Avant Scène 281 (February 1, 1963), 9-36. In French.

1277. _____. La Grande Oreille. 2 acts, comedy. Sipario, 18 (October, 1963), 57-78. Ettore Capriolo, translator. In Italian.

1278. _____. Les Hussards. 3 acts, tragi-comedy. L'Avant Scène, 86, 5-32. In French.

1279. _____. Jules. 3 acts, comedy. L'Avant Scène, 126, 1-33. In French.

1280. _____. Les Suisses. 2 parts. L'Avant Scène, 396 (February 1, 1968), 7-34. In French.

1281. Brecht, Bertolt, 1898-1956. Baal. 1 act. Spectaculum 6 (1963), 23-68. In German.

1282. _____. The Baby-Elephant. 1 act. Wake, 8 (1949), 9-19. Gerhard Nellhous, translator.

1283. _____. Baden Lehrstuck. 1 act. Tulane Drama Review, 4 (May, 1960), 118-133. Lee Baxandall, translator.

1284. _____. The Begger, or The Dead Dog. 1 act. Drama Review (TDR), 12 (Winter, 1968), 120-123. Michael Hamburger, translator.

1285. _____. The Days of the Commune. 14 scenes. Massachusetts Review, 12 (Summer, 1971), supplement. Leonard Lehrman, translator.

1286. _____. "Deutschland--Ein Greuelmärchen." 1 act. Das Wort, 8 (July, 1938), 35-39. In German.

1287. _____. Dialogues d'Exilés. 18 parts. L'Avant Scène, 432 (September 1, 1969), 7-41. Gilbert Badia and Jean Baudrillard, translators. In French.

1288. _____. The Elephant Calf. 1 act. Evergreen Review, 7 (March-April, 1963), 27-39. Eric Bentley, translator.

1289. _____. The Exception and the Rule. New Directions, 15 (1955), 45-69. Eric Bentley, translator.

1290. _____. Exercices pour les Comédiens. 2 parts. L'Avant Scène, 432 (September 1, 1969), 44-49.

1291. _____. Furcht und Elend des III Reiches. Sipario, 4 (January, 1949), 37-58. F. E. de Rici, translator. In Italian.

1292. _____. Furcht und Elend des Dritten Reiches. 1 act. Spectaculum, 4 (1963), 7-77. In German.

1293. _____. Des Güte Mensch von Sezuan. 1 act. Spectaculum, 1 (1962), 7-87. In German.

1294. _____. He Who Says No. 1 act. Accent, 7 (Autumn, 1946), 20-24. Gerhard Nellhaus, translator.

1295. _____. He Who Says Yes. 1 act. Accent, 7 (Autumn, 1946), 15-20. Gerhard Nellhaus, translator.

1296. _____. Die Heilige Johanna der Schlachthofe. 1 act. Spectaculum, 2 (1959), 43-125. In German.

1297. _____. The Horatians and the Curatians, A Play for School-Children. 1 act. Accent, 8 (Autumn, 1947), 3-22. H. R. Hayes, translator.

1298. _____. In the Jungle of Cities. 1 act. Theatre Arts, 45 (August, 1961), 25-56. Gerhard Nellhaus, translator.

1299. _____. The Informer. 1 act. Living Age, 355 (September, 1938), 35-42.

1300. _____. The Informer. 1 act. Penguin New Writing, 6 (1941), 105-115.

1301. _____. Leben des Galilei. 1 act. Spectaculum, 1 (1962), 89-165. In German

1302. _____. The Life of Confucius. (A scene from a posthumous fragment). Kenyon Review, 20 (Summer, 1958), 393-398. H. E. Rank, translator.

1303. _____. Macbeth: Murder at the Gate-Keeper's House. 1 act. Drama Review (TDR), 12 (Fall, 1967), 110-111.

1304. _____. Mother Courage. 2 acts. New Directions, 6 (1941), 1-80. H. R. Hayes, translator.

1305. _____. Der Prozess der Jeanne D'Arc zu Rouen 1431. 1 act. Spectaculum, 5 (1963), 33-68. In German.

1306. _____. Rechtsfindung, 1934. 1 act. Das Wort, 7 (June, 1938), 6-17. In German.

1307. _____. Romeo and Juliet: The Servants. 1 act. Drama Review (TDR), 12 (Fall, 1967), 108-110.

1308. _____. Schweyk im Zweiten Weltkrieg, 1 act. Spectaculum, 3 (1960), 67-124. In German.

1309. _____. The Seven Deadly Sins of the Lower Middle Class. 1 act, ballet cantata. Tulane Drama Review, 6 (September, 1961), 123-129. W. H. Auden and Chester Kallman, translators.

1310. _____. Der Spitzel. 1 act. Das Wort, 6 (March, 1938), 3-10. In German.

1311. _____. La vera vita di Jacob Ceherda. Sipario, 26 (August-September, 1971), 77-83. Carlo Formigoni, translator. In Italian.

1312. _____. Yes, I'm Going Away. 1 act. Living Age, 356 (May, 1939), 238-242. Ruth Norden, translator.

_____, adapter see Moliere 6113

_____, adapter see Shakespeare, W. 8176

1313. Breene, R. Simmons. The Heed o' the Heep. 1 act. Dublin Magazine, 2 (May, 1925), 650-653.

1314. Breffort, Alexandre. Irma la Dolce. 2 act, comedy. Sipario, 13 (December, 1958), 93-112. Vittorio Gassman and Luciano Lucignani, translators. In Italian.

Breit, Harvey, 1913- see Schulberg, B. 8089

Bremer, Claus, translator see Ionesco, E. 4394

1315. Brenman, Morris. Paris Interlude. 1 act. Scholastic, 28 (March 28, 1936), 11-12.

1316. Brennan, M. M. One Hundred Pounds Reward. 1 act, comedy. One-Act Play Magazine, 1 (April, 1938), 1043-1056.

1317. Brenner, Elizabeth. The Fearless Knight and the Dragon. 1 act. Plays, 19 (February, 1960), 59-66.

1318. _____. Four Letters Home. 1 act. Plays, 18 (November, 1958), 54-60.

_____, adapter see Clemens, S. L. 1887

1319. Brenton, Howard and David Hare. Brassneck. 1 act. Plays and Players, 21 (October, 1973), I-XVI, 43-45.

1320. _____, Brian Clark, Trevor Griffiths, David Hare, Steven Poliakoff, Hugh Stoddart, and Snoo Wilson. Lay By. 1 act. Plays and Players, 19 (November, 1971), 65-75.

1321. Bricaire, Jean-Jacques and Maurice Lasaygues. Les Deux Vierges. 2 acts, comedy. L'Avant Scène, 579 (January 15, 1976), 3-35. In French.

1322. _____. Folie Douce. 2 acts, comedy. L'Avant Scène, 495 (May 15, 1972), 7-37. In French.

1323. _____. L'Honneur des Cipolino. 4 acts, comedy. L'Avant Scène, 530 (December 1, 1973), 7-35. In French.

Bridges, Madeline, pseud. see DeVere, Mary Ainge 2388

1324. Bridgman, Betty. Bargains in Bonds. 1 act. Plays, 4 (January, 1945), 66-71.

Bridie, James, pseud. see Mavor, O. H. 5695

1325. Brieux, Eugène, 1858-1932. The School for Mothers-In-Law. 1 act. Smart Set, 41 (September, 1913), 1-16. Willard Huntington Wright, translator.

Briffault, Herma, translator see Picasso, P. 7144

1326. Brighouse, Harold, 1882- . The Boy: What Will He Become? 1 act. One-Act Play Magazine, 1 (August, 1937), 291-303.

1327. _____. The Night of "Mr. H." 1 act. Scholastic, 15 (November 2, 1929), 5-6, 12, 29.

1328. Brignetti, Raffaello. Altri equipaggi. 1 act. Il Dramma, (July, 1971), 64-76. In Italian.

1329. Brill, Beatrice. Straw in the Wind. 1 act. One-Act Play Magazine, 3 (May-June, 1940), 315-335.

1330. Bringer, Rudolphe. La cremazione del cugino passoire. 3 acts. Il Dramma, 102 (November 15, 1930), 41-43. In Italian.

1331. Brink, Carol Ryrie. Salute Mr. Washington. 1 act. Plays, 35 (March, 1976), 61-76.

1332. Brinker, Evva. The Magic Bread. 1 act. Plays, 17 (January, 1958), 63-66.

1333. Briscoe, Margaret Sutton. An I.O.U. 2 acts. Scribner's, 14 (September, 1893), 305-313.

1334. Brissoni, Alessandro. La casa sopra le nuvole. 1 act. Il Dramma, 359 (August 1, 1941), 40-44. In Italian.

_____, translator see Molière 6121

_____, translator see Obey, A. 6739

_____, translator see Tellez, G. 8740

Brissoni, Sandro, translator see Priestley, J. B. 7291

Britto, Edgardo R. de, translator see Alencar, J. M. de 124

1335. Brodsky, Ruth. No Hats, No Banquets. 3 acts. First Stage, 2 (Spring, 1963), 133-159.

1336. Brody, Alter. Rapunzel. 1 act. Theatre Arts, 9 (April, 1925), 257-266.

1337. Bron, Jacques. Le Dernier Juge. 1 act. L'Avant Scène, 428 (June 15, 1969), 39-43. In French.

1338. Brontë, Charlotte, 1816-1855. Jane Eyre. 1 act. Plays, 19 (October, 1959), 29-38. Lewy Olfson, adapter AND Plays, 27 (October, 1967), 89-96. Lewy Olfson, adapter.

1339. Brontë, Emily, 1818-1848. La voce nella tempesta. 3 acts. Il Dramma, 393/394 (January 1/15, 1943), 37-56. Adelchi Moltedo, translator. In Italian.

1340. _____. Wuthering Heights. 1 act. Plays, 24 (October, 1964), 83-95. AND Plays, 27 (January, 1968), 87-96. Lewy Olfson, adapter.

Brooke, Eleanor see Kerr, J. 4604

1341. Brookman, Katharine Barron. Interpolated. 1 act. Poet Lore, 35 (Spring, 1924), 78-88.

1341a. Brooks, Charlotte K. Firm Foundations. 1 act. Negro History Bulletin, 17 (March, 1954), 128-131. AND Negro History Bulletin, 23 (April, 1960), 157-160.

1342. Brooks, Elbridge S. The Children's Crusade. 1 act. St. Nicholas, 14 (April, 1887), 460-469.

1343. _____. Dicky Dot and Dotty Dick. 1 act. St. Nicholas, 13 (February, 1886), 285-287.

1344. _____. The False Sir Santa Claus. 1 act. St. Nicholas, 10 (November, 1882), 65-72.

1345. _____. Friends or Foes? 1 act. St. Nicholas, 17 (March, 1890), 419-426.

1346. _____. Lord Malapert of Moonshine Castle. 1 act. St. Nicholas, 9 (April, 1882), 490-495.

1347. _____. The New Red Riding-Hood. 1 act. St. Nicholas, 9 (May, 1882), 572-575.

1348. Brophy, Brigid, 1929- . The Waste Disposal Unit. 1 act. London Magazine, n.s., 4 (April, 1964), 35-58.

1349. Brophy, Edward Piert. Hollywood Zoo. 1 act. One-Act Play Magazine, 3 (September-October, 1940), 469-481.

1350. Broszkiewicz, Jerzy. Dwie Przygodny Lemuela Guillivera. 2 acts. Sipario, 18 (August-September, 1963), 79-87. A. M. Raffo, translator. In Italian.

1351. Brotherton, Alice Williams. The Talisman. 1 act. Poet Lore, 40 (1929), 153-157.

1352. Broughton, James, 1913- . The Last Word; or, What to Say About It. 1 act. San Francisco Review, 1 (Spring, 1959), 19-25.

1353. _____. The Playground, A Dance Drama of Our Precarious Time. 1 act. Theatre Arts, 30 (August, 1946), 450-460.

Broun, May Heywood, translator see Valle Inclan, R. del 8998

1354. Brower, Brock, 1931- . The Tender Edge. 1 act. New World Writing, 11 (1957), 42-70.

1355. Brown, Alice. The Loving Cup. 1 act. Woman's Home Companion, 40 (May, 1913), 11-12, 55-56.

1356. Brown, Alice V. Getting Ready for Winter. 1 act. Plays, 5 (January, 1946), 63-66.

1357. _____. Mrs. Sniffit's Christmas. 1 act. Plays, 10 (December, 1950), 62-64.

1358. _____. My Own Self. 1 act. Plays, 4 (December, 1944), 61-62.

1359. _____. The Trees Go to School. 1 act. Plays, 3 (December, 1943), 55-58.

1360. Brown, B. S. Snake Chief. 1 act. Negro History Bulletin, 34 (March, 1971), 70-71.

1361. Brown, Carol J. The Constitution Is Born. 1 act. Plays, 35 (December, 1975), 63-68.

1362. Brown, Charles. The Screen. 1 act. Scholastic, 10 (April 30, 1927), 15, 28.

1363. Brown, Cynthia. The Selfish Giant. 1 act. Plays, 3 (April, 1944), 58-60.

1364. Brown, Ivor, 1891- . Smithfield Preserv'd, or The Divill a Vegetarian. 1 act. London Mercury, 12 (September, 1925), 477-491.

1365. Brown, John Mason, 1900-1969, adapter. The Pageant of the Shearmen and Tailors. 1 act. Theatre Arts, 9 (December, 1925), 824-835.

1366. Brown, Joyce. The Tables Turned. 1 act. Plays, 26 (May, 1967), 78-80.

1367. Brown, Kenneth H., 1936- . The Brig. 2 acts. Tulane Drama Review, 8 (Spring, 1964), 222-259.

1368. Brown, Laura Norton. Kissing Goes by Favor. 1 act. Drama, 16 (October, 1925), 14-15, 33.

1369. Brown, Lennox. I Have to Call My Father. 1 act. <u>Drama and Theatre</u>, 8 (Winter, 1969-1970), 118-129.

1370. ———. The Meeting. 1 act. <u>Performing Arts in Canada</u>, 7 (Winter, 1970), 20-27.

1371. Brown, Manuel W. George Washington Carver, the Wizard of Tuskegee. 3 acts. <u>Negro History Bulletin</u>, 3 (May, 1940), 119-120.

Brown, Martha see Very, A. 9134

1372. Brown, Nathaniel, Andre Lawrence, Angelo Manqual, and Michael Wells. Hallowishes. 1 act. <u>Scripts</u>, 1 (October, 1972), 71-75.

1373. Brown, Thelma Lucille. The Talent Tree. 1 act. <u>Plays</u>, 2 (March, 1943), 41-45.

1374. Brown, Thomas Gilbert. A Children's Librarian Is Guest on "What's My Line?" 1 act. <u>Wilson Library Bulletin</u>, 27 (May, 1953), 740-743.

1375. Browne, Maurice. The King of the Jews. 1 act. <u>Drama</u>, 24 (November, 1916), 496-529.

1376. Browning, Robert, 1812-1889. The Pied Piper of Hamelin. 1 act. <u>Plays</u>, 27 (April, 1968), 79-86. Michael T. Leech, adapter.

1377. ———. The Pied Piper of Hamelin. 1 act. <u>Plays</u>, 32 (December, 1972), 67-70. Lewis Mahlmann, adapter.

1378. ———. The Pied Piper of Hamelin. 1 act. <u>Plays</u>, 21 (November, 1961), 37-47. Adele Thane, adapter.

1379. Bruck, Edith, 1932- . Sulla porta. 2 acts. <u>Il Dramma</u>, 46, no. 7 (July, 1970), 55-69. In Italian.

1380. Bruckner, Ferdinand, 1891-1958. Elisabeth d'Angleterre. 5 acts. <u>L'Avant Scène</u> (OST), 14 (December, 1949), 1-57. Rénée Cave, translator. In French.

1381. ———. Gioventu' malata. 3 acts. <u>Il Dramma</u>, n.s., 31/32 (February 15/March 1, 1947), 96-119. Grazia di Giammatteo and Fernaldo di Giammatteo, translators. In Italian.

1382. ———. Les Races. 3 acts. <u>Petite Illustration</u>, 188 (May 5, 1934), 1-34. Rénée Cave, adapter. In French.

Bruder, Lou, adapter see Buchner, G. 1402

1383. Brule, Claude. Le Siecle des Lumieres. 2 acts. L'Avant Scène, 449 (March 1, 1975), 20-54. In French.

1384. Bruller, Jean, 1902- . Zoo, ou l'Assassin Philantrope, Comedie Judiciaire Zoologique et Morale. 3 acts. L'Avant Scène, 316 (August 1, 1964), 9-35. In French.

Brunacci, Giorgio, translator see Inge, W. 4374

1385. Brune, Jean. Maître Francois est Mort. 1 act. L'Avant Scène, 142, 40-46. In French.

1386. Brunelli, Bruno, 1885- . L'ombrellino verde. 1 act. Il Dramma, 43 (June 1, 1928), 33-40. In Italian.

1387. Bruno, Pierrette. L'Arnacoeur. 3 acts. L'Avant Scène, 545 (July 15, 1974), 7-39. In French.

1388. Brunori, Andrea. La vocazione. 1 act. Il Dramma, 44, no. 2 (November, 1968), 65-69. In Italian.

1389. Brunson, Beverly. A Bastard of the Blood. 1 act. New World Writing, 10 (1956), 195-211.

1390. Brusati, Franco. La fastidiosa. 3 acts. Sipario, 18 (May, 1963), 50-70. In Italian.

1391. _____. La pieta di novembre. 2 acts. Sipario, 21 (May, 1966), 97-120. In Italian.

1392. _____ and Fabio Mauri. Il benessere. 3 acts. Sipario, 14 (May, 1959), 34-56. In Italian.

1393. Bruyère, Jean de la, 1645-1696. Les Dialogues du Sieur. 6 dialogs. L'Avant Scène, 431 (August 1, 1969), 29-43. Jean Rougerie, adapter. In French.

Bryan, G. S., translator see Hauptmann, G. 3971

1394. Bryant, Patricia. The Night the Angels Sang. 1 act. Resource, 14 (December, 1972), 7-9.

1395. Brydon, Margaret Wylie and Esther Ziegler. The Dreadful Dragon. 1 act. Plays, 10 (January, 1951), 35-47. AND Plays, 18 (February, 1959), 63-75.

1396. _____. May Witch. 1 act. Plays, 22 (May, 1963), 69-78.

1397. _____. The Reluctant Ghost. 1 act. Plays, 11 (May, 1952), 42-48. AND Plays, 17 (October, 1957), 59-65.

Buben, Zdenka, translator see Zeyer, J. 9646

Bucalossi, Marcella, translator see Mercer, D. 5757

1398. Buchan, Susan. The Wife of Flanders. 1 act. Bookman [London], 87 (December, 1934), 179-183.

1399. Buchanan, Fannie R. The Lighting of the Torch. 1 act. Drama, 10 (July-September, 1920), 350-354.

1400. Buchanan, George. An Irish Pastoral. 1 act. Dublin Magazine, 2 (September, 1924), 112-117.

1401. Büchner, Georg, 1913-1837. Leonzio e Lena. 3 acts. Il Dramma, 419/420 (February 1/15, 1944), 59-67. Agar Pampanini, translator. In Italian.

1402. _____. Woyzeck. L'Avant Scène, 246 (July 1, 1961), 44-51. Lou Bruder, adapter. In French.

1403. _____. Woyzeck. Gambit, 6 (No. 23), 87-126. Charles Marowitz, translator and adapter.

1404. _____. Woyzeck. New Directions, 12 (1950), 415-441. Henry Schnitzler and Seth Ulman, translators.

1405. Buck, Doris Pitkin. The Traitor's Wife. 1 act. Plays, 3 (March, 1944), 9-20.

_____ see Foulk, C. W. 3236

1406. Buck, Gertrude, 1868- . Mother-love. 1 act. Drama, 33 (February, 1919), 1-30.

1407. Buck, Pearl S., 1892- . China Speaks to America. 1 act. Asia, 43 (July, 1943), 418-422.

1408. _____. Chinese Incident. 1 act. Asia, 42 (May, 1942), 303-306.

1409. _____. Chinese Incident. 1 act. Scholastic, 41 (October 26-31), 17-19.

1410. _____. Sun Yat-Sen. 1 act. Asia, 44 (April, 1944), 170-174.

1411. _____. Will This Earth Hold? 1 act. Asia, 44 (November, 1944), 506-510.

Buckman, Thomas R., translator see Lagerkvist, P. 4765

1412. Buechler, James. Stone Soup. 1 act. Plays, 30 (October, 1970), 67-70.

1413. Bulgakov, Mikhail A. Ivan Vasilievich. 3 acts, comedy. Modern International Drama, 7 (Spring, 1974), 51-83. Laurence Senelick, translator.

1414. Bullins, Ed. The Fabulous Miss Marie. 1 act. Scripts, 1 (February, 1972), 56-80.

1415. _____. It Bees Dat Way: A Confrontation Ritual. 1 act. Theatre, 2 (1968-69), 120-124.

Bullock, Michael, 1918- , translator see Frisch, M. 3320

Bulwer-Lytton, Edward see Lytton, E. B. 5105, 5106, 5107

1416. Bumstead, Eudora S. Waiting for Santa Claus. 1 act. St. Nicholas, 16 (January, 1889), 222-226.

1417. Buntain, Ruth Jaeger. The Boo-Hoo Princess. 1 act. Plays, 12 (January, 1953), 63-67.

1418. Burack, Abraham Saul, 1908- . Line-up for Victory. 1 act. Plays, 2 (October, 1942), 58-62.

1419. Burckhardt, Rudolph. Love in Three Acts. Locus Solus, 1 (Winter, 1961), 156-162.

1420. Burgess, Jackson, 1927- . Dyer Day, A Redemption Play. 1 act. First Stage, 4 (Winter, 1965-66), 222-225.

1421. Burghlie, James. A Lawyer's Mistake. 1 act. Smart Set, 31 (May, 1910), 125-136.

1422. Burgos y Sarragoiti, Francisco Javier de, 1842-1937. The Bullies. 1 act. Poet Lore, 43 (No. 4, 1937), 339-359. Willis Knapp Jones, translator.

1423. Buridan, Giorgio. I più cari affetti. 1 act. Sipario, 175 (November, 1960), 58-62. In Italian.

1424. Burke, Kenneth, 1897- . Prince Ilan, an Ethical Masque in Seven Parts, Including a Prologue and a Coda. Broom, 6 (January, 1924), 12-22.

1425. Burleson, Bob. The Shouting Head of Prophet John. 4 parts. City Lights Journal, 3 (1966), 84-107.

1426. Burleson, Charlotte. Honey Thieves. 1 act. Plays, 28 (April, 1969), 71-73.

1427. _____. See Wee the Octopus. 1 act. Plays, 28 (March, 1969), 84-86.

1428. ———. The Teddy Bears. 1 act. Plays, 28 (January, 1969), 79-90.

1429. Burley, John. "Chop and Change." 1 act. Coterie, 6/7 (Winter, 1920/1921), 6-22.

1430. Burlingame, Cora. A Gram of Radium. 1 act. Plays, 3 (April, 1944), 1-7.

1431. ———. Rubber. 1 act. Plays, 5 (November, 1945), 11-19.

1432. ———. The Son of a Tanner. 1 act. Plays, 4 (March, 1945), 20-28.

1433. ———. The Three Wishes, A St. Patrick's Day Play. 1 act. Plays, 3 (March, 1944), 44-49. AND Plays, 27 (March, 1968), 75-79.

1434. ———. The Wizard of the Wireless. 1 act. Plays, 5 (March, 1946), 27-33.

1435. ———. Yellow Fever. 1 act. One-Act Play Magazine, 4 (November-December, 1941), 427-438.

1436. Burman, Barbara. History Lesson for Today. 1 act. Dramatika, 10 (1973), n.p.

1437. Burnett, Dana, 1888- . Impromptu. 1 act, comedy. Bookman [New York], 57 (May, 1923), 267-273.

1438. ———. Rain. 1 act. Drama, 14 (October, 1923), 20-23.

1439. Burnett, Frances Hodgson, 1849-1924. The Little Princess. 1 act. Plays, 17 (January, 1958), 87-96. Lewy Olfson, adapter.

1440. ———. The Little Princess. 1 act. Plays, 22 (February, 1963), 33-44. Adele Thane, adapter.

1441. ———. Racketty-Packetty House. 1 act. Plays, 24 (May, 1965), 75-78. Ruth Putnam Kimball, adapter.

1442. ——— and W. H. Gillette. Esmeralda. 4 acts. Century, 23 (February, 1882), 513-531.

1443. Burnett, Whit, 1899- . Home Edition. 1 act. Transition, 13 (Summer, 1928), 199-204.

1444. Burr, Amelia Josephine, 1878- . Judgment. 1 act, tragedy. The Poetry Journal, (May, 1913), 201-217; (June, 1913), 258-278; 2 (July, 1913), 6-25.

Burrell, Randall Cayford, adapter see The Nativity 6461

Burrows, John see Harding, J. 3903

1445. Burtle, Gerry Lynn. The Mystery of the Gumdrop Dragon. 1 act. Plays, 19 (May, 1960), 35-46. AND Plays, 28 (May, 1969), 51-62.

1446. Burton, Richard, 1861-1940. Tatters; A Character Sketch. 1 act. Drama, 12 (March, 1922), 206-208.

1447. Burtt, Theodore C., Jr. The Interview. 1 act. Drama and Theatre, 8 (Winter, 1969-1970), 142-148.

1448. Bush, Stephen. Once a Giant. 1 act. Performing Arts in Canada, 11 (Summer, 1974), 47-50.

1449. Bush-Fekete, Ladislao, 1898- . Bocciate in amore. 3 acts. Il Dramma, 274 (January 15, 1938), 4-29. In Italian.

1450. _____. Ferika. 3 acts. Il Dramma, 173 (November 1, 1933), 4-37. Ada Salvatore, translator. In Italian.

1451. _____. La tabaccheria della generalessa. 3 acts. Il Dramma, 157 (March 1, 1933), 4-33. In Italian.

Buttafava, Giovanni, translator see Aksjonov, V. 94

1452. Butterfield, Walton. Tea for Six. 1 act, comedy. Drama, 16 (January, 1926), 134-136, 155-159.

1453. Buttitta, Anthony. Singing Piedmont. 1 act. One-Act Play Magazine, 1 (August, 1937), 344-360. 1906-1972.

1454. Buzzati, Dino, 1906-1972. Un Cas Interessant. 2 parts. L'Avant Scène, 105, 1-24. Albert Camus, adapter. In French.

1455. _____. Il mantello. 1 act. Il Dramma, n.s., 285 (June, 1960), 37-47. In Italian.

1456. _____. L'uomo che andra' in America. 2 parts. Il Dramma, n.s., 309 (June, 1962), 8-36. In Italian.

1457. _____. Un verme al ministero. 3 acts. Il Dramma, n.s., 283 (April, 1960), 16-48. In Italian.

Buzzi, Mario, translator see Strindberg, A. 8565

1458. Buzzi, Paolo, 1874-1956. La fitta. Sipario, 260 (December, 1967), 92. In Italian.

1459. Buzzichini, Mario. Due ladri e una ballerina. 1 act. Il Dramma, 191 (August 1, 1934), 29-35. In Italian.

1460. _____ and Alberto Casella. Anche a Chicago nascon le violette. 3 acts. Il Dramma, 287 (August 1, 1938), 4-28. In Italian.

1461. Buzzolan, Ugo. Domenica d' un fidanzato. 1 act. Il Dramma, n.s., 203/204 (April 15/May 1, 1954), 52-72. In Italian.

1462. Byers, Jean M. And the Stars Heard. 1 act. Journal of the National Education Association, 30 (November, 1941), 243-246.

1463. Bynner, Witter, 1881-1968. The Little King. 1 act. Forum, 51 (April, 1914), 605-632.

1464. _____. Tiger. 1 act, comedy. Forum, 49 (May, 1913), 522-547.

1465. Byrne, Evelyn B. Books Alive! 1 act. Plays, 34 (November, 1974), 47-54.

C

1466. Caballo, Ernesto. Il pascolo dell' Alpino matteo. 3 acts. Il Dramma, 364 (October 15, 1941), 8-21. In Italian.

1467. Cabell, James Branch, 1879-1958. The Jewell Merchants. 1 act, comedy. Golden Book, 12 (September, 1930), 88-96.

1468. _____. The Jewell Merchants. 1 act. Smart Set, 65 (July, 1921), 67-81.

1469. Cable, Harold. Another Man's Family. 3 acts. Plays, 25 (December, 1965), 1-14.

1470. _____. Bailey, Go Home. 1 act, comedy. Plays, 28 (March, 1969), 27-37.

1471. _____. The Best of Sports. 1 act. Plays, 26 (May, 1967), 1-14.

1472. _____. Big Red Riding Hood. 1 act. Plays, 29 (March, 1970), 11-21.

1473. _____. A Deputy for Broken Bow. 1 act, comedy. Plays, 27 (November, 1967), 13-22.

1474. _____. The Fairest Pitcher of Them All. 4 acts.

Plays, 25 (March, 1966), 27-41. AND Plays, 32 (May, 1973), 27-40.

1475. _____. Last Stop. 1 act. Plays, 24 (May, 1965), 15-29.

1476. _____. Little Jackie and the Beanstalk. 1 act. Plays, 27 (April, 1968), 1-15.

1477. _____. Peace, Pilgrim. 1 act. Plays, 26 (November, 1966), 1-14.

1478. _____. The Reform of Sterling Silverheart. 1 act. Plays, 29 (November, 1969), 27-37.

1479. _____. The Reluctant Columbus. 1 act. Plays, 29 (October, 1969), 1-13.

1480. _____. That Time of Year. 1 act. Plays, 31 (December, 1971), 23-30.

1481. _____. Way, Way Down South. 1 act. Plays, 30 (November, 1970), 14-24.

1482. _____. The Way-Out Cinderella. 1 act. Plays, 23 (May, 1964), 23-35.

1483. _____. Young Forever. 1 act. Plays, 26 (October, 1966), 1-14.

1484. Cabridens, Max-Henri. La Fin du Monde, Drame Atomique. 1 act. L'Avant Scène, 194 (April 1, 1959), 31-36. In French.

Cadot, Michel, translator see Brecht, B. 1290

1485. Cady, Kathryn. Five Dances and a Supper, Comedy or Tragedy. 1 act. Overland, 24 (July, 1894), 94-96.

1486. Cagli, Bruno. Crudele intromissione. 2 acts. Sipario, 344 (January, 1975), 68-80. In Italian.

1487. Càglieri, Emilio. Notte d' avventure. 3 acts. Il Dramma, 316 (October 15, 1939), 4-20. In Italian.

1488. Cahoon, Herbert, 1918- . Phoenices. 1 act. The Chimera, 2 (Summer, 1944), 18-21.

1489. _____. Three Verse Plays: Three Wars; The Market; The Removal of the Academy. 1 act each. New Directions, 9 (1946), 235-242.

1490. Caillavet, G.-A. de, Robert de Flers, and Emmanuel Arène.

Le Roi. 4 acts, comedy. L'Avant Scène (OST), 7 (June, 1949), 1-41. In French.

Caillol, Maryse, translator see Houweninge, C. van 4198

Caillol, Michel J., 1943- , translator see Houweninge, C. van 4198

1491. Caillol, Pierrette. L'Homme Qui Se Taisait. 1 act. L'Avant Scène, 279 (January 1, 1963), 37-43. In French.

1492. Cain, James M., 1892-1977. Hemp. 1 act. American Mercury, 10 (April, 1927), 404-409.

1493. _____. The Hero. 1 act. American Mercury, 6 (September, 1925), 52-56.

1494. _____. Red, White and Blue. 1 act. American Mercury, 12 (October, 1927), 129-134.

1495. _____. Servants of the People. 1 act. American Mercury, 4 (April, 1925), 393-398.

1496. _____. Trial by Jury. 1 act. American Mercury, 13 (January, 1928), 30-34.

1497. _____. The Will of the People. 1 act. American Mercury, 16 (April, 1929), 394-398.

1498. Cajoli, Vladimiro. Quattro Giovani sonore. 3 acts. Sipario, 17 (May, 1962), 29-40. In Italian.

1499. Calaferte, Louis, 1928- . Chez les Titch. L'Avant Scène, 557 (February 1, 1975), 3-20. In French.

1500. _____. Trafic. 1 act. L'Avant Scène, 557 (February 1, 1975), 23-29. In French.

Calasso, Gian Pietro, translator see Zeami, M. 9638

Calder, John, translator see Arrabal, F. 377

1501. Calderon de la Barca, Pedro, 1600-1681. L'Alcade de Zalamea. 3 parts. L'Avant Scène, 263 (April 15, 1962), 11-27. Georges Pillement, translator. In French.

1502. _____. A House with Two Doors Is Difficult to Guard. 3 acts, comedy. Tulane Drama Review, 8 (Autumn, 1963), 157-217. Kenneth Muir, translator.

1503. _____. La Vie est un Songe, Drama en Trois Journées. L'Avant Scène, 258 (February 1, 1962), 39-54. Marie-Claire Valène and André Charpak, adapters. In French.

Calderone, Gianni see Marinetti, F. T. 5549

1503a. Caldwell, Ben. The Wall. Scripts, 1 (May, 1972), 91-92.

1504. Caldwell, Erskine, 1903- , and Jack Kirkland, 1902- . Tobacco Road. 3 acts. Il Dramma, n.s., 89 (July 15, 1949), 7-36. Gigi Cane, translator. In Italian.

1505. Caleffi, Fabrizio, 1952- . I tagliatori di teste. 2 parts. Sipario, 332 (January, 1974), 70-80. In Italian.

1506. Calhoun, Dorothy D. Pretties (All Her Life). 1 act. Touchstone, 6 (October, 1919), 26-31.

1507. Callaghan, Barry. Politics of Passion. 1 act. Performing Arts in Canada, 9 (Summer, 1972), 24-31.

1508. Callanan, Cecelia. Cupid and Company. 1 act. Plays, 12 (February, 1953), 11-18.

1509. Callegari, Gian Paolo, 1909- . Cristo ha ucciso. 3 acts. Il Dramma, n.s., 72 (November 1, 1948), 11-38. In Italian.

1510. _____. Irene fra due rive. 3 acts. Il Dramma, n.s., 265 (October, 1958), 14-49. In Italian.

1511. _____. Le ragazze bruciate verdi. 3 acts. Il Dramma, n.s., 243 (December, 1956), 47-87. In Italian.

1512. Calmo, Andrea. Il saltuzza. 1 act. Il Dramma, 373 (March 1, 1942), 35-41. Michelangelo Muraro, translator. In Italian.

Calvi, Carina, translator see Nash, N. R. 6437

_____, translator see Patrick, J. 6999

_____, translator see Rattigan, T. 7425

1513. Calvino, Vittorio. Ancora addio. 1 act. Il Dramma, n.s., 239/240 (August/September, 1956), 35-44. In Italian.

1514. _____. Un' anima per Giulia. 1 act. Il Dramma, n.s., 15 (June 15, 1946), 47-53. In Italian.

1515. _____. L'Arciere. 1 act. Il Dramma, n.s., 67/68/69 (August 15/September 1/15, 1948), 95-102. In Italian.

1516. _____. La cometa si fermò. 1 act. Il Dramma, n.s., 147/148 (December 15, 1951/January 1, 1952), 110-116. In Italian.

1517. _____. Confessione a Francesca. Sipario, 7 (August-September, 1952), 58-62. In Italian.

1518. _____. Cosí ce ne andremo. 1 act. Il Dramma, n.s., 41 (July 1, 1947), 54-63. In Italian.

1519. _____. La torre sul pollaio. 3 acts. Il Dramma, n.s., 81 (March 15, 1949), 9-37. In Italian.

Camerino, Aldo, translator see Chesterton, G. K. 1790

1520. Cami. Fedeltà e dovere. 1 act. Il Dramma, 131 (February 1, 1932), 42-44. In Italian.

1521. _____. Prestigiazione. 1 act. Il Dramma, 20 (June 15, 1927), 44-45. In Italian.

1522. _____. Il tragico affare dei sonnambuli. 3 acts. Il Dramma, 30 (November 15, 1927), 26-28. In Italian.

1523. Cammaerts, Emile, 1878-1953. Le Mystère des Trois Rois. 2 acts. English Review, 20 (July, 1915), 438-450. In French.

1524. Camoletti, Marc, 1923- . L'Amour-Propre. 3 acts. L'Avant Scène, 426 (May 15, 1969), 7-38. In French.

1525. _____. Boeing-Boeing. 3 acts, comedy. L'Avant Scène, 240 (April 1, 1961), 7-37. In French.

1526. _____. Secretissimo. 3 acts. L'Avant Scène, 344 (November 1, 1965), 9-41. In French.

1527. _____. Semiramis. 3 acts, comedy. L'Avant Scène, 297 (October 15, 1963), 8-36. In French.

1528. Camp, André. Un Homme Averti en Vaut Quatre. 1 act. L'Avant Scène, 233, 48-51. In French.

1529. _____. Nuit de Gel. 1 act. L'Avant Scène, 221, 33-36. In French.

_____ see also Aub, M. 435

_____, adapter see Casona, A. 1636, 1637, 1638, 1639, 1640, 1641, 1642

_____, adapter see Castro, G. de 1657

_____, adapter see Madern, J.-M. 5422

_____, adapter see Vallejo, A. B. 8999

    _____, translator see Arauz, A. 312

    _____, translator see Garcia Lorca, F. 3383

1530. _____ and Francisco Puig-Espert. Le Comte de Gomara. 1 act. L'Avant Scène, 125, 33-37. In French.

1531. _____. L'Enfant de la "Barraca". 1 act. L'Avant Scène, 99, 30-35.

Camp, Jean, 1891- , adapter see Alvarez Quintero, S. and J. Alvarez Quintero 165

    _____, adapter see Deza, E. S. de 2395

    _____, adapter see Valle-Inclan, R. de 8999

    _____, translator see Casona, A. 1635

    _____, translator see Lorca, F. G. 5042, 5048

    _____, translator see Martinez Sierra, G. and M. Martinez Sierra 5632

    _____, translator see Mora, J.-M. de 6211

    _____, translator see Vilalta, M. 9143

Campa, Odoardo, translator see Gorky, M. 3648

    _____, translator see Heiberg, G. 4027

1532. Campana, Domenico. I giorni dell' amore. 2 parts. Il Dramma, n.s., 336 (September, 1964), 10-39. In Italian.

Campanella, Paolo, translator see Obey, A. 6736, 6738, 6741

1533. Campanile, Achille, 1900- . Povero Piero. 3 acts, comedy. Sipario, 16 (July, 1961), 31-47. In Italian.

1534. _____. Tragedie in due battate. Il Dramma, 14 (January, 1927), 31-33. In Italian.

1535. Campbell, Alistair. The Suicide. 1 act. Landfall, 28 (December, 1974), 307-325.

1536. Campbell, Camilla. The Bell of Dolores. 1 act. Plays, 11 (October, 1951), 17-26. AND Plays, 28 (April, 1969), 75-85.

1537. _____. Sharing the Circus. 1 act. Plays, 9 (May, 1950), 64-65.

1538. _____, adapter. The Morning Maker. 1 act. Plays, 9 (January, 1950), 64-66.

Campbell, Jane Paxton, translator see Ostrovsky, A. 6911

1539. Campbell, John A. The Case of the Missing Parents. 1 act. Plays, 17 (March, 1958), 61-62.

1540. Campbell, Joseph, 1881- . Tower of Marl. 1 act. Dublin Magazine, n.s., 20 (July-September, 1945), 1-8.

1541. _____. The Turn-Out. 1 act. Irish Review, 2 (August, 1912), 317-335.

1542. Campbell, Josephine E. Guest of Honor. 1 act. Plays, 4 (May, 1945), 20-27.

1543. _____. Pink Roses for Christmas. 1 act. Plays, 4 (December, 1944), 14-19.

1544. _____. St. Patrick's Eve. 1 act. Plays, 4 (March, 1945), 15-20. AND Plays, 28 (March, 1969), 39-44.

1545. Campbell, Ken. Anything You Say Will Be Twisted. Plays and Players, 16 (August, 1969), 33-44, 76-81.

1546. _____. The Great Caper. Plays and Players, 21 (October-November, 1974), 51-58; 44-50.

1547. Campbell, Lawton. The Girl Who Slipped. 1 act, comedy. Drama, 17 (April, 1927), 203-205.

1548. Campbell, Paddy and William Skolnik. Under the Arch. 1 act. Canadian Theatre Review, 10 (Spring, 1976), 46-85.

1549. Campton, David. Mutatis mutandis. Sipario, 249 (January, 1967), 61-64. Laura del Bono, translator. In Italian.

1550. Camus, Albert, 1913-1960. Caligula. 4 acts. Sipario, 1 (June, 1946), 15-31. Cesare Vico Lodovici, translator. In Italian.

1551. _____. Caligula. Spectaculum, 6 (1963), 71-121. Guido G. Meister, translator. In German.

1552. _____. L'Etat de Siège. 3 parts. L'Avant Scène, 413-414 (November 1-15, 1968), 37-65. In French.

1553. _____. Le malentendu. 3 acts, tragedy. Sipario, 12 (October, 1957), 40-52. Vito Pandolfi, translator. In Italian.

1554. _____. Révolte Dans les Asturies. 4 acts. L'Avant

Scène, 413-414 (November 1-15, 1968), 27-34. In French.

_____, adapter see Buzzati, D. 1454

_____, adapter see Faulkner, W. 2943, 2944

Can, Jean, adapter see Albee, E. 100

Cancogni, Franca, translator see Fry, C. 3332

_____, translator see Leonard, H. 4926

_____, translator see MacNeice, L. 5280

_____, translator see Waterhouse, K. and W. Hall
9216

Candoni, Luigi, translator see Williams, T. 9429

Cane, Gigi, translator see Achard, M. 24

_____, translator see Anderson, M. 210

_____, translator see Caldwell, E. and J. Kirkland
1504

_____, translator see Corwin, N. 2049

_____, translator see Eliot, T. S. 2852

_____, translator see Euripides 2880

_____, translator see George, G. S. and E. Leontovich
3440

_____, translator see Giraudoux, J. 3564, 3568, 3570

_____, translator see Home, W. D. 4152

_____, translator see Mogin, J. 6103

_____, translator see Osborn, P. 6889

_____, translator see Priestley, J. B. 7292

_____, translator see Rattigan, T. 7430

_____, translator see Richardson, H. and W. Berney
7530

_____, translator see Roussin, A. 7759

_____, translator see Supervielle, J. 8621

Cane

_____, translator see Valency, M. J. 8994

_____, translator see Welles, O. 9281

_____, translator see Williams, T. 9426, 9431, 9444

Cane, Luciana, translator see Achard, M. 24

_____, translator see Mogin, J. 6103

1555. Cangiulla, Francesco, 1888- . Decisione. Sipario, 260 (December, 1967), 93. In Italian.

1556. _____. Detonazione. Sipario, 260 (December, 1967), 92. In Italian.

1557. _____. Il donnaiuolo e le 4 stagioni. Sipario, 260 (December, 1967), 93. In Italian.

1558. _____. No c'e un cane. Sipario, 260 (December, 1967), 92. In Italian.

1559. _____. L'ora precisa. Sipario, 260 (December, 1967), 93. In Italian.

1560. _____. Ritornero. 2 acts. Sipario, 260 (December, 1967), 93. In Italian.

1561. _____. Di tutti i colori. Sipario, 260 (December, 1967), 93. In Italian.

1562. _____ and Rodolfo De Angelis, 1893- . Stornelli vocali. Sipario, 260 (December, 1967), 93-94. In Italian.

Canitano, Anna, translator see Wilder, T. 9400

1563. Cann, Louise Gebhard. Life Is Always the Same. 1 act. Drama, 34 (May, 1919), 1-20.

Cannac, Genia, adapter see Evreinoff, N. 2891

1564. Cannan, Denis. Dear Daddy. 2 acts. Plays and Players, 24 (October-November, 1976), 39-49; 41-49.

1565. _____. Gerani per la guerra. 3 acts. Il Dramma, n.s., 141 (September 15, 1951), 7-37. Ada Salvatore, translator. In Italian.

1566. Cannan, Gilbert, 1884- . Gloves--A Fragment of the Eternal Duet. 1 act, comedy. Theatre Arts, 4 (April, 1920), 160-165.

1567. _____. James and John. 1 act. The Open Window, 8

(May, 1911), 101-127.

1568. Cannarozzo, Franco. Appuntamento nel Michigan. 1 act. Il Dramma, n. s., 183 (June 15, 1953), 31-38. In Italian.

1569. Cannon, Melissa. Will. 1 act. Literary Review, 17 (Spring, 1974), 333-342.

1570. Canolle, Jean. Hamlet de Trascon. 4 acts, comedy. L'Avant Scène, 92, 1-27. In French.

1571. _____. L'Impromptu d'Amsterdam, ou "La Parade". 1 act. L'Avant Scène, 132, 31-39. In French.

1572. _____. Lady Godiva. 3 acts. L'Avant Scène, 177 (July 1, 1958), 7-29. In French.

1573. Canovaccio dei comici dell'arte. 4 parts. Il Dramma, 356 (June 15, 1941), 33-42. In Italian.

1574. Cantini, Guido. Questo non è l'amore. 3 acts. Il Dramma, 284 (June 15, 1938), 4-23. In Italian.

1575. Canton, Wilberto. We Are God. 2 acts. Drama and Theatre, 10 (Spring, 1972), 139-160. S. Samuel Trifilo and Luis Soto Ruiz, translators.

1576. Capek, Karel M., 1890-1938. Bila nemoc. 3 acts. Sipario, 21 (December, 1966), 41-57. Gianlorenzo Pacini, translator. In Italian.

1577. _____. The Pistol of the Beg. 3 acts. Poet Lore, 34 (Winter, 1924), 475-523. E. D. Schonberger, translator.

1578. _____. R.U.R. 4 acts. Il Dramma, 68 (June 15, 1929), 9-42. In Italian.

1579. Caplan, Lydia. So Long, Miss Jones. 1 act. Journal of the National Education Association, 33 (March, 1944), 67-68.

1580. Capo, Gian. L'uomo in maschera. 3 acts. Il Dramma, 69 (July 1, 1929), 4-25. In Italian.

_____, translator see Begovic, M. 721

1581. Capote, Truman, 1924- . The Grass Harp. 2 acts. Theatre Arts, 36 (September, 1952), 34-64.

1582. Cappelli, Salvato. Il diavolo Peter. 3 parts. Il Dramma, n. s., 245 (February, 1957), 11-34. In Italian.

1583. _____. Duecentomila e uno. 2 parts. Il Dramma, n. s.,

358 (July, 1966), 9-32. In Italian.

1584. _____. Esame del comportamento in un matrimonio di grupa. 2 acts. Il Dramma, (March, 1975), 25-47. In Italian.

1585. _____. Incontro a Babele. 2 parts. Il Dramma, n. s., 319 (April, 1963), 12-37. In Italian.

1586. _____. Morte di Flavia e delle sue bambole. 2 parts. Il Dramma, n. s., 378/379 (March/April, 1968), 9-30. In Italian.

Capria, Raffaele La, translator see Green, J. 3699

_____ see Soldati, M. 8366

Capriolo, Ettore, translator see Arden, J. 320, 323

_____, translator see Billetdoux, F. 930

_____, translator see Breal, P. A. 1277

_____, translator see Delaney, S. 2289

_____, translator see Donleavy, J. P. 2535

_____, translator see Dos Passos, J. 2560

_____, translator see Genet, J. 3436

_____, translator see Gilroy, F. D. 3547

_____, translator see Hansberry, L. 3899

_____, translator see John, E. 4472

_____, translator see Jones, L. 4509, 4510

_____, translator see Lawler, R. 4846

_____, translator see McClure, M. 4136

_____, translator see Murdoch, I. 6304

_____, translator see Rudkin, D. 7781

_____, translator see Sanchez, S. 7902

_____, translator see Schisgal, M. 8034, 8036

_____, translator see van Itallie, J-C. 9031

1587. Capriolo, Gino. Terra sconosciuta. 3 acts. Il Dramma, 391/392 (December 1/15, 1942), 11-30. In Italian.

1588. Capron, Marcelle. Le Tabique Taboque. 1 act. L'Avant Scène, 330 (March 15, 1965), 33-43. In French.

1589. Capuana, Luigi. Giacinta. 4 acts. Il Dramma, 414/415/416 (November 15/December 1/15, 1943), 7-22. In Italian.

1590. Capus, Alfred, 1858-1922. The Adventurer. 4 acts, comedy. Drama 16 (November, 1914), 528-615. Benedict Papot, translator.

1591. _____. My Taylor. 1 act, comedy. Smart Set, 54 (February, 1918), 75-84. Barrett H. Clark, translator.

1592. Caragiale, Ioan Luca, 1852-1912. Un Lettre Perdue. 4 acts, comedy. L'Avant Scène, 120, 1-31. Edmond Bernard, translator. In French.

1593. _____. Mr. Leonida Face to Face with the Reaction. 1 act. Drama and Theatre, 10 (Winter, 1971/72), 77-95. Jules Noel Wright, translator.

1594. _____. Il signor Leonida e la reazione. 1 act. Il Dramma, n.s., 310 (July, 1962), 56-60. Ferdinando Ghilardi, translator. In Italian.

1595. Caramello, Michele. Le tre Marie. 3 acts. Il Dramma, 385 (September 1, 1942), 5-19. In Italian.

Caravette, N.A., translator see Tellez, G. 8741

1596. Carballido, Emilio. I Too Speak to the Rose. 1 act. Drama and Theatre, 8 (No. 1, 1969), 47-60. William I. Oliver, translator.

Carbuccia, Horace de, 1891- , adapter see Maugham, W.S. 5669, 5672, 5676

_____, translator see Veiller, B. 9060

Carcano, Gianfilippa, translator see Druon, M. 2610

1597. Carette, Louis, 1913- . Le Barbour. 2 parts. L'Avant Scène, 445 (March 15, 1970), 7-32. In French.

1598. _____. La Bonne Soupe. 2 parts, comedy. Sipario, 14 (February, 1959), 33-56. Belisario Randone, translator. In Italian.

1599. _____. L'ecole des Moroses. 1 act. Il Dramma, n.s., 208 (July 1, 1954), 44-50. Gian Renzo Morteo, translator.

In Italian.

1600. _____. L'Etouffe-Chrétien. 2 parts. L'Avant Scène, 238 (March 1, 1961), 8-27. In French.

1601. _____. L'Homme en Question. 2 parts. L'Avant Scène, 546 (August, 1974), 7-35. In French.

1602. _____. L'Oeuf. 2 acts, comedy. L'Avant Scène, 160, 4-26. In French.

1603. _____. L'Oeuf. 2 acts, comedy. Sipario, 13 (February, 1958), 37-52. Luciano Salce, translator. In Italian.

1604. _____. La Preuve par Quatre. 2 parts. L'Avant Scène, 360, (July 1, 1966), 9-34. In French.

1605. _____. Le Preuve par Quatre. 2 parts. Sipario, 20 (December, 1965), 111-128. Elena Reina, translator. In Italian.

1606. _____. Les Secrets de la Comedie Humaine. 2 acts. L'Avant Scène, 563 (May 1, 1975), 3-29. In French.

_____ see also Randone, B. L. 7404

Carlson, Harry G., translator see Forssell, L. 3226, 3227

1607. Carmer, Carl. Confab with Crockett. 1 act. Scholastic, 41 (October 12-17, 1942), 17-19.

1608. _____. Taps Is Not Enough. 1 act. Senior Scholastic, 47 (October 1, 1945), 17-18, 24.

1609. _____. Your Neck o' the Woods. Scholastic, 31 (September 25, 1937), 17-19E.

1610. Carmontelle, Louis, 1717-1806. Le Veuf, ou Il n'y a pas d'Eternelles Douleurs. 1 act. L'Avant Scène, 123, 35-38. In French.

Carne-Ross, D. S., translator see Pavese, C. 7018

Carner, Jose, adapter see Cervantes Saavedra, M. de 1692

Caro, Alexander, translator see Schnitzler, A. 8077

1611. Carpenter, Grant. The Dragon's Claws. 1 act. Smart Set, 42 (April, 1914), 135-141.

1612. Carpenter, Margaret Haley. Moon Miracle. 1 act. Plays,

Carpi, Annamaria, translator see Bachmann, I. 483

1613. Carpi, Attilio. Si accorciano le distanze. 3 acts. Il Dramma, n.s., 162 (August 1, 1952), 6-28. In Italian.

1614. _____. La sonata in do minore. 1 act. Il Dramma, 354 (May 15, 1941), 45-51. In Italian.

Carpinteri, Lino, adapter see Grum, S. 3764

Carpitella, Alberto, translator see Chekov, A. P. 1764

Carra, Marguerita, translator see Filippo, E. de 3019

1615. Carre, Michel, 1819-1872. L'Enfant Prodigue. 3 acts. Theatre Arts, 26 (September, 1942), 591-597. Ashley Dukes, adapter.

1616. Carrière, Jean-Claude, 1935- . L'Aide-Mémoire. 1 act. L'Avant Scène, 415 (December 1, 1968), 10-30. In French.

_____, adapter see Higgins, C. 4096

1617. Carrion, Miguel Ramos and Vital Aza. Zaragueta. 2 acts, comedy. Poet Lore, 33 (No. 1, 1922), 1-57. Stephen Scatori and Roy Temple House, translators.

1618. Carroll, John. The Enchanted Bicycle. 1 act. Plays, 27 (October, 1967), 83-87.

1619. _____. European Escapade. 1 act. Plays, 33 (November, 1973), 1-12.

Carroll, Lewis, pseud. see Dodgson, C. L. 2515-2518

1620. Carroll, Paul Vincent, 1900- . Conflitti. 3 acts. Il Dramma, n.s., 30 (February 1, 1947), 11-35. Enrico Raggio, translator. In Italian.

1621. _____. Interlude. 1 act. Dublin Magazine, n.s., 12 (April-June, 1937), 16-28.

1622. _____. We Have Ceased to Live. 1 act. Journal of Irish Literature, 1 (January, 1972), 15-70.

1623. _____. The White Steed. 3 acts. Il Dramma, 414/415/416 (November 15/December 1/15, 1943), 43-65. Vinicio Marinucci, translator. In Italian.

1624. Carsana, Ermanno, 1923- . Diapason ovvero l'ultimo paziente. 1 act. Il Dramma, n.s., 268 (May, 1967), 43-48.

1625. _____. L'importanza del latino. 1 act. Il Dramma, n.s., 355/356 (April/May, 1966), 77-83. In Italian.

1626. _____. Jeronimo. 1 act. Il Dramma, n.s., 373 (October, 1967), 62-69. In Italian.

1627. _____. Il valzer del defunto signor Giobatta. 1 act. Il Dramma, n.s., 361 (October, 1966), 57-64. In Italian.

1628. Carter, Lonnie. Iz She Izzy or Iz He Ain'tzy or Iz They Both. Scripts, 1 (May, 1972), 46-71.

1629. Cartwright, David. It's 1984 and the Sheep Have Fleas. 1 act. DeKalb Literary Arts Journal, 8 (Winter, 1975), 1-5.

Casassa, Claudina, translator see Birabeau, A. 951

_____, translator see Blondel, J. 1013

1630. Casella, Alberto, 1891- . Mio figlio ha un grande avvenire. 1 act. Il Dramma, n.s., 166 (October 1, 1952), 46-54. In Italian.

1631. _____. La morte in vacanza. 3 acts. Il Dramma, 120 (August 15, 1931), 4-39. In Italian.

1632. _____. Parentsi chiusa. 1 act. Il Dramma, 21 (July 11, 1927), 36-45. In Italian.

_____, translator see Achard, M. 23

_____, translator see Faure, G. 2945

_____ see also Buzzichini, M. 1460

1633. _____ and Tatiana Pavlova. Imperatrice di diverte. 4 acts. Il Dramma, 226 (January 15, 1936), 3-28. In Italian.

1634. Casey, Bill. The Fastest Insight Alive. 1 act. Contact, 3 (1959), 71-76.

Caslon, Denis, translator see Babel, I. 478

1635. Casona, Alejandra, 1903- . La Barque Sans Pecheur. 3 acts, comedy. L'Avant Scène (ROST), 65 (July, 1952), 1-23. Jean Camp, translator. In French.

1636. _____. Cocu, Battu et Content. 1 act, farce. L'Avant Scène, 75 (March 20, 1953), 25-33. André Camp, adapter. In French.

1638. _____. La Farce du Galant Qui Epousé une Forte Femme. 1 act. L'Avant Scène, 83 (November 5, 1953), 35-38. André Camp, adapter. In French.

1639. _____. Ines de Portugal. 3 acts. L'Avant Scène, 343 (October 15, 1965), 11-35. André Camp, adapter. In French.

1640. _____. La Justice du Corregidor. 1 act, farce. L'Avant Scène, 140, 37-41. André Camp, adapter. In French.

1641. _____. La Molinera d'Arcos. 1 act, farce. L'Avant Scène, 95, 19-37. André Camp, translator. In French.

1642. _____. Sancho Panza dans Son Ile. 1 act. L'Avant Scène, 263 (April 15, 1962), 29-35. André Camp, adapter. In French.

1643. Casper, Leonard, 1923- . Purloined. 1 act. Plays, 5 (October, 1945), 24-34.

Cassel, Federico, translator see Luke, P. 5091

1644. Cassieri, Giuseppe, 1926- . La cocuzza. 1 act. Sipario, 18 (February, 1963), 41-51. In Italian.

1645. _____. L'orecchio di Dionisio, 1 act. Sipario, 319 (December, 1972), 71-76. In Italian.

1646. _____. Il salto mortale. 1 act. Sipario, 17 (March, 1962), 50-57. In Italian.

1647. Castellaneta, Carlo, 1930- . La marcia di Radetzky. 2 parts. Il Dramma, 46, no. 4 (April, 1970), 95-111. In Italian.

Castellani, Emilio, translator see Giraudoux, J. 3571

_____, translator see Horvath, O. von 4177

1648. Castelli, Carlo. Ballatta per Tim pescatore di Trote. 1 act. Il Dramma, n.s., 244 (January, 1957), 44-54. In Italian.

1649. _____. Lamento e rabbia per i gatti. Il Dramma, 51 (November, 1975), 25-32. In Italian.

Castello, Giulio Cesare, translator see Anouilh, J. 267

_____, translator see Archibald, W. 318

_____, translator see Ayme, M. 471

_____, translator see Cronin, A. J. 2119

_____, translator see Greene, G. 3715

_____, translator see Hellman, L. 4045, 4048

_____, translator see Huxley, A. 4346

_____, translator see Nivoix, P. 6607

_____, translator see Salacrou, A. 7868

1650. Castelot, Andre. Napoleon III a la Barre de L'Histoire. L'Avant Scène, 568 (July 15, 1975), 3-28. In French.

1651. Castillo, Barbara Nunez del, 1943- . L'esempio. 2 acts. Il Dramma, 51 (November, 1975), 33-49. In Italian.

1652. _____. I giorni della notte. 3 acts. Il Dramma, n.s., 378/379 (March/April, 1968), 32-53. In Italian.

1653. Castillo, Carlos C., translator see Alvarez Quintero, S. and J. Alvarez Quintero 158

1654. Castle-Builder, The. 1 act. Smart Set, 5 (December, 1901), 29-58.

1655. Castri, Massimo. E' arrivato Pietro Gori, anarchico pericoloso e gentile. Sipario, 346 (March, 1975), 64-80. With Emilio Jona and Sergio Liberovici. In Italian.

1656. _____. Per uso di memoria. Sipario, 31 (April, 1976), 59-80. In Italian.

1657. Castro, Guillen de, 1569-1621. Le Cid de Lepreux. 1 act. L'Avant Scène, 184 (November 1, 1958), 31-33. André Camp, adapter. In French.

1658. Castro, Juan Antonio. Only a Man in Black. 2 acts. Modern International Drama, 6 (Fall, 1972), 13-42. Marcia Cobourn Wellworth, translator.

1659. _____. The Visit. 1 act. Modern International Drama, 5 (Fall, 1971), 61-69. Patricia W. O'Connor, translator.

1660. Cataldo, Gaspare, 1902- . Buon viaggio Paolo! 3 acts. Il Dramma, n.s., 16/17 (July 1/15, 1946), 83-101. In Italian.

1661. _____. La signora è partita. 3 acts. Il Dramma, 302

(March 15, 1939), 4-23. In Italian.

_____ see also de Stefani, A. 2381

1662. Catastrophe! 1 act. Smart Set, 17 (November, 1905), 151-153.

1663. Catron, Louis E. At a Beetle's Pace. 1 act. Dramatics, 42 (May, 1971), 4-8.

1664. _____. Touch the Blue Bird's Song. 1 act. Dramatics, 43 (December, 1971), 5-8.

1665. _____. Where Have All the Lightning Bugs Gone? 1 act. Dramatics, 43 (November, 1971), 5-9.

1666. Catteau, François. Le Par. 1 act. L'Avant Scène, 310 (May 1, 1964), 38-42. In French.

1667. Cau, Jean. Les Parachutistes. Sipario, 19 (May, 1964), 35-48. Elio Ceretti, translator. In Italian.

1668. Cauman, Sarah. Alice in Bookland. 1 act. Wilson Library Bulletin, 9 (October, 1934), 81-84, 95.

1669. Cavacchioli, Enrico. Cerchio della morte. 3 acts. Il Dramma, 89 (May 1, 1930), 4-29. In Italian.

1670. _____. Corte de miracoli. 3 acts. Il Dramma, 43 (June 1, 1928), 5-32. In Italian.

1671. Cavalier miseria, Il. 1 act. Il Dramma, n.s., 322/323 (July/August, 1963), 54-58. Enrico Fulchignoni, translator. In Italian.

1672. Cavalieri, Grace. Hush, No One Is Listening. 1 act. Dramatics, 43 (February, 1972), 4-7.

1673. Cavallotti, Cesare. Il capoufficio. 1 act. Il Dramma, 339 (October 1, 1940), 45-49. In Italian.

1674. Cavander, Kenneth. Godbug. 1 act. First Stage, 6 (Winter, 1967-68), 249-259.

1675. Cavazza, E. When Angry, Count a Hundred. 1 act. Century, 44 (August, 1892), 597-602.

Cave, Renée, adapter see Bruckner, F. 1380, 1382

1676. Cavendish, Lady Jane and Lady Elizabeth Brackley. The Concealed Fansyes. 5 acts. PMLA, 46 (September, 1931), 802-838.

1677. Ceccaldi, Daniel, 1927- . Mais qu-est-ce Que Fait Courir les Femmes, la Nuit a Madrid? 2 acts, comedy. L'Avant Scène, 528 (November 1, 1973), 7-38. In French.

_____, adapter see Goldoni, C. 3606

Cecchi, Emilio, translator see Kilty, J. 4623

Celebrini, Stelio, translator see Goldoni, C. 3604

1678. Celli, Giorgio, 1935- . Il sonno di carnefici. Sipario, 332 (January, 1974), 61-69. In Italian.

Cenalino, Sergio, translator see Achard, M. 39

_____, translator see Bernard, J.-J. 827

_____, translator see Cocteau, J. 1913

_____, translator see Corwin, N. 2047

_____, translator see Genet, J. 3437

_____, translator see Gorelik, M. 3642

_____, translator see Green, P. E. 3712

_____, translator see Hughes, R. 4308

_____, translator see Morris, T. B. 6238

_____, translator see Priestley, J. B. 7297

_____, translator see Williams, E. 9410

_____, translator see Williams, T. 9443

Centurier, Albert see Bernard, T. 855

1679. Cenzato, Giovanni, 1885- . Dopo la gioia. 3 acts. Il Dramma, 179 (February 1, 1934), 4-29. In Italian.

1680. _____. Ho perduto mio marito!... 3 acts. Il Dramma, 215 (August 1, 1935), 5-29. In Italian.

1681. _____. Il ladro sono io! 3 acts. Il Dramma, 255 (April 1, 1937), 2-24. In Italian.

1682. _____. La maniera forte. 3 acts. Il Dramma, 103 (December 1, 1930), 4-29. In Italian.

1683. _____. La moglie innamorata. 3 acts. Il Dramma, 65 (May 1, 1929), 4-31. In Italian.

1684.	_____. Noi che restiamo. 3 acts. Il Dramma, 224 (December 15, 1935), 2-22. In Italian.
1685.	_____. L'occhio del re. 3 acts. Il Dramma, 23 (August 1, 1927), 5-34. In Italian.
1686.	_____. Il sole negli occhi. 3 acts. Il Dramma, 298 (January 15, 1939), 4-23. In Italian.
1687.	_____. Il viaggio di astolfo. 3 acts. Il Dramma, n.s., 224 (May, 1955), 36-55. In Italian.
1688.	_____. La vita in due. 3 acts. Il Dramma, 86 (March 15, 1930), 8-32. In Italian.

Ceretti, Elio, translator see Cau, J. 1667

Cerio, F. Ferruccio see de Stefani, A. 2382

1689.	Cervantes Saavedra, Miguel de, 1547-1616. Don Quixote. 1 act. Plays, 20 (March, 1961), 85-94. Lewy Olfson, adapter.
1690.	_____. The Entremes of the Cave of Salamanca. 1 act. Poet Lore, 39 (Spring, 1928), 120-131. Willis Knapp Jones, translator.
1691.	_____. The Faithful Dog. 1 act, farce. Poet Lore, 46 (Autumn, 1940), 195-207. Angel Flores and Joseph Liss, translators.
1692.	_____. Le Gardien Zélé. 1 act. L'Avant Scène, 204 (September 15, 1959), 30-34. Jose Carner, adapter. In French.
1693.	_____. Il giudice dei divorzi. 1 act, intermezzo. Il Dramma, 45, no. 10 (July, 1969), 45-48. Vittorio Bodini, translator. In Italian.
1694.	_____. The Judge of the Divorce Court. 1 act. Poet Lore, 45 (No. 2, 1939), 117-126. Willis Knapp Jones, translator.
1695.	_____. Le Rétable des Merveilles. 1 act. L'Avant Scène, 146, 33-40. Paul Delon, adapter. In French.
1696.	_____. El Retablo de las Maravillas. 2 acts. Poet Lore, 32 (Summer, 1921), 234-243. Edith Fahnstock and Florence Donnell White, translators.

Cesareo, Giovanni, translator see Edmonds, R. 2816

1697.	Cesco, Bruno De. Scena in Montagna. 1 act. Il Dramma,

336 (August 15, 1940), 47-51. In Italian.

1698. Chabannes, Jacques, 1900- . Le Compagnon de Voyage. 3 acts. L'Avant Scène (OST), 20 (March, 1950), 3-32. In French.

1699. _____. "Halte au Destin". 1 act. L'Avant Scène (OST), 52 (November, 1951), 1-39. In French.

1700. _____. Monsieur et Madame Molière. 1 act. L'Avant Scène, 408 (August, 1968), 9-34. In French.

1701. _____. Quella che passa. 1 act. Il Dramma, 133 (March 1, 1932), 38-39. In Italian.

1702. Chadwick, Julia H. Joan of Arc. 1 act. Woman's Home Companion, 39 (May, 1912), 35, 64.

Chaine, Pierre see Lorde, A. de 5053, 5054

1703. Chalfi, Raquel. Felicidad. 1 act. Drama and Theatre, 12 (Fall, 1974), 85-100.

1704. Chalmers, Roy Melbourne. The Quest for an Ancestor. 1 act. Smart Set, 7 (June, 1902), 160.

1705. _____. Seeing the Pictures. 1 act. Smart Set, 8 (November, 1902), 84.

1706. Chaloner, Gwen. The Bookworm. 1 act. Plays, 20 (November, 1960), 35-40.

1707. _____. The Court of King Arithmetic. 1 act. Plays, 23 (March, 1964), 35-40.

1708. _____. The Magic Wishing Ring. 1 act. Plays, 23 (October, 1963), 49-54.

1709. _____. The Thankful Elf. 1 act. Plays, 23 (November, 1963), 73-77.

Champagne, Lenora, translator see Song of Songs of Solomon 8375

1710. Chance, Julie Grinnell. A Modern Child. 1 act. Smart Set, 1 (May, 1900), 79-85.

1711. _____. A Modern Daughter. 1 act. Smart Set, 1 (April, 1900), 77-82.

1712. _____. A Modern Mother. 1 act. Smart Set, 1 (March, 1900), 79-86.

1713. Chandler, Anna Curtis. A Chinese Rip Van Winkle. 1 act. Plays, 5 (January, 1946), 51-56.

1714. Chandler, Dale. Surface and Shadows. 1 act. One-Act Play Magazine, 3 (May-June, 1940), 355-359.

1715. Chang Feng-chao and Tiao Cheng-Kuo. Camping in the Snow. 1 act, comic dialogue. Chinese Literature, 2 (1973), 83-90.

Chang Feng-yi see Li Huang 4976

1716. Changing Willie's Mind. 1 act. Negro History Bulletin, 4 (April, 1941), 165-167.

Chanu, Jacques see Truffier, J. 8944

1717. Chao Shu-jen. Taking Goods to the Countryside. comedy. Chinese Literature, 1 (1966), 3-17. Gladys Yang, translator.

1718. Chapin, Harold, 1886-1915. The Autocrat of the Coffee Stall. 1 act. Theatre Arts, 5 (April, 1921), 125-141.

1719. _____. The Philosopher of Butterbiggins. 1 act, comedy. Golden Book, 9 (January, 1929), 87-90.

1720. Chapin, Marguerite. Who Scared Whom? 1 act. Plays, 15 (October, 1955), 58-59.

Chapman, Frederic, translator see France, A. 3241

Chapman, John R., 1927- see Cooney, R. 2001

Chapman, Robert see Coxe, L. O. 2086

1721. Chappell, Eric. The Banana Box. 2 acts. Plays and Players, 20 (June, 1973), I-XVI.

1722. _____. The Man Who Walked in a Beam of Sunlight. 1 act. Quarterly Review of Literature, 17 (1-2), 38-47. Lane Dunlop, translator.

1723. Char, Rene, 1907- . The Man Who Walked in a Ray of Sunshine. 1 act. Botteghe Oscure, 19 (Spring, 1957), 62-74. Roger Shattuck, translator.

1724. Charasson, Henriette, 1884- . En Chemin de Fer. 1 act. Petite Illustration, 186 (December 9, 1933), 1-6. In French.

1725. _____. Une Robe de Soie. 1 act. Petite Illustration, 186 (December 9, 1933), 1-6. In French.

1726. _____. Separation. 1 act. Petite Illustration, 186 (December 9, 1933), 1-6. In French.

Charles, Elaine see Bonacci, A. 1168

1727. Charpak, André, 1930- . La Femme d'un Autre, ou le Mari Sans le Lit. 1 act, comedy. L'Avant Scène, 298 (November 1, 1963), 38-43. In French.

1728. _____. Humilies et Offenses. 4 acts. L'Avant Scène, 179 (August, 1958), 7-24. In French.

1729. _____. Un Joueur. 4 acts. L'Avant Scène, 208 (November 15, 1959), 7-27. In French.

1730. _____. Monsieur Vautrin. 4 acts, comedy. L'Avant Scène, 298 (November 1, 1963), 11-36. In French.

_____, translator see Calderon de la Barca, P. 1503

1731. Charras, Charles. Cinquante Minutes d'Attente. 1 act, comedy. L'Avant Scène, 226, 27-37. In French.

1732. _____. L'Homme a l'Ombrelle Blanche. 1 act. L'Avant Scène, 226, 8-25. In French.

1733. _____. Onze Degres d'Aptitude. 1 act. L'Avant Scène, 489 (February 15, 1972), 31-37. In French.

1734. _____. Trois Cents Mètres D'Elévation. 1 act. L'Avant Scène, 417 (January 1, 1969), 29-36. In French.

_____, adapter see Schiller, J. C. F. von 8026, 8027

1735. Chartreux, Bernard and Jean Jourdheuil. Ah Kiou. tragedy. L'Avant Scène, 581 (February 15, 1976), 3-26. In French.

1736. Charvet, Phillippe. L'Ecole des Morte. 1 act. L'Avant Scène, 312 (June 1, 1964), 28-37. In French.

1737. Chase, Mary Coyle, 1907- . Bernadine. 2 acts, comedy. Theatre Arts, 38 (March, 1954), 34-65.

1738. _____. Harvey. 3 acts, comedy. Sipario, 6 (June, 1951), 33-55. Gian Gaspare Napolitano, translator. In Italian.

1739. Chatelain, Yves. Feu! 1 act, comedy. L'Avant Scène, 233 (December 15, 1 960), 40-47. In French.

1740. _____. Souper Intime. 1 act. L'Avant Scène, 213, 40-46. In French.

1741. Chatterji, Tapanmohan. Light-bearer. 1 act. Drama, 31 (August, 1918), 383-389.

1742. Chaucer, Geoffrey, 1340?-1400. The Canterbury Tales. 1 act. Plays, 22 (May, 1963), 97-107. Lewy Olfson, adapter.

Chauffard, R. J., adapter see Whiting, J. 9332

1743. Chayefsky, Paddy, 1923- . Gideon. 2 acts. Esquire, 56 (December, 1961), 215-230, 234, 236, 238, 240.

1744. _____. The Goddess. 1 act, screenplay. Esquire, 49 (March, 1958), 96-129.

1745. _____. The Latent Heterosexual. 1 act. Esquire, 51 (August, 1967), 49-56, 113, 116-120, 122.

1746. _____. The Tenth Man. 3 acts. L'Avant Scène, 251 (October 15, 1961), 7-27. Jose Andre Lacour, adapter. In French.

1747. _____. The Tenth Man. 3 acts. Sipario, 17 (November, 1962), 38-60. C. D. Marisi, translator. In Italian.

1748. _____. The Tenth Man. 3 acts. Theatre Arts, 45 (January, 1961), 25-56.

1749. Cheatham, Val R. Cinderella and Friends. 1 act. Plays, 30 (December, 1970), 78-82.

1750. _____. Dr. Frankenstein and Friends. 1 act. Plays, 35 (November, 1975), 61-65.

1751. _____. Goldilocks and Friends. 1 act. Plays, 34 (December, 1974), 81-84.

1752. _____. Hansel, Gretel and Friends. 1 act. Plays, 36 (November, 1976), 73-78.

1753. _____. The Hero. 1 act. Plays, 35 (April, 1976), 15-22.

1754. _____. Jack, Beanstalk and Friends. 1 act. Plays, 33 (May, 1974), 69-73.

1755. _____. PTA Triumphs Again. 1 act. Plays, 33 (December, 1973), 69-72.

1756. _____. Pinocchio and Friends. 1 act. Plays, 33 (March, 1974), 43-47.

1757. _____. Red Riding Hood and Friends. 1 act. Plays,

33 (February, 1974), 36-40.

1758. _____. Robin Hood and Friends. 1 act. Plays, 35 (March, 1976), 77-82.

1759. _____. Snow White and Friends. 1 act. Plays, 27 (December, 1967), 42-48.

1760. _____. The Tortoise, the Hare, and Friends. 1 act. Plays, 36 (October, 1976), 63-70.

1761. Chedid, Andree. Le Dernier Candidat. 1 act. L'Avant Scène, 515 (April 1, 1973), 39-47. In French.

1762. _____. Le Montreur, Deux Périodes. L'Avant Scène, 469/470 (April 1/15, 1971), 45-59. In French.

1763. _____. Le Personnage. 1 act. L'Avant Scène, 401 (April 15, 1968), 31-35. In French.

1764. Chekhov, Anton Pavlovich, 1860-1904. Gli amori di Platonov. 5 acts. Il Dramma, n.s., 268 (January, 1959), 12-35. Alberto Carpitella, translator. In Italian.

1765. _____. The Boor. 1 act, comedy. Golden Book, 2 (November, 1925), 654-660. Hilmar Baukage, translator.

1766. _____. The Brute. 1 act, comedy. L'Avant Scène, 299 (November 15, 1963), 38-43. Elsa Triolet, translator. In French.

1767. _____. The Cherry Orchard. 3 acts. L'Avant Scène, 218, 10-30. AND L'Avant Scène, 596 (October 15, 1976), 37-63. Georges Neveux, translator.

1768. _____. La Demande en Mariage. 1 act. L'Avant Scène, 110, 31-36. Georges Pitoeff and Ludmilla Pitoeff, adapters. In French.

1769. _____. Ivanov. 4 acts. L'Avant Scène, 275 (November 1, 1962), 9-33. Antoine Vitez, translator. In French.

1770. _____. The Jubilee. 1 act, farce. Poet Lore, 31 (Winter, 1920), 616-628. Olive Frances Murphy, translator.

1771. _____. La Mouette. 4 acts, comedy. L'Avant Scène, 108, 1-20. George Pitoeff and Ludmilla Pitoeff, adapters. In French.

1772. _____. On the High Road. 1 act. Il Dramma, 6 (May, 1926), 43-48. In Italian.

1773. _____. On the Highway. 1 act. Drama, 22 (May, 1916),

294-322. David A. Modell, translator.

1774. _____. The Proposal. 1 act. Golden Book, 13 (February, 1931), 70-75.

1775. _____. A Proposal of Marriage. 1 act. Il Dramma, 396 (February 15, 1943), 37-41. I. Vitaliano, translator. In Italian.

1776. _____. A Proposal of Marriage. 1 act. Plays, 29 (May, 1970), 83-92. Paul T. Nolan, adapter.

1777. _____. The Sea-Gull. 4 acts. Poet Lore, 24 (No. 1 1913), 1-41. Fred Eisemann, translator.

1778. _____. Summer in the Country, Not a Farce but a Tragedy. 1 act. Tulane Drama Review, 2 (February, 1958), 52-56. Eric Bentley, translator.

1779. _____. Tatyana Riepin. 1 act. London Mercury, 12 (October, 1925), 579-597. S. S. Koteliansky, translator.

1780. _____. The Three Sisters. 4 acts. L'Avant Scène, 100 35-61. Georges Pitoeff and Ludmilla Pitoeff, adapters. In French.

1781. _____. The Tobacco Evil. 1 act. Theatre Arts, 7 (January, 1923), 77-82. Henry James Forman, translator.

1782. _____. The Tragedian in Spite of Himself, a Farce of Suburban Life in One Act. Poet Lore, 33 (Summer, 1922), 268-273. Olive Frances Murphy, translator.

1783. _____. Uncle Vanya. 4 acts. L'Avant Scène, 202 (August 1, 1959), 8-36. Georges Pitoeff and Ludmilla Pitoeff, adapters. In French.

1784. _____. Uncle Vanya. 4 acts. Il Dramma, 421-427 (March 1-June 1, 1944), 41-55. Enzo Ferrieri, translator. In French.

1785. _____. Uncle Vanya. 4 acts. Poet Lore, 33 (Fall, 1922), 317-361. Frances Arno Shaphro, translator.

1786. _____. The Wood Demon. 4 acts. The Calendar of Modern Letters, 2 (December, 1925), 217-243; (January, 1926), 289-316. S. S. Koteliansky, translator.

Chen, Chin Lin see Chin Lin Chen 1804

Chen, Kwei, translator see Three Chinese Folk-Dramas . . . 8855

1787. Cheney, John Vance, 1848-1922. Columbus. 1 act. Overland, 21 (May, 1893), 550-554.

1788. _____. The Mad Piper, An Idyl. 1 act. Cosmopolitan, 12 (December, 1891), 143-154.

1789. Chermak, Sylvia, adapter. Peter and the Wolf. 1 act. Plays, 30 (April, 1971), 67-70.

_____, adapter see Moore, C. C. 6198

1790. Chesterton, Gilbert Keith, 1874-1936. Magic. 3 acts, fantastic comedy. Sipario, 12 (July-August, 1957), 41-53. Aldo Camerino, translator. In Italian.

1791. _____. Time's Abstract and Brief Chronicle. 1 act. Fortnightly, 82 (October, December, 1904), 705-714; 1096-1103.

1792. Chew, Samuel Claggett, 1888-1960. Mr. Moore and Mr. Chew. 1 act. American Mercury, 1 (January, 1924), 39-47.

1793. Chi piu sa manco sa. 3 acts. Il Dramma, n.s., 218/219 (December 1/15, 1954), 71-86. In Italian.

Chiappelli, Bice, translator see Kelly, G. 4578

_____, translator see O'Neill, E. 6862

1794. Chiara, Piero, 1913- . Il trigamo, o la spartizione. 2 acts. Il Dramma, 46, no. 11/12 (November/December, 1970), 91-103. In Italian.

1795. Chiarelli, Luigi, 1886-1947. L'alfabeto. 1 act. Il Dramma, 190 (July 15, 1934), 32-37. In Italian.

1796. _____. Il ciclo delle noci di cocco. 1 act. Il Dramma, 16 (March, 1927), 32-35. In Italian.

1797. _____. Fuochi d'artificio. 3 acts. Il Dramma, 85 (March 1, 1930), 4-29. In Italian.

1798. _____. Le lacrime e le stelle. 3 acts. Il Dramma, 85 (March 1, 1930), 4-29. In Italian.

1799. _____. La Morte degli amanti. 3 acts. Il Dramma, 58 (January 15, 1929), 4-28. In Italian.

1800. _____. Troppo tardi. 1 act. Il Dramma, 19 (June 1, 1927), 33-35. In Italian.

_____, translator see Mauriac, F. 5688

1801. Chiarelli, Ugo and Vittorio Curti. S.O.S. isola felice. 2 acts. Il Dramma, 332 (June 15, 1940), 34-46. In Italian.

Chiavarelli, Lucio, translator see Green, J. 3698

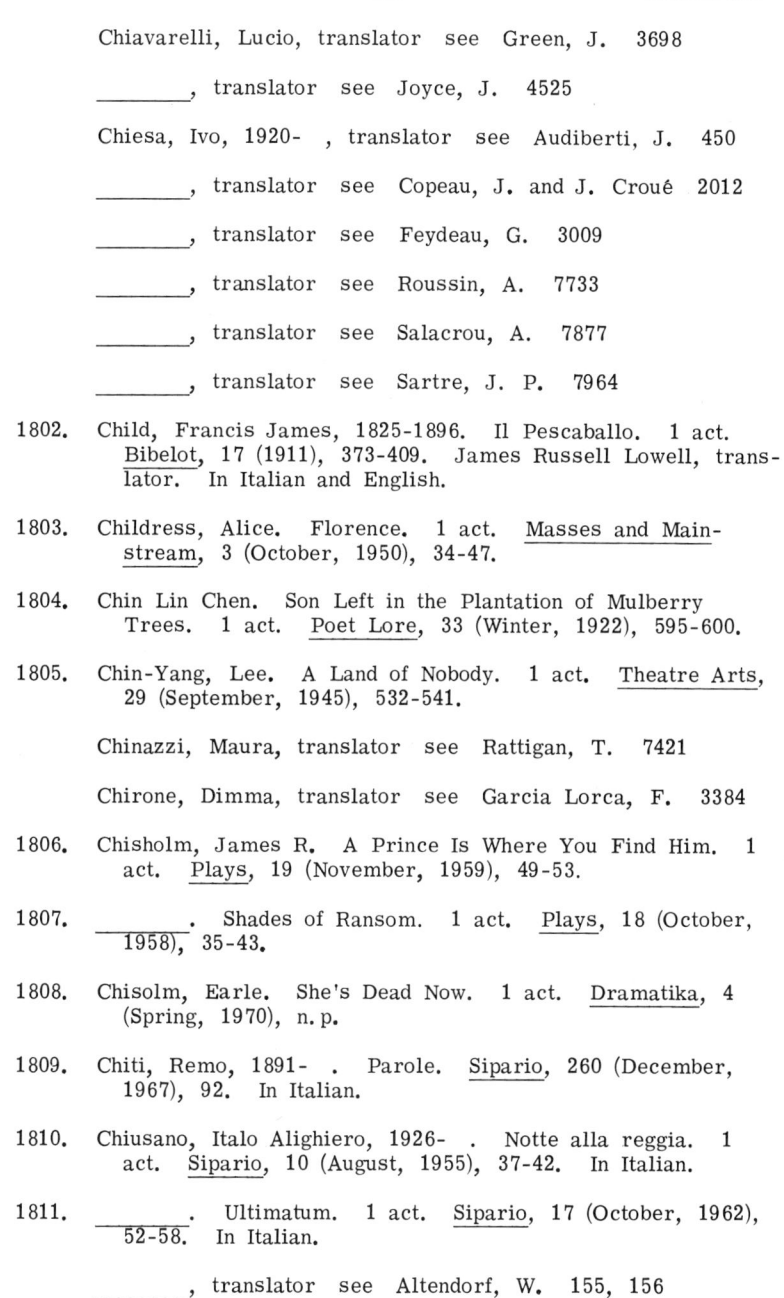

_____, translator see Joyce, J. 4525

Chiesa, Ivo, 1920- , translator see Audiberti, J. 450

_____, translator see Copeau, J. and J. Croué 2012

_____, translator see Feydeau, G. 3009

_____, translator see Roussin, A. 7733

_____, translator see Salacrou, A. 7877

_____, translator see Sartre, J. P. 7964

1802. Child, Francis James, 1825-1896. Il Pescaballo. 1 act. Bibelot, 17 (1911), 373-409. James Russell Lowell, translator. In Italian and English.

1803. Childress, Alice. Florence. 1 act. Masses and Mainstream, 3 (October, 1950), 34-47.

1804. Chin Lin Chen. Son Left in the Plantation of Mulberry Trees. 1 act. Poet Lore, 33 (Winter, 1922), 595-600.

1805. Chin-Yang, Lee. A Land of Nobody. 1 act. Theatre Arts, 29 (September, 1945), 532-541.

Chinazzi, Maura, translator see Rattigan, T. 7421

Chirone, Dimma, translator see Garcia Lorca, F. 3384

1806. Chisholm, James R. A Prince Is Where You Find Him. 1 act. Plays, 19 (November, 1959), 49-53.

1807. _____. Shades of Ransom. 1 act. Plays, 18 (October, 1958), 35-43.

1808. Chisolm, Earle. She's Dead Now. 1 act. Dramatika, 4 (Spring, 1970), n. p.

1809. Chiti, Remo, 1891- . Parole. Sipario, 260 (December, 1967), 92. In Italian.

1810. Chiusano, Italo Alighiero, 1926- . Notte alla reggia. 1 act. Sipario, 10 (August, 1955), 37-42. In Italian.

1811. _____. Ultimatum. 1 act. Sipario, 17 (October, 1962), 52-58. In Italian.

_____, translator see Altendorf, W. 155, 156

_____, translator see Böll, H. 1153

_____, translator see Dürrenmatt, F. 2741, 2747, 2749

_____, translator see Eisenreich, H. 2835

_____, translator see Forster, F. 3228

_____, translator see Hochwälder, F. 4121, 4122

_____, translator see Hofmannstahl, H. von 4138

_____, translator see Mund, W. M. 6295

_____, translator see Sylvanus, E. 8659

1812. Chkvarkine, V. La Petite Datcha. 3 acts, comedy. L'Avant Scène, 228, 8-30. Georges Soria, translator. In French.

1813. Chlumberg, Hans von, 1897-1930. Si recita come si può. 5 scenes. Il Dramma, 78 (November 15, 1929), 4-21. Lucio Ridenti and Otto Eisenschitz, translators. In Italian.

1814. Chodorov, Jerome, 1911- and Joseph Fields, 1895- . Anniversary Waltz. 3 acts, comedy. Theatre Arts, 39 (February, 1955), 34-58.

1815. Chomette, Réné, 1898- . Porte des Lilas. Screenplay. L'Avant Scène, 159, 6-39. In French.

1816. Chose, Raymond. La Farce Blanche, ou La Plus Rusée. 1 act. L'Avant Scène, 186 (December 1, 1958), 44-49. In French.

1817. _____. La Farce de L'Auberge. 1 act. L'Avant Scène, 422 (March 15, 1969), 31-38. In French.

1818. _____. La Farce Jaune, ou de Qui se Moque-T-on? 1 act. L'Avant Scène, 167, 35-41. In French.

1819. _____. La Farce Pouge, ou le Dernier Vivant. 1 act. L'Avant Scène, 286 (April 15, 1963), 39-44. In French.

1820. _____. Liseron, ou Le Destin de la Fille. 1 act. L'Avant Scène, 105, 33-39. In French.

Chotkowski, Z., translator see Mrozek, S. 6284

1821. Chrisholm, James R. Enchanted, I'm Sure. 1 act. Plays, 18 (January, 1959), 35-44.

1822. Christie, Agatha, 1890-1976. The Hollow. 3 acts. Sipario,

1823. _____. The Mousetrap. 2 acts. Il Dramma, n. s., 191 (October 15, 1953), 33-62. Ada Salvatore, translator. In Italian.

1824. _____. Ten Little Indians. 3 acts. Il Dramma, n. s., 34 (April 1, 1947), 8-37. Enrico Raggio, translator. In Italian.

1825. _____. Witness for the Prosecution. 3 acts. L'Avant Scène, 136, 1-29. Paule de Beaumont and Henry Torres, adapters. In French.

1826. Christmas, Joyce S. Three Little Kittens' Christmas. 1 act. Plays, 31 (December, 1971), 73-76.

1827. _____, adapter. The Lion and the Mouse. 1 act. Plays, 31 (March, 1972), 67-71.

1828. Christmas Pageant. 1 act. Learning With ... 2 (December, 1974), 26-27.

1829. Christmas with Martin and Katie. 1 act. Resource, 10 (November, 1968), 6-9, 30.

Chu Tsu-yi see Li Huang 4976

Chu Ya-nan see Wang Fa 9201

1830. Chubb, Percival, 1860-1960. The Old Year and the New. 1 act. Drama, 10 (December, 1919), 110-111.

1831. Church, Henry. Le Savant. 1 act. Mesures, 4 (July 15, 1938), 49-76. In French.

1832. Church, Virginia. Pierrot by the Light of the Moon. 1 act. Drama, 33, 139-148.

1833. _____. Very Social Service. 1 act, satire. Drama, 15 (December, 1924), 54-56, 70.

1934. _____. What Men Live By. 1 act. Drama, 12 (October-November, 1921), 33-38.

1935. Churchill, Caryl. Owners. 2 acts. Plays and Players, 20 (January, 1973), I-XVI.

1836. Churchill, Mary P. Hooray for Thanksgiving. 1 act. Plays, 30 (November, 1970), 67-68.

Clair, René, pseud. see Chomette, René 1815

8 (March, 1953), 33-57. Ada Salvatore, translator. In Italian.

1837. Clapp, Patricia. Christmas in Old New England. 1 act. Plays, 23 (December, 1963), 37-44.

1838. _____. The Do-Nothing Frog. 1 act. Plays, 27 (April, 1968), 69-73.

1839. _____. The Friendship Bracelet. 1 act. Plays, 23 (November, 1963), 43-50.

1840. _____. The Girl Whose Fortune Sought Her. 1 act. Plays, 14 (May, 1955), 53-60.

1841. _____. The Magic Bookshelf. 1 act. Plays, 19 (November, 1959), 35-42. AND Plays, 32 (November, 1972), 47-54.

1842. _____. The Other Side of the Wall. 1 act. Plays, 22 (February, 1963), 45-52.

1843. _____. The Signpost. 1 act. Plays, 22 (May, 1963), 53-59.

1844. _____. Susan and Aladdin's Lamp. 1 act. Plays, 19 (October, 1959), 53-61.

1845. _____. Yankee Doodle Came to Cranetown. 1 act. Plays, 35 (February, 1976), 65-77.

1846. Clark, Andrew. Pinter's Main Course. 1 act. North American Review, 261 (Spring, 1976), 60-65.

1847. Clark, Barrett Harper, 1890- . Fires at Valley Forge. 1 act. Plays, 2 (January, 1943), 1-13.

_____, translator see Augier, E. 456

_____, translator see Capus, A. 1591

_____, translator see Renard, J. 7480

_____, translator see Rolland, R. 7662

_____, translator see Wolff, P. 9533

Clark, Bertha W., translator see Nooshich, B. 6687

Clark, Brian see Brenton, H. 1320

1848. Clark, China. Perfection in Black. Scripts, 1 (May, 1972), 81-85.

1849. Clark, Ina Kitson. Outside the Gate; an Easter Mystery Play. 4 parts. Bookman [London], 86 (April, 1934), 27-33.

1850. Clark, Melissa. Let's Speak Vietnamese. 1 act. Dramatika, 10 (1973), n. p.

1851. Clarke, Austin, 1896- . The Flame. 1 act. Dublin Magazine, n. s., 4, 5 (October-December, 1929; January-March, 1930), 15-22; 15-25.

1852. _____. The Kiss. 1 act, comedy. Dublin Magazine, n. s., 17 (July-September, 1942), 5-18.

1853. _____. The Second Kiss. 1 act, comedy. Dublin Magazine, n. s., 21 (April-June, 1946), 5-19.

1854. _____. Sister Eucharia. 1 act. Dublin Magazine, n. s., 13 (July-September, 1938), 1-25.

1955. _____. The Son of Learning. 2 acts, comedy. Dublin Magazine, n. s., 1 (July-September, 1926), 33-50.

1856. Clarke, Ednah Proctor. The Revolt of Santa Claus. 1 act. Ladies' Home Journal, 19 (December, 1901), 19.

1857. Clarke, Helen Archibald, 1860-1926. Balaustion's Euripides, A Dramatic Version of 'Balaustion's Adventure' and 'Aristophanes' Apology' by Robert Browning. 4 acts. Poet Lore, 26 (New Year, 1915), 1-37.

_____, translator see Maeterlinck, M. 5424, 5425, 5431, 5432

Clarke, Hugh A., adapter see Wildenbruch, E. von 9387

1858. Clarke, Mary Cowden, 1809-1898. Puck's Pranks; or, Good for Evil. 1 act. St. Nicholas, 10 (February, 1883), 297-303.

1859. Clarke, Sebastien. Helliocentric World. Scripts, 1 (May, 1972), 86-90.

1860. Clarke, Violet. The Power of Flattery. 1 act. Smart Set, 8 (October, 1902), 143-145.

1861. Claudel, Paul, 1868-1955. Conversation dans le Loir-et-Cher. L'Avant Scène, 531 (December 15, 1973), 7-23. In French.

1862. _____. Crusts. 3 acts. Poet Lore, 50 (Autumn, 1944), 195-258. John Heard, translator.

1863. _____. The Hostage. 3 acts. Poet Lore, 50 (Summer, 1944), 100-175. John Heard, translator.

1864. _____. The Humiliation of the Father. 4 acts. Poet

Lore, 50 (Winter, 1944), 291-360. John Heard, translator.

1865. _____. L'Otage. 3 acts. L'Avant Scène, 356 (May 1, 1966), 6-20, 45-58. In French.

1866. _____. Le pain dur. 3 acts. Sipario, 6 (January, 1951), 45-64. Suzanne Rochat, translator. In Italian.

1867. _____. Partage de Midi. 3 acts. Il Dramma, n.s., 91/92 (August 15/September 1, 1949), 11-36. Piero Jahier, translator. In Italian.

1868. _____. La Père Humilié. 4 acts. Il Dramma, n.s., 99/100 (January 1, 1950), 39-61. Carlo Lari, translator. In Italian.

1869. _____. Proteo. 2 acts. satire. Il Dramma, n.s., 108 (May 1, 1950), 9-25. Suzanne Rochat, translator. In Italian.

1870. _____. Proteus, A Satiric Drama. 2 acts. Broom, 1 (December, 1921; January, February, 1922), 124-136; 268-278; 316-346. John Strong Newberry, translator.

1871. _____. Le Ravissement de Scapin. 1 act. L'Avant Scène (OST), 55 (January, 1952), 1-19. In French.

1872. _____. Le Ravissement de Scapin. 1 act. Il Dramma, n.s., 215 (October 15, 1954), 37-49. Gian Renzo Morteo, translator. In Italian.

1873. _____. Verkundigung. Der Sturm, 4 (No. 184/185, November, 1913), 122-125. In German

1874. Claus, Hugo. Friday. 2 acts. Plays and Players, 19 (February, 1972), 71-81. Translated by the author and Christopher Logue.

Clauser, Suzanne, translator see Schnitzler, A. 1872

1875. Clavel, Bernard, 1921- . Saint Euloge de Cordone. 3 acts, tragedy. L'Avant Scène, 353 (March 15, 1966), 10-44. In French.

Clavel, Maurice, 1920- , adapter see Shakespeare 8179

_____, translator see Betti, U. 892

_____, translator see Strindberg, A. 8577

Cleaver, Dale G., 1928- , translator see Ghelderode, M. de 3461

1876. Clemenceau, Georges, 1841-1929. Le Voile du Bonheur. 1 act. Petite Illustration, 88 (January 4, 1930), 1-41. In French.

1877. Clemens, Samuel Langhorne, 1835-1910. The Adventures of Tom Sawyer. 1 act. Plays, 14 (November, 1954), 91-96. AND Plays, 18 (November, 1968), 107-112. Lewy Olfson, adapter.

1878. _____. A Connecticut Yankee in King Arthur's Court. 1 act. Plays, 14 (May, 1955), 84-92.

1879. _____. A Connecticut Yankee in King Arthur's Court. 1 act. Plays, 28 (May, 1969), 99-107. Lewy Olfson, adapter.

1880. _____. Huckleberry Finn. 1 act. Plays, 30 (April, 1971), 71-80. Graham DuBois, adapter.

1881. _____. The Man That Corrupted Hadleyburg. 1 act. Plays, 28 (February, 1969), 75-89. Paul T. Nolan, adapter.

1882. _____. Meisterschaft. 3 acts. Century, 35 (January, 1888), 456-467.

1883. _____. The Million Pound Bank Note. 1 act. Plays, 9 (November, 1949), 80-92. Walter Hackett, adapter.

1884. _____. The Miraculous Eclipse. 1 act. Plays, 31 (April, 1972), 87-95. Joellen Bland, adapter.

1885. _____. On the Trail of Injun Joe. 1 act. Plays, 31 (January, 1972), 85-95. Joellen Bland, adapter.

1886. _____. The Prince and the Pauper. 1 act. Plays, 12 (February, 1953), 62-76. Celia Gordon, adapter.

1887. _____. The Prince and the Pauper. 1 act. Plays, 19 (January, 1960), 47-56. Elizabeth Brenner, adapter.

1888. _____. The Prince and the Pauper. 1 act. Plays, 26 (October, 1966), 81-95. Deborah Newman, adapter.

1889. _____. The Prince and the Pauper. 1 act. Plays, 30 (October, 1970), 85-96. Joellen Bland, adapter.

1890. _____. Tom Sawyer and Injun Joe. 1 act. Plays, 18 (April, 1959), 87-95. Lewy Olfson, adapter.

1891. _____. Tom Sawyer, Pirate. 1 act. Plays, 23 (March 1964), 77-84. AND Plays, 33 (April, 1974), 51-57. Adele Thane, adapter.

Clementelli, Elena, translator see Baroja, P. 612

1892. Clements, Claudine E. Troubadour's Dream; A Play for Christmas-tide in One Act and Three Episodes and an Epilogue. Drama, 16 (November, 1925), 57-58.

1893. Clements, Colin Campbell, 1894- . A Modern Harlequinade in Three Plays: Harlequinade; Columbine; The Return of Harlequin. 1 act each. Poet Lore, 31 (Winter, 1920), 579-603.

1894. _____. Seven Plays of Old Japan: The Cherry-Blossom River; By the Sumida River; Growing Old Together; The Star Dust Path; The Father; A Man and His Wife; Life Is a Dream. 1 act each. Poet Lore, 31 (Summer, 1920), 159-209.

1895. _____. You, a Play with a Happy Ending. 3 acts. Poet Lore, 29 (Summer, 1918), 472-485.

_____ see also Macintire, E. 5218

_____ see also Ryerson, F. 7827, 7828

_____, translator see Love in a French Kitchen 5060

1896. Clerc, Henri. Le Beau Metier. 4 acts. Petite Illustration, 88 (February 1, 1930), 1-30. In French.

Clerge, Claude, translator see Goldoni, C. 3604

1897. Clervers, Jean and Guillaume Hanoteau. La Belle Rombière. 3 acts, comedy. L'Avant Scène (OST), 54 (December, 1951), 1-51. In French.

1898. Cleugh, Dennis. The Violet Under the Snow. 1 act. Drama, 13 (November, 1922), 52-58.

1899. Clifford, Lucy Lane, d. 1929. Likeness of the Night. 4 acts. Anglo-Saxon Review, 4 (March, 1900), 38-93.

1900. _____. Long Duel; A Serious Comedy. 4 acts. Fortnightly, 76 Supplement (September, 1901).

1901. _____. The Search-Light. 1 act. 19th Century, 53 (January, 1903), 159-176.

1902. _____. A Supreme Moment. 1 act. 19th Century, 46 (July, 1899), 153-172.

1903. _____. A Woman Alone. 3 acts. 19th Century, 75 (May, 1914), 1144-1184.

1904. Clinton, Craig. A Shared Thing. 1 act. Dramatika, 9 (Spring, 1972), n. p.

1905. Cloquemin, Paul. The Lighthouse Keepers. 1 act. One-Act Play Magazine, 2 (November, 1938), 477-488. Max Wylie, translator.

Close, Upton, pseud. see Hall, J. W. 3844

Closson, Hermann, translator see L'Office de L'Etoile 6777

1906. Clot, Rene-Jean. La revelation. 4 acts. Sipario, 19 (May, 1964), 49-79. Giancarlo Galassi Beria, translator. In Italian.

1907. Cluny, James B. The Bed of Caesar, A Dramatic Fantasy. 1 act. Double Dealer, 4 (November, 1922), 232-233.

Clurman, Harold, 1901- , translator see Sartre, J. P. 7966

Cobelli, Giancarlo see Badessi, G. 489

Cocco, Cesco, translator see Beolco, A. 811

1908. Cochran, Betty Holmes. The Secret the Bell Told Boston. 1 act. Plays, 36 (December, 1976), 75-82.

1909. Cochrane, Alfred. Death and the Hyacinths. 1 act. Living Age, 210 (September, 1896), 706.

1910. Cocteau, Jean, 1889-1963. Le Bel Indifferent. 1 act. L'Avant Scène, 80 (July 25, 1953), 6-10. In French.

1911. _____. Les Chevaliers de la Table Ronde. 3 acts. L'Avant Scène, 365/6 (October 1-15, 1966), 34-59.

1912. _____. L'Ecole des Vevues. 1 act. L'Avant Scène, 102, 37-42. In French.

1913. _____. L'Ecole des Veuves. 1 act. Il Dramma, n. s., 189 (September 15, 1953), 7-11. Sergio Cenalino, translator. In Italian.

1914. _____. La machine a ecrire. 3 acts. Sipario, 5 (February, 1950), 53-72. Adolfo Franci, translator. In Italian.

1915. _____. Les Maries de la Tour Eiffel. 1 act. L'Avant Scène, 365/6 (October 1-15, 1966), 7-12. In French.

1916. _____. Les Mariés de la Tour Eiffel. 1 act. Il Dramma, n. s., 8 (March 1, 1946), 39-43. Carlo Fruttero,

Cocteau

1917. _____. Le Mariés de la Tour Eiffel. New Directions, 2 (1937), n.p. Dudley Fitts, translator. In Italian.

1918. _____. Over the Wire. 1 act. Atlantic, 146 (October, 1930), 581-589.

_____, adapter see Kilty, J. 4622

Coddington, Hester, translator see Prydz, A. 7321

Codecasa, Maria Silvia, translator see Barnes, P. 610

_____, translator see Bond, E. 1172

_____, translator see Coward, N. 2077

_____, translator see Gatti, A. 3423

_____, translator see Halliwell, D. 3867

_____, translator see Hampton, C. 3881

_____, translator see Nichols, P. 6543

Codey, Emile see Conty, J. 1991

1919. Codignola, Luciano. Giro d'Italia. 2 parts. Sipario, 20 (October, 1965), 27-46. In Italian.

1920. _____. La scatola. 1 act. Sipario, 20 (March, 1965), 56-62. In Italian.

_____, translator see Jellicoe, A. 4453

_____, translator see Kopit, A. 4687

_____, translator see Marowitz, C. 5574

Coen, Fabio, translator see Shaw, I. 8224

Coester, Alfred, translator see Sanchez, F. 7901

1921. Coffey, Charles. The Devil to Pay, or, The Wives Metamorphs'd. 1 act, farce. Baltimore Repertory, 1 supplement (1811), 33-43.

Coggio, Roger, 1934- see Luneau, S. 5092

1922. Coghill, Nevill, 1899- . The Tudor Touch. 1 act. London Mercury, 25 (April, 1932), 526-534.

1923. Cognets, Jean des. Cinemania. 1 act. Il Dramma, 4 (March, 1926), 41-48. In Italian.

1924. Cohan, George Michael, 1878-1942. The Farrell Case. 1 act. Smart Set, 63 (October, 1920), 63-68.

1925. Colbert, Mildred. Judge Monkey. 1 act. Plays, 14 (May, 1955), 77-79.

1926. _____. The Salt in the Sea. 1 act. Plays, 2 (October, 1942), 28-37.

Colbron, Grace Isabel, translator see Schnitzler, A. 8067

1927. Colby, Eleanor. A Vision of Youth. 1 act. Ladies' Home Journal, 30 (March, 1913), 91, 102.

Colby, Inez Sachs, translator see Ostrovsky, A. 6916

1928. Cole, E. R. April Is the Cruelest Month. 1 act. Poet Lore, 64 (Spring, 1970), 57-65.

1929. Cole, Eva. Welcome, Parents. 1 act. Plays, 25 (November, 1965), 56-59.

1930. Cole, Margaret H. Jesus Christ Is Born. 1 act. Resource, 4 (November, 1962), 13-14.

Colecchia, Francesca, translator see Solorzano, C. 8371

1931. Coleman, Lucille. From Where I Sit . . . 1 act. Poet Lore, 56 (Winter, 1951), 345-359.

1932. Colette, Sidonie Gabrielle Claudine, 1873-1954. Gigi. 1 act. L'Avant Scène (OST), 11 (October, 1949), 1-24. In French.

1933. _____. Gigi. 3 acts. Sipario, 10 (June, 1955), 31-52. Anita Loos, adapter. Maria Pia D'Arborio and Lucia Sampieri, translators. In Italian.

1934. _____ and Leopold Marchand. Cheri. 3 acts. Il Dramma, n. s., 147/148 (December 15, 1951/January 1, 1952), 11-42. Ada Salvatore, translator. In Italian.

1935. _____. La vagabonda. 4 acts. Il Dramma, 41 (May 1, 1928), 6-45. In Italian.

_____, adapter see Hartog, J. de 3951

Coline, Constance, adapter see Winter, K. 9476

_____, translator see Blackmore, P. 980

1936. Collaci, Mario. Ming-Y; A Love Story of Enchantment. 1 act. Poet Lore, 44 (No. 2, 1938), 160-175.

Collier, John, 1908- , adapter see Anderson, L. 205

1937. Collins, Bessie F. The Happy Gardener. 1 act. Plays, 15 (May, 1956), 57-58.

1938. Collins, David R. I'd Rather Do It Myself. 1 act. Plays, 29 (March, 1970), 35-46.

1939. Collins, Edward F. The Rainbow Walkers: Carnation Day. 1 act. Dramatika, 5 (Spring, 1970), n.p.

1940. Collins, Louise. The Modern Autocrat. A Comedy of Cross-Purposes. 1 act. Smart Set, 8 (December, 1902), 157-158.

1941. Collins, Wilkie, 1824-1889. The Moonstone. 1 act. Plays, 31 (May, 1972), 79-89. Adele Thane, adapter.

Collodi, Carlo, pseud. see Lorenzini, C. 5055, 5056

1942. Collon, Robert. Trencavel. 2 acts. L'Avant Scène, 295 (September 15, 1963), 8-30. In French.

1943. Colman, Morris. Philosophers, A Satirical Play in One Act. Smart Set, 60 (October, 1919), 87-94.

Colpi, Henri, 1921- see Rivemale, A. 7599

Colquist, Helga, translator see Hedberg, T. H. 4022, 4023

1944. Colson, John G. Baron Barnaby's Box. 1 act. Plays, 14 (March, 1955), 73-78. AND Plays, 30 (April, 1971), 57-62.

1945. _____. Black Ivo. 1 act. Plays, 12 (January, 1953), 40-50.

1946. _____. Bow to the Queen. 1 act. Plays, 11 (April, 1952), 47-54.

1947. _____. Ebenezer Neverspend. 1 act. Plays, 12 (December, 1952), 65-67.

1948. _____. A Message from Robin Hood. 1 act. Plays, 12 (October, 1952), 39-47.

1949. _____. Robin Hood in Sherwood Forest. 1 act. Plays, 15 (January, 1956), 49-58. AND Plays, 34 (January, 1975), 63-72.

1950. _____. Top of the Bill. Plays, 12 (March, 1953), 32-44.

1951. Colton, John, 1889-1946. Sciangai. 4 acts. Il Dramma, 150 (November 15, 1932), 4-30. In Italian.

1952. Colum, Padraic, 1881-1972. The Betrayal; A Melodrama in One Act. Drama, 11 (October, 1920), 3-7.

1953. _____. The Betrayal. 1 act. Dublin Magazine, 2 (July, 1925), 774-878.

1954. _____. Children of Lir. 1 act, tragedy. Journal of Irish Literature, 2 (January, 1973), 109-123.

1955. _____. Cloughoughter. 1 act. Journal of Irish Literature, 2 (January, 1973), 124-143.

1956. _____. The Miracle of the Corn. 1 act. Theatre Arts, 5 (October, 1921), 323-332.

1957. _____. Prologue to Balloon: A Comedy. 1 act. Dial, 85 (December, 1928), 490-500.

1958. _____. Swift's Pastoral. 1 act. Poetry, 17 (January, 1921), 175-180.

_____, translator see Blok, A. 1010

1959. Colvin, Ian. The Sequel. 1 act. Living Age, 331 (October 1, 1926), 72-74.

1960. Combs, Robert. Killer on the Prowl. 1 act. Plays, 18 (March, 1959), 36-48.

1961. _____. The Valiant Villain. 1 act. Plays, 18 (April, 1959), 1-12. AND Plays, 33 (May, 1974), 17-28.

1962. Comden, Betty and Adolph Green. Bells Are Ringing. 2 acts. Theatre Arts, 43 (April, 1959), 24-51.

1963. Commedia di dieci vergine. 1 act. Il Dramma, n.s., 279 (December, 1959), 21-36. In Italian.

1964. Comnene, Marie-Anne. Clorinde, ou le Mariage Interrompu. 1 act, comedy. L'Avant Scène, 280 (January 15, 1963), 29-43. In French.

_____, translator see Pirandello, L. 7181, 7183, 7185, 7188, 7190, 7201, 7206

1965. Compton, Dorothy M. A Hallowe'en Brew. 1 act. Nature Magazine, 32 (October, 1939), 463-465.

1966. Conacher, W. M. In County Mayo. 1 act. Queen's Quarterly, 40 (November, 1933), 599-611.

1967. Conboy, Frank J. The Century Plant. 1 act. Plays, 17 (January, 1958), 43-49.

Condon, Emilie Honzik, translator see Kvapil, J. 4742

1968. Cone, Molly, 1918- , adapter. Paul Bunyan and His Blue Ox. Plays, 26 (January, 1967), 69-74.

1969. Cone, Thomas. Veils. 2 acts. Performing Arts in Canada, 11 (Spring, 1974), 40-46.

1970. Confortes, Claude. Les Amours de la Marchande d'Epices. 1 act, comedy. L'Avant Scène, 416 (December 15, 1968), 43-50. In French.

1971. Conkle, Ellsworth Prouty, 1899- . Day's End. 1 act, monologue. Plays, 28 (February, 1969), 91-95.

1972. _____. If You Can't Eat Fish Without Tenderloin! 1 act. One-Act Play Magazine, 2 (March, 1939), 787-793.

1973. _____. 'Lection. 1 act. Scholastic, 32 (March 19, 1938), 17E-18E, 20E.

1974. _____. Madge. 1 act, comedy. One-Act Play Magazine, 1 (February, 1938), 892-898.

1975. _____. What D' You Call It? 1 act. One-Act Play Magazine, 2 (August-September, 1928), 269-289.

1976. Connelly, Marc, 1890- . Ex Cathedra, A Monophonic Pantomime. 1 act. Theatre Arts, 10 (December, 1926), 844-848.

1977. _____. The Green Pastures. 2 parts. Sipario, 1 (August-September, 1946), 19-45. Bruno Viano, translator. In Italian.

_____ see also Kaufman, G. S. 4559

1978. Conners, Barry, 1882-1933. Roxy. 3 acts. Il Dramma, 170 (September 15, 1933), 4-32. Evelina Levi, translator. In Italian.

1979. Connor, Patricia. Death of an Old Woman. 1 act. Irish Writing, 25 (December, 1953), 57-59.

1980. Conrad, Joseph, 1857-1924. One Day More. 1 act. English Review, 15 (August, 1913), 16-35.

1981. _____. One Day More. 1 act. Smart Set, 42 (February, 1914), 125-141.

1982. Constant. Frederic General. 1 act, comedy. L'Avant Scène, (OST), 13 (October, 1949), 1-28. In French.

1983. Contarello, Agostino. Italia sabato sera. 2 parts. Sipario, 10 (November, 1955), 32-53. In Italian.

Conte, Tonino see Trionfo, A. 8935

1984. Conti, Antonio. Che è di scena? 1 act. Il Dramma, 348 (February 15, 1941), 43-48. In Italian.

1985. _____. L'esame. 1 act. Il Dramma, 69 (July 1, 1929), 29-36. In Italian.

1986. _____. No a tutti. 2 parts. Il Dramma, n.s., 352/353 (January/February, 1966), 77-96. In Italian.

1987. _____. Il problema del quarto atto. 1 act. Il Dramma, 96 (August 15, 1930), 32-41. In Italian.

1988. _____. Ragazzi miei. 1 act. Il Dramma, 333 (July 1, 1940), 43-49. In Italian.

1989. _____. Sabbie mobili. 3 acts. Il Dramma, 242 (September 15, 1936), 2-22. In Italian.

1990. _____. Un uomo da niente. 3 acts. Il Dramma, 202 (January 15, 1935), 4-34. In Italian.

1991. Conty, Jean and Emile Codey. Sposami! 3 acts. Il Dramma, 21 (November, 1926), 7-30. Lucio Ridenti, translator. In Italian.

1992. _____ and Georges de Vissant. Mon bèguin piazzato e vincente. Il Dramma, 35 (February 1, 1928), 4-38. In Italian.

Convalli, Enzo, translator see Tre "No" Giapponesi 8924

1993. Converse, Florence, 1871- . Thy Kingdom Come. 1 act. Atlantic, 127 (March, 1921), 352-362.

1994. Conway, Edward Harold. The Windy Shot. 1 act. Smart Set, 45 (April, 1915), 367-377.

1995. Cook, Albert. The Death of Trotsky. 3 parts. Drama and Theatre, 9 (Fall, 1970), 32-50.

1996. Cook, Alice Carter. Komateekay. 1 act. Poet Lore, 43 (No. 2, 1936), 151-160.

1997. Cook, Leroy James, translator see Moineaux, G. 6107

1998. Cook, Michael. Head, Guts and Sound Bone Dance. 2 acts. Canadian Theatre Review, 1 (Winter, 1974), 72-110.

1999. Cook, Richard. The Inheritors. 1 act. Drama and Theatre, 7 (Winter, 1968-69), 159-172.

2000. Cooke, Nicilos. Dangling from Two Second Rate Tragedies; An Absurd Play in Five Scenes. Poet Lore, 59 (No. 3), 222-246.

Coolidge, Susan, pseud. see Woolsey, S. C. 9554

Coolus, Romain, pseud. see Weill, Rene 9265

2001. Cooney, Ray, 1932- , and John Chapman, 1927- . Le Saut du lit. 2 acts, comedy. L'Avant Scène, 506 (November 15, 1972), 7-39. Marcel Mithois, adapter. In French.

2002. Cooper, Esther. Little White Cloud. 1 act. Plays, 2 (November, 1942), 50-52.

2003. ———. The Magic Broom. 1 act. Plays, 2 (October, 1942), 53-55.

2004. ———. The Magic Spell. 1 act. Plays, 3 (October, 1943), 56-58.

2005. ———. Strawberry Cottage. 1 act. Plays, 2 (February, 1943), 51-53.

2006. ———. The Witch's Pumpkin. 1 act. Plays, 5 (October, 1945), 40-42.

2007. Cooper, Giles. Happy Family. 2 acts. Plays and Players, 14 (May, 1967), 27-42, 64-65.

2008. Cooper, James Fenimore, 1789-1851. The Spy. 1 act. Plays, 9 (March, 1950), 83-95. Walter Hackett, adapter.

Cooperman, Chasye, translator see Miller, L. 6054

2009. Copani, Peter. A Secret. 1 act. The Falcon, 7 (Spring, 1976), 63-71.

2010. Copeau, Jacques, 1879-1949. The House into Which We Are Born. 3 acts. Theatre Arts, 8 (July, 1924), 459-488. Ralph Roeder, translator.

2011. ——— and Jean Croué. Les Frères Karamazov. 5 acts. L'Avant Scène, 481 (October 15, 1971), 7-44. In French.

2012. _____. Les Frères Karamazov. 5 acts. Il Dramma, n.s., 192 (November 1, 1953), 9-42. Ivo Chiesa, translator. In Italian.

2013. Copeland, Jennie F. Pageant of Boston. 3 parts. New England Magazine, 54 (March, 1916), 115-126.

2014. Copi, 1939- . L'homosexuel, ou, La difficulte de s'exprimer. Sipario, 315-316 (August-September, 1972), 75-82. Emanuele Vacchetto, translator. In Italian.

2015. Coppee, François, 1842-1908- . The Passer-By. 1 act, comedy. Poet Lore, 34 (Autumn, 1923), 461-470.

Coppotelli, Arthur A., translator see Pincherle, A. 7156

2016. Corbett, Elizabeth F., 1887- . The After-glow. 1 act. Poet Lore, 36 (Summer, 1925), 311-316.

2017. _____. The Hanger Back. 1 act. Poet Lore, 41 (Spring, 1930), 91-104.

Corey, Caroline H., adapter see Grimm, J. and W. Grimm 3750

2018. Corkery, Daniel, 1878-1965. Fohnam the Sculptor. 3 acts. Journal of Irish Literature. 2 (May-September, 1973), 101-138.

2019. _____. Resurrection. 1 act. Theatre Arts, 8 (April, 1924), 259-272.

Corman, Cid, 1924- , translator see Zeami Motokiyo 9639

2020. Cormenzana, Jose Maria Bellido, 1922- . Train to H. 1 act. Modern International Drama, 1 (March, 1968), 218-228. Ronald C. Flores, translator.

2021. Corneau, Perry Boyer. Masks. 1 act, satire. Drama, 12 (April, 1922), 234-236.

2022. Corneilson, Edward N. Prepare the Way of the Lord. 1 act. Resource, 12 (November, 1970), 6, 31.

2023. Cornell, Mary. I Thank You. Canadian Forum, 12 (September, 1932), 454-458.

2024. Cornish, Roger N. Open Twenty-Four Hours. 1 act. Drama and Theatre, 7 (Fall, 1968), 39-55.

2025. _____. A World Without Words. 1 act. Dramatika, 2 (October, 1968), 28-34.

Corra, Bruno see Corradini, B. 2028-2035

2026. Corradini, Arnaldo and Bruno Corradini. Alternazione di Carattere. Sipario, 260 (December, 1967), 91. In Italian.

2027. ———— and Emilio Settimelli, 1891-1954. Dalla finestra. Sipario, 260 (December, 1967), 91-92. In Italian.

2028. Corradini, Bruno, 1892- . La trovata dell'avvocato Max. 1 act. Il Dramma, 334 (July 15, 1940), 42-47. In Italian.

———— see Corradini, A. 2026

———— see Marinetti, F. T. 5554

2029. ———— and Giuseppe Achille. Il cuore di allora. 3 acts. Il Dramma, 356 (June 15, 1941), 9-29.

2030. ————. Le donne sono cosî. 3 acts. Il Dramma, 288 (August 15, 1938), 4-26. In Italian.

2031. ————. Il pozzo dei miracoli. 3 acts. Il Dramma, 262 (July 15, 1937), 2-25. In Italian.

2032. ————. Traversata nera. 3 acts. Il Dramma, 244 (October 15, 1936), 2-24. In Italian.

2033. ———— and Emilio Settimelli, 1891-1954. Atto negativo. Sipario, 260 (December, 1967), 91. In Italian.

2034. ————. Davanti all'infinito. Sipario, 260 (December, 1967), 91. In Italian.

2035. ————. Passatismo. Sipario, 260 (December, 1967), 91. In Italian.

2036. Corrie, Joe, 1897- . And So to War. 1 act, satire. One-Act Play Magazine, 1 (June, 1937), 120-139.

Corsi, Mario, translator see Sardou, V. 7930

2037. Corso, Gregory, 1930- . In This Hung-Up Age. 1 act, farce. Encounter, 18 (January, 1962), 83-90.

2038. ————. In This Hung-Up Age. 1 act, farce. New Directions, 18 (1964), 149-161.

2039. ————. Standing on a Streetcorner, a Little Play. 1 act. Evergreen Review, 6 (March-April, 1962), 63-78.

2040. Corson, Hazel W., 1906- . Triumph for Two. 1 act.

Plays, 26 (March, 1967), 37-44.

2041. ———. Wanted: A House to Haunt. 1 act. Plays, 30 (October, 1970), 78-82.

2042. ———, adapter. The Clever Peasant. 1 act. Plays, 28 (October, 1968), 63-68.

2043. ———, adapter. Dame Fortune and Don Money. 1 act. Plays, 26 (April, 1967), 55-61.

2044. ———, adapter. Fish in the Forest. 1 act. Plays, 27 (October, 1967), 43-49.

2045. ———, adapter. The Green Glass Ball. 1 act. Plays, 27 (January, 1968), 43-49.

Cortese, Leonardo, 1916- , translator see Roblès, E. 7630

2046. Corthis, Andrè. La chiave. 1 act. Il Dramma, 155 (February 1, 1933), 36-42. In Italian.

2047. Corwin, Norman, 1910- . Descent of the Gods. 1 act. Il Dramma, n.s., 162 (August 1, 1952), 47-52. Sergio Cenalino, translator. In Italian.

2048. ———. Il mio cliente Ricciolo. 1 act. Il Dramma, n.s., 94 (October 1, 1949), 41-46. In Italian.

2049. ———. L'odissea di Runyon Jones. 1 act. Il Dramma, n.s., 80 (March 1, 1949), 31-37. Gigi Cane, translator. In Italian.

2050. ———. The Plot to Overthrow Christmas. 1 act, comedy. Senior Scholastic, 43 (December 13-18, 1943), 17-20, 24.

2051. ———. Samson. 1 act. Theatre Arts, 26 (September, 1942), 548-564.

2052. ———. Untitled. 1 act. Senior Scholastic, 45 (September 18, 1944), 17-20, 24.

2053. Cosmos, Jean, 1923- . Monsieur Alexandre. 2 parts, comedy. L'Avant Scène, 345 (November 15, 1965), 12-39. In French.

———, adapter see Hacks, P. 3810

———, translator see Shaw, G. B. 8209

Costanzo, Maurizio see Simongini, F. 8297

Costes, Cyrus de, translator see Sastre, A. 7970

2054. Costine, Jacques. Pile et Face, ou La Poutre et la Paille. 1 act. L'Avant Scène, 458 (October 15, 1970), 41-43. In French.

2055. ———. Le Prestige Male. 1 act. L'Avant Scène, 532 (January 1, 1974), 42-45. In French.

2056. Cote, Carol K. Walt Whitman: Poet of Democracy. 1 act. Plays, 30 (February, 1971), 77-84.

2057. ———, adapter. The Tortoise and the Hare. 1 act. Plays, 32 (January, 1973), 47-52.

2058. Cotterell, A. F. Social Service or All Creatures Great and Small. 1 act. Gambit, 4 (No. 16), 69-102.

2059. Courant, Paul. Thérèse, ou L'Ecole des Vocations. 1 act, comedy. L'Avant Scène, 449 (May 15, 1970), 37-42. In French.

Cournos, John, 1881- , translator see Teternikov, F. K. 8778

Courteline, Georges, pseud. see Moineaux, Georges 6104-6108

2060. Courtney, William Leonard, 1850-1928. 'Gaston Bonnier'; or 'Time's Revenges'. 2 acts, comedy. Anglo-Saxon Review, 8 (March, 1901), 103-124.

2061. ———. Undine: A Dream Play. 3 acts. Fortnightly, 77 (June, 1902), 1092-1116.

2062. Cousin, Gabriel. La Descente sur Recife. 1 act. L'Avant Scène, 469/470 (April 1/15, 1971), 79-84. In French.

Covaz, Tullio, translator see Wilde, O. 9375

2063. Cowan, Fletcher. Rose Leaves and Asparagus Tips, or Romance and Reality. A Symbolic Poem, Treating of a Present-Day Problem. 1 act. Smart Set, 8 (December, 1902), 33-40.

2064. Cowan, Sada. In the Morgue. 1 act. Forum, 55 (April, 1916), 399-407.

2065. Coward, Noel Pierce, 1899-1973. After the Ball. 2 parts, comedy. Il Dramma, n.s., 113 (July 15, 1950), 53-59. Mario Beltramo, translator. In Italian.

2066. ———. The Astonished Heart. 6 parts, comedy. Il

Dramma, n.s., 50/51 (December 1/15, 1947), 109-121. Mario Beltramo, translator. In Italian.

2067. _____. Blithe Spirit. 3 acts, comedy. Il Dramma, n.s., 14 (June 1, 1946), 9-40. Vinicio Marinucci, translator. In Italian.

2068. _____. Brief Encounter. 5 parts, comedy. Il Dramma, n.s., 135 (June 15, 1951), 39-50. Mario Beltramo, translator. In Italian.

2069. _____. Family Album. 1 act. Il Dramma, n.s., 131 (April 15, 1951), 49-54. In Italian.

2070. _____. Intermezzo. 3 acts, comedy. Il Dramma, 306 (May 15, 1939), 4-25. In Italian.

2071. _____. Present Laughter. 3 acts, comedy. Il Dramma, n.s., 64 (July 1, 1948), 7-36. Ada Salvatore, translator. In Italian.

2072. _____. Present Laughter. 3 acts. Theatre Arts, 33 (August, 1949), 57-96.

2073. _____. Primavera di San Martino. 3 acts, comedy. Il Dramma, n.s., 201 (March 15, 1954), 5-24. In Italian.

2074. _____. Private Lives. 3 acts, comedy. Il Dramma, 140 (June 15, 1932), 4-35. Ada Salvatore, translator. In Italian.

2075. _____. Quadrille. 3 acts, comedy. Sipario, 9 (April, 1954), 33-58. Ada Salvatore, translator. In Italian.

2076. _____. Relative Values. 3 acts, comedy. Sipario, 7 (May, 1952), 33-54. Ada Salvatore, translator. In Italian.

2077. _____. A Song at Twilight. Sipario, 255 (July, 1967), 37-52. Maria Silvia Codecasa, translator. In Italian.

2078. _____. Waiting in the Wings. 3 acts, comedy. Il Dramma, n.s., 352/353 (January/February, 1966), 5-35. Renzo Nissim, translator. In Italian.

2079. _____. Week End. 3 acts, comedy. Petite Illustration, 86 (November 17, 1928), 1-26. Andree Mery and Antoine Bibesco, adapters. In French.

2080. Cowl, Jane and Jane Murfin. Catene. 3 acts. Il Dramma, 386 (September 15, 1942), 7-27. Vinicio Marinucci, translator. In Italian.

Cowl, R. P., translator see Kivi, A. 4653

2081. Cox, Nancy Barney. Tugging. 1 act. Drama, 15 (February, 1925), 107-109.

2082. Cox, Palmer, 1840-1924. The Brownies in Fairyland. 2 acts. St. Nicholas, 21 (March-April, 1894), 462-465; 535-538.

2083. Cox, William Norment. The Scuffletown Outlaws. Scholastic, 14 (May 11, May 25, 1929), 6-7, 30-32; 8-9, 28.

2084. _____. The Scuffletown Outlaws; A Carolina Folk-Play. 1 act. Southwest Review, 11 (April, 1926), 179-204.

2085. Coxe, Clovis. Three Ghosts Walk. 1 act. Sewanee Review, 31 (July, 1923), 281-284.

2086. Coxe, Louis O., 1918- , and Robert Chapman. Billy Budd. 3 acts, tragedy. Theatre Arts, 36 (February, 1952), 50-69.

2087. Coyle, Rollin W. A Matter of Conscience. 1 act. Plays, 17 (January, 1958), 51-56.

2088. Craig, Anne Throop, 1869- . Passing of Dana's People; A Dramatic Cantata. 1 act. Poet Lore, 35 (Winter, 1924), 605-611.

2089. _____. The Well of Hazels. 1 act. Poet Lore, 34 (Autumn, 1923), 429-444.

2090. Craig, Edward Gordon, 1872-1966. School (An Interlude for Marionettes). 1 act. English Review, 26 (January, 1918), 24-28.

_____, editor see Fool, T. 3211

2091. Craigie, Pearl Mary Teresa, 1867-1906. Osbern and Ursyne. 3 acts. Anglo-Saxon Review, 1 (June, 1899), 124-175.

2092. _____ and George Moore, 1852-1933. The Fool's Hour. 1 act. Yellow Book, 1 (April, 1894), 253-272.

2093. Cramped Homes, Cramped Lives. 1 act. Scholastic, 35 (January 15, 1940), 21E-23E.

2094. Crane, Frank Dougall. Purple Cobwebs. 1 act. Poet Lore, 43 (No. 4, 1937), 372-381.

2095. Crane, William D., 1892- . Joan of Domremy. 1 act. Plays, 2 (March, 1943), 11-19.

2096. Craven, Arthur Scott and John Davys Beresford, 1873- . The Perfect Machine. 1 act, comedy. English Review,

26 (May, 1918), 393-408.

2097. Craven, Eleanor and Mildred Sandison Fenner. "Let the Next Generation Be My Client". 1 act. Journal of the National Education Association, 26 (February, 1937), 45-46.

2098. Craven, John V., Jr. Monsieur Galespard and Mademoiselle Jeanne. 1 act. Smart Set, 70 (March, 1923), 69-73.

2099. _____. Peach Marmalade. 1 act. Smart Set, 73 (February, 1924), 63-68.

2100. Crawford, John W., 1914- . The Dregs, A Monologue. 1 act. New Mexico Quarterly, 33 (Winter, 1963-64), 396-403.

2101. Creegan, George R. The Brementown Litterbug. 1 act. Plays, 26 (March, 1967), 82-84.

2102. _____. Hansel and Gretel Go Back to School. 1 act. Plays, 25 (February, 1966), 89-92.

2103. _____. Snow White's Rescue. 1 act. Plays, 26 (January, 1967), 92-94.

2104. _____, adapter. Snow White and Rose Red. 1 act. Plays, 30 (February, 1971), 74-76.

Creighton, Anthony see Osborne, J. J. 6897, 6898

Cremieux, Benjamin, translator see Pirandello, L. 7184, 7192, 7206

2105. Crichton, Madge. Pinocchio Strikes It Rich. 1 act. Plays, 35 (November, 1975), 53-60.

2106. _____. Silent Night. 1 act. Plays, 32 (December, 1972), 31-36.

2107. Crichton, Marion Carrie. The Revolt of the Vegetables. 1 act. Plays, 24 (October, 1964), 69-74.

2108. Crivelli, Fabio Maria. Questi nostri figli. 3 acts. Il Dramma, n.s., 149 (January 15, 1952), 8-25. In Italian.

2109. Crockett, Otway. The Burial Committee. 2 acts. First Stage, 5 (Winter, 1966-67), 199-220.

2110. Croisset, Francis de, 1877-1937. Il Etait une Fois . . . 3 acts. Petite Illustration, 182 (July 30, 1932), 1-34. In French.

2111. _____. La Livrée de M. Le Comte. 3 acts, comedy. Petite Illustration, 86 (January 7, 1928), 1-26. In French.

2112. _____. Pierre ou Jack ...? 3 acts, comedy. Petite Illustration, 181 (February 20, 1932), 1-37. In French.

2113. _____. Le Vol Nuptial. 3 acts, comedy. Petite Illustration, 186 (November 11, 1933), 1-34. In French.

2114. Crommelynck, Fernand, 1885- . Les Amants Puerils. 3 acts. L'Avant Scène, 132, 1-29. In French.

2115. _____. Chand et Froid, ou L'Idée de Monsieur Dom. 3 acts. Il Dramma, n.s., 25 (November 15, 1946), 9-42. Lorenzo Gigli, translator. In Italian.

2116. _____. Le Sculpteur de Masques. 3 acts. Il Dramma, 91 (June 1, 1930), 4-26. In Italian.

2117. _____. Tripes d'or. 3 acts, comedy. Sipario, 7 (June, 1952), 37-58. Massimo Bontempelli, translator. In Italian.

2118. _____. Une femme qu'a le coeur trop petit. 3 acts. Sipario, 8 (June, 1953), 29-60. Camillo Sbarbaro, translator. In Italian.

_____, adapter see Shakespeare, W. 8178

2119. Cronin, A. J. Jupiter Laughs. 3 acts. Sipario, 4 (July, 1949), 41-61. Giulio Cesare Castello, translator. In Italian.

2120. Cronin, Anthony. The Shame of It. 2 acts. Dublin Magazine, 9 (Autumn, 1971), 29-67.

2121. Crothers, Rachel, 1878-1958. Katy Did. 1 act. Smart Set, 27 (January, 1909), 129-136.

2122. _____. Mrs. Molly. 1 act. Smart Set, 27 (March, 1909), 104-113.

2123. _____. Nice People. 1 act, comedy. Everybody's Magazine, 45 (November, 1921), 87-94.

2124. _____. Peggy. 1 act. Scribner's, 76 (August, 1924), 175-183.

2125. _____. What They Think. 1 act. Ladies' Home Journal, 40 (February, 1923), 12-13, 126, 128, 131.

Croué, Jean see Copeau, J. 2011, 2012

Crouse, Russel, 1893- see Lindsay, H. 4987, 4988

2126. Crovi, Raffaele and Enrico Vaime. Uomini e no. Sipario, 228 (April, 1965), 44-53. In Italian.

2127. Crowell, Anne. Snow White. 3 acts. The Delineator, 93 (July, 1918), 32, 42.

2128. _____. The Wild Swans. 2 acts. The Delineator, 93 (October, 1918), 27.

2129. Crowell, Chester T. The Afternoon Orator. 1 act. The New Republic, 39 (June 11, 1924), 72-75.

2130. Crowley, Mart. The Boys in the Band. 2 acts. Sipario, 25 (October, 1970), 43-64. Miro Silvera, translator. In Italian.

2131. Crozière, Alphonse. Il dentista improvvisato. 1 act. Il Dramma, 115 (June 1, 1931), 41-43. In Italian.

Crumbaugh, Margaret S., adapter see Potter, B. 7262

2132. Csokor, Franz Theodor, 1885- . Kalypso. 7 parts. Il Dramma, n.s., 50/51 (December 1/15, 1947), 55-70. Grazio di Giammatteo and Fernaldo di Giammatteo, translators. In Italian.

2133. Cucchetti, Gino. Francesco Caracciolo. 7 parts. Il Dramma, 431/435 (August 1/October 1, 1955), 39-56. In Italian.

Cugno, Marco, translator see Sorescu, M. 8385, 8386

2134. Culbertson, Ernest Howard. Across the Jordan. 1 act. Theatre Arts, 13 (December, 1929), 931-939.

2135. _____. The End of the Trail. 1 act, tragedy. Theatre Arts, 8 (May, 1924), 326-340.

2136. Cullen, Countee, 1903-1946, and Owen Dodson. The Third Fourth of July. 1 act. Theatre Arts, 30 (August, 1946), 488-493.

2137. Cummings, E. E., 1894-1962. Santa Claus. A Morality. 1 act. Wake, 5 (Spring, 1946), 10-19.

2138. Cummings, Parke, 1902- . Economics Are Fun. 1 act. Esquire, 9 (May, 1928), 45, 119.

2139. Cunningham, Leon. The Dralda Bloom. 1 act. Poet Lore, 30 (Winter, 1919), 553-566.

2140. _____. The Wondership. 1 act. Poet Lore, 30 (Autumn, 1919), 362-376.

2141. Cunningham, Phyllis Fenn. Henry Duck's Christmas. 1 act. Plays, 34 (December, 1974), 77-80.

2142. Cunningham, Will J. Matron of Ephesus. 1 act. Poet Lore, 46 (Autumn, 1940), 258-278.

2143. Cuomo, Franco, 1938- . Caterina della misericordie. Sipario, 27 (January, 1972), 65-96. In Italian.

2144. _____. Storia di Giovanna, vergine di guerra e strega innamorata dell' arcangelo Michele e amata dal barone Gilles de Rais suo capitano ad Orleans. 1 act. Sipario, 351-352 (August-September, 1975), 76-112. In Italian.

2145. Cuppy, Elizabeth Overstreet. Mollusk or Suffragette? 1 act. Putnam's Magazine, 7 (November, 1909), 172-181.

2146. Curcio, Armando, 1900- . A che servono questi quattrini? 3 acts. Il Dramma, 336 (August 15, 1940), 4-21. In Italian.

2147. _____. Ci penso io! 3 acts. Il Dramma, 346 (January 15, 1941), 8-23. In Italian.

Curcio, Louis L., translator see Gorostiza, C. 3654

2148. Curel, François de, 1854-1928. The Beat of the Wing. 3 acts, comedy. Poet Lore, 20 (September-October, 1909), 321-375. Alice Van Kaathoven, translator.

2149. Curie, Eve, 1902- . 145, Wall Street. 3 acts. Petite Illustration, 184 (March 4, 1933), 1-38. In French.

2150. Curnow, Allen, 1911- . Resident of Nowhere. 1 act. Landfall, 23 (June, 1969), 148-175.

Curti, Vittorio see Chiarelli, U. 1801

Curtis, Jean-Louis, adapter see Luke, P. 5089

_____, translator see Shakespeare, W. 8188

Cutler, Sharon Vail, translator see Zemme, O. 9641

2151 Cutting, Mary Stewart. A Good Dinner. 1 act. Ladies' Home Journal, 22 (February, 1905), 5, 58.

2152. Cuvelier, Marcel. Oblomov. 2 parts, comedy. L'Avant Scène, 299 (November 15, 1963), 9-35. In French.

Czerniawski, Adam, translator see Rozewicz, T. 7775

Czerwinski, Edward J., translator see Karpowicz, T. 4551

_____, translator see Popovic, A. 7243

D

2153. D., S. J. Christmas Eve at Mother Hubbard's. 1 act. St. Nicholas, 25 (January, 1898), 254-259.

Dabadie, Jean-Loup, 1938- see Athayde, R. 427

_____ see Bedos, G. 715

_____, adapter see Fitzgerald, F. S. 3137

2154. Dabney, Julia Parker. Children of the Sunrise. 1 act. Poet Lore, 26 (November-December, 1915), 653-693.

2155. Dabril, Lucien and Léone Diétrich. L'Honneur des Dupont. 1 act, melodrama. L'Avant Scène, 445 (March 15, 1970), 35-42. In French.

2156. _____. De zero a vingt. 1 act. L'Avant Scène, 580 (February 1, 1976), 29-34. In French.

2157. Da Costa, Bernard, 1942- . Le Bal des Cuisinieres. 5 acts. L'Avant Scène, 507 (December 1, 1972), 5-24, 29-41. In French.

_____, adapter see Eyen, T. 2893

2158. Dadie, Bernard, 1916- . Assemien Dehyle. 1 act. L'Avant Scène, 343 (October 15, 1965), 37-43. In French.

2159. Daggett, James. Goodnight Please! 1 act, farce. One-Act Play Magazine, 1 (November, 1937), 597-611.

D'Agostino, Maria Luisa, translator see Kroetz, F. K. 4726

2160. Daiches, David, 1912- . A Cambridge Dialogue. 1 act. 20th Century, 157 (February, 1955), 179-190.

2161. Daix, Didier. La Fée. 1 act. L'Avant Scène, 187 (December 15, 1958), 36-43. In French.

2162. Dalbray, Muse. Tragédie de l'Absence. 1 act. L'Avant Scène, 323 (December 1, 1964), 37-39. In French.

2163. Daley, Guilbert A. Kiss the Book, A One-Act Farce-Comedy. Carolina Quarterly, 13 (Winter, 1960), 38-63.

2164. Dallagiacoma, Angelo, 1940- . Vita di William Shakespeare. 3 acts. Sipario, 300 (May, 1971), 60-80. In Italian.

2165. Dalrymple, Jean, 1910- , and Phillip Bloom, 1918- . Forever Now. 1 act. One-Act Play Magazine, 4 (September-October, 1941), 408-423.

2166. Daly, Maureen. Sixteen. 1 act. Scholastic, 37 (September 16, 1940), 32-34, 41.

2167. D'Ambra, Lucio. Fantasia. 1 act. Il Dramma, 49 (September 1, 1928), 28-45. In Italian.

2168. _____. Montecarlo. 3 acts. Il Dramma, 97 (September 1, 1930), 4-30. In Italian.

2169. _____. Solitudine. 3 acts. Il Dramma, 258 (May 15, 1937), 3-19. In Italian.

_____, translator see Amiel, D. 188

2170. _____ and Alberto Donaudy. Monzù. 3 acts. Il Dramma, 300 (February 15, 1939), 4-23. In Italian.

D'Amico, Maria Luisa Aguirre, translator see Larreta, A. 4822

_____, translator see Olmo, L. 6826

_____, translator see Sastre, A. 7972, 7973

_____, translator see Valle-Inclan, R. 9002

_____, translator see Vallejo, A. B. 9003

D'Amico, Masolino, translator see Adamov, A. 62

D'Amico, Suso Cecchi, translator see Lindsay, H. 4988

2171. Damon, S. Foster, 1893- . Kiri No Meijiyama. 1 act. Dial, 68 (February, 1920), 205-213.

2172. _____. Persephone in Eden. 1 act. Dial, 78 (June, 1925), 445-464.

2173. D'Amora, Ferdinando. La coltre. 1 act. Il Dramma, 16 (March, 1927), 29-31. In Italian.

2174. _____. Il cugino di Arsenio Lupin. 1 act. Il Dramma, 35 (February 1, 1928), 39-45. In Italian.

2175. _____. I due segreti. 1 act. Il Dramma, 37 (March 1, 1928), 35-36. In Italian.

2176. _____. La pellicola de Re del Siam. 1 act. Il Dramma, 20 (June 15, 1927), 35-43. In Italian.

2177. Danaud, Jean-Claude. Comment les Choses Arrivent. 1 act. L'Avant Scène, 523 (August 1, 1973), 31-36. In French.

2178. _____. Dimanche. 1 act. L'Avant Scène, 553 (December 1, 1974), 41-43. In French.

2179. Dane, Clemence, 1887-1975. A Bill of Divorcement. 1 act. Everybody's Magazine, 46 (February, 1922), 92-98.

Danesi, Lea, translator see Inge, W. 4374

Danesi, Natalia, translator see Hamilton, P. 3878

2180. Dangerfield, Trelawney. Old Stuff. 1 act. Smart Set, 52 (June, 1917), 77-82.

Daniel, Georges, 1935- , adapter see Gorky, M. 3644

Daniels, Camilla Chapin, translator see Ostrovsky, A. 6913

2181. D'Annunzio, Gabriele, 1863-1938. The Daughter of Jorio. 3 acts, tragedy. Poet Lore, 18 (No. 1, 1907), 1-88. Charlotte Porter, Pietro Isola, Alice Henry, translators.

2182. _____. The Dream of a Spring Morning. 1 act. Poet Lore, 14 (No. 1, 1903), 6-36. Anna Schenck, translator.

2183. _____. The Dream of an Autumn Sunset. 1 act, tragedy. Poet Lore, 15 (No. 1, 1904), 6-29. Anna Schenck, translator.

D'Anza, Daniele, translator see Harris, E. 3920

2184. Da Ponte, Lorenzo, 1749-1838. Cosi fan tutte. 2 acts. Theatre Arts, 40 (January, 1956), 36-57. Ruth Martin and Thomas Martin, translators.

D'Arborio, Maria Pia, translator see Arout, G. 365

_____, translator see Colette, S. G. C. 1933

D'Arborio, Silvana, translator see Achard, M. 29

_____, translator see Birabeau, A. 953

_____, translator see Salacrou, A. 7872

2185. D'Arcy, Alice. Cinderella. 1 act. Plays, 3 (December, 1943), 45-52.

2186. ———. Wonders of Storybook Land. 1 act. Plays, 3 (April, 1944), 47-54.

D'Arcy, Margaretta see Arden, J. 325, 326, 327

2187. Dard, Frederic, 1921- . L'Homme Traqué. 3 acts. L'Avant Scène, 97, 5-26. In French.

2188. ———. Jesus la Caille. L'Avant Scène (ROST), 62 (June, 1952), 1-30. In French.

Daskam, Josephine Dodge see Bacon, Josephine Dodge 486-488

2189. Datta, Jyotirmoy. The Dramatist Digested, A Prologue. Drama Review, 15 (Spring, 1971), 246-251.

Daugherty, George H., Jr., translator see Becquer, G. 714

2190. Daugherty, Sonia. The Sacred Cup. 1 act. Plays, 2 (December, 1942), 18-29.

2191. ———. The Way of an Eagle. 1 act. Plays, 2 (April, 1943), 1-10.

Dauli, Gian, translator see London, J. 5022, 5023

2192. Dautun, Paul. Dingos. 1 act. Petite Illustration, 192 (October 26, 1935), 1-9. In French.

2193. Dave, Arlette. Dans la Loge de Molière. 3 acts. L'Avant Scène, 93, 1-24. In French.

David, Charlotte Genney, translator see Donnay, C. M. 2541

2194. David, Michael Robert. The Justice Box. 1 act. Drama and Theatre, 11 (Fall, 1972), 15-30.

2195. Davidson, Gustav. The Great Adventure, A Dramatic Fantasy. 3 acts. Poet Lore, 51 (Autumn, 1945), 195-255.

2196. ———. The Man from Kiriot. 1 act. Poet Lore, 59 (No. 2), 139-148.

———, adapter see Meneses, E. de 5749

2197. ——— and Joseph Auslander, 1897- . "One Man Escapes". 1 act. Poet Lore, 44 (No. 2, No. 3, 1938),

97-125; 193-231.

2198. Davidson, John, 1857-1909. Fleet Street Eclogue, St. George's Day. 1 act. Yellow Book, 5 (April, 1895), 299-317.

2199. Davidson, Madeline. Finally I Am Born. 3 acts. First Stage, 1 (Spring, 1962), 49-78.

Daviel, François translator see Kazantzakis, N. 4563

2200. Davis, James. Taken. 1 act. Dramatika, 10 (1973), n.p.

2201. Davis, Lavinia R. Americans Every One. 1 act. Plays, 2 (May, 1943), 35-40.

2202. _____. David and the Second Lafayette. 1 act. Plays, 2 (January, 1943), 28-35.

2203. _____. The Happy Valentine. 1 act. Plays, 21 (February, 1962), 59-62.

2204. _____. St. Patrick and the Last Snake in Ireland. 1 act. Plays, 2 (March, 1943), 46-49.

2205. _____. A Turtle, a Flute and the General's Birthday. 1 act. Plays, 21 (February, 1962), 35-40.

2206. Davis, Robert Hobart, 1869- . The Room Without a Number. 1 act, farce. Smart Set, 51 (April, 1917), 201-207.

2207. Dawson, Elizabeth W. 'Twas the Night After Christmas-- 1776. 1 act. Plays, 36 (December, 1976), 65-74.

2208. Day, Blanche. The Victory Garden. 1 act. Plays, 3 (May, 1944), 74-76.

2209. Day, Curtiss La Q. The Booklegger. 1 act. Smart Set, 66 (December, 1921), 75-80.

2210. Day, Frederic Lansing. Heaven Is Deep. 3 acts. Drama & Theatre, 12 (Fall, 1974), 49-83.

Dazey, Charles Turner, 1855-1938 see Dazey, L. H. 2211

2211. Dazey, L. H. and Charles Turner Dazey, 1855-1938. A Woman's Choice. 1 act. Smart Set, 30 (April, 1910), 123-129.

De Acosta, Mercedes see Benson, S. 807

Deak, Frantisek, translator see Mayakovsky, V. 5701

Deak, Norma Jean, translator see Song of Songs of Solomon 8375

2212. De Alarcon, Pedro. Il cappello a tre punte. 1 act. Il Dramma, 399 (April 1, 1943), 35-42. In Italian.

2213. Dean, Alexander, 1893- . Just Neighborly. 1 act, satire. Drama, 12 (October-November, 1921), 10-12, 56-62.

Dean, Basil see Kennedy, M. 4596

2214. Dean, Ruth. Non-Fiction Party. 1 act. Wilson Library Bulletin, 10 (November, 1935), 200-204, 206.

2215. De Angelis, Augusto. L'attesa. 1 act. Il Dramma, 91 (June 1, 1930), 31-40. In Italian.

2216. _____. La giostra dei peccati. 3 acts. Il Dramma, 71 (August 1, 1929), 4-37. In Italian.

2217. De Angelis, Raoul Maria, 1908- . Alberto Durer, ovverossia Il mostro marino. 1 act. Il Dramma, 49 (March-April, 1973), 77-84. In Italian.

2218. _____. Il fuoco dei Marziani. 1 act, comedy. Il Dramma, (July, 1974), 25-41. In Italian.

2219. _____. Il numero sbagliato. 1 act. Il Dramma, 45, no. 9 (June, 1969), 83-88. In Italian.

De Angelis, Rodolfo, 1893- see Cangiullo, F. 1562

2220. Death of Me, The. 1 act, comedy. The Laughing Horse, 5 (1923), 30-34.

2221. De Baggis, Romeo. Fallo! 2 acts. Il Dramma, 51 (August-September, 1975), 25-40. In Italian.

_____, translator see Adamov, A. 61

_____, translator see Behan, B. 724, 728

_____, translator see Pinter, H. 7179

2222. De Benedetti, Aldo, 1892- . Buonanotte patrizia! 3 acts. Il Dramma, n.s., 242 (November, 1956), 8-38. In Italian.

2223. _____. Due dozzine di rose scarlatte. 3 acts. Il Dramma, 234 (May 15, 1936), 2-24. In Italian.

2224. _____. Un giorno d'Aprile. 1 act. Il Dramma, n.s., 368 (May, 1967), 22-31. In Italian.

2225. _____. Da giovedi a giovedi. 2 parts. Il Dramma, n.s., 272 (May 1959), 6-28. In Italian.

2226. _____. Lohengrin. 3 acts. Il Dramma, 185 (May 1, 1934), 4-36. In Italian.

2227. _____. M. T. 3 acts. Il Dramma, 164 (June 15, 1933), 4-38. In Italian.

2228. _____. No ti conosco più. 3 acts. Il Dramma, 153 (January 1, 1933), 4-35. In Italian.

2229. _____. Trenta secondi d'amore. 3 acts. Il Dramma, 272 (December 15, 1937), 4-27. In Italian.

2230. _____. Gli ultimi cinque minuti. 3 a cts. Il Dramma, n.s., 132 (May 1, 1951), 7-31. In Italian.

_____ see also Bonelli, L. 1187

2231. _____ and Guglielmo Zorzi. La resa di titi. 3 acts. Il Dramma, 129 (January 1, 1932), 4-34. In Italian.

De Benedetti, Giacomo, 1901- , translator see Sartre, J. P. 7962

De Boysson, Pascale, adapter see Schisgal, M. 8029, 8030, 8031

2232. DeBra, Elsa. Magic in the Deep Woods. 1 act. Plays, 20 (October, 1960), 73-76.

2233. _____. The Miracle Flower. 1 act. Plays, 20 (December, 1960), 67-70.

2234. De Burea, Seamus. Limpid River. 3 acts. First Stage, 5 (Spring, 1966), 30-55.

2235. Decaux, Alain, 1925- . Dumas le Magnifique. L'Avant Scène, 518 (May 15, 1973), 41-70. In French.

2236. _____. Les Rosenberg ne Doivent pas Mourir. 2 parts. L'Avant Scène, 411 (October 1, 1968), 10-32. In French.

_____ see Gavoty, B. 3429

2237. De Cespedes, Alba and Agostino Degli Espinosa. Gli affetti di famiglia. 3 acts, comedy. Sipario, 7 (July, 1952), 37-56. In Italian.

Decharte, Philippe, pseud. see Duprat-Geneau, J. 2732

2238. De Chiara, Ghigo. Antonello capobrigante. 2 parts, comedy. Sipario, 16 (August-September, 1961), 69-79. In Italian.

2239. _____. Itaca, itaca! Sipario, 336 (May, 1974), 62-80. In Italian.

2240. Declercq, Aimé. L'Envers Vaut l'Endroit. 3 acts. Petite Illustration, 185 (July 15, 1933), 1-30. In French.

De Dominicis, Giacinta Jovio, translator see Leonov, L. M. 4929

2241. Deemer, Charles. Above the Fire. 1 act. Dramatics, 44 (January, 1973), 5-9.

2242. Deevy, Teresa. "A Disciple". 1 act, comedy. Dublin Magazine, n.s., 12 (January-March, 1937), 29-47.

2243. _____. The Enthusiast. 1 act. One-Act Play Magazine, 1 (January, 1938), 771-785.

2244. _____. Going Beyond Alma's Glory. 1 act. Irish Writing, 17 (December, 1951), 21-32.

2245. _____. The King of Spain's Daughter. 1 act. Dublin Magazine, n.s., 11 (January-March, 1936), 13-25.

2246. _____. The King of Spain's Daughter. 1 act. Theatre Arts, 19 (June, 1935), 459-465.

2247. _____. Strange Birth. 1 act. Irish Writing, 1 (1946), 40-48.

2248. _____. Strange Birth. 1 act. Life and Letters, 61 (April, 1949), 22-30.

2249. DeFelice, James. The Elixir. 1 act. First Stage, 3 (Winter, 1963-64), 46-58.

2250. De Filippo, Eduardo, 1900- . Amicizia. 1 act, comedy. Sipario, 11 (March, 1956), 54-57. In Italian.

2251. _____. Le bugie con le gambe lunghe. 3 acts. Il Dramma, n.s., 60 (May 1, 1948), 9-32. In Italian.

2252. _____. Il figlio di Pulcinella. 3 acts. Sipario, 15 (June, 1960), 41-68. In Italian.

2253. _____. Filosoficamente. 1 act, comedy. Sipario, 11 (March, 1956), 58-63. In Italian.

2254. _____. Filumana Marturano. 3 acts. Il Dramma, n.s., 35/36 (May, 1947), 11-32. In Italian.

2255. _____. La grande magia. 3 acts. Il Dramma, n.s., 105 (March 15, 1950), 11-31. In Italian.

2256. _____. Mia famiglia. 3 acts, comedy. <u>Sipario</u>, 11 (March, 1956), 36-53. In Italian.

2257. _____. I morti non fanno paura. 1 act, comedy. <u>Sipario</u>, 11 (March, 1956), 64-68. In Italian.

2258. _____. Natale in casa Cupiello. 3 acts. <u>Il Dramma</u>, 397/398 (March 1/15, 1943), 72-86. In Italian.

2259. _____. La parte di Amleto. 1 act. <u>Il Dramma</u>, 331 (June 1, 1940), 45-51. In Italian.

2260. _____. La paura numero uno. 3 acts. <u>Il Dramma</u>, n.s., 133 (May 15, 1951), 11-32. In Italian.

2261. _____. Quasti fantasmi. 3 acts. <u>Il Dramma</u>, n.s., 16/17 (July 1/15, 1946), 13-32. In Italian.

2262. _____. Sabato, domenica e lunedi. 3 acts. <u>Sipario</u>, 14 (October, 1959), 37-63. In Italian.

2263. _____. Il sindaco del rione sanita. 3 acts. <u>Sipario</u>, 16 (February, 1961), 41-60. In Italian.

2264. _____. Tommaso d'Amalfi. 2 parts. <u>Il Dramma</u>, n.s., 326 (November, 1963), 18-58. In Italian.

2265. _____. Le voci di dentro. 3 acts. <u>Il Dramma</u>, n.s., 82 (April 1, 1949), 5-20. In Italian.

2266. De Filippo, Luigi, 1930- . Come e perche crollo il colosseo. 2 acts, comedy. <u>Il Dramma</u> (December, 1974), 25-55. In Italian.

2267. _____. La commedia del re buffone e del buffone re. <u>Il Dramma</u>, 51 (December, 1975), 25-52. In Italian.

2268. De Filippo, Peppino. Aria paesana. 1 act. <u>Il Dramma</u>, 360 (August 15, 1941), 32-39. In Italian.

2269. _____. Caccia grossa! 1 act. <u>Il Dramma</u>, 410/411 (September 15/October 1, 1943), 54-59. In Italian.

2270. _____. A coperchia è caduta una stella. 2 acts. <u>Il Dramma</u>, 395 (February 1, 1943), 31-42. In Italian.

2271. _____. Don Raffaele il trombone. 1 act. <u>Il Dramma</u>, 350 (March 15, 1941), 29-33. In Italian.

2272. _____. Il grande attore. 1 act. <u>Il Dramma</u>, 360 (August 15, 1941), 40-44. In Italian.

2273. _____. Le metamorfosi di un suanatore ambulante. 2

De Filippo

parts, farce. Il Dramma, (May, 1975), 25-61. In Italian.

2274. _____. Miseria bella. 1 act. Il Dramma, 350 (March 15, 1941), 39-43. In Italian.

2275. _____. Una persona fidata. 1 act. Il Dramma, 374 (March 15, 1942), 37-41. In Italian.

2276. _____. Un povero ragazzo. 3 acts. Il Dramma, 299 (February 1, 1939), 4-19. In Italian.

2277. _____. Pranziamo assieme. 1 act, farce. Sipario, 9 (August-September, 1954), 62-66. In Italian.

2278. _____. Quale onore! 1 act. Il Dramma, 370 (January 15, 1942), 35-40. In Italian.

2279. _____. Il ramoscello d'olivo. 1 act. Il Dramma, 360 (August 15, 1941), 25-31. In Italian.

2280. _____. Spacca il centesimo. 1 act. Il Dramma, 350 (March 15, 1941), 34-38. In Italian.

2281. De Filippo, Titina. Vivata di Bordo. 3 acts. Sipario, 175 (November, 1960), 37-52.

2282. De Flers, Robert. Il dottor Faust. 1 act. Il Dramma, 110 (March 15, 1931), 44-46. Vittorio Guerriero, translator. In Italian.

_____ see also Caillavet, G. A. de 1490

2283. De Ford, Miriam Allen, 1888- . Shelley. 5 acts. Poet Lore, 64 (Summer, 1969), 158-214.

2284. De Grazia, Edward. The Swings. 1 act. Evergreen Review, 6 (September-October, 1962), 50-66. Ursule Molinaro, translator.

2285. Deiber, Paul Emile. La Troupe du Roy. 1 act. L'Avant Scène, 269 (July 15, 1962), 9-15. In French.

Deisen, Dagmar, adaptor see Toller, E. 8874

Dejoux, Jean see Valmain, F. 9008

2286. Dekobra, M. La chiave del mistero. 1 act. Il Dramma, 10 (September, 1926), 34-39. Nennele Maccini, translator. In Italian.

2287. De La Mare, Walter, 1873-1956. The Stranger. 1 act. London Magazine, 1 (September, 1954), 13-19.

Delamotte, Jean-Paul, translator see Horovitz, I. 4172

2288. Delance, Georges. Bluff. 3 acts, comedy. Petite Illustration, 181 (January 16, 1932), 1-29. In French.

2289. Delaney, Shelagh, 1939- . The Lion in Love. 3 acts. Sipario, 19 (January, 1964), 58-78. Ettore Capriolo, translator. In Italian.

2290. _____. A Taste of Honey. 2 acts. L'Avant Scène, 217 9-29. Gabriel Arout Cheff and Françoise Mallet-Jorris, adapters.

2291. _____. A Taste of Honey. 2 acts. Sipario, 15 (April, 1960), 29-47. Gigi Lunari, translator. In Italian.

2292. _____. A Taste of Honey. 2 acts. Theatre Arts, 47 (January, 1963), 25-56.

Delano, Aline, translator see Gorky, M. 3651

2293. Delaquis, Georges. Mia moglie. 3 acts. Il Dramma, 16 (March, 1927), 7-28. Lucio Ridenti, translator. In Italian.

2294. _____. La Naissance de Tristan. 3 parts. Petite Illustration, 196 (February 20, 1937), 1-34. In French.

_____ see also Blum, R. 1019

2295. Delavaux, Robert. Triple Saut. 1 act, comedy. L'Avant Scène, 217, 31-35. In French.

Del Bono, Laura, translator see Campton, D. 1549

_____, translator see England, B. 2866

_____, translator see Herbert, F. H. 4063

_____, translator see Nichols, P. 6545

_____, translator see Pinter, H. 7174

_____, translator see Rattigan, T. 7424, 7429

_____, translator see Shaffer, P. 8168

_____, translator see Van Druten, J. 9027

2296. Del Buono, Oreste. L'infedele. 1 act. Sipario, 18 (February, 1963), 52-58. In Italian.

De Letraz, Jean see Eger, R. 2831

2297. Delgado, Ramon. Omega's Ninth. 1 act. First Stage, 3 (Winter, 1963-64), 7-12.

2298. Dell, Floyd, 1887-1969. A Long Time Ago. 1 act. Forum, 51 (February, 1914), 261-277.

2299. Dell, Jack Holton. The Duel. 2 acts. Plays and Players, 15 (June, 1968), 27-43, 60.

2300. Dell, Jeffrey. Karma. 3 acts. Petite Illustration, 185 (May 20, 1933), 1-30. Juliette Ralph-Mylo, adapter. In French.

2301. Della Corte, Francesco, 1913- . Atene anno zero. 2 parts. Il Dramma, n.s., 317 (February, 1963), 8-30. In Italian.

2302. Della Porta, Giovanni Battista. La cintia. 3 acts. Il Dramma, 355 (June 1, 1941), 11-28. In Italian.

2303. ———. I due fratelli rivali. 3 acts. Il Dramma, 408/409 (August 15/September 1, 1943), 31-49. In Italian.

2304. ———. La tabernaria. 3 acts, comedy. Sipario, 9 (August-September, 1954), 17-31. Camillo Bonanni, adapter. In Italian.

2305. Della Pura, E. Quello che ci voleva. 1 act. Il Dramma, 178 (January 15, 1934), 36-42. In Italian.

2306. Della Seta, Fabio. Un uomo arrivato. 1 act. Sipario, 10 (May, 1955), 50-56. In Italian.

2307. Dello Siesto, Andrea. Le due leggi di Maud. 3 acts. Il Dramma, 246 (November 15, 1936), 2-22. In Italian.

2308. ———. Evelina, zitella per bene. 3 acts. Il Dramma, 311 (August 1, 1939), 4-20. In Italian.

2309. ———. Mascherata di San Silvestro. 3 acts. Il Dramma, 292 (October 15, 1938), 4-18. In Italian.

2310. ———. Il "Signore di Tebe." 1 act. Il Dramma, 299 (February 1, 1939), 27-33. In Italian.

Delogu, Ignazio, translator see Sastre, A. 7971

Delon, Paul, adapter see Cervantes Saavedra, M. de 1695

2311. Delprat, Serge. La vie a l'envers. 1 act. Il Dramma, n.s., 217 (November 15, 1954), 40-47. Gian Renzo Morteo, translator. In Italian.

2312. De Maria, Alberto and Giuseppe Possenti. A ciascuno il suo. 1 act. Il Dramma, n.s., 268 (January, 1959), 58-63. In Italian.

2313. Demasy, Paul. La Tragedie D'Alexandre. 1 act. Petite Illustration, 180 (December 19, 1931), 1-25. In French.

2314. DeMay, Amy J. The Digits. 1 act. Plays, 2 (January, 1943), 53-56.

2315. De Mille, William Churchill, 1878- . The Martyrs. A Life-Study in One Scene. Smart Set, 18 (February, 1906), 159-160.

2316. _____. The Starveling. A Tragedy after Maeterlinck. 1 act. Smart Set, 8 (November, 1902), 123-125.

2317. _____ and John Erskine, 1879-1951. "Noblesse Oblige." 1 act. Smart Set, 21 (January, 1907), 72-81.

2318. Deming, Dorothy. Crisscross Streets. 1 act. Plays, 10 (May, 1951), 58-61.

2319. _____. The Defense Never Rests. 1 act. Plays, 9 (January, 1950), 31-36.

2320. _____. Eyes Right! 1 act. Plays, 12 (March, 1953), 67-70.

2321. _____. Fashion Show. 1 act. Plays, 9 (March, 1950), 25-30.

2322. _____. First Aid First. 1 act. Plays, 11 (November, 1951), 56-57.

2323. _____. Ghost-Layers, Incorporated. 1 act. Plays, 9 (November, 1949), 49-54.

2324. _____. Howard's Forward Pass. 1 act. Plays, 9 (October, 1949), 21-25.

2325. _____. The Mermaid Club. 1 act. Plays, 11 (November, 1951), 52-55.

2326. _____. Mister Catchy Cold. 1 act. Plays, 10 (March, 1951), 63-65.

2327. _____. A Narrow Squeak. 1 act. Plays, 9 (April, 1950), 21-25.

2328. _____. Salesmanship. 1 act. Plays, 11 (October, 1951), 62-68.

2329. De Moratin, Leandro Fernando. Il si delle fanciulle. 3 acts. Il Dramma, 421/427 (March 1/June 1, 1944), 91-104. In Italian.

Dempsey, F. O., translator see Blok, A. 1009

2330. Demuth, Charles. The Azure Adder. 1 act. Glebe, 1 (No. 3, 1913), 5-31.

Denes, Max, translator see Marlowe, C. 5564

Denis, Lilly, translator see Babel, I. 477

2331. Denker, Henry, 1912- . A Far Country. 3 acts. Theatre Arts, 46 (December, 1962), 25-56.

2332. _____ and Ralph Berkey, 1912- . Time Limit! 3 acts. Theatre Arts, 41 (April, 1957), 33-57.

2333. Denney, Reuel, 1913- . September Lemonade. 1 act. New World Writing, 7 (1955), 17-30.

2334. Dennis, Alice. The Wind Wand. 1 act. Plays, 4 (April, 1945), 44-48.

2335. Dennis, Ellen Dudley. I'm Nobody. 1 act. Dramatics, 45 (May, 1974), 8-16.

2336. Dennis, O. M. His Honor. 1 act. Smart Set, 35 (November, 1911), 129-134.

2337. Dennis, Ralph. Walking Berg. 1 act. Carolina Quarterly, 11 (Summer, 1960), 23-35.

2338. Dennison, George. The Operation. 1 act. Scripts, 1 (October, 1972), 5-11.

2339. _____. The Service for Joseph Axminster: A Vaudeville Play. Scripts. 1 (May, 1972), 29-45.

2340. Dennler, Florence E. Calling All Planets. 1 act. Plays, 19 (February, 1960), 79-82.

Denny, Norman, adapter see Ayme, M. 470

_____, translator see Shaw, G. B. 8215

2341. Depero, Fortunato, 1892-1960. Colori. Sipario, 260 (December, 1967), 96. In Italian.

2342. DePue, Elva. Hattie. 1 act. Touchstone, 1 (August, 1917), 361-369; 415-416.

2343. De Richaud, Andre. Les Reliques. 1 act, comedy. L'Avant Scène, 505 (November 1, 1972), 31-37. In French.

De Rici, F. E., translator see Brecht, B. 1291

2344. De Roberto, Federico. Rosario. 1 act. Il Dramma, 325 (March 1, 1940), 35-41. In Italian.

2345. D'Errico, Ezio. L'assedio. 2 parts. Il Dramma, n.s., 290 (November, 1960), 8-36. In Italian.

2346. _____. Balthazar. 3 acts. Il Dramma, n.s., 341 (February, 1965), 15-41. In Italian.

2347. _____. Best-Seller. 3 acts. Il Dramma, n.s., 234 (March, 1956), 9-28. In Italian.

2348. _____. Dove siamo. 1 act. Il Dramma, n.s., 308 (May, 1962), 21-32. In Italian.

2349. _____. La foresta. 2 parts. Il Dramma, n.s., 278 (November, 1959), 8-33. In Italian.

2350. _____. Le Forze. 3 acts. Il Dramma, n.s., 249 (June, 1957), 5-27. In Italian.

2351. _____. L'incidente. 1 act. Il Dramma, n.s., 365/366 (February/March, 1967), 88-94. In Italian.

2352. _____. Incontro col gentleman. 1 act. Il Dramma, n.s., 273 (June, 1959), 60-65. In Italian.

2353. _____. Qualcuno al cancello. 3 acts. Il Dramma, n.s., 299/300 (August/September, 1961), 65-90. In Italian.

2354. _____. La sedia a dondolo. 1 act. Il Dramma, n.s., 318 (March, 1963), 54-60. In Italian.

2355. _____. Tempo di cavallette. 2 parts. Il Dramma, n.s., 261 (June, 1958), 8-37. In Italian.

2356. Descaves, Lucien, 1861-1949. Les Fruits de l'Amour. 3 acts. Petite Illustration, 86 (May 5, 1928), 1-30. In French.

_____ see also Donnay, C. M. 2544

2357. De Selincourt, Hugh. Beastie. 1 act. The Open Window, 12 (September, 1911), 294-317.

2358. _____. Saint John and the Orphan. 1 act. The Open Window, 5 (February, 1911), 304-324.

2359. Deseo, Lydia May Glover, 1898- . Never the Twain. 1 act. Poet Lore, 41 (Summer, 1930), 272-292.

2360. Des Presles, Claude. L'Object. 1 act. L'Avant Scène, 503 (October 1, 1972), 49-52. In French.

2361. Dessi, Giuseppe. La Giustizia. 3 acts. Botteghe Oscure, 20 (Autumn, 1957), 533-601. In Italian.

2362. _____. La giustizia. 3 acts. Sipario, 14 (March, 1959), 38-55. In Italian.

2363. De Stefani, Alessandro, 1891- . L'amica di tutti e di nessuno. 3 acts. Il Dramma, 309 (July 1, 1939), 4-24. In Italian.

2364. _____. L'amore canta. 3 acts. Il Dramma, 142 (July 15, 1932), 4-34. In Italian.

2365. _____. L'angelo del miracolo. 3 acts. Il Dramma, 439/440 (December 1/31, 1944), 45-63. In Italian.

2366. _____. La barca viene dal lago. 1 act. Il Dramma, n.s., 358 (July, 1966), 57-65. In Italian.

2367. _____. Dopo divorzieremo. 3 acts. Il Dramma, 296 (December 15, 1938), 4-24. In Italian.

2368. _____. Equatore. 3 acts. Il Dramma, 184 (April 15, 1934), 4-36. In Italian.

2369. _____. Gran turismo. 3 acts. Il Dramma, 324 (February 15, 1940), 4-22. In Italian.

2370. _____. Il grande attore. 3 acts. Il Dramma, n.s., 193 (November 15, 1953), 5-26. In Italian.

2371. _____. Mattinate d'Aprile. 4 acts. Il Dramma, 268 (October 15, 1937), 2-25. In Italian.

2372. _____. Metropoli. 3 acts. Il Dramma, 293 (November 1, 1938), 4-24. In Italian.

2373. _____. Olimpiadi. 3 acts. Il Dramma, 201 (January 1, 1935), 4-30. In Italian.

2374. _____. L'ombra dietro la porta. 3 acts. Il Dramma, 193 (September 1, 1934), 4-36. In Italian.

2375. _____. I pazzi sulla montagna. 3 acts. Il Dramma, 240 (August 15, 1936), 2-24. In Italian.

2376. _____. La scoperta dell'Europa. 3 acts. Il Dramma,

348 (February 15, 1941), 6-25. In Italian.

2377. _____. Signora dalle camelie. 1 act. Il Dramma, n. s., 368 (May, 1967), 10-21. In Italian.

2378. _____. Triangolo magico. 3 acts. Il Dramma, 228 (February 15, 1936), 2-27. In Italian.

2379. _____. Una notte a Barcellona. 3 acts. Il Dramma, 264 (August 15, 1937), 2-23. In Italian.

2380. _____. Gli uomini non sono ingrati. 3 acts. Il Dramma, 259 (June 1, 1937), 2-24. In Italian.

_____, translator see Amiel, D. 189

_____, translator see Birabeau, A. 959

_____, translator see Boularan, J. 1226

_____, translator see Mourguet, M. 6277

_____, translator see Natanson, J. 6448

_____, translator see Nozière, F. 6704

2381. _____ and Gaspare Cataldo. Ecco la fortuno. 3 acts. Il Dramma, 286 (July 15, 1938), 4-24. In Italian.

2382. _____ and F. Ferruccio Cerio. L'urlo. 3 acts. Il Dramma, 207 (April 1, 1935), 4-30. In Italian.

2383. _____ and Mino Doletti. L'ultimo romanzo di Domenico Barnaba. 3 acts. Il Dramma, 428/429/430 (June 15/July 1/15, 1944), 9-26. In Italian.

D'Estor, Pol see Hellem, C. 4042

2384. Deutsch, Leon. Les Imprudentes. 1 act, comedy. L'Avant Scène, 163, 34-42. In French.

2385. _____. Pas d'Histoiries . . . 1 act, comedy. L'Avant Scène, 220, 46-51. In French.

2386. _____. Le Soleil et les Parapluies. 1 act, comedy. L'Avant Scène, 143, 39-47. In French.

2387. _____. Les Vagues Etaient Trop Fortes . . . 1 act, comedy. L'Avant Scène, 367 (November 1, 1966), 43-48. In French.

Deval, Jacques, pseud. see Boularan, J. 1216-1230

De Vecchis, Maripiera, translator see Bergman, H. 815

_____, translator see Bergman, I. 817

_____, translator see Vian, B. 9135

De Vellis, Mario, translator see Duvernois, H. 2787

_____, translator see Fodor, L. 3178, 3180, 3182

_____, translator see Herczeg, F. 4068

_____, translator see Molnar, F. 6151

_____, translator see Szecsen, S. 8679

2388. De Vere, Mary Ainge. A Nowadays Call. 1 act. Smart Set, 23 (October, 1907), 119-120.

2389. Devin, Lee. The Pointed Stick. 1 act. Poet Lore, 59 (No. 2), 174-182.

2390. Dewey, Kenneth G., 1934- . Mart of Addenda. 1 act. Contact, 3 (September, 1961), 130-136.

2391. Dewey, Priscilla B. Cinderella Swings. 1 act. Plays, 33 (November, 1973), 69-74.

2392. _____. Rumpelstiltskin Revisited. 1 act. Plays, 31 (December, 1971), 81-87.

2393. _____, adapter. The Fisherman and His Wife. 1 act. Plays, 31 (February, 1972), 67-70.

2394. Dey, James. What Did You Say "What" For? 1 act. Players Magazine, 40 (October, 1963), 13-17, 20.

2395. Deza, Enrique Suarez de. El Pelele. 3 acts. L'Avant Scène, 134, 27-41. Jean Camp, adapter. In French.

2396. _____. El Pelele. 3 acts. Il Dramma, n.s., 168 (November 1, 1952), 7-19. Ernesto Romagna Manoja, translator. In Italian.

2397. Diament, Mario. Story of a Kidnapping. Modern International Drama, 9 (Fall, 1975), 25-49. Marcia Cobourn Wellworth, translator.

2398. Diamond, Jeff. Back Stage. 1 act. Dramatika, 7 (1971), 36-37.

2399. Diamond, William. The Doubtful Son, or, Secrets of a Place. 5 acts. Baltimore Repertory, 1 supplement (1811), 45-72.

2400. _____. The Foundling in the Forest. 3 acts. The Mirror of Taste, 1 (January, 1810), supplement, 3-20.

2401. Dias, Earl J. Abner Crane from Hayseed Lane, An Old-Fashioned Melodrama. 1 act. Plays, 16 (October, 1956), 11-24. AND Plays, 30 (March, 1971), 25-38.

2402. _____. Another Redskin Bit the Dust. 1 act. Plays, 30 (October, 1970), 1-12.

2403. _____. A Ballad for the Shy. 1 act. Plays, 26 (December, 1966), 21-31.

2404. _____. The Ballad of Simon-Pure Sam. 1 act. Plays, 33 (March, 1974), 15-28.

2405. _____. The Beatnik and the Bard. 1 act. Plays, 20 (October, 1960), 1-12.

2406. _____. Beauty and the Ballot, A Comic Melodrama. 1 act. Plays, 26 (November, 1966), 29-30.

2407. _____. The Bow-Wow Blues. 1 act. Plays, 19 (October, 1959), 17-28.

2408. _____. The Case of the Missing Pearls. 1 act. Plays, 16 (March, 1957), 37-47.

2409. _____. Cast Up by the Sea. 1 act. Plays, 20 (May, 1961), 33-43. AND Plays, 34 (November, 1974), 25-34.

2410. _____. The Christmas Starlet. 1 act. Plays, 23 (December, 1963), 15-26.

2411. _____. The Cleanest Town in the West. 1 act. Plays, 20 (November, 1960), 13-24.

2412. _____. Collector's Item. 1 act. Plays, 22 (January, 1963), 1-12.

2413. _____. Dear Lottie. 1 act. Plays, 19 (April, 1960), 13-23.

2414. _____. Don't Tell the Folks Back Home. 1 act. Plays, 23 (January, 1964), 27-37.

2415. _____. Enter Mr. Poe. 1 act. Plays, 29 (November, 1969), 39-47.

2416. _____. Express to Valley Forge. 1 act. Plays, 9 (February, 1950), 54-63. AND Plays, 17 (February, 1958), 51-59.

Dias

2417. _____. The Face Is Familiar. 1 act. Plays, 19 (January, 1960), 1-13.

2418. _____. Feud at Squirrel Hollow. 1 act, comedy. Plays, 31 (January, 1972), 1-12.

2419. _____. Feudin' Fun. 1 act. Plays, 15 (November, 1955), 21-30. AND Plays, 32 (March, 1973), 21-30.

2420. _____. The General's Letter. 1 act. Plays, 18 (February, 1959), 1-10.

2421. _____. The Ghost from Genoa. 1 act. Plays, 15 (October, 1955), 23-31. AND Plays, 30 (October, 1970), 53-60.

2422. _____. The Gift of Laughter. 1 act. Plays, 19 (February, 1960), 1-12.

2423. _____. Greed for Gold. 1 act. Plays, 36 (November, 1976), 1-12.

2424. _____. Griselda the Governess. 1 act. Plays, 32 (December, 1972), 11-22.

2425. _____. Hold Back the Redskins. 1 act. Plays, 19 (November, 1959), 23-34.

2426. _____. Horse Sense. 1 act. Plays, 35 (October, 1975), 69-78.

2427. _____. The Knights of the Square Table. 1 act, comedy. Plays, 25 (December, 1965), 51-62.

2428. _____. The Lake Darby Monster. 1 act. Plays, 34 (December, 1974), 24-35.

2429. _____. Landslide for Shakespeare. 1 act. Plays, 16 (April, 1957), 1-11.

2430. _____. The Little Man Who Wasn't There. 1 act. Plays, 21 (January, 1962), 25-36. AND Plays, 33 (December, 1973), 25-36.

2431. _____. Madison Avenue Merry-Go-Round. 1 act. Plays, 21 (November, 1961), 13-24.

2432. _____. The Mantle. 1 act. Plays, 19 (May, 1960), 23-34.

2433. _____. Martha Washington's Spy. 1 act. Plays, 12 (February, 1953), 41-49. AND Plays, 26 (February, 1967), 59-67.

Dias

2434. ———. Mountain Madness. 1 act. Plays, 24 (February, 1965), 17-27.

2435. ———. My Fair Monster. 1 act. Plays, 26 (February, 1967), 1-11.

2436. ———. The Natives Are Restless Tonight. 1 act. Plays, 17 (January, 1958), 1-14. AND Plays, 32 (April, 1973), 1-14.

2437. ———. Not for Publication. 1 act. Plays, 22 (October, 1962), 15-25.

2438. ———. Out of This World. 1 act. Plays, 22 (February, 1963), 13-21.

2439. ———. Printer's Devil. 1 act. Plays, 16 (January, 1957), 27-36.

2440. ———. The Purloined Portrait. 1 act. Plays, 27 (November, 1967), 23-34.

2441. ———. The Sand Dune Hillbillies. 1 act. Plays, 26 (May, 1967), 15-26.

2442. ———. The Sands of Time. 1 act. Plays, 15 (March, 1956), 1-10.

2443. ———. See You in the Funnies. 1 act. Plays, 26 (January, 1967), 1-12.

2444. ———. Shades of Shakespeare. 1 act. Plays, 25 (April, 1966), 1-12.

2445. ———. Some of My Best Friends Are Spies. 1 act. Plays, 29 (January, 1970), 1-9.

2446. ———. Sophia the Seamstress. 1 act. Plays, 24 (April, 1965), 1-13.

2447. ———. Stage Bore. 1 act. Plays, 18 (May, 1959), 1-12.

2448. ———. Stop the Presses! 1 act. Plays, 17 (November, 1957), 17-27.

2449. ———. Strong and Silent. 1 act. Plays, 15 (May, 1956), 23-31.

2450. ———. Summer Stock à la Carte. 1 act. Plays, 21 (May, 1962), 1-12.

2451. ———. The Tall Stranger. 1 act. Plays, 22 (March,

1963), 1-12.

2452. _____. Thar She Blows. 1 act, comedy. Plays, 25 (November, 1965), 37-46.

2453. _____. The Touch of Genius. 1 act. Plays, 21 (April, 1962), 19-30.

2454. _____. Treasure at Bentley Inn. 1 act. Plays, 21 (March, 1962), 1-14.

2455. _____. Troy Was Never Like This. 1 act. Plays, 36 (December, 1976), 11-23.

2456. _____. Unsuspected Fruit. 1 act. Plays, 10 (April, 1951), 7-16.

2457. _____. Video Christmas. 1 act. Plays, 18 (December, 1958), 1-12.

2458. _____. Visitor to Gettysburg. 1 act. Plays, 11 (February, 1952), 30-38.

2459. _____. Way, Way Down East. 1 act. Plays, 14 (March, 1955), 1-10. AND Plays, 23 (May, 1964), 99-107.

2460. _____. What Ho! 1 act. Plays, 17 (May, 1958), 1-14.

2461. Diaz, Abby Morton. May-Day Indoors; or, The Yotopski Family's Rehearsal. 1 act. St. Nicholas, 3 (May, 1876), 459-460.

2462. _____. A Surprise Party. 1 act. St. Nicholas, 9 (October, 1882), 956-958.

2463. Dibble, Warren. How with This Rage, A Television Play Without Dialogue. 1 act. Landfall, 22 (December, 1968), 351-363.

Di Boyon, Enrico Leotardi, translator see Fayard, J. 2955

2464. Di Carpenetto, Daisy. Il fauno stanco. 1 act. Il Dramma, 140 (June 15, 1932), 39-45. In Italian.

2465. _____. Un uomo e una donna. 1 act. Il Dramma, 135 (April 1, 1932), 38-43. In Italian.

2466. Dickens, Charles, 1812-1870. Christmas at the Cratchits. 1 act. Plays, 12 (December, 1952), 45-50. Deborah Newman, adapter.

2467. _____. A Christmas Carol. 1 act. Plays, 10 (December, 1950), 65-77. AND Plays, 22 (December, 1962), 83-95. AND Plays, 27 (December, 1967), 81-90. AND Plays, 30 (December, 1970), 83-95. AND Plays, 32 (December, 1972), 81-90. AND Plays, 33 (December, 1973), 77-89. AND Plays, 34 (December, 1974), 85-95. AND Plays, 36 (December, 1976), 83-95. Walter Hackett, adapter.

2468. _____. Christmas Carol. 1 act. Senior Scholastic, 51 (December 8, 1947), 17-20. Frederich Garrigus, adapter.

2469. _____. A Christmas Carol. 1 act. Plays, 16 (December, 1956), 87-95. Lewy Olfson, adapter.

2470. _____. The Conspiracy. 1 act. Plays, 30 (February, 1971), 85-96. Adele Thane, adapter.

2471. _____. David Copperfield and Uriah Heep. 1 act. Plays, 17 (January, 1958), 77-86. Lewy Olfson, adapter.

2472. _____. The Fall of Uriah Heep. 1 act. Plays, 31 (March, 1972), 85-96. Joellen Bland, adapter.

2473. _____. Great Expectations. 1 act. Plays, 21 (March, 1962), 85-96. Edward Golden, adapter.

2474. _____. The Lamplighter. 1 act, farce. Golden Book, 3 (January, 1926), 69-80.

2475. _____. The Magic Fishbone. 1 act. Plays, 20 (October, 1960), 51-56. Mary Nygaard Peterson, adapter.

2476. _____. Martin Chuzzlewit. 1 act. Plays, 20 (May, 1961), 97-107. Lewy Olfson, adapter.

2477. _____. Mr. Scrooge Finds Christmas. 1 act. Plays, 35 (December, 1975), 73-83. Aileen Fisher, adapter.

2478. _____. Oliver Twist. 1 act. Plays, 30 (November, 1970), 85-96. AND Plays, 34 (March, 1975), 85-96. Joellen Bland, adapter.

2479. _____. Oliver Twist. 1 act. Plays, 20 (January, 1961), 90-96. Lewy Olfson, adapter.

2480. _____. Oliver Twist. 1 act. Plays, 24 (May, 1965), 87-98. Ronald K. Side, adapter.

2481. _____. The Pickwick Papers. 1 act. Plays, 16 (November, 1956), 89-95. Lewy Olfson, adapter.

2482. _____. A Tale of Two Cities. 1 act. Plays, 10 (February, 1951), 65-77. AND Plays, 26 (November, 1966), 99-111. Walter Hackett, adapter.

2483. _____. A Tale of Two Cities. 1 act. Plays, 29 (January, 1970), 81-95. Adele Thane, adapter.

Dickerman, Elizabeth S., translator see Botrel, T. J. M. 1200

2484. Dickinson, Trisha. The Christmas Present. 1 act. Dramatika, 7 (1971), 34-35.

2485. Diderot, Denis, 1713-1784. Les Amours de Jacques le Fataliste. 2 parts. L'Avant Scène, 466 (February 15, 1971), 7-21. Francis Huster, adapter. In French.

2486. _____. Est-il Bon? Est-il Méchant? 4 acts. L'Avant Scène, 123, 1-29. In French.

2487. _____. Le Neveu de Rameau. 1 act, satire. L'Avant Scène, 303 (January 15, 1964), 15-27. In French.

2488. Didier, Pierre. Le Français Tel Qu'On le Parle. 1 act. L'Avant Scène, 420 (February 15, 1969), 39-41. In French.

2489. _____. Mon Fils. 1 act, comedy. L'Avant Scène, 139, 35-41. In French.

2490. _____. Le Retour de Lumière. 1 act. L'Avant Scène, 443 (February 15, 1970), 35-41. In French.

2491. Diers, Theodore. Silent Night. 1 act. Prairie Schooner, 13 (Winter, 1939), 244-252.

Dietrich, Léone see Dabril, L. 2155, 2156

Dietz, Howard, 1896- , adapter see Puccini, G. 7323

2492. Dieudonne, Albert. Moi, Napoleon! 1 act, dramatic comedy. L'Avant Scène, 153, 31-40. In French.

2493. Dieudonné, Robert. Informazioni. 1 act. Il Dramma, 100 (October 15, 1930), 40-41. Giuseppe Faraci, translator. In Italian.

2494. Diez, Bernard. Amphitryon 1968. 1 act. L'Avant Scène, 396 (February 1, 1968), 37-43. In French.

2495. _____. Rue de Richelieu. 1 act. L'Avant Scène, 251 (October 15, 1961), 29-35. In French.

2496. _____. Le Tartuffe Repenti. 1 act. L'Avant Scène,

270 (August 1, 1962), 35-43. In French.

2497. Di Giacomo, Salvatore. Assunta spina. 2 acts. Il Dramma, n. s., 282 (March, 1960), 12-32. In Italian.

Di Giammatteo, Fernaldo, translator see Bruckner, F. 1381

_____, translator see Csokor, F. T. 2132

_____, translator see Evreinov, N. N. 2889

_____, translator see Toller, E. 8875

Di Giammatteo, Grazia, translator see Bruckner, F. 1381

_____, translator see Csokor, F. T. 2132

_____, translator see Evreinov, N. N. 2889

_____, translator see Toller, E. 8875

2498. Diller, Marion E. Thorpe. The Christmas Mouse. 1 act. Plays, 2 (December, 1942), 63-67.

2499. _____. The Singing Lesson. 1 act. Plays, 5 (May, 1946), 61-63.

2500. Di Luca, Dino. Primo premio all'amore. 1 act. Il Dramma, 352 (April 15, 1941), 47-51. In Italian.

2501. _____. Sognare insieme. 1 act. Il Dramma, 378 (May 15, 1942), 33-35. In Italian.

2502. Di Mattia, Vincenzo. I confessori. 2 parts. Il Dramma (June, 1974), 25-55. In Italian.

2503. _____. La lanzichenecca. 3 acts. Sipario, 20 (March, 1965), 24-55. In Italian.

2504. _____. Luce sul letto matrimoniale. 1 act. Sipario, 17 (November, 1962), 61-63. In Italian.

Dimond, Sid see Anderson, D. 222, 223

2505. Dinner, William and William Morum. L'Homme au Parapluie. 3 acts. L'Avant Scène, 79 (June 10, 1953), 5-40. Pol Quentin, adapter. In French.

2506. Di Salle, Glauco, 1920- . Fine dell'uomo. 1 act. Il Dramma, n. s., 82 (April 1, 1949), 51-55. In Italian.

2507. _____. Un matrimonio probabile. 1 act. Il Dramma,

47 (November/December, 1971), 129-132. In Italian.

2508. Dix, Beulah Marie, 1876- . A Legend of Saint Nicholas. 1 act. Poet Lore, 25 (Autumn, 1914), 473-495.

Dixon, Flora see Greene, A. 3714

2509. Dixon, M. Q. The Blue Pincushion. 1 act. Smart Set, 4 (May, 1901), 137-139.

Djurichick, Luka, translator see Nooshich, B. 6687

Doan, Robe J., translator see Adamov, A. 64

2510. Dobie, Charles Caldwell, 1881- . Immortals; A Slavic Fantasy. 1 act. Overland, n. s., 84 (March, 1926), 74-76, 94.

2511. Dobson, Austin, 1840-1921. A Dialogue to the Memory of Mr. Pope. 1 act. Scribner's, 3 (May, 1888), 548-550.

2512. _____. Proverbs in Porcelain, "Rein en Relief". 1 act. Bibelot, 7 (1901), 297-322.

2513. Docquois, George, 1863- . After the Opera. 1 act. Smart Set, 20 (December, 1906), 103-116.

2514. Dodge, Flora Bigelow. Mrs. Mack's Example. 1 act. Smart Set, 5 (September, 1901), 51-66.

2515. Dodgson, Charles Lutwidge, 1832-1898. Alice in Wonderland. 1 act. Plays, 26 (January, 1967), 81-97. AND Plays, 31 (April, 1972), 51-60. Rochelle Hill, adapter.

2516. _____. Alice in Wonderland. 1 act. Plays, 22 (January, 1963), 85-95. Lewy Olfson, adapter.

2517. _____. Alice's Adventures in Wonderland. 1 act. Plays, 33 (March, 1974), 77-82. Lewis Mahlmann, adapter.

2518. _____. Through the Looking-Glass. 1 act. Plays, 25 (May, 1966), 95-105. Lewy Olfson, adapter.

1519. Dodson, Owen, 1914- . Everybody Join Hands. 1 act. Theatre Arts, 27 (August, 1943), 555-565.

_____ see also Cullen, C. 2136

2520. Dohner, Irvin R. The Christmas Surprise. 1 act. Learning With ... 3 (November, 1975), 26-29.

2521. Doletti, Mino. Un allegro furfante. 1 act. Il Dramma, 28 (October 15, 1927), 40-45. In Italian.

2522. _____. I miserabili sono due. 1 act. Il Dramma, 9 (August, 1926), 41-45. In Italian.

_____ see also De Stefani, A. 2383

2523. Dolf, B. Der "Saujud." 1 act. Das Wort, 9 (November, 1938), 138-141. In German.

2524. Dolley, Georges. Cinematografo. 3 acts. Il Dramma, 44 (June 15, 1928), 34-35. Vittorio Guerriero, translator. In Italian.

_____ see Birabeau, A. 960

2525. Dominguez, Franklin, 1932- . Un Amigo Desconocida nos Aguarda. 1 act. L'Avant Scène, 339 (August, 1965), 53-60. Henri Premont, adapter. In French.

2526. _____. Un Portrait Sur les Bras. 1 act, comedy. L'Avant Scène, 444 (March 1, 1970), 27-37. In French.

2527. Donaghy, Lyle. Aristaeus. A Mask. 1 act. Dublin Magazine, n.s., 9 (January-March, 1934), 24-40.

2528. Donahue, Patricia M. The Bear's Nest. 1 act, comedy. One-Act Play Magazine, 1 (June, 1937), 100-118.

2529. _____. Stormy Passage. 1 act. One-Act Play Magazine, 2 (December, 1938), 525-541.

Donati, Luciano, translator see Molnar, F. 6146

2530. Donati, Paolo Luca. Robinson, venerdi e domenica. Sipario, 345 (February, 1975), 67-75. In Italian.

2531. Donaudy, Alberto. A moglie di entrambi. 3 acts. Il Dramma, 79 (December 1, 1929), 4-38. In Italian.

_____ see also D'Ambra, L. 2170

2532. Dondo, Mathurin Marius, 1884- . Two Blind Men and a Donkey; A Play for Marionettes. 1 act. Poet Lore, 32 (August, 1921), 391-402.

Dongo, Angelica, translator see Pasternak, B. L. 6997

2532. Donini, Alberto. L'orologia a cuccù. 3 acts. Il Dramma, 254 (March 15, 1937), 2-24. In Italian.

2534. Donizetti, Pino. Il chirugo inverosimile. 1 act. Sipario, 17 (July, 1962), 50-51. In Italian.

2535. Donleavy, J. P. Fairy Tales of New York. 4 acts. Sipario, 17 (July, 1962), 29-46. Ettore Capriolo, translator. In Italian.

2536. Donnay, Charles Maurice, 1859-1945. Confessioni. 1 act. Il Dramma, 53 (November 1, 1928), 42-44. In Italian.

2537. _____. Facciamo economia. 1 act. Il Dramma, 150 (November 15, 1932), 44-45. In Italian.

2538. _____. Il gioco dell'amore. 1 act. Il Dramma, 126 (November 15, 1931), 43-44. In Italian.

2539. _____. Il matrimonio. 1 act. Il Dramma, 132 (February 15, 1932), 42-43. In Italian.

2540. _____. Una moglie preziosa. 1 act. Il Dramma, 15 (February, 1927), 40-45. In Italian.

2541. _____. The Other Danger. 4 acts, comedy. Drama, 11 (August, 1913), 14-118. Charlotte Genney David, translator.

2542. _____. Prima pagare, e poi.... 1 act. Il Dramma, 107 (February 1, 1931), 36-41. In Italian.

2543. _____. Le Retour de Jerusalem. 4 acts. Petite Illustration, 87 (March 2, 1929), 1-38. In French.

2544. _____ and Lucien Descaves, 1861-1949. L'Ascension de Virginie. 3 acts, comedy. Petite Illustration, 87 (November 23, 1929), 1-38. In French.

2545. Doplicher, Fabio. Della notte. Sipario, 357 (February, 1976), 66-80. In Italian.

2546. Dorand, John. Surprise Party. 1 act. Plays, 14 (January, 1955), 18-26. AND Plays, 26 (January, 1967), 25-33.

2547. _____. Teen and Twenty. 1 act. Plays, 14 (March, 1955), 19-34. AND Plays, 18 (November, 1958), 13-28. AND Plays, 31 (March, 1972), 25-38.

2548. Dorey, Joseph Milnor, 1876- . Under Conviction. 1 act. Drama, 33 (February, 1919), 115-127.

2549. Dorgan, Howard. The First and Last Opinion of Solomon Goldstein. 1 act. DeKalb Literary Arts Journal, 5 (No. 4, 1972), 68-86.

Dorian, Cosentino, 1948- see Logan, S. 5018

2550. Dorin, Françoise. Les Bonshommes. 4 acts. L'Avant Scène, 459 (November 1, 1970), 7-42. In French.

2551. _____. Comme au Théatre. 3 acts, comedy. L'Avant Scène, 446 (April 1, 1970), 39-67. In French.

2552. _____. La Facture. 4 acts, comedy. L'Avant Scène, 416 (December 15, 1968), 10-41. In French.

2553. _____. Un Sale Egoiste. 4 acts, comedy. L'Avant Scène, 446 (April 1, 1970), 7-38. In French.

2554. _____. Le Tournant. 4 acts. L'Avant Scène, 555 (January 1, 1975), 3-39. In French.

2555. _____. Le Tube. 2 acts, comedy. L'Avant Scène, 572 (October 1, 1975), 3-39. In French.

2556. Dorin, Michel. L'Autre Valse. 3 acts. L'Avant Scène, 583 (March 15, 1976), 3-40. In French.

2557. Dorly, Pierre-Alain. Amis. 1 act. Petite Illustration, 192 (November 30, 1935), 1-10. In French.

2558. Dornac, Charles. Célébrité, Discretion. 1 act. Petite Illustration, 192 (December 21, 1935), 1-8. In French.

2559. Dornes, Roger. Va Faire un Tour au Bois. 3 acts, comedy. L'Avant Scène (OST), 25 (May, 1950), 3-36. In French.

2560. Dos Passos, John, 1896-1970, and Paul Shyre. U.S.A. 2 acts. Sipario, 176 (December, 1960), 77-96. Ettore Capriolo, translator. In Italian.

2561. _____. U.S.A. 2 acts. Theatre Arts, 44 (June 1960), 23-49.

2562. Dostoevski, Fedor, 1821-1881. Crime and Punishment. 4 acts. Il Dramma, n.s., 203/204 (April 15/May 1, 1954), 13-44. Lucio Ridenti, translator. In Italian.

2563. _____. The Demons. 3 parts. Il Dramma, n.s., 255 (December, 1957), 20-67. Diego Fabbri, translator. In Italian.

2564. _____. L'Eternel Mari. 2 acts. L'Avant Scène, 118, 1-15. Jacques Mauclair, adapter. In French.

2565. _____. Memorie del sottosuolo. Sipario, 9 (July, 1954), 38-46. Ettore Settanni, translator. In Italian.

2566. _____. Les Nuits Blanches. 1 act. L'Avant Scène, 245 (June 15, 1961), 7-17. Gil Sandier, translator. In French.

2567. Douglas, Barry. From Hearse to Eternity. 1 act. Plays, 35 (January, 1976), 13-20.

2568. Douglas, Ford. The Return Trip. 1 act. Smart Set, 70 (April, 1923), 71-74.

2569. _____. The Two Barrels. 1 act. Smart Set, 64 (April, 1921), 65-71.

2570. Dow, Hilda. The Preparation. 1 act. Resource, 7 (November, 1965), 11-12.

2571. Down Below the Rio Grande. 1 act. Scholastic, 32 (April 9, 1938), 17E-19E.

2572. Downey, June Etta, 1875- . Arrow. 1 act. Poet Lore, 38 (1927), 297-306.

2573. _____. A Study in the Nude. 1 act, tragedy. Poet Lore, 31 (Summer, 1920), 253-260.

2574. Downing, Robert. Jimmy Six. 1 act. Plays, 22 (November, 1962), 25-34.

2575. _____. The Second Sunday in May. 1 act. Plays, 16 (May, 1957), 1-11.

2576. _____. The Shop Girl's Revenge. 1 act. Plays, 15 (January, 1956), 25-34. AND Plays, 34 (October, 1974), 27-36.

2577. _____. Sticks and Stones. 1 act. Plays, 21 (May, 1962), 25-38. AND Plays, 33 (November, 1973), 23-32.

2578. Doyle, Sir Arthur Conan, 1859-1930. Sherlock Holmes and the Red-Headed League. 1 act. Plays, 19 (October, 1959), 87-96. Lewy Olfson, adapter.

2579. _____. Sherlock Holmes and "The Second Stain." 1 act. Plays, 31 (October, 1971), 83-96. Olive J. Marley, adapter.

2580. _____. Sherlock Holmes and the Stockbroker's Clerk. 1 act. Plays, 23 (October, 1963), 85-95. Lewy Olfson, adapter.

2581. Doyle, Louis F., S. J. Dark Roses. 1 act. Catholic World, 121 (May, 1925), 158-162.

2582. _____. France. 1 act. Catholic World, 124 (March, 1927), 788-797.

2583. Dozer, David. Ol-Dopt; or, The Adventures of Charles and

Emily Ann Andrews; a Radio Serial. <u>Scripts</u>, 1 (June, 1972), 56-84.

2584. Drachmann, Holger Henrik Herholdt, 1846-1908. Renaissance. 1 act. <u>Poet Lore</u>, 19 (Winter, 1908), 369-419. Lee M. Hollander, translator.

2585. Dragan, Olive Tilford. The Woods of Ida. 1 act. <u>Century</u>, 74 (August, 1907), 590-604.

2586. Drago-Bracco, Adolfo, 1894- . Colombine Wants Flowers. 1 act. <u>Poet Lore</u>, 55 (Summer, 1950), 144-162. Willis Knapp Jones, translator.

2587. Drain, Richard. The Tiger in the Rockery. 1 act. <u>First Stage</u>, 6 (Winter, 1967-68), 260-272.

2588. Draper, Cena Christopher. The Emperor's Daughters. 1 act. <u>Plays</u>, 10 (May, 1951), 43-54.

2589. _____. The Paper Princess. 1 act. <u>Plays</u>, 10 (February, 1951), 46-49.

2590. _____. Thankless Tate. 1 act. <u>Plays</u>, 14 (November, 1954), 62-68.

2591. Dreiser, Theodore, 1871-1945. The Blue Sphere. 1 act. <u>Smart Set</u>, 44 (December, 1914), 245-252.

2592. _____. The Dream. 1 act. <u>Seven Arts</u>, 2 (July, 1917), 319-333.

2593. _____. The Girl in the Coffin. 1 act. <u>Smart Set</u>, 41 (October, 1913), 127-140.

2594. _____. In the Dark. 1 act. <u>Smart Set</u>, 45 (January, 1915), 419-425.

2595. _____. Laughing Gas. 1 act. <u>Smart Set</u>, 45 (February, 1915), 85-94.

2596. _____. The Spring Recital. 1 act. <u>Little Review</u>, 2 (December, 1915), 28-35.

2597. Drennan, Marie. The Slippers That Broke of Themselves. 1 act. <u>Poet Lore</u>, 38 (1927), 258-273.

2598. _____. The Valley of Gloom. 1 act. <u>Poet Lore</u>, 34 (August, 1923), 449-457.

2599. Dresser, Jasmine Stone Van. Young D'Arcy. 1 act. <u>The Delineator</u>, 99 (August, 1921), 24-25, 50-52.

2600. Drexler, Rosalyn. Message from Garcia. 1 act. Fiction, 1 (1972), 3-4.

2601. Dreyer, Max, 1862-1946. On Probation. 4 acts. Poet Lore, 14 (No. 1, 1903), 40-113. Mary Harned, translator.

2602. Drinking Academy, or the Cheater's Holiday. 5 acts. PMLA, 39 (December, 1924), 837-871.

2603. Drinkwater, John, 1882-1937. Little Johnny. 1 act, comedy. English Review, 33 (October, 1921), 292-309.

2604. ———. The Storm. 1 act. New Numbers, 1 (August, 1914), 119-131.

2605. ———. The Storm. 1 act. Theatre Arts, 4 (July, 1920), 191-199.

2606. Driscoll, Louise. The Child of God. 1 act. Seven Arts, 1 (November, 1916), 34-46.

2607. ———. The Great Garden of the West. 1 act. Poetry, 13 (December, 1918), 138-145.

2608. ———. A Pageant of Women. 1 act. Drama, 14 (May-June, 1924), 263-265.

2609. ———. The Poor House. 1 act. Drama, 27 (August, 1917), 448-460.

Driussi, Luciana, translator see Mallet, R. 5475

2610. Druon, Maurice. La contessa, o "La voluttà di essere." 3 acts. Il Dramma, n.s., 364 (January, 1967), 11-36. Gianfilippa Carcano, translator. In Italian.

2611. Dryland, Gordon. Brothers in Mourning, A Dialogue. 1 act. Landfall, 7 (March, 1953), 13-18.

2612. Duberman, Martin, 1930- . History. 1 act. Evergreen Review, 13 (April, 1969), 49-55.

2613. Dubeux, Albert. Le Visiteur. 1 act. L'Avant Scène, 131, 37-40. In French.

——— see also Renard, M.-C. 7490

2614. Dubillard, Roland. Si Camille me Voyait.... 1 act. L'Avant Scène, 469/470 (April 1/15, 1971), 23-33.

2615. Du Bois, Albert. Notre Déesse. 5 acts. Petite Illustration, 193 (February 22, 1936), 1-30. In French.

2616. DuBois, Graham. Ay, There's the Rub. 1 act. Plays, 9 (February, 1950), 10-19.

2617. _____. Bind Up the Nation's Wounds. 1 act. Plays, 16 (February, 1957), 13-22.

2618. _____. Birthplace for a King. 1 act. Plays, 22 (December, 1962), 15-24.

2619. _____. Bonds of Affection. 1 act. Plays, 15 (January, 1956), 14-24.

2620. _____. The Brave But Once. 1 act. Plays, 5 (April, 1946), 10-18.

2621. _____. Cause for Gratitude. 1 act. Plays, 15 (November, 1955), 14-20.

2622. _____. A Cause to Serve. 1 act. Plays, 4 (December, 1944), 20-27.

2623. _____. A Child of Destiny. 1 act. Plays, 5 (October, 1945), 16-24.

2624. _____. Corn Meal and Poetry. 1 act. Plays, 9 (February, 1950), 31-39.

2625. _____. The Darkest Hour. 1 act. Plays, 5 (November, 1945), 34-38.

2626. _____. The Daughter of the Gods. 1 act. Plays, 9 (October, 1949), 11-21.

2627. _____. The Empty Room at the Inn. 1 act. Plays, 25 (December, 1965), 23-31.

2628. _____. The End of the Road. 1 act. Plays, 4 (January, 1945), 27-35.

2629. _____. Every Day Is Thanksgiving. 1 act. Plays, 11 (November, 1951), 11-20. AND Plays, 20 (November, 1960), 41-50.

2630. _____. Full Measure of Devotion. 1 act. Plays, 20 (February, 1961), 1-11.

2631. _____. The Glory and the Dream. 1 act. Plays, 11 (February, 1952), 12-21.

2632. _____. Glory Road. 1 act. Plays, 5 (January, 1946), 19-28.

2633. _____. The Good Egg. 1 act. Plays, 11 (April, 1952), 20-29. AND Plays, 27 (April, 1968), 27-36.

2634. _____. Good Out of Nazareth. 1 act. Plays, 18 (December, 1958), 13-20.

2635. _____. Governor Bradford's Scissors. 1 act. Plays, 21 (November, 1961), 25-35.

2636. _____. His Hand and Pen. 1 act. Plays, 4 (February, 1945), 29-35.

2637. _____. The Humblest Place. 1 act. Plays, 15 (December, 1955), 15-24.

2638. _____. A Just and Lasting Peace. 1 act. Plays, 23 (February, 1964), 25-34.

2639. _____. Known But to God. 1 act. Plays, 16 (November, 1956), 79-88.

2640. _____. The Last Laugh. 1 act. Plays, 9 (March, 1950), 13-24.

2641. _____. A Light in Darkness. 1 act. Plays, 10 (February, 1951), 23-33.

2642. _____. The Man Who Stayed at Home. 1 act. Plays, 14 (December, 1954), 33-42.

2643. _____. The Most Important Guests. 1 act. Plays, 20 (December, 1960), 15-24.

2644. _____. Night of Decision. 1 act. Plays, 21 (February, 1962), 1-10.

2645. _____. None So Blind. 1 act. Plays, 9 (March, 1950), 31-40.

2646. _____. The Perfect Gift. 1 act. Plays, 3 (December, 1943), 12-19. AND Plays, 28 (December, 1968), 11-18.

2647. _____. Poison Ivy. 1 act. Plays, 22 (April, 1963), 23-34.

2648. _____. Rain and Rebellion. 1 act. Plays, 10 (November, 1950), 18-26.

2649. _____. The Road to Bethlehem. 1 act. Plays, 11 (December, 1951), 11-19. AND Plays, 23 (December, 1963), 27-35.

2650. _____. Road to Valley Forge. 1 act. Plays, 29 (February, 1970), 11-18.

2651. _____. A Room for a King. 1 act. Plays, 12 (December, 1952), 27-37. AND Plays, 31 (December, 1971), 13-22.

2652. _____. St. Patrick Saves the Day. 1 act. Plays, 11 (March, 1952), 38-47. AND Plays, 29 (March, 1970), 53-62.

2653. _____. Shelter for the Night. 1 act. Plays, 17 (December, 1957), 23-32.

2654. _____. So Shines a Good Deed. 1 act. Plays, 5 (May, 1946), 24-32.

2655. _____. A Song in the Night. 1 act. Plays, 16 (December, 1956), 31-39. AND Plays, 34 (December, 1974), 36-44.

2656. _____. Spring Will Come. 1 act. Plays, 4 (January, 1945), 10-18.

2657. _____. Star over Bethlehem. 1 act. Plays, 19 (December, 1959), 15-24.

2658. _____. They Banish Our Anger. 1 act. Plays, 4 (May, 1945), 11-20.

2659. _____. Tulips and Two Lips. 1 act. Plays, 12 (April, 1953), 15-26.

2660. _____. Two Strangers from Nazareth. 1 act. Plays, 21 (December, 1961), 44-50.

2661. _____. What's In a Name? 1 act. Plays, 14 (November, 1954), 13-23.

2662. _____. The Winter of Our Discontent. 1 act. Plays, 5 (February, 1946), 8-16.

2663. _____. With Malice Toward None. 1 act. Plays, 14 (February, 1955), 1-12. AND Plays, 31 (February, 1972), 25-36.

_____, adapter see Clemens, S. L. 1880

DuBois, Marcel, translator see Rand, A. 7402

2664. Dubosc, Isabelle. L'Ile Irréelle. 1 act. L'Avant Scène, 429 (July 1, 1969), 37-44. In French.

2665. DuBreuilh, Simone. Une Demande en Mariage. 1 act, comedy. L'Avant Scène, 222, 30-38. In French.

2666. _____. L'Heure de Thé. 1 act. L'Avant Scène, 211, 41-49. In French.

2667. _____. Le Naufrage ou Miss Ann Saunders. 1 act, comedy. L'Avant Scène, 191 (February 15, 1959), 31-37. In French.

Duc, Hélène, adapter see Mihura, M. 5826

Duc, Marcel Le, translator see Guth, P. 3787

_____, translator see Labiche, E. 4748-4751

Ducceschi, Mirella, translator see Odets, C. 6771

_____, translator see Rattigan, T. 7420

_____, translator see Sherriff, R. C. 8251

2668. Ducreux, Louis, 1911- . L'Amour en Papier. Comedy. L'Avant Scène, (OST), 59 (April, 1952), 1-32. In French.

2669. _____. Le Roi Est Mort. 3 acts, comedy. L'Avant Scène (OST), 5 (May, 1949), 1-41. In French.

2670. _____. Le Roi Est Mort. 3 acts. Il Dramma, n. s., 115/116 (August 15/September 1, 1950), 59-87. B. L. Randone, translator. In Italian.

2671. _____. Vieux Soleil. 1 act, comedy. L'Avant Scène, 223, 37-42. In French.

2672. Duer, Caroline. The Ambassador's Burglar. 1 act. Smart Set, 5 (November, 1901), 49-57.

2673. _____. Mr. Shakespeare at School. 1 act. Smart Set, 7 (June, 1902), 65-73.

2674. Duff, Annis. A Play for Christmas Eve. 1 act. Horn Book, 14 (November, 1938), 355-362.

2675. Duffy, Maureen, 1933- . Rites. Plays and Players, 17 (October, 1969), 57-66.

2676. Duffy, Richard, 1873- . The Night of the Wedding. 1 act. Smart Set, 25 (May, 1908), 80-90.

2677. _____. The Tragic Spark. 2 acts, comedy. Smart Set, 7 (May, 1902), 63-79.

2678. Duggar, Frances. December's Gift. 1 act. Plays, 12 (December, 1952), 60-64.

2679. Duhamel, Georges, 1884- . The Combat. 5 acts. Poet Lore, 26 (Vacation, 1915), 409-487. Sasha Best, translator.

2680. _____. In the Shadow of Statues. 3 acts. Poet Lore, 25 (Autumn, 1914), 371-438. Sasha Best, translator.

2681. _____. The Light. 4 acts. Poet Lore, 25 (Summer, 1914), 161-203. Sasha Best, translator.

2682. _____. La Lumiere. 4 acts. Vers et Prose, 26 (July-September, 1911), 137-157; 27 (October-December, 1911), 76-90. In French.

_____, translator see Steinbeck, J. 8493

2683. Dukes, Ashley, 1885-1959. The Players' Dressing-Room, A Tragic Comedy. 1 act. Theatre Arts, 20 (June, 1936), 473-480.

2684. _____. Tyl Ulenspiegel, or The Song of Drums. 3 acts, heroic comedy. Theatre Arts, 10 (May, June, July, 1926), 240-253; 312-324; 385-395; 481-486.

_____, adapter see Carre, M. 837, 1615

_____, translator see Kaiser, G. 4531

2685. Dumas, Alexandre, 1803-1870. The Count of Monte Cristo. 1 act. Plays, 18 (May, 1959), 97-105. Lewy Olfson, adapter.

2686. _____. The Three Musketeers. 1 act. Plays, 12 (April, 1953), 87-93.

2687. Dumas, Alexandre, 1824-1895. L'amico delle donne. 3 acts. Il Dramma, 372 (February 15, 1942), 7-31. Giuseppe Achille, translator. In Italian.

2688. _____. La Dame aux Camelias. 3 acts. Sipario, 8 (October, 1953), 34-53. Carlo Terron, translator. In Italian.

2689. _____. The Money-Question. 5 acts, comedy. Poet Lore, 26 (Spring, 1915), 129-227.

2690. _____. Une Visite de Noces. 1 act, comedy. L'Avant Scène, 269 (July 15, 1962), 18-30. In French.

2691. Dumas, André. The Eternal Presence, A Nocturne. 1 act. Poet Lore, 29 (Summer, 1918), 459-468. Carree Horton Blackman, translator.

2692. Dumas, Rene-Louis. Pretez-moi Votre Fils. 1 act. L'Avant Scène, 541 (May 15, 1974), 37-43. In French.

2693. DuMaurier, Daphne, 1907- . Rebecca. 3 acts. Il Dramma, n.s., 48 (November 1, 1947), 9-43. Paola Ojetti, translator. In Italian.

2694. _____. September Tide. 3 acts. Il Dramma, n.s., 143 (October 15, 1951), 7-37. Ada Salvatore, translator. In Italian.

2695. Dumur, Louis and Virgile Josz. Don Juan en Flandre. 1 act. Vers et Prose, 33 (April-June, 1913), 75-86. In French.

2696. Dunbar, Alice. The Author's Evening at Home. 1 act. Smart Set, 2 (September, 1900), 105-106.

2697. Dunbar, Newell. The Ever Womanly. 1 act. Arena, 31 (February, 1904), 180-198.

2698. Dunbar, Olivia Howard. Blockade. 1 act. Theatre Arts, 7 (April, 1923), 127-142.

2699. Duncan, Frances and Elsie D. Yale. Save the Wild Flowers. 1 act. Woman's Home Companion, 54 (May, 1927), 49.

2700. Duncan, George. A Proposal. 1 act. Harper's, 108 (April, 1904), 796-801.

2701. Duncan, Kunigunde, 1886- . Atla. 1 act. Poet Lore, 60 (Spring, 1965), 3-19.

2702. Duncan, Ronald, 1914- . The Gift. 1 act. Gambit, 3 (No. 11), 93-110.

2703. Duncan, Winifred. The Classic Dancing School. 1 act. Drama, 17 (May, 1927), 235-242.

2704. Dunham, Curtis. Mademoiselle Plato, An Unplatonic Object Lesson. 1 act. Smart Set, 40 (August, 1913), 133-140.

Dunlop, Lane, translator see Char, R. 1723

2705. Dunne, Douglas. Two of a Kind. 1 act. Smart Set, 2 (October/November, 1900), 78-80.

2706. Dunning, Ralph Cheever. The Home-Coming. 1 act. Poetry, 7 (January, 1916), 179-181.

2707. Dunsany, Edward John Moreton Drax Plunket, Lord, 1878-1957. Il cristallo magico. 4 acts. Il Dramma, 373 (March 1, 1942), 7-25. Carlo Linati, translator. In Italian.

2708. _____. Fame and the Poet. 1 act, comedy. Atlantic, 124 (August, 1919), 175-184.

2709. _____. Fame and the Poet. 1 act, comedy. Golden Book, 12 (November, 1930), 87-89.

2710. _____. The Glittering Gate, A One-Act Comedy of Heaven. Golden Book, 16 (November, 1932), 464-468.

2711. _____. The Gods of the Mountain. 4 acts. Irish Review, 1 (December, 1911), 486-504.

2712. _____. The Golden Doom. 1 act. Il Dramma, 384 (August 15, 1942), 35-39. Vinicio Marinucci, translator. In Italian.

2713. _____. The Golden Doom. 1 act. Poetry and Drama, 1 (December, 1913), 431-442.

2714. _____. A Good Bargain. 1 act. Smart Set, 63 (September, 1920), 73-78.

2715. _____. If Shakespeare Lived Today. 1 act, satire. Atlantic, 126 (October, 1920), 497-508.

2716. _____. The Jest of Hahalaba. 1 act. Atlantic, 139 (January, 1927), 58-62.

2717. _____. King Argimenes and the Unknown Warrior. 1 act. Irish Review, 1 (September, 1911), 336-351.

2718. _____. The Laughter of the Gods. 1 act. Il Dramma, 391/392 (December 1/15, 1942), 75-83. Vinicio Marinucci, translator. In Italian.

2719. _____. The Laughter of the Gods. 3 acts. Golden Book, 8 (October, 1928), 496-507.

2720. _____. The Lost Silk Hat. 1 act. Golden Book, 10 (August, 1929), 89-91.

2721. _____. A Matter of Honour. 1 act. Esquire, 2 (July, 1934), 56.

2722. _____. A Night at an Inn. 1 act. Golden Book, 4 (September, 1926), 377-381.

2723. _____. The Pumpkin. 1 act. London Mercury, 24 (June, 1931), 122-129.

2724. _____. The Queen's Enemies. 1 act. Il Dramma, 382 (July 15, 1942), 39-43. Vinicio Marinucci, translator. In Italian.

2725. _____. The Queen's Enemies. 1 act. Golden Book, 6 (August, 1927), 258-267.

2726. _____. The Tents of the Arabs. 1 act. Il Dramma, 414/415/416 (November 15/December 1/15, 1943), 85-89. Vinicio Marinucci, translator. In Italian.

2727. _____. The Tents of the Arabs. 2 acts. Golden Book, 1 (June, 1925), 849-855.

2728. _____. The Tents of the Arabs. 1 act. Smart Set, 45 (March, 1915), 229-239.

2729. Dunster, Mark. Dialog. 1 act. Drama and Theatre, 9 (Winter, 1970/71), 102-105.

2730. _____. Skelton. 1 act. Drama and Theatre, 7 (Winter, 1968/69), 141-149.

2731. _____. Sojourner Truth. 1 act. Dramatika, 6 (Fall, 1970), 1-15.

2732. Duprat-Géneau, Jean, 1919- . Attila, ou le Fleau de Dieu. 1 act. L'Avant Scène, 228, 41-43. In French.

2733. Durafour, Michel, 1920- . Les Demoniaques. 3 acts. L'Avant Scène (OST), 29 (September, 1950), 3-30. In French.

Duran, Michel, pseud. see Durand, M. 2734.

2734. Durand, Michel, 1900- . Liberté Provisoire. 4 acts, comedy. Petite Illustration, 188 (June 30, 1934), 1-34. In French.

2735. Duranty, Louis. La Malle de Berlingue. 1 act, farce. Sipario, 11 (December, 1956), 17-19, 46. Sergio Morando, translator. In Italian.

2736. Duras, Marguerite, 1914- . L'Amante Anglaise. 2 parts. L'Avant Scène, 422 (March 15, 1969), 5-24. In French.

2737. _____. Ganze Tage in den Baumen. 3 acts. Spectaculum, 9 (1966), 15-54. Werner Spies, translator. In German.

2738. _____. Des Journées Entières dans les Arbres. 3 acts. L'Avant Scène, 348/9 (January 1, 15, 1966), 57-77. In French.

_____, translator see Gibson, W. 3502

2739. Durden, Mae. The Case of the Easter Villains. 1 act. Plays, 35 (April, 1976), 74-78.

Durer, C. S., translator see Witkiewicz, S. I. 9513, 9515, 9521

2740. Durrell, Lawrence, 1912- . Acte, or, The Prisoners of Time. 3 acts. Show, 1 (December, 1961), 45-55, 95-105.

2741. Dürrenmatt, Friedrich, 1921- . Abendstunde im Spätherbst. 1 act. Il Dramma, n.s., 270 (March, 1959), 67-76. Italo Alighiero Chiusano, translator. In Italian.

2742. _____. Der Besuch der Alten Dame. 3 acts, tragi-comedy. Spectaculum, 2 (1959), 126-196. In German.

2743. _____. Frank der Funfte. 1 act, comedy. L'Avant Scène, 285 (April 1, 1963), 8-28. Jean-Pierre Porret, adapter. In French.

2744. _____. Le Mariage de M. Mississippi. 2 parts, comedy. L'Avant Scène, 232 (December 1, 1960), 8-31. Jean-Pierre Porret, translator. In French.

2745. _____. Der Meteor. 2 acts. Sipario, 265 (May, 1968), 45-56. Aloisio Rendi, translator. In Italian.

2746. _____. The Mission of the Vega. 1 act. Texas Quarterly, 5 (Spring, 1962), 125-149. Alfred Schild, translator.

2747. _____. Die panne. 1 act. Il Dramma, n.s., 267 (December, 1958), 47-61. Italo Alighiero Chiusano, translator. In Italian.

2748. _____. Die Physiker. 2 acts, comedy. Spectaculum, 7 (1964), 105-147. In German.

2749. _____. Der Prozess um des Esels Schatten. 1 act. Il Dramma, n.s., 294 (March, 1961), 32-48. Italo Alighiero Chiusano, translator. In Italian.

2750. _____. Romulus. 4 acts, comedy. L'Avant Scène, 319 (October 1, 1964), 12-31. Jean-Pierre Porret, translator. In French.

2751. _____. Romulus. 1 act. Esquire, 57 (January, 1962), 47-54. Gore Vidal, adapter.

2752. _____. Romulus der Grosse. 4 acts, comedy. Spectaculum, 4 (1963), 81-134. In German.

2753. _____. The Visit. 3 acts. Theatre Arts, 43 (December, 1959), 33-64. Maurice Valency, adapter.

2754. _____. La Visite de la Vieille Dame. 3 acts, tragi-comedy. L'Avant Scène, 249 (September 15, 1961), 10-33. Jean-Pierre Porret, translator. In French.

2755. Dursi, Massimo, 1902- . La balena bianca. 1 act, farce. Sipario, 21 (April, 1966), 53-64. In Italian.

2756. _____. Narciso. 1 act. Sipario, 20 (November, 1965), 60-61.

2757. _____. Nessuno. 2 acts. Sipario, 267 (July, 1968), 51-64. In Italian.

2758. _____. I Posteri. 1 act. Sipario, 8 (November, 1953), 48-53. In Italian.

2759. _____. Stefano Pelloni Called the Ferryman. Drama and Theatre, 8 (No. 1, 1969), 14-46.

2760. _____. La strado morta. 1 act. Sipario, 18 (November, 1963), 69-72. In Italian.

2761. _____. Il tumulto dei ciompi. 2 parts. Sipario, 318 (November, 1972), 55-80. In Italian.

_____, translator see Obaldia, R. de 6721

2762. Durtain, Luc. Le Mari Singulier. 3 acts. Petite Illustration, 197 (July 3, 1937), 1-30. In French.

2763. _____. L'Oracle à Parlé. 3 acts. L'Avant Scène, 81 (September 20, 1953), 7-30. In French.

2764. Duse, Carlo V. Il dono della notte. 1 act. Il Dramma, 39 (April 1, 1928), 38-45. In Italian.

2765. Duse, Enzo, 1901- . C'è anche un fidanzato. 1 act. Il Dramma, 367 (December 1, 1941), 29-33. In Italian.

2766. _____. Introduzione alla vita eroica. 6 parts. Il Dramma, 280 (April 15, 1938), 4-15. In Italian.

2767. _____. Ladri. 3 acts. Il Dramma, 260 (June 15, 1937), 2-18. In Italian.

2768. _____. Maddalena, occhi di menta. 3 acts. Il Dramma, 307 (June 1, 1939), 4-23. In Italian.

2769. _____. Nemici dell'amore. 3 acts. Il Dramma, 337 (September 1, 1940), 31-44. In Italian.

2770. _____. Quelle oneste signore. 1 act. Il Dramma, 327 (April 1, 1940), 46-48. In Italian.

2771. D'Usseau, Arnaud, 1916- and James Ellis Gow, 1907-1952. Deep Are the Roots. 3 acts. Il Dramma, n.s., 106 (April 1, 1950), 7-35. Franca Savioli, translator. In Italian.

2772. Dutourd, Jean, 1920- . L'Arbre. 1 act. L'Avant Scène, 145, 1-25. In French.

2773. Duvall, Lucille Miller. April Fool's Day. 1 act. Plays, 19 (April, 1960), 47-52.

2774. _____. Autumn's Visit. 1 act. Plays, 17 (October, 1957), 75-78.

2775. _____. The Chosen One. 1 act. Plays, 16 (December, 1956), 41-50.

2776. _____. The Christmas Shoe. 1 act. Plays, 19 (December, 1959), 67-71.

2777. _____. Gunther Groundhog. 1 act. Plays, 17 (February, 1958), 60-66.

2778. _____. Little Chip's Christmas Tree. 1 act. Plays, 16 (December, 1956), 79-82.

2779. _____. Spring Is Here! 1 act. Plays, 18 (May, 1959), 71-74.

2780. _____. Valentine's Day. 1 act. Plays, 15 (February, 1956), 71-77.

2781. Duvernois, Henri, 1875-1937. I cadetti. 2 acts. Il Dramma, 161 (May 1, 1933), 30-45. Lucio Ridenti, translator. In Italian.

2782. _____. La clementina Piéfaroux. 1 act. Il Dramma, 166 (July 15, 1933), 38-45. Lucio Ridenti, translator. In Italian.

2783. _____. Cuore. 4 acts. Il Dramma, 122 (September 15, 1931), 4-38. Lucio Ridenti and Vittorio Guerriero, translators. In Italian.

2784. _____. L'esperimento di televisione. 1 act. Il Dramma, 153 (January 1, 1933), 40-45. In Italian.

2785. _____. La fuga. 3 acts. Il Dramma, 102 (November 15, 1930), 4-35. Lucio Ridenti, translator. In Italian.

2786. _____. La Fugue. 3 acts, comedy. Petite Illustration, 87 (October 19, 1929), 1-26. In French.

2787. _____. L'illusione di Giacomina. 3 acts. Il Dramma, 222 (November 15, 1935), 2-26. Mario De Vellis, translator. In Italian.

2788. _____. Jeanne. 3 acts, comedy. Petite Illustration, 184 (January 7, 1933), 1-30. In French.

2789. _____. La Professeur. 1 act, comedy. Petite Illustration, 86 (October 13, 1928), 1-9. In French.

2790. _____. Rouge! 3 acts, comedy. Petite Illustration, 191, (May 11, 1935), 1-33. In French.

2791. _____. Il sigaro. 1 act. Il Dramma, 8 (July, 1926), 39-45. Nennele Maccini, translator. In Italian.

2792. _____. Solo. 1 act. Il Dramma, 117 (July 1, 1931), 34-42. In Italian.

2793. D'Vorian, Jacques Mariel, 1942- . L'Etrange aventure. 1 act. L'Avant Scène, 537 (March 15, 1974), 35-42. In French.

2794. Dyer, Charles, 1928- . L'Escalier. 2 acts. L'Avant Scène, 395 (January 15, 1968), 7-30. Louis Velle, adapter. In French.

2795. _____. Il sottoscala. 2 acts. Sipario, 24 (August, 1969), 47-64. In Italian.

2796. _____. Staircase. 2 acts. Plays and Players, 14 (January, 1967), 31-46.

2797. Dyk, Victor. The Ninth Night. 1 act, comedy. Poet Lore, 29 (Spring, 1918), 90-101. Cyril Jeffrey Hrbek, translator.

Dyson, John P., translator see Perez, J. C. 7067

E

2798. Earle, Dorothy Kirchner. You're Such a Respectable Person, Miss Morrison. 1 act. Smart Set, 46 (August, 1915), 87-94.

2799. East, Dann. The Grunt. 1 act. the new renaissance, 2 (No. 2, 1976), 44.

2800. Eastman, Fred. God or Caesar? 1 act. Christian Century, 49 (October 12, 1932), 1240-1243.

2801. Eberhart, Richard, 1904- . The Apparition. 1 act. Poetry, 77 (March, 1951), 311-321.

2802. _____. Choosing a Monument. 1 act. Western Review, 14 (Autumn, 1949), 58-62.

2803. _____. Devils and Angels. 1 act. Tulane Drama Review, 6 (June, 1962), 15-32.

2804. _____. A Dialogue. 1 act. Discovery, 6 (1955), 77-86.

2805. _____. The Mad Musician. 1 act. Tulane Drama Review, 6 (June, 1962), 33-53.

2806. _____. Triptych. 1 act. The Chimera, 2 (Autumn, 1943), 15-25.

2807. _____. The Visionary Farms. 1 act. New World Writing, 3 (1953), 63-97.

2808. Ebner-Eschenbach, Marie von, 1830-1916. A Man of the World. 1 act. Poet Lore, 22 (Spring, 1911), 128-133. Roy Temple House, translator.

2809. Echegaray y Eizaguirre, Jose, 1835-1916. Always Ridiculous. 3 acts, comedy. Poet Lore, 27 (Summer, 1917), 233-325. T. Walter Gilkyson, translator.

2810. _____. The Madman Divine. 4 acts. Poet Lore, 19 (Spring, 1908), 3-86. Elizabeth Howard West, translator.

2811. _____. Madman or Saint. 3 acts. Poet Lore, 23 (Summer, 1912), 161-220. Ruth Lansing, translator.

2812. _____. Street Singer. 1 act. Drama, 25 (February, 1917), 62-76. John Garrett Underhill, translator.

2813. _____. Street Singer. 1 act. Golden Book, 5 (February, 1927), 192-196. John Garrett Underhill, translator.

2814. Eckart, Walter. Les Femmes de Kalatas. 1 act. L'Avant Scène, 308 (April 1, 1964), 31-35. Paul Sonnendrucker, translator. In French.

2815. Eckersley, Arthur, 1875-1921. A Tabloid. 1 act. Smart Set, 44 (October, 1914), 135-142.

2816. Edmonds, Randolph. Un uomo cattivo. 1 act. Il Dramma, n. s., 156 (May 1, 1952), 45-52. Giovanni Cesareo, translator. In Italian.

2817. Edson, Russell. The Crawlers. 1 act. New Directions, 26 (1974), 39-49.

2818. _____. Ketchup. New Directions, 23 (1971), 27-42.

2819. Edwards, Doris L. The New-Old Christmas. 1 act. Plays, 14 (December, 1954), 75-80.

2820. Edwards, Margaret Bunel. Turnabout. 1 act. Plays, 31 (December, 1971), 31-34.

2821. Eger, Rodolfo and Jean De Letraz. 13 a tavola. 3 acts. Il Dramma, 152 (December 15, 1932), 4-31. In Italian.

2822. Eggleston, Edward, 1837-1902. The House of Santa Claus. 1 act. St. Nicholas, 4 (December, 1876), 131-134.

2823. _____. Mother Goose and Her Family. 1 act. St. Nicholas, 7 (December, 1879), 146-149.

2824. Egloga de la Résurrection. 1 act. PMLA, 47 (December, 1932), 960-974. In Spanish.

2825. Ehlert, Fay. The Undercurrent. 1 act. Drama, 18 (January, 1928), 111-114.

2826. Ehni, Réné. Que Ferez-vous en Novembre? 2 acts. L'Avant Scène, 412 (October 15, 1968), 9-34. In French.

2827. _____. Que ferez-vous en novembre. 2 acts. Sipario, 24 (April, 1969), 46-64. Ornella Volta, translator. In Italian.

2828. Ehrlich, Ida Lublenski. Snaring the Lion. 1 act. Drama, 34 (May, 1919), 60-83.

2829. Ehrmann, Max, 1872- . David and Bathsheba. 3 acts. Drama, 28 (November, 1917), 492-569.

2830. Eich, Gunter, 1907-1972. Dreams. 1 act. Evergreen Review, 5 (November-December, 1961), 80-92.

2831. _____. The Girls from Viterbo. Prism International, 13 (Summer, 1973), 23-64. Michael Hamburger, translator.

2832. _____. The Year Lacertis. 1 act. Quarterly Review of Literature, 13 (No. 3/4, 1965), 314-356. Michael Hamburger, translator.

2833. Eifler, Millicent Spaulding. Dialogue of a Democracy, A Confrontation. Poet Lore, 64 (Autumn, 1969), 314-335.

2834. Einarsson, Indridi. Sword and Crozier. 5 acts. Poet Lore, 23 (Vacation, 1912), 224-283. Lee M. Hollander, translator.

Eisemann, Fred, translator see Chekhov, A. P. 1777

2835. Eisenreich, Herbert. Wovon Wir Leben und Woran Wir Sterben. 1 act. Il Dramma, n.s., 255 (December, 1957), 102-113. Italo Alighiero Chiusano, translator. In Italian.

Eisenschitz, Otto, translator see Chlumberg, H. von 1813

Ekeram, Catherine, adapter see Bergman, I. 816

Ekeram, Ulf, adapter see Bergman, I. 816

2836. Elder, Judith. The Road to London. 1 act. Plays, 2 (October, 1942), 9-14.

2837. Eldridge, Paul, 1888- . The Carnival, A Divine Comedy in One Act. Double Dealer, 5 (January, 1923), 4-29.

2838. _____. The Loser. 1 act. Drama, 11 (February, 1921), 166-170.

2839. Elfenbein, Josef A. Adam Goodfellow and the Jill Fish. 1 act. Plays, 32 (April, 1973), 67-72.

2840. _____. The April Elves. 1 act. Plays, 14 (April, 1955), 63-69.

2841. _____. The King Who Couldn't be Fooled. 1 act. Plays, 14 (March, 1955), 57-66.

2842. _____. Puss-in-Boots. 1 act. Plays, 29 (February, 1970), 67-73.

2843. _____. The Ten-Penny Tragedy. 1 act. Plays, 16 (October, 1956), 37-46. AND Plays, 26 (May, 1967), 27-35.

2844. Eliot, Annie. As Strangers; A Comedietta in One Act. Scribner's, 20 (August, 1896), 189-204.

2845. _____. From Four to Six; A Comedietta in One Act. Scribner's, 6 (July, 1889), 121-128.

2846. Eliot, George, 1819-1880. Armgart. 1 act. Atlantic, 28 (July, 1871), 94-105.

Eliot, Samuel A., Jr., translator see Wedekind, F. 9253, 9257

2847. Eliot, Thomas Stearns, 1888-1965. The Cocktail Party. 3 acts. Sipario, 7 (March, 1952), 33-55. Salvatore Rosati, translator. In Italian.

2848. _____. The Cocktail Party. 3 acts. Spectaculum, 1 (1962), 209-287. In German.

2849. _____. The Elder Statesman. 3 acts. Sipario, 14 (December, 1959), 77-93. Desideria Pasilini, translator. In Italian.

2850. _____. The Elder Statesman. 3 acts. Spectaculum, 3 (1960), 125-181. In German.

2851. _____. The Family Reunion. 2 parts. Sipario, 9 (January, 1954), 34-50. Salvatore Rosati, translator. In Italian.

2852. _____. Fragment of an Agon. Il Dramma, n. s., 90 (August 1, 1949), 46-47. Gigi Cane, translator. In Italian.

2853. _____. Murder in the Cathedral. 2 acts. Spectaculum, 1 (1962), 167-207. In German.

2854. Eliraz, Israël, 1936- . La Banane. 1 act. L'Avant Scène, 454 (August 1, 1970), 40-44. In French.

2855. _____. Loin de la Mer ... Loin de l'Eté. 1 act. L'Avant Scène, 355 (April 15, 1966), 38-43. Ahouva Lion, translator. In French.

Elka, pseud. see Kerautem, L. de 4600, 4601

Elliott, D. H. see Sassoon, R. L. 7969

2856. Elliott, William D. The Replacement. 1 act. Poet Lore, 65 (Winter, 1970), 407-424.

2857. Elness, Warren P. The Sound of Christmas. 1 act. Resource, 11 (November, 1969), 6-8, 30-31.

2858. Elton, Richard. Il re jazz. 1 act. Il Dramma, 29 (November 1, 1927), 37-39. In Italian.

2859. Elton, Richard D. The Handy Man. 1 act. Industrial Arts and Vocational Education, 33 (June, 1944), 226.

2860. Emery, Gilbert. The Hero. Everybody's Magazine, 46 (March, 1922), 123-130.

2861. Emig, Evelyn. The China Pig. 1 act. Poet Lore, 33 (Autumn, 1922), 439-450.

2862. _____. The Old Order. 1 act. Poet Lore, 32 (Winter, 1921), 586-595.

2863. Emmons, Myra. Visiting Mamma. 1 act. Harper's Bazaar, 43 (September, 1909), 860-864.

2864. Emory, William Closson. Love in the West. 2 parts. Transition, 13 (Summer, 1928), 33-41.

Ende, Amelia von, translator see Hauptmann, C. 3969

_____, translator see Wiegand, J. and W. Scharrelmann 9346

Enderiz, Ezequiel see Gabirondo, V. 3343

2865. Engel, Alexander and Alfred Grunwald. Dolly e il suo ballerino. 3 acts. Il Dramma, 113 (May 1, 1931), 4-28. In Italian.

2866. England, Barry. Conduct Unbecoming. 3 acts. Sipario, 25 (November, 1970), 38-64. Laura del Bono, translator. In Italian.

2867. England, George Allen, 1877-1936. "Under Their Skins." 1 act. Smart Set, 44 (November, 1914), 107-113.

2868. Ensana, Joel A. Please, No Flowers. 1 act. First Stage, 5 (Spring, 1966), 17-22.

Ephron, Henry, 1912- see Ephron, P. 2869

2869. Ephron, Phoebe, 1916- and Henry Ephron, 1912- . Take Her, She's Mine. 2 acts, comedy. Theatre Arts, 47 (July, 1963), 37-70.

Epstein, Stephane, translator see Hofmannsthal, H. von 4341

2870. Eremburg, Ilja. Il leone della piazza. 3 acts. Il Dramma, n.s., 74 (December 1, 1948), 9-31. Andrea Jamma, translator. In Italian.

Erlih, Devy, adapter see Ramuz, C. F. 7401

2871. Ernst, Alice Henson. Nightingale; An Arabian Night's Fantasy. 1 act. Poet Lore, 38 (1927), 293-314.

2872. _____. Spring Sluicing. 1 act. Theatre Arts, 12 (February, 1928), 125-138.

2873. _____. The Valley of Lost Men. 1 act. Theatre Arts, 14 (May, 1930), 430-440.

Ernst, Myron, translator see Adamov, A. 58

2874. Erskine, John, 1879-1951. Helen Retires. 3 acts. Golden Book, 19 (May, June, 1934), 537-548; 749-760.

_____ see De Mille, W. C. 2317

_____, translator see Petit, V. P. 7106

2875. Ervine, St. John, 1883- . She Was No Lady. 1 act, comedy. Golden Book, 13 (July, 1931), 81-85.

Escudero, Carlos, translator see Gutierrez, E. and J. J. Podesta 3791

Espinosa, Agostino Degli see De Cespedes, A. 2237

2876. Espriu, Salvador, 1913- . Entremes da Ronda de Mort a Sinera. 1 act. Sipario (August-September, 1967), 77-80. Adele Faccio, translator. In Italian.

Estrada, Jose, adapter see Mihura, M. 5826

2877. Estrin, Marc. Four Infiltration Pieces: Cost Plus and American Imperialism; City Limits Ripoff; 31 Flavors and Law 'n' Order; Take, Eat, This Is My Body. Scripts, 1 (March, 1972), 23-29.

———, translator see Jodorowsky, A. 4470

Eszterhazy, Matyas, translator see Karinthy, F. 4550

2878. Eubanks, Thelma. The Spirit of Negro History. 1 act. Negro History Bulletin, 15 (May, 1952), 171-172.

2879. Euripides, 5th cent. B.C. The Cyclops. 1 act. Hudson Review, 5 (Spring, 1952), 7-30. William Arrowsmith, translator.

2880. ———. Medea. 2 parts, tragedy. Il Dramma, n.s., 87 (June 15, 1949), 7-22. Robinson Jeffers, adapter. Gigi Cane, translator. In Italian.

2881. ———. Medea. 2 acts. Theatre Arts, 32 (August-September, 1948), 71-97. Robinson Jeffers, adapter.

Evans, Calvin, translator see Prins, P. de 7302

Evans, F. Cridland, translator see Hennique, L. 4058

2882. Evans, Gladys La Due. The Little Moral Child. 1 act. Poet Lore, 32 (Autumn, 1921), 409-415.

2883. Evans, Margaret. Faith. 1 act. Poet Lore, 33 (Spring, 1922), 132-137.

Evans, Oliver W., 1915- , translator see Pirandello, L. 7186

2884. Eveling, Stanley. Oh Starlings! 1 act. Plays and Players, 18 (March, 1971), 76-79.

2885. ———. Sweet Alice. 1 act. Plays and Players, 18 (March, 1971), 79-85.

2886. Evreinoff, Nikolai Nikolajevic, 1879-1953. La Comédie du Bonheur. 3 acts. Petite Illustration, 86 (January 28, 1928), 1-34. Fernand Noziere, translator.

2887. _____. Les Coulisses de L'Ame. 1 act. L'Avant Scène, 544 (July 1, 1974), 39-42. In French.

2888. _____. La morte lieta. 1 act. Il Dramma, n. s., 5 (January 15, 1946), 41-47. Lorenzo Gigli, translator. In Italian.

2889. _____. Le quinte dell'anima. 1 act. Il Dramma, n. s., 23/24 (October 15/November 1, 1946), 96-100. Grazia Di Giammatteo and Fernaldo Di Giammatteo, translators. In Italian.

2890. _____. Stiopic et Mania. 1 act. L'Avant Scène, 516 (April 15, 1973), 31-35. In French.

2891. _____. Le Triangle Immortel. 1 act. L'Avant Scène, 566 (June 15, 1975), 47-52. Genia Cannac, adapter. In French.

2892. Exton, Clive. Have You Any Dirty Washing, Mother Dear? 2 acts. Plays and Players, 16 (May, 1969), 35-50.

2893. Eyen, Tom, 1946- . Pourquoi la Rob d'Anna ne Veut pas Redescendre. L'Avant Scène, 549 (October 1, 1974), 3-18. Bernard Da Costa, adapter. In French.

F

2894. F., H. B. O, That Way Madness Lies; A Play for Marionettes. 1 act. Chap-Book, 4 (December 1, 1895), 71-80.

2895. Fabbri, Diego, 1911- . L'avvenimento. 2 parts. Il Dramma, n. s., 374/375 (November/December, 1967), 17-57. In Italian.

2896. _____. La bugiarda. 3 acts. Il Dramma, n. s., 236 (May, 1956), 13-48. In Italian.

2897. _____. Lascio alle mie donne. 2 parts. Il Dramma, 47 (November/December, 1971), 65-90. In Italian.

2898. _____. La libreria del sole. 3 acts. Il Dramma, n. s., 27/28 (December 15, 1946/January 1, 1947), 59-79. In Italian.

2899. _____. Procès à Jesus. 2 parts. L'Avant Scène, 171 (March 31, 1958), 4-31. Jacques Talagrand, translator. In French.

2900. _____. Processo a Gesú. 2 parts. Il Dramma, n. s., 223 (April, 1955), 6-42. In Italian.

2901. ———. Processo di famiglia. 2 parts. Il Dramma, n. s., 197 (January 15, 1954), 11-42. In Italian.

2902. ———. Rancore. 3 acts. Sipario, 5 (April, 1950), 53-69. In Italian.

2903. ———. Le Seducteur. 3 acts, comedy. L'Avant Scène, 124, 1-31. Michel Arnaud, adapter. In French.

2904. ———. Le Signe du Feu. 4 acts. L'Avant Scène, 236. (February 1, 1961), 9-31. Jacques Talagrand and Costa du Rels, adapters. In French.

2905. ———. Teresa Desqueyroux. 3 acts. Il Dramma, n. s., 296 (May, 1961), 12-38. In Italian.

2906. ———. Veglia d'armi. 2 parts. Il Dramma, n. s., 246 (March, 1957), 4-38. In Italian.

———, translator see Achard, M. 36

———, translator see Dostoevski, F. 2563

Fabbri, Jacques, pseud. see Fabbricotti, Jacques

Fabbricotti, Jacques, 1925- , adapter see Scarpetta 8010

2907. Fabré, Emile, 1870-1955. La Rabouilleuse. 4 acts. Petite Illustration, 195 (December 26, 1936), 1-30. In French.

Faccio, Adele, translator see Espriu, S. 2879

Faehl, Dietrich, translator see Wedekind, F. 9258

2908. Faggi, Vico. Un certo giorno di un certo anno in Aulide. 3 acts. Il Dramma, n. s., 345/346 (June/July, 1965), 40-56. In Italian.

2909. Fagin, Mary. Room 226. 1 act. Poet Lore, 36 (Winter, 1925), 610-614.

Fahnestock, Edith, translator see Cervantes Saavedra, M. de 1696

2910. ——— and Florence Donnell White. The Magic Theatre. 1 act. Poet Lore, 32 (No. 2, 1921), 234-243.

2911. Faier, Joan Sari. The Sage of Monticello. 1 act. Plays, 36 (November, 1976), 87-95.

2912. Fair, Felix. Tickets Please! 1 act. One-Act Play Magazine, 1 (July, 1937), 219-236.

2913. Falconi, Dino. Joe il rosso. 3 acts. Il Dramma, 172 (October 15, 1933), 4-35. In Italian.

2914. _____. Lieto fine. 3 acts. Il Dramma, 231 (April 1, 1936), 2-25. In Italian.

2915. _____. Paparino. 3 acts. Il Dramma, n.s., 85 (May 15, 1949), 7-32. In Italian.

2916. _____. Rollo il grande. 3 acts. Il Dramma, 250 (January 15, 1937), 2-25. In Italian.

2917. _____. La strada. 1 act. dialogue. Il Dramma, 53 (November 1, 1928), 40-41. In Italian.

2918. _____. I tre maurizi. 3 acts. Il Dramma, 276 (February 15, 1938), 4-23. In Italian.

_____, translator see Ridenti, L. 7574

_____, translator see Sturges, P. 8592

2919. _____ and Oreste Biancoli. L'uomo di Birzulàh. 3 acts. Il Dramma, 56 (December 15, 1928), 7-33. In Italian.

2920. Falena, Ugo. Il buon lodrone. 3 acts. Il Dramma, 3 (February, 1926), 5-40. In Italian.

2921. _____. La corona di Strass. 3 acts. Il Dramma, 130 (January 15, 1932), 4-25. In Italian.

2922. _____. Il Duca di Mantova. 3 acts. Il Dramma, 115 (June 1, 1931), 4-33. In Italian.

2923. _____. Il favorito. 3 acts. Il Dramma, 84 (February 15, 1930), 6-32. In Italian.

2924. _____. La regina pomaré. 3 acts. Il Dramma, 53 (November 1, 1928), 5-36. In Italian.

2925. Fallon, Padriac. Dialogue Between Raftery and Death. 1 act. Dublin Magazine, n.s., 27 (October-December, 1952), 1-7.

2926. _____. The Fallen Saint. 1 act. Dublin Magazine, n.s., 11 (July-September, 1936), 16-32.

2927. Fanny's Second Play. 1 act. Bookman [New York], 36 (November, 1912), 284-286.

2928. Faraci, Giuseppe. Celebrità. 1 act. Il Dramma, 55 (December 1, 1928), 41-44. In Italian.

2929. _____. La piu bella avventura. 1 act, fantasy. Il Dramma, 43 (June 1, 1928), 41-45. In Italian.

_____, translator see Bernard, T. 854

_____, translator see Dieudonné, R. 2493

_____, translator see Savoir, A. 8001

2930. Faramond, Maurice de. Diane de Poitiers. 3 acts. tragicomedy. Vers et Prose, 32 (January-March, 1913), 5-54. In French.

2931. _____. Nabuchodonsor. 1 act, tragedy. Vers et Prose, 26 (July-September, 1911), 105-115. In French.

2932. Farce of the Worthy Master Pierre Palelin the Lawyer. 1 act. Poet Lore, 28 (Summer, 1917), 343-364. Maurice Relonde, translator.

Farnsworth, Oliver, translator see Florian, J.-P. C. de 3161

2933. Farrar, John Chipman, 1896- . The House Gnomes. 1 act. Bookman [New York], 56 (December, 1922), 449-459.

2934. _____. The Magic Sea Shell. 1 act. Bookman [New York], 57 (July, 1923), 511-520.

Farrell, Hortense see Farrell, J. T. 2936

2935. Farrell, James Thomas, 1904- . A Lesson in History. 1 act. Quarterly Review of Literature, 2 (No. 2, 1944), 110-120.

2936. _____ and Hortense Farrell. Clifford and William. 1 act. Decision, 1 (April, 1941), 59-63.

2937. Farrington, James. The Hulks. 1 act. Smart Set, 33 (January, 1911), 123-132.

2938. Fassbinder, Rainer Werner. Pre-Paradise Sorrow Now. 4 scenes. Gambit, 6, no. 21, 5-76. Peter Zander, translator.

2939. Fast, Howard, 1914- . Tomorrow Will Be Ours. 1 act. Plays, 4 (February, 1945), 71-74.

2940. _____. Tomorrow Will Be Ours. 1 act. Senior Scholastic, 44 (May 8-13, 1944), 13-14.

2941. Fauchois, Réné, 1882- . La Dame aux Gants Verts. 3 acts, comedy. Petite Illustration, 190 (February 2, 1935), 1-38. In French.

2942. _____. Prenez Garde à la Peinture. 3 acts, comedy. Petite Illustration, 181 (April 23, 1932), 1-38. In French.

2943. Faulkner, William, 1897-1962. Requiem for a Nun. 2 parts. L'Avant Scène, 407 (July 15, 1968), 11-30. Albert Camus, adapter. In French.

2944. _____. Requiem for a Nun. 2 parts. Sipario, 14 (January, 1959), 37-54. Albert Camus, adapter. Luciano Lucignani, translator. In Italian.

2945. Faure, Gabrielle. Un giorno di festa. 1 act. Il Dramma, 125 (November 1, 1931), 32-38. Alberto Casella, translator. In Italian.

2946. _____. Heureux qui Comme Ulysse, ou Le Couple Parfait. 1 act. L'Avant Scène, 333 (May 1, 1965), 38-42. In French.

2947. Faure, Michel. Le Diable en Eté. 1 act. L'Avant Scène, 450 (June 1, 1970), 43-50. In French.

2948. Faux, Damally. The Littlest Month. 1 act. Plays, 10 (February, 1951), 62-64. AND Plays, 21 (February, 1962), 63-65.

Fava, Ada, translator see Sinclair, U. 8306

2949. Favart, Robert. "Cucendron," ou La Pure Agathe. 3 acts. L'Avant Scène (OST), 48 (September, 1951), 1-36. In French.

2950. Fawcett, Margaret Georgia. The Talking Christmas Tree. 1 act. Plays, 17 (December, 1957), 67-69.

Fay, Frances C., translator see Lemaitre, J. 4908

2951. Fay, Maxine. Saving the Old Homestead. 1 act. Plays, 12 (February, 1953), 19-22.

2952. Fayad, Samy. Come si rapina una banca. 3 acts. Il Dramma, n.s., 359/360 (August/September, 1966), 5-33. In Italian.

2953. _____. Don Giovanni innamorato. 1 act. Il Dramma, n.s., 211/212 (August 15/September 1, 1954), 87-104. In Italian.

2954. _____. Il marziano. 1 act. Sipario, 10 (February, 1955), 48-56. In Italian.

2955. Fayard, Jean. Il folle amore che non esiste. 1 act. Il Dramma, 1 (December, 1925), 39-44. Enrico Leotardi Di Boyon, translator. In Italian.

2956. _____. Tredici a tavola. 1 act. Il Dramma, 127 (December 1, 1931), 4-46. Vittorio Guerriero, translator. In Italian.

_____, adapter see Storm, L. 8540

Fazio, Gaetano, translator see Steinbeck, J. 8494

2957. Feather, Jean. The Dressmaker and the Queen. 1 act. Plays, 29 (January, 1970), 65-68.

2958. _____. If You Meet a Leprechaun. 1 act. Plays, 29 (March, 1970), 72-74.

2959. _____. The Poor Man's Clever Daughter. 1 act. Plays, 29 (May, 1970), 62-66.

2960. _____, adapter. The Boy Who Went to the North Wind. 1 act. Plays, 28 (January, 1969), 69-75.

2961. _____, adapter. Cap o'Rushes. 1 act. Plays, 28 (May, 1969), 75-81.

2962. _____, adapter. The Clever Cobbler. 1 act. Plays, 29 (January, 1970), 75-79.

2963. _____, adapter. The Long Leather Bag. 1 act. Plays, 30 (March, 1971), 71-75.

2964. _____, adapter. One Wish Too Many. 1 act. Plays, 30 (February, 1971), 69-73.

2965. _____, adapter. Quick-Witted Jack. 1 act. Plays, 30 (January, 1971), 57-64.

2966. _____, adapter. Tom and the Leprechaun. 1 act. Plays, 31 (March, 1972), 55-59.

2967. _____, adapter. Who Is Strongest? 1 act. Plays, 28 (February, 1969), 72-74.

Federici, Federico, translator see Gide, A. 3504

_____, translator see Schnitzler, A. 8076

2968. Federici, Mario, 1900- . Brocclin-Bar. 1 act. Il Dramma, 342 (November 15, 1940), 43-48. In Italian.

2969. _____. Chilometri bianchi. 3 acts. Il Dramma, 319 (December 1, 1939), 4-17. In Italian.

2970. _____. ...Ovvero, Il commendatore. 2 parts. Il Dramma, n.s., 217 (November 15, 1954), 6-28. In Italian.

2971. Fedo, Michael W. Blest Be the Bind That Ties. 1 act. De Kalb Literary Arts Journal, 3 (No. 3, 1969), 53-71.

2972. Feeney, Martin and James Rusilka. Eighteenth Noel. 1 act. Dramatics, 43 (January, 1972), 5-9.

2973. Feiffer, Jules, 1929- . Cohn of Arc. 1 act. Partisan Review, 40 (No. 2, 1973), 218-242.

2974. _____. Crawling Arnold. 1 act. Horizon, 4 (November, 1961), 49-56.

2975. _____. God Bless. 2 acts. Plays and Players, 16 (January, 1969), 35-50.

2976. Feinstein, Alan S. A Basket of Acorns. 1 act. Plays, 17 (March, 1958), 68-71.

2977. Feinstein, Joe. Cooking Up a Storm. 1 act. Plays, 26 (January, 1967), 13-23.

2978. Feldhaus-Weber, Mary. The Prodigal. 1 act. Minnesota Review, 7 (No. 1, 1967), 43-76.

2979. _____. The Virgin, the Lizard, and the Lamb. New Directions, 20 (1968), 20-29.

2980. Feliu y Condina, Jose. Maria del Carmen. 3 acts. Petite Illustration, 88 (November 8, 1930), 1-28. Carlos de Batlle and Antonin Lavergne, adapters. In French.

2981. Fellows, Malcolm Stuart. Ou Vivrez-Vous Demain? 1 act. L'Avant Scène, 435 (October 15, 1969), 45-51. Pierre Roudy, adapter. In French.

2982. Fenn, Frederick, 1868-1924 and Richard Pryce. The Love Child. 1 act. English Review, 4 (February, 1910), 409-420.

Fenner, Mildred Sandison see Craven, E. 2097

_____ see Fishburn, E. 3035

2983. Fenollosa, Mary McNeil. The Lady of the Hair-Pins. 1 act. Smart Set, 25 (August, 1908), 140-149.

Feral, Roger, adapter see Knott, F. 4670

Ferber, Edna, 1887-1968 see Kaufman, G. 4560

2984. Ferber, Maurice. The Wanderers. 1 act. Poet Lore, 43 (No. 4, 1937), 364-371.

2985. Ferdinand, Roger, 1898- . Le Bonheur de Suzanne. 1 act, comedy. L'Avant Scène, 302 (January 1, 1964), 39-43. In French.

2986. ———. La Foire Aux Sentiments. 3 acts, comedy. L'Avant Scène, 302 (January 1, 1964), 10-37. In French.

2987. ———. Mon Mari et Toi. 3 acts, comedy. L'Avant Scène, 90, 5-34. In French.

2988. ———. Il privilegio dell'amicizia. 1 act. Il Dramma, 150 (November 15, 1932), 34-40. In Italian.

2989. ———. Le Signe de Kikota. 4 acts, comedy. L'Avant Scène, 237 (February 15, 1961), 8-35. In French.

2990. ———. Six Heures, Chaussée d'Antin. 1 act, comedy. L'Avant Scène, 237 (February 15, 1961), 37-42. In French.

2991. ———. Trois Garçons et une Fille. 3 acts. Il Dramma, n.s., 114 (August 1, 1950), 7-29. Silvano D'Arborio, translator. In Italian.

2992. ———. Un uomo d'oro. 3 acts. Il Dramma, 19 (June 1, 1927), 7-32. In Italian.

———, adapter see Anderson, R. 216

———, adapter see O'Brien, L. 6748

2993. Ferguson, David. A Most Special Dragon. 1 act. Plays, 27 (January, 1968), 50-54.

Feriani, Vidusso, translator see 1789-La revolution... 8157

Ferioli, Daniella, translator see Boal, A. and G. Guarnieri 1029

2994. Ferlinghetti, Lawrence, 1919- . Servants of the People. New Directions, 18 (1964), 257-266.

2995. ———, translator see Artaud, A. 383

2996. Fermaud, Michel. Les Portes Claquent. 3 acts, comedy. L'Avant Scène, 189 (January 15, 1959), 7-31. In French.

Feroule, Henri see Mirande, Y. 6078

2997. Ferrari, Paolo. Amore senza stima. 4 acts. Il Dramma, 314 (September 15, 1939), 5-24. In Italian.

2998. _____. Il ridicolo. 5 acts. Il Dramma, n. s., 57/58/59 (March 15/April 1/15, 1948), 59-110. In Italian.

Ferrero, Clara, translator see Giraudoux, J. 3567

2999. Ferrero, Leo, 1903-1933. Angelica. 3 acts. Il Dramma, n. s., 274 (July, 1959), 5-27. In Italian.

Ferri, Liana C., translator see Bradbury, R. 1258

_____, translator see Grumberg, J.-C. 3768

_____, translator see Kozlenko, W. 4703

_____, translator see Robinson, L. 7623

_____, translator see Sauvajon, M. G. 7989

3000. Ferrier, Paul, 1843-1920. The Codicil. 1 act, comedy. Poet Lore, 19 (Summer, 1908), 193-206. Elizabeth Lester Mullin, translator.

Ferrieri, Enzo, 1897- , translator see Anouilh, J. 254

_____, translator see Chekhov, A. P. 1784

_____, translator see Renard, J. 7488

_____, translator see Supervielle, J. 8620

Ferro, Lida, translator see Amiel, D. 187

3001. Ferson, Alessandro. Le diavolerie. Sipario, 255 (July, 1967), 53-63. In Italian.

3002. _____. Pioggia, stato d'animo. 1 act. Sipario, 19 (November, 1964), 56-63. In Italian.

3003. Feuchtwanger, Lion, 1884-1958. Bürge Gutmann Schliesst Sonderfrieden. 1 act. Das Wort, 1 (August, 1936), 6-18. In German.

3004. Feuerstein, Arthur. Which, Three R's or Three R's Plus Industrial Arts and Domestic Science? 2 acts. Industrial Arts and Vocational Education, 19 (July, 1930), 254-256.

3005. Feuillet, Octave, 1821-1890. Scylla and Charybdis; A Lesson for Husbands. 1 act. Cosmopolitan, 4 (February, 1888), 490-497.

3006. Feydeau, Georges, 1862-1921. Chat en Poche. 3 acts, comedy. L'Avant Scène, 329 (March 1, 1965), 9-33. In French.

3007. _____. Le dindon. 3 acts. Il Dramma, n.s., 254 (November, 1957), 12-47. Leon Fini, translator. In Italian.

3008. _____. Going to Pot. 1 act. Tulane Drama Review, 5 (September, 1960), 127-168. Norman R. Shapiro, translator.

3009. _____. La puce a l'oreille. 3 acts. Sipario, 6 (November, 1951), 29-63. Ivo Chiesa, translator. In Italian.

3010. _____. Il tacchino. 3 acts, comedy. Sipario, 10 (October, 1955), 29-56. Laura Solari, translator. In Italian.

Ficke, Arthur Davison, 1883-1945, translator see Roelvink, H. C. J. 7647

3011. Fiedler, Leslie Aaron, 1917- . The Bearded Virgin and the Blind God. 1 act. Kenyon Review, 15 (Autumn, 1953), 540-551.

3012. Field, Etta Dexter. The Wooing of Penelope, An Incident of Depravity. 5 acts. Chap-Book, 3 (August 15, 1895), 224-260.

3013. Field, Eugene, 1850-1894. The Coming of the Prince. 1 act. Plays, 14 (December, 1954), 88-94. Jane McGowan, adapter.

3014. Field, Rachel Lyman, 1894-1942. The Bad Penny. 1 act. Scholastic, 24 (March 24, 1934), 7-10, 25.

3015. _____. Everygirl. 1 act. St. Nicholas, 40 (October, 1913), 1115-1117.

Fields, Joseph, 1895- see Chodorov, J. 1814

3016. Fife, Evelyn Henderson. We Are Three. 1 act. Drama, 16 (October, 1925), 17-18, 36.

3017. Fighting on the Plain. Chinese Literature (No. 5, 1974), 3-54.

3018. Filippo, Eduardo de. Madame Filoume. 3 acts. L'Avant Scène (ROST), 69 (November, 1952), 1-28. Jacques Audiberti, translator. In French.

3019. _____. Oh, These Ghosts! 3 acts. Tulane Drama Review, 8 (Spring, 1964), 118-162. Marguerita Carra and Louise H. Warner, translators.

3020. Filippone, Vincenzo. Ichneit on a Holiday. Drama and Theatre, 7 (No. 3, 1969), 203-206. Adrienne S. Mandel, translator.

3021. Fillia. Sensualita meccanica. Sipario, 260 (December, 1967), 96. In Italian.

3022. Finch, Lucine. At the Sign of the Silver Spoon. 1 act. Smart Set, 38 (October, 1912), 73-77.

3023. _____. The Butterfly. 3 acts. Poet Lore, 21 (September-October, 1910), 401-414.

3024. Finch, Robert. From Paradise to Butte. 1 act, comedy. One-Act Play Magazine, 4 (May-June, 1941), 224-241.

_____ see also Smith, B. 8330

3025. Fine, Sylvia and Max Liebman, 1902- . Local Board Makes Good. 1 act. Theatre Arts, 26 (September, 1942), 576-583.

3026. Fineberg, Larry, 1945- . Death. 1 act. Performing Arts in Canada, 10 (Summer, 1973), 48-51.

Fini, Leon, translator see Feydeau, G. 3007

3027. Finkel, Donald. The Jar. 3 acts. Quarterly Review of Literature, 12 (No. 1/2, 1962), 15-54.

Finney, Robert V., translator see Alarcon y Mendoza, J. R. de 96

3028. Firkins, Oscar W., 1864-1932. After Twenty-Five Years. 1 act. Drama, 15 (February, 1925), 99-101, 109.

3029. _____. The Looking-Glass. 1 act. Drama, 16 (February, 1926), 171-173.

3030. _____. The Reference. 1 act, comedy. Drama, 14 (March-April, 1924), 215-216, 238.

3031. _____. The Reticent Convict. 1 act. Drama, 18 (February, 1928), 141-143, 160.

3032. _____. Two Passengers for Chelsea. 1 act, comedy. Golden Book, 11 (January, 1930), 95-103.

3033. _____. The Unbidden Guest. 1 act. Poet Lore, 35 (1924), 276-297.

Fischer, Alex see Fischer, M. 3034

3034. Fischer, Max and Alex Fischer. Una "Première." 1 act. Il Dramma, 11 (October, 1926), 35-43. In Italian.

3035. Fishburn, Eleanor and Mildred Sandison Fenner. They Dared

Fishburn

to Teach. 1 act. Journal of the National Education Association, 29 (April, 1940), 123-124.

3036. Fisher, Aileen, 1906- . Abe's Winkin' Eye. 1 act. Plays, 11 (February, 1952), 39-49. AND Plays, 30 (February, 1971), 55-63.

3037. _____. All on a Day in May. 1 act. Plays, 14 (May, 1955), 73-76.

3038. _____. Angel in the Looking-Glass. 1 act. Plays, 9 (December, 1949), 33-39. AND Plays, 16 (December, 1956), 51-57.

3039. _____. Black Blizzard. 1 act. Plays, 10 (October, 1950), 39-44.

3040. _____. Calling All Christmases. 1 act. Plays, 21 (December, 1961), 89-96.

3041. _____. The Carved Symbol. 1 act. Plays, 34 (May, 1975), 91-92.

3042. _____. Caught at the Narrows. 1 act. Plays, 9 (January, 1950), 45-52.

3043. _____. The Christmas Cake. 1 act. Plays, 10 (December, 1950), 60-61.

3044. _____. Christmas in Court. 1 act. Plays, 22 (December, 1962), 47-52.

3045. _____. The Christmas Tablecloth. 1 act. Plays, 23 (December, 1963), 45-48.

3046. _____. A Christmas Tree for Kitty. 1 act. Plays, 19 (December, 1959), 84-86.

3047. _____. Courting Trouble. 1 act. Plays, 32 (January, 1973), 53-59.

3048. _____. Ghosts on Guard. 1 act. Plays, 9 (October, 1949), 36-41.

3049. _____. Hearts, Tarts and Valentines. 1 act. Plays, 9 (February, 1950), 48-54.

3050. _____. Hidden Meanings. 1 act. Plays, 24 (February, 1965), 79-80.

3051. _____. The Inn at Bethlehem. 1 act. Plays, 19 (December, 1959), 47-56.

3052. _____. Jack Straw. 1 act. Plays, 9 (November, 1949), 71-73.

3053. _____. Long Live Father! 1 act. Plays, 33 (January, 1974), 68-72.

3054. _____. Look to a New Day. 1 act. Plays, 20 (May, 1961), 83-96.

3055. _____. Luck Takes a Holiday. 1 act. Plays, 12 (May, 1953), 40-48.

3056. _____. The Mail Goes Through. 1 act. Plays, 10 (January, 1951), 53-58.

3057. _____. Many a Slip. 1 act. Plays, 10 (February, 1951), 50-54.

3058. _____. The Merry Christmas Elf. 1 act. Plays, 10 (December, 1950), 36-42.

3059. _____. Mother Goose's Party. 1 act. Plays, 21 (December, 1961), 80-84.

3060. _____. Murder in the Kitchen. 1 act. Plays, 9 (March, 1950), 46-52.

3061. _____. New Hearts for Old. 1 act. Plays, 10 (February, 1951), 34-40.

3062. _____. Nine Cheers for Christmas. 1 act. Plays, 15 (December, 1955), 53-56.

3063. _____. On Strike. 1 act. Plays, 10 (May, 1951), 35-42.

3064. _____. On Such a Night. 1 act. Plays, 12 (December, 1952), 50-53.

3065. _____. Once Upon a Time. 1 act. Plays, 10 (November, 1950), 70-78.

3066. _____. Our 49th State. 1 act. Plays, 23 (January, 1964), 83-95.

3067. _____. A Play Without a Name. 1 act. Plays, 10 (October, 1950), 12-19.

3068. _____. The Plot Thickens. 1 act. Plays, 9 (April, 1950), 44-50.

3069. _____. The Safety Parade. 1 act. Plays, 26 (April, 1967), 62-64.

Fisher

3070. _____. Setting Santa Straight. 1 act. Plays, 18 (December, 1958), 55-61.

3071. _____. Shoes and Stockings and Solomon. 1 act. Plays, 20 (December, 1960), 59-60.

3072. _____. Sing the Songs of Christmas. 1 act. Plays, 17 (December, 1957), 75-86. AND Plays, 36 (December, 1976), 25-35.

3073. _____. Sing the Songs of Cowboys. 1 act. Plays, 22 (October, 1962), 41-57.

3074. _____. Sing the Songs of Freedom. 1 act. Plays, 19 (May, 1960), 85-98.

3075. _____. Sing the Songs of Lincoln. 1 act. Plays, 21 (February, 1962), 79-95.

3076. _____. Sing the Songs of Pioneers. 1 act. Plays, 22 (January, 1963), 35-47.

3077. _____. Sing the Songs of Springtime. 1 act. Plays, 19 (April, 1960), 75-80.

3078. _____. Sing the Songs of Thanksgiving. 1 act. Plays, 18 (November, 1958), 76-85. AND Plays, 31 (November, 1971), 69-78.

3079. _____. Sing the Songs of Travel. 1 act. Plays, 21 (April, 1962), 54-60.

3080. _____. Songs of America Growing. 1 act. Plays, 21 (May, 1962), 75-84.

3081. _____. Special Edition. 1 act. Plays, 22 (May, 1963), 61-68.

3082. _____. The Spirit of Christmas. 1 act. Plays, 9 (December, 1949), 75-77.

3083. _____. The Squander Bug's Christmas Carol. 1 act. Plays, 4 (December, 1944), 66-71.

3084. _____. Standing Up for Santa. 1 act. Plays, 30 (December, 1970), 66-68.

3085. _____. Thanksgiving Feast. 1 act. Plays, 9 (November, 1949), 60-63.

3086. _____. Three and the Dragon. 1 act. Plays, 25 (May, 1966), 87-94.

3087. _____. Time for Mom. 1 act. Plays, 15 (May, 1956), 53-56. AND Plays, 29 (May, 1970), 67-70.

3088. _____. Treasure Hunt. 1 act. Plays, 9 (November, 1949), 55-59.

3089. _____. A Tree to Trim. 1 act. Plays, 19 (December, 1959), 1-13.

3090. _____. Up a Christmas Tree. 1 act. Plays, 28 (December, 1968), 83-84.

3091. _____. An Up-and-Doing Day. 1 act. Plays, 14 (April, 1955), 81-82.

3092. _____. The Voice of Liberty. 1 act. Plays, 23 (April, 1964), 57-64.

3093. _____. The Weaver's Son. 1 act. Plays, 12 (October, 1952), 33-39. AND Plays, 33 (October, 1973), 46-52.

3094. _____. The Week Before Christmas. 1 act. Plays, 14 (December, 1954), 87.

3095. _____. What Happened in Toyland. 1 act. Plays, 22 (December, 1962), 57-65.

3096. _____. What Happened on Clutter Street. 1 act. Plays, 24 (October, 1964), 47-52.

3097. _____. What Makes Thanksgiving. 1 act. Plays, 14 (November, 1954), 72.

3098. _____. What Now, Planet Earth? 1 act. Plays, 33 (March, 1974), 1-14.

3099. _____. Why the Sleepy Dormouse. 1 act. Plays, 23 (February, 1964), 75-78.

3100. _____. Yankee Doodle Dandy. 1 act. Plays, 25 (January, 1966), 61-62. AND Plays, 35 (November, 1975), 79-81.

3101. _____. Young Abe Lincoln. 1 act. Plays, 22 (February, 1963), 1-12. AND Plays, 32 (February, 1973), 43-53.

3102. _____, adapter. Mr. Scrooge Finds Christmas. 1 act. Plays, 20 (December, 1960), 75-85.

_____, adapter see Dickens, C. 2477

3103. _____ and Olive Rabe. Alice in Puzzleland. 1 act. Plays, 14 (January, 1955), 65-70.

Fisher and Rabe

3104. _____. Birthday Party for UNICEF. 1 act. Plays, 26 (October, 1966), 47-58.

3105. _____. Bringing Up Father. 1 act. Plays, 15 (November, 1955), 51-55.

3106. _____. Cavalcade of Human Rights. 1 act. Plays, 15 (October, 1955), 63-85. AND Plays, 24 (May, 1965), 99-122.

3107. _____. The Clean-up Club. 1 act. Plays, 16 (January, 1957), 82-84.

3108. _____. A Dish of Green Peas. 1 act. Plays, 15 (February, 1956), 55-63.

3109. _____. Famous Nickname. 1 act. Plays, 15 (January, 1956), 77-78.

3110. _____. Honest Abe Lincoln. 1 act. Plays, 16 (February, 1957), 37-42.

3111. _____. Johnny Appleseed's Vision. 1 act. Plays, 24 (January, 1965), 65-68.

3112. _____. Johnny on the Spot. 1 act. Plays, 25 (March, 1966), 75-80.

3113. _____. Our Great Declaration. 1 act. Plays, 34 (April, 1975), 85-95.

3114. _____. Rocket to Freedom. 1 act. Plays, 23 (May, 1964), 53-58.

3115. _____. Sing, America, Sing. 1 act. Plays, 15 (May, 1956), 73-82.

3116. _____. A Star for Old Glory. 1 act. Plays, 24 (April, 1965), 57-61.

3117. _____. The Sterling Silver Tree. 1 act. Plays, 14 (May, 1955), 39-43.

3118. _____. Trouble in the Air. 1 act. Plays, 27 (February, 1968), 79-95. AND Plays, 32 (May, 1973), 1-16.

3119. _____. Turning the Tables. 1 act. Plays, 14 (October, 1954), 77-86.

3120. _____. Uncle Tom's Cabin. 1 act. Plays, 15 (March, 1956), 24-30.

3121. _____. West to the Indies. 1 act. Plays, 17 (October, 1957), 14-22.

3122. _____. What Is a Patriot? 1 act. Plays, 15 (April, 1956), 23-30.

3123. _____. Wheels Within Wheels. 1 act. Plays, 24 (February, 1965), 61-64.

3124. Fisher, Dorothy Canfield, 1879-1958. The Woman Who Never Gets Any Sympathy. 1 act. Harper's Bazaar, 40 (November, 1906), 1002-1005.

Fisher, Martha A., translator see Reinecker, H. 7470

3125. Fisk, May Isabel. Another Point of View. A Monologue. 1 act. Smart Set, 11 (November, 1903), 115-116.

3126. _____. The Biter Bitten. 1 act. Harper's, 145 (August, 1922), 419-422.

3127. _____. Dressing for the Play, a Monologue. 1 act. Harper's, 126 (January, 1913), 317-320.

3128. _____. An Evening Musicale. 1 act. Smart Set, 10 (July, 1903), 111-114.

3129. _____. Shopping, A Monologue. 1 act. Harper's, 133 (October, 1916), 793-797.

3130. Fiske, Isabella Howe. Clouds of the Sun. 3 acts. Poet Lore, 15 (No. 2, 1904), 52-74.

3131. _____. A Comedy of the Exile. 1 act. Poet Lore, 17 (No. 1, 1906), 51-58.

Fiske, Richard see Levitt, A. 4965

Fitts, Dudley, 1903- , translator see Cocteau, J. 1917

_____, translator see Odio, E. 6774

3132. Fitzgerald, Betty. The Master in the House. 1 act. Scholastic, 24 (April 28, 1934), 11-13.

3133. Fitzgerald, F. Scott, 1896-1940. The Débutante. 1 act. Smart Set, 60 (November, 1919), 85-96.

3134. _____. Mr. Icky, The Quintessence of Quaintness in One Act. Smart Set, 61 (March, 1920), 93-98.

3135. _____. Porcelain and Pink. 1 act. Smart Set, 61 (January, 1920), 77-85.

3136. _____. "Send Me In, Coach." 1 act. Esquire, 6 (November, 1936), 55, 218-221.

3137. ———. The Vegetable. 2 parts. L'Avant Scène, 515 (April 1, 1973), 7-36. Jean-Loup Dabadie, adapter. In French.

3138. FitzGibbon, Constantine. Music Far Away: Intermezzo. Dublin Magazine, 10 (Autumn/Winter, 1973/74), 10-15.

3139. Fitzmaurice, George. The Coming of Ewn Andzale. 1 act. Dublin Magazine, n.s., 30 (July-September, 1954), 20-40.

3140. ———. The Enchanted Land. 3 acts. Dublin Magazine, n.s., 32 (January-March, 1957), 6-35.

3141. ———. The Linnaun Shee. 1 act, comedy. Dublin Magazine, 2 (October, 1924), 194-206.

3142. ———. One Evening Gleam. 1 act. Dublin Magazine, n.s., 24 (January-March, 1949), 5-21.

3143. ———. The Terrible Baisht. 1 act. Dublin Magazine, n.s., 30 (October-December, 1954), 14-34.

3144. ———. There are Tragedies and Tragedies. 1 act. Dublin Magazine, n.s., 23 (July-September, 1948), 13-25.

3145. ———. 'Twixt the Giltinans and the Carmodys. 1 act. Dublin Magazine, n.s., 18 (January-March, 1943), 11-33.

Fitzsimmons, Thomas, translator see Naghiu, I. 6431

3146. Fitzsimon, Shaun. The Great Sad. 1 act. Botteghe Oscure, 8 (1951), 159-164.

3147. Fiume, Salvatore, 1915- . Entra in casa una montagna. Sipario, 31 (June/July, 1976), 104-112. In Italian.

3148. Flaiano, Ennio. Il caso papaleo. 1 act. Sipario, 15 (July, 1960), 28-31.

3149. ———. La donna nell'armadio. 1 act, farce. Sipario, 13 (October, 1958), 50-54. In Italian.

3150. ———. La guerra spiegata ai poveri. 1 act. Il Dramma, n.s., 19/20 (August 15/September 1, 1946), 101-112. In Italian.

3151. Flanagan, Hallie F. The Curtain. 1 act. Drama, 13 (February, 1923), 167-169.

3152. Flanders, Florence Reiter. The Flight of the Moon Witches. 1 act. Plays, 26 (October, 1966), 67-71.

3153. Flavin, Martin A. 1883-1969. Calbe Stone's Death Watch. 1 act. Drama, 14 (January, 1924), 143-147.

3154. Fleming, B. J. Escape. 1 act. Negro History Bulletin, 3 (May, 1940), 120-122.

3155. Fleming, Berry, 1899- . The Acrobats. 1 act, comedy. First Stage, 1 (Winter, 1961-62), 11-40.

Fletcher, Ian, translator see Aristophanes 336

3156. Fletcher, Lucille. The Hitch Hiker. 1 act. Senior Scholastic, 51 (October 21, 1947), 18-21.

3157. Flexner, Hortense, 1885- . The Faun. 1 act. Drama, 11 (June, 1921), 311-318.

3158. _____. Voices. 1 act. Seven Arts, 1 (December, 1916), 135-143.

3159. Flokos, N. G. Hippocrates Dying. 1 act. Poet Lore, 58 (Winter, 1964), 328-331.

3160. Florance, Richard. It, The Usual Play With an Unusual Ending. 1 act. Smart Set, 47 (December, 1915), 85-90.

Flores, Angel, translator see Cervantes Saavedra, M. de 1691

_____, translator see Rueda, L. 7783

Flores, Ronald C., translator see Cormenzana, J. M. B. 2020

3161. Florian, Jean-Pierre Claris de, 1755-1794. The Twins of Bergamo. 1 act. Drama, 31 (August, 1918), 350-368. Oliver Farnsworth, translator.

3162. Flower, Elliot. His Imitation Sweetheart. 1 act. Ladies' Home Journal, 25 (February, 1908), 12, 55.

3163. Flynn, Claire Wallace. The String of Pearls. Woman's Home Companion, 37 (February, 1910), 8-9, 59.

3164. Fo, Dario. Aveva due pistole con gli occhi bianchi e neri. 3 acts. Sipario, (August-September, 1960), 33-56. In Italian.

3165. _____. I cadaveri si spediscono e le donne si spogliano. 1 act, farce. Sipario, 13 (August-September, 1958), 66-72. In Italian.

3166. _____. Chi ruba un piede e fortunato in amore. 2 parts. Sipario, 186 (October, 1961), 29-56. In Italian.

3167. _____. La colpa e sempre del diavolo. 2 parts. Sipario, 20 (October, 1965), 45-72. In Italian.

3168. _____. Gli arcangeli non giocano al flipper. 3 acts, comedy. Sipario, 14 (September, 1959), 38-58. In Italian.

3169. _____. Grande pantomima con bandiere e pupazzi piccoli e medi. 2 parts. Sipario, 24 (January, 1969), 44-59. In Italian.

3170. _____. Isabella, tre caravelle e un cacciaballe. 2 parts, comedy. Sipario, 18 (October, 1963), 33-52. In Italian.

3171. _____. Settimo: ruba un po' meno. 2 parts. Sipario, 19 (August-September, 1964), 40-71. In Italian.

3172. _____. La signora e dal buttare. Sipario, 22 (October, 1967), 45-64. In Italian.

Foa, Betty, translator see Wesker, A. 9304

3173. Fodor, John. Awkward-Hander Orpheus. Chelsea, 10 (September, 1961), 99-108.

3174. _____. The Locker Room. 1 act. Chelsea, 11 (March, 1962), 118-120.

3175. _____. The Sentimental Materialist. 2 acts. Chelsea, 14 (January, 1964), 150-153.

3176. Fodor, Laszlo, 1898- . Altalena della vita. 1 act. Il Dramma, 80 (December 15, 1929), 41-44. Corrado Rossi, translator. In Italian.

3177. _____. Amo un'attrice. 3 acts. Il Dramma, 22 (July 15, 1927), 6-35. In Italian.

3178. _____. L'amore non è tanto semplice. 7 parts. Il Dramma, 232 (April 15, 1936), 2-24. Ignazio Balla and Mario De Vellis, translators. In Italian.

3179. _____. Il bacio davanti allo specchio. 3 acts. Il Dramma, 154 (January 15, 1933), 4-31. Ada Salvatore, translator. In Italian.

3180. _____. Esami di maturatà. 3 acts. Il Dramma, 238 (July 15, 1936), 6-30. Ignazio Balla and Mario De Vellis, translators. In Italian.

3181. _____. Europa und der Stier. 3 acts. Il Dramma, n.s., 210 (August 1, 1954), 5-44. Ada Salvatore, translator. In Italian.

3182. _____. Un gioco di società. 3 acts. Il Dramma, 270 (November 15, 1937), 2-28. Ignazio Balla and Mario De Vellis, translators. In Italian.

3183. _____. Margherita di Navarra. 3 acts. Il Dramma, 123 (October 1, 1931), 5-34. In Italian.

3184. _____. Roulette. 3 acts. Il Dramma, 143 (August 1, 1932), 4-39. Ada Salvatore, translator. In Italian.

3185. _____. Signora, vi ho gia vista in qualche luogo! 3 acts. Il Dramma, 13 (December, 1926), 7-34. In Italian.

3186. Foissy, Guy, 1932- . Coeur a Deux. dialogue. L'Avant Scène, 469/470 (April 1/15, 1971), 61-66. In French.

3187. _____. Le Discours du Père. 1 act, dialogue. L'Avant Scène, 480 (October 1, 1971), 51-54. In French.

3188. _____. En Regardant Tomber les Murs, Un Dialogue. 1 act. L'Avant Scène, 350 (February 1, 1966), 38-43. In French.

3189. _____. Il Faut Viser la Pierre. 1 act. L'Avant Scène, 530 (December 1, 1973), 39-43. In French.

3190. _____. Je M'Appelle Rhubarbe. 1 act, dialogue. L'Avant Scène, 471 (May 1, 1971), 39-42. In French.

3191. Foley, Marie Agnes. The Emperor's New Robes. 1 act. Plays, 23 (March, 1964), 41-51.

3192. Folgore, Luciano. Allegria. 1 act. Il Dramma, 322 (January 15, 1940), 26-29. In Italian.

3193. _____. Il mago moderno. 1 act. Il Dramma, 275 (February 1, 1938), 21-24. In Italian.

3194. _____. La notte fatidica. 1 act. Il Dramma, 313 (September 1, 1939), 29-34. In Italian.

3195. Folmsbee, Beulah. Goblin Parade. 1 act. Plays, 2 (October, 1942), 37-43.

3196. _____. The Princess and the Crystal Pipe. 1 act. St. Nicholas, 48 (November, 1920), 61-65.

3197. Fontaine, Robert. Androcles and His Pal. 1 act. Plays, 24 (May, 1965), 83-86.

3198. _____. Another Cinderella. 1 act. Plays, 25 (January, 1966), 91-95.

3199. _____. The Efficiency Expert. 1 act. Plays, 24 (October, 1964), 77-81.

3200. _____. Fair Today, Followed by Tomorrow. 1 act.

Plays, 24 (April, 1965), 81-84. AND Plays, 32 (October, 1972), 65-68.

3201. _____. Graduation Address. 1 act. Plays, 26 (May, 1967), 91-92.

3202. _____. Great Caesar! 1 act. Plays, 27 (April, 1968), 75-78.

3203. _____. Is There a Monster in the House? 1 act. Plays, 25 (December, 1965), 83-86.

3204. _____. Let Sleeping Beauties Lie. 1 act. Plays, 24 (February, 1965), 91-95.

3205. _____. Ride Your Hobby. 1 act. Plays, 25 (October, 1965), 83-86.

3206. _____. The Supermarket Blues. 1 act. Plays, 24 (December, 1964), 83-86.

3207. _____. To the Moon. 1 act. Plays, 25 (February, 1966), 93-95.

3208. _____. United Spies. 1 act. Plays, 25 (May, 1966), 106-108.

3209. _____. Where Banking Is a Pleasure. 1 act. Plays, 33 (January, 1974), 79-82.

3210. Fontanelli, Giorgio. Cape Kennedy chiama sferracavallo. 1 act. Sipario, 355 (December, 1975), 64-75. In Italian.

3211. Fool, Tom. Blue Sky, A Sketch for a Little Farce for Marionettes. 1 act. English Review, 32 (March, 1921), 198-212. Gordon Craig, editor.

3212. Foote, Samuel. The Liar. 3 acts, farce. Baltimore Repertory, 1 (1811), supplement, 73-95.

3213. Ford, Ford Madox, 1873-1939. A House. 1 act. Chapbook [London] 21 (March, 1921), 1-24.

3214. _____. A House. 1 act. Poetry, 17 (March, 1921), 291-310.

3215. _____. Mister Bosphorus and the Muses. 4 acts. Poet Lore, 34 (Winter, 1924), 532-613.

3216. _____. The Mother, A Song-Drama. 1 act. Fortnightly, 75 (April, 1901), 740-746.

3217. Ford, John, 1586-c1640. 'Tis Pity She's a Whore. 5 acts.

L'Avant Scène, 565 (June 1, 1975), 3-28. Christiane Barry, adapter. In French.

3218. _____. 'Tis Pity She's a Whore. 5 acts. Il Dramma, n.s., 299/300 (August/September, 1961), 14-41. George Baume, translator. In Italian.

3219. Foreman, Richard. The Cliffs. 2 acts. Performance, 6 (May/June, 1973), 51-64.

3220. _____. Hotel China. 2 parts. Dramatika, 9 (Spring, 1972), n.p.

3221. Foreman, Stephen H. The Resolution of Mossie Wax: A TV Documentary. Scripts, 1 (June, 1972), 4-29.

3222. Forman, Henry James, 1879-1966, translator see Chekhov, A. P. 1781

Formigoni, Carlo, translator see Brecht, B. 1311

_____, translator see Moliere 6113

Forni, Mario, translator see O'Neill, E. 6840

3223. Forrest, Belford. Failures, An Episode in a Tragedy. 1 act. Smart Set, 49 (July, 1916), 223-232.

3224. _____. Honors Even. 1 act. Smart Set, 53 (December, 1917), 71-79.

3225. _____. Lost Sheep. 1 act. Smart Set, 50 (October, 1916), 71-75.

3226. Forssell, Lars, 1928- . Charlie McDeath. 1 act, tragedy. Literary Review, 9 (Winter, 1965-66), 314-325. Harry G. Carlson, translator.

3227. _____. The Coronation. 1 act. Players Magazine, 40 (November, 1963), 41-56. Harry G. Carlson, translator.

3228. Forster, Friedrich, 1895-1958. Der Grane. 4 acts. Il Dramma, n.s., 187/188 (September 1, 1953), 15-39. Italo Alighiero Chiusano, translator. In Italian.

3229. Forsyth, James, 1913- . Heloise. 3 acts. Theatre Arts, 43 (January, 1959), 26-49.

Forte, Mario, 1932- see Logan, S. 5018

3230. Fortuno, Claude. Apprenez a conduire par correspondence. 1 act. L'Avant Scène, 579 (January 15, 1976), 37-40. In French.

3231. _____. Confrontation. 1 act. L'Avant Scène, 451 (June 15, 1970), 35-43. In French.

3232. _____. Filigrane. 1 act. L'Avant Scène, 507 (December 1, 1972), 42-44. In French.

3233. _____. La Victime. 1 act. L'Avant Scène, 422 (March 15, 1969), 39-44. In French.

3234. Forzano, Giovacchino. A Gust of Wind. 3 acts. Gambit, 7, 58-105. Robert Rietty, translator.

3235. _____. To Live in Peace. 3 acts. Gambit, 7, 3-57. Victor Rietti, translator.

Forzi, Guglielmo, translator see Amiel, D. and M. A. Petry 191

Foster, Joseph G., translator see Obaldia, R. de 6734

3236. Foulk, C. W. and Doris P. Buck. The Floating Stone. 1 act. Plays, 2 (January, 1943), 43-46.

Foulke, Adrienne, translator see Sarment, J. 7941

3237. Four Lunatics, The. A Scenario of the Commedia dell'Arte. 3 acts. The Mask, 4 (October, 1911), 116-121.

3238. Fox, Hugh. The Wings of It Cast Wide Dark Shadows. 1 act. Dramatika, 4 (Fall, 1969), n.p.

3239. Fox's Grave. 1 act, farce. Outlook, 133 (February 14, 1923), 306-308. Michio Itow and Louis V. Ledoux, translator.

3240. France, Anatole, 1844-1924. Alla ventura. 1 act. Il Dramma, 419/420 (February 1/15, 1944), 51-58. Giovanni Marcellini, translator. In Italian.

3241. _____. Come What May. 1 act, comedy. Golden Book, 6 (November, 1927), 631-641. Frederic Chapman and J. Lewis May, translators.

3242. _____. La commedia di colui che sposò una donna muta. 2 acts. Il Dramma, 360 (August 15, 1941), 7-15. In Italian.

3243. _____. The Juggler of Our Lady. 1 act. Plays, 9 (December, 1949), 78-83. AND Plays, 31 (December, 1971), 89-94. Walter Hackett, adapter.

3244. _____. The Man Who Married a Dumb Wife. 2 acts, comedy. Golden Book, 1 (January, 1925), 41-53.

3245. _____. The Man Who Married a Dumb Wife. 1 act. Plays, 33 (April, 1974), 85-95. Paul T. Nolan, adapter.

3246. _____. Il processo crainiquebille. 3 acts. Il Dramma, 365 (November 1, 1941), 9-19. Giovanni Marcellini, translator. In Italian.

Franci, Adolfo, translator see Anouilh, J. 247, 258

_____, translator see Cocteau, J. 1914

_____, translator see Giraudoux, J. 3561

3247. Franciosa, Massimo. Il mio miglior nemico. 1 act. Sipario, 10 (August, 1955), 28-36. In Italian.

3248. Francis, J. O. The Poacher. 1 act, comedy. Theatre Arts, 9 (May, 1925), 327-337.

3249. Francis, Robert, 1901- . On a Theme by Thoreau. 1 act. Forum, 107 (April, 1947), 362-366.

3250. Francisco de Madrid. Egloga Hecha. 1 act. Hispanic Review, 11 (October, 1943), 282-293. In Spanish.

3251. Franck, Marcel. Le Congrès de Clermont-Ferrand. 3 acts, comedy. L'Avant Scène (OST), 56 (February, 1952), 1-38. In French.

3252. _____. Isabelle et le Pelican. 4 acts, comedy. L'Avant Scène, 109, 1-30. In French.

3253. Franck, Pierre. Les Deux Augures. 1 act. L'Avant Scène, 558 (February 1, 1975), 22-25. In French.

3254. _____. L'Inconnue. 1 act, comedy. L'Avant Scène, 558 (February 15, 1975), 26-28. In French.

3255. _____. Monsieur Teste. 1 act. L'Avant Scène, 558 (February 15, 1975), 3-17. In French.

3256. _____ and Rene Bergil. L'Amour Quelquefois. 1 act. L'Avant Scène, 418 (January 15, 1969), 7-17. In French.

3257. François, Roger. La Reine Faustine. 2 acts. L'Avant Scène, 206 (October 15, 1959), 40-49. In French.

3258. Frank, Bruno, 1887-1945. Toto. 3 acts. Il Dramma, 118 (July 15, 1931), 4-36. Carlotta Vesci-Baum, translator. In Italian.

3259. Frank, Christopher, 1942- . La Morte de Lord Chatterley. 1 act. L'Avant Scène, 538 (April 1, 1974), 33-37. In French.

Frank

_____ see Bedos, G. 715

3260. Frank, Florence Kiper, 1886?- . Garden. 1 act. Drama, 32 (November, 1918), 471-493.

3261. _____. Over the Hills and Far Away. 3 acts. Drama, 11 (December, 1920), 80-89.

3262. _____. The Return of Proserpine. 3 acts. Drama, 11 (August-September, 1921), 423-427.

3263. _____. The Three Spinners. 3 acts. Drama, 16 (February, 1926), 179-180, 194-198.

3264. Frank, Leonhard, 1882-1961. Karl et Anna. 4 acts. Petite Illustration, 87 (July 6, 1929), 1-18. Jean-Richard Bloch, translator. In French.

3265. Frank, Maude Morrison. A Friend in Need; or, How "The Vicar of Wakefield" Found a Publisher. 1 act. St. Nicholas, 42 (March, 1915), 447-451.

Frank, Nino, 1904- see Gilson, P. 3548

3266. _____, and Paul Gilson. Ex-Napoleon. 4 acts. L'Avant Scène, 225, 8-31. In French.

3267. Frankel, Marvin. The Ventriloquist. 1 act. Chicago Review, 22 (January/February, 1971), 77-100.

3268. Frankenstein, A Dramatic Spectacle Created by the Living Theatre Company. City Lights Journal, 3 (1966), 58-70.

3269. Franklin, June. Welcome, Baby Dear. 1 act. Performing Arts in Canada, 7 (No. 3, 1970), 33-39.

3270. Franzero, Carlo Maria, 1892- . Chez Maurice. 1 act. Il Dramma, 179 (February 1, 1934), 32-37. In Italian.

3271. _____. La lettera smarrita. 1 act. Il Dramma, 232 (April 15, 1936), 27-29. In Italian.

3272. _____. Le porte di giada. 1 act. Il Dramma, 201 (January 1, 1935), 33-38. In Italian.

3273. _____. Spiritismo. 1 act. Il Dramma, 189 (July 1, 1934), 32-37. In Italian.

3274. Fraschetti, Vincenzo. Mettiamoci d'accordo. 1 act. Il Dramma, 30 (November 15, 1927), 40-44. In Italian.

3275. Frattarelli, Emilio, translator see Salacrou, A. 7874

3276. Fratti, Mario. Betrozali. 2 acts. Drama and Theatre, 7 (No. 3, 1969), 207-227. Julius G. Rothenberg, translator.

3277. _____. Dolls No More. 1 act. Drama and Theatre, 11 (Winter, 1972/73), 114-117.

3278. _____. The Doorbell. 1 act. Ohio Review, 12 (Winter, 1970), 15-32.

3279. _____. Flowers from Lidice. 1 act. Dramatics, 44 (October, 1972), 5-8.

3280. _____. Gatta bianca al Greenwich. 1 act. Il Dramma, n.s., 306 (March, 1962), 51-59. In Italian.

3281. _____. The Refrigerators. 3 acts. Modern International Drama, 3 (September, 1969), 53-79.

3282. _____. Il rifiuto. 1 act. Il Dramma, n.s., 349 (October, 1965), 33-37. In Italian.

3283. _____. Il ritorno. 1 act. Il Dramma, n.s., 321 (June, 1963), 36-43. In Italian.

3284. _____. The Third Daughter. 3 acts. First Stage, 5 (Fall, 1966), 139-157. Adrienne S. Mandel, translator.

3285. _____. Waiting. 1 act. Poet Lore, 63 (Autumn, 1968), 330-342.

_____, translator see Stavis, B. 8476

3286. Frattini, Angelo, 1896- . Gli amanti indivisibili. 3 acts. Il Dramma, 113 (May 1, 1931), 31-33. In Italian.

3287. Frebe, C. W. In Garrison. 1 act. Poet Lore, 26 (Vacation, 1915), 499-511.

Frechtman, Bernard, translator see Ionesco, E. 4383

3288. Freda, Frank. The Comer. 1 act. Drama and Theatre, 7 (No. 3, 1969), 228-240.

3289. Frederick, John T. Twelfth Night at Fisher's Crossing. 1 act. Midland, 2 (January, 1916), 18-24.

3290. Freeman, Barbara. Potpourri. 1 act. Plays, 34 (March, 1975), 75-83.

3291. Freeman, Mary Eleanor Wilkins, 1852-1930. Eglantina. 3 acts. Ladies' Home Journal, 27 (July, 1910), 13-14, 38.

3292. _____. Giles Corey, Yeoman. 6 acts. Harper's, 86 (December, 1892), 20-40.

3293. _____. The Pumpkin Giant. 1 act. Plays, 21 (October, 1961), 61-66. Adele Thane, adapter.

Fremont, H. see Bernard, O. 835

3294. French, Burt. Chowder and Cherries. 1 act. Dramatics, 44 (March, 1973), 4-13.

3295. French, Down and Marshall French. Mud Pack Madness. 1 act. Plays, 18 (January, 1959), 27-34.

3296. French, Helen. Charlie Who? 1 act. Performing Arts in Canada, 8 (Summer, 1971), 27-33.

French, Marshall see French, D. 3295

Fresnay, Pierre, pseud. see Laudenbach, P.-J.

3297. Freund, Philip, 1909- . Simon Simon, A Pragmatic Comedy. 1 act. One-Act Play Magazine, 1 (May, 1937), 42-52.

3298. Freytag, Gustav, 1816-1895. Journalists. 4 acts, comedy. Drama, 9 (February, 1913), 30-140. Roy Temple House, translator.

Friar, Kimon, translator see Kazantzakis, N. 4564, 4565

3299. Frida, Emil Bohnslav, 1853-1912. At the Chasm. 1 act. Poet Lore, 24 (Autumn, 1913), 289-308. Charles Recht, translator.

3300. _____. The Vengeance of Catullus. 1 act. Poet Lore, 25 (Winter, 1914), 526-544. Charles Recht, translator.

3301. _____. The Witness. 1 act. Poet Lore, 25 (Winter, 1914), 546-558. Charles Recht, translator.

3302. Fried, Emanuel. The Dodo Bird. 1 act. Drama and Theatre, 11 (Winter, 1972/73), 118-131.

Fried, Erich, translator see Thomas, D. 8827

3303. Friedman, Charles. My Darlin' Aida. 2 acts. Theatre Arts, 37 (June, 1953), 35-61.

3304. Friel, Brian. The Enemy Within. 3 acts. Journal of Irish Literature, 4 (May, 1975), 3-64.

3305. Frink, Charles. The Human Accident. 3 acts. First Stage, 1 (Summer, 1962), 53-67.

3306. Frisby, Terence. There's a Girl in My Soup. 3 acts.

L'Avant Scène, 464 (January 15, 1971), 7-35. Marcel Moussy, adapter. In French.

3307. _____. There's a Girl in My Soup. 3 acts. Plays and Players, 13 (September, 1966), 31-46, 72.

3308. Frisch, Max, 1911- . Andorra; Stuck in Swölf Bildern. 1 act. Spectaculum, 5 (1963), 69-147. In German.

3309. _____. Biedermann und die Brandstifter. 1 act. L'Avant Scène, 587 (May 15, 1976), 3-28. Philippe Pilliod, adapter. In French.

3310. _____. Biedermann und die Brandstifter. 1 act. Il Dramma, n.s., 287/288 (August/September, 1960), 66-78. Aloisio Rendi, translator. In Italian.

3311. _____. Biedermann und die Brandstifter. 1 act. Spectaculum, 2 (1959), 197-265. In German.

3312. _____. Biografie: Ein Spiel. 2 parts. Spectaculum, 12 (1969), 9-79. In German.

3313. _____. The Chinese Wall. 1 act. Theatre Arts, 47 (August-September, 1963), 32-60. James L. Rosenberg, translator.

3314. _____. Don Juan oder Die Liebe zur Geometrie. 4 acts, comedy. Spectaculum, 1 (1962), 331-382. In German.

3315. _____. Graf Oderland. 1 act. L'Avant Scène, 493 (April 15, 1972), 13-36. Henry Bergerot, translator. In French.

3315a. _____. Graf Oderland. 1 act. Spectaculum, 4 (1963), 135-193. In German.

3316. _____. La Grande Muraille. 23 scenes, farce. L'Avant Scène, 512 (February 15, 1973), 7-34. Arthur Adamov, Jacqueline Autrusseau and Henry Bergerot, translators. In French.

3317. _____. Nun Singen Sie Wieder; Versuch eines Requiems. 2 acts. Sipario, 2 (January/February, 1947), 37-53. Fantasio Piccoli, translator. In Italian.

3318. _____. Nun Singen Sie Wieder; Versuch eines Requiems. 2 acts. Spectaculum, 1 (1962), 289-330. In German.

3319. _____. Phillip Hotz's Fury. 1 act. Esquire, 58 (October, 1962), 109-110, 174, 176-180.

3320. _____. Phillip Hotz's Fury. 1 act. Gambit (No. 4, 1963), 75-98. Michael Bullock, translator.

3321. Frith, Walter. Brothers-In-Arms. 1 act. Living Age, 281 (April 18, 1914), 166-175.

3322. Frog Prince, The. 1 act. Dramatics, 42 (April, 1971), 7-8.

3323. Frondaie, Pierre. Les Amants de Paris. 4 acts. Petite Illustration, 86 (January 14, 1928), 1-34. In French.

3324. Froome, John Redhead, Jr. Listening. 1 act. Poet Lore, 28 (Vacation, 1917), 422-431.

3325. Frost, L. Annie. Apron; An Acting Charade. 1 act. St. Nicholas, 2 (April, 1875), 364-367.

3326. Frost, Robert, 1875-1963. A Masque of Mercy. 1 act. Atlantic, 180 (November, 1947), 68-76.

3327. _____. A Way Out. 1 act. Seven Arts, 1 (February, 1917), 347-362.

3328. Fruchter, M. J. Rats. 1 act. Poet Lore, 37 (Spring, 1926), 154-157.

3329. Fruttero, Carlo. Una donna uccisa per deduzione. Sipario, 8 (August/September, 1953), 60-66. In Italian.

_____, translator see Cocteau, J. 1916

3330. Fry, Christopher, 1907- . Curtmantle. 3 acts. Sipario, 19 (March, 1964), 34-50, 62. Laura Dalla Rosa, translator. In Italian.

3331. _____. The Lady's Not for Burning. 3 acts, comedy. L'Avant Scène, 301 (December 15, 1963), 10-38. Philippe de Rothschild, adapter. In French.

3332. _____. A Phoenix Too Frequent. 1 act, comedy. Il Dramma, n.s., 189 (September 15, 1953), 12-22. Franca Cancogni and Ettore Violani, translators. In Italian.

3333. _____. A Phoenix Too Frequent. 1 act, comedy. Hudson Review, 3 (Summer, 1950), 165-202.

3334. _____. Le Prince d'Egypte. 3 acts. L'Avant Scène, 115, 1-23. Jacques Talagrand, adapter. In French.

Fu To see Sha Seh 8163

3335. Fuenter, Ernesto. The Eagle and the Serpent. 1 act. Drama and Theatre, 11 (Spring, 1973), 159-170.

3336. Fugard, Athol, John Kani and Winston Ntshona. Sizwe Bansi Is Dead. 1 act. Plays and Players, 21 (November, 1973), I-X.

3337. Fuji-ko. The Vampire Cat of Nabeshima. 1 act. Smart Set, 30 (January, 1910), 127-134.

3338. Fulchignoni, Enrico. Ognuno la sua croce. 1 act. Il Dramma, 391/392 (December 1/15, 1942), 61-64. In Italian.

_____, translator see Cavalier miseria, Il 1671

_____, translator see Kiyotsuga, K. 4654

_____, translator see Lettiga deserta, La 4942

_____, translator see Motokiyo, K. 6268

_____, translator see Roussin, A. 7760

_____, translator see Wilder, T. 9395

3339. Fulda, Ludwig, 1862- . The Blockhead. 5 acts. Poet Lore, 39 (Spring, 1928), 3-93. Anna Emilia Bagstad, translator.

3340. _____. By Ourselves. 1 act, comedy. Poet Lore, 23 (January-February, 1912), 1-24. Haya Wally, translator.

3341. Fulham, William H. The Devil Comes to Alcaraz. 1 act. Theatre Arts, 14 (September, 1930), 797-803.

Fuller, Dean see Thompson, J. 8847

Furness, Edna Lue, translator see Usigli, R. 8981

3342. Furniss, Grace Livingston. His Unbiased Opinion. 1 act. Cosmopolitan, 15 (October, 1893), 674-676.

Fuzellier, E. see Taladoire, B. 8692

Fuzier, J., translator see Webster, J. 9250

G

3343. Gabirondo, Victor and Ezequiel Enderiz. Luna di Miele. 1 act. Il Dramma, 66 (May 15, 1929), 39-44. Amilcare Quarra, translator. In Italian.

Gable, J. Harris, translator see Bernard, T. 839

3344. Gàbor, Andor. L'ora azzurra. 3 acts. Il Dramma, 54 (November 15, 1928), 5-28. In Italian.

Gage, Edward see Springer, T. G. 8455

3345. Gaillard, Roger. A-Propos de la Champmesle. 1 act. L'Avant Scène, 134, 43-47. In French.

3346. _____. La Reine et le Sorcier. 1 act. L'Avant Scène, 260 (March 1, 1962), 31-35. In French.

3347. _____. La Sibylle de la Rue de Tournon. 1 act. L'Avant Scène, 224, 30-36. In French.

3348. Galahad, Joseph Andrew. Sic Passim. 1 act. Poetry, 19 (October, 1921), 20-21.

Galassi, Giancarlo, translator see MacLiammoir, M. 5269

Galassi-Beria, G., translator see O'Casey, S. 6757

3349. Gale, Zona, 1874-1938. The Appreciators: A Wooing. 1 act. Smart Set, 14 (December, 1904), 105-107.

3350. _____. Uncle Jimmy. 1 act. Ladies' Home Journal, 38 (October, 1921), 18-19, 98, 101-104.

3351. Galeazzi, Galeazzo A. Colloquio col topolino. Monologue. Sipario, 17 (July, 1962), 47-49. In Italian.

3352. _____. Simili a dio. 2 parts, comedy. Sipario, 11 (April, 1956), 29-45. In Italian.

Galey, Matthieu, 1934- , adapter see Albee, E. 98

_____, adapter see Gray, S. 3696

_____, translator see Albee, E. 102

3353. Gallico, Paul. The Snow Goose. 1 act. Scholastic, 42 (March 8-13, 1943), 15-17.

Gallinaro, Maria Bianca, translator see O'Neill, E. 6837, 6845, 6864

Gallo, Daniel see Silvain, J. 8280

Galloni, Giannino, translator see Gide, A. 3506

_____, translator see Marcel, G. 5529, 5530

3354. Galsworthy, John, 1867-1933. Hall-Marked. 1 act, satire. Atlantic, 113 (June, 1914), 845-851.

3355. _____. The Little Dream. 1 act. Scribner's, 49 (May, 1911), 531-540.

3356. _____. Loyalties. 1 act. Everybody's Magazine, 48 (February, 1923), 96-103.

3357. _____. Sekhet: A Dream. 1 act. Scribner's, 57 (April, 1915), 445-451.

3358. _____. The Sun. 1 act. Scribner's, 65 (May, 1919), 513-516.

3359. Galtier, Charles. Farces et Attrapes. 1 act, comedy. L'Avant Scène, 200 (July 1, 1959), 35-42. In French.

3360. Gambaro, Griselda. Il campo. 2 acts. Sipario, 25 (August-September, 1970), 87-100. Anna Scriboni, translator. In Italian.

3361. Gamble, Hazel V. Little Fish. 1 act, comedy. Drama, 14 (February, 1924), 185-187.

3362. Gamble, Mary R. Aunt Columbia's Dinner Party. 1 act. Ladies' Home Journal, 34 (June, 1917), 28.

3363. Gandera, Felix. I due signori della signora. 3 acts. Il Dramma, 10 (September, 1926), 7-33. In Italian.

3364. _____ and C. Gever. L'amante immaginaria. 3 acts. Il Dramma, 7 (June, 1926), 6-38. In Italian.

Gandini, Umberto, translator see Horvath, O. von 4177

_____, translator see Kroetz, F. X. 4728

3365. Ganly, Andrew. The Dear Queen. 1 act. Journal of Irish Literature, 5 (May, 1976), 93-111.

3366. Gantillon, Simon, 1890- . Bifur. 3 parts. Il Dramma, n.s., 37 (May 15, 1947), 9-34. Ines Ghiron, translator. In Italian.

3367. _____. Cyclone. 1 act. One-Act Play Magazine, 1 (September, 1937), 424-460. D. L. Orna, translator.

3368. _____. Mille et Quatre. 1 act. L'Avant Scène, 152, 29-39. In French.

Garatti, Wanda, translator see Triana, J. 8932

Garber, Frederick, translator see Aichinger, I. 84

3369. Garcia, David. He-He. Trace, 59 (1966), 394-395.

3370. Garcia, Heduardo. The Death and Re-erection of Dr. Franklin. 1 act. The Scene, 1 (1972), 181-207.

3371. Garcia, Jesus Campos. The Marriage of Drama and Censorship. 1 act. Modern International Drama, 8 (Fall, 1974), 13-41. Ramon Layera, translator.

3372. Garcia-Alvarez, E. and P. Munoz-Seca. Il boia di Siviglia. 3 acts. Il Dramma, 2 (January, 1926), 6-35. Gilberto Beccari, translator. In Italian.

3373. _____. I milioni dello zio Peteroff. 3 acts. Il Dramma, 145 (September 1, 1932), 4-31. Gilberto Beccari and Amilcare Quarra, translators. In Italian.

3374. Garcia Lorca, Federico, 1898-1936. Blood Wedding. 3 acts, tragedy. Il Dramma, 410/411 (September 15/October 1, 1943), 29-44. Giuseppe Valentini, translator. In Italian.

3375. _____. Blood Wedding. 3 acts, tragedy. New Directions, 4 (1939), 1-61. Gilbert Neiman, translator.

3376. _____. La casa de Bernarda Alba. 3 acts. L'Avant Scène, 452/453 (July 1/15, 1970), 29-54. Andre Belamich, adapter. In French.

3377. _____. La casa de Bernarda Alba. 3 acts. Il Dramma, n.s., 19/20 (August 15/September 1, 1946), 13-29. Amedeo Recanati, translator. In Italian.

3378. _____. Chimera. 1 act. New Directions, 8 (1944), 382-384. Edwin Honig, translator.

3379. _____. Dialogue of Amargo. New Directions, 8 (1944), 390-394. Edwin Honig, translator.

3380. _____. Episode of the Lieutenant Colonel of the Civil-Guard. New Directions, 8 (1944), 394-396. Edwin Honig, translator.

3381. _____. In the Frame of Don Cristobal, a Puppet Farce. New Directions, 8 (1944), 396-407. Edwin Honig, translator.

3382. _____. Mariana Pineda. 3 parts. Il Dramma, n.s., 12/13 (May 1/15, 1946), 15-34. Nardo Languasco, translator. In Italian.

3383. _____. Le Petit Retable de Don Cristobal. 1 act, farce. L'Avant Scène, 452/453 (July 1/15, 1970), 21-27. Andre Camp, translator. In French.

3384. _____. Quadretto di Don Cristobal. 1 act, farce. Il Dramma, n.s., 12/13 (May 1/15, 1946), 63-67. Dimma Chirone, translator. In Italian.

3385. _____. La zapatera prodigiosa. 2 acts, farce. Il Dramma, n. s., 12/13 (May 1/15, 1946), 37-60. Nardo Languasco, translator. In Italian. See also Lorca, F. G. 5042-5049.

3386. Gardener, Eden. Behind the Purdah. 1 act. Asia, 20 (April, 1920), 273-276.

3387. Gardner, Herb, 1936- . A Thousand Clowns. 3 acts. Theatre Arts, 48 (January, 1964), 33-64.

Gardner, Mercedes, adapter see Pandora 6949

3388. _____, adapter, and Jean Shannon Smith, adapter. King Midas. 1 act. Plays, 28 (March, 1969), 59-67.

3389. Gargi, Balwant, 1918- . The Mango Tree. 3 acts, tragedy. Literary Review, 6 (Summer, 1963), 503-556.

3390. Gariffo, Enzo. Le cicogne. 1 act. Il Dramma, 95 (August 1, 1930), 30-37. In Italian.

_____, translator see Bernard, J.-J. 828

_____, translator see Bisson, A. 971

_____, translator see Kaiser, G. 4532

_____, translator see Lenormand, H. R. 4916

_____, translator see Sée, E. 8133

_____, translator see Wachthausen, R. 9177

Garineri, translator see Anderson, R. 219

3391. Garland, Robert, 1895- . At Night All Cats Are Gray. 1 act. Smart Set, 48 (March, 1916), 247-259.

3392. _____. The Double Miracle. 1 act. Forum, 53 (April, 1915), 511-527.

3393. _____. Love's Young Dream. 1 act. Smart Set, 40 (August, 1913), 83-87.

3394. Garnett, Louise Ayres, d. 1937. Hilltop, 1 act. Drama, 11 (May, 1921), 277-283.

3395. _____. The Pig Prince. 2 acts. Drama, 12 (April, 1922), 240-246.

3396. Garnung, Francis, 1926- . Les Membres de la Famille. 1 act. L'Avant Scène, 488 (February 1, 1972), 41-44. In French.

Garrel, Maurice, adapter see Schisgal, M. 8031

Garrigus, Frederich, adapter see Dickens, C. 2468

3397. Garrison, Christian B. A Rhyme in Time Saves Nine. 1 act. Plays, 32 (May, 1973), 55-61.

3398. Garrison, Theodosia, 1874- . At the Sign of the Cleft Heart. 1 act. Smart Set, 4 (July, 1901), 91-96.

3399. _____. An Hour of Earth. 1 act. Smart Set, 9 (March, 1903), 153-157.

3400. _____. The Literati. 1 act. Smart Set, 13 (May, 1904), 149-150.

3401. Garro, Elena. A Solid House. 1 act. Evergreen Review, 2 (Winter, 1959), 62-74. Lysander Kemp, translator.

3402. Garson, Barbara. Macbird. 4 acts. City Lights Journal, 3 (1966), 7-50.

Garten, Hugh F., 1904- , translator see Kaiser, G. 4533

3403. Garver, Juliet. Be-Bop and Beethoven. 1 act. Plays, 21 (October, 1961), 1-11.

3404. _____. Cave Man, Brave Man. 1 act. Plays, 19 (May, 1960), 13-22.

3405. _____. Charlie and the Six Chicks. 1 act. Plays, 34 (January, 1975), 19-31.

3406. _____. Debbie the Dreamer. 1 act. Plays, 31 (December, 1971), 1-12.

3407. _____. Father Hits the Jackpot. 1 act. Plays, 15 (April, 1956), 55-62. AND Plays, 26 (May, 1967), 65-72.

3408. _____. Father of the Year. 1 act. Plays, 15 (January, 1956), 35-44.

3409. _____. For Love or Money. 1 act, melodrama. Plays, 32 (May, 1973), 17-26.

3410. _____. A Howling Success. 1 act. Plays, 15 (May, 1956), 1-10. AND Plays, 24 (January, 1965), 15-24.

3411. _____. I Want to Talk to You. 1 act. Plays, 33 (March, 1974), 85-87.

3412. _____. Marla the Mechanic. 1 act. Plays, 34 (April, 1975), 1-13.

3413. _____. The Money Tree. 1 act. Plays, 20 (April, 1961), 1-11. AND Plays, 33 (April, 1974), 40-50.

3414. _____. My Fair Linda. 1 act. Plays, 22 (May, 1963), 1-13.

3415. _____. The Nerve of Napoleon. 1 act. Plays, 16 (October, 1956), 1-10.

3416. _____. Space Suit with Roses. 1 act. Plays, 20 (October, 1960), 27-36.

3417. _____. Turkey, Anyone? 1 act. Plays, 15 (November, 1955), 41-50. AND Plays, 29 (November, 1969), 59-68.

3418. Gasc, Yves. La Folie Rostanov. 4 acts, comedy. L'Avant Scène, 271 (September 1, 1962), 9-34. In French.

3419. Gaskill, William, adapter. The Speakers. 1 act. Gambit 7 (No. 25, 1974), 11-81. Max Stafford-Clark, joint adapter.

3420. Gass, Ken. The Boy Bishop. 3 acts. Canadian Theatre Review, 12 (Fall, 1976), 42-122.

Gassman, Vittorio, translator see Anouilh, J. 271

_____, translator see Breffort, A. 1314

Gaster, Bertha, translator see Gorgey, G. 3643

_____, translator see Karinthy, F. 4550

3421. Gatti, Armand, 1924- . Passion du General Franco. L'Avant Scène, 586 (May 1, 1976), 3-35. In French.

3422. _____. La Vie Imaginaire de l'Eboueur Auguste Geai. 2 parts. L'Avant Scène, 272 (September 15, 1962), 10-30. In French.

3423. _____. La Vie Imaginaire de l'Eboueur Auguste Geai. 4 acts. Sipario, (August-September, 1968), 54-69, 88. Maria Silvia Codecasa, translator.

3424. Gatti, Giulio. Antigone lo cascio. 3 acts. Il Dramma, n.s., 318 (March, 1963), 6-39. In Italian.

Gauthier, Guy. Manitoba. 2 acts. The Scène, 1 (1972), 65-78.

3425. Gavi, Valentino. Che c'entra l'amore? 1 act. Il Dramma, 206 (March 15, 1935), 34-41. In Italian.

3426. ———. Regali a Nelly. 1 act. Il Dramma, 48 (August 15, 1928), 32-40. In Italian.

3427. ———. Un signore in poltrona. 1 act. Il Dramma, 163 (June 1, 1933), 34-39. In Italian.

3428. ———. Tra due signori per bene. 1 act. Il Dramma, 176 (December 15, 1933), 35-41. In Italian.

Gavin, Mary see Head, C. 3998

3429. Gavoty, Bernard and Alain Decaux. Beaumarchais L'Innombrable. 1 act. L'Avant Scène, 457 (October 1, 1970), 41-54. In French.

3430. Gay, C. M. The Knock on the Door. 1 act. Learning With ..., 2 (November, 1974), 8-9.

3431. Gay, Robert M. Peace, Good Tickle-Brain. 1 act. Atlantic, 149 (May, 1932), 580-585.

3432. Gazzo, Michael V. A Hatful of Rain. 3 acts. Sipario, 11 (November, 1956), 32-56. Mino Roli, translator. In Italian.

3432a. ———. Hatful of Rain. 3 acts. Theatre Arts, 40 (December, 1956), 33-56.

3433. Gehri, Alfredo. Sesto piano. 3 acts. Il Dramma, 389 (November 1, 1942), 5-32. Lorenzo Ruggi, translator. In Italian.

3434. Geijerstam, Gustav, 1858-1909. Criminals; An Unpleasant Play. 1 act. Poet Lore, 34 (Summer, 1923), 186-209. Roy W. Swanson, translator.

3435. Gelindo. 1 act. Il Dramma, n.s., 291 (December, 1960), 32-44. In Italian.

3436. Genet, Jean, 1910- . Les bonnes. Sipario, 230 (June, 1965), 36-44. Ettore Capriolo, translator. In Italian.

3437. ———. Haute Surveillance. 1 act. Il Dramma, n. s., 184/185 (July 1/15, 1953), 51-62. Sergio Cenalino, translator. In Italian.

3438. ———. Die Neger. 1 act. Spectaculum, 8 (1965), 73-133. Katarina Hock and Ben Poller, translators. In German.

3439. George, Charles. When Shakespeare's Ladies Meet. 1 act. Scholastic, 42 (April 19-24, 1943), 15-16.

3440. George, George S. and Eugenie Leontovich. Civiale per il generale. 3 acts. Il Dramma, n.s., 83 (April 15, 1949), 7-37. Gigi Cane, translator. In Italian.

3441. Georges, Rene. Les Berlingots. 1 act. L'Avant Scène, 556 (January 15, 1975), 34-40. In French.

Geraldy, Paul, pseud. see Lefevre-Geraldy, P. 4892, 4893

Gerbidon, Marcel see Armont, P. 341

3442. Germoz, Alain. Le Temoin. 1 act. L'Avant Scène, 292 (July 15, 1963), 33-35. In French.

3443. Gerould, Daniel C. Candanles, Commissioner. 1 act. First Stage, 4 (Fall, 1965), 150-167.

3444. _____. Explosion. 1 act. Drama and Theatre, 9 (Spring, 1971), 169-176.

3445. _____. Tripstych: Three Short Plays for Dummies: Night Stick; Stick Up; Big Stick. Drama and Theatre, 11 (Winter, 1972/73), 108.

_____, translator see Olyesha, Y. 6831

_____, translator see Witkiewicz, S. I. 9511, 9513, 9515, 9517, 9520, 9521

Gerould, Eleanor S., translator see Olyesha, Y. 6831

_____, translator see Witkiewicz, S. I. 9511

3446. Gerry, Margarita Spalding. An Interruption. Harper's Bazaar, 40 (May, 1906), 398-403.

3447. Gerrymander. 1 act. Plays, 27 (May, 1968), 107-108.

3448. Gerstenberg, Alice. Ever Young. 1 act, comedy. Drama, 12 (February, 1922), 167-173.

3449. _____. Fourteen. 1 act, comedy. Drama, 10 (February, 1920), 180-184.

3450. Getchell, Margaret Colby. Birthday Candles. Woman's Home Companion, 44 (August, 1917), 23.

3451. Gevel, Claude, 1886- . Dans l'Histoire du Coeur. 1 act, comedy. L'Avant Scène, 105, 26-32. In French.

3452. _____. Mon Mari S'endort. 1 act, comedy. L'Avant Scène, 141, 33-39. In French.

Gevel

3453. ———. Tuez-Moi. 1 act, comedy. L'Avant Scène, 173 (May 1, 1958), 38-43. In French.

3454. ———. Le Vase Etrusque. 1 act. L'Avant Scène, 248 (September 1, 1961), 38-43. In French.

Gever, C. see Gandera, F. 3364

3455. Geyer, Sigfried. Sera d'inverno. 3 acts. Il Dramma, 49 (September 1, 1928), 4-24. In Italian.

3456. Ghelderode, Michel de, 1898-1962. Les aveugles. 1 act. Sipario, 8 (November, 1953), 34-36. Gianni Nicoletti, translator. In Italian.

3457. ———. Barabbas. 3 acts. Il Dramma, n.s., 259 (April, 1958), 13-32. Guido Guarda, translator. In Italian.

3458. ———. Christopher Columbus, A Dramatic Fairy Tale in Three Scenes. Tulane Drama Review, 3 (March, 1959), 83-98. George Hauger, translator.

3459. ———. La morte del dottor Faust. 3 acts. Il Dramma, n.s., 129 (March 15, 1951), 12-25. Anton Giulio Bragaglia, adapter. In Italian.

3460. ———. Pantagleize; A Farce to Make You Sad. 3 acts. Theatre Arts, 46 (August, 1962), 25-56. George Hauger, translator.

3461. ———. A Strange Rider. 1 act. Chicago Review, 9 (Winter, 1956), 96-108. Lucie T. Horner and Dale G. Cleaver, translators.

3462. Ghéon, Henri, 1875-1944. Le Chemin de la Croix. 14 parts. Il Dramma, n.s., 270 (March, 1959), 10-18. Guido Guarda, translator. In Italian.

3463. ———. Le Noël sur la Place. 3 parts. Il Dramma, n.s., 243 (December, 1956), 16-32. Guido Guarda, translator. In Italian.

3464. ———. L'uomo di Dio. 3 episodes. Il Dramma, n.s., 327 (December, 1963), 30-42. In Italian.

3465. Gherardi, Gherardo, 1890-1949. Autunno. 3 acts. Il Dramma, 303 (April 1, 1939), 4-24. In Italian.

3466. ———. Il burattino. 3 acts. Il Dramma, 38 (March 15, 1928), 7-31. In Italian.

3467. ———. Il drago volante. 4 acts. Il Dramma, 421-427 (March 1-June 1, 1944), 13-31. In Italian.

3468.	_____. Il nostro viaggio. 3 acts. Il Dramma, n.s., 61/62 (May 15/June 1, 1948), 11-31. In Italian.
3469.	_____. Ombre Cinesi. 3 acts. Il Dramma, 131 (February 1, 1932), 4-31. In Italian.
3470.	_____. Questi Ragazzi. 3 acts. Il Dramma, 199 (December 1, 1934), 4-30. In Italian.
3471.	_____. Truccature. 3 acts. Il Dramma, 271 (December 1, 1937), 3-27. In Italian.
3472.	Ghiglia, Diego and Claudio Siro. Giulio Cesare. 1 act. Il Dramma, 51 (October, 1975), 25-38. In Italian.

Ghilardi, Ferdinando, translator see Caragiale, I. L. 1594

Ghiron, Ines, translator see Gantillon, S. 3366

3473.	Giachetti, Cipriano. Il cavallo di Troia. 3 acts. Il Dramma, 4 (March, 1926), 6-32. In Italian.
3474.	_____. Il mio dente e il tuo cuore. 3 acts. Il Dramma, 52 (October 15, 1928), 5-31. In Italian.
3475.	Not used.
3476.	Giacosa, Giuseppe, 1847-1906. As the Leaves. 4 acts, comedy. Drama, 1 (February, 1911), 9-97.
3477.	_____. The Stronger. 3 acts, comedy. Drama, 10 (May, 1913), 32-156.

Giagni, Gian Domenico see Pratolini, V. 7274

Giampaoli, M., translator see Huxley, A. 4346

3478.	Giancapo and Rossato. Delitto e castigo. 3 acts. Il Dramma, 77 (November 1, 1929), 4-29. In Italian.
3479.	Gianesi, Raffaello. I sentimentali. 2 parts. Sipario, 17 (February, 1962), 52-68. In Italian.

Giannini, Clemente, translator see Strindberg, A. 8572

3480.	Giannini, Guglielmo, 1891- . L'abito nero. 1 act. Il Dramma, n.s., 161 (July 15, 1952), 11-19. In Italian.
3481.	_____. "Anonima fratelli Roylott." 3 acts. Il Dramma, 219 (October 1, 1935), 5-40. In Italian.
3482.	_____. L'attessa dell'angelo. 3 acts. Il Dramma, n.s., 173 (January 15, 1953), 5-21. In Italian.

3483. _____. Avrebbe potuto essere! 3 acts. Il Dramma, 304 (April 15, 1939), 4-26. In Italian.

3484. _____. La donna rossa. 1 act. Il Dramma, 335 (August 1, 1940), 40-48. In Italian.

3485. _____. Eva in vetrina. 3 acts. Il Dramma, 312 (August 15, 1939), 4-28. In Italian.

3486. _____. Mani in alto. 3 acts. Il Dramma, 263 (August 1, 1937), 2-33. In Italian.

3487. _____. Il nemico. 3 acts. Il Dramma, 357 (July 1, 1941), 9-43. In Italian.

3488. _____. Il pretore de Minimis. 3 acts. Il Dramma, n.s., 127 (February 15, 1951), 9-30. In Italian.

3489. _____. I rapaci. 3 acts. Il Dramma, 267 (October 1, 1937), 2-31. In Italian.

3490. _____. Ritorno del re. 3 acts. Il Dramma, n.s., 155 (April 15, 1952), 5-28. In Italian.

3491. _____. Lo schiavo impazzito. 3 acts. Il Dramma, 320 (December 15, 1939), 4-22. In Italian.

3492. _____. La sera del sabato. 3 acts. Il Dramma, 338 (September 15, 1940), 4-37. In Italian.

3493. _____. Ti voglio tanto bene. 1 act. Il Dramma, 340 (October 15, 1940), 39-48. In Italian.

Giannini, Jole, translator see Renard, J. 7484, 7485

Giapa, Ettore, translator see Hacks, P. 3812

Giardini, Bianca, translator see Lavedan, H. L. E. 4839

Giardini, Cesare, translator see Salacrou, A. 7881

3494. Gibbs, Wolcott, 1902-1958. Season in the Sun. 2 acts, comedy. Theatre Arts, 35 (June, 1951), 60-85.

3495. Gibson, H. The Babes in the Wood. 3 acts. Dublin Magazine, 1 (March, 1924), 684-698. Gerald MacNamara, translator.

3496. Gibson, Morgan. Madame C.I.A. 1 act. Dramatika, 2 (October, 1968), 21-26.

3497. Gibson, Pauline. Sir Robin of Locksley. 1 act. Scholastic, 32 (May 14, 1938), 30-33.

Gibson

———— see Schmitt, G. 8057

3498. ———— and Martin Rudd. Fill 'er Up. 1 act. Scholastic, 31 (October 16, 1937), 17E-18E, 20E.

3499. Gibson, Wilfried Wilson, 1878-1962. Bloodybush Edge. 1 act. New Numbers, 1 (February, 1914), 5-26.

3500. ————. Hoops. 1 act. New Numbers, 1 (August, 1914), 135-152.

3501. ————. The Queen's Crags. 1 act. English Review, 13 (January, 1913), 169-182.

3502. Gibson, William, 1914- . The Miracle Worker. 3 acts. L'Avant Scène, 279 (January 1, 1963), 10-34. Marguerite Duras and Gerard Jurlot, translators. In French.

3503. Gide, Andre, 1869-1951. Bethsabe. Vers et Prose, 16 (December, 1908; January-February, 1909), 1-17. In French.

3504. ————. Le caves du Vatican. 3 acts, comedy-farce. Sipario, 6 (March, 1951), 41-64. Federico Federici, translator. In Italian.

3505. ————. Le Treizième Arbre. 1 act, farce. Mesures, 1 (April 15, 1935), 97-129. In French.

3506. ———— and Jean-Louis Barrault. Il processo. 2 parts. Sipario, 3 (July, 1948), 33-50. Giannino Galloni, translator. In Italian.

3507. Gifford, Franklin Kent, 1861- . All or None. 1 act, comedy. Drama, 16 (March, 1926), 207-209, 237-238.

Gigli, Lorenzo, 1889- , translator see Crommelynck, F. 2115

————, translator see Evreinov, N. N. 2888

————, translator see Junichiro, T. 4527

Gignoux, R. see Luchaire, J. 5076, 5077

3508. Gilbert, Helen. The Good Sainte Anne. 1 act. Poet Lore, 35 (1924), 576-586.

3509. ————. The Spot on the Porch. 1 act. Poet Lore, 42 (Spring, 1933), 81-91.

3510. Gilbert, Mary Haines. Kitten. 1 act. St. Nicholas, 1 (April, 1874), 373-374.

3511. Gilbert, W. Stephen. There Goes the West End; A Playlet for Shaftsbury Avenue. 1 act. Plays and Players, 22 (November, 1974), 22-23.

3512. Gilbert, William Schwenck, 1836-1911. Sweethearts, 2 acts, comedy. Golden Book, 4 (December, 1926), 763-772.

3513. ———. Trial by Jury. 1 act, comedy. Golden Book, 9 (April, 1929), 102-106.

3514. ———. Trying a Dramatist. 1 act, comedy. Century, 83 (December, 1911), 179-189.

3515. ——— and Sir Arthur Seymour Sullivan, 1842-1900. H. M. S. Pinafore. 1 act. Plays, 33 (May, 1974), 81-92. Adele Thane, adapter.

3516. ———. Iolanthe, or, The Peer and the Peri. 1 act. Plays, 35 (October, 1975), 83-95. Adele Thane, adapter.

3517. ———. The Mikado. 1 act. Plays, 34 (November, 1974), 83-96. Adele Thane, adapter.

3518. ———. The Pirates of Penzance; or, The Slave of Duty. 1 act. Plays, 32 (May, 1973), 79-88. Adele Thane, adapter.

3519. ———. Ruddigore, or, The Witch's Curse. 1 act. Plays, 35 (April, 1976), 85-96. Adele Thane, adapter.

3520. ———. Trial by Jury. 1 act. Plays, 33 (December, 1973), 90-96. Adele Thane, adapter.

3521. ———. The Yoemen of the Guard. 1 act. Plays, 34 (April, 1975), 67-80. Adele Thane, adapter.

3522. Gilbreath, Alice. The Mysterious Mix-up. 1 act. Plays, 35 (April, 1976), 52-54.

3523. Gilchrist, Theo E. A Fish Tale from the Arctic. 1 act. Plays, 32 (March, 1973), 74-76.

Gilkyson, T. Walter, translator see Echegaray y Eizaguirre, J. 2809

3524. Gill, Peter. Over Gardens Out. 1 act. Plays and Players, 17 (January, 1970), 62-68.

3525. ———. The Sleepers Den. 3 acts. Plays and Players, 17 (January, 1970), 68-78.

3526. ———. Small Change. 2 acts. Plays and Players, 23 (August, September, 1976), 43-50; 53-60.

Gille, Andre, adapter see Ruzzante 7817

3527. Gilles, Ange. Il y a une Vertu dans le Soleil. 1 act. L'Avant Scène, 468 (March 15, 1971), 29-32. In French.

3528. _____. Un Lache. 1 act. L'Avant Scène, 545 (July 15, 1974), 43-50. In French.

3529. _____. Noces d'Argent. 1 act. L'Avant Scène, 525 (September 15, 1973), 37-41. In French.

3530. _____. Rimailho. 1 act. L'Avant Scène, 235 (January 15, 1961), 38-42. In French.

3531. Gillespie, C. Richard. The Burial. 1 act. Dramatics, 44 (February, 1973), 5-6, 8.

Gillespie, Gerald, translator see Valle-Inclan, R. M. del 9000

3532. Gillette, William Hooker, 1855-1937. Electricity. 3 acts, comedy. Drama, 12 (November, 1913), 12-123.

_____ see also Burnett, F. H. 1442

Gilliland, Herbert, translator see Pedrolo, M. de 7037

3533. Gillois, Andre, 1902- . En Correctionnelle. 1 act. L'Avant Scène, 254 (December 1, 1961), 32-35. In French.

3534. _____. Le Dessous des Cartes. 4 acts. L'Avant Scène, 194 (April 1, 1959), 7-29. In French.

3535. _____. Frère Jacques. 4 acts, comedy. L'Avant Scène, 84, 2-34. In French.

3536. _____. Kessa Gozène. 1 act. L'Avant Scène, 117, 43-46. In French.

3537. _____. Polydora. 3 acts. L'Avant Scène, 150, 1-30. In French.

3538. Gilmore, Alice F. Our Library, A Dewey Decimal Play. 1 act. Wilson Library Bulletin, 5 (November, 1930), 186-191.

3539. Gilmore, Louis. Affairs of Catherine, I. The Grand Duchess Receives. 1 act. Double Dealer, 2 (November, 1921), 191-200.

3540. _____. Affairs of Catherine, II. Long Live the Empress. 1 act. Double Dealer, 3 (January, 1922), 26.

3541. _____. Affairs of Catherine, III. Prince Petiomkin. 1 act. Double Dealer. 3 (March, 1922), 144-154.

3542. _____. Affairs of Catherine, IV. A Tenor. 1 act. Double Dealer, 3 (June, 1922), 301-310.

3543. _____. Affairs of Catherine, V. Widowed. 1 act. Double Dealer, 4 (October, 1922), 177-186.

3544. _____. Bagatelle. 1 act. Double Dealer, 1 (February, 1921), 51-57.

3545. Gilroy, Frank D. Les Jeux de la Nuit. 2 acts, comedy. L'Avant Scène, 554 (December 15, 1974), 3-32. Marcel Mithois, adapter. In French.

3546. _____. The Subject Was Roses. Sipario, 30 (November, 1975), 45-59. Benedetta Galassi Berio, translator. In Italian.

3547. _____. Who'll Save the Plowboy? Sipario, 225 (January, 1965), 51-64. Ettore Capriolo, translator. In Italian.

Gilson, Paul see Frank, N. 3266

3548. _____ and Nino Frank, 1904- . Portrait de Famille. 1 act. L'Avant Scène, 98, 1-7. In French.

Giltene, Jean see Joffe, A. 4471

3549. Gingerbread House, The. 1 act. Learning With ..., 2 (November, 1974), 19-20.

3550. Ginzburg, Natalia. Teresa. 3 acts. L'Avant Scène, 444 (March 1, 1970), 7-24. Michel Arnaud, adapter. In French.

Giomar, translator see Strindberg, A. 8578

3551. Giono, Jean, 1895- . La Femme du Boulanger. 3 acts. Il Dramma, n.s., 93 (September 15, 1949), 9-42. Ivo Senesi, translator. In Italian.

3552. Giordana, Gian Pietro. Faustina e la realtà. 1 act. Il Dramma, 215 (August 1, 1935), 36-42. In Italian.

3553. _____. Il richiamo. 3 acts. Il Dramma, 191 (August 1, 1934), 4-23. In Italian.

Gioseffi, Guido, adapter see Mastello, Il 5649

3554. Giovaninetti, Silvio, 1901- . L'abisso. 3 acts. Sipario, 3 (October, 1948), 37-58. In Italian.

3555. _____. Carne unica. 3 acts. Il Dramma, n.s., 269 (February, 1959), 6-36. In Italian.

3556. _____. Cio che non sai. 1 act. Sipario, 1 (November-December, 1946), 73-81. In Italian.

3557. _____. Lidia o l'infinito. 3 acts. Sipario, 5 (March, 1950), 53-75. In Italian.

3558. _____. I lupi. 3 acts. Il Dramma, n.s., 305 (February, 1962), 10-43. In Italian.

3559. _____. Il sangue verde. 3 acts. Il Dramma, n.s., 199 (February 15, 1954), 9-37. In Italian.

_____, translator see Anouilh, J. 246

Giovannini, Jole, translator see Anderson, R. 219

_____, translator see Renard, J. 7484, 7485

3560. Girardeau, Claude Monica, 1860- . The God of the Wood. 1 act. Drama, 10 (June, 1920), 305-307.

3561. Giraudoux, Jean, 1882-1944. Amphitryon 38. 3 acts. Il Dramma, n.s., 84 (May 1, 1949), 7-33. Adolfo Franci, translator. In Italian.

3562. _____. L'Apollon de Bellac. 1 act. Il Dramma, n.s., 182 (June 1, 1953), 33-43. Bruno Arcangeli, translator. In Italian.

3563. _____. The Enchanted. 3 acts. Theatre Arts, 34 (October, 1950), 55-88. Maurice Valency, adapter.

3564. _____. La Folle de Chaillot. 2 acts. Il Dramma, n.s., 99/100 (January 1, 1950), 103-132. Gigi Cane, translator. In Italian.

3565. _____. La Folle de Chaillot. 2 acts. L'Avant Scène, 352 (March 1, 1966), 8-20, 45-58. In French.

3566. _____. La Guerre de Troie N'Aura pas Lien. 2 acts. L'Avant Scène, 479 (September 15, 1971), 7-33. In French.

3567. _____. La Guerre de Troie N'Aura pas Lien. 2 acts. Il Dramma, n.s., 2/3 (December 1/15, 1945), 57-80. Clara Ferrero, translator. In Italian.

3568. _____. Impromptu de Paris. 1 act, comedy. Il Dramma, n.s., 108 (May 1, 1950), 45-57. Gigi Cane, translator. In Italian.

3569. _____. Impromptu de Paris. 1 act, comedy. Theatre Arts, 22 (March, 1938), 218-230.

3570. _____. Intermezzo. 3 acts. Il Dramma, n.s., 78 (February 1, 1949), 7-32. Gigi Cane, translator. In Italian.

3571. _____. Judith. 3 acts. Il Dramma, n.s., 137 (July 15, 1951), 7-38. Emilio Castellani, translator. In Italian.

3572. _____. The Madwoman of Chaillot. 2 acts. Theatre Arts, 33 (November, 1949), 57-92. Maurice Valency, adapter.

3573. _____. Ondine. 3 acts, comedy. Sipario, 11 (October, 1956), 28-56. Sergio Morando, translator. In Italian.

3574. _____. Ondine. 3 acts. Theatre Arts, 38 (December, 1954), 34-63. Maurice Valency, adapter.

3575. _____. Paris Impromptu. 1 act, comedy. Tulane Drama Review, 3 (May, 1959), 107-128. Rima Drell Reck, translator.

3576. _____. The Song of Songs. 1 act. Tulane Drama Review, 3 (May, 1959), 88-106. John Raikes, translator.

_____, adapter see Kennedy, M. and B. Dean 4596

3577. Girette, Marcel. Il creatore d'illusione. 1 act. Il Dramma, 99 (October 1, 1930), 37-46. Virgilio Marchesini, translator. In Italian.

Giuliani, Alfredo, translator see Michaux, H. 5806, 5807

3578. Givens, Helen M. The Bull Terrier and the Baby. 1 act, comedy. Ladies' Home Journal, 23 (October, 1906), 15, 90.

3579. _____. Improving Husbands. 1 act, comedy. Ladies' Home Journal, 24 (March, 1907), 10, 67.

3580. Glaenzer, Richard Butler. The Louis Quinze Salon, or, A Friend of Mrs. Robinson. 1 act. Smart Set, 24 (February, 1908), 102-104.

3581. Glaspell, Susan, 1882-1948. Bernice. 3 acts. Theatre Arts, 3 (October, 1919), 264-300.

Glazer, Benjamin F., translator see Lengyel, M. 4914

_____, translator see Molnar, F. 6147, 6156

Gleason, Anne see Gleason, E. 3582

3582. Gleason, Elizabeth and Anne Gleason. Signal Service. 1 act. New England Magazine, 7 (September, 1892), 101-106.

3583. Glick, Carl, 1890- . Outclassed, A Melodramatic Comedy in One Act. Smart Set, 56 (September, 1918), 83-93.

3584. _____. Prologue. 1 act. Poet Lore, 33 (Winter, 1922), 553-562.

3585. _____. Ten Days Later. 1 act, comedy. Drama, 11 (February, 1921), 159-165.

3586. _____ and Bernard Sobel, 1887-1964. The Immortal. 1 act. Poet Lore, 32 (Autumn, 1921), 441-453.

Glickman, Will, 1910- see Stein, J. 8490

3587. Gloria in Excelsis Deo Pro Nativitate Domini. 1 act. Il Dramma, n.s., 267 (December, 1958), 19-26. In Italian.

3588. Gobineau, Joseph Arthur, Count de, 1816-1882. The Renaissance. 1 act. Smart Set, 56 (October, 1918), 83-90.

3589. Goddard, Felicia. On With the New. A Dialogue. 1 act. Smart Set, 9 (February, 1903), 83-85.

3590. _____. What Society Is Coming To. 1 act. Smart Set, 11 (October, 1903), 55-57.

Godfernaux, André see Bernard, T. 856

3591. Godsey, Townsend. A Meeting in the Woods. 1 act. Players Magazine, 38 (March, 1962), 191-194.

3592. Goering, Reinhard. Navel Engagement. Drama and Theatre, 10 (Fall, 1971), 15-30. Elrich Weisstein, translator.

Goetz, Augustus see Goetz, R. 3596, 3597

3593. Goetz, Curt, 1888-1960. Il gallo di Amleto. 1 act. Il Dramma, 269 (November 1, 1937), 30-35. Goffredo Pautassi, translator. In Italian.

3594. _____. Giuochi di prestigio. 3 acts. Il Dramma, 48 (August 15, 1928), 4-28. In Italian.

3595. _____. Ingeborg. 3 acts. Il Dramma, 5 (April, 1926), 6-30. Ada Salvatore, translator. In Italian.

3596. Goetz, Ruth and Augustus Goetz. L'erediteira. 2 parts.

Il Dramma, n.s., 123/124 (December 15, 1950/January 1, 1951), 11-41. Ada Salvatore, translator. In Italian.

3597. _____. L'Héritière. 2 acts. L'Avant Scène (OST), 45 (July, 1951), 1-48. In French.

3598. Gogol, Nickolai, 1809-1852. After the Play. 1 act. Tulane Drama Review, 4 (December, 1959), 121-144. David Magarshack, translator.

3599. _____. Il diario di un passo. Sipario, 8 (August-September, 1953), 67-71. Antonio Santoni Rugiu, adapter.

3600. _____. Gamblers. 1 act, comedy. Tulane Drama Review, 2 (November, 1957), 7-32. Eric Bentley, translator.

3601. _____. The Inspector General. 1 act. Plays, 35 (November, 1975), 82-96. Michael T. Leech, adapter.

3602. _____. The Mysterious Portrait. 1 act. Plays, 34 (May, 1975), 77-86. Michael T. Leech, adapter.

3603. _____. Le Revizor. 5 acts, comedy. L'Avant Scène, 398 (March 1, 1968), 12-42. Arthur Adamov, translator. In French.

Golden, Edward, adapter see Dickens, C. 2473

_____, adapter see Goldsmith, O. 3611

_____, adapter see Scott, Sir W. 8113

_____, adapter see Swift, J. 8647

_____, adapter see Wilde, O. 9364

Goldman, Jean, 1921- , translator see Seymour, A. 8161

Goldman, Madeleine, translator see Seymour, A. 8161

3604. Goldoni, Carlo, 1707-1793. Il Campiello. 5 acts. L'Avant Scène, 596 (October 15, 1976), 3-35. Stelio Celebrini, Claude Clerge, and Eveline Perloff, translators. In French.

3605. _____. La dama prudente. 3 acts. Il Dramma, 431-435 (August 1-October 1, 1944), 9-33. In Italian.

3606. _____. L'Eventail. 2 acts. L'Avant Scène, 570 (September 1, 1975), 3-36. Daniel Ceccaldi, adapter. In French.

3607. _____. Le Menteur. 3 acts. L'Avant Scène, 451 (June 15, 1970), 7-31. Pierre Sabatier, translator. In French.

3608. _____. The Servant of Two Masters. 1 act, farce. Plays, 32 (November, 1972), 85-96. Paul T. Nolan, adapter.

3609. _____. The Squabbles of Chioggia. 3 acts, comedy. Drama, 15 (August, 1914), 347-433. Charles Lemmi, translator.

3610. Goldsmith, Oliver, 1728-1774. She Stoops to Conquer. 5 acts, comedy. Harper's, 70, 71, 72, 73 (December, 1884, January, October, November, 1885, January, February, March, April, May, June, July, August, 1886), 38-48; 291-297; 747-761; 917-926; 275-281; 357-362; 518-526; 707-715; 844-849; 66-70; 227-233; 415-416.

3611. _____. She Stoops to Conquer. 1 act. Plays, 16 (March, 1957), 83-94. Edward Golden, adapter.

3612. _____. She Stoops to Conquer. 1 act. Plays, 30 (January, 1971), 79-91. Paul T. Nolan, adapter.

3613. Goldsmith, Sophie L. Louisa Alcott's Wish. 1 act. Plays, 2 (November, 1942), 45-49.

3614. Goldstein, Malcolm. Death Poem. 1 act. Dramatika, 8 (Fall, 1971), 41-54.

3615. Golea, Antoine. La Prison. 3 acts. L'Avant Scène, 590 (July 1, 1976), 29-54. In French.

3616. Goll, Yuan, 1891-1950. The Chaplinade, A Film Poem. Massachusetts Review, 6 (Spring/Summer, 1965), 497-514. Clinton J. Atkinson and Arthur S. Wensinger, translators.

3617. Gombrowicz, Witold, 1904- . Operette. 3 acts. L'Avant Scène, 449 (May 15, 1970), 7-35. Français de Kot Jelenski and Genevieve Serreau, translators. In French.

3618. Gomes, Dias. Journey to Bahia. 3 acts. Players Magazine, 40 (January, 1964), 106-122. Stanley Richards, adapter.

3619. Gomez-Arcos, Agustin. Pré-Papa. 1 act, farce. L'Avant Scène, 434 (October 1, 1969), 37-44. Rachel Salik, adapter. In French.

3620. Gonne, Maud, 1866-1953. Dawn! 1 act. Shenandoah, 16 (Summer, 1965), 67-77.

3621. Gonthie, Max H. Maria et Les Isles. 1 act, comedy. L'Avant Scène, 316 (August 1, 1964), 37-44. In French.

3622. Gooch, Steve. Female Transport. Plays and Players, 21 (January-February, 1974), 31-37; 21-37.

3623. Good Witch, The. 1 act. St. Nicholas, 67 (November, 1939), 14-15.

3624. Goodale, (Mrs.) D. H. R. Quite Private: A Drawing-Room Commedietta. 3 acts. Harper's, 67 (July, 1883), 240-244.

3625. Goodell, Patricia. Bears, Bears, Bears. 1 act. Plays, 15 (February, 1956), 81-85.

3626. Goodlander, Mabel Ray. The Visit of the Tomter. 1 act. Woman's Home Companion, 41 (December, 1914), 66.

3627. Goodman, Kenneth Sawyer. Dust of the Road. 1 act. Scholastic, 27 (December 14, 1935), 7-8, 27.

3628. Goodman, Paul, 1911-1972. The Cave at Machpelah. 1 act. Commentary, 25 (June, 1958), 512-517.

3629. _____. Faustina, Ritual Tragedy. 2 acts. Quarterly Review of Literature, 11 (No. 2/3, 1961), 69-116. AND Quarterly Review of Literature, 19 (No. 3/4, 1975), 225-270.

3630. _____. Theory of Tragedy. 2 parts. Quarterly Review of Literature, 5 (No. 4, 1950), 318-338. AND Quarterly Review of Literature, 19 (No. 1/2, 1974), 105-112.

3631. _____. The Tower of Babel. 3 parts. New Directions, 5 (1940), 19-38.

Goodman, Randolph, 1908- , translator see Aspenstrom, W. 423

_____, translator see Bergman, I. 818

3632. Goodrich, Frances and Albert Hackett, 1900- . Diary of Ann Frank. 2 parts. L'Avant Scène, 192 (March 1, 1959), 11-37. Georges Neveux, adapter. In French.

3633. Gordin, Giacomo. Oltre l'oceano. 4 acts. Il Dramma, 146 (September 15, 1932), 6-26. Giacomo Lwow and Eligio Possenti, translators. In Italian.

3634. Gordon, Celia. A Compass for Christopher. 1 act. Plays, 12 (October, 1952), 61-64.

Gordon

3635. ———. Models for Health. 1 act. Plays, 11 (January, 1952), 67-70.

3636. ———. The Way to the Inn. 1 act. Plays, 11 (December, 1951), 53-56.

3637. ———. The Yorktown Lass. 1 act. Plays, 10 (February, 1951), 40-45.

———, adapter see Clemens, S. L. 1886

3638. Gordon, Charles. The Last Party; A Street Ritual. Dramatika, 5 (Spring, 1970), n. p.

3639. ———. Willie Bignigga; A Street Ritual. Dramatika, 5 (Spring, 1970), n. p.

Gordon, Denise, translator see Kroetz, F. X. 4727

3640. Gordon, Homer King. In the Fog. 1 act, comedy. Sunset, 58 (February, 1927), 28-31.

Gordon, Julien, pseud. see Chance, J. G. 1710-1712

3641. Gordon, Ruth, 1896- . The Leading Lady. 3 acts. Theatre Arts, 34 (February, 1950), 57-88.

3642. Gorelik, Mordecai. Paul Thompson Forever. 1 act. Il Dramma, n. s., 187/188 (September 1, 1953), 88-95. Sergio Cenalino, translator. In Italian.

3643. Gorgey, Gabor, 1902- . Afternoon Tea. 1 act. Modern International Drama, 2 (March, 1969), 43-51. Jeno Kovacs and Bertha Gaster, translators.

3644. Gorky, Maxim, 1868-1936. Children of the Sun. 4 acts. L'Avant Scène, 317 (September 1, 1964), 13-44. Georges Daniel, adapter. In French.

3645. ———. Children of the Sun. 4 acts. Poet Lore, 17 (No. 2, 1906), 1-77. Archibald John Wolfe, translator.

3646. ———. Enemies. 3 acts. L'Avant Scène, 475 (July 1, 1971), 7-38. Arthur Adamov, translator. In French.

3647. ———. A Night's Lodging. 4 acts. Poet Lore, 16 (Winter, 1905), 5-64. Edwin Hopkins, translator.

3648. ———. Il pane amaro. 3 acts. Il Dramma, n. s., 12/13 (May 1/15, 1946), 81-96. Odoardo Campa, translator. In Italian.

3649. ———. Les Petits Bourgeois. 4 acts. L'Avant Scène,

206 (October 15, 1959), 8-38. Arthur Adamov, adapter. In French.

3650. ———. The Smug Citizen. 4 acts. Poet Lore, 17 (No. 4, 1906), 1-74. Edwin Hopkins, translator.

3651. ———. Summer-folk; Scenes from Life. 4 acts, comedy. Poet Lore, 16 (No. 3, 1905), 1-90. Aline Delani, translator.

3652. Gorman, Arthur J. The Youth of Don Juan. 1 act. Scholastic, 24 (March 3, 1934), 7-8, 11.

3653. Gorman, Herbert S., 1893- . The Death of Nero. 1 act. Theatre Arts, 8 (March, 1924), 195-204.

3654. Gorostiza, Carlos, d. 1968. Neighbors. 1 act. Drama and Theatre, 9 (Winter, 1970/71), 106-132. Louis L. Curcio, translator.

3655. Gorostiza, Celestino. The Color of Our Skin. 3 acts. Drama and Theatre, 9 (Spring, 1971), 151-168; (Fall, 1971), 46-56. S. Samuel Trifilo and Luis Soto-Ruiz, translators.

3656. Gorsh, Carl. Two Oranges. 1 act. San Francisco Review, 1 (September, 1960), 42-47.

3657. Gotta, Salvatore, 1887- . Alta Montagna. 3 acts. Il Dramma, 279 (April 1, 1938), 4-16. In Italian.

3658. ———. Ombra, la moglie bella. 3 acts. Il Dramma, 134 (March 15, 1932), 4-26. In Italian.

3659. ———. Il primo peccato. 4 acts. Il Dramma, 297 (January 1, 1939), 4-21. In Italian.

3660. ——— and Mario Mortara. Filosofia di Ruth. 1 act. Il Dramma, 204 (February 15, 1935), 31-38. In Italian.

Goudiss, A., translator see Andreyev, L. N. 239

Gough, Margaret, translator see Turgenev, I. 8952

3661. Gouin, Ollivier Mercier, 1928- . Les demi-fous. 1 act. L'Avant Scène, 502 (September 15, 1972), 49-53. In French.

3662. Gould, Elizabeth Lincoln, adapter. Little Men. 2 acts. Ladies' Home Journal, 18 (December, 1900), 3-4, 40-41.

3663. ———, adapter. The "Little Women" Play. 2 acts. Ladies' Home Journal, 18 (January, 1901), 3-4, 36-37.

3664. Gould, Jean, 1919- . Attic Treasure. 1 act. Plays, 11 (February, 1952), 81-84.

3665. _____. New Worlds. 1 act. Plays, 10 (October, 1950), 45-52. AND Plays, 28 (October, 1968), 55-61.

3666. _____. The Seven Little Seeds. 1 act. Plays, 11 (March, 1952), 69-72.

3667. _____. Thanksgiving Is for Everybody. 1 act. Plays, 11 (November, 1951), 49-52.

3668. Gourgue, Jean, 1924- . Big-Ben. 1 act. L'Avant Scène, 462 (December 15, 1970), 7-35. In French.

3669. Gourmont, Remy de, 1858-1915. Histoire Tragique de la Princesse Phenissa; Expliquee en Quatre Episodes. Vers et Prose, 25 (April-June, 1911), 40-50. In French.

3670. _____. Lilith. 1 act. Poet Lore, 51 (Winter, 1945), 298-344. John Heard, translator.

3671. _____. The Old King. 1 act, tragedy. Drama, 22 (May, 1916), 206-231. Richard Aldington, translator.

3672. _____. The Shadow of a Woman. 1 act. Poet Lore, 55 (Spring, 1950), 3-17. Joy Hausmann, translator.

3673. _____. Theodat. 1 act. Drama, 22 (May, 1916), 184-205. Richard Aldington, translator.

3674. _____. Le Vieux Roi. Tragedy. Vers et Prose, 32 (January-March, 1913), 55-67. In French.

Gow, James Ellis, 1907-1952 see D'Usseau, A. 2771

Goyert, Georg, translator see O'Casey, S. 6758

3675. Grafton, Samuel. In His Image. 1 act. One-Act Play Magazine, 3 (March-April, 1940), 249-264.

3676. Graham, Manta S. Adjustment. 1 act. Plays, 4 (April, 1945), 17-29.

3677. _____. Crusade for Liberty. 1 act. Plays, 3 (October, 1943), 38-45.

3678. _____. The Unusual Flower. 1 act. Plays, 2 (March, 1943), 30-36.

3679. Graham, Mary. Idyll. 1 act. Drama, 16 (April, 1926), 255-256.

3680. Graham, Samuel. American Document. 1 act. Theatre Arts, 26 (September, 1942), 566-574.

Graham-Lujan, J., trans. see Lorca, F. G. 5044, 5046

3681. Not used.

3682. Grahame, Kenneth, 1859-1932. The Reluctant Dragon. 1 act. Plays, 22 (March, 1963), 51-60. Adele Thane, adapter.

3683. _____. The Reluctant Dragon. 1 act. Plays, 33 (May, 1974), 74-80. Lewis Mahlmann and David Cadwalader Jones, adapters.

3684. Grainger, Tom. The Action Tonight. 1 act. Prism International, 4 (Winter, 1965), 35-64.

Granata, Mario, translator see Gsell, P. 3772

_____, translator see Provins, M. 7318

3685. Grand Reopening, The. Learning With ..., 3 (November, 1975), 5-7.

3686. Granick, Harry. Witches' Sabbath. 2 acts. First Stage, 1 (Winter, 1961-62), 51-79.

3687. Grant, Robert, 1852-1940. The Lambs, A Tragedy. 1 act. Century, 24 (August, 1882), 537-547.

3688. Granville-Barker, Harley, 1877-1946. Farewell to the Theatre. 1 act. English Review, 29 (November, 1917), 390-410.

3689. Grass, Gunter, 1927- . Der Kuckuck. 1 act. Botteghe Oscure, 21 (Spring, 1958), 413-424. In German.

3690. Grassi, Ernesto, 1900- . Appuntamento in Paradisco. 2 parts. Il Dramma, n.s., 275/276 (August/September, 1959), 53-77. In Italian.

3691. _____. Commissario di notturna. 1 act. Il Dramma, n.s., 202 (April 1, 1954), 46-57. In Italian.

3692. _____. I sonnambali. 3 acts. Il Dramma, n.s., 295 (April, 1961), 8-28. In Italian.

3693. _____. Ventiquattr'ore di un uomo qualunque. 3 acts. Il Dramma, n.s., 225 (June, 1955), 7-30. In Italian.

3694. Grau, Giacinto. Il signor Pigmalione. 3 acts. Il Dramma, 428/429/430 (June 15/July 1/15, 1944), 31-51. In Italian.

Gray, Albert see Richard, H.-C. 7522

Gray, Madeleine see Roussin, A. 7762, 7763

3695. Gray, Marshall, pseud. The Milky Way Conference. 1 act. The Saturday Review of Literature, 30 (August 2, 1947), 18-19.

3696. Gray, Simon, 1936- . Butley. 2 acts. L'Avant Scène, 547 (September 1, 1974), 3-32. Matthieu Galey, adapter. In French.

3697. _____. Butley. 2 acts. Plays and Players, 19 (August, 1972), I-XV.

Grazni, Ivan, adapter see Aristophanes 334

Greco, Adriana, translator see Obaldia, R. de 6717

Gredy, Jean-Pierre, 1920- see Barillet, P. 584, 585, 586, 587, 588, 589, 590, 591, 592, 593, 594

_____, adapter see Shaffer, P. 8165, 8170

_____, adapter see Sheridan, R. B. 8247

_____, adapter see Slade, B. 8310

Green, Adolph see Comden, B. 1962

3697a Green, Carolyn. Janus. 3 acts. Theatre Arts, 41 (October, 1957), 34-58.

3698 Green, Julien, 1900- . Adrienne Mesurat. 3 acts. Il Dramma, n.s., 343/344 (April/May, 1965), 6-25. Lucio Chiavarelli, translator. In Italian.

3699. _____. Sud. 3 acts, comedy. Sipario, 11 (May, 1956), 37-56. Raffaele la Capria, translator. In Italian.

3700. Green, Paul Eliot, 1894- . The End of the Row. 1 act. Poet Lore, 35 (1924), 58-74.

3701. _____. Granny Boling. 1 act. Drama, 11 (August-September, 1921), 389-394.

3702. _____. The Hot Iron. 1 act. Poet Lore, 35 (1924), 48-57.

3703. _____. The Lord's Will. 1 act. Poet Lore, 33 (Autumn, 1922), 366-384.

3704. _____. The No 'Count Boy. 1 act. Scholastic, 22 (February 18, 1933), 7-9, 28, 33-34.

3705. _____. The No 'Count Boy. 1 act. Theatre Arts, 8 (November, 1924), 773-784.

3706. _____. Old Wash Lucas. 1 act. Poet Lore, 35 (1924), 254-270.

3707. _____. The Prayer-Meeting. 1 act. Poet Lore, 35 (1924), 232-253.

3708. _____. Roses for Johnny Johnson. 1 act, comedy. One-Act Play Magazine, 1 (March, 1938), 963-979.

3709. _____. Sam Tucker. 1 act. Poet Lore, 34 (Summer, 1923), 220-246.

3710. _____. Saturday Night. 1 act. Scholastic, 16 (May 10, 1930), 6-8. AND Scholastic, 30 (February 13, 1937), 5-7, 25.

3711. _____. A Saturday Night. 1 act. Senior Scholastic, 45 (January 22, 1945), 13-14, 20.

3712. _____. White Dresses. 1 act. Il Dramma, n.s., 195/196 (December 15, 1953/January 1, 1954), 63-68. Sergio Cenalino, translator. In Italian.

_____ see Wright, R. 9575

_____, translator see Ludwig, O. 5084

3713. Green, Roger Lancelyn, 1918- . Morwynion, A Lyric Play. 1 act. Dublin Magazine, n.s., 23 (April-June, 1948), 4-22.

3714. Greene, Alfreda M. and Flora Dixon. Miss Gloom's Dream. 1 act. Wilson Library Bulletin, 23 (May, 1949), 694, 696.

3715. Greene, Graham, 1904- . The Living Room. 2 acts. Sipario, 12 (June, 1957), 35-52. Giulio Cesare Castello, translator. In Italian.

3715a. _____. The Potting Shed. 3 acts. Theatre Arts, 42 (March, 1958), 24-48.

3716. _____. The Power and the Glory. Sipario, 10 (September, 1955), 37-56. Denis Cannan and Pierre Bost, adapters. Luigi Squarzina, translator. In Italian.

3717. Greene, Lida Lisle. Beyond Thule. 1 act. Plays, 9 (October, 1949), 41-48.

3718. Greenland, Bill. We Three, You and I. 1 act. Prism International, 9 (Summer, 1969), 80-90.

3719. Greenough, James Bradstreet, 1833-1901. The Blackbirds. 3 acts, comedy. Atlantic, 39 (January, 1877), 31-43.

3720. Gregor, Arthur. Continued Departure. 1 act. Accent, 11 (Spring, 1951), 153-160.

3721. Gregory, Lady Augusta, 1859?-1932. The Bogie Man. 1 act, comedy. Forum, 49 (January, 1913), 28-40.

3722. _____. Dervorgilla. 1 act, tragedy. Samhain (November, 1908), 13-27.

3723. _____. Hanrahan's Oath. 1 act, comedy. Little Review, 4 (November, 1917), 6, 33-38.

3724. _____. Hyacinth Halvey. 1 act, comedy. Samhain (December, 1906), 15-35.

3725. _____. McDonough's Wife. 1 act, comedy. Outlook, 99 (December 16, 1911), 920-925.

3726. _____. On the Racecourse. 1 act. Golden Book, 8 (September, 1928), 364-368.

3727. _____. The Rising of the Moon. 1 act, comedy. Samhain (December, 1904), 45-52.

3728. _____. Spreading the News. 1 act, comedy. Golden Book, 2 (September, 1925), 355-362.

3729. _____. Spreading the News. 1 act, comedy. Samhain (November, 1905), 15-28.

3730. _____. The Traveling Man. A Miracle Play. 1 act. Golden Book, 14 (October, 1913), 274-279.

3731. _____. The Traveling Man. 1 act. Scholastic, 25 (December 15, 1934), 9-10, 22.

3732. _____. The Workhouse Ward. 1 act. Golden Book, 9 (June, 1929), 100-103.

_____, translator see Hyde, D. 4350, 4351, 4353, 4355

3733. Gregory, Horace, 1898- . Beyond the Pyramid; Heard in the Protestant Cemetery. 1 act. Quarterly Review of Literature, 11 (No. 2/3, 1961), 155-162.

3734. Grella, Edoardo. L'àncora. 1 act. Il Dramma, 112 (April 15, 1931), 40-46. In Italian.

3735. _____. Luna di miele. 1 act. Il Dramma, 123 (October 1, 1931), 38-44. In Italian.

3736. _____. Presca notturna. 1 act. Il Dramma, 26 (September 15, 1927), 36-45. In Italian.

3737. _____. L'ultimo fiore. 1 act. Il Dramma, 368 (December 15, 1941), 38-42. In Italian.

3738. Gressieker, Hermann. Royal Gambit. 3 acts. Theatre Arts, 43 (July, 1959), 27-50. George White, translator and adapter.

3739. Greth, Roma. Rip's Wrinkle. 1 act. Plays, 27 (May, 1968), 1-12.

3740. _____. Two Masks. 1 act. Plays, 25 (February, 1966), 15-25.

3741. _____. Worms. 1 act. The Scene, 1 (1972), 33-64.

3742. _____. The Would-Be Swingers. 1 act. Plays, 30 (January, 1971), 1-10.

3743. Grieg, Nordahl, 1902-1943. Die Niederlage. Das Wort, 6 (January, 1938), 49-66; (March, 1938), 50-74; 7 (April, 1938), 56-81. In German.

3744. Griffi, Giuseppe Patroni. Il mio cuore e' nel sud. Sipario, 7 (August-September, 1952), 54-57. In Italian.

3745. Griffith, Alice Mary Matlock. Whither. 1 act. Poet Lore, 35 (1924), 140-147.

3746. Griffiths, Trevor. Apricots. 1 act. Gambit, 8 (No. 29, 1976), 37-47.

3747. _____. Sam, Sam. Plays and Players, 19 (April, 1972), 65-79.

Griffiths, Trevor see Brenton, H. 1320

3748. Grillo, John. Hello Goodbye Sebastian. 1 act. Gambit, 4 (No. 16), 11-68.

3749. Grimm, Jacob, 1785-1863 and Wilhelm Grimm, 1786-1859. The Brave Little Tailor. 1 act. Plays, 36 (December, 1976), 50-58. Adele Thane, adapter.

3750. _____. The Dancing Princesses. 1 act. Plays, 12 (May, 1953), 49-54. Caroline H. Corey, adapter.

3751. _____. The Four Accomplished Brothers. 1 act. Plays, 33 (March, 1974), 59-63. Margaret Hall, adapter.

3752. _____. The Frog Prince. 1 act. Plays, 30 (May, 1971),

66-72. Lewis Mahlmann and David Cadwalader Jones, adapters.

3753. _____. The Golden Goose. 1 act. Plays, 29 (April, 1970), 71-82. Ruth Vickery Holmes, adapter.

3754. _____. Snow White and the Seven Dwarfs. 1 act. Plays, 34 (October, 1974), 74-79. Lewis Mahlmann and David Cadwalader Jones, adapters.

3755. _____ The Spindle, the Shuttle, and the Needle. 1 act. Plays, 33 (November, 1973), 75-81. Gladys V. Smith, adapter.

Grimm, Wilhelm, 1786-1859 see Grimm, J. 3749-3755

3756. Grinins, Tekla A. To Test the Truth. 1 act. Plays, 34 (February, 1975), 41-46. AND Plays, 35 (May, 1976), 79-82.

3757. Gripari, Pierre. Lieutenant Tenant. 3 acts, comedy. L'Avant Scène, 277 (December 1, 1962), 9-31. In French.

3758. _____. Le No de Saint Denis. 1 act. L'Avant Scène, 535 (February 15, 1974), 36-43. In French.

3759. Grismondi, Giannino Antona-Traversi. La pelliccia di martora. 1 act. Il Dramma, 160 (April 15, 1933), 39-45. In Italian.

3760. Grissom, Herbert. An Easy Victim. 1 act. Smart Set, 8 (November, 1902), 109-110.

Grol-Prokopczyk, Regina, translator see Gruza, J. and K. T. Toeplitz 3771

3761. Gronowicz, Antoni. The United Animals. Kansas Quarterly, 2 (Winter, 1969/70), 133-151.

3762. Gross, Nathalie F. Indian Brave. 1 act. Plays, 14 (January, 1955), 75-78.

3763. _____. The Mystery Ring. 1 act. Plays, 16 (January, 1957), 77-81.

Gross, Sevilla, translator see Ballesteros, A. M. 536

_____, translator see Mendoza, J. R. de A. y 5747

3764. Grum, Slavko, 1901-1949. Dogodek v mestu Gogi. 2 acts. Sipario, 26 (December, 1971), 73-92. Lino Carpinteri and Frencesco Macedonio, adapters. Sergio Pacor and Liciania Pacor, translators. In Italian.

3765. Grumberg, Jean-Claude, 1939- . Amorphie d'Ottenburg. L'Avant Scène, 485 (December 15, 1971), 7-31. In French.

3766. _____. Demain, Une Fenetre Sur Rue ... 3 acts. L'Avant Scène, 405 (June 15, 1968), 7-29. In French.

3767. _____. Dreyfus. L'Avant Scène, 543 (June 15, 1974), 7-36. In French.

3768. _____. Dreyfus. 1 act. Il Dramma, (February, 1975), 25-53. Liana C. Ferri, translator. In Italian.

3769. _____. Michu. 1 act. L'Avant Scène, 543 (June 15, 1974), 39-41. In French.

3770. _____. Rixe. 1 act. L'Avant Scène, 469/470 (April 1/15, 1971), 87-92. In French.

Grummann, Paul H., translator see Bernstein, E. P. 861

_____, translator see Halbe, M. 3833

Grunwald, Alfred see Engel, A. 2865

3771. Gruza, Jerza, 1932- and Krzysztof T. Toeplitz, 1933- . Aquarium 2. 1 act, farce. Modern International Drama, 7 (Fall, 1973), 33-72. Regina Grol-Prokopczyk, translator.

3772. Gsell, Paul. Gémier a tu per tu con melpomene. 1 act. Il Dramma, 91 (June 1, 1930), 43-46. Mario Granata, translator. In Italian.

Guacci, Angelo see Luizet, J. 5088

3773. Guaita, Giovanni. Incontro fuori del tempo. 4 acts. Sipario, 21 (February, 1966), 54-64. In Italian.

Guarda, Guido, translator see Ghelderode, M. de 3457

_____, translator see Ghéon, H. 3462, 3463

_____, translator see Regnard, J.-F. 7463

3774. Guare, John. The House of Blue Leaves. 3 acts. L'Avant Scène, 509 (January 1, 1973), 7-30. Jacques Sigurd, adapter. In French.

Guarnieri, Gianfrancesco, 1936- see Boal, A. 1029

Guerney, Bernard Guilbert, translator see Averchenko, A. 464

3775. Guerra, Alicia, 1938- . Bebecheri et la Petite Fille Perverse. 1 act. L'Avant Scène, 536 (March 1, 1974), 43-45. In French.

Guerrieri, Gerardo, translator see Miller, A. 5846

_____, translator see Pawley, T. D. 7020

_____, translator see Warren, R. P. 9213

_____, translator see Wilder, T. 9393

_____, translator see Williams, T. 9421, 9435, 9441

Guerriero, Vittorio, translator see Bernard, T. 843, 846, 850

_____, translator see Birabeau, A. 958

_____, translator see DeFlers, R. 2282

_____, translator see Dolley, G. 2524

_____, translator see Duvernois, H. 2783

_____, translator see Fayard, J. 2956

_____, translator see Pujel, R. 7337

_____, translator see Reboux, P. 7454

_____, translator see Renard, J. 7482, 7487

_____, translator see Sarment, J. 7937

_____, translator see Zimmer, B. 9652

Guicciardini, Roberto, 1933- see Palazzeschi, A. 6938

Guidi, Guidarino, translator see Orton, J. 6885

_____, translator see Osborne, J. 6892, 6896

3776. Guidotti, Mario. Violenza no. 3 acts. Il Dramma, 48 (September-October, 1972), 72-83. In Italian.

Guimard, Paul, 1921- see Blondin, A. 1014

3777. Guinan, John. Black Oliver. 1 act. Dublin Magazine, n.s., 2 (July-September, 1927), 32-47.

3778. Guiney, Louise Imogen, 1861-1920. The Martyrs' Idyl. 1 act. Harper's, 98 (December, 1898), 130-141.

3779. Guinness, Bryan. Working the Dolls. 1 act. Dublin Magazine, 7 (Spring, 1968), 65-79.

3780. Guiterman, Arthur, 1871-1943. Christmas Stockings. 1 act. Ladies' Home Journal, 22 (December, 1904), 28.

_____ see Mendel, P. 5746

3781. Guitry, Sacha, 1885-1957. Mio padre aveva ragione. 3 acts. Il Dramma, 106 (January 15, 1931), 4-29. Alex Alexis, translator. In Italian.

3782. _____. Toa. 4 acts, comedy. L'Avant Scène, (OST), 15 (December, 1949), 1-29. In French.

3783. _____. Viaggio in Paradiso. 4 parts. Il Dramma, n.s., 136 (July 1, 1951), 7-27. Connie Ricono, translator. In Italian.

Gulack, Max, translator see Schehade, G. 8024

Gulick, James C., translator see Prelovsky, A. 7277

3784. Gunther, Otto. La signorina bionda. 1 act. Il Dramma, 95 (August 1, 1930), 41-43. Oskar Psichelio, translator. In Italian.

3785. Gurney, A. R., Jr. The Bridal Dinner. 3 acts. First Stage, 4 (Spring, 1965), 33-56.

3786. _____. Children. 2 acts. Plays and Players, 21 (May, June, 1974), 57-65; 61-65.

3787. Guth, Paul. Fugues. 1 act. Il Dramma, n.s., 161 (July 15, 1952), 41-51. Marcel Le Duc, translator. In Italian.

3788. Guthrie, Thomas Anstey, 1856-1934. Dramma in platea. 1 act. Il Dramma, 40 (April 15, 1928), 43-44. In Italian.

3789. _____. The Game of Adverbs. 1 act. Golden Book, 10 (December, 1929), 99-102.

3790. _____. Salted Almonds, or, Playing the Game. 1 act. Golden Book, 14 (November, 1931), 372-375.

3791. Gutierrez, Eduardo and José J. Podesta. Juan Moreira. 2 acts. Poet Lore, 51 (Summer, 1945), 101-116. Willis Knapp Jones and Carlos Escudero, translators.

Gutman, John, translator see Mussorgsky, M. 6422

3792. Gutzkow, Karl, 1811-1878. Uriel Acosta. 5 acts. Poet Lore, 7 (January-June, July, 1895), 6-18; 83-96; 140-149;

198-203; 263-270; 333-349. Richard Hovey and François Stewart Jones, translators.

3793. Guyan, Alexander. The Projectionist. 1 act. Landfall, 18 (March, 1964), 15-24.

3794. Gwynn, Frederick L. Requiem for Five Runs, With One Eye on William Faulkner's Latest Novel and the Other on the World Series. 3 acts. Furioso, 7 (Winter, 1952), 51-58.

Gwynn, S. L., translator see Musset, A. 6420

Gyp, pseud. see Martel de Janville, Sibylle Gabrielle Marie Antoinette de Riquetti de Mirabeau, Comptesse de 5584, 5585

H

3795. Haavikko, Paavo, 1931- . The Superintendent. 15 scenes. Literary Review, 14 (Fall, 1970), 96-113. Philip Binham, translator.

Hackett, Albert, 1900- see Goodrich, F. 3632

3796. Hackett, Walter, 1876-1944. Captain Applejack. 1 act, comedy. Everybody's Magazine, 47 (September, 1922), 130-137.

3797. _____. Facing the Future. 1 act. Plays, 5 (October, 1945), 56-65.

3798. _____. For the Duration. 1 act. Plays, 2 (January, 1943), 57-64.

3799. _____. Gentlemen from Virginia. 1 act. Plays, 4 (March, 1945), 72-75.

3800. _____. Henry Wallace's Experiment. 1 act. Plays, 2 (February, 1943), 1-12.

3801. _____. Incident at Valley Forge. 1 act. Plays, 3 (January, 1944), 4-12.

3802. _____. Luigi Steps Aside. 1 act. Plays, 16 (May, 1957), 12-20.

3803. _____. The Outgoing Tide. 1 act. Plays, 9 (May, 1950), 79-90.

3804. _____. Poor General Prescott. 1 act. Plays, 2 (April, 1943), 70-75.

3805. _____. Rhapsody in Blue; The Story of George Gershwin. 1 act. Plays, 4 (October, 1944), 74-79.

3806. _____. The Story of Samuel Slater. 1 act. Plays, 2 (October, 1942), 72-77.

3807. _____. Vacation: Limited. 1 act. Plays, 3 (February, 1944), 57-66.

3808. _____. Youth Day at the U.N. 1 act. Plays, 9 (May, 1950), 34-42.

3809. _____, adapter. The Glorious Whitewasher. 1 act. Plays, 27 (January, 1968), 55-60.

_____, adapter see Alcott, L. M. 112

_____, adapter see Clemens, S. L. 1883

_____, adapter see Cooper, J. F. 2008

_____, adapter see Dickens, C. 2467, 2482

_____, adapter see France, A. 3243

_____, adapter see Hawthorne, N. 3988

_____, adapter see Irving, W. 4404, 4405

_____, adapter see Maupassant, G. de 5679

_____, adapter see Stevenson, R. L. 8518

_____, adapter see Stockton, F. 8528

_____, adapter see Wilde, O. 9360

3810. Hacks, Peter, 1928- . La Bataille de Lobositz. 2 parts, comedy. L'Avant Scène, 429 (July 1, 1969), 7-33. Jean-Charles Lombard, translator. Jean Cosmos, adapter. In French.

3811. _____. La battaglia di Lobositz. 3 acts. Sipario, 25 (December, 1970), 95-112. Emilio Picco, translator. In Italian.

3812. _____. Der Muller von Sans Souci. Comedy. Sipario, 186 (October, 1961), 63-76. Ettore Giapa. In Italian.

3813. _____. Opening of the Indian Era. Modern International Drama, 4 (Fall, 1970), 7-44. Jacques-Leon Rose, translator.

3814. _____. Das Volksbuch vorn Herzog Ernst. 3 acts. Spectaculum, 8 (1965), 137-180. In German.

3815. Hagedorn, Hermann, 1882- . The Heart of Youth. 1 act. Outlook, 111 (November 24, 1915), 744-756.

3816. _____. The Keeper of the Gate. 1 act. Outlook, 107 (August 29, 1914), 1056-1060.

3817. _____. The Pool of Bethesda. 1 act. Outlook, 108 (December 2, 1914), 782-785.

3818. Haguet, Andre, 1900- . Mon Ami Le Cambrioleur. 2 acts, comedy. L'Avant Scène (OST), 21 (March, 1950), 3-34. In French.

3819. Hagy, Loleta. Fire in a Paper. 1 act. Plays, 3 (January, 1944), 39-42. AND Plays, 24 (May, 1965), 79-82.

3820. _____. The Owl's Answer. 1 act. Plays, 3 (October, 1943), 59-61.

3821. Hailey, Oliver. Hey You, Light Man! 1 act. Players Magazine, 38 (October, 1961), 15-30.

3822. Haim, Victor, 1935- . Abraham et Samuel. L'Avant Scène, 548 (September 15, 1974), 33-46. In French.

3823. _____. Comment Harponner le Requin. L'Avant Scène, 548 (September 15, 1974), 7-29. In French.

3824. _____. Isaac et la Sage-Femme. L'Avant Scène, 600 (December 15, 1976), 3-21. In French.

3825. _____. La Visite. 1 act. L'Avant Scène, 562 (April 15, 1975), 3-19. In French.

3825a. Haines, William H. Command Decision. 3 acts. Theatre Arts, 32 (June-July, 1948), 61-89.

3826. Haire, Wilson John. Within Two Shadows. 2 acts. Plays and Players, 19 (June, 1972), 61-82.

3827. _____. Within Two Shadows. 2 acts. Scripts, 1 (September, 1972), 52-103.

3828. Haitov, Nicolai. The Boat in the Forest. 1 act. Gambit, 3 (No. 12), 15-38. Donna Ireland and Kevin Ireland, translators.

3829. Hakim, Eleanor. Elephant and Flamingo Vaudeville. 1 act. Scripts, 1 (October, 1972), 93-105.

3830. Hakim, Tawfiq Al. The Death of Mohammed. 1 act. New Directions, 15 (1955), 274-283. William R. Polk, translator.

3831. Halàsz, Americo. Un bacio e nulla più! 3 acts. Il Dramma, 247 (December 1, 1936), 2-21. In Italian.

3832. _____. Mi amerai sempre? 3 acts. Il Dramma, 148 (October 15, 1932), 4-34. Ada Salvatore, translator. In Italian.

3833. Halbe, Max, 1865-1944. The Rosenhagens. 3 acts. Poet Lore, 21 (January-February, 1910), 1-87. Paul H. Grummann, translator.

3834. Hale, Edward Everett, 1822-1909. The Man Without a Country. 1 act. Plays, 29 (April, 1970), 41-46. Lewy Olfson, adapter.

3835. _____. The Man Without a Country. 1 act. Scholastic, 38 (February 17, 1941), 17-18, 22. Ann Barley, adapter.

3836. _____. Shot Through the Head; A Musical Drama of 1864 after the Fashion of a French Vaudeville. 4 acts. Harper's, 76 (December, 1887), 159-164.

3837. Hale, John. The Black Swan Winter. 2 acts. Plays and Players, 16 (July, 1969), 35-47, 74-79.

3838. Hale, Louise Closser, 1872-1933. The Other Woman. 1 act. Smart Set, 34 (June, 1911), 107-113.

3839. _____. Paste Cut Paste. 1 act. Smart Set, 36 (January, 1912), 125-132.

3840. Hale, William Gardner, 1849-1928. The Master. 2 acts. Drama, 2 (March, April, 1913), 113-131; 179-193.

3841. _____. Paris and Oenone. 1 act. Contemporary Review, 94 (November, 1908), 1-5.

3842. Halet, Pierre. Votre Silence, Cooper? 1 act. L'Avant Scène, 405 (June 15, 1968), 31-38. In French.

3843. Half a Basket of Peanuts. Chinese Literature, 5 (1973), 21-40.

Hall, Holworthy, pseud. see Porter, H. E. 7251, 7252

3844. Hall, Josef Washington, 1894- . The Joy Lady. 1 act. Drama, 18 (May, 1928), 250-252, 268-269.

3845. Hall, Kay DeBard. The Unquiet Warriors. 1 act. Poet Lore, 53 (Summer, 1947), 110-118.

3846. Hall, Kirk K. The Improvisation. 1 act. Dramatics, 42 (October, 1970), 8-9.

3847. Hall, Margaret C. Ali's Reward. 1 act. Plays, 27 (March, 1968), 71-74.

3848. _____. Doctor Know-It-All. 1 act. Plays, 27 (April, 1968), 65-68.

3849. _____. King Horn. 1 act. Plays, 18 (January, 1959), 60-66.

3850. _____. Reggie the Ghost. 1 act. Plays, 24 (October, 1964), 65-68.

3851. _____. The Tiger Who Wanted a Boy. 1 act. Plays, 16 (March, 1957), 72-76.

3852. _____, adapter. The Cherries of Sir Cleges. 1 act. Plays, 24 (December, 1964), 73-76.

3853. _____, adapter. How the Indian Found His Game. 1 act. Plays, 28 (January, 1969), 76-78.

3854. _____, adapter. Simpleton Peter. 1 act. Plays, 28 (March, 1969), 81-83.

_____, adapter see Grimm, J. and W. Grimm 3751

3855. Hall, Marjory. The Antique Trap. 1 act. Plays, 31 (February, 1972), 15-24.

3856. _____. Molly Meets the General. 1 act. Plays, 30 (February, 1971), 47-54.

3857. _____. The Pilgrim Rebel. 1 act. Plays, 31 (November, 1971), 13-24.

3858. Hall, May Emery. The Flying Horseshoe. 1 act. Plays, 3 (November, 1943), 1-6.

3859. _____. Hearts of Oak. 1 act. Plays, 3 (February, 1944), 38-43.

3860. _____. A New Compass. 1 act. Plays, 4 (April, 1945), 29-36.

3861. _____. The Wishing-Well. 1 act. Plays, 3 (March, 1944), 28-31. AND Plays, 21 (March, 1962), 47-50.

3862. Hall, Mazie. The Language Shop. 1 act. Plays, 3 (March, 1944), 32-36. AND Plays, 24 (January, 1965), 49-54.

3863. _____. The Square Box. 1 act. Plays, 16 (April, 1957), 47-51.

3864. Hall, Nick. Pastiche. 1 act, farce. DeKalb Literary Arts Journal, 3 (No. 1, 1968), 1-29.

3865. Hall, Roger. Desert Men. 1 act. Dramatics, 45 (November, 1973), 5-9.

Hall, Willis, 1929-   see Waterhouse, K. 9216, 9217, 9218

Halleux, Pierre, translator see Lagerkvist, P. 4766

3866. Halliwell, David. Little Malcolm and His Struggle Against the Eunuchs. Plays and Players, 13 (April, 1966), 31-46, 71-73.

3867. _____. Little Malcolm and His Struggle Against the Eunuchs. 3 acts. Sipario, 21 (August-September, 1966), 71-90. Maria Silvia Codecasa, translator. In Italian.

Halls, Aliki, translator see Anagnostaki, L. 192

3868. Halman, Doris F. Ceiling. 1 act. Plays, 2 (February, 1943), 54-64.

3869. _____. We, the Tools. 1 act. Plays, 2 (April, 1943), 59-65.

3870. Halpern, Martin. Mrs. Middleman's Descent. 1 act, comedy. First Stage, 5 (Fall, 1966), 158-171.

3871. _____. Reservations. 1 act, comedy. First Stage, 5 (Winter, 1966-67), 221-237.

3872. Halsey, Forrest, 1878- . The Empty Lamp. 1 act. Smart Set, 34 (May, 1911), 123-130.

Halty, Nuria, translator see Mossi, P. 6267

3873. Halverson, Bruce. Butterfly Buffet. 1 act. Dramatics, 45 (April, 1974), 4-10.

Hamburger, Michael, 1924- , translator see Brecht, B. 1284

_____, translator see Eich, G. 2831, 2832

_____, translator sèe Holderlin, F. 4141

_____, translator see Kokoschka, O. 4683

3874. Hamby, Roy. The Home of Our Government. 1 act. Plays, 2 (March, 1943), 73-78.

3875. _____. The Mayflower Passengers. 1 act. Plays, 2 (November, 1942), 79-82.

3876. _____. Sutter's San Francisco. 1 act. Plays, 3 (October, 1943), 78-84.

Hamilton, Edith, 1867-1963 see Aeschylus 79

3877. Hamilton, George. The Field of Honor. 1 act. Plays, 11 (February, 1952), 21-29.

3878. Hamilton, Patrick, 1904-1962. Gaslight. 3 acts. Il Dramma, n.s., 42/43/44 (August 1/15, September 1, 1947), 85-106. Natalia Danesi, translator. In Italian.

Hamon, Augustin, translator see Shaw, G. B. 8217

3879. Hamon, Franck. La Chasse au Dahut. 3 acts. L'Avant Scène, 540 (May 1, 1974), 7-36. In French.

Hamon, Henriette, translator see Shaw, G. B. 8217

3880. Hamon, Rene, 1944- . Epitelioma. 1 act, monologue. L'Avant Scène, 508 (December 15, 1972), 42-43. In French.

3881. Hampton, Christopher, 1946- . The Philanthropist. Sipario, 27 (June, 1972), 62-80. Maria Silvia Codecasa, translator. In Italian.

3882. Handke, Peter, 1942- . Calling for Help. 1 act. Drama Review, 15 (Fall, 1970), 84-87. Michael Roloff, translator.

3883. _____. Kaspar. Spectaculum, 12 (1969), 115-181. In German.

3884. _____. My Foot My Tutor. 1 act. Drama Review, 15 (Fall, 1970), 62-83. Michael Roloff, translator.

3885. _____. The Ride Across Lake Constance. Scripts, 1 (March, 1972), 30-65. Michael Roloff, translator.

3886. Hankin, St. John, 1869-1909. The Constant Lover. 1 act. Smart Set, 38 (October, 1912), 133-142.

3887. _____. The Constant Lover. 1 act, comedy. Theatre Arts, 3 (April, 1919), 67-77.

3888. _____. A New Wing at Elsinore. 1 act, comedy. Golden Book, 16 (October, 1932), 361-364.

3889. Hanley, William. Mrs. Dolly. 2 acts. Sipario, (January-February, 1968), 85-96. Paola Ojetti, translator. In Italian.

3890. Hanlon, John. Pan Passes Northward. 1 act. Smart Set, 61 (April, 1920), 67-72.

3891. ———. The Seeker of a Secret. 1 act. Smart Set, 63 (November, 1920), 115-116.

3892. Hanna, Helen. Becky, the Half-Witch. 1 act. Plays, 33 (October, 1973), 39-45.

3893. ———. The Miracle of Spring. 1 act. Plays, 23 (March, 1964), 71-76.

3894. Hanna, Tacie May. The House Beautiful. 1 act, comedy. Drama, 15 (February, 1925), 112-114.

3895. ———. Hyacinths. 1 act. Drama, 12 (September, 1922), 338-341.

3896. ———. Upon the Waters. 1 act. Drama, 14 (November, 1923), 58-62, 69.

3897. Hanoteau, Guillaume. La Grande Roue. 3 acts. L'Avant Scène (ROST), 67 (October, 1952), 1-39. In French.

3898. ———. La Tour Eiffel Qui Tué. 1 act. L'Avant Scène, 95, 1-17. In French.

——— see also Clervers, Jean 1897

3899. Hansberry, Lorraine, 1930-1965. A Raisin in the Sun. 3 acts. Sipario, 17 (June, 1962), 17-40. Ettore Capriolo, translator. In Italian.

3900. ———. A Raisin in the Sun. 3 acts. Theatre Arts, 44 (October, 1960), 27-58.

3901. Hanshew, Thomas W., 1857-1914. The Harvest. 1 act. Smart Set, 26 (November, 1908), 118-133.

Hanson, Daniel L., translator see Bjørnson, B. 977

3902. Harber, Beth. The Gentleman from Philadelphia. 1 act. Plays, 10 (January, 1951), 72-78.

Harburg, E. Y., 1898- see Saidy, F. 7852

3903. Harding, John and John Burrows. The Golden Pathway Annual. 2 acts. Plays and Players, 21 (August, September, 1974), 57-66; 51-58.

3904. Hardt, Ernst, 1876-1947. Tristram the Jester. 5 acts. Poet Lore, 43 (Nos. 3, 4, 1937), 229-278; 289-327. John Heard, translator.

3905. Hardy, Connie. Angels We Have Heard on High; A Chancel Play. 1 act. Learning With ..., 2 (November, 1974), 10-12.

3906. Hardy, Thomas, 1840-1928. Far from the Madding Crowd. 1 act. Plays, 32 (March, 1973), 83-96. Adele Thane, adapter.

3907. ———. Tony Kytes, the Arch Deceiver. 1 act. Plays, 22 (February, 1963), 87-94. Paul T. Nolan, adapter.

3908. Hare, David. Fanshen. 2 acts. Plays and Players, 22 (September, 1975), 43-50.

3909. ———. The Great Exhibition. 2 acts. Plays and Players, 19 (May, 1972), 63-81.

3910. ———. How Brophy Made Good. 1 act. Gambit, 17, 83-125.

3911. ———. Slag. 2 acts. Plays and Players, 17 (June, 1970), 61-77.

———— see also Brenton, H. 1319, 1320

Hark, Mildred see McQueen, Mildred Hark 5284-5419

3912. Harkins, Peter J. The Miracle of Paper. 1 act. Plays, 3 (March, 1944), 68-78.

Harmon, A. M., translator see Lucian 5079

Harned, Mary, translator see Bernstein, E. P. 860

————, translator see Dreyer, M. 2601

————, translator see Hauptmann, C. 3968

————, translator see Hauptmann, G. 3970, 3973, 3975

————, translator see Strindberg, A. 8562, 8563, 8570, 8575

————, translator see Sudermann, H. 8602, 8603

Harned, W. H., translator see Sudermann, H. 8602

3913. Harnwell, Anna Jane, 1872- , and Isabelle Meeker. Sojourners. 1 act. Drama, 10 (July-September, 1920), 357-364.

3914. Harper, James Macpherson. The First Cat on Mars. 1 act. Plays, 15 (February, 1956), 47-54.

3915. Harris, Allena. Old Walnut. 1 act. Scholastic, 21 (January 7, 1933), 9-11.

3916. Harris, Andrew B. Tausk. 2 acts. Drama and Theatre, 12 (Spring, 1975), 167-185.

3917. Harris, Claudia Lucas. It's Spring. 1 act. Drama, 11 (April, 1921), 245-250.

3918. _____. Young Mr. Santa Claus. 1 act. Drama, 12 (October-November, 1921), 42-47.

Harris, David, translator see Benn, G. 766

3919. Harris, Edna May, 1900- . Windblown. 1 act. Poet Lore, 38 (1927), 426-434.

3920. Harris, Elmer. Johnny Belinda. 3 acts. Il Dramma, n.s., 145 (November 15, 1951), 7-30. Bruno Arcangeli and Daniele D'Anza, translators. In Italian.

3921. Harris, Frank, 1854-1931. Joan La Romee. 2 acts. Two Worlds, 3 (April, May-June, 1927), 75-86; 145-148.

3922. _____. The King of the Jews. 1 act. English Review, 8 (April, 1911), 8-12.

3923. _____. The King of the Jews. 1 act. Two Worlds, 2 (January, 1927), 137-140.

3924. Harris, Hazel Harper. When a Man Wanders. 1 act. Poet Lore, 40 (1929), 602-609.

3925. Harris, Helen Webb. Frederick Douglass. 3 acts. Negro History Bulletin, 15 (February, March, April, 1952), 97-102; 123-127; 144-150.

3926. Harris, Lillian. Marriage Is so Difficult. 1 act, farce. Poet Lore, 38 (1927), 452-463.

3927. _____. Publicity. 1 act. Poet Lore, 38 (1927), 590-602.

3928. Harris, May. The Open Door. 1 act. Smart Set, 20 (October, 1906), 60-67.

3929. _____. A Poet's Wife. 1 act. Smart Set, 44 (October, 1914), 55-59.

3930. Harris, Neil. Cop and Blow. Scripts, 1 (May, 1972), 72-80.

3931. Harris, Pulaski. Road of Dreams. 1 act. Dramatics, 41 (March, 1970), 6-7, 28-29.

3932. Harris, Richard W. The Spineless Drudge. 1 act. First Stage, 2 (Winter, 1962-63), 42-45.

3933. Harrity, Richard, 1907- . Gone Tomorrow. 1 act. Theatre Arts, 30 (August, 1946), 472-487.

3934. _____. Hope Is a Thing with Feathers. 1 act. Theatre Arts, 29 (September, 1945), 503-514.

3935. Harrold, William. The Moosical Comedy. 3 acts. Dramatika, 7 (1971), 48-58.

3936. Hart, A. and M. Braddel. Nelle migliori famiglie. 3 acts. Il Dramma, 141 (July 1, 1932), 4-38. Ada Salvatore, translator. In Italian.

3937. Hart, Joseph. The Ghost Dance. 2 acts. Drama and Theatre, 11 (Winter, 1972/73), 80-99.

3938. _____. Sonata for Mott Street: Three One Act Plays. Slow Night on Spring Street; Clockwork; Election Night. Drama and Theatre, 11 (Fall, 1972), 41-59.

3939. Hart, Mary T. The Enchanted Chimney. 1 act. Woman's Home Companion, 37 (December, 1910), 46-47.

3940. Hart, Moss, 1904-1961. The Climate of Eden. 2 acts. Theatre Arts, 38 (May, 1954), 34-65.

3941. _____. Light Up the Sky. 3 acts. Theatre Arts, 33 (October, 1949), 57-88.

_____ see Kaufman, G. S. 4561

3942. _____ and George S. Kaufman, 1889-1961. Dream On, Soldier. 1 act. Theatre Arts, 27 (September, 1943), 533-537.

3943. _____. The Man Who Came to Dinner. 3 acts, comedy. Sipario, 3 (August, 1948), 29-52. Ada Salvatore, translator. In Italian.

3944. Hartleben, Otto Erich, 1864-1905. Hanna Jagert. 3 acts. Poet Lore, 24 (Winter, 1913), 369-418. Sarah Elizabeth Holmes, translator.

3945. Hartley, Roland English. All Things Considered. 1 act. Poet Lore, 42 (Autumn, 1934), 165-175.

3946. _____. The Course of True Love. 1 act. Poet Lore, 55 (Summer, 1950), 163-175.

3947. _____. An Hour at Noon. 1 act. Poet Lore, 42 (Autumn, 1934), 176-185.

3948. _____. Portrait of the Artist's Wife. 1 act. Poet Lore, 48 (Summer, 1942), 121-141.

3949. _____. What's Right. 1 act. Poet Lore, 43 (No. 2, (1936), 169-182.

3950. _____ and Caroline Marguerite Power. The Two of Them. 1 act. Golden Book, 21 (April, 1935), 355-358.

3951. Hartog, Jean de, 1914- . Le Ciel de Lit. 3 acts. L'Avant Scène, 477 (August 1, 1971), 7-36. Sidonie Gabrielle Claudine Colette, adapter. In French.

3952. _____. The Fourposter. 3 acts. Il Dramma, n.s., 181 (May 15, 1953), 9-30. Ada Salvatore, translator. In Italian.

3953. _____. Mort d'un Rat. 3 acts. L'Avant Scène (OST), 47 (August, 1951), 1-38. Jean Mercure, translator. In French.

3954. _____. Skipper Next to God. 3 acts. Il Dramma, n.s., 195/196 (December 15, 1953/January 1, 1954), 29-52. Nicoletta Neri, translator. In Italian.

3955. Hartweg, Norman L. The Pit. 1 act. Tulane Drama Review, 9 (Spring, 1965), 231-253.

3956. Hartzell, Gladys. In Those 12 Days. 1 act. Resource, 4 (November, 1962), 7-11.

Harvey, John, translator see Anouilh, J. 257

3957. Harwood, Harold March, 1874-1959. La via delle Indie. 3 acts. Il Dramma, 138 (May 15, 1932), 4-31. Ada Salvatore, translator. In Italian.

3958. Hasenclever, Walter, 1890-1940. The Plague; A Moving-Picture. Smart Set, 70 (January, 1923), 75-84.

3959. Hastings, Bruce Macdonald. Twice One. 1 act. Smart Set, 39 (January, 1913), 129-142.

3960. Hastings, Michael. Don't Destroy Me! 3 acts. Nimbus, 3 (Summer, 1956), 41-62.

Hatem, Huguette, adapter see Betti, U. 888

3961. Hatteras, Owen. Pertinent and Impertinent. 1 act. Smart Set, 41 (October, 1913), 63-67.

3962. Hatvany, Luli. Questa sera o mai. 3 acts. Il Dramma, 116 (June 15, 1931), 4-37. Oreste Biancoli, translator. In Italian.

Hauger, George, translator see Ghelderode, M. de 3458, 3460

3963. Haugh, Gerry Lynn. The Case of the Toy Town Clown. 1 act. Plays, 30 (December, 1970), 69-75.

3964. ———. The Most Unusual Ghost. 1 act. Plays, 28 (October, 1968), 77-81.

3965. ———. The Unhoppy Bunny. 1 act. Plays, 34 (March, 1975), 47-51.

3966. Hauptman, William. Shearwater. 1 act. Performance, 5 (March/April, 1973), 97-105.

3967. Hauptmann, Carl. The Dead Are Singing. 1 act. Texas Review, 1 (April, 1916), 250-256.

3968. ———. Ephraim's Breite. 5 acts. Poet Lore, 12 (No. 4, 1900), 465-536. Mary Harned, translator.

3969. ———. War--A Te Deum. 4 parts. Drama, 24 (November, 1916), 597-653. Amelia Von Ende, translator.

Hauptmann, Elizabeth, adapter see Molière 6113

3970. Hauptmann, Gerhart, 1862-1946. And Pippa Dances; A Mystical Tale of the Glass-Works. 4 acts. Poet Lore, 18 (No. 3, 1907), 289-341. Mary Harned, translator.

3971. ———. The Assumption of Hannele, A Dream Poem. 2 acts. Poet Lore, 20 (May-June, 1909), 161-191. G. S. Bryan, translator.

3972. ———. Before Dawn, A Social Drama. 5 acts. Poet Lore, 20 (July-August, 1909), 241-315. Leonard Bloomfield, translator.

3973. ———. Elga. 1 act. Poet Lore, 17 (No. 1, 1906), 1-35. Mary Harned, translator.

3974. ———. The Reconciliation. 3 acts. Poet Lore, 21 (September-October, 1910), 337-390. Roy Temple House, translator.

3975. ———. The Sunken Bell. 5 acts. Poet Lore, 10 (No. 2, 1898), 161-234. Mary Harned, translator.

Hausmann, Joy, translator see Gourmont, R. de 3672

3976. Havas, Nelly. Budapest 1930. 1 act. Il Dramma, 92 (June 15, 1930), 43-44. Taulero Zulberti, translator. In Italian.

3977. ———. I conti dell'attrice. 1 act. Il Dramma, 75 (October 1, 1929), 40-41. Taulero Zulberti, translator. In Italian.

3978. ———. Donne intelligenti. 1 act. Il Dramma, 77 (November 1, 1929), 40-42. Taulero Zulberti, translator. In Italian.

3979. ———. La preda. 1 act. Il Dramma, 90 (May 15, 1930), 39-44. Taulero Zulberti, translator. In Italian.

3980. Havel, Václav, 1936- . Das Gartenfest. 4 parts. Spectaculum, 12 (1969), 257-290. August Scholtis, translator. In German.

3981. ———. Le Rapporot Dont Vous Etes l'Object. L'Avant Scène, 486 (January 1, 1972), 7-33. Milan Kepel, adapter. In French.

3982. ———. Vyrozumeni. 1 act. Sipario, 21 (December, 1966), 59-78. Gianlorenzo Pacini, translator. In Italian.

3983. ———. Zahradni Slavnost. 4 acts. Sipario, 270 (October, 1968), 48-60. Gianlorenzo Pacini, translator. In Italian.

3984. ———. Ztizena Moznost Soustredeni. 2 acts. Sipario, 25 (April, 1970), 55-68. Gianlorenzo Pacini, translator. In Italian.

3985. "Haven't Got a Fitten' Book to Read". 1 act. Wilson Library Bulletin, 29 (October, 1954), 177.

3986. Hawkridge, Winifred. The Price of Orchids, A Sentimental Comedy. 1 act. Smart Set, 47 (October, 1915), 103-119.

3987. Hawthorne, Nathaniel, 1804-1864. Feathertop. 1 act. Plays, 28 (March, 1969), 87-96. Adele Thane, adapter.

3988. ———. The Great Stone Face. 1 act. Plays, 25 (November, 1965), 85-94. Walter Hackett, adapter.

3989. ———. The House of the Seven Gables. 1 act. Plays, 14 (March, 1955), 87-95. Lewy Olfson, adapter.

3990. ———. The House of the Seven Gables. 1 act. Plays, 33 (February, 1974), 84-96. Adele Thane, adapter.

3991. Hay, Julius, 1900- . Tanjka macht die Augen Auf. 3 acts, comedy. Das Wort, 5 (November, 1937), 59-107. In German.

Hayashi, Tsugako, translator see Zeami 9638

Hayes, H. R., translator see Brecht, B. 1297, 1304

3992. Hayes, John J. The Moment After. A Thought. 1 act. Dublin Magazine, 3 (August, 1925), 26-31.

3993. Hayes, Joseph. Calculated Risk. 3 acts. Theatre Arts, 47 (December, 1963), 20-54.

3994. Haymon, David, 1927- . Sounding Brass. 1 act, comedy. One-Act Play Magazine, 4 (September-October, 1941), 349-380.

3995. Hazam, Lou. Partners in Velvet. 1 act. Senior Scholastic, 58 (March 21, 1951), 12-13, 28, 30.

3996. Hazeltine, Alice Isabel. Madelon, a Little Shepherdess at Bethlehem. 1 act. Horn Book, 21 (November, 1945), 482-490.

3997. Head, Cloyd. Grotesques, a Decoration in Black and White. 1 act. Poetry, 9 (October, 1916), 1-30.

3998. _____ and Mary Gavin. The Curtains. 1 act. Poetry, 16 (April, 1920), 1-11.

3999. Head, Faye E. Fable Frolic. 1 act. Plays, 33 (May, 1974), 63-68.

4000. _____. A Spouse for Susie Mouse. 1 act. Plays, 29 (April, 1970), 61-64.

4001. _____, adapter. The Second Shepherd's Play. 1 act. Plays, 30 (December, 1970), 37-42.

4002. Head, Robert. Sancticity. 1 act. Tulane Drama Review, 8 (Winter, 1963), 187-203.

4003. Heal, Edith, 1903- . Into the Everywhere, A Play for the Mind's Eye. 1 act. Poet Lore, 38 (1927), 466-472.

4004. Healey, Joseph P. The Drama of the Future. 1 act. Smart Set, 7 (August, 1902), 147-148.

4005. Healy, Cahir. Self-Respect. 1 act. Catholic World, 128 (October, 1928), 43-51.

4006. Heard, John, adapter. "Whom God Hath Joined." 1 act. Poet Lore, 44 (No. 3, 1938), 232-239.

_____, translator see Claudel, P. 1862, 1863, 1864

_____, translator see Gourmont, R. de 3670

_____, translator see Hardt, E. 3904

_____, translator see Hofmannsthal, H. von 4130

_____, translator see Hrotsvitha 4261, 4263

_____, translator see Maupassant, G. de 5682

_____, translator see Yushkevich, S. 9627

4007. Hearn, Lafcadio, 1850-1904. The Great Wave. 1 act. Plays, 34 (April, 1975), 81-83. Jan Acord, adapter.

4008. Heaster, Dale. How to Trap a Husband. 1 act, comedy. Plays, 32 (March, 1973), 11-20.

4009. Heath, Anna Lenington. The Gypsy Look. 1 act. Plays, 12 (January, 1953), 33-39.

4010. _____. Much Ado About Ants. 1 act. Plays, 24 (December, 1964), 61-66.

4011. _____. Rhetoric and Rhymes. 1 act. Plays, 4 (November, 1944), 21-28.

4012. Heath, James. Home Sports. 1 act. Industrial Arts and Vocational Education, 30 (May, 1941), 199-200.

4013. Hebbel, Christian Friedrich, 1813-1863. Agnes Bernauer. 5 acts. L'Avant Scène, 364 (September 15, 1966), 9-31. Pierre Sabatier, translator.

4014. _____. Agnese Bernauer. 2 acts. Il Dramma, 419/420 (February 1/15, 1944), 31-45. In Italian.

4015. _____. Agnes Bernauer. 5 acts. Poet Lore, 20 (January-February, 1909), 1-60. Loueen Pattee, translator.

4016. _____. Herod and Marianne. 5 acts, tragedy. Drama, 6 (May, 1912), 20-168. Edith J. R. Isaacs and Kurt Rahlson, translators.

4017. _____. Maria Maddalena. 3 acts. Il Dramma, 395 (February 1, 1943), 5-22. Rafaello Melani, translator. In Italian.

4018. Hecht, Ben, 1894-1964. Blue Sunday. 1 act. Double Dealer, 1 (May, 1921), 190-192.

___ see Bodenheim, M. 1041

4019. ___ and Charles MacArthur, 1895-1956. Front Page. 2 acts, comedy. L'Avant Scène, 262 (April 1, 1962), 7-42. Jacques Boylaran, translator. In French.

4020. ___. Fun to Be Free, A Pageant. 1 act. Plays, 2 (March, 1943), 59-67.

4021. Hed. Kill Viet Cong. 1 act. Tulane Drama Review, 10 (Summer, 1966), 153.

4022. Hedberg, Tor Harold, 1862-1931. Borga Gard. 4 acts. Poet Lore, 32 (No. 4, 1921), 317-374. Helga Colquist, translator.

4023. ___. Johan Ulfstjerna. 5 acts. Poet Lore, 32 (No. 1, 1921), 1-63. Helga Colquist, translator.

4024. Hedges, Bertha. The Dead Saint. 1 act. Drama, 12 (June-August, 1922), 305-309.

4025. Heggen, Thomas, 1919- and Joshua Logan, 1908- . Mister Roberts. 2 acts, comedy. Theatre Arts, 34 (March, 1950), 57-104.

4026. Heiberg, Gunner Edward Rode, 1857-1929. Balcony. 3 acts. Poet Lore, 33 (Autumn, 1922), 475-496. Edwin Johan Vicknes and Glenn Hughes, translators.

4027. ___. Tragedia d'amore. 4 acts. Il Dramma, 421-427 (March 1-June 1, 1944), 61-77. Irina Lonska and Odoardo Campa, translators. In Italian.

4028. Heijermans, Herman, 1864-1924. Ahasverus. 1 act. Drama, 19 (February, 1929), 145-147. Caroline Heijermans-Houwink and J. J. Houwink, translators.

4029. ___. Good Hope, A Drama of the Sea. 4 acts. Drama, 8 (November, 1912), 17-104. Harriet Gampert Higgins, translator.

4030. ___. The Good Hope. 4 acts. Il Dramma, n. s., 15 (June, 1946), 9-29. Adelchi Moltedo, translator. In Italian.

4031. ___. Jubilee. 1 act. Drama, 13 (July, 1923), 325-331. Lilian Saunders and Caroline Heijermans-Houwink, translators.

4032. ___. Links. 4 acts. Poet Lore, 38 (1927), 1-76. Howard Peacey and W. R. Brandt, translators.

4033. _____. Saltimbank. 1 act. Drama, 13 (August-September, 1923), 363-367. Lilian Saunders and Caroline Heijermans-Houwink, translators.

4034. Heine, Heinrich, 1797-1856. The Flying Dutchman. 1 act. Plays, 29 (October, 1969), 85-95. Lewy Olfson, adapter.

4035. Heinegg, Peter. Dante Ammazzato. 3 acts, fantasy. Trace, 58 (No. 3, 1965), 269-275.

4036. Heinzen, Barbara Brem. Double-Ditto Dream Date. 1 act. Plays, 34 (October, 1974), 53-58.

4037. _____. Miss Cast. 1 act. Plays, 28 (January, 1969), 23-32.

4038. _____. Scholarship Shenanigans. 1 act. Plays, 33 (May, 1974), 45-52.

4039. _____. Teen Tycoon. 1 act. Plays, 29 (March, 1970), 1-9.

4040. Helias, Pierre. L'Autre. 1 act. L'Avant Scène, 106, 34-38. In French.

4041. _____. Les Fous de la Mer. 1 act. L'Avant Scène, 338 (July 15, 1965), 35-42. In French.

4042. Hellem, Charles, W. Valcros and Pol D'Estor. Sabotage. 1 act. Smart Set, 41 (November, 1913), 135-141. André Tridon, translator.

Heller, Mary M. see Stump, A. L. 8586

Heller, Otto, translator see Wildenbruch, E. von 9387

4043. Hellman, Lillian, 1905- . Another Part of the Forest. 3 acts. Sipario, 3 (March, 1948), 29-56. Ada Salvatore, translator. In Italian.

4044. _____. The Autumn Garden. 3 acts. Theatre Arts, 35 (September, October, November, 1951), 62-71; 62-73; 56-64.

4045. _____. The Children's Hour. 3 acts. Sipario, 5 (September, 1950), 43-66. Giulio Cesare Castello, translator. In Italian.

4046. _____. The Children's Hour. 3 acts. Theatre Arts, 37 (May, 1953), 34-63.

4047. _____. The Little Foxes. 3 acts. Il Dramma, n. s., 73 (November 15, 1948), 9-35. Ada Salvatore, translator. In Italian.

4048. _____. The Searching Wind. 2 parts. Sipario, 3 (September, 1948), 37-60. Giulio Cesare Castello, translator. In Italian.

4049. _____. Toys in the Attic. 3 acts. Theatre Arts, 45 (October, 1961), 25-56.

_____, adapter see Anouilh, J. 266

4050. Heltai, Eugenio. Le ragazze Tunderlak. 3 acts. Il Dramma, 210 (May 15, 1935), 4-36. Ada Salvatore, translator. In Italian.

4051. Heltai, Jenoe. Beneficenza. 1 act. Il Dramma, 88 (April 15, 1930), 43-45. Corrado Rossi, translator. In Italian.

4052. _____. Ricordi. 1 act. Il Dramma, 44 (June 15, 1928), 40-41. Taulero Zulberti, translator. In Italian.

4053. Henderson, Bonnie Jo. There's Some Milk in the Icebox. 1 act. Mademoiselle, 62 (November, 1965), 176-177, 228-229, 235, 237.

4054. Henderson, John, 1915- , adapter. Three Against Death. 1 act. Plays, 19 (April, 1960), 1-11.

4055. Henderson, Keith and Geoffrey Whitworth. The Qualm. 1 act. The Open Window, 5 (February, 1911), 265-294.

4056. Hendry, Thomas. That Boy, Call Him Back. 1 act. Performing Arts in Canada, 9 (Winter, 1972), 44-47.

Henley, William Ernest, 1849-1903 see Stevenson, R. L. 8521, 8522

4057. Hennefeld, Edmund B. The Cave. 3 acts. First Stage, 4 (Summer, 1965), 108-136.

4058. Hennique, Leon, 1851- . The Death of the Duc D'Enghien. 1 act. Poet Lore, 20 (November-December, 1909), 401-431. F. Cridland Evans, translator.

Henry, Alice, translator see D'Annunzio, G. 2181

4059. Herbert, Alan Patrick, 1890- . The Book of Jonah as Almost Any Modern Irishman Would Have Written It. 1 act, farce. London Mercury, 3 (April, 1921), 601-605.

4060. _____. Two Gentlemen of Soho. 1 act. Atlantic, 139 (May, 1927), 577-592.

4061. _____. Two Gentlemen of Soho. 1 act. London Mercury, 16 (September, 1927), 490-503.

4062. Herbert, Frederick Hugh, 1897-1958. For Love or Money. 3 acts. Il Dramma, n. s., 180 (May 1, 1953), 4-36. Ada Salvatore, translator.

4063. _____. The Moon Is Blue. 3 acts, comedy. Il Dramma, n. s., 209 (July 15, 1954), 5-34. Laura Del Bono, translator. In Italian.

4064. _____. The Moon is Blue. 3 acts, comedy. Theatre Arts, 36 (January, 1952), 50-74.

4065. Herbert, John. Omphale and the Hero. 3 acts. Canadian Theatre Review, 3 (Summer, 1974), 46-116.

4066. Herczeg, Ferenc. Giulia Szendrey. 3 acts. Il Dramma, 213 (July 1, 1935), 5-29. Ignazio Balla and Cesare Vico Lodovici, translators. In Italian.

4067. _____. Il segreto di famiglia. 1 act. Il Dramma, 23 (August 1, 1927), 43-45. Taulero Zulberti, translator. In Italian.

4068. _____. Trovar marito. 3 acts. Il Dramma, 436/437/438 (October 15/November 1/15, 1944), 9-32. Mario De Vellis, translator. In Italian.

4069. _____. La volpe azzurra. 3 acts. Il Dramma, 114 (May 15, 1931), 4-30. In Italian.

4070. Herford, Beatrice. The Bride's Christmas Tree. 1 act. Ladies' Home Journal, 28 (December, 1911), 14, 64.

4071. Herford, Oliver, 1863-1935. Fox and Geese. 1 act. St. Nicholas, 26 (December, 1898), 136-139.

4072. _____. A Modern Dialogue. 1 act. Smart Set, 7 (August, 1902), 53-54.

4073. _____. Sir Rat. 1 act. St. Nicholas, 17 (November, 1889), 65-67.

4074. _____. A Three-Sided Question, A Woodland Comedy. 1 act. St. Nicholas, 24 (June, 1897), 637-638.

Herman, Bernice, translator see Jirasek, A. 4469

4075. Herman, George, 1925- . The Hat Rack. 1 act. First Stage, 1 (Fall, 1962), 50-52.

4076. Herman, Stephen J. Four Variations on a Scene. 1 act. Dramatics, 43 (October, 1971), 5-8.

4077. Herndon, Venable. Bag of Flies. 1 act. Chelsea, 15 (June, 1964), 20-37.

4078. Heroes of Democracy. 1 act. Negro History Bulletin, 4 (March, 1941), 129-130, 134-135, 139-140.

4079. Herondas. Mime I (The Matchmaker). Arion, 2 (Winter, 1963), 58-61. Richard Braun, translator.

4080. Herr, Louis Albert. A Mechanical-Drawing Broadcast. 1 act. Industrial Education Magazine, 40 (March, 1938), 77-80.

4081. Herring, Robert, 1868-1938. Life and Deaths of St. George of Lydda. Life and Letters, 47 (December, 1945), 182-196.

Herry, Ginette, translator see Svevo, I. 8641

4082. Herschberger, Ruth. A Dream Play. 1 act. Botteghe Oscure, 19 (Spring, 1957), 250-269.

4083. Hershey, Mary B. The Third Lamb. 1 act. Resource, 12 (November, 1970), 9-11, 32.

4084. Hervey, Michael, 1920- . Virtue Is Her Own Reward. 2 acts. Plays, 25 (April, 1966), 27-35.

4085. Hervieu, Paul, 1857-1915. Enchained. 3 acts. Dramatist, 1 (April, 1910), 58-89. Ysidor Asckenasy, translator.

4086. _____. In Chains. 3 acts. Poet Lore, 20 (March-April, 1909), 81-112. Ysidor Asckenasy, translator.

Hervilliez, Gabriel d' see Roland, C. 7658

Herzberger, David, translator see Arrabal, F. 379

4087. Heshmati, Leota B. Abdul and the Caliph's Treasure. 1 act. Plays, 31 (November, 1971), 63-65.

4088. _____. The Old Man Minds His Wife. 1 act. Plays, 31 (October, 1971), 63-66.

4089. _____. Secret of the Roman Stairs. 3 acts. Plays, 25 (April, 1966), 37-42.

Hewitt, James, translator see Arrabal 374

4090. Hewlett, Maurice Henry, 1861-1923. A Masque of Dead Florentines. 2 parts. Bibelot, 10 (1904), 5-41.

4091. Heym, Stefan. Gestern--Hente--Morgen. 1 act. Das Wort, 3 (March, 1937), 35-45. In German.

Heyward, Dorothy see Heyward, DuBose 4091a

4091a. Heyward, DuBose and Dorothy Heyward. Porgy. 4 acts. Theatre Arts, 39 (October, 1955), 35-64.

4092. Hibbard, George Abiah, 1858- . The Marvels of Science. 1 act. Scribner's, 29 (April, 1901), 476-482.

4093. _____. A Matter of Opinion. 1 act, comedy. Scribner's, 28 (August, 1900), 233-245.

4094. Hicks, Wilson. Before the Dawn. 1 act, melodrama. Smart Set, 61 (February, 1920), 71-75.

4095. _____. Trickery. 1 act. Smart Set, 66 (September, 1921), 79-85.

4096. Higgins, Colin. Harold and Maude. 2 acts. L'Avant Scène 537 (March 15, 1974), 7-31. Jean-Claude Carriere, adapter. In French.

4097. Higgins, Dick, 1938- . Twenty-One Episodes for the Aquarian Theater. Chelsea, 11 (March, 1962), 128-139.

4098. Higgins, Frederick Robert, 1896-1941. A Deuce O'Jacks. 1 act. Dublin Magazine, n.s., 11 (April-June, 1936), 24-47.

Higgins, Harriet Gampert, translator see Heijermans, H. 4029

4099. Higgins, Helen Boyd. Making Room for the Little King. 1 act. Plays, 5 (December, 1945), 29-33.

Highet, Gilbert, 1906- , translator see Menander 5742

4100. Higley, Philo. First Freedom. 1 act. One-Act Play Magazine, 3 (February, 1940), 159-171.

4101. Higuera, Pablo de la, 1932- . Le Miroir. 1 act. L'Avant Scène, 498 (July 1, 1972), 29-35. In French.

4102. _____. Les Trois Musiciens, Fantaisie Interlude, d'Après le Tableau de Pablo Picasso. 1 act. L'Avant Scène, 341 (September 15, 1965), 27-33. In French.

4103. Hijo que Nego a su Padre. 1 act. PMLA, 25 (No. 2, 1910), 268-273. In Spanish.

4104. Hildesheimer, Wolfgang, 1916- . Mary Stuart. Scripts, 1 (January, 1972), 31-95. Christopher Holme, translator.

4105. _____. The Sacrifice of Helen. 1 act. Modern Drama, 2 (September, 1968), 7-29. Jacques Leon Rose, translator.

4106. _____. Die Verspätung. 2 acts. Spectaculum, 6 (1963), 125-172. In German.

4107. Hill, Kay, 1917- . Midnight Burial. 1 act. Plays, 16 (April, 1957), 53-55.

Hill, Lucienne, translator see Anouilh, J. 259, 280

Hill, Rochelle, adapter see Dodgson, D. L. 2515

4108. Hiller, Kurt. Der Sinn des Lebens und die Reichstagswahl. 1 act. Der Sturm, 2 (January, 1912), 740-741. In German.

4109. Hillyer, Robert Silliman, 1895- . The Masquerade. 1 act. One-Act Play Magazine, 4 (March-April, 1941), 123-136.

4110. Hilton, Charles. Broken Pines. 1 act. Poet Lore, 40 (1929), 461-473. AND Poet Lore, 42 (Winter, 1935), 276-288.

4111. Hine, Daryl, 1936- . The Death of Seneca. 1 act. Chicago Review, 22 (Autumn, 1970), 5-87.

Hinks, K. W., adapter see Wangenheim, A. 9203

Hirsch, Robin, translator see Hochwalder, F. 4123

4112. Hirshberg, Bernard. Brave Admiral. 1 act. Plays, 4 (October, 1944), 27-31.

4113. _____. Peter Tomorrow. 1 act. Plays, 4 (March, 1945), 54-55.

4114. Hitchcock, George. The Busy Martyr. 3 acts. First Stage, 2 (Winter, 1962-63), 46-68.

4115. _____. The Housewarming. 1 act. Mainstream, 11 (July, 1958), 27-41.

4116. _____. Prometheus Found. 2 acts. Mainstream, 12 (November, 1959), 32-59.

4117. _____. Prometheus Found. 2 acts. San Francisco Review, 1 (Winter, 1958), 39-59.

4118. _____. The Ticket. 1 act. Chelsea, 8 (October, 1960), 118-150.

4119. _____. Upward, Upward. 3 acts, comedy. First Stage, 3 (Summer-Fall, 1964), 142-166.

Hobart, Michel, translator see O'Casey, S. 6753

4120. Hochwalder, Fritz, 1911- . L'Accusateur Public. 3 acts. L'Avant Scène, 331 (April 1, 1965), 11-36. Richard Thieberger, translator. In French.

4121. _____. Ester. 5 acts. Sipario, 17 (April, 1962), 45-62. Italo Alighiero Chiusano. In Italian.

4122. _____. Hotel du Commerce. 5 parts. Il Dramma, n.s., 232 (January, 1956), 15-40. Italo Alighiero Chiusano, translator. In Italian.

4123. _____. The Order. 3 acts. Modern International Drama, 3 (March, 1970), 7-37. Robin Hirsch, translator.

4124. _____. Sacro esperimento. 2 parts. Sipario, 10 (May, 1955), 31-49. In Italian.

Hock, Katarina, translator see Genet, J. 3438

4125. Hodkinson, Ken. How Long. 1 act. Prism International, 2 (Spring, 1961), 48-71.

Hoff, Frank, translator see Motoyazu, K. Z. 6274

4126. Hoffman, Charles H. Ring on Her Finger. 1 act, comedy. The American Magazine, 125 (June, 1938), 24-25, 123-127.

4127. Hoffman, Phoebe. Martha's Mourning. 1 act. Drama, 29 (February, 1918), 111-121.

4128. Hofmann, Gert. Our Man in Madras. 1 act. Evergreen Review, 13 (February, 1969), 55-61.

4129. Hofmannsthal, Hugo von, 1874-1929. Death and the Fool. 1 act. Poet Lore, 24 (Vacation, 1913), 253-267. Elizabeth Walter, translator.

4130. _____. Death and the Fool. 1 act. Poet Lore, 45 (No. 1, 1939), 5-21. John Heard, translator.

4131. _____. Elektra. 1 act. Vers et Prose, 12 (December, January-February, 1908), 62-81; 15 (September-November, 1908), 91-104; 17 (April-June, 1909), 86-95; 18 (July-September, 1909), 73-88. Paul Strozzi and Stephane Epstein, translators. In French.

4132. _____. Fear, A Dialogue. 1 act. Poet Lore, 60 (Autumn, 1965), 244-250. Mariana Scott, translator.

4133. _____. Idyll. 1 act. Drama, 26 (May, 1917), 169-175. Charles Wharton Stork, translator.

4134. _____. Idyll. 1 act. Poet Lore, 52 (Autumn, 1946), 141-148. Mariana Scott, translator.

4135. _____. Prologue. 1 act. Living Age, 322 (July 5, 1924), 33-37.

4136. _____. Prologue to Brecht's Baal. 1 act. Tulane Drama Review, 6 (September, 1961), 111-120. Alfred Schwarz, translator.

4137. _____. Der Unbestechliche. 5 acts. Il Dramma, n.s., 220 (January, 1955), 7-28. Italo Alighiero Chiusano, translator. In Italian.

4138. _____. The White Fan, An Intermezzo. 1 act. Poet Lore, 54 (Summer, 1948), 120-138. Mariana Scott, translator.

Hohenemser, Rolf, translator see Izumo, T. 4415

Holbrook, Mary Sibyl, translator see Lavedan, H. 4838, 4841

4139. Holck, Timothy M. The Prodigal Son: A Modern Version. 3 acts. Learning With ..., 1 (February, 1973), 5-8.

4140. Holdas, A. He Lives. 1 act. Poet Lore, 52 (Summer, 1946), 117-126. Moshe Spiegel, translator.

4141. Holderlin, Friedrich, 1770-1843. The Death of Empedicles (Uncompleted Play). Quarterly Review of Literature, 13 (No. 1/2, 1964), 97-121. Michael Hamburger, translator.

Hollander, Lee M., 1880- , translator see Bjørnson, B. 978

_____, translator see Drachmann, H. H. H. 2584

_____, translator see Einarsson, I. 2834

_____, translator see Scholz, W. von 8081, 8082

4142. Holler, Rose M. Brave Little Indian Brave. 1 act. Plays, 11 (April, 1952), 36-46.

4143. Hollingsworth, Leslie. America the Beautiful. 1 act. Plays, 4 (October, 1944), 80-86.

4144. _____. Lincoln: Hero Unlimited. 1 act. Plays, 4 (January, 1945), 80-85.

4145. _____. Mark Twain. 1 act. Plays, 4 (November, 1944), 72-76.

4146. _____. A Modern Cinderella. 1 act. Plays, 15 (February, 1956), 21-30.

4147. _____. On the Air. 1 act. Plays, 4 (December, 1944), 79-84.

4148. _____. Silent Night. 1 act. One-Act Play Magazine, 4 (November-December, 1941), 461-468.

4149. _____. Silent Night. 1 act. Plays, 27 (December, 1967), 91-96.

Holme, Christopher, translator see Hildesheimer, W. 4104

4150. Holmes, Ruth Vickery. The Cats and the Monkey. 1 act. Plays, 2 (October, 1942), 44-46.

_____, adapter see Grimm, J. and W. Grimm 3753

Holmes, Sarah Elizabeth, translator see Hartleben, O. E. 3944

4151. Holt, Will. The First. 1 act. L'Avant Scène, 466 (February 15, 1971), 33-41. Dominique Minot, adapter. In French.

4152. Home, William Douglas, 1912- . Now Barabbas. 2 parts. Il Dramma, n.s., 66 (August 1, 1948). Gigi Cane, translator. In Italian.

4152a. _____. The Reluctant Debutante. 2 acts. Theatre Arts, 41 (May, 1957), 34-63.

4153. _____. The Secretary Bird. comedy. L'Avant Scène, 480 (October 1, 1971), 7-39. Marc-Gilbert Sauvajon, adapter. In French.

4154. _____. Yes, M'Lord. 3 acts, comedy. Theatre Arts, 34 (April, 1950), 57-88.

4155. Homer. The Iliad. 1 act. Plays, 19 (April, 1960), 88-96. Lewy Olfson, adapter.

4156. _____. The Odyssey. 1 act. Plays, 20 (October, 1960), 83-93. Lewy Olfson, adapter.

4157. Hong, Mrs. Howard V. A Festival of Responses. 1 act. Resource, 7 (November, 1965), 20-24.

4158. Honig, Edwin, 1919- . Orpheus Below. 4 acts. New Directions, 24 (1972), 74-97.

4159. _____. The Widow. 1 act. Western Review, 16 (Summer, 1952), 309-319.

_____, translator see Garcia Lorca, F. 3378, 3379, 3380, 3381

4160. Hood, Charles Newton. While You Wait. 1 act. Smart Set, 1 (June, 1900), 100-106.

4161. Hope, Anthony, 1863-1933. The Prisoner of Zenda. 1 act. Plays, 22 (October, 1962), 85-95. Lewy Olfson, adapter.

4162. Hopkins, Arthur, 1878-1950. Moonshine. 1 act. Golden Book, 10 (November, 1929), 102-105.

4163. _____. Moonshine. 1 act. Theatre Arts, 3 (January, 1919), 51-62.

Hopkins, Edwin, translator see Gorky, M. 3647, 3650

4164. Hopkins, John. Find Your Way Home. 2 acts. Plays and Players, 17 (July, 1970), 57-76.

4165. _____. This Story of Yours. 3 acts. Plays and Players, 16 (February, 1969), 31-46, 56-69.

4166. Hoppenstedt, Elbert M., 1917- . Poet's Nightmare. 1 act. Plays, 9 (January, 1950), 37-44. AND Plays, 30 (January, 1971), 41-48.

4167. _____. Shoe Fly Pudding. 1 act. Plays, 31 (January, 1972), 13-23.

4168. _____. The Two Faces of Liberty. 1 act. Plays, 35 (November, 1975), 67-75.

4169. _____. Which Witch Is Which? 1 act. Plays, 33 (October, 1973), 53-59.

_____ see also Waite, H. E. 9186, 9187, 9188

4170. Horgan, Paul, 1903- . A Tree on the Plains. 3 parts. Southwest Review, 28 (Summer, 1943), 345-376.

4171. Horne, Richard Hengist, 1803-1884. The Death of Marlowe. 1 act, tragedy. Bibelot, 3 (1897), 367-398.

Horner, Lucie T., translator see Ghelderode, M. de 3461

4172. Horovitz, Israel. Acrobats. 1 act. L'Avant Scène, 529 (November 15, 1973), 31-35. Jean-Paul Delamotte, adapter. In French.

4173. _____. Acrobats. 1 act. Show, 1 (May, 1970), 61-68.

4174. _____. Line. 1 act. L'Avant Scène, 529 (November 15, 1973), 7-28. Claude Roy, adapter. In French.

4175. Horvath, Odon von, 1901- . La Foi, l'Esperance et la Charite. L'Avant Scène, 590 (July 1, 1976), 3-25. Renee Laurel, translator. In French.

4176. _____. Kasimir und Karoline, Ein Volksstuck. 1 act. Spectaculum, 8 (1965), 183-229. In German.

4177. _____. Notte Italiana. 1 act. Sipario, 327-328 (August-September, 1973), 89-112. Umberto Gandini and Emilio Castellani, translators. In Italian.

4178. Hosain, Khwaja Shahid. The Square Peg, A Dramatic Exercise in Verse. 1 act. New Mexico Quarterly, 31 (Winter, 1961-62), 331-338.

Hossein, Robert, pseud. see Hosseinoff, R. 4408

4179. Hosseinoff, Robert, 1927- . Responsabilité Limitée. 3 acts. L'Avant Scène, 99, 1-28. In French.

4180. Hostetter, Van Vechten. Peace on Earth.... 1 act. Smart Set, 62 (July, 1920), 93-95.

4181. Houghton, Stanley, 1881-1913. Fanny Hawthorn. 1 act. Everybody's Magazine, 47 (October, 1922), 128-134.

4182. House Party, A. 1 act. Living Age, 220 (February, 1899), 458-463. Katherine Vincent, translator.

House, Roy Temple, translator see Carrion, M. R. and V. Aza 1617

_____, translator see Ebner-Eschenbach, M. von
2808

_____, translator see Freytag, G. 3298

_____, translator see Hauptmann, G. 3974

_____, translator see Lavedan, H. L. E. 4843

_____, translator see Martel de Janville, Comtesse de
5585

4183. Housman, Laurence, 1865-1959. Aims and Objects, 1849. A Palace Play. 1 act. 19th Century, 115 (May, 1934), 596-602.

4184. _____. Ashes to Ashes, A Palace Epilogue. 1 act. Life and Letters, 10 (June, 1934), 273-279.

4185. _____. Bethlehem. 1 act. Senior Scholastic, 47 (December 10, 1945), 17-20.

4186. _____. Brother Wolf. 1 act. 19th Century, 88 (November, 1920), 813-823.

4187. _____. Charles! Charles! 1 act, comedy. 19th Century, 105 (January, 1929), 127-142.

4188. _____. The Christmas Tree. 1 act. Drama, 11 (December, 1920), 75-76.

4189. _____. The Fire-Lighters. A Dialogue on a Burning Topic. 1 act. London Mercury, 19 (January, 1929), 263-277.

4190. _____. The Messengers. 1 act. 19th Century, 105 (February, 1929), 269-285.

4191. _____. The Order of Release. 1 act. Fortnightly Review, 126 (September, 1926), 289-297.

4192. _____. The Revellers. 1 act. 19th Century, 90 (October, 1921), 616-628.

4193. _____. Ruling Powers. 1 act. Yale Review, 29 (June, 1940), 689-705.

4194. _____. This Is the Heir. 1 act. One-Act Play Magazine, 3 (September-October, 1940), 427-438.

_____ see also Paull, H. 7016

4195. Houston, James D. Time to Kill. 1 act. Dust, 3 (Fall, 1966), 13-20.

4196. Houston, Noel, 1909- . According to Law. 1 act. One-Act Play Magazine, 3 (January, 1940), 29-53.

4197. Houston, Sally, adapter. Three Golden Hairs. 1 act. Plays, 35 (January, 1976), 41-46.

4198. Houweninge, Chiem van, 1940- . Le Dernier Train. 1 act. L'Avant Scène, 589 (June, 1976), 37-43. Maryse Caillol and Michel Caillol, translators. In French.

Houwick, Caroline Heijermans, translator see Heijermans, H. 4028, 4031, 4033

Houwick, J., translator see Heijermans, H. 4028

4199. Hovey, Richard, 1864-1900. Taliesin: A Masque. 3 parts. Poet Lore, 8 (January, February, June-July, 1896), 1-14; 63-78; 292-306.

_____, translator see Gutzkow, K. 3792

Hovis, Jacques F., translator see Quillard, P. 7367

4200. How Billy Helped Things Along. 1 act. Quarterly Journal of Speech, 4 (October, 1918), 437-447.

4201. Howard, Helen Littler. Betty Blue's Shoe. 1 act. Plays, 5 (May, 1946), 58-60.

4202. _____. Bohboh, Beebee, and Booboo. 1 act. Plays, 5 (March, 1946), 54-56.

4203. _____. Bo-Peep's Valentine. 1 act. Plays, 5 (February, 1946), 61-63.

4204. _____. Doctor Know All. 1 act. Plays, 9 (October, 1949), 54-58. AND Plays, 32 (March, 1973), 69-73.

4205. _____. Gallop Away! 1 act. Plays, 4 (May, 1945), 60-62.

4206. _____. Hip Hip Ho. 1 act. Plays, 5 (January, 1946), 57-60.

4207. _____. The Magic Jack-O-Lantern. 1 act. Plays, 5 (October, 1945), 51-53.

4208. _____. Mother's Gift. 1 act. Plays, 3 (May, 1944), 34-36.

4209. _____. The Pixy Jester's Joke. 1 act. Plays, 3 (October, 1943), 45-50.

4210. _____. Ronny, Donny, and Susy. 1 act. Plays, 4 (April, 1945), 53-58.

4211. _____. The Stranger's Choice. 1 act. Plays, 5 (December, 1945), 50-52.

4212. _____. Thankful Indeed. 1 act. Plays, 5 (November, 1945), 55-57.

4213. _____. Thanks to Sammy Scarecrow. 1 act. Plays, 19 (November, 1959), 65-67.

4214. _____. This Little Pig Went to Market. 1 act. Plays, 2 (April, 1943), 54-56.

4215. Not used

Howard, Helen L., adapter see Ramée, L. de la 7394

4216. Howard, Homer Hildreth. The Child in the House. 1 act. Poet Lore, 24 (Winter, 1913), 433-444.

4217. Howard, Mary Warner. At the End of the Rainbow. 1 act. Plays, 18 (October, 1958), 59-64.

Howard, Richard, translator see Adamov, A. 57, 66

4218. Howard, Roger. Three Short Plays: The Travels of Yi Yuk-Sa to the Caves at Yenan; Episodes From the Fighting in the East; Returning to the Capital. Scripts, 1 (February, 1972), 45-55.

4218a. Howard, Sidney. Madame, Will You Walk. 3 acts. Theatre Arts, 41 (February, 1957), 33-60.

4219. Howard, Vernon. The Backward-Jumping Frog. 1 act. Plays, 15 (April, 1956), 73-74.

4220. _____. The Bird Court. 1 act. Plays, 15 (November, 1955), 62-64.

4221. _____. The Blackbird. 1 act. Plays, 14 (January, 1955), 84-87.

4222. _____. Danger--Pixies at Work. 1 act. Plays, 14 (May, 1955), 80-83.

4223. _____. The Happy Poet. 1 act. Plays, 15 (February, 1956), 86-88.

4224. _____. The Lazy Fox. 1 act. Plays, 15 (January, 1956), 74-76.

4225. _____. A Rest for Mr. Winkle. 1 act. Plays, 14 (October, 1954), 74-76.

4226. _____. The Scarecrow Party. 1 act. Plays, 16 (October, 1956), 75-76.

4227. _____. The Singing Shark. 1 act. Plays, 16 (May, 1957), 77-78.

4228. _____. Song of the Forest. 1 act. Plays, 15 (March, 1956), 84-86.

4229. _____. Vegetable Salad. 1 act. Plays, 15 (February, 1956), 78-80.

4230. _____. The Wrong Time. 1 act. Plays, 16 (January, 1957), 74-76.

4231. Howarth, Donald. A Hearts and Minds Job. 2 acts. Plays and Players, 18 (August, 1971), 61-81.

4232. _____. A Lilly in Little India. 3 acts. Plays and Players, 13 (May, 1966), 31-43.

4233. _____. Three Months Gone. 2 acts. Plays and Players, 17 (April, 1970), 57-77.

4234. Howeis, Lionel. The Rose of Persia. 3 acts. Drama, 11 (March, 1921), 200-213.

4235. Howells, William Dean, 1837-1920. After the Wedding. 1 act. Harper's 114 (December, 1906), 64-69.

4236. _____. Bride Roses. 1 act. Harper's, 87 (August, 1893), 424-430.

4237. _____. Christmas Every Day. 1 act. Plays, 12 (December, 1952), 68-76. AND Plays, 23 (December, 1963), 87-95. Jane McGowan, adapter.

4238. _____. Christmas Every Day. 1 act. Plays, 19 (December, 1959), 57-65. Adele Thane, adapter.

4239. _____. A Counterfeit Presentment. 3 parts, comedy. Atlantic, 40 (August, September, October, 1877), 148-161; 296-305; 448-460.

4240. _____. The Elevator. 1 act, farce. Harper's, 70 (December, 1884), 111-125.

4241. _____. Evening Dress. 3 acts, farce. Cosmopolitan, 13 (May, 1892), 116-127.

4242. _____. Father and Mother. 1 act. Harper's, 100 (May, 1900), 869-874.

4243. _____. Five O'Clock Tea. 1 act, farce. Harper's, 76 (December, 1887), 86-96.

4244. _____. The Garroters. 1 act, farce. Harper's, 72 (December, 1885), 146-162.

4245. _____. The Impossible. 1 act. Harper's, 122 (December, 1910), 116-125.

4246. _____. Indian Giver. 1 act, comedy. Harper's, 94 (January, 1897), 235-252.

4247. _____. A Letter of Introduction. 1 act, farce. Harper's, 84 (January, 1892), 243-256.

4248. _____. A Likely Story. 1 act, farce. Harper's, 78, (December, 1888), 26-38.

4249. _____. A Masterpiece of Diplomacy. 1 act, farce. Harper's, 88 (February, 1894), 371-385.

4250. _____. The Mother. 1 act. Harper's, 106 (December, 1902), 21-26.

4251. _____. The Mouse-Trap. 1 act, farce. Harper's, 74 (December, 1886), 64-75.

4252. _____. The Night Before Christmas. 1 act. Harper's, 120 (January, 1919), 207-216.

4253. _____. Out of the Question. 6 acts, comedy. Atlantic, 39 (February, March, April, 1877), 195-208; 317-329; 447-461.

4254. _____. The Parlor Car. 1 act, farce. Atlantic, 38 (September, 1876), 290-300.

4255. _____. Parting Friends. 1 act. Harper's, 121 (October, 1910), 670-677.

4256. _____. A Previous Engagement. 1 act, comedy. Harper's, 92 (December, 1895), 29-44.

4257. _____. The Register. 3 acts. Harper's, 68 (December, 1883), 70-86.

4258. _____. Self-Sacrifice; A Farce-Tragedy. 1 act. Harper's, 122 (April, 1911), 748-757.

4259. _____. A True Hero; Melodrama. 1 act. Harper's, 119 (November, 1909), 866-875.

4260. _____. The Unexpected Guests. 1 act, farce. Harper's, 86 (January, 1893), 211-225.

Hrbek, Cyril Jeffrey, translator see Dyk, V. 2797

Hrbkova, Sarka B., translator see Kvapil, J. 4743

_____, translator see Subert, F. A. 8598

4261. Hrotsvitha. Abraham. 1 act. Poet Lore, 42 (Spring, 1935), 299-313. John Heard, translator.

4262. _____. Callimachus. Allegorica, 1 (Spring, 1976), 7-51.

Lariss Bonfante and Marianna de Vinci Nichols, translators. In Latin and English.

4263. _____. Gallicanus. 1 act. Poet Lore, 42 (Spring, 1935), 314-328. John Heard, translator.

4264. Hsiung, Cheng-Chin. The Marvelous Romance of Wen Chun-Chin. 1 act. Poet Lore, 35 (1924), 298-313.

4265. _____. The Thrice Promised Bride. 1 act. Golden Book 2 (August, 1925), 230-236.

4266. _____. The Thrice Promised Bride. 1 act. Theatre Arts, 7 (October, 1923), 329-347.

4267. Huber, Mary B. The Dreammaker's Tree. 1 act. Plays, 5 (December, 1945), 55-56.

4268. Hubert, Philip G., Jr. A Railway Tragedy--Perhaps. 1 act. Bookman [New York], 24 (December, 1906), 340-343.

4269. Huff, Betty Tracy. Arts and Parts. 1 act. Plays, 28 (December, 1968), 19-29.

4270. _____. Beat That Bongo. 1 act. Plays, 24 (November, 1964), 13-21.

4271. _____. The Case of the Missing Masterpiece. 1 act. Plays, 21 (January, 1962), 15-24.

4272. _____. The Copper Farthing. 1 act. Plays, 19 (March, 1960), 73-76.

4273. _____. Cracker Barrel Circus. 1 act. Plays, 35 (December, 1975), 1-12.

4274. _____. A Day at the Store. 1 act. Plays, 32 (November, 1972), 27-40.

4275. _____. Everybody Loves Gladys. 1 act. Plays, 34 (May, 1975), 1-12.

4276. _____. The Feast of the Thousand Lanterns. 1 act. Plays, 19 (April, 1960), 60-64.

4277. _____. Flora of the Flower Shop. 1 act. Plays, 26 (February, 1967), 23-32. AND Plays, 36 (October, 1976), 27-36.

4278. _____. Gertie, the Greeting Card Girl. 1 act. Plays, 26 (May, 1967), 37-47.

4279. _____. The Girl and the Gold Mine: An Old-Fashioned Melodrama. 1 act. Plays, 26 (October, 1966), 29-39.

4280. _____. The Great Contest. 1 act. Plays, 26 (April, 1967), 15-27.

4281. _____. The Gypsie's Secret. 1 act. Plays, 27 (December, 1967), 23-32.

4282. _____. The Heiress of Harkington Hall. 1 act. Plays, 34 (April, 1975), 25-35.

4283. _____. Hillbilly Blues. 1 act. Plays, 27 (January, 1968), 1-10.

4284. _____. A Houseful of Elves. 1 act. Plays, 19 (January, 1960), 65-68.

4285. _____. Last of the Ghastleys. 1 act. Plays, 30 (February, 1971), 1-11.

4286. _____. Lily of the Label Department. 1 act. Plays, 33 (February, 1974), 1-12.

4287. _____. Meet Mr. Murchinson. 1 act. Plays, 20 (May, 1961), 1-10.

4288. _____. Mr. Efficiency. 1 act. Plays, 28 (January, 1969), 1-11.

4289. _____. The Mystery of the Seventh Witch. 1 act. Plays, 34 (October, 1974), 37-46.

4290. _____. Penelope, Pride of the Pickle Factory. 1 act. Plays, 25 (February, 1966), 39-49. AND Plays, 31 (April, 1972), 31-41.

4291. _____. Professor Hobo. 1 act. Plays, 23 (November, 1963), 1-14.

4292. _____. Recipe for Rain. 1 act. Plays, 25 (November, 1965), 15-25.

4293. _____. Ride the Gooberville State! 1 act, melodrama. Plays, 29 (April, 1970), 1-10.

4294. _____. The Sea People. 1 act. Plays, 19 (January, 1960), 75-78.

4295. _____. Spy for a Day. 1 act. Plays, 27 (March, 1968), 13-22.

4296. _____. A Street in Samarkand. 1 act. Plays, 19 (October, 1959), 62-66.

4297. _____. Tessie, the Tea Bag Maker. 1 act. Plays, 30 (May, 1971), 13-24.

4298. _____. Too Many Cooks. 1 act. Plays, 23 (May, 1964), 1-12.

4299. _____. Way, Way Off Broadway. 1 act, comedy. Plays, 27 (October, 1967), 29-41. AND Plays, 34 (January, 1975), 32-44.

4300. Hughes, Glenn, 1894-1964. Babbitt's Boy. 1 act. Scholastic, 21 (October 8, 1932), 9-10, 14.

4301. _____. Bottled in Bond: A Tragic Farce in One Act. Drama, 13 (February, 1923), 170-173.

_____, translator see Heiberg, G. 4026

4302. Hughes, Langston, 1902-1967. Battezzato de solo. 1 act. Il Dramma, n.s., 181 (May 15, 1953), 49-53. In Italian.

4303. _____. "Don't You Want to Be Free?". 1 act. One-Act Play Magazine, 2 (October, 1938), 359-393.

4304. _____. Mulatto. 2 acts. Sipario, 3 (January-February, 1948), 45-58. Enrico Maseda, translator. In Italian.

4305. _____. Private Jim Crow. 1 act. Negro Story, 1 (May-June, 1945), 3-9.

4306. _____. Soul Gone Home. 1 act. One-Act Play Magazine, 1 (July, 1937), 196-200.

4307. Hughes, Richard, 1900-1976. A Comedy of Danger. 1 act. Golden Book, 14 (August, 1931), 82-87.

4308. _____. The Man Born to Be Hanged. 1 act. Il Dramma, n.s., 158 (June 1, 1952), 43-47. Sergio Cenalino, translator. In Italian.

4309. Hughes, Riley. Anne Bradstreet. 1 act. Plays, 2 (May, 1943), 79-84.

4310. _____. The Boy Bowditch. 1 act. Plays, 3 (May, 1944), 77-81.

4311. _____. Illustrious Voyager. 1 act. Plays, 2 (October, 1942), 22-27.

4312. _____. Nathan Hale. 1 act. Plays, 3 (October, 1943), 33-37.

4313. _____. Philosopher in Grain: Michael Faraday. 1 act. Plays, 4 (November, 1944), 16-20.

4314. _____. Tin to Win. 1 act. Plays, 2 (November, 1942), 68-70.

Hughes, Ted, adapter see Seneca 8153

4315. Hugo, Victor, 1802-1885. The Bishop's Candlesticks. 1 act. Plays, 16 (February, 1957), 89-96. AND Plays, 22 (December, 1962), 25-33. Lewy Olfson, adapter.

4316. _____. Little Cosette and Father Christmas. 1 act. Plays, 29 (December, 1969), 85-96. Adele Thane, adapter.

4317. _____. Lucrece Borgia. 2 acts. L'Avant Scène, 574 (November 1, 1975), 3-31. In French.

4318. _____. Mille Francs de Récompense. 4 acts. L'Avant Scène, 248 (September 1, 1961), 10-36. In French.

4319. _____. Ruy Blas. 3 parts. Il Dramma, n. s., 362/363 (November/December, 1966), 99-125. Carlo Terron, translator. In Italian.

4320. Hull, Helen Rose. The Idealists. 1 act. Touchstone, 1 (September, 1917), 457-463.

4321. _____. Release. 1 act. Touchstone, 6 (December, 1919), 122-127.

4322. Hummell, Violet. Easter Reminders. 1 act. Plays, 16 (April, 1957), 56-58.

4323. Hung, Shen. The Wedded Husband. 3 acts. Poet Lore, 32 (No. 1, 1921), 110-135.

4324. Hunt, Livingston. Naming the Novel; A Dialogue Between Two Well-Known Authors. 1 act. Smart Set, 4 (July, 1901), 159-160.

4325. Hunt, Sylvia. Treasure! 1 act. Wilson Library Bulletin, 8 (October, 1933), 107-110.

4326. Hunter, Norman C., 1908- . Waters of the Moon. 3 acts. Il Dramma, n. s., 214 (October 1, 1954), 7-34. Ada Salvatore, translator. In Italian.

Huntzbuchler, translator see Kataiev, V. 4553

4327. Husson, Albert, 1912- . Claude de Lyon. 3 acts. L'Avant Scène, 255 (December 15, 1961), 8-29. In French.

4328. _____. La Cuisine des Anges. 3 acts, comedy. L'Avant Scène (ROST), 70 (December, 1952), 1-31. In French.

4329. _____. La Cuisine des Anges. 3 acts. Il Dramma, n.s., 184/185 (July 1/15, 1953), 81-109. Paola Ojetti, translator. In Italian.

4330. _____. L'Impromptu des Collines. 1 act. L'Avant Scène, 255 (December 15, 1961), 32-37. In French.

4331. _____. L'Ombre du Cavalier. 3 acts. L'Avant Scène, 128, 1-25. In French.

4332. _____. Le Système Fabrizzi. 4 acts, comedy. L'Avant Scène, 300 (December 1, 1963), 9-35. In French.

_____, adapter see Murray, J. and A. Boretz 6407

_____, adapter see Pincherle, A. 7155

_____, adapter see Wallach, I. 4952, 9194

4333. Huster, Francis. Hamlet. 1 act. L'Avant Scène, 578 (January 1, 1976), 27-37. In French.

_____, adapter see Diderot, D. 2485

4334. Hutchins, Maude Phelps. The Case of Astrolable. New Directions, 8 (1944), 87-103.

4335. _____. The Marriage of Toto. 1 act. Accent, 5 (Spring, 1945), 145-152.

4336. _____. Mary Play. 1 act. Quarterly Review of Literature, 3 (No. 2, 1946), 142-155.

4337. _____. A Play: The Wandering Jew. 2 parts. New Directions, 13 (1951), 21-31.

4338. _____. A Short Play about Joseph Smith, Jr. New Directions, 9 (1946), 361-367.

4339. Hutchins, Will. Jeanne D'Arc at Vaucouleurs. 1 act. Poet Lore, 21 (March-April, 1910), 97-148.

4340. Hutten, Baroness von. Ten Years After (With Apologies to Dumas, père). 1 act. Smart Set, 11 (October, 1903), 75-77.

4341. Hutton, Michael Clayton. Power Without Glory. 3 acts. Il Dramma, n.s., 111 (June 15, 1950), 11-33. Ada Salvatore, translator. In Italian.

4342. Huxley, Aldous Leonard, 1894-1963. Albert: Prince Consort. 1 act. Golden Hind, 1 (July, 1923), 13-19.

4343. _____. Ambassador of Capripedia. 1 act. Golden Hind, 1 (April, 1923), 9-13.

4344. _____. Among the Nightingales. 1 act. Smart Set, 63 (November, 1920), 71-88.

4345. _____. The Gioconda Smile. 3 acts. Theatre Arts, 35 (May, 1951), 51-88.

4346. _____. Mortal Coils. 3 acts. Sipario, 3 (November-December, 1948), 45-68. Giulio C. Castello and M. Giampaoli, translators. In Italian.

4347. _____. Permutations Among the Nightingales. 1 act. Coterie, 4 (Easter, 1920), 68-93.

4348. Hyakuzo, Kurata. Il maestro e il discepolo. 2 parts. Il Dramma, 417/418 (January 1/15, 1944), 37-60. Vinicio Marinucci, translator. In Italian.

4349. Hyde, Douglas, 1860-1949. Casadh an Tsùgàin. 1 act. Il Dramma, n.s., 277 (October, 1959), 36-40. Gigi Lunari, translator. In Italian.

4350. _____. The Lost Saint. 1 act. Samhain (October, 1902), 14-23. In Irish and English. Lady Augusta Gregory, translator.

4351. _____. The Marriage. 1 act. Golden Book, 6 (September, 1927), 327-332. Lady Augusta Gregory, translator.

4352. _____. The Marriage. 1 act. Poet Lore, 20 (March-April, 1909), 135-140.

4353. _____. The Poorhouse. 1 act, comedy. Samhain (September, 1903), 13-24. In Irish and English. Lady Augusta Gregory, translator.

4354. _____. The Twisting of the Rope. 1 act, comedy. Poet Lore, 16 (Spring, 1905), 12-22.

4355. _____. The Twisting of the Rope. 1 act, comedy. Samhain (October, 1901), 20-38. In Irish and English. Lady Augusta Gregory, translator.

4356. Hyde, Walter Woodburn. A Day in Alexandria at the Festival of Adonis. 1 act, farce. Sewanee Review, 30 (April, 1922), 174-178.

4357. Hyman, Marcus. A Spatial Episode. 1 act. Bermondsey Book, 2 (March, 1925), 81-85.

I

4358. Iannelli, Richard A. Plan C. 1 act. Dramatics, 46 (January, 1975), 8-11.

4359. Ibbitson, John. The Ritual. 1 act. Performing Arts in Canada, 11 (Fall, 1974), 43-46.

4360. Ibsen, Henrik, 1828-1906. An Enemy of the People. 1 act. Plays, 29 (March, 1970), 86-96. Paul T. Nolan, adapter.

4361. _____. Hedda Gabler. 4 acts. L'Avant Scène, 143, 3-36. Counte Prozor, translator. In French.

4362. _____. The Lady From the Sea. 5 acts. Il Dramma, 439/440 (December 1/15, 1944), 11-36. Tèrésah, translator. In Italian.

4363. _____. Little Eyolf. 3 acts. Il Dramma, 400 (April 15, 1943), 7-24. Eligio Possenti, translator. In Italian.

4364. _____. Love's Comedy. 3 acts. Il Dramma, 342 (November 15, 1940), 6-25. In Italian.

4365. _____. When We Dead Awaken. 3 acts. L'Avant Scène, 599 (December 1, 1976), 3-26. Comte Prozor, translator. In French.

4366. Ickler, Lyda M. Kitty Hawk--1903. 1 act. Plays, 5 (February, 1946), 72-76.

4367. _____. Walk Proudly Here--Americans. 1 act. Plays, 5 (November, 1945), 71-75.

4368. Ilf, Ilya and Evgeny Petrov. The Power of Love. 1 act. Modern International Drama, 8 (Fall, 1974), 73-85. Laurence Senelick, translator.

4369. Indick, Benjamin P. Apples. 1 act. Players Magazine, 41 (April, 1965), 177-178.

4370. _____. Books Have Wings. 1 act. Plays, 24 (November, 1964), 63-66.

4371. Ingannati, Gli. 3 acts. Sipario, 19 (June, 1964), 69-88. Gigi Lunari, adapter. In Italian.

4372. Inge, William, 1913-1973. Bus Stop. 3 acts. Theatre Arts, 40 (October, 1956), 33-56.

4373. _____. Come Back, Little Sheba. 2 acts. Theatre Arts, 34 (November, 1950), 57-88.

4374. _____. Dark at the Top of the Stairs. 3 acts. Sipario, 14 (June, 1959), 37-57. Lea Danesi and Giorgio Brunacci, translators. In Italian.

4375. _____. The Dark at the Top of the Stairs. 3 acts. Theatre Arts, 43 (September, 1959), 33-60.

4376. _____. A Loss of Roses. 2 acts. Esquire, 53 (January, 1960), 119-132, 134, 137-144.

4377. _____. The Mall. 1 act. Esquire, 51 (January, 1959), 75-78.

4378. _____. Picnic. 3 acts. Il Dramma, n.s., 231 (December, 1955), 16-44. Mino Roli, translator. In Italian.

4379. _____. Picnic. 3 acts. Theatre Arts, 38 (April, 1954), 34-61.

4380. Ingelow, Jean. An Anniversary: December 10, 1688. 1 act, dialogue. Longman's Magazine, 15 (December, 1889), 142-148.

4381. Ingham, Travis. Crosstown Manhattan! 1 act. One-Act Play Magazine, 2 (March, 1939), 815-829.

4382. Ionesco, Eugene, 1912- . The Bald Soprano. 1 act. New World Writing, 9 (1956), 198-224. Donald Allen, translator.

4383. _____. Bedlam Galore, For Two or More. 1 act. Tulane Drama Review, 7 (Spring, 1963), 221-242. Bernard Frechtman, translator.

4384. _____. La Cantatrice Chauve. 1 act. Spectaculum, 5 (1963), 149-175. Serge Stauffer, translator. In German.

4385. _____. Ce Formidable Bordel! L'Avant Scène, 542 (June, 1, 1974), 7-33. In French.

4386. _____. The Chairs, A Tragic Farce. 1 act. Theatre Arts, 42 (July, 1958), 28-38. Donald Watson, translator.

4387. _____. Foursome. 1 act. Evergreen Review, 4 (May-June, 1960), 46-53. Donald Allen, translator.

4388. _____. Frenzy for Two. 1 act. Evergreen Review, 9 (June, 1965), 31-39, 85-87. Donald Watson, translator.

4389. _____. The Gap. 1 act. Massachusetts Review, 10 (Winter, 1969), 119-127. Rosette Lamont, translator.

4390. _____. Improvisation, or The Shepherd's Chameleon. 1 act. Horizon, 3 (May, 1961), 92-97.

4391. _____. Une Jeune Fille a Marier. 1 act. L'Avant Scène, 472 (May 15, 1971), 45-49. In French.

4392. _____. Jeux de Massacre. 1 act. L'Avant Scène, 472 (May 15, 1971), 7-39. In French.

4393. _____. Jeux de Massacre. 1 act. Il Dramma, 46, no. 10 (October, 1970), 100-102. Gian Renzo Mortea, translator. In Italian.

4394. _____. Der König Stirbt. 1 act. Spectaculum, 7 (1964), 152-195. Claus Bremer and Hans Rudolf Stauffacher, translators. In German.

4395. _____. La Leçon. 1 act, comedy. L'Avant Scène, 156, 29-39. AND L'Avant Scène, 472 (May 15, 1971), 41-44. In French.

4396. _____. La Leçon. 1 act. Il Dramma, n.s., 213 (September 15, 1954), 47-58. Gian Renzo Mortea, translator. In Italian.

4397. _____. La Leçon. 1 act. Theatre Arts, 42 (July, 1958), 39-48. Donald Watson, translator.

4398. _____. Macbett. L'Avant Scène, 501 (September 1, 1972), 7-34. In French.

4399. _____. The Motor Show. 1 act. Evergreen Review, 8 (April-May, 1964), 65-66.

4400. _____. Rhinoceros. 3 acts. Theatre Arts, 46 (July, 1962), 25-61.

4401. _____. Scène à Quatre. 1 act. L'Avant Scène, 210 (December 15, 1959), 44-46. In French.

4402. _____. Tueur sans Gages. 3 acts. L'Avant Scène, 510 (January 15, 1973), 7-32. In French.

Ireland, Donna, translator see Haitov, N. 3828

Ireland, Kevin, translator see Haitov, N. 3828

4403. Irvine, Clyde. Yet They Endure ...! 1 act. One-Act Play Magazine, 3 (January, 1940), 3-18.

4404. Irving, Washington, 1783-1859. The Legend of Sleepy Hollow. 1 act. Plays, 10 (October, 1950), 67-78. Walter Hackett, adapter.

4405. _____. Rip Van Winkle. 1 act. Plays, 9 (April, 1950), 72-82. Walter Hackett, adapter.

4406. _____. Rip Van Winkle. 1 act. Plays, 19 (February, 1960), 13-23. Lewy Olfson, adapter.

4407. _____. Rip Van Winkle. 3 acts. Plays, 25 (April, 1966), 53-61. Adele Thane, adapter.

4408. Irwin, Margaret. The Three Visitors. 1 act. Bermondsey Book, 3 (September, 1926), 81-93.

4409. Isaac, Dan. Auntie Hamlet. 1 act. Dramatika, 9 (Spring, 1972), n. p.

Isaacs, Edith J. R., translator see Hebbel, F. 4016

Isanz, Tanja, translator see Ugrjumov, D. 8965

Isanz, Tatiana, translator see Arbuzov, A. 314

Isherwood, Christopher, 1904- see Auden, W. H. 439

4410. Isherwood, Claire and Lawrence Nelson. Salvation's Story. 1 act. Resource, 3 (November, 1961), 13-15.

4411. Isle-Adam, Villiers de l', 1838-1889. Axel, "Le Monde Passionnel". 4 parts. L'Avant Scène, 261 (March 15, 1962), 37-46. In French.

Isola, Pietro, 1864- , translator see D'Annunzio, G. 2181

4412. Isom, Joan Shaddox. Free Spirits. 1 act. Plays, 34 (March, 1975), 16-29.

4413. Isom, Louise Metcalfe. The Boy with the Bagpipe. 1 act. Plays, 18 (May, 1959), 49-54.

Itow, Michio, translator see The Fox's Grave 3239

_____, translator see She Who Was Fished 8230

_____, translator see Somebody-Nothing 8373

4414. Ivan, Rosalind. Fantasie Impromptu. 1 act. Drama, 11 (April, 1921), 233-236.

Ivernel, Philippe, translator see Weiss, P. 9274

4415. Izumo, Takeda. Terakoya. 1 act. Il Dramma, 402/403 (May 15/June 1, 1943), 64-73. Rolf Hohenemser, translator. In Italian.

J

Jacchia, Umberto, translator see Shaw, I. 8223

4416. Jackson, Douglas. The Gentle Genius. 1 act. Plays, 29 (December, 1969), 27-37.

4417. _____. A Kiss for Madeline. 1 act. Plays, 32 (February, 1973), 11-24.

4418. Jackson, Patricia M. Rainbow. 1 act. Plays, 35 (March, 1976), 83-86.

4419. Jacob, Eva. The Crowded House. 1 act. Plays, 16 (April, 1957), 59-64.

4420. _____. Robin Hood Tricks the Sheriff. 1 act. Plays, 16 (October, 1956), 77-81.

4421. _____, adapter. Snow White. 1 act. Plays, 17 (March, 1958), 72-78.

4422. Jacobbi, Ruggero. Il Cobra alle caviglie. 1 act. Il Dramma, 45, no. 13 (October, 1969), 83-89. In Italian.

4423. Jacobs, M. G. Into the Tents of Men, A Verse Play for Reading or Acting. 1 act. Poet Lore, 58 (Winter, 1964), 336-351.

4424. Jacobson, Katherine Virginia. God Keeps Trying. 1 act. Resource, 14 (November, 1972), 3-4.

4425. Jacquemard, Yves, 1944- and Jean Michel Senecal. Angelo. 1 act. Sipario, 348 (May, 1975), 71-80. In Italian.

4426. Jaeger, C. Stephen. The Compromise. 2 acts. Drama and Theatre, 8 (Winter, 1969-70), 130-142.

4427. Jaffe, Bernard. Science in a Democracy. 1 act. Scholastic, 36 (March 11, 1940), 17-19, 24.

4428. Jagendorf, Moritz, 1888- . Cinderella of New Hampshire. 1 act. Plays, 2 (April, 1943), 23-30.

4429. _____. M'Lord of Massachusetts. 1 act. Plays, 2 (December, 1942), 43-52.

_____, adapter see Master Patelin . . . 5649a

_____, translator see Schnitzler, A. 8066

_____, translator see Vega, L. de 9057

Jahier, Piero, 1884- , translator see Claudel, P. 1867

Jahn, Lila, translator see Musil, R. 6414

4430. Jahnn, Hans-Henny. Thomas Chatterton; eine tragödie. 5 acts. Spectaculum, 2 (1959), 267-333. In German.

4431. Jakobi, Paula. Chinese Lily. 1 act. Forum, 54 (November, 1915), 551-566.

4432. Jalabert, Pierre. La Farce des Bossus. 1 act, comedy. Petite Illustration, 184 (February 25, 1933), 1-12. In French.

4433. James, Bartlett Burleigh. Santa's Lost Sack. 1 act. Ladies' Home Journal, 22 (December, 1904), 28.

James, Grace see Barr, B. and G. Stevens 613

4434. James, Henry, 1843-1916. A Change of Heart. 1 act. Atlantic, 29 (January, 1872), 49-60.

4435. _____. Daisy Miller. 3 acts, comedy. Atlantic, 51 (April, May, June, 1883), 433-456; 577-597; 721-740.

4436. _____. Washington Square. 1 act. Plays, 24 (March, 1965), 85-94. Lewy Olfson, adapter.

4437. James, Patricia. When Mozart Was Sixteen. 1 act. Plays, 20 (January, 1961), 14-20.

4438. Jamiaque, Yves. Acapulco Madame. 2 parts. L'Avant Scène, 598 (November 15, 1976), 3-48. In French.

4439. _____. Les Cochons d'Inde. 2 parts. L'Avant Scène, 235 (January 15, 1961), 8-36. In French.

4440. _____. Monsieur Amiliar. 2 acts, comedy. L'Avant Scène, 560 (March 15, 1975), 3-47. In French.

4441. _____. Point H. 2 acts. L'Avant Scène, 370 (December 15, 1966), 9-36. In French.

Jamin, Georges, adapter see Kearney, P. 4567

4442. Jandl, Ernst, 1925 and Friedericke Mayrocker, 1924- . The Giant. 1 act. Literary Review, 17 (Summer, 1974), 511-525. Christopher Middleton, translator.

4443. Janey, Sue Ellen. The Million-Dollar Quiz Show. 1 act, comedy. Plays, 25 (April, 1966), 92-95.

4444. Janusch, Mildred June. Haym Salomon. 1 act. Scholastic, 34 (May 6, 1939), 33-35, 42.

4445. Jappolo, Beniamino. L'ultima stazione. 1 act. Il Dramma, 375 (April 1, 1942), 35-40. In Italian.

4446. Jaquine, Jacques. Raphael ... Fais Tourner le Monde. 1 act. L'Avant Scène, 497 (June 15, 1972), 40-43. In French.

Jarka, Horst, translator see Soyfer, J. 8395, 8396

4447. Jarrell, Myra Williams. Case of Mrs. Kantsey Know. 1 act, comedy. Drama, 12 (March, 1922), 210-212.

4448. Jarry, Alfred, 1873-1907. Fear Visits Love. Fiction, 2 (No. 1, 1973), 23-24. John Ashbery, translator.

4449. _____. Ubu Bound. 5 acts. Works, 1 (Spring, 1968), 70-87. Ron Padgett, translator.

4450. _____. Ubu Cocu. 5 acts. Works, 3 (Spring/Winter, 1972), 54-74. Albert Bermel, translator.

Jasienko, Jean-Michel, adapter see Saroyan, W. 7950

4451. Jasudowicz, Dennis, 1940- . Five Plays: It Ain't Tea. The Stuff a Writer Is Made Out Of. The Jig Is Up. The Last Capitalist. The Folk Singer. 1 act each. City Lights Journal, 2 (1964), 227-246.

4452. _____. Slumming. 1 act. Tulane Drama Review, 9 (Winter, 1964), 212-229.

Jeffers, Robinson, 1887-1962, adapter see Euripides 2880, 2881

Jelenski, F. de K., translator see Gombrowicz, W. 3617

4453. Jellicoe, Ann, 1928- . The Knack. 3 acts. Sipario, 19 (January, 1964), 42-57. Luciano Codignola, translator. In Italian.

Jemma, Andrea, translator see Eremburg, I. 2870

_____, translator see Leonov, L. M. 4928

_____, translator see Simonov, K. 8299

_____, translator see Sofronov, A. 8362

4454. Jenks, Tudor. Quits. 1 act. Century, 46 (October, 1893), 957-960.

4455. _____. Thanksgiving Dinner, A Modern Farce. 1 act. The Independent, 61 (November 29, 1906), 1258-1260.

4456. _____. Waiting for the Ring, A Monologue. 1 act. Century, 64 (June, 1902), 303-304.

4457. Jennings, Anne. The Little Evergreen Tree. 1 act. Plays, 28 (December, 1968), 77-81.

4458. _____. The Visit of Mother Cloud. 1 act. Plays, 28 (March, 1969), 76-80.

4459. Jennings, Edith. The Finger Fairies. 1 act. Wilson Library Bulletin, 15 (October, 1940), 152-153.

4460. Jennings, George. Elijah Lovejoy. 1 act. Scholastic, 40 (March 23-28, 1942), 17-19, 24.

4461. _____. Mississippi ... Father of Waters. 1 act. Scholastic, 38 (May 5, 1941), 17-19.

4462. Jens, Arlene J. Christmas Pathway. 1 act. Resource, 7 (November, 1965), 5-8.

4463. Jensen, Stanley C. North Pole Confidential. 1 act. Plays, 14 (December, 1954), 81-86.

4464. Jerome, Jerome Klapka, 1859-1927. Alla deriva. 1 act. Il Dramma, 119 (August 1, 1931), 44-46.

4465. _____. Fanny è i suoi domestici. 3 acts. Il Dramma, 40 (April 15, 1928), 7-36. In Italian.

4466. _____. The Passing to the Third Floor Back. 3 acts. Petite Illustration, 185 (August 12, 1933), 1-26. Andree Mery, translator. In French.

4467. _____. Robina in Search of a Husband. 3 acts. Il Dramma, 155 (February 1, 1933), 4-33. In Italian.

Jikramov, K. see Tendrjakov, V. 8742

4468. Jimenez Rueda, Julio. The Unforeseen. 3 acts. Poet Lore, 35 (1924), 1-42. Gino V. M. de Solenni, translator.

4469. Jirasek, Aloïs, 1851-1930. Dobromila Rettig. 3 acts, comedy. Poet Lore, 31 (Winter, 1920), 475-537.

4470. Jodorowsky, Alexandro. Sacramental Melodrama. City Lights Journal, 3 (1966), 75-83. Marc Estrin, translator.

4471. Joffe, Alex, 1918- , and Jean Giltene. Florence et le Dentiste. 3 acts, comedy. L'Avant Scène (ROST), 61 (May, 1952), 1-30. In French.

4472. John, Errol. Moon on a Rainbow Shawl. 3 acts. Sipario, 17 (March, 1962), 33-49. Ettore Capriolo, translator. In Italian.

4473. John, Gwen. Ambrosia. 1 act. Dublin Magazine, 2 (August, 1924), 7-13.

4474. _____. "Edge O'Dark." 1 act. English Review, 12 (November, 1912), 592-603.

4475. _____. Little Decameron. 1 act. Dublin Magazine, n.s., 1 (April-June, 1926), 27-33.

4476. _____. Mr. Jardyne, A Mystery. 1 act. Dublin Magazine, 2 (November, 1924), 246-256.

4477. Johns, Orrick, 1887- . Eclipse. 1 act. Others, 5 (March, 1919), 1-11.

4478. _____. The Hero in Pink, A Greek Tragedy. 1 act. Smart Set, 48 (March, 1916), 201-202.

4479. _____. Shadow. 1 act. Others, 5 (February, 1919), 1-13.

4480. Johnson, B. S., 1933- . Not Counting the Savages. Transatlantic Review, 45 (Spring, 1973), 55-75.

4481. _____. You're Human Like the Rest of Them. 1 act. Transatlantic Review (London), 19 (Autumn, 1965), 37-43.

4482. Johnson, D. H. The Last Boat. 1 act. Scholastic, 40 (April 27-May 2, 1942), 17-19.

4483. _____. The Man from Cemetery Ridge. 1 act. Scholastic, 40 (February 9-14, 1942), 17-18, 24.

4484. Johnson, Gail. The Guess-for-Fun Alphabet. 1 act. Plays, 28 (April, 1969), 67-70.

4485. Johnson, Georgia Douglas. Plumes. 1 act. Opportunity, 5 (June, 1927), 200-201, 217-218.

Johnson, Jakobina, translator see Kvaran, E. 4744

_____, translator see Sigurjonsson, J. 8274

4486. Johnson, Larry E. Un signore che passava. 3 acts. Il Dramma, 200 (December 15, 1934), 4-40. Goffredo Pautassi, translator. In Italian.

4487. Johnson, Martyn. Mr. and Mrs. P. Roe. 1 act, comedy. Drama, 13 (December, 1922), 92-95.

4488. Johnson, Pamela Hansford, 1912- . The Duchess at Sunset. 1 act. Midway (January, 1961), 67-101.

4489. Johnson, Thelma H. The Story of Benjamin Banneker. 1 act. Negro History Bulletin, 15 (April, 1952), 137-140.

4490. Johnson, Wallace. Don't Leave Me Alone. 1 act. Drama and Theatre, 11 (Winter, 1972/73), 100-107.

4491. _____. What Did You Learn in School Today? 1 act. Players' Magazine, 41 (January, 1965), 99-102.

4492. Jokai, Maurus, 1825-1904. Nine Times Christmas. 1 act. Plays, 19 (December, 1959), 37-46. Lewy Olfson, adapter.

4493. _____. Which of the Nine? 1 act. Plays, 15 (December, 1955), 77-84. Lewy Olfson, adapter.

4494. Jolas, Eugene, 1897?- . Flight Into Geography, A Scenario. Transition, 10 (January, 1928), 76-85.

Jolivet, Alfred, 1885- , translator see Strindberg, A. 8564

4495. Jolly, Andrew. Quintila. 3 acts. First Stage, 1 (Fall, 1962), 53-79.

4496. Jolly Old Abbot of Canterbury. 1 act. St. Nicholas, 3 (December, 1875), 123-124.

4497. Jona, Anselmo. La pistola a tamburo. 1 act. Il Dramma, 17 (April, 1927), 38-45. In Italian.

4498. _____. Il sangue del padrone delle ferriere. 1 act. Il Dramma, 19 (June 1, 1927), 45-46. In Italian.

4499. Jona, Emilio. Atomtod. 2 parts. Sipario, 19 (December, 1964), 72-80. In Italian.

_____ see Castri, M. 1655

_____ see Liberovici, S. 4977

4500. Jones, David Cadwalader. The Magic Mushrooms. 1 act. Plays, 30 (April, 1971), 63-65.

4501. _____, adapter. The Enchanted Well. 1 act. Plays, 34 (April, 1975), 61-65.

4502. _____, adapter. The Magic Shoes. 1 act. Plays, 33 (January, 1974), 73-78.

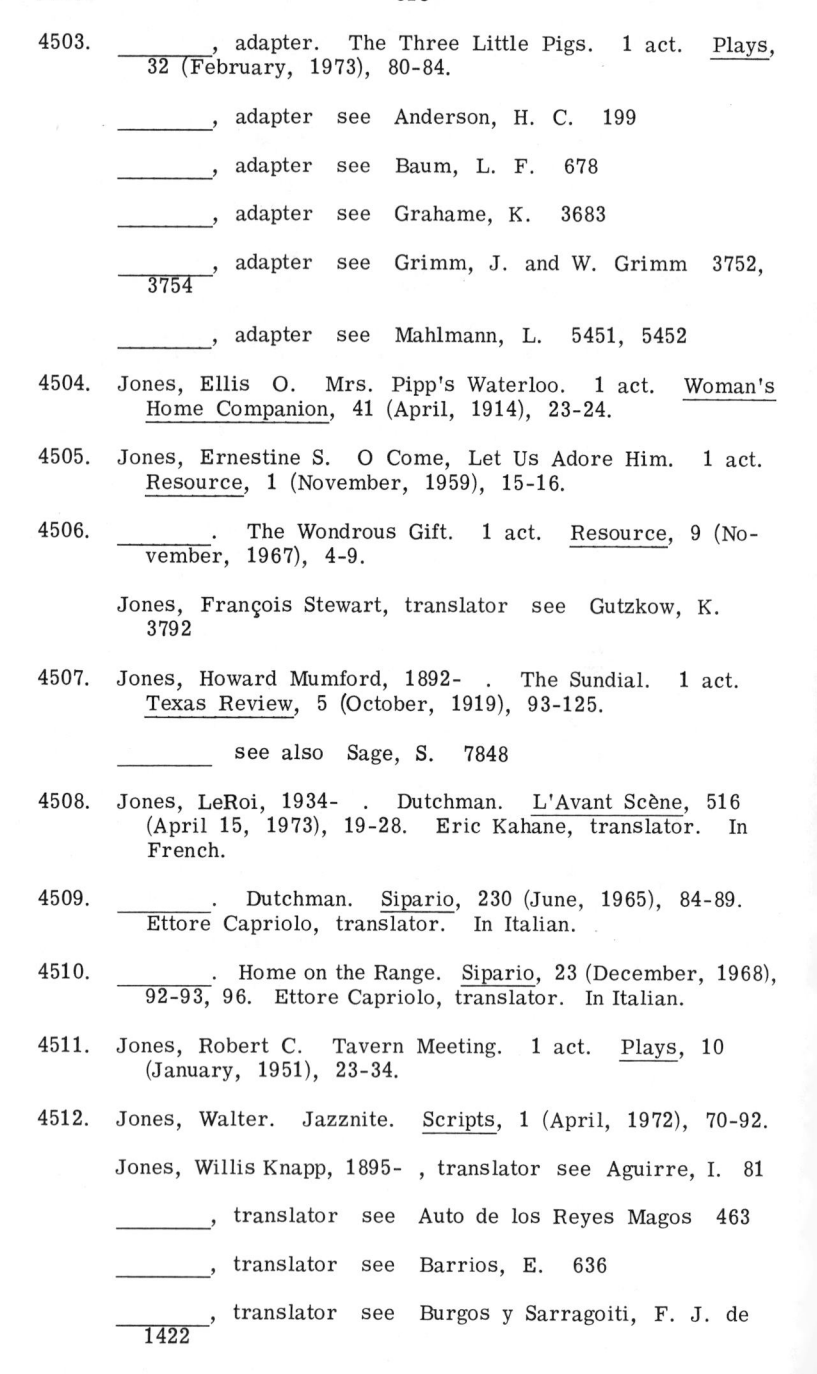

4503. _____, adapter. The Three Little Pigs. 1 act. Plays, 32 (February, 1973), 80-84.

_____, adapter see Anderson, H. C. 199

_____, adapter see Baum, L. F. 678

_____, adapter see Grahame, K. 3683

_____, adapter see Grimm, J. and W. Grimm 3752, 3754

_____, adapter see Mahlmann, L. 5451, 5452

4504. Jones, Ellis O. Mrs. Pipp's Waterloo. 1 act. Woman's Home Companion, 41 (April, 1914), 23-24.

4505. Jones, Ernestine S. O Come, Let Us Adore Him. 1 act. Resource, 1 (November, 1959), 15-16.

4506. _____. The Wondrous Gift. 1 act. Resource, 9 (November, 1967), 4-9.

Jones, François Stewart, translator see Gutzkow, K. 3792

4507. Jones, Howard Mumford, 1892- . The Sundial. 1 act. Texas Review, 5 (October, 1919), 93-125.

_____ see also Sage, S. 7848

4508. Jones, LeRoi, 1934- . Dutchman. L'Avant Scène, 516 (April 15, 1973), 19-28. Eric Kahane, translator. In French.

4509. _____. Dutchman. Sipario, 230 (June, 1965), 84-89. Ettore Capriolo, translator. In Italian.

4510. _____. Home on the Range. Sipario, 23 (December, 1968), 92-93, 96. Ettore Capriolo, translator. In Italian.

4511. Jones, Robert C. Tavern Meeting. 1 act. Plays, 10 (January, 1951), 23-34.

4512. Jones, Walter. Jazznite. Scripts, 1 (April, 1972), 70-92.

Jones, Willis Knapp, 1895- , translator see Aguirre, I. 81

_____, translator see Auto de los Reyes Magos 463

_____, translator see Barrios, E. 636

_____, translator see Burgos y Sarragoiti, F. J. de 1422

_____, translator see Cervantes Saavedra, M. de
1690, 1694

_____, translator see Drago-Bracco, A. 2586

_____, translator see Gutierrez, E. and J. J. Podesta
3791

_____, translator see Marivaux, P. C. de 5558

_____, translator see Marques, R. 5575

_____, translator see Matto, J. M. R. 5662

_____, translator see Moock, A. 6195, 6196

_____, translator see Navarro, F. 6454

_____, translator see Pena, M. 7042

_____, translator see Petit, V. P. 7106

_____, translator see Vazquez, J. A. 9051

_____, translator see Vega, L. de 9059

_____, translator see Vilalta, M. 9144

_____, translator see Zorilla y Moral, J. 9655

4513. Jonquille, Nepomucene. Le Vie de Polichinelle. Sipario, 8 (August-September, 1953), 46-59. Alberto Perrini, translator. In Italian.

4514. Joppolo, Beniamino, 1906-1963. L'acqua di diverte a far morire di sete. Sipario, 27 (February, 1972), 60-72. In Italian.

4515. _____. I carabinieri. 3 parts. Sipario, 24 (May, 1969), 47-64. In Italian.

4516. Jordan, Elizabeth D. A Confidence. Harper's Bazaar, 43 (May, 1909), 447-450.

Jorio, Casimiro, translator see Priestley, J. B. 7294

4517. Jornet, Josep Benet I. The Ship. 1 act. Modern International Drama, 8 (Fall, 1974), 45-70. George E. Wellwarth, translator.

4518. Jose San Martin, South American Hero. 1 act. Plays, 3 (April, 1944), 73-77.

4519. Josset, Andre. Elizabeth, La Femme Sans Homme. 2 parts. L'Avant Scène, 111, 1-28. In French.

4520. _____. Elizabeth, La Femme Sans Homme. 2 parts. Petite Illustration, 193 (February 9, 1936), 1-26. In French.

4521. _____. Premier Amour. 2 parts. L'Avant Scène, 134, 1-25. In French.

4522. _____. Primo amore. 2 parts. Il Dramma, n.s., 152 (March 1, 1952), 7-31. G. V. Sampieri, translator. In Italian.

Josz, Virgile see Dumur, L. 2695

Joudheuil, Jean see Chartreux, B. 1735

4523. Jovinelli, Gerardo. L'esperimento del dottor Brandley. 3 acts. Il Dramma, 339 (October 1, 1940), 6-27. In Italian.

Joxe, Francois, adapter see Toller, E. 8874

4524. Joyce, James, 1882-1941. Exiles. 3 acts. Il Dramma, 353 (May 1, 1941), 9-31. Carlo Linati, translator. In Italian.

4525. _____. The Sister. 1 act. Il Dramma, n.s., 347/348 (August/September, 1965), 96-103. Lucio Chiavarelli, translator. In Italian.

4526. Jung, Franz. Puppenspiel. 1 act. Der Sturm, 2 (January, 1912), 750. In German.

4527. Junichiro, Tanizaki. Poichè io l'amo. 3 acts. Il Dramma, 344 (December 15, 1940), 5-29. Lorenzo Gigli, translator. In Italian.

Jurlot, Gerard, translator see Gibson, W. 3502

4528. Justema, William, Jr. Chi-Fu, A Play With Masks. 1 act. Drama, 13 (August-September, 1923), 356, 370.

K

4529. Kachigan, Samuel, 1941- . The Game. 1 act. Transatlantic Review, (London), 37/38 (Autumn/Winter, 1970/1971), 208-217.

4530. Kafka, Franz, 1883-1924. Guardiano alla tomba. 1 act. Il Dramma, n.s., 70 (October 1, 1948), 53-56. In Italian.

Kahane, Eric, adapter see Ayckbourn, A. 467

———, translator see Jones, L. 4508

———, adapter see Miller, A. 5845

———, adapter see Orton, J. 6884

———, adapter see Pinter, H. 7172

———, translator see Tabori, G. 8682

4531. Kaiser, Georg, 1878-1945. From Morn to Midnight. 1 act. Poet Lore, 31 (Autumn, 1920), 317-363. Ashley Dukes, translator.

4532. ———. Giovanna. 1 act. Il Dramma, 135 (April 1, 1932), 31-36. Enzo Gariffo, translator. In Italian.

4533. ———. The Protagonist. 1 act. Tulane Drama Review, 5 (December, 1960), 133-144. H. F. Garten, translator.

4534. ———. The Raft of the Medusa. 1 act. First Stage, 1 (Spring, 1962), 35-48. Ulrich Weisstein, translator.

4535. Kallas, Aino, 1878-1956. Bathsheba of Saaremaa. 1 act. One-Act Play Magazine, 2 (March, 1939), 771-786. Alex Matson, translator.

Kallman, Chester, 1921- see Auden, W. H. 440

———, translator see Brecht, B. 1309

4536. Kalos, Pete. The Solution Is the Window to the Soul. 1 act. Dramatika, 7 (1971), 32-33.

Kaminka, Didier see Rego, L. 7467

4537. Kaminsky, Stuart M. Here Comes the Interesting Part. 1 act. First Stage, 6 (Fall, 1967), 169-176.

4538. Kandel, Aben. Hey Scrub-A-Drudge! 1 act. One-Act Play Magazine, 2 (December, 1938), 542-559.

Kane, Alice see Kane, R. 4543

4539. Kane, Eleanora Bowling. The Children of Chocolate Street. 1 act. Plays, 10 (December, 1950), 54-59. AND Plays, 29 (December, 1969), 73-78.

4540. ———. Paul Revere of Boston. 1 act. Plays, 28 (April, 1969), 53-60.

4541. _____. The Princess and the Greenies. 1 act. Plays, 29 (October, 1969), 74-78.

4542. _____. Two Against Napoleon. 1 act. Plays, 5 (January, 1946), 72-76.

4543. Kane, Ralph and Alice Kane. A Christmas Greeting. 1 act. Resource, 10 (November, 1968), 2-5, 31-32.

Kani, John see Fugard, A. 3336

4544. Kanin, Garson. Born Yesterday. 3 acts. Sipario, 4 (November, 1949), 53-73. Ada Salvatore, translator. In Italian.

4545. Kanjincho, A Kabuki Play. 1 act. Evergreen Review, 4 (September-October, 1960), 28-51. James R. Brandon and Tamako Niwa, translators.

4546. Kao Hung. Storm Warning. 1 act. Chinese Literature, 8 (1973), 35-60.

4547. Kaplan, Ysabel De Witte, 1877- . Madonna and the Scarecrow. 3 acts. Poet Lore, 34 (Summer, 1923), 254-270.

4548. _____. Princess Weaver of the Skies. 1 act. Poet Lore, 32 (No. 3, 1921), 267-278.

4549. Kaprow, Allan. Five Happenings. New Writers, 4 (1967), 81-106.

4550. Karinthy, Ferenc, 1921- . Steinway Grand. 1 act. Modern International Drama, 1 (March, 1968), 138-152. Bertha Gaster, editor; Matyas Eszterhazy, translator.

4551. Karpowicz, Tymoteusz. The Strange Passenger. 1 act. Drama and Theatre, 7 (Winter, 1968-69), 116-140. Edward J. Czerwinski, translator.

Kass, Henry, translator see Nikl, P. 6602a

4552. Kataev, Valentin, 1897- . Path of Flowers. 4 acts. Il Dramma, 375 (April 1, 1942), 7-24. M. Rakowska, translator. In Italian.

4553. _____. La Quadrature du Cercle. 3 acts, comedy. L'Avant Scène (OST), 12 (October, 1949), 1-30. Huntzbuchler, translator.

4554. Kattan, Naim, 1928- . La Discretion. 1 act. L'Avant Scène, 520 (June 15, 1973), 35-40. In French.

4555. _____. Le Trajet. 1 act. L'Avant Scène, 557 (February 1, 1975), 31-33. In French.

4556. Kauffman, George. Fool a Fool. 1 act. Dust, 1 (Spring, 1964), 41-48.

4557. _____. The Social Worker and the Alcoholic. 1 act. First Stage, 3 (Winter, 1963-64), 42-45.

4558. Kauffman, Stanley, 1916- . The More the Merrier. 1 act, satire. One-Act Play Magazine, 2 (January, 1939), 650-663.

4559. Kaufman, George S., 1889-1961 and Marc Connelly, 1890- . A Christmas Carol. 3 acts. Bookman [New York], 56 (December, 1922), 409-419.

4560. _____ and Edna Ferber, 1887-1968. Dinner at Eight. 3 acts, comedy. Petite Illustration, 185 (July 29, 1933), 1-42. Jacques Boularan, adapter. In French.

4561. _____ and Moss Hart, 1904-1961. Once in a Lifetime. 3 acts. Il Dramma, n.s., 10 (April 1, 1946), 7-36.

Vinicio Marinucci, translator. In Italian.

_____ see also Hart, M. 3942, 3943

_____ see also Teichmann, H. 8738

Kaufman, Kenneth C., translator see Larra, M. J. de 4821

4562. Kaufman, S. Jay. Kisses. 1 act. Smart Set, 47 (November, 1915), 259-266.

Kayden, Eugene M., translator see Andreyev, L. N. 233

4563. Kazantzakis, Nikos, 1885-1957. Le Christ Recrucifie. 2 parts, tragedy. L'Avant Scène, 264 (May 1, 1962), 9-34. François Daviel, adapter. In French.

4564. _____. Comedy: A Tragedy in One Act. Literary Review, 18 (Summer, 1975), 417-454. Kimon Friar, translator.

4565. _____. Sodom and Gomorrah. 2 acts. Literary Review, 19 (Winter, 1976), 126-356. Kimon Friar, translator.

4566. Kearney, Patrick. The Great Noontide. 1 act, satire. Drama, 11 (January, 1921), 109-113.

4567. _____. A Man's Man. 4 acts. Petite Illustration, 187 (March 10, 1934), 1-26. Georges Jamin, adapter. In French.

4568. _____. The Murder of Marat. 1 act. Drama, 18 (April, 1928), 208-210.

4569. _____. Tongues of Fire. 1 act. Drama, 11 (August-September, 1921), 397-401.

4570. Kearns, John. The Enchanted Thorn. 1 act. Drama, 11 (June, 1921), 324-325.

4571. Keats, Mark. Peter Salem. Minuteman. 1 act. Plays, 35 (April, 1976), 55-64.

4572. Kedrov, V. The Mad Dog. 1 act. Poet Lore, 58 (Spring, 1963), 55-64. Moshe Spiegel, translator.

4573. Keeler, Charles. A Pagoda Slave. 1 act. Drama, 12 (February, 1922), 163-166.

4574. Keenan, Martha. The Princess with the Broken Heart. 1 act. Plays, 28 (February, 1969), 63-66.

Keene, Donald, 1922- , translator see Mishima, Y. 6080

_____, translator see Yukio, M. 9625

Keene, Frances, translator see Sarment, J. 7941

4575. Keith, Joseph Joel. Black Lilacs. 1 act. Fantasy, 4 (Summer, 1934), 28-31.

4576. Kelleher, D. L. Her Dowry. 1 act. Dublin Magazine, 1 (April, 1924), 815-821.

4577. Kelley, Ethel. Paging John Harvard. 1 act. Bookman [New York], 65 (April, 1927), 163-166.

4578. Kelly, George Edward, 1887- . Craig's Wife. 3 acts. Il Dramma, 406/407 (July 15/August 1, 1943), 39-69. Bice Chiappelli, translator. In Italian.

4579. _____. Finders-Keepers. 1 act. Scholastic, 26 (March 16-23, 1935), 8-10, 27; 10-13.

4580. _____. The Show-Off. 3 acts, comedy. Scholastic, 17 (November 1, 15, 29, December 13, 1930, January 3, 17, 1931), 6-8, 10; 10-12, 15, 18; 9-10, 12, 19, 28; 11-12, 28-31; 11-12, 26, 28, 31; 8-10, 25.

4581. Kelly, Mollie. More Than a Million. 1 act, comedy. Scholastic, 25 (November 24, 1934), 5-7, 16.

4582. Kelly, Thomas, 1909- . The Golden Brew. 1 act. Dublin Magazine, n.s., 31 (July-September, 1955), 18-34.

4583. Kelly, Tim. A Tale That Wagged the Dog. 1 act. Dramatics, 47 (January, 1976), 16-21.

4584. Kelsey, Alice Geer. The Wise Man and the Hodja. 1 act. Plays, 31 (January, 1972), 39-44.

4585. Kemp, Harry, 1883- . The Dramatic Art, A Viennese Fantasy. 1 act. Smart Set, 74 (May, 1924), 41-50.

4586. _____. The Prodigal Son. 1 act. Smart Set, 52 (July, 1917), 83-93.

Kemp, Lysander, translator see Garro, E. 3401

_____, translator see Villaurrutia, X. 9148

4587. Kenan, Amos. The Balloon. 1 act. First Stage, 2 (Summer, 1963), 187-193. Rosette Lamont, translator.

4588. _____. Jesus, As Seen by His Friends. 2 acts. Drama and Theatre, 11 (Spring, 1973), 148-158.

4589. _____. The Lion. 1 act. First Stage, 4 (Spring, 1965), 8-13. Rosette Lamont, translator.

4590. Kennard, Marietta C. The Flight of the Herons. 1 act. Drama, 14 (December, 1923), 97-98, 107.

4591. Kennedy, Adrienne. The Owl Answers. 1 act. Poet Lore, 60 (Autumn, 1965), 195-211.

4592. Kennedy, Charles Rann. The Servant in the House. 5 acts. Golden Book, 2 (December, 1925), 795-815.

4593. Kennedy, Lucy. No One's Safe. 1 act. One-Act Play Magazine, 4 (March-April, 1941), 137-163.

4594. _____. The Pied Piper of Hamelin. 1 act. Plays, 12 (April, 1953), 47-56.

4595. _____. Tom Paine. 1 act. Plays, 4 (March, 1945), 10-14.

4596. Kennedy, Margaret, 1896- and Basil Dean. The Constant Nymph. 3 acts, comedy. Petite Illustration, 189 (December 22, 1934), 1-42. Jean Giraudoux, adapter. In French.

4597. Kenney, Francis L., Jr. Lady Lawyer. 1 act, satire. One-Act Play Magazine, 3 (March-April, 1940), 265-271.

4598. Kenny, Maurice. Forked Tongues. 1 act. Drama and Theatre, 12 (Spring, 1975), 143-153.

Kent, David see Bond, N. 1177

4599. Kent, Priscilla. Ellen Comes Through. 1 act. Senior Scholastic, 43 (September 27-October 2, 1943), 15-16.

Kepel, Milan, adapter see Havel, V. 3981

———, adapter see Topol, J. 8888

4600. Kerautem, Louis de. Le Centenaire. 1 act. L'Avant Scène, 494 (May 1, 1972), 35-42. In French.

4601. ———. Le Roti de Veau. 1 act. L'Avant Scène, 506 (November 15, 1972), 41-51. In French.

4602. Kerley, Rosialee. The Wedding Guest. 1 act. Poet Lore, 33 (Summer, 1922), 232-238.

Kern, Gary, translator see Lunts, L. 5093

4603. Kernan, Mary Anne. Book Week Birthday Party. 1 act. Wilson Library Bulletin, 15 (October, 1940), 154-156.

4604. Kerr, Jean, 1923- and Eleanor Brooke. King of Hearts. 3 acts, comedy. Theatre Arts, 39 (July, 1955), 35-62.

4605. Keskin, Yildirim. Le Lointain. 1 act. L'Avant Scène, 229, 41-46. In French.

4606. Kesselring, Joseph, 1902-1967. Arsenic and Old Lace. 3 acts, comedy. Il Dramma, n.s., 11 (April 15, 1946), 9-38. Vinicio Marinucci, translator. In Italian.

4607. Kester, Katharine. Penny a Flower. 1 act. Drama, 15 (December, 1924), 59-63.

4608. Ketchum, Arthur. Bethlehem. 1 act. Hornbook, 19 (November-December, 1943), 435-443.

4609. ———. The Maid's Prologue. 1 act. Poet Lore, 25 (Summer, 1924), 206-209.

4610. Ketchum, Philip L. Breadline. 1 act. Survey Graphic, 22 (August, 1933), 414-416.

4611. ———. The Whistle Blows. 1 act. The Survey, 67 (January 1, 1932), 361-363, 397.

4612. Keyser, Frank. Count the Days I'm Gone. 1 act. One-Act Play Magazine, 3 (July-August, 1940), 403-415.

4613. Kezich, Tullio. Una burla riuscita. Sipario, 17 (April, 1962), 31-44. In Italian.

4614. _____. La coscienza di Zeno. 2 parts. Sipario, 19 (November, 1964), 30-55. In Italian.

4615. _____. Lo stanzone. 2 acts. Sipario, 266 (June, 1968), 65-80. In Italian.

4616. _____ and Luigi Squarzina. Bouvard e Picuchet. 2 acts. Sipario, 271 (November, 1968), 48-71. In Italian.

4617. Khaytov, Nikolay. Paths. 1 act. Literary Review, 16 (Winter, 1972-73), 203-214. Anastasia D. Moser, translator.

4618. Kielland, Alexander Lange, 1849-1906. Three Couples. 3 acts, comedy. Drama, 26 (May, 1917), 240-324. Henry Lindanger, translator.

4619. Kiggins, William R. "I Don't Understand..." 1 act. Resource, 8 (June, 1967), 18-22.

4620. Kihm, Jean-Jacques. Oedipe, ou Le Silence des Dieux. 2 parts. L'Avant Scène, 567 (July 1, 1975), 39-61. In French.

4621. Kildare, George. The Watchers. 1 act. This Quarter, 1 (No. 1, 1925), 89-96.

4622. Kilty, Jerome, 1922- . Dear Liar. 2 acts, comedy. L'Avant Scène, 242 (May 1, 1961), 10-25. Jean Cocteau, adapter. In French.

4623. _____. Dear Liar. 2 acts, comedy. Sipario, 17 (January, 1962), 33-45. Emilio Cecchi, translator. In Italian.

4624. Kilvert, Margaret Cameron, 1867- . A Christmas Chime. 1 act. McClure's, 22 (December, 1903), 174-184.

4625. _____. The Committee on Matrimony. 1 act, comedy. McClure's, 21 (October, 1903), 659-665.

4626. Kimball, Kathleen. The Meat Rack. Scripts, 1 (May, 1972), 4-28.

4627. Kimball, Ruth Putnam. Where Is Phronsie Pepper? 1 act. Plays, 24 (March, 1965), 51-59.

_____, adapter see Burnett, F. H. 1441

4628. Kimmel, H. B. Radio Felicity. 1 act. Literary Review, 15 (Fall, 1971), 101-119.

4629. King, Florence. Cross My Palm with Silver. 1 act. Wilson Library Bulletin, 11 (October, 1936), 119-120.

4630. King, Grace Elizabeth, 1852- . A Splendid Offering. 1 act, comedy. Drama, 16 (March, 1926), 213-215, 235-237.

4631. King, Peggy Cameron. The Lonely Little Old Lady. 1 act. Plays, 24 (December, 1964), 29-38.

4632. King, Walter. Little Snow White. 1 act. Plays, 23 (January, 1964), 79-82.

4633. King and the Vowels, The. 1 act. Plays, 3 (January, 1944), 50-52.

4634. Kingman, Lee, 1919- . Mr. Thanks Has His Day. 1 act. Plays, 3 (November, 1943), 37-42.

4635. ———. A Time from Now. 1 act. Plays, 3 (December, 1943), 1-11.

4636. Kingsbury, Sara. Christmas Guest. 1 act. Drama, 32 (November, 1918), 455-461.

4637. Kingsley, Sidney, 1906- . Darkness at Noon. 3 acts, tragedy. Theatre Arts, 37 (April, 1953), 34-64.

4638. Kipling, Rudyard, 1865-1936. Captains Courageous. 1 act. Plays, 15 (April, 1956), 79-87. Lewy Olfson, adapter.

4639. ———. Kim. 1 act. Plays, 35 (May, 1976), 83-92. Adele Thane, adapter.

4640. ———. The Lamentable Comedy of Willow Wood. 1 act. Fortnightly, 53 (May, 1890), 670-681.

4641. Kipphardt, Heinar, 1922- . In Der Sache J. Robert Oppenheimer. 1 act. Spectaculum, 7 (1964), 199-280. In German.

4642. ———. Shakespeare Dringend Gesucht. 3 acts, satiric comedy. Sipario, 11 (July-August, 1956), 70-88. Simonetta Martini, translator. In Italian.

Kirby, Victoria Nes, translator see Kruchenykh, A. 4733

———, translator see Marinetti, F. T. 5549

———, translator see Mayakovsky, V. 5702

———, translator see Ribemont-Dessaignes, G. 7507

4643. Kirker, Katherine. The Lady Compassionate. 1 act. Poet Lore, 33 (Summer, 1922), 239-245.

Kirkland, Jack, 1902- see Caldwell, E. 1504

4644. Kish, Jack. Man and a Computer Machine. 1 act. Dramatika, 10 (1973), n.p.

4645. Kishida, Kunio, 1890-1954. Adoration. 1 act. Literary Review, 6 (Autumn, 1962), 122-143. Richard McKinnon, translator.

4646. Kishon, Ephraim. The Blaumilch Canal. 1 act. Il Dramma, n.s., 308 (May, 1962), 49-57. Elio Piattelli, translator. In Italian.

4647. _____. The Blaumilch Canal. 1 act. Gambit, 3 (No. 12), 69-88.

4648. Kistemaekers, Henri. L'istinto. 3 acts. Il Dramma, 125 (November 1, 1931), 4-23. In Italian.

4649. Kitaif, Theodore. Confessions. 1 act. Trace, 68 (1968), 328-329.

4650. _____. Learning the Ropes. 1 act. Dramatika, 6 (Fall, 1970), 28-31.

4651. _____. A Way Out. 1 act. Dust, 4 (Summer, 1969), 32-36.

4652. Kitani, Shigeo. The Sound of Night. 1 act. Players' Magazine, 41 (October, 1964), 13-20. Andrew T. Tsubaki, translator.

4653. Kivi, Aleksis, 1834-1872. Eva. 1 act. Dublin Magazine, n.s., 1 (October-December, 1926), 15-30. R. P. Cowl, translator.

4654. Kiyotsugu, Kwannami, 1334-1384. La donna di Eguchi. 1 act. Il Dramma, n.s., 322/323 (July/August, 1963), 63-66. Enrico Fulchignoni, translator. In Italian.

Klancar, Anthony J., translator see Murnik, R. 6308

4655. Klauber, Adolph. The Green-Eyed Monster. 1 act. Smart Set, 42 (January, 1914), 133-141.

4656. Klauber, Amy Josephine. The Exile. 1 act. Poet Lore, 33 (Summer, 1922), 246-254.

4657. Kleibacker, Frederick. Lady Wildcat. 1 act. American Prefaces, 2 (February, 1937), 67-72. ALSO 5 (June, 1940), 171-176.

4658. Klein, Elaine. Moving Day. 1 act. Plays, 23 (May, 1964), 37-44.

4659. Klein, Johanne. Le Laitier. 1 act. L'Avant Scène, 426 (May 15, 1969), 40-44. In French.

4660. _____. Silences. 1 act, comedy. L'Avant Scène, 328 (February 15, 1965), 42-47. In French.

4661. Kleist, Heinrich von, 1777-1811. The Broken Jug. 1 act. Poet Lore, 45 (No. 2, 1939), 146-209. John T. Krumpelmann, translator.

4662. _____. The Feud of the Schroffensteins. 5 acts. Poet Lore, 27 (Autumn, 1916), 457-576. Mary J. Price and Laurance M. Price, translators.

4663. _____. Robert Guiscard, Duke of the Normans. 1 act, tragedy. Tulane Drama Review, 6 (March, 1962), 178-192. L. R. Scheuer, translator.

4664. _____. Der Zerbrochene Krug. 1 act, comedy. L'Avant Scène, 296 (October 1, 1963), 9-29. Michel Arnaud, adapter. In French.

4665. Kliewer, Warren. The Daughters of Lot. Kansas Quarterly, 3 (Winter, 1970-71), 91-132.

Knapp, Bettina L., translator see Arrabal, F. 372, 373, 376, 378

_____, translator see Vauthier, J. 9049

4666. Knee, Allan. Ephraim. 1 act. First Stage, 5 (Spring, 1966), 23-29.

4667. Knight, Elizabeth Lou. Shrimp! 1 act. Plays, 3 (November, 1943), 81-85.

4668. Knight, Lee. Flibber Turns the Tables. 1 act. Plays, 9 (November, 1949), 63-68.

4669. Knight, Ruth Adams, 1898- . No Medals. 1 act. Plays, 2 (November, 1942), 62-66.

4670. Knott, Frederick. Dial M for Murder. 3 acts. L'Avant Scène, 88, 1-31. Roger Feral, adapter. In French.

4671. _____. Dial M for Murder. 3 acts. Theatre Arts, 39 (March, 1955), 35-63.

Knowlton, Beatrice see Knowlton, D. 4672

4672. Knowlton, Don and Beatrice Knowlton. The Way the Noise Began. 1 act, comedy. Drama, 12 (October-November, 1921), 20-21.

4673. Knox, Alexander, 1907- . The Closing Door. 2 acts. Theatre Arts, 34 (May, 1950), 61-68.

4674. Knox, Margaret and Anna M. Lutkenhaus. America, the Beautiful, Democracy's Goal: A Pageant. 1 act. St. Nicholas, 47 (June, 1920), 738-744.

4675. Koch, Kenneth, 1925- . Bertha. 1 act. Evergreen Review, 4 (November-December, 1960), 42-45.

4676. _____. Seven Plays: The Academic Murders; Easter; Mexico City; The Lost Feed; The Gold Standard; The Building of Florence. 1 act each. Art and Literature, 6 (Autumn, 1965), 44-52.

Koeckert, translator see Martinez Sierra, G. and M. Martinez Sierra 5631

4677. Koenig, Eleanor C. The Grave Woman. 1 act. Poetry, 32 (July, 1928), 206-209.

4678. _____. Two Dialogues: The Shade; Two on an Old Pathway. Poetry, 35 (November, 1929), 87-91.

4679. Koestler, Arthur, 1905- . Twilight Bar. 2 parts. Il Dramma, n.s., 45 (September 15, 1947), 9-33. Vinicio Marinucci, translator. In Italian.

4680. Kojiro, Kanze, 1435-1516. A Butterfly. 2 parts. Prairie Schooner, 33 (Fall, 1959), 221-224. Makoto Ueda, translator.

3681. Kokoschka, Oscar, 1886- . Assassino, speranza delle donne. 1 act. Sipario, 326 (July, 1973), 57-59. Lia Secci, translator. In Italian.

4682. _____. Morder, Hoffnung der Frauen. 1 act. Der Sturm, 1 (July 14, 1910), 155-156. In German.

4683. _____. Murderer, The Women's Hope. 1 act. Tulane Drama Review, 2 (May, 1958), 71-74. Michael Hamburger, translator.

4684. Konick, Marcus. The Atom and Oak Ridge, Tennessee. 1 act. Plays, 5 (May, 1946), 71-75.

4685. Koon, Helene, adapter. Pierre Patelin. 1 act. Plays, 24 (January, 1965), 37-48.

4686. Kopit, Arthur. The Conquest of Everest. 1 act. Mademoiselle (November, 1964), 159, 207-209.

4687. _____. The Conquest of Everest. 1 act. Sipario, 21 (January, 1966), 62-64. Luciano Codignola, translator. In Italian.

4688. _____. La Conquête de L'Everest. 1 act. L'Avant Scène, 404 (June 1, 1968), 40-43. Renée Rosenthal, adapter. In French.

4689. _____. Indians. 2 acts. Sipario, 25 (August-September, 1970), 68-85. Mario Maffi, translator. In Italian.

4690. Kops, Bernard, 1926- . David, It Is Getting Dark. 3 acts. L'Avant Scène, 454 (August 1, 1970), 7-38. Edith Zetline, translator. In French.

4691. _____. The Hamlet of Stepney Green. 3 acts. Il Dramma, n.s., 280 (January, 1960), 12-38. In Italian.

4692. Koselka, Fritz. Uno strano tè in casa Halden. 3 acts. Il Dramma, 349 (March 1, 1941), 8-27. Vincenzo Tieri, translator. In Italian.

Kosicka, Jadwiga, translator see Witkiewicz, S. I. 9517

Koteliansky, S. S., translator see Chekhov, A. P. 1779, 1786

4693. Kotzebue, August von, 1761-1819. The Deserter. 1 act, farce. Golden Book, 7 (February, 1928), 193-202. Beatrice B. Beebe, translator.

4694. _____. The House by the Side of the Road. 1 act. Golden Book, 10 (July, 1929), 89-93. Beatrice B. Beebe, translator.

4695. _____. The Man Who Couldn't Talk. 1 act, comedy. Poet Lore, 40 (1929), 223-236. Beatrice B. Beebe, translator.

4696. _____. The Nightcap of the Prophet Elias. 1 act, farce. Poet Lore, 40 (1929), 391-406. Beatrice B. Beebe, translator.

4697. _____. Pharaoh's Daughter. 1 act, comedy. Golden Book, 8 (July, 1928), 53-59. Beatrice B. Beebe, translator.

Kovacs, Jeno, translator see Gorgey, C. 3643

4698. Kozak, Primož, 1929- . Il congresso. 3 acts. Il Dramma, 45, no. 5 (February, 1969), 49-68. Alessio Lokar, translator. In Italian.

4699. Kozlenko, William, 1907- . The Devil Is a Good Man. 1 act. One-Act Play Magazine, 3 (March-April, 1940), 195-229.

4700. _____. It Takes a Thief. 1 act, comedy. First Stage, 4 (Winter, 1965-66), 232-236.

4701. _____. Jacob Comes Home. 1 act. One-Act Play Magazine, 2 (December, 1938), 515-524.

4702. _____. The Street Attends a Funeral. 1 act. One-Act Play Magazine, 2 (May, 1938), 58-66.

4703. _____. This Earth Is Ours. 5 parts. Il Dramma, 381 (July 1, 1942), 34-43. Liana Ferri, translator. In Italian.

4704. _____. This Earth Is Ours. 1 act. One-Act Play Magazine, 1 (June, 1937), 153-179.

4705. _____. The Trumpets of Wrath. 1 act. One-Act Play Magazine, 1 (November, 1937), 627-663.

4706. Krakauer, Daniel. Jack Who Yawned. 2 acts. Locus Solus, 2 (Summer, 1961), 132-143.

4707. Kramme, Walter. Outline for a Pageant. 1 act. Resource, 2 (February, 1961), 18-19.

4708. Kranz, Heinrich B. Il masseur. 1 act. Il Dramma, 39 (April 1, 1928), 36-37. Taulero Zulberti, translator. In Italian.

4709. Krasna, Norman, 1909- . Dear Ruth. 3 acts. Il Dramma, n.s., 126 (February 1, 1951), 9-34. Ada Salvatore, translator. In Italian.

4710. Kraus, Karl, 1875-1936. Ultima notte dell'uomo. 1 act. Il Dramma, n.s., 115/116 (August 15/September 1, 1950), 112-119. In Italian.

4711. Krauss, Carol. For the Love of Mike. 1 act. Learning With..., 3 (February, 1975), 21.

4712. Kreymborg, Alfred, 1883-1966. Brother Bill, A Little Play from Harlem. 1 act, comedy. Theatre Arts, 11 (April, 1927), 299-306.

4713. _____. Helpless Herberts. 1 act, comedy. Theatre Arts, 8 (February, 1924), 119-132.

4714. _____. I'm Not Complaining, A Kaffeeklatsch. 1 act. Theatre Arts, 15 (June, 1931), 493-498.

4715. _____. Monday, A Lame Minuet. 1 act. Drama, 10 (May, 1920), 264-271.

4716. _____. No More War; An Ode to Peace. 1 act. Esquire, 29 (February, 1948), 72-73.

4717. _____. Pianissimo; An Intermezzo. 1 act. Poetry, 20 (July, 1922), 175-186.

4718. _____. Privilege and Privation, A Playful Affair. 1 act. One-Act Play Magazine, 1 (June, 1937), 141-152.

4719. _____. Slow Blue; A Feminine Fantasia. 1 act. Poetry, 54 (July, 1939), 197-201.

4720. _____. There's a Nation. 1 act. Senior Scholastic, 44 (April 3-8, 1944), 15-16.

4721. _____. Trap Door--A Travesty for Slow as Well as for Quick Feet. 1 act. Theatre Arts, 9 (November, 1925), 742-751.

4722. _____. Trap Doors. 1 act. Scholastic, 22 (April 1, 1933), 8-9, 13, 18, 24.

4723. _____. Uneasy Street (A Village Play). 1 act. One-Act Play Magazine, 2 (June-July, 1938), 83-104.

4724. _____. When the Willow Nods, A Dance-Play for Poem-mimes. 1 act. Poetry, 11 (March, 1918), 287-297.

4725. Kring, Hilda Adam. The Bird Who Couldn't Sing. 1 act. Plays, 16 (April, 1957), 65-66.

4726. Kroetz, Franz Xaver, 1946- . La corte delle stalle. 2 acts. Sipario, 319 (December, 1972), 60-70. Maria Luisa D'Agostino, translator. In Italian.

4727. _____. Michi's Blood; A Requiem. Partisan Review, 43 (No. 3, 1976), 427-438. Michael Roloff and Denise Gordon, translators.

4728. _____. Oberosterreich. 3 acts. Sipario, 336 (May, 1974), 48-61. Umberto Gandini, translator. In Italian.

4729. Kroll, Francis Lynde, 1904- . The Great Golden Nugget. 1 act. Plays, 21 (March, 1962), 58-64.

4730. _____. Halloween Brew. 1 act. Plays, 16 (October, 1956), 82-86.

4731. _____. The Hiding Place. 1 act. Plays, 19 (April, 1960), 53-59.

4732. _____. The Jester and the King's Tarts. 1 act. Plays, 17 (February, 1958), 72-76.

4733. Kruchenykh, Alexei. Victory Over the Sun. 2 acts. Drama Review, 15 (Fall, 1971), 107-124. Ewa Bartos and Victoria Nes Kirby, translators.

4734. Krum, Charlotte. The Shoemaker's Guest. 1 act. Horn Book, 16 (November-December, 1940), 467-473.

Krumpelmann, John T., translator see Kleist, H. 4661

_____, translator see Sachs, H. 7841

4735. Krushel, Kenneth, adapter. The Exploits of Mullah Nasrudin. 1 act. Plays, 35 (March, 1976), 39-46.

4736. Kummer, Clare. The Inspiration of the Play; Some Confessions of a Woman Playwright. 1 act. Forum, 61 (March, 1919), 307-316.

4737. Kummer, Frederic Arnold, 1873- . The Love of Women. 1 act. Smart Set, 28 (August, 1909), 123-130.

4738. Kuo, Mo-Jo. Chu Yuan. 5 acts. Sipario, 13 (December, 1957), 49-72. Maria Tchou Mamo, translator. In Italian.

4739. Kurnitz, Harry, 1908- . The Reclining Figure. 3 acts, comedy. Theatre Arts, 40 (June, 1956), 33-55.

Kurtz, Maurice, adapter see Miller, A. 5848

4740. Kuyumjian, Dikran, 1895- . The Ci-divant. 1 act. Dial, 69 (August, 1920), 125-131.

4741. Kvapil, Jaroslav, 1868-1950. The Clouds. 3 acts. Poet Lore, 21 (November-December, 1910), 417-466. Charles Recht, translator.

4742. _____. The Princess Pampelishka. 3 acts. Poet Lore, 54 (Spring, 1948), 3-69. Emilie Honzik Condon, Ingeborg E. Smith, Dorothea Prall Radin, and George Rapall Noyes, translators.

4743. _____. The Will o' the Wisp. 4 acts. Poet Lore, 27 (New Year's, 1916), 1-75. Sarka B. Hrbkova, translator.

4744. Kvaran, Einar H. Governor Lenhard. 5 acts. Poet Lore, 43 (No. 1, 1936), 3-55. Jakobina Johnson, translator.

Kwei Chen see Chen, Kwei

L

4745. L., Y. The Dark Wood. 1 act. Dublin Magazine, n.s., 17 (October-December, 1942), 7-10.

4746. Labiche, Eugene, 1815-1888. Les Chemins de Fer. 5 acts. Sipario, 21 (January, 1966), 41-61. Gigi Lunari, translator. In Italian.

4747. _____. The Man Who Set Fire to a Lady. 1 act, comedy. Tulane Drama Review, 4 (December, 1959), 145-162. Fred Partridge, translator.

4748. _____. Le Plus Heureux Des Trois. 3 acts. Il Dramma, n.s., 355/356 (April/May, 1966), 15-39. Marcel le Duc, translator. In Italian.

4749. _____. Si deve dire? 3 acts. Il Dramma, n.s., 369/370 (June/July, 1967), 52-76. Marcel le Duc, translator. In Italian.

4750. _____. 29 gradi all'ombra. 1 act. Il Dramma, n.s., 355/356 (April/May, 1966), 40-48. Marcel le Duc, translator. In Italian.

4751. _____. Il viaggio de Signor Perrichon. 4 acts. Il Dramma, n.s., 369/370 (June/July, 1967), 25-49. Marcel le Duc, translator. In Italian.

4752. _____. Voyage autour de ma Marmite. 1 act. vaudeville. L'Avant Scène, 562 (April 15, 1975), 23-40. In French.

4753. _____ and Marc Michel, 1812-1868. La fille bien gardee. 1 act, comedy. L'Avant Scène, 503 (October 1, 1972), 33-45. In French.

4754. _____. A Leghorn Hat. 5 acts, comedy. Poet Lore, 28 (New Year's, 1917), 1-53. Clair Vincent Chesley, translator.

4755. _____. La station Champbandet. 3 acts, comedy. L'Avant Scène, 503 (October 1, 1972), 7-32. In French.

4756. Labrenn, Theodore. The Grass's Springing. 3 acts. First Stage, 2 (Fall, 1963), 365-389.

4757. Lacey, Jackson. The Prince, the Wolf and the Firebird. 2 acts. Gambit, 4 (No. 14), 5-107.

4758. Lackmann, Ronald. The Crooked Jar. 1 act. Plays, 17 (February, 1958), 77-80.

4759. _____. Why the Indians Wear Moccasins. 1 act. Plays, 17 (November, 1957), 61-64.

4760. Lacour, Jean. Mascarin. 3 acts, comedy. L'Avant Scène, 207 (November 1, 1959), 6-34. In French.

4761. Lacour, Jose-Andre, 1919- . L'Annee du Bac. 3 acts. L'Avant Scène, 187 (December 15, 1958), 7-34. In French.

4762. _____. Club. 1 act. L'Avant Scène (OST), 27 (June, 1950), 23-29. In French.

4763. _____. Notre Peau. 3 acts. L'Avant Scène (OST), 27 (June, 1950), 3-20. In French.

_____, adapter see Chayefsky, P. 1746

_____, translator see Wouk, H. 9571

4764. Lagerkvist, Pär, 1891- . Bödeln. 1 act. Il Dramma, n.s., 166 (October 1, 1952), 9-24. Giacomo Oreglia, translator. In Italian.

4765. _____. The Difficult Hour, Three One-Act Plays. Tulane Drama Review, 6 (November, 1961), 32-58. Thomas R. Buckman, translator.

4766. _____. Il Tunnel. 1 act. Il Dramma, n.s., 170/171/172 (December 1/15, 1952/January 1, 1953), 115-118. Pierre Halleaux, translator. In Italian.

4767. La Guma, Alex, 1925?- . The Man in the Tree. 1 act. Literary Review, 15 (Fall, 1971), 19-30.

Lahaye, Michelle, adapter see Wilde, O. 9371

4768. Lahr, Georgiana Lieder. The Enchanted Broom. 1 act. Plays, 26 (October, 1966), 72-74.

4769. Lakatos, Fodor. L'Affare Kubinski. 3 acts. Il Dramma, 192 (August 15, 1934), 4-33. Ada Salvatore, translator. In Italian.

4770. Lakatos, Laszlo. Miracolo d'amore. 1 act. Il Dramma, 22 (July 15, 1927), 44-45. Taulero Zulberti, translator. In Italian.

4771. _____. A quattr' occhi. 1 act. Il Dramma, 92 (June 15, 1930), 40-42. Corrado Rossi, translator. In Italian.

4772. _____. Sogni di minorenni. 1 act. Il Dramma, 97 (September 1, 1930), 44-45. Corrado Rossi, translator. In Italian.

4773. Lamb, A. C. Portrait of a Pioneer. 1 act. Negro History Bulletin, 12 (April, 1949), 162-164.

4774. Lamb, Esther Hill. Land Ho! 1 act. Drama, 21 (June, 1931), 13-14, 30.

4775. Lambeck, Frederick. Uncle Tertius on the Home Front. 1 act. Publishers' Weekly, 143 (January 23, 1943), 342-346.

Lamont, Rosette, translator see Ionesco, E. 4389

_____, translator see Kenan, A. 4589

4776. Lamoureux, Robert, 1920- . La Brune Que Voila. 3 acts, comedy. L'Avant Scène, 174 (May 15, 1958), 7-35. In French.

4777. _____. La soupiere. 2 acts, comedy. L'Avant Scène, 504 (October 15, 1972), 7-32. In French.

4778. Lampell, Millard. The Lonesome Train. 1 act. Senior Scholastic, 46 (February 5, 1945), 17-19.

4779. _____. Talk Their Language. 1 act. Senior Scholastic, 46 (April 9, 1945), 13-15.

4780. Lampton, W. J. A Pair of Them. 1 act. Smart Set, 1 (May, 1900), 141-142.

4781. Landi, Stefano. I Bambini. 1 act. Il Dramma, 358 (July 15, 1941), 43-49. In Italian.

4782. _____. Ciò che non si dice. 1 act. Il Dramma, 361/362 (September 1/15, 1941), 92-96. In Italian.

4783. _____. Il falco d'argento. 3 acts. Il Dramma, 301 (March 1, 1939), 4-22. In Italian.

4784. _____. Un gradino più giù. 3 acts. Il Dramma, 380 (June 15, 1942), 7-24. In Italian.

4785. _____. In questo solo mondo. 3 acts. Il Dramma, 417/418 (January 1/15, 1944), 5-27.

4786. _____. L'uccelliera. 1 act. Il Dramma, 365 (November 1, 1941), 31-41. In Italian.

4787. Landor, Walter Savage, 1775-1864. The Empress Catharine and Princess Dashkof; An Imaginary Conversation. 1 act. Golden Book, 14 (September, 1931), 172-176.

4788. Lane, Kenneth Westmacott. Creation; A Phantasy. 1 act. Palms, 2 (Early Fall, 1924), 72-74.

4789. Lane, Marion. Is There Life on Other Planets? 1 act. Plays, 24 (March, 1965), 60.

4790. Lang, André, 1893- . Fragile. 3 acts, comedy. Petite Illustration, 87 (March 16, 1930), 1-30. In French.

4791. _____. Les Trois Henry. 4 acts. Petite Illustration, 88 (July 19, 1930), 1-33. In French.

4792. Lang, Andrew, 1844-1912. The New Pygmalion, or the Statue's Choice. 1 act. Longman's Magazine, 1 (January, 1883), 299-302.

4793. _____. La voce dell'amore. 1 act. Il Dramma, 89 (May 1, 1930), 39-44. Corrado Rossi, translator. In Italian.

4794. Lang, L. Lockhart. On the Hire System. 1 act. Blackwood's Magazine, 170 (November, 1901), 591-612.

4795. Langer, Frantisek. Die Uhr. Der Sturm, 5 (July, 1914), 62-63. In German.

4796. Langford, Ernest. The Snake. 1 act. Prism International, 1 (Winter, 1959), 5-30.

4797. Langley, Noel, 1911- . Little Lambs Eat Ivy. 3 acts. Il Dramma, n.s., 103 (February 15, 1950), 11-38. Ada Salvatore, translator. In Italian.

_____ see also Morley, R. 6232, 6233, 6234

4798. Langner, Lawrence. Wedded: A Social Comedy. 1 act. Little Review, 1 (November, 1914), 8-18.

4799. Langston, Lucile E. Footprints. 1 act. Plays, 19 (February, 1960), 73-78.

4800. _____. The Whistler. 1 act. Plays, 17 (April, 1958), 75-77.

Languasco, Nardo, translator see Garcia Lorca, F. 3382, 3385

4801. Languirand, Jacques. The Departures. 3 acts. Gambit, 5 41-74. Albert Bermel, translator.

4802. Lanoux, Armand, 1913- and Jacques Rutman. Le Commandant Watrin. L'Avant Scène, 334 (May 15, 1965), 20-52. In French.

4803. Lanoux, Victor, 1936- . Le Peril Bleu, ou, Mefiez-Vous des Autobus. 2 acts, comedy. L'Avant Scène, 556 (January 15, 1975), 5-33. In French.

4804. _____. Le Tourniquet. L'Avant Scène, 520 (June 15, 1973), 7-31. In French.

Lansing, Ruth, translator see Echegaray y Eizaguirre, J. 2811

4805. Lanza, Francesco. Giorno di festa. 1 act. Il Dramma, 330 (May 15, 1940), 29-32. In Italian.

4806. Lanza, Giuseppe. Il binocolo alla rovescia. 3 acts. Il Dramma, 181 (March 1, 1934), 4-27. In Italian.

4807. _____. Un mondo mai visto. 1 act. Il Dramma, n.s., 313 (October, 1962), 49-55. In Italian.

4808. _____. Il peccato. 3 acts. Il Dramma, 63 (April 1, 1929), 4-25. In Italian.

4809. _____. Il profumo delle magnolie. 1 act. Il Dramma, 211 (June 1, 1935), 30-38. In Italian.

4810. _____. Zuda. 3 acts. Il Dramma, 261 (July 1, 1937), 2-24. In Italian.

4811. Laparcerie-Richepin, Cora. La Vraie Carmen. 2 parts. Petite Illustration, 192 (October 12, 1935), 1-25. In French.

4812. Lapena, Amelia. Sepang Loca. 1 act. Literary Review, 3 (Summer, 1960), 592-611.

4813. La Porte, René. C'era una volta un bola.... 1 act. Il Dramma, n.s., 119 (October 15, 1950), 45-49. B. L. Randone, translator. In Italian.

4814. _____. Federigo. 3 acts. Il Dramma, n.s., 115/116, (August 15/September 1, 1950), 7-32. Luciana Cane and Gigi Cane, translators. In Italian.

4815. _____. La Fleur d'Oubli. 2 acts. L'Avant Scène (ROST), 64 (July, 1952), 1-32. In French.

4816. Larger, Dominique-Pierre, 1945- . Le Gage. 1 act. L'Avant Scène, 427 (June 1, 1969), 49-50. In French.

4817. Larguier, Leo. Les Bonaparte. 3 acts, tragedy. Petite Illustration, 86 (February 18, 1928), 1-22. In French.

Lari, Carlo, translator see Achard, M. 17, 34

_____, translator see Amiel, D. 185

_____, translator see Claudel, P. 1868

4818. Larkin, Margaret. El Cristo. 1 act. The Laughing Horse, 12 (August, 1925), 1-3, 24-32.

4819. Larra, Carlos. L'Accident. 1 act, farce. L'Avant Scène, 168 (February 15, 1958), 34-41. Maribel Montaner, translator. In French.

4820. _____. Sur une Plage de l'Ouest. 1 act, farce. L'Avant Scène, 191 (February 15, 1959), 38-41. Maribel Montaner, translator. In French.

4821. Larra, Mariano Jose de, 1809-1837. Quitting Business. 5 acts, comedy. Poet Lore, 35 (1924), 159-209. Kenneth C. Kaufman, translator.

4822. Larreta, Antonio, 1928- . Juan Palmieri Tupamaro. Sipario, 322 (March, 1973), 63-80. Maria Luisa Aguirre D'Amico, translator. In Italian.

4823. Larson, Edith. Safety First, Safety Last, Safety Always, 1 act. Plays, 27 (May, 1968), 35-41.

4824. _____, adapter. All Around the Town. 1 act. Plays, 29 (March, 1970), 63-71.

4825. Larson, Emma Mauritz. May Baskets New. 1 act. Woman's Home Companion, 45 (May, 1918), 39.

Lasaygues, Maurice see Bricaire, J.-J. 1321, 1322, 1323

Laudenbach, Pierre-Jules, 1897- , translator see Rattigan, T. 7423

4826. Laudenbach, Roland, 1921- . Bille en Tete. 2 acts, comedy. L'Avant Scène, 157, 6-34. In French.

_____ see also Anouilh, J. 282

4827. Launcelot and Elaine. 3 acts. The Delineator, 94 (May, 1919), 51.

4828. Laure, Katherine. Drums in the Dusk. 1 act. Plays, 10 (April, 1951), 17-30.

4829. _____. The Golden Door. 1 act. Plays, 4 (December, 1944), 48-51.

Laurel, Renee, translator see Horvath, O. von 4175

4830. Laurents, Arthur, 1920- . Invitation to a March. 3 acts. Theatre Arts, 46 (January, 1962), 25-56.

4831. ———. The Time of the Cuckoo. 2 acts. Theatre Arts, 37 (November, 1953), 34-60.

4832. ———. West Side Story. 2 acts. Theatre Arts, 43 (October, 1959), 33-54.

4833. ——— and Stephen Sondheim, 1930- . Gypsy. 2 acts. Theatre Arts, 46 (June, 1962), 25-56.

4834. Lauwick, Harvé. Non mi sposate! 1 act. Il Dramma, 2 (January, 1926), 44-48. In Italian.

4835. ———. Il ritorno di Ulisse. 1 act. Il Dramma, 100 (October 15, 1930), 42-46. In Italian.

4836. Lavedan, Henri Leon Emile, 1859-1940. Amour des Bêtes. 1 act. Smart Set, 9 (April, 1903), 131-133. In French.

4837. ———. Deux Ménages. 1 act. Smart Set, 19 (June, 1906), 108-112. In French.

4838. ———. Five Little Plays: Along the Quays; For Ever and Ever; Where Shall We Go?; The Afternoon Walk; Not at Home. 1 act each. Poet Lore, 28 (Vacation, 1917), 385-413. Mary Sibyl Holbrook, translator.

4839. ———. Il metodo per diventar celebi. 1 act. Il Dramma, 103 (December 1, 1930), 43-45. Bianca Giardini, translator. In Italian.

4840. ———. The Pearl. 1 act. Dramatist, 3 (January, 1912), 229-232.

4841. ———. Sunday on Sunday Goes By. 1 act. Poet Lore, 27 (Spring, 1916), 185-189. Mary Sibyl Holbrook, translator.

4842. ———. Their Heart. 6 parts, comedy. Poet Lore, 30 (Spring, 1919), 1-34. William V. Silverberg, translator.

4843. ———. Two Husbands. 1 act, comedy. Poet Lore, 19 (Summer, 1908), 207-211. Roy Temple House, translator.

Lavergne, Antonin, adapter see Feliu y Condina, J. 2980

Laville, Pierre, adapter see Rojas, F. de 7657

4844. Lawler, Lillian B., 1898- . The Gifts of Mother Lingua. 1 act. Classical Journal, 19 (October, 1923), 36-39.

4845. ———. Rex Helvetiorum. 1 act. Classical Journal, 15 (March, 1920), 365-367. In Latin.

4846. Lawler, Ray, 1921- . The Summer of the Seventeenth Doll. 3 acts. Sipario, 17 (June, 1962), 41-68. Ettore Capriolo, translator. In Italian.

4847. _____. Summer of the Seventeenth Doll. 3 acts. Theatre Arts, 43 (August, 1959), 25-56.

Lawrence, Andre see Brown, N. 1372

4848. Lawrence, Charles Edward, 1870-1940. The Caged Eagle. 1 act. Bookman [London], 84 (September, 1933), 277-279.

4849. _____. The Hour of Prospero. 1 act. 19th Century, 92 (October, 1922), 685-696.

4850. _____. The Message of Lazarus. 1 act. 19th Century, 91 (January, 1922), 170-176.

4851. Lawrence, David Herbert, 1885-1930. Altitude, the first Scene of an Unfinished Play. Laughing Horse, 20 (Summer, 1938), 13-34.

4852. _____. The Daughter-in-Law. 4 acts. Plays and Players, 14 (June, 1967), 23-38.

4853. _____. The Married Man. 4 acts. Virginia Quarterly Review, 16 (Autumn, 1940), 523-547.

4854. _____. The Merry-Go-Round. 5 acts. Virginia Quarterly Review, 17 (Winter, 1941, Supplement), 1-44.

4855. _____. The Widowing of Mrs. Holyoyd. 3 acts. New Editions, 1 (Fall, 1956), 5-27.

4856. Lawrence, Jerome, 1915- and Robert E. Lee, 1918- . Auntie Mame. 2 acts, comedy. Theatre Arts, 42 (November, 1958), 27-62.

4857. _____. The Gang's All Here. 3 acts. Theatre Arts, 44 (November, 1960), 25-56.

4858. _____. Inherit the Wind. 3 acts. Theatre Arts, 41 (August, 1957), 35-62.

4859. Lawrence, Joan. Somebody's Valentine. 1 act. Plays, 12 (February, 1953), 50-53.

4860. Laws, Anna Cantrell. A Twice-Told Tale. 1 act. Drama, 31 (August, 1918), 400-413.

4861. Lawson, John Howard, 1895- . Blockade. 1 act. One-Act Play Magazine, 2 (October, 1938), 405-420.

4862. Lawson, Wayne. Reflexions. 1 act. Hudson Review, 8 (Autumn, 1955), 388-404.

4863. Lay Confessional, A. 1 act. Living Age, 146 (August 7, 1880), 367-376.

Layera, Ramon, translator see Garcia, J. C. 3371

4864. Leacock, Stephen, 1869-1944. The Two Milords or the Blow of Thunder. 1 act. Atlantic, 159 (May, 1937), 597-599.

4865. Learsi, Rufus. The Triumph of Instinct. 1 act, comedy. Drama, 14 (October, 1923), 26-28.

4866. Leautier, Gilbert. La Jacassiere. 1 act. L'Avant Scène, 584 (April 1, 1976), 31-40. In French.

4867. Lebesque, Maurice, 1911- . L'Amour Parmi Nous. 2 parts, tragi-comedy. L'Avant Scène, 175 (June 1, 1958), 7-23. In French.

4868. _____. Les Fiancés de la Seine. 1 act. L'Avant Scène, 110, 1-7. In French.

4869. _____. La Nouvelle Amusette. 1 act. L'Avant Scène, 145, 27-39. In French.

4870. Lechlitner, Ruth. We Are the Rising Wing. 1 act. New Directions, 3 (1938), n.p.

4871. Ledoux, Louis Vernon, 1880- . A Sicilian Idyl. 1 act. Yale Review, 3 (October, 1913), 91-101.

_____, translator see The Fox's Grave 3239

_____, translator see She Who Was Finished 8230

_____, translator see Somebody-Nothing 8373

4872. Lee, Agnes. The Asphodel. 4 acts. North American Review, 182 (May, 1906), 770-776.

4873. _____. The Blunted Age. 1 act. Poetry, 19 (November, 1921), 71-73.

4874. _____. Eastland Waters. 1 act. Poetry, 7 (February, 1916), 234-235.

4875. Lee, Albert. A Prearranged Accident. 2 acts, comedy. Harper's, 95 (August, 1897), 475-483.

4876. Lee, Emma. At the Sign of the "Bible and Sun." 1 act. Wilson Library Bulletin, 9 (November, 1934), 120-129, 148

4877. Lee, Hobart. The Marriage Lease. 1 act. Smart Set, 38 (December, 1912), 133-141.

4878. Lee, James, 1923- . Career. 3 acts. Theatre Arts, 41 (November, 1957), 36-61.

4879. Lee, Jesse. Castaway on Polywolynesia. 1 act. Plays, 33 (January, 1974), 13-23.

4880. _____. Westward Ho! Ho! Ho! 1 act. Plays, 35 (October, 1975), 1-11.

4881. Lee, Mary Elizabeth. The Black Death, or Ta-Un, A Persian Tragedy. 1 act. Poet Lore, 28 (Winter, 1917), 691-702.

4882. _____. The Honor Cross. 1 act. Poet Lore, 27 (Winter, 1916), 702-706.

Lee, Robert E., 1918- see Lawrence, J. 4856, 4857, 4858

4883. Lee, Sylvia. The Green Piper. 1 act. Plays, 15 (April, 1956), 75-78.

4884. _____. Moonbeam Dares. 1 act. Plays, 16 (April, 1957), 67-71.

4885. _____. Spring Secrets. 1 act. Plays, 11 (March, 1952), 80-84.

4886. _____. The Whirlwind Comes. 1 act. Plays, 11 (October, 1951), 58-61.

Lee, Vernon, pseud. see Paget, Violet 6927, 6928

Lee Chin-Yang see Chin-Yang, Lee 1805

4887. Leech, Michael T. Galileo. 1 act. Plays, 27 (October, 1967), 13-27.

4888. _____. King to Be. 1 act. Plays, 31 (January, 1972), 45-56.

4889. _____. Punch and Judy; A Play for Puppets and People. 1 act. Plays, 26 (November, 1966), 91-98.

4890. _____. The Story of Gilbert and Sullivan. 1 act. Plays, 27 (November, 1967), 83-96.

4891. _____, adapter. Beauty and the Beast. 1 act. Plays, 27 (March, 1968), 85-94.

_____, adapter see Anderson, H. C. 193, 201

_____, adapter see Browning, R. 1376

_____, adapter see Gogol, N. 3601, 3602

_____, adapter see Tolstoy, L. N. 8876

4892. Lefevre-Geraldy, Paul, 1885- . Gilbert et Marcellin. 1 act. L'Avant Scène, 161, 36-42. In French.

4893. _____. Una storia d'amore. 4 acts. Il Dramma, 251 (February 1, 1937), 2-21. Enrico Raggio, translator. In Italian.

4894. Lefrancq, Germaine. Monsieur et Mesdames Kluck. 3 acts, comedy. L'Avant Scène, 118, 17-45. In French.

Le Grand, Maurice, pseud. see Nohain, F. 6623

4895. Lehan, Robert R. Lifeguards. 1 act. Dramatics, 45 (October, 1973), 6-10.

4896. Lehman, John F. Biskie the Snowman. 1 act. Plays, 4 (February, 1945), 51-54.

4897. _____. Good Health Trolley. 1 act. Plays, 4 (October, 1944), 53-55.

4898. _____. Pinkie and the Robins. 1 act. Plays, 3 (March, 1944), 55-56.

4899. _____. Two-Penny Show. 1 act. Plays, 4 (May, 1945), 57-60.

4900. _____. The Witch's Pattern. 1 act. Plays, 10 (October, 1950), 60-63.

Lehrman, Leonard, translator see Brecht, B. 1285

4901. Leinster, Murray and George B. Jenkins, Jr. The Beautiful Thing. 1 act. Smart Set, 59 (August, 1919), 89-95.

4902. Leitner, Irving A. Excitement at the Circus. 1 act. Plays 27 (November, 1967), 79-82.

4903. _____. The Thump-ity Bump-ity Box. 1 act. Plays, 27 (February, 1968), 65-68.

4904. Lelli, Renato, 1899- . All' insegna della sorelle Kadàr. 3 acts. Il Dramma, 295 (December 1, 1938), 4-25. In Italian.

347   Lelli

4905. _____. Sulle strade di notte. 3 acts. Il Dramma, n.s., 239/240 (August/September, 1956), 47-67. In Italian.

4906. Lello, Elizabeth. The Mystery at Tumble Inn. 1 act. Plays, 25 (May, 1966), 15-25.

4907. Lem, André. Le Premier Jour. 3 acts. L'Avant Scène (OST), 30 (October, 1950), 3-24. In French.

4908. Lemaitre, Jules, 1853-1914. Forgiveness. 3 acts, comedy. Poet Lore, 24 (Vacation, 1913), 209-236. Frances C. Fay, translator.

4909. Lemasson, Sophie and Jean-Claude Penchenat. 1789. The French Revolution, Year One. Gambit, 20, 9-52. Alexander Trocchi, translator.

Lemmi, Charles, translator see Goldoni, C. 3609

4910. Lengyel, Cornel Adam, 1915- . The Atom Clock. Poet Lore, 64 (Winter, 1969), 435-457.

4911. _____. The World's My Village, A Rustic Comedy. 1 act. Poet Lore, 55 (Autumn, 1950), 195-229.

4912. Lengyel, Melchior, 1880- . Beniamino. 3 acts. Il Dramma, 92 (June 15, 1930), 4-31. In Italian.

4913. _____. Ninotchka. 3 acts, comedy. L'Avant Scène (OST), 26 (June, 1950), 3-42. In French.

4914. _____. The Soiree on the Neva. 1 act. Smart Set, 67 (January, 1922), 69-78. Benjamin Glazer, translator.

4915. Lenormand, Henri René, 1882-1951. Crépuscule du Théatre. 3 acts. Petite Illustration, 190 (January 26, 1935), 1-26. In French.

4916. _____. L'innocente. 1 act. Il Dramma, 145 (September 1, 1932), 36-43. Enzo Gariffo, translator. In Italian.

4917. _____. L'Innocente. 1 act. Petite Illustration, 86 (October 13, 1928), 1-9. In French.

4918. Lent, Evangeline M. A Rag Doll. 1 act. Smart Set, 28 (May, 1909), 100-110.

4919. Lenz, Leo. Il profumo di mia moglie. 3 acts. Il Dramma, 126 (November 15, 1931), 4-27. In Italian.

4920. Lenz, Siegfried. Time of Innocence. Modern International Drama, 4 (Spring, 1971), 15-55. Michael Bachem, translator.

4921. ———. Zeit der Schuldlosen. 2 parts. Sipario, 20 (May, 1965), 36-54. Gigi Lunari, translator. In Italian.

4922. Leonard, Hugh. The Au Pair Man. 3 acts. Plays and Players, 16 (December, 1968), 35-50.

4923. ———. DA. 2 acts. Plays and Players, 21 (December, 1973), I-XVI, 39.

4924. ———. Mick and Mick. 2 acts. Plays and Players, 14 (November, 1966), 31-46.

4925. ———. The Patrick Pearse Motel. 2 acts. Plays and Players, 18 (May, 1971), 63-85.

4926. ———. Stephen D. 2 acts. Sipario, 20 (August-September, 1965), 8-22. Franca Cancogni, translator. In Italian.

4927. Leonardi, Alfred. The Beanstalk Trial. 1 act. Plays, 36 (October, 1976), 52-62.

4928. Leonov, Leonid Maximovich, 1899- . Obyknovenny Celovek. 4 acts. Il Dramma, n.s., 86 (June 1, 1949), 7-35. Andrea Jemma, translator. In Italian.

4929. ———. Zdotuaja Kareta. 4 acts. Sipario, 16 (December, 1961), 73-93. Giacinta Jorio de Dominicis, translator. In Italian.

Leontovich, Eugenie see George, G. S. 3440

Lepelletier, Georges de Bouheilier see Bouhelier, S-G. de 1212, 1213, 1214, 1215

4930. Lerici, Roberto. Libere stanze: Il gioco dei quattro cantoni; Un fatto di assassinio. 1 act each. Sipario, 21 (November, 1966), 41-53, 62. In Italian.

4931. Lerner, Allan Jay, 1918- . Brigadoon. 2 acts. Theatre Arts, 36 (August, 1952), 48-65, 80-87.

4932. ———. Paint Your Wagon. 2 acts. Theatre Arts, 36 (December, 1952), 36-60.

4933. Lerner, W. Zollev. Kaddish. 1 act. Prairie Schooner, 6 (Spring, 1932), 132-143.

4934. Lery, Maxime. Certain Général Bonaparte. 1 act, comedy. Petite Illustration, 198 (September 25, 1937), 1-7. In French.

4935. ——— and Guy D'Abzac. Un Mari sur Mesure. 1 act.

Petite Illustration, 192 (December 21, 1935), 1-7. In French.

4936. Lesage, Alain-René, 1668-1747. The Rival of His Master. 1 act, comedy. Tulane Drama Review, 6 (June, 1962), 130-155. W. S. Merwin, translator.

4937. Lescure, Pierre. A Son Image. 3 acts. L'Avant Scène, 110, 9-30. In French.

4938. Lessay, Jean. Le Costume. 1 act. L'Avant Scène, 165, 31-41. In French.

4939. Leto, Alfonso, 1920- . La raggazza di stoccolma. 2 parts. Il Dramma, n.s., 371/372 (August/September, 1967), 64-100. In Italian.

4940. Letraz, Jean de. Bichon. 3 acts, comedy. Petite Illustration, 193 (January 18, 1936), 1-38. In French.

4941. _____. Nous Avons Tous Fait la Meme Chose. 3 acts, comedy. L'Avant Scène (OST), 3 (April, 1949), 1-36. In French.

4942. Lettiga deserta, La. 1 act. Il Dramma, n.s., 322/323 (July/August, 1963), 60-63. Enrico Fulchignoni, translator. In Italian.

4943. Lettres de la Religieuse Portugaise. L'Avant Scène, 519 (June 1, 1973), 23-28. In French.

4944. Leuser, Eleanore. The Broth of Christkindli. 1 act. Plays, 9 (December, 1949), 50-54.

4945. _____. The Christmas Sampler. 1 act. Plays, 11 (December, 1951), 57-61.

4946. _____. The Five Brothers. 1 act. Plays, 12 (January, 1953), 68-69.

4947. _____. The Honored One. 1 act. Plays, 22 (November, 1962), 35-39.

4948. _____. The King's Jester. 1 act. Plays, 12 (April, 1953), 66-70.

4949. _____. The Legend of the Christmas Rose. 1 act. Plays, 16 (December, 1956), 83-86.

4950. _____. Little Bird in the Tree. 1 act. Plays, 9 (January, 1950), 53-56.

4951. _____. The Little Witch Who Tried. 1 act. Plays, 9 (October, 1949), 59-62.

4952. _____. The Magic Grapes. 1 act. Plays, 12 (October, 1952), 57-61.

4953. _____. The Magic Well. 1 act. Plays, 12 (March, 1953), 62-66. AND Plays, 22 (May, 1963), 91-95.

4954. _____. The Wise People of Gotham. 3 acts. Plays, 25 (February, 1966), 79-84.

_____, adapter see Ruskin, J. 7800

4955. Levate li occhi e resguardate. 1 act. Il Dramma, n.s., 283 (April, 1960), 9-14. In Italian.

4956. Leverson, Ada. Gentlemen v. Players. A Critic Match. 1 act. English Review, 34 (April, 1922), 331-334.

Levi, Evelina, translator see Achard, M. 38

_____, translator see Conners, B. 1978

4957. Levi, Paolo, 1919- . Lastrico d'inferno. 3 acts. Il Dramma, n.s., 271 (April, 1959), 6-34. In Italian.

4958. _____. The Pinedus Affair. 2 acts. Gambit, 2 (1963), 6-56. Robert Rietty, translator.

4959. _____. Unpublished Story. 2 acts. Gambit, 3 (No. 11), 3-91. Robert Rietty, translator.

_____, adapter see Quoirez, F. 7370

4960. Levi, Shelley. Achilles' Heel. 1 act. Plays, 25 (May, 1966), 69-72.

4961. Levick, Milnes. Wings in the Mesh, A Colloquy in One Act. Smart Set, 59 (July, 1919), 95-103.

4962. Levin, Carole. One Day in the Life of a Fairy Tale Princess. 1 act. Dramatika, 3 (March, 1969), 17-18.

4963. Levin, Ron. By the Sea. 1 act. December, 4 (Winter, 1963), 86-104.

4964. Levinger, Elma Ehrlich. The Tenth Man. 1 act. Drama, 19 (April, 1929), 204-206, 220-221.

4965. Levitt, Alfred and Richard Fiske. Herman's No Angel. 1 act. The Clipper, 2 (November, 1941), 22-27.

4966. Levitt, Paul M. Act the Second: The Norwich Incident. 1 act. Ohio Review, 17 (Fall, 1975), 25-40.

4967. Levitt, Saul, 1913- . The Andersonville Trial. 2 acts. Theatre Arts, 45 (May, 1961), 27-53.

4968. Levoy, Myron. Eli and Emily. 1 act. North American Review, n.s., 2 (July, 1965), 9-15.

4969. _____. The Sun Is a Red Dwarf. 1 act. Dramatika, 7 (1971), 69-77.

4970. Levy, Benn W., 1900- . The Rape of the Belt. 3 acts. Theatre Arts, 45 (March, 1961), 25-56.

4971. Lewis, Matthew Gregory, 1775-1818. Alfonso, King of Castile. 5 acts, tragedy. The Mirror of Taste, 1 (May, 1810), supplement, 3-22.

4972. _____. Venoni; or, The Novice of St. Mark's. 3 acts. The Mirror of Taste, 1 (March, 1810), supplement, 3-16.

4973. Lewis, Wyndham, 1884-1957. The Ideal Giant. 1 act. Little Review, 5 (May, 1918), 1-18.

4974. _____. Noel: A Fragment. 1 act. Living Age, 333 (December 15, 1927), 1090-1096.

4975. Lewisohn, Ludwig, 1882-1955. The Lie. 1 act. Smart Set, 41 (December, 1913), 127-142.

Li Chi-huang see Sha Seh 8163

4976. Li Huang, Chang Feng-yi, Lin Yin-wu. War Drums on the Equator. Chinese Literature, 7 (1965), 3-72.

Liberovici, Sergio see Castri, M. 1655

4977. _____ and Emilio Jona. Il 29 luglio di 1900; vita e morte di Gaetano Bresci. Sipario, 321 (February, 1973), 61-80. In Italian.

4978. Lieberman, Herbert Henry, 1933- . Matty, the Moron and the Madonna. 3 acts. Chicago Review, 16 (Autumn, 1963), 17-64.

Liebman, Max, 1902- see Fine, S. 1529

4979. Liese, El Frieda. What a Man! 1 act. Plays, 33 (March, 1974), 65-69.

4980. Lilli, Virgilio, 1907- . Il figlio di laboratorio. 3 acts. Il Dramma, n.s., 321 (June, 1963), 8-35. In Italian.

Lima, Robert, translator see Ballesteros, A. M. 537

4981. Limbour, Georges. La Nuit Close. 1 act. Botteghe Oscure, 3 (1949), 358-380. In French.

Lin Yin-wu see Li Huang 4976

Linati, Carlo, translator see Dunsany, E. J. M. D. P. 2707

_____, translator see Joyce, J. 4524

_____, translator see Synge, J. M. 8666, 8669, 8671, 8675

_____, translator see Yeats, W. B. 9589, 9601, 9606

4982. Lind, Jakov. Audioplay 1: Voices. Scripts, 1 (February, 1972), 34-44. Jack D. Zipes, translator.

4983. _____. Audioplay 2: Safe. Scripts, 1 (June, 1972), 30-38.

Lindanger, Henry, translator see Kielland, A. L. 4618

4984. Lindenberger, Herbert, 1929- . Victims: No Sunset on Sounion; Man and Dog; The Boys; Improvisation on a Naturalist Play; A Gift for the Great Man. 1 act each. Players' Magazine, 42 (November, December, 1965, Spring-Summer, 1966), 41-44; 67-73; 95-96.

4985. Lindquist, Jack. Road Blocks to the Gospel. 1 act. Resource, 6 (June, 1965), 10-13.

4986. Lindsay, Donald. Truce. 1 act. Scholastic, 29 (November 7, 1936), 16, 21.

4987. Lindsay, Howard, 1889- , and Russel Crouse, 1893- . The Great Sebastions. 3 acts. Theatre Arts, 41 (July, 1957), 35-69.

4988. _____. Life with Father. 3 acts. Sipario, 15 (July, 1960), 32-55. Suso Cecchi d'Amico, translator. In Italian.

4989. Lindsay, Jack. The Damned Dieties. 1 act. The London Aphrodite, 1 (August, 1928), 54-64.

4990. _____. The Failure. 1 act. The London Aphrodite, 2 (October, 1928), 151-159.

4991. _____. Hate. 1 act. The London Aphrodite, 4 (February, 1929), 298-313.

4992. Linebarger, J. M. The Meeting. 1 act. Cimarron Review, 3 (March, 1968), 38-54.

4993. Lineberger, James. A Song for All Saints. 2 acts. Tulane Drama Review, 9 (Fall, 1964), 156-196.

Lion, Ahouva see Sates, C. 7977

_____, translator see Eliraz, J. 2855

4994. Lipnick, Esther. Angel of Mercy. 1 act. Plays, 5 (November, 1945), 28-33.

4995. _____. Son of Liberty. 1 act. Plays, 3 (April, 1944), 34-40.

4996. Lipscomb, G. D. Frances. 1 act. Opportunity, 3 (May, 1925), 148-153.

Liss, Felicia, translator see Saluron, A. 7894

4997. Liss, Florence. Adventures in Bookland. 1 act. Plays, 18 (November, 1958), 61-66.

4998. _____ and Nova G. Nestrick. Joy of Giving Thanks. 1 act. Plays, 19 (November, 1959), 55-60.

4999. Liss, Joseph. Rebirth in Barrows Inlet. 1 act. Theatre Arts, 30 (August, 1946), 465-471.

_____, translator see Cervantes Saavedra, M. de 1691

_____, translator see Rueda, L. de 7783

5000. Litchfield, Grace Denio. Women As Advocates. 1 act. Independent, 55 (July 9, 1903), 1627-1630.

5001. Littlewood, Joan. Oh What a Lovely War. 2 parts. Sipario, 18 (December, 1963), 113-132. Gigi Lunari, translator. In Italian.

5002. Litvack, Barry. A Naked Lady Is Abare: Bears, Spears and People. 1 act. Dramatika, 7 (1971), 12-16.

5003. _____. A Play About Somebody Who Just Wanted Something to Happen to Him: A Body Politic. 1 act. Dramatika, 7 (1971), 17-18.

5004. Living Newspaper. Injunction Granted. Minnesota Review, n.s. 1 (Fall, 1973), 46-101.

5005. Living Theatre Collective. The Money Tower. Drama Review, 18 (June, 1974), 20-25.

Livingston, Arthur, translator see Pirandello, L. 7193, 7194

5006. Livingston, Francis M. The Dark Man at the Feast. 1 act. Smart Set (April, 1901), 114-118.

5007. _____. The Double Negative; A Problem Playlet. 1 act. Smart Set, 7 (May, 1902), 158-160.

5008. _____. A Sentimental Journey, 1902. 1 act. Smart Set, 6 (January, 1902), 105-110.

Locher, Jean see Aroutcheff, G. 369

5009. Locke, Charlie. Gutlibi, il massacratore. 3 acts. Il Dramma, 7 (June, 1926), 45-47. In Italian.

5010. Locke, Kay. The Sleeping Chinese Beauty. 1 act. Plays, 26 (May, 1967), 81-84.

5011. Lodovici, Cesare Vico, 1885- . L'Eroica. 1 act. Poet Lore, 34 (Summer, 1923), 159-176. Petronelle Sombart, translator.

5012. _____. Guerrin meschino agli alberi del sole. 2 parts. Il Dramma, n.s., 327 (December, 1963), 44-64. In Italian.

5013. _____. The Idiot. 3 acts. Poet Lore, 30 (Autumn, 1919), 317-355. Petronelle Sombart, translator.

5014. _____. Ruota. Prologue, monologue, epilogue. Il Dramma, 158 (March 15, 1933), 4-26. In Italian.

5015. _____. Woman, of No One. 3 acts. Poet Lore, 32 (No. 2, 1921), 159-200. Petronelle Sombart, translator.

_____, translator see Anouilh, J. 279

_____, translator see Ayme, M. 474

_____, translator see Camus, A. 1550

_____, translator see Herczeg, F. 4066

_____, translator see Martens, G. M. and A. Obey 5623

_____, translator see Mauriac, F. 5689

_____, translator see Montherlant, H. de 6190

_____, translator see Patrick, J. 7000

_____, translator see Salacrou, A. 7875

5016. Loesser, Frank, 1910- . The Most Happy Fella. 3 acts. Theatre Arts, 42 (October, 1958), 26-53.

5017. Loew, Ralph W. Christmas in the Shadows. 1 act. Resource, 10 (December, 1968), 2-7.

Logan, Joshua, 1908- see Heggen, T. 4025

5018. Logan, S. [Cosentino Dorian, 1948- , Mario Forte, 1932- , and Enrico Ventura, 1936- .] Gli operativi, dramma sociologico. Il Dramma, 48 (April, 1972), 44-67. In Italian.

Lo Gatto, Ettore, translator see Zamjatin, E. I. 9632

Logue, Christopher, translator see Claus, H. 1874

5019. Lohman, Fran. The Telegram. 1 act. The Scene, 1 (1972), 140-147.

5020. Loiseau, Georges. L'Envol de l'Aigle. 1 act. Petite Illustration, 184 (February 25, 1933), 1-8. In French.

Lokar, Alessio, translator see Kozak, P. 4698

5021. Loki's Flyting. 1 act. The Quest, 2 (Spring, 1968), 273-282. Paul B. Taylor and W. H. Auden, translators.

Lombard, Jean-Charles, translator see Hacks, P. 3810

Lombard, Suzanne, adapter see Saunders, J. 7981

Lombardi, M., translator see Stevenson, R. L. 8519

5022. London, Jack, 1876-1916. L'incontro. 1 act. Il Dramma, 130 (January 15, 1932), 29-36. Gian Dauli, translator. In Italian.

5023. _____. Uccidere un uomo. 1 act. Il Dramma, 128 (December 15, 1931), 40-44. Gian Dauli, translator. In Italian.

5024. Longfellow, Henry Wadsworth, 1807-1882. Michael Angelo. 3 parts. Atlantic, 51 (January, February, March, 1883), 1-35; 145-170; 289-319.

5025. Longhi, Vincent. Climb the Greased Pole. 3 acts. Plays and Players, 15 (February, 1968), 21-36.

5026. Longstreth, T. Morris, 1886- . The Junior Partisans. 1 act. Plays, 2 (January, 1943), 19-27.

5027. _____. The Little Lion. 1 act. Plays, 3 (March, 1944), 21-27.

5028. Lonsdale, Frederick, 1881-1954. Aria nuova. 3 acts. Il Dramma, 163 (June 1, 1933), 4-31. Ada Salvatore, translator. In Italian.

5029. _____. The Day After Tomorrow. 3 acts, comedy. Theatre Arts, 35 (April, 1951), 57-88.

5030. _____. The Last of Mrs. Cheney. 3 acts. Il Dramma, 83 (February 1, 1930), 4-34. Goffredo Pautassi, translator. In Italian.

5031. _____. Ma non la siamo un poco tutti? 3 acts. Il Dramma, 278 (March 15, 1938), 4-21. In Italian.

Lonska, Irina, translator see Heiberg, G. 4027

5032. Loomis, Charles Battell, 1861-1911. An Evening of Truth. 1 act. Smart Set, 14 (November, 1904), 93-96.

5033. _____. Piazza Parleys. 1 act. Smart Set, 11 (December, 1903), 95-97.

5034. Loos, Anita, 1893- . Gigi. 2 acts, comedy. Theatre Arts, 36 (July, 1952), 41-69.

5035. Lopez, Guido, 1924- . Fiducia. 1 act. Il Dramma, n.s., 53 (January 15, 1948), 51-55. In Italian.

5036. Lopez, Sabatino, 1867-1951. Il destino. 1 act. Il Dramma, n.s., 168 (November 1, 1952), 27-32. In Italian.

5037. _____. Luce. 1 act. Il Dramma, 258 (May 15, 1937), 28-33. In Italian.

5038. _____. Questa o quella. 3 acts. Il Dramma, 217 (September 1, 1935), 5-28. In Italian.

5039. _____ and Eligio Possenti. Pigrizia. 3 acts. Il Dramma, 180 (February 15, 1934), 4-31. In Italian.

5040. Lopez Diaz, Grace P. A Foreign-Language Teacher's Dream. 1 act. Modern Language Journal, 23 (January, 1939), 265-269.

5041. Lo Presti, Carlo. Il ritorno di Gorgia. 2 parts. Il Dramma, n.s., 376/377 (January/February, 1968), 103-113. In Italian.

5042. Lorca, Federico Garcia, 1898-1936. Amour de Don Perlimplin. 1 act. L'Avant Scène, 154, 21-29. Jean Camp, adapter. In French.

5043. _____. The Audience. 1 act. Evergreen Review, 2 (Autumn, 1958), 93-107. Ben Belitt, translator.

5044. _____. The House of Bernard Alba. 3 acts. Theatre Arts, 36 (March, 1952), 51-63. James Graham-Lujan and Richard O'Connell, translators.

5045. _____. Mariana Pineda. 3 acts. Chicago Review, 16 (No. 4, 1964), 5-56. Marion L. Miller and Anne K. Blodgett, translators.

5046. _____. Mariana Pineda. 3 acts. Tulane Drama Review, 7 (Winter, 1962), 18-75. James Graham-Lujan, translator.

5047. _____. The Tragicomedy of Don Cristobita and Dona Rosita. 1 act, puppet play. New World Writing, 8 (1955), 187-219. William I. Oliver, translator.

5048. _____. Yerma. 3 acts, tragedy. L'Avant Scène, 98, 14-30. Jean Camp, translator. In French.

5049. _____. Yerma. 3 acts, tragedy. Spectaculum, 3 (1960), 183-219. In German.

_____. see also Garcia Lorca, F. 3374-3385.

5050. Lord, Daniel A. The Road to Connaught. 1 act. Catholic World, 110 (December, 1919), 382-394.

5051. Lord, Katherine. The Minister's Dream. 1 act. The Delineator, 80 (November, 1912), 358-359.

5052. Lorde, Andre de. The System of Doctor Gourdon and Professor Plume. 1 act. Drama Review, 18 (March, 1974), 44-52. John Towsen, translator.

5053. _____ and Pierre Chaine. Mon Cure Chez les Pauvres. 5 acts. Petite Illustration, 88 (November 15, 1930), 1-30. In French.

5054. _____. Mon Cure Chez les Riches. 5 acts. Petite Illustration, 86 (August 4, 1928), 1-38. In French.

5055. Lorenzini, Carlo, 1826-1890. Pinocchio. 1 act. Plays, 30 (November, 1970), 47-53. Lewis Mahlmann, adapter.

5056. _____. Pinocchio Goes to School. 1 act. Plays, 20 (January, 1961), 63-70. Adele Thane, adapter.

Loreti, Enzo, translator see Sadoveanu, I. M. 7846

5057. Lothar, Rodolfo. Il lupo mannara. 3 acts. Il Dramma, 14 (January, 1927), 7-30. In Italian.

5058. Louki, Pierre. La Petite Cuiller. monologue. L'Avant Scène, 576 (December 1, 1975), 27-34. In French.

5059. Lourson, Laurent, 1926- . Narcissus. 1 act. Gambit, 2 (1963), 72-97. Donald Watson, translator.

5060. Love in a French Kitchen, a Mediaeval Farce. 1 act. Poet Lore, 28 (Winter, 1917), 722-729. Colin C. Clements and John M. Saunders, translators.

5061. Love Test, The. 1 act. Smart Set, 2 (December, 1900), 144-156.

5062. Lovell, Caroline C. Prince Charming's Fate. 3 acts. St. Nicholas, 30 (February, 1903), 350-359.

5063. ———. The War Woman. 1 act. Drama, 13 (October, 1922), 23-26.

5064. Lovett, Howard Meriwether. Silverheels. 1 act. Plays, 2 (November, 1942), 22-30.

5065. Lovett, Robert Morse, 1870-1956. Cowards. 4 acts. Drama, 27 (August, 1917), 330-403.

5066. Lovinfosse, Henri-Marie. L'aurora verde. 1 act. Il Dramma, n.s., 181 (May 15, 1953), 53-56. In Italian.

5067. Loving, Pierre, 1893- . Autumn. 1 act. Drama, 13 (November, 1922), 61-63.

5068. Lowe, Lucy. The Bitterly Reviled. 1 act. Poet Lore, 33 (Summer, 1922), 300-307.

Lowell, James Russell, 1819-1891, translator see Child, F. J. 1802

5069. Lowell, Robert, 1917-1977. Benito Cereno. 1 act. Show, 4 (August, 1964), 82-96.

5070. ———. My Kinsman, Major Molineux. 1 act. Partisan Review, 31 (Fall, 1964), 495-514, 566-583.

5071. ———. The Violent Wedding. 2 acts, tragedy. Poet Lore, 58 (Spring, 1963), 3-43.

5072. Loy, Mina. The Pamperers. 1 act. Dial, 69 (July, 1920), 65-78.

5073. Lubicz-Milosz, Oscar Vladislas de, 1877-1939. Rebezahl, Scenes de Don Juan. L'Avant Scène, 534 (February 1, 1974), 13-21. In French.

Lubimov, Nicholas, translator see Pushkin, A. 7345

5074. Luc, Jean Bernard. Le complexe de Philemon. 3 acts.

Sipario, 7 (October, 1952), 29-51. Bruno Arcangeli, translator. In Italian.

5075. Luce, Clare Boothe, 1903- . Women. 3 acts. Il Dramma, n.s., 2/3 (December 1/15, 1945), 11-42. Vinicio Marinucci, translator. In Italian.

5076. Luchaire, Julien. Altitude 3.200. 3 acts, comedy. Petite Illustration, 197 (May 1, 1937), 1-30. In French.

5077. _____. Le Cheval Arabe. 1 act, comedy. L'Avant Scène, 212, 35-41. In French.

5078. Lucian, Dialogue of the Dead. 1 act. Golden Book, 13 (January, 1931), 61-62.

5079. _____. The Judgment of Paris. 1 act. Golden Book, 6 (July, 1927), 49-52. A. M. Harmon, translator.

5080. Luciani, Mario. Il Marinaio Flip. 3 acts. Il Dramma, 330 (May 15, 1940), 6-23. In Italian.

_____, translator see Salacrou, A. 7869

_____, see also Montanelli, I. 6179

Lucignani, Luciano, translator see Breffort, A. 1314

_____, translator see Faulkner, W. 2944

5081. Lude, Christian. L'Age Canonique. 4 acts, comedy. L'Avant Scène, 74 (March 5, 1953), 9-32. In French.

5082. Ludlam, Charles. Eunuchs of the Forbidden City. 4 acts. Scripts, 1 (April, 1972), 28-57.

5083. _____. Hot Ice. 2 acts. Drama Review, 18 (June, 1974), 87-102.

5084. Ludwig, Otto, 1813-1865. The Forest Warden. 5 acts, tragedy. Poet Lore, 24 (Summer, 1913), 129-198. Paul Green, translator.

5085. Luftig, Richard. Abracadabra. 1 act. Plays, 34 (April, 1975), 37-41.

5086. _____. Herman the Hatman. 1 act. Plays, 33 (April, 1974), 59-63.

5087. Luizet, Jean. Inquietudes. 1 act. L'Avant Scène, 136, 31-38. In French.

5088. _____ and Angelo Guacci. Faux Depart. 1 act. L'Avant Scène, 256 (January 1, 1962), 31-35. In French.

Lujan, James Graham, translator see Lorca, F. G. 5044, 5046

5089. Luke, Peter, 1919- . Hadrian VII. 2 acts. L'Avant Scène, 471 (May 1, 1971), 7-35. Jean-Louis Curtis, adapter. In French.

5090. _____. Hadrian VII. 2 acts. Plays and Players, 15 (May, 1968), 27-42.

5091. _____. Hadrian VII. 2 acts. Sipario, 302 (July, 1971), 55-77. Federico Cassel, translator. In Italian.

Lunari, Gigi, translator see Bond, E. 1175

_____, translator see Delaney, S. 2291

_____, translator see Hyde, D. 4349

_____, translator see Ingannati, Gli 4371

_____, translator see Labiche, E. 4746

_____, translator see Lenz, S. 4921

_____, translator see Littlewood, J. 5001

_____, translator see Morris, E. 6235

_____, translator see Mortimer, J. 6246

_____, translator see Nash, N. R. 6436

_____, translator see Schisgal, M. 8032

5092. Luneau, Sylvie and Roger Coggio, 1934- . Le Journal d'un Fou. 1 act. L'Avant Scène, 278 (December 15, 1962), 10-19. In French.

5093. Lunts, Lev, 1901-1924. Bertran de Born. 5 acts, tragedy. Drama and Theatre, 9 (Fall, 1970), 51-65. Gary Kern, translator.

5094. Luther, Lester. Law. 1 act. Forum, 53 (June, 1915), 776-779.

Lutkenhaus, Anna M. see Knox, M. 4674

5095. Lutz, Gertrude May. Secular Trilogy: Salome and the Head; David Laments; Ruth and Boaz. 1 act each. Poet Lore, 55 (Autumn, 1950), 275-280.

5096. _____. Yet Not As One. 1 act. Poet Lore, 60 (Spring, 1965), 77-86.

5097. Luzi, Gian Francesco, 1912- . L'ansia cieca. Sipario, 9 (July, 1954), 47-56. In Italian.

5098. _____. La bugiarda meravigliosa. Sipario, 7 (August-September, 1952), 46-53. In Italian.

5099. _____. Il quarto arriva. Il Dramma, n.s., 33 (March 15, 1947), 55-63. In Italian.

Lwow, Giacomo, translator see Gordin, G. 3633

_____, translator see Ostrovsky, A. 6915

Lyday, Leon F., translator see Ballesteros, A. M. 538

5100. Lynch, May. Finn MacCool. 1 act. Plays, 26 (March, 1967), 55-59.

5101. _____. The Royal Dog. 1 act. Plays, 34 (January, 1975), 52-56.

5102. _____. Scheherazade. 1 act. Plays, 18 (March, 1959), 59-63.

5103. Lyttleton, Edith Sophy, 1865-1948. Dame Julian's Window. 1 act. 19th Century, 73 (February, 1913), 435-449.

5104. _____. The Thumbscrew. 1 act. 19th Century, 69 (May, 1911), 938-960.

_____, translator see Nyanysa 6712

5105. Lytton, Edward Bulwer, 1803-1873. The Death of Clytemnestra. 1 act. Living Age, 3 (December, 1844), 338-343.

5106. _____. The Rightful Heir. 5 acts. Harper's, 38 (December, 1868), 129-143.

5107. _____. Walpole; or, Every Man Has His Place. A Comedy in Rhyme. 3 acts. Harper's, 40 (February, 1870), 438-449.

M

5108. M., A. A. Fair Mistress Dorothy. 1 act. Living Age, 268 (March 25, 1911), 744-746.

5109. _____. A Slight Misunderstanding. 1 act. Living Age, 269 (April 1, 1911), 52-54.

5110. _____. William Smith, Editor. 2 acts. Living Age, 264 (February 5, 1910), 370-372.

Ma Yung see Sha Seh 8163

5111. Maastricht Play, A Christmas Miracle. 1 act. Theatre Arts, 11 (December, 1927), 947-952. Donald Fay Robinson, adapter.

5112. MacArdle, Dorothy. The Red Man's Call. 1 act. One-Act Play Magazine, 1 (April, 1938), 1101-1117.

MacArthur, Charles, 1895-1956 see Hecht, B. 4019, 4020

5113. McArthur, Jean. Fiesta. 1 act. Plays, 16 (May, 1957), 53-59.

5114. ———. Fiesta the First. 1 act. Plays, 19 (May, 1960), 47-51.

5115. McBride, Doris. The Horrible Humpy Dragon. 1 act. Plays, 20 (January, 1961), 77-80.

5116. ———. The Meanest Witch. 1 act. Plays, 20 (October, 1960), 68-72.

5117. McBrown, Gertrude Parthenia. Africa Sings. 1 act. Negro History Bulletin, 17 (February, 1954), 113-114.

5118. ———. The Birthday Surprise. 1 act. Negro History Bulletin, 16 (February, 1953), 102-104.

5119. ———. Bought with Cookies. 1 act. Negro History Bulletin, 12 (April, 1949), 155-156, 165-166.

5120. ———. New Pages for Our History Textbooks. 1 act. Negro History Bulletin, 21 (February, 1958), 113-115.

5121. McCallum, Phyllis. No Christmas Here. 1 act. Plays, 33 (December, 1973), 61-68.

5122. MacCampbell, Donald. Squaring the Family Circle. 1 act. Poet Lore, 43 (No. 1, 1936), 71-83.

MacCario, Ermanno, translator see Arnold, P. 355

5123. McCarthy, Ethna. The Uninvited. 1 act. Dublin Magazine, n.s., 26 (July-September, 1951), 10-25.

5124. McCarthy, Mary B. First Aid, Library Style; or SOS to the Rescue. 1 act. Wilson Library Bulletin, 28 (April, 1954), 680-681, 685.

5125. McCarty, E. Clayton, 1901- . The Little Cake. 1 act. Plays, 2 (December, 1942), 30-36.

5126. McCarty, Sara Sloane. Roly-Poly Freckle-Face. 1 act. Plays, 18 (March, 1959), 16-26.

5127. _____. The Tree Friends. 1 act. Plays, 20 (May, 1961), 73-76.

5128. McCauley, Clarice Vallette. The Queen's Hour. 1 act. Drama, 10 (June, 1920), 295-300.

5129. McChesney, Dora Greenwell, 1871-1912. Outside the Gate. 1 act. Fortnightly, 80 (December, 1903), 1035-1040.

Maccini, Nennele, translator see Dekobra, M. 2286

_____, translator see Duvernois, H. 2791

5130. McClellan, Walter. The Delta Wife. 1 act. Double Dealer, 4 (December, 1922), 271-278.

5131. McClure, John, 1893- . The Alchemist. 1 act. Double Dealer, 7 (April, 1925), 136-139.

5132. _____. The Great Prognostic. 1 act. Double Dealer, 8 (July, 1925), 223-224.

5133. _____. The Madhouse at Cairo; A Fantasy in Dialectics. 1 act. Smart Set, 68 (May, 1922), 80-82.

5134. _____. The Rebellion of Women; A Dramatic Fantasy. 1 act. Smart Set, 70 (February, 1923), 65-66.

5135. _____. Two Curtain Raisers: The Doom of Metrodorus; The Cruet of Marigolds. 1 act each. Smart Set, 66 (November, 1921), 71-75.

5136. McClure, Michael. The Beard. 1 act. Sipario, 25 (December, 1970), 81-90. Ettore Capriolo, translator. In Italian.

5137. _____. The Feast. Floating Bear, 14 (1961), 1-13.

5138. _____. The Masked Choir. 1 act. Performing Arts Journal, 1 (Fall, 1976), 106-126.

5139. McCourt, Edna Wahlert. Jill's Way. 1 act. Seven Arts, 1 (February, 1917), 328-335.

5140. _____. The Truth. 1 act. Seven Arts, 1 (March, 1917), 475-492.

5141. McCoy, Paul S. Briefly Speaking. 1 act. Plays, 17 (February, 1958), 81-86.

McCoy

5142. _____. Cicero the Great. 1 act. Plays, 17 (October, 1957), 79-86.

5143. _____. Double Talk. 1 act. Plays, 20 (January, 1961), 84-89.

5144. _____. Farewell to Calvin. 1 act. Plays, 19 (March, 1960), 11-22.

5145. _____. Greetings from the Fultons. 1 act. Plays, 17 (December, 1957), 11-22.

5146. _____. Hold Your Hat! 1 act. Plays, 17 (March, 1958), 1-11.

5147. _____. Johnny Nightmare. 1 act. Plays, 18 (January, 1959), 1-11.

5148. _____. Keep It Under Cover. 1 act. Plays, 18 (May, 1959), 23-33.

5149. _____. The Lieutenant Pays His Respects. 1 act. Plays, 3 (March, 1944), 57-67.

5150. _____. Luncheon for Three. 1 act. Plays, 15 (March, 1956), 31-42.

5151. _____. Miss Fix-It. 1 act. Plays, 15 (April, 1956), 31-42. AND Plays, 26 (April, 1967), 37-48. AND Plays, 34 (November, 1974), 55-65.

5152. _____. No Garden This Year. 1 act. Plays, 17 (April, 1958), 81-85.

5153. _____. No Treat for Gilbert. 1 act. Plays, 18 (October, 1958), 13-24.

5154. _____. She's Not Talking. 1 act. Plays, 17 (April, 1958), 23-36.

5155. _____. Take Care, Anne! 1 act. Plays, 19 (January, 1960), 29-41.

5156. _____. Two for the Show. 1 act. Plays, 18 (October, 1958), 79-84.

5157. _____. Word of Honor. 1 act. Plays, 19 (November, 1959), 77-83.

5158. _____. You Don't Belong to Me! 1 act. Plays, 14 (October, 1954), 13-25. AND Plays, 24 (April, 1965), 15-27. AND Plays, 33 (January, 1974), 35-46.

5159. _____. You'd Never Think It! 1 act. Plays, 18 (May, 1959), 75-80.

5160. McCoy, Samuel D. Mrs. Potiphar Pays a Call. 1 act. Smart Set, 37 (May, 1912), 123-125.

5161. McCracken, Wycliffe. Vengeance in Leka. 1 act. One-Act Play Magazine, 1 (December, 1937), 698-712.

5162. MacDonagh, Donagh, 1912- . The Happy Day. 1 act. Botteghe Oscure, 24 (Autumn, 1959), 73-98.

5163. _____. Happy As Larry. 1 act. New World Writing, 6 (1954), 95-146.

5164. MacDonagh, John. Author! Author! 1 act. Dublin Magazine, 1 (February, 1924), 621-728.

5165. _____. Just Like Shaw. 1 act. Dublin Magazine, 1 (September, 1923), 141-148.

5166. MacDonagh, Thomas, 1817-1917. Metempsychosis; or, A Mad World. 1 act. Irish Review, 1 (February, 1912), 585-599.

5167. MacDonald, Leila. The Love of the Poor. 1 act. The Savoy, 2 (April, 1896), 139-144.

5168. MacDonald, Zillah K., 1885- . Circumventin' Sandy. 1 act, comedy. Drama, 17 (February, 1927), 145-146, 157-159.

5169. _____. The Feather Fisher, Keeper of Pure Waters. 1 act. Touchstone, 4 (November, 1918), 120-128.

5170. _____. Light Along the Rails. 1 act. Touchstone, 3 (June, 1918), 229-236.

5171. _____. The Long Box. 1 act. Drama, 14 (February, 1924), 180-182, 200.

5172. MacDougall, Ranald. The Death of Aunt Aggie. 1 act. Theatre Arts, 27 (September, 1943), 538-554.

5173. MacDougall, Roger, 1910- and Ted Allan. Gog et Magog. 3 acts, comedy. L'Avant Scène, 229, 8-39. Gabriel Aroutcheff, translator. In French.

Macedonio, Francesco, adapter see Grum, S. 3764

5174. McEnroe, Robert E. The Silver Whistle. 3 acts. Theatre Arts, 33 (July, 1949), 57-92.

5175. McFarlan, Ethel. The Day of the Dragon. 1 act. Plays, 20 (November, 1960), 51-57.

5176. ———. The Great One. 1 act. Plays, 14 (March, 1955), 79-83.

5177. ———. The Olive Jar. 1 act. Plays, 29 (November, 1969), 76-84.

5178. ———. The Pear Tree. 1 act. Plays, 22 (April, 1963), 71-73.

5179. ———. The Secret Island. 1 act. Plays, 31 (April, 1972), 79-82.

5180. ———. When the Cat's Away. 1 act. Plays, 15 (May, 1956), 47-52.

5181. ———. The Winter Garden. 1 act. Plays, 23 (January, 1964), 75-78.

5182. ———, adapter. The Tiger Catcher. 1 act. Plays, 26 (January, 1967), 65-68.

5183. MacFarlane, Anne. Slippers. 1 act. Poet Lore, 32 (Autumn, 1921), 425-430.

5184. McGaughan, Geraldine E. Afterwards. 1 act. Scholastic, 28 (March 7, 1936), 7-9.

5185. ———. Afterwards. 1 act. Senior Scholastic, 55 (January 18, 1950), 5-7, 16.

5186. ———. Spring, 1943. 1 act. Scholastic, 42 (February 22-27, 1943), 15-16, 20.

5187. McGowan, Jane. The Admiral's Nightmare. 1 act. Plays, 22 (October, 1962), 58-64.

5188. ———. Aloha, Mother. 1 act. Plays, 21 (May, 1962), 61-64.

5189. ———. The Birthday Pie. 1 act. Plays, 23 (February, 1964), 79-83.

5190. ———. A Broadway Turkey. 1 act. Plays, 20 (November, 1960), 1-12.

5191. ———. The Christmas Umbrella. 1 act. Plays, 14 (December, 1954), 43-52. AND Plays, 24 (December, 1964), 51-60.

5192. ———. Crosspatch and Cupid. 1 act. Plays, 16 (February, 1957), 71-76.

5193. _____. Cupid in Command. 1 act. Plays, 23 (February, 1964), 71-74.

5194. _____. Cupid on the Loose. 1 act. Plays, 2 (February, 1943), 23-30.

5195. _____. Damsels in Distress. 1 act. Plays, 17 (November, 1957), 71-79.

5196. _____. The Iron Queen of Cornwall. 1 act. Plays, 3 (February, 1944), 13-23.

5197. _____. The Lincoln Cupboard. 1 act. Plays, 15 (February, 1956), 31-41.

5198. _____. A Matter of Health. 1 act. Plays, 24 (April, 1965), 70-76.

5199. _____. The Miraculous Tea Party. Plays, 16 (November, 1956), 53-60.

5200. _____. Smokey Wins His Star. 1 act. Plays, 22 (October, 1962), 75-80.

5201. _____. Squeaknibble's Christmas. 1 act. Plays, 19 (December, 1959), 79-83.

5202. _____. The Talking Flag. 1 act. Plays, 17 (November, 1957), 37-40.

5203. _____. The Teddy Bear Hero. 1 act. Plays, 19 (May, 1960), 68-72.

5204. _____. The Tree of Hearts. 1 act. Plays, 16 (February, 1957), 57-65. AND Plays, 33 (February, 1974), 53-61.

5205. _____. A Visit to Goldilocks. 1 act. Plays, 19 (November, 1959), 61-64.

_____, adapter see Blackmore, R. 982

_____, adapter see Field, E. 3013

_____, adapter see Howells, W. D. 4237

5206. McGrath, John. Events While Guarding the Bofors Gun. 2 acts. Plays and Players, 13 (June, 1966), 31-46, 71.

5207. _____. Fish in the Sea. Plays and Players, 22 (April, May, 1975), 35-49; 39-50.

5208. _____. Plugged In: Angel of the Morning; Plugged in to

History; They're Knocking Down the Pie-Shop. 1 act each. Plays and Players, 20 (November, 1972), I-XII.

5209. McGregor, Don. Sir Osbert and Lester. 1 act. Plays, 28 (October, 1968), 73-76.

5210. McGuire, Harry. When the Ship Goes Down. 1 act. Drama, 18 (December, 1927), 82-84, 94.

5211. Machado, Maria Clara. Plouft, Le Petit Fantome. 1 act. L'Avant Scène, 232 (December 1, 1960), 33-41. Michel Simon, translator. In French.

5212. McHale, Ethel Kharasch. The Tiger's Promise. 1 act. Plays, 35 (November, 1975), 49-52.

5213. Machard, Alfred. La Chambre Nuptiale. 1 act, comedy. L'Avant Scène, 179 (August, 1958), 26-45. In French.

5214. McHugh, Martin J. A Minute's Wait. 1 act, comedy. One-Act Play Magazine, 1 (April, 1938), 1063-1085.

5215. McHugh, Vincent. Song for American Union. 1 act. Plays, 2 (May, 1943), 63-70.

5216. MacInnis, Charles Pattison. Immortality. 1 act. Drama, 16 (April, 1926), 258-260.

5217. McInroy, Harl. Honorable Togo. 1 act, comedy. Drama, 11 (August-September, 1921), 410-413.

Macintire, Elizabeth J., translator see Topelius, Z. 8887

5218. _____ and Colin Clements. The Ivory Tower. 1 act. Poet Lore, 30 (Spring, 1919), 127-137.

5219. MacKay, Constance D'Arcy. The Boston Tea Party. 1 act. Woman's Home Companion, 38 (June, 1911), 13, 55-56.

5220. _____. The Festival of Pomona. 1 act. Drama, 17 (February, 1915), 161-171.

5221. _____. The First Noel. 1 act. St. Nicholas, 56 (December, 1928), 108-109, 154-155.

5222. _____. In the Days of Piers Ploughman. 1 act. Scholastic, 13 (November 3, November 17, 1928), 6-7, 10; 6-7.

5223. _____. A Little Pilgrim's Progress. 1 act. St. Nicholas, 37 (November, 1909), 60-63.

5224. _____. The Snow Witch. 1 act. The Delineator, 77 (February, 1911), 161-164.

5225. _____. The Spirit of Christmas Joy. 1 act. The Delineator, 78 (December, 1911), 514-516.

5226. _____. Young Michael Angelo. 1 act. Horn Book, 5 (August, 1929), 3-13.

5227. MacKay, Edward T. Whistler's Mother, An Episode in the Life of the Artist. 1 act. One-Act Play Magazine, 4 (September-October, 1941), 331-348.

5228. MacKay, Katherine. Gabrielle; A Dream from the Treasures Contained in the Letters of Abelard and Heloise. 3 acts. North American Review, 176 (April, 1903), 610-633.

5229. MacKaye, Percy, 1875-1956. Napoleon Crossing the Rockies. 1 act. Century, 107 (April, 1924), 867-882.

5230. _____. Sanctuary, A Bird Masque. 1 act. Century, 87 (February, 1914), 547-557.

5231. MacKaye, Robert Keith. The Swamp. 1 act. Drama, 21 (March, 1931), 19-20, 22.

5232. MacKeown, M. J. J. Cuckoo. 1 act, comedy. One-Act Play Magazine, 1 (April, 1938), 1086-1100.

5233. McKinney, Isabel, 1879- . Mud. 1 act. Poet Lore, 30 (Autumn, 1919), 417-427.

5234. McKinney, Jean Brabham. The Book Hospital. 1 act. Plays, 21 (November, 1961), 73-76.

5235. _____. The Witch with the Golden Hair. 1 act. Plays, 21 (October, 1961), 75-78.

McKinnon, Richard, translator see Kishida, K. 4648

5236. McKnight, Robert Wilson. The Pigeon. 3 acts. Poet Lore, 30 (Winter, 1919), 579-587.

5237. McLane, Fannie Moulton. Behind the Khaki of the Scouts. 1 act. St. Nicholas, 50 (February, 1923), 386-389.

5238. McLaurin, Kate. A Discussion with Interruptions. 1 act. Smart Set, 26 (December, 1908), 125-127.

5239. MacLeish, Archibald, 1892- . Air Raid. 1 act. Scholastic, 35 (November 6, 1939), 21E-25E.

5240. _____. The Fall of the City. 1 act. Scholastic, 31 (November 13, 1937), 17E-20E, 22E-23E.

5241. _____. J. B. 1 act. Spectaculum, 3 (1960), 221-302.

5242. _____. J. B. 2 acts. Theatre Arts, 44 (February, 1960), 33-64.

5243. _____. The Secret of Freedom. 1 act. Esquire, 52 (October, 1959), 153-154, 156, 158, 160, 162, 164, 167-173.

5244. _____. This Music Crept by Me on the Wafer. 1 act. Botteghe Oscure, 11 (1953), 172-225.

5245. MacLellan, Esther and Catherine V. Schroll. Best Friends. 1 act. Plays, 16 (March, 1957), 61-65. AND Plays, 29 (January, 1970), 69-74.

5246. _____. Birthday Gift. 1 act. Plays, 9 (February, 1950), 75-78.

5247. _____. A Cat for Halloween. 1 act. Plays, 12 (October, 1952), 48-52.

5248. _____. Circus Parade. 1 act. Plays, 11 (May, 1952), 52-55.

5249. _____. The Cross Princess. 1 act. Plays, 12 (February, 1953), 35-40.

5250. _____. A Flower for Mother's Day. 1 act. Plays, 12 (May, 1953), 70-73.

5251. _____. Help Wanted for Easter. 1 act. Plays, 12 (April, 1953), 70-73.

5252. _____. House for Rent. 1 act. Plays, 16 (January, 1957), 63-68.

5253. _____. The Lamp in the Forest. 1 act. Plays, 9 (March, 1950), 62-65.

5254. _____. More Than Courage. 1 act. Plays, 17 (October, 1957), 51-58.

5255. _____. A Needle Fights for Freedom. 1 act. Plays, 10 (February, 1951), 59-61.

5256. _____. The Pilgrim Spirit. 1 act. Plays, 17 (November, 1957), 48-54.

5257. _____. Pilgrims and Pebbles. 1 act. Plays, 11 (November, 1951), 40-44.

5258. _____. Piñata. 1 act. Plays, 9 (December, 1949), 54-62.

5259. _____. The Princess from Norway. 1 act. Plays, 17 (May, 1958), 59-64.

5260. _____. Return of the Nina. 1 act. Plays, 10 (October, 1950), 56-59.

5261. _____. The Secret of the Princess. 1 act. Plays, 15 (March, 1956), 61-66.

5262. _____. The Secret of the Windmill. 1 act. Plays, 21 (May, 1962), 39-44.

5263. _____. Ship's Boy to the Indies. 1 act. Plays, 11 (October, 1951), 35-39.

5264. _____. Small Shoes and Small Tulips. 1 act. Plays, 12 (May, 1953), 61-65.

5265. _____. Swiss Mystery. 1 act. Plays, 17 (March, 1958), 47-54.

5266. _____. Test for a Witch. 1 act. Plays, 15 (October, 1955), 43-48. AND Plays, 29 (October, 1969), 79-84.

5267. _____. Umbrella Magic. 1 act. Plays, 11 (January, 1952), 56-60.

5268. _____. Witches' Delight. 1 act. Plays, 14 (October, 1954), 49-54.

MacLeod, Fiona, pseud. see Sharp, W. 8197, 8198, 8199

5269. MacLiammoir, Michael. Ill Met by Moonlight. 3 acts. Sipario, 3 (November-December, 1948), 69-87. Giancarlo Galassi and O. Olivet, translators. In Italian.

5270. McMahon, Bernice. Careless Ness, the Dragon. 1 act. Plays, 27 (March, 1968), 81-84.

5271. MacMahon, Bryan. The Death of Biddy Early. 1 act. Journal of Irish Literature, 1 (May, 1972), 30-44.

5272. _____. Jack Furey. 1 act. Journal of Irish Literature, 1 (May, 1972), 45-62.

5273. MacManus, L. The Cromwellian. 2 acts. Dublin Magazine, n.s., 11 (October-December, 1936), 18-47.

5274. McMeekin, Isabel McLennan, 1895- . Mother Goose's Sleeping Cap. 1 act. Plays, 2 (November, 1942), 56-61.

5275. _____. The Runaway Balloon. 1 act. Plays, 2 (January, 1943), 47-50.

5276. _____. Two Nights Before Christmas. 1 act. Plays, 2 (December, 1942), 52-55.

5277. MacMillan, Mary Louise. The Gate of Wishes. 1 act. Poet Lore, 22 (Winter, 1911), 469-476.

McMurray, David Arthur, translator see Adoum, J. E. 77

5278. MacNamara, Gerald, 1866-1958. Who Fears to Speak? 1 act. Dublin Magazine, n.s., 4 (January-March, 1929), 30-52.

_____, translator see Gibson, H. 3495

_____, translator see Tcinderella 8736

McNeel, June Thompson see Searcy, K. and C. Oliver 8120

5279. MacNeice, Louis, 1907-1963. The Crash Landing. 1 act. Botteghe Oscure, 4 (1949), 378-385.

5280. _____. The Nosebag. Sipario, 7 (August-September, 1952), 63-70. Franca Cancogni, translator. In Italian.

5281. _____. One for the Grave. A Modern Morality Play. 2 acts. Massachusetts Review, 8 (Winter, 1967), 13-92.

5282. Macphail, Sir Andrew. The Last Rising. Queen's Quarterly, 37 (April, 1930), 246-258.

5283. MacQueen, Laurence I. Sacrifice. 1 act. Drama, 11 (March, 1921), 216-219.

5284. McQueen, Mildred Hark, 1908- . The Christmas Bear. 1 act. Plays, 23 (December, 1963), 69-74.

5285. _____. Mother's Choice. 1 act. Plays, 20 (May, 1961), 61-68.

5286. _____. Who's the President? 1 act. Plays, 20 (January, 1961), 47-55.

5287. _____ and Noel McQueen. Advice to the Lovelorn. 1 act. Plays, 4 (March, 1945), 1-9.

5288. _____. Aladdin, Incorporated. 1 act. Plays, 5 (February, 1946), 33-41. AND Plays, 24 (February, 1965), 51-60.

5289. _____. Aladdin Steps Out. 1 act. Plays, 16 (November, 1956), 25-36.

5290. _____. All Aboard for Christmas. 1 act. Plays, 15 (December, 1955), 1-14.

5291. _____. All Is Not Gold. 1 act. Plays, 9 (October, 1949), 25-35.

5292. _____. Author of Liberty. 1 act. Plays, 11 (January, 1952), 20-32.

5293. _____. Bake a Cherry Pie. 1 act. Plays, 12 (February, 1953), 1-10. AND Plays, 32 (February, 1973), 25-34.

5294. _____. The Best Year. 1 act. Plays, 16 (January, 1957), 57-62. AND Plays, 29 (January, 1970), 59-64.

5295. _____. Beware of Rumors. 1 act. Plays, 3 (November, 1943), 76-80.

5296. _____. A Book a Day. 1 act. Plays, 11 (November, 1951), 58-67.

5297. _____. The Book Revue. 1 act. Plays, 14 (November, 1954), 85-89.

5298. _____. Books à la Mode. 1 act. Plays, 17 (November, 1957), 80-94.

5299. _____. Books to the Rescue. 1 act. Plays, 14 (November, 1954), 73-84.

5300. _____. Boy with a Future. 1 act. Plays, 5 (January, 1946), 39-44.

5301. _____. The Bremen Town Musicians. 1 act. Plays, 21 (January, 1962), 79-84.

5302. _____. A Bunch of Keys. 1 act. Plays, 5 (November, 1945), 60-66.

5303. _____. Cabana Blues. 1 act. Plays, 14 (April, 1955), 20-30.

5304. _____. The Case for Books. 1 act. Plays, 10 (November, 1950), 57-69. AND Plays, 26 (November, 1966), 15-28.

5305. _____. Christmas Eve Letter. 1 act. Plays, 18 (December, 1958), 21-32.

5306. _____. Christmas Eve News. 1 act. Plays, 10 (December, 1950), 43-49. AND Plays, 28 (December, 1968), 61-67.

5307. _____. Christmas in the Woods. 1 act. Plays, 16 (December, 1956), 75-78.

5308. _____. Christmas Party. 1 act. Plays, 9 (December, 1949), 63-67.

5309. _____. Christmas Recaptured. 1 act. Plays, 11 (December, 1951), 20-31. AND Plays, 19 (December, 1959), 25-36.

5310. _____. Christmas Shopping Early. 1 act. Plays, 27 (December, 1967), 49-58.

5311. _____. The Christmas Snowman. 1 act. Plays, 9 (December, 1949), 39-50. AND Plays, (December, 1965), 41-50.

5312. _____. Civilians Stay Put. 1 act. Plays, 4 (April, 1945), 59-66.

5313. _____. Cupies and Hearts. 1 act. Plays, 14 (February, 1955), 47-55.

5314. _____. A Date with Washington. 1 act. Plays, 26 (February, 1967), 33-42.

5315. _____. A Day for Trees. 1 act. Plays, 12 (May, 1953), 66-69.

5316. _____. A Dish for the King. 1 act. Plays, 17 (January, 1958), 35-42.

5317. _____. Doctor Manners. 1 act. Plays, 10 (April, 1951), 67-72. AND Plays, 26 (January, 1967), 75-80.

5318. _____. Double Exposure. 1 act. Plays, 4 (December, 1944), 1-9.

5319. _____. Enter George Washington. 1 act. Plays, 22 (February, 1963), 53-61.

5320. _____. Exit Glamour. 1 act. One-Act Play Magazine, 3 (November-December, 1940), 514-522.

5321. _____. Father Keeps House. 1 act. Plays, 14 (May, 1955), 19-29. AND Plays, 28 (May, 1969), 25-35.

5322. _____. Father's Easter Hat. 1 act. Plays, 14 (April, 1955), 41-48. AND Plays, 29 (April, 1970), 53-60.

5323. _____. February Heroes. 1 act. Plays, 20 (February, 1961), 39-48.

5324. _____. First in Peace. 1 act. Plays, 4 (February, 1945), 21-28.

5325. _____. Forest Fantasy. A Play for Arbor Day. 1 act. Plays, 3 (May, 1944), 43-49.

5326. _____. G for Gettysburg. 1 act. Plays, 14 (February, 1955), 21-31. AND Plays, 31 (February, 1972), 45-54.

5327. _____. The Glory He Deserves. 1 act. Plays, 5 (October, 1945), 35-39.

5328. _____. Going Up. 1 act. Plays, 4 (May, 1945), 63-69.

5329. _____. Halloween Magic. 1 act. Plays, 16 (October, 1956), 68-74.

5330. _____. Happy Easter to Margy. 1 act. Plays, 15 (March, 1956), 79-83.

5331. _____. Happy Haunts. 1 act. Plays, 10 (October, 1950), 20-30.

5332. _____. Happy Hearts. 1 act. Plays, 9 (February, 1950), 20-30.

5333. _____. Happy New Year. 1 act. Plays, 9 (January, 1950), 19-30.

5334. _____. Hats and Rabbits. 1 act. Plays, 9 (April, 1950), 11-21.

5335. _____. Heart Trouble. 1 act. Plays, 10 (February, 1951), 1-10. AND Plays, 18 (February, 1959), 11-20.

5336. _____. Hearts and Flowers for Mother. 1 act. Plays, 18 (May, 1959), 81-88.

5337. _____. The Homecoming. 1 act. Plays, 10 (January, 1951), 12-22. AND Plays, 25 (October, 1965), 37-47.

5338. _____. Hometown Halloween. 1 act. Plays, 12 (October, 1952), 1-11. AND Plays, 23 (October, 1963), 31-41.

5339. _____. The Homiest Room. 1 act. Plays, 3 (March, 1944), 1-9.

5340. _____. The House Is Haunted. A Halloween Mystery. 1 act. Plays, 27 (October, 1967), 50-56.

5341. _____. If We Only Could Cook. 1 act. Plays, 11 (November, 1951), 1-10.

5342. _____. It's Greek to Me. 1 act. Plays, 5 (April, 1946), 1-10.

5343. _____. Jingle Bells. 1 act. Plays, 29 (December, 1969), 48-56.

5344. _____. Junction Santa Claus. 1 act. Plays, 11 (December, 1951), 43-52. AND Plays, 20 (December, 1960), 37-46.

5345. _____. Just Relax, Mother. 1 act. Plays, 17 (May, 1958), 35-45.

5346. _____. The Late Mr. Scarface. 1 act. One-Act Play Magazine, 3 (September-October, 1940), 482-488.

5347. _____. Let George Do It. 1 act. Plays, 25 (February, 1966), 61-70. AND Plays, 34 (February, 1975), 55-63.

5348. _____. Let's Go Formal. 1 act. Plays, 3 (February, 1944), 24-32.

5349. _____. Let's Go Formal. 1 act. Senior Scholastic, 44 (March 20-25, 1944), 13-15, 18.

5350. _____. The Life for Mother. 1 act. Plays, 22 (May, 1963), 43-52.

5351. _____. Lincoln Reminders. 1 act. Plays, 14 (February, 1955), 75-79. AND Plays, 28 (February, 1969), 67-71.

5352. _____. The Lincoln Umbrella. 1 act. Plays, 9 (February, 1950), 40-47. AND Plays, 23 (February, 1964), 55-63.

5353. _____. Living Up to Lincoln. 1 act. Plays, 19 (February, 1960), 49-57.

5354. _____. Love from Bud. 1 act. Plays, 2 (October, 1942), 14-21.

5355. _____. The Magic Egg. 1 act. Plays, 4 (March, 1945), 29-36.

5356. _____. Many Thanks. 1 act. Plays, 14 (November, 1954), 53-61. AND Plays, 30 (November, 1970), 39-46.

5357. _____. Mementos of Our Ancestors. 1 act. Plays, 17 (November, 1957), 1-15.

5358. _____. Merry Christmas, Crawfords! 1 act. Plays, 16 (December, 1956), 15-29. AND Plays, 34 (December, 1974), 10-23.

5359. _____. Merry Christmas Customs. 1 act. Plays, 17 (December, 1957), 63-66.

5360. _____. Mind Your P's and Q's. 1 act. Plays, 12 (March, 1953), 51-57. AND Plays, 22 (March, 1963), 44-50.

5361. _____. Minority of Millions. 1 act. Plays, 17 (February, 1958), 1-12. AND Plays, 29 (May, 1970), 71-82.

5362. _____. Mr. Owl's Advice. 1 act. Plays, 17 (April, 1958), 69-71.

5363. _____. Mom's a Grandma Now. 1 act. Plays, 9 (May, 1950), 1-14.

5364. _____. The Moon Keeps Shining. 1 act. Plays, 10 (May, 1951), 1-10.

5365. _____. Mother Earth's New Dress. 1 act. Plays, 5 (March, 1946), 34-42.

5366. _____. Mother's Admirers. 1 act. Plays, 5 (May, 1946), 33-42. AND Plays, 27 (May, 1968), 43-52.

5367. _____. Mother's V.I.P.'s. 1 act. Plays, 15 (May, 1956), 11-22. AND Plays, 32 (May, 1973), 45-53.

5368. _____. Music Hath Charms. 1 act. Plays, 12 (March, 1953), 1-8.

5369. _____. Neighbors to the North. 1 act. Plays, 22 (November, 1962), 79-82.

5370. _____. New-Fangled Thanksgiving. 1 act. Plays, 33 (November, 1973), 55-62.

5371. _____. Not Fit for Man or Beast. 1 act. Plays, 23 (January, 1964), 59-67.

5372. _____. Nothing to Be Thankful for. 1 act. Plays, 26 (November, 1966), 53-62.

5373. _____. Nursery Rhyme Diet. 1 act. Plays, 11 (October, 1951), 50-54.

5374. _____. An Ode to Spring. 1 act. Plays, 12 (April, 1953), 1-14. AND Plays, 25 (May, 1966), 41-53.

5375. _____. Off the Shelf. 1 act. Plays, 4 (November, 1944), 29-35.

5376. _____. Our Famous Ancestors. 1 act. Plays, 25 (November, 1965), 27-36.

5377. _____. Our Own Four Walls. 1 act. Plays, 5 (April, 1946), 40-46.

5378. _____. Pleasant Dreams. 1 act. Plays, 4 (January, 1945), 50-53.

5379. _____. Portrait of an American. 1 act. Plays, 12 (May, 1953), 14-22. AND Plays, 23 (May, 1964), 13-22.

5380. _____. The Princess and the Rose-Colored Glasses. 1 act. Plays, 26 (April, 1967), 75-82.

5381. _____. Princess of Hearts. 1 act. Plays, 20 (February, 1961), 73-78.

5382. _____. Putting Pop in His Place. 1 act. Plays, 20 (January, 1961), 35-45.

5383. _____. A Quiet Christmas. 1 act. Plays, 10 (December, 1950), 1-14. AND Plays, 24 (December, 1964), 15-28.

5384. _____. Rainbow Colors. 1 act. Plays, 9 (January, 1950), 66-69.

5385. _____. Reindeer on the Roof. 1 act. Plays, 12 (December, 1952), 13-26. AND Plays, 31 (December, 1971), 45-57.

5386. _____. A Rival for Dad. 1 act. Plays, 3 (December, 1943), 20-26.

5387. _____. Soldiers on the Home Front. 1 act. Plays, 3 (May, 1944), 70-73.

5388. _____. The Sparrow Family. 1 act. Plays, 18 (February, 1959), 83-86.

5389. _____. Spring Daze. 1 act. Plays, 10 (March, 1951), 1-9. AND Plays, 18 (March, 1959), 27-35.

5390. _____. Spring Fever. 1 act. Plays, 9 (March, 1950), 1-12. AND Plays, 24 (April, 1965), 45-56.

5391. _____. Spring Tonic. 1 act. Plays, 24 (March, 1965), 71-76.

5392. _____. The Star in the Window. 1 act. Plays, 21 (December, 1961), 33-43.

5393. _____. Stretch a Point. 1 act. Plays, 3 (January, 1944), 63-66.

5394. _____. Surprise Guests. 1 act. Plays, 9 (November, 1949), 1-10. AND Plays, 19 (November, 1959), 1-10.

5395. _____. Sweet Sixteen. 1 act. Plays, 3 (April, 1944), 8-15.

5396. _____. Television-itis. 1 act. Plays, 9 (May, 1950), 24-34.

5397. _____. Tempest in a Teapot. 1 act. Plays, 5 (November, 1945), 19-27.

5398. _____. Thanks to Billy. 1 act. Plays, 9 (November, 1949), 40-49.

5399. _____. Thanks to George Washington. 1 act. Plays, 16 (February, 1957), 23-35.

5400. _____. Thanksgiving Postscript. 1 act. Plays, 18 (November, 1958), 1-12. AND Plays, 31 (November, 1971), 47-56.

5401. _____. Thanksgiving Wishbone. 1 act. Plays, 16 (November, 1956), 61-63.

5402. _____. That Christmas Feeling. 1 act. Plays, 18 (December, 1958), 45-54.

5403. _____. Three Wishes for Mother. 1 act. Plays, 11 (May, 1952), 55-59.

5404. _____. Through You I Live. 1 act. One-Act Play Magazine, 4 (March-April, 1941), 176-190.

5405. _____. To Be or Not to Be. 1 act. Plays, 5 (January, 1946), 11-19.

5406. _____. Too Many Kittens. 1 act. Plays, 14 (January, 1955), 49-58. AND Plays, 28 (January, 1969), 59-68.

5407. _____. Turkey Gobblers. 1 act. Plays, 23 (November, 1963), 29-41. AND Plays, 35 (November, 1975), 25-38.

5408. _____. 'Twas the Night Before Christmas. 1 act. Plays, 5 (December, 1945), 1-11.

5409. _____. Unaccustomed As I Am. 1 act. One-Act Play Magazine, 4 (May-June, 1941), 213-223.

5410. _____. Unaccustomed As I Am. 1 act. Scholastic, 39 (October 20, 1941), 17-19.

5411. _____. Under the Harvest Moon. 1 act. Plays, 4 (October, 1944), 32-37.

5412. _____. A Visit to the White House. 1 act. Plays, 24 (January, 1965), 83-95.

5413. _____. Voices of America. 1 act. Plays, 4 (November, 1944), 41-44.

5414. _____. Vote for Uncle Sam. 1 act. Plays, 10 (November, 1950), 11-18.

5415. _____. We Want Mother. 1 act. Plays, 15 (May, 1956), 33-40.

5416. _____. What, No Santa Claus? 1 act. Plays, 5 (December, 1945), 43-49.

5417. _____. What, No Venison? 1 act. Plays, 15 (November, 1955), 1-13. AND Plays, 32 (November, 1972), 13-26.

5418. _____. When Do We Eat? 1 act. Plays, 14 (October, 1954), 39-48. AND Plays, 26 (March, 1967), 45-53.

5419. _____. Who's Old-Fashioned? 1 act. Plays, 11 (May, 1952), 21-31. AND Plays, 16 (May, 1957), 21-30.

McQueen, Noel see McQueen, M. H. 5287-5419.

Madany, translator see Martinez Sierra, G. and M. Martinez Sierra 5631

5420. Madden, David, 1933- . Cassandra Singing. 3 acts. First Stage, 2 (Spring, 1963), 99-132.

5421. _____. In My Father's House. 1 act. First Stage, 5 (Summer, 1966), 119-131.

5422. Madern, Jose-Maria. La Chemise de Nylon. 1 act. L'Avant Scène, 486 (January 1, 1972), 35-44. Andre Camp, adapter. In French.

5423. Madis, Alex. Presa al laccio! 3 acts. Il Dramma, 25 (September 1, 1927), 6-40. In Italian.

_____ see also Mirande, Y. 6079

Madrid, Francisco de see Francisco de Madrid 3250

5424. Maeterlinck, Maurice, 1862-1949. Aglavaine and Selysette. 5 acts, tragedy. Poet Lore, 14 (No. 4, 1903), 11-64. Charlotte Porter and Helen A. Clarke, translators.

5425. _____. Alladine and Palomides. 5 acts. Poet Lore, 7 (June-July, 1895), 281-301. Charlotte Porter and Helen A. Clarke, translators.

5426. _____. Il dolore giunge dall'altra parte. 1 act. Il Dramma, n.s., 49 (November 15, 1947), 33-41. Micaela De Pastrovich Pampanini, translator. In Italian.

5427. _____. The Intruder. 1 act. Golden Book, 16 (December, 1932), 543-553.

5428. _____. Joyzelle. 5 acts. Poet Lore, 16 (Summer, 1905), 1-45. Clarence Stratton, translator.

5429. _____. Monna Vanna. 3 acts. Poet Lore, 15 (No. 3, 1904), 1-52. Charlotte Porter, translator.

5430. _____. Pelleas and Melisande. 5 acts, tragedy. Poet Lore, 6 (August-September, 1894), 413-452.

5431. _____. The Seven Princesses. 1 act. Poet Lore, 6 (January-March, 1894), 29-32, 87-93, 150-161. Charlotte Porter and Helen A. Clarke, translators.

5432. _____. The Sightless. 1 act. Poet Lore, 5 (No. 3-8 & 9, 1893), 159-163, 218-221, 273-277, 442-452. Charlotte Porter and Helen A. Clarke, translators.

5433. _____. Sister Beatrice. 3 acts. Anglo-Saxon Review, 6 (September, 1900), 90-119. A. Bernard Miall, translator.

_____, translator see Shakespeare, W. 8183

5434. Maevius. A Masque for Democrats. 1 act. Landfall, 4 (March, 1950), 79-84.

5435. Maffei, Mario. Zutik il processo di Burgos. Sipario, 356 (January, 1976), 62-80. In Italian.

_____, translator see Kopit, A. 4689

Magarshack, David, 1899- , translator see Gogol, N. 3598

5436. Magnan, Jean-Marie. La Coexistence. 1 act. L'Avant Scène, 400 (April 1, 1968), 37-39. In French.

5437. _____. L'Oeil du Maître. 1 act. L'Avant Scène, 346 (December 1, 1965), 48-52. In French.

5438. _____. Le Songe de la Nuit d'un Couple. 1 act. L'Avant Scène, 400 (April 1, 1968), 40-42. In French.

5439. Magnier, Claude. Herminie. 2 acts, comedy. L'Avant Scène, 448 (May 1, 1970), 7-42. In French.

5440. _____. Léon, ou la Bonne Formule. 4 acts, comedy. L'Avant Scène, 448 (May 1, 1970), 43-72. In French.

5441. _____. Monsieur Masure. 5 acts. L'Avant Scène, 490 (March 1, 1972), 45-75. In French.

5442. _____. Monsieur Masure. 2 parts, farce. Il Dramma, n.s., 248 (May, 1957), 6-33. B. L. Randone, translator. In Italian.

5443. _____. Oscar. 3 acts, comedy. L'Avant Scène, 173 (May 1, 1958), 6-36. AND L'Avant Scène, 490 (March 1, 1972), 5-38. In French.

5444. Magnoni, Bruno. Il costo di una vita. 2 parts. Il Dramma, n.s., 320 (May, 1963), 8-42. In Italian.

5445. _____. Le nozze di Giovanna Phile. 1 act. Il Dramma, n.s., 183 (June 15, 1953), 20-30. In Italian.

5446. Magnus, Julian. A Cloud on the Honey-Moon. 1 act, comedy. Harper's, 69 (September, 1884), 580-583.

5447. Magnuson, James. Pecos Bill Meets the Trickster (A Jungian Western). 1 act. Dramatika, 8 (Fall, 1971), n.p.

5448. Mahar, Ethel. Evergreen. 1 act. Plays, 5 (December, 1945), 40-42.

5449. Mahieu, Charles. Sur un Banc. 1 act, comedy. L'Avant Scène, 247 (August 1, 1961), 37-44. In French.

5450. Mahlmann, Lewis. Rumpelstiltskin. 1 act. Plays, 32 (October, 1972), 74-80.

_____, adapter see Andersen, H. C. 199

_____, adapter see Baum, L. F. 678

_____, adapter see Browning, R. 1377

_____, adapter see Dodgson, C. L. 2517

_____, adapter see Grahame, K. 3683

_____, adapter see Grimm, J. and W. Grimm 3752, 3754

_____, adapter see Lorenzini, C. 5055

_____, adapter see Perrault, C. 7071

_____, adapter see Ruskin, J. 7801

5451. _____ and David Cadwalader Jones. Jack and the Beanstalk. 1 act. Plays, 31 (May, 1972), 63-68.

5452. _____. Why the Sea Is Salt. 1 act. Plays, 33 (October, 1973), 75-80.

5453. Mai, Fabiene. Volodia. 1 act. L'Avant Scène, 499 (July 15, 1972), 34-37. In French.

5454. Maiakovski, Vladimir. Les Bains. 6 acts. L'Avant Scène, 401 (April 15, 1968), 13-29. Elsa Triolet, translator. In French.

5455. _____. Banja. 6 acts. Sipario, 266 (June, 1968), 53-64. Giuseppe Mariano, translator. In Italian.

5456. _____. Die Wanze. 1 act. Spectaculum, 2 (1959), 335-377. In German.

5457. Mainardi, Renato, 1931- . Antonio von Elba. 2 acts. Sipario, 349-350 (June-July, 1975), 92-112. In Italian.

5458. _____. Pas de deux. 2 parts. Il Dramma, n.s., 380/381 (May/June, 1968), 4-27. In Italian.

5459. _____. Per non morire. 2 parts. Il Dramma, n.s., 361 (October, 1966), 6-30. In Italian.

5460. _____. Per una giovanetta che nessuno piange. 2 parts. Il Dramma, n.s., 347/348 (August/September, 1965), 16-40. In Italian.

5461. _____. Una Strana quiete. 2 acts. Il Dramma, (July, 1975), 25-49. In Italian.

5462. Majeski, Bill. Murder at Mother Goose's Place. 1 act. Plays, 35 (May, 1976), 43-48.

5463. _____. Whatever Happened to Good Old Ebenezer Scrooge? 1 act. Plays, 36 (December, 1976), 1-10.

5464. Major, Mike. Chalk and Slate. 1 act. Dramatics, 45 (February, 1974), 6-11.

5465. _____. Simon Sez. 1 act. Dramatics, 42 (March, 1971), 4-10.

5466. _____. Squawk of a Distant Gull. 1 act. Dramatics, 44 (November, 1972), 5-9.

5467. Malanga, Gerard. The Rubber Heart, a One-Act Soap Opera. Art and Literature, 9 (Summer, 1966), 172-191.

5468. Malaparte, Curzio. Du Côté de Chez Proust. 1 act. L'Avant Scène (OST), 1 (March, 1949), 27-41. In French.

5469. Malcolm, Ian. God Save McQueen. 1 act. Performing Arts in Canada, 6 (Fall, 1969), 27-33.

5470. Malerba, Luigi, 1927- . Ossido di Carbonio. 1 act. Sipario, 353-354 (October, November, 1975), 105-112. In Italian.

5471. Males, U. Harold. The Professional Attitude. 3 acts. First Stage, 1 (Fall, 1962), 8-34.

Malina, Judith see Beck, J. 693

5472. Malkind, Margaret. Sweet Liberty. 1 act. Plays, 36 (November, 1976), 79-86.

Mallan, Lloyd, translator see Montellano, B. O. de 6180

5473. Mallarme, Stephane, 1842-1898. Herodiade. 1 act. Poet Lore, 32 (Autumn, 1921), 458-462. Joseph Twadell Shipley, translator.

5474. Mallet, Robert, 1915- . L'Equipage au Complet. 1 act, comedy. L'Avant Scène, 149, 1-25. In French.

5475. _____. L'Equipage au Complet. Il Dramma, n.s., 257 (February, 1958), 16-43. Luciana Driussi, translator. In Italian.

5476. _____. Satire en Trois Temps, Quatre Mouvements. 1 act. L'Avant Scène, 149, 27-38. In French.

Mallet-Jorris, Françoise, 1930- , translator see Delaney, S. 2290

5477. Mallock, William Hurrell, 1849-1923. Women in Parliament. 3 acts. 19th Century, 72 (August, 1912), 292-318.

5478. Mallory, Jay. Il dolce aloe. 3 acts. Il Dramma, 248 (December 15, 1936), 2-27. In Italian.

5479. Malone, Mary. The Groundhog's Shadow. 1 act. Plays, 16 (February, 1957), 66-70.

5480. _____. The Last Snake in Ireland. 1 act. Plays, 16 (March, 1957), 55-60.

5481. _____. A Letter for Charlotte. 1 act. Plays, 9 (January, 1950), 10-18.

5482. _____. The President's Bride. 1 act. Plays, 17 (May, 1958), 27-34.

5483. Maloon, James. Feedback. 1 act. Dramatika, 8 (Fall, 1971), n.p.

5484. _____. The Simon Game. 1 act. Dramatika, 8 (Fall, 1971), n. p.

5485. Maltz, Albert, 1908- . Mr. Togo and His Friends. 1 act. Plays, 2 (December, 1942), 70-72.

5486. _____. Rehearsal. 1 act. One-Act Play Magazine, 1 (March, 1938), 994-1020.

Mamo, Maria Tchou, translator see Kuo, Mo-Jo 4738

_____, translator see Vendetta del pescatore, La 9062

5487. Mancuso, Umberto, 1890- and Giuseppe Zucca. Interno 1, interno 5, interno 7. 3 acts. Il Dramma, 98 (September 15, 1930), 4-35. In Italian.

Mandel, Adrienne Schizzano, translator see Bellido, J. M. 735

_____, translator see Filippone, V. 3020

_____, translator see Fratti, M. 3284

_____, translator see Zerboni, R. 9643

5488. Mandel, Oscar, 1926- . The Cage Opened, and Out Flew a Coward. Minnesota Review, 4 (Spring, 1964), 308-331.

5488a. _____. The Fatal French Dentist. 1 act. First Stage, 4 (Summer, 1965), 90-96.

5489. _____. General Audax. 1 act. First Stage, 6 (Fall, 1967), 146-168.

5490. _____. Honest Urubamba, a Puppet Play Without Strings. 1 act. Literary Review, 9 (Autumn, 1965), 120-160.

5491. _____. Island. Massachusetts Review, 2 (Winter, 1961), 265-300.

5492. _____. Living Room with 6 Oppressions. 1 act. Drama and Theatre, 8 (Spring, 1970), 189-195.

5493. _____. The Monk Who Wouldn't. 1 act. First Stage, 1 (Summer, 1962), 27-40.

5494. _____. Professor Snaffle's Polypon. 5 acts. First Stage, 5 (Summer, 1966), 65-89.

5495. _____. The Virgin and the Unicorn, a Comic Miracle Play. 3 acts. Minnesota Review, 7 (No. 1, 1967), 15-41.

5496. Mandich, Francesco. I sassi ne le scarpe. 3 parts. Sipario, 13 (December, 1958), 39-53. In Italian.

5497. Manet, Eduardo, 1927- . Les Nonnes. 2 parts, parable. L'Avant Scène, 431 (August 1, 1969), 5-27. In French.

Mangual, Angelo see Brown, N. 1372

5498. Manhoff, Bill, 1920- . L'Amour, Vous Connaissez? 3 acts, comedy. L'Avant Scène, 355 (April 15, 1966), 9-35. France Roche, adapter. In French.

5499. Manners, John Hartley, 1870-1928. Ministers of Grace. 1 act. Smart Set, 38 (September, 1912), 129-142.

5500. ———. The Woman Intervenes. 1 act. Smart Set, 36 (April, 1912), 113-123.

5501. Manning, Marie. Nervous Prostration. 1 act. Harper's, 125 (September, 1912), 641-644.

5502. Manning, Susan. Background for Nancy. 1 act. Plays, 27 (January, 1968), 27-35.

5503. Manning-Sanders, George. The Choice. 1 act, comedy. Dublin Magazine, 2 (February, 1925), 448-458.

Manoja, Ernesto Romagna, translator see Deza, E. S. de 2396

5504. Manrique, Gómez. Della nativita di nostro Signore. 1 act. Il Dramma, n.s., 255 (December, 1957), 13-16. In Italian.

5505. Manson, H. W. D. The Magnolia Tree. 3 acts. Gambit, 8, 69-130.

5506. Mantle, Margaret. Beatrice and Benedick. 1 act. Plays, 14 (May, 1955), 13-18.

5507. ———. A Doctor for Lucinda. 1 act. Plays, 14 (January, 1955), 59-64.

5508. Manzari, Nicola, 1909- . Dio salvi la Scozia. 3 acts. Il Dramma, n.s., 270 (March, 1959), 22-48. In Italian.

5509. ———. La gabbia vuota. 3 acts. Il Dramma, n.s., 310 (July, 1962), 20-50. In Italian.

5510. ———. Le gatte. 1 act. Il Dramma, n.s., 272 (May, 1959), 45-50. In Italián.

5511. _____. Miracolo. 3 acts. Il Dramma, n. s., 61/62 (May 15/June 1, 1948), 95-112. In Italian.

5512. _____. I nostri cari bambini. 3 acts. Il Dramma, n. s., 244 (January, 1957), 11-33. In Italian.

5513. _____. I poeti servono a qualche cosa. 3 acts. Il Dramma, 322 (January 15, 1940), 4-20. In Italian.

5514. _____. Pudore. 3 acts. Il Dramma, n. s., 226 (July, 1955), 5-34. In Italian.

5515. _____. I ragazzi se ne vanno.... 1. act. Il Dramma, 213 (July 1, 1935), 37-43. In Italian.

5516. _____. Il salotto della signora Bihàr. 3 acts. Il Dramma, 412/413 (October 15/November 1, 1943), 5-24. In Italian.

5517. _____. Salud. 3 acts. Il Dramma, n. s., 347/348 (August/September, 1965), 60-76. In Italian.

5518. _____. Il trionfo del diritto. 3 acts. Il Dramma, 345 (January 1, 1941), 8-26. In Italian.

5519. _____. Tutto per la donna. 3 acts. Il Dramma, 310 (July 15, 1939), 4-19. In Italian.

5520. Mapp, Frances, adapter. The Golden Bird. 1 act. Plays, 28 (December, 1968), 51-60.

5521. _____. The Ogre Who Built a Bridge. 1 act. Plays, 28 (November, 1968), 77-82.

_____, adapter see Andersen, H. C. 197

_____, adapter see Baum, L. F. 677

5522. Maraini, Dacia. Don Juan. Sipario, 358 (March, 1976), 57-80. In Italian.

5523. _____. La famiglia normale. 1 act. Sipario, 21 (October, 1966), 47-51. In Italian.

5524. _____. Il ricatto a teatro. 2 acts. Sipario, 23 (March, 1968), 38-52. In Italian.

_____, translator see Witkiewicz, S. I. 9512

5525. Marais, Claude and Carlos d'Aguila. Le Nuit Blanche de Monsieur de Musset. 1 act, comedy. L'Avant Scène, 97, 28-34. In French.

5526. Marais, Jean-Bernard. La Galette des Rois. 1 act. L'Avant Scène, 547 (September 1, 1974), 36-39. In French.

5527. Marasco, Robert, 1936- . Child's Play. 6 scenes. L'Avant Scène, 484 (December 1, 1971), 7-31. Pol Quentin, adapter. In French.

5528. Marble, Annie. Faith of Our Fathers. 2 acts. Drama, 10 (July-September, 1920), 373-377.

Marceau, Felicien, pseud. see Carette, L. 1597-1609

5529. Marcel, Gabriel, 1889- . Le chemin de Crete. 4 acts. Sipario, 5 (May, 1950), 49-77. Giannino Galloni, translator. In Italian.

5530. _____. Un homme de Dieu. 4 acts. Sipario, 1 (October, 1946), 11-32. Giannino Galloni, translator. In Italian.

5531. _____. La Prune et la Prunelle. 1 act. L'Avant Scène, 225, 32-37. In French.

5532. Marcelle-Maurette, 1903- . Anastasia. 3 acts. Theatre Arts, 40 (May, 1956), 35-61. Guy Bolton, adapter.

5533. _____. La Nuit de Feu. 1 act. L'Avant Scène, 304 (February 1, 1964), 35-42. In French.

5534. _____. Printemps. 1 act. L'Avant Scène, 228, 32-39. In French.

5535. Marcellini, Giovanni. Rosso e nero. 4 acts. Il Dramma, 352 (April 15, 1941), 9-31. In Italian.

_____, translator see France, A. 3240, 3246

_____, translator see Masao, K. 5637

_____, translator see Mérimée, P. 5770

_____, translator see Molière 6122

_____, translator see Renard, J. 7483, 7486

_____, translator see Vega Carpio, L. F. de 9054

5536. Marchand, Leopold. J'ai Tué. 3 acts. Petite Illustration, 86 (December 15, 1928), 1-26. In French.

5537. _____. Durand, Bijoutier. 3 acts. Petite Illustration, 88 (February 8, 1930), 1-34. In French.

5538. _____ and Albert Willemetz. Trois Valses. 3 acts, comedy. Petite Illustration, 198 (October 9, 1937), 1-47. In French.

_____ see Colette, S. G. C. 1934, 1935

5539. Marchandeau, François. Angustias. 1 act. L'Avant Scène, 337 (July 1, 1965), 39-45. In French.

Marchesini, Virgilio, translator see Girette, M. 3577

Marciano, Paolo Angioletti, translator see Naum, G. 6452

5540. Marcus, Frank, 1928- . Cleo and Max. 1 act. London Magazine, n.s., 5 (February, 1966), 55-64.

5541. _____. The Killing of Sister George. 3 acts. Esquire, 66 (November, 1966), 118-129, 152-153.

5542. _____. Mrs. Mouse, Are You Within? 3 acts. Plays and Players, 15 (July, 1968), 29-44, 63-65.

5543. _____. Notes on a Love Affair. 2 acts. Plays and Players, 19 (July, 1972), 35-50.

5544. Marcus, Irving H. To You the Torch. 1 act. Plays, 2 (May, 1943), 18-25. AND Plays, 18 (May, 1959), 89-96.

5545. Marcus, Joseph. Judgment of Paris. 1 act. Journal of Irish Literature, 5 (May, 1976), 18-48.

Mariana, Emilio, translator see Schiller, J. C. F. von 8026

5546. Mariani, Federico. Sunbeam. 1 act. Smart Set, 29 (October, 1909), 130-138.

Mariano, Ettore, translator see Saroyan, W. 7945

Mariano, Giuseppe, translator see Maiakovsky, V. 5455

5547. Marie, André. Tartuffe--Acte VI. 1 act, comedy. L'Avant Scène, 290 (June 15, 1963), 38-43. In French.

5548. Marinetti, Filippo Tommaso, 1876-1944. Le Basi. Sipario, 260 (December, 1967), 89. In Italian.

5549. _____. Short Plays: The Arrest; The Little Theatre of Love; Simultaneity; Lights; The Tactile Quartet; Indecision; The Battle of the Backdrops; Public Gardens (with Francesco Cangiullo); Music of the Toilette (with Gianni Calderone). 1 act each. Drama Review, 17 (December, 1973), 116-125. Victoria Nes Kirby, translator.

Marinetti

5550. _____. Simultaneita. <u>Sipario</u>, 260 (December, 1967), 89-90. In Italian.

5551. _____. Il suggeritore nudo. <u>Sipario</u>, 260 (December, 1967), 83-88. In Italian.

5552. _____. Il teatrino dell'amore. <u>Sipario</u>, 260 (December, 1967), 90. In Italian.

5553. _____. Vengono. <u>Sipario</u>, 260 (December, 1967), 89. In Italian.

5554. _____ and Bruno Corradini, 1892- . Le mani. <u>Sipario</u>, 260 (December, 1967), 90-91. In Italian.

Marinucci, Vinicio, translator see Anderson, M. 212

_____, translator see Barry, P. 638

_____, translator see Carroll, P. V. 1623

_____, translator see Coward, N. 2067, 2080

_____, translator see Cowl, J. and J. Murfin 2080

_____, translator see Dunsany, E. J. M. D. P. 2712, 2718, 2724, 2726

_____, translator see Hyakuzo, K. 4348

_____, translator see Kaufman, G. S. and M. Hart 4561

_____, translator see Kesselring, J. 4606

_____, translator see Koestler, A. 4679

_____, translator see Luce, C. B. 5075

_____, translator see Mérimée, P. 5772

_____, translator see O'Neill, E. 6841

_____, translator see Priestley, J. B. 7298

_____, translator see Printzlau, O. 7305

_____, translator see Shaw, I. 8225

_____, translator see Suzuki, S. 8638, 8639

Marisi, C. D., translator see Cheyefsky, P. 1747

Marisi

_____, translator see Whiting, J. 9330

5555. Marivaux, Pierre, 1688-1793. La Colonie. 1 act, comedy. L'Avant Scène, 269 (July 15, 1962), 35-42. In French.

5556. _____. La Commère. 1 act. Il Dramma, n.s., 354 (March, 1966), 69-76. Costanza Andreucci, translator. In Italian.

5557. _____. Les Serments Indiscrets. 5 acts, comedy. L'Avant Scène, 133, 1-25. In French.

5558. _____. The Test. 1 act. Poet Lore, 35 (1924), 533-561. Willis Knapp Jones, translator.

5559. Markham, Catharine. How Christmas Was Saved, or The Sorrows of Santa Claus. 2 acts. St. Nicholas, 36 (December, 1908), 153-157.

5560. Marks, Jeannette, 1875- . Dragon. 1 act. Double-Dealer, 2 (August-September, 1921), 54-66.

5561. _____. The Merry, Merry Cuckoo. 1 act. The Dramatist, 4 (October, 1912), 291-300.

5562. _____. A Welsh Honeymoon. 1 act. Smart Set, 38 (November, 1912), 135-141.

Marks, Lionel Simeon (Mrs.) see Peabody, J. P. 7023, 7024

Marley, Olive J., adapter see Doyle, Sir A. C. 2579

5563. Marlowe, Alan. A Play. Floating Bear, 30 (1964), 2-3.

5564. Marlowe, Christopher, 1564-1593. The Jew of Marlowe. 5 acts. L'Avant Scène, 588 (June 1, 1976), 3-33. Max Denes and Francois Rey, translators. In French.

Marni, Jeanne, pseud. see Marniere, J. M. F. 5565, 5566

5565. Marniere, Jeanne Marie François, 1854-1910. Amis? 1 act. Smart Set, 26 (November, 1908), 134-136. In French.

5566. _____. Premier Jeudi. 1 act. Smart Set, 16 (July, 1905), 135-137. In French.

5567. Marotta, Giaseppe. Un ladro in paradiso. 2 parts. Sipario, 56 (December, 1950), 65-83. In Italian.

5568. _____ and Belisario Randone. Bello di papa. 3 acts, comedy. Sipario, 12 (November, 1957), 34-60. In Italian.

5569. _____. Don Vincenzino. 1 act. Sipario, 16 (June, 1961), 63-67. In Italian.

5570. _____. Il generale dei Teddy boys. 2 parts, comedy. Sipario, 17 (December, 1962), 81-99. In Italian.

5571. _____. Il terrore di Roma. 1 act. Sipario, 187 (November, 1961), 64-66. In Italian.

5572. _____. Vado per vedove. 3 acts, farce. Sipario, 17 (February, 1962), 33-51. In Italian.

5573. _____. Veronica e gli ospiti. 3 acts, comedy. Sipario, 14 (July-August, 1959), 26-49. In Italian.

5574. Marowitz, Charles. Amleto. Sipario, 230 (June, 1965), 52-57. Luciano Codignola, translator. In Italian.

_____, translator see Buchner, G. 1403

_____, translator see Shakespeare, W. 8184

_____, translator see Wilde, O. 9361

5575. Marques, Rene. The House of the Setting Sun; A Puerto Rican Tragedy. 2 acts. Poet Lore, 59 (No. 2), 99-131. Willis Knapp Jones, translator.

Marquez, Robert, translator see Adoum, J. E. 77

5576. Marquis, Marjorie. The First Christmas. 1 act. Ladies' Home Journal, 47 (December, 1930), 14-15, 51, 53.

5577. Marra, Dorothy Brandt. "Woof" for the Red, White and Blue. 1 act. Plays, 34 (May, 1975), 87-90.

Marrast, Robert, translator see Aub, M. 433

5578. Marsan, Jean. Aux Quatre Coins. 3 acts, comedy. L'Avant Scène (OST), 31 (October, 1950), 3-40. In French.

5579. _____. Interdit au Public. 3 acts. L'Avant Scène, 394 (January 1, 1968), 10-39. In French.

5580. Marsh, Janet. The Long-Haired Warriors. 1 act. Plays, 2 (November, 1942), 31-36.

5581. Marshall, Sheila L. February on Trial. 1 act. Plays, 32 (February, 1973), 63-71.

5582. _____. A Thanksgiving Dream. 1 act. Plays, 35 (November, 1975), 45-48.

5583. Marston, John Westland, 1819-1890. A Hard Struggle. 1 act. Living Age, 51 (April 17, 1858), 213-221.

5584. Martel de Janville, Sibylle Gabrielle Marie Antoinette de Riquetti de Mirabeau, comtesse de, 1850-1932. Innamorati, l'amore attraverso le etá. 1 act. Il Dramma, 4 (March, 1926), 38-40. In Italian.

5585. _____. Little Blue Guienea-Hen. 1 act, comedy. Poet Lore, 30 (Spring, 1919), 60-80. R. T. House, translator.

5586. Martens, Anne Coulter. The Age of Precarious. 1 act. Plays, 30 (May, 1971), 35-42.

5587. _____. The American Way. 1 act. Plays, 23 (February, 1964), 13-24.

5588. _____. The Comeback Caper. 1 act. Plays, 33 (May, 1974), 1-15.

5589. _____. The Costume Caper. 1 act. Plays, 27 (October, 1967), 1-12.

5590. _____. A Cue for Cleopatra. 1 act. Plays, 23 (October, 1963), 1-15. AND Plays, 35 (February, 1976), 21-34.

5591. _____. The Cupid Computer. 1 act. Plays, 27 (February, 1968), 1-12.

5592. _____. The Dragon with the Squeaky Roar. 1 act. Plays, 30 (November, 1970), 55-59.

5593. _____. Fit to Be Tied. 1 act. Plays, 27 (November, 1967), 1-11.

5594. _____. Fitness Is the Fashion. 1 act. Plays, 23 (April, 1964), 1-11.

5595. _____. George Slept Here, Too. 1 act. Plays, 28 (February, 1969), 1-8.

5596. _____. The Go-Go Gophers. 1 act. Plays, 26 (March, 1967), 1-12.

5597. _____. Granny from Killarney. 1 act. Plays, 23 (March, 1964), 1-14.

5598. _____. Green Men, Go Home. 1 act. Plays, 28 (April, 1969), 45-52.

5599. _____. Hobgoblin House. 1 act. Plays, 36 (October, 1976), 37-45.

5600. _____. Is Cupid Stupid? 1 act. Plays, 29 (February, 1970), 1-10.

5601. _____. It's a Woman's World. 1 act. Plays, 31 (February, 1972), 1-11.

5602. _____. Jury Duty. 1 act. Plays, 35 (March, 1976), 11-24.

5603. _____. The Magic Hat. 1 act. Plays, 30 (October, 1970), 71-77.

5604. _____. My Swinging Swain. 1 act. Plays, 25 (October, 1965), 1-12.

5605. _____. The Mystery of the Missing Money. 1 act. Plays, 36 (November, 1976), 13-26.

5606. _____. Nor Long Remember. 1 act. Plays, 22 (May, 1963), 15-28.

5607. _____. One Life to Lose. 1 act. Plays, 27 (May, 1968), 13-22.

5608. _____. Open House. 1 act. Plays, 24 (October, 1964), 17-28.

5609. _____. Over the River. 1 act. Plays, 25 (November, 1965), 1-14.

5610. _____. The Road Ahead. 1 act. Plays, 27 (February, 1968), 57-64.

5611. _____. Roscoe the Robot. 1 act. Plays, 28 (October, 1968), 1-10.

5612. _____. Rosemary for Remembrance. 1 act. Plays, 23 (April, 1964), 27-36.

5613. _____. Runaway. 1 act. Plays, 21 (October, 1961), 25-35.

5614. _____. Santa Claus Is Twins. 1 act. Plays, 29 (December, 1969), 39-47.

5615. _____. Springtime for Dan. 1 act. Plays, 20 (March, 1961), 39-49. AND Plays, 29 (April, 1970), 30-40.

5616. _____. Star of Bethlehem. 1 act. Plays, 24 (December, 1964), 1-14. AND Plays, 35 (December, 1975), 13-25.

5617. _____. Telephonitis. 1 act. Plays, 31 (April, 1972), 21-30.

5618. _____. That Franklin Boy. 1 act. Plays, 29 (March, 1970), 47-52.

5619. _____. Thirteen. 1 act. Plays, 16 (October, 1956), 47-56. AND Plays, 30 (March, 1971), 55-64.

5620. _____. Turnabout in Time. 1 act. Plays, 23 (January, 1964), 1-13.

5621. _____. Visions of Sugar Plums. 1 act. Plays, 26 (December, 1966), 33-45.

5622. _____. Which Is Witch? 1 act. Plays, 29 (October, 1969), 15-24.

5623. Martens, G. M. and André Obey. Pezzenti in paradiso. 3 acts. Il Dramma, n.s., 101 (January 15, 1950), 3-21. Cesare Vico Lodovici, translator. In Italian.

Martin, Allan Langdon, pseud. see Cowl, J. and J. Murfin 2080

5624. Martin, John Joseph, 1893- . Charlie Barringer, the Second of Five Sketches from a County Poor Farm. 1 act. Theatre Arts, 5 (July, 1921), 242-248.

5625. _____. The Wife of Usher's Well, a Tragedy of the Fantastic. 1 act. Poet Lore, 30 (Spring, 1919), 94-111.

Martin, Ruth, translator see Da Ponte, L. 2184

Martin, Thomas, translator see Da Ponte, L. 2184

Martinelli, Milly, translator see Arbuzov, A. 314, 315

_____, translator see Volodin, A. M. 9170

5626. Martinez Sierra, Gregorio, 1881-1947. The Cradle Song. 2 acts, comedy. Poet Lore, 28 (Winter, 1917), 625-679. John Garrett Underhill, translator.

5627. _____. Dobbiamo esser felici. 3 acts. Il Dramma, 94 (July 15, 1930), 4-33. Gilberto Beccari, translator. In Italian.

5628. _____. Love Magic. 1 act, comedy. Drama, 25 (February, 1917), 40-61. John Garrett Underhill, translator.

5629. _____. Noi tre (Triangolo). 3 acts. Il Dramma, 107 (February 1, 1931), 4-32. In Italian.

5630. _____. Poor John. 1 act, comedy. Drama, (February, 1920), 172-180. John Garrett Underhill, translator.

5631. _____ and Maria Martinez Sierra. The Cradle Song. 2 acts, comedy. Petite Illustration, 179 (July 4, 1931), 1-21. Koeckert and Madany, translators. In French.

5632. _____. Des Femmes dans L'Orage. 1 act. L'Avant Scène, 115, 33-40. Jean Camp, translator. In French.

5633. _____ and Carlos Semprun Maura. Giulietta compra un figlio. 3 acts. Il Dramma, 21 (July 1, 1927), 5-30. Gilberto Beccari, translator. In Italian.

Martinez Sierra, Maria see Martinez Sierra, G. 5631, 5632

5634. Martini, Dario G. Qualcosa comunque. 3 acts. Il Dramma, n.s., 314 (November, 1962), 12-38. In Italian.

_____ see also Bassano, E. 657

Martini, Simonetta, translator see Kipphardt, H. 4642

Martone, Maria, translator see Romains, J. 7671

Marx, Henry, translator see Stramm, A. 8549, 8550

5635. Marz, Roy. After Closing. 1 act. First Stage, 1 (Summer, 1962), 41-51.

5636. _____. O'Fallon's Cup. 3 acts. First Stage, 5 (Summer, 1966), 90-118.

5637. Masao, Koumé. La fortuna. 1 act, farce. Il Dramma, 412/413 (October 15/November 1, 1943), 81-86. Giovanni Marcellini, translator. In Italian.

5638. Masciola, Charles. The Hunting of the Snark. 1 act. Dramatika, 10 (1973), n.p.

Masdea, Enrico, translator see Hughes, L. 4304

5639. Masefield, John, 1878-1967. Good Friday. 1 act. Fortnightly, 104 (December, 1915), 993-1018.

5640. _____. Sweeps of Ninety-Eight; A Drama of the Irish Wars. 1 act. Golden Book, 17 (June, 1933), 550-556.

5641. _____. A Word with Sir Francis Drake During His Last Night in London. 1 act. Atlantic, 208 (July, 1961), 50-54.

Mason, Bryna E., translator see Bernard, J.-J. 830

5642. Mason, Miriam E., 1900- . Mary Elizabeth's Wonderful Dream. 1 act. Plays, 9 (November, 1949), 33-40.

5643. Massa, Mario. Idem idem. 2 acts. Il Dramma, 61 (March 1, 1929), 23-34. In Italian.

5644. _____. L'osteria degli immortali. 3 acts. Il Dramma, 44 (June 15, 1928), 5-20. In Italian.

5645. _____. Questo danaro. 3 acts. Il Dramma, 332 (June 15, 1940), 6-21. In Italian.

5646. Massinger, Philip, 1583-1640. New Way to Pay Old Debts. 5 acts, comedy. The Mirror of Taste, 1 (April, 1810), supplement, 3-21.

5647. Masson, Andre, 1921- . Les Voyageurs de l'espoir. 1 act. L'Avant Scène, 600 (December 15, 1976), 23-26. In French.

5648. Masson, Tom, 1866-1934. A Sad Mistake (With Asides). 1 act. Smart Set, 16 (July, 1905), 159-160.

5649. Mastello, Il. 1 act. Sipario, 5 (July, 1950), 65-68. Guido Gioseffi, adapter. In Italian.

5649a. Master Patelin, The Lawyer. 1 act, farce. Golden Book, 13 (March, 1931), 74-79. M. Jagendorf, adapter.

5650. Masterman, Margaret. Misunderstanding in the Lady-Chapel. 1 act. London Mercury, 35 (January, 1937), 308-313.

5651. Masters, Edgar Lee, 1869-1950. The Conversation. 1 act. Poetry, 7 (November, 1915), 55-59.

5652. Masters, Helen Geneva. The Bozeman Trail. 1 act. Scholastic, 12 (March 31, 1928), 6-8, 13.

5653. Masterson, Kate, 1870- . A Man to Order. 1 act. Smart Set, 4 (May, 1901), 155-157.

5654. Mathews, Frances Aymar. Lady Jane's Highwayman. 1 act. Harper's Weekly, 47 (December 12, 1903), 15-17.

5655. Matilla, Luis. Post-Mortem. 1 act. Modern International Drama, 7 (Spring, 1974), 23-47. Marcia C. Wellworth, translator.

5656. Matsas, Nestor. Les crocodiles. 1 act. L'Avant Scène, 504 (October 15, 1972), 34-39. In French.

5657. _____. Les Morts Vivent le Dimanche, ou Etude Expérimentale sur le Cannibalisme du Dimanche. 1 act. L'Avant Scène, 370 (December 15, 1966), 39-43. In French.

Matson, Alex, translator see Kallas, A. 4535

5658. Matson, Charlotte. If Worse Comes to Worst, or Times

Are Getting Harder and Harder. 1 act. Wilson Library Bulletin, 7 (February, 1933), 353-355.

5659. Matthews, Edith V. Brander. At the Eleventh Hour. Harper's Bazaar, 38 (March, 1904), 232-239.

5660. Matthews, Marie. The Dragon and the Century Plant. 1 act. Plays, 28 (December, 1968), 74-76.

5661. Mattinata a Kurosawa. 1 act. Il Dramma, 317 (November 1, 1939), 14-17. In Italian.

5662. Matto, Jose Maria Rivarola. The End of Chipi Gonzalez, A Modern Miracle Play of Paraguay. 3 acts. Poet Lore, 60 (Summer, 1965), 99-146. Willis Knapp Jones, translator.

5663. Mattolini, Mario and Mauro Pezzati. Dies Irae. 1 act. Sipario, 10 (November, 1955), 54-55. In Italian.

Mauclair, Jacques, adapter see Dostoevski, F. 2564

Maude, Aylmer, translator see Tolstoy, L. N. 8878

Maude, Louise, translator see Tolstoy, L. N. 8878

5664. Maugham, Robert Cecil Romer, 1916- . Enemy! 2 acts. Plays and Players, 17 (March, 1970), 61-76.

5665. Maugham, William Somerset, 1874-1965. The Breadwinner. 3 acts. Il Dramma, 139 (June 1, 1932), 4-40. In Italian.

5666. ———. Caroline. 3 acts, comedy. L'Avant Scène, 310 (May 1, 1964), 11-36. Pol Quentin, adapter. In French.

5667. ———. The Circle. 3 acts. Il Dramma, 132 (February 15, 1932), 4-31. In Italian.

5668. ———. The Circle. 3 acts, comedy. Everybody's Magazine, 46 (January, 1922), 91-97.

5669. ———. The Circle. 3 acts, comedy. Petite Illustration, 86 (December 29, 1928), 1-22. H. de Carbuccia, adapter. In French.

5670. ———. The Explorer. 4 acts. Il Dramma, 175 (December 1, 1933), 4-37. In Italian.

5671. ———. Home and Beauty. 3 acts. Il Dramma, 119 (August 1, 1931), 4-38. Ada Salvatore, translator. In Italian.

5672. ———. The Letter. 3 acts. Petite Illustration, 88 (April 26, 1930), 1-22. H. de Carbuccia, adapter. In French.

5673. _____. A Man of Honour. 4 acts. Fortnightly, 79 (March, 1903, Supplement), 1-50.

5674. _____. Our Betters. 3 acts. Il Dramma, 149 (November 1, 1932), 4-36. In Italian.

5675. _____. Penelope. 3 acts. Il Dramma, 108 (February 15, 1931), 4-42. Ada Salvatore, translator. In Italian.

5676. _____. The Sacred Flame. 3 acts. Petite Illustration, 181 (April 9, 1932), 1-25. H. de Carbuccia, adapter. In French.

5677. _____. Theatre. 3 acts. Il Dramma, n. s., 39 (June 15, 1947), 7-38. Enrico Raggio, translator. In Italian.

_____, adapter see Molière 6110

5678. Maule, C. Cypress, Rita and Doreen. 1 act. Dramatika, 6 (Fall, 1970), 32-41.

Maulnier, Thierry, pseud. see Talagrand, J. 8693-8697

5679. Maupassant, Guy de, 1850-1893. The Necklace. 1 act. Plays, 9 (January, 1950), 76-87. Walter Hackett, adapter.

5680. _____. The Necklace. 1 act. Plays, 21 (October, 1961), 87-96. Earl J. Dias, adapter.

5681. _____. The Necklace. 1 act. Plays, 30 (May, 1971), 51-57. Lewy Olfson, adapter.

5682. _____. Peace at Home--At Any Price. 2 acts, comedy. Poet Lore, 47 (Autumn, 1941), 195-234. John Heard, translator.

5683. Maura, Carlos Semprun. L'Homme Couché. 1 act. L'Avant Scène, 474 (June 15, 1971), 7-42. In French.

_____ see also Martinez Sierra, G. 5633

5684. Maurey, Max. Le Chauffeur. 1 act, comedy. L'Avant Scène, 85, 25-37. In French.

5685. _____. La Delaissée. 1 act, comedy. L'Avant Scène, 80 (July 25, 1953), 11-22. In French.

_____ see also Bernard, T. 857

5686. Mauri, Fabio. Lezione di inglese. 2 parts. Sipario, 25 (March, 1970), 42-64. In Italian.

_____ see Brusati, F. 1392

Mauri, Silvana Ottieri, translator see Anouilh, J. 262

5687. Mauriac, François, 1885-1970. Asmodée. 5 acts. L'Avant Scène, 247 (August 1, 1961), 8-35. In French.

5688. ───────. Asmodee. 5 acts. Sipario, 7 (January-February, 1952), 41-61. Luigi Chiarelli, translator. In Italian.

5689. ───────. Les mal aimes. 3 acts. Sipario, 2 (June, 1947), 37-55. Cesare Vico Lodovici, translator. In Italian.

5690. Mauro, Gianni. La Sua Breve ora Felice. 4 acts. Botteghe Oscure, 22 (Autumn, 1958), 491-536. In Italian.

5691. Mauroc, Daniel. Sand Is My Uniform. 2 acts. First Stage, 3 (Summer-Fall, 1964), 174-178.

5692. ───────. The Snow Steals Down. 2 acts. Works, 1 (Summer, 1968), 71-83.

5693. Maurri, Enzo. L'Arcivescovo. 2 acts, comedy. Il Dramma, (January, 1975), 25-65. In Italian.

5694. Mauton, Margaret. The Backward Lady. 1 act. Poet Lore, 53 (Winter, 1947), 291-307.

5695. Mavor, Osborne Henry, 1888-1951. Dafne Laureola. 4 acts. Il Dramma, n.s., 139/140 (August 15/September 1, 1951), 10-36. Lella Ajmerito, translator. In Italian.

5696. Mawson, Harry P. Placing a Play. 1 act. Smart Set, 22 (May, 1907), 121-124.

5697. Max, Alan. Mission to Athens. 1 act. Masses and Mainstream, 4 (August, 1951), 32-44.

5698. Maxwell, Gerald. A Morning's Work. 1 act, comedy. 19th Century, 52 (July, 1902), 167-176.

5699. ───────. Who Goes Home? 1 act. 19th Century, 60 (September, 1906), 508-520.

5700. May, Elaine. Not Enough Rope. 1 act. Mademoiselle, 66 (November, 1967), 152-153, 201-204.

May, J. Lewis, translator see France, A. 3241

5701. Mayakovsky, Vladimir Vladimirovich, 1893-1930. The Championship of the Universal Class Struggle. 1 act. Drama Review, 17 (March, 1973), 55-63. Frantisek Deak, translator.

5702. ───────. Moscow Is Burning. 2 parts. Drama Review, 17

(March, 1973), 69-89. Ewa Bartos, Victoria Nes Kirby and Helen Wilga, translators.

5703. _____. Vladimir Mayakovsky. 2 acts, tragedy. Chicago Review, 20/21 (May, 1969), 5-21. Pierre Sokolsky, translator.

5704. Mayhall, Jane, 1921- . Eclogue. 1 act. Quarterly Review of Literature, 8 (No. 2, 1955), 127-139.

Mayne, Rutherford, pseud. see Waddell, S. 9179, 9180

5705. Mayr, Grace Alicia. One Man in His Time. 1 act. Plays, 32 (April, 1973), 15-23.

5706. _____. Paul Revere, Rider to Lexington. 1 act. Plays, 34 (February, 1975), 85-95.

5707. _____. The Printer in Queen Street. 1 act. Plays, 33 (October, 1973), 25-37.

5708. _____. Swap-Shop Special. 1 act. Plays, 31 (February, 1972), 63-66.

Mayrocker, Friederike, 1924- see Jandl, E. 4442

5709. Mazaud, Emile. The Holiday. 1 act. Theatre Arts, 6 (January, 1922), 33-61. Ralph Roeder, translator.

5710. Mazure, Joseph. L'Homicide Involontaire. 1 act. L'Avant Scène, 249 (September 15, 1961), 35-38. In French.

5711. Mazzetti, Lorenza. L'ora di religione. 1 act. Il Dramma, n.s., 313 (October, 1962), 56-58. In Italian.

5712. Mazzolotti, Piero. La colonnella. 3 acts. Il Dramma, 351 (April 1, 1941), 9-30. In Italian.

5713. _____. La felicità. 3 acts. Il Dramma, 216 (August 15, 1935), 5-30. In Italian.

5714. _____. Sei tu l'amore? 3 acts. Il Dramma, 73 (September 1, 1929), 4-35. In Italian.

5715. _____. La signorina Chimera. 3 acts. Il Dramma, 136 (April 15, 1932), 4-33. In Italian.

5716. Mazzoni, Cesare. Giuochi di societá. 1 act. Il Dramma, 197 (November 1, 1934), 31-39. In Italian.

Mazzucchetti, Lavinia, translator see Zweig, S. 9662

5717. Mazzucco, Roberto. Cristina, ovvero l'Italiano geloso. Il

Dramma, n.s., 376/377 (January/February, 1968), 28-50. In Italian.

5718. _____. Freedom Left Out in the Rain. 1 act. Drama and Theatre, 7 (No. 3, 1969), 196-201. R. N. L. Absalom, translator.

5719. _____. Un Italiano tra noi. 3 acts. Il Dramma, n.s., 337 (October, 1964), 9-34. In Italian.

5720. _____. Piove sulla libertá. 1 act. Il Dramma, n.s., 342 (March, 1965), 45-50. In Italian.

5721. Meano, Cesare, 1899- . Amleto è morto. 1 act. Il Dramma, 333 (July 1, 1940), 29-32. In Italian.

5722. _____. Bella. 3 acts. Il Dramma, n.s., 237 (June, 1956), 7-30. In Italian.

5723. _____. Melisenda per me. 3 acts. Il Dramma, 343 (December 1, 1940), 6-25. In Italian.

5724. _____. Millesima seconda. 3 acts. Il Dramma, 359 (August 1, 1941), 7-32. In Italian.

5725. _____. La morte di Ulisse. 1 act. Il Dramma, 384 (August 15, 1942), 30-31. In Italian.

5726. _____. Spettacolo fuori programma. 3 acts. Il Dramma, 327 (April 1, 1940), 6-28. In Italian.

_____, translator see Rolland, G. 7660

Medina, Johnnie see Barker, C. 600

5727. Mee, Charles Louis, Jr., 1938- . God Bless Us, Every One. 2 acts. Tulane Drama Review, 10 (Fall, 1965), 162-206.

5728. Meehan, Barry. Game. 1 act. Dramatics, 46 (March, 1975), 4-10.

5729. _____. Mrs. Belfiore. 1 act. Dramatics, 45 (January, 1974), 7-12.

5730. Meeker, Arthur. Hardy Perennials. 1 act, comedy. Drama, 13 (May-June, 1923), 292-296.

Meeker, Isabelle see Harnwell, A. J. 3913

5731. Megrue, Roi Cooper, 1883-1927. Double Cross. 1 act. Smart Set, 34 (August, 1911), 123-128.

5732. _____. Interviewed. 1 act. Smart Set, 32 (November, 1910), 121-130.

5733. _____. The Same Old Thing. 1 act. Smart Set, 29 (November, 1909), 128-135.

5734. Meigs, Cornelia Lynde, 1884- . Primrose Lane. 1 act. St. Nicholas, 46 (May, 1919), 641-647.

5735. Meili, Janet. There Was an Old Woman. 1 act. Plays, 32 (November, 1972), 41-46.

5736. Meillant, Henry, 1924- . Jeux d'Enfants. 1 act. L'Avant Scène, 461 (December 1, 1970), 29-34. In French.

Meister, Guida G., translator see Camus, A. 1551

5737. Mejerchol'd, Vsevolod and Juriz Bondi. Alinur. 3 acts. Il Dramma, (August/September, 1971), 80-88. In Italian.

Mekota, Beatrice M., translator see Shpazhinsky, I. V. 8263

_____ see Subert, F. A. 8595, 8596, 8597, 8599

Melani, Raffaello, translator see Hebbel, C. F. 4017

5738. Melchior, Hathaway Kale. Little Ki and the Serpent. 1 act. Plays, 17 (April, 1958), 37-44.

5739. _____. Visit to the Planets. 1 act. Plays, 16 (May, 1957), 37-44.

5740. Meldon, Maurice, 1928- . Purple Path to the Poppy Field. 1 act. New World Writing, 5 (1954), 146-179.

5741. Melmoth, D. The Great American Light War. 4 acts. Drama Review, 12 (Winter, 1968), 74-102.

5742. Menander, 343?-?291. The Curmudgeon. 5 acts. Horizon, 1 (July, 1959), 80-88. Gilbert Highet, translator.

5743. Mencken, Henry Louis, 1880-1956. The Artist, A Drama Without Words. 1 act. Smart Set, 49 (August, 1916), 79-84.

5744. _____. Il pianista sentimentale. 1 act. Il Dramma, 121 (September 1, 1931), 45-46. In Italian.

5745. _____. Il virtuoso. 1 act. Il Dramma, 105 (January 1, 1931), 45-46. In Italian.

5746. Mendel, Paula and Arthur Guiterman. Journeys End in

Lovers' Meeting. 1 act. Ladies' Home Journal, 19 (February, 1902), 9.

5747. Mendoza, Juan Ruiz de Alacon y. The Suspected Truth. First Stage, 6 (Spring, Summer, 1967), 37-50; 133-139. Sevilla Gross and Henry F. Salerno, translators.

5748. Meneghini, Anna Luisa, 1924- . Andrea. 1 act. Il Dramma, n.s., 125 (January 15, 1951), 50-60. In Italian.

5749. Meneses, Enrique de. The Glittering Highway. 4 acts. Poet Lore, 38 (1927), 317-357. Gustav Davidson, translator.

5750. Menestrel, Marie. On tue toujours celle qu'on aime. 1 act. L'Avant Scène, 546 (August, 1974), 39-42. In French.

Mengarini, Bice, translator see Millar, R. 5831

Mengers, Marie C., translator see Regnier, H. 7464

5751. Menken, John. The Yellow Season. 1 act. Chelsea, 10 (September, 1961), 123-146.

5752. Menotti, Gian Carlo, 1911- . Martin's Lie. Show, 4 (December, 1964), 44-45, 82-83, 86, 89.

5753. _____. Vanessa. 4 acts. Esquire, 48 (December, 1957), 114-122.

5754. Mensio, Cesare. L'ocenao. 1 act. Il Dramma, 212 (June 15, 1935), 32-43. In Italian.

5755. Menthon, Henri de. Les Larbins. 3 acts. L'Avant Scène, 567 (July 1, 1975), 3-30. In French.

5756. Menuau, Georges. Choc en Retour. 1 act, comedy. Petite Illustration, 192 (October 26, 1935), 1-13. In French.

5757. Mercer, David, 1928- . After Haggerty. 2 acts. Sipario, 330 (November, 1973), 50-80. Marcella Bucalossi, translator. In Italian.

5758. _____. Belcher's Luck. 2 acts. Plays and Players, 14 (February, 1967), 31-46.

5759. _____. On the Eve of Publication. Scripts, 1 (June, 1972), 39-50.

5760. Mercier, Maurice. L'Affaire Victor. 1 act. L'Avant Scène 332 (April 15, 1965), 43-50. In French.

5761. _____. Jamais Trois ... Sans Quatre. 1 act. L'Avant Scène, 268 (July 1, 1962), 39-43. In French.

5762. _____. Le Reve de L'Infante. 1 act. L'Avant Scène, 331 (April 1, 1965), 38-43. In French.

5763. Mercier, Vivian. Common Ground, or, Bridge in the Afternoon. 1 act. Journal of Irish Literature, 2 (May-September, 1973), 45-78.

Mercure, Jean, adapter see Ardrey, R. 329

_____, adapter see Miller, A. 5841

_____, translator see Hartog, J. de 3953

5764. Mere, Charles, 1883- . Le Carnaval de l'Amour. 4 acts. Petite Illustration, 86 (May 26, 1928), 1-34. In French.

5765. _____. Un Homme du Nord. 4 acts, comedy. Petite Illustration, 186 (December 30, 1933), 1-38. In French.

5766. Meredith, Burgess, 1908- . The Adventures of Mr. Bean. 1 act. One-Act Play Magazine, 1 (December, 1937), 675-684.

5767. _____. Oliver Bean. 1 act. Scholastic, 31 (January 22, 1938), 21E-22E, 27E.

5768. _____. Screen Test. 1 act. Senior Scholastic, 52 (March 22, 1948), 17-19.

5769. Meredith, George, 1828-1909. The Sentimentalists; An Unfinished Comedy. 1 act. Scribner's, 48 (August, 1910), 129-141.

5770. Mérimée, Prosper, 1803-1870. La carrozza del Santo Sacramento. 1 act. Il Dramma, 371 (February 1, 1942), 36-46. Giovanni Marcellini, translator. In Italian.

5771. _____. The Conspirators. 1 act, comedy. Golden Book, 1 (April, 1925), 537-553.

5772. _____. Ines Mendo, o la sconfitta del pregiudizio. 1 act. Il Dramma, 406/407 (July 15/August 1, 1943), 77-83. Vinicio Marinucci, translator. In Italian.

5773. _____. La Jacquerie. 3 acts. L'Avant Scène (ROST), 73 (February, 1953), 1-34. Georges Arest, adapter. In French.

5774. Merington, Marguerite. Father Time and His Children. 1 act. St. Nicholas, 36 (January, 1909), 236-240.

5775. _____. The Gibson Play. 2 acts, comedy. The Ladies' Home Journal, 18 (March, 1901), 7-8, 40-41.

5776. _____. Grouse Out of Season. 1 act, comedy. Harper's Bazaar, 37 (November, 1903), 1018-1027.

5777. _____. A Lover's Knot. 1 act, comedy. Harper's Bazaar, 44 (June, 1910), 384-386.

5778. _____, adapter. The "Cranford" Play. 3 acts. The Ladies' Home Journal, 18 (February, 1901), 5-6, 50-51.

5779. Merow, Erva Loomis. The Terrible Turkey. 1 act. Plays, 17 (November, 1957), 69-70.

5780. Merrick, William, 1915- . Forgot in the Rains. 1 act. One-Act Play Magazine, 2 (February, 1939), 731-745.

5781. Merrill, Fenimore, d. 1919. The Avenue. 1 act, comedy. Drama, 10 (November, 1919), 53-57.

5782. Merrill, James, 1920- . The Bait. 1 act. Quarterly Review of Literature, 8 (No. 2, 1955), 81-98.

5783. Merritt, Robert. Togetherness. 1 act. Tulane Drama Review, 7 (Winter, 1962), 206-219.

Mervent, Maria, pseud. see Soler, A. 8368

Merwin, W. S., 1927- , translator see Lesage, A. 4936

_____. Rueda, L. de 7784

5784. Mery, Andree. Cinq à Sept. 3 acts, comedy. Petite Illustration, 184 (January 14, 1933), 1-30. In French.

5785. _____. Les Jeux Sont Faits! 3 acts, comedy. Petite Illustration, 189 (September 29, 1934), 1-30. In French.

_____, adapter see Coward, N. 2079

_____, translator see Jerome, J. K. 4466

5786. Messager, Charles, 1882- . La Belette. 1 act. L'Avant Scène, 238 (March 1, 1961), 29-35. In French.

5787. _____. La Brouille. 3 acts. Il Dramma, n. s., 229 (October, 1955), 6-29. Suzanne Rochat, translator. In Italian.

5788. _____. La Brouille. 3 acts, comedy. Petite Illustration, 178 (February 28, 1931), 1-26. In French.

5789. _____. Les Pères Ennemis. 1 act, farce. L'Avant Scène, 318 (September 15, 1964), 29-35. In French.

5790. _____. The Pilgrim. 1 act. One-Act Play Magazine, 1 (October, 1937), 483-509. Ruth C. Allen, translator.

5791. _____. The Steamer Tenacity. 3 acts, comedy. Poet Lore, 32 (1921), 463-496. John Strong Newberry, translator.

5792. _____. Trois Mois de Prison. 4 acts. Il Dramma, n. s., 134 (June 1, 1951), 9-38. Suzanne Rochat, translator. In Italian.

5793. Messenger, Bill. Man in the Red Suit. 1 act. Plays, 26 (December, 1966), 81-87.

5794. Messina, Paolo. Il muro di silenzio. 3 acts. Il Dramma, n. s., 304 (January, 1962), 12-37. In Italian.

5795. Metamorfosi di Pulcinella, Le. Scenario della Commedia dell'Arte. 3 acts. Sipario, 9 (August-September, 1954), 32-34. In Italian.

5796. Metastasio, Pietro, 1698-1782. Componimento sacro per la festività del SS. Natale. 2 parts. Il Dramma, n. s., 99/100 (January 1, 1950), 77-96. In Italian.

5797. Mew, Tommie. Blue. 1 act. Dramatika, 3 (March, 1969), 15.

5798. _____. Earthjoy. 1 act. Dramatika, 10 (1973), n. p.

5799. _____. Karma. 1 act. Dramatika, 3 (March, 1969), 16.

5800. Meyer, Adelph E. The Little Fool. 1 act, comedy. Drama, 17 (October, 1926), 13-14, 29-30.

5801. Meyer, Annie Nathan, 1867-1951. The Scientific Mother. 1 act. Bookman [New York], 5 (July, 1897), 381-382.

5802. Meyer, Josephine A. To Be Perfectly Frank. 1 act, comedy. Smart Set, 65 (June, 1921), 69-79.

Mezirka, Vera, translator see Zeyer, J. 9645

Miall, A. Bernard, translator see Maeterlinck, M. 5433

5803. Micallef, Lexie. Tripe. 1 act. Gambit, 7 (No. 25, 1974), 83-104.

5804. Michaelson, L. W. The Tenth Circle. 1 act. Poet Lore, 59 (No. 1), 36-57.

5805. "Michal." The Furniture. 1 act. Coterie, 5 (Autumn, 1920), 41-52.

5806. Michaux, Henri. Catene. 1 act. Sipario, 26 (February, 1971), 56-61. Alfredo Giuliani, translator. In Italian.

5807. _____. Dramma dei costruttori. 1 act. Sipario, 26 (February, 1971), 61-64. Alfredo Giuliani, translator. In Italian.

Michel, Marc, 1812-1868 see Labiche, E. 4753, 4754, 4755

5808. Michelotti, Gigi, 1879- . Lei e il suo ritratto. 2 acts. Il Dramma, 169 (September 1, 1933), 34-44. In Italian.

5809. Michelsen, Hans Gunter, 1920- . Feierabend 1 und 2 Spectaculum, 6 (1963), 175-208.

_____, translator see Shaw, G. B. 8212

5810. Michelson, Max. The Haunted Hat-Shop. 1 act. Poetry, 17 (February, 1921), 233-237.

5811. Michelson, Miriam, 1870- . Bygones. 1 act. Smart Set, 51 (March, 1917), 81-92.

5812. _____. The Curiosity of Kitty Cochraine. 1 act. Smart Set, 37 (May, 1912), 133-142.

5813. Mick, Hettie Louise. The Maid Who Wouldn't Be Proper; A Puppett Play. 3 acts. Drama, 12 (September, 1922), 351-357.

Micozzi, Amleto, translator see Beckett, S. 696

_____, translator see O'Neill, E. 6847, 6854, 6857, 6863

_____, translator see Osborne, J. 6893

Middlemass, Robert see Porter, H. E. 7251, 7252

Middleton, Christopher, translator see Jandl, E. and F. Mayrocker 4442

5814. Middleton, George, 1880- . Among the Lions, A Social Satire in One Act. Smart Set, 51 (February, 1917), 327-336.

5815. _____. The Gargoyle. 1 act. Smart Set, 27 (April, 1909), 97-103.

5816. _____. In His House. 1 act. Smart Set, 29 (September, 1909), 124-132.

5817. _____. On Bail. 1 act. Smart Set, 39 (March, 1913), 135-141.

5818. _____. The Reason. 1 act. Smart Set, 53 (September, 1917), 89-97.

5819. Middleton, Richard Barham, 1882-1911. The District Visitor. 1 act. English Review, 15 (November, 1913), 497-505.

5820. Middleton, Thomas, 1580-1627. A Game of Chess. 5 acts. Sipario, 334 (March, 1974), 58-80. Ugo Tessitore, translator. In Italian.

5821. _____ and William Rowley, 1585?-1642. Les Amants Maléfiques. 1 act, tragedy. L'Avant Scène, 362 (August, 1966), 9-25. Georges Arout, adapter. In French.

5822. Mierow, Herbert Edward. Alexander the Great. 3 acts. Poet Lore, 55 (Summer, 1950), 99-128.

5823. _____. The Dream. 4 acts. Poet Lore, 58 (Summer, 1963), 123-145.

5824. _____. The Hill. 3 acts. Poet Lore, 52 (Spring, 1946), 3-29.

5825. _____. The Portal. 4 acts. Poet Lore, 56 (Autumn, 1951), 238-262.

Mihalakeas, T. see Vandenberghe, P. 9022

5826. Mihura, Miguel. Trois Chapeaux Claque. 3 acts, comedy. L'Avant Scène, 191 (February 15, 1959), 9-28. Hélène Duc and José Estrada, adapters. In French.

5827. Milano nel 1848 e Milano nel 1859. 5 acts. Sipario, 16 (August-September, 1961), 42-49. In Italian.

5828. Mildren, Nan L. Hiawatha. 3 acts. Ladies' Home Journal, 30 (March, 1913), 93.

5829. Miles, Josephine, 1911- . House and Home. 1 act. First Stage, 4 (Fall, 1965), 196-202.

5830. Milhaud, Darius, 1892-1974. Passagio. Sipario, 19 (December, 1964), 62-71. In Italian.

5831. Millar, Ronald, 1933- . The Affair. 3 acts. Sipario, 231 (July, 1965), 45-64. Bice Mengarini, translator. In Italian.

5832. _____. The Affair. 3 acts. Theatre Arts, 47 (March, 1963), 25-56.

5833. _____ and Nigel Balchin. Comme un Oiseau. 3 acts. L'Avant Scène, 330 (March 15, 1965), 9-31. Pol Quentin, translator. In French.

5834. Millaud, Fernand. L'Abonne. 1 act, comedy. L'Avant Scène, 309 (April 15, 1964), 38-43. In French.

5835. _____. Au Paradis. 1 act, comedy. L'Avant Scène, 158, 41-48. In French.

5836. Millay, Edna St. Vincent, 1892-1950. Aria da Capo. 1 act. Chapbook [London], 14 (August, 1920), 1-24.

5837. Millay, Kathleen. Flatlanders. 1 act. Scholastic, 26 (April 6, 1935), 9, 20.

5838. Miller, Agnes. The Finding of the First Arbutus. 1 act. St. Nicholas, 47 (April, 1920), 550-553.

5839. _____. The First Thanksgiving Day. 1 act. St. Nicholas, 40 (November, 1912), 61-64.

5840. Miller, Arthur, 1915- . After the Fall. 2 acts. Saturday Evening Post, 237 (February 1, 1964), 34-58.

5841. _____. The Creation of the World and Other Business. 3 acts. L'Avant Scène, 552 (November 15, 1974), 3-36. Jean Mercure, adapter. In French.

5842. _____. The Crucible. 4 acts. L'Avant Scène, 112, 1-38. Marcel Ayme, adapter. In French.

5843. _____. The Crucible. 4 acts. Sipario, 11 (January, 1956), supplement. 35-68. Luchino Visconti and Gino Bardi, translators. In Italian.

5844. _____. The Crucible. 4 acts. Theatre Arts, 37 (October, 1953), 35-67.

5845. _____. Death of a Salesman, Certain Private Conversations in Two Acts and a Requiem. L'Avant Scène, 354 (April 1, 1966), 12-50. Eric Kahane, adapter. In French.

5846. _____. Death of a Salesman. 2 parts. Sipario, 6 (April, 1951), 41-67. Gerardo Guerrieri, translator. In Italian.

5847. _____. Death of a Salesman, Certain Private Conversations in Two Acts and a Requiem. Theatre Arts, 35 (March, 1951), 49-51.

5848. _____. Incident at Vichy. L'Avant Scène, 489 (February 15, 1972), 11-28. Maurice Kurtz, adapter. In French.

5849. _____. A View from the Bridge, Consisting of Two One-Act Plays. L'Avant Scène, 204 (September 15, 1959), 7-28. Marcel Ayme, adapter. In French.

5850. _____. A View from the Bridge, Consisting of Two One-Act Plays. Theatre Arts, 40 (September, 1956), 33-68.

5851. Miller, Helen Louise. The ABC's Thanksgiving. 1 act. Plays, 21 (November, 1961), 77-80.

5852. _____. An All-American Thank You. 1 act. Plays, 28 (November, 1968), 45-51.

5853. _____. Angel Child. 1 act. Plays, 2 (December, 1942), 1-7.

5854. _____. Attic Treasure. 1 act. Plays, 24 (January, 1965), 1-13.

5855. _____. Band Aid. 1 act. Plays, 4 (October, 1944), 58-66.

5856. _____. Bandit Ben Rides Again. 1 act. Plays, 21 (March, 1962), 65-71.

5857. _____. The Bar-None Trading Post. 1 act. Plays, 23 (April, 1964), 77-85.

5858. _____. Bartholomew's Joyful Noise. 1 act. Plays, 22 (November, 1962), 65-71.

5859. _____. The Bashful Bunny. 1 act. Plays, 15 (March, 1956), 53-60.

5860. _____. Baskets or Bonnets. 1 act. Plays, 21 (April, 1962), 77-83.

5861. _____. Beany's Private Eye. 1 act. Plays, 15 (January, 1956), 1-13. AND Plays, 30 (January, 1971), 21-32.

5862. _____. The Best Policy. 1 act. Plays, 11 (February, 1952), 1-11.

5863. _____. Bewitched and Bewildered. 1 act. Plays, 10 (October, 1950), 1-11.

5864. _____. The Booby Trap. 1 act. Plays, 3 (April, 1944), 63-72.

5865. _____. Boomerang. 1 act. Plays, 9 (January, 1950), 1-10. AND Plays, 16 (April, 1957), 25-33.

5866. _____. The Bread and Butter Shop. 1 act. Plays, 24 (January, 1965), 69-77.

5867. _____. The Broken Broomstick. 1 act. Plays, 18 (October, 1958), 69-73. AND Plays, 31 (October, 1971), 67-71.

5868. _____. The Broomstick Beauty. 1 act. Plays, 30 (October, 1970), 23-32.

5869. _____. Bunnies and Bonnets. 1 act. Plays, 12 (April, 1953), 77-86. AND Plays, 25 (April, 1966), 43-52. AND Plays, 33 (April, 1974), 64-74.

5870. _____. The Busy Barbers. 1 act. Plays, 17 (March, 1958), 63-67.

5871. _____. Call Washington 1776. 1 act. Plays, 24 (February, 1965), 3-15.

5872. _____. Captain Castaway's Captives. 1 act. Plays, 27 (May, 1968), 59-68.

5873. _____. The Case of the Forgetful Easter Rabbit. 1 act. Plays, 24 (April, 1965), 63-69.

5874. _____. The Case of the Giggling Goblin. 1 act. Plays, 28 (October, 1968), 47-54.

5875. _____. The Case of the Silent Caroler. 1 act. Plays, 11 (December, 1951), 1-11. AND Plays, 17 (December, 1957), 33-43. AND Plays, 30 (December, 1970), 1-11.

5876. _____. The Christmas Cowboy. 1 act. Plays, 10 (December, 1950), 26-35.

5877. _____. The Christmas Oboe. 1 act. Plays, 14 (December, 1954), 1-12.

5878. _____. The Christmas Peppermints. 1 act. Plays, 23 (December, 1963), 49-57.

5879. _____. A Christmas Promise. 1 act. Plays, 12 (December, 1952), 1-12. AND Plays, 29 (December, 1969), 1-12.

5880. _____. The Christmas Runaways. 1 act. Plays, 14 (December, 1954), 63-70.

5881. _____. Circus Daze. 1 act. Plays, 26 (May, 1967), 49-57.

5882. _____. Comic Valentine. 1 act. Plays, 4 (February, 1945), 55-65.

5883. _____. The Country Store Cat. 1 act. Plays, 19

(March, 1960), 77-83. AND Plays, 31 (March, 1972), 73-79.

5884. _____. Cry Witch. 1 act. Plays, 21 (January, 1962), 37-47.

5885. _____. Cupid on the Loose. 1 act. Plays, 14 (February, 1955), 13-20. AND Plays, 30 (February, 1971), 31-38.

5886. _____. Cupid's Golden Key Ring. 1 act. Plays, 29 (February, 1970), 75-81.

5887. _____. The Curious Quest. 1 act. Plays, 14 (March, 1955), 49-56. AND Plays, 34 (March, 1975), 61-68.

5888. _____. The Curse of Hog Hollow. 1 act. Plays, 21 (October, 1961), 13-24.

5889. _____. A Day to Remember. 1 act. Plays, 9 (May, 1950), 15-23.

5890. _____. Dial M for Mother. 1 act. Plays, 21 (May, 1962), 13-24.

5891. _____. Dick Whittington and His Cat. 1 act. Plays, 15 (January, 1956), 83-89.

5892. _____. Doctor's Daughter. 1 act. Plays, 4 (May, 1945), 27-35. AND Plays, 15 (May, 1956), 83-91.

5893. _____. Dolly Saves the Day. 1 act. Plays, 2 (January, 1943), 36-43.

5894. _____. Father Talks Turkey. 1 act. Plays, 4 (November, 1944), 1-8. AND Plays, 28 (November, 1968), 25-34.

5895. _____. A February Failure. 1 act. Plays, 14 (February, 1955), 43-46.

5896. _____. The Forgotten Hero. 1 act. Plays, 17 (November, 1957), 41-47.

5897. _____. The Friendship Wheel. 1 act. Plays, 26 (November, 1966), 47-52.

5898. _____. Garden Hold-Up. 1 act. Plays, 18 (May, 1959), 55-59.

5899. _____. Gathering Sticks. 1 act. Plays, 21 (May, 1962), 85-89.

5900. ──────. The Gentle Giant-Killer. 1 act. Plays, 26 (October, 1966), 59-66.

5901. ──────. Ghost in the House. 1 act. Plays, 12 (October, 1952), 70-81. AND Plays, 32 (October, 1972), 23-35.

5902. ──────. Gifts for the New Year. 1 act. Plays, 23 (January, 1964), 69-74.

5903. ──────. Girls in Books. 1 act. Plays, 24 (November, 1964), 55-62.

5904. ──────. The Glass Slippers. 1 act. Plays, 21 (March, 1962), 77-83.

5905. ──────. Good Enough for Lincoln. 1 act. Plays, 9 (February, 1950), 1-9. AND Plays, 17 (February, 1958), 25-33.

5906. ──────. The Greedy Goblin. 1 act. Plays, 32 (October, 1972), 37-45.

5907. ──────. The Half-Pint Cowboy. 1 act. Plays, 18 (January, 1959), 67-72. AND Plays, 30 (January, 1971), 73-78.

5908. ──────. The Haunted Clothesline. 1 act. Plays, 9 (October, 1949), 1-10. AND Plays, 22 (October, 1962), 27-36. AND Plays, 33 (October, 1973), 15-24.

5909. ──────. The Haunted High School. 1 act. Plays, 16 (October, 1956), 87-93.

5910. ──────. Haunts for Hire. 1 act. Plays, 18 (October, 1958), 1-12. AND Plays, 35 (October, 1975), 37-46.

5911. ──────. Heart Throbs. 1 act. Plays, 16 (February, 1957), 1-12.

5912. ──────. Hello, Mr. Groundhog. 1 act. Plays, 24 (February, 1965), 65-74.

5913. ──────. Hero's Homecoming. 1 act. Plays, 15 (November, 1955), 81-94.

5914. ──────. Homework. 1 act. Plays, 4 (January, 1945), 1-10. AND Plays, 11 (March, 1952), 85-93. AND Plays, 33 (December, 1973), 51-60.

5915. ──────. A Hooky Holiday. 2 acts. Plays, 25 (March, 1966), 15-26.

5916. ──────. Horn of Plenty. 1 act. Plays, 24 (November, 1964), 1-12.

5917. _____. Horrors, Incorporated. 1 act. Plays, 28 (October, 1968), 11-19.

5918. _____. Hotel Santa Claus. 1 act. Plays, 23 (December, 1963), 1-13.

5919. _____. The Hound of the Maskervilles. 1 act. Plays, 26 (October, 1966), 15-27.

5920. _____. I'll Eat My Hat. 1 act. Plays, 15 (November, 1955), 69-80.

5921. _____. Jiminy Cinders. 1 act. Plays, 16 (January, 1957), 49-56.

5922. _____. The Judge's Diary. 1 act. Plays, 11 (May, 1952), 10-20. AND Plays, 18 (May, 1959), 13-22.

5923. _____. Jump for George. 1 act. Plays, 15 (February, 1956), 1-12.

5924. _____. Just What the Doctor Ordered. 1 act. Plays, 9 (November, 1949), 11-20. AND Plays, 16 (November, 1956), 1-10. AND Plays, 29 (November, 1969), 17-26.

5925. _____. Lacey's Last Garland. 1 act. Plays, 16 (May, 1957), 45-52.

5926. _____. The Left-Over Reindeer. 1 act. Plays, 15 (December, 1955), 25-38.

5927. _____. The Library Circus. 1 act. Plays, 20 (November, 1960), 65-70. AND Plays, 33 (November, 1973), 63-68.

5928. _____. The Lincoln Heart. 1 act. Plays, 28 (February, 1969), 9-18.

5929. _____. A Lincoln Museum. 1 act. Plays, 33 (February, 1974), 41-47.

5930. _____. Lincoln's Library Fine. 1 act. Plays, 21 (February, 1962), 53-58.

5931. _____. A Link with Lincoln. 1 act. Plays, 25 (February, 1966), 1-14.

5932. _____. The Little Nut Tree. 1 act. Plays, 21 (April, 1962), 67-72.

5933. _____. The Lost Christmas Cards. 1 act. Plays, 18 (December, 1958), 71-75.

5934. _____. The Magic Carpet Sweeper. 1 act. Plays, 16 (May, 1957), 69-76.

5935. _____. The Magic Cookie Jar. 1 act. Plays, 2 (November, 1942), 36-44. AND Plays, 15 (October, 1955), 49-57.

5936. _____. The Magic Pencils. 1 act. Plays, 22 (May, 1963), 79-84.

5937. _____. The Magic Telephone. 1 act. Plays, 23 (February, 1964), 65-69.

5938. _____. A Man Like Lincoln. 1 act. Plays, 23 (February, 1964), 1-12.

5939. _____. A Marine for Mother. 1 act. Plays, 3 (May, 1944), 61-69.

5940. _____. Mary's Invitation. 1 act. Plays, 19 (November, 1959), 69-75.

5941. _____. May Day for Mother. 1 act. Plays, 19 (May, 1960), 63-67.

5942. _____. Meet Mr. Muffin. 1 act. Plays, 21 (January, 1962), 69-73.

5943. _____. Melody for Lincoln. 1 act. Plays, 17 (February, 1958), 43-50.

5944. _____. Merry-Go-Round for Mother. 1 act. Plays, 20 (May, 1961), 45-52.

5945. _____. Miss Frankenstein. 1 act. Plays, 25 (October, 1965), 13-22.

5946. _____. Miss Lonelyheart. 1 act. Plays, 3 (February, 1944), 1-13. AND Plays, 9 (February, 1950), 83-95.

5947. _____. The Missing "Linc". 1 act. Plays, 5 (January, 1946), 1-10.

5948. _____. The Missing Link. 1 act. Plays, 26 (February, 1967), 13-22.

5949. _____. Mr. Snow White's Thanksgiving. 1 act. Plays, 15 (November, 1955), 31-40.

5950. _____. The Mistletoe Mystery. 1 act. Plays, 21 (December, 1961), 1-11.

5951. _____. Monsieur Santa Claus. 1 act. Plays, 17 (December, 1957), 1-10.

5952. _____. Mother Beats the Band. 1 act. Plays, 14 (May, 1955), 1-11. AND Plays, 27 (May, 1968), 23-33.

5953. _____. Mother for Mayor. 1 act. Plays, 12 (May, 1953), 1-13. AND Plays, 24 (May, 1965), 31-43. AND Plays, 34 (May, 1975), 53-64.

5954. _____. The Mother Goose Bakeshop. 1 act. Plays, 19 (January, 1960), 69-74.

5955. _____. Mother's Apron Strings. 1 act. Plays, 10 (May, 1951), 21-29.

5956. _____. Mother's Big Day. 1 act. Plays, 5 (May, 1946), 1-11.

5957. _____. A Mother's Day Treasure Hunt. 1 act. Plays, 28 (May, 1969), 69-74.

5958. _____. Mother's Fairy Godmother. 1 act. Plays, 16 (May, 1957), 31-36.

5959. _____. The Mount Vernon Cricket. 1 act. Plays, 28 (February, 1969), 35-43.

5960. _____. The Mouse That Soared. 1 act. Plays, 23 (October, 1963), 61-66.

5961. _____. Mystery at Knob Creek Farm. 1 act. Plays, 18 (February, 1959), 55-61.

5962. _____. The Mystery of Turkey-Lurkey. 1 act. Plays, 17 (November, 1957), 55-60.

5963. _____. "N" for Nuisance. 1 act. Plays, 12 (January, 1953), 1-12.

5964. _____. New Shoes. 1 act. Plays, 26 (May, 1967), 85-89.

5965. _____. Not for Girls. 1 act. Plays, 14 (May, 1955), 44-52.

5966. _____. Nothing to Wear. 1 act. Plays, 5 (March, 1946), 1-11.

5967. _____. Old Glory Grows Up. 1 act. Plays, 19 (February, 1960), 83-87.

5968. _____. One to Grow On. 1 act. Plays, 24 (April, 1965), 35-44.

5969. _____. Open House for Shakespeare. 1 act. Plays, 30 (November, 1970), 25-37.

5970. _____. Papa Pepper--Patriot. 1 act. Plays, 2 (March, 1943), 1-10.

5971. _____. Papa Pepper's Bombshell. 1 act. Plays, 12 (March, 1953), 9-17.

5972. _____. The Paper Bag Mystery. 1 act. Plays, 25 (November, 1965), 47-55. AND Plays, 34 (December, 1974), 67-75.

5973. _____. The Parrot and the Pirates. 1 act. Plays, 23 (November, 1963), 51-56.

5974. _____. Party Line. 1 act. Plays, 17 (March, 1958), 29-38.

5975. _____. Paul Revere Rides Again. 1 act. Plays, 14 (April, 1955), 49-57.

5976. _____. The Pennsylvania Parakeet. 1 act. Plays, 15 (February, 1956), 42-46.

5977. _____. Peter Rabbit Volunteers. 1 act. Plays, 27 (April, 1968), 59-64.

5978. _____. The Petrified Prince. 1 act. Plays, 14 (January, 1955), 39-48. AND Plays, 27 (February, 1968), 47-56.

5979. _____. Pilgrim Parting. 1 act. Plays, 14 (November, 1954), 45-52.

5980. _____. The Pilgrim Who Didn't Care. 1 act. Plays, 29 (November, 1969), 69-75.

5981. _____. Pin-Up Pals. 1 act. Plays, 29 (February, 1970), 31-38.

5982. _____. The Pink Parasol, A Play for Memorial Day. 1 act. Plays, 3 (May, 1944), 11-20.

5983. _____. The Polka Dot Pup. 1 act. Plays, 14 (October, 1954), 55-61.

5984. _____. Princess Lonely Heart. 1 act. Plays, 22 (February, 1963), 81-86.

5985. _____. Puppy Love. 1 act. Plays, 9 (December, 1949), 10-18. AND Plays, 26 (December, 1966), 11-19.

5986. _____. The Rabbit Who Refused to Run. 1 act. Plays, 25 (April, 1966), 75-80. AND Plays, 32 (April, 1973), 73-78.

5987. _____. Rabbit's Foot. 1 act. Plays, 9 (April, 1950), 1-11. AND Plays, 17 (April, 1958), 13-22. AND Plays, 30 (April, 1971), 9-18.

5988. _____. The Rabbits Who Changed Their Minds. 1 act. Plays, 18 (March, 1959), 69-73. AND Plays, 29 (March, 1970), 75-79.

5989. _____. Red Carpet Christmas. 1 act. Plays, 22 (December, 1962), 1-13.

5990. _____. The Red Flannel Suit. 1 act. Plays, 20 (December, 1960), 1-13.

5991. _____. The Return of Bobby Shafto. 1 act. Plays, 27 (October, 1967), 69-76.

5992. _____. Right of Adoption. 1 act. Plays, 15 (January, 1956), 59-66.

5993. _____. Rummage for Victory. 1 act. Plays, 4 (March, 1945), 56-66.

5994. _____. The Runaway Toys. 1 act. Plays, 22 (December, 1962), 71-76.

5995. _____. The Runaway Unicorn. 1 act. Plays, 21 (November, 1961), 67-72.

5996. _____. S.O.S. from Santa. 1 act. Plays, 28 (December, 1968), 31-39.

5997. _____. Sandy Scarecrow's Halloween. 1 act. Plays, 29 (October, 1969), 53-60.

5998. _____. Santa Calls a Conference. Christmas Customs Round the World. 1 act. Plays, 26 (December, 1966), 49-58.

5999. _____. Santa Claus for President. 1 act. Plays, 11 (December, 1951), 66-69. AND Plays, 20 (December, 1960), 71-74. AND Plays, 32 (December, 1972), 57-60.

6000. _____. Say It With Flowers. 1 act. Plays, 5 (February, 1946), 1-8. AND Plays, 11 (February, 1952), 85-92.

6001. _____. A School for Scaring. 1 act. Plays, 17 (October, 1957), 69-74.

6002. _____. Season's Greetings. 1 act. Plays, 16 (December, 1956), 1-13.

6003. _____. Sergeant Santa Claus. 1 act. Plays, 4 (December, 1944), 1-13.

6004. _____. The Shady Shadows. 1 act. Plays, 2 (April, 1943), 38-44.

6005. _____. The Shakespearean Touch. 1 act. Plays, 14 (November, 1954), 1-12.

6006. _____. Shirley Holmes and the FBI. 1 act. Plays, 24 (May, 1965), 45-53. AND Plays, 33 (March, 1974), 49-58.

6007. _____. The Shower of Hearts. 1 act. Plays, 19 (February, 1960), 67-72. AND Plays, 31 (February, 1972), 71-76.

6008. _____. Simple Simon's Reward. Plays, 27 (November, 1967), 65-74.

6009. _____. Snoop's Scoop. 1 act. Plays, 3 (January, 1944), 23-32.

6010. _____. So Long at the Fair. 1 act. Plays, 22 (May, 1963), 85-90.

6011. _____. The Soft Hearted Ghost. 1 act. Plays, 5 (October, 1945), 1-8. AND Plays, 11 (October, 1951), 10-17.

6012. _____. Softy the Snow Man. 1 act. Plays, 12 (December, 1952), 38-44. AND Plays, 16 (December, 1956), 63-69.

6013. _____. Sourdough Sally. 1 act. Plays, 22 (January, 1963), 61-67.

6014. _____. Spooks in Books. 1 act. Plays, 15 (October, 1955), 1-8.

6015. _____. Spooky Spectacles. 1 act. Plays, 14 (October, 1954), 1-12.

6016. _____. Spunky Punky. 1 act. Plays, 19 (October, 1959), 67-71.

6017. _____. Strictly Puritan. 1 act. Plays, 22 (November, 1962), 51-58.

6018. _____. A Surprise for Mother. 1 act. Plays, 2 (April, 1943), 11-22. AND Plays, 29 (May, 1970), 35-44.

6019. _____. Ten Pennies for Lincoln. 1 act. Plays, 18 (February, 1959), 79-82.

6020. _____. Thankful's Red Beads. 1 act. Plays, 19 (November, 1959), 43-48.

6021. _____. Thanks to Butter-Fingers. 1 act. Plays, 27 (November, 1967), 35-44.

6022. _____. Thanksgiving à la Carte. 1 act. Plays, 10 (November, 1950), 1-10. AND Plays, 20 (November, 1960), 25-34.

6023. _____. Thanksgiving for Frieda. 1 act. Plays, 3 (November, 1943), 26-36.

6024. _____. A Thanksgiving Riddle. 1 act. Plays, 18 (November, 1958), 71-75. AND Plays, 32 (November, 1972), 55-59.

6025. _____. Three Cheers for Mother. 1 act. Plays, 4 (May, 1945), 1-10.

6026. _____. Three Little Kittens. 1 act. Plays, 23 (April, 1964), 69-72.

6027. _____. The Tomboy and the Dragon. 1 act. Plays, 27 (December, 1967), 73-80.

6028. _____. Too Many Angels. 1 act. Plays, 29 (December, 1969), 65-71.

6029. _____. The Toy Scout Jamboree. 1 act. Plays, 24 (December, 1964), 67-72.

6030. _____. A Travel Game. 1 act. Plays, 23 (May, 1964), 77-82.

6031. _____. The Trial of Mother Goose. 1 act. Plays, 26 (April, 1967), 65-72.

6032. _____. Trouble in Tick Tock Town. 1 act. Plays, 19 (April, 1960), 65-70.

6033. _____. Turkey Turns the Tables. 1 act. Plays, 5 (November, 1945), 1-11.

6034. _____. Turning the Tables. 1 act. Plays, 18 (November, 1958), 37-46.

6035. _____. The Uninvited Guests. 1 act. Plays, 2 (May, 1943), 1-7. AND Plays, 17 (May, 1958), 77-82.

6036. _____. A Valentine for Kate. 1 act. Plays, 24 (February, 1965), 29-39. AND Plays, 34 (February, 1975), 15-25.

6037. _____. The Vanishing Easter Egg. 1 act. Plays, 26 (March, 1967), 27-36.

Miller

6038. _____. Vicky Gets the Vote. 1 act. Plays, 16 (November, 1956), 37-44.

6039. _____. Wake Up! Santa Claus! 1 act. Plays, 19 (December, 1959), 73-78.

6040. _____. The Washington Shilling. 1 act. Plays, 16 (February, 1957), 43-52.

6041. _____. Washington's Leading Lady. 1 act. Plays, 16 (February, 1957), 81-87.

6042. _____. Washington's Lucky Star. 1 act. Plays, 22 (February, 1963), 75-80.

6043. _____. The Washingtons Slept Here. 1 act. Plays, 4 (February, 1945), 1-12. AND Plays, 21 (February, 1962), 23-34.

6044. _____. The Weatherman on Trial. 1 act. Plays, 19 (May, 1960), 73-78.

6045. _____. What Makes It Tick? 1 act. Plays, 31 (November, 1971), 25-36.

6046. _____. What's Cooking? 1 act. Plays, 2 (February, 1943), 12-22. AND Plays, 5 (October, 1945), 65-75. AND Plays, 28 (January, 1969), 13-22.

6047. _____. Which Way to Halloween? 1 act. Plays, 22 (October, 1962), 65-71.

6048. _____. The White House Rabbit. 1 act. Plays, 22 (March, 1963), 37-43.

6049. _____. Who's Who at the Zoo. 1 act. Plays, 23 (March, 1964), 65-70.

6050. _____. The Wishing Stream. 1 act. Plays, 20 (January, 1961), 71-76.

6051. _____. The Youngest Witch. 1 act. Plays, 3 (October, 1943), 15-24.

_____, adapter see Andersen, H. C. 198

_____ see Wiggin, K. D. 9348

6052. Miller, Jane V. Don't Be Just a File Clerk. 1 act. Plays, 34 (February, 1975), 73-78.

6053. _____. Robots for Sale. 1 act. Plays, 34 (May, 1975), 66-68.

6054. Miller, Louis, 1889- . Mr. Man. 4 acts. Poet Lore, 40 (Winter, 1929), 475-543. S. K. Padover and Chasye Cooperman, translators.

Miller, Maria Ossipovna, translator see Narodny, I. 6435

6055. Miller, Marion L. Cry Witch. 1 act. Plays, 10 (January, 1951), 1-11. AND Plays, 33 (April, 1974), 29-39.

6056. _____. Not Worth a Continental. 1 act. Plays, 12 (January, 1953), 12-20.

_____, translator see Lorca, F. G. 5045

6057. Miller, Paul Vincent. The Red, the Pink, and the True Blue. 1 act. First Stage, 5 (Spring, 1966), 8-16.

6058. Miller, Stephanie. The Dangerous Game. 1 act. Plays, 27 (March, 1968), 48-58.

6059. Mills, Grace Evelyn. Christmas Comes to Hamelin. 1 act. Plays, 4 (December, 1944), 36-44. AND Plays, 15 (December, 1955), 39-47. AND Plays, 30 (December, 1970), 53-60.

6060. Milne, Alan Alexander, 1882-1956. The Dover Road. 1 act. Everybody's Magazine, 46 (May, 1922), 157-163.

6061. _____. The Man in the Bowler Hat. 1 act. Ladies' Home Journal, 40 (April, 1923), 5, 106, 108, 111-112.

6062. _____. Miss Marlow at Play. 1 act. One-Act Play Magazine, 1 (May, 1937), 6-22.

6063. _____. The Truth about Blayds. 1 act. Everybody's Magazine, 47 (August, 1922), 76-82.

6064. Milne, J. R. The Dardanelles Puff-Box. 1 act. Smart Set, 62 (May, 1920), 77-83.

6065. _____. Melodrama, a One-Act Sketch. Smart Set, 60 (September, 1919), 95-99.

6066. Milner, Roger, 1925- . How's the World Treating You? 3 acts. Plays and Players, 13 (March, 1966), 31-46, 71-72.

6067. Milosz, O. W., 1877-1939. Mephiboseth. Vers et Prose, 35 (October-December, 1913), 76-93. In French.

6068. _____. Miguel Manara. 1 act. Poet Lore, 30 (Summer, 1919), 224-264. Edward J. O'Brien, translator.

6069. Milton, Nerissa Long. The Challenge. 4 parts, fantasy. Negro History Bulletin, 17 (October, November, December, 1953, January, 1954), 15-16; 43-44; 66-68; 87-88.

6070. Minervini, Roberto. Maison Clarette. 1 act. Il Dramma, 92 (June 15, 1930), 35-39. In Italian.

6071. ———. Mattuntino. 1 act. Il Dramma, 54 (November 15, 1928), 28-33. In Italian.

6072. ———. Preludio per una vita galante. 1 act. Il Dramma, 45 (July 1, 1928), 40-43. In Italian.

6073. ———. Ritiro del divino amore. 1 act. Il Dramma, 167 (August 1, 1933), 36-41. In Italian.

6074. Minnucci, Vittorio. Vestiti su misura. 3 acts. Il Dramma, 204 (February 15, 1935), 4-24. In Italian.

Minot, Dominique, adapter see Holt, W. 4151

6075. Miquette's First Dinner Party. 1 act. Living Age, 218 (August, 1898), 557-560.

6076. Miraglia, Giuseppe Nicola. Tempo di mezzo. 1 act. Sipario, 5 (April, 1950), 71-74. In Italian.

6077. Miranda, Julian E. Cornerstone of Civil Rights. 1 act. Plays, 34 (March, 1975), 31-36.

6078. Mirande, Yves and Henri Feroule. La collana di perle. 1 act. Il Dramma, 114 (May 15, 1931), 40-45. In Italian.

6079. ——— and Alex Madis. Simona è fatta così. 3 acts. Il Dramma, 31 (December 1, 1927), 6-32. In Italian.

Mirza, Gail, translator see Sampaio, S. 7897

Miserocchi, Manilio, 1898- , translator see Noè, I. 6613

6080. Mishima, Yukio. Sotoba Komachi, a Modern No Play. 1 act. Virginia Quarterly Review, 33 (Spring, 1957), 270-288. Donald Keene, translator.

Missiroli, Mario, translator see Panizza, O. 6951

6081. Mitchell, Earle. The Bookmaker's Shoes. 1 act. Smart Set, 30 (March, 1910), 131-136.

6082. Mitchell, Ken. This Train. 1 act. Performing Arts in Canada, 10 (Spring, 1973), 45-51.

6083. Mitchell, Lynn B. The Women of Alexandria. 1 act. New Mexico Quarterly, 1 (February, 1931), 43-49.

6084. Mitchell, Ronald Elwy, 1905- . A Husband for Breakfast. 1 act, comedy. One-Act Play Magazine, 1 (October, 1937), 510-526.

6085. _____. Resurrection Ezra, a Pennsylvania Comedy. 1 act. One-Act Play Magazine, 2 (August-September, 1938), 253-268.

6086. Mitchell, Susan L., editor. Leaguers and Peelers; or The Apple Cart. 2 acts. Irish Review, 1 (October, 1911), 390-406.

6087. Mitchell, W. O. Ladybug Ladybug. 1 act. Edge, 5 (Fall, 1966), 44-51.

Mitford, Nancy, 1904- , adapter see Roussin, A. 7747

6088. Mithois, Marcel, 1922- . L'Accompagnateur. 1 act, monologue. L'Avant Scène, 231, 33-34. In French.

6089. _____. L'Arc de Triomphe. 4 acts, comedy. L'Avant Scène, 535 (February 15, 1974), 7-33. In French.

6090. _____. Les Coups de Théatre. 1 act, comedy. L'Avant Scène, 240 (April 1, 1961), 39-43. In French.

6091. _____. Croque-Monsieur. 2 acts, comedy. L'Avant Scène, 325 (January 1, 1965), 11-33. In French.

6092. _____. Cruelle Galejade. 1 act, comedy. L'Avant Scène, 209 (December 1, 1959), 37-42. In French.

6093. _____. Elisabeth est Morte. 1 act. L'Avant Scène, 182 (October 1, 1958), 30-33. In French.

6094. _____. Isabelle et le General. 1 act. L'Avant Scène, 174 (May 15, 1958), 41-48. In French.

6095. _____. Le Passe-Temps. 1 act. L'Avant Scène, 253 (November 15, 1961), 32-36. In French.

6096. _____. La Troisième Agnes. 1 act, comedy. L'Avant Scène, 300 (December 1, 1963), 37-41.

6097. _____. Les Vacances Revées. 1 act, comedy. L'Avant Scène, 325 (January 1, 1965), 35-40. In French.

_____, adapter see Cooney, R. and J. Chapman 2001

_____, adapter see Gilroy, F. D. 3545

6098. Mixon, Ada. Peace on Earth. 1 act. Poet Lore, 28 (New Year's, 1917), 65-77.

6099. Mnacko, Ladislav, 1919- . In principio erano i marescialli. 5 acts. Il Dramma, 45, no. 11 (August, 1969), 29-50. Ela Ripellino, translator. In Italian.

6100. Mobert, Helen L. The Singing Pool. 1 act. Poet Lore, 30 (Summer, 1919), 275-288.

Modell, David A., translator see Chekhov, A. P. 1773

6101. Moessinger, William. He Won't Be Home for Christmas. 1 act. Plays, 34 (December, 1974), 59-66.

6102. Mogherini, Isa. La seggiola. Sipario, 9 (July, 1954), 33-37. In Italian.

6103. Mogin, Jean. A Chacun Selon Sa Faim. 3 acts. Il Dramma, n.s., 113 (July 15, 1950), 9-27. Luciana Cane and Gigi Cane, translators. In Italian.

6104. Moineaux, Georges, 1860-1929. Les Gaités de L'Escadron. L'Avant Scène (OST), 10 (September, 1949), 1-37. In French.

6105. _____. La lettera raccomandata. 1 act. Il Dramma, 60 (February 15, 1929), 44-45. Alex Alexis, translator. In Italian.

6106. _____. Mentons bleus. 1 act, comedy. Sipario, 12 (June, 1957), 53-56. Manlio Vergoz, translator. In Italian.

6107. _____. Peace at Home. 1 act, comedy. Poet Lore, 29 (Spring, 1917), 217-230. Leroy James Cook, translator.

6108. _____. A Rule Is a Rule, Four Playlets: The Torn Transfer; The Registered Letter; Article 330; The Scales of Justice. 1 act each. Tulane Drama Review, 3 (October, 1958), 62-80. Jacques Barzun, translator.

6109. Moise a Mao, De. L'Avant Scène, 539 (April 15, 1974), 3-38. In French.

6110. Molière, 1622-1673, pseud. Le Bourgeois Gentilhomme. 2 acts, comedy. Theatre Arts, 39 (November, 1955), 49-64. William Somerset Maugham, adapter.

6111. _____. Il cornuto immaginario. 1 act, farce. Il Dramma, 366 (November 15, 1941), 38-43. In Italian.

6112. _____. The Doctor in Spite of Himself. 1 act. Plays, 16 (April, 1957), 73-80. Lewy Olfson, adapter.

6113. _____. Don Giovanni. Sipario, 219 (July, 1964), 28-43. Bertolt Brecht, Benno Besson and Elizabeth Hauptmann, adapters; Carlo Formigoni, Giovanna Acampora, Franco Parenti, translators.

6114. _____. Don Juan. 5 acts. L'Avant Scène, 593 (September 1, 1976), 29-72. In French.

6115. _____. Les Femmes Savantes. 5 acts, comedy. L'Avant Scène, 409-410 (September, 1968), 7-48. In French.

6116. _____. The Flying Doctor. 1 act. Golden Book, 1 (May, 1925), 672-677.

6117. _____. The Foolish Snobs. 1 act. Plays, 34 (October, 1974), 86-96. Paul T. Nolan, adapter.

6118. _____. The Forced Marriage. 1 act, comedy. Tulane Drama Review, 8 (Winter, 1963), 155-174. Albert Bermel, translator.

6119. _____. George Dandin, or The Discomfited Husband. 3 acts, comedy. Theatre Arts, 8 (September, 1924), 605-621. Stark Young, translator.

6120. _____. The Imaginary Invalid. 1 act. Plays, 33 (November, 1973), 83-95. Joellen Bland, adapter.

6121. _____. La Mariage Forcé. 1 act. Il Dramma, 391/392 (December 1/15, 1942), 67-74. A. Brissoni, translator. In Italian.

6122. _____. Il medico volante. 1 act, farce. Il Dramma, 383 (August 1, 1942), 36-39. Giovanni Marcellini, translator. In Italian.

6123. _____. The Romantic Ladies. 1 act, comedy. Golden Book, 11 (April, 1930), 103-108, 110, 112.

6124. _____. The School for Wifes. 1 act. Plays, 31 (November, 1971), 85-96. Paul T. Nolan, adapter.

6125. _____. Le Tartuffe, ou l'Imposteur. 5 acts. L'Avant Scène, 368 (November 15, 1966), 16-51. In French.

6126. _____. The Would-Be Gentleman. 1 act. Plays, 19 (May, 1960), 99-107. Lewy Olfson, adapter.

Molina, Tirso de, pseud. see Tellez, G. 8740, 8741

6127. Molinaro, Ursule. After the Wash. 1 act. Chelsea, 17 (August, 1965), 109-133.

6128. _____. Breakfast Past Noon. 1 act. Works, 1 (Summer, 1968), 49-64.

6129. _____. The Engagement. 1 act. San Francisco Review, 1 (June, 1960), 15-27.

6130. _____. The Sundial. 1 act. Chelsea, 12 (September, 1962), 40-52.

6131. _____. The Thirteenth Christmas. 1 act. Chelsea, 8 (October, 1960), 88-98.

6132. _____. The Tourniquet. 1 act. Chelsea, 10 (September, 1961), 28-41.

_____, translator see DeGrazia, E. 2284

6133. Molnar, Ferenc, 1878-1952. Amore sacro e amor profano. 1 act. Il Dramma, 53 (November 1, 1928), 37-39. Stefano Rokk-Richter, translator. In Italian.

6134. _____. Armonia. 3 acts. Il Dramma, 160 (April 15, 1933), 4-34. Ada Salvatore, translator. In Italian.

6135. _____. Attori. 1 act. Il Dramma, 71 (August 1, 1929), 41-43. Ignazio Balla and Borgomaneri, translators. In Italian.

6136. _____. La celebre cantante. 1 act. Il Dramma, 120 (August 15, 1931), 40-42. In Italian.

6137. _____. La commedia del buon cuore. 3 acts. Il Dramma, 24 (August 15, 1927), 6-43. Stefano Rokk-Richter, translator. In Italian.

6138. _____. Dinner. 1 act. Smart Set, 67 (February, 1922), 73-82.

6139. _____. Discrezione. 1 act. Il Dramma, 79 (December 1, 1929), 43-44. In Italian.

6140. _____. Due donne. 1 act. Il Dramma, 69 (July 1, 1929), 40-41. Ignazio Balla and Borgomaneri, translators. In Italian.

6141. _____. Girono di nozze. 1 act. Il Dramma, 203 (February 1, 1935), 23-32. Ada Salvatore, translator. In Italian.

6142. _____. The Guardsman. 3 acts. Il Dramma, 8 (July, 1926), 6-34. In Italian.

6143. ———. The Guardsman. 1 act. Living Age, 323 (October 4, 1924), 68-78.

6144. ———. Heavenly and Earthly Love. 1 act, comedy. Golden Book, 22 (August, 1935), 187-189.

6145. ———. The Host. 1 act. Golden Book, 7 (June, 1928), 781-786. Joseph Szebenyei, translator.

6146. ———. L'imperdonabile peccato. 1 act. Il Dramma, 39 (April 1, 1928), 31-32. Luciano Donati, translator. In Italian.

6147. ———. Lies, a Comedy of the Eternal Feminine. 1 act. Golden Book, 11 (February, 1930), 101-102. Benjamin Glazer, translator.

6148. ———. Liliom. 7 parts. Il Dramma, 253 (March 1, 1937), 2-27. In Italian.

6149. ———. Liliom. 1 act. Everybody's Magazine, 45 (October, 1921), 57-64.

6150. ———. Il nemico del teatro. 1 act, dialogue. Il Dramma, 31 (December 1, 1927), 43-45. Taulero Zulberti, translator. In Italian.

6151. ———. Olimpia, o gli occhi azzurri dell'imperatore. 3 acts. Il Dramma, 233 (May 1, 1936), 2-24. Ignazio Balla and Mario de Vellis, translators. In Italian.

6152. ———. 1, 2, 3. 1 act. Il Dramma, 104 (December 15, 1930), 4-28. Ada Salvatore, translator. In Italian.

6153. ———. Pasticceria Kiss. 1 act. Il Dramma, 203 (February 1, 1935), 4-22. Ada Salvatore, translator. In Italian.

6154. ———. La piacevole menzogna. 1 act. Il Dramma, 23 (August 1, 1927), 35-37. In Italian.

6155. ———. The Play's the Thing. 3 acts, comedy. Theatre Arts, 33 (March, 1949), 67-90.

6156. ———. The Putty Club. 1 act. Theatre Arts, 7 (July, 1923), 251-256. Benjamin Glazer, translator.

6157. ———. Qualcuno. 3 acts. Il Dramma, 135 (April 1, 1932), 4-29. In Italian.

6158. ———. La ragazza del porto. 3 acts. Il Dramma, 218 (September 15, 1935), 5-29. In Italian.

6159. ———. Reparto scandali. 1 act. Il Dramma, 63 (April 1, 1929), 39-40. Corrado Rossi, translator. In Italian.

6160. ———. Restituitemi mio marito. 1 act. Il Dramma, 16 (March, 1927), 36-38. In Italian.

6161. ———. Souper. 1 act. Il Dramma, 104 (December 15, 1930), Ada Salvatore, translator. In Italian.

6162. ———. Spunti per commedie. 1 act. Il Dramma, 18 (May, 1927), 40-42. Taulero Zulberti, translator. In Italian.

6163. ———. Street and Number, a Comedy of Marriage. 1 act. Golden Book, 17 (April, 1933), 367-369.

6164. ———. The Swan. 3 acts. Il Dramma, 55 (December 1, 1928), 6-40. In Italian.

6165. ———. Two Slaps in the Face. 1 act. Golden Book, 2 (July, 1925), 65-67.

6166. ———. L'uomo-corno. 1 act. Il Dramma, 93 (July 1, 1930), 45-46. Ignazio Balla and Borgomaneri, translators. In Italian.

6167. ———. Il valore dell' intervista. 1 act. Il Dramma, 38 (March 15, 1928), 32-33. Sandro Sandri, translator. In Italian.

6168. ———. Il viveur e il cocchiere. 1 act. Il Dramma, 80 (December 15, 1929), 38-40. Taulero Zulberti, translator. In Italian.

6169. ——— and Joseph Teleki. The Actress. 1 act. Smart Set, 33 (March, 1911), 119-122.

———, translator see Heijermans, H. 4030

6170. Monaghan, Katherine. Christmas Concert. 1 act. Scholastic, 37 (September 16, 1940), 17-18, 22.

6171. Monicelli, Franco. Leonida non è qui. 3 acts. Il Dramma, n.s., 178 (April 1, 1953), 9-35. In Italian.

6172. Monkhouse, Allan Noble, 1853- . The Grand Cham's Diamond. 1 act. Scholastic, 23 (September 30, 1933), 4-6, 30-31.

6173. Monnier, Henry. L'Enterement. 1 act. L'Avant Scène, 456 (September 15, 1970), 45-54. In French.

6174. ——— and Gustave Vaez. Monsieur Prudhomme. 5 acts.

L'Avant Scène, 456 (September 15, 1970), 7-40. Nicole Parrot, adapter. In French.

6175. Monro, Harold, 1879-1932. One Day Awake. 1 act. Chapbook [London], 32 (December, 1922), 1-32.

6176. Monroe, Harriet, 1861?-1936. After All. 1 act. Poet Lore, 12 (July, 1900), 321-326.

6177. Montague, Clifford M. Tropics. 1 act. Poet Lore, 40 (1929), 414-419.

6178. Montanelli, Indro, 1909- . Evviva. 1 act. Il Dramma, n. s., 284 (May, 1960), 14-49. In Italian.

6179. _____ and Mario Luciani. L'illustre concittadino. 3 acts. Il Dramma, n. s., 96 (November 1, 1949), 7-27. In Italian.

Montaner, Maribel, translator see Larra, C. 4819, 4820

6180. Montellano, Bernardo Ortiz de. Salome's Head. 1 act. New Directions, 8 (1944), 328-332. Lloyd Mallan, translator.

6181. Montemayor, George de, 1521?-1561. Al Serenissimo Principe de Castilla. 3 parts. PMLA, 43 (December, 1928), 953-989. In Spanish.

6182. Montenegro, Ramón Maria del Valle Inclán, 1869-1936. Le corna di Don Friolera. 3 acts. Il Dramma, 347 (February 1, 1941), 7-24. In Italian.

6183. Monterde, Francisco. She Who Returned to Life. 3 acts, comedy. Poet Lore, 55 (Winter, 1950), 291-335. Louis G. Zelson, translator.

6184. Montgomery, George Edgar. A Gentle Maniac, a Study in Love and Insanity. 1 act. Cosmopolitan, 9 (February, 1890), 479-490.

6185. Montgomery, James. Nothing But the Truth. 3 acts. Il Dramma, 252 (February 15, 1937), 2-30. In Italian.

6186. Montgomery, Robert. Subject to Fits: A Response to Dostoevski's The Idiot. 2 acts. Scripts, 1 (February, 1972), 4-33.

6187. Montherlant, Henri Marie Joseph Millon de, 1896- . Celles Qu'on Prend dans Ses Bras. 3 acts. L'Avant Scène, 147, 1-27. In French.

6188. _____. Demain il Fera Jour. 3 acts. L'Avant Scène, (OST), 9 (July, 1949), 23-37. In French.

6189. _____. Fils de Personne. 4 acts. L'Avant Scène, (OST), 9 (July, 1949), 1-22. In French.

6190. _____. Le Maître de Santiago. 3 acts. Sipario, 5 (January, 1950), 53-66. Cesare Vico Lodovici, translator. In Italian.

6191. _____. Port Royal. Sipario, 11 (December, 1956), 54-73. Camillo Sbarbaro, translator. In Italian.

6192. _____. Quelle che prendiamo tra le braccia. 3 acts. Sipario, 6 (July, 1951), 37-53. In Italian.

6193. _____. La regina morta. 3 acts. Sipario, 7 (January-February, 1952), 62-80. Massimo Bontempelli, translator. In Italian.

6194. _____. La Ville Dont le Prince est un Enfant. 3 acts. L'Avant Scène, 436 (November 1, 1969), 7-30. In French.

Monticelli, Milly de, translator see Arbuzov, A. 314, 315

_____, translator see Pogodin, N. 7224

_____, translator see Svartz, E. L. 8640

_____, translator see Tendrjakov, V. and K. Jikramov 8742

_____, translator see Ugrjumov, D. 8965

_____, translator see Virta, N. 9155

6195. Moock, Armando. Don Juan's Women. 1 act. Poet Lore, 46 (Spring, 1940), 45-75. Willis Knapp Jones, translator.

6196. _____. Songbook of the Baby Jesus. 1 act. Poet Lore, 45 (No. 1, 1939), 23-42. Willis Knapp Jones, translator.

6197. Moon, Ilanon. Final Appearance, A Drama of the Death of a Free Public. 1 act. Classical Journal, 42 (May, 1947), 497-504.

Moore, Carroll see Barasch, N. 552, 553

6198. Moore, Clement Clarke, 1779-1863. A Visit from St. Nicholas. 1 act. Plays, 33 (December, 1973), 73-76. Sylvia Chermak, adapter.

6199. Moore, Edna G. Mr. Longfellow Observes Book Week. 1 act. Plays, 3 (November, 1943), 53-57.

6200. Moore, George, 1852-1933. The Apostle. 3 acts. Dial, 74, 75 (June, July, 1923), 537-561; 43-72.

6201. _____. The Coming of Gabrielle. 3 acts, comedy. English Review, 30 (March, April, May, 1920), 202-216; 296-310; 392-403.

6202. _____ and William Butler Yeats, 1865-1939. Diarmaid and Grania. 3 acts. Dublin Magazine, n.s., 26 (April-June, 1951), 1-41.

6203. Moore, Helen Lippincott. What the Animals Say at Christmas. 1 act. Resource, 13 (November, 1971), 8-13.

6204. Moore, Jocelyn and Heather G. Thorpe. How the World Began. 2 acts. Horn Book, 17 (March-April, 1941), 130-141.

Moore, Lou Wall, adapter see Wilde, O. 9366

6205. Moore, Mavor. The Argument. 1 act. Performing Arts in Canada, 10 (Winter, 1973), 40-44.

6206. Moore, Thomas Sturge, 1870-1944. Orpheus and Eurydice. 3 acts. Fortnightly, 92 (December, 1901), 1-26.

_____, translator see Tagore, R. 8685

Moore, William Dyer, translator see Alvarez Quintero, S. and J. Alvarez Quintero 159

6207. Moore, William H. The Magic Box. 1 act. Plays, 22 (November, 1962), 59-63.

6208. Mor, Enzo. La porta della fortuna. 1 act. Il Dramma, 242 (September 15, 1936), 29-33. In Italian.

6209. _____ and Borghesio. L'autore della commedia. 1 act. Il Dramma, 257 (May 1, 1937), 34-38. In Italian.

6210. _____. Mezze maniche. 1 act. Il Dramma, 234 (May 15, 1936), 27-30. In Italian.

6211. Mora, Juan-Miguel de. Avant Tout la Lumière. 1 act. L'Avant Scène, 395 (January 15, 1968), 33-68. Jean Camp, translator. In French.

6212. Moran, Irene. The Kingdom of Oceanus. 1 act. Plays, 17 (April, 1958), 45-50.

6213. Morand, Paul, 1888- . Le Voyageur et l'Amour. 1 act. Petite Illustration, 181 (March 5, 1932), 1-12. In French.

Morando, Sergio, translator see Duranty, L. 2735

_____, translator see Giraudoux, J. 3573

_____, translator see Salacrou, A. 7870

6214. Moratin, Jose. Fanny's Consent. 3 acts, comedy. Poet Lore, 40 (1929), 159-214. Anna Emilio Bagstad, translator.

Moravia, Alberto, pseud. see Pincherle, A. 7153-7156

Morel, J., translator see Webster, J. 9250

6215. Moreno, Virginia R. Straw Patriot. 1 act. Literary Review, 3 (Summer, 1960), 573-591.

Moreto, Gian Renzo, translator see Adamov, A. 59

Morgan, Bayard Quiney, 1883- , translator see Schnitzler, A. 8073

6216. Morgan, Charles D., 1894-1958. Search Me! 1 act. Smart Set, 45 (January, 1915), 379-388.

6217. Morgan, Edward J. The Return. 1 act. Drama, 11 (January, 1921), 119-121.

6218. Morgan, J. L. The Obsequies. 1 act. Smart Set, 55 (June, 1918), 81-86.

6219. Morgan, Jacques. At the Club. 1 act. Smart Set, 47 (September, 1915), 251-254.

Moriconi, Adolfo, translator see Shaffer, P. 8171

6220. Morin, Etienne Christophe, 1899- . Suzanne. 3 acts, comedy. Petite Illustration, 87 (March 23, 1929), 1-34. In French.

6221. Morley, Christopher Darlington, 1890-1957. Abandoned Husbands. 1 act. Saturday Review of Literature, 5 (October 20, 1928), 269-270.

6222. _____. Bedroom Suite. 1 act, comedy. Outlook, 133 (January 10, 1923), 78-92.

6223. _____. East of Eden: Genesis IV.16. 1 act. The New Republic, 39 (August 13, 1924), 318-323.

6224. _____. Good Theatre. 1 act. Scholastic, 25 (October 13, 1934), 7-9.

6225. _____. "In Modern Dress." 1 act. Scholastic, 13 (September 22, 1928), 6, 9.

6226. _____. Really, My Dear .... 1 act. Forum, 79 (May, 1928), 723-735.

6227. _____. The Sun Machine. 1 act. Saturday Review of Literature, 5 (December 8, 1928), 401.

6228. _____. Walt, a One-Act Portrait. Bookman [New York] 59 (August, 1924), 646-662.

6229. Morley, Olive J. King Arthur and His Knights. 1 act. Plays, 29 (April, 1970), 83-95.

6230. _____. O Little Town of Bethlehem. 1 act. Plays, 15 (December, 1955), 57-62. AND Plays, 32 (December, 1972), 45-50.

6231. _____, adapter. Robin Hood and the Gentle Knight. 1 act. Plays, 30 (March, 1971), 45-54.

_____, adapter see Alcott, L. M. 110, 113

_____, adapter see Austen, J. 458

_____, adapter see Thackeray, W. M. 8782

6232. Morley, Robert, 1908- and Noel Langley, 1933- . Edward My Son. 3 acts, comedy. L'Avant Scène, 291 (July 1, 1963), 10-36. Pierre Sabatier, adapter. In French.

6233. _____. Edward My Son. 3 acts. Il Dramma, n.s., 107 (April 15, 1950), 9-33. Paola Ojetti, translator. In Italian.

6234. _____. Edward My Son. 3 acts, comedy. Theatre Arts, 33 (September, 1949), 57-96.

6235. Morris, Edmund. The Wooden Dish. 2 parts. Il Dramma, n.s., 218/219 (December 1/15, 1954), 29-59. Gigi Lunari, translator. In Italian.

6236. Morris, May. Lady Griselda's Dream. 1 act. Longman's Magazine, 32 (June, 1898), 145-157.

Morris, Richard see Willson, M. 9454

6237. Morris, Thomas Baden, 1900- . Beyond Illusion. 1 act, comedy. One-Act Play Magazine, 2 (November, 1938), 453-476.

6238. _____. I Will Arise. 1 act. Il Dramma, n.s., 144 (November 1, 1951), 44-55. Sergio Cenalino, translator. In Italian.

6239. Morris, William, 1834-1896. Sir Peter Harpdon's End. 1 act, tragedy. Bibelot, 20 (1914), 247-289.

6240. Morse, Corinne. The Queen of Sew-and-Sew. 1 act. Plays, 15 (May, 1956), 41-46.

6241. _____. Tarts for the King. 1 act. Plays, 19 (February, 1960), 45-48.

6242. Morse, Katharine D. The Nativity. 1 act. Poetry, 37 (December, 1930), 126-129.

6243. Morse, Richard M., 1922- . The Narrowest Street. 1 act. Theatre Arts, 29 (September, 1945), 523-531.

Mortara, Mario see Gotta, S. 3660

6244. Mortari, Curio. La sedicesima notte. 1 act. Il Dramma, 181 (March 1, 1934), 29-36. In Italian.

Morteo, Gian Renzo, translator see Adamov, A. 59

_____, translator see Carette, L. 1599

_____, translator see Claudel, P. 1872

_____, translator see Delprat, S. 2311

_____, translator see Ionesco, J. 4393, 4396

Mortier, Alfred, adapter see Ruzzante 7817

6245. Mortier, Pietro. Il verbo amare. 3 acts. Il Dramma, 197 (November 1, 1934), 4-26. In Italian.

6246. Mortimer, John, 1923- . The Dock Brief. 1 act. Il Dramma, n.s., 267 (December, 1958), 29-45. Gigi Lunari, translator. In Italian.

6247. _____. I, Claudius. 2 acts. Plays and Players, 19 (September, 1972), I-XVI.

6248. _____. Une Heure pour Dejeuner. 1 act. L'Avant Scène, 399 (March 15, 1968), 37-43. Pol Quentin, adapter. In French.

6249. _____. A Voyage Round My Father. 2 acts. Plays and Players, 18 (February, 1971), 68-85.

6250. Morton, Frances McKinnon. The Three Friends. 1 act. St. Nicholas, 51 (March, 1924), 530-533.

6251. Morucchio, Umberto, 1893- . Passaggio dell' Equatore.

3 acts. Il Dramma, 358 (July 15, 1941), 9-33. In Italian.

Morum, William see Dinner, W. 2505

6252. Mosca, Giovanni. L'Angelo e il commendatore. 3 acts. Il Dramma, n. s., 80 (March 1, 1949), 7-24. In Italian.

6253. _____. L'Anticamera. 1 act. Il Dramma, 399 (April 1, 1943), 17-22. In Italian.

6254. _____. La campana delle tentazioni. 2 parts. Il Dramma, n. s., 298 (July, 1961), 8-39. In Italian.

6255. _____. L'ex alunno. 3 acts. Il Dramma, 381 (July 1, 1942), 7-22. In Italian.

6256. _____. La giostra. 1 act. Il Dramma, 399 (April 1, 1943), 12-16. In Italian.

6257. _____. La sommossa. 1 act. Il Dramma, 399 (April 1, 1943), 7-11. In Italian.

6258. Mosca, Vito. Giuliano senza vocasione. 1 act. Sipario, 5 (January, 1950), 67-74. In Italian.

6259. Mosel, Tad. All the Way Home. 3 acts. Theatre Arts, 46 (October, 1962), 25-56.

Moser, Anastasia D., translator see Khaytov, N. 4617

6260. Mosher, John Chapin. The Beanstalk. 1 act. Smart Set, 60 (December, 1919), 83-87.

6261. _____. Fee Fo Fum. 1 act. Seven Arts, 1 (April, 1917), 602-615.

6262. _____. The Quay of Magic Things. 1 act, comedy. Drama, 10 (February, 1920), 188-191.

6263. _____. Sauce for the Emperor. 1 act, comedy. Smart Set, 51 (January, 1917), 199-208.

6264. Moss, Howard. No Strings Attached. 1 act. New Directions, 8 (1944), 200-209.

6265. _____. The Palace at 4 A.M. 2 acts. Quarterly Review of Literature, 18 (Nos. 3 & 4, 1973), 379-424.

6266. Moss, Louis Quentin. "An Ounce of Safety--." 1 act. Industrial Education Magazine, 37 (November, 1935), 242-247.

6267. Mossi, Padre. Ollantay. 1 act. First Stage, 6 (Spring, 1967), 12-36. Nuria Halty and Howard Richardson, translator.

6268. Motokiyo, Kwanze. Il tamburo di panno. 1 act. Il Dramma, n. s., 322/323 (July/August, 1963), 58-60. Enrico Fulchignoni, translator. In Italian.

6269. Motokiyo, Zeami, 1363-1444. Akogi, a Noh Play. 2 parts. Sewanee Review, 67 (1959), 87-93. Makoto Ueda, translator.

6270. _____. Kanawa, a Crown of Iron Spikes. 1 act. Poet Lore, 23 (Summer, 1912), 222-224. T. Ochiai, translator.

6271. _____. Koyoi Komachi: The Nightly Courting of Komachi. 1 act. Texas Quarterly, 7 (Summer, 1964), 132-142. Roy E. Teele, translator.

6272. _____. Sotoba Komachi. 1 act. New Mexico Quarterly, 25 (Spring, 1955), 57-65. Sam Houston Brock, translator.

_____ see also Zeami Motokiyo

6273. Motoyazu, Komparu Zembo, 1453-1532. Early Snow, a Noh Play. 1 act. Poetry, 15 (March, 1920), 317-320. Arthur Waley, translator.

6274. _____. Ikkaku Sennin. 1 act. Players Magazine, 41 (March, 1965), 149-155. Frank Hoff, translator. William Packard, adapter.

6275. Mouloudji, Marcel. Quattro donne. 3 acts. Il Dramma, n. s., 52 (January 1, 1948), 7-30. Bruno Arcangeli, translator. In Italian.

6276. _____. Les Sargasses. 2 parts. Il Dramma, n. s., 260 (May, 1958), 47-59. Umberto Allemandi, translator. In Italian.

6277. Mourguet, Michel. Amicizia. 3 acts. Il Dramma, 159 (April 1, 1933), 4-36. Alessandro De Stefani, translator. In Italian.

6278. _____. Amitiè. 3 acts, comedy. Petite Illustration, 181 (March 12, 1932), 1-29. In French.

6279. Mousheng, Lin. The Easiest Language to Learn. 1 act. Asia (January, 1945), 21-22.

6280. Moussy, Marcel. Trois Hommes sur un Cheval. 3 acts, comedy. L'Avant Scène, 427 (June 1, 1969), 7-47. In French.

_____, adapter see Frisby, T. 3306

6281. Mowery, William Byron. Election of the Roulette, a Play of Russian Life, 1850. 1 act. Poet Lore, 33 (Winter, 1922), 525-536.

6282. Mowrer, Paul Scott, 1887- . Forest Bride. 1 act. Poet Lore, 60 (Autumn, 1965), 219-242.

Moyes, Patricia, 1923- , translator see Anouilh, J. 275

6283. Mozo, Jeronimo Lopez. The Testament. Modern International Drama, 4 (Fall, 1970), 47-60. Alexander Olynes, translator.

6284. Mrozek, Slawomir, 1930- . Un caso fortunato. 3 acts. Sipario, 315-316 (August-September, 1972), 83-98. A. Chotkowski and P. Statuit, translators. In Italian.

6285. _____. Policjy. 3 acts. Spectaculum, 4 (1963), 195-226. In German.

6286. _____. Tango. 3 acts. Sipario, 259 (November, 1967), 40-59. Anton Maria Ruffo, translator. In Italian.

6287. _____. Tango. 3 acts. Spectaculum, 9 (1966), 59-119. Ludwig Zimmerer, translator. In German.

6288. Mughini, Renata. I figli. 3 acts. Il Dramma, 283 (June 1, 1938), 4-19. In Italian.

Muir, Kenneth, 1907- , translator see Calderon de la Barca, P. 1502

6289. Mulet, Paul. The Scabs. 1 act. First Stage, 1 (Fall, 1962), 35-49.

6290. Müller, Erik. Furia d'amore. 1 act. Il Dramma, n.s., 195/196 (December 15, 1953/January 1, 1954), 99-106. In Italian.

6291. Müller, Heiner, 1929- . Philoktet. Spectaculum, 12 (1969), 225-254. In German.

6292. Muller, Peter. Spudorata verita. 2 acts. Sipario, 26 (January, 1971), 43-64. Magda Zalan, translator. In Italian.

Mullin, Elizabeth Lester, translator see Ferrier, P. 3000

6293. Mullins, Helene. Truth About Liars. 1 act, comedy. Poet Lore, 34 (Spring, 1923), 145-155.

6294. Mulock-Craik, Dinah, 1826-1887. Magnus and Morna: A Shetland Fairy Tale. 1 act. Harper's, 53 (November, 1876), 801-808.

6295. Mund, Wilhelm Michael. Der Tod Julius des Zweiten. 1 act. Il Dramma, n.s., 184/185 (July 1/15, 1953), 35-46. Italo Alighiero Chiusano, translator. In Italian.

6296. Muni, Ann. Chief Halloween Spirit. 1 act. Plays, 17 (October, 1957), 66-68.

6297. Munoz-Seca, Pedro. La lettura del copione. 1 act. Il Dramma, 159 (April 1, 1933), 41-45. Gilberto Beccari, translator. In Italian.

_____ see also Garcia-Alvarez, E. 3372, 3373

6298. Munro, Hector Hugh, 1870-1916. The Baker's Dozen, a Comedy on Shipboard. 1 act. Golden Book, 15 (June, 1932), 553-556.

6299. _____. The Miracle Merchant, a Sketch in One Act. Scholastic, 30 (April 17, 1937), 9-10, 13.

6300. Munro, Helen Waite. Pom-Pom. 1 act. Plays, 2 (May, 1943), 48-51.

6301. Mura. L'amante di tutti. 1 act. Il Dramma, 73 (September 1, 1929), 38-45. In Italian.

6302. _____. L'amore e l'avventura. 1 act. Il Dramma, 131 (February 1, 1932), 34-41. In Italian.

6303. _____. Le derubate. 1 act. Il Dramma, 128 (December 15, 1931), 28-37. In Italian.

Muraro, Michelangelo, translator see Calmo, A. 1512

6304. Murdoch, Iris, 1919- and John B. Priestley. The Severed Head. 3 acts. Sipario, 225 (January, 1965), 31-50. Ettore Capriolo, translator. In Italian.

6305. _____ and James Saunders. The Italian Girl. 2 acts. Plays and Players, 15 (March, 1968), 27-42, 53-60, 62, 65.

6306. Murdoch, Marion. The Cuckoo. 1 act. Plays, 5 (March, 1946), 11-27. AND Plays, 14 (April, 1955), 1-19.

6307. Murdock, Charles A. A 16th-Century Christmas. 1 act. St. Nicholas, 16 (December, 1888), 145-149.

Murfin, Jane see Cowl, J. 2080

6308. Murnik, Radoslav. Napoleon's Samovar. 1 act, comedy. Poet Lore, 48 (Autumn, 1942), 195-219. Anthony J. Klancar, translator.

6309. Murphy, Elinor. I'll Try. 1 act. St. Nicholas, 48 (January, 1921), 256-260.

Murphy, Olive Frances, translator see Blok, A. 1012

_____, translator see Chekhov, A. P. 1770, 1782

6310. Murphy, Thomas. The Orphans. 3 acts. Journal of Irish Literature, 3 (September, 1974), supplement, 1-44.

6311. Murray, John, 1906- . Airport Adventure. 1 act. Plays, 28 (February, 1969), 19-33. AND Plays, 35 (April, 1976), 23-37.

6312. _____. Badlands Ballyhoo. 1 act. Plays, 21 (January, 1962), 1-13. AND Plays, 32 (January, 1973), 11-22. AND Plays, 35 (January, 1976), 21-32.

6313. _____. Be My Ghost. 1 act. Plays, 14 (October, 1954), 27-38.

6314. _____. The Belles of Horsefly Gulch. 1 act. Plays, 21 (April, 1962), 31-43. AND Plays, 35 (March, 1976), 25-37.

6315. _____. The Big Top Murders. 1 act. Plays, 34 (January, 1975), 1-17.

6316. _____. The Boy Next Door. 1 act. Plays, 14 (November, 1954), 25-38.

6317. _____. A Case for Mrs. Hudson. 1 act. Plays, 11 (April, 1952), 1-14.

6318. _____. A Case for Two Detectives. 1 act. Plays, 15 (April, 1956), 13-22. AND Plays, 18 (October, 1958), 25-34. AND Plays, 28 (April, 1969), 13-22. AND Plays, 35 (February, 1976), 11-20.

6319. _____. A Case for Two Spies. 1 act. Plays, 30 (May, 1971), 25-34.

6320. _____. A Case of Mistaken Identity. 1 act. Plays, 22 (March, 1963), 13-24.

6321. _____. The Case of the Missing Poet. 1 act. Plays, 12 (April, 1953), 27-37.

6322. _____. The Case of the Wall Street. 1 act. Plays, 20 (January, 1961), 21-33.

6323. _____. City of Fear. 1 act. Plays, 19 (May, 1960), 1-12.

6324. _____. Colossal, Stupendous. 1 act. Plays, 16 (April, 1957), 13-24.

6325. _____. Come to the Fair! 1 act. Plays, 30 (May, 1971), 1-12.

6326. _____. The Customs Caper. 1 act. Plays, 30 (March, 1971), 1-13.

6327. _____. Dead of Night. 1 act. Plays, 15 (March, 1956), 11-23.

6328. _____. The Devonshire Demons. 1 act. Plays, 33 (January, 1974), 1-12.

6329. _____. Dig That Mastodon! 1 act. Plays, 32 (March, 1973), 1-10.

6330. _____. Do or Diet. 1 act, monologue. Plays, 32 (January, 1973), 60-62.

6331. _____. Don't Call Us--We'll Call You. 1 act. Plays, 21 (February, 1962), 11-22.

6332. _____. Don't Pet My Rock! 1 act. Plays, 36 (October, 1976), 1-16.

6333. _____. The Door. 1 act. Plays, 10 (March, 1951), 10-18.

6334. _____. The End of the Line. 1 act. Plays, 16 (October, 1956), 25-36.

6335. _____. Every Room with Bath. 1 act. Plays, 19 (November, 1959), 11-22.

6336. _____. Fabre's Little World. 1 act. Plays, 11 (March, 1952), 17-27.

6337. _____. The Final Curtain. 1 act. Plays, 17 (October, 1957), 1-13.

6338. _____. The Five Buttons. 1 act. Plays, 14 (March, 1955), 35-48.

6339. _____. Fulfillment. 1 act. Plays, 30 (April, 1971), 19-28.

6340. _____. A Game of Chess. 1 act. Plays, 12 (October, 1952), 23-32.

6341. _____. Gray Flannel Blues. 1 act. Plays, 24 (May, 1965), 1-13.

6342. _____. The Greatest Christmas Gift. 1 act. Plays, 33 (December, 1973), 37-49.

6343. _____. The Happy Hollidays. 1 act. Plays, 30 (December, 1970), 13-24.

6344. _____. The Haunting of Hathaway House. 1 act. Plays, 31 (November, 1971), 1-12.

6345. _____. Healthy, Wealthy and Wild. 1 act. Plays, 29 (May, 1970), 13-24.

6346. _____. Hear No Evil, Speak No Evil. 1 act. Plays, 23 (March, 1964), 15-25.

6347. _____. His and Hers. 1 act. Plays, 18 (February, 1959), 35-47.

6348. _____. Honest Injun! 1 act. Plays, 16 (March, 1957), 1-13.

6349. _____. Hot Line to Destruction. 1 act. Plays, 34 (May, 1975), 13-28.

6350. _____. House of Horrors. 1 act. Plays, 21 (October, 1961), 37-47.

6351. _____. How High Is Your Fi? 1 act. Plays, 18 (April, 1959), 23-37.

6352. _____. I Love You, Mr. Klotz! 1 act. Plays, 21 (March, 1962), 25-38.

6353. _____. I Want to Report a Murder. 1 act. Plays, 19 (January, 1960), 15-28.

6354. _____. "Icarus Is Coming." 1 act, melodrama. Plays, 28 (March, 1969), 13-25.

6355. _____. The Impossible Room. 1 act. Plays, 31 (January, 1972), 25-38.

6356. _____. Invisible Inventions, Incorporated. 1 act. Plays, 23 (April, 1964), 13-25.

6357. _____. Kid Avalanche. 1 act. Plays, 20 (February, 1961), 13-25.

6358. _____. Lights! Camera! Action! 1 act. Plays, 33 (March, 1974), 29-42.

6359. _____. Like Mother Used to Make. 1 act. Plays, 24 (November, 1964), 23-35.

6360. _____. Lock, Stock, and Barrel. 1 act. Plays, 16 (November, 1956), 11-24.

6361. _____. The Looking Glass Murder. 1 act. Plays, 27 (January, 1968), 11-25.

6362. _____. Love's in Fashion. 1 act. Plays, 22 (May, 1963), 29-41.

6363. _____. Mad About Art. 1 act. Plays, 27 (February, 1968), 13-28.

6364. _____. The Mechanical Man. 1 act. Plays, 28 (November, 1968), 89-96.

6365. _____. Midnight Crossing. 1 act. Plays, 17 (May, 1958), 15-26.

6366. _____. The Mish-Mash Bird. 1 act. Plays, 16 (January, 1957), 15-26.

6367. _____. Miss Forsythe Is Missing. 1 act. Plays, 23 (January, 1964), 15-26.

6368. _____. Miss Hepplewhite Takes Over. 1 act. Plays, 23 (November, 1963), 15-28.

6369. _____. Mr. Filbert's Claim to Fame. 1 act. Plays, 18 (January, 1959), 13-26.

6370. _____. Mister Twister. 1 act. Plays, 22 (January, 1963), 13-26.

6371. _____. Mulvaney's First Case. 1 act. Plays, 17 (January, 1958), 23-33.

6372. _____. My Host--the Ghost. 1 act. Plays, 24 (January, 1965), 25-36.

6373. _____. The Mystery in the Lab. 1 act. Plays, 12 (January, 1953), 20-32.

6374. _____. Mystery Liner. 1 act. Plays, 31 (April, 1972), 1-12.

6375. _____. Mystery Manor. 1 act. Plays, 28 (October, 1968), 33-46.

6376. _____. The National Everything. 1 act. Plays, 28 (November, 1968), 1-12.

6377. _____. Old Ghosts at Home. 1 act. Plays, 19 (October, 1959), 1-15.

6378. _____. Once Upon a Midnight Dreary. 1 act. Plays, 34 (November, 1974), 1-13.

6379. _____. One in a Million. 1 act. Plays, 30 (February, 1971), 21-29.

6380. _____. The Perfect Couple. 1 act. Plays, 19 (April, 1960), 24-36.

6381. _____. Publisher's Choice. 1 act. Plays, 30 (November, 1970), 1-13.

6382. _____. Quiz Biz. 1 act. Plays, 18 (March, 1959), 1-15.

6383. _____. Really Rural. 1 act. Plays, 31 (March, 1972), 39-48.

6384. _____. Scaredy Cat. 1 act. Plays, 17 (April, 1958), 1-12.

6385. _____. Shadow-of-Death. 1 act. Plays, 35 (December, 1975), 27-40.

6386. _____. Shiver My Timbers. 1 act. Plays, 22 (October, 1962), 1-13.

6387. _____. The Sixth Juror. 1 act. Plays, 30 (October, 1970), 33-45.

6388. _____. Spies and Dolls. 1 act. Plays, 26 (March, 1967), 13-25.

6389. _____. Stage Set for Murder. 1 act. Plays, 20 (March, 1961), 1-15.

6390. _____. Strange Inheritance. 1 act. Plays, 32 (October, 1972), 1-15.

6391. _____. The Super-Duper Market. 1 act, monologue. Plays, 32 (November, 1972), 81-83.

6392. _____. The Swiss Chalet Mystery. 1 act. Plays, 14 (January, 1955), 27-38. AND Plays, 29 (March, 1970), 23-34.

6393. _____. Take My Advice. 1 act. Plays, 25 (October, 1965), 23-35.

6394. _____. The Tarot Terrors. 1 act. Plays, 34 (March, 1975), 1-15.

6395. ———. Terror on the Island. 1 act. Plays, 22 (November, 1962), 13-24.

6396. ———. That's the Spirit. 1 act. Plays, 15 (October, 1955), 9-22.

6397. ———. The Third Richest Man in the World. 1 act. Plays, 33 (October, 1973), 1-14.

6398. ———. A Triumph for Trimbly. 1 act. Plays, 29 (November, 1969), 49-58.

6399. ———. Two for the Money. 1 act. Plays, 24 (March, 1965), 17-30.

6400. ———. The Vagabond Vampires. 1 act. Plays, 35 (May, 1976), 1-16.

6401. ———. Visitor from Outer Space. 1 act. Plays, 24 (October, 1964), 1-16.

6402. ———. Vote for Miss Checkout. 1 act. Plays, 20 (May, 1961), 11-23.

6403. ———. What Happened on Center Street. 1 act. Plays, 35 (October, 1975), 13-27.

6404. ———. When the Hurlyburly's Done. 1 act. Plays, 20 (October, 1960), 13-25.

6405. ———. Will-O'-Wisp. 1 act. Plays, 11 (January, 1952), 8-20.

6406. ———. The Woman Who Owned the West. 1 act. Plays, 34 (October, 1974), 1-14.

6407. ——— and Allen Boretz, 1900- . Adieu Berthe! 3 acts, comedy. L'Avant Scène, 404 (June 1, 1968), 7-38. Albert Husson and Francis Blanche, adapters. In French.

6408. Murray, T. C. The Green Branch. 1 act. Dublin Magazine, n.s., 18 (July-September, 1943), 15-34.

6409. ———. The Pipe in the Fields. 1 act. Dublin Magazine, n.s., 2 (April-June, 1927), 7-30.

6410. ———. A Spot in the Sun. 1 act. Dublin Magazine, n.s., 13 (April-June, 1938), 14-36.

Murray, William, adapter see Pirandello, L. 7202

6411. Musaphia, Joseph, 1935- . Free. 1 act. Landfall, 17 (December, 1963), 348-369.

6412. Musatescu, Tudor. Sogno di una notte d'inverno. 3 acts. Il Dramma, 412/413 (October 15/November 1, 1943), 53-77. Paolo Soldati, translator. In Italian.

6413. Muse, Violet. The Town Mouse and His Country Cousin. 1 act. Plays, 3 (January, 1944), 42-47.

6414. Musil, Robert. Die Schwarmer. 3 acts. Sipario, 11 (July-August, 1956), 19-38. Lila Jahn, translator. In Italian.

6415. Musil, Rosemary Gabbert. The Invisible Dragon of Winn Sinn Tu. 1 act. Plays, 19 (March, 1960), 37-49.

6416. _____. The Peach Tree Kingdom. 1 act. Plays, 23 (January, 1964), 38-48.

6417. Musselman, N. H. Mila Whendle, an Unpleasant Play. 4 acts. Poet Lore, 13 (Number 1, 1901), 22-53.

6418. Musset, Alfred de, 1810-1857. Un Caprice. 1 act, comedy. L'Avant Scène, 409-410 (September, 1968), 79-94. In French.

6419. _____. A Caprice. 1 act, comedy. Poet Lore, 33 (Autumn, 1922), 395-419. Anne Grace Wirt, translator.

6420. _____. A Door Must Be Either Open or Shut; A Proverb in One Act. Golden Book, 4 (July, 1926), 67-74. S. L. Gwynn, translator.

6421. Musso, L. Il Pleut Bergère. 1 act, comedy. L'Avant Scène, 171 (March 31, 1958), 35-39. In French.

6422. Mussorgsky, Modest, 1835-1881. Boris Godunov. 4 acts. Theatre Arts, 43 (March, 1959), 25-43. John Gutman, translator.

6423. Myall, Charles A. Ships on the Sand. 1 act. Drama, 12 (February, 1922), 153-156.

6424. Myers, Henry. The First Fifty Years. 1 act. Everybody's Magazine, 47 (July, 1922), 105-112.

6425. Myers, Irvin H. Socrates Up to Date. 1 act. Atlantic, 143 (January, 1929), 78-83.

6426. Mygatt, Tracy Dickinson. The Aino Puku. 1 act. World Outlook, 4 (June, 1918), 20-21.

6427. _____. The Noose. 1 act. Drama, 20 (November, 1929), 42-48.

6428. _____. Seventy-three Voted Yes. World Outlook, 4 (September, 1918), 18-19.

Myrick, Arthur B., translator see Banville, T. de 549

6429. Myrick, Norman. The Day Is Brick. 1 act. Plays, 2 (May, 1943), 8-17.

N

6430. Nadin, Marilyn C. Jack Frost and the Scarecrow. 1 act. Plays, 28 (November, 1968), 83-85.

6431. Naghiu, Iosif. Petrescu Is My Name. 1 act. Dramatika, 8 (Fall, 1971), n.p. Thomas Fitzsimmons and Stefan Stoenescu, translators.

6432. Nakazawa, Ken. The Persimmon Thief. 1 act, comedy. Drama, 16 (December, 1925), 97-98.

6433. Napolitano, Gian Gaspare, 1907- . Il venditore di fumo. Il Dramma, 80 (December 15, 1929), 6-26. In Italian.

_____, translator see Chase, M. C. 1738

6434. Nardelli, Federico V. and Fabrizio Sarazani. Antitragica. 3 acts. Il Dramma, 187 (June 1, 1934), 4-21. In Italian.

6435. Narodny, Ivan. Fortune Favors Fools. 1 act, comedy. Poet Lore, 23 (Autumn, 1912), 305-319. Maria Ossipovna Miller, translator.

6436. Nash, N. Richard, 1913- . Girls of Summer. 3 acts. Il Dramma, n.s., 275/276 (August/September, 1959), 5-37. Gigi Lunari, translator. In Italian.

6437. _____. The Rainmaker. 3 acts. Il Dramma, n.s., 247 (April, 1957), 7-35. Carina Calvi, translator. In Italian.

6438. _____. The Rainmaker. 3 acts. Theatre Arts, 40 (March, 1956), 34-62.

6439. _____. See the Jaguar. 3 acts. Theatre Arts, 37 (August, 1953), 34-64.

6440. _____. The Young and Fair. 3 acts. Theatre Arts, 33 (May, 1949), 57-88.

6441. Nash, Ogden, 1902-1971. It's All Wrong. 1 act, comedy. Golden Book, 17 (February, 1933), 137-138.

6442. Nass, Elyse. Love from the Madhouse. 1 act. DeKalb Literary Arts Journal, 8 (Winter, 1975), 36-54.

6443. Natale del mondo. 1 act. Il Dramma, n.s., 350/351 (November/December, 1965), 8-9. In Italian.

Natanson, Irene, translator see Witkiewicz, S. I. 9516

6444. Natanson, Jacques, 1901- . L'Eté. 3 acts, comedy. Petite Illustration, 190 (January 12, 1935), 1-34. In French.

6445. _____. Gli amanti eccezionali. 3 acts. Il Dramma, 75 (October 1, 1929), 4-39. In Italian.

6446. _____. Je T'Attendais. 3 acts, comedy. Petite Illustration, 87 (December 28, 1929), 1-34. In French.

6447. _____. Letteratura. 1 act. Il Dramma, 136 (April 15, 1932), 43-46. Piceno, translator. In Italian.

6448. _____. Michel. 3 acts. Il Dramma, 186 (May 15, 1934), 4-33. Alessandro de Stefani, translator. In Italian.

6449. Nathan, Bertha. If Wishes Were Horses. 1 act. Plays, 5 (April, 1946), 33-39.

6450. Nathan, George Jean, 1882- . The Eternal Mystery. 1 act. Smart Set, 39 (April, 1913), 137-142.

6451. Nativity, The. 1 act. Golden Book, 12 (December, 1930), 77-80. Randall Cayford Burrell, adapter.

6452. Naum, Gellu, 1915- . L'orologeria Taus. 2 parts. Il Dramma, 48 (June, 1972), 75-92. Paola Angioletti Marciano, translator. In Italian.

6453. Naumburg, Margaret. Cleavage. 1 act. One-Act Play Magazine, 1 (January, 1938), 803-820.

6454. Navarro, Francisco, 1902- . The City. 1 act. Poet Lore, 54 (Spring, 1948), 71-82. Willis Knapp Jones, translator.

6455. Negis, André. Un Visite. 1 act. L'Avant Scène, 242 (May 1, 1961), 27-33. In French.

6456. Neihardt, John Gneisenan, 1881- . Eight Hundred Rubles. 1 act. Forum, 53 (March, 1915), 393-402.

6457. Neilson, Francis, 1867-1961. The Bath Road. 3 acts, comedy. Drama, 13 (February, March, April, 1923), 175-183; 222-228; 260-266.

Neiman, Gilbert, translator see Lorca, F. G. 3375

6458. Nel quartiere dei piaceri. 3 acts. Il Dramma, 317 (November 1, 1939), 5-11. In Italian.

Nellhaus, Gerhard, translator see Brecht, B. 1282, 1294, 1295, 1298

6459. Nellie's Fishy Fate. 1 act. Plays, 31 (March, 1972), 13-24.

Nelson, Lawrence see Isherwood, C. 4410

6460. Nelson, Ralph. Mail Call. 1 act. Theatre Arts, 27 (August, 1943), 515-523.

6461. Nelson, Rodney. Pity on the Wapentake: A Folk Play. 1 act. South Dakota Review, 12 (Autumn, 1974), 41-57.

6462. Nelson, Stanley. The Harrison Progressive School. 1 act. The Scene, 1 (1972), 86-105.

6463. Nemerov, Howard, 1920- . Cain. 1 act. Tulane Drama Review, 4 (December, 1959), 12-26.

Neri, Nocoletta, translator see Aroutcheff, G. 363

_____, translator see Hartog, J. de 3954

6464. Neruda, Pablo, 1904- . Radiance and Death of Joaquin Murieta. Modern International Drama, 10 (Fall, 1976), 11-38. Willis Barnstone, translator.

6465. Nerval, Gerard de, 1808-1855. Nicolas Flamel. 1 act. Dublin Magazine, 1 (January, 1924), 503-512. J. S. Starkey, translator.

Nes, Nancy, translator see Aragon, L. 311

6466. Nessesson, Elsa Behaim. In the Secret Places. 1 act. Drama, 17 (November, 1926), 43-45, 62-63.

Nestrick, Nova G. see Liss, F. 4998

6467. Nestroy, Johann, 1801-1862. Liberty Comes to Krahwinkel. 3 acts, farce. Tulane Drama Review, 5 (June, 1961), 135-174. Sybil Welch and Colin Welch, translators.

6468. Nethercot, Arthur Hobart, 1895- . The Funeral March of a Marionette. 1 act. Poet Lore, 31 (Summer, 1920), 232-242.

6469. _____. The Grecian Urn. 1 act. Poet Lore, 33 (Spring, 1922), 142-147.

6470. _____. Peter Gink. 1 act. Poet Lore, 35 (1924), 118-126.

6471. Nettleford, W. T. and W. A. Rathkey. This Is the Worst News. 1 act, satire. One-Act Play Magazine, 2 (February, 1939), 726-730.

6472. Neumann, Sara. The Old Order. 1 act. Drama, 11 (February, 1921), 147-150.

6473. Neven, Charlotte. The Barretts of Wimpole Street. 3 acts. Petite Illustration, 189 (November 24, 1934), 3-34. Rudolf Besier, translator. In French.

6474. Neveux, Georges, 1900- . Le Chien du Jardinier. 3 acts, comedy. L'Avant Scène, 119, 1-24. In French.

6475. _____. Ma Chance et Ma Chanson. 1 act, comedy. L'Avant Scène, 170, 27-38. In French.

6476. _____. Plainte Contre Inconnu. 2 parts, comedy. L'Avant Scène, 170, 4-24. In French.

6477. _____. Plainte Contre Inconnu. 2 parts. Sipario, 2 (August-September, 1947), 43-60. Giancarlo Vigorelli, translator. In Italian.

6478. _____. Robert Macaire. 4 acts. L'Avant Scène, 578 (January 1, 1976), 3-25. In French.

6479. _____. Le Systeme Deux. 1 act, comedy. L'Avant Scène, 119, 25-39. In French.

6480. _____. Le Systeme Deux. 1 act, comedy. Sipario, 12 (July-August, 1957), 63-72. Lilia Silvestri, translator. In Italian.

6481. _____. Theatre dans une Bouteille: La Canari; Les Nuits de Chicago; Les Quatre Operations. 3 sketches. L'Avant Scène, 94, 27-36. In French.

6482. _____. Le Vampire de Bougival. 1 act. L'Avant Scène, 239 (March 15, 1961), 36-41. In French.

6483. _____. La Voleuse de Londres. 3 acts. L'Avant Scène, 239 (March 15, 1961), 9-34. In French.

6484. _____. Zamore. 1 act. L'Avant Scène, 94, 1-23. In French.

6485. _____. Zamore. 1 act. Sipario, 11 (April, 1956), 46-60. In Italian.

_____, adapter see Goodrich, F. and A. Hackett 3632

_____, translator see Chekov, A. P. 1767

Newberry, John Strong, translator see Claudel, P. 1870

_____, translator see Messager, C. 5791

6486. Newburge, David. Bang! Bang! 1 act. The Scene, 1 (1972), 10-32.

6487. Newman, Benjamin W. Underground. 1 act. Poet Lore, 38 (1927), 571-578.

6488. Newman, Deborah. The All-American Tour. 1 act. Plays, 23 (May, 1964), 71-75.

6489. _____. The Best Part of Christmas. 1 act. Plays, 16 (December, 1956), 58-62.

6490. _____. Bunny of the Year. 1 act. Plays, 9 (April, 1950), 59-62.

6491. _____. The Christmas Question. 1 act. Plays, 21 (December, 1961), 85-88.

6492. _____. The Christmas Tree Surprise. 1 act. Plays, 11 (December, 1951), 73-76. AND Plays, 24 (December, 1964), 77-80.

6493. _____. Cinderella. 1 act. Plays, 18 (April, 1959), 65-73.

6494. _____. A Compass for Christopher. 1 act. Plays, 24 (October, 1964), 73-76.

6495. _____. Election Day in the U.S.A. 1 act. Plays, 11 (November, 1951), 35-39.

6496. _____. The Enchanted Cottage. 1 act. Plays, 20 (October, 1960), 63-67.

6497. _____. The First Thanksgiving. Plays, 26, 27 (November, 1967), 75-77.

6498. _____. A Gift for the World. 1 act. Plays, 15 (November, 1955), 57-61.

6499. _____. Green Leaf's Lesson. 1 act. Plays, 9 (October, 1949), 66-69.

6500. _____. The Halloween Spell. 1 act. Plays, 19 (October, 1959), 47-52.

6501. _____. Happy Holidays. 1 act. Plays, 12 (January, 1953), 59-63.

6502. _____. In Honor of Trees. 1 act. Plays, 10 (May, 1951), 61-65.

6503. _____. Kachoo! 1 act. Plays, 11 (January, 1952), 61-64.

6504. _____. The Keys to Peace. 1 act. Plays, 18 (November, 1958), 67-70.

6505. _____. Long Ago in Bethlehem. 1 act. Plays, 26 (December, 1966), 44-48.

6506. _____. Looking for Lincoln. 1 act. Plays, 21 (February, 1962), 41-45.

6507. _____. The Magic Goose. 1 act. Plays, 10 (January, 1951), 68-71.

6508. _____. Memorial Day for the Blue and Gray. 1 act. Plays, 11 (May, 1952), 48-51. AND Plays, 18 (May, 1959), 67-70.

6509. _____. The Message of the Hearts. 1 act. Plays, 11 (February, 1952), 70-73.

6510. _____. Mr. Lincoln's Beard. 1 act. Plays, 16 (February, 1957), 53-56. AND Plays, 35 (February, 1976), 41-44.

6511. _____. Mrs. Santa's Christmas Gift. 1 act. Plays, 9 (December, 1949), 67-70.

6512. _____. The New Washington. 1 act. Plays, 14 (February, 1955), 67-70.

6513. _____. One Night in Bethlehem. 1 act. Plays, 20 (December, 1960), 47-51.

6514. _____. Plum Blossom and the Dragon. 1 act. Plays, 22 (January, 1963), 49-54.

6515. _____. A Present from Abe. 1 act. Plays, 10 (February, 1951), 55-58. AND Plays, 24 (February, 1965), 75-78.

6516. _____. The Prize Shamrock. 1 act. Plays, 12 (March, 1953), 58-61. AND Plays, 18 (March, 1959), 73-78.

6517. _____. The Pumpkineaters' Pumpkin. 1 act. Plays, 10 (October, 1950), 53-56.

6518. _____. Rabbits, Rabbits, Rabbits. 1 act. Plays, 20 (March, 1961), 79-83.

6519. _____. The Rebellious Robots. 1 act. Plays, 21 (November, 1961), 59-65.

6520. _____. Roses for Mother. 1 act. Plays, 10 (May, 1951), 55-58.

6521. _____. Somebody's Valentine. 1 act. Plays, 26 (February, 1967), 75-78.

6522. _____. Something New for Halloween. 1 act. Plays, 12 (October, 1952), 53-57. AND Plays, 23 (October, 1963), 73-77.

6523. _____. Spring Neighbors. 1 act. Plays, 10 (April, 1951), 59-62.

6524. _____. Spring to the Rescue. 1 act. Plays, 10 (March, 1951), 56-59.

6525. _____. The Stars and Stripes. 1 act. Plays, 12 (February, 1953), 53-57. AND Plays, 27 (February, 1968), 73-77.

6526. _____. The Stolen Heart. 1 act. Plays, 9 (February, 1950), 79-82. AND Plays, 25 (February, 1966), 85-88.

6527. _____. Thanks for Thanksgiving. 1 act. Plays, 17 (November, 1957), 65-68.

6528. _____. Thanks to the Indians. 1 act. Plays, 11 (November, 1951), 44-48.

6529. _____. Thanksgiving Farm. 1 act. Plays, 20 (November, 1960), 59-64.

6530. _____. Washington's Gold Button. 1 act. Plays, 9 (February, 1950), 71-74. AND Plays, 20 (February, 1961), 84-88.

6531. _____. The Way to the Inn. 1 act. Plays, 22 (December, 1962), 53-56.

6532. _____. The Wonderful Halloween Cape. 1 act. Plays, 20 (October, 1960), 45-50.

6533. _____. The Wonderful World of Hans Christian Andersen. 1 act. Plays, 21 (January, 1962), 55-61.

6534. _____. The Yankee Doodle Kitten. 1 act. Plays, 23 (November, 1963), 67-71.

_____, adapter see Andersen, H. C. 194, 200

_____, adapter see Austen, J. 459

_____, adapter see Clemens, S. L. 1888

_____, adapter see Dickens, C. 2466

6535. Newton, Douglas. Lights with Us, a Dialogue. 1 act. Botteghe Oscure, 15 (1955), 163-199.

6536. Niccodemi, Dario, 1877-1934. Dawn, Day, Night. 3 acts. Gambit, 6, 3-32. Robert Rietty, translator.

6537. _____. Vera Mirzewa. 4 acts. Il Dramma, 60 (February 15, 1929), 4-36. In Italian.

6538. Nichol, James W. The House on Chestnut Street. 1 act. Performing Arts in Canada, 10 (Fall, 1973), 48-51.

6539. _____. Tub. 1 act. Performing Arts in Canada, 7 (No. 1, 1970), 21-27.

6540. Nichols, Content S. Everychild, a School Morality Play. 1 act. St. Nicholas, 42 (February, 1915), 358-359.

6541. Nichols, Dudley. The Informer. Theatre Arts, 35 (August, 1951), 59-82.

Nichols, Marianna da Vinci, translator see Hrotsvitha 4262

6542. Nichols, Peter, 1927- . A Day in the Death of Joe Egg. 3 acts. L'Avant Scène, 442 (February 1, 1970), 7-36. Claude Roy, translator. In French.

6543. _____. A Day in the Death of Joe Egg. 3 acts. Sipario, 24 (November, 1969), 40-62. Maria Silvia Codecasa, translator. In Italian.

6544. _____. Forget-Me-Not. 2 acts. L'Avant Scène, 497 (June 15, 1972), 7-37. Claude Roy, adapter. In French.

6545. _____. Servizio Sanitario Nazionale, ovvero Il Grande Amore di Sorella Cleo. 2 parts, comedy. Il Dramma (April, 1974), 25-68. Laura del Bono, translator. In Italian.

6546. Nichols, Robert. Minding the Store. 1 act. Scripts, 1 (October, 1972), 62-70.

6547. _____. The Wax Engine. Scripts, 1 (March, 1972), 67-88.

6548. Nicholson, Jessie. A Beau for Nora. 4 acts. Plays, 25 (March, 1966), 1-14.

Nicholson

6549. _____. A Castle in Spain. 1 act. Plays, 21 (November, 1961), 1-12.

6550. _____. Conversation Piece. 1 act. Plays, 28 (May, 1969), 1-12.

6551. _____. The Ghost Walks Tonight. 1 act. Plays, 11 (October, 1951), 27-35. AND Plays, 18 (October, 1958), 45-53.

6552. _____. The Handwriting on the Wall. 1 act. Plays, 28 (February, 1969), 51-62.

6553. _____. The Haunted Bookshop. 1 act. Plays, 27 (November, 1967), 55-63.

6554. _____. Holiday for Santa. 1 act. Plays, 17 (December, 1957), 51-58.

6555. _____. Mind over Matter. 1 act. Plays, 20 (March, 1961), 17-26.

6556. _____. The Mysterious Stranger. 1 act. Plays, 11 (May, 1952), 32-41. AND Plays, 18 (April, 1959), 47-56. AND Plays, 32 (March, 1973), 47-55.

6557. _____. The Mystery of Patriot Inn. 1 act. Plays, 17 (February, 1958), 35-42.

6558. _____. The Nautical Sheep. 1 act. Plays, 10 (January, 1951), 59-63.

6559. _____. Sugar and Spice. 1 act. Plays, 11 (January, 1952), 48-55. AND Plays, 20 (May, 1961), 53-60.

6560. _____. Teapot Trouble. 1 act. Plays, 10 (March, 1951), 47-55. AND Plays, 24 (March, 1965), 61-69.

6561. _____. Valentine Stardust. 1 act. Plays, 11 (February, 1952), 50-57. AND Plays, 34 (February, 1975), 65-72.

6562. Nicholson, Kenyon, 1894- . The Anonymous Letter. 1 act. Smart Set, 65 (May, 1921), 73-83.

6563. _____. The Casino Gardens. 1 act. Smart Set, 64 (March, 1921), 77-83.

6564. _____. The Gentle Assassin. 1 act. Smart Set, 62 (June, 1920), 83-89.

6565. _____. The Marriage of Little Eva. 1 act, comedy. Smart Set, 65 (August, 1921), 75-85.

6566. _____. Meet the Wife. 1 act, comedy. Smart Set, 68 (August, 1922), 85-93.

6567. _____. White Elephants. 1 act, comedy. Smart Set, 66 (October, 1921), 63-74.

6568. Nicholson, Mary Ann. Ben Franklin Plays Cupid. 1 act. Plays, 28 (May, 1969), 63-67.

6569. _____. The Crying Clown. 1 act. Plays, 14 (November, 1954), 69-71.

6570. _____. The Fearless One. 1 act. Plays, 17 (January, 1958), 57-62.

6571. _____. The Laughing Princess. 1 act. Plays, 15 (April, 1956), 69-72.

6572. _____. The Price of Eggs. 1 act. Plays, 14 (February, 1955), 71-74.

6573. _____. Princess Nimble-Wit. 1 act. Plays, 15 (January, 1956), 45-48.

6574. _____. A Princess Too Little. 1 act. Plays, 22 (April, 1963), 79-82.

6575. _____. Washington's Paper Army. 1 act. Plays, 30 (February, 1971), 65-68.

6576. _____. The Wise Wife. 1 act. Plays, 15 (April, 1956), 63-68.

6577. Nicol, Eric. Citizens of Calais. 2 acts. Canadian Theatre Review, 7 (Summer, 1975), 52-114.

Nicolaeff, Ariadne, translator see Arbusov, A. N. 316

6578. Nicolai, Aldo, 1887-1967. Aquarium. 2 acts, comedy. L'Avant Scène, 336 (June 15, 1965), 10-40. Georges Sonnier, translator. In French.

6579. _____. Ce Qui Est Dit Est Dit.... 1 act. L'Avant Scène, 336 (June 15, 1965), 42-46. Georges Sonnier, translator. In French.

6580. _____. Una famiglia molto unita. 1 act. Il Dramma, n.s., 364 (January, 1967), 81-88. In Italian.

6581. _____. Farfalla ... farfalla.... 2 parts. Il Dramma, n.s., 365/366 (February/March, 1967), 47-67. In Italian.

6582. _____. Formiche. 3 acts. Il Dramma, n.s., 253 (October, 1957), 5-28. In Italian.

6583. _____. Il mondo d'acqua. 2 parts. Il Dramma, n.s., 306 (March, 1962), 6-42. In Italian.

6584. _____. Nero come un canarino. 2 parts. Il Dramma, n.s., 376/377 (January/February, 1968), 5-26. In Italian.

6585. _____. Il pendolo. 2 parts. Il Dramma, n.s., 322/323 (July/August, 1963), 16-41. In Italian.

6586. _____. Die Zwiebel. 2 parts. Il Dramma, n.s., 342 (March, 1965), 5-26. In Italian.

6587. Nicolai, Aldo, 1920- . Haute Sensibilité. 1 act, monologue. L'Avant Scène, 436 (November 1, 1969), 33-34. Georges Sonnier, adapter. In French.

6588. _____. Il soldato piccicó. 3 acts. Il Dramma, n.s., 273 (June, 1959), 24-48. In Italian.

6589. _____. Teresina. 2 acts. Il Dramma, n.s., 213 (September 15, 1954), 5-23. In Italian.

Nicoletti, Gianni, translator see Achard, M. 22

_____, translator see Ghelderode, M. de 3456

_____, translator see Simenon, G. 8282

6590. Nicolosi, Vito Mar. Ospizio "La pace." 1 act. Il Dramma, 85 (March 1, 1930), 33-38. In Italian.

_____. Sole. 1 act. Il Dramma, 121 (September 1, 1931), 35-41. In Italian.

6591. Nidess, Daniel Ary. My Chosen People. 1 act. One-Act Play Magazine, 3 (February, 1940), 144-158.

6592. Niedecker, Lorine. Fancy Another Day Gone. 1 act. New Directions, 1 (1936), 91-96.

6593. _____. The President of the Holding Company. 1 act. New Directions, 1 (1936), 89-90.

6594. Niggli, Josephina, 1911- . The Red Velvet Goat. 1 act. One-Act Play Magazine, 1 (July, 1937), 250-270.

6595. _____. Sunday Costs Five Pesos. 1 act, comedy. One-Act Play Magazine, 1 (January, 1938), 786-802.

6596. _____. This Is Villa! 1 act. One-Act Play Magazine, 2 (January, 1939), 611-638.

6597. Nightingale, E. M. Ariadne Exposed. 1 act. Plays, 25 (January, 1966), 15-20.

6598. _____. Arise, Sparta! 1 act. Plays, 32 (November, 1972), 75-79.

6599. _____. Incident Before Troy. 1 act. Plays, 26 (November, 1966), 86-90.

6600. Nightingale, E. M. The Truth About Croesus. 1 act, farce. Plays, 31 (November, 1971), 79-83.

_____, adapter see Aristophanes 335

6601. Nigond, Gabriel. La Nuit d'Augerge. 1 act. Petite Illustration, 87 (November 16, 1929), 1-10. In French.

6602. Nikl, Peter. Bessie Bosch. 1 act. Das Wort, 2 (December, 1936), 12-24. In German.

6602a. _____. On the Border. 1 act. One-Act Play Magazine, 2 (August-September, 1938), 298-314. Henry Kass, translator.

6603. Nilssen, Jerome. The Homecoming. 1 act. Resource, 7 (April, 1966), 13-17.

6604. Ninchi, Annibale. L'Ultima notte di Marlowe. 3 acts. Sipario, 187 (November, 1961), 49-63. In Italian.

6605. Nissen, Patricia J. The True Gift of Christmas. 1 act. Learning With ..., 3 (December, 1975), 7-8.

Nissim, Elio, translator see Osborne, J. 6894

_____, translator see Pinter, H. 7174, 7175, 7176, 7178

Nissim, Renzo, translator see Coward, N. 2078

6606. Nivoix, Paul. Amours. 3 acts. Petite Illustration, 87 (February 2, 1929), 1-30. In French.

6607. _____. Les Nouveaux Maîtres. 3 acts. Sipario, 4 (May, 1949), 41-63. Giulio Cesare Castello, translator. In Italian.

Niwa, Tamako, translator see Kanjincho 4545

6608. Noah, Robert, 1926- . The Advocate. 3 acts. Theatre Arts, 47 (November, 1963), 33-64.

Noakes, David, translator see Arnaud, G. 347

6609. Noble, Charles C. "There Is Room." 1 act. Christian Century, 47 (December 10, 1930), 1525-1526.

6610. Noblston, Allen. Sacrifice. 1 act. One-Act Play Magazine, 1 (September, 1937), 409-422.

6611. Noe, Yvan. Christian. 3 acts, comedy. Petite Illustration, 196 (January 16, 1937), 1-34. In French.

6612. _____. Ne Faisons pas un Reve. 1 act. L'Avant Scène, 176 (June 15, 1958), 45-48. In French.

6613. _____. Teddy e il suo partner. 3 acts. Il Dramma, 182 (March 15, 1934), 4-31. Manilio Miserocchi, translator. In Italian.

6614. _____. Teddy and Partner. 3 acts, comedy. Petite Illustration, 184 (March 11, 1933), 1-33. In French.

6615. Noguchi, Yone, 1875-1947. The Demon's Shell. 1 act. Poet Lore, 17 (No. 3, 1906), 44-49.

6616. _____. The Everlasting Sorrow. 1 act. The Egoist, 4 (October, 1917), 141-143.

6617. _____. The Melon Thief. 1 act. Poet Lore, 15 (Spring, 1904), 40-42.

6618. _____. The Mountain She-Devil. 1 act. Poet Lore, 29 (Autumn, 1918), 447-451.

6619. _____. The Perfect Jewel Maiden. 1 act. Poet Lore, 28 (Summer, 1917), 334-337.

6620. _____. The Shower: The Moon. 1 act. Poet Lore, 29 (Autumn, 1918), 455-458.

6621. _____. The Tears of the Birds. 1 act. Poet Lore, 29 (Autumn, 1918), 451-455.

6622. _____. The Willow Tree. 1 act. The Open Window, 9 (June, 1911), 129-135.

6623. Nohain, Franc. Le Chapeau Chinois. 1 act, comedy. Petite Illustration, 88 (September 6, 1930), 1-11. In French.

6624. Nohain, Jean, 1900- . Le Carnaval de Juillet. 2 acts, comedy. L'Avant Scène (OST), 6 (June, 1949), 1-38. In French.

6625. Nolan, Jeannette Covert, 1897- . Happy Christmas to All. 1 act. Plays, 3 (December, 1943), 27-34. AND Plays, 18 (December, 1958), 63-70.

6626. _____. Judge Douglas Presides. 1 act. Plays, 2 (January, 1943), 13-18.

6627. _____. Miss Barton Is Needed. 1 act. Plays, 10 (March, 1951), 19-32.

6628. Nolan, Paul Thomas, 1919- . America Is a Song. 1 act. Plays, 22 (March, 1963), 61-68.

6629. _____. And Christmas Is Its Name. 1 act. Plays, 19 (December, 1959), 87-95.

6630. _____. An Anton Chekhov Sort of Evening. 1 act. Plays, 27 (March, 1968), 1-12.

6631. _____. The Awakening of Granville. 1 act. Plays, 30 (December, 1970), 25-35.

6632. _____. The Awards Graduation. 1 act. Plays, 33 (May, 1974), 29-36.

6633. _____. The Beanstalk Kid. 1 act. Plays, 35 (March, 1976), 1-9.

6634. _____. Boshibari and the Two Thieves. 1 act. Plays, 19 (October, 1959), 83-86.

6635. _____. Cinderfellow. 1 act. Plays, 34 (December, 1974), 1-9.

6636. _____. The Courters. 1 act. Plays, 22 (January, 1963), 27-34.

6637. _____. The Double Nine of Chih Yvan. 1 act. Plays, 23 (October, 1963), 78-84.

6638. _____. Emma and the Professor's Coat. 1 act. Plays, 35 (March, 1976), 87-95.

6639. _____. Exit the Hero. 1 act. Plays, 33 (November, 1973), 13-22.

6640. _____. Four Letters from Algernon. 1 act. Plays, 29 (February, 1970), 19-29.

6641. _____. The French Cabinetmaker. 1 act. Plays, 22 (October, 1962), 37-44.

6642. _____. The Frog Who Wouldn't Be Kissed. 1 act. Plays, 35 (October, 1975), 28-36.

6643. _____. The Gates of Dinkelsbuehl. 1 act. Plays, 20 (April, 1961), 89-96.

6644. _____. Going Steady. 1 act. Plays, 23 (March, 1964), 27-34.

6645. _____. The Golden Voice of Erik. 1 act. Plays, 21 (November, 1961), 81-86.

6646. _____. Graduation Forecast. 1 act. Plays, 31 (May, 1972), 27-34.

6647. _____. The Happiest Hat. 1 act. Plays, 28 (April, 1969), 1-12.

6648. _____. Happy Ending. 1 act. Plays, 27 (April, 1968), 17-26.

6649. _____. Hi Down There. 1 act. Plays, 28 (October, 1968), 21-31.

6650. _____. Hidebound. 1 act. Plays, 33 (January, 1974), 24-33.

6651. _____. The Highland Fling. 1 act. Plays, 20 (February, 1961), 89-96.

6652. _____. The In-Group. 1 act. Plays, 27 (May, 1968), 93-103. AND Plays, 35 (May, 1976), 27-37.

6653. _____. Johnny Appleseed. Plays, 21 (March, 1962), 39-46.

6654. _____. A Leak in the Dike. 1 act. Plays, 19 (May, 1960), 79-84.

6655. _____. Licha's Birthday Serenade. 1 act. Plays, 20 (October, 1960), 77-82.

6656. _____. The Magic of Salamanca. 1 act. Plays, 21 (January, 1962), 48-54.

6657. _____. Masks of Various Colors. 1 act. Plays, 34 (May, 1975), 29-38.

6658. _____. Mr. Luck and Little Chance. 1 act. Plays, 33 (December, 1973), 13-24.

6659. _____. The Moon's Up There. 1 act. Plays, 22 (April, 1963), 1-10.

6660. _____. Our Sister, Sitya. 1 act. Plays, 19 (February, 1960), 91-96.

6661. _____. The Perils of Prophecy. 1 act. Plays, 32 (February, 1973), 1-10.

6662. _____. Pygmalion Tries Again. 1 act. Plays, 31 (April, 1972), 13-20.

6663. _____. Robin Hood and the Match at Nottingham. 1 act. Plays, 21 (October, 1961), 53-60.

6664. _____. The Skill of Pericles. 1 act. Plays, 21 (May, 1962), 54-60.

6665. _____. The Son of William Tell. 1 act. Plays, 19 (April, 1960), 81-87.

6666. _____. Stanislaw and the Wolf. 1 act. Plays, 19 (January, 1960), 79-84.

6667. _____. Strangers and Neighbors. 1 act. Plays, 32 (November, 1972), 1-12.

6668. _____. The Straw Boy. 1 act. Plays, 17 (November, 1957), 29-36.

6669. _____. Sunshine and Smiles. 1 act. Plays, 34 (March, 1975), 37-46.

6670. _____. Take It from the Beginning. 1 act. Plays, 28 (May, 1969), 13-23.

6671. _____. Temporary Job. 1 act. Plays, 29 (October, 1969), 25-36.

6672. _____. The Test. 1 act. Plays, 34 (April, 1975), 15-24.

6673. _____. This Younger Generation. 1 act. Plays, 28 (May, 1969), 89-98.

6674. _____. Trash and Treasure. 1 act. Plays, 28 (January, 1969), 33-44.

6675. _____. Tree to the Sky. 1 act. Plays, 25 (May, 1966), 27-39.

6676. _____. The Trial of Peter Zenger. 2 acts. Plays, 25 (April, 1966), 13-25. AND Plays, 32 (April, 1973), 84-96.

6677. _____. The Trouble with Christmas. 1 act. Plays, 32 (December, 1972), 1-10.

6678. _____. Tug-of-War. 1 act. Plays, 32 (January, 1973), 1-10.

6679. _____. A View of the Sea. 1 act. Plays, 24 (March, 1965), 31-41.

6680. _____. What's Zymurgy with You? 1 act. Plays, 28 (March, 1969), 1-12.

6681. _____. Where You Are. 1 act. Plays, 34 (February, 1975), 26-34.

6682. _____. The Whole City's Down Below. 1 act. Plays, 27 (December, 1967), 12-22.

6683. _____. Who's Compatible? 1 act. Plays, 31 (October, 1971), 27-35.

6684. _____. Wishing Well or Ill. 1 act. Plays, 29 (December, 1969), 13-25.

6685. _____. A Young Man of Considerable Value. 1 act. Plays, 28 (November, 1968), 13-24.

_____, adapter see Chekhov, A. P. 1776

_____, adapter see Clemens, S. L. 1881

_____, adapter see France, A. 3245

_____, adapter see Goldoni, C. 3608

_____, adapter see Goldsmith, O. 3612

_____, adapter see Hardy, T. 3907

_____, adapter see Ibsen, H. 4360

_____, adapter see Molière 6117, 6124

_____, adapter see Poe, E. A. 7222

_____, adapter see Smith, R. P. 8351

_____, adapter see Wells, H. G. 9289

_____, adapter see Wilde, O. 9359

6686. Nono, Luigi. Intolleranza. 2 parts. Sipario, 19 (December, 1964), 57-60. In Italian.

6687. Nooshich, Branislav. The Prince of Semberia. 1 act. Poet Lore, 33 (Spring, 1922), 85-96. Luka Djurichick and Bertha W. Clark, translators.

6688. Norcross, E. Blanche. Pied Piper's Land. 1 act. Plays, 35 (January, 1976), 47-53.

Norden, Ruth, translator see Brecht, B. 1312

6689. Nordseth, Mary. The Evening. 1 act. Trace, 67 (1968), 110-113.

6690. _____. The Game. 1 act. Trace, 64 (1967), 94-99.

6691. Norman, Charles, 1904- . Faustus. 1 act. Theatre Arts, 13 (April, 1930), 309-312.

6692. _____. Telemachus. 1 act. Theatre Arts, 12 (December, 1928), 879-884.

6693. Norman, Frank, 1930- . Insideout. 2 acts. Plays and Players, 17 (February, 1970), 61-78.

6694. Norman, Mrs. George. Green Cushions. 1 act. Living Age, 256 (February 29, 1908), 554-557.

Norsa, Angelo, translator see Alvarez Quintero, S. and J. Alvarez Quintero 173

6695. Norse, Julian. The Throne. 1 act. Dramatika, 3 (March, 1969), 46.

6696. Nothnagle, Claribel. Jack Just Anybody. 1 act. Plays, 3 (February, 1944), 53-56.

6697. _____. Mother Goose's Children. 1 act. Plays, 2 (January, 1943), 50-52.

6698. _____. Sally Ann Remembers. 1 act. Plays, 2 (May, 1943), 60-62.

6699. Novac, Anna. Match a la une. 1 act. L'Avant Scène, 568 (July 15, 1975), 31-40. In French.

6700. _____. Un Peu de Tendresse.... Ou le Complexe de la Soupe. 2 acts. L'Avant Scène, 442 (February 1, 1970), 38-45. In French.

6701. Novas, Himilce. Free This Day: A Trial in Seven Exhibits. Scripts, 1 (April, 1972), 58-69.

6702. Novelli, Claudio. I condottieri. 2 parts. Il Dramma, n.s., 334/335 (July/August, 1964), 58-82. In Italian.

6703. Novelli, Enrico. L'assassino. 1 act. Il Dramma, 439/440 (December 1/31, 1944), 71-77. In Italian.

Noyes, George Rapall, translator see Blok, A. 1011

_____, translator see Jirasek, A. 4469

_____, translator see Kvapil, J. 4742

_____, translator see Ostrovsky, A. 6911, 6913, 6916

_____, translator see Vojnovich, I. 9169

_____, translator see Yushkevich, S. 9627

_____, translator see Zeyer, J. 9645, 9646

6704. Nozière, Ferdinando. Quella vecchia canaglia.... 3 acts. Il Dramma, 162 (May 15, 1933), 4-37. Alessandro de Stefani, translator. In Italian.

Nozière, Fernand, translator see Evreinoff, N. N. 2886

Ntshona, Winston see Fugard, A. 3336

Nugent, Elliott, 1899- see Nugent, J. C. 6705

6705. Nugent, John Charles, 1878-1947 and Elliott Nugent, 1899- . Kempy. 1 act, comedy. Everybody's Magazine, 47 (November, 1922), 83-88.

6706. Nulli, Edoardo. Il tempo el la signoria angoscia. 1 act. Il Dramma, n.s., 96 (November 1, 1949), 41-50. In Italian.

6707. Nuttall, Jeff. The People Show. 1 act. Gambit, 4 (No. 16), 103-110.

6708. Nutter, Carolyn F., adapter. Red Riding Hood and the Wolf. 1 act. Plays, 11 (April, 1952), 62-66.

6709. Nutting, Herbert Chester. Fovea. 2 acts. Classical Journal, 14 (December, 1918), 176-184. In Latin.

6710. _____. Passer. 1 act. Classical Journal, 11 (April, 1916), 418-427. In Latin.

6711. _____. Situalae. 2 acts. Classical Journal, 15 (June, 1920), 535-545. In Latin.

6712. Nyanysa, a Zulu Play. 1 act. 19th Century, 70 (August, 1911), 321-338. Edith Lyttleton, translator.

O

6713. Oates, Joyce Carol, 1938- . Ontological Proof of My Existence. 1 act. Partisan Review, 37 (No. 4, 1970), 471-497.

6714. Obaldia, Réné de, 1918- . L'Air du Large. 1 act. L'Avant Scène, 324 (December 15, 1964), 20-31. In French.

6715. _____. La Baby-Sitter. L'Avant Scène, 487 (January 15, 1972), 21-24, 29-31, 33-39. In French.

6716. _____. Classe Terminale. L'Avant Scène, 519 (June 1, 1973), 7-16. In French.

6717. _____. Un coniglio molto caldo. Il Dramma, n.s., 262 (July, 1958), 51-55. Adriana Greco, translator. In Italian.

6718. _____. Cosmonaute Agricole. L'Avant Scène, 418 (January 15, 1969), 27-36. In French.

6719. _____. Le Dammé. 1 act. L'Avant Scène, 324 (December 15, 1964), 32-35. In French.

6720. _____. Le Defunt. 1 act. L'Avant Scène, 169, 38-41. In French.

6721. _____. Del vento tra i rami del sassafrasso. Sipario, 251 (March, 1967), 49-64. Massimo Dursi, adapter. In Italian.

6722. _____. Deux Femmes Pour un Fantome. L'Avant Scène, 487 (January 15, 1972), 7-20. In French.

6723. _____. Du Vent dans les Branches de Sassafras. 2 acts, comedy. L'Avant Scène, 350 (February 1, 1966), 11-36. In French.

6724. _____. An Edinburgh Impromptu. 1 act. New Writers, 4 (1967), 75-79.

6725. _____. Edouard et Agrippine. 1 act. L'Avant Scène, 230, 29-33. In French.

6726. _____. Edward and Agrippina. 1 act. Gambit, 2, 58-67. Donald Watson, translator.

6727. _____. ...Et a la Fin Etait le Bang. 2 acts, comedy. L'Avant Scène, 551 (November 1, 1974), 3-39. In French.

6728. _____. Le Général Inconnu. 1 act. L'Avant Scène, 324 (December 14, 1964), 9-18. AND L'Avant Scène, 469/470 (April 1/15, 1971), 95-106. In French.

6729. _____. Genousie. 2 acts, comedy. L'Avant Scène, 230, 8-27. In French.

6730. _____. The Guillotine Mazurka. 1 act. Chelsea, 13 (June, 1963), 32-48. Robert Cordier, translator.

6731. _____. Monsieur Klebs et Rozalie. 2 acts, comedy. L'Avant Scène, 573 (October 15, 1975), 3-32. In French.

6732. _____. Petite Suite Poetique Resolument Optimiste. L'Avant Scène, 487 (January 15, 1972), 43-45. In French.

6733. _____. Le Satyre de la Villette. 2 acts, comedy. L'Avant Scène, 288 (May 15, 1963), 10-36. In French.

6734. _____. Wind in the Branches of the Sassafras. 2 acts, comedy. Modern International Drama, 1 (March, 1968), 154-180. Joseph G. Foster, translator.

6735. Obata, Shigeyoshi. The Melon Thief. 1 act. Drama, 10 (December, 1919), 104-107.

6736. Obey, André, 1892- . Une Fille Pour du Vent. Il Dramma, n. s., 293 (February, 1961), 8-28. Paolo Campanella, translator. In Italian.

6737. _____. L'Homme de Cendres. 3 acts. L'Avant Scène (OST), 16 (January, 1950), 3-42. In French.

6738. _____. Maria. 2 parts. Il Dramma, n. s., 118 (October 1, 1950), 7-32. Paolo Campanella, translator. In Italian.

6739. _____. Noè. 5 acts. Il Dramma, n. s., 53 (January 15, 1948), 7-27. Alessandro Brissoni, translator. In Italian.

6740. _____. Les Trois Coups de Minuit. 2 acts. L'Avant Scène, 188 (January 1, 1959), 7-36. In French.

6741. _____. L'uomo di cenere. 3 acts. Il Dramma, n. s., 138 (August 1, 1951), 7-42. Paolo Campanella, translator. In Italian.

_____, adapter see Rose, R. 7699

_____ see also Martens, G. M. 5623

6742. Oboler, Arch. I Have No Prayer. 1 act. Dramatika, 8 (Fall, 1971), n. p.

6743. O'Brien, Edna. The Wedding Dress. 1 act. Mademoiselle, 58 (November, 1963), 134-135, 190-199.

6744. O'Brien, Edward Joseph Harrington, 1890-1941. At the Flowing of the Tide. 1 act. Forum, 52 (September, 1914), 375-386.

_____, translator see Milosz, O. W. 6068

6745. O'Brien, Flann. The Insect Play. 1 act. Journal of Irish Literature, 3 (January, 1974), 24-39.

6746. _____. The Man with Four Legs. 1 act. Journal of Irish Literature, 3 (January, 1974), 40-55.

6747. O'Brien, Kate, 1898- . That Lady. 3 acts. Theatre Arts, 34 (June, 1950), 59-88.

6748. O'Brien, Liam, 1913- . The Remarkable Mr. Pennypacker. 3 acts, comedy. L'Avant Scène, 198 (June 1, 1959), 8-34. Roger-Ferdinand, adapter. In French.

6749. _____. The Remarkable Mr. Pennypacker. 3 acts, comedy. Theatre Arts, 39 (April, 1955), 36-65.

6750. O'Brien, Seumas, 1880- . The Black Bottle. 1 act. Senior Scholastic, 50 (March 17, 1947), 17-18, 22-23.

6751. _____. The Wild Boar. 1 act. Poet Lore, 38 (1927), 536-550.

6752. O'Byrne, Dermot. On the Hill. 1 act. Irish Review, 2 (February, 1913), 648-663.

6753. O'Casey, Sean, 1884-1964. Bedtime Story. 1 act, satire. L'Avant Scène, 230, 35-43. Michel Hobart, translator. In French.

6754. _____. The Drums of Father Ned. 3 acts, comedy. Theatre Arts, 44 (May, 1960), 23-52.

6755. _____. Juno and the Paycock. 3 acts. Il Dramma, 397/398 (March 1/15, 1943), 40-62. Alessandra Scalero, translator.

6756. _____. Kathleen Listens In. 1 act. Tulane Drama Review, 5 (June, 1961), 36-50.

6757. _____. The Plough and the Stars. 4 acts. Il Dramma, n.s., 56 (March 1, 1948), 9-36. G. Galassi-Beria and O. Olivet, translators. In Italian.

6758. _____. The Plough and the Stars. 4 acts. Spectaculum, 6 (1963), 211-263. Georg Goyert, translator. In German.

Ochiai, T., translator see Motokiyo, Z. 6270

O'Connell, Richard L., translator see Lorca, F. G. 5044

6759. O'Connell, Thomas Edward. Alfie. 1 act. One-Act Play Magazine, 4 (November-December, 1941), 487-509.

6760. _____. Carolette, a Little Song for Christmas Eve. 1 act. One-Act Play Magazine, 3 (November-December, 1940), 538-557.

6761. _____. Interim. 1 act. One-Act Play Magazine, 3 (January, 1940), 57-71.

6762. _____. Mr. Lincoln's Grave. 1 act. Plays, 3 (January, 1944), 67-75.

6763. _____. A Question of Understanding. 1 act. One-Act Play Magazine, 3 (March-April, 1940), 272-277.

6764. O'Connor, Frank, 1903-1966. At the Wakehouse. 1 act. Theatre Arts, 10 (June, 1926), 412-414.

6765. _____. The Statue's Daughter. 3 acts, fantasy. Journal of Irish Literature, 4 (January, 1975), 59-117.

O'Connor, Oleta Joan, translator see Blok, A. 1011

6766. O'Connor, Patricia. My Dear! 1 act, comedy. Drama, 14 (February, 1924), 188-189.

O'Connor, Patricia W., translator see Castro, J. A. 1659

6767. O'Connor, Patrick, 1915- . Nothing Very Much Thank You. 1 act. First Stage, 7 (Winter, 1967-1968), 230-248.

6768. _____. The Wooden Box. 1 act. First Stage, 4 (Spring, 1965), 26-32.

Oddera, translator see Shaw, I. and J.-P. Aumont 8227

6769. Odea, Mark Leland Hill. Shivaree. 1 act, comedy. Drama, 11 (October, 1920), 11-15.

6770. _____. The Song of Solomon. 1 act. Drama, 11 (February, 1921), 154-157.

O'Dempsey, F., translator see Blok, A. 1009

6771. Odets, Clifford, 1906-1963. The Country Girl. 2 acts. Il Dramma, n.s., 235 (April, 1956), 13-44. Mirella Ducceschi, translator. In Italian.

6772. Odets, Clifford, 1906-1963. The Country Girl. 2 acts. Theatre Arts, 36 (May, 1952), 58-86.

6773. _____. Waiting for Lefty. Sipario, 1 (August-September, 1946), 47-57. Bruno Archangeli, translator. In Italian.

6774. Odio, Eunice, 1922- . Transit of Fire (Fragments). 1 act. New World Writing, 14 (1958), 102-113. Dudley Fitts, translator.

6775. O'Donnell, Mark. Three Short Plays: Bricks; Neck and Neck; The 1812 Overalls. Dramatics, 43 (May, 1972), 4-9.

6776. O'Farachain, Rosbeard. Lost Light. 1 act. Dublin Magazine, n.s., 19 (October-December, 1944), 16-55.

6777. Office de L'Etoile, L'. 1 act. Mesures, 4 (July 15, 1938), 173-185. Hermann Closson, translator. In French.

6778. O'Flaherty, Liam. Darkness. 3 acts, tragedy. New Coterie, 3 (Summer, 1926), 42-68.

6779. Ogden, Ruth. Among the Pines. 2 acts. St. Nicholas, 11 (November, 1883), 58-65.

6780. Oglesbee, Delle Houghton. Ten Fingers of François; Christmas Play of Old Provence. 1 act. Drama, 14 (November, 1923), 65-69.

6781. Oglesbee, Frank W. Windfalls and Grand Designs. 1 act. Dramatika, 3 (March, 1969), 39-44.

6782. O'Grady, Moira. Symphony in O Flat. 1 act. Dramatika, 6 (Fall, 1970), 24-27.

6783. O'Hara, Frank, 1926-1966. The General Returns from One Place to Another. Art and Literature, 4 (Spring, 1965), 125-155.

Ojetti, Paola, 1911- , translator see Albee, E. 99

_____, translator see Barillet, P. and J. P. Grédy 584

_____, translator see Blackmore, P. 981

_____, translator see DuMaurier, D. 2693

_____, translator see Hanley, W. 3889

_____, translator see Husson, A. 4329

_____, translator see Morley, R. and N. Langley 6233

_____, translator see Shaw, G. B. 8210, 8221

6784. O'Keefe, John. Wild Oats, or, The Strolling Gentleman. 5 acts. Baltimore Repertory, 1 (1811), supplement, 1-32.

6785. O'Kelly, Seumas, 1881-1920. Driftwood. 1 act, comedy. Dublin Magazine, 1 (November, 1923), 287-306.

6786. _____. The Matchmakers. 1 act, comedy. One-Act Play Magazine, 1 (February, 1938), 867-891.

Oland, Edith, translator see Strindberg, A. 8579

Oland, Warner, translator see Strindberg, A. 8579

6787. Oldmeadow, Katherine L. St. Nicholas. 1 act. St. Nicholas, 65 (December, 1937), 14-17, 37, 41, 50.

6788. Olfson, Lewy. Avon Calling! 1 act. Plays, 31 (May, 1972), 73-78.

6789. _____. A Birthday Anthem for America. 1 act. Plays, 35 (November, 1975), 77-78.

6790. _____. The Bride of Gorse-Bracken Hall. 1 act. Plays, 34 (February, 1975), 35-40.

6791. _____. Cause for Celebration. 1 act. Plays, 35 (January, 1976), 79-84.

6792. _____. Christmas Coast to Coast. 1 act. Plays, 21 (December, 1961), 23-32.

6793. _____. Cinderella Revisited. 1 act. Plays, 32 (December, 1972), 23-29.

6794. _____. A Couple of Right Smart Fellers. 1 act. Plays, 32 (February, 1973), 91-96.

6795. _____. Equal Frights. 1 act. Plays, 32 (October, 1972), 69-73.

6796. _____. La Forza del Miss Muffet. 1 act. Plays, 32 (January, 1973), 63-66.

6797. _____. Great Caesar's Ghost! 1 act. Plays, 31 (January, 1972), 81-84.

6798. _____. Happy Haunting! 1 act. Plays, 33 (October, 1973), 87-92.

6799. _____. Hen Party. 1 act. Plays, 32 (March, 1973), 77-81.

6800. _____. The Incredible Housing Shortage. 1 act. Plays, 31 (March, 1972), 80-84.

6801. _____. Joanna Livermore Parrot. 1 act. Plays, 32 (May, 1973), 69-72.

6802. _____. A King Is Born. 1 act. Plays, 18 (December, 1958), 87-95.

Olfson

6803. _____. The Last Time I Saw Paris. 1 act. Plays, 33 (February, 1974), 79-83.

6804. _____. Meet Miss Stone-Age! 1 act. Plays, 32 (April, 1973), 79-83.

6805. _____. My Son, the Prince. 1 act. Plays, 30 (January, 1971), 92-96.

6806. _____. The Once and Future Frog. 1 act. Plays, 33 (April, 1974), 75-79.

6807. _____. Once I Chased a Butterfly. 1 act. Plays, 33 (May, 1974), 37-43.

6808. _____. The Saga of John Trueheart. 1 act. Plays, 34 (March, 1975), 69-74.

6809. _____. Sail On! Sail On! 1 act. Plays, 31 (October, 1971), 77-81.

6810. _____. Second Chance. 1 act. Plays, 34 (November, 1974), 35-46.

6811. _____. Sing a Song of Holiday! 1 act. Plays, 35 (December, 1975), 69-71.

6812. _____. The Sky's the Limit! 1 act. Plays, 35 (October, 1975), 59-64.

6813. _____. Spying High. 1 act. Plays, 30 (October, 1970), 61-65.

6814. _____. The Ten-Year-Old Detective. 1 act, melodrama. Plays, 29 (May, 1970), 57-61.

6815. _____. Three Fables from a Broken Fortune Cookie. 1 act. Plays, 34 (May, 1975), 69-75.

6816. _____. The Three Swine of Most Small Stature. 1 act. Plays, 30 (March, 1971), 91-95.

6817. _____. Try Data-Date! 1 act. Plays, 30 (May, 1971), 77-80.

6818. _____, adapter. Christmas for Cosette. 1 act. Plays, 20 (December, 1960), 87-95.

6819. _____, adapter. The Crowning of King Arthur. 1 act. Plays, 24 (December, 1964), 87-96.

_____, adapter see Alcott, L. M. 111

Olfson

_____, adapter see Aldrich, T. B. 121

_____, adapter see Barrie, J. M. 627

_____, adapter see Brontë, C. 1338

_____, adapter see Brontë, E. 1340

_____, adapter see Burnett, F. H. 1439

_____, adapter see Cervantes Saavedra, M. de 1689

_____, adapter see Chaucer, G. 1742

_____, adapter see Clemens, S. L. 1877, 1879, 1890

_____, adapter see Dickens, C. 2469, 2471, 2476, 2479, 2481

_____, adapter see Dodgson, C. L. 2516, 2518

_____, adapter see Doyle, A. C. 2578, 2580

_____, adapter see Dumas, A. 2685

_____, adapter see Hale, H. H. 3834

_____, adapter see Hawthorne, N. 3989

_____, adapter see Heine, H. 4034

_____, adapter see Homer 4155, 4156

_____, adapter see Hope, A. 4161

_____, adapter see Hugo, V. 4315

_____, adapter see Irving, W. 4406

_____, adapter see James, H. 4436

_____, adapter see Jokai, M. 4492, 4493

_____, adapter see Kipling, R. 4638

_____, adapter see Maupassant, G. de 5681

_____, adapter see Molière 6112, 6126

_____, adapter see Poe, E. A. 7221

_____, adapter see Rostand, E. 7717

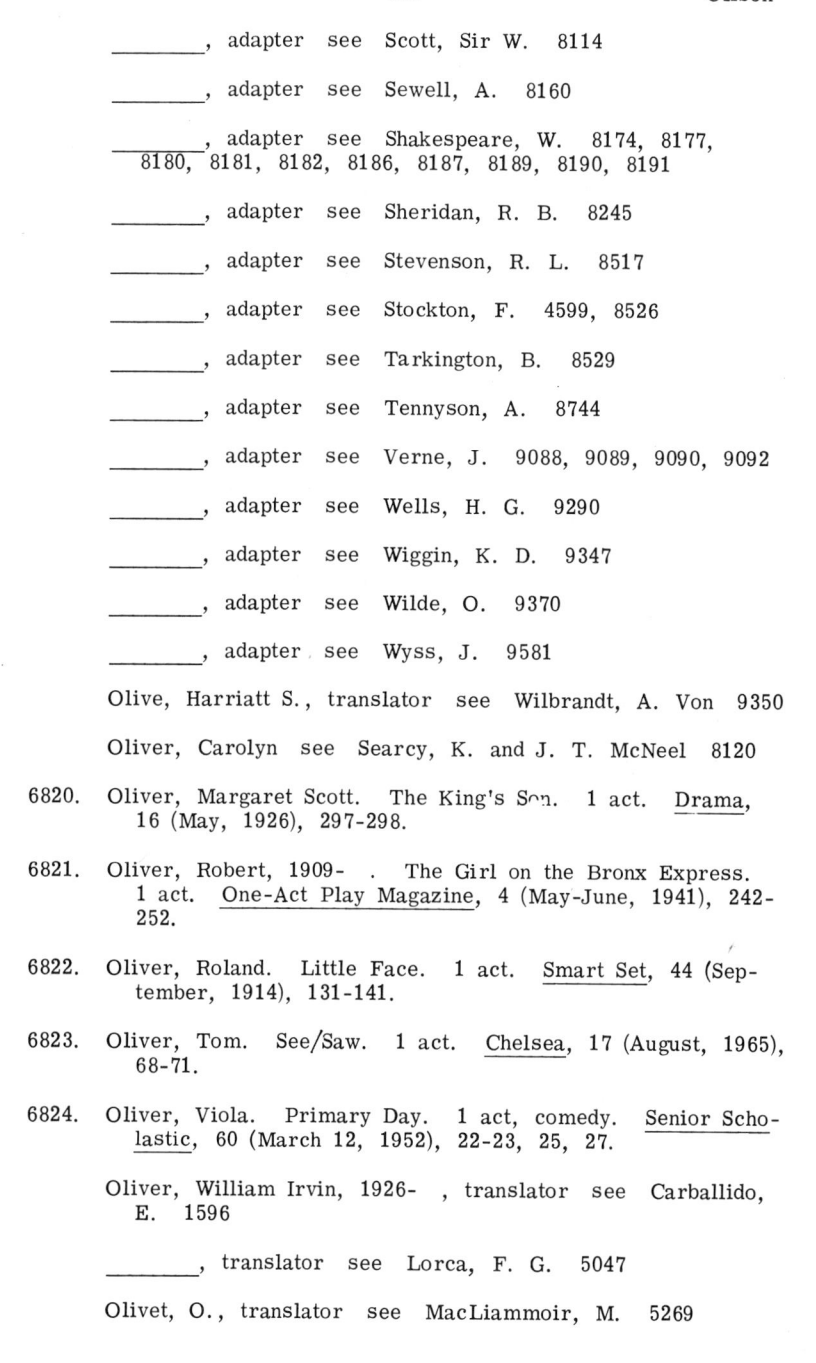

_____, adapter see Scott, Sir W. 8114

_____, adapter see Sewell, A. 8160

_____, adapter see Shakespeare, W. 8174, 8177, 8180, 8181, 8182, 8186, 8187, 8189, 8190, 8191

_____, adapter see Sheridan, R. B. 8245

_____, adapter see Stevenson, R. L. 8517

_____, adapter see Stockton, F. 4599, 8526

_____, adapter see Tarkington, B. 8529

_____, adapter see Tennyson, A. 8744

_____, adapter see Verne, J. 9088, 9089, 9090, 9092

_____, adapter see Wells, H. G. 9290

_____, adapter see Wiggin, K. D. 9347

_____, adapter see Wilde, O. 9370

_____, adapter see Wyss, J. 9581

Olive, Harriatt S., translator see Wilbrandt, A. Von 9350

Oliver, Carolyn see Searcy, K. and J. T. McNeel 8120

6820. Oliver, Margaret Scott. The King's Son. 1 act. Drama, 16 (May, 1926), 297-298.

6821. Oliver, Robert, 1909- . The Girl on the Bronx Express. 1 act. One-Act Play Magazine, 4 (May-June, 1941), 242-252.

6822. Oliver, Roland. Little Face. 1 act. Smart Set, 44 (September, 1914), 131-141.

6823. Oliver, Tom. See/Saw. 1 act. Chelsea, 17 (August, 1965), 68-71.

6824. Oliver, Viola. Primary Day. 1 act, comedy. Senior Scholastic, 60 (March 12, 1952), 22-23, 25, 27.

Oliver, William Irvin, 1926- , translator see Carballido, E. 1596

_____, translator see Lorca, F. G. 5047

Olivet, O., translator see MacLiammoir, M. 5269

_____, translator see O'Casey, S. 6757

6825. Olivieri, Egisto. La casa lontana. 3 acts. Il Dramma, 190 (July 15, 1934), 4-29. In Italian.

6826. Olmo, Lauro. La noticia. 1 act. Sipario, 256-257 (August-September, 1967), 70-71. Maria Luisa Aguirre d'Amico, translator. In Italian.

6827. Olson, Elder, 1909- . The Abstract Tragedy--A Comedy of Masks. 1 act. First Stage, 2 (Summer, 1963), 166-186.

6828. _____. A Crack in the Universe. 3 acts. First Stage, 1 (Spring, 1962), 9-33.

6829. _____. The Sorcerer's Apprentices. 1 act, comedietina. Western Review, 21 (Autumn, 1956), 5-14.

6830. Oltramare, Georges. L'Escalier de Service. 4 acts, comedy. Petite Illustration, 88 (February 15, 1930), 1-26. In French.

6831. Olyesha, Yuri. The Conspiracy of Feelings. 4 acts. Drama and Theatre, 7 (Fall, 1968), 20-38. Daniel C. Gerould and Eleanor S. Gerould.

Olynes, Alexander, translator see Mozo, J. L. 6283

6832. On the Docks, a Peking Opera. Chinese Literature, 1 (1969), 3-53. AND revised edition. Chinese Literature, 5 (1972), 52-98.

6833. O'Neil, George, 1898-1940. Ladies at Twelve. 1 act, comedy. Smart Set, 55 (July, 1918), 73-80.

6834. O'Neill, Eugene, 1888-1953. Ah, Wilderness. 4 acts. Il Dramma, 388 (October 15, 1942), 5-31. In Italian.

6835. _____. All God's Chillun Got Wings. 2 acts. American Mercury, 1 (February, 1924), 129-148.

6836. _____. Anna Christie. 4 acts. Il Dramma, 384 (August 15, 1942), 7-23. Alessandra Scalero, translator. In Italian.

6837. _____. Before Breakfast. 1 act. Il Dramma, 401 (May 1, 1943), 37-40. Maria Bianca Gallinaro, translator. In Italian.

6838. _____. Before Breakfast. 1 act, tragedy. Golden Book, 15 (February, 1932), 151-156.

6839. _____. Beyond the Horizon. 3 acts. Il Dramma, 376/

377 (April 15/May 1, 1942), 13-62. Alessandra Scalero, translator. In Italian.

6840. _____. Days Without End. 4 acts. Il Dramma, n.s., 23/24 (October 15/November 1, 1946), 11-39. Mario Forni, translator. In Italian.

6841. _____. Diff'rent. 2 acts. Il Dramma, 412/413 (October 15/November 1, 1943), 29-46. Vinicio Marinucci, translator. In Italian.

6842. _____. The Dreamy Kid. 1 act. Theatre Arts, 4 (January, 1920), 41-56.

6843. _____. The Emperor Jones. 1 act, tragedy. Golden Book, 3 (April, 1926), 517-530.

6844. _____. The Emperor Jones. 1 act, tragedy. Theatre Arts, 5 (January, 1921), 29-59.

6845. _____. The First Man. 4 acts. Il Dramma, n.s., 1 (November 15, 1945), 7-28. Bianca Gallinaro, translator. In Italian.

6846. _____. The Great God Brown. 4 acts. Il Dramma, 391/392 (December 1/15, 1942), 37-55. Alessandra Scalero, translator. In Italian.

6847. _____. Hughie. 1 act. Sipario, 16 (March, 1961), 52-58. Amleto Micozzi, translator. In Italian.

6848. _____. Hughie. 1 act. Spectaculum, 3 (1960), 303-327. In German.

6849. _____. The Iceman Cometh. 4 acts. Il Dramma, n.s., 75/76 (January 1, 1949), 14-76. In Italian.

6850. _____. Ile. 1 act. Golden Book, 9 (February, 1929), 87-93.

6851. _____. Ile. 1 act. Scholastic, 28 (February 15, 1936), 4-6, 8, 20.

6852. _____. Ile. 1 act. Smart Set, 55 (May, 1918), 89-100.

6853. _____. In the Zone. 1 act. Scholastic, 38 (January 27, 1941), 17-21, 27.

6854. _____. Long Day's Journey Into Night. 4 acts. Sipario, 12 (May, 1957), 34-76. Amleto Micozzi, translator. In Italian.

6855. _____. The Long Voyage Home. 1 act. Il Dramma, 180 (February 15, 1934), 34-41. In Italian.

O'Neill   478

6856. _____. The Long Voyage Home. 1 act. Smart Set, 53 (October, 1917), 83-94.

6857. _____. A Moon for the Misbegotten. 4 acts. Il Dramma, n.s., 251/252 (August/September, 1957), 12-47. Amleto Micozzi, translator. In Italian.

6858. _____. The Moon of the Caribbees. 1 act. Il Dramma, 174 (November 15, 1933), 36-43. In Italian.

6859. _____. The Moon of the Caribbees. 1 act. Smart Set, 55 (August, 1918), 73-86.

6860. _____. Mourning Becomes Electra. 3 parts, tragedy. Il Dramma, 361/362 (September 1/15, 1941), 16-68. In Italian.

6861. _____. The Rope. 1 act. Il Dramma, 414/415/416 (November 15/December 1/15, 1943), 67-74. Franco Rossi, translator. In Italian.

6862. _____. Strange Interlude. 2 parts, 9 acts. Il Dramma, n.s., 6/7 (February 1/15, 1946), 13-75. Bice Chiappelli, translator. In Italian.

6863. _____. A Touch of the Poet. 4 acts. Sipario, 13 (November, 1958), 37-58. Amleto Micozzi, translator. In Italian.

6864. _____. Welded. 3 acts. Il Dramma, 402/403 (May 15/June 1, 1943), 37-52. Maria Bianca Gallinaro, translator. In Italian.

6865. _____. Where the Cross Is Made. 1 act. Scholastic, 16 (February 1, 1930), 6-8, 12, 28.

6866. O'Neill, Mary Devenport. Cain. 1 act. Dublin Magazine, n.s., 13 (October-December, 1938), 30-36.

6867. _____. Out of the Darkness. 1 act. Dublin Magazine, n.s., 22 (July-September, 1947), 1-24.

6868. O'Neill, Michael, 1913- and Jeremy Seabrook. The Bosom of the Family. 2 acts. Plays and Players, 18 (September, 1971), 71-84.

6869. _____. Life Price. 1 act. Plays and Players, 16 (March, 1969), 31-43.

6870. Oost, Regina. Living Water. 1 act. Learning With..., 3 (December, 1975), 25-26.

6871. Open Theater, The. Terminal, a Collective Work Created by the Open Theater Ensemble, Text by Susan Yankowitz. Scripts, 1 (November, 1971), 17-45.

6872. Oppenheim, James, 1882-1932. Prelude. 1 act. Seven Arts, 1 (January, 1917), 240-259.

6873. _____. The Shadow in the White House. 1 act. Seven Arts, 2 (July, 1917), 263-269.

6874. Orczy, Baroness Emmuska, 1865-1947. The Scarlet Pimpernel. 1 act. Plays, 26 (May, 1967), 93-108. Michael T. Leech, adapter.

6875. Ordway, Sally. Three Short Sketches: Cross-Country, West Coast; Crabs; Cross-Country, East Coast. Scripts, 1 (December, 1971), 26-35.

Oreglia, Giacomo, translator see Bergman, H. 815

_____, translator see Lagerkvist, P. 4764

O'Rell, Max, pseud. see Blouet, P. 1017

6876. Ori, Luciano. Il clinofilo. 1 act. Il Dramma, 44, no. 2 (November, 1968), 80-83. In Italian.

6877. O'Riordan, Conal Holmes O'Connell, 1874-1948. His Majesty's Pleasure. 3 acts, comedy. Irish Review, 2 (September, October, November, 1912), 355-369; 431-443; 481-493.

6878. Orkeny, Istvan. Totek. 2 acts. Sipario, 25 (July, 1970), 48-64. Magda Zalan, translator. In Italian.

6879. Orlovitz, Gil. Gray. 1 act. Literary Review, 2 (Winter, 1958-59), 206-308.

6880. _____. Stevie Guy. 3 acts. Quarterly Review of Literature, 6 (No. 1, 3, 1950, 1951), 24-49; 245-298.

6881. Ormandy, Edith. Little Ida and the Flowers. Plays, 11 (May, 1952), 60-63.

6882. Orme, Frank. Graduation Present. 1 act. Plays, 3 (May, 1944), 21-27.

Orna, D. L., translator see Gantillon, S. 3367

6883. Ortmayer, Roger. How to Get to the End of the Fourth of July. 1 act. Southwest Review, 48 (Autumn, 1963), 313-322.

6884. Orton, Joe, 1933-1967. Le Locataire. 2 acts. L'Avant

Scène, 483 (November 15, 1971), 7-35. Eric Kahane, translator. In French.

6885. _____. Loot. 2 acts. Sipario, (April, 1968), 44-58. Guidarino Guidi. In Italian.

6886. _____. Until She Screams. 1 act. Evergreen Review, 14 (May, 1970), 51-53.

6887. Osborn, Carolyn. The Somebodies. 1 act. Plays, 31 (January, 1972), 73-76.

6888. Osborn, Paul, 1901- . On Borrowed Time. 2 parts. Il Dramma, n. s., 46 (October 1, 1947), 11-37. Gigi Cane, translator. In Italian.

6889. _____. Point of No Return. 3 acts. Theatre Arts, 37 (March, 1953), 34-64.

6890. Osborne, Duffield. Xanthippe on Woman Suffrage. 1 act. Yale Review, 4 (April, 1915), 590-607.

6891. Osborne, Hubert. Shore Leave. 1 act. Everybody's Magazine, 48 (January, 1923), 150-156.

6892. Osborne, John James, 1929- . L'albergo di Amsterdam. 2 parts, comedy. Il Dramma, (August-September, 1974), 25-55. Guidarino Guidi, translator. In Italian.

6893. _____. The Entertainer. Sipario, 13 (August-September, 1958), 39-65. Amleto Micozzi, translator. In Italian.

6894. _____. Un Luogo che vuol chiamarsi Roma. Il Dramma, 50 (January, 1974), 25-51. Elio Nissim, translator. In Italian.

6895. _____. Luther. 3 acts. L'Avant Scène, 338 (July 15, 1965), 11-33. Pol Quentin, translator. In French.

6896. _____. Un Patriota per me. 3 acts. Il Dramma, (May, 1974), 25-67. Guidarino Guidi, translator. In Italian.

6897. _____ and Anthony Creighton. Epitaph for George Dillon. 3 acts. Sipario, 17 (August-September, 1962), 56-76. Remo Priolo, translator. In Italian.

6898. _____. Epitaph for George Dillon. 3 acts. Theatre Arts, 46 (March, 1962), 25-56.

Osbourne, Lloyd, 1868-1947 see Strong, A. 8584

6899. Oser, Janice Auritt. Fren's Friends. 1 act. Plays, 15 (January, 1956), 67-73.

6900. ———. The King's Calendar. 1 act. Plays, 31 (May, 1972), 43-48.

6901. ———. The King's Weather. 1 act. Plays, 16 (March, 1957), 49-54.

6902. ———. The Lost Note. 1 act. Plays, 17 (May, 1958), 54-58.

6903. ———. Professor Willy's Wisher-Switcher. 1 act. Plays, 12 (April, 1953), 56-60.

6904. ———. Running the Country. 1 act. Plays, 29 (November, 1969), 85-88.

6905. ———. A Small World. 1 act. Plays, 14 (March, 1955), 67-71.

6906. Osgood, Phillips Endecott. Midwinter-Eve Fire. 1 act. Horn Book, 15 (November, 1939), 359-367.

6907. ———. Midwinter-Eve Fire. 1 act. Scholastic, 35 (December 18, 1939), 17E-19E.

6908. O'Shea, Monica Barry. The Rushlight. 1 act. Drama, 28 (November, 1917), 602-615.

6909. Osness, Miriam S. Green Shutters. 1 act. Scholastic, 22 (April 29, 1933), 12-13.

6910. Ostertag, Donald E. Killing Frost. 1 act. Dramatics, 44 (April, 1973), 5-9.

6911. Ostrovsky, Alexander, 1823-1886. A Cat Has Not Always Carnival; Scenes from Moscow Life. 4 acts. Poet Lore, 40 (1929), 317-372. Jane Paxton Campbell and George Rapall Noyes, translators.

6912. ———. Colpevoli senza colpa. 3 acts. Il Dramma, 88 (April 15, 1930), 4-25. Sergio Strenkowsky and Lucio Ridenti, translators. In Italian.

6913. ———. Fairy Gold. 5 acts, comedy. Poet Lore, 40 (1929), 1-80. Camilla Chapin Daniels and George Rapall Noyes, translators.

6914. ———. La Forêt. 5 acts, comedy. L'Avant Scène, 447 (April 15, 1970), 7-35. Andre Barsacq, adapter. In French.

6915. ———. Signorina senza dote. 4 acts. Il Dramma, 72 (August 15, 1929), 6-42. Giacomo Lwow, translator. In Italian.

6916. _____. Wolves and Sheep. 5 acts, comedy. Poet Lore, 38 (1927), 159-253. Inez Sachs Colby and George Rapall Noyes, translators.

O'Sullivan, Seumas, pseud. see Starkey, J. S.

6917. Ottieri, Ottiero. L'assemblea deserta. 1 act. Sipario, 17 (January, 1962), 46-54. In Italian.

Ottina, Dada, translator see Priestley, J. B. 7292

6918. Ouellet, Elizabeth. Dialogue for Strangers. 1 act. One-Act Play Magazine, 4 (January-February, 1941), 88-94.

6919. Oulmont, Charles. Trois Couverts. 1 act. L'Avant Scène, 528 (November 1, 1973), 41-45. In French.

Overman, E. L., translator see Alvarez Quintero, S. and J. Alvarez Quintero 158

6920. Overton, Gwendolen, 1876- . First Love--And Second. 1 act. Smart Set, 3 (January, 1901), 140-146.

6921. Owen, Philip. Perseus and Andromeda. 1 act. Drama, 6 (May-June, 1915), 251-261.

6922. _____. Shirt of Rain. 1 act. The London Aphrodite, 5 (April, 1929), 393-399.

6923. _____. The Widow of Ephesus. 1 act. The London Aphrodite, 6 (July, 1929), 488-496.

6924. Owens, Rochelle, 1936- . Emma Instigated Me. 1 act. Performing Arts Journal, 1 (Spring, 1976), 71-94.

6925. _____. Kontraption. 1 act. Scripts, 1 (December, 1971), 4-25.

6926. Oyono, Guillaume. Trois Prétendants, un Mari. 4 acts. L'Avant Scène, 302 (January 1, 1964), 44-60. In French.

P

Pacini, Gianlorenzo, translator see Capek, K. 1576

_____, translator see Havel, V. 3982, 3983, 3984

_____, translator see Smocek, L. 8357

Packard, William, 1933- , translator and adapter see Motoyazu, K. Z. 6274

Pacor, Liciana, translator see Grum, S. 3764

Pacor, Sergio, translator see Grum, S. 3764

Pacuvio, Giulio, translator see Adam, A. R. 48

_____, translator see Salacrou, A. 7873

Padgett, Ron, translator see Jarry, A. 4449

Padover, S. K., translator see Miller, L. 6054

6927. Paget, Violet, 1856-1935. Ariadne in Mantua. 5 acts. Bibelot, 12 (1906), 5-75.

6928. _____. Ariane a Mantoue. 5 acts. Vers et Prose, 22 (July-September, 1910), 23 (October-December, 1910), 77-90; 88-98. A. Foulon de Vaulx, translator. In French.

6929. Pagnol, Marcel, 1895- . Fanny. 4 acts, comedy. Petite Illustration, 187 (February 3, 1934), 1-38. In French.

6930. _____. Judas. 5 acts. L'Avant Scène, 122, 1-38. In French.

6931. _____. Marius. 4 acts. Petite Illustration, 179 (May 16, 1931), 1-38. In French.

6932. _____. Merlusse. Petite Illustration, 191 (June 1, 1935), 1-30. In French.

6933. _____. Topaze. 4 acts. Petite Illustration, 178 (January 17, 1931), 1-40. In French.

6934. Pailleron, Edouard Jules Henri, 1834-1899. The Spark. 1 act, comedy. Poet Lore, 38 (1927), 373-400. Abbie Findlay Potts, translator.

6935. Paine, Albert Bigelow, 1861-1937. An Easter Soliloquy. Smart Set, 1 (April, 1900), 75-76.

6936. Pakots, Giuseppe. Il liquore dell'amore. 1 act. Il Dramma, 48 (August 15, 1928), 43-45. Taulero Zulberti, translator. In Italian.

6937. Palazzeschi, Aldo, 1885- . Roma. 3 acts. Sipario, 10 (April, 1955), 33-52. Alberto Perrini, adapter. In Italian.

6938. _____ and Roberto Guicciardini, 1933- . Perela' uomo di fumo. 2 parts. Sipario, 299 (March-April, 1971), 57-80. In Italian.

6939. Pallavicini, Roberto. Olimpia o del mestiere. 3 acts. Il Dramma, n.s., 359/360 (August/September, 1966), 45-75. In Italian.

6940. Palm, Carla L. The Perplexing Pirandello. 1 act, comedy. Drama, 15 (February, 1925), 102-104.

6941. _____. Schnitzleresque. 1 act, satire. Drama, 14 (March-April, 1924), 210-212, 238.

6942. Palmer, Frederick. Killing Them All. 1 act. Colliers, 68 (October 21, 1921), 9-10.

6943. Palmer, George. His Old Sweethearts. 1 act. Ladies' Home Journal, 26 (November, 1909), 13, 82.

6944. Palmer, Helen M. New Year's Day. 1 act, comedy. Harper's Bazaar, 35 (May, 1901), 43-48.

6945. Palmer, John. Over the Hills. 1 act, comedy. Smart Set, 46 (June, 1915), 227-235.

6946. Palmieri, Ferdinando. I lazzaroni. 3 acts. Sipario, 13 (December, 1958), 25-38. In Italian.

6947. Paluel-Marmont, Albert. Sud. 3 acts. Petite Illustration, 188 (August 4, 1934), 1-26. In French.

Pampanini, Agar, translator see Buchner, G. 1401

_____, translator see Yeats, W. B. 9588, 9594, 9608

Pampanini, Micaela De Pastrovich, translator see Maeterlinck, M. 5426

_____, translator see Yeats, W. B. 9604, 9605

Pandolfi, Laura, translator see Wedekind, F. 9256

6948. Pandolfi, Vito, 1917- . Processo a Giovanna. 1 act. Il Dramma, n. s., 136 (July 1, 1951), 50-59. In Italian.

_____, translator see Camus, A. 1553

6949. Pandora. 1 act. Plays, 34 (March, 1975), 53-60. Mercedes Gardner and Jean Shannon Smith, adapters.

6950. Panitz, Sol. Among Ourselves. 1 act. Senior Scholastic, 52 (February 23, 1948), 15-19.

6951. Panizza, Oscar, 1853-1921. Das Leibeskonzil. 5 acts. Sipario, 27 (March, 1972), 74-88. Paolo Bonacelli and Mario Missiroli, translators. In Italian.

6952. Paolieri, Ferdinando. L'odore del sud. 3 acts. Il Dramma, 39 (April 1, 1928), 7-30. In Italian.

Papot, Benedict, translator see Augier, E. 455

_____, translator see Becque, H. 712

_____, translator see Capus, A. 1590

6953. Paquin, Dorian. La Combinaison. 1 act. L'Avant Scène, 437 (November 15, 1969), 37-42. In French.

6954. Paradis, Marjorie B. The Admiral's Daughter. 1 act. Plays, 11 (January, 1952), 1-8. AND Plays, 19 (October, 1959), 39-46.

6955. _____. Alpha Kappa. 1 act. Plays, 12 (October, 1952), 12-23. AND Plays, 29 (January, 1970), 33-44.

6956. _____. Cupid's Partner. 1 act. Plays, 14 (May, 1955), 30-38.

6957. _____. The Diamond Earring. 1 act. Plays, 16 (January, 1957), 1-13.

6958. _____. Midge Rings the Bell. 1 act. Plays, 3 (May, 1944), 1-10.

6959. _____. Mister A. Lincoln. 1 act. Plays, 15 (February, 1956), 13-20.

6960. _____. None But the Fair. 1 act. Plays, 14 (December, 1954), 24-32.

6961. _____. Party Dress. 1 act. Plays, 5 (February, 1946), 16-23.

6962. _____. The Pinch-Hitter. 1 act. Plays, 9 (December, 1949), 26-32.

6963. _____. Santa Goes to Town. 1 act. Plays, 5 (December, 1945), 18-28.

6964. _____. She Also Serves. 1 act. Plays, 10 (April, 1951), 1-6.

6965. _____. She Laughs Last. 1 act. Plays, 10 (May, 1951), 10-21. AND Plays, 22 (March, 1963), 25-35.

6966. _____. Socrates Saves the Day. 1 act. Plays, 16 (November, 1956), 45-52.

6967. _____. Super-Sleuths, Inc. 1 act. Plays, 17 (January, 1958), 15-21.

6968. _____. Up in the Air. 1 act. Plays, 14 (March, 1955), 11-18.

6969. _____. Was Her Face Red! 1 act, comedy. Plays, 26 (April, 1967), 29-36.

6970. Paredes, Pedro Sanchez. The Castle and the Plain. 2 acts. Drama and Theatre, 8 (Spring, 1970), 161-167. Calvin C. Smith, translator.

Parenti, Franco, translator see Molière 6113

Paris, Jean, adapter see Behan, B. 725

6971. Parise, Goffredo. Le Manège Conjugal. 1 act. L'Avant Scène, 196 (October 1, 1963), 31-38. In French.

Parker, Douglass, translator see Aristophanes 332

6972. Parker, Louis Napoleon, 1852-1944. A Minuet. 1 act. Century, 89 (January, 1915), 370-376.

6973. _____. The Monkey's Paw. 1 act. Golden Book, 5 (April, 1927), 511-519.

6974. Parker, Marilynn, adapter. The Brahman, the Tiger and the Jackal. 1 act. Plays, 31 (March, 1972), 61-66.

6975. Parker, Stewart. Spokesong, or, the Common Wheel. 2 acts. Plays and Players, 24 (December, 1976; January, 1977), 43-50; 43-50.

6976. Parkhurst, Winthrop. Beggar and the King. 1 act. Drama, 33 (February, 1919), 62-74.

6977. _____. Getting Unmarried. 1 act. Smart Set, 54 (April, 1918), 91-99.

6978. _____. The Importance of Being Early. 1 act. Smart Set, 50 (November, 1916), 229-240.

6979. _____. It Never Happens, a Comedy of the Somewhat Improbable. 1 act. Smart Set, 57 (December, 1918), 77-87.

6980. _____. Morraca. 1 act. Drama, 32 (November, 1918), 536-574.

6981. Parlakian, Nishan. Plagiarized. 3 acts. First Stage, 1 (Summer, 1962), 5-26.

6982. _____. What Does Greta Garbo Mean to You? 1 act. Drama and Theatre, 11 (Spring, 1973), 145-147.

6983. Parnac, Jean-Maurice. Poisons. 1 act, comedy. L'Avant Scène, 127, 33-38. In French.

6984. Parodi, Anton Gaetano. Adolfo, o della magia. 2 parts. Il Dramma, n.s., 349 (October, 1965), 6-32. In Italian.

6985. _____. L'ex maggiore Hermann Grotz. 3 acts. Il Dramma, n.s., 277 (October, 1959), 6-22. In Italian.

6986. Parrella, Ida. The Knock on the Door. 1 act. Plays, 30 (January, 1971), 65-68.

6987. Parrish, Herbert. In the Andes. 2 acts. Atlantic, 140 (August, 1927), 231-238.

Parrot, Nicole, adapter see Monnier, H. and G. Vaez 6174

6988. Parsons, Chris. Waiting for Santa. 1 act. Plays, 18 (December, 1958), 76-80.

6989. Parsons, Mrs. Clement. The Lesson in Acting, an Imagined Dialogue. 1 act. Life and Letters, 7 (August, 1931), 96-106.

6990. Parsons, Florence Mary. Matters of Taste. A Conversation Piece. 1 act. 19th Century, 112 (August, 1932), 227-235.

6991. Parsons, G. Lewis. Your Opportunity. 2 acts. Industrial Arts Magazine, 18 (February, 1929), 51-54.

6992. Parsons, Mary Ruth. Cookbook. 1 act. Mademoiselle, 64 (November, 1966), 164-165, 204-205.

Partridge, Fred, translator see Labiche, E. 4747

6993. Pascal, André. Le Grand Patron. 3 acts, comedy. Petite Illustration, 179 (May 9, 1931), 1-37. In French.

6994. Pascal, Floy. Facing Reality. 1 act, farce. Poet Lore, 33 (Autumn, 1922), 451-457.

6995. Paschall, Alma. When the Bugle Blows. 1 act. Poet Lore, 55 (Spring, 1950), 39-49.

Pasolini, Desideria, translator see Eliot, T. S. 2839

6996. Pasqualino, Fortunato. Abelardo. 1 act. Il Dramma, 44, no. 2 (November, 1968), 70-74. In Italian.

Pasquier, H. Du, translator see Swinburne, A. C. 8648

Passeur, Steve, pseud. see Morin, E. C. 6220

6997. Pasternak, Boris Leonidovich, 1890-1960. La bellezza cieca. Il Dramma, 45, no. 6 (March, 1969), 37-52. Angelica Dongo, translator. In Italian.

Pasvolsky, Leo, translator see Andreyev, L. N. 232

6998. Pathiraja, Dharmasena, 1943- . L'Aveugle et le Paralytique. 1 act. L'Avant Scène, 477 (August 1, 1971), 39-42. In French.

6999. Patrick, John, 1907- . The Curious Savage. 3 acts. Il Dramma, n.s., 250 (July, 1957), 7-36. Carina Calvi, translator. In Italian.

7000. _____. The Teahouse of the August Moon. 3 acts, comedy. Il Dramma, n.s., 216 (November 1, 1954), 6-38. Cesare Vico Lodovici, translator. In Italian.

7001. _____. The Teahouse of the August Moon. 3 acts, comedy. Theatre Arts, 39 (June, 1955), 34-61.

7002. Patrick, Robert, 1907- . Kennedy's Children; An Afternoon in a Bar. 2 acts. Plays and Players, 22 (February; March, 1975), 45-50; 43-49.

7003. _____. Un bel di. 1 act. Performance, 5 (March/April, 1973), 106-113.

7004. Patroni-Griffi, Giuseppe. D'amore si muore. 3 parts. Il Dramma, n.s., 263/264 (August/September, 1958), 8-39. In Italian.

Pattee, Loueen, translator see Hebbel, F. 4015

7005. Patterson, Emma L. No Room at the Inn. 1 act. Plays, 2 (December, 1942), 37-43. AND Plays, 9 (December, 1949), 19-25.

7006. Patterson, Frederick C. Jeanette. 1 act. Smart Set, 31 (August, 1910), 129-134.

7007. _____. On the Veldt. 1 act. Smart Set, 29 (December, 1909), 113-117.

7008. Patti, Ercole. Un Amore a Roma. 2 parts, comedy. Sipario, 14 (July/August, 1959), 50-64. In Italian.

7009. _____. Una sceneggiatura. 1 act. Sipario, 11 (June, 1956), 55-56. In Italian.

7010. Patton, Marion Keep. The Gift of Gifts. 1 act. The Delineator, 85 (December, 1914), 20-21.

7011. Paul, Elliot, 1891-1958. The Ninety and Nine. 3 parts. Transition, 11 (February, 1928), 51-58.

7012. Paull, Harry Major, 1854- . A Bolt from the Blue. 1 act. 19th Century, 94 (December, 1923), 843-855.

7013. _____. The Other Room. 1 act. 19th Century, 90 (November, 1921), 807-818.

7014. _____. The Painter and the Millionaire. 2 acts. Fortnightly, 92 (December, 1909), 1115-1136.

7015. _____. The Vision. 2 acts. 19th Century, 89 (January, 1921), 175-188.

7016. _____ and Laurence Housman, 1865- . The Unknown Star. 3 acts. 19th Century, 86 (December, 1919), 1065-1095.

7017. Paulus, Margaret. Sherlock Holmes and the Gorgon's Head. 1 act. Scholastic, 41 (November 9-14, 1942), 17-19.

Pautassi, Goffredo, translator see Apel, P. 307

_____, translator see Beith, J. H. 730

_____, translator see Goetz, C. 3593

_____, translator see Johnson, L. E. 4486

_____, translator see Lonsdale, F. 5030

_____, translator Wexley, J. 9313

7018. Pavese, Cesare. Six Dialogues with Leuco. Arion, 2 (Summer, 1963), 80-104; [Six More Dialogues] 3 (Summer, 1964), 67-85. William Arrowsmith and D. S. Carne-Ross, translators.

Pavlova, Tatiana, 1896- see Casella, A. 1633

7019. Pavoni, Lao. Amalassunta. 3 acts. Sipario, 265 (May, 1968), 57-64. In Italian.

_____ see Squarzina, L. 8461

7020. Pawley, Thomas D. Judgment Day. 1 act. Sipario, 3 (January-February, 1948), 59-63. Gerardo Guerrieri, translator. In Italian.

7021. Payne, George Henry. A Man of Science. 1 act, comedy. Everybody's Magazine, 3 (July, 1900), 50-58.

7022. Pea, Enrico. Trealberi. 3 acts. Botteghe Oscure, 7 (1951), 134-181. In Italian.

7023. Peabody, Josephine Preston, 1874-1922. The Wings. 1 act. Harper's, 110 (May, 1905), 947-956.

7024. _____. The Wings. 1 act. Poet Lore, 25 (Vacation, 1914), 352-369.

Peacey, Howard, translator see Heijermans, H. 4032

7025. Peacock, Mary. Keeping Christmas. 1 act. Plays, 10 (December, 1950), 50-53.

7026. _____. Little Friend. 1 act. Plays, 18 (December, 1958), 81-85.

7027. Peacocke, Leslie T. The Penultimate Test. 1 act. Smart Set, 37.(June, 1912), 135-142.

7028. _____. The Victorious Surrender of Lady Sybil. 1 act. Smart Set, 32 (October, 1910), 127-133.

Pearson, John, translator see Ruibal, J. 7787, 7789

7029. Pech, Claude-Henri. Les Animateurs du Jour. 1 act. Comedy-tragedy. L'Avant Scène, 424 (April 15, 1969), 29-33. In French.

7030. _____. Passe-porc, ou Le Confessionnal. 1 act. L'Avant Scène, 564 (May 15, 1975), 27-31. In French.

7031. _____. Strange Morning. 1 act. L'Avant Scène, 475 (May 15, 1975), 27-31. In French.

7032. Pecorelli, Nicola. I benpensati. 3 acts. Sipario, 16 (April, 1961), 32-55. In Italian.

7033. Pedder, D. C. Between Two Trains. 1 act. 19th Century, 58 (October, 1905), 649-656.

7034. _____. Primavera. 3 acts. Living Age, 269 (June 10, 1911), 672-678.

Peden, Margaret S., translator see Wolff, E. 9530

7035. Pedrolo, Manuel de, 1918- . Cruma. Modern International Drama, 6 (Spring, 1973), 59-80. George E. Wellworth, translator.

7036. _____. Full Circle. Modern International Drama, 4 (Fall, 1970), 63-94. B. D. Steel, translator.

7037. _____. Men and No. 2 acts. Modern International Drama, 10 (Fall, 1976), 41-74. Herbert Gilliland, translator.

7038. _____. The Room. 3 acts. Modern International Drama, 5 (Spring, 1972), 21-59. Jill R. Webster, translator.

7039. Pelee, Lillian Sutton. At the Little Pipe. 1 act. Poet Lore, 31 (Autumn, 1920), 422-431.

7040. _____. Ties of Blood. 1 act. Poet Lore, 32 (Winter, 1921), 573-580.

7041. Pelland, Louis. Le Veridique Procès de Barbe-Bleue. 1 act, comedy. L'Avant Scène, 194 (April 1, 1959), 37-40. In French.

7042. Pena, Martins, 1815-1848. A Rural Justice of the Peace. 1 act, comedy. Poet Lore, 54 (Summer, 1948), 99-119. Willis Knapp Jones, translator.

Penchenat, Jean-Claude, translator see Lemasson, S. 4909

7043. Pendered, Mary L. Hymen a la Mode. 1 act. Smart Set, 32 (September, 1910), 127-130.

7044. Pendleton, Edrie. ABC for Safety. 1 act. Plays, 10 (April, 1951), 63-66.

7045. _____. Bobby and the Lincoln Speech. 1 act. Plays, 14 (February, 1955), 56-65.

7046. _____. Cupid's Post Office. 1 act. Plays, 3 (February, 1944), 33-38.

7047. _____. Ghosts in the Library. 1 act. Plays, 9 (November, 1949), 21-32. AND Plays, 30 (November, 1970), 73-84.

7048. _____. Hearts and Flowers for Mother. 1 act. Plays, 12 (May, 1953), 32-39.

7049. _____. In Honor of Washington. 1 act. Plays, 9 (February, 1950), 63-70. AND Plays, 19 (February, 1960), 37-44.

7050. _____. Mom's Perfect Day. 1 act. Plays, 11 (May, 1952), 1-10.

7051. _____. Nothing to Be Thankful for. 1 act. Plays, 10 (November, 1950), 27-35.

7052. _____. The Santa Claus Parade. 1 act. Plays, 11 (December, 1951), 70-72.

7053. _____. The Star in the Window. 1 act. Plays, 10 (December, 1950), 15-25.

7054. _____. The Stuff of Heroes. 1 act. Plays, 5 (November, 1945), 39-44.

7055. _____. Thanks to George Washington. 1 act. Plays, 10 (February, 1951), 11-23.

7056. _____. To Mother, with Love. 1 act. Plays, 3 (May, 1944), 27-33.

7057. _____. Vote for Your Hero. 1 act. Plays, 20 (November, 1960), 77-86.

7058. Peneau, Yves. Deux Gros Lots. 1 act, comedy. L'Avant Scène, 301 (December 15, 1963), 41-49. In French.

7059. _____. Un Mauvais Jour! 1 act. L'Avant Scène, 198 (June 1, 1959), 37-42. In French.

7060. Pensa, Carlo Maria. Gli altri ci uccidono. 3 acts. Il Dramma, n.s., 205 (May 15, 1954), 24-38. In Italian.

7061. Peple, Edward. The Girl. 1 act. Golden Book, 7 (April, 1928), 495-500.

7062. Peralopez Ranjel. Farca a Honor & Reverencia del Glorioso Nascimiento. 1 act. PMLA, 41 (December, 1926), 860-890. In Spanish.

7063. Percival, William. A Conversation in Hades. 1 act. Sewanee Review, 4 (May, 1896), 377-380.

7064. Perez Galdos, Benito, 1845-1920. Electra. 5 acts. Drama, 2 (May, 1911), 13-138.

7065. _____. The Grandfather. 5 acts. Poet Lore, 21 (May-June, 1910), 161-233. Elizabeth Wallace, translator.

7066. _____. Un Joven de Provecho. 4 acts, comedy. PMLA, 50 (September, 1935), 833-896. In Spanish.

7067. Perez, Jose Cid. The Comedy of the Dead. 1 act. First Stage, 6 (Spring, 1967), 68-80. John P. Dyson, translator.

7068. Perkins, E. B. Stage Struck. 1 act, comedy. Harper's Bazaar, 36 (February, 1902), 108-113.

7069. Perks, Albert E. Spiropanosome: A Bacteriological Tragedy. 1 act. Trace, 67 (1968), 114-120.

7070. Perlmutter, Ruth. Kidnapped by the Indians. 1 act. Plays, 5 (January, 1946), 29-38.

Perloff, Eveline, translator see Goldoni, C. 3604

7071. Perrault, Charles, 1628-1703. Puss in Boots. 1 act.

Perrault

Plays, 36 (October, 1976), 71-75. Lewis Mahlmann, adapter.

7072. _____. Puss in Boots. 1 act. Plays, 23 (May, 1964), 59-69. Adele Thane, adapter.

7073. _____. The Sleeping Beauty. 3 acts. Plays, 25 (March, 1966), 67-73. Adele Thane, adapter.

7074. Perreault, John, 1937- . Oedipus. Drama Review, 15 (Summer, 1971), 141-147.

7075. Perret, Jacques, 1901- . Le Couteau. 1 act, comedy. L'Avant Scène, 341 (September 15, 1965), 9-25. In French.

7076. _____. La Mort de Maximilien d'Autriche. 1 act. L'Avant Scène, 108, 23-39. In French.

7077. Perrin, Michel. Le Café de Pomone. 3 acts, comedy. L'Avant Scène (OST), 34 (December, 1950), 4-35. In French.

7078. Perrini, Alberto, 1919- . Coincidenza secondo binario. 1 act. Il Dramma, n.s., 368 (May, 1967), 32-42. In Italian.

7079. _____. Giuda. 1 act. Il Dramma, n.s., 160 (July 1, 1952), 49-59. In Italian.

7080. _____. Non si dorme a Karkwall. 2 parts, farce. Sipario, 12 (September, 1957), 42-60. In Italian.

7081. _____. Sola su questa mare. 2 parts. Il Dramma, n.s., 325 (October, 1963), 8-36. In Italian.

_____, adapter see Palazzeschi, A. 6937

_____, translator see Jonquille, N. 4513

7082. Perrucci, Andrea. La contata dei pastori. 3 acts. Il Dramma, n.s., 123/124 (December 15, 1950/January 1, 1951), 64-111. In Italian.

7083. Perry, Lucia. King Tutankhamon's Ruin. 1 act. Bookman [New York], 58 (January, 1924), 604-605.

7084. Pertwee, Roland. Evening Dress Indispensable. 1 act. Ladies' Home Journal, 41 (November, 1924), 10-11, 123, 125, 164.

7085. _____. The Loveliest Thing. 1 act. Ladies' Home Journal, 39 (December, 1922), 10-11, 150, 152-154, 157-158.

7086. Pessoa, Fernando. O marinheiro. Il Dramma, 46, no. 8 (August, 1970), 35-38. Antonio Tabucchi, translator. In Italian.

7087. Peters, Rollo. The Dream Assassins. 1 act. Forum, 54 (July, 1915), 117-118.

7088. Petersen, Ruth I. Late Spring. 1 act. Plays, 14 (May, 1955), 69-72.

7089. Petersen, Saralice. Christmas Tree Legend. 1 act. Resource, 8 (November, 1966), 16-17.

7090. ———. Variations on the Theme of Jonah. 1 act. Resource, 8 (April, 1967), 19-22.

Petersen, Will, 1928- , translator see Zeami Motokiyo 9639

7091. Peterson, Agnes Emelie. In the Light of the Star. 1 act. Drama, 21 (November, 1930), 19-20, 22, 31-32.

7092. ———. The Wind. 1 act. Drama, 15 (May, 1925), 174-177, 184.

7093. Peterson, Frederick, 1859-1938. Two Doctors at Akragas. 1 act. Atlantic, 107 (June, 1911), 816-819.

7094. Peterson, Mary Nygaard. Abe Buys a Barrel. 1 act. Plays, 15 (February, 1956), 64-70.

7095. ———. Adobe Christmas. 1 act. Plays, 17 (December, 1957), 45-50.

7096. ———. Beyond Mutiny. 1 act. Plays, 16 (October, 1956), 57-62. AND Plays, 29 (October, 1969), 61-66.

7097. ———. The Elf of the Woods. 1 act. Plays, 18 (March, 1959), 79-86.

7098. ———. Fairy Gold. 1 act. Plays, 17 (March, 1958), 55-60.

7099. ———. The Gift That Won the Princess. 1 act. Plays, 19 (March, 1960), 59-67.

7100. ———. Old Four-Legs. 1 act. Plays, 17 (May, 1958), 65-68.

7101. ———. Pedro and the Burro. 1 act. Plays, 18 (April, 1959), 39-46.

7102. ———. Simple Sam. 1 act. Plays, 17 (January, 1958), 71-76.

7103. _____. The Soup Stone. 1 act. Plays, 16 (March, 1957), 67-71.

7104. _____. The Wonderful, Beautiful Day. 1 act. Plays, 20 (January, 1961), 57-62.

7105. _____, adapter. The Magic Box. 1 act. Plays, 29 (February, 1970), 39-45.

_____, adapter see Dickens, C. 2475

7106. Petit, Victor Perez. Moonlight Sonata. 1 act. Poet Lore, 51 (Winter, 1945), 353-368. Willis Knapp Jones and Carlos Escudero, translators.

7107. Not used.

Petitjean, Armand, translator see Auden, W. H. and C. Isherwood 439

7108. Petrea, Raymond A. The Story of Christmas. 1 act. Resource, 1 (November, 1959), 12-14.

7109. Petresco, Julia. La Cite du Soleil. 1 act. L'Avant Scène, 510 (January 15, 1973), 35-42. In French.

7110. _____. Il Faut Murer la Fenêtre. 1 act. L'Avant Scène, 430 (July 15, 1969), 37-43. In French.

7111. _____. Règlement de Comptes. 1 act. L'Avant Scène, 465 (February 1, 1971), 34-39. In French.

Petrov, Evgeny see Ilf, I. 4368

7112. Petrova, Olga. Myrrha. 3 acts. Poet Lore, 60 (Winter, 1965), 291-344.

7113. _____. Refuge. 3 acts. Poet Lore, 58 (Autumn, 1963), 195-257.

Petry, M. Amiel see Amiel, D. 191

7114. Pettinato, Concetto. Il pomo di Paride. 6 acts. Il Dramma, 101 (November 1, 1930), 30-33. In Italian.

7115. Peyrou, Pierre. Le Meunier de Delft. 1 act, comedy. L'Avant Scène, 157, 36-40. In French.

Pezzani, Mireille, translator see Arauz, A. 313

_____, translator see Vilalta, M. 9145

7116. Pezzati, Mauro. Imputato Riccardo. 1 act. Sipario, 10 (January, 1955), 51-56. In Italian.

　　　　　　　———　see Mattolini, M. 5663

　　　　　　　Phelps, Elizabeth Stuart see Ward, E. S. 9205

7117.　Phelps, Sydney K. The Fairy Prince. 1 act. 19th Century, 63 (January, 1908), 138-143.

7118.　Philipott, Michel. Survivre. 3 acts. L'Avant Scène, (OST), 51 (November, 1951), 1-30. In French.

7119.　Philips, F. C. Partita vinta. 1 act. Il Dramma, 130 (January 15, 1932), 38-44. Maria Pia Biancoli, translator. In Italian.

7120.　Phillips, Charles. The Fool of God. 1 act. Catholic World, 108 (December, 1918), 358-377.

7121.　Phillips, Ernestine. Aesop, Man of Fables. 1 act. Plays, 22 (April, 1963), 43-52.

7122.　———. The Three Wishes. 1 act. Plays, 20 (March, 1961), 65-70.

7123.　Phillips, Louis, 1942- . The Banquet. 1 act. Drama and Theatre, 9 (Winter, 1970/71), 90-101.

7124.　———. God Have Mercy on the June-Bug. 2 acts. Modern International Drama, 7 (October, 1973), 65-108.

7125.　Phillips, Marguerite Kreger. All Because of a Scullery Maid. 1 act. Plays, 21 (March, 1962), 15-24. AND Plays, 35 (May, 1976), 49-58.

7126.　———. Ask the Library Lady. 1 act. Plays, 14 (April, 1955), 31-40.

7127.　———. The Crimson Glory Rose. 1 act. Plays, 12 (May, 1953), 23-31.

7128.　———. A Flair for Fashion. 1 act. Plays, 11 (October, 1951), 1-9.

7129.　———. The Green Thumb. 1 act. Plays, 14 (May, 1955), 65-68.

7130.　———. A Hat for Mother. 1 act. Plays, 24 (May, 1965), 65-70.

7131.　———. The Inn of the Blue Rose. 1 act. Plays, 21 (December, 1961), 13-22.

7132.　———. Johnny Did Try. 1 act. Plays, 11 (March, 1952), 48-54.

7133. _____. Moving on Tomorrow. 1 act. Plays, 16 (March, 1957), 15-24.

7134. _____. A Real April Fool's Day. 1 act. Plays, 17 (April, 1958), 51-55.

7135. _____. Strictly for Relatives. 1 act. Plays, 12 (March, 1953), 18-31.

7136. _____. Violets for Christmas. 1 act. Plays, 11 (December, 1951), 32-42.

7137. _____. Young Irving. 1 act. Plays, 10 (April, 1951), 31-40.

7138. Phillips, Olive. The Cardboard Star. 1 act. Plays, 27 (December, 1967), 1-11.

7139. Phillips, Stephen, 1868-1915. The Adversary. 1 act. Contemporary Review, 102 (September, 1912), 407-412.

7140. _____. No. 6. 1 act. Scribner's, 58 (August, 1915), 130-138.

7141. _____. The Unfinished Masterpiece. 1 act. British Review, 34 (January, 1922), 21-28.

7142. Phipps, A. H. More About Apples. 1 act. Poet Lore, 40 (1929), 144-149.

Piachaud, Réné-Louis, translator see Shakespeare, W. 8175

Piattelli, Elio, translator see Kishon, E. 4645

7143. Picasso, Pablo, 1881-1973. Le desir attrape par la queue. 6 acts. L'Avant Scène, 500 (August, 1972), 9-20. In French.

7144. _____. Desire Trapped by the Tail. 5 acts. New World Writing, 2 (1952), 70-86. Herma Briffault, translator.

7145. _____. Les quatres petites filles. 6 acts. L'Avant Scène, 500 (August, 1972), 27-42. In French.

Picco, Emilio, translator see Hacks, P. 3811

Piccoli, Fantasio, translator see Frisch, M. 3317

Piceno, translator see Natanson, J. 6447

7146. Picton-Warlow, Tod. Alec and Joey. 1 act. Drama at Calgary, 3 (No. 3, 1969), 78-84.

7147. Piechaud, Martial. Le Favori. 3 acts. Petite Illustration, 184 (January 21, 1933), 1-29. In French.

7148. _____. Le Quatrième. 1 act. Petite Illustration, 86 (May 19, 1928), 1-11. In French.

7149. Pieterse, Cosmo. Feat Accomplished and Hero Completely Defeated. 1 act. Literary Review, 15 (Fall, 1971), 84-93.

Pignet, Henri, adapter see Wilde, O. 9362

7150. Pillement, Georges, 1898- . Ah! Que D'Amour Gaché sans Profit Pour Personne! 1 act. Transatlantic Review (Paris), 1 (February, 1924), 46-52. In French.

7151. _____. L'Amour est mon Cercueil, Prologue et Epilogue. Transatlantic Review (Paris), 1 (No. 6, 1924), 424-439. In French.

_____, translator see Calderon de la Barca, P. 1501

Pilliod, Philippe, adapter see Frisch, M. 3309

7152. Pillot, E. The Young Wonder. A One-Act Play of Modern Hero-Worship. 1 act, comedy. Drama, 11 (February, 1921), 151-153.

7153. Pincherle, Alberto, 1907- . Beatrice Cenci. 1 act. Botteghe Oscure, 16 (1955), 363-461. In Italian.

7154. _____. Gli indifferenti. 2 parts. Sipario, 2 (May, 1947), 33-56. In Italian.

7155. _____. Il mondo e quello che e. 2 acts, comedy. L'Avant Scène, 440 (January 1, 1970), 7-30. Albert Husson, adapter. In French.

7156. _____. Il mondo e quello che e. 2 acts, comedy. Salmagundi, 14 (Fall, 1970), 39-104. Arthur A. Coppotelli, translator.

7157. Pinelli, Tullio, 1908- . Il ciarlatano meraviglioso. 2 parts. Il Dramma, n.s., 365/366 (February/March, 1967), 6-38. In Italian.

7158. _____. Il ciarlatano meraviglioso. 2 parts. Sipario, 17 (May, 1962), 41-61. In Italian.

7159. _____. Gorgonio. 3 acts. L'Avant Scène, 241 (April 15, 1961), 7-32. Claude Santelli, adapter. In French.

7160. _____. L'inferno. 1 act. Il Dramma, n.s., 206 (June 1, 1954), 37-40. In Italian.

7161. _____. Lotta con l'angelo. 3 acts. Il Dramma, 393/394 (January 1/15, 1943), 13-31. In Italian.

7162. _____. Mattutino. 1 act. Il Dramma, n. s., 207 (June 15, 1954), 52-55. In Italian.

7163. _____. Pegaso. 3 acts. Il Dramma, 323 (February 1, 1940), 4-16. In Italian.

7164. _____. La sacra rappresentazione di Santa Marina. Il Dramma, 46, no. 5 (May, 1970), 41-51. In Italian.

7165. _____. Lo stilita. 1 act. Il Dramma, 276 (February 15, 1938), 26-30. In Italian.

7166. Pinget, Robert, 1919- . Architruc. 1 act. L'Avant Scène, 313 (June 15, 1964), 32-38. AND L'Avant Scène, 469/470 (April 1/15, 1970), 69-76. In French.

7167. _____. L'Hypothèse. 1 act. L'Avant Scène, 313 (June 15, 1964), 26-31. In French.

7168. _____. La Manivelle. New Writers, 2 (1962), 96-127. Adapted by Samuel Beckett as "The Old Tune." In French and English.

7169. _____. The Old Tune. 1 act. Evergreen Review, 5 (March-April, 1961), 47-60. Samuel Beckett, translator.

7170. Pink, Claire. The Safety Pup. 1 act. Plays, 19 (April, 1960), 71-74.

7171. Pinner, David. Fanghorn. 3 acts. Plays and Players, 15 (January, 1968), 23-37.

7172. Pinter, Harold, 1930- . The Caretaker. 2 parts. L'Avant Scène, 441 (January 15, 1970), 7-28. Eric Kahane, adapter. In French.

7173. _____. The Caretaker. 3 acts. Spectaculum, 8 (1965), 233-282. Willy H. Thiem, translator. In German.

7174. _____. The Collection. 1 act. Sipario, 18 (April, 1963), 56-63. Elio Nissim and Laura del Bono, translator. In Italian.

7175. _____. The Dumb Waiter. 1 act. Sipario, 16 (July, 1961), 48-54. Elio Nissim, translator. In Italian.

7176. _____. Four Sketches. Sipario, 27 (April, 1972), 86-88. Elio Nissim, translator. In Italian.

7177. _____. Landscape. 1 act. Evergreen Review, 13 (July, 1969), 55-61.

Pinter 500

7178. _____. The Lover. 1 act. Sipario, 19 (April, 1964), 45-51. Elio Nissim, translator. In Italian.

7179. _____. Old Times. Sipario, 27 (April, 1972), 76-85. Romeo de Baggis, translator. In Italian.

7180. Piper, Edwin Ford. The Land of the Aiouwas, a Masque. 1 act. Midland, 8 (February, 1922), 59-77.

7181. Pirandello, Luigi, 1867-1936. Bellavita. 1 act. L'Avant Scène, 106, 27-32. Marie-Anne Comnene, adapter. In French.

7182. _____. Ciascuno a Suo Modo. 2 acts. L'Avant Scène, 399 (March 15, 1968), 7-34. Michel Arnaud, translator. In French.

7183. _____. Comme Avant, Mieux qu'Avant. 3 acts. L'Avant Scène, 130, 1-32. Marie-Anne Comnene, adapter. In French.

7184. _____. Cosi E (Se Vi Pare). 3 acts. Petite Illustration, 197 (June 5, 1937), 1-22. Benjamin Cremieux, translator. In French.

7185. _____. Le Devoir du Médecin. 1 act. L'Avant Scène, 166, 38-42. Marie-Anne Comnene, translator. In French.

7186. _____. The Doctor's Duty. 1 act. Poet Lore, 48 (Winter, 1942), 291-304. Oliver W. Evans, translator.

7187. _____. Dream (but perhaps not). 1 act. This Quarter, 2 (April/June, 1930), 605-629. Samuel Putnam, translator.

7188. _____. L'Etau. 1 act. L'Avant Scène, 130, 35-40. Marie-Anne Comnene, adapter. In French.

7189. _____. I fantasmi. 1 act. Il Dramma, 134 (March 15, 1932), 27-40. In Italian.

7190. _____. La Fleur a la Bouche. 1 act. L'Avant Scène, 109, 33-37. Marie-Anne Comnene, adapter. In French.

7191. _____. I giganti della montagna. 1 act. Il Dramma, n. s., 362/363 (Nov./Dec., 1966), 18-40. In Italian.

7192. _____. Henri IV. 3 acts, tragedy. L'Avant Scène, 162, 13-36. Benjamin Cremieux, translator. In French.

7193. _____. The Jar. 1 act. One-Act Play Magazine, 2 (October, 1938), 339-358. Arthur Livingston, translator.

7194. _____. The Man with the Flower in His Mouth. 1 act. Dial, 75 (October, 1923), 313-322. Arthur Livingston, translator.

7195. _____. The Man with the Flower in His Mouth. 1 act. Tulane Drama Review, 1 (June, 1957), 15-21. Eric Bentley, translator.

7196. _____. Non si Sa Come. 3 acts. L'Avant Scène, 267 (June 15, 1962), 9-34. Michel Arnaud, translator. In French.

7197. _____. Pari. 1 act. Il Dramma, n. s., 26 (December 1, 1946), 41-48. In Italian.

7198. _____. Pari. Sipario, 7 (December, 1952), 53-59. In Italian.

7199. _____. Questa Sera Si Recita a Soggetto. 3 acts, comedy. L'Avant Scène, 333 (May 1, 1965), 10-36. Michel Arnaud, translator. In French.

7200. _____. Qui si insegna a rubare. 1 act, comedy. Sipario, 11 (June, 1956), 48-54. In Italian.

7201. _____. La Raison des Autres. 3 acts. L'Avant Scène, 106, 3-26. Marie-Anne Comnene, adapter. In French.

7202. _____. The Rules of the Game. 3 acts. Theatre Arts, 45 (April, 1961), 27-52. William Murray, adapter.

7203. _____. Sicilian Limes. 1 act. Theatre Arts, 6 (October, 1922), 329-344. Elisabeth Abbott, translator.

7204. _____. Six Characters in Search of an Author. 2 acts, comedy. Broom, 2, 3 (June, July, August, 1922), 186-204; 321-337; 44-54. Edward Stores, translator.

7205. _____. Six Characters in Search of an Author. 2 acts, comedy. Spectaculum, 6 (1963), 262-316. Georg Richert, translator. In German.

7206. _____. Tutto per Bene. 3 acts. L'Avant Scène, 280 (January 15, 1963), 8-27. Benjamin Cremieux and Marie-Anne Comnene, translators. In French.

7207. _____. Vestire gli ignudi. 3 acts. Il Dramma, 249 (January 1, 1937), 8-30. In Italian.

7208. Pistilli, Gennaro, 1920- . Il momento due. 1 act. Sipario, 314 (July, 1972), 71-80. In Italian.

Pitoeff, Georges, adapter see Chekhov, A. P. 1768, 1771, 1780, 1783

Pitoeff, Ludmilla, adapter see Chekhov, A. P. 1768, 1771, 1780, 1783

7209. Pizzinelli, Corrado. La mamma del diavolo. 1 act. Sipario, 16 (May, 1961), 48-56. In Italian.

Platt, Pat, adapter see Ruskin, J. 7801

7210. Plescia, Gillian L. A Brush with Danger. 1 act, melodrama. Plays, 32 (March, 1973), 43-46.

7211. _____. Trouble in Dental City. 1 act. Plays, 33 (February, 1974), 48-52.

7212. _____, adapter. Big Cat, Little Cat, Old Man Monkey. 1 act. Plays, 34 (May, 1975), 49-52.

7213. _____, adapter. Jack and the Sillies. 1 act. Plays, 33 (October, 1973), 67-74.

7214. _____, adapter. The Strange and Wonderful Object. 1 act. Plays, 35 (May, 1976), 39-42.

7215. Plichta, Dalibor, 1920- . Finale della superparata. 1 act. Sipario, 270 (October, 1968), 61-72. Pier Francesco Poli, translator. In Italian.

7216. Plimmer, Denis. In Heaven and Earth. 1 act. One-Act Play Magazine, 1 (August, 1937), 323-343.

7217. Plimpton, Harriet. Dark Window. 1 act. Poet Lore, 48 (Winter, 1942), 336-357.

7218. _____. I Will Not Have It So. 1 act. Poet Lore, 46 (Autumn, 1940), 213-245.

7219. _____. So Much of Light. 1 act. Poet Lore, 51 (Spring, 1945), 3-41.

Podesta, Jose J. see Gutierrez, E. 3791

7220. Poe, Edgar Allan, 1809-1849. The Gold Bug. 1 act. Plays, 33 (March, 1974), 88-95. Adele Thane, adapter.

7221. _____. The Masque of the Red Death. 1 act. Plays, 15 (January, 1956), 90-94. Lewy Olfson, adapter.

7222. _____. Three Sundays in a Week. 1 act. Plays, 22 (November, 1962), 89-95. Paul T. Nolan, adapter.

7223. Poetic Licenses: A Forecast. 1 act. Living Age, 183 (November 23, 1889), 509-511.

7224. Pogodin, Nicolaj. Cernye Pticy. 3 acts. Sipario, 18 (June, 1963), 91-108. Milly de Monticelli, translator. In Italian.

7225. Pohl, Frederick Julius, 1889- . Varnishing Day. 1 act, satire. Poet Lore, 38 (1927), 128-140.

7226. Poiret, Jean. La Cage aux Folles. 4 acts, comedy. L'Avant Scène, 518 (May 15, 1973), 7-38. In French.

7227. Poley, Irvin C. The End of This Day's Business. 1 act. One-Act Play Magazine, 3 (March-April, 1940), 230-248.

Poli, Pier Francesco, translator see Plichta, D. 7215

7228. Poliakoff, Stephen. City Sugar. 2 acts. Plays and Players, 23 (January; February, 1976), 41-50; 41-50.

Poliakoff, Steven see Brenton, H. 1320

7229. Poliziano, Angelo Ambrogini, 1454-1494. Orfeo. 1 act. Bibelot, 6 (1900), 7-27. John Addington Symonds, translator.

Polk, William R., translator see Hakim, T. A. 3830

Poller, Ben, translator see Genet, J. 3438

7230. Pollock, Alice Leal. Wireless, a Modern Episode in One Act. Smart Set, 24 (March, 1908), 96-103.

7231. _____ and Aura Woodin Brantzell. The Resemblance. 1 act. Smart Set, 33 (February, 1911), 127-134.

7232. Pollock, Channing, 1880-1946. The Enemy. 4 acts. Scholastic, 9 (October 30; November 13, 27, December 11, 1926, January 8, 22, 1927), 7-9, 26; 8-10, 28; 8-10; 10-11, 26-27; 10-11; 10-11, 31.

7233. _____. The Fool. 1 act. Everybody's Magazine, 48 (March, 1923), 120-126.

7234. Pollock, Henry. Hotel Ritz, alle Ottol. 3 acts. Il Dramma, 100 (October 15, 1930), 4-36. In Italian.

Pollock, Walter Harries see Besant, W. 881

7235. Pomerance, Bernard. High in Vietnam, Hot Damn. 1 act. Gambit, 6 (1972), 69-80.

7236. _____. Hospital. 1 act. Gambit, 6 (1972), 81-88.

7237. _____. Thanksgiving Before Detroit. 1 act. Gambit, 6 (1972), 89-105.

7238. Pommeret, Xavier. La Grande Enquête de Francois-Felix Kulpa. 70 sequences, melodrama. L'Avant Scène, 460 (November 15, 1970), 7-34. In French.

7239. Pompei, Mario. La lampada dell'orco. 1 act. Il Dramma, 23 (August 1, 1927), 38-42. In Italian.

7240. _____. Se vincessi.... 1 act. Il Dramma, 78 (November 15, 1929), 36-40. In Italian.

7241. _____. La signora che rubava i cuori. 3 acts. Il Dramma, 67 (June 1, 1929), 8-24. In Italian.

7242. _____. Le tre figliole di Pinco Pallino. 3 acts. Il Dramma, 58 (January 15, 1929), 30-39. In Italian.

Pons, Maurice, 1925- , translator see Arden, J. 322

7243. Popovic, Aleksandar. Second Door Left. 2 acts. Drama and Theatre, 8 (Winter, 1969-70), 102-117. E. J. Czerwinski, translator.

Poquelin, Jean Baptiste see Molière 6110-6126

7244. Poray, Aniela. The High School Library of the Future. 1 act. Wilson Library Bulletin, 4 (May, 1930), 447-448, 466.

7245. Porche, François, 1877-1944. La Race Errante. 3 acts. Petite Illustration, 182 (June 18, 1932), 1-38. In French.

7246. _____. Un Roi, Deux Dames et un Valet. 4 acts, comedy. Petite Illustration, 190 (March 16, 1955), 1-33. In French.

7247. Poretto, Liva. Il ciarlatano. 1 act. Il Dramma, 436/437/438 (October 15/November 1/15, 1944), 65-69. In Italian.

Porret, Jean-Pierre, translator see Durrenmatt, F. 2744, 2750, 2754

7248. Porta, Elvio, 1945- , and Armando Pugliese, 1947- . Masaniello. 3 parts. Sipario, 343 (December, 1974), 56-77. In Italian.

Porter, Charlotte, translator see D'Annunzio, G. 2181

_____, translator see Maeterlinck, M. 5424, 5425, 5429, 5431, 5432

_____, translator see Sudermann, H. 8604

7249. Porter, Ella Williams. Callie Goes to Camp. 1 act. Plays, 9 (May, 1950), 52-58.

7250. _____. Who's Necessary? 1 act. Plays, 9 (March, 1950), 41-46.

Porter, H. C., translator see Sudermann, H. 8604

7251. Porter, Harold Everett, 1887-1936 and Robert Middlemass. The Valiant. 1 act. McClure's, 53 (March, 1921), 8-11, 47-49.

7252. _____. The Valiant. 1 act. Senior Scholastic, 52 (February 16, 1948), 16-18.

Porter, Helen Tracy, translator see Schnitzler, A. 8069, 8074

_____, translator see Sudermann, H. 8606

7253. Porto-Riche, Georges de, 1849-1930. La Marchand d'Estampes. 3 acts. Petite Illustration, 88 (September 13, 1930), 1-40. In French.

7254. _____. Les Vrais Dieux. 2 parts. Petite Illustration, 88 (January 4, 1930), 1-15. In French.

7255. Portor, Laura Spencer. The Light of Other Days. 1 act. Ladies' Home Journal, 23 (December, 1905), 20.

7256. _____. To Bethlehem. 1 act. Woman's Home Companion, 58 (December, 1931), 21-22, 103-104.

7257. Porzio, Domenico. Vangelo secondo Borges. 2 parts. Il Dramma, 48 (January, 1972), 42-55. In Italian.

Posin, Jack A., 1900- , translator see Yushkevich, S. 9627

7258. Possenti, Eligio, 1886- . La lontana parente. 3 acts. Il Dramma, n.s., 61/62 (May 15/June 1, 1948), 63-82. In Italian.

7259. _____. La nostra fortuna. 1 act. Il Dramma, n.s., 121 (November 15, 1950), 5-25. In Italian.

7260. _____. Villetta alla periferia. 3 acts. Il Dramma, 436/437/438 (October 15/November 1/15, 1944), 41-58. In Italian.

_____, translator see Gordin, G. 3633

_____, translator see Ibsen, H. 4363

_____, translator see Lopez, S. 5039

Possenti, Giuseppe see De Maria, A. 2312

7261. Post, Edward. Tower. 1 act. One-Act Play Magazine, 3 (July-August, 1940), 363-384.

7262. Potter, Beatrix, 1866-1943. Timothy the Tailor's Christmas. 1 act. Plays, 32 (December, 1972), 51-55. Margaret S. Crumbaugh, adapter.

7263. Potter, Rowland S. The Scars of Zalagai. 1 act. One-Act Play Magazine, 4 (September-October, 1941), 391-407.

Potts, Abbie Findlay, translator see Pailleron, E. J. H. 6934

7264. Pound, Ezra, 1885-1972. An Anachronism at Chinon. 1 act. Little Review, 4 (June, 1917), 14-21.

_____, translator see Sophocles 8381

7265. Power, Arthur. The Drapier Letters. 1 act. Transition, 11 (February, 1928), 71-89.

Power, Caroline Marguerite see Hartley, R. 3950

7266. Power, Victor. The Escape. 2 acts. Drama and Theatre, 10 (Winter, 1971/72), 96-112.

7267. Praga, André. Ecrire Pour le Théatre. 1 act, satire. L'Avant Scène, 464 (January 15, 1971), 37-42. In French.

7268. _____. Les Frères. 1 act. L'Avant Scène, 495 (May 15, 1972), 40-43. In French.

7269. _____. Histoire d'Une Chemise et d'Un Violon. 1 act. L'Avant Scène, 295 (September 15, 1963), 32-34. In French.

7270. _____. Ombres. 1 act. L'Avant Scène, 320 (October 15, 1964), 40-43. In French.

7271. _____. Salle d'attente. 1 act, satire. L'Avant Scène, 581 (February 15, 1976), 29-31. In French.

Prampolini, Giacomo, 1898- , translator see Wedekind, F. 9254

7272. Pratella, Francesco Balilla, 1880-1955. Notturno. Sipario, 260 (December, 1967), 94. In Italian.

7273. _____. Teropia. Sipario, 260 (December, 1967), 94. In Italian.

7274. Pratolini, Vasco and Gian Domenico Giagni. La domenica della buona gente. Sipario, 7 (August-September, 1952), 34-45. In Italian.

7275. Praxy, Raoul, 1891- . La Victime. 1 act, comedy. L'Avant Scène, 155, 35-44. In French.

7276. Preis, Arthur L. The Clown and the Undertaker. 1 act. Scholastic, 12 (April 28, 1928), 30-32.

7277. Prelovsky, Anatoly. A Common Man. 1 act. Literary Review, 13 (Spring, 1970), 303-317. James C. Gulick, translator.

7278. Premoisan, Alain. Tu Crois au Père Noël. 1 act. L'Avant Scène, 360 (July 1, 1966), 37-43. In French.

Premont, Henri, adapter see Dominguez, F. 2525

7279. Presles, Claude des. Les Beaux-Parents, ou Il ne Faut pas Se Fier aux Apparences. 1 act, comedy. L'Avant Scène, 103, 34-39. In French.

7280. _____. Billets-Doux. 1 act. L'Avant Scène, 135, 37-39. In French.

7281. _____. Les Bois du Colonel. 1 act. L'Avant Scène, 329 (March 1, 1965), 35-42. In French.

7282. _____. Les Groseilles. 1 act. L'Avant Scène, 245 (June 15, 1961), 37-40. In French.

7283. _____. Les Impondérables. 1 act. L'Avant Scène, 474 (June 15, 1971), 36-37. In French.

7284. _____. L'Oncle. 1 act. L'Avant Scène, 419 (February 1, 1969), 31-35. In French.

7285. Press, Steve, 1934- . We Need Another Man. 2 acts. Modern International Drama, 7 (October, 1973), 37-61.

7286. Price, Doris. Two Gods. 1 act. Opportunity (December, 1932), 380-383, 389.

Price, Laurence M., translator see Kleist, H. 4662

Price, Mary J., translator see Kleist, H. 4662

7287. Price We Pay, The. 1 act. Scholastic, 33 (September 24, 1938), 19E-20E, 24E.

7288. Priest, Paul. Prelimbo--A Closet Drama. 1 act. Carolina Quarterly, 11 (Spring, 1960), 54-56.

7289. Priestley, Horace. Ivan the Terrible. 3 acts. Drama, (July-August, 1915), 331-403.

7290. Priestley, John Boynton, 1894- . Dangerous Corner. 3 acts. L'Avant Scène, 182 (October 1, 1958), 7-28. Michel Arnaud, adapter. In French.

7291. _____. Dangerous Corner. 3 acts. Il Dramma, n. s., 158 (June 1, 1952), 7-32. Sandro Brissoni, translator. In Italian.

7292. _____. Eden End. 3 acts. Il Dramma, n. s., 120 (November 1, 1950), 7-32. Dada Ottina and Gigi Cane, translators. In Italian.

7293. _____. Eden End. 3 acts. Sipario, 3 (November-December, 1948), 25-44. Ada Salvatore, translator. In Italian.

7294. _____. I Have Been Here Before. 3 acts. Il Dramma, n. s., 71 (October 15, 1948), 13-35. Casimiro Jorio, translator. In Italian.

7295. _____. An Inspector Calls. 3 acts. Il Dramma, n. s., 35/36 (May 1, 1947), 71-95. Giuliano Tomei, translator. In Italian.

7296. _____. An Inspector Calls. Theatre Arts, 33 (April, 1949), 65-86.

7297. _____. The Linden Tree. 2 parts. Il Dramma, n. s., 170/171/172 (December 1/15, 1952/January 1, 1953), 35-66. Sergio Cenalino, translator. In Italian.

7298. _____. The Long Mirror. 3 acts. Il Dramma, n. s., 54 (February 1, 1948), 9-35. Vinicio Marinucci, translator. In Italian.

7299. _____. Music at Night. 3 acts. Il Dramma, n. s., 27/28 (December 15, 1946/January 1, 1947), 91-117. Mario Beltramo, translator. In Italian.

7300. _____. Time and the Conways. 3 acts. Il Dramma, n. s., 26 (December 1, 1946), 11-37. Alessandra Scalero, translator. In Italian.

_____ see Murdoch, I. 6304

7301. Prin, Claude, 1932- . Candidat. 1 act. L'Avant Scène, 474 (June 15, 1971), 25-33. In French.

7302. Prins, Peter de. The Ear of Malchus. 3 acts. Gambit, 4 (No. 13), 5-97. Calvin Evans, translator.

7303. Prins, Pierre de. La Chaise. 1 act. L'Avant Scène, 208 (November 15, 1959), 29-33. In French.

7304. _____. Les Vautours. 1 act. L'Avant Scène, 257 (January 15, 1962), 28-35. Jean Verlain, translator. In French.

7305. Printzlau, Olga. I vetri appannati. 1 act. Il Dramma, 378 (May 15, 1942), 9-27. Vinicio Marinucci, translator. In Italian.

Priolo, Remo, translator see Osborne, J. 6897

7306. Pritchard, Barry. The Audition. 1 act. Prism International, 4 (Summer, 1964), 48-67.

7307. _____. Visions of Sugar Plums. 2 acts. First Stage, 4 (Fall, 1965), 176-195.

7308. Privacky, Augusta Hutson. Grey Squirrel and the White Buffalo. 1 act. Plays, 16 (May, 1957), 61-68.

Proclemer, Anna, translator see Ustinov, P. 8983

Pronko, Leonard, translator see Sastre, A. 7974, 7975

7309. Prosperi, Carola. Sera di pioggia. 1 act. Il Dramma, 436/437/438 (October 15/November 1/15, 1944), 37-39. In Italian.

7310. Prosperi, Giorgio. La congiura. 3 acts, tragedy. Sipario, 15 (May, 1960), 31-56. In Italian.

7311. Provins, Michel. L'articolo 252. 1 act. Il Dramma, 40 (April 15, 1928), 40-42. In Italian.

7312. _____. Avant et Après. 1 act. Smart Set, 3 (April, 1901), 130-133. In French.

7313. _____. Basta una donna. 1 act. Il Dramma, 101 (November 1, 1930), 43-46. In Italian.

7314. _____. Cendrillon. 1 act. Smart Set, 5 (September, 1901), 149-152. In French.

7315. _____. Crisi coniugali. 1 act. Il Dramma, 69 (July 1, 1929), 42-43. Alex Alexis, translator. In Italian.

7316. _____. Deux Ecoles. 1 act. Smart Set, 24 (January, 1908), 141-145. In French.

7317. _____. La dolce vita. 1 act. Il Dramma, 106 (January 15, 1931), 42-45. In Italian.

7318. _____. Le gioie dell'estate: Il mare. 1 act. Il Dramma, 95 (August 1, 1930), 26-29. Mario Granata, translator. In Italian.

7319. _____. Idylle. 1 act. Smart Set, 33 (April, 1911), 141-144. In French.

Provins 510

7320. _____. La Lumière. 1 act. Smart Set, 26 (September, 1908), 119-123. In French.

Prozor, Counte, translator see Ibsen, H. 4361, 4365

Pryce, Richard, 1864-1942 see Fenn, F. 2982

7321. Prydz, Alvilde. He Is Coming. 1 act. Poet Lore, 25 (Summer, 1914), 230-244. Hester Coddington, translator.

7322. Pshibishevsky, Stanislav, 1868- . For Happiness. 3 acts. Poet Lore, 23 (Spring, 1912), 81-110. Lucille Bacon, translator.

Psichelio, Oskar, translator see Gunther, O. 3784

7323. Puccini, Giacomo, 1858-1924. La Bohème. 4 acts. Theatre Arts, 37 (December, 1953), 34-60. Howard Dietz, adapter.

7324. Puget, Claude-André, 1900- . Le Coeur Volant. 2 acts. L'Avant Scène, 164, 4-33. In French.

7325. _____. Un Facheux Etat d'Esprit. 1 act. L'Avant Scène, 96, 28-37. In French.

7326. _____. La Ligne de Coeur. 3 acts, comedy. Petite Illustration, 181 (January 2, 1932), 1-30. In French.

7327. _____. Le Roi de la Fete. 3 acts. Il Dramma, n.s., 177 (March 15, 1953), 9-38. Ada Salvatore, translator. In Italian.

_____, adapter see Shakespeare, W. 8185

_____, adapter see Taylor, S. and C. O. Skinner 8734, 8735

7328. _____ and Pierre Bost. Un Nomme Judas. 3 acts. L'Avant Scène, 96, 1-24. In French.

7329. _____. Un Nommé Juda. 3 acts. Il Dramma, n.s., 233 (February, 1956), 13-38. Icilio Ripamonti, translator. In Italian.

7330. Puggioni, Pino. Yutzy Brown. 1 act. Il Dramma, n.s., 337 (October, 1964), 59-67. In Italian.

Pugliese, Armando, 1947- see Porta, E. 7248

7331. Pugliese, Sergio, 1908- . L'arca di Noè. 3 acts. Il Dramma, 408/409 (August 15/September 1, 1943), 9-27. In Italian.

7332. _____. Cugino Filippo. 3 acts. Il Dramma, 257 (May 1, 1937), 3-20. In Italian.

7333. _____. Trampoli. 3 acts. Il Dramma, 212 (June 15, 1935), 5-29. In Italian.

7334. Pugnetti, Gino. Le domeniche di Angiola e Bortolo. 1 act. Il Dramma, n.s., 197 (January 15, 1954), 63-71. In Italian.

7335. _____. La ragazza e i soldati. 1 act. Il Dramma, n.s., 229 (October, 1955), 46-56. In Italian.

7336. _____. L'ultimo sogno della signora Catri. 1 act. Il Dramma, n.s., 127 (February 15, 1951), 48-53. In Italian.

Puig-Espert, Francisco see Camp, André 1530, 1531

7337. Pujel, René. La comparsa. 1 act. Il Dramma, 141 (July 1, 1932), 41-43. Vittorio Guerriero, translator. In Italian.

7338. _____. Intervallo di manovella. 1 act. Il Dramma, 165 (July 1, 1933), 45-46. In Italian.

7339. Pulman, Jack. The Happy Apple. 3 acts. Plays and Players, 17 (May, 1970), 54-77.

7340. Pumphrey, Byron. Sadco. 1 act. First Stage, 6 (Fall, 1967), 187-194.

7341. Purcell, Margaret Barbrick. Flight. 1 act. Poet Lore, 65 (Summer, 1970), 180-193.

7342. Purdy, James, 1923- . Children Is All. 1 act. Mademoiselle, 56 (November, 1962), 108-109, 164-165, 167-173, 184-186.

7343. _____. Wedding Finger. 1 act. New Directions, 28 (1974), 77-98.

Purnal, Roland. Maïe. 1 act. Mesures, 31 (July 15, 1937), 37-71. In French.

7344. Pushkin, Alexander, 1799-1837. L'Invité de Pierre. 1 act. L'Avant Scène, 150, 33-40. Michel Arnaud, adapter. In French.

7345. _____. Mozart and Salieri. 1 act. Poet Lore, 31 (Summer, 1920), 297-304. Nicholas Lubimov, translator.

7346. Puss-In-Boots. 3 acts. St. Nicholas, 9 (January, 1882), 217-221.

7347. Putnam, Mrs. Nina Wilcox, 1888-1962. Orthodoxy. 1 act, satire. Forum, 51 (June, 1914), 801-820.

Putnam, Samuel, translator see Pirandello, L. 7187

7348. Pyle, Howard, 1853-1911. The Apple of Contentment. 1 act. Plays, 23 (November, 1963), 57-65. Adele Thane, adapter.

7349. _____. Hope and Memory. 1 act. Century, 63 (November, 1901), 108-110.

7350. Pyle, Katherine. The Magic Sword. 3 acts. St. Nicholas, 1 (November, 1897), 78-82.

7351. Pyle, Mary Thurman. Bright Stream. 1 act. Plays, 11 (March, 1952), 55-62.

7352. _____. Halloween Gets a New Look. 1 act. Plays, 10 (October, 1950), 31-38.

7353. _____. Mrs. Gibbs Advertises. 1 act. Plays, 10 (November, 1950), 36-43.

7354. _____. The Perambulating Pie. 1 act. Plays, 9 (December, 1949), 1-9.

7355. _____. The Three Royal R's: A Play for American Education Week. 1 act. Plays, 2 (November, 1942), 1-10. AND Plays, 16 (November, 1956), 69-78.

Pyros, John see Tucetsky, D. 8947

7356. Pyrrhic Victory. 1 act. Plays, 27 (May, 1968), 105-106.

Q

7357. Quackenbush, Jan. Still Fires. 1 act. Gambit, 3 (No. 11), 111-116.

7358. Quality of Mercy, The. 1 act. Plays, 3 (February, 1944), 67-78.

7359. Quarella, David. Rounding the Triangle. 1 act. Smart Set, 40 (May, 1913), 131-140.

Quarra, Amilcare, translator see Gabirondo, V. and E. Enderiz 3343

_____, translator see Garcia-Alvarez, E. and P. Munoz-Seca 3373

_____, translator see Sevilla, L. F. de and R. Sepulreda 8159

7360. Quasimodo, Salvatore, 1901-1968. L'amore di Galatea. 3 acts. Sipario, 19 (December, 1964), 89-95. In Italian.

7361. Queenes Majesties Entertainment. 1 act. PMLA, 26 (No. 1, 1911), 92-127.

7362. Quentin, Pol. Sammy. 2 acts. L'Avant Scène, 245 (June 15, 1961), 19-36. In French.

_____, adapter see Dinner, W. and W. Morum 2505

_____, adapter see Marasco, R. 5527

_____, adapter see Maugham, W. S. 5666

_____, adapter see Mortimer, J. 6248

_____, translator see Bolt, R. 1158

_____, translator see Millar, R. and N. Balchin 5833

_____, translator see Osborne, J. J. 6895

7363. _____ and Georges Bellak. Football. 3 acts. L'Avant Scène, 256 (January 1, 1962), 7-28. In French.

7364. Quiles, Eduardo. The Bridal Chamber. 1 act. Modern International Drama, 7 (Fall, 1973), 21-29. Marcia Cobourn Wellworth, translator.

7365. _____. The Employee. 2 acts. Modern International Drama, 9 (Fall, 1975), 53-87. Laurie Taylor, translator.

7366. _____. The Refrigerator. 1 act. Modern International Drama, 7 (Fall, 1973), 7-18. George E. Wellworth, translator.

7367. Quillard, Pierre. The Girl With Cut-Off Hands, a Passion Play. Drama Review, 20 (September, 1976), 122-128. Jacques F. Hovis, translator.

Quintero, Joaquin Alvarez see Alvarez Quintero, J. 157-174

Quintero, Serafin Alvarez see Alvarez Quintero, S. 157-174

7368. Quoirez, Françoise, 1935- . Chateau en Suède. 4 acts, comedy. L'Avant Scène, 234, 7-29. In French.

7369. _____. La Robe Mauve de Valentine. 2 acts. L'Avant Scène, 318 (September 15, 1964), 8-27. In French.

7370. _____. Tra un mese tra un anno. Sipario, 15 (April, 1960), 48-67. Paolo Levi, adapter. In Italian.

7371. _____. Les Violons Parfois. 2 acts. L'Avant Scène, 265 (May 15, 1962), 8-29. In French.

R

7372. Rabe, David. The Basic Training of Pavlo Hummel. 2 acts. Scripts, 1 (November, 1971), 56-92.

7373. Rabe, Margaret. The Princess' Choice. 1 act. Quarterly Journal of Speech, 5 (May, 1919), 279-286.

7374. Rabe, Olive Hanson. To the Rescue. 1 act. Plays, 4 (November, 1944), 57-65.

_____ see also Fisher, A. 3103-3123

7375. Rabenhorst, Loretta Capell. Spring Is Coming. 1 act. Plays, 2 (April, 1943), 51-53.

7376. _____. The Test. 1 act. Plays, 2 (May, 1943), 40-47.

7377. Raborg, Frederick A., Jr. Ramon and the Artist. 1 act. Dramatics, 47 (May, 1976), 28-34.

7378. Racine, Jean Baptiste, 1639-1699. Phèdre. 5 acts, tragedy. L'Avant Scène, 342 (October 1, 1965), 21-61. In French.

7379. Radford, Dollie. The Ransom. 3 acts. Drama, 6 (March-April, 1915), 117-153.

Radin, Dorothea P., translator see Kvapil, J. 4742

7380. Radin, Max. Dumnorix. 3 acts. Classical Journal, 13 (February, 1918), 314-342. In Latin.

Raffo, A. M., translator see Broszkiewicz, J. 1350

_____, translator see Rozewicz, T. 7776

7381. Raggio, Enrico. Autori. 1 act. Il Dramma, 83 (February 1, 1930), 35-38. In Italian.

7382. _____. Barbara. 1 act. Il Dramma, 94 (July 15, 1930), 37-45. In Italian.

7383. _____. Colloquio. 1 act. Il Dramma, 91 (June 1, 1930), 41-42. In Italian.

7384. _____. L'età delle attrici. 1 act. Il Dramma, 85 (March 1, 1930), 39-43. In Italian.

7385. _____. Fine d'anno. 1 act. Il Dramma, 81 (January 1, 1930), 40-44. In Italian.

7386. _____. Il pasto dell'attore. 1 act. Il Dramma, 78 (November 15, 1929), 30-31. In Italian.

7387. _____. Il prisma. 1 act. Il Dramma, 88 (April 15, 1930), 38-42. In Italian.

7388. _____. Sera di novità. 1 act. Il Dramma, 80 (December 15, 1929), 29-32. In Italian.

7389. _____. Le tre vie. 1 act. Il Dramma, 86 (March 15, 1930), 33-35. In Italian.

7390. _____. I vestiti della donna amata. 3 acts. Il Dramma, 229 (March 1, 1936), 2-28. In Italian.

7391. _____. Il vestito di Gisella. 1 act. Il Dramma, 79 (December 1, 1929), 29-30. In Italian.

_____, translator see Carroll, P. V. 1620

_____, translator see Christie, A. 1824

_____, translator see Lefevre-Geraldry, P. 4893

_____, translator see Maugham, W. S. 5677

_____, translator see Vane, S. 9034

Rahlson, Kurt, translator see Hebbel, C. F. 4016

7392. Rahn, Suzanne, adapter. Night of the Trolls. 1 act. Plays, 35 (February, 1976), 45-48.

7393. Raid on the White Tiger Regiment. Chinese Literature, 10 (1967), 13-58. AND Chinese Literature, 3 (1973), 3-54.

Raikes, John, translator see Giraudoux, J. 3576

Raimondi, Piero, translator see Asturias, M. A. 425

Raiteri, Dante, translator see Bauer, J. M. 675

_____, translator see Wessel, O. 9308

Rakowska, M., translator see Kataev, V. 4552

Ralph-Mylo, Juliette, adapter see Dell, J. 2300

7394. Ramée, Louise de la. The Nurnberg Stove. 1 act. Plays, 31 (December, 1971), 35-43. Helen L. Howard, adapter.

7395. Ramsey, Alicia. Henkers Mahlzeit. 1 act. Smart Set, 30 (February, 1910), 123-131.

7396. Ramsey, Helen. The Day the Indians Came. 1 act. Plays, 20 (November, 1960), 71-76.

7397. _____. The Feathered Dream. 1 act. Plays, 20 (April, 1961), 23-30.

7398. _____. The Grateful Gobbles. 1 act. Plays, 16 (November, 1956), 64-66.

7399. _____. In the Name of Miles Standish. 1 act. Plays, 14 (November, 1954), 39-44.

7400. _____. Names to Remember. 1 act. Plays, 16 (November, 1956), 67-68.

7401. Ramuz, Charles Ferdinand. L'Histoire du Soldat. 1 act. L'Avant Scène, 574 (November 1, 1975), 35-42. Devy Erlih, adapter. In French.

7402. Rand, Ayn. La notte del 16 Gennaio. 3 acts. Il Dramma, n. s., 47 (October 15, 1947), 7-35. Marcel DuBois, translator. In Italian.

Randall, Elinor, translator see Sender, R. 8152

7403. Randolph, Edith. Lamma's Eve. 1 act. Poet Lore, 32 (Summer, 1921), 288-306.

Randone, B. L., translator see Ducreux, L. 2670

_____, translator see La Porte, R. 4813

_____, translator see Magnier, C. 5442

_____, translator see Marceau, F.

_____, translator see Roussin, A. 7738, 7739, 7744, 7751, 7753, 7757

_____, translator see Sarment, J. 7937

_____ see also Marotta, G. 5568-5573

7404. _____ and Louis Carette. Eduardo e Carolina. 3 acts. Il Dramma, n. s., 186 (August 1, 1953), 9-33. In Italian.

7405. Rangoni, Riccardo. La Seppia. 3 acts. Sipario, 177 (January, 1961), 35-64. In Italian.

Rank, H. E., translator see Brecht, B. 1302

7406. Ransan, André. Le Bal des Bourreaux. 1 act. L'Avant Scène, 317 (September 1, 1964), 47-53. In French.

7407. _____. La Monnaie des ses Reves. 1 act, comedy. L'Avant Scène, 126, 35-42. In French.

7408. _____. Phryne. 1 act. L'Avant Scène, (OST), 49 (October, 1951), 1-30. In French.

7409. _____. La Posterité. 1 act, comedy. L'Avant Scène, 208 (November 15, 1959), 34-41. In French.

7410. _____. Réprouvée. 1 act. L'Avant Scène, 273 (October 1, 1962), 29-34. In French.

7411. _____. La Traversée. 1 act. L'Avant Scène, 107, 33-40. In French.

7412. Ransley, Peter. Disabled. 3 acts. Plays and Players, 18 (June, 1971), 70-85.

7413. _____. Ellen. 2 acts. Plays and Players, 18 (April, 1971), 68-85.

7414. Raphael, Alice. Dormer Windows. 1 act. Drama, 11 (August-September, 1921), 418-420.

7415. _____. An Interlude in the Life of St. Francis. 1 act. Drama, 11 (November, 1920), 37-40.

7416. Rappopport, David. Ode to a Scenic Northwest. 1 act. Dramatics, 45 (December, 1973), 12-16.

7417. Ratcliffe, Michael. Alexander II, or, Something for Every-One. 1 act. Works, 1 (Winter, 1968), 84-93.

Rathkey, W. A. see Nettleford, W. T. 6471

7418. Ratkowski, Thomas M. Apples, Oranges, Strawberries. 1 act. Plays, 35 (October, 1975), 65-68.

7419. Rattigan, Terence, 1911-1977. A Bequest to the Nation. 2 acts. Plays and Players, 18 (January, 1971), 60-85.

7420. _____. The Browning Version. Il Dramma, n.s., 135 (June 15, 1951), 7-25. Mirella Ducceschi, translator. In Italian.

7421. _____. The Deep Blue Sea. 3 acts, comedy. Sipario, 9 (February, 1954), 35-55. Maura Chinazzi, translator. In Italian.

7422. _____. The Deep Blue Sea. 3 acts. Theatre Arts, 37 (July, 1953), 34-59.

7423. _____. French Without Tears. 3 acts, comedy. Petite Illustration, 198 (September 4, 1937), 1-34. Pierre-Jules Laudenbach and Maurice Sachs, translators. In French.

7424. _____. O Mistress Mine. 3 acts. Il Dramma, n.s., 159 (June 15, 1952), 5-35. Laura Del Bono, translator. In Italian.

7425. _____. Ross. 2 acts. Sipario, 18 (January, 1963), 41-67. Carina Calvi, translator. In Italian.

_____. Ross. 2 acts. Theatre Arts, 47 (April, 1963), 25-58.

7426. _____. Separate Tables. 2 episodes. Il Dramma, n.s., 258 (March, 1958), 6-38. In Italian.

7427. _____. Separate Tables; Table Number Seven, a Play in Two Scenes; Table by the Window, a Play in Three Scenes. Theatre Arts, 42 (May, 1958), 35-63.

7428. _____. The Sleeping Prince. 2 acts, comedy. Theatre Arts, 41 (December, 1957), 35-65.

7429. _____. Who's Silvia? 3 acts, comedy. Sipario, 10 (January, 1955), 29-50. Laura Del Bono, translator. In Italian.

7430. _____. The Winslow Boy. 2 parts. Il Dramma, n.s., 88 (July 1, 1949), 7-40. Gigi Cane, translator. In Italian.

7431. _____. The Winslow Boy. Theatre Arts, 32 (October, 1948), 63-90.

7432. Rau, Santha Rama, 1923- . A Passage to India. 3 acts. Theatre Arts, 46 (April, 1962), 25-56.

7433. Ravegnani, Giuseppe, 1895- . Chiamami becco. 1 act. Il Dramma, 5 (April, 1926), 36-45. In Italian.

_____, translator see Soldevila, C. 8367

7434. Ravetch, Herbert. Abra-Kadabra-Kadoo!!! 1 act. Plays, 17 (October, 1957), 35-44.

7435. _____. The Big Difference. 1 act. Plays, 18 (March, 1959), 64-68.

7436. _____. The Secret of Pinchpenny Manor. 1 act. Plays, 17 (March, 1958), 39-45.

7437. _____. The Words We Live By. 1 act. Plays, 17 (May, 1958), 47-53.

7438. _____. You Can't Run Away From It. 1 act. Plays, 18 (November, 1958), 29-35.

7439. Rawe, Marcella. The Camelia Costumes. 1 act. Plays, 20 (March, 1961), 27-38.

7440. _____. Halfway to Concord. 1 act. Plays, 18 (April, 1959), 13-22.

7441. _____. The Kindly Little Tailor. 1 act. Plays, 29 (February, 1970), 61-66.

7442. _____. There Is a Tide. 1 act. Plays, 27 (February, 1968), 29-38.

7443. _____. A Time for Purpose. 1 act. Plays, 25 (February, 1966), 27-38.

7444. Rawls, James. The Pilgrim Painting. 1 act. Plays, 18 (November, 1958), 47-53. AND Plays, 36 (November, 1976), 52-58.

7445. Raylambert, Jeannine. Ombrages. 1 act. L'Avant Scène, 175 (June 1, 1958), 30-41. In French.

7446. Raynal, Paul, 1890- . Au Soleil de l'Instinct. 3 acts, tragedy. Petite Illustration, 181 (April 16, 1932), 1-29. In French.

7447. _____. Napoleon Unique. 3 acts, comedy. Petite Illustration, 197 (May 8, 1937), 1-34. In French.

7448. Reaching for the Moon. 2 acts. Industrial Arts Magazine, 18 (June, 1929), 210-214.

7449. Reaney, James. Sticks and Stones: The Donnellys, Part Two. 3 acts. Canadian Theatre Review, 2 (Spring, 1974), 40-114.

7450. Reay, Nina Butler. Good Old Summer Time. 1 act. Plays, 14 (May, 1955), 61-64.

7451. _____. Mr. Bates Goes to the Polls. 1 act. Plays, 10 (November, 1950), 48-50. AND Plays, 24 (November, 1964), 76-78.

7452. Rebello, Luiz Francisco. Il giorno dopo. 1 act. Il Dramma, 44, no. 3 (December, 1968), 42-48. Arrigo Repetto, translator. In Italian.

7453. Rebora, Roberto. Il corridore che canta. 1 act. Sipario, 21 (March, 1966), 60-63. In Italian.

_____, translator see Usigli, R. 8980

7454. Reboux, Paul. Il baro. 3 acts. Il Dramma, 118 (July 15, 1931), 38-42. Vittorio Guerriero, translator. In Italian.

Recanati, Amedeo, translator see Garcia Lorca, F. 3377

Recht, Charles, translator see Biro, L. 965, 967

_____, translator see Frida, E. B. 3299, 3300, 3301

_____, translator see Kvapil, J. 4741

Reck, Rima Drell, translator see Giraudoux, J. 3575

7455. Redentin Easter Play, The. 2 acts. Poet Lore, 47 (Spring, 1941), 8-39. A. E. Zucker, H. K. Russell, and Mary Margaret Russell, translator.

7456. Redgrave, Michael. The Aspern Papers. 3 acts. Sipario, 16 (March, 1961), 29-50. Alvise Sapori, translator. In Italian.

7457. Reed, Dena. The Critic Was a Lady. 1 act. One-Act Play Magazine, 4 (July-August, 1941), 309-324.

7458. _____. Lucilla's Proposal. 1 act. Plays, 30 (January, 1971), 11-20.

7459. Reed, Ethelyn. The Intruder. 1 act. Smart Set, 36 (March, 1912), 133-138.

7460. Reed, John, 1887-1920. Freedom, a Satirical Episode. 1 act. One-Act Play Magazine, 2 (May, 1938), 34-46.

7461. Reely, Mary Katharine. Flittermouse. 1 act, comedy. Drama, 14 (December, 1923), 104-107.

7462. Regan, Sylvia. The Fifth Season. 3 acts, comedy. Theatre Arts, 38 (July, 1954), 34-63.

7463. Regnard, Jean-François, 1655-1709. L'erede universale. 1 act. Il Dramma, n. s., 263/264 (August/September, 1958), 69-80. Guido Guarda, translator. In Italian.

7464. Regnier, Henri de, 1864-1936. The Guardian. 1 act. Poet Lore, 46 (Winter, 1940), 291-302. Marie C. Mengers, translator.

7465. Regnier, Max, 1907- . Champagne et Whisky. 2 acts, comedy. L'Avant Scène, 167, 4-33. In French.

7466. _____. Les Petites Têtes. 2 acts, comedy. L'Avant Scène, 117, 1-41. In French.

7467. Rego, Luis and Didier Kaminka. Viens chez moi J'Habite chez un Copine. 3 acts. L'Avant Scène, 564 (May 15, 1975), 3-23. In French.

Regy, Claude, translator see Wesker, A. 9305

Reina, Elena, translator see Carette, L. 1605

_____, translator see Shaffer, P. 8172

_____, translator see Shepard, S. 8241

_____, translator see Story, D. 8539

7468. Reinach, Marco. Una donnina senza logica. 1 act. Il Dramma, 79 (December 1, 1929), 31-38. In Italian.

7469. _____. Un posticino molto tranquillo. 1 act. Il Dramma, 88 (April 15, 1930), 28-35. In Italian.

7470. Reinecker, Herbert, 1914- . Night Train. 2 acts. Modern International Drama, 1 (September, 1967), 65-102. Martha A. Fisher, translator.

7471. Reines, Bernard J. Citizen Franklin of Philadelphia. 1 act. Plays, 2 (October, 1942), 1-8.

7472. _____. Gerrymander. 1 act. Plays, 2 (November, 1942), 67-71.

7473. _____. Horace Mann, American Educator. 1 act. Plays, 3 (November, 1943), 7-18.

7474. _____. Letter to Private Smith. 1 act. Plays, 3 (December, 1943), 62-69.

7475. _____. Rizal of the Philippines. 1 act. Plays, 3 (October, 1943), 1-14.

7476. _____. So Precious a Gift. 1 act. One-Act Play Magazine, 4 (September-October, 1941), 381-390.

7477. _____. Woman Courageous, the Story of Lucy Stone. 1 act. One-Act Play Magazine, 4 (January-February, 1941), 68-87.

7478. _____. Young Franklin Takes Over. 1 act. Plays, 4 (October, 1944), 9-19.

7479. Reinhold, Robert. The Heist. 1 act. The Scene, 1 (1972), 148-180.

Relonde, Maurice, translator see Farce of the Worthy Master... 2932

Rels, Costa du, translator see Fabbri, D. 2904

7480. Rènard, Jules, 1864-1910. Good-Bye! 1 act, comedy. Smart Set, 49 (June, 1916), 81-93. Barrett H. Clark, translator.

7481. _____. Monsieur Vernet. 2 acts, comedy. Petite Illustration, 186 (October 14, 1933), 1-22. In French.

7482. _____. Non cerco un amante. 1 act. Il Dramma, 126 (November 15, 1931), 36-42. Vittorio Guerriero, translator. In Italian.

7483. _____. Il pane di casa. 1 act. Il Dramma, 364 (October 15, 1941), 33-39. Giovanni Marcellini, translator. In Italian.

7484. _____. Il piacere di dirsi addio. 1 act. Il Dramma, 404 (June 15, 1943), 37-42. Jole Giannini, translator. In Italian.

7485. _____. Il piacere di dirsi addio. 1 act. Sipario, 9 (October, 1954), 51-55. Jole Giannini, translator. In Italian.

7486. _____. Rosso malpelo. 1 act. Il Dramma, 376/377 (April 15/May 1, 1942), 72-82. Giovanni Marcellini, translator. In Italian.

7487. _____. Il Signor Vernet. 2 acts. Il Dramma, 111 (April 1, 1931), 4-22. Vittorio Guerriero, translator. In Italian.

7488. _____. Il Signor Vernet. 2 acts. Sipario, 9 (October, 1954), 35-50. Enzo Ferrieri, translator. In Italian.

7489. _____. L'ultima visita. 1 act. Il Dramma, 116 (June 15, 1931), 40-45. In Italian.

7490. Renard, Maurice-Charles, 1888- and Albert Dubeux. Sans Temoin. 1 act. L'Avant Scène, 172 (April 15, 1958), 36-41. In French.

Rendi, Aloisio, translator see Durrenmatt, F. 2745

_____, translator see Frisch, M. 3310

7491. Renn, Ludwig. Mein Maultier, Meine Frau und Meine Ziege. 1 act. Das Wort, 8 (September, 1938), 74-80. In German.

7492. Renoir, Jean, 1894-1979. Carola. 3 acts. L'Avant Scène, 597 (November 1, 1976), 3-44. In French.

7493. Rèpaci, Leonida, 1898- . L'attesa. 3 acts. Il Dramma, 93 (July 1, 1930), 4-41. In Italian.

7494. _____. L'inaugurazione. 1 act. Il Dramma, 102 (November 15, 1930), 36-40. In Italian.

Repetto, Arriga, translator see Rebello, L. F. 7452

7495. Representation of the Holy Ghost, The. 1 act. Mirror of Taste, 3 (January, 1811), 10-14.

7496. Resurrezione di Cristo. 1 act. Il Dramma, 294 (March, 1961), 6-8. In Italian.

7497. Rexroth, Kenneth, 1905- . Beyond the Mountains. 1 act. Quarterly Review of Literature, 4 (No. 3, 1948), 255-292.

7498. _____. Iphigenia at Aulis, a Dance Play. New Directions, 11 (1949), 266-288.

7499. _____. Phaedra, a Dance Play. New Directions, 9 (1946), 156-186.

Rey, François translator see Marlowe, C. 5564

7500. Rey, Henri-François, 1919- . La Bande à Bonnot. 3 parts, tragi-comedy. L'Avant Scène, 100, 65-91. In French.

7501. Reyher, Ferdinand. "The Play's the Thing," a Dramatic Nightmare. 1 act. Smart Set, 46 (May, 1915), 99-110.

7502. Reynolds, Frederick. The Five Knights; or, The Edict of Charlemagne. 3 acts. The Mirror of Taste, 1 (June, 1810), supplement, 3-16.

7503. Reynosa, Rodrigo de. Coplas de Unos Tres Pastores. 1 act. Philological Quarterly, 21 (January, 1942), 29-37. In Spanish.

7504. Rhapsody in Blue. 1 act. Senior Scholastic, 52 (April 26, 1948), 14-16.

7505. Ribeiro, Gomez Duharte. Le sorelle di Segovia. 3 acts. Il Dramma, n.s., 122 (December 1, 1950), 9-31. Bruno Rovere, translator. In Italian.

7506. Ribemont-Dessaignes, Georges, 1884- . A Poet's Day. 1 act. Life and Letters, 57 (June, 1948), 227-252. M. Merlin Thomas, translator.

7507. _____. Le Serin Muet. 1 act. Drama Review, 16 (March, 1972), 110-116. Victoria Nes Kirby, translator.

7508. Ribes, Jean-Michel, 1946- . Il Faut Que le Sycomore Coule. 2 parts. L'Avant Scène, 595 (October 1, 1976), 39-65. In French.

7509. _____. Omphalos Hotel. L'Avant Scène, 575 (November 15, 1975), 3-38. In French.

7510. _____. On Loge la Nuit-Cafe a l'Eau. L'Avant Scène, 575 (November 15, 1975), 39-57. In French.

7511. _____. Par Dela les Marronniers. L'Avant Scène, 513 (March 1, 1973), 7-23. In French.

7512. _____. Tout Contre un Petit Bois. L'Avant Scène, 595 (October 1, 1976), 3-28. In French.

7513. Ribulsi, Enrico. Il ritorno. 1 act. Sipario, 2 (November, 1947), 51-55. In Italian.

Ricard, André, translator see Aub, M. 434

7514. Riccora, Paola. C'era una volta.... 1 act. Il Dramma, 347 (February 1, 1941), 39-46. In Italian.

7515. _____. Fine mese. 3 acts. Il Dramma, 273 (January 1, 1938), 4-27. In Italian.

7516. _____. Io e te. 3 parts. Il Dramma, 282 (May 15, 1938), 4-24. In Italian.

7517. _____. Se tu non m'ami.... 1 act. Il Dramma, 330 (May 15, 1940), 39-47. In Italian.

7518. _____. Sera di pioggia. 3 acts. Il Dramma, 294 (November 15, 1938), 4-26. In Italian.

7519. Rice, Cale Young, 1872-1943. The Avengers. 1 act. Bookman [New York], 53 (December, 1917), 102.

7520. Rice, Elmer, 1892-1967. Dream Girl. 2 parts. Il Dramma, n.s., 63 (June 15, 1948), 9-40. Mino Roli, translator. In Italian.

7521. Rice, Katharine McDowell. Mrs. Tubbs's Telegram. 1 act, comedy. St. Nicholas, 32 (February, 1905), 344-351.

7522. Richard, Henri-Charles and Albert Gray. Danse Sans Musique. 3 acts. L'Avant Scène (OST), 58 (March, 1952), 1-29. In French.

Richard, Roger, adapter see Bergman, H. 814

7523. Richards, Max, 1942- . Cripple Play. Landfall, 29 (December, 1975), 282-294.

7524. Richards, Milton. The Boy Who Voted for Lincoln. 1 act. Plays, 2 (January, 1943), 72-77.

7525. Richards, Stanley. District of Columbia. 1 act. Negro Story, 2 (December, 1944-January, 1945), 54-58.

7526. _____. District of Columbia. 1 act. Opportunity, 23 (April-June, 1945), 88-91.

_____, adapter see Gomes, D. 3618

7527. Richardson, Anna Steese. Christmas Conspiracy. 1 act. Woman's Home Companion, 37 (December, 1910), 25, 60.

7528. _____. "Mlle. Mystic." 1 act, comedy. Woman's Home Companion, 37 (August, 1910), 8, 37-38.

7529. Richardson, Grace. You Are the Only WASP I Know. 1 act. Performing Arts in Canada, 6 (Summer, 1969), 20-26.

Richardson, Howard, 1917- , translator see Mossi, P. 6267

7530. _____ and William Berney. Eclisse di luna. 2 parts. Il Dramma, n.s., 110 (June 1, 1950), 7-32. Gigi Cane, translator. In Italian.

7531. Richardson, Margaret C. Daylight Wishing Time. 1 act. Plays, 14 (April, 1955), 58-62.

7532. Richardson, Paul. The Salesman. 1 act. Dramatics, 44 (May, 1973), 4-10.

Richert, Georg, translator see Pirandello, L. 7205

Richetti, Giorgio, translator see Shamir, M. 8194

7533. Richman, Arthur, 1886-1944. Ambush. 1 act. Everybody's Magazine, 46 (April, 1922), 137-144.

7534. Richmond, Grace S. Honor and the Girl. 1 act. Ladies' Home Journal, 10 (February, 1903), 13.

7535. Richmond, M. C. Blind Alley. 1 act. Industrial Arts Magazine, 17 (July, 1928), 238-241.

7536. _____. Fads and Frills. 1 act. Industrial Arts Magazine, 19 (March, 1930), 91-93.

7537. Richmond, Samuel S. Ace Navigator. 1 act. Plays, 4 (November, 1944), 11-15.

7538. ———. Big Banker. 1 act. Plays, 9 (October, 1949), 74-79.

7539. ———. The Big Idea. 1 act. Plays, 5 (October, 1945), 76-82.

7540. ———. Bluebird's Children. 1 act. Plays, 4 (May, 1945), 70-73.

7541. ———. Born to the Soil. 1 act. Plays, 4 (December, 1944), 72-78.

7542. ———. Business Is Business. 1 act. Plays, 4 (January, 1945), 72-79.

7543. ———. Buster Picks a Winner. 1 act. Plays, 10 (April, 1951), 73-78.

7544. ———. A Career for Ralph. 1 act. Plays, 2 (December, 1942), 73-78.

7545. ———. The Case of Mr. X. 1 act. Plays, 9 (April, 1950), 66-71.

7546. ———. Caught--One Snipe. 1 act. Plays, 5 (January, 1946), 67-71.

7547. ———. The Corner Store. 1 act. Plays, 5 (March, 1946), 65-72.

7548. ———. The Crisis. 1 act. Plays, 2 (March, 1943), 68-72.

7549. ———. Cub Reporter. 1 act. Plays, 4 (March, 1945), 67-71.

7550. ———. Engineering a Bid. 1 act. Plays, 9 (February, 1950), 70-75.

7551. ———. Flag the Limited. 1 act. Plays, 5 (November, 1945), 67-70.

7552. ———. For Art's Sake. 1 act. Plays, 9 (March, 1950), 74-82.

7553. ———. For the Welfare of All. 1 act. Plays, 10 (May, 1951), 66-73.

7554. ———. Glamour and Grease. 1 act. Plays, 5 (December, 1945), 60-64.

7555. _____. Hail--The Genie. 1 act. Plays, 2 (May, 1943), 73-78.

7556. _____. The Highway Trail. 1 act. Plays, 9 (October, 1949), 70-74.

7557. _____. Highways of Tomorrow. 1 act. Plays, 2 (February, 1943), 65-70.

7558. _____. Hilltop House. 1 act. Plays, 5 (April, 1946), 76-86.

7559. _____. His First Patient. 1 act. Plays, 4 (November, 1944), 66-71. AND Plays, 24 (April, 1965), 29-43.

7560. _____. The House That Jack Built. 1 act. Plays, 5 (May, 1946), 66-70.

7561. _____. Joan Makes a Sale. 1 act. Plays, 2 (October, 1942), 69-71.

7562. _____. The Legacy. 1 act. Plays, 2 (April, 1943), 66-69.

7563. _____. No Sale. 1 act. Plays, 4 (February, 1945), 66-70.

7564. _____. On Trial. 1 act. Plays, 5 (February, 1946), 67-71.

7565. _____. Prescription for Success. 1 act. Plays, 2 (January, 1943), 68-71.

7566. _____. Service for Hubert. 1 act. Plays, 4 (October, 1944), 67-73.

7567. _____. Wanted--A Stenographer. 1 act. Plays, 2 (November, 1942), 72-78.

7568. _____. We But Teach. 1 act. Plays, 4 (April, 1945), 67-71.

7569. Richter, Charles de. La Confession de Mendon. 1 act, comedy. L'Avant Scène, 195 (April 15, 1959), 37-41. In French.

7570. _____. Le Plus Saisi des Trois. 1 act, comedy. L'Avant Scène, 353 (March 15, 1966), 46-51. In French.

Ricono, Connie, translator see Boudousse, J. 1211

_____, translator see Guitry, S. 3783

Ricono

_____, translator see Shaw, I. and J.-P. Aumont
8227

_____, translator see Verneuil, L. 9100

7571. Riddell, Stewart. The Gate of Blue. 1 act. Bookman [New York], 58 (January, 1924), 605-606.

7572. Ridenour, Louis N. Pilot Lights of the Apocalypse. 1 act. Senior Scholastic, 48 (April 29, 1946), 17-19, 28. AND Senior Scholastic, 52 (April 12, 1948), 18-20.

7573. Ridenti, Lucio. La poltrona di teatro, Monologue for Elsa Merlini. 1 act. Il Dramma, 323 (February 1, 1940), 30-31. In Italian.

_____, translator see Bernard, T. 843, 850

_____, translator see Chlumberg, H. von 1813

_____, translator see Delaquis, G. 2293

_____, translator see Dostoevski, F. 2562

_____, translator see Duvernois, H. 2781, 2782, 2783, 2785

_____, translator see Ostrovsky, A. 6912

7574. _____ and Dino Falconi. 100 donne nude. 3 acts. Il Dramma, 17 (April, 1927), 2-37. In Italian.

7575. Rieder, Rolla. Mutcrogpro. 1 act. Dramatika, 7 (1971), 7-11.

7576. Rietmann, Carlo Marcello, 1905- . Il consulto. 1 act. Il Dramma, n.s., 201 (March 15, 1954), 39-46. In Italian.

7577. _____. La grande speranza. 3 acts. Il Dramma, n.s., 289 (October, 1960), 12-42. In Italian.

7578. _____. Maschere scandalizzate. 1 act. Il Dramma, n.s., 374/375 (November/December, 1967), 58-68. In Italian.

7579. _____. Il vento sotto la porta. 3 acts. Il Dramma, n.s., 350/351 (November/December, 1965), 58-113. In Italian.

Rietti, Victor, translator see Bracco, R. 1255

_____, translator see Forzano, G. 3235

Rietty, Robert, translator see Forzano, G. 3234

————, translator see Levi, P. 4958, 4959

————, translator see Niccodemi, D. 6536

Rieux, Albert, 1906- see Vattier, R. 9047

7580. Riggs, Lynn. We Speak for Ourselves. 1 act. Theatre Arts, 27 (December, 1943), 752-757.

7581. Rigoir, Vincent, 1935- . Le Grand Autobus. 1 act. L'Avant Scène, 509 (January 1, 1973), 33-38. In French.

7582. Riley, Alice C. D. The Mandarin Coat. 1 act, comedy. Drama, 13 (January, 1923), 132-135, 141-143.

7583. ————. Taxi. 1 act, comedy. Drama, 16 (February, 1926), 177-178.

7584. ————. Their Anniversary. 1 act, comedy. Drama, 12 (February, 1922), 157-162.

7585. Rimanelli, Giosè, 1926- . Il corno Francese. 1 act. Il Dramma, n.s., 303 (December, 1961), 32-44. In Italian.

7586. ————. Lares. 1 act. Il Dramma, n.s., 341 (February, 1965), 46-50. In Italian.

7587. ————. Te' in casa Picasso. 2 parts. Il Dramma, n.s., 338/339 (November/December, 1964), 41-64. In Italian.

7588. Ringwood, Gwen Pharis. Dark Harvest. 3 acts. Canadian Theatre Review, 5 (Winter, 1975), 70-128.

7589. Riollet, Marius. La Bête. 1 act. L'Avant Scène, 275 (November 1, 1962), 35-43. In French.

Ripamonti, Icilio, translator see Puget, C.-A. and P. Bost 7329

Ripellino, Ela, translator see Mnacko, L. 6099

7590. Rit, Gaston. La Rencontre. 1 act. L'Avant Scène, 406 (July 1, 1968), 31-35. In French.

7591. Ritchie, Estelle. Flowers in May. 1 act. Plays, 3 (May, 1944), 49-51.

7592. ————. Ricky and the Eggs. 1 act. Plays, 15 (March, 1956), 75-78.

7593. Rittenhouse, Charles. Children of the Sun. 1 act. Plays, 5 (April, 1946), 57-66.

7594. _____. A Family in Space, a Comedy. About the Solar System. 1 act. Plays, 18 (March, 1959), 49-58.

7595. Ritter, Mary L. Silent. 3 acts. St. Nicholas, 1 (January, 1874), 124-128.

7596. Rittner, Thaddäus. Theatre pare. 1 act. Der Sturm, 1 (June 9, 1910), 116-117. In German.

7597. Rivemale, Alexandre. Hier à Andersonville. 3 acts. L'Avant Scène, 363 (September 1, 1966), 7-30. In French.

7598. _____. Le Mobile. 3 acts, comedy. L'Avant Scène, 233 (December 15, 1960), 9-38. In French.

7599. _____ and Henri Colpi. L'Eléphant dans la Maison. L'Avant Scène (ROST), 68 (October, 1952), 1-21. In French.

7600. Rives, Amelie, 1863-1945. Athelwold. 5 acts. Harper's, 84 (February, 1892), 394-424.

Rizzardi, Alfredo, translator see Borgese, E. M. 1198

7601. Roam, Pearl. The Magic Smile. 1 act. Plays, 21 (October, 1961), 67-70.

Robbins, Aileen, translator see Tzara, T. 8962

7602. Robbins, Jean. Magnus the Magnificent. 1 act. Plays, 21 (January, 1962), 75-78.

7603. Robbins, Kenneth. A Good and Dandy World. 1 act. Dramatics, 42 (November, 1970), 5-9.

7604. Robecchi-Brivio, Erminio. La figlia del Re. 1 act. Il Dramma, 353 (May 1, 1941), 43-50. In Italian.

7605. Roberts, Edward Barry. The Secret Life of Dan Ingram. 1 act. Plays, 29 (April, 1970), 11-19.

7606. Roberts, Helen M. Betsy Ross. 1 act. Plays, 3 (January, 1944), 33-38. AND Plays, 29 (February, 1970), 46-52.

7607. _____. The Boy Dreamer. 1 act. Plays, 3 (October, 1943), 25-32.

7608. _____. The Builder of the Wall. 1 act. Plays, 4 (May, 1945), 41-48.

7609. _____. The Ducal Bonnet. 1 act. Plays, 2 (February, 1943), 31-36.

7610. _____. For the Glory of Spain. 1 act. Plays, 4 (October, 1944), 37-43. AND Plays, 32 (October, 1972), 59-64.

7611. _____. The Lonely Fir Tree. 1 act. Plays, 4 (December, 1944), 52-56.

7612. _____. The Tomboy Princess. 1 act. Plays, 4 (March, 1945), 42-46.

7613. Roberts, Walter, adapter. The Musicians of Bremen Town. 1 act. Plays, 27 (January, 1968), 71-74.

7614. Robertson, O. J. The Animals' Christmas Tree. 1 act. Plays, 27 (December, 1967), 67-69.

7615. _____. The Sleepy Little Elf. 1 act. Plays, 27 (December, 1967), 70-72.

7616. _____. Toys for Santa. 1 act. Plays, 26 (December, 1966), 69-71.

7617. Robinson, Christina. The Boat Club Dance. 1 act. Plays, 22 (April, 1963), 11-22.

Robinson, Donald Fay, adapter see Maastricht Play 5111

7618. Robinson, Edwin Arlington, 1869-1935. Demos and Dionysus. 1 act. Theatre Arts, 9 (January, 1925), 32-42.

7619. Robinson, Gertrude. Paul Revere's Cloak. 1 act. Plays, 3 (April, 1944), 15-24.

7620. _____. President Lincoln's Shawl Pin. 1 act. Plays, 4 (February, 1945), 12-20.

7621. _____. School's Done. 1 act. Plays, 2 (March, 1943), 20-29.

7622. _____. Scribe to George Washington. 1 act. Plays, 3 (January, 1943), 12-23.

7623. Robinson, Lennox, 1886-1958. Church Street. 1 act. Il Dramma, 385 (September 1, 1942), 27-40. Liana Ferri, translator. In Italian.

7624. _____. Crabbed Youth and Age. 1 act, comedy. Theatre Arts, 8 (January, 1924), 51-63.

7625. _____. Never the Time and the Place. 1 act. Dublin Magazine, 1 (May, 1924), 856-867.

7626. Robinson, Miriam. The Image-Makers Take Over. 1 act. Plays, 32 (October, 1972), 16-22.

Robinson 532

7627. _____. A New Look at American History. 1 act. Plays, 32 (April, 1973), 53-58.

7628. _____, adapter. A Father's Pride. 1 act. Plays, 34 (November, 1974), 71-74.

7629. _____, adapter. A Mother's Burden. 1 act. Plays, 33 (January, 1973), 56-66.

7630. Roblès, Emmanuel, 1913- . Montserrat. 3 acts. Il Dramma, n.s., 119 (October 15, 1950), 7-27. Leonardo Cortese, translator. In Italian.

Robson, Cecil, adapter see Whiting, J. 9332

7631. Robson, William N. Open Letter on Race Hatred. 1 act. Theatre Arts, 28 (September, 1944), 537-552.

7632. Rocca, Guido. I coccodrilli. 3 acts, comedy. Sipario, 12 (January, 1957), 41-57. In Italian.

7633. _____. Mare e whisky. 3 acts, comedy. Sipario, 14 (November, 1959), 37-56. In Italian.

7634. _____. Una montagna di carta. 3 acts, comedy. Sipario, 146 (June, 1958), 37-56. In Italian.

7635. Rocca, Robert. Un Certain Monsieur Blot. 3 acts. L'Avant Scène, 252 (November 1, 1961), 7-40. In French.

7636. Rocco, Gino. "Mezzo gaudio." 3 acts. Il Dramma, 15 (February, 1927), 7-34. In Italian.

7637. _____. Niente. 1 act. Il Dramma, 208 (April 15, 1935), 19-32. In Italian.

7638. _____. Ricevimento di gala. 1 act. Il Dramma, 279 (April 1, 1938), 23-31. In Italian.

7639. _____. Tragedia senza eroe. 3 acts. Il Dramma, 82 (January 15, 1930), 6-32. In Italian.

7640. _____. Troppo equali. 1 act. Il Dramma, 305 (May 1, 1939), 23-28. In Italian.

7641. _____. Tutto. 1 act. Il Dramma, 208 (April 15, 1935), 4-18. In Italian.

7642. _____. Il velo impigliato. 1 act. Il Dramma, 56 (December 15, 1928), 34-40. In Italian.

Rochat, Suzanne, translator see Achard, M. 21

_____, translator see Claudel, P. 1866, 1869

_____, translator see Messager, C. 5787, 5792

Roche, France, translator see Manhoff, B. 5498

7643. Roda, Roda. Odio balcanico. 1 act. Il Dramma, 44 (June 15, 1928), 36-39. Taulero Zulberti, translator. In Italian.

7644. _____. La scatola dei gioielli. 1 act. Il Dramma, 46 (July 15, 1928), 40-41. Taulero Zulberti, translator. In Italian.

7645. Rody, Alberto, 1933- . Tic-Tac (Hoquet Pour Deux Vieillards). 1 act. L'Avant Scène, 459 (November 1, 1970), 45-50. In French.

7646. Roedel, Reto. Monologo alla radio. 1 act. Il Dramma, n. s., 190 (October 1, 1953), 38-48.

Roeder, Ralph, translator see Copeau, J. 2010

_____, translator see Mazaud, E. 5709

7647. Roelvink, Herman C. J. The Stormbird. 4 acts. Poet Lore, 24 (Spring, 1913), 65-107. Arthur Davison Ficke, translator.

7648. Roger-Ferdinand. La Galette des Rois. 3 acts, comedy. L'Avant Scène (OST), 18 (February, 1950), 3-41. In French.

7649. _____. Le President Houdecoeur. 4 acts, comedy. L'Avant Scène, (OST), 37 (February, 1951), 3-50. In French.

_____, adapter see Anderson, R. 216

_____, adapter see O'Brien, L. 6748

7650. Roger-Marx, Claude, 1888- . Dimanche. 1 act, comedy. Petite Illustration, 184 (February 25, 1933), 1-9. In French.

7651. Rogers, John William, Jr., 1894- . Bumblepuppy, a Comedy of Climate. 1 act. Theatre Arts, 10 (September, 1926), 604-612.

7652. _____. Judge Lynch. 1 act. Southwest Review, 10 (October, 1924), 3-23.

7653. _____. Westward People: A Drama of Mary Austin

Holley's First Visit to Texas. 1 act. Southwest Review, 20 (October, 1934), 87-109.

7654. Rognoni, Angelo. La fiaba di Namu'. 3 acts. Il Dramma, n. s., 215 (October 15, 1954), 7-29. In Italian.

7655. Roguish Tricks of Coviello, The. A Scenario of the Commedia dell'arte. 3 acts. The Mask, 6 (April, 1914), 353-356.

Roinard, P. N., adapter see Song of Songs of Solomon 8375

7656. Rojas, Fernando de. La celestina. 2 parts. Il Dramma, n. s., 307 (April, 1962), 5-47. Carlo Terron, translator. In Italian.

7657. _____. La Celestine. L'Avant Scène, 566 (June 15, 1975), 3-45. Pierre Laville, adapter. In French.

Rokk-Richter, Stefano, translator see Molnar, F. 6133, 6137

7658. Roland, Claude and Gabriel d'Hervilliez. Les Assureurs. 1 act, comedy. Petite Illustration, 191 (July 20, 1935), 1-9. In French.

Roli, Mino, translator see Gazo, M. V. 3432

_____, translator see Inge, W. 4378

_____, translator see Rice, E. 7520

_____, translator see Williams, T. 9418, 9430

7659. _____ and Giancarlo Sbragia. La confessioni della Signora Elvira. Sipario, 226 (February, 1965), 19-36. In Italian.

7660. Rolland, Georges. Coltiviamo in pace i nostri giardini. 3 acts. Il Dramma, n. s., 146 (December 1, 1951), 6-28. Cesare Meano, translator. In Italian.

7661. Rolland, Romain, 1866-1944. Le Jeu de l'Amour et la Mort. 1 act. Petite Illustration, 86 (March 10, 1928), 1-22. In French.

7662. _____. The Wolves. 3 acts. Drama, 32, 578-636. Barrett H. Clark, translator.

7663. Rollins, Alice W. Dealing in Futures. 1 act. Cosmopolitan, 16 (November, 1893), 90-101.

Roloff, Michael, translator see Handke, P. 3882, 3884, 3885

_____, translator see Kroetz, F. X. 4727

7664. Roma, Enrico. La corsa dietro l'ombra. 3 acts. Il Dramma, 161 (May 1, 1933), 4-26. In Italian.

7665. _____. Il fantoccio irresistibile. 3 acts. Il Dramma, 235 (June 1, 1936), 2-26. In Italian.

7666. _____. Una parte difficile. 1 act. Il Dramma, 171 (October 1, 1933), 18-31. In Italian.

7667. Romains, Jules, 1885-1972. Boen, ou La Possession des Biens. 3 acts, comedy. Petite Illustration, 180 (October 21, 1931), 1-33. In French.

7668. _____. Donogoo. 3 parts. Petite Illustration, 178 (February 7, 1931), 1-40. In French.

7669. _____. Knock, ou, Le Triomphe de la Medecine. 3 acts, comedy. L'Avant Scène, 521-522 (July, 1973), 23-54. In French.

7670. _____. La Scintillante. 1 act, comedy. L'Avant Scène, 521-522 (July, 1973), 57-69. In French.

7671. _____. Il signore le Trouhadec si lascia traviare. 5 acts. Il Dramma, 66 (May 15, 1929), 4-24. Maria Martone, translator. In Italian.

7672. Romualdi, Giuseppe. La casa del parco. 3 acts. Il Dramma, 256 (April 15, 1937), 2-21. In Italian.

7673. _____. Glisenti.... Calibro 9. 3 acts. Il Dramma, 209 (May 1, 1935), 4-27. In Italian.

7674. _____. Le montagne. 3 acts. Il Dramma, 333 (July 1, 1940), 6-26. In Italian.

7675. _____. Una notte. 3 acts. Il Dramma, 269 (November 1, 1937), 2-17. In Italian.

7676. _____. Primavera sulla veve. 3 acts. Il Dramma, 245 (November 1, 1936), 2-22. In Italian.

7677. _____. L'ultima carta. 3 acts. Il Dramma, 188 (June 15, 1934), 4-30. In Italian.

7678. Ronan, Robert. The Missing Gift. 1 act. Plays, 20 (March, 1961), 71-74.

7679. Ronchi, Teresa. Es ist Krieg. Sipario, 347 (April, 1975), 67-80. In Italian.

7680. Ronchini, Roberto. Binario morto. 1 act. Sipario, 19 (October, 1964), 60-64. In Italian.

7681. Ronco, Mario. Il piatto d'argento. 10 parts. Il Dramma, n. s., 50/51 (December 1/15, 1947), 93-103. In Italian.

7682. Roncoroni, Jean-Louis, 1926- . Un Bourgeois de Calais. 1 act. L'Avant Scène, 321 (November 1, 1964), 38-44. In French.

7683. _____. Les Hommes du Dimanche. 3 acts. L'Avant Scène, 181 (September 15, 1958), 24-46. In French.

7684. _____. La Petite Bête. 1 act. L'Avant Scène, 563 (May 1, 1975), 31-42. In French.

7685. _____. Rebrousse-Poil. 3 acts. L'Avant Scène, 321 (November 1, 1964), 9-34. In French.

7686. _____. Le Temps de Cerises. 4 acts. L'Avant Scène, 261 (March 15, 1962), 8-32. In French.

7687. _____. Le Tir Clara. 3 acts. L'Avant Scène, 201 (July 15, 1959), 7-31. In French.

7688. Rondi, Brunello, 1924- . Gli amanti. 3 acts. Il Dramma, n. s., 373 (October, 1967), 5-29. In Italian.

7689. _____. La camera degli ospiti. 2 parts. Il Dramma, n. s., 254 (March, 1966), 24-40. In Italian.

7690. _____. Il capitano d'industria. 2 parts, comedy. Sipario, 16 (May, 1961), 35-74. In Italian.

7691. Ronfani, Ugo. I fiori di un anno lontano. 1 act. Il Dramma, n. s., 324 (September, 1963), 43-54. In Italian.

7692. _____. Nebbie. 1 act. Il Dramma, n. s., 337 (October, 1964), 79-90. In Italian.

_____, translator see Saurraute, N. 7960

Rongel, Carlos, translator see Valéry, P. 8997

7693. Roof, Katharine Metcalf. Christmas Tryst. 1 act. Touchstone, 6 (December, 1919), 83-89, 151-158.

7694. _____. Edge of the Wood. 1 act. Drama, 10 (February, 1920), 196-199.

7695. _____. The Secret. 1 act. Smart Set, 19 (August, 1906), 108-111.

7696. _____. The Wanderer. 1 act. Smart Set, 23 (November, 1907), 130-133.

7697. Rooney, James R. The Demon Cat. 1 act. Journal of Irish Literature, 3 (May, 1974), supplement, 1-16.

Rosa, Laura Dalla, translator see Fry, C. 3330

Rosada, Guido, translator see Shelley, E. 8235

Rosada, Rolandi, translator see Shelley, E. 8235

7698. Rosano, Rene. L'Idiot du Miracle. 1 act. L'Avant Scène, 594 (September 15, 1976), 31-40. In French.

Rosati, Salvatore, translator see Eliot, T. S. 2847, 2851

Rose, Jacques-Leon, translator see Hacks, P. 3813

_____, translator see Hildesheimer, W. 4105

7699. Rose, Reginald, 1920- . Twelve Angry Men. L'Avant Scène, 184 (November 1, 1958), 8-27. André Obey, adapter. In French.

Rosenberg, James L., 1921- , translator see Frisch, M. 3313

Rosenthal, Renée, adapter see Kopit, A. 4688

Rosi, Giuseppina, translator see Aroutcheff, G. 359

Rosmer, Ernst, pseud. see Bernstein, E. P. 860, 861

7700. Ross, Arthur R. Dialogue from a Garden. 1 act. New Mexico Quarterly, 32 (Autumn-Winter, 1962-63), 145-155.

7701. Ross, Clarendon. The Avenger. 1 act. Drama, 31 (August, 1919), 329-339.

7702. _____. The Prisoner. 1 act. Poet Lore, 29 (Winter, 1918), 590-595.

7703. _____. Reconsiderations: The Murderer; The Derelict. 1 act, each. Poet Lore, 30 (Winter, 1919), 596-607.

7704. Ross, Fannie R. As Grandmother Told It. 1 act. Plays, 3 (November, 1943), 58-62.

7705. _____. It Happened in Egypt. 1 act. Plays, 10 (March, 1951), 41-46.

7706. Ross, Hugh. --After the Event. 1 act. Bookman [London], 84 (September, 1933), 280-284.

7707. Ross, Kenneth, 1908- . Mr. Kilt and the Great I Am. 3 acts. Plays and Players, 17 (September, 1970), 67-86.

7708. _____. Under the Skin. 2 acts. Plays and Players, 15 (August, 1968), 27-46.

7709. Ross, Sari. Spinning a Spider's Tale. 1 act. Plays, 34 (January, 1975), 57-61.

Rossato see Giancapo 3478

7710. Rossato, Arturo. Uno qualunque. 3 parts. Sipario, 13 (December, 1958), 17-24. In Italian.

7711. Rosselson, Leon. Le Primitif. 1 act. L'Avant Scène, 542 (June 1, 1974), 36-43. Anne Bocquet-Roudy, adapter. In French.

7712. Rossi, Corrado. Infedelta. 1 act. Il Dramma, 69 (July 1, 1929), 37-39. In Italian.

_____, translator see Fodor, L. 3176

_____, translator see Heltai, J. 4051

_____, translator see Lakatos, L. 4771, 4772

_____, translator see Lang, A. 4793

_____, translator see Molnar, F. 6159

Rossi, Franco, translator see O'Neill, E. 6861

7713. Rosso, Renzo. La Gabbia. 2 acts. Sipario, 267 (July, 1968), 35-50. In Italian.

7714. Rosso di San Secondo, Piermaria, 1887-1956. Copecchia e Marianorma. 1 act. Il Dramma, 400 (April 15, 1943), 33-37. In Italian.

7715. _____. Le esperienze di Giovanni Arce, filosofo. 3 acts. Il Dramma, 95 (August 1, 1930), 4-24. In Italian.

7716. _____. Trappola per vecchia letteratura. 3 parts. Il Dramma, 178 (January 15, 1934), 4-16. In Italian.

7717. Rostand, Edmond, 1868-1918. Cyrano de Bergerac. 1 act. Plays, 15 (October, 1955), 87-96. Lewy Olfson, adapter.

7718. _____. La Princesse Lointaine. 4 acts. Petite Illustration, 87 (November 9, 1929), 1-40. In French.

7719. _____. The Romancers. 3 acts, comedy. Poet Lore, 32 (1921), 520-561. Anna E. Bagstad, translator.

7720. Rostand, Maurice, 1891- . Le Général Boulanger. 2 parts. Petite Illustration, 180 (December 12, 1931), 1-50. In French.

7721. _____. Une Jeune Fille Espagnole. 3 acts, comedy. Petite Illustration, 181 (March 26, 1932), 1-41. In French.

7722. _____. Napoleon IV. 4 acts. Petite Illustration, 86 (October 20, 1928), 1-38. In French.

7723. Rosten, Norman. Miss Liberty Goes to Town. 1 act. Senior Scholastic, 43 (January 17-22, 1944), 13-15.

7724. Roth, Philip, 1933- . Heard Melodies Are Sweeter. 1 act. Esquire, 50 (August, 1958), 58. AND Esquire, 80 (October, 1973), 315, 498.

Rothenberg, Julius G., translator see Fratti, M. 3276

Rothschild, Philippe de, 1902- see Fry, C. 3331

7725. Rouchet, Pierre. Crime au Village. 1 act. L'Avant Scène, 291 (July 1, 1963), 37-44. In French.

7726. Roudy, Pierre, 1927- . Elle Etait Rousse. 1 act. L'Avant Scène, 491 (March 15, 1972), 33-36. In French.

7727. _____. Le Numero. 1 act. L'Avant Scène, 412 (October 15, 1968), 37-43. In French.

7728. _____. Les Oeufs a la Moutarde. 1 act. L'Avant Scène, 561 (April 1, 1975), 27-33. In French.

_____, translator see Fellows, M. S. 2981

_____, translator see Wesker, A. 9305

7729. Rougerie, Jean, 1929- . Entretiens avec le Professeur Y. L'Avant Scène, 584 (April 1, 1976), 3-23. In French.

_____, adapter see Bruyère, J. de la 1393

Rougeul, Jean, translator see Scarnicci, G. and R. Tarabusi 8009

Rouleau, Raymond, 1904- , adapter see Williams, T. 9434

7730. Rouquette, Max. La Comédie du Miroir. 1 act. L'Avant Scène, 164, 35-42. In French.

7731. _____. Le Medecin de Cucugnan. 1 act, farce. L'Avant Scène, 111, 31-40. In French.

7732. Roussel, Raymond, 1877- . L'Etoile au Front. 3 acts. L'Avant Scène, 476 (July 15, 1971), 7-33. In French.

7733. Roussin, Andre, 1911- . Am Stram Gram. 3 acts. Sipario, 3 (April, 1948), 33-52. Ivo Chiesa, translator. In Italian.

7734. _____. L'Amour Fou, ou, La Premiere Surprise. 4 acts, comedy. L'Avant Scène, 569 (August, 1975), 3-36. In French.

7735. _____. Un Amour Qui ne Finit Pas. 2 parts, comedy. L'Avant Scène, 289 (June 1, 1963), 9-33. In French.

7736. _____. Les Barbes Nobles. 1 act, comedy. L'Avant Scène, 75 (March 20, 1953), 7-17. In French.

7737. _____. Bobosse. 3 acts, comedy. L'Avant Scène (OST), 28 (July, 1950), 3-34. In French.

7738. _____. Bobosse. 3 acts. Il Dramma, n.s., 156 (May 1, 1952), 7-28. B. L. Randone, translator. In Italian.

7739. _____. La cicogna si diverte. 4 acts. Il Dramma, n.s., 150 (February 1, 1952), 6-36. B. L. Randone, translator. In Italian.

7740. _____. La Claque. 2 acts, comedy. L'Avant Scène, 525 (September 15, 1973), 7-35. In French.

7741. _____. La Coquine. 2 parts, comedy. L'Avant Scène, 254 (December 1, 1961), 8-30. In French.

7742. _____. L'Ecole des Autres. 1 act. L'Avant Scène, 289 (June 1, 1963), 35-41. In French.

7743. _____. L'Ecole des Dupes. 1 act, comedy. L'Avant Scène, 137, 33-41. In French.

7744. _____. L'Ecole des Dupes. 1 act. Il Dramma, n.s., 187/188 (September 1, 1953), 40-48. B. L. Randone, translator. In Italian.

7745. _____. Une Femme Qui Dit la Verité. 1 act, comedy. L'Avant Scène, 234, 31-39. In French.

7746. _____. Les Glorieuses. 2 acts, comedy. L'Avant Scène, 250 (October 1, 1961), 8-29. In French.

7747. _____. The Little Hut. 3 acts, comedy. Theatre Arts, 38 (October, 1954), 34-60. Nancy Mitford, adapter.

7748. _____. Lorsque l'Enfant Parait. 4 acts, comedy. L'Avant Scène (ROST), 60 (May, 1952), 1-37. In French.

7749. _____. La Mamma. 2 acts, comedy. L'Avant Scène, 153, 1-28. In French.

7750. _____. Le Mari, Le Femme et la Mort. 3 acts, comedy. L'Avant Scène, 544 (July 1, 1974), 7-37. In French.

7751. _____. Le Mari, la Femme et la Mort. 3 acts. Il Dramma, n. s., 221 (February, 1955), 3-30. B. L. Randone, translator. In Italian.

7752. _____. Nina. 3 acts, comedy. L'Avant Scène (OST), 22 (April, 1950), 3-37. In French.

7753. _____. Nina. 3 acts. Il Dramma, n. s., 104 (March 1, 1950), 11-37. B. L. Randone, translator. In Italian.

7754. _____. La Nuit d'Avril. 1 act. L'Avant Scène, 501 (September 1, 1972), 37-40. In French.

7755. _____. Les Oeufs de L'Autruche. 2 acts, comedy. L'Avant Scène (OST), 1 (March, 1949), 3-25. In French.

7756. _____. On Ne Sait Jamais. 2 acts, comedy. L'Avant Scène, 439 (December 15, 1969), 7-35. In French.

7757. _____. La Petite Hutte. 3 acts. Il Dramma, n. s., 90 (August 1, 1949), 7-30. B. L. Randone, translator. In Italian.

7758. _____. Rupture. 1 act. L'Avant Scène, 306 (March 1, 1964), 31-36. In French.

7759. _____. Le uova della struzzo. 2 parts. Il Dramma, n. s., 98 (December 1, 1949), 7-27. Gigi Cane, translator. In Italian.

7760. _____. Le Uova di Struzzo. 2 acts, comedy. Il Dramma (November, 1974), 25-53. Enrico Fulchignoni, translator. In Italian.

7761. _____. La Voyante. 2 acts, tragi-comedy. L'Avant Scène, 306 (March 1, 1964), 9-29. In French.

_____, adapter see Williams, E. 9412

_____, translator see Simon, N. 8283

7762. ———— and Madeleine Gray. Hélène, ou La Joie de Vivre. 3 acts, comedy. L'Avant Scène, 77 (April 25, 1953), 3-30. In French.

7763. ————. The Private Life of Helen of Troy. 3 acts. Il Dramma, n.s., 200 (March 1, 1954), 5-25. B. L. Randone, translator. In Italian.

7764. Rouveyrol, Aurania. The Price of Love. 1 act, comedy. Drama, 16 (March, 1926), 219-220, 238-239.

Rovere, Bruno, translator see Ribeiro, G. D. 7505

7765. Roversi, Roberto. Il crack. 3 parts. Sipario, 24 (March, 1969), 49-64. In Italian.

7766. Rowell, Adelaide Corinne, 1887- . The High Heart. 1 act. Drama, 17 (March, 1927), 173-176, 190-191.

7767. ————. The Last Frontier. 1 act. Drama, 15 (April, 1925), 157-160, 163.

7768. ————. The Silly Ass. 1 act, comedy. Drama, 12 (September, 1922), 344-350.

7769. ————. Unto the Least of These. 1 act. Drama, 18 (November, 1927), 43-46, 59-62.

7770. Rowland, Elsie. Hans, Who Made the Princess Laugh. 1 act. Plays, 2 (April, 1943), 45-50.

7771. ————. A Precedent in Pastries. 1 act. Plays, 4 (March, 1945), 37-41.

7772. ————. The Three Aunts. 1 act. Plays, 3 (March, 1944), 37-43. AND Plays, 27 (May, 1968), 77-84.

7773. Rowley, Richard. River in Spate. 1 act. Dublin Magazine, n.s., 17 (January-March, 1942), 18-41.

Rowley, William, 1585?-1642 see Middleton, T. 5821

Roy, Claude, 1915- , adapter see Nichols, P. 6542, 6544

————, translator see Barnes, P. 609

————, translator see Horovitz, I. 4174

Roy, Jessie H. see Turner, G. C. 8956

7774. Royle, Edwin Milton, 1862-1942. The Squaw-man, An Idyl of the Ranch. 1 act. Cosmopolitan, 34 (August, 1904), 411-418.

7775. Rozewicz, Tadeusz, 1921- . The Interrupted Act. 1 act. Gambit, 3 (No. 12), 39-67. Adam Czerniawski, translator.

7776. _____. Kartoteka. 1 act. Sipario, 18 (August-September, 1963), 69-77. A. M. Raffo, translator. In Italian.

7777. _____. Die Zeugen, oder Unsere Kleine Stabilisierung. 1 act. Spectaculum, 7 (1964), 283-309. Ilka Boll, translator. In German.

7778. Rubber Won't Stretch. 1 act. Plays, 3 (November, 1943), 73-76.

7779. Rubinstein, H. F. "Revanche"--A Mystery. New Coterie, 1 (November, 1925), 71-85.

7780. Rubio, Emery and Miriam Balf. Sunday Breakfast. 2 parts. Il Dramma, n.s., 170/171/172 (December 1/15, 1952/ January 1, 1953), 79-110. Ada Salvatore, translator. In Italian.

Rudd, Martin see Gibson, P. 3498

7781. Rudkin, David, 1937- . Afore Night Come. 2 acts. Sipario, 230 (June, 1965), 58-74. Ettore Capriolo, translator. In Italian.

7782. _____. Ashes. 3 parts. Plays and Players, 21 (March, April, 1974), 57-65; 63-65.

7783. Rueda, Lope de, 1510?-1565. Cuckholds Go to Heaven. 1 act. Poet Lore, 46 (Autumn, 1940), 208-212. Angel Flores and Joseph Liss, translators.

7784. _____. Eufemia. 1 act, comedy. Tulane Drama Review, 3 (December, 1958), 57-79. W. S. Merwin, translator.

7785. _____. The Olives. 1 act. Modern Language Journal, 31 (February, 1947), 100-102. Frank E. Snow, translator.

Ruffo, Anton Mario, translator see Mrozek, S. 6286

7786. Rugg, Minnie M. and Morton Sonnenfeld. We Pledge Ourselves. 1 act. Senior Scholastic, 43 (November 8-13, 1943), 17-19.

Ruggi, Lorenzo, 1883- , translator see Gehri, A. 3433

Rugiu, Antonio Santoni, adapter see Gogol, N. 3599

7787. Ruibal, Jose. The Beggars. 1 act. Drama and Theatre, 7 (Fall, 1968), 56-63. John Pearson, translator.

7788. _____. The Begging Machine. Modern International Drama, 9 (Spring, 1976), 7-45. J. S. Bernstein, translator.

7789. _____. The Codfish. Modern International Drama, 5 (Spring, 1972), 7-18. John Pearson, translator.

7790. _____. The Jackass. 1 act. Modern International Drama, 2 (September, 1968), 33-56. Thomas Seward, translator.

7791. Ruinet, Gerard, 1944- . Le Droit Chemin. 1 act. L'Avant Scène, 517 (May 1, 1973), 45-49. In French.

7792. _____. Le Grand Jeu. 1 act. L'Avant Scène, 493 (April 15, 1972), 41-43. In French.

Ruiz, Luis Soto, translator see Canton, W. 1575

_____, translator see Gorostiza, C. 3655

7793. Ruiz, Raul. Changing of the Guard. 1 act. First Stage, 5 (Winter, 1966-67), 238-243. Miller Williams, translator.

7794. Rulkotter, Frederick. Poor Oliver. 1 act. One-Act Play Magazine, 4 (July-August, 1941), 259-273.

7795. Rumpelstiltskin. 1 act. Plays, 14 (January, 1955), 79-83. Rowena Bennett, adapter.

7796. Runnette, Helen V. Christmas Quest. 1 act. Plays, 28 (December, 1968), 41-49.

7797. _____. Touchstone. 1 act. Plays, 14 (December, 1964), 53-61.

7798. _____. The Way. 1 act. Plays, 15 (December, 1955), 48-52.

Rusilka, James see Feeney, M. 2972

7799. Rusinol y Prats, Santiago, 1861-1931. Prodigal Doll. 1 act, comedy. Drama, 25 (February, 1917), 90-116. John Garrett Underhill, translator.

7800. Ruskin, John, 1819-1900. The King of the Golden River. 1 act. Plays, 11 (January, 1952), 71-77. Eleanor Leuser, adapter.

7801. _____. The King of the Golden River. 1 act. Plays, 34 (February, 1975), 79-84. Lewis Mahlmann and Pat Platt, adapters.

7802. Russ, Joanna. Scenes from Domestic Life. 1 act. Little Magazine, 5 (Spring, 1971), 32-47.

7803. _____. Window Dressing. Confrontation, 6 (Spring, 1973), 57-67.

Russell, H. K., translator see The Redentin Easter Play 7455

7804. Russell, Mary Margaret. The Devil's Doll. 1 act. Poet Lore, 42 (Spring, 1935), 338-355.

_____, translator see The Redentin Easter Play 7455

7805. Russo, Ferdinando. Luciella Catena. 2 acts, comedy. Sipario, 9 (August-September, 1954), 35-42. In Italian.

7806. Ruth, Leon. Le Flambeau. 3 acts. L'Avant Scène, 227, 35-42. In French.

7807. _____. Il n'y a pas d'Automne Sans Eté. 1 act, comedy. L'Avant Scène, 144, 41-51. In French.

7808. _____. Le "Oui" des Jeunes Filles. 1 act, comedy. L'Avant Scène, 177 (July 1, 1958), 30-40. In French.

7809. _____. Poison. 1 act, comedy. L'Avant Scène, 271 (September 1, 1962), 36-42. In French.

7810. _____. Trio en Sol Majeur. 1 act, comedy. L'Avant Scène, 121, 39-46. In French.

7811. Ruthenberg, G. Hutchinson. The Children. 1 act. Drama, 15 (March, 1925), 131-132, 136.

7812. Ruthenburg, Grace Dorcas. The Gooseberry Mandarin, a Semi-Tragedy for Puppets. 1 act. Theatre Arts, 12 (July, 1928), 501-504.

7813. _____. Hans Burlow's Last Puppet. 1 act. Scholastic, 20 (March 5, 1932), 17-18, 48.

7814. Rutherford, Eric. Notice to Quit. 1 act. Dramatika, 9 (Spring, 1972), n. p.

7815. Rutherford, Margery C. Albert Einstein, Schoolboy. 1 act. Plays, 27 (April, 1968), 51-57.

7816. _____. Sam Clemens of Hannibal. 1 act. Plays, 28 (January, 1969), 53-58.

Rutman, Jacques see Lanoux, A. 4802

7817. Ruzzante, 1502-1542. Les Vilains. 3 parts, farce. L'Avant Scène, 514 (March 15, 1973), 7-31. Andre Gille and Alfred Mortier, adapters. In French.

7818. Ryan, Elaine. Now I Lay Me Down to Sleep. 3 acts, comedy. Theatre Arts, 34 (July, 1950), 57-88.

7819. Ryan, Roberta M. Snow White or the Modern School Girl. 1 act. Wilson Library Bulletin, 13 (April, 1939), 554-555.

7820. Rybak, Rose Kacherian. Bicentennial Bonanza. 1 act. Plays, 35 (January, 1976), 69-78.

7821. _____. The Day the Marsmen Landed. 1 act. Plays, 30 (April, 1971), 37-42.

7822. _____. The Day the Moonmen Landed. 1 act. Plays, 22 (October, 1962), 45-50.

7823. _____. Election Day in Spooksville. 1 act. Plays, 24 (October, 1964), 29-39. AND Plays, 36 (November, 1976), 27-38.

7824. _____. History Hits the Jackpot. 1 act. Plays, 36 (October, 1976), 17-26.

7825. _____. Rufus Robin's Day in Court. 1 act. Plays, 22 (April, 1963), 74-78.

7826. Ryerson, Florence, 1892- . Letters. 1 act, comedy. Drama, 16 (April, 1926), 253-254.

7827. _____ and Colin Clements, 1894- . Farewell to Love. 1 act. One-Act Play Magazine, 1 (November, 1937), 579-596.

7828. _____. On the Lot, a Fantastic Comedy. 1 act. Drama, 19 (November, 1928), 46-47.

7829. Ryga, George. Indian. 1 act. Performing Arts in Canada, 8 (Fall, 1971), 17-23.

7830. _____. Paracelsus and the Hero. 3 acts. Canadian Theatre Review, 4 (Fall, 1974), 36-126.

7831. Ryner, Han. La Promesse. Vers et Prose, 24 (January-March, 1911), 75-79. In French.

7832. Ryton, Royce. The Other Side of the Swamp. 2 acts. Plays and Players, 23 (June, July, 1976), 41-50; 44-50.

7833. Sabath, Bernard. Lady of Eternal Springtime. 3 acts, comedy. First Stage, 2 (Spring, 1963), 81-97.

7834. Sabatier, Pierre, 1897- . Charmante Enfant. 1 act, comedy. L'Avant Scène, 176 (June 15, 1958), 39-44. In French.

7835. _____. Fait divers. 1 act. L'Avant Scène, 588 (June 1, 1976), 37-40. In French.

7836. _____. Histoire de Fours. 1 act. L'Avant Scène, 484 (December 1, 1971), 33-38. In French.

7837. _____. Psychiatrie. 1 act. L'Avant Scène, 531 (December 15, 1973), 31-34. In French.

7838. _____. Le Souper de Venise. 1 act. L'Avant Scène, 120, 33-38. In French.

7839. _____. Surprise-Partie. 1 act. L'Avant Scène, 328 (February 15, 1965), 48-51. In French.

_____, adapter see Morley, R. and N. Langley 6232

_____, translator see Goldoni, C. 3607

_____, translator see Hebbel, C. F. 4013

7840. Sabin, Edwin L. The Dinner Table. 1 act. Century, 90 (May, 1915), 159-160.

7841. Sachs, Hans, 1494-1576. Brooding Calves. 1 act. Poet Lore, 38 (1927), 435-446. John Krumpelmann, translator.

Sachs, Maurice, translator see Rattigan, T. 7423

7842. Sachs, Nelly, 1891- . Eli; Ein Mysterienspiel vom Leiden Israels. 1 act. Spectaculum, 5 (1963), 177-221. In German.

7843. Sackville, Margaret. The Coming of Hippolytus. 1 act. Poetry, 3 (November, 1913), 40-45.

7844. Sackville-West, Edward Charles, 1901-1965. Flaubert and Madame Bovary. 1 act. The Windmill, 1 (1946), 12-25.

7845. Sade, Donatien-Alphonse-François de, 1740-1814. Oxtiern, ovvero le sventure del libertinaggio. 3 acts. Il Dramma, n.s., 380/381 (May/June, 1968), 32-40. Luigi Bàccolo, translator. In Italian.

7846. Sadoveanu, Ion Marin. Anno Domini. 1 act. Il Dramma, 390 (November 15, 1942), 33-39. Enzo Loreti, translator. In Italian.

7847. Saffold, Virginia, 1912- . The Last Mrs. Blakely. 1 act, comedy. One-Act Play Magazine, 1 (January, 1938), 821-842.

Sagan, François, pseud. see Quoirez, F. 7368-7371

7848. Sage, Selwin and Howard Mumford Jones. The Fascinating Mr. Denby, a Feminine Comedy. 1 act. Drama, 14, 175-177, 187.

7849. Sagoff, Maurice. A Library Operetta. 1 act. Wilson Library Bulletin, 12 (December, 1937), 243-247.

7850. Sagoff, Sara E. Hand-Me-Down Hildy. 1 act. Plays, 21 (December, 1961), 51-56.

7851. _____. The Switch-About Shopkeepers. 1 act. Plays, 22 (March, 1963), 69-76.

7852. Saidy, Fred, 1907- , and E. Y. Harburg, 1898- . Finian's Rainbow. 2 acts. Theatre Arts, 33 (January, 1949), 55-76.

7853. St. Clair, Robert, 1925- . Bus Trip. 1 act. Plays, 19 (February, 1960), 25-36.

7854. _____. Carol's Christmas Cards. 1 act. Plays, 20 (December, 1960), 25-36.

7855. _____. Fire Trap. 1 act. One-Act Play Magazine, 4 (July-August, 1941), 291-308.

7856. _____. The Gay Pretenders. 1 act. Plays, 20 (January, 1961), 1-13.

7857. _____. The Spirit of Christmas. 1 act. Plays, 2 (December, 1942), 79-85.

7858. _____. The Sun Bride. 1 act. Plays, 17 (March, 1958), 13-27.

7859. _____. The Tinker's Christmas. 1 act. Plays, 18 (December, 1958), 33-44.

St. Cyr, Dirce, translator see Bracco, R. 1254, 1257

7860. Saint-Granier and Philippe Bonnieres. L'Hotel du Bon Repas. 3 acts. Sipario, 8 (May, 1953), 33-51. Olga de Vellis Aillaud, translator. In Italian.

7861. Saint-Martin, Anne. Les Zakouskis. 1 act. L'Avant Scène, 305 (February 15, 1964), 33-35. In French.

7862. Sàito, Nello. I cattedratici. 2 parts. Il Dramma, 45, no. 4 (January, 1969), 81-96. In Italian.

7863. _____. Copione, la rivoluzione e finita. farce. Sipario, 306 (November, 1971), 57-71. In Italian.

7864. _____. Fix. 2 parts. Il Dramma (March, 1974), 25-58. In Italian.

7865. Saitta, Achille. I figli degli antenati. 3 acts, comedy. Sipario, 10 (July, 1955), 29-56. In Italian.

7866. _____. Non c'e regola, ahime! 3 acts, comedy. Sipario, 9 (March, 1954), 34-54. In Italian.

Saki, pseud. see Munro, H. H. 6298-6299.

7867. Salacrou, Armand, 1899- . Atlas-Hotel. 3 acts, comedy. Petite Illustration, 197 (July 24, 1937), 1-30. In French.

7868. _____. Dieu le savait. 3 acts. Sipario, 6 (August-September, 1951), 49-71. Diulio Cesare Castello, translator. In Italian.

7869. _____. Un Femme Libre. 3 acts. Il Dramma, n. s., 23/24 (October 15/November 1, 1946), 59-93. Mario Luciani, translator. In Italian.

7870. _____. Une femme trop honnete. 3 acts, comedy. Sipario, 12 (April, 1957), 40-60. Sergio Morando, translator. In Italian.

7871. _____. Les Fiancés du Havre. 3 acts, comedy. L'Avant Scène, 348-349 (January 1, 1966), 10-39. In French.

7872. _____. Les Fiancées du Havre. 3 acts. Il Dramma, n. s., 38 (June 1, 1947), 9-36. Silvana D'Arborio, translator. In Italian.

7873. _____. Les frenetiques. Sipario, 4 (April, 1949), 41-60. Giulio Pacuvio, translator. In Italian.

7874. _____. Un Homme Comme les Autres. 3 acts. Il Dramma, n. s., 21 (September 15, 1946), 9-41. Emilio Frattarelli, translator. In Italian.

7875. _____. L'Inconnue d'Arras. 3 acts. Il Dramma, 328 (April 15, 1940), 7-31. Cesare Vico Lodovici, translator. In Italian.

7876. _____. Le Miroir. 4 acts. L'Avant Scène, 139, 3-31. In French.

7877. _____. Les nuits de la colere. Sipario, 2 (July, 1947), 33-51. Ivo Chiesa, translator. In Italian.

7878. _____. Poof. 1 act. L'Avant Scène (OST), 33 (November, 1950), 3-28. In French.

7879. _____. Pourquoi pas Moi? 1 act. L'Avant Scène (OST), 33 (November, 1950), 31-46. In French.

7880. _____. Sens Interdit, Psychodrame. 1 act. L'Avant Scène, 348-349 (January 1, 1966), 45-55. In French.

7881. _____. Sens interdit. Sipario, 8 (June, 1953), 75-83. Cesare Giardini, translator. In Italian.

7882. _____. Le soldat et la sorciere. 2 parts. Sipario, 2 (December, 1947), 29-53. Berto Terzolo, translator. In Italian.

7883. Salaya, Alonso de. Farsa Hecha. 1 act. PMLA, 52 (March, 1937), 23-54. In Spanish.

7884. Salce, Luciano. Don Jack. 1 act. Sipario, 13 (October, 1958), 42-49. In Italian.

_____, translator see Anouilh, J. 250

_____, translator see Carette, L. 1603

Salemson, Harold J., translator see Vitrac, R. 9158

7885. Salerno, Henry F. The Trap. 1 act. Drama and Theatre, 11 (Fall, 1972), 60-66.

_____, translator see Ballesteros, A. M. 536

_____, translator see Mendoza, J. R. de A. y 5747

Salik, Rachel, adapter see Gomez-Arcos, A. 3619

Salkeld, Blanaid, translator see Blok, A. 1008

7886. Salsa, Carlo, 1898- . L'ora blu. 1 act. Il Dramma, 138 (May 15, 1932), 38-45. In Italian.

7887. _____. Quartetto per corni. 1 act. Il Dramma, 142 (July 15, 1932), 36-44. In Italian.

7888. _____. La regola del 3. 1 act. Il Dramma, 14 (January, 1914), 34-40. In Italian.

7889. _____. Il sole di Austerlitz. 1 act. Il Dramma, 146 (September 15, 1932), 30-39. In Italian.

7890. Salt, Jim. The Bird. 1 act. Edge, 3 (Autumn, 1964), 64-76.

7891. _____. The Worm. 1 act. Edge, 1 (Autumn, 1963), 93-107.

7892. Salt, Peter Sydney. The Bell of Freedom. 1 act. Poet Lore, 59 (No. 1), 3-32.

7893. Saltus, Edgar, 1855-1921. After the Ball. 1 act. Smart Set, 67 (March, 1922), 93-99.

7894. Saluron, Armand, 1899- . Poof. 1 act. Modern International Drama, 1 (September, 1967), 105-131. Felicia Liss, translator.

7895. Salutin, Rick. 1837: The Farmer's Revolt. 2 acts. Canadian Theatre Review, 6 (Spring, 1975), 58-115.

7896. Salvatore, Ada. Trent'anni di servizio. 2 parts. Il Dramma, 441/442/443 (January 1/15/February 1, 1945), 8-19. In Italian.

_____, translator see Barrie, Sir J. M. 626

_____, translator see Besier, R. 882

_____, translator see Boularan, J. 1217

_____, translator see Bush-Fekete, L. 1450

_____, translator see Cannan, D. 1565

_____, translator see Christie, A. 1822, 1823

_____, translator see Colette, S. G. C. 1934

_____, translator see Coward, N. 2071, 2074, 2075, 2076

_____, translator see DuMaurier, D. 2694

_____, translator see Fodor, L. 3179, 3181, 3184

_____, translator see Goetz, C. 3595

_____, translator see Goetz, R. 3596

_____, translator see Halasz, A. 3832

Salvatore

_____, translator see Hart, A. and M. Braddel 3936
_____, translator see Hart, M. 3943
_____, translator see Hartog, J. de 3952
_____, translator see Harwood, H. M. 3957
_____, translator see Hellman, L. 4043, 4047
_____, translator see Heltai, E. 4050
_____, translator see Herbert, F. H. 4062
_____, translator see Hunter, N. C. 4326
_____, translator see Hutton, M. C. 4341
_____, translator see Karrin, G. 4544
_____, translator see Krasna, N. 4709
_____, translator see Lakatos, F. 4769
_____, translator see Langley, N. 4797
_____, translator see Lonsdale, F. 5028
_____, translator see Maugham, W. S. 5671, 5675
_____, translator see Molnar, F. 6134, 6141, 6152, 6153, 6161
_____, translator see Priestley, J. B. 7293
_____, translator see Puget, C.-A. 7327
_____, translator see Rubio, E. and M. Balf 7780
_____, translator see Savoir, A. 7999
_____, translator see Schnitzler, A. 8075
_____, translator see Spewack, S. 8446
_____, translator see Taylor, S. 8731
_____, translator see Vajda, E. 8991
_____, translator see Verneuil, L. 9093

7897. Sampaio, Silveira. The Need for Polygamy. 3 acts. Modern International Drama, 9 (Spring, 1976), 49-63. Gail Mirza, translator.

Sampieri, G. V., translator see Josset, A. 4522

Sampieri, Lucia, translator see Colette, S. G. C. 1933

7898. Sampson, Elizabeth. The World Is in Your Hands. 1 act. Scholastic, 34 (April 29, 1939), 27-29.

Samuel, Horace B., translator see Schnitzler, A. 8068

7899. Samuels, Gertrude. Judas the Maccabee and Me. 1 act. DeKalb Literary Arts Journal, 3 (No. 4, 1969), 73-93.

7900. Sanavio, Piero, 1930- . Le apparenze inquiuete. 1 act. Il Dramma, (August/September, 1971), 144-150. In Italian.

—————, translator see Adamov, A. 68

7901. Sanchez, Florencia. The Foreign Girl. 4 acts. First Stage, 6 (Spring, 1967), 51-67. Alfred Coester, translator.

7902. Sanchez, Sonia. The Bronx Is the Next. Sipario, 23 (December, 1968), 94-96. Ettore Capriolo, translator. In Italian.

7903. —————. Dirty Hearts. Scripts, 1 (November, 1971), 46-50.

7904. Sanderlin, Owenita, 1916- . Follow the North Star. 1 act. Plays, 2 (May, 1943), 57-60.

7905. Sanderson, Toni. This Is Only Wednesday. 1 act. Dramatics, 41 (October, 1969), 4-5.

Sandier, Gil, adapter see Dostoevski, F. 2566

Sandison, Mildred see Fenner, Mildred Sandison

7906. Sandor, Ugo. Il giocatore. 4 acts. Il Dramma, 368 (December 15, 1941), 7-27. In Italian.

Sandri, Sandro, translator see Molnar, F. 6167

7907. Sands, Leslie. Un Remède de Cheval! 3 acts, comedy. L'Avant Scène, 163, 4-32. Frederic Valmain, adapter. In French.

7908. Sanesi, Andrea. Commedia senza adulterio. 3 acts. Il Dramma, 431-435 (August 1-October 1, 1944), 61-83. In Italian.

Sanesi, Roberto, translator see Thomas, D. 8825

7909. Sani, Massimo, 1929- . Settembre 1920: Occupazione delle fabbriche. 2 parts. Il Dramma, 46, no. 9 (September, 1970), 60-79. In Italian.

7910. Sankey, Tom. The Golden Screw. 2 acts. Works, 1 (Autumn, 1967), 49-94.

7911. _____. The Taming of the Screw: An Afterword. 3 acts. Works, 1 (Autumn, 1967), 95-98.

7912. Sanquineti, Edoardo. Orlando Furioso. Sipario, 24 (June-July, 1969), 74-96. In Italian.

7913. Sansom, Clive. A December Evening, 1817. 1 act. Fortnightly, 72 (December, 1949), 400-407.

7914. Santel, César. L'Emprunt. 1 act, comedy. L'Avant Scène, 185 (November 15, 1958), 29-34. In French.

7915. Santelli, Cesar, 1889- . Monsieur Corbillon veut Rompre en Beauté. 1 act, comedy. L'Avant Scène, 267 (June 15, 1962), 36-39. In French.

7916. Santelli, Claude, 1923- . Chambre à Part. 1 act, comedy. L'Avant Scène, 266 (June 1, 1962), 33-36. In French.

7917. _____. Le Fantome. 5 acts, farce. L'Avant Scène, 100, 3-33. In French.

7918. _____. Jusqu'a Minuit. 1 act. L'Avant Scène, 241 (April 15, 1961), 34-38. In French.

7919. _____. Lope de Vega. 2 parts, heroic-comedy. L'Avant Scène, 176 (June 15, 1958), 7-37. In French.

_____, translator see Pinelli, T. 7159

7920. Santi, Leone. La gloria negli eccelsi. 2 parts. Il Dramma, n.s., 303 (December, 1961), 7-12. In Italian.

7921. Santucci, Luigi. Giosafat. 4 parts. Il Dramma, 49 (January-February, 1973) 85-97. In Italian.

7922. _____. Oratorio scenico alla memoria di Bob Kennedy. Il Dramma, 45, no. 6 (March, 1969), 59-62. In Italian.

7923. Saphier, William and Maxwell Bodenheim, 1895-1954. The Kitchen Absurd. 1 act. Others, 4 (February, 1918), 18-29.

7924. Sapin, Louis. Papa Bon Dieu. 1 act. L'Avant Scène, 168 (February 15, 1958), 7-32. In French.

Sapinsley, Alvin, adapter see Ayme, M. 470

7925. Saponaro, Nicola. Erasmo. Il Dramma, 45, no. 14/15 (November/December, 1969), 95-112. In Italian.

Sapori, Alvise, translator see Bond, E. 1170, 1176

———, translator see Redgrave, M. 7456

7926. Sarazani, Fabrizio, 1905- . La grande famiglia. 3 acts. Il Dramma, n. s., 260 (May, 1958), 6-24. In Italian.

7927. ———. Personaggi al caffè. 1 act. Il Dramma, 265 (September 1, 1937), 28-31. In Italian.

——— see Nardelli, F. V. 6434

7928. Sardeson, Charles T. Love Is Stronger Than Walls. 1 act. Resource, 11 (February, 1970), 2-4.

7929. Sardou, André. L'Instinct. 1 act. Smart Set, 12 (February, 1904), 145-151. In French.

7930. Sardou, Victorien, 1831-1908. Marchesa! 3 acts. Il Dramma, 133 (March 1, 1932), 4-34. Mario Corsi, trans. In Italian.

7931. Sarment, Jean, 1897- . Bobard. 4 acts, comedy. Petite Illustration, 88 (August 23, 1930), 1-45. In French.

7932. ———. Le Collier de Jade. 1 act. L'Avant Scène, 113, 35-39. In French.

7933. ———. La Couronne de Carton. 4 acts. Petite Illustration, 188 (May 12, 1934), 1-38. In French.

7934. ———. Discours des Prix. 3 acts, comedy. Petite Illustration, 189 (December 15, 1934), 3-38. In French.

7935. ———. L'Impromptu de Paris. 1 act. Petite Illustration, 192 (December 21, 1935), 1-7. In French.

7936. ———. Madame Quinze. 3 acts. Petite Illustration, 190 (April 27, 1935), 1-38. In French.

7937. ———. Mamouret. 3 acts. Il Dramma, n. s., 153 (March 15, 1952), 6-32. Vittorio Guerriero and B. L. Randone, translators. In Italian.

7938. ———. Le Pavillon des Enfants. 2 parts. L'Avant Scène, 113, 1-33. In French.

7939. ———. Peau d'Espagne. 4 acts, comedy. Petite Illustration, 185 (June 10, 1933), 1-34. In French.

7940. ———. Le Plancher des Vaches. 4 acts, comedy. Petite Illustration, 182 (June 11, 1932), 1-38. In French.

7941. _____. Rude Awakening. 4 acts. Poet Lore, 45 (No. 3-4, 1939), 231-306. Frances Keene and Adrienne Foulke, trans.

7942. _____. Sur Mon Beau Navire. 3 acts, comedy. Petite Illustration, 87 (January 5, 1929), 1-34. In French.

7943. _____. Le Voyage à Biarritz. 1 act. Petite Illustration, 195 (November 7, 1936), 1-14. In French.

7944. Saroyan, William, 1908- . The Accident. 1 act. Contact (No. 1, 1958), 156-160.

7945. _____. Across the Board on Tomorrow-Morning. 1 act. Il Dramma, n. s., 19/20 (August 15/September 1, 1946), 43-54. Ettore Mariano, translator. In Italian.

7946. _____. The Beautiful People. 2 acts. Sipario, 1 (November-December, 1946), 57-71. Bruno Arcangeli, translator. In Italian.

7947. _____. Cat, Mouse, Man, Woman. 1 act. Contact (No. 1, 1958), 147-155.

7948. _____. The Cave Dwellers. 2 acts. Theatre Arts, 42 (December, 1958), 27-42.

7949. _____. Four Plays: The Playwright and the Public; The Handshakers; The Doctor and the Patient; This I Believe. 1 act each. Atlantic, 211 (April, 1963), 50-52.

7950. _____. L'Huitre et la Perle. 1 act. L'Avant Scène, 92, 29-37. Jean-Michel Jasienko, adapter. In French.

7951. _____. The Man With the Heart in the Highlands. 1 act. One-Act Play Magazine, 1 (December, 1937), 685-697.

7952. _____. My Heart's In the Highlands. Sipario, 3 (June, 1948), 33-43. Bruno Arcangeli, translator. In Italian.

7953. _____. Once Around the Block. 1 act. American Mercury, 69 (December, 1949), 663-675.

7954. _____. The Oyster and the Pearl. 1 act. Perspectives, USA, 4 (Summer, 1953), 86-104. (Issued in British, French, German and Italian editions.)

7955. _____. The People with Light Coming Out of Them. 1 act. Scholastic, 38 (March 24, 1941), 17-19, 28.

7956. _____. The Slaughter of the Innocents. 2 acts, tragedy. Theatre Arts, 36 (November, 1952), 33-56.

7957. _____. There's Something I Got to Tell You. 1 act. Scholastic, 41 (December 14-19, 1942), 18-20.

7958. _____. Three Entertainments: I. A Number of Absurd and Poetic Events in the Life of the Great American Goof. A Ballet-Play; II. The Poetic Situation in America since Alexandre Dumas and Several Others. A Ballet-Poem; III. Opera, Opera. 1 act each. Twice a Year, 5/6 (Fall/ Winter, 1940/Spring/Summer, 1941), 164-193.

7959. Sarr, Kenneth. The Passing. 1 act, tragedy. One-Act Play Magazine, 1 (April, 1938), 1057-1062.

7960. Sarraute, Nathalie, 1902- . Le mensonge. 1 act. Il Dramma, 45, no. 8 (May, 1969), 79-83. Ugo Ronfani, translator. In Italian.

7961. Sartre, Jean-Paul, 1905- . Le Diable et le Bon Dieu. 3 acts. L'Avant Scène, 402-403 (May, 1968), 37-87. In French.

7962. _____. Le Diable et le Bon Dieu. 3 acts. Il Dramma, n. s., 316 (January, 1963), 13-46. Giacomo DeBenedetti, translator. In Italian.

7963. _____. Morts Sans Sépulture. 4 acts. Spectaculum, 4 (1963), 227-269. In German.

7964. _____. Les Mouches. 3 acts. Sipario, 1 (May, 1946), 13-34. Ivo Chiesa, translator. In Italian.

7965. _____. La Putain Respectueuse. 1 act. L'Avant Scène, 402-403 (May, 1968), 19-31. In French.

7966. _____. The Respectful Prostitute. 1 act. Twice a Year, 16/17 (1948), 17-64. Harold Clurman, translator.

7967. Sarzano, Luigi. Si dira delle misere donne. Sipario, 253 (May, 1967), 50-63. In Italian.

7968. Sassoon, R. L. The Crowded Bedroom. 1 act. Chicago Review, 16 (Summer, 1963), 29-40.

7969. _____ and D. H. Elliott. Up. 1 act. First Stage, 2 (Fall, 1963), 363-364.

7970. Sastre, Alfonso, 1926- . The Condemned Squad. 1 act. Players Magazine, 38 (November, 1961), 57-68. Cyrus de Costes, translator.

7971. _____. Cronache romane. 2 parts. Il Dramma, 46, no. 1 (January, 1970), 95-113. Ignazio Delogu, translator. In Italian.

7972. _____. Il dottor Frankenstein a Hortaleza. Sipario, 306 (November, 1971), 72-79. Maria Luisa Aguirre D'Amico, translator. In Italian.

7973. _____. Guilermo Tell tiene los ojos tristes. Sipario, 256-257 (August-September, 1967), 37-50. Maria Luisa Aguirre d'Amico, translator. In Italian.

7974. _____. In the Net. 3 acts. Modern International Drama, 8 (Spring, 1975), 11-44. Leonard Pronko, translator.

7975. _____. Pathetic Prologue. 1 act. Modern International Drama, 1 (March, 1968), 196-215. Leonard Pronko, translator.

7976. Satchell, Mary. Daniel Hale Williams, Pioneer Surgeon. 1 act. Plays, 33 (February, 1974), 13-21.

7977. Sates, Claude and Ahouva Lion. La Princesse Turandot. 2 parts. L'Avant Scène, 394 (Jan. 1, 1968), 41-52. In French.

Satz, Evelina, translator see Svartz, E. L. 8640

7978. Sauer, Kenneth. Time Tunnel to Christmas. 1 act. Resource, 9 (November, 1967), 10-12.

7979. Saul, Milton. A Girl for Buddy. 2 acts, comedy. Drama and Theatre, 9 (Fall, 1970), 14-31.

7980. Saul's Jealousy. 1 act. Learning With..., 3 (March, 1975), 27.

7981. Saunders, James, 1925- . Neighbours. 1 act. L'Avant Scène, 534 (February 1, 1974), 25-36. Suzanne Lombard, adapter. In French.

7982. _____. Neighbours. 1 act. Plays and Players, 14 (September, 1967), 19-27.

_____ see also Murdoch, I. 6305

Saunders, John M., translator see Love in a French Kitchen 5060

7983. Saunders, Lilian. The Bee. 1 act. Drama, 14 (February, 1924), 170-172, 189.

7984. _____. Night Brings a Counselor. 1 act. Drama, 13 (April, 1923), 251-253.

7985. _____. Sob Sister. 1 act. Drama, 11 (July, 1921), 354-357.

_____, translator see Bessey, R. M. S. 885

_____, translator see Heijermans, H. 4031, 4033

7986. Saunders, Louise, 1893- . Our Kind. 1 act, comedy. Smart Set, 64 (February, 1921), 73-84.

7987. Sauti, Insan. The Installment Plan. 1 act. Drama and Theatre, 11 (Fall, 1972), 31-40.

7988. Sauvajon, Marc-Gilbert, 1909- . Adorable Julia. 3 acts. L'Avant Scène, 138, 1-39. In French.

7989. _____. Tapage Nocturne. 2 parts. Il Dramma, n. s., 238 (July, 1956), 8-36. Liana Ferri, translator. In Italian.

7990. _____. Tchao! 2 acts, comedy. L'Avant Scène, 435 (October 15, 1969), 7-42. In French.

7991. _____. Tredici a tavola. 3 acts. Il Dramma, n. s., 207 (June 15, 1954), 5-26. In Italian.

_____, adapter see Home, W. D. 4153

_____, adapter see Ustinov, P. 8982, 8984

7992. Savary, Jerome. Les Derniers Jours de Solitude de Robinson Crusoe; 20 Ans d'Aventures et d'Amour. L'Avant Scène, 496 (June 1, 1972), 9-38. In French.

7993. Savelli, Anthony. Never Say Diet. 1 act. Smart Set, 4 (May, 1901), 103-105.

7994. Savinio, Alberto. La famiglia Mastinu. Sipario, 3 (June, 1948), 45-50. In Italian.

Savioli, Franca, translator see D'Usseau, A. and J. E. Gow 2771

7995. Saviotti, Gino. Il buon Silvestro. 3 acts. Il Dramma, 61 (March 1, 1929), 4-22. In Italian.

7996. _____. Cocorita. 1 act. Il Dramma, 12 (November, 1926), 40-44. In Italian.

7997. _____. Un po' d'amore. 1 act. Il Dramma, 30 (November 15, 1927), 29-36. In Italian.

7998. Savoir, Alfred. Le Figurant de la Gaité. 4 acts, comedy. L'Avant Scène (OST), 2 (March, 1949), 1-29. In French.

7999. _____. Guardian Angel. 3 acts, comedy. Sipario, 8 (December, 1953), 59-81. Ada Salvatore, translator. In Italian.

8000. _____. Passy 08-45. 3 acts. Il Dramma, 50 (September 15, 1928), 6-42. In Italian.

8001. _____. Presso i cani. 1 act. Il Dramma, 56 (December 15, 1928), 41-44. Giuseppe Faraci, translator. In Italian.

8002. Sawyer, Ruth, 1880- . The Sidhe of Ben-Mor. 1 act. Poet Lore, 21 (July-August, 1910), 300-310.

8003. Sax, Carol and Morris Christie. Questions. 1 act. Touchstone, 5 (May, 1919), 111-114.

8004. Sayers, Frances Clarke. Rootabaga Processional. 1 act. puppet play. Horn Book, 8 (May, 1932), 124-130.

8005. Sayre, George Wallace. Final Edition. 1 act. Plays, 15 (April, 1956), 1-12.

Sbarbaro, Camillo, translator see Crommelynck, F. 2118

_____, translator see De Montherlant, H. 6191

8006. Sbragia, Alberto. Le ombre. 1 act. Il Dramma, 101 (November 1, 1930), 34-42. In Italian.

8007. Sbragia, Giancarlo, 1926- . Le veglie inutili. 1 act. Il Dramma, n.s., 183 (June 15, 1953), 10-19. In Italian.

_____ see Roli, M. 7659

8008. Scabia, Giuliano. Scontri generali. Sipario, 24 (October, 1969), 44-60. In Italian.

Scalero, Alessandra, translator see O'Casey, S. 6755

_____, translator see O'Neill, E. 6836, 6839, 6846

_____, translator see Priestley, J. B. 7300

_____, translator see Sherwood, R. 8257

Scanlan, David, translator see Strindberg, A. 8561

8009. Scarnicci, Giulio and Renzo Tarabusi. Caviar ou Lentilles. 3 acts, comedy. L'Avant Scène, 347 (December 15, 1965), 11-47. Jean Rougeul, translator. In French.

8010. Scarpetta. Misère et Noblesse. 3 acts, comedy. L'Avant Scène, 141, 3-32. Jacques Fabbricotti, adapter. In French.

Scatori, Stephen, translator see Carrion, M. R. and V. Aza 1617

8011. Schaaf, Albert K. Hassle in the Castle. 1 act. Plays, 34 (November, 1974), 75-79.

8012. ──────. Jump for Joy. 1 act. Plays, 19 (March, 1960), 23-35.

8013. ──────. Sorry, No Answer. 1 act. Plays, 34 (January, 1975), 73-76.

8014. ──────. A Touch Too Much. 1 act. Plays, 35 (January, 1976), 55-61.

8015. ──────. Wolfe at the Door. 1 act. Plays, 34 (October, 1974), 81-85.

8016. ──────. Your Money Cheerfully Refunded. 1 act. Plays, 30 (October, 1970), 83-84.

8017. Schaaf, Stany. Cette Petite Ville. 1 act. L'Avant Scène, 259 (February 15, 1962), 35-39. In French.

Scharrelmann, Wilhelm see Wiegand, J. 5036

8018. Schary, Dore, 1905- . Sunrise at Campobello. 2 acts. Theatre Arts, 43 (November, 1959), 33-58.

8019. Schawinsky, Xanti. Play, Life, Illusion. 4 parts. Drama Review, 15 (Summer, 1971), 45-59.

8020. Scheerbart, Paul. Herr Kammerdiener Kneetschke. Der Sturm, 4 (156/157, April, 1913), 10-14. In German.

8021. Schehade, Georges. Monsieur Bob'le. 3 acts. L'Avant Scène (OST), 38 (February, 1951), 1-40. In French.

8022. ──────. Vasco. 1 act. Gambit, 1 (1963), 5-67. Robert Baldick, translator.

8023. ──────. Les Violettes. Comedy. Sipario, 187 (November, 1961), 30-47. Laurice Benzoni Schehade. In Italian.

8024. ──────. Violets. Modern International Drama, 3 (March, 1970), 41-74. Max Gulack, translator.

Schehade, Laurice Benzoni, translator see Schehade, G. 8023

Schenck, Anna, translator see D'Annunzio, G. 2182, 2183

Schering, Emil, translator see Strindberg, A. 8563, 8575

Scheuer, L. R., translator see Kleist, H. von 4663

Schild, Alfred, translator see Durrenmatt, F. 2746

8025. Schiller, Johann Christoph Friedrich von, 1759-1805. Don

Schiller

Carlos. 5 acts. L'Avant Scène, 140, 3-35. Charles Charras, adapter. In French.

8026. _____. Maria Stuarda. 5 acts, tragedy. Il Dramma, n.s., 279 (December, 1959), 44-76. Emilio Mariana, translator. In Italian.

8027. _____. Marie Stuart. 5 acts, comedy. L'Avant Scène, 304 (February 1, 1964), 11-33. Charles Charras, adapter. In French.

8028. _____. Wallenstein. 3 acts. Sipario, 19 (December, 1964), 96-101. Lilyan Zafred and Mario Zafred, adapters. In Italian.

8029. Schisgal, Murray, 1926- . Les Chinois. 1 act. L'Avant Scène, 421 (March 1, 1969), 25-40. Pascale de Boysson, adapter. In French.

8030. _____. Fragments. 1 act. L'Avant Scène, 421 (March 1, 1969), 5-18. Pascale de Boysson, adapter. In French.

8031. _____. Love. 2 acts. L'Avant Scène, 369 (December 1, 1966), 11-34. Pascale de Boysson and Maurice Garrel, adapters. In French.

8032. _____. Luv. 2 parts. Sipario, 21 (February, 1966), 33-53. Gigi Lunari, translator. In Italian.

8033. _____. The Tiger. 1 act. L'Avant Scène, 312 (June 1, 1964), 20-27. Laurent Terzieff, adapter. In French.

8034. _____. The Tiger. 1 act. Sipario, 19 (October, 1964), 53-59. Ettore Capriolo, translator. In Italian.

8035. _____. The Typists. 1 act. L'Avant Scène, 312 (June 1, 1964), 10-19. Laurent Terzieff, adapter. In French.

8036. _____. The Typists. 1 act. Sipario, 19 (October, 1964), 44-52. Ettore Capriolo, translator. In Italian.

8037. _____. Windows. 1 act. Show, 5 (April, 1965), 73-87.

8038. Schlumberger, Jean. Cesaire. 1 act. Living Age, 312 (January 14, 1922), 106-115.

8039. _____. Le Visiteur de Minuit. 1 act. L'Avant Scène, 166, 44-49. In French.

8040. Schmidt, Godfrey P., Jr. I Did But Jest. 1 act. Poet Lore, 35 (1924), 130-139.

Schmidt-Wartenberg, H. M., editor see Tiroler Passionsspiel 8870

8041. Schmitt, Gladys. The Desert Blooms. Senior Scholastic, 51 (November 17, 1947), 18-20.

8042. _____. The Doctor Turns into a Poet. 1 act. Scholastic, 24 (May 5, 1934), 7-8.

8043. _____. Dusky Singing. 1 act. Scholastic, 32 (April 30, 1938), 21E-22E, 24E.

8044. _____. Fiesta for Juanita. 1 act. Scholastic, 32 (March 13, 1938), 21E-23E.

8045. _____. The Man Who Discovered the Sun. 1 act. Scholastic, 27 (October 5, 1935), 7-8, 27.

8046. _____. A Man's a Man for a'That. 1 act. Scholastic, 32 (February 12, 1938), 17E-18E.

8047. _____. Mark Twain Digs for Gold. 1 act. Scholastic, 27 (November 23, 1935), 9-10.

8048. _____. Mark Twain Digs for Gold. 1 act. Senior Scholastic, 52 (May 10, 1948), 23-25.

8049. _____. Miracle in Louisiana. 1 act. Scholastic, 35 (October 23, 1939), 21E-23E.

8050. _____. Mr. Elliot's Crazy Notion. 1 act. Scholastic, 26 (May 18, 1935), 8-9, 11, 27.

8051. _____. Not for Ladies. 1 act. Scholastic, 30 (May 15, 1937), 8-9.

8052. _____. The Raven's First Flight. 1 act. Scholastic, 26 (February 2, 1935), 7-8.

8053. _____. The Records Show. 1 act. Scholastic, 31 (October 30, 1937), 21E-23E.

8054. _____. The Secret Weapon. 1 act. Scholastic, 37 (September 16, 1940), 17-20, 28.

8055. _____. The State Versus Joe Miller. 1 act. Scholastic, 29 (January 9, 1937), 9-10.

8056. _____. The Vicar Saves the Day. 1 act. Scholastic, 27 (January 11, 1936), 7-8, 12.

8057. _____ and Pauline Gibson. The Petticoat Brigade. Scholastic, 29 (October 10, 1936), 15-16, 23.

8058. Schneider, Edouard. L'Exaltation. 3 acts. Petite Illustration, 86 (April 14, 1928), 1-22. In French.

8059. Schnittkind, Henry T. Shambles, a Sketch of the Present War. 1 act. Poet Lore, 25 (Winter, 1914), 559-571.

8060. Schnitzler, Arthur, 1862-1931. Agonia d'amore. 1 act. Il Dramma, 90 (May 15, 1930), 35-38. Umberto Barbaro, translator. In Italian.

8061. ———. Il burattinaio. 1 act. Il Dramma, 136 (April 15, 1932), 36-42. Umberto Barbaro, translator. In Italian.

8062. ———. Cena d'addio. 1 act. Il Dramma, 78 (November 15, 1929), 41-44. Umberto Barbaro, translator. In Italian.

8063. ———. Dissolution, a Viennese Comedy of Love. 1 act. Golden Book, 16 (August, 1932), 175-180.

8064. ———. The Duke and the Actress. 1 act. Poet Lore, 21 (July-August, 1910), 257-284. Hans Weysz, translator.

8065. ———. Episode. 1 act. Golden Book, 17 (January, 1933), 70-77.

8066. ———. Gallant Cassian. 1 act. Poet Lore, 33 (Winter, 1922), 507-520. Moritz A. Jagendorf, translator.

8067. ———. The Green Cockatoo. 1 act. Golden Book, 4 (November, 1926), 637-653. Grace Isabel Colbron, translator.

8068. ———. The Lady with the Dagger. 1 act. Fortnightly, 91 (June, 1909), 1179-1191. Horace B. Samuel, translator.

8069. ———. The Lady with the Dagger. 1 act. Poet Lore, 15 (Summer, 1904), 1-18. Helen Tracy Porter, translator.

8070. ———. The Legacy. 3 acts. Poet Lore, 22 (Vacation, 1911), 241-308. Mary L. Stephenson, translator.

8071. ———. Letteratura. 1 act. Il Dramma, 158 (March 15, 1933), 34-44. Umberto Barbaro, translator. In Italian.

8072. ———. Liebelei. 3 acts. Petite Illustration, 186 (November 4, 1933), 1-20. Suzanne Clauser, translator. In French.

8073. ———. Light-o'-Love. 3 acts. Drama, 7 (August, 1912), 15-77. Bayard Quincy Morgan, translator.

8074. ———. Living Hours. 1 act. Poet Lore, 17 (No. 1, 1906), 36-45. Helen Tracy Porter, translator.

8075. _____. Al pappagallo verde. 1 act. Il Dramma, 46 (July 15, 1928), 17-35. Ada Salvatore, translator. In Italian.

8076. _____. Reicen. 10 parts. Sipario, 5 (November, 1950), 49-69. Federico Federici, translator. In Italian.

8077. _____. The Vast Domain. 5 acts, tragedy. Poet Lore, 34 (Autumn, 1923), 317-407. Edward Woticky and Alexander Caro, translators.

Schnitzler, Henry, translator see Buchner, G. 1404

8078. Schoenewolf, Gerald. Poof! 1 act. Esquire, 73 (December, 1969), 209.

8079. Schoenfeld, Bernard C. Johnny Appleseed. 1 act. Scholastic, 37 (September 16, 1940), 17-19.

8080. Scholl, Ralph. A Fable. 1 act. First Stage, 6 (Fall, 1967), 177-186.

Scholtis, August, translator see Havel, V. 3980

8081. Scholz, Wilhelm von, 1874- . The Jew of Constance. 5 acts, tragedy. Poet Lore, 57 (October, 1962), 387-472. Lee M. Hollander, translator.

8082. _____. Souls Exchanged; The Comedy of Resurrections. 2 acts. Poet Lore, 52 (Autumn; Winter, 1946), 202-255; 291-352. Lee M. Hollander, translator.

Schonberger, E. D., translator see Capek, K. M. 1577

8083. Schreiber, Isabelle Georges. Une Affaire Exceptionnelle. 1 act. L'Avant Scène, 197 (May 15, 1959), 38-41. In French.

8084. _____. Dialogue des Inconnus. 1 act. L'Avant Scène, 315 (July 15, 1964), 33-43. In French.

8085. _____. Lune ou l'Autre. 1 act. L'Avant Scène, 281 (February 1, 1963), 39-44. In French.

8086. Schroeder, Charles. To You This Day. 2 acts. Resource, 8 (November, 1966), 18-26.

Schroll, Catherine V. see MacLellan, E. 5245-5268

8087. Schroll, Francis L. Some Tricks Are Treats. 1 act. Plays, 14 (October, 1954), 62-66.

8088. Schuchert, Herman. The Critics' Catastrophe, a Probable

Possibility. 1 act. Little Review, 2 (April, 1915), 20-27.

8089. Schulberg, Budd, 1914- and Harvey Breit, 1913- . The Disenchanted. 3 acts. Theatre Arts, 44 (August, 1960), 21-47.

8090. Schuman, Howard. Censored Scenes from King Kong. 1 act. Gambit, 7 (No. 26/27, 1975), 65-116.

8091. Schumann, David. Leave Us Blow. 1 act. Dramatika, 3 (March, 1969), 9-14.

8092. Schwartz, Delmore, 1913-1966. Paris and Helen, an Entertainment. New Directions, 6 (1941), 193-219.

8093. ———. Shenandoah, or The Naming of the Child. 1 act. Kenyon Review, 3 (Summer, 1941), 271-292.

8094. ———. Shenandoah. New Directions, 32 (1976), 24-45.

8095. Schwartz, Esther Dresden. Three Souls in Search of a Dramatist. 1 act, farce. Drama, 16 (April, 1926), 247-248, 260.

8096. Schwartz, Lynne Sharon. King Arthur and His Sword. 1 act. Plays, 21 (March, 1962), 51-57.

———, adapter see Baum, L. F. 676

8097. Schwartz, Morton K. All in Favor. 1 act. Plays, 5 (March, 1946), 47-53.

8098. ———. The Auction. 1 act. Plays, 10 (April, 1941), 53-58.

8099. ———. The Loud Speaker. 1 act. Plays, 10 (November, 1950), 43-47.

8100. ———. Somewhat Forgetful. 1 act. Plays, 9 (April, 1950), 51-56.

8101. Schwartz, Paula. Parcel Pick-Up. 1 act. Dramatics, 46 (November, 1974), 8-11.

Schwarz, Alfred, translator see Hofmannsthal, H. von 4136

Scialpi, Lucio, translator see Bernard, J.-J. 824

8102. Sciascia, Leonardo. I mafiosi. 2 parts. Il Dramma, 48 (November-December, 1972), 51-72. In Italian.

Sclafani, G. see Zorzi, G. 9658

8103. Scoff, Alain. Jesus-fric Supercrack. 2 parts. L'Avant Scène, 505 (November 1, 1972), 7-28. In French.

Scot, Michael, translator see Verlaine, P. 9085

8104. Scot-Heron, Gil. Enigma of College Black. 1 act. Dramatika, 7 (1971), 23-31.

8105. Scott, Alexander, 1920- . Killer Crusade; A Poem for Voices. Akros, 6 (April, 1971), 10-33.

8106. Scott, Christine E. Then Came the Good Harvest. 1 act. Plays, 26 (November, 1966), 70-74.

8107. Scott, Gladys Giulford. The Silly Citizens of Happy Valley. 1 act. Plays, 19 (May, 1960), 53-62.

8108. Scott, Margretta. The Bag O' Dreams. 1 act. Drama, 11 (January, 1921), 131-132.

8109. ──────. Heart of Pierrot. 1 act. Drama, 10 (February, 1920), 200-202.

8110. ──────. Three Kisses. 1 act. Drama, 10 (October, 1919), 15-21.

8111. ──────. The Tragedy. 1 act. Poet Lore, 53 (Autumn, 1947), 195-213.

Scott, Mariana, translator see Hofmannsthal, H. von 4132, 4137, 4143

8112. Scott, Natalie Vivian. Zombi. 1 act. Theatre Arts, 13 (January, 1929), 53-61.

8113. Scott, Sir Walter, 1771-1832. The Lady of the Lake. 1 act. Plays, 16 (January, 1957), 85-94. Edward Golden, adapter.

8114. ──────. Quentin Durward. 1 act. Plays, 15 (February, 1956), 89-96. Lewy Olfson, adapter.

8115. Scott, Winfield Townley, 1910- . Noon Hour. 1 act. Smoke, 1 (May, 1931), 7-9.

8116. Scribe, Eugene, 1791-1861. Le Verre d'Eau, ou Les Effets et les Causes. 5 acts. L'Avant Scène, 591 (July 15, 1976), 3-30. In French.

Scriboni, Anna, translator see Gambaro, G. 3360

8117. Sea Battle at Night. Chinese Literature, 3 (1968), 13-60; 4 (1968), 49-89.

Seabrook, Jeremy see O'Neill, M. 6868, 6869

8118. Sealock, Thelma W. The Lincoln Coat. 1 act. Plays, 4 (January, 1945), 36-43. AND Plays, 12 (February, 1953), 27-34.

8119. Seaman's Pipe!, or, The Battle and the Breeze. 3 acts. Living Age, 10 (August 8, 1846), 295-296.

8120. Searcy, Katherine, June Thompson McNeel and Carolyn Oliver. A Visit to the Library. 1 act. Wilson Library Bulletin, 24 (October, 1949), 166-167.

8121. Sears, John V. The Sleeping Princess. 5 acts. St. Nicholas, 7 (January, 1880), 267-271.

8122. Sebastian, Mihail. Edition de Midi. 3 acts, comedy. L'Avant Scène, 186 (December 1, 1958), 7-42. Pierre Hechter, adapter. In French.

8123. Seborga, Guido. Cristo degli abissi. 3 acts. Il Dramma, n. s., 343/344 (April/May, 1965), 28-45. In Italian.

Seca, P. Munoz see Munoz-Seca, P. 6297

Secci, Lia, translator see Kokoschka, O. 4681

_____, translator see Stramm, A. 8552

8124. Second, Louis. Apollinaris. New Directions, 7 (1942), 225-232.

8125. Sedgwick, Henry Dwight, 1861-1957. The Classics Again. 1 act. Atlantic, 112 (July, 1913), 34-47.

8126. See, Edmond, 1875- . Un Ami de Jeunesse. 1 act, comedy. L'Avant Scène, 201 (July 15, 1959), 33-41. In French.

8127. _____. L'Elastique. 1 act. Petite Illustration, 88 (August 9, 1930), 1-12. In French.

8128. _____. L'Indiscret. 3 acts, comedy. Petite Illustration, 188 (July 21, 1934), 1-30. In French.

8129. _____. Le Métier d'Amant. 1 act. Petite Illustration, 86 (May 19, 1928), 1-15. In French.

8130. _____. Les Miettes. 2 acts, comedy. Petite Illustration, 88 (August 9, 1930), 1-18. In French.

8131. _____. Il n'y a pas Que l'Amour. 1 act. L'Avant Scène, 244 (June 1, 1961), 43-49. In French.

8132. _____. Les Retours Imprévus. 1 act. L'Avant Scène, 160, 29-37. In French.

8133. _____. Il volto nuovo. 1 act. Il Dramma, 171 (October 1, 1933), 34-38. Enzo Gariffo, translator. In Italian.

8134. Seeley, F. P. International Art. 1 act. 19th Century, 60 (July, 1906), 152-157.

Segala, Amos, translator see Asturias, M. A. 426

8135. Seiffer, David. The Compromise. 1 act. Dramatika, 1 (1968), n. p.

8136. Seiffert, Marjorie Allen. Noah's Ark, a Play for Toys. 1 act, Poetry, 37 (April, 1928), 1-14.

8137. _____. The Old Woman. 2 parts. Poetry, 13 (January, 1919), 204-208. AND Poetry, 15 (November, 1919), 111-113.

8138. Seiler, Conrad. Excitement to Order. 1 act, comedy. One-Act Play Magazine, 3 (July-August, 1940), 385-402. AND One-Act Play Magazine, 4 (January-February, 1941), 3-18.

8139. _____. How to Be Happy Though Married. 1 act, farce. One-Act Play Magazine, 4 (March-April, 1941), 110-122.

8140. _____. Let's End It All. 1 act, comedy. One-Act Play Magazine, 3 (February, 1940), 99-121. AND One-Act Play Magazine, 4 (January-February, 1941), 31-51.

8141. _____. Mistress Shakespeare. 1 act, tragi-comedy. Poet Lore, 43 (No. 2, 1936), 119-130.

8142. _____. Permanent Anaesthesia, a Comedy of the Near Future. 1 act. One-Act Play Magazine, 3 (September-October, 1940), 439-455.

8143. _____. Relief. 1 act. One-Act Play Magazine, 2 (January, 1939), 639-649.

8144. _____. Why I Am a Bachelor. 1 act, comedy. One-Act Play Magazine, 1 (March, 1938), 980-993.

8145. Seitz, George B. Hildetua. 1 act. Smart Set, 32 (September, 1910), 143-150.

8146. Selincourt, Hugh de, 1878-1951. The Dream of Death. 1 act. Two Worlds, 2 (December, 1926), 25-32.

8147. Sellers, Irma P. The Adored One. 1 act. Drama, 14 (May-June, 1924), 253-261.

8148. Selnick, Eugene. The Gold Machine. 1 act. Drama, 20 (March, 1930), 173-175, 190.

Seltzer, Thomas, translator see Andreyev, L. N. 234, 235, 237

_____, translator see Artsybashev, M. P. 389

Semprun, Carlos, adapter see Andreyev, L. N. 236

8149. Sender, Ramon Jose, 1902- . The House of Lot. 1 act. New Mexico Quarterly, 20 (Spring, 1950), 27-40.

8150. _____. The Key. 1 act. Kenyon Review, 5 (Spring, 1943), 201-218.

8151. _____. The Secret. 1 act. One-Act Play Magazine, 1 (November, 1937), 612-626.

8152. _____. The Wind. 1 act. New Mexico Quarterly, 33 (Summer, 1963), 185-212. Elinor Randall, translator.

8153. Seneca. Oedipus. 5 acts. Arion, 7 (Summer, 1968), 325-371. Ted Hughes, adapter.

Senecal, Jean Michel see Jacquemard, Y. 4425

Senelick, Laurence, translator see Bulgakov, M. A. 1413

_____, translator see Ilf, I. and E. Petrov 4368

Senesi, Ivo, 1893- , translator see Giono, J. 3551

Sepulveda, R. see Sevilla, L. F. de 8159

8154. Serlen, Bruce. Appomattox. 1 act. Dramatics, 43 (March, 1972), 4-7.

8155. Serrano, Nina and Judith Binder. The Chicken Made of Rags. 1 act. Scripts, 1 (October, 1972), 42-53.

Serreau, Genevieve, translator see Gombrowicz, W. 3617

8156. Serretta, Enrico. Un sogno. 1 act. Il Dramma, 105 (January 1, 1931), 40-44. In Italian.

Settanni, Ettore, translator see Dostoevski, F. 2565

_____, translator see Tolstoy, L. 8877

Setti, Lorenza, translator see Wilder, T. 9392

Settimelli, Emilio, 1891-1954 see Corradini, A. 2027

─────── see Corradini, B. 2033, 2034, 2035

8157. 1789--La Revolution doit s'arreter a la Perfection du Nonheur (Saint-Just). Sipario, 26 (August-September, 1971), 88-97. Marga Vidusso Ferriani, translator. In Italian.

8158. 1789/1793. L'Avant Scène, 526/527 (October 1, 15, 1973), 19-59. In French.

8159. Sevilla, Luigi F. De and R. Sepulveda. Madre Allegria. 3 acts. Il Dramma, 382 (July 15, 1942), 7-28. Gilberto Beccari and Amilcare Quarra, translators. In Italian.

Seward, Thomas, translator see Ruibal, J. 7790

8160. Sewell, Anna, 1820-1878. Black Beauty. 1 act. Plays, 17 (March, 1958), 89-96. Lewy Olfson, adapter.

8161. Seymour, Alan, 1927- . L'Unique Jour de l'Année. 3 acts. L'Avant Scène, 361 (July 15, 1966), 13-40. Jean Goldman and Madeleine Goldman, translators.

8162. Seymour, Judith. The Lincoln Lady. 1 act. Plays, 20 (February, 1961), 79-83.

8163. Sha Seh, Fu To, Ma Yung, and Li Chi-huang. Letters from the South. Chinese Literature, 3 (1966), 3-64. Sidney Shapiro, translator.

8164. Shachiapang, a Peking Opera. Chinese Literature, 11 (1967), 3-53. AND Chinese Literature, 11 (1970), 3-62.

8165. Shaffer, Peter, 1926- . Black Comedy. 1 act. L'Avant Scène, 397 (February 15, 1968), 7-30. Barillet and Gredy, adapters. In French.

8166. ─────── . Black Comedy. 1 act. Plays and Players, 15 (April, 1968), 42-46, 59-66, 68-73.

8167. ─────── . Black Comedy. 1 act. Sipario, 249 (January, 1967), 41-57. In Italian.

8168. ─────── . Five Finger Exercise. 2 acts. Sipario, 17 (June, 1962), 69-90. Laura del Bono, translator. In Italian.

8169. ─────── . Five Finger Exercise. 2 acts. Theatre Arts, 45 (February, 1961), 27-56.

8170. _____. L'Oeil Anonyme. 1 act, comedy. L'Avant Scène, 397 (February 15, 1968), 33-46. Barillet and Gredy, adapters. In French.

8171. _____. Public Eye. 1 act. Sipario, 19 (April, 1964), 52-62. Adolfo Moriconi, translator. In Italian.

8172. _____. The Royal Hunt of the Sun. 2 acts. Sipario, 21 (June, 1966), 45-63. Elena Reina, translator. In Italian.

8173. _____. The White Liars. 1 act. Plays and Players, 15 (April, 1968), 31-42.

8174. Shakespeare, William, 1564-1616. As You Like It. 1 act. Plays, 17 (February, 1958), 87-96. Lewy Olfson, adapter.

8175. _____. Coriolanus. 5 acts, tragedy. Petite Illustration, 187 (February 10, 1934), 1-38. René-Louis Piachaud, translator. In French.

8176. _____. Coriolanus. 5 acts, tragedy. Spectaculum, 8 (1965), 9-70. Bertolt Brecht, adapter. In German.

8177. _____. Hamlet. 1 act. Plays, 18 (November, 1958), 86-96. Lewy Olfson, adapter.

8178. _____. Henry IV, Part I. 4 acts. Sipario, 9 (December, 1954), 42-64. Fernand Crommelynck, adapter; Corrado Alvaro, translator. In Italian.

8179. _____. Julius César. 5 acts, tragedy. L'Avant Scène, 323 (December 1, 1964), 11-34. Maurice Clavel, adapter. In French.

8180. _____. Julius Caesar. 1 act. Plays, 14 (January, 1955), 88-96. AND Plays, 24 (February, 1965), 81-90. AND Plays, 35 (January, 1976), 85-95. Lewy Olfson, adapter.

8181. _____. King Lear. 1 act. Plays, 21 (November, 1961), 87-96. Lewy Olfson, adapter.

8182. _____. Macbeth. 1 act. Plays, 14 (April, 1955), 87-95. AND Plays, 25 (January, 1966), 79-90. AND Plays, 34 (January, 1975), 85-96. Lewy Olfson, adapter.

8183. _____. Macbeth. 5 acts, tragedy. Vers et Prose, 18 (July-September, 1909), 5-40. Maurice Maeterlinck, translator. In French.

8184. _____. Measure for Measure. Plays and Players, 22 (June, 1975), 41-50. Charles Marowitz, adapter.

8185. _____. The Merchant of Venice. 2 acts, comedy. L'Avant Scène, 253 (November 15, 1961), 8-30. Claude-André Puget, adapter. In French.

8186. _____. A Midsummer Night's Dream. 1 act. Plays, 18 (February, 1959), 87-96. Lewy Olfson, adapter.

8187. _____. Much Ado about Nothing. 1 act. Plays, 17 (April, 1958), 87-96. Lewy Olfson, adapter.

8188. _____. Richard III. 5 acts. L'Avant Scène, 502 (September 15, 1972), 7-45. Jean-Louis Curtis, translator. In French.

8189. _____. Romeo and Juliet. 1 act. Plays, 16 (May, 1957), 79-90. AND Plays, 23 (May, 1964), 87-98. AND Plays, 33 (January, 1974), 83-95. Lewy Olfson, adapter.

8190. _____. The Taming of the Shrew. 1 act. Plays, 19 (January, 1960), 85-96. Lewy Olfson, adapter.

8191. _____. The Tempest. 1 act. Plays, 20 (November, 1960), 87-96. Lewy Olfson, adapter.

8192. _____. Twelfth Night, comedy. L'Avant Scène, 243 (May 15, 1961), 9-29. Nichole Anouilh and Jean Anouilh, adapters. In French.

8193. Shakespeare's Funeral. 1 act. Living Age, 117 (May, 1873), 387-404.

8194. Shamir, Moshe, 1921- . La guerra dei figli della luce. 4 parts. Il Dramma, n.s., 301 (October, 1961), 10-40. Giorgio Richetti, translator. In Italian.

Shaphro, Frances Arno, translator see Chekhov, A. P. 1785

Shapiro, Norman R., translator see Feydeau, G. 3008

Shapiro, Sidney, translator see Sha Seh 8163

8195. Sharma, Partap. A Touch of Brightness. 7 scenes. Gambit, 3 (No. 9), 3-54.

8196. Sharp, H. Sutton. Germs. 1 act. Drama, 16 (February, 1926), 167-168, 170.

8197. Sharp, William, 1856?-1905. The Birth of a Soul. 1 act. Chapbook, 1 (September 15, 1894), 224-228.

8198. _____. The Immortal Hour. 2 acts. Fortnightly, 74 (November, 1900), 867-896.

Sharp

8199. _____. A Northern Night. 1 act. Chapbook, 1 (June 15, 1894), 60-71.

Shattuck, Roger Whitney, 1923- , translator see Char, R. 1722

8200. Shaw, Charles G., 1892- . The Gay Night Life of New York. 1 act. Smart Set, 68 (June, 1922), 86-88.

8201. Shaw, Frances. The Person in the Chair, a Revelation. 1 act. Drama, 11 (February, 1921), 171-174.

8202. Shaw, George Bernard, 1856-1950. Androcles and the Lion. 3 acts, comedy. Everybody's Magazine, 31 (September, 1914), 289-311.

8203. _____. The Apple Cart. 3 acts. Spectaculum, 4 (1963), 271-333. In German.

8204. _____. Back to Methuselah. 1 act. Everybody's Magazine, 46 (June, 1922), 141-148.

8205. _____. Caesar and Cleopatra. 5 acts, comedy. Theatre Arts, 34 (September, 1950), 51-88.

8206. _____. The Dark Lady of the Sonnets. English Review, 7 (January, 1911), 258-269.

8207. _____. Don Juan in Hell (Section from Man and Superman). 1 act. Theatre Arts, 36 (April, 1952), 50-66.

8208. _____. Great Catherine. 1 act. Everybody's Magazine, 32 (February, 1915), 193-212.

8209. _____. Major Barbara. 4 acts. L'Avant Scène, 450 (June 1, 1970), 7-41. Jean Cosmos, adapter. In French.

8210. _____. Man and Superman: Intermezzo--Don Juan in Hell. Il Dramma, n.s., 294 (March, 1961), 13-20. Paola Ojetti, translator. In Italian.

8211. _____. Misalliance. 1 act, farce. Theatre Arts, 37 (September, 1953), 35-63.

8212. _____. O'Flaherty. 1 act. Spectaculum, 9 (1966), 123-140. Hans Gunter Michelsen, translator. In German.

8213. _____. Overruled; A Dramatic Study. 1 act. English Review, 14 (May, 1913), 179-197.

8214. _____. Overruled. 1 act. Hearst's Magazine, 23 (May, 1913), 681-696.

8215. _____. Un Petit Drame. 1 act. Esquire, 52 (December, 1959), 172-174. Norman Denny, translator. In English and French.

8216. _____. Pygmalion. 5 acts. Everybody's Magazine, 31 (November, 1914), 577-612.

8217. _____. Saint Joan, Chronicle in 6 Scenes and an Epilogue. Petite Illustration, 86 (July 28, 1928), 1-41. Augustin Hamon and Henriette Hamon, translators. In French.

8218. _____. Saint Joan, Chronicle in 6 Scenes and an Epilogue. Spectaculum, 1 (1962), 383-471. In German.

8219. _____. The War Indemnities. 1 act. American Mercury, 35 (August, 1935), 395-397.

8220. _____. Why She Would Not. 1 act, comedy. London Magazine, 3 (August, 1956), 11-20.

8221. _____. Why She Would Not. 1 act, comedy. Sipario, 11 (December, 1956), 50-53. Paola Ojetti, translator. In Italian.

8222. _____. Why She Would Not. 1 act, comedy. Theatre Arts, 40 (August, 1956), 24-57.

8223. Shaw, Irwin, 1930- . The Assassin. 3 acts. Sipario, 3 (May, 1948), 29-51. Umberto Jacchia, translator. In Italian.

8224. _____. Bury the Dead. 1 act. Sipario, 1 (July, 1946), 15-30. Fabio Coen, translator. In Italian.

8225. _____. The Gentle People. 3 acts. Il Dramma, n.s., 4 (January 1, 1946), 9-40. Vinicio Marinucci, translator. In Italian.

8226. _____. Second Mortgage. 1 act. One-Act Play Magazine, 2 (May, 1938), 47-57.

8227. _____ and Jean-Pierre Aumont. Lucy Crown. 3 acts. Il Dramma, n.s., 281 (February, 1960), 6-38. Connie Ricono and Oddera, translators. In Italian.

8228. Shaw, Robert, 1927-1978. Cato Street. 2 acts. Plays and Players, 19 (December, 1971), 61-84.

8229. _____. The Man in the Glass Booth. 2 acts. Plays and Players, 15 (November, 1967), 23-34.

8230. She Who Was Fished. 1 act, farce. Outlook, 133 (January 31, 1923), 218-219. Michio Itow and Louis V. Ledoux, translators.

8231. Shea, Gordon F. Treasure. 1 act. Plays, 30 (March, 1971), 76-78.

8232. Shedd, Harrison Graves. Cottonwood Court (A Drama of Early Nebraska). 1 act. Prairie Schooner, 3 (Spring, 1929), 107-124.

8233. Sheehan, Perley Poore. Efficiency. 1 act. McClure's, 49 (August, 1917), 33, 56-58.

8234. Shein, Brian. Kafka, a Ritual. Prism International, 7 (Spring, 1968), 105-126.

8235. Shelley, Elsa. Pick-Up Girl. 3 acts. Il Dramma, n.s., 27/28 (December 15, 1946/January 1, 1947), 11-43. Rolandi Rosada and Guido Rosada, translators. In Italian.

8236. Shen Hung. The Cow-Herd and the Weaving Maid. 1 act. Drama, 11 (August-September, 1921), 404-408.

8237. Shenk, Esther. Washington at Home. 1 act. Wilson Library Bulletin, 6 (May, 1932), 611-615.

8238. Shepard, Sam, 1943- . Operation Sidewinder. 2 acts. Esquire, 71 (May, 1969), 152, 160, 210, 212, 214, 216-218, 220, 222-228, 230-234.

8239. _____. The Rock Garden. Scripts, 1 (January, 1972), 24-30.

8240. _____. The Tooth of Crime. 2 acts. Performance, 5 (March/April, 1973), 67-91.

8241. _____. La turista. 2 acts. Sipario, 25 (February, 1970), 50-64. Elena Vegliani Reina, translator. In Italian.

8242. _____. The Unseen Hand. 1 act. Plays and Players, 20 (May, 1973), I-XI.

8243. Shepherd, Edmund. The Closed Door. 1 act. Smart Set, 31 (June, 1910), 131-137.

8244. Sheridan, Emma. The Wind and the Lady Moon. 1 act. Drama, 12 (June-August, 1922), 314-318.

8245. Sheridan, Richard Brinsley, 1751-1816. The Rivals. 1 act. Plays, 15 (March, 1956), 87-95. AND Plays, 22 (March, 1963), 87-96. Lewy Olfson, adapter.

8246. _____. St. Patrick's Day, or, The Scheming Lieutenant. 1 act. Golden Book, 7 (March, 1928), 351-360.

8247. _____. The School for Scandal. 5 acts, comedy.

Sheridan

L'Avant Scène, 274 (October 15, 1962), 7-35. Pierre Barillet and Jean-Pierre Gredy, adapters. In French.

8248. Sherman, Lucius Adelno. Ecce Germania. 3 acts. Prairie Schooner, 2 (Fall, 1928), 235-241.

8249. _____. The Interrupted Experiment. 3 acts. Prairie Schooner, 2 (Spring, 1928), 97-102.

8250. _____. Shakespeare 1564-1616; A Spectacle. 1 act. Prairie Schooner, 1 (April, 1927), 117-139.

8251. Sherriff, Robert Cedric, 1896- . Home at Seven. 3 acts. Il Dramma, n.s., 117 (September 15, 1950), 5-32. Mirella Ducceschi, translator. In Italian.

8252. _____. Journey's End. 3 acts. Petite Illustration, 87 (November 2, 1929), 1-34. Lucien Besnard and Virginia Vernon, adapters. In French.

8253. Sherry, Ruth Forbes. Seize on Tragic Time. 1 act. Poet Lore, 58 (Summer, 1963), 99-117.

8254. Sherwin, Louis. A Cure for Authors. 1 act. American Mercury, 11 (July, 1927), 365-368.

8255. Sherwood, Geralding. "Ens." 1 act. Dramatika, 3 (March, 1969), 5-7.

8256. Sherwood, Margaret, 1864-1955. Vittoria. 5 acts. Scribner's, 37 (April, 1905), 497-504.

8257. Sherwood, Robert Emmet, 1896-1955. The Petrified Forest. 2 parts. Sipario, 1 (November-December, 1946), 9-29. Alessandra Scalero, translator. In Italian.

8258. _____. Reunion in Vienna. 3 acts. Il Dramma, 236 (June 15, 1936), 2-27. In Italian.

8259. _____. Small War on Murray Hill. 3 acts, comedy. Theatre Arts, 42 (August, 1958), 26-47.

Shipley, Joseph Twadell, 1893- , translator see Mallarme, S. 5473

8260. Shoemaker, Carole. 10-10 Till We Read You Again, Good Buddy. 1 act. Plays, 36 (December, 1976), 59-64.

8261. Shore, Maxine. Catastrophe Clarence. 1 act. Plays, 15 (March, 1956), 43-52. AND Plays, 31 (October, 1971), 37-46.

8262. _____. Watch Out for Aunt Hattie. 1 act. Plays, 11 (March, 1952), 28-38.

8263. Shpazhinsky, Ippolit Vasilievich. Madame Major. 5 acts. Poet Lore, 28 (Summer, 1917), 257-324. Francis H. Snow and Beatrice M. Mekota, translators.

8264. Shriner, Fleming. The Admiral Leads On. 1 act. Plays, 25 (October, 1965), 79-82.

8265. Shulman, Max, 1919- and Robert Paul Smith, 1915- . The Tender Trap. 3 acts, comedy. Theatre Arts, 40 (February, 1956), 36-61.

8266. Shyre, Paul, adapter. A Whitman Portrait; A Dramatic Narrative in Two Acts. Nassau Review, 1 (Spring, 1965), 19-79.

_____ see also Dos Passos, J. 2560, 2561

8267. Siciliano, Enzo, 1934- . La mama com'e. 1 act. Sipario, 264 (April, 1968), 59-64. In Italian.

8268. _____. La tazza. 1 act. Sipario, 21 (October, 1966), 42-46. In Italian.

8269. _____. Vita e morte di Cola di Rienzo. Sipario, 324 (May, 1973), 61-80. In Italian.

8270. Sickels, Eleanor. Dare All for Liberty. 1 act. Plays, 4 (January, 1945), 43-49.

8271. _____. The Spelling Match. 1 act. Plays, 3 (October, 1943), 51-55.

Side, Ronald K., adapter see Dickens, C. 2480

8272. Sifton, Claire G. Ernie. 1 act. One-Act Play Magazine, 3 (January, 1940), 19-28.

8273. _____ and Paul Sifton. Kate Larsen. 1 act. One-Act Play Magazine, 2 (June-July, 1938), 161-175.

Sifton, Paul see Sifton, C. G. 8273

Sigurd, Jacques, adapter see Guare, J. 3774

_____, adapter see Wasserman, D. 9215

8274. Sigurjonsson, Johann, 1880-1919. Loft's Wish. 3 acts. Poet Lore, 46 (Summer, 1940), 99-146. Jakobina Johnson, translator.

8275. Silone, Ignazio, 1900- . L'avventura d'un povero Cristiano. 3 parts. Il Dramma, 45, no. 12 (September, 1969), 29-51. In Italian.

8276. Silori, Luigi. Stagione sulle baracche. 1 act. Sipario, 10 (August, 1955), 43-49. In Italian.

Silva, Carlo see Vergani, O. 9083

8277. Silvain, Jean. De l'Eau Sous les Ponts. 1 act. L'Avant Scène, 344 (November 1, 1965), 42-45. In French.

8278. _____. Mandoline. 1 act. L'Avant Scène, 262 (April 1, 1962), 45-51. In French.

8279. _____. Le Père Damien. 3 acts. L'Avant Scène (OST), 39 (March, 1951), 1-42. In French.

8280. _____ and Daniel Gallo. Comme les Chats. 1 act. L'Avant Scène, 447 (April 15, 1970), 37-42. In French.

Silvera, Miro, translator see Crowley, M. 2130

Silverberg, William V., translator see Lavedan, H. 4842

8281. Silverman, Stanley H. Isaiah and the United Nations. 1 act. Senior Scholastic, 51 (October 6, 1947), 19-21.

Silvestri, Ilia, translator see Neveux, G. 6480

8282. Simenon, Georges, 1903- . La Neige Etait Sale. 3 acts. Il Dramma, n.s., 142 (October 1, 1951), 9-32. Gianni Nicoletti, translator. In Italian.

Simon, Michel, 1895- , translator see Machado, M. C. 5211

8283. Simon, Neil, 1927- . Barefoot in the Park. 2 acts, comedy. L'Avant Scène, 328 (February 15, 1965), 10-40. André Roussin, translator. In French.

8284. Simon, Shirley, 1921- . The Baking Contest. 1 act. Plays, 18 (February, 1959), 49-54.

8285. _____. Cure for a King. 1 act. Plays, 18 (April, 1959), 61-66.

8286. _____. Doctor Farmer. 1 act. Plays, 18 (April, 1959), 75-80.

8287. _____. The Rock. 1 act. Plays, 19 (January, 1960), 42-46.

8288. _____. The Smell of New Bread. 1 act. Plays, 21 (May, 1962), 69-74.

8289. _____. Taffy and Sylvie. 1 act. Plays, 19 (October, 1959), 75-80.

8290. _____. The Tiger and the Brahman. 1 act. Plays, 17 (May, 1958), 69-72.

8291. _____. The Town That Learned. 1 act. Plays, 18 (January, 1959), 77-82.

8292. _____. William Rob Attacks a Problem. 1 act. Plays, 18 (October, 1958), 65-68.

8293. Simonds, Natalie. Hansel and Gretel. 1 act. Plays, 3 (December, 1943), 58-61. AND Plays, 21 (April, 1962), 73-76.

8294. _____. Peter Rabbit. 1 act. Plays, 2 (November, 1942), 53-56.

8295. _____. The Unhappy Santa. 1 act. Plays, 2 (December, 1942), 61-62.

8296. Simonetta, Umberto. Un lancio riuscito proprio bene. 1 act. Sipario, 24 (March, 1969), 65-69. In Italian.

8297. Simongini, Franco and Maurizio Costanzo. Quell' angelo azzurro che si chiamo TV. 1 act. Il Dramma, 44, no. 2 (November, 1968), 83-85. In Italian.

8298. Simoni, Renato. Carlo Gozzi. 4 acts. Il Dramma, n.s., 163/164 (August 15/September 1, 1952), 83-114. In Italian.

8299. Simonov, Konstantin. La Questione Russa. 3 acts. Sipario, 2 (October, 1947), 38-54. Andrea Jemma, translator. In Italian.

8300. Simons, Beverley. Leela Means to Play. 2 acts. Canadian Theatre Review, 9 (Winter, 1976), 30-161.

8301. Simpson, Fred M. The Dedication. 1 act. Yellow Book, 1 (April, 1894), 159-184.

8302. Simpson, Louis, 1923- . Andromeda. 1 act. Hudson Review, 8 (Winter, 1956), 499-518.

8303. _____. The Father Out of the Machine; A Masque. 1 act. Chicago Review, 5 (Winter, 1951), 3-13.

8304. Simpson, Mary. The Christmas Story. 1 act. Resource, 1 (November, 1959), 20-21.

8305. Simpson, Norman Frederick, 1919- . The Cresta Run. 2 acts. Plays and Players, 13 (February, 1966), 29-43.

8306. Sinclair, Upton, 1878-1968. La forza di un gigante. 3 acts.

Il Dramma, n.s., 91/92 (August 15/September 1, 1949), 59-92. Ada Fava, translator. In Italian.

8307. Singer, Felix. The Final Play. 1 act. Trace, 62/63 (1967), 418-424.

Singer, Leslie, adapter see Tzara, T. 8961

8308. Siro, Claudio. Kitsch. 2 acts. Il Dramma, 51 (October, 1975), 39-57. In Italian.

_____ see Ghiglia, D. 3472

Sjoberg, Leif, translator see Aspenstrom, W. 423

8309. Skinner, Ada M. The New New Year. 1 act. St. Nicholas, 45 (January, 1918), 257-262.

Skinner, Cornelia Otis, 1901- see Taylor, S. 8734, 8735

Skolnik, William see Campbell, P. 1548

8310. Slade, Bernard. Meme Heure l'Annee Prochaine. 2 acts, comedy. L'Avant Scène, 594 (September 15, 1976), 3-29. Pierre Barillet and Jean-Pierre Gredy, adapters. In French.

8311. Slater, Montagu, 1902- . The Seven Ages of Man. 1 act. Life and Letters, 17 (Winter, 1937), 109-119.

8312. Slattery, Margaret E. Don't Send for Hector. 1 act. Plays, 25 (January, 1966), 1-13.

8313. _____. The Golden Hearts. 1 act. Plays, 22 (February, 1963), 63-71.

8314. _____. The King in the Kitchen. 1 act. Plays, 11 (March, 1952), 62-68. AND Plays, 23 (March, 1964), 53-59.

8315. _____. The Patchwork Princess. 1 act. Plays, 11 (April, 1952), 30-36.

8316. _____. The Peppermint Easter Egg. 1 act. Plays, 22 (April, 1963), 35-42.

8317. _____. The Queen's Mirror. 1 act. Plays, 20 (April, 1961), 45-52.

8318. _____. Rainbow Palace. 1 act. Plays, 19 (January, 1960), 57-64.

8319. _____. Royal Magic. 1 act. Plays, 12 (May, 1953), 54-60.

8320. _____. The Shipwrecked King. 1 act. Plays, 25 (May, 1966), 55-61.

8321. _____. The Silent Prince. 1 act. Plays, 18 (April, 1959), 57-64.

8322. _____. The Silly Princesses. 1 act. Plays, 20 (March, 1961), 57-64.

8323. _____. The Stolen Cook. 1 act. Plays, 24 (November, 1964), 67-75.

8324. Smalley, Webster. The Man with the Oboe. 2 acts, comedy. Players' Magazine, 40 (February, 1964), 142-158.

8325. Smith, Beatrice S. Adams for the Defense. 1 act. Plays, 35 (May, 1976), 67-77.

8326. Smith, Betty, 1904- . The Boy, Abe. 1 act. One-Act Play Magazine, 4 (March-April, 1941), 99-109.

8327. _____. First Sorrow. 1 act. Plays, 3 (January, 1944), 1-3.

8328. _____. So Gracious Is the Time. 1 act. One-Act Play Magazine, 2 (June-July, 1938), 143-160.

8329. _____. Story Told in Indiana. 1 act. Theatre Arts, 28 (November, 1944), 677-680.

8330. _____ and Robert Finch. The Package for Ponsonby. 1 act. One-Act Play Magazine, 4 (January-February, 1941), 52-67.

8331. _____ and Clemon White. West from the Panhandle. 1 act, tragedy. One-Act Play Magazine, 2 (February, 1939), 703-725.

Smith, Calvin C., translator see Bellido, J. M. 734, 736

_____, translator see Paredes, P. S. 6970

8332. Smith, Gladys V. The Catnip Patch. 1 act. Plays, 20 (March, 1961), 75-78.

8333. _____. Easter Bunny on Pleasant Street. 1 act. Plays, 19 (March, 1960), 69-72.

8334. _____, adapter. The Tiger, the Brahman, and the Jackal. 1 act. Plays, 26 (November, 1966), 75-78.

8335. Smith, Hyacinthe Stoddart. Cordia. 3 acts. Poet Lore, 19 (Summer, 1908), 165-192.

Smith, Ingeborg, E., translator see Kvapil, J. 4742

8336. Smith, J. Kinchin. The Mummers' Play. 1 act. Theatre Arts, 7 (January, 1923), 63-68.

8337. Smith, Jacqueline V. Summer Soldier. 1 act. Plays, 35 (October, 1975), 79-82.

8338. Smith, Janet K. The Ballad of Hynd Horn. 1 act. Scholastic, 28 (February 15, 1936), 14-15.

Smith, Jean Shannon, adapter see Pandora 6949

--------- see also Gardner, M. 3388

8339. Smith, Mardee. The Book Week Assembly. 1 act. Wilson Library Bulletin, 22 (October, 1947), 156-158.

8340. Smith, Maria W. Exitium Caesaris. 1 act. Classical Journal, 16 (December, 1920), 157-164. In Latin.

8341. Smith, Mary F. Wait and See. 1 act. Plays, 17 (January, 1958), 67-70.

8342. Smith, Miriam Spencer. An American Grandfather. 1 act. Poet Lore, 35 (1924), 443-455.

8343. ---------. Good Night. 1 act. Drama, 16 (February, 1926), 174, 199.

8344. ---------. The Hamburger King. 1 act. Drama, 15 (March, 1925), 125-127, 136.

8345. ---------. Slow but Sure. 1 act, comedy. Drama, 17 (February, 1927), 138-140.

8346. ---------. The Wedding Anniversary. 1 act. Drama, 17 (April, 1927), 206-207.

8347. Smith, N. K. Budge, Budge Not. 1 act. One-Act Play Magazine, 1 (July, 1937), 201-218.

8348. Smith, Nora Archibald. What Happened to the Tarts. 1 act. St. Nicholas, 47 (August, 1920), 936-940.

8349. Smith, Peter J. The Enlightenment of Others by Will Skuffel. 2 acts. Drama and Theatre, 8 (No. 1, 1969), 61-79.

8350. ---------. The Gas Tank. 1 act. First Stage, 6 (Winter, 1967-1968), 216-229.

8351. Smith, Richard Penn, 1799-1854. The Last Eligible Man. 1 act, farce. Plays, 31 (February, 1972), 85-96. Paul T. Nolan, adapter.

Smith, Robert Paul, 1915- see Shulman, M. 8265

8352. Smith, S. Decatur, Jr. Jack and Jill. 1 act. Ladies' Home Journal, 24 (December, 1906), 14, 73.

8353. _____. A Mother Goose Christmas. 1 act. Ladies' Home Journal, 25 (December, 1907), 19, 75.

8454. _____. "The Princess Aline" Play. 2 acts, comedy. Ladies' Home Journal, 18 (April, 1901), 3-4, 40-41.

8355. Smith, Terence. Eyes and No Eyes. 1 act. Irish Writing, 4 (April, 1948), 61-71.

8356. Smith, Warren. The Day! 1 act. American Prefaces, 3 (October, 1937), 3-9.

8357. Smocek, Ladislav, 1932- . Podivne odpoledne dr. Zvonka Burkeho. 1 act. Sipario, 21 (December, 1966), 81-88. Gianlorenzo Pacini, translator. In Italian.

8358. Snelling, Dorothy. Winning Combination. 1 act. Plays, 28 (April, 1969), 23-33.

8359. Snider, Charles Lee. Jonah in the Bible Country. 1 act. American Mercury, 30 (October, 1933), 165-171.

Snow, Francis H., translator see Shpazhinsky, I. V. 8263

_____, translator see Subert, F. A. 8596

Snow, Frank E., translator see Rueda, L. de 7785

Sobel, Bernard, 1887-1964 see Glick, C. 3586

8360. Socorri, Claude. C'Est Mon Mari. 1 act, comedy. Petite Illustration, 195 (November 7, 1936), 1-10. In French.

8361. Soffici, Ardengo, 1879- . Una serata in famiglia. 1 act. Il Dramma, 351 (April 1, 1941), 39-42. In Italian.

8362. Sofronov, Anatol Vladimirovic, 1911- . Moskovsky Charakter. 4 acts. Il Dramma, n.s., 97 (November 15, 1949), 7-34. Andrea Jemma, translator. In Italian.

Sogard, Thyge, translator see Bjørnson, B. 975

Sokolsky, Pierre, translator see Mayakovsky, V. V. 5703

Solari, Laura, translator see Feydeau, G. 3010

8363. Solari, Pietro. Pamela divorziata. 4 acts. Il Dramma, 36 (February 15, 1928), 6-33. In Italian.

8364. _____. Radio-Intermezzo per Microfono. Il Dramma, 205 (March 1, 1935), 34-35. In Italian.

8365. _____. Ritorno di Ulisse. 1 act. Il Dramma, 207 (April 1, 1935), 38-39. In Italian.

8366. Soldati, Mario and Raffaele la Capria. La Finestra. 1 act. Sipario, 18 (February, 1963), 59-69. In Italian.

Soldati, Paolo, translator see Musatescu, T. 6412

8367. Soldervila, Carlo. Una data eccezionale. 1 act. Il Dramma, 402/403 (May 15/June 1, 1943), 79-82. Giuseppe Ravegnani, translator. In Italian.

Solenni, Gino V. M. de, translator see Jimenez Rueda, J. 4468

8368. Soler, Anita. Le Solitaire. 1 act. L'Avant Scène, 297 (October 15, 1963), 37-42. In French.

Sollar, Fabien see Willemetz, A. 9406

Sologub, Fedor, pseud. see Teternikov, F. K. 8778

8369. Soloman, Norman. A Passion Play. 1 act. The Floating Bear, 21 (1962), 234-235.

8370. Solon, Israel. The Biteless Dog. 1 act. Smart Set, 42 (January, 1914), 97-102.

8371. Solorzano, Carlos. The Puppets. 1 act. Modern International Drama, 7 (Spring, 1974), 7-19. Francesca Colecchia, translator.

8372. Solzhenitsyn, Aleksandr Isayevich, 1918- . Sveca Na Vetru. Il Dramma, 46, no. 3 (March, 1970), 42-57. Pietro Zveteremich, translator. In Italian.

Sombart, Petronelle, translator see Lodovici, C. 5011, 5013, 5015

8373. Somebody-Nothing; An Ancient Japanese Farce. 1 act. Asia, 21 (December, 1921), 1011-1012. Michio Itow and Louis V. Ledoux, translators.

Sommaripas, François, 1928- , translator see Wesker, A. 9300

8374. Sommer, Lucien. Les Vitraux. 1 act. L'Avant Scène, 293 (August 1, 1963), 39-45. In French.

Sondheim, Stephen, 1930- see Laurents, A. 4833

8375. Song of Songs of Solomon, The. Drama Review, 20 (September, 1976), 129-135. P. N. Roinard, adapter; Lenora Champagne and Norma Jean Deak, translators.

8376. Song of the Dragon River. Revised edition. Chinese Literature, 7 (1972), 3-52.

Sonnendrucker, Paul, translator see Eckart, W. 2814

Sonnenfeld, Morton see Rugg, M. M. 7786

8377. Sonnier, Georges, 1918- . L'Impromptu de Rome, ou Le Septième Personnage. 1 act, comedy. L'Avant Scène, 369 (December 1, 1966), 39-44.

8378. ———. La Pelisse. 2 acts, farce. L'Avant Scène, 278 (December 15, 1962), 21-37. In French.

———, translator see Nicolai, A. 6578, 6579

———, translator see Nicolai, A., Jr. 6587

8379. Soper, Mark J. Of You and Me. 1 act. Dramatics, 43 (April, 1972), 5-7.

8380. Sophocles, 496?-406 B. C. Antigone. Massachusetts Review, 9 (Spring, 1968), 297-330. Theodore Stinchecum, translator.

8381. ———. Women of Trachis. 1 act, tragedy. Hudson Review, 6 (Winter, 1954), 487-523. Ezra Pound, translator.

8382. Sorabji, Cornelia, 1866-1954. Gold Mohur Tune: "To Remember." 5 acts. 19th Century, 106 (July, 1929), 133-142.

8383. Sorbets, Gaston. La Colombe Poignardée. 3 acts. Petite Illustration, 181 (March 19, 1932), 1-30. In French.

8384. ———. La Moisson Verte. 4 acts. Petite Illustration, 185 (June 17, 1933), 1-34. In French.

8385. Sorescu, Marin. La cattedrale. 3 parts. Il Dramma, 45, no. 10 (July, 1969), 76-79. Mario Cugno, translator. In Italian.

8386. ———. I nervi esistono. 2 acts. Il Dramma, 49 (January-February, 1973), 121-136. Marco Cugno, translator. In Italian.

8387. Soria, Georges, 1914- . L'Etrangère dans l'Ile. 2 parts. L'Avant Scène, 185 (November 15, 1958), 7-27. In French.

8388. ———. Les Passions Contraires. 3 acts. L'Avant Scène, 315 (July 15, 1964), 10-32. In French.

8389. _____. Les Témoins. 2 acts. L'Avant Scène, 259 (February 15, 1962), 9-33. In French.

_____, translator see Chkvarkine, V. 1812

8390. Sos, Gyorgy. A True Legend. 1 act. Mainstream, 14 (August, 1961), 43-60.

8391. Soule, George. The Logical Extreme. 1 act. Little Review, 1 (January, 1915), 3-6.

8392. _____. The Last Woman. 1 act. Little Review, 1 (February, 1915), 20-25.

8393. Southgate, Patricia. Freddy. 1 act. Evergreen Review, 6 (July-August, 1962), 27-39.

_____, translator see Aron, J.-P. 357

8394. Souza, Antonio. Pascualina. 1 act. Americas, 9 (December, 1957), 22-25.

8395. Soyfer, Jura. Eddie Lechner's Trip to Paradise. Modern International Drama, 4 (Spring, 1971), 59-78. Horst Jarka, translator.

8396. _____. The End of the World. Modern International Drama, 5 (Spring, 1972), 63-80. Horst Jarka, translator.

8397. Soyinka, Wole, 1934- . The Road. 2 acts. Gambit (No. 4, 1963), 5-69.

8398. Spaak, Claude. Le Pain Blanc. 4 acts. L'Avant Scène, 148, 1-21. In French.

8399. _____. La Rose des Vents. 2 parts. L'Avant Scène, 85, 1-23. In French.

8400. _____. Trois Fois le Jour. 3 acts. L'Avant Scène, 260 (March 1, 1962), 8-29. In French.

Spagnol, Mario, translator see Zuckmayer, C. 9660

8401. Spain, Leona. This Might Happen to You. 1 act. Plays, 2 (February, 1943), 44-47.

8402. Spaini, Alberto, 1892- . Il giramondo. 1 act. Il Dramma, 65 (May 1, 1929), 35-44. In Italian.

8403. Spamer, Claribel. April Showers. 1 act. Plays, 9 (April, 1950), 62-65.

8404. _____. The Blushing Bunny. 1 act. Plays, 17 (April 1958), 78-80.

Spamer

8405. _____. The Bunny Who Was Always Late. 1 act. Plays, 9 (April, 1950), 57-59.

8406. _____. The Dream Maker's Workshop. 1 act. Plays, 3 (February, 1944), 49-53.

8407. _____. The Dwarfs' Beards. 1 act. Plays, 5 (April, 1946), 70-73.

8408. _____. The First Butterfly. 1 act. Plays, 16 (March, 1957), 77-78.

8409. _____. Halloween Scarecrow. 1 act. Plays, 15 (October, 1955), 60-61.

8410. _____. Hop, Jump and Skip. 1 act. Plays, 9 (May, 1950), 68-78.

8411. _____. Jack Frost's Goodbye Gift. 1 act. Plays, 14 (March, 1955), 84-86.

8412. _____. Jack-O-Lantern. 1 act. Plays, 9 (October, 1949), 63-66.

8413. _____. Jack's Friends. 1 act. Plays, 11 (January, 1952), 64-66.

8414. _____. King Cole's Blues. 1 act. Plays, 3 (October, 1943), 62-64.

8415. _____. Little February. 1 act. Plays, 11 (February, 1952), 79-81.

8416. _____. Little Forget-Me-Not. 1 act. Plays, 4 (December, 1944), 63-65.

8417. _____. The Little Prop Boy. 1 act. Plays, 4 (March, 1945), 51-53.

8418. _____. The Little Witch Who Forgot. 1 act. Plays, 4 (October, 1944), 55-57.

8419. _____. The Man in the Moon. 1 act. Plays, 5 (March, 1946), 56-57.

8420. _____. Mary's Cake. 1 act. Plays, 10 (November, 1950), 51-53.

8421. _____. Mary's Garden. 1 act. Plays, 5 (May, 1946), 55-58.

8422. _____. The Mayor of Burgville. 1 act. Plays, 18 (October, 1958), 54-58.

8423. ———. The Mirror Children. 1 act. Plays, 4 (April, 1945), 50-52.

8424. ———. Miss Robin's School. 1 act. Plays, 9 (March, 1950), 71-73.

8425. ———. Mister Owl. 1 act. Plays, 9 (November, 1949), 68-71.

8426. ———. Not So Simple Simon. 1 act. Plays, 4 (November, 1944), 45-46.

8427. ———. The Pop-Up Books. 1 act. Plays, 11 (November, 1951), 68-70.

8428. ———. The Pot of Gold. 1 act. Plays, 5 (March, 1946), 58-60.

8429. ———. Pussy Pleases. 1 act. Plays, 9 (January, 1950), 62-64.

8430. ———. The Shy Prince. 1 act. Plays, 3 (November, 1943), 65-69.

8431. ———. Topsy-Turvy Weather. 1 act. Plays, 20 (January, 1961), 81-83.

8432. ———. Twinkle. 1 act. Plays, 12 (December, 1952), 54-56.

8433. ———. The Uncolored Easter Egg. 1 act. Plays, 10 (March, 1951), 60-62.

8434. ———. The Useful Scarecrow. 1 act. Plays, 5 (November, 1945), 57-59.

8435. ———. Wispy. 1 act. Plays, 14 (October, 1954), 71-73.

8436. [Spanish Farce of the 16th Century]. 1 act. PMLA, 24 (No. 1, 1909), 1-31. J. P. Wickersham Crawford, editor. In Spanish.

8437. Spark, Muriel, 1918- . The Interview. 1 act. Transatlantic Review (London), 4 (Summer, 1960), 69-88.

8438. Speare, Dorothy. Romeo and Juliet. 1 act. Bookman [New York], 57 (March, 1923), 7-17.

8439. Speare, Elizabeth George, 1908- . The Forest of Arden. 1 act. Plays, 11 (April, 1952), 14-19.

8440. Speirs, Russell. A Change of Mind. 1 act. Drama, 20 (October, 1929), 13-14.

8441. _____. The Grave. 1 act. Poet Lore, 40 (1929), 113-118.

8442. _____. Hogan's Successor. 1 act. Drama, 19 (May, 1929), 233-234.

8443. Spencer, Colin. Spitting Image. 2 acts. Plays and Players, 16 (November, 1968), 27-45.

8444. Sperr, Martin, 1944- . Jagdszenen aus Niederbayern. Sipario, 27 (February, 1972), 76-88. Marga Feriani Vidusso, translator. In Italian.

8445. _____. Jagdszenen aus Niederbayern. 1 act. Spectaculum, 9 (1966), 143-190. In German.

Spewack, Bella, 1899- see Spewack, S. 8448-9

8446. Spewack, Samuel, 1899- . Sotto il sicomoro. 3 acts. Sipario, 8 (April, 1953), 33-54. Ada Salvatore, translator. In Italian.

8447. _____. Two Blind Mice. 3 acts. Theatre Arts, 33 (December, 1949), 57-90.

8448. _____ and Bella Spewack, 1899- . Kiss Me, Kate. 2 acts, comedy. Theatre Arts, 39 (January, 1955), 34-57.

8449. _____. My 3 Angels. 3 acts, comedy. Theatre Arts, 38 (June, 1954), 35-61.

8450. Speyer, Lady. Love Me, Love My Dog. 1 act. Smart Set, 58 (January, 1919), 73-82.

Spiegel, Moshe, translator see Holdas, A. 4140

_____, translator see Kedrov, V. 4572

_____, translator see Zoschenko, M. 9659

Spies, Werner, translator see Duras, M. 2737

8451. Spigelgass, Leonard, 1908- . A Majority of One. 3 acts. Theatre Arts, 44 (September, 1960), 27-56.

8452. Spiraux, Alain. La Démangeaison. 1 act, farce. L'Avant Scène, 439 (December 15, 1969), 37-42. In French.

8453. _____. Le Roi Borgne. 1 act. L'Avant Scène, 483 (November 15, 1971), 39-43. In French.

8454. Spofford, Harriet Prescott, 1835-1921. The Changeling. 1 act. St. Nicholas, 26 (April, 1899), 501-512.

Sprinchorn, Evert, translator see Strindberg, A. 8573

8455. Springer, Thomas Grant, 1873- and Edward Gage. The Luckiest Man. 1 act. Smart Set, 37 (July, 1912), 135-141.

8456. Spurling, John. Macrune's Guevara. Plays and Players, 16 (September, 1969), 33-48, 75-78.

8557. Spyri, Johanna, 1827-1901. Heidi. 1 act. Plays, 26 (March, 1967), 85-96. Adele Thane, adapter.

8458. _____. Heidi Finds the Way. 1 act. Plays, 18 (January, 1957), 51-59. Karin Asbrand, adapter.

8459. Squarzina, Luigi. Un epilogo entomologico, ovvero l'incomunicabilita degli esseri. 1 act, dialogue. Sipario, 17 (May, 1962), 62-66. In Italian.

8460. _____. Romagnola. 3 parts. Sipario, 14 (April, 1959), 30-67. In Italian.

_____, translator see Anderson, R. 217

_____, translator see Anouilh, J. 264

_____, translator see Greene, G. 3716

_____ see also Kezich, T. 4616

8461. _____ and Lao Pavoni. Lo squarciagola. 1 act. Sipario, 21 (October, 1966), 55-64. In Italian.

8462. Squire, John Collings, 1884-1958. The Best Hand. 1 act. London Mercury, 13 (January, 1926), 251-254.

8463. _____. Clown of Stratford. 1 act, comedy. London Mercury, 7 (November, 1922), 18-25.

8464. _____. The Shortest Play in the World, Act One and Only. London Mercury, 13 (January, 1926), 250.

8465. Squires, Edith Lombard. Queen Jezebel. 1 act. Poet Lore, 40 (1929), 615-626.

8466. Sroda, Anne. The Castlebury Clock. 1 act. Plays, 35 (March, 1976), 47-53.

8467. _____. The Easter Geese. 1 act. Plays, 35 (April, 1976), 39-44.

8468. _____. The Happiness Box. 1 act. Plays, 35 (October, 1975), 53-58.

8469. ———. Janet the Janitress. 1 act. Plays, 35 (January, 1976), 1-11.

8470. ———. Santa Changes His Mind. 1 act. Plays, 35 (December, 1975), 41-44.

8471. ———. Wings for the King. 1 act. Plays, 35 (November, 1975), 39-44.

Stafford-Clark, Max, adapter see Gaskill, W. 3419

Stankiewicz, Marketa Goetz, translator see Barlach, E. 604

8472. Stansbury, Mary. Easter Egg Magic. 1 act. Plays, 16 (April, 1957), 41-46.

8473. Stanwood, Louise Rogers. The Progress of Mrs. Alexander. 3 acts, comedy. New England Magazine, n.s., 43 (February, 1911), 529-560, 655-663.

Starkey, James Sullivan, 1879-1958, translator see Nerval, G. de 6465

8474. Starling, Lynn. For Heaven's Sake. 1 act. Plays, 3 (October, 1943), 70-77.

8475. States, Bert O. A Rent in the Universe. 1 act, farce. First Stage, 6 (Summer, 1967), 103-111.

Statuti, P., translator see Mrozek, S. 6284

Stauffacher, Hans Rudolf, translator see Ionesco, E. 4394

Stauffer, Serge, translator see Ionesco, E. 4384

8476. Stavis, Barrie. Joe Hill Is Not Dead. 3 acts. Sipario, 21 (March, 1966), 36-59. Mario Fratti, translator. In Italian.

8477. Stead, C. K. Dialogue on a Northern Shore. 1 act. Landfall, 12 (September, 1958), 38-43.

8478. Stechhan, H. O. and Maverick Terrell. Branded Mavericks. 1 act. Smart Set, 42 (March, 1914), 133-142.

——— see also Terrell, M. 8748, 8749

8479. Steckler, Stuart. Barf! 1 act. Dramatika, 7 (1971), 19-22.

8480. Stedman, Adelaide. The Substitute Bride. 1 act. Smart Set, 35 (October, 1911), 129-136.

Steel, B. D., translator see Pedrolo, M. de 7036

8481. Steele, Jack. Design for Loving. 1 act. One-Act Play Magazine, 4 (March-April, 1941), 164-175.

8482. _____. Groom's Biscuits. 1 act, farce. One-Act Play Magazine, 4 (November-December, 1941), 439-460.

8483. _____. Moon-Struck. 1 act, comedy. One-Act Play Magazine, 4 (July-August, 1941), 274-290.

8484. _____. Visiting Uncles. 1 act, comedy. One-Act Play Magazine, 4 (May-June, 1941), 195-212.

8485. Steele, Wilbur Daniel, 1886- . Ropes. 1 act. Harper's, 142 (January, 1921), 193-208.

8486. _____. Terrible Woman. 1 act. Pictorial Review, 26 (November, 1924), 6-7.

8487. Steelsmith, Mary. This Isn't Exactly How I Expected It. 1 act. Dramatics, 46 (September/October, 1974), 4-8.

8488. Stein, Gertrude, 1874-1946. Daniel Webster, Eighteen in America: A Play. New Directions, 2 (1937), n.p.

8489. _____. Four Saints in Three Acts, an Opera to Be Sung. Transition, 16-17 (June, 1929), 39-72.

8490. Stein, Joseph, 1912- and Will Glickman, 1910- . Plain and Fancy. 2 acts, comedy. Theatre Arts, 40 (July, 1956), 33-57.

8491. Steinbeck, John, 1902-1968. The Aerial Engineer from Bombs Away. Senior Scholastic, 43 (December 6-11, 1943), 17-18.

8492. _____. The Moon Is Down. 2 parts. Il Dramma, n.s., 18 (August 1, 1946), 11-39. Pilade Vecchietti and Paolina Vecchietti, translators. In Italian.

8493. _____. Of Mice and Men. 3 acts. L'Avant Scène, 589 (June 15, 1976), 3-33. Marcel Duhamel, translator. In French.

8494. _____. Of Mice and Men. 3 acts. Il Dramma, n.s., 165 (September 15, 1952), 7-28. Gaetano Fazio, translator. In Italian.

8495. Steiner, Barbara A. Damian and the Wooden Flute. 1 act. Plays, 33 (April, 1974), 80-84.

8496. _____. The First Ride of Willow Witch. 1 act. Plays, 28 (October, 1968), 69-72.

8497. _____. Topsy-Turvy Foodland. 1 act. Plays, 28 (February, 1969), 45-50.

8498. Steingold, Rita Whitman. The Parrot Who Would Not Talk. 1 act. Plays, 28 (November, 1968), 73-76.

Steno, Flavia, translator see Blanchon, J. 994

8499. Stephens, James, 1882-1950. The Demi-Gods. 3 acts. Journal of Irish Literature, 4 (September, 1975), 10-46.

8500. Stephens, Nan Bagby. Charivari. 1 act. Theatre Arts, 12 (November, 1928), 814-822.

Stephenson, Mary L., translator see Schnitzler, A. 8070

8501. Sterling, George, 1869-1926. The Dryad. 1 act. Overland, n.s., 84 (September, 1926), 293-294.

8502. _____. The Dryad. 1 act. Smart Set, 58 (February, 1919), 81-86.

8503. _____. La ninfa immortale. 1 act. Il Dramma, 191 (August 1, 1934), 42-44. In Italian.

8504. _____. The Rabbit-Hutch. 1 act. Smart Set, 60 (September, 1919), 123-124.

8505. Sternheim, Carl, 1881-1943. Burger Schippel. 1 act, comedy. Spectaculum, 9 (1966), 193-229. In German.

8506. _____. A Pair of Drawers. 4 acts. Transition, 6 (September, 1927), 16-39; 7 (October, 1927), 88-102; 8 (November, 1927), 97-113; 9 (December, 1927), 102-119. Eugene Jolas, translator.

8507. Stettner, Louis. An Evening in an Important Asylum. 1 act. First Stage, 6 (Summer, 1967), 119-132.

8508. Stevens, Caroline D. Elopements While You Wait. 1 act, farce. Drama, 13 (February, 1923), 184-187.

8509. Stevens, David. Melilotte. 1 act. St. Nicholas, 41 (March, 1914), 434-448.

Stevens, Gould see Barr, B. 613

8510. Stevens, Wallace, 1879-1955. Bowl, Cat and Broomstick. 1 act. Quarterly Review of Literature, 16 (Nos. 1/2, 1969), 236-247.

8511. _____. Carlos Among the Candles. 1 act. Poetry, 11 (December, 1917), 115-123.

8512. _____. Three Travelers Watch a Sunrise. 1 act. Poetry, 8 (July, 1916), 163-179.

8513. Stevenson, Dorothy, 1892- . Flight from Destiny. 1 act. Players' Magazine, 42 (October, 1965), 9-24, 32.

8514. Stevenson, Philip. Art in the Home. 1 act. Southwest Review, 13 (No. 2, 1927), 217-233.

8515. _____. Transit. 1 act. One-Act Play Magazine, 1 (October, 1937), 527-556.

8516. Stevenson, Robert Louis, 1850-1894. Kidnapped. 1 act. Plays, 28 (January, 1969), 87-96. Adele Thane, adapter.

8517. _____. The Kidnapping of David Balfour. 1 act. Plays, 15 (April, 1956), 88-96. Lewy Olfson, adapter.

8518. _____. The Sire de Maletroit's Door. 1 act. Plays, 27 (April, 1968), 87-95. Walter Hackett, adapter.

8519. _____. Lo specchio. 1 act. Sipario, 1 (July, 1946), 39-42. M. Lombardi, translator. In Italian.

8520. _____. Treasure Island. 1 act. Plays, 11 (April, 1952), 77-84. AND Plays, 25 (March, 1966), 87-94. Marjorie Ann York, adapter.

8521. _____ and William Ernest Henley, 1849-1903. Macaire, a Melodramatic Farce in Three Acts. Chapbook 3 (June 1, June 15, 1895), 45-71; 92-101.

8522. _____. Macaire, a Melodramatic Farce in Three Acts. Golden Book, 6 (December, 1927), 796-810.

8523. Stevenson, William Adell, III. One the Two of Us. Scripts, 1 (May, 1972), 93-98.

8524. Stigler, W. A. The Soup Stone. 1 act, comedy. Poet Lore, 35 (1924), 91-99.

8525. Stiles, George. General Bullet. 1 act. Mainstream, 11 (March, 1958), 16-27.

Stimson, F. J., adapter see Wagner, R. 9183

Stinchecum, Theodore, translator see Sophocles 8380

8526. Stockton, Frank R., 1834-1902. The Lady or the Tiger? 1 act. Plays, 21 (May, 1962), 99-107. Lewy Olfson, adapter.

8527. _____. Old Pipes and the Dryad. 1 act. Plays, 23 (January, 1964), 49-58. Adele Thane, adapter.

8528. ———. The Transferred Ghost. 1 act. Plays, 9 (October, 1949), 75-85. Walter Hackett, adapter.

8529. ———. The Transferred Ghost. 1 act. Plays, 20 (April, 1961), 13-22. Lewy Olfson, adapter.

8530. Stockton, Richard F. The Casket-Maker. 1 act. Cimarron Review, 2 (December, 1967), 23-38.

Stoddart, Hugh see Brenton, H. 1320

Stoenescu, Stefan, translator see Naghiu, I. 6431

8531. Stone, John A. The Chorus Girl. 1 act. First Stage, 1 (Winter, 1961-1962), 41-49.

8532. ———. The Nose. 3 acts. First Stage, 3 (Summer-Fall, 1964), 179-219.

Stone, Steven, translator see Ylirnusi, T. 9609, 9610

8533. Stone, Weldon. We Write a Play. 1 act, comedy. One-Act Play Magazine, 2 (June-July, 1938), 125-142.

8534. Stoppard, Tom, 1937- . Albert's Bridge. Plays and Players, 15 (October, 1967), 21-30.

8535. Storer, Edward. Helen. 1 act. Poetry and Drama, 2 (June, 1914), 153-165.

Stores, Edward, translator see Pirandello, L. 7204

8536. Storey, David, 1933- . The Contractor. 3 acts. Plays and Players, 17 (December, 1969), 63-86.

8537. ———. Home. 2 acts. Plays and Players, 17 (August, 1970), 61-77.

8538. ———. In Celebration. 2 acts. Plays and Players, 16 (June, 1969), 35-55.

8539. ———. The Restoration of Arnold Middleton. 3 acts. Sipario, 268-269 (August-September, 1968), 70-88. Elena Reina, translator. In Italian.

Stork, Charles Wharton, 1881- , translator see Hofmannsthal, H. von 4133

8540. Storm, Lesley. Paolino ha disegnato un cavallo. 3 acts, comedy. Sipario, 10 (December, 1955), 39-63. Gaetano Fazio, adapter. In Italian.

8541. Stott, Mike. Funny Peculiar. 2 acts, farce. Plays and Players, 23 (April, May, 1976), 43-50; 43-49.

8542. Stow, Clara. The Party of the Third Part. 1 act, comedy. Drama, 15 (February, 1925), 110-111.

8543. Strachan, Edna Higgins. The Chinese Water Wheel. 1 act. Drama, 21 (October, 1930), 15-16, 22-23.

8544. Stramm, August, 1874-1915. The Bride of the Moor. 1 act. Poet Lore, 25 (Winter, 1914), 499-513. Edward J. O'Brien, translator.

8545. _____. Erwachen. Der Sturm, 5 (No. 13/14, October, 1914), 90-93. In German.

8546. _____. Die Haidebrant. Der Sturm, 5 (No. 10/11, August/September, 1914), 74-76. In German.

8547. _____. Krafte. Der Sturm, 5 (No. 23/24, March, 1915), 150-156. In German.

8548. _____. Rudimentar. Der Sturm, 5 (No. 7, July, 1914), 50-53. In German.

8549. _____. Rudimentar. Drama Review, 19 (September, 1975), 24-33. Henry Marx, translator.

8550. _____. Sancta Susanna. 1 act. Drama Review, 19 (September, 1975), 18-23. Henry Marx, translator.

8551. _____. Sancta Susanna, the Song of a May Night. 1 act. Poet Lore, 25 (Winter, 1914), 514-522. Edward J. O'Brien, translator.

8552. _____. Sancta Susanna. 1 act. Sipario, 326 (July, 1973), 60-63. Lia Secci, translator. In Italian.

8553. _____. Sancta Susanna. Der Sturm, 5 (No. 4, May, 1914), 26-28. In German.

8554. Strange, Joanna Gleed. Today? 1 act. The Survey, 36 (June 10, 1916), 287-289.

8555. Stratton, Charles. The Coda. 1 act. Drama, 30 (May, 1918), 215-232.

8556. Stratton, Clarence. Afternoon in Arcady. 1 act. House and Garden, 39 (June, 1921), 34-35.

8557. _____. Ruby Red, an Oriental Satire. 1 act. Drama, 10 (February, 1920), 192-195.

_____, translator see Maeterlinck, M. 5428

8558. Streacker, Lucille. Bob's Armistice Parade. 1 act. Plays, 5 (November, 1945), 44-47.

8559. _____. The Roaring March Lion. 1 act. Plays, 11 (March, 1952), 78-79.

Strenkowsky, Sergio, translator see Ostrovsky, A. 6912

8560. Stricker, Carol J. Beside Thy Cradle, Here I Stand. 1 act. Resource, 2 (November, 1960), 12-15.

8561. Strindberg, August, 1849-1912. Coram Populo! De Creatione et Sententia Vera Mundi, a Mystery. 6 acts. Tulane Drama Review, 6 (November, 1961), 128-131. David Scalan, translator.

8562. _____. The Creditor. 1 act, tragi-comedy. Poet Lore, 22 (Spring, 1911), 81-116. Mary Harned, translator.

8563. _____. Debit and Credit. 1 act. Poet Lore, 17 (Autumn, 1906), 28-44. Emil Schering and Mary Harned, translators.

8564. _____. Dödsdansen. 4 acts. L'Avant Scène, 305 (February 15, 1964), 11-30. Alfred Jolivet and Frederic Bart, translators. In French.

8565. _____. Ebbrezza. 4 acts. Il Dramma, 441/442/443 (January 1/15/February 1, 1945), 27-47. Mario Buzzi, translator. In Italian.

8566. _____. Equals. 1 act. Golden Book, 7 (January, 1928), 85-91.

8567. _____. Erik XIV. 4 acts. L'Avant Scène, 224, 9-28. Carl-Gustaf Bjurstrom and Boris Vian, translators. In French.

8568. _____. Facing Death. 1 act. The Dramatist, 2 (July, 1911), 173-184.

8569. _____. Julie. 1 act, tragedy. Poet Lore, 22 (Summer, 1911), 161-194. Arthur Swan, translator.

8570. _____. The Outcast. 1 act. Poet Lore, 17 (Autumn, 1906), 8-21. Mary Harned, translator.

8571. _____. La Paria. 1 act. L'Avant Scène, 127, 25-31. Michel Arnaud, adapter. In French.

8572. _____. Pask. 3 acts. Il Dramma, n.s., 87 (June 15, 1949), 33-49. Clemente Giannini, translator. In Italian.

8573. _____. The Pelican. 1 act. Tulane Drama Review, 4 (March, 1960), 117-143. Evert Sprinchorn, translator.

Strindberg

8574. _____. Simoom. 1 act. Current Literature, 39 (October, 1905), 438-440. Francis J. Ziegler, translator.

8575. _____. Simoom. 1 act. Poet Lore, 17 (No. 3, 1906), 21-28. Emil Schering and Mary Harned, translators.

8576. _____. Simoom. 1 act. Smart Set, 40 (July, 1913), 135-141. Edwin Björkman, translator.

8577. _____. Le Songe. Prologue and 15 scenes. L'Avant Scène, 465 (February 1, 1971), 7-32. Maurice Clavel, adapter. In French.

8578. _____. The Stronger. 1 act. Il Dramma, 37 (March 1, 1928), 37-39. Giomar, translator. In Italian.

8579. _____. The Stronger. 1 act. International, 4 (September, 1911), 58-59. Edith Oland and Warner Oland, translators.

8580. _____. The Stronger. 1 act. Poet Lore, 17 (Spring, 1906), 47-50. F. I. Ziegler, translator.

8581. _____. The Stronger Woman. 1 act. Two Worlds, 1 (No. 2, 1926), 185-188.

8582. _____. To Damascus; A Dream Trilogy. 3 parts, 4 acts each. Poet Lore, 42 (Spring, 1933); (Autumn, 1934); (Winter, 1935), 1-70; 99-150; 195-264.

8583. Strong, Austin. The Drums of Oude. 1 act. Golden Book, 10 (October, 1929), 103-110.

8584. _____ and Lloyd Osbourne. Little Father of the Wilderness, a One-Act Play to Touch the Heart of Cynics. Golden Book, 18 (October, 1933), 353-362.

8585. Strong, Leonard Alfred George, 1896- . Over the Toast. 1 act. Esquire, 2 (September, 1934), 44, 141-142.

Strozzi, Paul, translator see Hofmannsthal, H. von 4131

8586. Stuart, Dorothy Margaret. The Death-Mask; A Regency Conversation-Piece. 1 act. The Wind and the Rain, 3 (Spring, 1947), 206-216.

8587. _____. The Taper and the Torch, Windsor, 1808. 1 act. 19th Century, 140 (September, 1946), 140-146.

8588. _____. The Transparency; Conversation Piece at Kew, 1789. 19th Century, 139 (February, 1946), 76-84.

8589. Stuart, Muriel. Andromeda Unfettered. 1 act. English Review, 32 (June, 1921), 483-492.

8590. Stübs, Albin. Der Rattenfänger bei den Schildbürgen. 1 act. Das Wort, 9 (October, 1938), 65-73. In German.

8591. Stump, Anna L. and Mary M. Heller. Between Book Covers. 1 act. Library Journal, 77 (February 15, 1952), 286-289.

8592. Sturges, Preston, 1898-1959. Poco per bene. 3 acts. Il Dramma, 105 (January 1, 1931), 4-34. Dino Falconi, translator. In Italian.

8593. Sturgis, Julian. Crossroads. 1 act, comedy. Blackwoods Magazine, 171 (February, 1902), 194-204.

Sturzenegger, Yvonne, translator see Triana, J. 8933

8594. Suares, Andre. Achille Vengeur. Vers et Prose, 11 (September-November, 1907), 5-51. In French.

8595. Subert, Frantisek Adolf, 1849- . The Awakening. 5 acts. Poet Lore, 33 (Summer, 1922), 159-227. Beatrice M. Mekota, translator.

8596. _____. The Four Bare Walls. 4 acts. Poet Lore, 28 (Autumn, 1917), 497-552. Beatrice M. Mekota and Francis H. Snow, translators.

8597. _____. The Great Freeholder. 3 acts. Poet Lore, 35 (1924), 317-379. Beatrice M. Mekota, translator.

8598. _____. Jan Vyrava. 5 acts. Poet Lore, 26 (Summer, 1915), 281-350. Sarka B. Hrbkova, translator.

8599. _____. Petr Vok Rozmberk. 5 acts. Poet Lore, 31 (Spring, 1920), 1-68. Beatrice M. Mekota, translator.

8600. Sudekum, Fred. The Cooped Coup. Drama and Theatre, 10 (Fall, 1971), 31-36.

8601. Sudermann, Hermann, 1857-1928. The Far-away Princess. 1 act, comedy. Golden Book, 5 (May, 1927), 625-633.

8602. _____. Johannes. 5 acts, tragedy. Poet Lore, 11 (No. 2, 1899), 161-236. W. H. Harned and Mary Harned, translators.

8603. _____. Morituro: Teias. 1 act. Poet Lore, 9 (No. 3, 1897), 330-352. Mary Harned, translator.

8604. _____. Saint John's Fire. 4 acts. Poet Lore, 15 (No. 4, 1904), 1-71. Charlotte Porter and H. C. Porter, translators.

8605. _____. Teja. 1 act. Golden Book, 6 (October, 1927), 493-503. Archibald Alexander, translator.

8606. _____. The Three Heron's Feathers. 5 acts. Poet Lore, 12 (No. 2, 1900), 161-234. Helen Tracy Porter, translator.

8607. Sudman, Dean. Holiday or Holy Day? 1 act. Resource, 5 (November, 1963), 16-18.

8608. Suffran, Michel. Les Approches du Soir. 1 act. L'Avant Scène, 250 (October 1, 1961), 31-37. In French.

8609. _____. La Balle au Chasseur. 1 act. L'Avant Scène, 463 (January 1, 1971), 35-43. In French.

8610. _____. Savonarole, ou le Plaisir de Dieu Seul. 11 scenes. L'Avant Scène, 463 (January 1, 1971), 7-33. In French.

8611. _____. Le Seuil du Jardin. 1 act. L'Avant Scène, 307 (March 15, 1964), 43-51. In French.

8612. Sukosky, Donald G. The World Resounds. 1 act. Resource, 2 (November, 1960), 18-21.

8613. Sulliotti, Italo, 1894- . L'armata del silenzio. 3 acts. Il Dramma, 128 (December 15, 1931), 4-25. In Italian.

8614. Sullivan, A. M. Transcontinental. 1 act. Scholastic, 40 (May 18-23, 1942), 17-18.

Sullivan, Sir Arthur Seymour, 1842-1900 see Gilbert, G. S. 3515-3521

8615. Sullivan, Frank, 1892- . Life Is a Bowl of Eugene O'Neills: A Dramatic Satire in One Act. Golden Book, 18 (July, 1933), 60-62.

8616. Sullivan, Warren. The Fixer. 1 act. Scholastic, 26 (April 27, 1935), 8-11.

8617. Sumner, John. The Frightful Forest. 1 act. Plays, 11 (October, 1951), 40-49.

8618. Sumner, McVay. "An Amethyst Remembrance." 1 act. Smart Set, 3 (February, 1901), 56-60.

8619. Sundell, Carl. The Bone Shop. 1 act. Poet Lore, 64 (Spring, 1969), 49-64.

Sundstrom, Jacqueline, adapter see Behan, B. 725

8620. Supervielle, Jules, 1884-1960. Robinson, ou L'Amour Vient de Loin. 3 acts. Il Dramma, n. s., 285 (June, 1960), 12-31. Enzo Ferrieri, translator. In Italian.

8621. ———. Le Voleur d'Enfants. 3 acts. Sipario, 4 (December, 1949), 113-130. Gigi Cane, translator. In Italian.

8622. Surchi, Sergio. Il domatore. Sipario, 9 (January, 1954), 51-54. In Italian.

8623. ———. Giacinta, o l'evasione. 1 act. Sipario, 10 (April, 1955), 54-56. In Italian.

8624. ———. Nuvola. 1 act. Il Dramma, n. s., 214 (October 1, 1954), 51-56. In Italian.

8625. Sussmann, C. Julien, 1930- . Le Dernier Exemplaire. 1 act. L'Avant Scène, 407 (July 15, 1968), 32-35. In French.

8626. ———. Le Voyage. 1 act. L'Avant Scène, 474 (June 15, 1971), 35-36. In French.

8627. Sutherland, Donald, 1931- . My Sister, My Spouse, a Sacred Comedy. 2 acts. Prairie Schooner, 34 (Winter, 1960-61), 285-356.

8628. Sutphen, William Gilbert Van Tassel, 1861- . Cherry Blossoms. 1 act. Harper's, 105 (August, 1902), 366-376.

8629. ———. First Aid to the Injured. 1 act, farce. Harper's, 92 (May, 1896), 965-970.

8630. ———. A House of Cards. 1 act, comedy. Harper's, 109 (November, 1904), 901-910.

8631. ———. Intermezzo. 1 act. Harper's, 106 (May, 1903), 896-902.

8632. ———. Special Delivery. 1 act. Harper's, 108 (February, 1904), 458-462.

8633. ———. Two Minds in the Matter. 1 act. Harper's, 133 (June, 1916), 153-157.

8634. ———. An Unequal Triangle. 1 act. Smart Set, 36 (February, 1912), 127-132.

8635. Sutro, Alfred, 1863-1933. A Marriage Has Been Arranged. 1 act, comedy. Golden Book, 12 (July, 1930), 98-101.

8636. Sutton, Donald. Black Tomorrow. 1 act. Dramatika, 7 (1971), 40-47.

8637. Sutton, Vida Ravenscroft. Mantle of the Virgin. 1 act. Drama, 12 (December, 1921), 71-79, 99-100.

8638. Suzuki, Sinzaburo, 1893-1923. La dama della montagna. 1 act. Il Dramma, n. s., 305 (February, 1962), 62-65. Vinicio Marinucci, translator. In Italian.

8639. _____. Vendetta. 1 act. Il Dramma, n. s., 305 (February, 1962), 65-67. Vinicio Marinucci, translator. In Italian.

8640. Svartz, Evgenij Lvovic. Ten'. 3 acts. Sipario, 18 (June, 1963), 71-89. Milly de Monticelli and Evelina Satz, translators. In Italian.

8641. Svevo, Italo, 1861-1929. La Comédie sans Titre, ou La Regeneration. 3 acts. L'Avant Scène, 545 (April 15, 1976), 3-41. Ginette Herry, adapter. In French.

8642. _____. A Husband. 3 acts. Modern International Drama, 6 (Fall, 1972), 45-88. Beno Weiss, translator.

8643. Swain, Corinne Rockwell. A Maeterlinckian Moving Day. 1 act. Smart Set, 37 (June, 1912), 117-120.

Swan, Arthur, translator see Strindberg, A. 8569

Swan, E. Leda, translator see Zolin, A. 9654

8644. Swanson, Brent. The Meaning of Christmas. 1 act. Learning With...., 2 (December, 1974), 22-23.

Swanson, Roy W., translator see Geijerstam, G. 3434

8645. Swanson, Walter S. J. Negerinde! The First Bad Sojourns of Young Miss Truth, the New York Slave. 2 acts. Massachusetts Review, 11 (Autumn, 1970), 687-740.

8646. Swenson, May, 1919- . The Floor. 1 act. First Stage, 6 (Summer, 1967), 112-118.

8647. Swift, Jonathan, 1667-1745. Gulliver's Travels in Lilliput Land. 1 act. Plays, 18 (January, 1959), 83-96. Edward Golden, adapter.

8648. Swinburne, Algernon Charles, 1837-1909. Atalante en Calyon. Vers et Prose, 30 (July-September, 1912), 146-182; 31 (October-December, 1912), 117-131; 32 (January-March, 1913), 98-116; 33 (April-June, 1913), 59-74. H. Du Pasquier, translator. In French.

8649. Swinley, E. Ion. The Lifting of the Dark. 1 act. Coterie, 6/7 (Winter, 1920/1921), 103-109.

8650. Swintz, Martha. The King's Creampuffs. 1 act. Plays, 5 (April, 1946), 46-56. AND Plays, 15 (April, 1956), 43-53. AND Plays, 27 (March, 1968), 59-69.

8651. _____. Panic in the Palace. 1 act. Plays, 11 (January, 1952), 33-42. AND Plays, 31 (January, 1972), 57-66.

8652. _____. Posies for the Potentate. 1 act. Plays, 25 (January, 1966), 45-53.

8653. _____. The Three Wishing Bags. 1 act. Plays, 9 (April, 1950), 26-37. AND Plays, 17 (April, 1958), 57-68.

8654. Sword of Damocles. 1 act. Plays, 28 (November, 1968), 86-88.

8655. Swortzell, Lowell. The Egyptian Cinderella. 1 act. Plays, 21 (February, 1962), 47-52.

8656. _____. London Bridge. 1 act. Plays, 28 (April, 1969), 61-66.

8657. _____. Why the Peacock Is Proud. 1 act. Plays, 31 (October, 1971), 47-51.

8658. _____, adapter. The Fisherman and His Wife. 1 act. Plays, 25 (May, 1966), 62-68.

8659. Sylvanus, Erwin. Jan Palach. Il Dramma, 49 (December, 1973), 47-69. Italo Aleghiera Chiusano, translator. In Italian.

Symonds, John Addington, 1840-1893, translator see Poliziano, A. A. 7229

8660. Symons, Arthur, 1865-1945. Barbara Roscorla's Child. 1 act, tragedy. Little Review, 4 (October, 1917), 25-36.

8661. _____. Cleopatra in Judaea. 1 act. Forum, 55 (June, 1916), 643-660.

8662. _____. Dance of the Seven Deadly Sins. 1 act. English Review, 30 (June, 1920), 481-485.

8663. _____. Iseult of Brittany. 1 act. The Poetry Journal, 5 (March, 1916), 41-51.

8664. _____. The Lover of the Queen of Sheba. 1 act. Dome, n.s., 5 (November, 1900), 5-12.

8665. Symons, James David. The Conscript Fathers: A Forecast. 1 act. English Review, 27 (September, 1918), 208-212.

8666. Synge, John Millington, 1871-1909. Deirdre of the Sorrows. 3 acts, tragedy. Il Dramma, 350 (March 15, 1941), 9-23. Carlo Linati, translator. In Italian.

8667. _____. Deirdre of the Sorrows. 3 acts, tragedy. Theatre Arts, 34 (August, 1950), 67-88.

8668. _____. In the Shadow of the Glen. 1 act. Bibelot, 19 (1913), 271-297.

8669. _____. In the Shadow of the Glen. 1 act. Il Dramma, 336 (August 15, 1940), 31-35. Carlo Linati, translator. In Italian.

8670. _____. In the Shadow of the Glen. 1 act. Samhain, (December, 1904), 34-44.

8671. _____. The Playboy of the Western World. 3 acts. Il Dramma, 340 (October 15, 1940), 4-24. Carlo Linati, translator. In Italian.

8672. _____. The Playboy of the Western World. 3 acts. Golden Book, 4 (October, 1926), 513-537.

8673. _____. The Playboy of the Western World. 3 acts. Spectaculum, 7 (1964), 313-354. Heinrich Boll and Annemarie Boll, translators. In German.

8674. _____. Riders to the Sea. 1 act, tragedy. Bibelot, 19 (July, 1913), 249-268.

8675. _____. Riders to the Sea. 1 act. Il Dramma, 323 (February 1, 1940), 19-23. Carlo Linati, translator. In Italian.

8676. _____. Riders to the Sea. 1 act, tragedy. Golden Book, 13 (June, 1931), 80-84.

8677. _____. Riders to the Sea. 1 act, tragedy. Poet Lore, 16 (Spring, 1905), 1-11.

8678. _____. Riders to the Sea. 1 act, tragedy. Samhain, (September, 1903), 25-33.

Szebenyei, Joseph, translator see Molnar, F. 6145

8679. Szecsen, Szantho. 120 all'ora. 3 acts. Il Dramma, 230 (March 15, 1936), 2-27. Ignazio Balla and Mario de Vellis, translators. In Italian.

8680. Szenes, B. Una sposa molto ricca. 3 acts. Il Dramma, 243 (October 1, 1936), 2-23. In Italian.

T

8681. Taber, Gladys Bagg, 1899- . Miss Manda. 1 act. Poet Lore, 38 (1927), 412-421.

8682. Tabori, George, 1914- . Niggerlovers. L'Avant Scène, 516 (April 15, 1973), 11-17. Eric Kahane, translator. In French.

Tabucchi, Antonio, translator see Pessoa, F. 7086

8683. Tagliabue, John. Mario in the Land of the Green Queen, a Puppet Play. 1 act. Carolina Quarterly, 16 (Summer, 1964), 45-55.

8684. ———. Mario in the Land of the Unicorn, a Puppet Play. 1 act. Carolina Quarterly, 16 (Spring, 1964), 54-60.

8685. Tagore, Rabindranath, 1861-1941. The Foundling Hero. 1 act. Golden Hind, 1 (January, 1923), 9-12. T. Sturge Moore, translator.

8686. ———. King of the Dark Chamber. 1 act. Drama, 14 (May, 1914), 177-237.

8687. ———. The Post Office. 2 acts. Forum, 51 (March, 1914), 455-471.

8688. Taikeff, Stanley. Solo Recital. 1 act. Dramatics, 45 (March, 1974), 3-6.

8689. Taketomo, Torao. Mulan. 1 act. Asia, 19 (December, 1919), 1258-1261.

8690. Taking the Bandit's Stronghold, a Peking Opera. Chinese Literature, 8 (1967), 129-181.

8691. Taking Tiger Mountain by Strategy, a Peking Opera. Chinese Literature, 1 (1970), 3-57.

8692. Taladoire, B. and E. Fuzeillier. Argo. 1 act. Mesures, 3 (July 15, 1937), 73-112. In French.

8693. Talagrand, Jacques, 1909- . La Condition Humaine. L'Avant Scène, 107, 1-31. In French.

8694. ———. La Maison de la Nuit. 3 acts. L'Avant Scène, 83 (November 5, 1953), 3-31. In French.

8695. _____. La Maison de la Nuit. 3 acts. Sipario, 10 (February, 1955), 29-47. Guglielmo Zorzi, translator. In Italian.

8696. _____. Le Profanateur. 4 acts. Sipario, 8 (June, 1953), 61-74. Giulia Veronesi, translator. In Italian.

8697. _____. Le Soir du Conquérant. 2 parts. L'Avant Scène, 467 (March 1, 1971), 7-29. In French.

_____, adapter see Fry, C. 3334

_____, translator see Fabbri, D. 2899, 2904

8698. Talarico, Elio. Dedalo e fuga. 3 acts. Il Dramma, 374 (March 15, 1942), 7-25. In Italian.

8699. _____. Prometheus. 3 acts. Il Dramma, n. s., 286 (July, 1960), 10-34. In Italian.

8700. Talk in a Taxi: A Dialogue in Fits. 1 act. Living Age, 258 (August 15, 1908), 445-456.

8701. Tamburo di panno, Il. 1 act. Il Dramma, 317 (November 1, 1939), 11-14. In Italian.

8702. Tanzi, Gastone. I timpani della verità. 1 act. Il Dramma, 97 (September 1, 1930), 36-43. In Italian.

Tarabusi, Renzo see Scarnicci, G. 8009

8703. Tardieu, Jean, 1903- . Hiver, ou Les Temps du Verbe. 2 acts. L'Avant Scène, 128, 27-38. In French.

8704. _____. Mi-Figue, Mi-Raisin. Four Comedies: Oswald et Zenaide; Faust et Yorick; Le Meuble; In Geste Pour un Autre. L'Avant Scène (OST), 55 (January, 1952), 20-36. In French.

8705. Tarkington, Booth, 1869-1946. Beauty and the Jacobin, an Interlude of the French Revolution. 2 parts. Harper's, 125 (August-September, 1912), 390-399, 539-553.

8706. _____. Bimbo, the Pirate. 1 act. Ladies' Home Journal, 41 (June, 1924), 18-19, 44, 46, 49, 51, 53.

8707. _____. The Ghost Story. 1 act. Ladies' Home Journal, 39 (March, 1922), 6-7, 126, 128-129, 131.

8708. _____. The Intimate Strangers. 3 acts. Harper's, 144, 145 (April, May, June, 1922), 599-610; 761-773; 75-86.

8709. _____. Mister Antonio. 4 acts, comedy. Harper's, 134 (January, February, 1917), 187-203; 374-387.

8710. _____. Monsieur Beaucaire. 1 act. Plays, 15 (May, 1956), 63-72. Lewy Olfson, adapter. AND Plays, 23 (November, 1963), 83-94. Lewy Olfson, adapter.

8711. _____. Station YYYY. 1 act. Ladies' Home Journal, 43 (May, 1926), 6-7, 200, 203-204, 207.

8712. _____. The Travelers. 1 act. Ladies' Home Journal, 43 (March, 1926), 16-17, 168, 171, 173-174, 176, 179, 181-182.

8713. _____. The Trysting Place. 1 act, farce. Ladies' Home Journal, 39 (September, 1922), 3-5, 137-138, 141-142, 145.

8714. Tassell, Mabel S. Van. The Enchanted Island. 1 act. St. Nicholas, 60 (May, 1933), 338-339, 354.

8715. Tausheck, Ruthe Massion. The Saga of Davey Rocket. 1 act. Plays, 21 (October, 1961), 79-85.

8716. Tavel, Ronald. Christina's World. 3 acts. Chicago Review, 16 (Winter-Spring, 1963), 1-79.

8717. _____. Kitchenette. 1 act. Partisan Review, 34 (Spring, 1967), 233-250.

8718. _____. Secrets of the Citizens Correction Committee. Scripts, 1 (January, 1972), 4-23.

8719. Taylor, Cecil P. Bread and Butter. Plays and Players, 14 (October, 1966), 31-46, 72.

8720. Taylor, J. Russell. The Posing of Vivette. 1 act. Scribner's, 22 (December, 1897), 693-700.

8721. Taylor, L. M. Cockcrow. 1 act. Poet Lore, 33 (Spring, 1922), 118-127.

Taylor, Laurie, translator see Quiles, E. 7365

8722. Taylor, Marion Ansel, 1904- . If Wishes Were Fishes. 1 act. Plays, 2 (March, 1943), 53-58.

8723. _____. Nathaniel Hawthorne and the Curse of the Pyncheons. 1 act. Plays, 19 (March, 1960), 84-96.

8724. _____. The White Whale. 1 act. Plays, 19 (November, 1959), 84-96.

Taylor, Paul B., translator see Loki's Flyting 5021

8725. Taylor, Peter, 1919- . The Death of a Kinsman. 1 act. Sewanee Review, 57 (No. 1, 1949), 86-119.

8726. _____. The Early Guest; a Sort of a Story, a Sort of a Play, a Sort of a Dream. 1 act. Shenandoah, 24 (Winter, 1973), 21-43.

8727. _____. A Stand in the Mountains. 1 act. Kenyon Review, 30 (No. 2, 1968), 169-264.

8728. _____. Tennessee Day in St. Louis. 1 act, comedy. Kenyon Review, 18 (Winter, 1956), 92-119.

8729. _____. Three Ghost Plays: Two Images; a Father and a Son; Missing Person. 1 act each. Shenandoah, 21 (Spring, 1970), 3-35.

8730. _____. The Whistler. 1 act. Virginia Quarterly Review, 46 (Spring, 1970), 248-263.

8731. Taylor, Samuel, 1912- . The Happy Time. 3 acts. Il Dramma, n. s., 130 (April 1, 1951), 5-34. Ada Salvatore, translator. In Italian.

8732. _____. The Happy Time. 3 acts, comedy. Theatre Arts, 35 (February, 1951), 53-90.

8733. _____. Sabrina Fair. 4 acts, comedy. Theatre Arts, 38 (November, 1954), 34-70.

8734. _____ and Cornelia Otis Skinner, 1901- . The Pleasure of His Company. 2 acts, comedy. L'Avant Scène, 209 (December 1, 1959), 7-35. Claude-André Puget, adapter. In French.

8735. _____. The Pleasure of His Company. 2 acts, comedy. Theatre Arts, 44 (April, 1960), 21-52.

8736. Tcinderella. 4 acts. Dublin Magazine, 2 (September, 1924), 118-128. Gerald MacNamara, translator.

Teele, Roy E., translator see Motokiyo, Z. 6271

8737. Teeple, Lou Rodman. Spartan Dorothy and Her Fox. 1 act, farce. Overland, n. s., 39 (January, 1902), 548-553.

Teglio, Paolo, 1883- , translator see Vandenberghe, P. 9020

8738. Teichmann, Howard, 1916- and George S. Kaufman, 1889- . The Solid Gold Cadillac. 2 acts, comedy. Theatre Arts, 40 (April, 1956), 34-57.

8739. Teitel, Irving. The Day Baseball Died. 1 act. Senior Scholastic, 50 (April 14, 1947), 21-23, 27.

Teleki, Joseph see Molnar, F. 6169

8740. Tellez, Gabriel, 1571?-1648. Don Gil dalle calze verdi. 3 parts. Il Dramma, 393/394 (January 1/15, 1943), 67-82. Alessandro Brissoni, translator. In Italian.

8741. _____. El Vergonzoso en Palacio. 3 acts. L'Avant Scène, 284 (March 15, 1963), 10-41. N. A. Caravette, adapter. In French.

8742. Tendrjakov, V. and K. Jikramov. Bandiera bianca. 2 acts. Sipario, 19 (February, 1964), 27-40. Milly de Monticelli, translator. In Italian.

8743. Tennen, Steven. The Plight of Farmer Jones. 1 act. Plays, 31 (November, 1971), 66-68.

8744. Tennyson, Alfred, Lord, 1809-1892. Enoch Arden. 1 act. Plays, 17 (March, 1958), 79-88. Lewy Olfson, adapter.

Térésah, translator see Ibsen, H. 4362

8745. Terrell, Maverick. Honi Soit, a Satire on Circumstantial Evidence. 1 act. Smart Set, 54 (January, 1918), 71-75.

8746. _____. Temperament. 1 act. Smart Set, 50 (September, 1916), 215-220.

8747. _____. When Greek Meets Greek. 1 act. Smart Set, 54 (April, 1918), 125-128.

_____ see also Stechhan, H. O. 8478

8748. _____ and H. O. Stechhan. The Real "Q." 1 act. Smart Set, 35 (September, 1911), 129-136.

8749. _____. You Never Can Tell about a Woman. 1 act. Smart Set, 37 (August, 1912), 133-141.

8750. Terron, Carlo Renato, 1914- . L'arrivista. 3 acts. Il Dramma, n.s., 350/351 (November/December, 1965), 11-44. In Italian.

8751. _____. Avevo piu stima dell' idrogeno. 3 acts, comedy. Sipario, 10 (March, 1955), 56-80. In Italian.

8752. _____. Colloquio col tango. Monologue. Sipario, 13 (July, 1958), 52-56. In Italian.

8753. _____. Il complesso dell' oblelisco, ovvero le risorse della psicanalisi. Il Dramma, n.s., 378/379 (March/April, 1968), 62-72. In Italian.

8754. _____. Il diamante del profeta. 3 acts. Il Dramma, n. s., 340 (January, 1965), 5-37. In Italian.

8755. _____. Il figlio del mare. 3 acts. Il Dramma, n. s., 357 (June, 1966), 4-39. In Italian.

8756. _____. Giuditta. 3 acts. Il Dramma, n. s., 94 (October 1, 1949), 7-25. In Italian.

8757. _____. Lavinia fra i dannati. 3 acts, tragedy. Sipario, 15 (January, 1960), 43-60. In Italian.

8758. _____. La libertà. 1 act. Il Dramma, n. s., 90 (August 1, 1949), 37-42. In Italian.

8759. _____. Le mamme. 1 act. Il Dramma, n. s., 308 (May, 1962), 10-20. In Italian.

8760. _____. Non c'e pace per l'antico fauno. 3 acts, vaudeville. Sipario, 8 (February, 1953), 34-56. In Italian.

8761. _____. Notti a Milano. 3 acts. Il Dramma, n. s., 324 (September, 1963), 6-42. In Italian.

8762. _____. Processo agli innocenti. 3 acts. Il Dramma, n. s., 125 (January 15, 1951), 9-29. In Italian.

8763. _____. Riso verde: Le piume ovvero una grande famiglia; La sposa Cristiana ovvero camera 337; L'amira della tigre o sennò i parti; I narcisi o anche dente per dente. 1 act each. Il Dramma, 328 (January, 1964), 5-57. In Italian.

8764. _____. Stasera arsenico ovvero la commedia de caffè. Il Dramma, n. s., 371/372 (August/September, 1967), 42-62. In Italian.

8765. _____. Il tempo addosso. 3 acts. Il Dramma, n. s., 367 (April, 1967), 14-53. In Italian.

8766. _____. La vedova nera. Monologue. Sipario, 14 (November, 1959), 57-60. In Italian.

8767. _____, adapter. Ippolito e la vendetta. 1 act. Sipario, 13 (February, 1958), 53-60. In Italian.

_____, adapter see Dumas, A. 2688

_____, translator see Hugo, V. 4319

_____, translator see Rojas, F. de 7656

8768. Terry, Megan. Keep Tightly Closed in a Cool Dry Place.

	1 act. Tulane Drama Review, 10 (Summer, 1966), 177-200.
8769.	_____. The Tommy Allen Show. Scripts, 1 (December, 1971), 36-61.
8770.	Terson, Peter. The Apprentices. 2 acts. Plays and Players, 16 (October, 1968), 27-55.
8771.	_____. But Fred Freud Is Dead. 3 acts. Plays and Players, 19 (March, 1972), 62-78.
8772.	_____. The Mighty Reservoy. 3 acts. Plays and Players, 14 (August, 1967), 19-32.
8773.	_____. The Samaritan. 1 act. Plays and Players, 18 (July, 1971), 72-84.
8774.	_____. Spring-Heeled Jack. 2 acts. Plays and Players, 18 (November, 1970), 62-85.
8775.	Tervagne, Georges de. Pique-Nique en Ville. 3 acts, comedy. L'Avant Scène, 362 (August, 1966), 27-56. In French.
	Terzieff, Laurent, 1935- , adapter see Schisgal, M. 8033, 8035
	Terzoli, Italo see Vergani, O. 9083
	Terzolo, Berto, translator see Salacrou, A. 7882
	Tessitore, Ugo, translator see Middleton, T. 5820
8776.	Testoni, Alfredo. L'equilibrico. 1 act. Il Dramma, 125 (November 1, 1931), 27-30. In Italian.
8777.	_____. Le piccole commedie. 3 acts. Il Dramma, 104 (December 15, 1930), 39-43. In Italian.
8778.	Teternikov, Fedor Kuzmich, 1863-1927. Triumph of Death. 3 acts, tragedy. Drama, 23 (August, 1916), 346-382. John Cournos, translator.
8779.	Teyssandier, Francois, 1944- . Des Voix Dans la Ville. 1 act. L'Avant Scène, 512 (February 15, 1973), 37-42. In French.
8780.	Thackeray, William Makepeace, 1811-1863. King Glumpus. 1 act. Bookman [New York], 8 (December, 1898), 342-346.
8781.	_____. The Rose and the Ring. 1 act. Plays, 30 (March, 1971), 79-90. Adele Thane, adapter.

Thackeray

8782. _____. Vanity Fair. 1 act. Plays, 32 (January, 1973), 67-80. Olive J. Morley, adapter.

8783. _____. The Wolves and the Lamb. 2 acts. Golden Book, 3 (February, 1926), 216-240.

8784. Thane, Adele, 1904- . Big Paul Bunyan. 1 act. Plays, 30 (April, 1971), 29-35.

8785. _____. The Brownie Who Found Christmas. 1 act. Plays, 20 (December, 1960), 53-58.

8786. _____. Dick Whittington and His Cat. 1 act. Plays, 21 (April, 1962), 45-53. AND Plays, 34 (April, 1975), 42-50.

8787. _____. A Gift for Hans Brinker. 1 act. Plays, 27 (January, 1968), 61-66.

8788. _____. The Least Gift. 1 act. Plays, 21 (December, 1961), 67-75.

8789. _____. The Lost Cherub. 1 act. Plays, 20 (December, 1960), 61-65.

8790. _____. The Magic Nutmeg-Grater. 1 act. Plays, 19 (April, 1960), 37-46.

8791. _____. A Place in the Family. 1 act. Plays, 30 (April, 1971), 51-56.

8792. _____. The Saucy Scarecrow. 1 act. Plays, 20 (October, 1960), 37-44.

8793. _____. The Travels of Marco Polo. 1 act. Plays, 30 (May, 1971), 81-92.

8794. _____, adapter. Aladdin and His Wonderful Lamp. 1 act. Plays, 23 (April, 1964), 45-56.

8795. _____, adapter. The Baker's Neighbor. 1 act. Plays, 30 (November, 1970), 61-66.

8796. _____, adapter. The Brave Little Tailor. 1 act. Plays, 26 (February, 1967), 49-57.

8797. _____, adapter. The Caliph's Journey. 1 act. Plays, 21 (January, 1962), 62-68.

8798. _____, adapter. The Christmas Nutcracker. 1 act. Plays, 22 (December, 1962), 35-45.

8799. _____, adapter. Cinderella. 1 act. Plays, 27 (October, 1967), 57-68.

8800. _____, adapter. Dummling and the Golden Goose. 1 act. <u>Plays</u>, 25 (January, 1966), 35-43.

8801. _____, adapter. The Elves and the Shoemaker. 4 acts. <u>Plays</u>, 25 (December, 1965), 33-40.

8802. _____, adapter. Hansel and Gretel. 1 act. <u>Plays</u>, 24 (February, 1965), 41-50.

8803. _____, adapter. The Hare, the Hippo, and the Elephant. 1 act. <u>Plays</u>, 30 (May, 1971), 59-65.

8804. _____, adapter. Jack and the Magic Beanstalk. 1 act. <u>Plays</u>, 24 (January, 1965), 55-63.

8805. _____, adapter. King Alfred and the Cakes. 1 act. <u>Plays</u>, 25 (May, 1966), 79-84.

8806. _____, adapter. King Thrushbeard. 1 act. <u>Plays</u>, 27 (November, 1967), 45-54.

8807. _____, adapter. The King Who Was Bored. 1 act. <u>Plays</u>, 30 (January, 1971), 49-55.

8808. _____, adapter. The Little Princess. 1 act. <u>Plays</u>, 22 (February, 1963), 33-44.

8809. _____, adapter. The Magic Spear. 1 act. <u>Plays</u>, 32 (October, 1972), 47-54.

8810. _____, adapter. Merry Tyll and the Three Rogues. 1 act. <u>Plays</u>, 27 (December, 1967), 33-41.

8811. _____, adapter. Pip Visits Miss Havisham. 1 act. <u>Plays</u>, 28 (October, 1968), 87-95.

8812. _____, adapter. Rapunzel. 1 act. <u>Plays</u>, 26 (February, 1967), 79-88.

8813. _____, adapter. Rumpelstiltskin. 1 act. <u>Plays</u>, 22 (April, 1963), 53-63.

8814. _____, adapter. The Three Wishes. 2 acts. <u>Plays</u>, 25 (April, 1966), 69-74.

8815. _____, adapter. The Twelve Dancing Princesses. 1 act. <u>Plays</u>, 24 (November, 1964), 37-46.

_____, adapter see Alcott, L. M. 109

_____, adapter see Anderson, H. C. 195, 202

_____, adapter see Barrie, Sir J. M. 625

_____, adapter see Browning, R. 1378

_____, adapter see Burnett, F. H. 1440

_____, adapter see Clemens, S. L. 1891

_____, adapter see Collins, W. 1941

_____, adapter see Dickens, C. 2470, 2483

_____, adapter see Freeman, M. E. W. 3293

_____, adapter see Gilbert, W. S. and A. S. Sullivan
3515-3521

_____, adapter see Grahame, K. 3682

_____, adapter see Grimm, J. and W. Grimm 3749

_____, adapter see Hardy, T. 3906

_____, adapter see Hawthorne, N. 3987, 3990

_____, adapter see Howells, W. D. 4238

_____, adapter see Hugo, V. 4316

_____, adapter see Irving, W. 4407

_____, adapter see Kipling, R. 4639

_____, adapter see Lorenzini, C. 5056

_____, adapter see Perrault, C. 7072, 7073

_____, adapter see Poe, E. A. 7220

_____, adapter see Pyle, H. 7348

_____, adapter see Spyri, J. 8457

_____, adapter see Stevenson, R. L. 8516

_____, adapter see Stockton, F. R. 8527

_____, adapter see Thackeray, W. M. 8781

_____, adapter see Verne, J. 9091

_____, adapter see Woolsey, S. C. 9554

8816. Thayer, John Adams. Sabotage. 1 act. Dramatist, 5 (January, 1914), 425-437.

8817. Theocritus. The Ladies Go to the Festival; an Idyll of the City. 1 act. Golden Book, 4 (October, 1926), 560-562.

Thieberger, Richard, translator see Hochwalder, F. 4120

Thiem, Willy H., translator see Pinter, H. 7173

8818. Tholy, Rene. L'Air des Bijoux. 1 act. L'Avant Scène, 554 (December 15, 1974), 35-38. In French.

8819. _____. Buroctopus. 1 act. L'Avant Scène, 466 (February 15, 1971), 23-32. In French.

8820. _____. Pollution. 1 act. L'Avant Scène, 587 (May 15, 1976), 33-36. In French.

8821. Thoma, Ludwig, 1867-1921. When You're Twenty-One! 1 act, comedy. One-Act Play Magazine, 1 (August, 1937), 304-322. Frank E. Washburn-Freud, translator.

8822. Thomas, Augustus, 1857-1934. Nemesis. 5 acts. Everybody's Magazine, 45 (July, 1921), 106-112.

8823. Thomas, Charles. Jenny in the Orchard. 1 act. Il Dramma, n. s., 155 (April 15, 1952), 52-58. Leon Fini, translator. In Italian.

8824. Thomas, Dylan, 1914-1953. Llareggub, a Piece for Radio Perhaps. 1 act. Botteghe Oscure, 9 (1952), 134-153.

8825. _____. Mussolini at Breakfast. Il Dramma, 46, no. 3 (March, 1970), 62-63. Roberto Sanesi, translator. In Italian.

8826. _____. Under Milk Wood. Mademoiselle, 38 (February, 1954), 110-122, 144-156.

8827. _____. Under Milk Wood. 1 act. Spectaculum, 5 (1963), 223-266. Erich Fried, translator. In German.

8828. Thomas, Elsie M. The Magic Pumpkin Patch. 1 act. Plays, 25 (October, 1965), 73-78.

Thomas, M. Merlin, translator see Ribemont-Dessaignes, G. 7506

8829. Thomas, Robert, 1930- . Un Ami ... Imprévu. 4 acts. L'Avant Scène, 430 (July 15, 1969), 7-36. In French.

8830. _____. Assassins Associés. 3 acts, comedy. L'Avant Scène, 346 (December 1, 1965), 10-42. In French.

8831. _____. La Chambre Mandarine. Comedy. L'Avant Scène, 553 (December 1, 1974), 3-39. In French.

8832. _____. Deux Chats et... Un Souris. 1 act. L'Avant Scène, 346 (December 1, 1965), 44-47. In French.

8833. _____. Le Deuxième Coup de Feu. 4 acts, comedy. L'Avant Scène, 327 (February 1, 1965), 10-31. In French.

8834. _____. Double Jeu. 5 acts, comedy. L'Avant Scène, 458 (October 15, 1970), 7-36, 39. In French.

8835. _____. Freddy. 4 acts, comedy. L'Avant Scène, 423 (April 1, 1969), 7-39. In French.

8836. _____. Huit Femmes. 3 acts, comedy. L'Avant Scène, 268 (July 1, 1962), 10-37. In French.

8837. _____. La Louve. 1 act, comedy. L'Avant Scène, 592 (August, 1976), 37-40. In French.

8838. _____. Piege Pour un Homme Seul. 4 acts, comedy. L'Avant Scène, 231, 8-31. In French.

8839. Thompson, Blanche Jenning. The Dream Maker. 1 act. Drama, 12 (March, 1922), 197-199.

8840. Thompson, Doris K. and Jane Assur. Salvage. 1 act. Drama, 21 (May, 1931), 17-18, 20, 39.

8841. Thompson, Dorothy F. Whose Birthday Is It? 1 act. Plays, 12 (March, 1953), 45-51.

8842. Thompson, Harlan. Geometrically Speaking. 1 act. Smart Set, 57 (November, 1918), 75-83.

8843. _____. The Man Hunt. 1 act, farce. Smart Set, 59 (June, 1919), 87-98.

8844. _____. One by One, a Morality Play, More or Less. 1 act. Smart Set, 59 (May, 1919), 93-107.

8845. _____. Pants and the Man. 1 act. Smart Set, 53 (November, 1917), 91-99.

8846. Thompson, Jay, 1927- . Double Entry: The Bible Salesman; the Oldest Trick in the World. 1 act each. Theatre Arts, 45 (July, 1961), 34-52.

8847. _____, Marshall Barer, 1923- and Dean Fuller, 1922- . Once upon a Mattress. 2 acts, comedy. Theatre Arts, 44 (July, 1960), 25-50.

8848. Thorne, Olive. Ten Dollars. 1 act. St. Nicholas, 6 (January, 1879), 194-197.

8849. Thorne-Thomsen, Gudrun. The Troll's Christmas. 1 act. Elementary School Teacher, 8 (December, 1907), 210-215.

8850. Thornton, Jane Foster. The King Who Hated Birthdays. 1 act. Plays, 32 (March, 1973), 57-62.

8851. _____. My Darling Clementine. 1 act. Plays, 34 (April, 1975), 57-60.

8852. _____. Planet Parade. 1 act. Plays, 32 (November, 1972), 60-62.

8853. _____. Santa's Magic Hat. 1 act. Plays, 35 (December, 1975), 57-62.

8854. _____. Wake Up, Aurora! 1 act. Plays, 33 (November, 1973), 33-38.

Thorpe, Heather G. see Moore, J. 6204

8855. Three Chinese Folk-Dramas: Princely Fortune; Meeting at the Well; Woman-Song. 1 act each. Theatre Arts, 14 (November, 1930), 967-978. Hartley Burr Alexander, editor. Kwei Chen, translator.

8856. Three Princes of Salerno, The. A Scenario of the Commedia dell'Arte. 3 acts. The Mask, 4 (April, 1912), 335-339.

8857. Thurston, Althea. A Pageant of Spring. 1 act. Drama, 12 (April, 1922), 251-252.

Tiao Cheng-Kuo see Chang Feng-Chao 1715

8858. Tieri, Vincenzo, 1895- . Amarsi così. 3 acts. Il Dramma, 410/411 (September 15/October 1, 1943), 7-24. In Italian.

8859. _____. La battaglia del trasimeno. 3 acts. Il Dramma, 370 (January 15, 1942), 7-25. In Italian.

8860. _____. Figaro II. 3 acts. Il Dramma, 419/420 (February 1/15, 1944), 7-24. In Italian.

8861. _____. Ingresso libero. 3 acts. Il Dramma, n.s., 182 (June 1, 1953), 9-31. In Italian.

8862. _____. Non tradire. 3 acts. Il Dramma, 404 (June 15, 1943), 5-23. In Italian.

8863. _____. La paura. 3 acts. Il Dramma, 211 (June 1, 1935), 4-26. In Italian.

8864. _____. Questi poveri amanti. 3 acts. Il Dramma, 281 (May 1, 1938), 4-21. In Italian.

_____, translator see Koselka, F. 4692

8865. Tilden, Freeman. Enter Dora--Exit Dad. 1 act. Ladies' Home Journal, 39 (May, 1922), 15, 53-55.

8866. Timmory, Gabriel. Interview. 1 act, comedy. One-Act Play Magazine, 2 (August-September, 1938), 290-297. Percival Wilde, adapter.

8867. _____. To Kill a Man. 1 act, comedy. One-Act Play Magazine, 1 (May, 1937), 24-40. Percival Wilde, adapter.

8868. Tinseau, Leon de. Ce Qui Fait le Plus Vite. Passer L'Heure. 1 act. Smart Set, 2 (June, 1900), 147-149. In French.

8869. Tipe, David. Snow Birds. 1 act. Performing Arts in Canada, 9 (Spring, 1972), 27-30.

8870. Tiroler Passionsspiel. 3 parts. PMLA, 5 (No. 3, 1890), 1-127. H. M. Schmidt-Wartenberg, editor. In German.

Tirso de Molina, pseud. see Tellez, G. 4718

8871. Toddi. Io non sono io. 1 act. Il Dramma, 3 (February, 1926), 41-48. In Italian.

Toeplitz, Krzysztof T., 1933- see Gruza, J. 3771

8872. Toles, Myriam. We, the People. 1 act. Plays, 22 (February, 1963), 23-32.

8873. Toller, Ernst, 1893-1939. Brokenbrow. 3 acts, tragedy. Two Worlds, 1 (No. 3, 1926), 321-352.

8874. _____. Hinkemann. 2 parts, tragedy. L'Avant Scène, 580 (February 1, 1976), 3-22. Dagmar Deiseu and François Joxe, adapters. In French.

8875. _____. Pastor Hall. 3 acts. Il Dramma, n. s., 67/68/ 69 (August 1/September 1/15, 1948), 13-31. Grazio Di Giammatteo and Fernaldo Di Giammatteo, translators. In Italian.

8876. Tolstoy, Leo Nikolaevich, 1828-1910. How Much Land Does a Man Need? 1 act. Plays, 27 (January, 1968), 75-77. Michael T. Leech, adapter.

8877. _____. The Kreutzer Sonata. 1 act. Sipario, 10

Tolstoy

(August, 1955), 50-56. Ettore Settanni, adapter. In Italian.

8878. _____. The Living Dead. 6 acts. Golden Book, 1 (March, 1925), 395-419. Louise Maude and Aylmer Maude, translators.

8879. _____. Traveller and Peasant. 1 act. English Review, 5 (July, 1910), 617-624.

8880. _____. Tutto il male vien di lî. 1 act. Il Dramma, 216 (August 15, 1935), 32-37. In Italian.

8881. Tom Tyler and His Wife. 1 act, comedy. PMLA, 15 (No. 3, 1900), 253-289.

Tomei, Giuliano, translator see Priestley, J. B. 7295

_____, translator see Wright, R. 9575

8882. Tomes, Margaret Otey. The Children of the Evangelists. 1 act. Drama, 11 (November, 1920), 58-60.

8883. Tomizza, Fulvio. Vera verk. 3 acts. Sipario, 18 (July, 1963), 63-75. In Italian.

8884. Tonelli, Giovanni. L'ospite inatteso. 1 act. Il Dramma, 30 (November 15, 1927), 19-25. In Italian.

8885. _____. Sognare!... 3 acts. Il Dramma, 90 (May 15, 1930), 4-32. In Italian.

8886. _____. Lo zio prete. 1 act. Il Dramma, 86 (March 15, 1930), 36-45. In Italian.

8887. Topelius, Zakarias, 1818-1898. Four Fairy Plays: The Stolen Prince; The Field of Enchantment; The Troll King's Breakfast; The Bride's Crown. 1 act each. Poet Lore, 28 (Autumn, 1917), 567-599. Elizabeth J. MacIntire, translator.

Tophoven, Elmar, translator see Beckett, S. 704, 705, 709

Tophoven, Erika, translator see Beckett, S. 704, 705, 709

8888. Topol, Josef, 1935- . Fin de Carnaval. L'Avant Scène, 438 (December 1, 1969), 7-36. Milan Kepel, adapter. In French.

8889. _____. Un ora d'amore. 1 act. Il Dramma, 45, no. 9 (June, 1969), 63-72. Serena Vitale, translator. In Italian.

8890. Torcross, John. Let the Law Take Its Course. 1 act. Smart Set, 69 (December, 1922), 58-60.

8891. _____. A Quiet Evening. 1 act. Smart Set, 70 (April, 1923), 85-86.

Toro, Julio del, translator see Alarcón y Mendoza, J. R. de 96

8892. Torphy, William. Brandywine. 12 parts. Drama and Theatre, 12 (Spring, 1975), 154-166.

8893. Torrence, Ridgely, 1875-1950. Danse Calinda--A Pantomime with Folk-Music. 1 act. Theatre Arts, 3 (July, 1919), 204-212.

8894. Torrero, Leo. La forza del destino. 1 act. Il Dramma, 441/443 (January 1/February 1/15, 1945), 61-71. In Italian.

8895. Torres, Henry, 1891- . Edition Speciale. 3 acts, comedy. Petite Illustration, 183 (December 24, 1932), 1-34. In French.

_____, adapter see Christie, A. 1825

_____, translator see Veiller, B. 9060

8896. Totheroh, Dan W. The Great Dark. 1 act. Drama, 21 (February, 1931), 19-20, 22.

8897. _____. The Lost Princess. 1 act. Drama, 19 (January, 1929), 107-109, 112.

8898. _____. Mirthful Marionettes. 1 act. Drama, 21 (April, 1931), 19-20, 22, 24.

8899. _____. Pearls. 1 act. Scholastic, 31 (October 9, 1937), 17E-19E.

8900. _____. The Stolen Prince. 1 act. Delineator, 116 (June, 1930), 12, 71-72, 74, 76.

8901. _____. The Stolen Prince. 1 act. Drama, 15 (October, 1924), 30-32.

8902. _____. Tune of a Tune. 1 act, comedy. Drama, 10 (February, 1920), 184-188.

8903. _____. While the Mushrooms Bubble, a Fantasy with or without Music, as You Please. 1 act. Poet Lore, 32 (Summer, 1921), 251-261.

8904. _____. The Widdy's Mite. 1 act, comedy. Drama, 13 (October, 1922), 13-15.

8905. Toudouze, Georges Gustave, 1877- . Le Fait du Prince. 1 act, comedy. Petite Illustration, 192 (November 30, 1935), 1-17. In French.

8906. Tourteau, Jean-Jacques. L'Ascenseur du Quai d'Orsay. 1 act. L'Avant Scène, 528 (November 1, 1973), 47-51. In French.

8907. Towles, Lena Ruth. The Pied Pier. 1 act. Wilson Library Bulletin, 11 (October, 1936), 135, 145.

8908. Towne, Charles Hanson, 1877-1949. The Aliens. 1 act. McClure's, 47 (May, 1916), 12-13, 76.

Towsen, John, translator see Lorde, A. de 5052

8909. Tozzi, Federigo, 1883-1970. L'uva. 1 act. Il Dramma, 45, nos. 14/15 (November/December, 1969), 63-68. In Italian.

8910. Trabucco, Carlo, 1898- . Agostino l'arcidiavolo. 1 act. Il Dramma, n.s., 367 (April, 1967), 79-86. In Italian.

8911. Tracy, Charles. HO to AA, a Stage Playlet in Two Scenes. Transition, 26 (1937), 134-140.

8912. Tragedia de los Amores de Eneas y de la Reyna Dido. PMLA, 46 (June, 1931), 353-431. In Spanish.

8913. Tragedy of True Love, The. A Warning to Those Contemplating Matrimony. 1 act. Smart Set, 3 (April, 1901), 143-144.

8914. Tragical Comedy, or Comical Tragedy, of Punch and Judy. 3 acts. Harper's, 42 (May, 1871), 833-847.

8915. Traill, Henry Duff, 1842-1900. Below the Opposition Gangway. 1 act. Fortnightly, 38 (December, 1882), 821-828.

8916. _____. Lord Westbury and Bishop Wilberforce; a Lucianic Dialogue. 1 act. Fortnightly, 39 (February, 1883), 197-204.

8917. _____. Our Learned Philhellenes. 1 act. Fortnightly, 67 (April, 1897), 504-512.

8918. _____. Our Learned Philhellenes. 1 act. Living Age, 213 (May, 1897), 367-371.

8919. _____. Parnell and Butt; a Dialogue in the Shades. 1 act. Fortnightly, 57 (January, 1892), 115-126.

8920. _____. South Kensington Hellenism. 1 act. Fortnightly, 40 (July, 1882), 111-119.

8921. Traversi, Camillo Antona. La Maschera. 1 act. Il Dramma, 126 (November 15, 1931), 31-35. In Italian.

8922. _____. Le rozeno. 4 acts. Il Dramma, 405 (July 1, 1943), 7-26. In Italian.

8923. Traversi, Giannino Antonia. I giorni più lieti. 3 acts. Il Dramma, 74 (September 15, 1929), 4-41. In Italian.

8924. Tre "No" Giapponesi del XV secolo: Il vecchio pino ed il Susino-Rosa; I due pini che sono invecchiati insieme; Lo specchio dell'illusione. 1 act each. Il Dramma, 414/415/416 (November 15/December 1/15, 1943), 79-84. Enzo Convalli, translator. In Italian.

8925. Tre "No" Giapponesi: I pini cantano; Il battipanni; Il vecchio soldato. 1 act each. Il Dramma, 344 (December 15, 1940), 32-40. In Italian.

8926. Treen, David A. Loose Ends. 1 act. Dramatics, 47 (September, 1975), 6-9.

8927. Treitel, Ralph. The Minyana's Daughter. 1 act, farce. Drama and Theatre, 7 (Winter, 1968-1969), 150-159.

8928. Treno, R. Eavesdropping on the Diplomats. 1 act. Living Age, 352 (June, 1937), 304-305.

8929. Tres Pasos de la Pasión. 1 act. PMLA, 47 (December, 1932), 952-960. In Spanish.

8930. Trevelyan, Robert Calvery, 1872-1951. Thersites. 1 act. Life and Letters, 11 (November, 1934), 202-210.

8931. Trevor, William, 1928- . Going Home. Transatlantic Review, 45 (Spring, 1973), 34-54.

Trezzini, Lamberto, translator see Witkiewicz, S. I. 9514, 9516

8932. Triana, Jose, 1931- . La Noche de les Asesinos. 2 acts. Sipario, 261-262 (January-February, 1968), 72-83. Wanda Garatti, translator. In Italian.

8933. _____. La Noche de les Asesinos. 2 acts. Spectaculum, 12 (1969), 185-222. Yvonne Sturzenegger, translator. In German.

Tridon, André, adapter see Wedekind, F. 9255, 9259

_____, translator see Hellem, C. 4042

8934. Trieste, Leopoldo, 1919- . Cronaca. 3 acts. Il Dramma, n.s., 31/32 (February 15/March 1, 1947), 58-75. In Italian.

Trifilo, S. Samuel, translator see Canton, W. 1575

_____, translator see Gorostiza, C. 3655

Triolet, Elsa, translator see Chekhov, A. 1766

_____, translator see Maiakovski, V. 5454

8935. Trionfo, Aldo and Tonino Conte. Sandokan. 2 acts. Sipario, 25 (April, 1970), 16-27. In Italian.

Trocchi, Alexander, 1925- , translator see Lemasson, S. and J.-C. Penchenat 4909

8936. Troisi, Dante, 1920- . Chiamata in giudizio. 3 acts. Sipario, 174 (October, 1960), 27-48. In Italian.

8937. _____. Il frutto dell'albero. 3 acts. Il Dramma, 48 (July-August, 1972), 51-86. In Italian.

8938. Troubetzkoy, Amelie Rives. Out of the Midst of Hatred. 1 act. Virginia Quarterly Review, 2 (April, 1926), 226-237.

8939. Trowbridge, Marjorie. A Christmas Play. 1 act. St. Nicholas, 51 (December, 1923), 194-200.

8940. Trowbridge, W. R. H. The Immortals Converse. 1 act. Living Age, 324 (March 7, 1925), 540-546.

8941. _____. The Library Come to Life. 1 act. Golden Book, 2 (August, 1925), 268-273.

8942. Troyat, Henri. Sebastien. 3 acts, comedy. L'Avant Scène (OST), 4 (April, 1949), 1-37. In French.

8943. Trudell, Barbara. A Salute to the Flag. 1 act. Plays, 35 (February, 1976), 79-83.

8944. Truffier, Jules and Jacques Chanu. Un Chatiment. 1 act. Petite Illustration, 87 (November 16, 1929), 1-8. In French.

8945. Trumbo, Dalton, 1905-1976. The Biggest Thief in Town. 3 acts, comedy. Theatre Arts, 34 (January, 1950), 57-88.

Trzcinski, Edmund, 1921- see Beven, D. 901

Tsubaki, Andrew T., translator see Kitani, S. 4652

8946. Tucci, Niccolo. Unconjugable Lives. Art and Literature, 3 (Autumn-Winter, 1964), 184-218.

8947. Tucetsky, David and John Pyros. Computerized Play. 1 act. Dramatika, 10 (1973), n.p.

8948. Tunberg, Karl A. Hang by Their Shoelaces. 2 acts. Drama and Theatre, 7 (Fall, 1968), 64-87.

8949. Tupper, Edith Sessions. Thou Shalt Not Steal. 1 act. Smart Set, 27 (February, 1909), 134-140.

8950. Turgenev, Ivan, 1818-1883. A Month in the Country. 5 acts, comedy. L'Avant Scène, 307 (March 15, 1964), 12-41. André Barsacq, adapter. In French.

8951. _____. A Month in the Country. 5 acts. Il Dramma, 198 (November 15, 1934), 4-25. Marta Abba, translator. In Italian.

8952. _____. One May Spin a Thread Too Finely. 1 act, comedy. Fortnightly, 91 (April, 1909), 786-804. Margaret Gough, translator.

8953. Turique, Berr de. A Door Must Be Either Open or Shut, a Drawing-Room Comedy. 1 act. Cosmopolitan, 3 (August, 1887), 417-422.

8954. Turnbull, Lucia. The Good Neighbors. 1 act. Plays, 18 (May, 1959), 42-48.

8955. _____. The Magic Shoes. 1 act. Plays, 15 (March, 1956), 67-73. AND Plays, 35 (March, 1976), 54-60.

8956. Turner, Geneva C. and Jessie H. Roy. Bridge the Gap. Negro History, 20 (March, 1957), 133-137.

8957. Turpin, François. Don Juan Malgré Lui. 1 act. L'Avant Scène, 425 (May 1, 1969), 39-42. In French.

8958. _____. Pastorale. 1 act. L'Avant Scène, 467 (March 1, 1971), 31-34. In French.

8959. _____. On Finit Quelquefois par ou l'On Devrait Toujours Commencer. 1 act. L'Avant Scène, 347 (December 15, 1965), 49-53. In French.

8960. _____. Sait-on Jamais! 1 act. L'Avant Scène, 190 (February 1, 1959), 37-41. In French.

Twain 626

Twain, Mark, pseud. see Clemens, S. L. 1877-1891

8961. Tzara, Tristan, 1896-1964. The Gas-Burning Heart. 1 act. Chicago Review, 20/21 (May, 1969), 48-64. Leslie Singer, adapter.

8962. _____. Handkerchief of Clouds. 15 acts, tragedy. Drama Review, 16 (December, 1972), 112-129. Aileen Robbins, translator.

U

8963. Udoff, Yale M. Shade. 1 act. Mademoiselle, 74 (April, 1972), 224-225, 253-254, 256-260, 262-263.

Ueda, Makoto, translator see Kojiro, K. 4680

_____, translator see Motokiyo, Z. 6269

8964. Ufficio della stella, L'. Il Dramma, (December, 1974), 16-20. In Italian.

8965. Ugrjumov, Dimitrij. Kreslo N. 16. 3 acts. Sipario, 188 (December, 1961), 94-112. Tanja Isanz and Milly de Monticelli, translators. In Italian.

8966. Uhler, John Earle. The Teache Comes. 1 act. Southwest Review, 20 (January, 1935), 191-216.

8967. Ullman, Samuel S. The Youth, Bolivar. 1 act. Plays, 3 (December, 1943), 38-45. AND Plays, 25 (March, 1966), 59-65.

Ulman, Seth, translator see Buchner, G. 1404

8968. Unamuno y Jugo, Miguel de, 1864-1936. The Other: A Mystery in Three Acts and an Epilogue. Poet Lore, 53 (Spring, 1947), 3-35. H. Alpern, translator.

Underhill, John Garrett, translator see Benavente y Martinez, J. 741, 743-747

_____, translator see Echegaray y Eizaguirre, J. 2812, 2813

_____, translator see Martinez Sierra, G. 5626, 5628, 5630

_____, translator see Rusinol y Prats, S. 7799

_____, translator see Vega L. de 9055

8969. Unger, Erich. Die Gehemmten. 1 act. Der Sturm, 1 (No. 43, December, 1910), 343, 344. In German.

8970. Unger, Robert. Chronicles of Bohikee Creek. 1 act. Dramatika, 5 (Spring, 1970), n. p.

8971. Upson, William Hazlett. The Master Salesman. 1 act. Senior Scholastic, 51 (January 12, 1948), 18-21.

Uraneff, Vadim, translator see Blok, A. 1010

8972. Urban, Catherine. Alice in Bookland. 1 act. Plays, 22 (November, 1962), 72-74.

8973. _____. Mrs. Claus' Christmas Present. 1 act. Plays, 15 (December, 1955), 67-70.

8974. _____. The Queen with the Broken Heart. 1 act. Plays, 5 (February, 1946), 58-60.

8975. _____. Santa and Priorities. 1 act. Plays, 4 (December, 1944), 45-47.

8976. _____. Santa and the Spacemen. 1 act. Plays, 22 (December, 1962), 67-70.

8977. _____. The Scarecrow's Hat. 1 act. Plays, 23 (October, 1963), 67-72.

8978. _____. The Timid Little Witch. 1 act. Plays, 14 (October, 1954), 67-70.

8979. Ursell, Geoffrey, 1943- . The Park. 1 act. Performing Arts in Canada, 9 (Fall, 1972), 22-27.

8980. Usigli, Rodolfo. El gesticulador. 3 acts. Sipario, 21 (July, 1966), 45-64. Roberto Rebora, translator. In Italian.

8981. _____. The Great Middle Class. 3 acts, comedy. Poet Lore, 63 (Summer, 1968), 156-232. Edna Lue Furness, translator.

8982. Ustinov, Peter, 1921- . Love of Four Colonels. 3 acts. L'Avant Scène, 155, 1-33. Marc-Gilbert Sauvejon, adapter. In French.

8983. _____. The Love of Four Colonels. 3 acts, comedy. Sipario, 7 (April, 1952), 33-53. Vitaliano Brancati and Anna Proclemer, translator. In Italian.

8984. _____. Romanoff and Juliet. 3 acts. L'Avant Scène,

169 (March 1, 1958), 4-36. Marc-Gilbert Sauvajon, adapter. In French.

8985. _____. Romanoff and Juliet. 3 acts. Theatre Arts, 43 (May, 1959), 25-40.

Utt, Ana Lee, translator see Quintero, S. A., Alvarez Quintero, S. and J. Alvarez Quintero 174

V

Vacchetto, Emanuele, translator see Copi 2014

Vaez, Gustave see Monnier, H. 6174

8986. Vahl, Rod. Circus Magic. 1 act. Plays, 25 (January, 1966), 63-66. AND Plays, 33 (May, 1974), 58-61.

8987. _____. The Indian Boy Without a Name. 1 act. Plays, (October, 1965), 55-60.

8988. Vail, Lawrence. Popopeeka. 1 act, comedy. Smart Set, 64 (January, 1921), 89-97.

8989. Vail, Walter J. The Death of Columbine. 3 acts, comedy. First Stage, 4 (Summer, 1965), 62-89.

8990. _____. Manny. 1 act. First Stage, 4 (Spring, 1965), 14-25.

Vailler see Bajard 510

Vaime, Enrico see Crovi, E. 2126

8991. Vajda, Ernst, 1887- . Una signora che vuol divorziare. 3 acts. Il Dramma, 109 (March 1, 1931), 4-33. Ada Salvatore, translator. In Italian.

8992. Valabrègne, Albin. La scienza dell'amore. 1 act. Il Dramma, 18 (May, 1927), 43-45. In Italian.

Valcros, W. see Hellem, C. 4042

8993. Valdarnini, Alfio, 1926- . Diario di una donna. 3 acts. Il Dramma, n.s., 313 (October, 1962), 20-48. In Italian.

8994. Valency, Maurice Jacques, 1903- . The Tracian Horses. 3 acts. Il Dramma, n.s., 70 (October 1, 1948), 11-41. Gigi Cane, translator. In Italian.

_____, adapter see Durrenmatt, F. 2753

8995. _____, translator see Giraudoux, J. 1801, 3563, 3572, 3574

Not used.

8996. Valène, Marie-Claire, translator see Calderon de la Barca, P. 1503

8996. Valentini, Giuseppe. Ettore. 4 acts. Il Dramma, 371 (February 1, 1942), 7-27. In Italian.

_____, translator see Garcia Lorca, F. 3374

8997. Valéry, Paul Ambroise, 1871-1945. Amphion. 1 act. Quarterly Review of Literature, 6 (No. 4, 1952), 327-344. Carlos Rongel, translator.

8998. Valle Inclan, Ramon del, 1870-1936. The Dragon's Head; A Fantastic Farce. 1 act. Poet Lore, 29 (Winter, 1918), 531-564. May Heywood Broun, translator.

8999. _____. Lien de Sang. 1 act. L'Avant Scène, 112, 41-45. Jean Camp, adapter. In French.

9000. _____. Lights of Bohemia. 1 act. Modern International Drama, 2 (March, 1969), 55-97. Anthony N. Zahareas and Gerald Gillespie, translators.

9001. _____. Luces de Bohemia. 1 act. L'Avant Scène, 292 (July 15, 1963), 10-31. Jeannine Worms, adapter. In French.

9002. _____. La rosa di carta. 1 act. Sipario, 314 (July, 1972), 65-69. Maria Luisa Aguirre D'Amico, translator. In Italian.

9003. Vallejo, Antonio Buero, 1916- . El Concierto de San Ovidio. 3 acts. Sipario, 256-257 (August-September, 1967), 51-69, 71. Maria Luisa Aguirre D'Amico, translator. In Italian.

9004. _____. The Concert at Saint Ovide. 3 acts. Modern International Drama, 1 (September, 1967), 9-61. Farris Anderson, translator.

9005. _____. Ecrit Sur le Sable. 1 act, tragedy. L'Avant Scène, 183 (October 15, 1958), 35-40. André Camp, adapter. In French.

9006. Valmain, Frederic. La Corde pour le Pendre. 1 act. L'Avant Scène, 124, 33-39. In French.

9007. _____. Meurtres en Fa Diésé. 3 acts. L'Avant Scène, 190 (February 1, 1959), 7-35. In French.

_____, adapter see Sands, L. 7907

9008. _____ and Jean Dejoux. Illégitime Defense, ou Lotus et Discretion...! 2 acts. L'Avant Scène, 270 (August 1, 1962), 7-34. In French.

9009. Valori, Gino, 1890- . L'amante di prima. 3 acts. Il Dramma, 223 (December 1, 1935), 2023. In Italian.

9010. _____. L'amor sincero. 1 act. Il Dramma, 341 (November 1, 1940), 41-44. In Italian.

9011. _____. L'argilla. 1 act. Il Dramma, 78 (November 15, 1929), 24-29. In Italian.

9012. _____. La rivencita delle mogli. 3 acts. Il Dramma, 189 (July 1, 1934), 4-28. In Italian.

Valoriani, Valerio, translator see Weiss, P. 9173

9013. Van Campen, Helen G. Life on Broadway, the Musical Comedy Rehearsal. 1 act. McClure's, 41 (May, 1913), 68-72.

9014. Vance, Daisy Melville. Over the Garden Wall. 1 act. Scholastic, 29 (January 30, 1937), 6-7, 14.

9015. Van Delden, Egbert H. Alice in Everydayland. 1 act. Poet Lore, 38 (1927), 96-105.

9016. _____. The Guy Upstairs. 1 act. Poet Lore, 40 (1929), 251-263.

9017. Vandenberghe, Paul, -1961. Une Cliente Perdue. 1 act. L'Avant Scène, 180 (September 1, 1958), 34-39. In French.

9018. _____. Un Coup de Soleil. 1 act, comedy. L'Avant Scène, 148, 25-39. In French.

9019. _____. Printemps Perdus. 4 acts. L'Avant Scène, 103, 1-32. In French.

9020. _____. La rabbia nel cuore. 3 acts. Il Dramma, n. s., 112 (July 1, 1950), Paolo Teglio, translator. In Italian.

9021. _____. Une Répétition Générale, ou La Pièce a Conviction. 1 act. L'Avant Scène, 264 (May 1, 1962), 37-40. In French.

9022. _____ and T. Mihalakeas. Mauvaise Semence. 4 acts. L'Avant Scène, 197 (May 15, 1959), 7-36. In French.

9023. Vandevere, J. Lilian. Mother Goose Gives a Dinner. 1 act. Plays, 5 (April, 1946), 73-75.

9024. Van Dresser, Jasmine. Eight-Thirty Sharp. 1 act, comedy. Delineator, 99 (January, 1922), 20-21, 68-69.

9025. Van Druten, John, 1901-1957. Bell, Book and Candle. 3 acts, comedy. Theatre Arts, 36 (June, 1952), 51-75.

9026. _____. I Am a Camera. 3 acts. Theatre Arts, 37 (January, 1953), 35-64.

9027. _____. I Remember Mama. 2 parts. Il Dramma, n.s., 128 (March 1, 1951), 9-35. Laura del Bono, translator. In Italian.

9028. Van Duyn, Mona, 1921- . Call Your People, America. 1 act. Senior Scholastic, 44 (February 21-26, 1944), 15, 20.

9029. Van Dyke, Henry, 1852-1933. The House of Rimmon. 4 acts. Scribner's, 44 (August-September, 1908), 129-147; 283-300.

9030. Van Itallie, Jean-Claude, 1936- . America Hurrah. Sipario, 23 (December, 1968), 55-71. Ettore Capriolo, translator. In Italian.

9031. _____. Eat Cake! 1 act. Performance, 5 (March/April, 1973), 91-96.

9032. _____. It's Almost Like Being. 1 act. Tulane Drama Review, 9 (Summer, 1965), 171-178.

9033. _____. Take a Deep Breath. 1 act. Toucan, 2 (No. 2/3, 1970), supplement, 8-10.

Van Kaathoven, Alice, translator see Curel, F. de 2148

9034. Vane, Sutton, 1888-1963. Outward Bound. 3 acts. Il Dramma, n.s., 77 (January 15, 1949), 7-32. Enrico Raggio, translator.

9035. Vanni, Alfredo. L'amante del sogno. 3 acts. Il Dramma, 37 (March 1, 1928), 7-34. In Italian.

9036. _____. Il carillon. 1 act. Il Dramma, 217 (September 1, 1935), 31-35. In Italian.

9037. _____. Una donna quasi onesta. 3 acts. Il Dramma, 26 (September 15, 1927), 6-35. In Italian.

9038. _____. Hollywood. 3 acts. Il Dramma, 59 (February 1, 1929), 4-32. In Italian.

9039. ———. Quattro di cuori. 3 acts. Il Dramma, 289 (September 1, 1938), 4-25. In Italian.

9040. ———. Sogno delle mille e una notte. 3 acts. Il Dramma, 194 (September 15, 1934), 4-34. In Italian.

9041. Varaldo, Alessandro. L'idea di Cora. 1 act. Il Dramma, 275 (February 1, 1938), 4-10. In Italian.

9042. ———. Partita in quattro. 1 act. Il Dramma, 328 (April 15, 1940), 42-49. In Italian.

9043. ———. Il tappeto verde. 2 acts. Il Dramma, 171 (October 1, 1933), 4-14. In Italian.

9044. Varney, Horace. The Garden of the Christmas Fairy. 1 act. Ladies' Home Journal, 29 (December, 1912), 85.

9045. ———. Watching for Santa Claus. 1 act. Ladies' Home Journal, 21 (December, 1903), 19.

9046. Vasilico, Giuliano, 1940- . Le 120 giornate di Sodoma; Dal Romanzo del marchese De Sade. Sipario, 324 (May, 1973), 54-60. In Italian.

9047. Vattier, Robert, 1914- and Albert Rieux, 1906- . Gonzalo Sent la Violette. 1 act. L'Avant Scène, 178 (July 15, 1958), 41-49. In French.

Vaughn, Eric, translator see Wedekind, F. 9258

Vaulx, A. Foulon de, translator see Paget, V. 6928

9048. Vauthier, Jean. Capitaine Bada. 3 acts. L'Avant Scène (OST), 57 (February, 1952), 1-34. In French.

9049. ———. The Prodigies. 1 act. First Stage, 4 (Winter, 1965-1966), 237-259. Bettina L. Knapp, translator.

9050. Vazart, Claude. La Balance d'Eros. 1 act, comedy. L'Avant Scène, 411 (October 1, 1968), 34-37.

9051. Vazquez, Jose Andres. With Chains of Gold. 1 act. Poet Lore, 34 (Autumn, 1923), 417-425. Willis Knapp Jones, translator.

9052. Veber, Francis. L'Enlèvement. 2 acts. L'Avant Scène, 420 (February 15, 1969), 7-37. In French.

Vecchietti, Paolina, translator see Steinbeck, J. 8492

Vecchietti, Pilade, translator see Steinbeck, J. 8492

Vega

9053. Vega, Lope de, 1562-1635. The Father Outwitted. Interlude. Mirror of Taste, 2 (October, 1810), 241-248.

9054. _____. L'indemoniata. 1 act. Il Dramma, 363 (October 1, 1941), 38-39. Giovanni Marcellini, translator. In Italian.

9055. _____. The King, the Greatest Alcade. 3 acts. Poet Lore, 29 (Summer, 1918), 379-446. John Garrett Underhill, translator.

9056. _____. The Outrageous Saint. 3 acts. Tulane Drama Review, 7 (Fall, 1962), 58-104. Willis Barnstone, translator.

9057. _____. The Pastrybaker. 1 act, farce. Theatre Arts, 19 (September, 1935), 713-721. M. Jagendorf, translator.

9058. _____. Sin Secreto no ay Amor. 3 acts, comedy. PMLA, 9 (No. 2, 1894), 182-311. In Spanish.

9059. _____. The Stupid Lady. 3 acts, comedy. Poet Lore, 57 (July, 1962), 291-354. Willis Knapp Jones, translator.

9060. Veiller, Bayard, 1869?-1943. The Trial of Mary Dugan. 3 acts. Petite Illustration, 87 (June 22, 1929), 1-34. Henry Torres and H. de Carbuccia, translators.

9061. Velle, Louis. A la Monnaie du Pape. 4 acts, comedy. L'Avant Scène, 131, 1-34. In French.

_____, adapter see Dyer, C. 2794

9062. Vendetta del pescatore, La. Chinese opera. Sipario, 13 (December, 1957), 74-80. Maria Tchou Mamo, translator. In Italian.

9063. Veneziani, Carlo. Alga Marina. 3 acts. Il Dramma, 20 (June 15, 1927), 7-34. In Italian.

9064. _____. L'antenato. 3 acts. Il Dramma, 101 (November 1, 1930), 4-27. In Italian.

9065. _____. Aprite le finestre. 3 acts. Il Dramma, 334 (July 15, 1940), 4-27. In Italian.

9066. _____. Un bimbo cosî.... 3 acts. Il Dramma, 285 (July 1, 1938), 4-23. In Italian.

9067. _____. La finestra sul mondo. 4 acts. Il Dramma, 124 (October 15, 1931), 4-31. In Italian.

9068. _____. L'innesto dell'eternità. 1 act. Il Dramma, 111 (April 1, 1931), 23-37. In Italian.

9069. _____. Il pescatore di Balene. 3 acts. Il Dramma, 291 (October 1, 1938), 4-26. In Italian.

9070. _____. Il reuccio malinconico. 1 act. Il Dramma, 31 (December 1, 1927), 33-39. In Italian.

9071. _____. Il signore è servito. 3 acts. Il Dramma, 33 (January 1, 1928), 6-32. In Italian.

9072. Vengeur de son Père, Le. 1 act. L'Avant Scène, 77 (April 25, 1953), 35-40. In French.

Ventura, Enrico, 1936- see Logan, S. 5018

9073. Venturini, Franco, 1937- . Chaino. Sipario, 24 (November, 1969), 64-66. In Italian.

9074. Verdot, Guy, 1918- . Avec Lui. 3 acts. L'Avant Scène, 540 (May 1, 1974), 37-51. In French.

9075. _____. Théodat. 1 act. L'Avant Scène, 476 (July 15, 1971), 35-39. In French.

9076. _____. Le Vieil Ulysse. 2 acts. L'Avant Scène, 433 (September 15, 1969), 33-46. In French.

9077. Verga, Giovanni, 1840-1922. Mastro Don Gesualdo. 3 acts. Il Dramma, 341 (November 1, 1940), 6-30. In Italian.

9078. Vergani, Orio. L'ispezione. 1 act. Il Dramma, n.s., 231 (December, 1955), 63-69. In Italian.

9079. _____. Li-Ma-Tong, nuvoletta rosa. 3 acts. Il Dramma, n.s., 224 (May, 1955), 6-24. In Italian.

9080. _____. Il primo amore. 1 act. Il Dramma, 280 (April 15, 1938), 24-31. In Italian. AND Il Dramma, 329 (May 1, 1940), 40-46. In Italian.

9081. _____. S'egli tornasse. 1 act. Il Dramma, 329 (May 1, 1940), 28-33. In Italian.

9082. _____. Un viglacco. 1 act. Il Dramma, 18 (May, 1927), 30-37. In Italian.

9083. _____, Carlo Silva and Italo Terzoli. Sette Scalini Azzurri. 2 parts. Il Dramma, n.s., 179 (April 15, 1953), 7-28. In Italian.

Vergoz, Manlio, translator see Moineaux, G. 6106

9084. Verhoeff, Caroline. The Sleeping Beauty. 5 acts. St. Nicholas, 40 (April, 1913), 548-552.

Verlain, Jean, translator see Prins, P. de 7304

9085. Verlaine, Paul, 1844-1896. Minuet: A Pastoral Absurdity. 1 act, comedy. Dublin Magazine, n.s., 26 (October-December, 1951), 25-46. Michael Scot, translator.

9086. Vermilye, Kate Jordan. The Pompadour's Protege. 1 act. Smart Set, 11 (September, 1903), 75-87.

9087. Vermorel, Claude, 1909- . Un Jardin Sur la Mer. 4 acts. L'Avant Scène, 314 (July 1, 1964), 10-35. In French.

9088. Verne, Jules, 1828-1905. Around the World in Eighty Days. 1 act. Plays, 18 (October, 1958), 85-95. Lewy Olfson, adapter.

9089. _____. The Black Indies. 1 act. Plays, 25 (April, 1966), 81-91. Lewy Olfson, adapter.

9090. _____. Five Weeks in a Balloon. 1 act. Plays, 23 (April, 1964), 87-95. Lewy Olfson, adapter.

9091. _____. Master Zacharius. 1 act. Plays, 28 (November, 1968), 97-106. Adele Thane, adapter.

9092. _____. Twenty Thousand Leagues Under the Sea. 1 act. Plays, 17 (May, 1958), 83-91. Lewy Olfson, adapter.

9093. Verneuil, Louis, 1893-1952. Affairs of State. 3 acts. Il Dramma, n.s., 198 (February 1, 1954), 9-42. Ada Salvatore, translator. In Italian.

9094. _____. L'Amant de Madame Vidal. 3 acts, comedy. Petite Illustration, 190 (April 20, 1935), 1-38. In French.

9095. _____. La Banque Nemo. 3 acts, comedy. Petite Illustration, 182 (June 4, 1932), 1-42. In French.

9096. _____. Dora Nelson. Petite Illustration, 192 (December 28, 1935), 1-38. In French.

9097. _____. Une Femme Ravie. 4 acts. Petite Illustration, 183 (December 17, 1932), 1-46. In French.

9098. _____. Pile ou Face. 5 acts, comedy. Petite Illustration, 189 (October 13, 1934), 1-46. In French.

9099. _____. Signorina, vi voglio sposare. 3 acts. Il Dramma, 9 (August, 1926), 7-28. In Italian.

9100. _____. I tre signori Chantrel. 3 acts. Il Dramma, n.s., 102 (February 1, 1950), 7-34. Connie Ricono, translator. In Italian.

9101. _____. Vive le Roi! Petite Illustration, 193 (January 25, 1936), 1-52. In French.

_____ see also Berr, Georges 866-868

9102. _____ and Georges Berr. L'Ecole des Contribuables. 3 acts, comedy. Petite Illustration, 188 (June 16, 1934), 1-42. In French.

Vernon, Lee, pseud. see Paget, V. 6927, 6928

Vernon, Virginia, translator see Sherriff, R. C. 8252

Veronesi, Giulia, translator see Talagrand, J. 8696

9103. Very, Alice. Abe Lincoln Goes to School. 1 act. Plays, 16 (February, 1957), 77-80.

9104. _____. Christmas in Old Boston. 1 act. Plays, 14 (December, 1954), 71-74. AND Plays, 35 (December, 1975), 53-56.

9105. _____. Christmas Joy. 1 act. Plays, 3 (December, 1943), 53-55.

9106. _____. Dancing Children. 1 act. Plays, 11 (October, 1951), 55-57.

9107. _____. Doctor Time's Office. 1 act. Plays, 4 (January, 1945), 57-60.

9108. _____. Easter Egg Rolling. 1 act. Plays, 5 (March, 1946), 61-64.

9109. _____. Everywhere Christmas. 1 act. Plays, 4 (December, 1944), 56-60. AND Plays, 15 (December, 1955), 71-75.

9110. _____. The Flower Garden. 1 act. Plays, 3 (April, 1944), 55-57.

9111. _____. The Frog and the Mouse. 1 act. Plays, 5 (February, 1946), 63-66.

9112. _____. General George. 1 act. Plays, 18 (February, 1959), 76-78.

9113. _____. A Golden Bell for Mother. 1 act. Plays, 3 (May, 1944), 52-55.

9114. _____. Highland Lad. 1 act. Plays, 4 (October, 1944), 20-26.

9115. _____. John Grumlie. 1 act. Plays, 5 (October, 1945), 48-50.

9116. _____. Jonathan's Thanksgiving. 1 act. Plays, 30 (November, 1970), 69-72.

9117. _____. The Little Fir Tree. 1 act. Plays, 16 (December, 1956), 70-74.

9118. _____. The Magic Mirror. 1 act. Plays, 12 (April, 1953), 74-76.

9119. _____. The Mayflower. 1 act. Plays, 15 (May, 1956), 59-62.

9120. _____. The Old Woman and Her Pig. 1 act. Plays, 3 (March, 1944), 53-55.

9121. _____. Planting Time. 1 act. Plays, 14 (April, 1955), 83-85.

9122. _____. President Lincoln's Children. 1 act. Plays, 4 (February, 1945), 36-38.

9123. _____. Return of Columbus. 1 act. Plays, 19 (October, 1959), 72-74.

9124. _____. The Snow Girl. 1 act. Plays, 2 (February, 1943), 48-51.

9125. _____. Thanksgiving Night. 1 act. Plays, 4 (November, 1944), 49-50.

9126. _____. The Three Sillies. 1 act. Plays, 4 (April, 1945), 37-40.

9127. _____. Tom Tit Tot. 1 act. Plays, 2 (May, 1943), 52-56.

9128. _____. The Trees at School. 1 act. Plays, 17 (May, 1958), 73-75.

9129. _____. The Twelve Months. 1 act. Plays, 2 (March, 1943), 49-53.

9130. _____. Valentine Antics. 1 act. Plays, 4 (February, 1945), 50-51.

9131. _____. Victory for Liberty. 1 act. Plays, 2 (January, 1943), 65-67.

9132. _____. Victory Gardens. 1 act. Plays, 4 (May, 1945), 55-57.

9133. _____. What Happened to the Cakes. 1 act. Plays, 3 (February, 1944), 47-49.

9134. _____ and Martha Brown. The Fairy Circus. 1 act. Plays, 2 (October, 1942), 47-52.

Vesci-Baum, Carlotta, translator see Frank, B. 3258

9135. Vian, Boris, 1920-1959. Les Batisseurs d'Empire. 3 acts. Il Dramma, n.s., 292 (January, 1961), 12-29. Maripiera de Vecchis, translator. In Italian.

9136. _____. L'Equarrissage Pour Tous. 1 act. L'Avant Scène, 406 (July 1, 1968), 10-28. In French.

_____, translator see Strindberg, A. 8567

Viano, Bruno, translator see Connelly, M. 1977

9137. Vibert, Jehan Georges, 1840-1902. The Sick Doctor. 1 act, comedy. Century, 51 (April, 1896), 945-947.

9138. Vicente, Gill, 1470-1536. Four Plays: The Three Wise Men; The Serenade; The Sailor's Wife; The Widower's Comedy. 1 act, each. Tulane Drama Review, 5 (March, 1961), 160-186. Jill Booty, translator.

Vicesvinci, C., translator see Alvarez Quintero, S. and J. Alvarez Quintero 170

9139. Vichnevski, Vsevolad. La Tragédie Optimiste. 3 acts. L'Avant Scène (OST), 50 (October, 1951), 1-32. Gabriel Aroutcheff and Georges Aroutcheff, translators.

Vicknes, Edwin Johan, translator see Heiberg, G. 4026

9140. Vidal, Gore, 1925- . The Best Man. 3 acts. Theatre Arts, 45 (September, 1961), 25-56.

9141. _____. Visit to a Small Planet. 3 acts, comedy. Theatre Arts, 42 (February, 1958), 33-56.

_____, adapter see Durrenmatt, F. 2751

9142. Vidalie, Albert, 1913- . Les Mystères de Paris. 1 act. L'Avant Scène, 102, 1-35. In French.

Vidusso, Marga Feriani, translator see Boal, A. 1028

_____, translator see Sperr, M. 8444

Vigorelli, Giancarlo, translator see Neveux, G. 6477

9143. Vilalta, Maruxa. Un Jour de Folie. 1 act. L'Avant Scène, 423 (April 1, 1969), 41-43. Jean Camp, adapter. In French.

9144. ____. Together Tonight. Modern International Drama, 6 (Spring, 1973), 7-38. Willis K. Jones, translator.

9145. ____. La Ultima Letra. 1 act, monologue. L'Avant Scène, 314 (July 1, 1964), 37-43. Mireille Pezzani, translator. In French.

9146. Vilas, Faith Van Valkenburgh. Tears of Dawn, a Medieval Fantasy. 1 act. Poet Lore, 33 (Spring, 1922), 105-113.

Vildrac, Charles, pseud. see Messager, C. 5786-5792

9147. Vilfrid, Jacques. L'Amour, Toujours l'Amour! 3 acts. L'Avant Scène (OST), 42 (May, 1951), 1-47. In French.

Villars, Meg see Bisson, A. 973

9148. Villaurrutia, Xavier, 1903-1950. What Are You Thinking About? 1 act. New World Writing, 14 (1958), 163-181. Lysander Kemp, translator.

9149. Villeroy, Auguste. La Double Passion. 3 acts. Petite Illustration, 88 (August 16, 1930), 1-26. In French.

9150. Villiers, Marie-Louise. Ne Dites pas: Fontaine. 1 act. L'Avant Scène, 236, 33-37. In French.

Vincent, Claude, adapter see Wilde, O. 9368

Vincent, Katherine, translator see A House Party 4182

9151. Viola, Cesare Giulio. Candido. 3 acts. Il Dramma, n.s., 266 (November, 1958), 14-38. In Italian.

9152. ____. Nora seconda. 3 acts. Il Dramma, n.s., 202 (April 1, 1954), 9-26. In Italian.

9153. ____. Poveri davanti a Dio. 3 acts. Il Dramma, n.s., 49 (November 15, 1947), 7-26. In Italian.

9154. ____. Venerdi' santo. 3 acts. Il Dramma, n.s., 239/240 (August/September, 1956), 10-28. In Italian.

Violani, Ettore, translator see Fry, C. 3332

9155. Virta, Nikolaj, 1906- . Zemlja. 5 acts. Sipario, 16 (December, 1961), 50-72. Milly de Monticelli, translator. In Italian.

Visconti, Luchino, translator see Miller, A. 5843

Vissant, Georges de see Conty, J. 1992

Vitale, Serena, translator see Topol, J. 8889

Vitaliano, I., translator see Chekhov, A. P. 1775

9156. Vitaly, Georges, 1927- . Guerre et Paix au Café Sneffle. 4 acts. L'Avant Scène, 428 (June 15, 1969), 7-37. In French.

9157. Vitamin "U". 1 act. Senior Scholastic, 43 (November 29-December 4, 1943), 15-16.

Vitez, Antoine, translator see Chekhov, A. P. 1769

9158. Vitrac, Roger, 1899-1952. The Ephemera. 1 act. This Quarter, 2 (January/March, 1930), 449-460. Harold J. Salemson, translator.

9159. ————. The Painter. 1 act. Broom, 3 (October, 1922), 223-229. Matthew Josephson, translator.

9160. ————. Poison; a Drama Without Words. 1 act. Broom, 5 (November, 1923), 226-228. Malcolm Cowley, translator.

9161. ————. Victor, ou Les Enfants au Pouvoir. 3 acts. L'Avant Scène, 276 (November 15, 1962), 9-28. In French.

9162. Viviani, Raffaele. L'imbroglione onesto. 3 acts. Il Dramma, 266 (September 15, 1937), 2-28. In Italian.

9163. ————. Mestiere di padre. 3 acts. Il Dramma, 318 (November 15, 1939), 4-17. In Italian.

9164. ————. La tavola dei poveri. 3 acts, comedy. Sipario, 9 (August-September, 1954), 43-61. In Italian.

9165. Viviani, Vittorio. Trio fulgor. 1 act. Il Dramma, 355 (June 1, 1941), 39-47. In Italian.

9166. Vivran. Alizon. 1 act. L'Avant Scène, 306 (March 1, 1964), 37-50. In French.

9167. Voaden, Herman. Murder Pattern. 1 act. Canadian Theatre Review, 5 (Winter, 1975), 44-60.

9168. Vogel, Joseph. Tonsillitis, an Impression. 1 act. This Quarter, 1 (Spring, 1929), 5-10.

9169. Vojnovich, Ivo, 1857-1929. A Trilogy of Dubrovnik; Allons Enfants; The Twilight; On the Terrace. Poet Lore, 56 (Summer, Autumn, Winter, 1951), 103-142; 195-218; 291-340. John J. Batistich and George Rapall Noyes, translators.

9170. Volodin, Aleksandr Moiseevic, 1919- . Le Due Frecce. Sipario, 331 (December, 1973), 63-76. Milli Martinelli, translator. In Italian.

Volta, Ornella, translator see Ehni, R. 2827

9171. Volzer, Marion. A Statue for Joey. 1 act. Senior Scholastic, 50 (January 23, 1947), 13-14.

9172. Vosatka, Helen. The Piggy Bank Helps Uncle Sam. 1 act. Plays, 2 (May, 1943), 70-72.

9173. Voteur, Ferdinand. My Unfinished Portrait. 3 acts. Poet Lore, 56 (Spring, 1951), 3-75.

9174. Voulet, Jacqueline, 1941- . L'Arret. 1 act, monologue. L'Avant Scène, 514 (March 15, 1973), 33-37. In French.

9175. _____. Entre Nous. 1 act, monologue. L'Avant Scène, 485 (December 15, 1971), 33-34. In French.

Vrchlicky, Jaroslav, pseud. see Frida, E. B. 3299-3301

9176. Vulpescu, Romulus, 1933- . Il perbene. 1 act. Il Dramma, 46, no. 6 (June, 1960), 36-42. Paola Angioletti, translator. In Italian.

W

9177. Wachthausen, René. Il talismano. 1 act. Il Dramma, 147 (October 1, 1932), 36-42. Enzo Gariffo, translator. In Italian.

9178. _____. Le Verre de Vin Blanc. 1 act, comedy. Petite Illustration, 88 (September 6, 1930), 1-8. In French.

9179. Waddell, Samuel, 1878- . Phantoms, a Comedy or Tragedy in One Act. Dublin Magazine, 1 (December, 1923), 382-391.

9180. _____. A Prologue. 1 act. Dublin Magazine, 2 (June, 1925), 722-725.

9181. Wade, Isaac W. Spring Harvest. 1 act. Southwest Review, 10 (July, 1925), 73-77.

9182. Wagner, Al. A Parabolic Quartet. 1 act. Resource, 7 (April, 1966), 18-25.

9183. Wagner, Richard, 1813-1883. Das Rheingold. 1 act. Scribner's, 24 (December, 1898), 693-720. F. J. Stimson, adapter.

9184. Wainwright, Fonrose. Safe for Today. 1 act. The Survey, 68 (July 1, 1932), 309-311, 317.

9185. Waite, Helen Elmira, 1903- . Cecily Entertains the Enemy. 1 act. Plays, 14 (February, 1955), 32-42.

9186. _____ and Elbert M. Hoppenstedt, 1917- . Christmas House. 1 act. Plays, 4 (December, 1944), 28-35. AND Plays, 25 (December, 1965), 15-22.

9187. _____. The Master of the Strait. 1 act. Plays, 5 (December, 1945), 12-18.

9188. _____. Not Only the Strong. 1 act. Plays, 2 (May, 1943), 26-35.

Waley, Arthur, 1889- , translator see Motoyazu, K. Z. 6273

9189. Walker, Stuart, 1888-1941. Lady of the Weeping Willow Tree. 3 acts. Drama, 29 (February, 1918), 10-52.

9190. _____. Sir David Wears a Crown. 1 act. Ladies' Home Journal, 38 (June, 1921), 6-7, 154, 157-159.

9191. Wallace, Edgar, 1875-1932. Il gran premio di Ascot. 3 acts. Il Dramma, 127 (December 1, 1931), 4-35. In Italian.

Wallace, Elizabeth, translator see Perez Galdos, B. 7065

9192. Wallace, Lew, 1827-1905. Commodus. 5 acts. Harper's, 78 (January, 1889), 169-193.

9193. Wallace, Ruth. The Case of the Frustrated Corpse. 1 act. Plays, 19 (February, 1960), 88-90.

9194. Wallach, Ira, 1913- . Absence of a Cello. 3 acts, comedy. L'Avant Scène, 351 (February 15, 1966), 9-36. Albert Husson, adapter. In French.

Wallop, Douglass, 1920- see Abbott, G. 5

Wally, Haya, translator see Fulda, L. 3340

9195. Walser, Martin, 1929- . Chêne et Lapins Angora, Chronique Allemande. L'Avant Scène, 434 (October 1, 1969), 7-33. Gilbert Badia, translator. In French.

9196. _____. Der Schwaze Schwan. 2 acts. Spectaculum, 8 (1965), 285-330. In German.

9197. _____. Die Zimmerschlacht. 1 act. Spectaculum, 12 (1969), 83-111. In German.

9198. Walsh, Thomas. Goya in the Cupola. 1 act. Century, 89 (March, 1915), 701-704.

_____, translator see Alvarez Quintero, S. and J. Alvarez Quintera 168

Walter, Elizabeth, translator see Hofmannsthal, H. von 4129

9199. Walter, Otto F. The Cat. 3 parts. Gambit, 4 (No. 15), 4-64. Derk Wynand, translator.

9200. _____. The Open Mind. 1 act. Dramatika, 8 (Fall, 1971), n. p.

9201. Wang Fa and Chu Ya-nan. One Big Family. 1 act. Chinese Literature, 2 (1973), 75-82.

9202. Wang Shu-yuan, and others. Azalea Mountain. Chinese Literature, 1 (1974), 3-69.

9203. Wangenheim, Alice. The Cave of Precious Things. 1 act. Journal of Home Economics, 11 (May, 1919), 215-220. K. W. Hinks, adapter.

9204. Wantling, William. Conversation Recorded in an East Village Coffee-House Between François Maria Arouet de Voltaire, Niccolo Machiavelli, and Jean-Jacques Rousseau. 1 act. Dramatika, 7 (1971), 59-68.

9205. Ward, Elizabeth Stuart, 1844-1911. Within the Gates. 3 acts. McClure's, 17 (May, June, July, 1901), 35-43; 142-149; 236-250.

9206. Ward, Muriel. A Family Affair. 1 act. Plays, 11 (November, 1951), 21-34. AND Plays, 25 (January, 1966), 21-34.

9207. _____. It's So Peaceful. 1 act. Plays, 5 (May, 1946), 12-23. AND Plays, 16 (March, 1957), 25-36.

9208. _____. Mr. Lazy Man's Family. 1 act. Plays, 10 (April, 1951), 41-52. AND Plays, 26 (January, 1967), 45-56.

9209. Ward, Theodore. Challenge. 1 act. Mainstream, 15 (February, March, 1962), 40-59; 39-52.

9210. Ward, Winifred Duncan. Babes in the Wood. 1 act. Touchstone, 5 (July, 1919), 281-285.

9211. Warner, Frances Lester. Christmas Eve, the Holly-Goblins. 1 act. St. Nicholas, 59 (December, 1931), 80-83, 114-115, 118.

Warner, Louise H., translator see Filippo, E. de 3019

9212. Warren, Robert Penn, 1905- . All the King's Men. 3 acts. Sewanee Review, 68 (April-June, 1960), 179-239.

9213. _____. All the King's Men. 3 acts. Sipario, 176 (December, 1960), 52-71. Gerardo Guerrieri, translator. In Italian.

9214. Warren, Rose. Rejected. 1 act. Touchstone, 1 (September, 1917), 506-509.

Washburn-Freund, Frank E., translator see Thoma, L. 8821

Washburn-Freund, Mrs. Frank E., translator see Bahr, H. 499

9215. Wasserman, Dale. One Flew Over the Cuckoo's Nest. 2 acts. L'Avant Scène, 536 (March 1, 1974), 7-40. Jacques Sigurd, adapter. In French.

9216. Waterhouse, Keith, 1929- and Willis Hall, 1929- . Billy Liar. 3 acts. Sipario, 19 (February, 1964), 45-63. Franca Cancogni, translator. In Italian.

9217. _____. Billy Liar. 3 acts. Theatre Arts, 46 (May, 1962), 27-56.

9218. _____. Who's How. 2 acts. Plays and Players, 20 (September, 1973), I-XVI, 39-41.

9219. Watkins, Martha Swintz. Nobody Believes in Witches. 1 act. Plays, 25 (October, 1965), 48-54.

9220. Not used.

Watson, Donald, translator see Ionesco, E. 4386, 4388, 4397

_____, translator see Lourson, L. 5059

_____, translator see Obaldia, R. 6726

9221. Watson, Robert, 1925- . The Plot in the Palace. 3 acts, comedy. First Stage, 3 (Spring, 1964), 65-91.

9222. Watts, Frances B. Arthur Bones, the Reading Dog. 1 act. Plays, 26 (November, 1966), 63-69.

9223. _____. The Barefoot Trader. 1 act. Plays, 26 (November, 1966), 79-85.

9224. _____. The Bridge to Killybog Fair. 1 act. Plays, 28 (March, 1969), 45-51.

9225. _____. Christmas Eve in Pine Cone Forest. 1 act. Plays, 26 (December, 1966), 75-79.

9226. _____. The Crimson Feather. 1 act. Plays, 22 (March, 1963), 81-85.

9227. _____. The Fairy Ring. 1 act. Plays, 29 (March, 1970), 80-85.

9228. _____. Finnegan at the Fair. 1 act. Plays, 30 (March, 1971), 39-44.

9229. _____. Grandma and the Pampered Boarder. 1 act. Plays, 29 (October, 1969), 37-45.

9230. _____. The Harvest Moon Supper. 1 act. Plays, 26 (October, 1966), 75-80.

9231. _____. Hurrah for Books. 1 act. Plays, 27 (March, 1968), 41-47.

9232. _____. Jill-in-the-Box. 1 act. Plays, 23 (December, 1963), 75-80.

9233. _____. The King's Valentine Tarts. 1 act. Plays, 30 (February, 1971), 39-46.

9234. _____. The Leprechaun Shoemaker. 1 act. Plays, 25 (March, 1966), 43-48.

9235. _____. The Leprechaun's Pot of Gold. 1 act. Plays, 24 (March, 1965), 43-50. AND Plays, 33 (March, 1974), 70-76.

9236. _____. The Littlest Elf. 1 act. Plays, 30 (December, 1970), 76-77.

9237. _____. The Log in the Bog. 1 act. Plays, 29 (December, 1969), 79-83.

9238. _____. The Magic Touchstone. 1 act. Plays, 32 (March, 1973), 63-68.

9239. ———. The Merry Mix-Up. 1 act. Plays, 26 (May, 1967), 73-77.

9240. ———. Miss Louisa and the Outlaws. 1 act. Plays, 23 (October, 1963), 55-60.

9241. ———. The Queen's Christmas Cake. 2 acts. Plays, 25 (December, 1965), 69-75.

9242. ———. The Runaway Genie. 1 act. Plays, 23 (October, 1963), 43-48.

9243. ———. Santa and the Efficiency Expert. 1 act. Plays, 27 (December, 1967), 59-64.

9244. ———. The Storybook Revolt. 1 act. Plays, 25 (November, 1965), 67-73.

9245. ———. The Tiniest Heart. 1 act. Plays, 20 (February, 1961), 56-62. AND Plays, 32 (February, 1973), 73-79.

9246. ———. The Witch in the Golden Hat. 1 act. Plays, 25 (October, 1965), 68-72.

9247. We Are There--At Christmas. 1 act. Resource, 14 (November, 1972), 13-14.

9248. Weathers, Winston. Vision of the Silver Bell. 1 act. Plays, 5 (December, 1945), 70-75.

9249. Weblowe, Ben. Little Devil Dought; If Ye Don't Give Me Monie I'll Sweepe Ye All Out. 5 acts, tragedy. Dublin Magazine, 2 (December, 1924; January, 1925), 312-321; 376-385.

Webster, Jill R., translator see Pedrolo, M. de 7038

9250. Webster, John, 1580?-1625. The White Devil. 5 acts. L'Avant Scène (OST), 46 (July, 1951), 1-43. J. Fuzier and J. Morel, translators. In French.

9251. ———. The White Devil. Il Dramma (February, 1974), 25-51. J. Rodolfo Wilcock, adapter. In Italian.

9252. Wedde, Alton H. The Congregation's Advent-Christmas Worship. 1 act. Resource, 8 (November, 1966), 11-15.

9253. Wedekind, Frank, 1864-1918. Erdgeist. 4 acts, tragedy. Giebe, 2 (No. 3, 1914), 3-93. Samuel A. Eliot, Jr., translator.

9254. ———. Fruhling's Erwachen. 3 acts, tragedy. Il Dramma, n.s., 16/17 (July 1/15, 1946), 57-80. Giacomo Prampolini, translator. In Italian.

9255. _____. The Heart of a Tenor. 1 act. Smart Set, 40 (June, 1913), 129-141. André Tridon, adapter.

9256. _____. Lulu. 5 acts, tragedy. Il Dramma, 42/43/44 (August 1/15/September 1, 1947), 14-44. Laura Pandolfi, translator. In Italian.

9257. _____. Pandora's Box. 3 acts, tragedy. Glebe, 2 (No. 4, 1914), 5-79. Samuel A. Eliot, Jr., translator.

9258. _____. The Solar Spectrum; Those Who Buy the Gods of Love, an Idyll from Modern Life. 1 act. Tulane Drama Review, 4 (September, 1959), 108-138. Dietrich Faehl and Eric Vaughn, translators.

9259. _____. The Tenor. 1 act. Golden Book, 5 (January, 1927), 65-73. André Tridon, translator.

9260. Wefer, Marion. In Gotham Meadow. 1 act. Plays, 5 (May, 1946), 48-54.

9261. _____. Little Known Louisa. 1 act. Plays, 5 (May, 1946), 75-80.

9262. Weidlich, Albert W. Why the Butterfly Reminds Us of Easter. 1 act. Learning With..., 4 (April, 1976), 31-32.

9263. Weidman, Jerome, 1913- and George Abbott, 1887- . Fiorello! 2 acts. Theatre Arts, 45 (November, 1961), 25-56.

9264. Weiger, Eugene. The Set Up. 3 acts. First Stage, 3 (Spring, 1964), 110-137.

Weill, Kurt, 1900-1950 see Anderson, M. 213

9265. Weill, René, 1868-1952 and André Rivoire. Pardon, Madame. 3 acts, comedy. Petite Illustration, 88 (June 7, 1930), 1-33. In French.

9266. Wein, Sadye B. The Secret Hiding Place. 1 act. Plays, 20 (April, 1961), 53-58.

9267. Weinberg, Albert. Lofty Motives. 1 act, comedy. Poet Lore, 38 (1927), 603-606.

9268. Weinberger, Mildred. Elaine. 1 act. Poet Lore, 34 (Spring, 1923), 72-110.

Weingarten, Joseph A., translator see Bjørnson, B. 974

9269. Weingarten, Romain. Alice, Dans les Jardins du Luxembourg. L'Avant Scène, 461 (December 1, 1970), 7-25. In French.

9270. ———. Comme la Pierre. 1 act. L'Avant Scène, 469/470 (April 1/15, 1971), 15-20. In French.

9271. Weinstein, Sheila. The Waiting Room. 1 act. Dramatika, 3 (March, 1969), 23-29.

9272. Weisenborn, Gunther, 1902- . The Man Without a Face. 2 acts. Modern International Drama, 2 (March, 1969), 7-39. Gabrielle Bingham, translator.

Weiss, Beno, translator see Svevo, I. 8642

9273. Weiss, Peter, 1916- . Come il Signor Mockinpott fu liberato dai suoi tormenti. 1 act. Sipario, 327-328 (August-September, 1973), 68-88. Valerio Valoriani, translator. In Italian.

9274. ———. Holderlin. 2 acts. L'Avant Scène, 550 (October 15, 1974), 3-41. Philippe Ivernel, translator. In French.

9275. ———. Die Verfolgung und Ermordung Jean Paul Marats Dargestellt Durch die Schauspielgruppe des Hospizer zu Charenton unter Anleitung des Herren de Sade. 2 acts. Spectaculum, 9 (1966), 233-304. In German.

Weisstein, Ulrich, translator see Goering, R. 3592

———, translator see Kaiser, G. 4534

9276. Weitz, Elissa Raquel. The Lansky Soliloquies. Modern International Drama, 7 (October, 1973), 9-33.

9277. Welburn, Vivienne C. Johnny So Long. 3 acts. Gambit, 8, 3-67.

Welch, Colin, translator see Nestroy, J. 6467

Welch, Sybil, translator see Nestroy, J. 6467

9278. Weller, Michael. And Now There's Just the Three of Us. 1 act. Plays and Players, 17 (November, 1969), 68-78.

9279. ———. Cancer. 3 acts. Plays and Players, 18 (December, 1970), 65-84.

9280. ———. Fishing. 2 acts. Plays and Players, 22 (July, August, 1975), 43-50; 45-50.

9281. Welles, Orson, 1915- . Columbus Day. 1 act. Il Dramma, n.s., 42/43/44 (August 1/15/September 1, 1947), 113-117. Gigi Cane, translator. In Italian.

9282. Wellman, Rita, 1890- . Dawn. 1 act. Drama, 33 (February, 1919), 89-102.

9283. _____. The Lady with the Mirror. 1 act. Drama, 31 (August, 1918), 299-316.

9284. Wells, Carolyn, -1942. April's Lady. 1 act. Ladies' Home Journal, 33 (April, 1916), 38.

9285. _____. Christmas Gifts of All Nations. 1 act. Ladies' Home Journal, 29 (December, 1912), 86, 91.

9286. _____. The Day Before Christmas. 1 act. Ladies' Home Journal, 21 (December, 1903), 16.

9287. _____. Dolly Dialogue. 1 act. St. Nicholas, 34 (December, 1906), 156-157.

9288. _____. The Glory of the World. 1 act. St. Nicholas, 44 (December, 1916), 151-157.

9289. Wells, Herbert George, 1866-1946. The Inexperienced Ghost. 1 act. Plays, 25 (October, 1965), 87-96.

9290. _____. The Invisible Man. 1 act. Plays, 24 (November, 1964), 83-93. Lewy Olfson, adapter.

Wells, Michael see Brown, N. 1372

Wellworth, George E., translator see Jornet, J. B. I. 4517

_____, translator see Pedrolo, M. de 7035

_____, translator see Quiles, E. 7366

Wellworth, Marcia Cobourn, translator see Bellido, J. M. 733

_____, translator see Castro, J. A. 1658

_____, translator see Diament, M. 2397

_____, translator see Matilla, L. 5655

_____, translator see Quiles, E. 7364

9291. Welsh, Robert Gilbert. Jezebel. 1 act. Forum, 53 (May, 1915), 647-660.

9292. Wendt, Frederick W. Dies Irae. 1 act. Smart Set, 34 (July, 1911), 117-121.

Wensinger, Arthur S., translator see Goll, Y. 3616

9293. Wentworth, Marion Craig, 1872- . War Brides. 1 act. Century, 89 (February, 1915), 527-544.

Wernaer, Robert M., translator see Wildenbruch, E. 9388

9294. Werner, Sally. The Choosing of Easter Rabbit. 1 act. Plays, 14 (April, 1955), 77-80. AND Plays, 31 (April, 1972), 83-86.

9295. _____. The King's Bean Soup. 1 act. Plays, 14 (January, 1955), 71-74.

9296. _____. Mr. Smooch's Trap. 1 act. Plays, 14 (February, 1955), 80-84.

9297. _____. A New Home for Mice. 1 act. Plays, 15 (November, 1955), 65-67.

9298. Wertmuller, Lina. Amore e magia nella cucina di mamma. 1 act. Sipario, 329 (October, 1973), 59-80. In Italian.

9299. _____. 2+2 non fa piu 4. 2 parts. Sipario, 24 (February, 1969), 39-53. In Italian.

9300. Wesker, Arnold, 1932- . Chips with Everything. 2 acts. L'Avant Scène, 494 (May 1, 1972), 11-31. François Sommaripas, translator. In French.

9301. _____. Chips with Everything. 2 acts. Theatre Arts, 47 (October, 1963), 33-57.

9302. _____. The Friends. 2 acts. Plays and Players, 18 (October, 1970), 67-82.

9303. _____. The Old Ones. 2 acts. Plays and Players, 20 (October, 1972), I-XV.

9304. _____. The Old Ones. 2 acts. Sipario, 320 (January, 1973), 63-80. Betty Foa, translator. In Italian.

9305. _____. Les Quatre Saisons. 4 acts. L'Avant Scène, 417 (January 1, 1969), 5-26. Pierre Roudy and Claude Regy, adapters. In French.

9306. _____. Their Very Own and Golden City. 2 acts. Plays and Players, 13 (August, 1966), 31-46, 71.

9307. Wesley, Richard. The Black Terror. Scripts, 1 (December, 1971), 71-101.

9308. Wessel, Oscar, 1899- . Hiroshima. 1 act. Il Dramma, n.s., 129 (March 15, 1951), 49-54. Dante Raiteri, translator. In Italian.

West, Elizabeth Howard, translator see Echegaray y Eizaguirre, J. 2810

9309. Weston, Effie. The Substitute. 1 act. Smart Set, 31 (July, 1910), 115-121.

9310. Westphal, Eric, 1929- . Mozartement votre. 1 act. L'Avant Scène, 570 (September 1, 1975), 39-51. In French.

9311. _____. Toi et Tes Nuages. 2 acts. Dramatic comedy. L'Avant Scène, 468 (March 15, 1971), 7-27. In French.

9312. Wexley, John, 1902- . Comes the Dreamer. 2 acts. First Stage, 2 (Winter, 1962-1963), 7-36.

9313. _____. Keystone (The Last Mile). 3 acts. Il Dramma, 112 (April 15, 1931), 4-36. Goffredo Pautassi, translator. In Italian.

Weysz, Hans, translator see Schnitzler, A. 8064

9314. Wharton, Edith, 1862-1937. Pomegranate Seed. 1 act. Scribner's, 51 (March, 1912), 284-291.

9315. Wheatcroft, John. Reprise. 1 act. Poet Lore, 63 (Spring, 1968), 60-81.

9316. _____. We Are the History of the U.S. 1 act. Drama and Theatre, 12 (Spring, 1975), 142.

9317. Wheeler, Hugh, 1916- . Big Fish, Little Fish. 3 acts. Theatre Arts, 46 (September, 1962), 25-56.

9318. Wheetley, Kim Alan. The Barefoot Boy. 1 act. Dramatics, 41 (January, 1970), 8-10, 28-34.

9319. Whipkey, Stella Dunaway. Door Mats. 1 act. Poet Lore, 40 (1929), 92-108.

9320. _____. Very Crude Oil. 1 act, comedy. Drama, 20 (May, 1930), 237-239.

9321. White, Arthur Corning. Two Black Sheep; a Satiric Dialogue. 1 act. Poet Lore, 35 (1924), 464-470.

9322. White, Clematis. A Convert. 1 act. Smart Set, 35 (November, 1911), 103-106.

White, Clemon see Smith, B. 8331

9323. White, Edgar. Dija. 1 act. Scripts, 1 (October, 1972), 15-17.

9324. ———. The Life and Times of J. Walter Sminthens. 2 acts. Scripts, 1 (April, 1972), 4-27.

9325. ———. The Rastifarian. 1 act. Scripts, 1 (October, 1972), 13-14.

White, Florence Donnell, translator see Cervantes Saavedra, M. de 1696

——— see also Fannstock, E. 2910

White, George, translator and adapter see Gressieker, H. 3738

9326. Whitehand, Robert. Derricks on a Hill. 1 act. American Prefaces, 1 (October, 1935), 12-16.

9327. Whitehouse, Josephine Henry. Daily Bread. 1 act. Poet Lore, 40 (1929), 129-141.

9328. Whiting, Eleanor Custis. Ashes. 1 act. Poet Lore, 33 (Autumn, 1922), 423-438.

9329. ———. Common Ground. 1 act. Poet Lore, 32 (1921), 140-148.

9330. Whiting, John. The Devils. 3 acts. Sipario, 17 (October, 1962), 30-51. C. D. Marisi, translator. In Italian.

9331. ———. No Why. 1 act. London Magazine, n.s., 1 (May, 1961), 52-62.

9332. ———. Saint's Day. 3 acts. L'Avant Scène, 180 (September 1, 1958), 7-32. Cecil Robson and R.-J. Chauffard, adapters. In French.

9333. Whitman, Constance. School for Jesters. 1 act. Plays, 23 (May, 1964), 45-52.

9334. ———. Straight from the Heart. 1 act. Plays, 23 (February, 1964), 35-43.

9335. Whitney, J. D. Mr. S. Claus's Predicament. 1 act. St. Nicholas, 43 (December, 1915), 164-167.

9336. Whiton, Harry E. The Very Nearest Room. 1 act. One-Act Play Magazine, 3 (September-October, 1940), 456-468.

9337. Whittaker, Helene. The Genie of the Bottle. 1 act. Plays, 25 (November, 1965), 79-84.

9338. _____. A Gift from Johnny Appleseed. 1 act. Plays, 25 (February, 1966), 71-77.

9339. _____. Mother Makes a Choice. 1 act. Plays, 25 (May, 1966), 73-78.

Whitworth, Geoffrey see Henderson, K. 4055

9340. Whitworth, Virginia Payne. The King and the Bee. 1 act. Plays, 18 (January, 1959), 73-76.

9341. _____. The Magic Cloak. 1 act. Plays, 27 (April, 1968), 37-43.

9342. _____. Master of All Masters. 1 act. Plays, 27 (May, 1968), 74-76.

9343. _____. The Mechanical Maid. 1 act. Plays, 20 (May, 1961), 24-32.

9344. Widdemer, Margaret, 1897- . The Baby Liked "Greensleeves." 1 act. Plays, 3 (December, 1943), 35-38.

9345. _____. Judith's Father. 1 act. Plays, 3 (April, 1944), 24-33.

9346. Wiegand, Johannes and Wilhelm Scharrelmann. The Wages of War. 3 acts. Poet Lore, 19 (Summer, 1908), 129-164. Amelia von Ende, translator.

9347. Wiggin, Kate Douglas, 1856-1923. The Birds' Christmas Carol. 1 act. Plays, 17 (December, 1957), 87-94. Lewy Olfson, adapter.

9348. _____. The Birds' Christmas Carol. 4 acts. Plays, 25 (December, 1965), 87-95. AND Plays, 32 (December, 1972), 71-80. Helen Louise Miller, adapter.

9349. Wight, Lawrence. The Handwriting on the Wall. 1 act. Plays, 11 (February, 1952), 59-69.

9350. Wilbrandt, Adolf von, 1837-1911. The Master of Palmyra. 5 acts. Poet Lore, 13 (1901), 161-248. Harriatt S. Olive, translator.

9351. Wilbur, Elene. The Table Set for Himself. 1 act. Scholastic, 23 (December 16, 1933), 9-11, 28.

9352. Wilcock, Rodolfo J. L'agonia di Luisa con leavventure di Gilgamesh alla televisione. 3 acts. Sipario, 253 (May, 1967), 40-49. In Italian.

9353. _____. Il Brasile. 1 act. Sipario, 175 (November, 1960), 53-57. In Italian.

9354. _____. La Caduta di un impero. 1 act. Il Dramma, (October, 1974), 43-51. In Italian.

9355. _____. Sei atti unici senza parole. Sipario, 259 (November, 1967), 60-63. In Italian.

_____, adapter see Webster, J. 9251

9356. Wilcox, Constance Grenelle. Told in a Chinese Garden. 1 act. Drama, 34 (May, 1919), 116-150.

9357. Wilde, Charles F. Junior Prom. 1 act. Plays, 12 (January, 1953), 70-77.

9358. _____. Susan Goes Hollywood. 1 act. Plays, 5 (March, 1946), 73-83.

9359. Wilde, Oscar, 1856-1900. The Birthday of the Infanta. 1 act. Plays, 24 (April, 1965), 85-95. Paul T. Nolan, adapter.

9360. _____. The Canterville Ghost. 1 act. Plays, 23 (March, 1964), 85-94. Walter Hackett, adapter.

9361. _____. The Critic as Artist. 1 act. Plays and Players, 19 (October, 1971), 64-72. Charles Marowitz, adapter.

9362. _____. A Florentine Tragedy. 1 act. L'Avant Scène, 138, 41-47. Henri Pignet, adapter. In French.

9363. _____. For Love of the King, a Burmese Masque. 3 acts. Century, 103 (December, 1921), 225-242.

9364. _____. The Happy Prince. 1 act. Plays, 14 (February, 1955), 85-93. AND Plays, 32 (April, 1973), 43-51. Edward Golden, adapter.

9365. _____. The Happy Prince. 1 act. Plays, 19 (March, 1960), 51-58. Virginia Bartholome, adapter.

9366. _____. The Happy Prince. 1 act. Poet Lore, 27 (Vacation, 1916), 406-410. Lou Wall Moore and Margaret F. Allen, adapters.

9367. _____. An Ideal Husband. 4 acts. Il Dramma, 408/409 (August 15/September 1, 1943), 57-78. Riccardo Aragno, translator. In Italian.

9368. _____. The Importance of Being Earnest. 3 acts, comedy. L'Avant Scène, 101, 1-25. Jean Anouilh and Claude Vincent, adapters. In French.

Wilde

9369. ———. The Importance of Being Earnest. 3 acts, comedy. Il Dramma, 337 (September 1, 1940), 6-22. In Italian.

9370. ———. The Importance of Being Earnest. 1 act. Plays, 14 (October, 1954), 87-95. AND Plays, 21 (January, 1962), 85-95. AND Plays, 28 (April, 1969), 87-95. AND Plays, 36 (October, 1976), 85-95. Lewy Olfson, adapter.

9371. ———. Lady Windermere's Fan. 4 acts. L'Avant Scène, 127, 1-23. Michelle Lahaye, adapter. In French.

9372. ———. Salome. 1 act, tragedy. Il Dramma, 326 (March 15, 1940), 31-41. In Italian.

9373. ———. Salome. 1 act, tragedy. Golden Book, 1 (February, 1925), 207-220.

7374. ———. Salome. 1 act, tragedy. Poet Lore, 18 (Summer, 1907), 199-223.

9375. ———. A Woman of No Importance. 3 acts, comedy. Il Dramma, 326 (March 15, 1940), 6-22. Tullio Covaz, translator. In Italian.

9376. Wilde, Percival, 1887-1953. According to Darwin. 1 act. Forum, 54 (October, 1915), 488-504.

9377. ———. Blood of the Martyrs. 1 act. One-Act Play Magazine, 1 (September, 1937), 387-407.

9378. ———. The Culprit. 1 act. Smart Set, 39 (February, 1913), 129-142.

9379. ———. Dawn. 1 act. Smart Set, 44 (November, 1914), 115-123.

9380. ———. Ordeal by Battle. 1 act. One-Act Play Magazine, 2 (June-July, 1938), 105-124.

9381. ———. A Question of Morality. 1 act, comedy. Century, 90 (August, 1915), 609-617.

9382. ———. Salt for Savor. 1 act, comedy. Esquire, 40 (December, 1953), 158-160, 162, 164-166.

9383. ———. Saved! A Grand Guignol Thriller. 1 act. Smart Set, 46 (July, 1915), 397-409.

9384. ———. The Short Cut. 1 act. Scholastic, 20 (April 16, 1932), 9-10, 12.

9385. ———. What Never Dies. 1 act. Drama, 21 (January, 1931), 21-24, 26.

9386. ———. A Wonderful Woman. 1 act. Smart Set, 67 (April, 1922), 79-91.

———, adapter see Timmory, G. 8866, 8867

9387. Wildenbruch, Ernst von, 1845-1909. Halold. 5 acts. Poet Lore, 3 (1891), 393-480. Otto Heller, translator. Hugh A. Clarke, adapter.

9388. ———. King Henry. 4 acts. Drama, 17 (February, 1915), 12-145. Robert M. Wernaer, translator.

9389. Wilder, Thornton Niven, 1897-1975. The Angel on the Ship. 1 act. Harper's, 157 (October, 1928), 564-565.

9390. ———. Childhood. 1 act. Atlantic, 206 (November, 1960), 78-84.

9391. ———. The Drunken Sisters. 1 act. Atlantic, 200 (November, 1957), 92-95.

9392. ———. 4 Plays in 3 Minutes: The Penny That Beauty Spent; Childe Roland to the Dark Tower Came; Mozart and the Grey Steward; The Angel That Troubled the Waters. 1 act each. Sipario, 1 (August-September, 1946), 59-64. Lorenza Setti, translator. In Italian.

9393. ———. The Happy Journey to Trenton and Camden. 1 act. Il Dramma, 327 (April 1, 1940), 37-42. Gerardo Guerrieri, translator. In Italian.

9394. ———. The Happy Journey to Trenton and Camden. 1 act. Scholastic, 33 (September 17, 1938), 17E-20E.

9395. ———. The Long Christmas Dinner. 1 act, comedy. Sipario, 10 (December, 1955), 64-68. Enrico Fulchignoni, translator. In Italian.

9396. ———. Love and How to Cure It. 1 act. Il Dramma, n.s., 4 (January 1, 1946), 53-56. Ricardo Aragno, translator. In Italian.

9397. ———. The Matchmaker. 4 acts, comedy. Theatre Arts, 42 (April, 1958), 32-58.

9398. ———. Mozart and the Gray Steward. 1 act. Harper's, 157 (October, 1928), 565-567.

9399. ———. Mozart and the Gray Steward. 1 act. Scholastic, 19 (October 3, 1931), 14-15.

9400. ———. Queens of France. 1 act. Il Dramma, n.s., 1 (November 15, 1945), 37-41. Riccardo Aragno and Anna Canitano, translators. In Italian.

9401. _____. Queens of France. 1 act. Yale Review, 21 (September, 1931), 72-85.

9402. _____. Such Things Only Happen in Books. 1 act, comedy. Golden Book, 15 (April, 1932), 369-373.

9403. Wildman, Eugene. Turns. 1 act. Dramatika, 3 (March, 1969), 31-37.

9404. _____. Viet Hut. 1 act. Dramatika, 2 (October, 1968), 38-39.

Wilga, Helen, translator see Mayakovsky, V. 5702

9405. Wilkes, Elizabeth. A Matter of Business. 1 act. Plays, 9 (April, 1950), 37-43.

Willemetz, Albert see Marchand, L. 5538

9406. _____ and Fabien Sollar. Phi-Phi. 3 acts. L'Avant Scène (OST), 8 (July, 1949), 1-34. In French.

9407. Willenberg, C. H. What Dreams May Come. 1 act. Plays, 35 (November, 1975), 14-24.

9408. Williams, Albert N. Festival. 1 act. One-Act Play Magazine, 2 (December, 1938), 560-583.

9409. Williams, Blanche Graham. The Land of Make-Believe. 1 act. Wilson Library Bulletin, 9 (October, 1934), 78.

Williams, Eleanor Winslow see Arnold, K. 353

9410. Williams, Emlyn, 1905- . The Corn Is Green. 3 acts. Il Dramma, n. s., 167 (October 15, 1952), 5-41. Sergio Cenalino, translator. In Italian.

9411. _____. Ritratto d'attore. 3 acts. Il Dramma, n. s., 65 (July 15, 1948), 7-41. In Italian.

9412. _____. Some One Waiting. 3 acts. L'Avant Scène, 121, 3-37. André Roussin, adapter. In French.

9413. Williams, George Llyonel. Snipe Hunt. 1 act. First Stage, 2 (Summer, 1963), 194-201.

9414. Williams, Gweneira M. A Kettle of Brains. 1 act. Plays, 3 (November, 1943), 69-72. AND Plays, 24 (April, 1965), 77-80.

Williams, Heathcote. AC/DC. Gambit, 18/19, 5-137.

9415. Williams, Jesse Lynch, 1807-1886. Why Marry? 3 acts, comedy. Golden Book, 3 (June, 1926), 789-826.

Williams, Miller, 1930- , translator see Ruiz, R. 7793

9416. Williams, Oscar, 1900-1964 and Jack Brady. The King Who Scoffed. 1 act, tragedy. Poet Lore, 34 (Spring, 1923), 139-144.

9417. Williams, R. E. The Mad Dutchman's Magic Eye. 1 act. Plays, 5 (April, 1946), 19-32.

9418. Williams, Tennessee, 1914- . Auto-da-Fé. 1 act, tragedy. Il Dramma, n.s., 63 (June 15, 1948), 61-66. Mino Roli, translator. In Italian.

9419. _____. Battle of Angels. 3 acts. Pharos, 1/2 (Spring, 1945), 3-109.

9420. _____. Camino Real. 3 acts. Theatre Arts, 38 (August, 1954), 36-65.

9421. _____. Cat on a Hot Tin Roof. 3 acts. Sipario, 13 (April, 1958), 41-58. Gerardo Guerrieri, translator. In Italian.

9422. _____. Cat on a Hot Tin Roof. 3 acts. Theatre Arts, 41 (June, 1957), 33-71.

9423. _____. The Demolition Downtown. 1 act. Esquire, 75 (June, 1971), 124-127, 152.

9424. _____. Dos Ranchos, or, The Purification. 3 parts. New Directions, 8 (1944), 230-256.

9425. _____. The Gnadiges Fraulein. 1 act. Esquire, 64 (August, 1965), 102, 130-134.

9426. _____. Hello from Bertha. 1 act. Il Dramma, n.s., 77 (January 15, 1949), 37-41. Gigi Cane, translator. In Italian.

9427. _____. I Can't Imagine Tomorrow. 1 act. Esquire, 65 (March, 1966), 76-79.

9428. _____. I Rise in Flame, Cried the Phoenix. 1 act. New World Writing, 1 (1952), 46-67.

9429. _____. I Rise in Flame, Cried the Phoenix. 1 act. Sipario, 12 (October, 1957), 53-56. Luigi Candoni, translator. In Italian.

9430. _____. The Lady of Larkspur Lotion. 1 act. Il Dramma, n.s., 65 (July 15, 1948), 55-57. Mino Roli, translator. In Italian.

9431. _____. Lord Byron's Love Letter. 1 act. Il Dramma, n.s., 85 (May 15, 1949), 53-54. Gigi Cane, translator. In Italian.

9432. _____. The Mutilated. 1 act. Esquire, 64 (August, 1965), 96-101.

9433. _____. The Night of the Iguana. 3 acts. Esquire, 57 (February, 1962), 47-62, 115-116, 118, 120, 123-124, 126-127, 130.

9434. _____. Orpheus Descending. 2 acts. L'Avant Scène, 200 (July 1, 1959), 8-33. Raymond Rouleau, adapter. In French.

9435. _____. Orpheus Descending. 3 acts. Sipario, 16 (June, 1961), 39-62. Gerardo Guerrieri, translator. In Italian.

9436. _____. Orpheus Descending. 3 acts. Theatre Arts, 42 (September, 1958), 26-55.

9437. _____. A Perfect Analysis Given by a Parrot. 1 act. Esquire, 50 (October, 1958), 131-134. AND Esquire, 80 (October, 1973), 288-290, 486, 488.

9438. _____. Period of Adjustment. 3 acts. Esquire, 54 (December, 1960), 210, 214-215, 218, 220, 223-224, 228, 230, 232, 234, 236, 238, 240, 242-246, 248-250, 254, 256, 258-261, 263-264, 266-276.

9439. _____. The Rose Tattoo. 3 acts. Theatre Arts, 39 (May, 1955), 35-65.

9440. _____. Small Craft Warnings. 2 acts. Plays and Players, 20 (April, 1973), I-XIII.

9441. _____. A Streetcar Named Desire. 3 acts. Sipario, 6 (December, 1951), 49-72. Gerardo Guerrieri, translator. In Italian.

9442. _____. Sweet Bird of Youth. 3 acts. Esquire, 51 (April, 1959), 114-130, 132-134, 136, 138, 140, 142-155.

9443. _____. This Property Is Condemned. 1 act. Il Dramma, n.s., 161 (July 15, 1952), 23-26. Sergio Cenalino, translator. In Italian.

9444. _____. 27 Wagons Full of Cotton. 1 act. Il Dramma, n.s., 67/68/69 (August 1/September 1/15, 1948), 79-88. Gigi Cane, translator. In Italian.

9445. Williams, William Carlos, 1883-1963. The Comic Life of Elia Brobitza. 1 act. Others, 5 (April/May, 1919), 1-16.

9446. _____. Many Loves. 3 acts. Theatre Arts, 46 (February, 1962), 25-56.

9447. _____. Trial Horse No. 1 (Many Loves); An Entertainment in Three Acts and Six Scenes. New Directions, 7 (1942), 233-305.

9448. Williamson, Bruce. The Fog Around Us. 1 act. First Person, 2 (Winter, 1961), 74-81.

9449. Willment, Frank. The Missing Missionary. 1 act. Plays, 34 (October, 1974), 15-25.

9450. _____. Swifty. 1 act. Plays, 31 (October, 1971), 1-15.

9451. _____. The Whites of Their Eyes. 1 act. Plays, 26 (February, 1967), 89-95.

9452. _____. Who's Got the Button? 1 act. Plays, 33 (April, 1974), 17-27.

9453. Willoughby, Edwin Eliot. The Last of Mr. Weekney. 1 act. Wilson Library Bulletin, 9 (May, 1935), 485-488.

9454. Willson, Meredith, 1902- and Richard Morris. The Unsinkable Molly Brown. 2 acts. Theatre Arts, 47 (February, 1963), 25-56.

9455. Wilner, Ortha. Cinerella. 2 acts. Classical Journal, 38 (November, 1942), 111-114. In Latin.

9456. Wilson, Angus, 1913- . Skeletons and Assegais. Family Reminiscences. 1 act. Transatlantic Review (London), 9 (Spring, 1962), 19-43.

9457. Wilson, Bernice. Earth Is for All. 1 act. Plays, 33 (January, 1973), 63-67.

9458. Wilson, Carolyn. What Can I Do? 1 act. St. Nicholas, 45 (May, 1918), 599-603.

9459. Wilson, Dorothy Clarke. No Room in the Hotel. 1 act. Scholastic, 39 (December 15-20, 1941), 17-19, 24.

9460. Wilson, Edmund, 1895-1972. Karl Marx: A Prolet-Play. 1 act. Partisan Review, 5 (June, 1938), 36-40.

9461. Wilson, Frank H. Sugar Cain. 1 act. Opportunity, 4 (June, 1926), 181-184, 201-203.

9462. Wilson, J. Raines. The Trial of a Heart. 1 act. Smart Set, 36 (February, 1912), 141-142.

9463. Wilson, Leisa Graeme. The Lady Loses Her Hoop--A Sad Tale in Sadder Verse. 1 act. Drama, 12 (March, 1922), 279-280.

9464. _____. Like Father Like Son; A Bit of Domesticity. 1 act. Drama, 13 (February, 1923), 188-191.

9465. Wilson, Marie Lyon. The First Flowers. 1 act. Plays, 3 (March, 1944), 50-52.

9466. Wilson, Snoo. The Beast. 2 acts. Plays and Players, 22 (December, 1974-January, 1975), 39-50; 39-50.

9467. _____. The Everest Hotel. 1 act. Plays and Players, 23 (March, 1976), 41-50.

9468. _____. Reason. 2 parts. Gambit, 8 (No. 29, 1976), 77-89.

9469. _____. Vampire. 3 acts. Plays and Players, 20 (July, 1973), V-XIV.

_____ see also Brenton, H. 1320

9470. Wilson, W. Lawler. The Hundred Days. 1 act. Fortnightly, 86 (November, 1906), 827-832.

9471. Wimsatt, Genevieve. Sheep Skin Po. 1 act. Plays, 12 (January, 1953), 51-58.

9472. Wincelberg, Shimon, 1924- . Kataki. 3 acts. Gambit, 5, 3-40.

9473. _____. The Windows of Heaven. 3 acts. Gambit, 3, 19-84.

9474. Windeler, B. Cyril. Daniel. 3 acts. Poet Lore, 45 (1939), 49-111.

9475. Winter, Jack, 1936- . The Wrecked Blackship. 1 act. Performing Arts in Canada, 7 (No. 2, 1970), 23-28.

9476. Winter, Keith. The Shining Hour. 3 acts. Petite Illustration, 196 (March 27, 1937), 1-30. Constance Coline, adapter. In French.

9477. Winter, Mary. The Ruling Class. 1 act, comedy. Drama, 15 (April, 1925), 150-152.

9478. Winther, Barbara. African Trio: Three Folk Tales from Africa. I. The Fierce Creature. II. When the Hare Brought the Sun. III. The Princess Who Was Hidden from the World. 1 act each. Plays, 29 (October, 1969), 46-52.

9479. ———. Fire Demon and South Wind. 1 act. Plays, 35 (October, 1975), 47-52.

9480. ———. A Gift for Pachacuti Inca. 1 act. Plays, 32 (December, 1972), 37-43.

9481. ———. The Great Samurai Sword. 1 act. Plays, 29 (January, 1970), 52-58.

9482. ———. The Greatest Treasure. 1 act. Plays, 31 (December, 1971), 59-66.

9483. ———. Japanese Trio. Plays, 36 (December, 1976), 43-49.

9484. ———. Listen to the Hodja. 1 act. Plays, 30 (January, 1971), 33-40.

9485. ———. Little Mouse-Deer. 1 act. Plays, 35 (December, 1975), 45-51.

9486. ———. Old Baba Yaga. 1 act. Plays, 29 (May, 1970), 49-55.

9487. ———. Shine On, Pecos Bill. 1 act. Plays, 30 (May, 1971), 43-50.

9488. ———. The Trolls of Glittertop Mountain. 1 act. Plays, 31 (May, 1972), 49-55.

9489. ———. Two Dilemma Tales. 1 act. Plays, 35 (February, 1976), 35-40.

9490. ———. The Villain and the Toy Shop. 1 act. Plays, 29 (December, 1969), 57-64.

9491. ———. White Elephant. 1 act. Plays, 35 (April, 1976), 45-51.

9492. ———, adapter. Ah Wing Fu and the Golden Dragon. 1 act. Plays, 34 (January, 1975), 79-84.

9493. ———, adapter. Anansi, the African Spider: Three Folk Tales from West Africa. Plays, 34 (April, 1975), 51-56.

9494. ———, adapter. The Boy Called Aesop: Three Greek Fables. Plays, 32 (April, 1973), 59-65.

9495. ———, adapter. Dinnetah. A Navaho Creation Myth. 1 act. Plays, 28 (May, 1969), 41-49.

9496. ———, adapter. Follow the River Lai. An Asian Legend. 1 act. Plays, 29 (February, 1970), 53-60.

9497. _____, adapter. The Maharajah Is Bored. 1 act. Plays, 31 (April, 1972), 71-78.

9498. _____, adapter. The Monkey Without a Tail. 1 act. Plays, 36 (October, 1976), 47-51.

9499. _____, adapter. Nikluk and the Loon. 1 act. Plays, 34 (February, 1975), 47-53.

9500. _____, adapter. Prince Rama. 1 act. Plays, 33 (February, 1974), 73-78.

9501. _____, adapter. The Sleeping Mountains. 1 act. Plays, 30 (April, 1971), 43-50.

9502. _____, adapter. The Terrible Gypsy Mala. A Gypsy Folk Tale. 1 act. Plays, 29 (April, 1970), 65-70.

9503. _____, adapter. Tyll's Clever Pranks. 1 act. Plays, 34 (December, 1974), 52-58.

9504. _____, adapter. Under the Mango Tree. 1 act. Plays, 32 (February, 1973), 55-61.

_____, adapter see Andersen, H. C. 196

Wirt, Anne Grace, translator see Musset, A. de 6419

9505. Wise, Conrad. La Sérénissime. 1 act. L'Avant Scène, 115, 27-32. In French.

9506. Wishengrad, Morton. The Rope Dancers. 3 acts. Theatre Arts, 44 (January, 1960), 33-64.

9507. Wissant, Georges de. Jours. 3 acts. L'Avant Scène, (ROST), 71 (December, 1952), 1-30. In French.

9508. _____. Pour Etre Joue. 1 act. L'Avant Scène, 110, 37-40. In French.

9509. Witherspoon, Frances. The Other Room. 1 act. Poet Lore, 38 (1927), 269-290.

9510. Witherspoon, Kathleen. Jute. 3 acts. Southwest Review, 16 (April, 1931), 384-436.

9511. Witkiewicz, Stanislaw Ignacy, 1885-1939. The Anonymous Work. 4 acts. Drama and Theatre, 12 (Fall, 1934), 23-48. Daniel Gerould and Eleanor Gerould, translators.

9512. _____. Commedia ripugnante di una madre. 3 acts. Sipario, 25 (January, 1970), 44-56. Dacia Maraini, translator. In Italian.

9513. _____. The Crazy Locomotive. 2 acts. First Stage, 6 (Winter, 1967-1968), 206-215. C. S. Durer and Daniel C. Gerould, translators.

9514. _____. In una casa di campagna. 3 acts. Il Dramma, 46, no. 10 (October, 1970), 44-54. Elena Barbaro and Lamberto Trezzini, translators. In Italian.

9515. _____. The Madman and the Nun, or There Is Nothing Bad Which Could Not Turn to Something Worse. 3 acts. First Stage, 4 (Winter, 1965-1966), 212-221. C. S. Durer and Daniel C. Gerould, translators.

9516. _____. La metafisica di un vitello a due teste. 3 acts. Sipario, 27 (May, 1972), 67-80. Irene Natanson and Lamberto Trezzini, translators. In Italian.

9517. _____. The New Deliverance. 1 act. New Directions, 30 (1975), 133-151. Daniel Gerould and Jadwiga Kosicka, translators.

9518. _____. La nuova liberazione. 1 act. Sipario, 24 (September, 1969), 55-58. In Italian.

9519. _____. I pragmatisti. 3 acts. Sipario, 24 (September, 1969), 59-64. In Italian.

9520. _____. The Pragmatists. 3 acts. Drama and Theatre, 10 (Fall, 1971), 37-45. Daniel Gerould, translator.

9521. _____. The Water Hen. 3 acts, tragedy. First Stage, 6 (Summer, 1967), 86-102. C. S. Durer and Daniel C. Gerould, translators.

9522. Wittlinger, Karl, 1922- . Do You Know the Milky Way? 2 acts. Theatre Arts, 47 (June, 1963), 37-60.

9523. Woeppel, Louise B. W. Christmas in Our Town. 1 act. Resource, 1 (November, 1959), 17-19.

9524. Wolas, Eva. Look Back on Today! 1 act, comedy. One-Act Play Magazine, 3 (May-June, 1940), 297-314. AND One-Act Play Magazine, 4 (November-December, 1941), 469-486.

9525. _____. Soap Opera. 1 act. Dramatics, 46 (May, 1975), 12-17.

9526. Wolf, Friedrich, 1888-1953. Die "Newa" Kommt! 1 act. Das Wort, 5 (November, 1937), 110-117. In German.

9527. Wolf, Friedrich. Professor Mamlock. 1 act. One-Act Play Magazine, 2 (November, 1938), 489-495.

Wolfe, Archibald John, translator see Gorky, M. 3645

9528. Wolfe, Thomas, 1900-1938. Welcome to Our City. 1 act. Esquire, 48 (October, 1957), 58-82.

9529. Wolff. L'allodola. 1 act. Il Dramma, 61 (March 1, 1929), 35-45. In Italian.

9530. Wolff, Egon. The Invaders. 2 acts. Modern International Drama, 8 (Spring, 1975), 47-79. Margaret S. Peden, translator.

9531. Wolff, Oscar M. Where But in America. 1 act. Smart Set, 54 (March, 1918), 79-87.

9532. Wolff, Pierre. La scuola degli amanti. 3 acts. Il Dramma, 110 (March 15, 1931), 4-35. In Italian.

9533. _____. Unhoodwinkable. 1 act, comedy. Smart Set, 58 (March, 1919), 85-93. Barrett H. Clark, translator.

9534. _____. Il velo strappato. 2 acts. Il Dramma, 82 (January 15, 1930), 33-45. In Italian.

9535. Wolfs, John. Der Dogmatiker und der Voraussetzungslose. Dialogue. Der Sturm, 1 (No. 52, February 25, 1911), 31. In German.

9536. Wolfys, Noel. The Princess and the Dragon. 1 act. Plays, 25 (March, 1966), 81-84.

9537. Wolinski. Le Roi des Cons. 2 parts. L'Avant Scène, 582 (March 1, 1976), 3-30. In French.

9538. Wolman, Diana. An Imaginary Trial of George Washington. 1 act. Plays, 20 (February, 1961), 26-38. AND Plays, 33 (February, 1974), 23-35.

9539. Woman's Luncheon, A. 1 act. Atlantic, 76 (August, 1895), 194-205.

9540. Wong Ou-hung, 1910- and Ah Chia, adapters. The Red Lantern, a Peking Opera. 10 scenes. Chinese Literature, 5 (1965), 3-48. AND revised edition, Chinese Literature, 8 (1970), 8-52. Yang Hsien-yi and Gladys Yang, translators.

9541. Woock, Clare C. Madame USA. 1 act. Works, 3 (Summer/Fall, 1971), 56-84.

9542. Wood, Charles, 1933- . Dingo. 2 acts. Plays and Players, 14 (July, 1967), 23-38.

9543. Woodbridge, Elizabeth. The Christmas Conspiracy. 2 acts. St. Nicholas, 39 (December, 1911), 163-169.

9544. Woodcock, George. Maskerman. 1 act. Prism International, 2 (Winter, 1961), 4-40.

9545. Woodford, Bruce P. The Prisoner. 1 act. Poet Lore, 57 (Summer, 1953), 195-217.

9546. Woodmeald, J. E. At the Sign of the Postboy's Horn. 2 acts. Dome, n.s., 1 (October-December, 1898), 45-62.

9547. _____. Cousin Frederick, a Conventional Comedy. 1 act. Dome, 2 (1897), 51-72.

9548. _____. The Lady Amaranth, a Conventional Farce. 1 act. Dome, 4 (1898), 43-57.

9549. _____. Near Nature's Heart, a Pastoral Play. 2 acts. Dome, 1 (1897), 37-60.

9550. _____. Snowed Up, a Conventional Comedy. 2 acts. Dome, n.s., 1 (October-December, 1898), 252-271.

9551. Woodruff, Robert W. Death: A Discussion. 1 act. Smart Set, 44 (December, 1914), 213-216.

9552. Woolf, Douglas, 1922- . The Love Letter. New Directions, 19 (1966), 232-243.

9553. Woolf, Edgar Allan. A Bit of the World. 1 act. Smart Set, 32 (December, 1910), 121-126.

9554. Woolsey, Sarah Chauncey, 1835-1905. Toinette and the Elves. 1 act. Plays, 23 (December, 1963), 59-68. Adele Thane, adapter.

9555. Worm Turns, The. 1 act. Plays, 3 (January, 1944), 55-62.

9556. Worms, Jeannine. Une Biche. 1 act, comedy. L'Avant Scène, 419 (February 1, 1969), 29. In French.

9557. _____. Un Chat Est un Chat. 1 act. L'Avant Scène, 492 (April 1, 1972), 25-36. In French.

9558. _____. Une Femme Admirable. 1 act. L'Avant Scène, 414 (December 1, 1968), 39. In French.

9559. _____. Un Fils a Maman. 1 act, comedy. L'Avant Scène, 416 (December 15, 1968), 51. In French.

9560. _____. Le Gouter. 1 act. L'Avant Scène, 492 (April 1, 1972), 9-14. In French.

9561. _____. Un Gros Gateau. 1 act. L'Avant Scène, 440 (January 1, 1970), 33-39. In French.

9562. _____. Le Journal. 1 act. L'Avant Scène, 414 (December 1, 1968), 41. In French.

9563. _____. Mougnou-Mougnou, ou Un Coeur de Mère. 1 act. L'Avant Scène, 480 (October 1, 1971), 41-49. In French.

9564. _____. Tout a L'Heure. 1 act, farce. L'Avant Scène, 492 (April 1, 1972), 15-23. In French.

9565. _____. Tout a L'Heure. 1 act, farce. Il Dramma, 48 (May, 1972), 37-46. Paola Angioletti, translator. In Italian.

_____, adapter see Valle Inclan, R. M. del 9001

9566. Wormser, Florine R. The Portrait. 1 act. Smart Set, 28 (June, 1909), 76-83.

9567. Wortis, Avi. A Little Rebellion. 1 act. Mainstream, 13 (April, 1960), 39-51.

9568. Woster, Alice. All Houses Are Haunted. 1 act. Plays, 9 (December, 1949), 71-74.

9569. _____. Hubbub on the Bookshelf. 1 act. Plays, 3 (November, 1943), 42-53. AND Plays, 28 (November, 1968), 61-72.

9570. _____. Panic in a Desk Drawer. A Historical Fantasy. 1 act. Plays, 29 (October, 1969), 67-73.

Woticky, Edward, translator see Schnitzler, A. 8077

9571. Wouk, Herman, 1915- . The Cain Mutiny. 3 acts. L'Avant Scène, 165, 4-28. José-André Lacour, translator. In French.

9572. Wraiths of Destiny. 1 act. Bookman [New York], 43 (June, 1916), 373-377.

9573. Wright, Clifford. Almost an Elopement. 1 act. Transatlantic Review (London), 5 (December, 1960), 142-155.

9574. Wright, Doris. The Twelve Days of Christmas. 1 act. Plays, 11 (December, 1951), 62-65. AND Plays, 17 (December, 1957), 59-62. AND Plays, 31 (December, 1971), 77-80.

Wright, Jules Noel, translator see Caragiale, I. L. 1593

9575. Wright, Richard, 1908-1960 and Paul Eliot Green, 1894- . Native Son. Sipario, 3 (January-February, 1948), 17-44. Giuliano Tomei, translator. In Italian.

Wright, Willard Huntington, 1888-1939, translator see Brieux, E. 1325

9576. Wuchter, Shirley D. The Baptism of Jesus. 1 act. Learning With..., 4 (January, 1976), 14-15.

9577. Wunderlich, Lawrence. 9 to 5 to 0, a Neofarce in Three Doses. Chelsea, 15 (June, 1964), 89-104.

9578. _____. Prometheus Rebound. 1 act. First Stage, 3 (Spring, 1964), 91-109.

Wylie, Max, translator see Cloquemin, P. 1905

9579. Wyllie, Nellie. The Frightened Witch. 1 act. Plays, 2 (October, 1942), 55-57.

9580. Wymark, Olwen. Lunchtime Concert. 1 act. Gambit, 3 (No. 10), 67-88.

Wynand, Derk, translator see Walter, O. F. 9199

9581. Wyss, Johann Rudolf, 1781-1830. The Swiss Family Robinson. 1 act. Plays, 23 (February, 1964), 85-96. Lewy Olfson, adapter.

X

9582. Xanrof. Fausse Manoeuvre. 1 act. Smart Set, 4 (May, 1901), 141-143. In French.

Y

Yale, Elsie D. see Duncan, F. 2699

Yambo, pseud. see Novelli, E. 6703

Yang Hsien-yi, translator see Wong Ou-hung 9540

Yang, Gladys, translator see Chao Shu-jen 1717

_____, translator see Wong Ou-hung 9540

9583. Yankowitz, Susan. The Ha-Ha Play. 1 act. Scripts, 1 (October, 1972), 81-92.

_____ see also Open Theatre, The 6871

9584. Yates, Elizabeth. A New Song. 1 act. Horn Book, 14 (November, 1938), 388-390.

9585. Yates, J. Michael. Night Freight. 1 act. Performing Arts in Canada, 8 (Spring, 1971), 27-33.

9586. Yeats, William Butler, 1865-1939. The Cat and the Moon, a Play for Dancers. 1 act. Criterion, 2 (July, 1924), 395-408.

9587. _____. The Cat and the Moon, a Play for Dancers. 1 act. Dial, 77 (July, 1924), 23-30.

9588. _____. The Cat and the Moon. 1 act. Il Dramma, 410/411 (September 15/October 1, 1943), 78-81. Agar Pampanini, translator. In Italian.

9589. _____. Cathleen ni Houlihan. 1 act. Il Dramma, 346 (January 15, 1941), 41-44. Carlo Linati, translator. In Italian.

9590. _____. Cathleen ni Hoolihan. 1 act. Samhain, (October, 1902), 24-31.

9591. _____. The Dreaming of the Bones. 1 act. Little Review, 6 (January, 1919), 1-14.

9592. _____. A Full Moon in March. 1 act. Poetry, 45 (March, 1935), 299-310.

9593. _____. The Green Helmet. 1 act. Forum, 46 (September, 1911), 301-321.

9594. _____. The Hour-Glass. 1 act. Il Dramma, 410/411 (September 15/October 1, 1943), 61-66. Agar Pampanini, translator. In Italian.

9595. _____. The Hour Glass, a Morality. 1 act. Golden Book, 3 (May, 1926), 641-646.

9596. _____. The Hour-Glass. 1 act. The Mask, 4 (April, 1913), 327-346.

9597. _____. The Hour Glass, a Morality. 1 act. North American Review, 177 (September, 1903), 445-456.

9598. _____. The King of the Great Clock Tower. 1 act. Life and Letters, 11 (November, 1934), 141-146.

9599. _____. Lady Cathleen. 4 parts. Il Dramma, 343 (December 1, 1940), 39-49. In Italian.

9600. _____. The Land of Heart's Desire. 1 act. Bibelot, 9 (1903), 184-213.

9601. ———. The Land of Heart's Desire. 1 act. Il Dramma, 339 (October 1, 1940), 33-36. Carlo Linati, translator. In Italian.

9602. ———. The Only Jealousy of Emer. 1 act. Poetry, 13 (January, 1919), 175-193.

9603. ———. Player Queen. 1 act, comedy. Dial, 73 (November, 1922), 486-506.

9604. ———. The Player-Queen. 1 act. Il Dramma, 410/411 (September 15/October 1, 1943), 67-77. Micaela De Pastrovich Pampanini, translator. In Italian.

9605. ———. The Pot of Broth. 1 act. Il Dramma, n.s., 10 (April 1, 1946), 47-50. Micaela De Pastrovich Pampanini, translator. In Italian.

9606. ———. The Shadowy Waters. 1 act. Il Dramma, 336 (August 15, 1940), 39-45. Carlo Linati, translator. In Italian.

9607. ———. The Shadowy Waters. 1 act. North American Review, 170 (May, 1900), 711-729.

9608. ———. The Unicorn from the Stars. 3 acts. Il Dramma, 367 (December 1, 1941), 7-20. Agar Pampanini, translator. In Italian.

——————— see also Moore, G. 6202

9609. Yliruusi, Tauno, 1927- . Lucian, the Mark Twain of Antiquity. 3 acts, comedy. Modern International Drama, 3 (September, 1969), 7-37. Steven Stone, translator.

9610. ———. A Woman's Place. 2 acts. Modern International Drama, 5 (Fall, 1971), 29-58. Steven Stone, translator.

9611. Yole, Jean. La Servante Sans Gages. 5 acts. Petite Illustration, 187 (March 24, 1934), 1-38. In French.

9612. Yordan, Philip, 1914- . Anna Lucasta. 3 acts. Il Dramma, n.s., 109 (May 15, 1950), 11-38. Franca Savioli, translator. In Italian.

Yorickson, translator see Boularan, J. 1220

9613. York, Marjorie Ann. Lincoln's Buckskin Breeches. 1 act. Plays, 11 (February, 1952), 74-78.

9614. ———. The Naming of the Flowers. 1 act. Plays, 11 (March, 1952), 73-77.

_____, adapter see Stevenson, R. L. 8520

9615. Young, Roland K. The Missing Guest, a Play in One Act and No Dialogue. Smart Set, 50 (December, 1916), 79-82.

9616. Young, Stanley, 1906- . Ship Forever Sailing. 1 act. Plays, 2 (November, 1942), 10-21.

9617. Young, Stark, 1881-1963. At the Shrine. 1 act. Golden Book, 16 (July, 1932), 77-82.

9618. _____. At the Shrine. 1 act. Theatre Arts, 3 (July, 1919), 196-203.

9619. _____. The Colonnade. 4 acts. Theatre Arts, 8 (August, 1924), 521-560.

9620. _____. The Leaves, an Eclogue. 1 act. North American Review, 118 (November, 1923), 641-645.

9621. _____. The Queen of Sheba. 1 act. Theatre Arts, 6 (April, 1922), 152-164.

9622. _____. Rose Windows. 1 act. Theatre Arts, 9 (October, 1925), 682-693.

_____, translator see Molière 6119

9623. Youri, 1927- . Le Vampire. 1 act. L'Avant Scène, 398 (March 1, 1968), 44-51. In French.

9624. Yu T'Ang Ch'un. 1 act. Il Dramma, (February, 1975), 63-82. Gica Bobich, translator. In Italian.

9625. Yukio, Mishima, 1925- . Hanjo. 1 act. Encounter, 8 (January, 1957), 45-51. Donald Keene, translator.

9626. Yung Chun. The Army and People Are One Family. Chinese Literature, 9 (1968), 93-104.

9627. Yushkevich, Semen, 1868-1927. In the City. 4 acts. Poet Lore, 47 (Summer, 1941), 99-174. J. A. Posin, G. R. Noyes and John Heard, translators.

Z

9628. Zacks, Robert. The Stranger. 1 act. One-Act Play Magazine, 3 (July-August, 1940), 417-423.

Zafred, Lilyan, translator see Schiller, F. 8028

Zafred, Mario, translator see Schiller, F. 8028

Zahareas, Anthony N., translator see Valle-Inclan, R. del 9000

9629. Zahn, Curtis, 1912- . An Albino Kind of Logic. 1 act. First Stage, 3 (Summer-Fall, 1964), 167-173.

9630. _____. Conditioned Reflex. 1 act, satirical tragedy. First Stage, 4 (Summer, 1965), 97-107.

Zalan, Magda, translator see Muller, P. 6292

_____, translator see Orkeny, I. 6878

9631. Zamacois, Miguel. L'inconsolabile. 1 act. Il Dramma, 125 (November 1, 1931), 39-44. In Italian.

9632. Zamjatin, Evgenij Ivanovic. La Pulce. 4 acts. Sipario, 8 (July, 1953), 30-43. Ettore Lo Gatto, translator. In Italian.

Zander, Peter, translator see Fassbinder, R. W. 2938

Zappa, P. F., translator see Bernard, T. and A. Godfernaux 856

9633. Zardi, Federico. Alla periferia. 1 act. Sipario, 13 (October, 1958), 33-41. In Italian.

9634. _____. Emma. 2 parts. Il Dramma, n.s., 154 (April 1, 1952), 7-36. In Italian.

9635. _____. I Marziani. 3 acts. Sipario, 15 (March, 1960), 37-71. In Italian.

9636. _____. Serata di gala. 3 acts. Sipario, 13 (May, 1958), 41-64. In Italian.

9637. _____. I tromboni. 4 acts, comedy. Sipario, 12 (February, 1957), 36-79. In Italian.

9638. Zeami Motokiyo, 1363-1443. Aoi no ue. 1 act. Sipario, 25 (October, 1970), 18, 20. Gian Pietro Calasio and Tsugako Hayashi, translators. In Italian.

9639. _____. Yashima, a Second Group of Shura-mono Noh. Origin, second series, 3 (October, 1961), 15-63. Cid Corman and Will Petersen, translators.

_____ see also Motokiyo, Z.

9640. Zeller, Winn. The Unsought Land. 1 act. American Prefaces, 1 (March, 1936), 83-86.

Zelson, Louis G., translator see Monterde, F. 6183

9641. Zemme, Oskar. The Arrival. Modern International Drama, 9 (Fall, 1975), 7-22. Sharon Vail Cutler, translator.

9642. Zerboni, Roberto. Antonio. 1 act. Il Dramma, n.s., 137 (July 15, 1951), 58-63. In Italian.

9643. _____. Antonio. 1 act. First Stage, 4 (Winter, 1965-66), 226-231. Adrienne Schizzano Mandel, translator.

9644. _____. Vicolo senza sole. 3 acts. Il Dramma, 390 (November 15, 1942), 7-23. In Italian.

Zetline, Edith, translator see Kops, B. 4690

9645. Zeyer, Julius. Diarmuid and Grainne. 4 acts. Poet Lore, 44 (No. 4, 1938), 289-343. George Rapall Noyes and Vera Mezirka, translators.

9646. _____. Raduz and Mahulena. 4 acts. Poet Lore, 34 (Spring, 1923), 1-62. Zdenka Buben and George Rapall Noyes, translators.

9647. Ziegelmaier, Gregory. The Archbishop. 1 act. Drama and Theatre, 10 (Spring, 1972), 161-185.

9648. _____. A Common for All Saints. 1 act. First Stage, 4 (Fall, 1965), 168-175.

9649. Ziegler, Esther E. Just in Time. 1 act. Plays, 12 (April, 1953), 38-46.

_____ see also Brydon, M. 1395, 1396, 1397

Ziegler, Francis I., translator see Strindberg, A. 8574, 8580

9650. Zilahy, Lajos, 1891- . Tuzmadar. 3 acts. Petite Illustration, 185 (June 3, 1933), 1-30. Denys Amiel, adapter. In French.

Zilboarg, Gregory, 1890- , translator see Andreyev, L. N. 230

9651. Zimmer, Bernard. Ion. 2 parts, tragi-comedy. L'Avant Scène, 82 (October, 1953), 5-28. In French.

9652. _____. La lettera. 1 act. Il Dramma, 156 (February 15, 1933), 40-45. Vittorio Guerriero, translator. In Italian.

Zimmerer, Ludwig, translator see Mrozek, S. 6287

9653. Zindel, Paul, 1937- . The Effect of Gamma Rays on Man-in-the-Moon Marigolds. 2 acts. Plays and Players, 20 (December, 1972), I-X.

Zipes, Jack D., translator see Lind, J. 4982

9654. Zolin, A. A Helpless Woman! 1 act, comedy. One-Act Play Magazine, 2 (June-July, 1938), 176-186. E. Leda Swan, translator.

Zorelli, Vittorio, translator see Birabeau, A. 956

9655. Zorrilla y Moral, José, 1817-1893. The Dagger of the Goth. 1 act. Poet Lore, 40 (1929), 426-442. Willis Knapp Jones, translator.

9656. Zorzi, Guglielmo, 1879- . Con loro. 3 acts. Il Dramma, n. s., 55 (February 15, 1948), 9-31. In Italian.

9657. _____. La Veine D'Or. 3 acts. Petite Illustration, 87 (December 14, 1929), 1-26. J. J. Bernard, translator. In French.

_____, translator see Talagrand, J. 8695

_____ see also De Benedetti, A. 2231

9658. _____ and G. Scalafani. La fiaba dei re magi. 3 acts. Il Dramma, 147 (October 1, 1932), 4-33. In Italian.

9659. Zoschenko, Michael, 1895- . Bad Business. 1 act, comedy. One-Act Play Magazine, 2 (February, 1939), 691-702. Moshe Spiegel, translator.

Zucca, Giuseppe see Mancuso, U. 5487

Zucker, A. E., translator see The Redentin Easter Play 7455

9660. Zuckmayer, Carl, 1896- . Der Hauptmann von Kopenick. 3 acts. Sipario, 11 (July-August, 1956), 40-69. Mario Spagnol, translator. In Italian.

Zulberti, Taulero, translator see Abony, A. 13

_____, translator see Havas, N. 3976-3979

_____, translator see Heltai, J. 4052

_____, translator see Herczeg, F. 4067

_____, translator see Kranz, H. B. 4708

_____, translator see Lakatos, L. 4770

_____, translator see Molnar, F. 6150, 6162, 6168

_____, translator see Pakots, G. 6936

_____, translator see Roda, R. 7643, 7644

Zveteremich, Pietro, translator see Solzhenitsyn, A. I. 8372

9661. Zweig, Arnold, 1887- . Das Spiel vom Herrn und vom Jockel. 1 act. Das Wort, 7 (May, 1938), 45-67. In German.

9662. Zweig, Stefan, 1881-1942. L'agnello del povero. 3 acts. Il Dramma, n. s., 151 (February 15, 1952), 8-32. Lavinia Mazzucchetti, translator. In Italian.

TITLE INDEX

A

A B C for Safety. Pendleton, E. 7044
A B C's Thanksgiving, The. Miller, H. L. 5851
A che servono questi quattrini? Curcio, A. 2146
A ognuno la sua croce. Fulchignoni, E. 892
A Wen. Bellow, S. 738
Abandoned Husbands. Morley, C. 6221
Abdul and the Caliph's Treasure. Heshmati, L. B. 4087
Abe Buys a Barrell. Peterson, M. N. 7094
Abe Lincoln Goes to School. Very, A. 9103
Abelardo. Pasqualino, F. 6996
Abendstunde im Spätherbst. Dürrenmatt, F. 2741
Abe's Winkin' Eye. Fisher, A. 3036
Abisso, L'. Giovaninetti, S. 3554
Abito Nero, L'. Giannini, G. 3480
Abner Crane from Hayseed Lane. Dias, E. J. 2401
Abonne. Millaud, F. 5834
Abortionist, The. Atkins, R. 431
Above the Fire. Deemer, C. 2241
Abracadabra. Luftig, R. 5085
Abraham. Hrotsvitha 4261
Abraham et Samuel. Haim, V. 3822
Abra-Kadabra-Kadoo!!! Ravetch, H. 7434
Absence of a Cello. Wallach, I. 9194
Abstract Tragedy, The. Olson, E. 6827
AC/DC. Williams, H. 2269
Academic Murders, The. Koch, K. 4676
Acapulco Madame. Jamiaque, Y. 4438
Accident, L'. Larra, C. 4819
Accident, The. Saroyan, W. 7944
Accompagnateur. Mithois, M. 6088
Accoppiamento, L'. Bona, G. 1165
According to Darwin. Wilde, P. 9376
According to Law. Houston, N. 4196
Accustateur Public. Hochwalder, F. 4120
Ace Navigator. Richmond, S. S. 7537
Achille Vengeur. Suares, A. 8594
Achilles' Heel. Levi, S. 4960
Acqua si diverte a far morire di sete, L'. Joppolo, B. 4514
Acrobats, The. Fleming, B. 3155
Acrobats. Horovitz, I. 4172
Across the Board on Tomorrow-Morning. Saroyan, W. 7945
Across the Jordan. Culbertson, E. H. 2134
Act the Second: The Norwich Incident. Levitt, P. M. 4966
Acte, or The Prisoners of Time. Durrell, L. 2740
Acting Charade, An 47
Action Tonight, The. Grainger, T. 3684
Actress, The. Molnar, F. and J. Teleki 6169
Adam. Achard, M. 17
Adam Goodfellow and the Jill Fish. Elfenbein, J. A. 2839
Adams for the Defense. Smith, B. S. 8325
Adder, The. Abercrombie, L. 10
Adieu Berthe! Murray, J. and A. Boretz 6407
Adjustment. Graham, M. S. 3676
Admiral Leads On, The. Shriner, F. 8264
Admiral's Daughter, The. Paradis, M. B. 6954
Admiral's Nightmare, The. McGowan, J. 5187

Adobe Christmas. Peterson, M. N. 7095
Adolfo o della magia. Parodi, A. G. 6984
Adorable Julia. Sauvajon, M. 7988
Adoration. Kishida, K. 4645
Adorazione de' re magi, L'. Adimari, A. 75
Adored One, The. Sellers, I. P. 8147
Adrienne Mesurat. Green, J. 3698
Adventurer, The. Capus, A. 1590
Adventures in Bookland. Liss, F. 4997
Adventures of Jo March, The. Alcott, L. M. 109
Adventures of Mr. Bean. Meredith, B. 5766
Adventures of Tom Sawyer, The. Clemens, S. L. 1877
Adversary, The. Phillips, S. 7139
Advice of the Lovelorn. McQueen, M. H. and N. McQueen 5287
Advocate, The. Noah, R. 6608
Aerial Engineer, The. Steinbeck, J. 8491
Aesop, Man of Fables. Phillips, E. 7121
Affair, The. Millar, R. 5831, 5832
Affaire Exceptionnelle, Une. Schreiber, I. G. 8083
Affaire Victor. Mercier, M. 5760
Affairs of Catherine, I. The Grand Duchess. Gilmore, L. 3539
Affairs of Catherine. II. Long Live the Empress. Gilmore, L. 3540
Affairs of Catherine. III. Prince Patiomkin. Gilmore, L. 3541
Affairs of Catherine. IV. A Tenor. Gilmore, L. 3542
Affairs of Catherine. V. Widowed. Gilmore, L. 3543
Affairs of State. Verneuil, L. 9093
Affare Kubinski, L'. Lakatos, F. 4769
Affetti di famiglia, Gli. De Cespedes, A. and A. D. Espinosa 2237
Afore Night Come. Rudkin, D. 7781
Africa Sings. McBrown, G. P. 5117

African Trio. Winther, B. 9478
After All. Monroe, H. 6175
After Closing. Marz, R. 5635
After-Dinner Speaker, The. Allen, L. 143
After Euripides's Electra. Baring, M. 595
After Glow. Corbett, E. F. 2016
After Haggerty. Mercer, D. 5757
After the Ball. Coward, N. 2065
After the Ball. Saltus, E. 7893
After the Event. Ross, H. 7706
After the Fall. Miller, A. 5840
After the Opera. Docquois, G. 2513
After the Play. Gogol, N. 3598
After the Wash. Molinaro, U. 6127
After the Wedding. Howells, W. D. 4235
After Twenty-Five Years. Firkins, O. W. 3028
Afternoon in Arcady. Stratton, C. 8556
Afternoon Orator, The. Crowell, C. T. 2129
Afternoon Tea. Gorgey, G. 3643
Afternoon Walk. Lavendan, H. 4838
Afterwards. McGaughan, G. E. 5184, 5185
Agamemnon. Alfred, W. 133
Age Canonique. Lude, C. 5081
Age du Fer. Amiel, D. 179
Age du Juliette. Boularan, J. 1216
Age of Accountability. Boatright, M. C. 1030
Age of Precarious, The. Martens, A. C. 5586
Aglavaine and Selysette. Maeterlinck, M. 5424
Agnello del povero, L'. Zweig, S. 9662
Agnese Bernauer. Hebbel, C. F. 4013, 4014, 4015
Agonia d'amore. Schnitzler, A. 8060
Agonia di Luisa con le avventure di Gilgamesh alla televisione, L'. Wilcock, R. J. 9352
Agostino l'arcidiavolo. Trabucco, C. 8910
Ah Kiou. Chartreux, B. and J. Jourdheuil 1735
Ah! Que D'Amour Gaché sans Profit pour Personne! Pillement, G. 7150

Ah See and the Six-Colored Heaven. Boiko, C. 1044
Ah, Wilderness. O'Neill, E. 6834
Ah Wing Fu and the Golden Dragon. Winther, B. 9492
Ahasverus. Heijermans, H. 4028
Aide-Mémoire. Carrière, J. 1616
Aims and Objects. Housman, L. 4183
Aino Puku, The. Mygatt, T. D. 6426
Air des Bijoux, L'. Tholy, R. 8818
Air du Large. Obaldia, R. de 6714
Air Raid. MacLeish, A. 5239
Airport Adventure. Murray, J. 6311
Ajax. Abel, L. 7
Akogi, a Noh Play. Motokiyo, Z. 6269
Al Adams and the Wonderful Lamp. Boiko, C. 1045
Al Pappagallo verde. Schnitzler, A. 8075
Aladdin and His Wonderful Lamp. Thane, A. 8794
Aladdin, Incorporated. McQueen, M. H. and N. McQueen 5288
Aladdin Steps Out. McQueen, M. H. and N. McQueen 5289
Albergo di Amsterdam, L'. Osborne, J. 6892
Albergo sul porto, Un. Betti, U. 887
Albert Einstein, Schoolboy. Rutherford, M. C. 7815
Albert: Prince Consort. Huxley, A. L. 4342
Alberto Durer, ovverossia Il mostro marino. De Angelis, R. M. 2217
Albert's Bridge. Stoppard, T. 8534
Albino Kind of Logic, An. Zahn, C. 9629
Alcade de Zalamea. Calderon de la Barca, P. 1501
Alchemist, The. McClure, J. 5131
Alec and Joey. Picton-Warlow, T. 7146
Alexander II, or, Something for Everyone. Ratcliffe, M. 7417
Alexander the Great. Mierow, H. E. 5822
Alfabeto, L'. Chiarelli, L. 1795
Alfie. O'Connell, T. E. 6759
Alfonso, King of Castile. Lewis, M. G. 4971

Alga Marina. Veneziani, C. 9063
Alice, Dans les Jardins du Luxembourg. Weingarten, R. 9269
Alice-Heidi's Secrets 135
Alice in Bookland. Cauman, S. 1668
Alice in Bookland. Urban, C. 8972
Alice in Everydayland. Van Delden, E. H. 9015
Alice in Puzzleland. Fisher, A. and O. Rabe 3103
Alice in Wonderland. Dodgson, C. L. 2515, 2516, 2517
Alice's Adventures in Wonderland. Dodgson, C. L. 2517
Aliens. Towne, C. H. 8908
Alinur. Mejerchol'd, V. and J. Bondi 5737
Ali's Reward. Hall, M. C. 3847
Alizon, Vivran 9166
All Aboard! Bengal, B. 762, 763
All Aboard for Christmas. McQueen, M. H. and N. McQueen 5290
All About Mothers. Boiko, C. 1046
All Around the Town. Larson, E. 4824
All Because of a Scullery Maid. Phillips, M. K. 7125
All God's Chillun Got Wings. O'Neill, E. 6835
All Hands on Deck. Boiko, C. 1047
All Houses are Haunted. Woster, A. 9568
All in Favor. Schwartz, M. K. 8097
All Is Not Gold. McQueen, M. H. and N. McQueen 5291
All on a Day in May. Fisher, A. 3037
All or None. Gifford, F. K. 3507
All Points West. Boiko, C. 1048
All Summer Long. Anderson, R. 214
All the King's Men. Warren, R. P. 9212, 9213
All the Way Home. Mosel, T. 6259
All Things Considered. Hartley, R. E. 3945
All This and Alan, Too. Allred, J. 148
Alla deriva. Jerome, J. K. 4464
Alla periferia. Zardi, F. 9633
Alla ventura. France, A. 3240

Alladine and Palomides. Maeterlinck, M. 5425
All-American Thank You, An. Miller, H. L. 5852
All-American Tour, The. Newman, D. 6488
Allegria. Folgore, L. 3192
Allegro furfante, Un. Doletti, M. 2521
All 'insegna delle sorelle Kadàr. Lelli, R. 4904
Allodola, L'. Wolff 9529
Allons Enfants! Vojnovich, I. 9169
Almost an Elopement. Wright, C. 9573
Almost Everyman. Austin, H. H. 460
Aloha, Mother. McGowan, J. 5188
Along the Quays. Lavendan, H. 4838
Alouette. Anouilh, J. 245, 246
Alpha Kappa. Paradis, M. B. 6955
Alpinistes. Aroutcheff, G. 358
Alta Montagna. Gotta, S. 3657
Altalena della vita. Fodor, L. 3176
Alternazione di carattere. Corradini, A. 2026
Altitude. Lawrence, D. H. 4851
Altitude 3.200. Luchaire, J. 5076
Altri equipaggi. Brignetti, R. 1328
Always Ridiculous. Echegaray, J. 2809
Am Stram Gram. Roussin, A. 7733
Amalassunta. Pavoni, L. 7019
Amant de Madame Vidal. Verneuil, L. 9094
Amante Anglaise, L'. Duras, M. 2736
Amante del sogno, L'. Vanni, A. 9035
Amante di prima, L'. Valori, G. 9009
Amante di tutti, L'. Mura 6301
Amante immaginaria, L'. Gandera, F. and C. Gever 3364
Amants de Paris. Frondaie, P. 3323
Amants Maléfiques, Les. Middleton, T. and W. Rowley 5821
Amants Puerils, Les. Crommelynck, F. 2114

Amarsi così. Tieri, V. 8858
Ambassador of Capripedia. Huxley, A. L. 4343
Ambassador's Burglar, The. Duer, C. 2672
Ambition 177
Ambrizione. Achille, G. 44
Ambrosia. John G. 4473
Ambush. Richman, A. 7533
America Hurrah. van Itallie, J.-C. 9030
America Is a Song. Nolan, P. T. 6628
America the Beautiful. Hollingsworth, L. 4143
America the Beautiful, Democracy's Goal. Knox, M. and A. M. Lutkenhaus 4674
American Answer. Birnbaum, P. 963
American Document. Graham, S. 3680
American Dream, An. Albee, E. 97
American Grandfather. Smith, M. S. 8342
American Way, The. Martens, A. C. 5587
Americans Every One. Davis, L. R. 2201
"Amethyst Remembrance, An." Sumner, M. 2053, 8618
Ami-Ami. Barillet, P. and J. P. Grédy 584
Ami D'Argentine. Bernard, T. and M. Maurey 857
Ami de Jeunesse, Un. See, E. 8126
Ami ... Imprevu, Un. Thomas, R. 8829
Amica di tutti, L'. De Stefani, A. 2363
Amicizia. De Filippo, E. 2250
Amicizia. Mourguet, M. 6277
Amicizie pericolose. Achard, P. 41
Amico delle donne, L'. Dumas, A. 2687
Amigo Desconocida nos Aguarda. Dominguez, F. 2525
Amis. Dorly, P. 5565
Amis? Marniere, J. M. F. 2557
Amitie. Mourguet, M. 6278
Amleto. Marowitz, C. 5574
Amleto e morto. Meano, C. 5721
Amo un'attrice. Fodor, L. 3177
Among Ourselves. Panitz, S. 6950

Among the Lions. Middleton, G. 5814
Among the Nightingales. Huxley, A. L. 4344
Among the Pines. Ogden, R. 6779
Amor sincero, L'. Valori, G. 9010
Amore a Roma, Un. Patti, E. 7008
Amore canta, L'. De Stefani, A. 2364
Amore deve nascere, L'. Antonelli, L. 296
Amore di Galatea, L'. Quasimodo, S. 7360
Amore e l'avventura, L'. Mura 6302
Amore e magia nella cucina di mamma. Wertmuller, L. 9298
Amore non è tanto semplice, L'. Fodor, L. 3178
Amore sacro e amor profano. Molnar, F. 6133
Amore senza stima. Ferrari, P. 2997
Amore si muore, D'. Patroni-Griffi, G. 7004
Amorphie d'Ottenburg. Grumberg, J.-C. 3765
Amour de Don Perlimplin. Lorca, F. G. 5042
Amour, Délices et Or. Berquier-Marinier, M. 865
Amour des Bêtes, L'. Lavedan, H. L. E. 4836
Amour en Papier, L'. Ducreux, L. 2668
Amour est mon Cercueil, L'. Pillement, G. 7151
Amour Fou, L'. Roussin, A. 7734
Amour Parmi Nous. Lebesque, M. 4867
Amour-Propre, L'. Camoletti, M. 1524
Amour Quelquefois, L'. Franck, P. and R. Bergil 3256
Amour Qui ne Finit pas. Roussin, A. 7735
Amour, Toujours L'Amour! Vilfrid, J. 9147
Amour, Vous Connaissez? Mannoff, B. 5498
Amoureuse Aventure. Armont, P. and M. Gerbidon 341
Amours. Nivoix, P. 6606
Amours de Jacques le Fataliste, Les. Diderot, D. 2485

Amours de la Marchande d'Epices, Les. Confortes, C. 1970
Amours du Poete. Blum, R. and G. Delaquys 1019
Ampelour, L'. Audiberti, J. 441
Amphion. Valéry, P. A. 8997
Amphitryon 1968. Diez, B. 2494
Amphitryon 38. Giraudoux, J. 3561
Anachronism at Chinon, An. Pound, E. 7264
Anansi, the African Spider. Winther, B. 9493
Anastasia. Marcelle-Maurette 5532
Anche a Chicago nascon le violette. Buzzichini, M. and A. Casella 1460
Anche i grassi hanno l'onore. Bompiani, V. 1160
Ancora, L'. Grella, E. 3734
Ancora addio. Calvino, V. 1513
And Christmas Is Its Name. Nolan, P. T. 6629
And Forbid Them Not. Bowman, L. M. 1245
And Now There's Just the Three of Us. Weller, M. 9278
And Pippa Dances. Hauptmann, G. 3970
And Sew On. Asbrand, K. 393
And So to War. Corrie, J. 2036
And the Stars Heard. Byers, J. M. 1462
And They Used to Star in Movies. Black, C. 979
Anders Paints a Picture. Asbrand, K. 394
Andersonville Trial. Levitt, S. 4967
Andirivieni, L'. Bertoli, P. B. 874
Andorra; Stuck in Zwölf Bildern. Frisch, M. 3308
Andrea. Meneghini, A. L. 5748
Androcles and His Pal. Fontaine, R. 3197
Androcles and the Lion. Shaw, G. B. 8202
Andromeda. Simpson, L. 8302
Andromeda Unfettered. Stuart, M. 8589
Angel Child. Miller, H. L. 5853
Angel in the Looking-Glass. Fisher, A. 3038
Angel of Mercy. Lipnick, E. 4994
Angel of the Morning. McGrath, J. 5208

Angel on the Ship. Wilder, T. 9389
Angel That Troubled the Waters, The. Wilder, T. 9392
Angelica. Ferrero, L. 2999
Angelo. Jacquemard, Y. 4425
Angelo del miracolo, L'. De Stefani, A. 2365
Angelo e il commendatore, L'. Mosca, G. 6252
Angels We Have Heard on High. Hardy, C. 3905
Angustias. Marchandeau, F. 5539
Anima per Giulia, Un'. Calvino, V. 1514
Animals Christmas Tree. Robertson, O. J. 7614
Animateurs du Jour. Pech, C. H. 7029
Anna Christie. O'Neill, E. 6836
Anna Lucasta. Yordan, P. 9612
Anne Bradstreet. Hughes, R. 4309
Anne of the Thousand Days. Anderson, M. 207
L'Annee du Bac. Lacour, J.-A. 4761
Anniversary: December 10, 1688, An. Ingelow, J. 4380
Anniversary Waltz. Chodorov, J. J. Fields 1814
Anno Domino. Sadoveanu, I. M. 7846
Announciation, The. Alexander, H. B. 127
"Anonima fratelli Roylott." Giannini, G. 3481
Anonymous Letter, The. Nicholson, K. 6562
Anonymous Work, The. Witkiewicz, S. 9511
Another Cinderella. Fontaine, R. 3198
Another Man's Family. Gable, H. 1469
Another Part of the Forest. Hellman, L. 4043
Another Point of View. Fisk, M. I. 3125
Another Redskin Bit the Dust. Dias, E. J. 2402
Another Way to Weigh an Elephant. Blumenfeld, L. 1020
Ansia cieca, L'. Luzi, G. F. 5097
Antenato, L'. Veneziani, C. 9064

Anticamera, L'. Mosca, G. 6253
Antigone. Anouilh, J. 247
Antigone. Sophocles 8380
Antigone lo cascio. Gatti, G. 3424
Antique Trap, The. Hall, M. 3855
Antitragica. Nardelli, F. V. and F. Sarazani 6434
Anton Chekhov Sort of Evening, An. Nolan, P. T. 6630
Antonello capobrigante. De Chiara, G. 2238
Antonio. Zerboni, R. 9642, 9643
Antonio von Elba. Mainardi, R. 5457
Anyone for the Moon? Alderman, E. R. 114
Anything You Say Will Be Twisted. Campbell, K. 1545
Anywhere and Everywhere. Boiko, C. 1049
Aoi no ue. Zeami, M. 9638
Apes Shall Inherit the Earth. Aspenstrom, W. 423
Apollinaris. Second, L. 8124
Apollon de Bellac, L'. Giraudoux, J. 3562
Apostle, The. Moore, G. 6200
Apparenze inquiete, Le. Sanavio, P. 7900
Apparition. Eberhart, R. 2801
Apple Cart, The. Shaw, G. B. 8203
Apple of Contentment, The. Pyle, H. 7348
Apples 310
Apples. Indick, B. 4369
Apples, Oranges, Strawberries. Ratkowski, T. M. 7418
Appomattox. Serlen, B. 8154
Appreciators, The. Gale, Z. 3349
Apprenez a conduire par correspondence. Fortuna, C. 3230
Apprentices, The. Terson, P. 8770
Approches du Soir. Suffran, M. 8608
Appuntamento in paradiso. Grassi, E. 3690
Appuntamento nel Michigan. Cannarozzo, F. 1568
Apricots. Griffiths, T. 3746
April Elves. Elfenbein, J. A. 2840
April Fool Surprise, An. Barr, J. 614
April Fool's Day. Duvall, L. M. 2773
April Is the Cruelest Month. Cole, E. R. 1928

April Showers. Spamer, C.
8403
April's Lady. Wells, C. 9284
Aprite le finestra. Veneziani,
C. 9065
Apron. Frost, L. A. 3325
Aquarium. Nicolai, A. 6578
Aquarium 2. Gruza, J. and
K. T. Toeplitz 3771
Arabian Knight, The. Boiko, C.
1050
Arbre, L'. Dutourd, J. 2772
Arc de Triomphe, L'. Mithois,
M. 6089
Arca di Noè, L'. Pugliese, S.
7331
Archbishop, The. Ziegelmaier,
G. 9647
Architecte et L'Empereur d'Assyrie. Arrabal, F. 370
Architruc. Pinget, R. 7166
Arciere, L'. Calvino, V. 1515
Arcivescovo, L'. Maurri, E.
5693
Ardèle, ou la Marguerite.
Anouilh, J. 248, 249
Are You Perfect? Ames, T.
178
Arena racconta. Boal, A. and
G. Guarnieri 1029
Argilla, L'. Valori, G. 9011
Argo. Taladoire, B. and E.
Fuzeillier 8692
Argument, The. Adams, P.-L.
70
Argument, The. Moore, M.
6205
Aria da Capo. Millay, E. St.
V. 5836
Aria nuova. Lonsdale, F. 5028
Aria paesana. De Filippo, P.
2268
Ariadne Exposed. Nightingale,
E. M. 6597
Ariadne in Mantua. Paget, V.
6927, 6928
Arise, Sparta! Nightingale, E.
M. 6598
Aristaeus. Donagby, L. 2527
Armata del silenzio, L'. Sulliotti, I. 8613
Arme Mensch, Der. Altendorf,
W. 155
Armgart. Eliot, G. 2846
Armoire Classique. Audiberti,
J. 442
Armonia. Molnar, F. 6134
Armstrong's Last Goodnight, The

Arden, J. 320
Army and People Are One Family,
The. Yung Chun 9626
Arnacoeur, L'. Bruno, P. 1387
Around the World in Eighty Days.
Verne, J. 9088
Arrest, The. Marinetti, F. T.
5549
Arret, L'. Voulet, J. 9174
Arrival, The. Zemme, O. 9641
Arrivato Pietro Gori. Castri, M.
1655
Arrivista, L'. Terron, C. R.
8750
Arrow, The. Downey, J. E. 2572
Arsenic and Old Lace. Kesselring,
J. 4606
Art in the Home. Stevenson, P.
8514
Artemisia. Banti, A. 548
Arthur Bones, The Reading Bag.
Watts, F. B. 9222
Article 330. Moineaux, G. 6108
Articolo 252, L'. Provins, M.
7311
Artist, The. Mencken, H. L.
5743
Arts and Parts. Huff, B. T. 4269
As Grandmother Told It. Ross, F.
R. 7704
As Strangers. Eliot, A. 2844
As the Leaves. Giacosa, G. 3476
As We Were. Adamov, A. 57
As You Like It. Shakespeare, W.
8174
Asaph. Bates, W. O. 669
Ascenseur du Quai d'Orsay, L'.
Tourteau, J.-J. 8906
Ascension de Virginie, L'. Donnay,
C. and L. Descaves 2544
Ashes. Rudkin, D. 7782
Ashes. Whiting, E. C. 9328
Ashes to Ashes. Housman, L.
4184
Ask the Library Lady. Phillips,
M. K. 7126
Asmodée. Mauriac, F. 5687, 5688
Aspern Papers, The. Redgrave, M.
7456
Asphodel, The. Lee, A. 4872
Assassin, The. Shaw, I. 8223
Assassino, L'. Novelli, E. 6703
Assassino speranza delle donne.
Kokoschka, O. 4681
Assassins Associes. Thomas, R.
8830
Assedio, L'. D'Errico, E. 2345
Assemblea deserta, L'. Ottieri, O.
6917

Assemien Dehyle. Dadie, B. 2158
Assumption of Hannele. Hauptmann, G. 3971
Assunta spina. Di Giacomo, S. 2497
Assureurs. Roland C. and G. D'Hervilliez 7658
Astonished Heart, The. Coward, N. 2066
At a Beetle's Pace. Catron, L. E. 1663
At a Lost Outpost. Aichinger, I. 84
At Night All Cats Are Gray. Garland, R. 3391
At the Chasm. Frida, E. B. 3299
At the Club. Morgan, J. 6219
At the Eleventh Hour. Matthews, E. V. B. 5659
At the End of the Rainbow. Howard, M. W. 4217
At the Flowing of the Tide. O'Brien, E. J. H. 6744
At the Little Pipe. Pelee, L. S. 7039
At the Shrine. Young, S. 9617, 9618
At the Sign of the "Bible and Sun." Lee, E. 4876
At the Sign of the Cleft Heart. Garrison, T. 3398
At the Sign of the Postboy's Horn. Woodmeald, J. E. 9546
At the Sign of the Silver Spoon. Finch, L. 3022
At the Wakehouse. O'Connor, F. 6764
At Whitsuntide. Bentley, L. D. G. 810
Atalante en Calyon. Swinburne, A. C. 8648
Atene anno zero. Della Corte, F. 2301
Athelwold. Rives, A. 7600
Atla. Duncan, K. 2701
Atlas-Hotel. Slacrou, A. 7867
Atom and Oak Ridge, Tennessee, The. Konick, M. 4684
Atom Clock, The. Lengyel, C. A. 4910
Atomtod. Jona, E. 4499
Attacco alla coscienza. Bagnara, M. 491
Attache d'ambasciata, L'. Bérnard, O. and H. Fremont 835

Attesa, L'. De Angelis, A. 2215
Attesa, L'. Règpaci, L. 7493
Attessa dell'angelo, L'. Giannini, G. 3482
Attic Treasure. Gould, J. 3664
Attic Treasure. Miller, H. L. 5854
Attila, ou le Fleau de Dieu. Duprat-Géneau, J. 2732
Atto negativo. Corra, B. 2033
Attori. Molnar, F. 6135
Au Clair de la Lune. Bouvelet, J. and E. J. Bradby 1241
Au Pair Man, The. Leonard, H. 4922
Au Paradis. Millaud, F. 5835
Au Pied du Mur. Aragon, L. 311
Au Soleil de L'Instinct. Raynal, P. 7446
Auction, The. Schwartz, M. K. 8098
Audace avventura. Armont, P. and M. Gerbidon 342
Audience. Lorca, F. G. 5043
Audioplay 1: Voices. Lind, J. 4982
Audioplay 2: Safe. Lind, J. 4983
Audition, The. Pritchard, B. 7306
Aunt Columbia's Dinner Party. Gamble, M. R. 3362
Aunt Lasmi. Basudeb, S. 659
Auntie Hamlet. Isaac, D. 4409
Auntie Mame. Lawrence, J. and R. E. Lee 4856
Auprès de ma blonde. Achard, M. 18
Aurora verde, L'. Lovinfosse, H. -M. 5066
Author! Author! MacDonagh, J. 5164
Author of Liberty. McQueen, M. H. and N. McQueen 5292
Author's Evening at Home, The. Dunbar, A. 2696
Auto-da-Fé. Williams, T. 9418
Auto de los Reyes Magos 463
Autocrat of the Coffee Stall. Chapin, H. 1718
Autore della commedia, L'. Mor, E. and Borghesio 6209
Autori. Raggio, E. 7381
Autre. Helias, P. 4040
Autre valse, L'. Dorin, M. 2556
Autumn. Loving, P. 5067
Autumn Garden. Hellman, L. 4044

Autumn's Visit. Duvall, L. M. 2774
Autunno. Gherardi, G. 3465
Aux Quatre Coins. Marsan, J. 5578
Avant et Après. Provins, M. 7312
Avant Tout la Lumière. Mora, J.-M. de 6211
Avec Lui. Verdot, G. 9074
Avenger, The. Ross, C. 7701
Avengers. Rice, C. Y. 7519
Avenue, The. Merrill, F. 5781
Aveu, L'. Bernhardt, L. S. 859
Aveugle et le Paralytique, L'. Pathiraja, D. 6998
Aveugles, Les. De Ghelderode, M. 3456
Aveva due pistole con gli occhi bianchi e neri. Fo, D. 3164
Avevo piu' stima dell' idrogeno. Terron, C. 8751
Avon Calling! Olfson, L. 6788
Avrebbe potuto essere! Giannini, G. 3483
Avvenimento, L'. Fabbri, D. 2895
Avventura d'un povero Cristiano, L'. Silone, I. 8275
Avventura sulla spiaggia. Antonelli, L. 297
Avventuriero davanti alla porta. Begovic, M. 721
Awakening. Subert, F. A. 8595
Awakening of Granville, The. Nolan, P. T. 6631
Awards Graduation, The. Nolan, P. T. 6632
Awkward-Hander Orpheus. Fodor, J. 3173
Axel, "Le Monde Passionnel". Isle-Adam, V. de L' 4411
Ay, There's the Rub. DuBois, G. 2616
Azalea Mountain. Wang Shu-yuan 9202
Azure Adder, The. Demuth, C. 2330

B

Baal. Brecht, B. 1281
Babbitt's Boy. Hughes, G. 4300
Babes in the Wood, The. Gibson, H. 3495
Babes in the Wood. Ward, W. D. 9210

Baby-Elephant, The. Brecht, B. 1282
Baby Liked "Greensleeves," The. Widdemer, M. 9344
Baby-Sitter, La. Obaldia, R. de 6715
Bacio davanti allo specchio, Il. Fodor, L. 3179
Bacio e nulla più, Un. Halàsz, A. 3831
Back Stage. Diamond, J. 2398
Back to Methuselah. Shaw, G. B. 8204
Background for Nancy. Manning, S. 5502
Backward-Jumping Frog, The. Howard, V. 4219
Backward Lady. Mauton, M. 5694
Bad Business. Zoschenko, M. 9659
Bad Day at Bleak Creek. Alderman, E. R. 115
Bad Penny, The. Field, R. 3014
Bad Seed. Anderson, M. 208
Baden Lehrstuck. Brecht, B. 1283
Badlands Ballyhoo. Murray, J. 6312
Bag O'Dreams, The. Scott, M. 8108
Bag of Flies. Herndon, V. 4077
Bagatelle, La. Achard, M. 19
Bagatelle. Gilmore, L. 3544
Bagi perduti. Birabeau, A. 945
Bagman, The. Arden, J. 321
Bailey, Go Home. Cable, H. 1470
Bains, Les. Maiakovski, V. 5454
Baisers Perdus. Birabeau, A. 946
Bait, The. Merrill, J. 5782
Bake a Cherry Pie. McQueen, M. H. and N. McQueen 5293
Baker's Dozen, The. Munro, H. H. 6298
Baker's Neighbor, The. Thane, A. 8795
Baking Contest, The. Simon, S. 8284
Bal des Bourreaux. Ransan, A. 7406
Bal des Cuisinieres, Le. Da Costa, B. 2157
Bal des voleurs, Le. Anouilh, J. 250
Balance d'Eros, La. Vazart, C. 9050
Balaustion's Euripides. Clarke,

H. A. 1857
Balcony. Heiberg, G. 4026
Bald Soprano, The. Ionesco, E. 4382
Balena bianca, La. Dursi, M. 2755
Ballad for the Shy, A. Dias, E. J. 2403
Ballad of Hynd Horn, The. Smith, J. K. 8338
Ballad of Simon-Pure Sam. Dias, E. J. 2404
Ballatta per Tim Pescatore di Trote. Castelli, C. 1648
Balle au Chasseur, La. Suffran, M. 8609
Ballo del tenente helt, Il. Aroutcheff, G. 359
Balloon, The. Kenan, A. 4587
Ballygombeen Bequest, The. Arden, J. and M. D'Arcy 325
Balthazar. D'Errico, E. 2346
Bambini, I. Landi, S. 4781
Banana Box, The. Chappell, E. 1721
Banane, La. Eliraz, I. 2854
Band Aid. Miller, H. L. 5855
Band Rotunda, The. Baxter, J. K. 681
Bande à Bonnot, La. Rey, H.-F. 7500
Bandiera bianco. Tendrjakov, V. and K. Jikramov 8742
Bandit Ben Rides Again. Miller, H. L. 5856
Bang! Bang! Newburge, D. 6486
Banja. Mayakovsky, V. 5455
Banque Nemo. Verneuil, L. 9095
Banquet, The. Phillips, L. 7123
Baptism of Jesus, The. Wuchter, S. D. 9576
Barabbas. Ghelderode, M. De 3457
Barbara. Raggio, E. 7382
Barbara Roscorla's Child. Symons, A. 8660
Barbara's Wedding. Barrie, J. M. 624
Barbes Nobles, Les. Roussin, A. 7736
Barbier de Seville, Le. Beaumarchais 690
Barbour, Le. Carette, L. 1597
Barca viene dal lago, La. De Stefani, A. 2366
Barefoot Bog, The. Wheetley, K. A. 9318

Barefoot in Athens. Anderson, M. 209
Barefoot in the Park. Simon, N. 8283
Barefoot Trader, The. Watts, F. B. 9223
Barf! Steckler, S. 8479
Bargains in Bonds. Bridgman, B. 1324
Bar-None Trading Post, The. Miller, H. L. 5857
Baro, Il. Reboux, P. 7454
Baron Barnaby's Box. Colson, J. G. 1944
Barque Sans Pecheur, La. Casona, A. 1635
Barretts of Wimpole Street, The. Besier, R. 882
Barretts of Wimpole Street. Neven, C. 6473
Bartholomew's Joyful Noise. Miller, H. L. 5858
Bashful Bunny, The. Miller, H. L. 5859
Basi, Le. Marinetti, F. T. 5548
Basic Training of Pavlo Hummel, The. Rabe, D. 7372
Basket of Acorns, A. Feinstein, A. S. 2976
Baskets or Bonnets. Miller, H. L. 5860
Basta una donna. Provins, M. 7313
Bastard of the Blood. Brunson, B. 1389
Bataille de Lobositz, La. Hacks, P. 3810, 3811
Bath Road, The. Neilson, F. 6457
Bathsheba of Saaremaa. Kallas, A. 4535
Batisseurs d'Empire, Les. Vian, B. 9135
Battaglio del trasimeno, La. Tieri, V. 8859
Battezzato da solo. Hughes, L. 4302
Battle of Angels. Williams, T. 9419
Battle of the Backdrops, The. Marinetti, F. T. 5549
Be My Ghost. Murray, J. 6313
Beanstalk, The. Mosher, J. C. 6260
Beanstalk Kid, The. Nolan, P. T. 6633
Beanstalk Trial, The. Leonardi, A. 4927

688

Beany's Private Eye. Miller, H. L. 5861
Bear, The. Barrington, M. 635
Beard, The. McClure, M. 5136
Bearded Virgin before the Blind God. Fiedler, L. A. 3011
Bears, Bears, Bears. Goddell, P. 3625
Bear's Nest. Donahue, P. M. 2528
Beast, The. Wilson, S. 9466
Beastie. De Selincourt, H. 2357
Beat of the Wing, The. Curel, F. de 2148
Beat That Bongo. Huff, B. T. 4270
Beatnik and the Bard, The. Dias, E. J. 2405
Beatrice and Benedick. Mantle, M. 5506
Beatrice Cenci. Pincherle, A. 7153
Beau Dimanche de Septembre. Betti, U. 888
Beau for Nora, A. Nicholson, J. 6548
Beau Métier. Clerc, H. 1896
Beaumarchais l'Innombrable. Gavoty, B. and A. Decaux 3429
Beautiful People, The. Saroyan, W. 7946
Beautiful Thing, The. Leinster, M. and G. B. Jenkins, Jr. 4901
Beauty and the Ballot. Dias, E. J. 2406
Beauty and the Beast. Leech, M. T. 4891
Beauty and the Jacobin. Tarkington, B. 8705
Beauty Sleeping Black. Boyajian, A. 1246
Beaux-Parents, ou Il ne Faut pas Se Fier aux Apparences. Presles, C. des 7279
Bebecheri et la Petite Fille Perverse. Guerra, A. 3775
Be-Bop and Beethoven. Garver, J. 3403
Becket. Anouilh, J. 251
Becky, the Half-Witch. Hanna, H. 3892
Bed, The. Adler, J. 76
Bed of Caesar, The. Cluny, J. B. 1907
Bedlam Galore, for Two or More. Ionesco, E. 4383

Bedroom Suite. Morley, C. 6222
Bedtime Story. O'Casey, S. 6753
Bee, The. Saunders, L. 7983
Before Breakfast. O'Neill, E. 6837, 6838
Before Dawn. Hauptmann, G. 3972
Before the Dawn. Hicks, W. 4094
Before Your Very Eyes. Boiko, C. 1051
Beggar and the King. Parkhurst, W. 6976
Beggar, or The Dead Dog. Brecht, B. 1284
Beggars, The. Ruibal, J. 7787
Begging Machine, The. Ruibal, J. 7788
Behind the Khaki of the Scouts. McLane, F. M. 5237
Behind the Purdah. Gardener, E. 3386
Bel Indifferent, Le. Cocteau, J. 1910
Belcher's Luck. Mercer, D. 5758
Belette. Messager, C. 5786
Bell, Book and Candle. Van Druten, J. 9025
Bell of Dolores, The. Campbell, C. 1536
Bell of Freedom, The. Salt, P. S. 7892
Bella. Meano, C. 5722
Bella Lucerto, La. Alvarez Quintero, S. and J. Alvarez Quintero 157
Bellavita. Pirandello, L. 7181
Belle Marinerie. Achard, M. 20
Belle Rombière, La. Clervers, and G. Hanoteau 1897
Belle Telephone, La. Boiko, C. 1052
Belles of Horsefly Gulch, The. Murray, J. 6314
Bellezza cieca, La. Pasternak, B. L. 6997
Bello di papa. Marotta, G. and B. Randone 5568
Bells Are Ringing. Comden, B. and A. Green 1962
Below the Opposition Gangway. Traill, H. D. 8915
Ben Franklin Plays Cupid. Nicholson, M. A. 6568
Beneficenza. Heltai, J. 4051
Benefit for the Seamen. Angoff, C. 241
Benessere, Il. Brusati, F. and F. Mauri 1392
Beniamino. Lengyel, M. 4912

Benito Cereno. Lowell, R. 5069
Benpensati, I. Pecorelli, N. 7032
Bequest to the Nation, A. Rattigan, T. 7419
Berlingots, Les. Georges, R. 3441
Bernardine. Chase, M. C. 1737
Bernice. Glaspell, S. 3581
Bertha. Koch, K. 4675
Bertran De Born. Lunts, L. 5093
Beside Thy Cradle, Here I Stand. Stricker, C. J. 8560
Bessie Bosch. Nikl, P. 6602
Best Friends. MacLellan, E. and C. V. Schroll 5245
Best Hand, The. Squire, J. C. 8462
Best Man, The. Vidal, G. 9140
Best of All Possible Worlds, The. Ballesteros, A. M. 536
Best of Sports, The. Cable, H. 1471
Best Part of Christmas, The. Newman, D. 6489
Best Policy, The. Miller, H. L. 5862
Best-Seller. D'Errico, E. 2347
Best Year, The. McQueen, M. H. and N. McQueen 5294
Besuch der Alten Dame, Der. Durrenmatt, F. 2742
Bete, La. Riollet, M. 7589
Bethlehem. Housman, L. 4185
Bethlehem. Ketchum, A. 4608
Bethsabe. Gide, A. 3503
Betrayal, The. Colum, P. 1952, 1953
Betrayed, The. 886
Betrozali. Fratti, M. 3276
Betsy Ross. Roberts, H. M. 7606
Betty Blue's Shoe. Howard, H. L. 4201
Betty de la Ponche. Barillet, P. and J. P. Gredy 592
Between Book Covers. Stump, A. L. and M. M. Heller 8591
Between the Acts. Bjornson, B. 974
Between Two Trains. Pedder, D. C. 7033
Beware of Rumors. McQueen, M. H. and N. McQueen 5295
Beware the Genies! Boiko, C. 1053
Bewitched and Bewildered. Miller, H. L. 5863
Beyond Illusion, Morris, T. B. 6237
Beyond Mutiny. Peterson, M. N. 7096
Beyond the Horizon. O'Neill, E. 6839
Beyond the Mountains. Rexroth, K. 7497
Beyond the Pyramid. Gregory, H. 3733
Beyond Thule. Greene, L. L. 3717
Bible Salesman. Thompson, J. 8846
Bicentennial Bonanza. Rybak, R. K. 7820
Biche, Une. Worms, J. 9556
Bichon. Letraz, J. de 4940
Bicyclers. Bangs, J. K. 540
Biedermann und die Brandstifter. Frisch, M. 3309, 3310, 3311
Bien Amicalement. Billetdoux, F. 928
Bifur. Gantillon, S. 3366
Big and the Little Maneuver, The. Adamov, A. 58
Big Banker. Richmond, S. S. 7538
Big-Ben. Gourgue, J. 3668
Big Cat, Little Cat, Old Man Monkey. Plescia, G. L. 7212
Big Difference, The. Ravetch, H. 7435
Big Fish, Little Fish. Wheeler, H. 9317
Big House, The. Behan, B. 722-724
Big Idea, The. Richmond, S. S. 7539
Big Paul Bunyan. Thane, A. 8784
Big Red Riding Hood. Cable, H. 1472
Big Shoo, The. Boiko, C. 1054
Big Stick. Gerould, D. Trypstych 3445
Big Top Murders, The. Murray, J. 6315
Biggest Thief in Town. Trumbo, D. 8945
Bila nemoc. Capek, K. 1576
Bill of Divorcement, A. Dane, C. 2179
Bille en Tete. Laudenbach, R. 4826
Billets-Doux. Presles, C. des 7280
Billy Budd. Coxe, L. O. and R. Chapman 2086

Billy Liar. Waterhouse K. and W. Hall 9216, 9217
Bimbo cosî..., Un. Veneziani, C. 9066
Bimbo, the Pirate. Tarkington, B. 8706
Binario morto. Ronchini, R. 7680
Bind Up the Nation's Wounds. DuBois, G. 2617
Binocolo alla rovescia, Il. Lanza, G. 4806
Biografie: Ein Spiel. Frisch, M. 3312
Bird, The. Salt, J. 7890
Bird Court, The. Howard, V. 4220
Bird Who Couldn't Sing, The. Kring, H. A. 4725
Bird's Christmas Carol, The. Wiggin, K. D. 9347, 9348
Birth of a Soul, The. Sharp, W. 8197
Birth of Christ, The. 968
Birthday Anthem for America, A. Olfson, L. 6789
Birthday Candles. Getchell, M. C. 3450
Birthday Gift. MacLellan, E. and C. V. Schroll 5246
Birthday of the Infanta, The. Wilde, O. 9359
Birthday Party for UNICEF. Fisher, A. and O. Rabe 3104
Birthday Pie, The. McGowan, J. 5189
Birthday Surprise, The. McBrown, G. P. 5118
Birthdays of Frances Willard. Ashman, J. 420
Birthplace for a King. DuBois, G. 2618
Bishop's Candlesticks, The. Hugo, V. 4315
Biskie the Snowman. Lehman, J. F. 4896
Bisogna non perdere il treno. Antonelli, L. 298
Bit of the World, A. Woolf, E. A. 9553
Biteless Dog, The. Solon, I. 8370
Biter Bitten, The. Fisk, M. I. 3126
Bitterly Reviled. Lowe, L. 5068
Black Beauty. Sewell, Anna 8160
Black Blizzard. Fisher, A. 3039
Black Bottle, The. O'Brien, S. 6750

Black Comedy. Shaffer, P. 8165, 8166, 8167
Black Death or Ta-Un. Lee, M. E. 4881
Black Indies, The. Verne, J. 9089
Black Ivo. Colson, J. G. 1945
Black Lilacs. Keith, J. J. 4575
Black Oliver. Guinan, J. 3777
Black Swan Winter, The. Hale, J. 3837
Black Terror, The. Wesley, R. 9307
Black Tomorrow. Sutton, D. 8636
Blackbird, The. Howard, V. 4221
Blackbirds, The. Greenough, J. B. 3719
Blanc et Rouge. Bommart, J. 1159
Blaumilch Canal, The. Kishon, E. 4646, 4647
Blest Be the Bind That Ties. Fedo, M. W. 2971
Blind Alley. Richmond, M. C. 7535
Blithe Spirit. Coward, N. 2067
Blockade. Dunbar, O. H. 2698
Blockade. Lawson, J. H. 4861
Blockhead. Fulda, L. 3339
Blood of the Martyrs. Wilde, P. 9377
Blood Wedding. Garcia Lorca, F. 3374, 3375
Bloodybush Edge. Gibson, W. W. 3499
Blue. Mew, T. 5797
Blue Jackets, The. 1018
Blue Pincushion, The. Dixon, M. Q. 2509
Blue Sphere, The. Dreiser, T. 2591
Blue Sky. Fool, Tom 3211
Blue Sunday. Hecht, B. 4018
Blue Toadstool, The. Bellah, M. 732
Bluebird's Children. Richmond, S. S. 7540
Bluff. Delance, G. 2288
Blunted Age, The. Lee, Agnes 4873
Blushing Bunny, The. Spamer, C. 8404
Boat Club Dance. Robinson, C. 7617
Boat in the Forest, The. Haitov, N. 3828
Bobard. Sarment, J. 7931
Bobby and the Lincoln Speech. Pendleton, E. 7045

Bobosse. Roussin, A. 7737, 7738
Bob's Armistice Parade. Streacker, L. 8558
Bocciate in amore. Bush-Fekete, L. 1449
Bödeln. Lagerkvist, P. 4764
Boeing-Boeing. Camoletti, M. 1525
Boen, ou La Possession des Biens. Romains, J. 7667
Bogie Man. Gregory, Lady A. 3721
Bohboh, Beebee, and Booboo. Howard, H. L. 4202
Bohème, La. Puccini, G. 7323
Boia di Siviglia, Il. Garcia Alvarez, E. and P. Munoz Seca 3372
Bois de Colonel, Les. Presles, C. des 7281
Bolt from the Blue. Paull, H. M. 7012
Bon Secours. Anstruther, E. 284
Bonaparte. Larguier, L. 4817
Bonds of Affection. DuBois, G. 2619
Bonds of Interest. Benavente y Martinez, J. 741
Bone Shop, The. Sundell, C. 8619
Bonheur de Suzanne. Ferdinand, R. 2985
Bonne Compagnie, La. Audouard, Y. 452
Bonne Planque. Andre, M. 224
Bonne Soupe, La. Carette, L. 1598
Bonnes, Les. Genet, J. 3436
Bonshommes, Les. Dorin, F. 2550
Booby Trap, The. Miller, H. L. 5864
Boo-Hoo Princess, The. Buntain, R. J. 1417
Book a Day, A. McQueen, M. H. and N. McQueen 5296
Book Hospital, The. McKinney, J. B. 5234
Book of Jonah as Almost Any Modern Irishman Would Have Written It. Herbert, A. P. 4059
Book Play for High Schools 1192
Book Revue, The. McQueen, M. H. and N. McQueen 5297
Book That Saved the Earth, The.

Boiko, C. 1055
Book Week Assembly, The. Smith, M. 8339
Book Week Birthday Party. Kernan, M. A. 4603
Booklegger, The. Day, C. La Q. 2209
Bookmaker's Shoes, The. Mitchell, E. 6081
Books à la Mode. McQueen, M. H. and N. McQueen 5298
Books Alive! Byrne, E. B. 1465
Books Have Wings. Indick, B. P. 4370
Books in the Woods. 1193
Books to the Rescue. McQueen, M. H. and N. McQueen 5299
Bookworm, The. Chaloner, G. 1706
Boomerang. Miller, H. L. 5865
Boor, The. Chekhov, A. P. 1765
Bo-Peep's Valentine. Howard, H. L. 4203
Borga Gard. Hedberg, T. H. 4022
Borghese romantio, Il. Blanchon, J. 994
Borinage. Bertolini, A. 877
Boris Godunov. Mussorgsky, M. 6422
Born to the Soil. Richmond, S. S. 7541
Born Yesterday. Kanin, G. 4544
Boshibari and the Two Thieves. Nolan, P. T. 6634
Bosom of the Family, The. O'Neill, M. and J. Seabrook 6868
Boston Tea Party, The. Barbee, L. 556
Boston Tea Party, The. MacKay, C. D'A. 5219
Bottled in Bond. Hughes, G. 4301
Bought with Cookies. McBrown, G. P. 5119
Boulanger, la Boulangère et le Petit Mitron, Le. Anouilh, J. 252
Boulder Bay. Ah Chien 82
Bourgeois de Calas. Roncoroni, J. L. 7682
Bourgeois Gentilhomme. Molière, 6110
Bouvard e Pecuchet. Kezich, T. and L. Squarzina 4616
Bow to the Queen. Colson, J. G. 1946
Bowl, Cat and Broomstick. Stevens, W. 8510

Bow-Wow Blues, The. Dias, E. J. 2407
Boy, Abe. Smith, B. 8326
Boy Bishop, The. Gass, K. 3420
Boy Bowditch, The. Hughes, R. 4310
Boy Called Aesop, The. Winther, B. 9494
Boy Dreamer, The. Roberts, H. M. 7607
Boy From Next Tuesday, The. Boiko, C. 1056
Boy Next Door, The. Murray, J. 6316
Boy: What Will He Become? Brighouse, H. 1326
Boy Who Voted for Lincoln, The. Richards, M. 7524
Boy Who Went to the North Wind, The. Feather, J. 2960
Boy with a Future. McQueen, M. H. and N. McQueen 5300
Boy With the Bagpipe, The. Isom, L. M. 4413
Boys in the Band, The. Crowley, M. 2130
Bozeman Trail, The. Masters, H. G. 5652
Brahman, the Tiger and the Jackal, The. Parker, M. 6974
Branded Mavericks. Stechhan, H. O. and M. Terrell 8478
Brandywine. Torphy, W. 8892
Brasile, Il. Wilcock, J. R. 9353
Brassneck. Brenton, H. and D. Hare 1319
Brave Admiral. Hirshberg, B. 4112
Brave and the Blind. Blankfort, M. 999
Brave But Once, The. DuBois, G. 2620
Brave Little Indian Brave. Holler, R. M. 4142
Brave Little Tailor, The. Grimm, J. and W. Grimm 3749
Brave Little Tailor, The. Thane, A. 8796
Brave Trudy and the Dragon. Boiko, C. 1057
Bread and Butter. Taylor, C. P. 8719
Bread and Butter Shop, The. Miller, H. L. 5866
Breadline. Ketchum, P. L. 4610

Breadwinner, The. Maugham, W. S. 5665
Breakfast Past Noon. Molinaro, U. 6128
Breath. Beckett, S. 694
Brementown Litterbug, The. Creegan, G. R. 2101
Bremen Town Musicians, The. McQueen, M. H. and N. McQueen 5301
Bricks. O'Donnell, M. Three short plays. 6775
Bridal Chamber, The. Quiles, E. 7364
Bridal Dinner, The. Gurney, A. R., Jr. 3785
Bride of Gorse-Bracken Hall, The. Olfson, L. 6790
Bride of the Moor. Stramm, A. 8544
Bride Roses. Howells, W. D. 4236
Bridegroom, The. Biro, L. 965, 966
Bride's Christmas Tree, The. Herford, B. 4070
Bride's Crown. Topelius, Z. 8887
Bridge to Killybog Fair, The. Watts, F. B. 9224
Bridging the Gap. Turner, G. C. and J. H. Roy 8956
Brief Encounter. Coward, N. 2068
Briefly Speaking. McCoy, P. S. 5141
Brig. Brown, K. H. 1367
Brigadoon. Lerner, A. J. 4931
Brigante e la diva, Il. Adami, G. 52
Bright Comes. Asbrand, K. 395
Bright Morning. Alvarez Quintero, S. and J. Alvarez Quintero 158
Bright Stream. Pyle, M. T. 7351
Bringing Up Father. Fisher, A. O. Rabe 3105
Broadway Turkey, A. McGowan, J. 5190
Brocclin-Bar. Federici, M. 2968
Broken Broomstick, The. Miller, H. L. 5867
Broken Jug, The. Kleist, H. von 4661
Broken Pines. Hilton, C. 4110
Brokenbrow. Toller, E. 8873
Bronx Is the Next, The. Sanchez, S. 7902
Brooding Calves. Sachs, H. 7841
Broomstick Beauty, The. Miller,

H. L. 1445
Broth of Christkindli, The. Leuser, E. 4944
Brother Bill. Kreymborg, A. 4712
Brother Wolf. Housman, L. 4186
Brothers-In-Arms. Frith, W. 3321
Brothers in Mourning. Dryland, G. 2611
Brouille, La. Messager, C. 5787, 5788
Brownie Who Found Christmas, The. Thane, A. 8785
Brownies in Fairyland, The. Cox, P. 2082
Browning Version, The. Rattigan, T. 7420
Brune Que Voila, La. Lamoureux, R. 4776
Brush with Danger, A. Plescia, G. 7210
Brute. Chekhov, A. 1766
Bud on Nantucket Island. Beer, T. 717
Budapest 1930. Havas, N. 3976
Budge, Budge Not. Smith, N. K. 8347
Bugiarda, La. Fabbri, D. 2896
Bugiarda meravigliosa, La. Luzi, G. F. 5098
Bugie con le gambe lunghe, Le. De Filippo, E. 2251
Builder of the Wall, The. Roberts, H. M. 7608
Building of Florence, The. Koch, K. 4576
Bull Terrier and the Baby, The. Givens, H. M. 3578
Bullies, The. Burgos y Sarragoiti, F. J. de 1422
Bumblepuppy. Rogers, J. W., Jr. 7651
Bunch of Keys, A. McQueen, M. H. and N. McQueen 5302
Bunnies and Bonnets. Miller, H. L. 5869
Bunny of the Year. Newman, D. 6490
Bunny Who Was Always Late, The. Spamer, C. 8405
Buon Iodrone, Il. Falena, U. 2920
Buon Silvestro, Il. Saviotti, G. 7995
Buon viaggio Paolo! Cataldo, G. 1660

Buonanotte patrizia! De Benedetti, A. 2222
Burattinaio, Il. Schnitzler, A. 8061
Burattino, Il. Gherardi, G. 3466
Bürge Gutmann schliesst Sonderfrieden. Feuchtwanger, L. 3003
Burger Schippel. Sternheim, C. 8505
Burial, The. Gillespie, C. R. 3531
Burial Committee, The. Crockett, O. 2109
Buried Treasure. Barr, J. 615
Burla riuscita, Una. Kezich, T. 4613
Buroctopus. Tholy, R. 8819
Bury the Dead. Shaw, I. 8224
Bus Stop. Inge, W. 4372
Bus Trip. St. Clair, R. 7853
Busby Berkeley at Dachau. Boyajian, A. 1247
Business Is Business. Richmond, S. S. 7542
Business Meeting, A. Bates, A. 666
Busmen. Allen, J. 142
Buster Picks a Winner. Richmond, S. S. 7543
Busy Barbers, The. Miller, H. L. 5870
Busy Martyr, The. Hitchcock, G. 4114
But Fred Freud Is Dead. Terson, P. 8771
Butley. Gray, S. 3696, 3697
Butterfly, The. Finch, L. 3023
Butterfly, A. Kojiro, K. 4680
Butterfly Buffet. Halverson, B. 3873
Buttons, Pirates, and Pearls! Boiko, C. 1058
By Ourselves. Fulda, L. 3340
By the Light of the Moon. Alvarez Quintero, S. and J. Alvarez Quintero 159
By the Sea. Levin, R. 4963
By the Sumida River. Clements, C. C. 1894
By Their Words Ye Shall Know Them. Alvarez Quintero, S. and J. Alvarez Quintero 160
Bygones. Michelson, M. 5811

C

C. C. Boatright, M. C. 1031

Cabana Blues. McQueen, M. H. and N. McQueen 5303
Caccia grossa! De Filippo, P. 2269
Cacciatore d'anitre, Il. Betti, U. 889
Cachette d'Harpagon. Aub, M. and A. Camp 435
Cadaveri si spediscono e le donne si spogliano, I. Fo, D. 3165
Cadetti, I. Duvernois, H. 2781
Caduta di un impero, La. Wilcock, J. R. 9354
Caesar and Cleopatra. Shaw, G. B. 8205
Cafe De Pomone, Le. Perrin, M. 7077
Cage aux Folles, La. Poiret, J. 7226
Cage Opened, and Out Flew a Coward, The. Mandel, O. 5488
Caged Eagle. Lawrence, C. E. 4848
Cages, The. Arrabal, F. 372
Cain. Nemerov, H. 6463
Cain. O'Neill, M. D. 6866
Caine Mutiny, The. Wouk, H. 9571
Caino. Venturini, F. 9073
Calculated Risk. Hayes, J. 3993
Caleb Stone's Death Watch. Flavin, M. A. 3153
Caligula. Camus, A. 1550, 1551
Caliph's Journey, The. Thane, A. 8797
Call Washington 1776. Miller, H. L. 5871
Call Your People, America. Van Duyn, M. 9028
Callie Goes to Camp. Porter, E. W. 7249
Callimachus. Hrotsvitha 4262
Calling All Christmases. Fisher, A. 3040
Calling All Planets. Dennler, F. E. 2340
Calling for Help. Handke, P. 3882
Calore del seno. Birabeau, A. 947
Calypso. Baring, M. 596
Cambridge Dialogue, A. Daiches, D. 2160
Camelia Costumes, The. Rawe, M. 7439
Camera degli ospiti, La. Rondi, B. 7689
Cameriere di Don Giovanni, Il. Benavente y Martinez, J. 742
Camino Real. Williams, T. 9420
Campana delle tentazioni, La. Mosca, G. 6254
Campiello, Il. Goldoni, C. 3604
Camping in the Snow. Chang Feng-Chao and Tiao Cheng-Kuo 1715
Campo, Il. Gambaro, G. 3360
Canale di Blaumilch, Il. Kishon, E. 1189, 1190
Cancer. Weller, M. 9279
Candanles, Commissioner. Gerould, D. C. 3443
Candidat. Prin, C. 7301
Candido. Viola, C. G. 9151
Conovaccio dei comici dell-arte. 1573
Cantata dei pastori, La. Perrucci, A. 1714
Cantatrice Chauve, La. Ionesco, E. 4384
Cantava per tutti, Uno. Bassano, E. 656
Canterbury Tales, The. Chaucer, G. 1742
Canterville Ghost, The. Wilde, O. 9360
Cap o'Rushes. Feather, J. 2961
Cape Kennedy chiama sferracavallo. Fontanelli, G. 3210
Capitaine Bada. Vauthier, J. 9048
Capitano d'industria, Il. Rondi, B. 7690
Capoufficio, Il. Cavallotti, C. 1673
Cappello a tre punte, Il. De Alarcon, P. 2212
Caprice. Musset, A. de 6418, 6419
Captain Applejack. Hackett, W. 3796
Captain Castaway's Captives. Miller, H. L. 5872
Captain Scrimshaw's Treasure. Boiko, C. 1059
Captains Courageous. Kipling, R. 4638
Cara ombra, La. Boularan, J. 1217
Carabinieri, I. Joppolo, B. 4515
Cardboard Star, The. Phillips, O. 7138
Care and Feeding of Mothers, The. Boiko, C. 1060
Career. Lee, J. 4878
Career for Ralph, A. Richmond,

S. S. 7544
Careless Ness, the Dragon.
	McMahon, B. 5270
Caretaker, The. Pinter, H.
	7172, 7173
Carillon, Il. Vanni, A. 9036
Carlo Gozzi. Simoni, R. 8298
Carlos Among the Candles.
	Stevens, W. 8511
Carnaval de Juillet. Nohain, J.
	6624
Carnaval de L'Amour. Mere,
	C. 5764
Carne unica. Giovaninetti, S.
	3555
Carnival, The. Eldridge, P.
	2837
Carnival Saturday. Arrufat, A.
	381
Carola. Renoir, J. 7492
Carolette. O'Connell, T. E.
	6760
Caroline. Maugham, W. S.
	5666
Carol's Christmas Cards. St.
	Clair, R. 7854
Carrozza del santo sacramento,
	La. Mérimée, P. 5770
Carry On, Cupid! Boiko, C.
	1061
Carved Symbol, The. Fisher,
	A. 3041
Cas Interessant, Un. Buzzati,
	D. 1454
Casa con dos Puertas Mala es de
	Guardar. Calderon de la
	Barca, P. 801
Casa de Bernarda Alba, La.
	Garcia Lorca, F. 3376, 3377
Casa del delitto, La. Bernard,
	T. 850
Casa del parco, La. Romualdi,
	G. 7672
Casa delle nubili, La. Bonacci,
	A. 1166
Casa lontana, La. Olivieri, E.
	6825
Casa sopra le nuvole, La. Brissoni, A. 1334
Casa sull'acqua, La. Betti, U.
	890
Casadh an Tsùgàin. Hyde, D.
	4349
Cascando. Beckett, S. 695
Case for Books, The. McQueen,
	M. H. and N. McQueen 5304
Case for Mrs. Hudson, A. Murray, J. 6317
Case for Two Detectives, A. Murray, J. 6318
Case for Two Spies, A. Murray,
	J. 6319
Case of Astrolable, The. Hutchins,
	M. P. 4334
Case of Mistaken Identity, A. Murray, J. 6320
Case of Mr. X, The. Richmond,
	S. S. 7545
Case of Mrs. Kantsey Know. Jarrell, M. W. 4447
Case of the Easter Villains, The.
	Durden, M. 2739
Case of the Forgetful Easter Rabbit, The. Miller, H. L. 5873
Case of the Frustrated Corpse, The.
	Wallace, R. 9193
Case of the Giggling Goblin, The.
	Miller, H. L. 5874
Case of the Missing Masterpiece,
	The. Huff, B. T. 4271
Case of the Missing Parents, The.
	Campbell, J. A. 1539
Case of the Missing Pearls, The.
	Dias, E. J. 2408
Case of the Missing Poet, The.
	Murray, J. 6321
Case of the Silent Caroler, The.
	Miller, H. L. 5875
Case of the Toy Town Clown, The.
	Haugh, G. L. 3963
Case of the Wall Street, The.
	Murray, J. 6322
Caserma della fate, La. Badessi,
	G. and G. Cobelli 489
Casino Gardens, The. Nicholson,
	K. 6563
Casket-Maker, The. Stockton, R.
	F. 8530
Caso fortunato, Un. Mrozek, S.
	6284
Caso papaleo, Il. Flaiano, E. 3148
Cassandra Singing. Madden, D.
	5420
Cast Up by the Sea. Dias, E. J.
	2409
Castaway on Polywolynesia. Lee,
	J. 4879
Castilla Vuelve à Castilla. Arauz,
	A. 312
Castle and the Plains, The. Paredes, P. S. 6970
Castle in Spain, A. Nicholson, J.
	6549
Castle-Builder, The. 1654
Castlebury Clock, The. Sroda, A.
	8466

Cat, The. Walter, O. F. 9199
Cat and the Moon, The. Yeats,
　W. B. 9586, 9587, 9588
Cat and the Queen, The. Bennett,
　R. 776
Cat for Halloween, A. MacLellan,
　E. and C. V. Schroll 5247
Cat Has Not Always Carnival.
　Ostrovsky, A. 6911
Cat, Mouse, Man, Woman. Saroyan, W. 7947
Cat on a Hot Tin Roof. Williams
　T. 9421, 9422
Catastrophe! 1662
Catastrophe Clarence. Shore, M.
　8261
Catene. Cowl, J. and J. Murfin.
　2080
Catene. Michaux, H. 5806
Caterina delle misericordie. Cuomo, F. 2143
Cathleen ni Hoolihan. Yeats, W.
　B. 9589, 9590
Catnip Patch, The. Smith, G. V.
　8332
Cato Street. Shaw, R. 8228
Cats and the Monkey, The.
　Holmes, R. V. 4150
Cattedrale, La. Sorescu, M.
　8385
Cattedratici, I. Sàito, N. 7862
Caught at the Narrows. Fisher,
　A. 3042
Caught--One Snipe. Richmond,
　S. S. 7546
Cause for Celebration. Olfson,
　L. 6791
Cause for Gratitude. DuBois, G.
　2621
Cause to Serve, A. DuBois, G.
　2622
Cavalcade of Human Rights.
　Fisher, A. and O. Rabe 3106
Cavalier miseria, Il. 1671
Cavalier Seul, Le. Audiberti,
　J. 443
Cavallo di Troia, Il. Giachetti,
　C. 3473
Cave, The. Hennefeld, E. B.
　4057
Cave at Machpelah, The. Goodman, P. 3628
Cave Dwellers. Saroyan, W.
　7948
Cave Man, Brave Man. Garver,
　J. 3404
Cave of Precious Things, The.
　Wagenheim, A. 9203

Caves du Vatican, Le. Gide, A.
　3504
Caviale per il generale. George,
　G. S. and E. Leontovich 3440
Caviar ou Lentilles. Scarnicci,
　G. and R. Tarabusi 8009
C'e anche un fidanzato. Duse, E.
　2765
Ce Formidable Bordel! Ionesco,
　E. 4385
Ce Qui Est Dit Est Dit. Nicolai,
　A. 6579
Ce Qui Fait le Plus Vite. Tinseau,
　L. de 8868
"... Ce Soir, A Samarcande."
　Boularan, J. 1218
Cécile, ou L'Ecole des Pères.
　Anouilh, J. 253, 254
Cecily Entertains the Enemy. Waite,
　H. E. 9185
Ceiling. Halman, D. F. 3868
Celebre cantante, La. Molnar, F.
　6136
Celebrità. Faraci, G. 2928
Célébrité, Discretion. Dornac,
　C. 2558
Celestina, La. Rojas, F. de
　7656, 7657
Celles Qu'on Prend dans Ses Bras.
　Montherlant, H. de 6187
Cena d'addio. Schnitzler, A. 8062
Cendrillon. Provins, M. 7314
Ceneri. Beckett, S. 696
Cenno, Il. Antonelli, L. 299
Censored Scenes from King Kong.
　Schuman, H. 8090
Centenaire, Le. Kerautem, L. de
　4600
Centenario, Il. Alvarez Quintero,
　S. and J. Alvarez Quintero 161
Century Plant, The. Conboy, F.
　J. 1967
C'era una volta un bola.... La
　Porte, R. 4813
C'era una volta.... Riccora, P.
　7514
Cerchio della morte. Cavacchioli,
　E. 1669
Cernye Pticy. Pogodin, N. 7224
Certain Général Bonaparte. Lery,
　M. 4934
Certain Monsieur Blot. Rocca, R.
　7635
Certo giorno di un certo anno in
　Aulide, Un. Faggi, V. 2908
Ces Messieurs de la Santé. Armont, P. 340
Césaire. Schlumberger, J. 8038

"C'Est mon Mari." Socorri, C. 8360
Cet Animal Etrange. Aroutcheff, G. 360, 361
Cette Petite Ville. Schaaf, S. 8017
Chacun Selon sa Faim, A. Mogin, J. 6103
Chafing-Dish Party, A. Bangs, J. K. 541
Chairs. Ionesco, E. 4386
Chaise, La. Prins, P. de 7303
Chalk and Slate. Major, M. 5464
Challenge, The. Milton, N. L. 6069
Challenge. Ward, T. 9209
Challenge to Young America, A. Baker, J. L. 518
Chambre à Part. Santelli, C. 7916
Chambre Mandarine, La. Thomas, R. 8831
Chambre Nuptiale, La. Machard, A. 5213
Champagne et Whisky. Regnier, M. 7465
Championship of the Universal Class Struggle, The. Mayakovsky, V. 5701
Chand et froid. Crommelynck, F. 2115
Change of Heart, A. James, H. 4434
Change of Mind. Speirs, R. 8440
Changeling, The. Spofford, H. P. 8454
Changing the Guard. Ruiz, R. 7793
Changing Willie's Mind. 1716
Chapeau Chinois. Nohain, F. 6623
Chaplinade, The. Goll, Y. 3616
Charivari. Stephens, N. B. 8500
Charles! Charles! Housman, L. 4187
Charlie and the Six Chicks. Garver, J. 3405
Charlie Barringer. Martin, J. J. 5624
Charlie McDeath. Forssell, L. 3226
Charlie Who? French, H. 3296
Charm, The. Besant, Sir W. and W. H. Pollock 881
Charmante Enfant. Sabatier, P. 7834

Charmante Soiree. Boularan, J. 1219
Chasse au Dahut, La. Hamon, F. 3879
Chat en Poche. Feydeau, G. 3006
Chat est un Chat, Un. Worms, J. 9557
Chateau en Suède. Quoirez, F. 7368
Chatelaine de Shenstone. Bisson, A. 970
Chatiment. Truffier, J. and Chanu, J. 8944
Chauffeur, Le. Maurey, M. 5684
Che c'entra l'amore? Gavi, V. 3425
Che servono questi quattrini? A. Curcio, A. 545
Chemin de Crete, Le. Marcel, G. 5529
Chemin de la Croix, Le. Ghéen, H. 3462
Chemins de fer, Les. Labiche, E. 4746
Chemise de Nylon, La. Madern, J. M. 5422
Chene et Lapins Angora. Walser, M. 9195
Cher Antoine, ou L'Amour Raté. Anouilh, J. 255
Cheri. Colette, S. G. C. and L. Marchand 1934
Cherries of Sir Cleges, The. Hall, M. 3852
Cherry-Blossom River. Clements, C. C. 1894
Cherry Blossoms. Sutphen, W. G. V. T. 8628
Cherry Orchard. Chekhov, A. 1767
Cheval Arabe. Luchaire, J. 5077
Chevaliers de la Table Ronde, Les. Cocteau, J. 1911
Chez les Titch. Calaferte, L. 1499
Chez Maurice. Franzero, C. M. 3270
Chi è di scena? Conti, A. 1984
Chi piu sa manco sa. 1793
Chi ruba un piede e fortunato in amore. Fo, D. 3166
Chiamami becco. Ravegnani, G. 7433
Chiamata in giudizio. Troisi, D. 8536
Chiave, La. Corthis, A. 2046

Chiave del mistero, La. Dekobra, M. 2286
Chic e moche. Bernard, J. J. 824
Chicken-Little. Barker, C. and J. Medina 600
Chicken Made of Rage, The. Serrano, N. and J. Binder 8155
Chief Halloween Spirit. Muni, A. 6296
Chien du Jardinier, Le. Neveux, G. 6474
Chien Sous la Peau, Le. Auden, W. H. and C. Isherwood 439
Chi-Fu. Justema, W., Jr. 4528
Child in the House. Howard, H. H. 4216
Child Is Born, A. Benet, S. V. 758
Child of Destiny, A. DuBois, G. 2623
Child of God, The. Driscoll, L. 2606
Child Who Was Made of Snow, The. Bennett, R. 802
Childe Roland to the Dark Tower Came. Wilder, T. 9392
Childhood. Wilder, T. 9390
Children. Gurney, A. R., Jr. 3786
Children, The. Ruthenberg, G. H. 7811
Children Is All. Purdy, J. 7342
Children of Chocolate Street, The. Kane, E. B. 4539
Children of Lir. Colum, P. 1954
Children of the Evangelists, The. Tomes, M. O. 8882
Children of the Sun. Gorky, M. 3644, 3645
Children of the Sun. Rittenhouse, C. 7593
Children of the Sunrise. Dabney, J. P. 2154
Children's Crusade, The. Brooks, E. S. 1342
Children's Hour. Hellman, L. 4045, 4046
Children's Librarian Is Guest on "What's My Line?". Brown, T. G. 1374
Child's Play. Marasco, R. 5527
Chilometri bianchi. Federici, M. 2969
Chimera. Garcia Lorca, F. 3378
China Comes to You. Asbrand, K. 396
China Pig. Emig, E. 2861

China Speaks to America. Buck, P. S. 1407
Chinese Incident. Buck, P. S. 1408, 1409
Chinese Lily. Jakobi, P. 4431
Chinese Rip Van Winkle, A. Chandler, A. C. 1713
Chinese Wall, The. Frisch, M. 3313
Chinese Water Wheel. Strachan, E. H. 8543
Chinita. Bessey, R. M. S. 885
Chinois. Barillet, P. and J.-P. Gredy 585
Chinois, Les. Schisgal, M. 8029
Chips with Everything. Wesker, A. 9300, 9301
Chiromante, Il. Bolla, N. 1154
Chirugo inverosimile, Il. Donizetti, P. 2534
Chit-Chat on a Rat. Atherton, C. S. 428
Choc en Retour. Menuau, G. 5756
Choice, The. Manning-Sanders, G. 5503
Choice of Giannetta. Applegate, A. E. 309
Choosing a Monument. Eberhart, R. 2802
Choosing of Easter Rabbit, The. Werner, S. 9294
Chop and Change. Burley, J. 1429
Chorus Girl, The. Stone, J. A. 8531
Chosen One, The. Duvall, L. M. 2775
Choutes, Les. Barillet, P. and J.-P. Gredy 586
Chowder and Cherries. French, B. 3294
Christ Recrucifie. Kazantzakis, N. 4563
Christian. Noe, Y. 6611
Christina's World. Tavel, R. 8716
Christmas at the Cratchits. Dickens, C. 2466
Christmas Bear, The. McQueen, M. H. 5284
Christmas Cake, The. Fisher, A. 3043
Christmas Carol, A. Dickens, C. 2467, 2468, 2469
Christmas Carol. Kaufman, G. S. and M. Connelly 4559
Christmas Cat, The. Anglund, B. 240
Christmas Chime, A. Kilvert, M.

C. 4624
Christmas Coast to Coast. Olfson, L. 6792
Christmas Comes to Hamelin. Mills, G. E. 6059
Christmas Concert. Monaghan, K. 6170
Christmas Conspiracy. Richardson, A. S. 7527
Christmas Conspiracy, The. Woodbridge, E. 9543
Christmas Cowboy, The. Miller, H. L. 5876
Christmas Eve at Mother Hubbard's. D., S. J. 2153
Christmas Eve in Pine Cone Forest. Watts, F. B. 9225
Christmas Eve Letter. McQueen, M. H. and N. McQueen 5305
Christmas Eve News. McQueen, M. H. and N. McQueen 5306
Christmas Eve, The Holly-Goblin's. Warner, F. L. 9211
Christmas Every Day. Howells, W. D. 4237, 4238
Christmas for Cosette. Olfson, L. 6818
Christmas Gifts of All Nations. Wells, C. 9285
Christmas Greeting, A. Kane, R. 4543
Christmas Guest. Kingsbury, S. 4636
Christmas House. Waite, H. E. and E. M. Hoppenstedt 9186
Christmas in Court. Fisher, A. 3044
Christmas in Old Boston. Very, A. 9104
Christmas in Old New England. Clapp, P. 1837
Christmas in Our Town. Woeppel, L. B. W. 9523
Christmas in the Shadows. Loew, R. W. 5017
Christmas in the Woods. McQueen, M. H. and N. McQueen 5307
Christmas Joy. Very, A. 9105
Christmas Mouse, The. Diller, M. E. T. 2498
Christmas Nutcracker, The. Thane, A. 8798
Christmas Oboe, The. Miller, H. L. 5877
Christmas Pageant. 1828
Christmas Party. McQueen, M. H. and N. McQueen 5308

Christmas Pathway. Jens, A. J. 4462
Christmas Peppermints, The. Miller, H. L. 5878
Christmas Play. Trowbridge, M. 8939
Christmas Present, The. Dickinson, T. 2484
Christmas Promise, A. Miller, H. L. 5879
Christmas Quest. Runnette, H. V. 7796
Christmas Question, The. Newman, D. 6491
Christmas Recaptured. McQueen, M. H. and N. McQueen 5309
Christmas Revel, The. Boiko, C. 1062
Christmas Runaways, The. Miller, H. L. 5880
Christmas Sampler, The. Leuser, E. 4945
Christmas Shoe, The. Duvall, L. M. 2776
Christmas Shopping Early. McQueen, M. H. and N. McQueen 5310
Christmas Snowman, The. McQueen, M. H. and N. McQueen 5311
Christmas Starlet, The. Dias, J. 2410
Christmas Stockings. Guiterman, A. 3780
Christmas Story, The. Simpson, M. 8304
Christmas Surprise, The. Dohner, I. R. 2520
Christmas Tablecloth, The. Fisher, A. 3045
Christmas Tree, The. Housman, L. 4188
Christmas Tree for Kitty, A. Fisher, A. 3046
Christmas Tree Legend. Petersen, S. 7089
Christmas Tree Surprise, The. Newman, D. 6492
Christmas Tryst. Roof, K. M. 7693
Christmas Umbrella, The. McGowan, J. 5191
Christmas Visitor, The. Bailey, A. H. 503
Christmas with Martin and Katie. 1829
Christopher Columbus. Ghelderode, M. de 3458

Chronicles of Bohikee Creek. Unger, R. 8970
Chu Yuan. Kuo, M.-J. 4738
Church Street. Robinson, L. 7623
Ci penso io! Curcio, A. 2147
Ciarlatano, Il. Poretto, L. 7247
Ciarlatano meraviglioso, Il. Pinelli, T. 7157, 7158
Ciascuno a Suo Modo. Pirandello, L. 7182
Ciascuno il suo, A. De Maria, A. and G. Possenti 2312
Cicero. Bonelli, L. 1180
Cicero the Great. McCoy, P. S. 5142
Ciclo delle noci di cocco, Il. Chiarelli, L. 1796
Cicogna si diverte, La. Roussin, A. 7739
Cicogne, Le. Gariffo, E. 3390
Cid le Lepreux, Le. Castro, G. de 1657
Ci-divant, The. Kuyumjian, D. 4740
Ciel de Lit, Le. Hartog, J. de 3951
Cinderella. Bland, E. N. 995
Cinderella. D'Arcy, A. 2185
Cinderella. Newman, D. 6493
Cinderella. Thane, A. 8799
Cinderella and Friends. Cheatham, V. R. 1749
Cinderella of New Hampshire. Jagendorf, M. 4428
Cinderella Revisited. Olfson, L. 6793
Cinderella Swings. Dewey, P. B. 2391
Cinderfellow. Nolan, P. T. 6635
Cinder-Rabbit. Baher, C. W. 493
Cinder-Riley. Boiko, C. 1063
Cinemania. Cognets, J. des 1923
Cinematografo. Dolley, G. 2524
Cinema-Verite. Boyajian, A. 1248
Cinerella. Wilner, O. 9455
Cinq à Sept. Mery, A. 5784
Cinquante Minutes d'Attente. Charras, C. 1731
Cintia, La. Della Porta, G. B. 2302
Cio che non sai. Giovaninetti, S. 3556
Ciò che non si dice. Landi, S. 4782

Circe's Auction. Baker, W. M. 523
Circle. Maugham, W. S. 5667, 5668, 5669
Circumventin' Sandy. MacDonald, Z. K. 5168
Circus Daze. Miller, H. L. 5881
Circus Magic. Vahl, R. 8986
Circus Parade. MacLellan, E. and C. V. Schroll 5248
Cirque aux Illusions, La. Aubert, R. 436
Cite du Soleil, La. Petresco, J. 7109
Citizen Franklin of Philadelphia. Reines, B. J. 7471
Citizens of Calais. Nicol, E. 6577
City. Navarro, F. 6454
City Lights Ripoff. Estrin, M. Four Infiltration Pieces. 2877
City of Fear. Murray, J. 6323
City Sugar. Poliakoff, S. 7228
Civiale per il generale. George, G. S. and Leontovich, E. 3440
Civilians Stay Put. McQueen, M. H. and N. McQueen 5312
Claque, La. Roussin, A. 7740
Classe Terminale. Obaldia, R. de 6716
Classic Dancing School, The. Duncan, W. 2703
Classics Again, The. Sedgwick, H. D. 8125
Claude de Lyon. Husson, A. 4327
Clean Sweep, A. Boiko, C. 1064
Clean Up, The. Abel, B. 6
Clean-up Club, The. Fisher, A. and O. Rabe 3107
Cleanest Town in the West, The. Dias, E. J. 2411
Cleavage. Naumburg, M. 6453
Clementina Piéfaroux, La. Duvernois, H. 2782
Cleo and Max. Marcus, F. 5540
Cleopatra in Judaea. Symons, A. 8661
Clerambard. Ayme, M. 468, 469, 470
Clever Cobbler, The. Feather, J. 2962
Clever Peasant, The. Corson, H. W. 2042
Cliente Perdue, Une. Vandenberghe, P. 9017
Clifford and William. Farrell, J. T. and H. Farrell 2936
Cliffs, The. Foreman, R. 3219
Climate of Eden. Hart, M. 3940

Climb the Greased Pole. Longhi, V. 5025
Clinofilo, Il. Ori, L. 6876
Clock Work. Hart, J. Sonata for Mott Street. 3938
Clorinde, ou Le Mariage Interrompu. Comnene, M. 1964
Close to the Wind. Barnes, E. 608
Closed Door, The. Shepherd, E. 8243
Closing Door. Knox, A. 4673
Cloud Descends, The. Bodenheim, M. 1036
Cloud on the Honey-Moon, A. Magnus, J. 5446
Clouds, The. Kvapil, J. 4741
Clouds of the Sun. Fiske, I. H. 3130
Cloughoughter. Colum, P. 1955
Clown and the Undertaker, The. Preis, A. L. 7276
Clown of Stratford. Squire, J. C. 8463
Club. Lacour, J.-A. 4762
Cobra alle caviglie, Il. Jacobbi, R. 4422
Coccodrilli, I. Rocca, G. 7632
Cochons d'Inde. Jamiaque, Y. 4439
Cockcrow. Taylor, L. M. 8721
Cocktail Party, The. Eliot, T. S. 2847, 2848
Cocorita. Saviotti, G. 7996
Cocu, Battu et Content. Casona, A. 1636
Cocuzza, La. Cassieri, G. 1644
Coda, The. Stratton, C. 8555
Codfish, The. Ruibal, J. 7789
Codicil. Ferrier, P. 3000
Coeur. Bernstein, H. 862
Coeur a Deux. Foissy, G. 3186
Coeur Volant, Le. Puget, C.-A. 7324
Coexistence, La. Magnan, J.-M. 5436
Cohn of Arc. Feiffer, J. 2973
Coincidenza secondo binario. Perrini, A. 7078
Collana di perle, La. Mirande, Y. and H. Feroule 6078
Collection, The. Pinter, H. 7174
Collector's Item. Dias, E. J. 2412
Collier de Jade, Le. Sarment, J. 7932
Colloquio. Raggio, E. 7383
Colloquio col tango. Terron, C. 8752
Colloquio col Topolino. Galeazzi, G. A. 3351
Colombe. Anouilh, J. 256
Colombe a Deux Têtes, La. Bacon, J. 484
Colombe Poignardée. Sorbets, G. 8383
Colombine. Clements, C. C. 977
Colombine Wants Flowers. Drago-Bracco, A. 2586
Colonie. Marivaux, P. 5555
Colonnade, The. Young, S. 9619
Colonnella, La. Mazzolotti, P. 5712
Color of Our Skin, The. Gorostiza, C. 3655
Colore dell'anima, Il. Alessi, R. 125
Colori. Depero, F. 2341
Colors Mean so Much. Asbrand, K. 397
Colossal, Stupendous. Murray, J. 6324
Colour-Blind. Aide, C. H. 85
Colpa e sempre del diavolo, La. Fo, D. 3167
Colpevoli senza colpa. Ostrovsky, A. 6912
Coltiviamo in pace i nostri giardini. Roland, G. 7660
Coltre, La. D'Amora, F. 2173
Colui che viveva la sua morte. Achard, M. 21
Columbus. Cheney, J. V. 1787
Columbus Day. Welles, O. 9281
Columbus Sails the Sea. Barbee, L. 557
Combat, The. Duhamel, G. 2679
Combinaison. Paquin, D. 6953
Come Back, Little Sheba. Inge, W. 4373
Come e perche crollo il colosseo. De Filippo, L. 2266
Come il Signor Mockpinpott fu liberato dai suoi tormenti. Weiss, P. 9273
Come si rapina una banca. Fayad, S. 2952
Come to the Fair! Murray, J. 6325
Come un ladro di notte. Bassano, E. 646
Come What May. France, A. 3241
Comeback Caper, The. Martens, A. C. 5588
Comédie du Bonheur. Evreinoff,

N. N. 2886
Comédie du Miroir, La. Rouquette, M. 7730
Comédie sans Titre, ou La Regeneration, La. Svevo, I. 8641
Comedy: A Tragedy in One Act. Kazantzakis, N. 4564
Comedy of Danger, A. Hughes, R. 4307
Comedy of the Dead, The. Perez, J. C. 7067
Comedy of the Exile. Fiske, I. H. 3131
Comer, The. Freda, F. 3288
Comes the Dreamer. Wexley, J. 9312
Cometa si fermò. Calvino, V. 1516
Comic Life of Elia Brobitza, The. Williams, W. C. 9445
Comic Valentine. Miller, H. L. 5882
Coming of Ewn Andzale, The. Fitzmaurice, G. 3139
Coming of Gabrielle, The. Moore, G. 6201
Coming of Hippolytus, The. Sackville, M. 7843
Coming of the Prince, The. Field, E. 3013
Command Decision. Haines, W. H. 3825a
Commandant Watrin. Lanoux, A. and J. Rutman 4802
Comme au Théatre. Dorin, F. 2551
Comme Avant, Mieux Qu'Avant. Pirandello, L. 7183
Comme la Pierre. Weingarten, R. 9270
Comme les Chats. Silvain, J. and D. Gallo 8280
Comme Nous Avons Eté. Adamov, A. 59
Comme un Oiseau. Millar, R. and N. Balchin 5833
Commedia del buon cuore, La. Molnar, F. 6137
Commedia del re buffone e de buffone re. De Filippo, L. 2267
Commedia di colui che sposò una donna muta. France, A. 3242
Commedia di dieci vergine. 1963
Commedia nella commedia. Bailly, A. 502
Commedia ripugnante di una madre. Witkiewicz, S. I. 9512

Commedia senza adulterio. Sanesi, A. 7908
Comment Harponner le Requin. Haim, V. 3823
Comment les Choses Arrivent. Danaud, J. C. 2177
Comment Va le Monde, Monsieur? Billetdoux, F. 929
Commère, La. Marivaux, P. 5556
Commissario di notturna. Grassi, E. 3691
Commissionnaire, Le. Boucherit, S. 1205
Committee on Matrimony, The. Kilvert, M. C. 4625
Commodus. Wallace, L. 9192
Common for All Saints, A. Ziegelmaier, G. 9648
Common Ground. Mercier, V. 5763
Common Ground. Whiting, E. C. 9329
Common Man, A. Prelovsky, A. 7277
Compagnon de Voyage, Le. Chabannes, J. 1698
Compagnons de la Marjolaine, Les. Achard, M. 22
Comparsa, La. Bodet, R. 1042
Comparsa, La. Pujel, R. 7337
Compass for Christopher, A. Gordon, C. 3634
Compass for Christopher, A. Newman, D. 6494
Complesso dell'obelisco. Terron, C. 8753
Complex de Philemon, Le. Luc, J. B. 5074
Complexe de Philemon, Le. Boudousse, J. 1207
Componimento sacro per la festivitá del SS. Natale. Metastasio, P. 5796
Comportement des Epoux Bredburry, Le. Billetdoux, F. 930
Comprendere il Pianto, Per. Balla, G. 535
Compromise, The. Jaeger, C. S. 4426
Compromise, The. Seiffer, D. 8135
Computerized Play. Tucetsky, D. and J. Pyros 8947
Comte de Gomara, Le. Camp, A. and F. Puig-Espert 1530
Con loro. Zorzi, G. 9656
Concealed Fansyes, The. Caven-

dish, Lady J. and Lady E. Brackley 1676
Concentric Circles. Bradford, B. 1259
Concert at Saint Ovide, The. Vallejo, A. B. 9004
Conchiglia all'orecchio, La. Bompiani, V. 1161, 1162
Concietro de San Ovidio, El. Vallejo, A. B. 9003
Condamne de Pichwickton. Antoine, A. -P. 285
Condemned Squad. Sastre, A. 7970
Condition Humaine, La. Talagrand, J. 8693
Conditioned Reflex. Zahn, C. 9630
Condottieri, I. Novelli, C. 6702
Conduct Unbecoming. England, B. 2866
Confab with Crockett. Carmer, C. 1607
Confession. Amiel, D. 180
Confession de Mendon, La. Richter, C. de 7569
Confessione a Francesca. Calvino, V. 1517
Confessioni. Donnay, C. M. 2536
Confessioni della Signora Elvira, La. Roli, M. and G. Sbragia 7659
Confessions. Kitaif, T. 4649
Confessori, I. Di Mattia, V. 2502
Confidence, A. Jordan, E. D. 4516
Confidences. Amiel, D. 181
Confiseur. Bonacci, A. and E. Charles 1168
Conflitti. Carroll, P. V. 1620
Confrontation. Fortuno, C. 3231
Congaree Sketches. Adams, E. C. L. 69
Congiura, La. Prosperi, G. 7310
Congregation's Advent-Christmas Worship, The. Wedde, A. H. 9252
Congres de Clermont-Ferrand, Le. Franck, M. 3251
Congresso, Il. Kozak, P. 4698
Congresswomen, The. Aristophanes 332
Coniglio molto caldo, Un. Obaldia, R. de 6717

Connecticut Yankee in King Arthur's Court, A. Clemens, S. L. 1878, 1879
Conquest of Everest, The. Kopit, A. 4686, 4687
Conquête de l'Everest, La. Kopit, A. 4688
Conscript Fathers, The. Symons, J. D. 8665
Conspiracy, The. Dickens, C. 2470
Conspiracy of Feelings, The. Olyesha, Y. 6831
Conspirators, The. Barbour, R. H. 575
Conspirators, The. Merimee, P. 5771
Constant Lover, The. Hankin, St. J. 3886, 3887
Constant Nymph, The. Kennedy, M. and B. Dean 4596
Constitution Is Born, The. Brown, C. J. 1361
Consulto, Il. Rietmann, C. M. 7576
Contata dei pastori, La. Perrucci, A. 7082
Contessa, La. Druon, M. 2610
Conti dell'attrice, I. Havas, N. 3977
Continued Departure. Gregor, A. 3720
Contractor, The. Storey, D. 8536
Contratto, Il. Birabeau, A. 948
Conversation, The. Masters, E. L. 5651
Conversation dans le Loir-et-Cher. Claudel, P. 1861
Conversation in Hades. Percival, W. 7063
Conversation Piece. Nicholson, J. 6550
Conversation Recorded in an East Village Coffee-House. Wantling, W. 9204
Convert, A. White, C. 9322
Cookbook. Parsons, M. R. 6992
Cooking Up a Storm. Feinstein, J. 2977
Cooped Coup, The. Sudekum, F. 8600
Cop and Blow. Harris, N. 3930
Copecchia e Marianorma. Rosso di San Secondo, P. 7714
Coperchia è caduta una stella, A. De Filippo, P. 2270
Copione, la rivoluzione e finita. Saito, N. 7863

Coplas de Unos Tres Pastores. Reynosa, R. de 7503
Copper Farthing, The. Huff, B. T. 4272
Coquine. Roussin, A. 7741
Coram Populo! Strindberg, A. 8561
Corde Pour le Pendre, La. Valmain, F. 9006
Cordia. Smith, H. S. 8335
Corinna Goes A-Maying. Boiko, C. 1065
Coriolanus. Shakespeare, W. 8175, 8176
Corn Is Green, The. Williams, E. 9410
Corn Meal and Poetry. DuBois, G. 2624
Corna di Don Friolera, Le. Montenegro, R. M. del V.I. 6182
Corner, The. Freda, F. 3288
Corner Store, The. Richmond, S. S. 7547
Cornerstone of Civil Rights. Miranda, J. E. 6077
Corno Francese, Il. Rimanelli, G. 7585
Cornuto immaginario, Il. Molière 6111
Corona di Strass, La. Falena, U. 2921
Coronation, The. Forssell, L. 3227
Corpo che sale, Il. Boccioni, U. 1034
Corpse, The. Atkins, R. 432
Correctionnelle, En. Gillois, A. 3533
Corridore che canta, Il. Rebora, R. 7453
Corruzione al palazzo di giustizia. Betti, U. 891
Corsa dietro l'ombra, La. Roma, E. 7664
Corsaro, Il. Achard, M. 23
Corte dei miracoli. Cavacchioli, E. 1670
Corte delle stalle, La. Kroetz, F. X. 4726
Coscienza di Zeno, La. Kezich, T. 4614
Cose piu grandi di loro, Le. Bertòli, P. B. 875
Cosi ce ne andremo. Calvino, V. 1518
Cosi è (Se Vi Pare). Pirandello, L. 7184

Cosi fan Tutte. Da Ponte, L. 2184
Cosma perduto. Bagnara, M. 492
Cosmonaute Agricole, Le. Obaldia, R. 6718
Cost Plus and American Imperialism. Estrin, M. Four Infiltration Pieces. 2877
Costo di una vita, Il. Magnoni, B. 5444
Costume, Le. Lessay, J. 4938
Costume Caper, The. Martens, A. C. 5589
Cote D'Azur. Birabeau, A. and G. Dolley 960
Cottonwood Court. Shedd, H. G. 8232
Coulisses de l'ame, Les. Evreinov, N. 2887
Count of Monte Cristo, The. Dumas, A. 2685
Count the Days I'm Gone. Keyser, F. 4612
Counterfeit Presentment, A. Howells, W. D. 4239
Country Girl. Odets, C. 6771, 6772
Country Store Cat, The. Miller, H. L. 5883
Coup de Cyrano. Bernard, T. 853
Coup de Soleil, Un. Vandenberghe, P. 9018
Coup d'Etat du 2 Decembre. Arnaud, R. 170
Couple of Right Smart Fellers, A. Olfson, L. 6794
Coups de Théatre. Mithois, M. 6090
Couronne de Carton. Sarment, J. 7933
Course of True Love, The. Hartley, R. E. 3946
Court of King Arithmetic, The. Chaloner, G. 1707
Courters, The. Nolan, P. T. 6636
Courting Trouble. Fisher, A. 3047
Courtroom of Terror, The. Blaine, B. G. 984
Cousin Frederick. Woodmeald, J. E. 9547
Couteau. Perret, J. 7075
Covetous Councilman, The. Bealmear, J. H. 687
Cowards. Lovett, R. M. 5065
Cow-herd and the Weaving Maid, The. Shen Hung 8236
Crabbed Youth and Age. Robinson, L. 7624

Crabs. Ordway, W. Three Short Sketches. 6875
Crack, Il. Roversi, R. 7765
Crack in the Universe. Olson, E. 6828
Cracker Barrel Circus. Huff, B. T. 4273
Cradle Song. Martinez Sierra, G. and M. Martinez Sierra 5626, 5631
Craig's Wife. Kelley, G. E. 4578
Cramped Homes, Cramped Lives. 2093
Cranford. Merington, M. 5778
Crash Landing, The. MacNeice, L. 5279
Crawlers, The. Edson, R. 2817
Crawling Arnold. Feiffer, J. 2974
Crazy Locomotive, The. Witkiewicz, S. I. 9513
Creation. Lane, K. W. 4788
Creation of the World and Other Business, The. Miller, A. 5841
Creatore d'illusione, Il. Girette, M. 3577
Creditor, The. Strindberg, A. 8562
Cremazione del cugino Passoire, La. Bringer, R. 1330
Crepuscule du Theatre. Lenormand, H. R. 4915
Cresta Run, The. Simpson, N. F. 8305
Crier by Night. Bottomley, G. 1201
Crime and Punishment. Dostoevski, F. 2562
Crime au Village. Rouchet, P. 7725
Crime et Châtiment. Aroutcheff, G. 362
Crime et Châtiment. Baty, G. 673
Criminals. Geijerstam, G. 3434
Crimson Feather, The. Watts, F. B. 9226
Crimson Glory Rose, The. Phillips, M. K. 7127
Cripple Play. Richards, M. 7523
Crise Ministerielle. Bernard, T. 837
Crisi coniugali. Provisn, M. 7315

Crisis, The. Richmond, S. S. 7548
Crisscross Streets. Deming, D. 2318
Cristallo magico, Il. Dunsany, E. J. M. D. P. 2707
Cristina. Mazzucco, R. 5717
Cristo, El. Larkin, M. 4818
Cristo degli abissi. Seborga, G. 8123
Cristo ha ucciso. Callegari, G. P. 1509
Critic as Artist, The. Wilde, O. 9361
Critic Was a Lady, The. Reed, D. 7457
Critics' Catastrophe, The. Schuchert, H. 8088
Crocodiles, Les. Matsas, N. 5656
Crocus Who Couldn't Bloom, The. Boiko, C. 1066
Crois au Père Noel. Premoisan, A. 7278
Cromwellian, The. MacManus, L. 5273
Cronaca. Trieste, L. 8934
Cronache romane. Sastre, A. 7971
Crooked Jar, The. Lackmann, R. 4758
Croque-Monsieur. Mithois, M. 6091
Cross-Country, East Coast. Ordway, W. Three Short Sketches. 6875
Cross-Country, West Coast. Ordway, W. Three Short Sketches. 6875
Cross My Palm with Silver. King, F. 4629
Cross of Gold, The. Anderson, D. and S. Dimond 222
Cross Princess, The. MacLellan, E. and C. V. Schroll 5249
Crosspatch and Cupid. McGowan, J. 5192
Crossroads. Sturgis, J. 8593
Crosstown Manhattan! Ingham, T. 4381
Crowded Bedroom. Sassoon, R. L. 7968
Crowded House, The. Jacob, E. 4419
Crowning of King Arthur, The. Olfson, L. 6819
Crowning of the Queen, The. Baker, J. M. 519
Crows, The. Becque, H. 712
Crucible, The. Miller, A. 5842, 5843, 5844

Crudele intromissione. Cagli, B. 1486
Cruelle Galejade. Mithois, M. 6092
Cruma. Pedrolo, M. de 7035
Crusade for Liberty. Graham, M. S. 3677
Crusts. Claudel, P. 1862
Cry Witch. Miller, H. L. 5884
Cry Witch. Miller, M. L. 6055
Crying Clown, The. Nicholson, M. A. 6569
Crystal Flask, The. Asbrand, K. 398
Cub Reporter. Richmond, S. S. 7549
"Cucendron," ou La Pure Agathe. Favart, R. 2949
Cuckolds Go to Heaven. Rueda, L. de 7783
"Cuckoo." MacKeown, M. J. J. 5232
Cuckoo, The. Murdoch, M. 6306
Cue for Cleopatra, A. Martens, A. C. 5590
Cugino di Arsenio Lupin, Il. D'Amora, F. 2174
Cugino Filippo. Pugliese, S. 7332
Cuisine des Anges, La. Husson, A. 4327, 4328
Culprit, The. Wilde, P. L. 9378
Cuor di Leone. Beith, J. H. 730
Cuore. Duvernois, H. 2783
Cuore alla mano. Alvarez Quintero, S. and J. Alvarez Quintero 162
Cuore di allora, Il. Corradini, B. and G. Achille 2029
Cupid and Company. Callanan, C. 1508
Cupid Computer, The. Martens, A. C. 5591
Cupid in Command. McGowan, J. 5193
Cupid on the Loose. McGowan, J. 5194
Cupid on the Loose. Miller, H. L. 5885
Cupid's Golden Key Ring. Miller, H. L. 5886
Cupid's Partner. Paradis, M. B. 6956
Cupid's Post Office. Pendleton, E. 7046
Cupies and Hearts. McQueen, M. H. and N. McQueen 5313
Cupivac. Boiko, C. 1067
Cure for a King. Simon, S. 8285
Cure for Authors. Sherwin, L. 8254
Curiosity of Kitty Cochraine, The. Michelson, M. 5812
Curious Quest, The. Miller, H. L. 5887
Curious Savage, The. Patrick, J. 6999
Curmudgeon, The. Menander 5742
Curse of Hog Hollow, The. Miller, H. L. 5888
Curtain, The. Flanagan, H. F. 3151
Curtains. Head, C. and M. Gavin 3998
Curtmantle. Fry, C. 3330
Customs Caper, The. Murray, J. 6326
Cybernella. Boiko, C. 1068
Cyclone. Gantillon, S. 3367
Cyclops. Euripides 2879
Cypress, Rita and Doreen. Maule, C. 5678
Cyrano de Bergerac. Rostand, E. 7717

D

DA. Leonard, H. 4923
Dacappo. Acquabona, P. 46
Daddy Violet. Birimisa, G. 962
Daddy's Gone A-Hunting. Akins, Z. 88
Dadi e l'archibugio, I. Balducci, A. 531
Dafne Laureola. Mavor, O. H. 5695
Dagger of the Goth, The. Zorrilla y Moral, J. 9655
Daily Bread. Whitehouse, J. H. 9327
Daisy Miller. James, H. 4435
Dalla finestra. Corradini, A. 2027
Dama della montagna, La. Suzuki, S. 8638
Dama prudente, La. Goldoni, C. 3605
Dame aux Camelias, La. Dumas, A. 2688
Dame aux Gants Verts. Fauchois, R. 2941
Dame de Coeur, La. Bernede, A. 858

Dame de Trèfle, La. Aroutcheff, G. 363
Dame Fortune and Don Money. Corson, H. W. 2043
Dame Julian's Window. Lyttleton, E. S. 5103
Damian and the Wooden Flute. Steiner, B. A. 8495
Damn Yankees. Abbott, G. and Wallop, D. 5
Damné. Obaldia, R. de 6719
Damned Dieties, The. Lindsay, J. 4989
Damsels in Distress. McGowan, J. 5195
Dance of the Seven Deadly Sins. Symons, A. 8662
Dancing Children, The. Very, A. 9106
Dancing Princesses, The. Grimm, J. and W. Grimm 3750
Danger--Pixies at Work. Howard, V. 4222
Dangerous Corner. Priestley, J. B. 7290, 7291
Dangerous Game, The. Miller, S. 6058
Dangling from Two Second Rate Tragedies. Cooke, N. 2000
Daniel. Windeler, B. C. 9474
Daniel Hale Williams, Pioneer Surgeon. Satchell, M. 7976
Daniel Webster, Eighteen in America. Stein, G. 8488
Daniele, Fille de Dieu. Beer, J. de 716
Dans l'Histoire du Coeur. Gevel, C. 3451
Dans la Loge de Molière. Dave, A. 2193
Danse Calinda. Torrence, R. 8893
Danse sans Musique. Richard, H.-C. and A. Gray 7522
Dante Ammazzato. Heinegg, P. 4035
Dardanelles Puff-Box, The. Milne, J. R. 6064
Dare All for Liberty. Sickels, E. 8270
Dark at the Top of the Stairs. Inge, W. 4374, 4375
Dark Harvest. Ringwood, G. P. 7588
Dark Lady of the Sonnets, The. Shaw, G. B. 8206
Dark Man at the Feast, The. Livingston, F. M. 5006

Dark Roses. Doyle, L. F. 2581
Dark Window. Plimpton, H. 7217
Dark Wood, The. L., Y. 4745
Darkest Hour, The. DuBois, G. 2625
Darkness. O'Flaherty, L. 6778
Darkness at Noon. Kingsley, S. 4637
Data eccezionale, Una. Soldevila, C. 8367
Date with Washington, A. McQueen, M. H. and N. McQueen 5314
Daughter of Jorio, The. D'Annunzio, G. 2181
Daughter of the Gods, The. DuBois, G. 2626
Daughter-in-Law, The. Lawrence, D. H. 4852
Daughters of Lot, The. Kliewer, W. 4665
Davanti all'infinito. Corra, B. 2034
David and Bathsheba. Ehrmann, M. 2829
David and the Second Lafayette. Davis, L. 2202
David Copperfield and Uriah Heep. Dickens, C. 2471
David, It Is Getting Dark. Kops, B. 4690
David Laments. Lutz, G. M. 5095
Dawn! Gonne, M. 3620
Dawn. Wellman, R. 9282
Dawn. Wilde, P. L. 9379
Dawn, Day, Night. Niccodemi, D. 6536
Day, The. Smith, W. 8356
Day After Tomorrow. Lonsdale, F. 5029
Day At the Store, A. Huff, B. T. 4274
Day Baseball Died, The. Teitel, I. 8739
Day Before Christmas, The. Wells, C. 9286
Day for Trees, A. McQueen, M. H. and N. McQueen 5315
Day in Alexandria at the Festival of Adonis. Hyde, W. W. 4356
Day in the Death of Joe Egg, A. Nichols, P. 6542, 6543
Day Is Brick, The. Myrick, N. 6429
Day of the Dragon, The. McFarlan, E. 5175
Day the Indians Came, The. Ramsey, H. 7396

Day the Marsmen Landed, The. Rybak, R. K. 7821
Day the Moonmen Landed, The. Rybak, R. K. 7822
Day to Remember, A. Miller, H. L. 5889
Daylight Wishing Time. Richardson, M. C. 7531
Day's End. Conkle, E. P. 1971
Days of the Commune. Brecht, B. 1285
Days Without End. O'Neill, E. 6840
Dead Are Singing, The. Hauptmann, C. 3967
Dead of Night. Murray, J. 6327
Dead Saint, The. Hedges, B. 4024
Dealing in Futures. Rollins, A. W. 7663
Dear Daddy. Cannon, D. 1564
Dear Liar. Kilty, J. 4622, 4623
Dear Lottie. Dias, E. J. 2413
Dear Queen, The. Ganly, A. 3365
Dear Ruth. Krasna, N. 4709
Death. Fineberg, L. 3026
Death: A Discussion. Woodruff, R. W. 9551
Death and Re-erection of Dr. Franklin, The. Garcia, E. 3370
Death and the Fool. Hofmannsthal, H. von 4129, 4130
Death and the Hyacinths. Cochrane, A. 1909
Death Knocks. Allen, W. 145
Death-Mask, The. Stuart, D. M. 8586
Death of a Kinsman. Taylor, P. 8725
Death of a Salesman. Miller, A. 5845, 5846, 5847
Death of an Old Woman. Connor, P. 1979
Death of Aunt Aggie. MacDougall, R. 5172
Death of Biddy, The. MacMahon, B. 5271
Death of Clytemnestra, The. Lytton, E. B. 5105
Death of Columbine, The. Vail, W. J. 8989
Death of Empedocles. Holderlin, F. 4141
Death of Marlowe. Horne, R. H. 4171
Death of Me, The. 2220
Death of Mohammed, The. Hakim, T. A. 3830
Death of Nero, The. Gorman, H. S. 3653
Death of Seneca, The. Hine, D. 4111
Death of the Duc D'Enghien, The. Hennique, L. 4058
Death of Trotsky, The. Cook, A. 1995
Death Poem. Goldstein, M. 3614
Débauche. Boularan, J. 1220
Debbie the Dreamer. Garver, J. 3406
Debit and Credit. Strindberg, A. 8563
Débutante, The. Fitzgerald, F. S. 3133
Decalage. Amiel, D. 182
December Evening, 1817, A. Sansom, C. 7913
December's Gift. Duggar, F. 2678
Decisione. Cangiullo, F. 1555
Decree Nisi, The. Bates, J. 668
Dedalo e fuga. Talarico, E. 8698
Dedication, The. Simpson, F. M. 8301
Deep Are the Roots. D'Usseau, A. and J. E. Gow 2771
Deep Blue Sea, The. Rattigan, T. 7421, 7422
Defense Never Rests, The. Deming, D. 2319
Defunt, Le. Obaldia, R. de 6720
Deirdre of the Sorrows. Synge, J. M. 8666, 8667
Dejeuner D'Amoureux. Birabeau, A. 949
Del vento tra i rami del sassafrasso. Obaldia, R. de 6721
Delaissée, La. Maurey, M. 5685
Delia, or A Masque of Night. Auden, W. H. and C. Kallman 440
Delicate Balance, The. Albee, E. 98
Delitto all' Isola della Capre. Betti, U. 892
Delitto e castigo. Giancapo and Rossato 3478
Della Natività di Nostro Signore. Manrique, G. 5504
Della notte. Doplicher, F. 2545
Delta Wife, The. McClellan, W. 5130
Demain il Fera Jour. Montherlant, H. de 6188

Demain, Une Fenetre Sur Rue....
Grumberg, J.-C. 3766
Demande en Mariage, La. Chekhov, A. P. 1768
Demande en Mariage, Une. Dubreuilh, S. 2665
Démangeaison, La. Spiraux, A. 8452
Demi-fous, Les. Gouin, O. M. 3661
Demigod, The. Bailey, H. C. 507
Demi-Gods, The. Stephens, J. 8499
Demoiselle de petite vertu, La. Achard, M. 24
Demolition Downtown, The. Williams, T. 9423
Demon Cat, The. Rooney, J. R. 7697
Demoniaques, Les. Durafour, M. 2733
Demons, The. Dostoevski, F. 2563
Demon's Shell. Noguchi, Y. 6615
Demos and Dionysus. Robinson, E. A. 7618
Dentista improvvisato, Il. Crozière, A. 2131
Departures, The. Languirand, J. 4801
Deputy for Broken Bow, A. Cable, H. 1473
Derelict. Ross, C. 5150
Dernier Candidat, Le. Chedid, A. 1761
Dernier Exemplaire, Le. Sussmann, J. 8625
Dernier Juge, Le. Bron, J. 1337
Dernier Train, Le. Houweninge, C. van 4198
Derniere Bande, Le. Beckett, S. 697
Derniers Jours de Solitude de Robinson Crusoe, Les. Savary, J. 7992
Derricks on a Hill. Whitehand, R. 9326
Derubate, Le. Mura 6303
Dervorgilla. Gregory, Lady A. 3722
Descent of the Gods. Corwin, N. 2047
Descente sur Recife, La. Cousin, G. 2062
Desert Blooms, The. Schmitt,
G. 8041
Desert Men. Hall, R. 3865
Deserter, The. Abercrombie, L. 11
Deserter, The. Kotzebue, A. von 4693
Desiderio, Il. Amiel, D. 183
Design for Loving. Steele, J. 8481
Desir, Attrape par la Queue. Picasso, P. 7143
Desire Trapped by the Tail. Picasso, P. 7144
Dessous des Cartes, Le. Gillois, A. 3534
Destination: Christmas! Boiko, C. 1069
Destino, Il. Lopez, S. 5036
Detonazione. Cangiullo, F. 1556
Deuce O'Jacks, A. Higgins, F. R. 4098
"Deutschland--Ein Greuelmärchen." Brecht, B. 1286
Deux Augures, Les. Franck, P. 3253
Deux Chats Et ... Un Souris. Thomas, R. 8832
Deux Ecoles. Provins, M. 7316
Deux Femmes Pour un Fantome. Obaldia, R. de 6722
Deux Gros Lots. Peneau, Y. 7058
Deux Ménages. Lavedan, H. 4837
Deux Vierges, Les. Bricaire, J.-J. and M. Lasaygues 1321
Deuxieme Coup de Feu, Le. Thomas, R. 8833
Devil Comes to Alcaraz, The. Fulham, W. H. 3341
Devil Is a Good Man. Kozlenko, W. 4699
Devil to Pay, The. Coffey, C. 1921
Devils, The. Whiting, J. 9330
Devils and Angels. Eberhart, R. 2803
Devil's Doll, The. Russell, M. M. 7804
Devoir du Medecin, Le. Pirandello, L. 7185
Devonshire Demons, The. Murray, J. 6328
Diable en Eté, Le. Faure, M. 2947
Diable et le Bon Dieu, Le. Sartre, J.-P. 7961, 7962
Dial M for Mother. Miller, H. L. 5890
Dial M for Murder. Knott, F. 4670, 4671

Dialog. Dunster, M. 2729
Dialogue. Eberhart, R. 2804
Dialogue About Love, Poetry and Government Service. Blok, A. 1008
Dialogue Between Raftery and Death. Fallon, P. 2925
Dialogue des Inconnus. Schreiber, I. G. 8084
Dialogue for Strangers. Ouellet, E. 6918
Dialogue from a Garden. Ross, A. R. 7700
Dialogue of a Democracy. Eifler, M. S. 2833
Dialogue of Amargo. Garcia Lorca, F. 3379
Dialogue of the Dead. Lucian 5078
Dialogue on a Northern Shore. Stead, C. K. 8477
Dialogue Pathetique. Adam, P. 50
Dialogue to the Memory of Mr. Pope. Dobson, A. 2511
Dialogues d'Exilés. Brecht, B. 1287
Dialogues des Carmelites. Bernanos, G. 823
Dialogues du Sieur. Bruyère, J. de la 1393
Diamante del profeta, Il. Terron, C. 8754
Diamond Erring, The. Paradis, M. B. 6957
Diane de Poitiers. Faramond, M. de 2930
Diapason. Carsana, E. 1624
Diari, I. Bertoli, P. B. 876
Diario di un pazzo, Il. Gogol, N. 3599
Diario di una donna. Valdarnini, A. 8993
Diarmuid and Grainne. Zeyer, J. 9645
Diarmuid and Grania. Moore, G. and W. B. Yeats 6202
Diary of Ann Frank. Goodrich, F. and A. Hackett 3632
Diavolerie, Le. Fersen, A. 3001
Diavolo Peter, Il. Capelli, S. 1582
Dichiarazione, La. Bataille, H. 661
Dick Whittington and His Cat. Miller, H. L. 5891
Dick Whittington and His Cat. Thane, A. 8786
Dicky Dot and Dotty Dick. Brooks, E. S. 1343
Did It Really Happen? Akins, Z. 89
Dies Irae. Mattolini, M. and M. Pezzati 5663
Dies Irae. Wendt, F. W. 9292
Dieu aboie-t-il? Boyer, F. 1252
Dieu le savait. Salacrou, A. 7868
Difficult Hour. Lagerkvist, P. 4765
Diff'rent. O'Neill, E. 6841
Dig That Mastadon! Murray, J. 6329
Digits, The. DeMay, A. J. 2314
Dija. White, E. 9323
Diluvio, Il. Betti, U. 893
Dimanche. Danaud, J.-C. 2178
Dimanche. Roger-Marx, C. 7650
Dindon, Le. Feydeau, G. 3007
Dingo. Wood, C. 9542
Dingos. Dautun, P. 2192
Dinner. Molnar, F. 6138
Dinner at Eight. Kaufman, G. S. and E. Ferber 4560
Dinner Table, The. Sabin, E. L. 7840
Dinnetah. Winther, B. 9495
Dio salvi la Scozia. Manzari, N. 5508
Direzione memorie. Augias, C. 453
Dirty Hearts. Sanchez, S. 7903
Disabled. Ransley, P. 7412
Disarmati, I. Barzini, L., Jr. 645
"Disciple, A." Deevy, T. 2242
Discours de Père, Le. Foissy, G. 3187
Discours des Prix. Sarment, J. 7934
Discretion, La. Kattan, N. 4554
Discrezione. Molnar, F. 6139
Discussion with Interruptions, A. McLaurin, K. 5238
Disenchanted, The. Schulberg, B. and H. Breit 8089
Dish for the Colonel, A. Baker, N. B. 520
Dish for the King, A. McQueen, M. H. and N. McQueen 5316
Dish of Green Peas, A. Fisher, A. and O. Rabe 3108
Dissolution. Schnitzler, A. 8063
District of Columbia. Richards, S. 7525, 7526
District Visitor, The. Middleton, R. B. 5819

Ditch. Andrews, M. R. S. 228
Do I Hear Twenty Thousand? Benchley, R. C. 751
Do or Diet. Murray, J. 6330
Do You Know the Milky Way? Wittlinger, K. 9522
Dobbiamo esser felici. Martinez Sierra, G. 5627
Dobromila Rettig. Jirasek, A. 4469
Dock Brief, The. Mortimer, J. 6246
Doctor and the Patient. Saroyan, W. 7949
Doctor Farmer. Simon, S. 8286
Doctor for Lucinda, A. Mantle, M. 5507
Dr. Frankenstein and Friends. Cheatham, V. R. 1750
Doctor in Spite of Himself, The. Molière 6112
Doctor Know All. Howard, H. L. 4204
Doctor Know-It-All. Hall, M. C. 3848
Dr. Leviticus and the Wicked Imp. Bealmear, J. H. 686
Doctor Manners. McQueen, M. H. and N. McQueen 5317
Doctor Time's Office. Very, A. 9107
Doctor Turns Into a Poet, The. Schmitt, G. L. 8042
Doctor's Daughter. Miller, H. L. 5892
Doctor's Duty, The. Pirandello, L. 7186
Dodo Bird, The. Fried, E. 3302
Dodsdansen. Strindberg, A. 8564
Dogmatiker und der Voraussetzungslose. Wolfs, J. 9535
Dogodek v mestu Gogi. Grum, S. 3764
Dolce aloe, Il. Mallory, J. 5478
Dolce vita, La. Provins, M. 7317
Dolls, A Christmas Nonsense Play. Armstrong, L. V. V. 344
Dolls No More. Fratti, M. 3277
Dolly Dialogue. Wells, C. 9287
Dolly e il suo ballerino. Engel, A. and A. Grunwald 2865
Dolly Saves the Day. Miller, H. L. 5893

Dolly Saves the Picture. Barbee, L. 558
Dolore giunge dall'altra parte, Il. Maeterlinck, M. 5426
Domatore, Il. Bassano, E. 647
Domatore, Il. Surchi, S. 8622
Domenica ci si riposa, La. Bompiani, V. 1163
Domenica d'un fidanzato. Buzzolan, U. 1461
Domenica della buona gente, La. Pratolini, V. and G. D. Giagni 7274
Domeniche di Angiola e Bortolo. Pugnetti, G. 7334
Domino. Achard, M. 25, 26
Don Carlos. Schiller, J. C. F. von 8025
Don Chisciotte. Bragaglia, A. G. 1265
Don D'Adele, Le. Barillet, P. and J.-P. Gredy 587
Don Gil dalle calzi verdi. Tellez, G. 8740
Don Giovanni. Molière 6113
Don Giovanni al rogo. Balducci, A. 532
Don Giovanni innamorato. Fayad, S. 2953
Don Giovanni Involontario. Brancati, V. 1270
Don Jack. Salce, L. 7884
Don Juan. Maraini, D. 5522
Don Juan. Molière 6114
Don Juan Duped. Boyesen, A. 1253
Don Juan en Flandre. Dumur, L. and V. Josz 2695
Don Juan in Hell. Shaw, G. B. 8207
Don Juan Malgré Lui. Turpin, F. 8957
Don Juan oder Die Leibe zur Geometrie. Frisch, M. 3314
Don Juan's Failure. Baring, M. 597
Don Juan's Women. Moock, A. 6195
Don Quixote. Cervantes, M. de 1689
Don Raffaele il trombone. De Filippo, P. 2271
Don Vincenzino. Marotta, G. and B. Randone 5569
Donna di Eguchi, La. Kiyotsuga, K. 4654
Donna dolce, Una. Adamov, A. 68

Donna quasi onesta, Una. Vanni, A. 9037
Donna Rossa, La. Giannini, G. 3484
Donna uccisa per deduzione, Una. Fruttero, C. 3329
Donnaiuolo, Il. Cangiullo, F. 1557
Donne intelligenti. Havas, N. 3978
Donne nell'armadio, La. Flaiano, E. 3149
Donne sono così, Le. Corradini, B. and G. Achille 2030
Donnina senza importanza, Una. Armont, P. and M. Gerbidon 343
Donnina senza logica, Una. Reinach, M. 7468
Dono della notte, Il. Duse, C. V. 2764
Donogoo. Romains, J. 7668
Do-Nothing Frog, The. Clapp, P. 1838
Don't Be Just a File Clerk. Miller, J. V. 6052
Don't Call Us--We'll Call You. Murray, J. 6331
Don't Destroy Me! Hasting, M. 3960
Don't Leave Me Alone. Johnson, W. 4490
Don't Pet My Rock! Murray, J. 6332
Don't Send for Hector. Slattery, M. E. 8312
Don't Tell the Folks Back Home. Dias, E. J. 2414
"Don't You Want to Be Free?" Hughes, L. 4303
Door, The. Murray, J. 6333
Door Mats. Whipkey, S. D. 9319
Door Must Be Either Open or Shut, A. Musset, A. de 6420
"Door Must Be Either Open or Shut." Turique, B. de 8953
Doorbell, The. Fratti, M. 3278
Dopo divorzieremo. De Stefani, A. 2367
Dopo la gioia. Cenzato, G. 1679
Dopo la recita. Baraldi, I. 551
Dora Nelson. Verneuil, L. 9096
Dormer Windows. Raphael, A. 7414
Dos Ranchos, or, The Purification. Williams, T. 9424
Dottor Faust, Il. De Flers, R. 2282
Dottor Frankenstein a Hortaleza, Il. Sastre, A. 7972
Double Cross. Megrue, R. C. 5731
Double-Ditto Dream. Heinzen, B. 4036
Double Entry. Thompson, J. 8846
Double Exposure. McQueen, M. H. and N. McQueen 5318
Double Game, The. Baring, M. 598
Double Jeu. Thomas, R. 8834
Double Miracle. Garland, R. 3392
Double Negative, The. Livingston, F. M. 5007
Double Nine of Chin Yuan. Nolan, P. T. 6637
Double Passion. Villeroy, A. 9149
Double Talk. McCoy, S. 5143
Doubtful Son, The. Diamond, W. 2399
Dove siamo. D'Errico, E. 2348
Dover Road, The. Milne, A. A. 6060
Down Below the Rio Grande 2571
Drago volante, Il. Gherardi, G. 3467
Dragon. Marks, J. 5560
Dragon and the Century Plant, The. Matthews, M. 5660
Dragon with the Squeaky Roar, The. Martens, A. C. 5592
Dragon's Claws, The. Carpenter, G. 1611
Dragon's Head. Valle Inclan, R. 8998
Dralda Bloom. Cunningham, L. 2139
Drama of the Future, The. Healey, J. P. 4004
Dramatic Art, The. Kemp, H. 4585
Dramatic Evening. Bangs, J. K. 542
Dramatist Digested, The. Datta, J. 2189
Dramma dei costruttori. Michaux, H. 5807
Dramma di sogni. Bonelli, L. 1181
Dramma in platea. Guthrie, T. A. 3788
Dramma, la commedia, la farsa, Il. Antonelli, L. 300
Drapier Letters, The. Power, A. 7265
Dreadful Dragon, The. Brydon, M. W. and E. Ziegler 1395

Dream, The. Dreiser, T. 2592
Dream. Mierow, H. E. 5823
Dream Assassins, The. Peters, R. 7087
Dream (but perhaps not). Pirandello, L. 7187
Dream Comes True, The. Barbee, L. 559
Dream Girl. Rice, E. 7520
Dream Maker, The. Thompson, B. J. 8839
Dream Maker's Workshop, The. Spamer, C. 8406
Dream of a Spring Morning. D'Annunzio, G. 2182
Dream of an Autumn Sunset. D'Annunzio, G. 2183
Dream of Death, The. Selincourt, H. de 8146
Dream on, Soldier. Hart, M. and G. S. Kaufman 3942
Dream Play, A. Herschberger, R. 4082
Dreaming of the Bones, The. Yeats, W. B. 9591
Dreammaker's Tree, The. Huber, M. B. 4267
Dreams. Eich, G. 2830
Dreamy Kid, The. O'Neill, E. 6842
Dregs. Crawford, J. W. 2100
Dressing for the Play. Fish, M. I. 3127
Dressmaker and the Queen, The. Feather, J. 2957
Dreyfus. Grumberg, J.-C. 3767, 3768
Driftwood. O'Kelly, S. 6785
Drinking Academy 2602
Droit Chemin, Le. Ruinet, G. 7791
Drums in the Dusk. Laure, K. 4828
Drums of Father Ned. O'Casey, S. 6754
Drums of Oude, The. Strong, A. 8583
Drunken Sisters. Wilder, T. 9391
Dryad, The. Sterling, G. 8501, 8502
Dryad and the Deacon. Bates, W. O. 670
Du Coté de Chez Proust. Malaparte, C. 5468
Du Guesclin. Botrel, T. J. M. 1200
Duca di Mantova, Il. Falena, U. 2922

Ducal Bonnet, The. Roberts, H. M. 7609
Duchess at Sunset. Johnson, P. H. 4488
Duchesse d'Algues, La. Blackmore, P. 980
Due donne. Molnar, F. 6140
Due dozzine di rose scarlatte. De Benedetti, A. 2223
Due fratelli rivali, I. Della Porta, G. B. 2303
Due Frecce, Le. Volodin, A. M. 9170
Due ladri e una ballerina. Buzzichini, M. 1459
Due leggi di Maud, Le. Dello Siesto, A. 2307
Due segreti, I. D'Amora, F. 2175
Due signori della signora, I. Gandera, F. 3363
Duecentomila e uno. Cappelli, S. 1583
Duel, The. Dell, J. H. 2299
Duke and the Actress, The. Schnitzler, A. 8064
Dulce Man, The. Blanton, C. 1000
Dumas le Magnifique. Decaux, A. 2235
Dumb Waiter, The. Pinter, H. 7175
Dummling and the Golden Goose. Thane, A. 8800
Dumnorix. Radin, M. 7380
Durand, Bijoutier. Marchand, L. 5537
Dusky Singing. Schmitt, G. 8043
Dust of the Road. Goodman, K. S. 3627
Dutchman. Jones, L. 4508, 4509
Dwarfs' Beards, The. Spamer, C. 8407
Dwie Przygodny Lemuela Gullivera. Broszkiewicz, J. 1350
Dyer Day. Burgess, J. 1420

E

...E dev'essere un maschio. Achille, G. 45
E facile per gli uomini. Barabas, P. 550
E passato qualcuno. Bassano, E. 651
Eagle and the Serpent, The. Fuentes, E. 3335

Ear of Malchus, The. Prins, P. de 7302
Early Guest, The. Taylor, P. 8726
Early Morning. Bond, E. 1169
Early Snow. Motoyazu, K. Z. 6273
Earth Is for All. Wilson, B. 9457
Earthjoy. Mew, T. 5798
Easiest Language to Learn, The. Mousheng, Lin 6279
East of Eden: Genesis IV.16. Morley, C. 6223
Easter. Koch, K. 4676
Easter Bunny on Pleasant Street. Smith, G. V. 8333
Easter Egg Magic. Stansbury, M. 8472
Easter Egg Rolling. Very, A. 9108
Easter Geese, The. Sroda, A. 8467
Easter Reminders. Hummell, V. 4322
Easter Soliloquy, An. Paine, A. B. 6935
Eastland Waters. Lee, A. 4874
Easy Victim, An. Grissom, H. 3760
Eat Cake! van Itallie, J.-C. 9031
Eau Sous les Ponts. Silvain, J. 8277
Eavesdropping on the Diplomats. Treno, R. 8928
Ebbrezza. Strindberg, A. 8565
Ebenezer Neverspend. Colson, J. G. 1947
Ecce Germania. Sherman, L. A. 8248
Ecco la fortuno. De Stefani, A. and G. Cataldo 2381
Eclipse. Johns, O. 4477
Eclisse di luna. Richardson, H. and W. Berney 7530
Eclogue. Mayhall, J. 5704
Ecole des Autres. Roussin, A. 7742
Ecole des Charlatans. Bernard, T. and A. Centurier 855
Ecole des Contribuables. Verneuil, L. and G. Barr 9102
Ecole des Dupes, L'. Roussin, A. 7743, 7744
Ecole des Moroses, L'. Carette, L. 1599
Ecole des Mortes. Charvet, P. 1736

Ecole des Vevues. Cocteau, J. 1912, 1913
Ecole du Piston. Bernard, T. 838
Economics Are Fun. Cummings, P. 2138
Ecrire Pour le Théatre. Praga, A. 7267
Ecrit Sur le Sable. Vallejo, A. B. 9005
Eddie Leuchner's Trip to Paradise. Soyfer, J. 8395
Eden End. Priestley, J. B. 7292, 7293
"Edge o'Dark." John, G. 4474
Edge of the Wood. Roof, K. M. 7694
Edinburgh Impromptu, An. Obaldia, R. de 6724
Edition de Midi. Sebastian, M. 8122
Edition Speciale. Torres, H. 8895
Editorial Conference. Angoff, C. 242
Edmee. Breal, P. A. 1275
Edouard et Agrippine. Obaldia, R. de 6725
Eduardo e Carolina. Randone, B. L. and L. Carette 7404
Edward and Agrippina. Obaldia, R. de 6726
Edward My Son. Morley, R. and N. Langley 6232, 6233, 6234
Effect of Gamma Rays on Man-in-the-Moon Marigolds. Zindel, P. 9653
Effet Glapion. Audiberti, J. 444
Efficiency. Sheehan, P. P. 8233
Efficiency Expert, The. Fontaine, R. 3199
Eglantina. Freeman, M. E. W. 3291
Egli tornasse, S'. Vergani, O. 9081
Egloga de la Resurrection. 2824
Egloga Hecha. Francisco de Madrid. 3250
Egoista, L'. Bertolazzi, C. 871
Egyptian Cinderella, The. Swortzell, L. 8655
Eh Joe. Beckett, S. 698
Eight Hundred Rubles. Neihardt, J. G. 6456
Eight O'Clock. Berkeley, R. C. 819
1837: The Farmers' Revolt. Salutin, R. 7895

715

1812 Overalls, The. O'Donnell, M. Three Short Plays. 6775
Eighteenth Noel. Feeney, M. and J. Rusilka 2972
Eight-Thirty Sharp. Van Dresser, J. 9024
Elaine. Weinberger, M. 9268
Elastique. See, E. 8127
Elder Statesman, The. Eliot, T. S. 2849, 2850
Election Day in Spooksville. Rybak, R. K. 7823
Election Day in the U.S.A. Newman, D. 6495
Election Night. Hart, J. Sonata for Mott Street. 3938
Election of the Roulette. Mowery, W. B. 6281
Electra. Perez Galdos, B. 7064
Electricity. Gillette, W. H. 3532
Elektra. Hofmannsthal, H. von 4131
Elephant and Flamingo Vaudeville. Hakim, E. 3829
Elephant Calf. Brecht, B. 1288
Elephant dans La Maison. Rivemale, A. and H. Colpi 7599
Eletto, L'. Binazzi, M. 937
Elevator. Howells, W. D. 4240
Elf of the Woods, The. Peterson, M. N. 7097
Elga. Hauptmann, G. 3973
Eli. Sachs, N. 7842
Eli and Emily. Levoy, M. 4968
Elijah Lovejoy. Jennings, G. 4460
Elisabeth d'Angleterre. Bruckner, F. 1380
Elisabeth est Morte. Mithois, M. 6093
Elixir, The. DeFelice, J. 2249
Elizabeth, La Femme Sans Homme. Josset, A. 4519, 4520
Elle Etait Rousse. Roudy, P. 7726
Ellen. Ransley, P. 7413
Ellen Comes Through. Kent, P. 4599
Elopements While You Wait. Stevens, C. D. 8508
Elves and the Shoemaker, The. Thane, A. 8801
Embers. Beckett, S. 699, 700
Emma. Zardi, F. 9634
Emma and the Professor's Coat. Nolan, P. T. 6638

Emma Instigated Me. Owens, R. 6924
Emperor and the Nightingale, The. Andersen, H. C. 193
Emperor Jones, The. O'Neill, E. 6843, 6844
Emperor's Daughters, The. Draper, C. C. 2588
Emperor's New Clothes, The. Andersen, H. C. 194
Emperor's New Robes, The. Foley, M. A. 3191
Emperor's Nightingale, The. Andersen, H. C. 195, 196
Employee, The. Quiles, E. 7365
Empress Catharine and Princess Dashkof, The. Lander, W. S. 4787
Emprunt. Santel, C. 7914
Empty Lamp, The. Halsey, F. 3872
Empty Room at the Inn, The. DuBois, G. 2627
En Chemin de Fer. Charasson, H. 1724
En Fiacre. Adamov, A. 60, 61
Encapsulated. Blumenfeld, L. 1021
Enchained. Hervieu, P. 4085
Enchanted. Giraudoux, J. 3563
Enchanted Bicycle, The. Carroll, J. 1618
Enchanted Broom, The. Lahr, G. L. 4768
Enchanted Chimney, The. Hart, M. T. 3939
Enchanted Cottage, The. Newman, D. 6496
Enchanted, I'm Sure. Chrisholm, J. R. 1821
Enchanted Island. Tassell, M. S. V. 8714
Enchanted Land, The. Fitzmaurice, G. 3140
Enchanted Princess, The. Baher, C. W. 494
Enchanted Thorn, The. Kearns, J. 4570
Enchanted Well, The. Jones, D. C. 4501
End of Chipi Gonzalez. Matto, J. M. R. 5662
End of the Line, The. Murray, J. 6334
End of the Road, The. DuBois, G. 2628
End of the Row. Green, P. 3700

End of the Trail, The. Culbertson, E. H. 2135
End of the World, The. Abercrombie, L. 12
End of the World, The. Soyfer, J. 8396
End of This Day's Business. Poley, I. C. 7227
Endgame. Beckett, S. 701
Enemies. Gorky, M. 3646
Enemy. Alexander, I. J. 130
Enemy! Maugham, R. C. R. 5664
Enemy, The. Pollock, C. 7232
Enemy of the People, An. Ibsen, H. 4360
Enemy Within, The. Friel, B. 3304
Enfant de la "Barraca." Camp, A. and F. Puig-Espert 1531
Enfant du Dimanche. Brasseur, P. 1273
Enfant Prodigue. Carre, M. 1615
Engagement, The. Molinaro, U. 6129
Engineering a Bid. Richmond, S. S. 7550
English As She Is Spoke. Bernard, T. 839
Enigma of College Black. Scot-Heson, G. 8104
Enlèvement, L'. Veber, F. 9052
Enlightenment of Others by Will Skuffel, The. Smith, P. J. 8349
Ennemie. Antoine, A. P. 286
Enoch Arden. Tennyson, A. 8744
"Ens." Sherwood, G. 8255
Enter Dora--Exit Dad. Tilden, F. 8865
Enter George Washington. McQueen, M. H. and N. McQueen 5319
Enter Mr. Poe. Dias, E. J. 2415
Enterement, L'. Monnier, H. 6173
Entertainer, The. Osborne, J. 6893
Enthusiast. Deevy, T. 2243
Entra in casa una montagna. Fiume, S. 3147
Entre Chien et Loup. Aroutcheff, G. 364
Entre Nous. Voulet, J. 9175
Entremes da Ronda de mort a sinera. Espriu, S. 2876
Entremes of the Cave of Salamanca. Cervantes Saavedre, M. 1690
Entretiens avec le Professeur Y. Rougerie, J. 7729
Envers Vaut L'Endroit. Declercq, A. 2240
Envol de L'Aigle, L'. Loiseau, G. 5020
Ephemera, The. Vitrac, R. 9158
Ephraim. Knee, A. 4666
Ephraim's Breite. Hauptmann, C. 3968
Epilogo entomologico ovvero l'incomunicabilita degli esseri, Un. Squarzina, L. 8459
Episode. Schnitzler, A. 8065
Episode from an Author's Life. Anouilh, J. 257
Episode of the Lieutenant Colonel of the Civil Guard. Garcia Lorca, F. 3380
Episodes from the Fighting in the East. Howard, R. Three Short Plays. 4218
Epitaph for George Dillon. Osborne, J. J. and A. Creighton 6897, 6898
Epitelioma. Hamou, R. 3880
Equal Frights. Olfson, L. 6795
Equals. Strindberg, J. A. 8566
Equarrissage Pour Tous. Vian, B. 9136
Equatore. De Stefani, A. 2368
Equilibrico, L'. Testoni, A. 8776
Equipage au complet, L'. Mallet, R. 5475
Erasmo. Saponaro, N. 7925
Erdgeist. Wedekind, F. 9253
Ere Quaternaire, L'. Bihan, M. le 925
Erede universale, L'. Regnard, J.-F. 7463
Ereditiera, L'. Goetz, R. and A. Goetz 3596
Erik XIV. Strindberg, A. 8567
Ernie. Sifton, C. G. 8272
Eroica. Lodovici, C. 5011
Erwachen. Stramm, A. 8545
Es Ist Krieg. Ronchi, T. 7679
Esame, L'. Conti, A. 1985
Esame del comportamento in un matrimonio di grupa. Cappelli, S. 1584
Esami di maturità. Fodor, L. 3180
Escalier. Dyer, C. 2794
Escalier de Service. Oltramare, G. 6830

Escape. Fleming, B. J. 3154
Escape, The. Power, V. 7266
Esempio, L'. Castillo, B. N. del 1651
Esmeralda. Burnett, F. H. and W. H. Gillette 1442
Esperienze di Giovanni Arce, filosofo, Le. Rosso di San Secondo, P. 7715
Esperimento del Dottor Brandley, L'. Jovinelli, G. 4523
Esperimento di televisione, L'. Duvernois, H. 2784
Espoir. Bernstein, H. 863
Ester. Hochwalder, F. 4121
Est-il Bon? Est-il Merchant? Diderot, D. 2486
Et a la Fin Etait le Bang. Obaldia, R. de 6727
Età delle attrici, L'. Raggio, E. 7384
Etait une Fois.... Croisset, F. 2110
Etat de Siège. Camus, A. 1552
Etau. Pirandello, L. 7188
Ete. Natanson, J. 6444
Eternal Mystery, The. Nathan, G. J. 6450
Eternal Presence, The. Dumas, A. 2691
Eternel Mari. Dostoevski, F. 2564
Ethiopia. Arent, A. 330
Etienne. Boularan, J. 1221
Etoile au Front, L'. Roussel, R. 7732
Etouffe-Chretien. Carette, L. 1600
Etrange aventure, L'. D'Vorian, J. M. 2793
Etrangère dans L'Ile. Soria, G. 8387
Ettore. Valentini, G. 8996
Eufemia. Rueda, L. de 7784
Eugenie Grandet. Arrault, A. 380
Eugenio, o il trionfo della salute. Bajini, S. 511
Eunuchs of the Forbidden City. Ludlam, C. 5082
Europa und der Stier. Fodor, L. 3181
European Escapade. Carroll, J. R. 1619
Eurydice. Anouilh, J. 258
Eva. Kivi, A. 4653
Eva in Veltrina. Giannini, G. 3485

Evangel. Barrett, W. A. 623
Evelina, zitella per bene. Dello Siesto, A. 2308
Evening, The. Nordseth, M. 6689
Evening Dress. Howells, W. D. 4241
Evening Dress Indispensable. Pertwee, R. 7084
Evening in an Important Asylum, An. Stettner, L. 8507
Evening Musicale, An. Fisk, M. I. 3128
Evening of Truth, An. Loomis, C. B. 5032
Eventail, L'. Goldoni, C. 3606
Events While Guarding the Bofors Gun. McGrath, J. 5206
Ever Womanly, The. Dunbar, N. 2697
Ever Young. Gerstenberg, A. 3448
Everest Hotel, The. Wilson, S. 9467
Evergreen. Mahar, E. 5448
Everlasting Sorrow, The. Noguchi, Y. 6616
Every Day Is Thanksgiving. DuBois, G. 2629
Every Room with Bath. Murray, J. 6335
Everybody Join Hands. Dodson, O. 2519
Everybody Loves Gladys. Huff, B. T. 4275
Everychild. Nichols, C. S. 6540
Everyday Fairies. Beatty, J. 689
Everygirl. Field, R. L. 3015
Everything in the Garden. Albee, E. 99
Everywhere Christmas. Very, A. 9109
Evviva. Montanelli, I. 6178
Ex alunno, L'. Mosca, G. 6255
Ex Cathedra. Connelly, M. 1976
Ex maggiore Hermann Grotz, L'. Parodi, A. G. 6985
Exaltation. Schneider, E. 8058
Examinatoire, L'. Barrier, M. 632
Exception and the Rule, The. Brecht, B. 1289
Excitement at the Circus. Leitner, I. A. 4902
Excitement to Order. Seiler, C. 8138
Exercices pour les Comédiens. Brecht, B. 1290
Exile. Klauber, A. J. 4656

Exiles. Joyce, J. 4524
Exit Glamour. McQueen, M. H. and N. McQueen 5320
Exit the Hero. Nolan, P. T. 6639
Exitium Caesaris. Smith, M. W. 8340
Ex-Napoleon. Frank, N. and P. Gibson 3266
Expedition Nocturne. Bernard, T. 853
Explication. Barrier, M. 633
Exploits of Mullah Nasrudin, The. Krushel, K. 4735
Explorer, The. Maugham, W. S. 5670
Explosion. Gerould, D. C. 3444
Express to Valley Forge. Dias, E. J. 2416
Exterior Decorator, The. Boiko, C. 1070
Extraordinaire Bonhomme de Neige, Un. Bourbon, A. 1232
Extreme Unction. Aldis, M. R. 119
Eyes and No Eyes. Smith, T. 8355
Eyes Right! Deming, D. 2320

F

Fable, A. Scholl, R. 8080
Fable du Secret Bien Garde, La. Casona, A. 1637
Fable Frolic. Head, F. 3999
Fabre's Little World. Murray, J. 6336
Fabulous Miss Marie, The. Bullins, E. 1414
Faccia del mostro, La. Anton, E. 288
Facciamo economia. Donnay, M. 2537
Face Is Familiar, The. Dias, E. J. 2417
Facheux Etat D'Esprit, Un. Puget, C.-A. 7325
Facing Death. Strindberg, A. 8568
Facing Reality. Pascal, F. 6994
Facing the Future. Hackett, W. 3797
Facture, La. Dorin, F. 2552
Fads and Frills. Richmond, M. C. 7536
Failure, The. Lindsay, J. 4990

Failures. Forrest, B. 3223
Fair Game. Nordseth, M. 6689
Fair Mistress Dorothy. M., A. A. 5108
Fair Today, Followed by Tomorrow. Fontaine, R. 3200
Fairest Pitcher of Them All, The. Cable, H. 1474
Fairy Circus, The. Very, A. and M. Brown 9134
Fairy Gold. Ostrovsky, A. 6913
Fairy Gold. Peterson, M. N. 7098
Fairy Prince, The. Phelps, S. K. 7117
Fairy Ring, The. Watts, F. B. 9227
Fairy Tales of New York. Donleavy, J. P. 2535
Faiseur, Le. Balzac, H. de 539
Fait divers. Sabatier, P. 7835
Fait du Prince. Toudouze, G. G. 8905
Faith. Evans, M. 2883
Faith of Our Fathers. Marble, A. 5528
Faithful Dog. Cervantes Saavedra, M. 1691
Falco d'argento, Il. Landi, S. 4783
Fall of the City, The. MacLeish, A. 5240
Fall of Uriah Heep, The. Dickens, C. 2472
Fallen Saint, The. Fallon, P. 2926
Fallo! De Baggis, R. 2221
False Sir Santa Claus, The. Brooks, E. S. 1344
Fame and the Poet. Dunsany, E. J. M. D. P. 2708, 2709
Famiglia. Amiel, D. and M. A. Petry 191
Famiglia Mastinu, La. Savinio, A. 7994
Famiglia molto unita, Una. Nicolai, A. 6580
Famiglia normale, La. Maraini, D. 5523
Family Affair, A. Ward, M. 9206
Family Album. Coward, N. 2069
Family in Space, A. Rittenhouse, C. 7594
Family Reunion, The. Eliot, T. S. 2851
Famous Nickname. Fisher, A. and O. Rabe 3109
Fancy Another Day Gone. Niedecker, L. 6592
Fanghorn. Pinner, D. 7171

Fanny. Pagnol, M. 6929
Fanny è i suoi domestici. Jerome, J. K. 4465
Fanny Hawthorne. Houghton, S. 4181
Fanny's Consent. Moratin, J. 6214
Fanny's Second Play 2927
Fanshen. Hare, D. 3908
Fantasia. D'Ambra, L. 2167
Fantasie Impromptu. Ivan, R. 4414
Fantasmi, I. Pirandello, L. 7189
Fantastic Suite. Bellido, J. M. 733
Fantoccio irresistibile. Roma, E. 7665
Fantome, Le. Santelli, C. 7917
Far Country, A. Denker, H. 2331
Far from the Madding Crowd. Hardy, T. 3906
Far-Away Princess, The. Sudermann, H. 8601
Farce Blanche, or La Plus Rusée. Chose, R. 1816
Farce de l'Auberge. Chose, R. 1817
Farce des Bossus. Jalabert, P. 4432
Farce du Galant Qui Epousa une Forte Femme. Casona, A. 1638
Farce Jaune, ou De Qui Se Moque-T-on? Chose, R. 1818
Farce of the Worthy Master Pierre Patelin the Lawyer 2932
Farce Pouge ou le Dernier Vivant, La. Chose, R. 1819
Farces et Attrapes. Galtier, C. 3359
Farwell to Calvin. McCoy, P. S. 5144
Farewell to Love. Ryerson, F. and C. Clements 7827
Farewell to the Theatre. Granville-Barker, H. 3688
Farfalla ... farfalla.... Nicolai, A. 6581
Farfalle dalle ali di fuoco, La. Bevilacqua, G. 902
Farrell Case, The. Cohan, G. M. 1924
Farsa Hecha. Salaya, A. 7883
Fascinating Mr. Denby, The. Sage, S. and H. M. Jones 7848

Fascinating Mrs. Osborne, The. Bigelow, J. H. 922
Fashion Show. Deming, D. 2321
Fastest Insight Alive, The. Casey, B. 1634
Fastest Thimble in the West, The. Boiko, C. 1071
Fastidiosa, La. Brusati, F. 1390
Fatal French Dentist, The. Mandel, O. 5488a
Fatal Message, The. Bangs, J. K. 543
Father. Clements, C. C. 1894
Father and a Son, A. Taylor, P. Three Ghost Plays. 8729
Father and Mother. Howells, W. D. 4242
Father Hits the Jackpot. Garver, J. 3407
Father Keeps House. McQueen, M. H. and N. McQueen 5321
Father of the Year. Garver, J. 3408
Father Out of the Machine. Simpson, L. M. 8303
Father Outwitted, The. Vega, L. de 9053
Father Talks Turkey. Miller, H. L. 5894
Father Time and His Children. Merington, M. 5774
Father's Day. Bland, P. 996
Father's Easter Hat. McQueen, M. H. and N. McQueen 5322
Father's Pride, A. Robinson, M. 7628
Fatto di assassinio, Un. Lerici, R. Libere stanze. 4930
Faun, The. Flexner, H. 3157
Fauno stanco, Il. Di Carpenetto, D. 2464
Fausse Manoeuvre. Xanrof 9582
Faustina. Goodman, P. 3629
Faustina e la realtà. Giordana, G. P. 3552
Faustus. Norman, C. 6691
Faut Murer la Fenêtre, Il. Petresco, J. 7110
Faut Passer Par les Nuages, Il. Billetdoux, F. 931
Faut Que le Sycomore Coule, Il. Ribes, J.-M. 7508
Faut Viser la Pierre, Il. Foissy, G. 3189
Faux Depart. Luizet, J. and A. Guacci 5088
Favori. Piechaud, M. 7147
Favorito, Il. Falena, U. 2923

Feaf. Hofmannsthal, H. von 4132
Fear Visits Love. Jarry, A. 4448
Fearless Knight and the Dragon. Brenner, E. 1317
Fearless One, The. Nicholson, M. A. 6570
Feast, The. Mc Clure, M. 5137
Feast of the Thousand Lanterns, The. Huff, B. T. 4276
Feat Accomplished and a Hero Completely Defeated. Pietrese, C. 7149
Feather Fisher; Keeper of Pure Waters. MacDonald, Z. K. 5169
Feathered Dream, The. Ramsey, H. 7397
Feathertop. Hawthorne, N. 3987
February Failure, A. Miller, H. L. 5895
February Heroes. McQueen, M. H. and N. McQueen 5323
February on Trial. Marshall, S. L. 5581
Fedeltà e dovere. Cami 1520
Federigo. La Porte, R. 4814
Fee, La. Daix, D. 2161
Fee Fo Fum. Mosher, J. C. 6261
Feedback. Maloon, J. 5483
Feierabend 1 und 2. Michelsen, H. G. 5809
Felicidad. Chalfi, R. 1703
Felicità, La. Mazzolotti, P. 5713
Felicita Colombo. Adami, G. 53
Female Transport. Gooch, S. 3622
Femme Admirable, Une. Worms, J. 9558
Femme de paille, La. Arley, C. 339
Femme du Boulanger, La. Giono, J. 3551
Femme d'un Autre. Charpak, A. 1727
Femme en Blanc. Achard, M. 27
Femme en Fleur. Amiel, D. 184
Femme libre, Un. Salacrou, A. 7869
Femme qu' a le Coeur Trop Petit, Une. Crommelynck, F. 2118
Femme Qui Dit la Verite. Roussin, A. 7745
Femme Ravie. Verneuil, L. 9097

Femme Trop Honnet, Une. Salacrou, A. 7870
Femmes dans L'Orage, Des. Martinez Sierra, G. and M. Martinez Sierra 5632
Femmes de Kalatas. Eckart, W. 2814
Femmes Parallèles. Billetdoux, F. 932
Femmes Savantes, Les. Molière 6115
Ferika. Bush-Fekete, L. 1450
Fern's Friends. Oser, J. A. 6899
Festival. Williams, A. N. 9408
Festival of Pomona, The. Mackay, C. D. 5220
Festival of Responses, A. Hong, Mrs. H. V. 4157
Feu! Chatelain, Y. 1739
Feud at Squirrel Hollow. Dias, E. J. 2418
Feud of the Schroffensteins. Kleist, H. von 4662
Feudin' Fun. Dias, E. J. 2419
Feuille de Vigne, La. Boudousse, J. 1208
Fiaba dei re magi, La. Zorzi, G. and G. Sclafani 9658
Fiaba di Namu', La. Rognoni, A. 7654
Fiacre. Adamov, A. 26
Fiammellina. Alvarez Quintero, S. and J. Alvarez Quintero 163
Fiancées du Havre, Les. Salacrou, A. 7871, 7872
Fiances de la Seine, Les. Lebesque, M. 4868
Fidanzata del Bersagliere, La. Antòn, E. 289
Fiducia. Lopez, G. 5035
Field of Enchantment. Topelius, Z. 8887
Field of Honor, The. Hamilton, G. 3877
Fierce Creature, The. Winther, B. African Trio. 9478
Fiesta. McArthur, J. 5113
Fiesta for Juanita. Schmitt, G. 8044
Fiesta the First. McArthur, J. 5114
15-Minute Red Revue. Bon, J. E. 1188
Fifth Commandment, The. Bierstadt, E. H. 921
Fifth Season. Regan, S. 7462
Figaro II. Tieri, V. 8860

721

Fighting Cock, The. Anouilh, J. 259
Fighting on the Plain. 3017
Figli, I. Mughini, R. 6288
Figli degli antenati, I. Saitta, A. 7865
Figlia del Re, La. Robecchi-Brivio, E. 7604
Figlio del mare, Il. Terron, C. 8755
Figlio di ettore, Il. Bacchelli, R. 479
Figlio di laboratorio, Il. Lilli, V. 4980
Figlio di Pulcinella, Il. De Filippo, E. 2252
Figurant de la Gaité, Le. Savoir, A. 7998
Filigrane. Fortuno, C. 3232
Fill 'er Up. Gibson, P. 3498
Fille Bien Gardee, La. Labiche, E. and Marc-Michel 4753
Fille Pour du Vent, Une. Obey, A. 6736
Filosofia di Ruth. Gotta, S. and M. Mortara 3660
Filosoficamente. De Filippo, E. 2253
Fils a Maman, Un. Worms, J. 9559
Fils de Personne. Montherlant, H. de 6189
Filumena Marturano. De Filippo, E. 2254
Fin da quando c'è il paradiso.... Priestley, J. B. 1759
Fin de Carnaval. Topol, J. 8888
Fin de Partie. Beckett, S. 702
Fin du Monde, La. Cabridens, M. -H. 1484
Final Appearance. Moon, I. 6197
Final Curtain, The. Murray, J. 6337
Final Edition. Sayre, G. W. 8005
Final Play, The. Singer, F. 8307
Finale della superparata. Plichta, D. 7215
Finally I Am Born. Davidson, M. 2199
Find Your Way Home. Hopkins, J. 4164
Finders-Keepers. Kelly, G. E. 4579
Finding Arthur's Organ. Benedikt, M. 755
Finding of the First Arbutus. Miller, A. 5838
Fine d'anno. Raggio, E. 7385
Fine dell'uomo. Di Salle, G. 2506
Fine mese. Riccora, P. 7515
Finestra, La. Soldati, M. and R. La Capria 8366
Finestra sul mondo, La. Veneziani, C. 9067
Finger Fairies. Jennings, E. 4459
Finian's Rainbow. Saidy, F. and E. Y. Harburg 7852
Finita la commedia. Adamov, A. 62
Finn MacCool. Lynch, M. 5100
Finnegan at the Fair. Watts, F. B. 9228
Fiore nel libro, Il. Alvarez Quintero, S. and J. Alvarez Quintero 164
Fiorello! Weidman, J. and G. Abbott 9263
Fiori di un anno lontano, I. Ronfani, U. 7691
Fiorina. Beolco, A. 811
Fire and Ice. Bier, R. 918
Fire Demon and South Wind. Winther, B. 9479
Fire in a Paper. Hagy, L. 3819
Fire Trap. St. Clair, R. 7855
Fire-Lighters, The. Housman, L. 4189
Fires at Valley Forge. Clark, B. H. 1847
Firm Foundations. Brooks, C. K. 1341a
First! Barbee, L. 560
First, The. Holt, W. 4151
First Aid First. Deming, D. 2322
First Aid, Library Style, or SOS to the Rescue. McCarthy, M. B. 5124
First Aid to the Injured. Sutphen, W. G. Van T. 8629
First and Last Opinion of Soloman Goldstein, The. Dorgan, H. 2549
First Butterfly, The. Spamer, C. 8408
First Cat on Mars, The. Harper, J. M. 3914
First Christmas, The. Marquis, M. 5576
First Day of April, The. Barbee, L. 561
First Easter Eggs, The. Bennett, R. 777

722

First Fifty Years, The. Myers, H. 6424
First Flowers, The. Wilson, M. L. 9465
First Freedom. Higley, P. 4100
First in Peace. McQueen, M. H. and N. McQueen 5324
First Lesson in Acting, The. Boleslawsky, R. 1152
First Love--And Second. Overton, G. 6920
First Man, The. O'Neill, E. 6845
First Noel, The. Mackay, C. D. 5221
First of October, The. Bacon, J. D. D. 486
First Ride of Willow Witch, The. Steiner, B. A. 8496
First Sorrow. Smith, B. 8327
First Thanksgiving, The. Newman, D. 6497
First Thanksgiving Day, The. Miller, A. 5839
Fish in the Forest. Corson, H. W. 2044
Fish in the Sea. McGrath, J. 5207
Fisherman and His Wife, The. Dewey, P. B. 2393
Fisherman and His Wife, The. Swortzell, L. 8658
Fishing. Weller, M. 9280
Fishy Tale from the Arctic, A. Gilchrist, T. E. 3523
Fiston. Birabeau, A. 950
Fit to Be Tied. Martens, A. C. 5593
Fitness Is the Fashion. Martens, A. C. 5594
Fitta, La. Buzzi, D. 1458
Five Brothers, The. Leuser, E. 4946
Five Buttons, The. Murray, J. 6338
Five Dances and a Supper. Cady, K. 1485
Five Finger Exercise. Shaffer, P. 8168, 8169
Five Happenings. Kaprow, A. 4549
Five Knights, The. Reynolds, F. 7502
Five Little Plays. Lavedan, H. 4838
Five O'Clock Tea. Howells, W. D. 4243
Five Plays. Jasudowicz, D. 4451

Five Weeks in a Balloon. Verne, J. 9090
Fix. Saito, N. 7864
Fixer, The. Sullivan, W. 8616
Flag of the United States, The. Barbee, L. 562
Flag Stop. Bach, M. 482
Flag the Limited. Richmond, S. S. 7551
Flair for Fashion, A. Phillips, M. K. 7128
Flambeau. Ruth, L. 7806
Flame, The. Clarke, A. 1851
Flatlanders. Millay, K. 5837
Flaubert and Madame Bovary. Sackville-West, E. C. 7844
Fleet Street Eclogue, St. George's Day. Davidson, J. 2198
Fleur à la Bouche, La. Pirandello, L. 7190
Fleur de Cactus. Barillet, P. and J.-P. Gredy 588
Fleur des Pois. Bourdet, E. 1233
Fleur d'Oubli, La. La Porte, R. 4815
Flibber Turns the Tables. Knight, L. 4668
Flight. Purcell, M. B. 7341
Flight from Destiny. Stevenson, D. 8513
Flight into Geography. Jolas, E. 4494
Flight of the Herons, The. Kennard, M. C. 4590
Flight of the Moon Witches, The. Flanders, F. R. 3152
Flittermouse. Reely, M. K. 7461
Floating Stone, The. Foulk, C. W. and D. P. Buck 3236
Floor, The. Swenson, M. 8646
Flora of the Flower Shop. Huff, B. T. 4277
Florence. Childress, A. 1803
Florence et le Dentiste. Joffe, A. and J. Giltene 4471
Florentine Tragedy, A. Wilde, O. 9362
Flower for Mother's Day, A. MacLellan, E. and C. V. Schroll 5250
Flower Garden, The. Very, A. 9110
Flowers from Lidice. Fratti, M. 3279
Flowers in May. Ritchie, E. 7591
Flowers That Grew Overnight, The. Albert, L. 104
Flying Doctor, The. Molière 6116

Flying Dutchman, The. Heine, H. 4034
Flying Horseshoe, The. Hall, M. E. 3858
Fog Around Us, The. Williamson, B. 9448
Fohnam the Sculptor. Corkery, D. 2018
Foi, La. Horvath, O. von. 4175
Foire Aux Sentiments. Ferdinand, R. 2986
Foire D'Empoigne. Anouilh, J. 260, 261
Folie Douce. Bricaire, J.-J. and M. Lasaygues 1322
Folie Rostanov. Gasc, Y. 3418
Folk Singer, The. Jasudowicz, D. 4451
Folle Amanda. Barillet, P. and J.-P. Gredy 589
Folle amore che non esiste, Il. Fayard, J. 2955
Folle de Chaillot, La. Giraudoux, J. 3564, 3565
Follow the North Star. Sanderlin, O. 7904
Follow the River Lai. Winther, B. 9496
Fontaines Lumineuses. Berr, G. and L. Verneuil 866
Fool, The. Pollock, C. 7233
Fool a Fool. Kauffman, G. 4556
Fool of God, The. Phillips, C. 7120
Foolish Mouse, The. Bailey, C. S. 505
Foolish Snobs, The. Molière 6117
Fool's Hour, The. Craigie, P. M. T. and G. Moore 2092
Football. Quentin, P. and G. Bellak 7363
Footprints. Langston, L. E. 4799
For Art's Sake. Richmond, S. S. 7552
For Ever and Ever. Lavedan, H. 4838
For France. Benson, S. and M. De Acosta 807
For Happiness. Pshibishevsky, S. 7322
For Heaven's Sake. Starling, L. 8474
For Lack of a Nail. Baumer, M. 679
For Love of the King. Wilde, O. 9363

For Love or Money. Garver, J. 3409
For Love or Money. Herbert, F. H. 4062
For the Duration. Hackett, W. 3798
For the Glory of Spain. Roberts, H. 7610
For the Love of Mike. Krauss, C. 4711
For the Welfare of All. Richmond, S. S. 7553
Forced Marriage. Molière 6118
Foreign Girl, The. Sanchez, F. 7901
Foreign-Language Teacher's Dream, A. Lopez Diaz, G. P. 5040
Forest Bride. Mowrer, P. S. 6282
Forest Fantasy. McQueen, M. H. and N. McQueen 5325
Forest of Arden, The. Speare, E. G. 8439
Forest Warden, The. Ludwig, O. 5084
Foresta, La. D'Errico, E. 2349
Forêt, La. Ostrovski, A. 6914
Forever Now. Dalrymple, J. and P. Bloom 2165
Forget-Me-Not. Nichols, P. 6544
Forgiveness. Lemaitre, J. 4908
Forgot in the Rains. Merrick, W. 5780
Forgotten Hero, The. Miller, H. L. 5896
Forked Tongues. Kenny, M. 4598
Formiche. Nicolai, A. 6582
Fortuna, La. Masao, K. 5637
Fortune Favors Fools. Narodny, I. 6435
Forza del destino, La. Torrero, L. 8894
Forza del Miss Muffet, La. Olfson, L. 6796
Forza di un gigante, La. Sinclair, U. 8306
Forze, Le. D'Errico, E. 2350
Foundling Hero, The. Tagore, R. 8685
Foundling in the Forest, The. Diamond, W. 2400
Four Accomplished Brothers, The. Grimm, J. and A. Grimm 3751
Four Antarctica. Andrews, J. W. 226
Four Bare Walls. Subert, F. A. 8596
Four Extra Valentines, The. Barbee, L. 563

Four Fairy Plays. Topelius, Z. 8887
Four Infiltration Pieces. Estrin, M. 2877
Four Keys to the Library. Boothman, M. L. 1194
Four Letters Home. Brenner, E. 1318
Four Letters from Algernon. Nolan, P. T. 6640
Four Lunatics, The. 3237
Four Plays. Saroyan, W. 7949
Four Plays. Vicente, G. 9138
4 Plays in 3 Minutes. Wilder, T. 9392
Four Saints in Three Acts. Stein, G. 8489
Four Sketches. Pinter, H. 7176
$4000. Bourjaily, V. 1239
Four Variations on a Scene. Herman, S. J. 4076
Fourposter, The. Hartog, J. De 3952
Foursome. Ionesco, E. 4387
Fourteen. Gerstenberg, A. 3449
Fous de la Mer. Helias, P. 4041
Fovea. Nutting, H. C. 6709
Fox and Geese. Herford, O. 4071
Fox's Grave 3239
Fragile. Lang, A. 4790
Fragment of an Agon. Eliot, T. S. 2852
Fragments. Schisgal, M. 8030
Français Tel Qu'On le Parle, Le. Didier, P. 2488
France. Doyle, L. F. 2582
Frances. Lipscomb, G. D. 4996
Francesco Caracciolo. Cucchetti, G. 2133
Frank der Funfte. Durrenmatt, F. 2743
Frankenstein 3268
Franklin Reversal, The. Boiko, C. 1072
Freddy. Southgate, P. 8393
Freddy. Thomas, R. 8835
Frederic General. Constant 1982
Frederick Douglass. Archer, L. C. 317
Frederick Douglass. Harris, H. W. 3925
Free. Musaphia, J. 6411
Free Spirits. Isom, J. S. 4412
Free This Day. Novas, H. 6701
Freedom. Reed, J. 7460
Freedom Left Out in the Rain.

Mazzucco, R. 5718
French Cabinetmaker, The. Nolan, P. T. 6641
French Doll's Surprise, The. Bennett, R. 778
French Without Tears. Rattigan, T. 7423
Frenetiques, Les. Salacrou, A. 7873
Frenzy for Two. Ionesco, E. 4388
Frère Jacques. Gillois, A. 3535
Frères, Les. Praga, A. 7268
Frères Karamazov, Les. Copeau, J. and J. Croué. 2011, 2012
Fric-Frac. Bourdet, E. 1234
Friday. Claus, H. 1874
Friend in Need; or, How "The Vicar of Wakefield" Found a Publisher. Frank, M. M. 3265
Friends, The. Wesker, A. 9302
Friends or Foes? Brooks, E. S. 1345
Friendship Bracelet, The. Clapp, P. 1839
Friendship Wheel, The. Miller, H. L. 5897
Frightened Witch, The. Wyllie, N. 9579
Frightful Forest, The. Sumner, J. N. 8617
Frog and the Mouse, The. Very, A. 9111
Frog Prince, The 3322
Frog Prince, The. Grimm, J. and W. Grimm 3752
Frog Who Wouldn't Be Kissed, The. Nolan, P. T. 6642
From Four to Six. Eliot, A. 2845
From Hearse to Eternity. Douglas, B. 2567
From Morn to Midnight. Kaiser, G. 4531
From Paradise to Butte. Finch, R. 3024
From Where I Sit.... Coleman, L. 1931
Front Page. Hecht, B. and C. MacArthur 4019
Fruhling's Erwachen. Wedekind, F. 9254
Fruits de L'Amour. Descaves, L. 2356
Frutto dell'albero, Il. Troisi, D. 8937
Fuga, La. Duvernois, H. 2785
Fugue, La. Duvernois, H. 2786
Fugues. Guth, P. 3787
Fulfillment. Murray, J. 6339

Full Circle.   Pedrolo, M. de
  7036
Full Measure of Devotion.   Du-
  Bois, G.   2630
Full Moon in March.   Yeats, W.
  B.   9592
Fun to Be Free.   Hecht, B. and
  C. MacArthur   4020
Funeral March of a Marionette.
  Nethercot, A. H.   6468
Funny Peculiar.   Stott, M.   8541
Fuochi d'artificio.   Chiarelli, L.
  1797
Fuoco dei Marziani, Il.   De An-
  gelis, R..M.   2218
Furcht und Elend Des Dritten
  Reiches.   Brecht, B.   1292
Furia d'amore.   Müller, E.   6290
Furie, Le.   Binazzi, M.   938
Furniture, The.   "Michal."   5805
Futility.   Allen, C. K.   137

G

G for Gettysburg.   McQueen, M.
  H. and N. McQueen   5326
Gabbia, La.   Rosso, R.   7713
Gabbia vuota, La.   Manzari, N.
  5509
Gabrielle.   MacKay, K.   5228
Gage, Le.   Larger, D.-P.   4816
Gaités de L'Escadron, Les.
  Moineaux, G.   6104
Gaités des Rois, La.   Roger-
  Ferdinand   7648
Galette des Rois, La.   Marais,
  J.-B.   5526
Galileo.   Leech, M. T.   4887
Gallant Cassian.   Schnitzler, A.
  8066
Gallicanus.   Hrotsvitha   4263
Gallo di Amleto, Il.   Goetz, C.
  3593
Gallop Away!   Howard, H. L.
  4205
Gambetta and Bismark.   Barclay,
  Sir T.   576
Gambetta and Dr. Stresemann.
  Barclay, Sir T.   577
Gambetta and Monsieur Poincare.
  Barclay, Sir T.   578
Gambetta Calls on Signor Musso-
  lini.   Barclay, Sir T.   579
Gambetta's Love Story.   Barclay,
  Sir T.   580
Gambetta's Shade and M. Poin-
  care Again.   Barclay, Sir T.
  581

Gamblers.   Gogol, N.   3600
Game, The.   Kachigan, S.   4529
Game.   Meehan, B.   5728
Game, The.   Nordseth, M.   6690
Game of Adverbs, The.   Guthrie,
  T. A.   3789
Game of Chess, A.   Middleton, T.
  5820
Game of Chess, A.   Murray, J.
  6340
Gang's All Here, The.   Lawrence,
  J. and R. E. Lee   4857
Ganze Tage in den Baumen.   Duras,
  M.   2737
Gap, The.   Ionesco, E.   4389
Garçon D'Honneur.   Blondin, A.
  and P. Guimard   1014
Garden.   Frank, F. K.   3260
Garden Hold-Up.   Miller, H. L.
  5898
Garden of the Christmas Fairy, The.
  Varney, H.   9044
Gardener.   Arlett, V. I.   337
Gardien des Oiseaux, Le.   Aman-
  Jean, F.   176
Gardien Zele, Le.   Cervantes Saa-
  vedra, M.   1692
Gargoyle, The.   Middleton, G.
  5815
Garroters.   Howells, W. D.   4244
Gartenfest, Das.   Havel, V.   3980
Gas Tank, The.   Smith, P. J.
  8350
Gas-Burning Heart, The.   Tzara,
  T.   8961
Gaslight.   Hamilton, P.   3878
"Gaston Bonnier"; or "Time's Re-
  venges."   Courtney, W. L.   2060
Gate of Blue, The.   Riddell, S.
  7571
Gate of Wishes.   MacMillan, M.
  L.   5277
Gates of Dinkelsbuehl, The.   Nolan,
  P. T.   6643
Gathering Sticks.   Miller, H. L.
  5899
Gatta bianca al Greenwich.   Fratti,
  M.   3280
Gatte, Le.   Manzari, N.   5510
Gay Night Life, The.   Shaw, C.
  G.   8200
Gay Pretenders, The.   St. Clair,
  R.   7856
Gehemmten, Die.   Unger, E.   8969
Gelindo.   3435
Gelsomino d'Arabia.   Aniante, A.
  243
Gémier a tu per tu con melpomene.
  Gsell, P.   3772

General Audax. Mandel, O. 5489
General Boulanger. Rostand, M. 7720
General Bullet. Stiles, G. 8525
General George. Very, A. 9112
General Goes Home, The. Barton, L. 644
Général Inconnu. Obaldia, R. de 6728
General Returns from One Place to Another, The. O'Hara, F. 6783
Generale dei Teddy boys, Il. Marotta, G. and B. Randone 5570
General's Letter, The. Dias, E. J. 2420
Genie of the Bottle, The. Whittaker, H. 9337
Genio e colura. Boccioni, U. 1035
Genousie. Obaldia, R. de 6729
Gentle Assassin, The. Nicholson, N. 6564
Gentle Furniture Shop, The. Bodenheim, M. 1037
Gentle Genius, The. Jackson, D. 4416
Gentle Giant-Killer, The. Miller, H. L. 5900
Gentle Maniac, A. Montgomery, G. E. 6184
Gentle People, The. Shaw, I. 8225
Gentleman from Philadelphia, The. Harber, B. 3902
Gentlemen All. Allen, R. A. 144
Gentlemen from Virginia. Hackett, W. 3799
Gentlemen v. Players; A Critic Match. Leverson, A. 4956
Geometric Progression. Bradford, B. 1260
Geometrically Speaking. Thompson, H. 8842
George Dandin, or The Discomfited Husband. Molière 6119
George Slept Here, Too. Martens, A. C. 5595
George Washington Carver; Wizard of Tuskegee. Brown, M. W. 1371
Gerani per la guerra. Cannan, D. 1565
Germs. Sharp, H. S. 8196
Gerrymander. 3447

Gerrymander. Reines, B. J. 7472
Gertie, the Greeting Card Girl. Huff, B. T. 4278
Gestern--Hente--Morgen. Heym, S. 4091
Gesticulador, El. Usigli, R. 8980
Getting On. Bennett, A. 769
Getting Ready for Winter. Brown, A. V. 1356
Getting Unmarried. Parkhurst, W. 6977
Ghibli. Bevilacqua, G. 903
Ghost Dance, The. Hart, J. 3937
Ghost from Genoa, The. Dias, E. J. 2421
Ghost in the House. Miller, H. L. 5901
Ghost Story, The. Tarkington, B. 8707
Ghost Walks Tonight, The. Nicholson, J. 6551
Ghost Wanted. Boiko, C. 1073
Ghost-Layers, Incorporated. Deming, D. 2323
Ghosts in the Library. Pendleton, E. 7047
Ghosts on Guard. Fisher, A. 3048
Giacinta o l'evasione. Surchi, S. 8623
Giancinta. Capuana, L. 1589
Giant, The. Jandl, E. and F. Mayrocker 4442
Gibigianna, La. Bertolazzi, C. 872
Giboyer's Son. Augier, E. 455
Gibson. Merington, M. 5775
Gideon. Chayefsky, P. 1743
Gift, The. Duncan, R. 2702
Gift for Hans Brinker, A. Thane, A. 8787
Gift for Pachacuti Inca, A. Winther, B. 9480
Gift for the World, A. Newman, D. 6498
Gift from Johnny Appleseed, A. Whittaker, H. 9338
Gift Horse, The. Blaine, B. G. 985
Gift of Gifts, The. Patton, M. K. 7010
Gift of Laughter, The. Dias, E. J. 2422
Gift That Won the Princess, The. Peterson, M. N. 7099
Gifts for the New Year. Miller, H. L. 5902

Gifts of Mother Lingua. Lawler, L. B. 4844
Giganti della montagna. Pirandello, L. 7181
Gigi. Colette, S. G. C. 1932, 1933
Gigi. Loos, A. 5034
Gilbert et Marcellin. Lefevre-Geraldy, P. 4892
Giles Corey, Yeoman. Freeman, M. E. W. 3292
Gingerbread House, The. 3549
Giocatore, Il. Sandor, U. 7906
Gioco dei quattro cantoni, Il. Lerici, R. Libere stanze 4930
Gioco dell'amore, Il. Donnay, C. 2538
Gioco di società, Un. Fodor, L. 3182
Gioconda Smile, The. Huxley, A. 4345
Gioie dell'estate, Le. Provins, M. 7318
Giorni della notte. Castillo, B. N. del 1652
Giorni dell'amore, I. Campana, D. 1532
Giorni piu leiti, I. Traversi, G. A. 8923
Giorno d'aprile, Un. De Benedetti, A. 2224
Giorno di festa, Un. Faure, G. 2945
Giorno di festa. Lanza, F. 4805
Giorno dopo, Il. Rebello, L. F. 7452
Giosafat. Santucci, L. 7921
Giostra, La. Mosca, G. 6256
Giostra dei peccati, La. De Angelis, A. 2216
Giovanna. Kaiser, G. 4532
Giovanni l'idealista. Apel, P. 307
Giovedi a giovedi, Da. De Benedetti, A. 2225
Gioventu' malata. Bruckner, F. 1381
Giramondo, Il. Spaini, A. 8402
Girandola. Bevilacqua, G. 904
Girl, The. Peple, E. 7061
Girl and the Gold Mine, The. Huff, B. T. 4279
Girl for Buddy, A. Saul, M. 7979
Girl in the Coffin, The. Dreiser, T. 2593
Girl on the Bronx Express, The.

Oliver, R. 6821
Girl That God Made, The. Blanchard, E. H. 993
Girl Who Slipped, The. Campbell, L. 1547
Girl Whose Fortune Sought Her, The. Clapp, P. 1840
Girl With Cut-Off Hands, The. Quillard, P. 7367
Girls from Viterbo, The. Eich, G. 2831
Girls in Books. Miller, H. L. 5903
Girls of Summer. Nash, N. R. 6436
Giro d'Italia. Codignola, L. 1919
Girono di nozze. Molnar, F. 6141
Giuda. Perrini, A. 7079
Giudice dei divorzi, Il. Cervantes Saavedra, M. de 1693
Giuditta. Terron, C. 8756
Giulia Szendrey. Herczeg, F. 4066
Giulia viene da lontano. Biagi, E. 912
Giuliano senza vocazione. Mosca, V. 6258
Giulietta compra un figlio. Martinez Sierra, G. and C. S. Maura 5633
Giulio Cesare. Ghiglia, D. and C. Siro 3472
Giuochi di prestigio. Goetz, C. 3594
Giuochi di società. Mazzoni, C. 5716
Giustizia, La. Dessi, G. 2361, 2362
Glamour and Grease. Richmond, S. S. 7554
Glass Slippers, The. Miller, H. L. 5904
Gleam in the Darkness, A. Aide, C. H. 86
Gli altri ci uccidono. Pensa, C. M. 7060
Gli amanti. Rondi, B. 7688
Gli amanti eccezionali. Natanson, J. 6445
Gli amanti indivisibili. Frattini, A. 3286
Gli amori di Platonov. Chekhov, A. P. 1764
Gli arcangeli non giocano al flipper. Fo, D. 3168
Gli estranei. Binazzi, M. 939
Gli operativi. Logan, S. 5018

Gli ultimi cinque minuti. De Benedetti, A. 2230
Gli uomini non sono ingrati. De Stefani, A. 2380
Glisenti ... Calibro 9. Romualdi, G. 7673
Glittering Gate, The. Dunsany, E. J. M. D. P. 2710
Glittering Highway, The. Meneses, E. de 5749
Gloria in Excelsis Deo Pro Nativitate Domini 3587
Gloria negli eccelsi, La. Santi, L. 7920
Glorieuses. Roussin, A. 7746
Glorious Whitewasher, The. Hackett, W. 3809
Glory and the Dream, The. DuBois, G. 2631
Glory He Deserves, The. McQueen, M. H. and N. McQueen 5327
Glory of the World, The. Wells, C. 9288
Glory Road. DuBois, G. 2632
Glove. Bjørnson, B. 975
Gloves. Cannon, G. 1566
Gnadiges Fraulein. Williams, T. 9425
Goblin Parade. Folmsbee, B. 3195
God and Texas. Ardrey, R. 328
God Bless. Feiffer, J. 2975
God Bless Us, Every One. Mee, C. L., Jr. 5727
God Have Mercy on the June-Bug. Phillips, L. 7124
God Keeps Trying. Jacobson, K. V. 4424
God of the Wood, The. Girardeau, C. M. 3560
God or Caesar? Eastman, F. 2800
God Save McQueen. Malcolm, I. 5469
Godbug. Cavander, K. 1674
Goddess, The. Chayefsky, P. 1744
God's Love Has Made It So. Bonea, S. 1179
Gods of the Mountain, The. Dunsany, E. J. M. D. P. 2711
Gog e magog. Arout, G. 365
Gog et Magog. MacDougall, R. and T. Allan 5173
Goglu. Barbeau, J. 554
Go-Go Gophers, The. Martens, A. C. 5596

Going Beyond Alma's Glory. Deevy, T. 2244
Going Home. Trevor, W. 8931
Going Steady. Nolan, P. T. 6644
Going to Pot. Feydeau, G. 3008
Going Up. McQueen, M. H. and N. McQueen 5328
Gold Bug, The. Poe, E. A. 7220
Gold in Your Garden. Asbrand, K. 399
Gold Machine. Selnick, E. 8148
Gold Mine at Jeremiah Flats, The. Anderson, R. A. 220
Gold Mohur Tune: "To Remember." Sorabji, C. 8382
Gold Standard, The. Koch, K. 4676
Golden Bell for Mother, A. Very, A. 9113
Golden Bird, The. Mapp, F. 5520
Golden Brew, The. Kelly, T. 4582
Golden Doom, The. Dunsany, E. J. M. D. P. 2712, 2713
Golden Door, The. Laure, K. 4829
Golden Goose, The. Grimm, J. and W. Grimm 3753
Golden Hearts, The. Slattery, M. E. 8313
Golden Pathway Annual, The. Harding, J. and J. Burrows 3903
Golden Screw, The. Sankey, T. 7910
Golden Voice of Erik, The. Nolan, P. T. 6645
Goldilocks and Friends. Cheatham, V. R. 1751
Golfiacs, The. Bangs, J. K. 544
Gone. Abse, D. 14, 15
Gone for a Soldier. Biel, N. 916
Gone Tomorrow. Harrity, R. 3933
Gonzalo Sent la Violette. Vattier, R. and A. Rieux 9047
Good and Dandy World, A. Robbins, K. 7603
Good and Obedient Young Man. Barr, B. and G. Stevens 613
Good Bargain, A. Dunsany, E. J. M. D. P. 2714
Good-Bye! Renard, J. 7480
Good Dinner, A. Cutting, M. S. 2151
Good Egg, The. DuBois, G. 2633
Good Enough for Lincoln. Miller, H. L. 5905
Good Friday. Masefield, J. 5639

Good Health Trolley. Lehman, J. F. 4897
Good Hope. Heijermans, H. 4029, 4030
Good Morning, Mr. Rabbit. Bennett, R. 779
Good Neighbors, The. Trumbull, L. 8954
Good Night. Smith, M. S. 8343
Good Old Summer Time. Reay, N. B. 7450
Good Out of Nazareth. DuBois, G. 2634
Good Sainte Anne, The. Gilbert, H. 3508
Good Theatre. Morley, C. 6224
Good Witch, The. 3623
Good Words for a Stirring Tune. Bakeless, K. L. 513
Goodbye, Dan Bailey. Bernard, K. 831
Goodnight Please! Daggett, J. 2159
Gooseberry Mandarin. Ruthenburg, G. D. 7812
Gorgonio. Pinelli, T. 7159
Gospel of the Gourmet, The. Benson, E. F. 805
Gouter, Le. Worms, J. 9560
Governor Bradford's Scissors. DuBois, G. 2635
Governor Lenhard. Kvaran, E. H. 4744
Governor's Wife, The. Benavente y Martinez 743
Goya in the Cupola. Walsh, T. 9198
Gradino più giù, Un. Landi, S. 4784
Graduation Address. Fontaine, R. 3201
Graduation Forecast. Nolan, P. T. 6646
Graduation Present. Orme, F. 6882
Graf Oderland. Frisch, M. 3315, 3315a
Gram of Radium, A. Burlingame, C. 1430
Gran premio di Ascot, Il. Wallace, E. 9191
Gran turismo. De Stefani, A. 2369
Grand Autobus, Le. Rigoir, V. 7581
Grand Cham's Diamond, The. Monkhouse, A. N. 6172
Grand Jeu, Le. Ruinet, G. 7792

Grand Patron. Pascal, A. 6993
Grand Reopening, The. 3685
Grande amore sta per incominciare, Un. Birabeau, A. 951
Grande attore, Il. De Filippo, P. 2272
Grande attore, Il. De Stefani, A. 2370
Grande Enquête de Francois-Felix Kulpa. Pommeret, X. 7238
Grande et la Petite Manoeuvre, La. Adamov, A. 63
Grande famiglia, La. Sarazani, F. 7926
Grande magia, La. De Filippo, E. 579
Grande Muraille, La. Frisch, M. 3316
Grande nave, La. Bassano, E. 648
Grande Oreille. Breal, P. A. 1276
Grande pantomima con bandiere e pupazzi piccoli e medi. Fo, D. 3169
Grande Roue, La. Hanoteau, G. 3897
Grande speranza, La. Rietmann, C. M. 7577
Grandfather, The. Perez Galdos, B. 7065
Grandma and the Pampered Boarder. Watts, F. B. 9229
Grandmother, The. Biro, L. 967
Grane, Der. Forster, F. 3228
Granny Boling. Green, P. 3701
Granny from Killarney. Martens, A. C. 5597
Granny Goodman's Christmas. Bennett, R. 780
Grass Harp, The. Capote, T. 1581
Grass's Springing, The. Labrenn, T. 4756
Grateful Gobbles, The. Ramsey, H. 7398
Grave. Speirs, R. 8441
Grave Woman, The. Koenig, E. C. 4676
Gray. Orlovitz, G. 6879
Gray Flannel Blues. Murray, J. 6341
Great Adventure. Davidson, G. 2195
Great American Light War, The. Melmoth, D. 5741
Great Caesar! Fontaine, R. 3202

730

Great Caesar's Ghost! Olfson, L. 6797
Great Caper, The. Campbell, K. 1546
Great Catherine. Shaw, G. B. 8208
Great Contest, The. Huff, B. T. 4280
Great Dark, The. Totheroh, D. 8896
Great Exhibition, The. Hare, D. 3909
Great Expectations. Dickens, C. 2473
Great Freeholder, The. Subert, F. A. 8597
Great Game, The. Berkman, A. 820
Great Garden of the West, The. Driscoll, L. 2607
Great God Brown, The. O'Neill, E. 6846
Great Golden Nugget, The. Kroll, F. L. 4729
Great Lexicographer, The. Bissell, W. L. 969
Great Middle Class, The. Usigli, R. 8981
Great Noontide, The. Kearney, P. 4566
Great One, The. McFarlan, E. 5176
Great Prognostic, The. McClure, J. 5132
Great Sad, The. Fitzsimon, S. 3146
Great Samurai Sword, The. Winther, B. 9481
Great Sebastions, The. Lindsay, H. and R. Crouse 4987
Great Silkie of Sule Skerry, The. Bate, L. 665
Great Stone Face, The. Hawthorne, N. 3988
Great Wave, The. Hearn, L. 4007
Greatest Christmas Gift, The. Murray, J. 6342
Greatest Treasure, The. Winther, B. 9482
Grecian Urn, The. Nethercot, A. H. 6469
Greed for Gold. Dias, E. J. 2423
Greedy Goblin, The. Miller, H. L. 5906
Green Branch, The. Murray, T. C. 6408

Green Cockatoo. Schnitzler, A. 8067
Green Cushions. Norman, Mrs. G. 6694
Green Glass Ball. Corson, H. W. 2045
Green Helmet, The. Yeats, W. B. 9593
Green Leaf's Lesson. Newman, D. 6499
Green Men, Go Home. Martens, A. C. 5598
Green Pastures, The. Connelly, M. 1977
Green Piper, The. Lee, S. 4883
Green Shutters. Osness, M. S. 6909
Green Thumb, The. Phillips, M. K. 7129
Green-Eyed Monster, The. Klauber, A. 4655
Greetings from the Fultons. McCoy, P. S. 5145
Grey Squirrel and the White Buffalo. Privacky, A. H. 7308
Gringoire, the Ballad Monger. Banville, T. de 549
Griselda the Governess. Dias, E. J. 2424
Groom's Biscuits. Steele, J. 8482
Gros Gateau, Un. Worms, J. 9561
Groseilles. Presles, C. des 7282
Grotesques. Head, C. 3997
Grotte, La. Anouilh, J. 262
Groundhog's Shadow, The. Malone, M. 5479
Grouse Out of Season. Merington, M. 5776
Growing Old Together. Clements, C. C. 1894
Grunt, The. East, D. 2799
Guaranteed Forever. Baker, G. 517
Guardian, The. Regnier, H. de 7464
Guardian Angel. Savoir, A. 7999
Guardiano alla tomba. Kafka, F. 4530
Guardsman, The. Molnar, F. 6142, 6143
Guerra dei figlia della luce, La. Shamir, M. 8194
Guerra spiegata ai poveri, La. Flaiano, E. 3150
Guerre de Troie N'Aura pas Lien, La. Giraudoux, J. 3566, 3567
Guerre et Paix au Café Sneffle. Vitaly, G. 9156

Guerrin meschino agli alberi del sole. Lodovici, C. V. 5012
Guess-for-Fun Alphabet, The. Johnson, G. 4484
Guest of Honor. Campbell, J. E. 1542
Guillaume le Confident. Aroutcheff G. and J. Locher 369
Guillermo Tell Tiene los Ojos Tristes. Sastre, A. 7973
Guillotine Mazurka, The. Obaldia, R. de 6730
Gulliver's Travels in Lilliput Land. Swift, J. 8647
Gunther Groundhog. Duvall, L. M. 2777
Gust of Wind, A. Forzano, G. 3234
Gute Mensch Von Sezuan, Der. Brecht, B. 1293
Gutlibi, il massacratore. Locke, C. 5009
Guy Bedos/Sophie Daumier; 29 Sketches. Bedos, G., J.-L. Dabadie, and C. Frank 715
Guy Upstairs, The. Delden, E. H. van 9016
Gypsie's Secret, The. Huff, B. T. 4281
Gypsy. Laurents, A. and S. Sondheim 4833
Gypsy Look, The. Heath, A. L. 4009

H

H. M. S. Pinafore. Gilbert, W. S. and Sir A. S. Sullivan 3515
Ha-Ha Play, The. Yankowitz, S. 9583
Habits. Boyajian, A. 1249
Hadrian VII. Luke, P. 5089, 5090, 5091
Haidebrant, Die. Stramm, A. 8546
Hail--The Geni. Richmond, S. S. 7555
Half a Basket of Peanuts. 3843
Half-Pint Cowboy, The. Miller, H. L. 5907
Halfway to Concord. Rowe, M. 7440
Hall-Marked. Galsworthy, J. 3354
Halloween Brew, A. Compton, D. M. 1965

Halloween Brew. Kroll, F. L. 4730
Halloween Gets a New Look. Pyle, M. T. 7352
Halloween Hullabaloo. Boiko, C. 1074
Halloween Magic. McQueen, M. H. and N. McQueen 5329
Halloween Scarecrow. Spamer, C. 8409
Halloween Spell, The. Newman, D. 6500
Hallowishes. Brown, N., A. Laurence, A. Mangual and M. Wells 1372
Halold. Wildenbruch, E. von 9387
"Halte au Destin." Chabannes, J. 1699
Hamburger King, The. Smith, M. S. 8344
Hamelot. Alderman, E. R. 116
Hamlet. Huster, F. 4333
Hamlet. Shakespeare, W. 8177
Hamlet de Trascon. Canolle, J. 1570
Hamlet of Stepney Green, The. Kops, B. 4691
Hand-Me-Down Hildy. Sagoff, S. E. 7850
Handkerchief of Clouds. Tzara, T. 8962
Handshakers. Saroyan, W. 7949
Handwriting on the Wall, The. Nicholson, J. 6552
Handwriting on the Wall, The. Wight, L. 9349
Handy Man, The. Elton, R. D. 2859
Hang by Their Shoelaces. Tunberg, K. A. 8948
Hanger Back. Corbett, E. F. 2017
Hanjo. Yukio, M. 9625
Hanna Jagert. Hartleben, O. E. 3944
Hanrahan's Oath. Gregory, Lady A. 3723
Hans Bulow's Last Puppet. Ruthenberg, G. D. 7813
Hans, Who Made the Princess Laugh. Rowland, E. 7770
Hansel and Gretel. Simonds, N. 8293
Hansel and Gretel. Thane, A. 8802
Hansel and Gretel Go Back to School. Creegan, G. 2102
Hansel, Gretel, and Friends. Cheatham, V. R. 1752

Happiest Hat, The. Nolan, P. T. 6647
Happiness Box, The. Sroda, A. 8468
Happy Apple, The. Pulman, J. 7339
Happy as Larry. MacDonagh, D. 5163
Happy Christmas to All. Nolan, J. C. 6625
Happy Day, The. MacDonagh, D. 5162
Happy Days. Beckett, S. 703, 704
Happy Easter to Margy. McQueen, M. H. and N. McQueen 5330
Happy Ending. Nolan, P. T. 6648
Happy Family. Cooper, G. 2007
Happy Gardener, The. Collins, B. F. 1937
Happy Haunting! Olfson, L. 6798
Happy Haunts. McQueen, M. H. and N. McQueen 5331
Happy Hearts. McQueen, M. H. and N. McQueen 5332
Happy Holidays, The. Murray, J. 6343
Happy Holidays. Newman, D. 6501
Happy Journey to Trenton and Camden, The. Wilder, T. N. 9393, 9394
Happy New Year. Barbee, L. 564
Happy New Year. McQueen, M. H. and N. McQueen 5333
Happy Poet, The. Howard, V. 4223
Happy Prince, The. Wilde, O. 9364, 9365, 9366
Happy Time, The. Taylor, S. 8731, 8732
Happy Valentine, The. Davis, L. R. 2203
Hard Struggle, A. Marston, J. W. 5583
Hardy Perennials. Meeker, A. 5730
Hare and the Tortoise, The. Bennett, R. 781
Hare, the Hippo, and the Elephant, The. Thane, A. 8803
Harlequinade. Clements, C. C. 1893
Harold and Maude. Higgins, C. 4096
Harrison Progressive School, The.

Nelson, S. 6462
Harvest, The. Hanshew, T. W. 3901
Harvest Moon Supper, The. Watts, F. B. 9230
Harvey. Chase, M. 1738
Hassle in the Castle. Schaaf, A. K. 8011
Hat for Mother, A. Phillips, M. K. 7130
Hat Rack, The. Herman, G. 4075
Hate. Lindsay, J. 4991
Hatful of Rain, A. Gazzo, M. V. 3432, 3432a
Hats and Rabbits. McQueen, M. H. and N. McQueen 5334
Hattie. De Pue, E. 2342
Haunted Bookshop, The. Nicholson, J. 6553
Haunted Clothesline, The. Miller, H. L. 5908
Haunted Hat-Shop, The. Michelson, M. 5810
Haunted High School, The. Miller, H. L. 5909
Haunting of Hathaway House, The. Murray, J. 6344
Haunts for Hire. Miller, H. L. 5910
Hauptmann von Kopenick, Der. Zuckmayer, C. 9660
Haute Sensibilité. Nicolai, A. 6587
Haute Surveillance. Genet, J. 3437
Hauteur de la Nuit, La. Bernard, R. 836
Have You Any Dirty Washing, Mother Dear? Exton, C. 2892
"Haven't Got a Fitten' Book to Read" 3985
Haym Salomon. Janusch, M. J. 4444
He Is Coming. Prydz, A. 7321
He Is Something! Andrews, J. W. 227
He Lives. Holdas, A. 4140
He Who Gets Slapped. Andreyev, L. N. 230, 231
He Who Says No. Brecht, B. 1294
He Who Says Yes. Brecht, B. 1295
He Won't Be Home for Christmas. Moessinger, W. 6101
He-He. Garcia, D. 3369
Head, Guts and Sound Bone Dance. Cook, M. 1998

Healthy, Wealthy and Wild. Murray, J. 6345
Hear No Evil, Speak No Evil. Murray, J. 6346
Heard Melodies Are Sweeter. Roth, P. 7724
Heart of a Tenor, The. Wedekind, F. 9255
Heart of Age, The. Bercovici, E. 812
Heart of Pierrot. Scott, M. 8109
Heart of Youth. Hagedorn, H. 3815
Heart Throbs. Miller, H. L. 5911
Heart Trouble. McQueen, M. H. and N. McQueen 5335
Hearts and Flowers for Mother. McQueen, M. H. and N. McQueen 5336
Hearts and Flowers for Mother. Pendleton, E. 7048
Hearts and Minds Job, A. Howarth, D. 4231
Hearts of Oak. Hall, M. E. 3859
Hearts, Tarts, and Valentines. Fisher, A. 3049
Heaven Is Deep. Day, F. L. 2210
Heavenly and Earthly Love. Molnar, F. 6144
Heaven's Little Ironies. Allen, J. L. 140
Hedda Gabler. Ibsen, H. 4361
Heed o' the Deep. Breene, R. S. 1313
Heidi. Spyri, J. 8457
Heidi Finds the Way. Spyri, J. 8458
Heilige Johanna, Die. Shaw, G. B. 5418
Heilige Johanna der Schlachthofe, Die. Brecht, B. 1296
Heiress of Harkington Hall, The. Huff, B. T. 4282
Heist, The. Reinhold, R. 7479
Helen. Storer, E. 8535
Helen Retires. Erskine, J. 2874
Hélène, ou La Joie de Vivre. Roussin, A. and M. Gray 7762
Helliocentric World. Clarke, S. 1859
Hello from Bertha. Williams, T. 9426
Hello Goodbye Sebastian. Grillo, J. 3748

Hello, Mr. Groundhog. Miller, H. L. 5912
Heloise. Forsyth, J. 3229
Help Wanted for Easter. MacLellan, E. and C. V. Schroll 5251
Helpful Cats, The. Adams, P. -L. 71
Helpless Herberts. Kreymborg, A. 4713
Helpless Woman! Zolin, A. 9654
Hemp. Cain, J. M. 1492
Hen Party. Olfson, L. 6799
Henkers Mahlzeit. Ramsey, A. 7395
Henri IV. Pirandello, L. 7192
Henry Duck's Christmas. Cunningham, D. F. 2141
Henry IV, Part I. Shakespeare, W. 8178
Henry Wallace's Experiment. Hackett, W. 3800
Her Dowry. Kelleher, D. L. 4576
Here Comes the Interesting Part. Kaminsky, S. M. 4537
Héritière, L'. Goetz, R. and A. Goetz 3597
Herman the Hatman. Luftig, R. 5086
Herman's No Angel. Levitt, A. and R. Fiske 4965
Herminie. Magnier, C. 5439
Hero, The. Cain, J. M. 1493
Hero, The. Cheatham, V. R. 1753
Hero, The. Emery, G. 2860
Hero Here at Heorot. Albert, R. 105
Hero in Pink, The. Johns, O. 4478
Herod and Marianne. Hebbel, F. 4016
Herodiade. Mallarme, S. 5473
Heroes of Democracy. 4078
Heroes of Labour. Barker, H. 602
Hero's Homecoming. Miller, H. L. 5913
Herr Biedermann und die Brandstifter. Frisch, M. 889
Herr Kammerdiener Kneetschke. Scheerbart, P. 8020
Heure de Thé, L'. Dubreuilh, S. 2666
Heureux qui Comme Ulysse. Fauré, G. 2946
Hey Scrub-a-Drudge! Kandel, A. 4538
Hey You, Light Man! Hailey, O. 3821

Hi Down There. Nolan, P. T. 6649
Hi, Neighbor. Asbrand, K. 400
Hiawatha. Mildren, N. L. 5828
Hibernatus. Boudousse, J. 1209
Hidden Meanings. Fisher, A. 3050
Hidden Spring, The. Bracco, R. 1254
Hidebound. Nolan, P. T. 6650
Hiding Place, The. Kroll, F. L. 4731
Hier à Andersonville. Rivemale, A. 7597
High Heart. Rowell, A. C. 7766
High in Vietnam, Hot Damn. Pomerance, B. 7235
High School Library of the Future, The. Poray, A. 7244
Highland Fling, The. Nolan, P. T. 6651
Highland Lad. Very, A. 9114
Highway Trail, The. Richmond, S. S. 7556
Highways of Tomorrow. Richmond, S. S. 7557
Hijo que Nego a su Padre. 4103
Hildetua. Seitz, G. B. 8145
Hill, The. Mierow, H. E. 5824
Hillbilly Blues. Huff, B. T. 4283
Hilltop. Garnett, L. A. 3394
Hilltop House. Richmond, S. S. 7558
Hinkemann. Toller, E. 8874
Hip Hip Ho. Howard, H. L. 4206
Hippocrates Dying. Flokos, N. G. 3159
Hiroshima. Wessel, O. 9308
His and Hers. Murray, J. 6347
His First Patient. Richmond, S. S. 7559
His Hand and Pen. DuBois, G. 2636
His Honor. Dennis, O. M. 2336
His Imitation Sweetheart. Flower, E. 3162
His Majesty's Pleasure. O'Riordan, C. H. O. 6877
His Old Sweethearts. Palmer, G. 6943
His Unbiased Opinion. Furniss, G. L. 3342
His Widow's Husband. Benavente y Martinez, J. 744
Histoire d'une Chemis et d'un Violon. Praga, A. 7269

Histoire de Fours. Sabatier, P. 7836
Histoire du Soldat, L'. Ramuz, C. F. 7401
Histoire Tragique de la Princesse Phenissa. Gourmont, R. de 3669
History. Duberman, M. 2612
History Hits the Jackpot. Rybak, R. K. 7824
History Lesson for Today. Burman, B. 1436
Hitch Hiker, The. Fletcher, L. 3156
Hiver, ou Les Temps du Verbe. Tardieu, J. 8703
HO to AA. Tracy, C. 8911
Ho perduto mio marito! Cenzato, G. 1680
Hobgoblin House. Martens, A. C. 5599
Hogan's Successor. Speirs, R. 8442
Hold Back the Redskins. Dias, E. J. 2425
Hold Your Hat! McCoy, P. S. 5146
Holderlin. Weiss, P. 9274
Holiday. Barry, P. 638
Holiday, The. Mazaud, E. 5709
Holiday for Santa. Nicholson, J. 6554
Holiday or Holy Day? Sudman, D. 8607
Hollow, The. Christie, A. 1822
Holly Hangs High, The. Barbee, L. 565
Hollywood. Vanni, A. 9038
Hollywood Zoo. Brophy, E. P. 1349
Home. Storey, D. 8537
Home and Beauty. Maugham, W. S. 5671
Home at Seven. Sherriff, R. C. 8251
Home Edition. Burnett, W. 1443
Home for Heroes, The. Bowering, G. 1242
Home of Our Government, The. Hamby, R. 3874
Home on the Range. Jones, L. 4510
Home Sports. Heath, J. 4012
Home-Coming, The. Dunning, R. C. 2706
Homecoming, The. McQueen, M. H. and N. McQueen 5337
Homecoming, The. Nilssen, J. 6603

Hometown Halloween. McQueen, M. H. and N. McQueen 5338
Homework. Miller, H. L. 5914
Homicide Involontaire. Mazure, J. 5710
Homiest Room, The. McQueen, M. H. and N. McQueen 5339
Homme a l'Ombrelle Blanche. Charras, C. 1732
Homme au Parapluie. Dinner, W. and W. Morum 2505
Homme Averti en Vaut Quatre. Camp, A. 1528
Homme Comme les Autres, Un. Salacrou, A. 7874
Homme Couche, L'. Maura, C. S. 5683
Homme de Cendres. Obey, A. 6737
Homme de Dieu, Un. Marcel, G. 5530
Homme du Nord. Mere, C. 5765
Homme en Question, L'. Carette, L. 1601
Homme et la Perruche. Allioux, A. 147
Homme qui se Taisait. Caillol, P. 1491
Homme Traque. Dard, F. 2187
Hommes de Haute Vertu. Aub, M. 433
Hommes du Dimanche, Les. Roncoroni, J. -L. 7683
Homosexuel, L'. Copi 2014
Honest Abe Lincoln. Fisher, A. and O. Rabe 3110
Honest Injun! Murray, J. 6348
Honest Urubamba. Mandel, O. 5490
Honey Thieves. Burleson, C. 1426
Honeymoon, The. Bennett, A. 770
Honi Soit. Terrell, M. 8745
Honneur des Cipolino, L'. Bricaire, J. -J. and M. Lasaygues 1323
Honneur des Dupont, L'. Dabril, L. and L. Diétrich 2155
Honor--and the Girl. Richmond, G. S. 7534
Honor Cross. Lee, M. E. 4882
Honorable Cat's Decision. Boiko, C. 1075
Honorable Togo. McInroy, H. 5217
Honored One, The. Leuser, E. 4947
Honors Even. Forrest, B. 3224

Hooky Holiday, A. Miller, H. L. 5915
Hoops. Gibson, W. W. 3500
Hooray for Thanksgiving. Churchill, M. P. 1836
Hop, Jump and Skip. Spamer, C. 8410
Hope and Memory. Pyle, H. 7349
Hope Is a Thing with Feathers. Harrity, R. 3934
Horace Mann, American Educator. Reines, B. J. 7473
Horatians and the Curatians, The. Brecht, B. 1297
Horn of Plenty. Miller, H. L. 5916
Horrible Humpy Dragon, The. McBride, D. 5115
Horrors, Incorporated. Miller, H. L. 5917
Horse Sense. Dias, E. J. 2426
Hospital. Pomerance, B. 7236
Host, The. Molnar, F. 6145
Hostage, The. Behan, B. 725, 726
Hostage, The. Claudel, P. 1863
Hot Ice. Ludlam, C. 5083
Hot Iron, The. Green, P. 3702
Hot Line to Destruction. Murray, J. 6349
Hotel China. Foreman, R. 3220
Hotel du Bon Repos, L'. Saint-Granier and P. Bonnieres 7860
Hotel du Commerce. Hochwälder, F. 4122
Hotel Oak. Boiko, C. 1076
Hotel Ritz, alle ottol. Pollock, H. 7234
Hotel Santa Claus. Miller, H. L. 5918
Hound of the Maskervilles, The. Miller, H. L. 5919
Hounded by Basketballs. Albert, R. 106
Hour at Noon, An. Hartley, R. E. 3947
Hour Glass, The. Yeats, W. B. 9594, 9595, 9596, 9597
Hour of Earth, An. Garrison, T. 3399
Hour of Prospero. Lawrence, C. S. 4849
House, A. Ford, F. M. 3213, 3214
House and Home. Miles, J. 5829
House Beautiful, The. Hanna, T. M. 3894
House by the Side of the Road, The. Kotzebue, A. von 4694

House for Rent. MacLellan, E. and C. V. Schroll 5252
House Gnomes. Farrar, J. C. 2933
House into Which We Are Born, The. Copeau, J. 2010
House Is Haunted, The. McQueen, M. H. and N. McQueen 5340
House of Bernarda Alba, The. Lorca, F. G. 5044
House of Blue Leaves, The. Guare, J. 3774
House of Cards. Sutphen, W. G. van T. 8630
House of Horrors. Murray, J. 6350
House of Lot, The. Sender, R. J. 8149
House of Rimmon, The. Van Dyke, H. 9029
House of Santa Claus, The. Eggleston, E. 2822
House of the Setting Suns, The. Marques, R. 5575
House of the Seven Gables, The. Hawthorne, N. 3989, 3990
House on Chestnut Street, The. Nichol, J. W. 6538
House Party, A. 4182
House That Jack Built, The. Richmond, S. S. 7560
House with Two Doors Is Difficult to Guard, A. Calderon de la Barca, P. 1502
Houseful of Elves, A. Huff, B. T. 4284
Housewarming, The. Hitchcock, G. 4115
How Billy Helped Things Along. 4200
How Brophy Made Good. Hare, D. 3910
How Christmas Was Saved, or The Sorrows of Santa Claus. Markham, C. 5559
How Come Christmas. Bradford, R. 1262, 1263
How High Is Your Fi? Murray, J. 6351
How Long. Hodkinson, K. 4125
How Many Dark Ships in the Forest? Arial, R. 331
How Mothers Came to Be. Boiko, C. 1077
How Much Land Does a Man Need? Tolstoy, L. N. 8876
How the Indian Found His Game. Hall, M. 3853

How the World Began. Moore, J. and H. G. Thorpe 6204
How to Be Happy Though Married. Seiler, C. 8139
How to Choose a Boy. Boiko, C. 1078
How to Get to the End of the Fourth of July. Ortmayer, R. 6883
How to Trap a Husband. Hester, D. 4008
How with This Rage. Dibble, W. 2463
Howard's Forward Pass. Deming, D. 2324
Howling Success, A. Garver, J. 3410
How's the World Treating You? Milner, R. 6066
Hubbub on the Bookshelf. Woster, A. 9569
Huckleberry Finn. Clemens, S. L. 1880
Hughie. O'Neill, E. 6847, 6848
Huit Femmes. Thomas, R. 8836
Huitre et la Perle. Saroyan, W. 7950
Hulks, The. Farrington, J. 2937
Human Accident, The. Frink, C. 3305
Humblest Place, The. DuBois, G. 2637
Humiliation of the Father. Claudel, P. 1864
Humilies et Offenses. Charpak, A. 1728
Humpty Dumpty. Bloch, B. 1002
Hundred Days, The. Wilson, W. L. 9470
Hundred Fires, A. Bobb, R. 1032
Hunt for the Violet. Barbee, L. 566
Hunting of the Snark, The. Masciola, C. 5638
Hurluberlu. Anouilh, J. 263, 264
Hurrah for Books. Watts, F. B. 9231
Hurray for Families. Anderson, Mary E. 206
Husband, A. Svevo, I. 8642
Husband for Breakfast. Mitchell, R. E. 6084
Hush, No One Is Listening. Cavalieri, G. 1672
Hussards, Les. Breal, P.-A. 1278
Hyacinth Halvey. Gregory, Lady A. 3724
Hyacinths. Hanna, T. M. 3895

Hymen a la Mode. Pendered, M. L. 7043
Hypothese. Pinget, R. 7167

I

I Am a Camera. Van Druten, J. 9026
I Can Get Along. Asbrand, K. 401
I Can't Imagine Tomorrow. Williams, T. 9427
I, Claudius. Mortimer, J. 6247
I Did But Jest. Schmidt, G. P., Jr. 8040
"I Don't Understand..." Kiggins, W. R. 4619
I Have Been Here Before. Priestley, J. B. 7294
I Have No Prayer. Oboler, A. 6742
I Have to Call My Father. Brown, L. 1369
I Love You, Mr. Klotz! Murray, J. 6352
I. O. U., An. Briscoe, M. S. 1333
I Remember Mama. Van Druten, J. 9027
I Rise in Flame, Cried the Phoenix. Williams, T. 9428, 9429
I Thank You. Cornell, M. 2023
I Too Speak to the Rose. Carballido, E. 1596
I Want to Report a Murder. Murray, J. 6353
I Want to Talk to You. Garver, J. 3411
I Will Arise. Morris, T. B. 6238
I Will Not Have It So. Plimpton, H. 7218
"Icarus Is Coming." Murray, J. 6354
Iceman Cometh, The. O'Neill, E. 6849
Ichheit on a Holiday. Filippone, V. 3020
I'd Rather Do It Myself. Collins, D. R. 1938
Idea di Cora, L'. Varaldo, A. 9041
Ideal Giant, The. Lewis, W. 4973
Ideal Husband, An. Wilde, O. 9367
Idealists, The. Hull, H. R. 4320
Idem idem. Massa, M. 5643

Idiot, L'. Barsacq, A. 640
Idiot. Lodovici, C. 5013
Idiot du Miracle, L'. Rosano, R. 7698
Idiote. Achard, M. 28, 29
Idyll. Graham, M. 3679
Idyll. Hofmannsthal, H. von 4133, 4134
Idylle. Provins, M. 7319
If Shakespeare Lived Today. Dunsany, E. J. M. D. P. 2715
If We Only Could Cook. McQueen, M. H. and N. McQueen 5341
If Wishes Were Fishes. Taylor, M. A. 8722
If Wishes Were Horses. Nathan, B. 6449
If Worse Comes to Worst or Times Are Getting Harder and Harder. Matson, C. 5658
If You Can't Eat Fish Without Tenderloin! Conkle, E. P. 1972
If You Meet a Leprechaun. Feather, J. 2958
Ikkaku Sennin. Motoyazu, K. Z. 6274
Il n'y a pas Que l'Amour. See, E. 8131
Il y a Une Vertu dans le Soleil. Gilles, A. 3527
Ile. O'Neill, E. 6850, 6851, 6852
Ile Irréelle, L'. Dubosc, I. 2664
Iliad, The. Homer 4155
I'll Eat My Hat. Miller, H. L. 5920
Ill Met by Moonlight. MacLiammoir, M. 5269
I'll Try. Murphy, E. 6309
Illegitime Defense. Valmain, F. and J. Dejoux 9008
Illusione di Giacomina, L'. Duvernois, H. 2787
Illustre concittadino, L'. Montanelli, I. and M. Luciani 6179
Illustrious Voyager. Hughes, R. 4311
I'm Nobody. Dennis, E. D. 2335
I'm Not Complaining. Kreymborg, A. 4714
Image-Makers Take Over, The. Robinson, M. 7626
Imaginary Invalid, The. Molière 6120
Imaginary Trial of George Washington, An. Wolman, D. 9538
Imbroglione onesto, L'. Viviani, R. 9162
Immortal. Glick, C. and B. Sobel 3586
Immortal Hour, The. Sharp, W. 8198

Immortality. MacInnis, C. P. 5216
Immortals. Dobie, C. C. 2510
Immortals Converse, The. Trowbridge, W. R. H. 8940
Imperatrice di diverte. Casella, A. and T. Pavlova 1633
Imperdonabile peccato, L'. Molnar, F. 6146
Impondérables, Les. Presles, C. des 7283
Importance of Being Early, The. Parkhurst, W. 6978
Importance of Being Earnest, The. Wilde, O. 9368, 9369, 9370
Importanza del latino, L'. Carsana, E. 1625
Impossible. Howells, W. D. 4245
Impossible Lover. Arrabal, F. 373
Impossible Room, The. Murray, J. 6355
Impromptu. Burnett, D. 1437
Impromptu d'Amsterdam, ou "La Parade." Canolle, J. 1571
Impromptu de Paris. Giraudoux, J. 3568, 3569
Impromptu de Paris. Sarment, J. 7935
Impromptu de Rome, ou Le Septième Personnage. Sonnier, G. 8377
Impromptu des Collines. Husson, A. 4330
Improving Husbands. Givens, H. M. 3579
Improvisation, The. Hall, K. K. 3846
Improvisation, or The Shepherd's Chameleon. Ionesco, E. 4390
Imprudentes, Les. Deutsch, L. 2384
Imputato Riccardo. Pezzati, M. 7116
In campagna è un'altra cosa. Bevilacqua, G. 905
In Celebration. Storey, D. 8538
In Chains. Hervieu, P. 4086
In collaborazione. Borg, W. 1196
In County Mayo. Conacher, W. M. 1966
In der Sache J. Robert Oppenheimer. Kipphardt, H. 4641
In Garrison. Freybe, C. E. 3287
In Gotham Meadow. Wefer, M. 9260
In Gremio Decorum. Barclay, Sir T. 582
In Heaven and Earth. Plimmer, D. 7216
In Hell with the Dramatists. Bartlett, R. 641
In His House. Middleton, G. 5816
In His Image. Grafton, S. 3675
In Honor of Trees. Newman, D. 6502
In Honor of Washington. Pendleton, E. 7049
"In Modern Dress." Morley, C. 6225
In My Father's House. Madden, D. 5421
In principio erano i marescialli. Mnacko, L. 6099
In Questo solo mondo. Landi, S. 4785
In the Andes. Parrish, H. 6987
In the City. Yushkevich, S. 9627
In the Dark. Dreiser, T. 2594
In the Days of Piers Ploughman. MacKay, D. D'A 5222
In the Fog. Gordon, H. K. 3640
In the Frame of Don Cristobal. Garcia Lorca, F. 3381
In the Jungle of Cities. Brecht, B. 1298
In the Light of the Manger. Bates, W. O. 671
In the Light of the Star. Peterson, A. E. 7091
In the Morgue. Cowan, S. 2064
In the Name of Miles Standish. Ramsey, H. 7399
In the Net. Sastre, A. 7974
In the Secret Places. Nessesson, E. B. 6466
In the Shade of the Old Apple Tree. Barker, G. 601
In the Shadow of Statues. Duhamel, G. 2680
In the Shadow of the Glen. Synge, J. M. 8668, 8669, 8670
In the Witch's House. Bennett, R. 782
In the Zone. O'Neill, E. 6853
In This Hung-Up Age. Corso, G. 2037, 2038
In Those 12 Days. Hartzell, G. 3956
In una casa di campagna. Witkiewicz, S. I. 9514
In verziere. Bertolazzi, C. 873
Inaugurazione, L'. Rèpaci, L. 7494

Incident. Andreyev, L. N. 232
Incident at Valley Forge. Hackett, W. 3801
Incident at Vichy. Miller, A. 5848
Incident Before Troy. Nightingale, E. M. 6599
Incidente, L'. D'Errico, E. 2351
Incidente al Caffè Minerva, Un. Berri, G. 869
Incidente del 7 aprile, L'. Bernard, T. 840
Incompetent Godmother, The. Adams, P.-L. 72
Inconnue, L'. Franck, P. 3254
Inconnue d'Arras, L'. Salacrou, A. 7875
Inconsolabile, L'. Zamacois, M. 9631
Incontro, L'. London, J. 5022
Incontro a babele. Cappelli, S. 1585
Incontro col gentleman. D'Errico, E. 2352
Incontro fuori del tempo. Guaita, G. 3773
Incontro sentimentale. Antonelli, L. 301
Incredible Housing Shortage, The. Olfson, L. 6800
Indecision. Marinetti, F. T. 5549
Indemoniata, L'. Vega Carpio, L. F. de 9054
Indian. Ryga, G. 7829
Indian Boy Without a Name, The. Vahl, R. 8987
Indian Brave. Gross, N. F. 3762
Indian Giver. Howells, W. D. 4246
Indians. Kipit, A. 4689
Indifferenti, Gli. Pincherle, A. 7154
Indiscret. See, E. 8128
In'ependence. Alger, E. M. 134
Ines de Portugal. Casona, A. 1639
Ines Mendo, or, Prejudice Vanquished. Mérimée, P. 5772
Inexperienced Ghost, The. Wells, H. G. 9289
Infedele, L'. Del Buono, O. 2296
Infedeltà. Rossi, C. 7712
Inferno, L'. Pinelli, T. 7160
Informazioni. Dieudonné, R. 2493

Informer, The. Brecht, B. 1299, 1300
Informer, The. Nichols, D. 6541
Ingannati, Gli. 4371
Ingeborg. Goetz, C. 3595
Ingresso libero. Tieri, V. 8861
In-Group, The. Nolan, P. T. 6652
Inherit the Wind. Lawrence, J. and R. E. Lee 4858
Inheritors, The. Cook, R. 1999
Injunction Granted. Living Newspaper. 5004
Inn at Bethlehem, The. Fisher, A. 3051
Inn of the Blue Rose, The. Phillips, M. K. 7131
Innamorati, l'amore attraverso le eta. Martel de Janville, S. G. M. A. de R. de M. 5584
Innesto dell'eternità, L'. Veneziani, C. 9068
Inno d'avvento. Apollonio, M. 308
Innocente, L'. Lenormand, H. R. 4916, 4917
Innocents. Archibald, W. 318, 319
Innocenza di Camilla. Bontempelli, M. 1191
Inquietudes. Luizet, J. 5087
Insatiable Dragon, The. Boiko, C. 1079
Insect Play, The. O'Brien, F. 6745
Insideout. Norman, F. 6693
Inspector Calls, An. Priestley, J. B. 7295, 7296
Inspector General, The. Gogol, N. 3601
Inspiration of the Play, The. Kummer, C. 4736
Installment Plan, The. Santi, I. 7987
Instinct, L'. Sardou, A. 7929
Interdit au Public. Marsan, J. 5579
Interim. O'Connell, T. E. 6761
Interlude. Carroll, P. V. 1621
Interlude in the Life of St. Francis, An. Raphael, A. 7415
Intermezzo. Coward, N. 2070
Intermezzo. Giraudoux, J. 3570
Intermezzo. Sutphen, Van T. 8631
International Art. Seeley, F. P. 8134
Interno 1, Interno 5, Interno 7. Mancuso, U. and G. Zucca 5487

Interpolated. Brookman, K. B. 1341
Interrogation, The. Bellido, J. M. 734
Interrupted Act, The. Rozewicz, T. 7775
Interrupted Experiment. Sherman, L. A. 8249
Interrupted Proposal, An. Bates, A. 667
Interruption, An. Gerry, M. S. 3446
Intervallo di manovella. Pujel, R. 7338
Interview, The. Burtt, T. C., Jr. 1447
Interview, The. Spark, M. 8437
Interview. Timmory, G. 8866
Interviewed. Megrue, R. C. 5732
Intimate Strangers. Tarkington, B. 8708
Into the Everywhere. Heal, E. 4003
Into the Tents of Men. Jacobs, M. G. 4423
Intolleranza. Nono, L. 6686
Introduzione alla vita eroica. Duse, E. 2766
Intruder, The. Maeterlinck, M. 5427
Intruder, The. Reed, E. 7459
Invaders, The. Wolff, E. 9530
Invasion, The. Adamov, A. 64
Investigation of a Chair. Ah Chien 83
Invisible Dragon of Winn Sinn Tu. Musil, R. G. 6415
Invisible Inventions, Incorporated. Murray, J. 6356
Invisible Man, The. Wells, H. G. 9290
Invitation au Chateau, L'. Anouilh, J. 265
Invitation to a March. Laurents, A. 4830
Invité de Pierre. Pushkin, A. 7344
Io e te. Riccora, P. 7516
Io fui, sono e sarò. Bevilacqua, G. 906
Io non sono io. Toddi 8871
Iolanthe. Gilbert, W. S. and Sir A. S. Sullivan 3516
Ion. Zimmer, B. 9651
Iphigenia at Aulis. Rexroth, K. 7498

Ippolito e la vendetta. Terron, C. 8767
Irene fra due rive. Callegari, G. P. 1510
Irish Pastoral, An. Buchanan, G. 1400
Irkutskaja Istorija. Arbuzov, A. 314
Irma la Dolce. Breffort, A. 1314
Iron Queen of Cornwall, The. McGowan, J. 5196
Is Cupid Stupid? Martens, A. C. 5600
Is There a Monster in the House? Fontaine, R. 3203
Is There Life on Other Planets? Lane, M. 4789
Isaac et la Sage-Femme. Haim, V. 3824
Isabella. Fo, D. 3170
Isabelle et le General. Mithois, M. 6094
Isabelle et le Pelican. Franck, M. 3252
Isaiah and the United Nations. Silverman, S. H. 8281
Iseult of Brittany. Symons, A. 8663
Island. Mandel, O. 5491
Island of the Mighty, The. Arden, J. and M. D'Archy 326, 327
Ispezione. Betti, U. 894
Ispezione, L'. Vergani, O. 9078
Istante prima, Un. Bassano, E. 649
Istinto, L'. Kistemaekers, H. 4648
It Ain't Tea. Jasudowicz, D. 4451
It All Depends. Braley, B. 1269
It Bees Dat Way. Bullins, E. 1415
It Happened in Egypt. Ross, F. R. 7705
It Never Happens. Parkhurst, W. 6979
It Takes a Thief. Kozlenko, W. 7100
It, The Usual Play with an Unusual Ending. Florance, R. 3160
Itaca, Itaca! De Chiara, G. 2239
Italia sabato sera. Contarello, A. 1983
Italian Girl, The. Murdoch, I. and J. Saunders 6305
Italiano tra noi, Un. Mazzucco, R. 5719
It's a Magic Time. Barbee, L. 567

It's a Woman's World. Martens,
  A. C. 5601
It's All Wrong. Nash, O. 6441
It's All (Y)ours! Beye, H. 910
It's Almost Like Being. Itallie,
  J. -C. van 9032
It's Greek to Me. McQueen, M.
  H. and N. McQueen 5342
It's 1984 and the Sheep Have Fleas.
  Cartwright, D. 1629
It's Really Quite Simple. Anderson, H. L. 204
It's So Peaceful. Ward, M. 9207
It's Spring. Harris, C. L. 3917
Ivan the Terrible. Priestley, H. 7289
Ivan Vasilievich. Bulgakov, M. A. 1413
Ivanov. Chekhov, A. 1769
Ivory Tower. Macintire, E. and Clements, C. 5218
Iz She Izzy or Iz He Ain'tzy or Iz They Both. Carter, L. 1628

J

J. B. MacLeish, A. 5241, 5242
Jacassiere, La. Leautier, G. 4866
Jack and Jill. Smith, S. D., Jr. 8352
Jack and the Beanstalk. Mahlmann, L. and D. C. Jones 5451
Jack and the Magic Beanstalk. Thane, A. 8804
Jack and the Sillies. Plescia, G. L. 7213
Jack, Beanstalk and Friends. Cheatham, V. R. 1754
Jack Frost and the Scarecrow. Nadin, M. C. 6430
Jack Frost's Goodbye Gift. Spamer, C. 8411
Jack Furey. MacMahon, B. 5272
Jack Jonette's Ride. Boiko, C. 1080
Jack Just Anybody. Nothnagle, C. 6696
Jack-O-Lantern. Spamer, C. 8412
Jack Straw. Fisher, A. 3052
Jack Who Yawned. Krakauer, D. 4706
Jack Winter's Dream. Baxter, J. K. 682

Jackass, The. Ruibal, J. 7790
Jack's Friends. Spamer, C. 8413
Jacob Comes Home. Kozlenko, W. 4701
Jacquerie, La. Merimee, P. 5773
Jagdszenen aus Niederbayern. Sperr, M. 8445
J'ai Tué. Marchand, L. 5536
Jamais Trois ... Sans Quatre. Mercier, M. 5761
James and John. Cannan, G. 1567
Jan Palach. Sylvanus, E. 8659
Jan Vyrava. Subert, F. A. 8598
Jane Eyre. Brontë, C. 1338
Janet the Janitress. Sroda, A. 8469
Janus. Green, C. 3697a
Japanese Trio. Winther, B. 9483
Jar, The. Finkel, D. 3027
Jar. Pirandello, L. 7193
Jardin Sur la Mer. Vermorel, C. 9087
Jazznite. Jones, W. 4512
Je M'Appelle Rhubarbe. Foissy, G. 3190
Je Suis Seule Ce Soir. Antoine, A. -P. 287
Je T'Attendais. Natanson, J. 6446
Je T'Enleve. Boudousse, J. 1210
Jealousy. Becquer, G. A. 714
Jean de la Lune. Achard, M. 30, 31
Jeanette. Patterson, F. C. 7006
Jeanne. Duvernois, H. 2788
Jeanne D'Arc at Vaucouleurs. Hutchins, W. 4339
Jeanne D'Arc, La Pucelle de France. Bouhelier, St. -G. de 1212
Jenny in the Orchard. Thomas, C. 8823
Jeronimo. Carsana, E. 1626
Jest of Hahalaba. Dunsany, E. J. M. D. P. 2716
Jester and the King's Tarts, The. Kroll, F. L. 4732
Jesuit. Alencar, J. de 124
Jesus, As Seen by His Friends. Kenan, A. 4588
Jesus Christ is Born. Cole, M. H. 1930
Jesus-fric Supercrack. Scoff, A. 8103
Jesus la Caille. Dard, F. 2188
Jeu de L'Amour et de la Mort. Rolland, R. 7661
Jeune Fille a Marier, Une. Ionesco, E. 4391

Jeune Fille Espagnole. Rostand, M. 7721
Jeunesse, La. Amiel, D. 185
Jeux d'Enfants. Meillant, H. 5736
Jeux de la Nuit, Les. Gilroy, F. D. 3545
Jeux de Massacre. Ionesco, J. 4392, 4393
Jeux Sont Faits! Mery, A. 5785
Jew of Constance. Scholz, W. van 8081
Jew of Malta, The. Marlowe, C. 5564
Jewell Merchants, The. Cabell, J. B. 1467, 1468
Jezebel. Welsh, R. G. 9291
Jig Is Up, The. Jasudowicz, D. 4451
Jill-In-the-Box. Watts, F. B. 9232
Jill's Way. McCourt, E. W. 5139
Jiminy Cinders. Miller, H. L. 5921
Jimmy Six. Downing, R. 2574
Jingle Bells. McQueen, M. H. and N. McQueen 5343
Joan la Romee. Harris, F. 3921
Joan Makes a Sale. Richmond, S. S. 7561
Joan of Arc. Chadwick, J. H. 1702
Joan of Domremy. Crane, W. D. 2095
Joan of Lorraine. Anderson, M. 210, 211
Joanna Livermore Parrot. Olfson, L. 6801
Joe Hill Is Not Dead. Stavis, B. 8476
Joe il rosso. Falconi, D. 2913
Joe White and the Seven Lizards. Boiko, C. 1081
Johan Ulfstjerna. Hedberg, T. H. 4023
Johannes. Sudermann, H. 8602
John Grumlie. Very, A. 9115
John Herkner. Bernstein, E. P. 860
John the Bastard. Abel, L. 8
Johnny Appleseed. Nolan, P. T. 6653
Johnny Appleseed. Schoenfeld, B. C. 8079
Johnny Appleseed's Vision. Fisher, A. and O. Rabe 3111

Johnny Belinda. Harris, E. 3920
Johnny Did Try. Phillips, M. K. 7132
Johnny Nightmare. McCoy, P. S. 5147
Johnny on the Spot. Fisher, A. and O. Rabe 3112
Johnny Question-Mark. Boiko, C. 1082
Johnny So Long. Welburn, V. C. 9277
Jolly Old Abbot of Canterbury. 4496
Jonah in the Bible Country. Snider, C. L. 8359
Jonathan's Thanksgiving. Very, A. 9116
Jose San Martin, South American Hero. 4518
Joueur, Un. Charpak, A. 1729
Jour de Folie, Un. Vilalta, M. 9143
Jour de Gloire. Bisson, A. and M. Villars 973
Joures. Wissant, G. de 9507
Journal, Le. Worms, J. 9562
Journal d'un Fou. Luneau, S. and R. Coggio 5092
Journalists. Freytag, G. 3298
Journées Entières dans les Arbres. Duras, M. 2738
Journey to Bahia. Gomes, D. 3618
Journey's End. Shirriff, R. C. 8252
Journeys End in Lovers' Meeting. Mendel, P. and A. Guiterman 5746
Joven de Provecho. Perez Galdos, B. 7066
Joy Lady, The. Hall, J. W. 3844
Joy of Giving Thanks. Liss, F. and N. G. Nestrick 4998
Joyeux Noel. Barillet, P. and J.-P. Gredy 592
Joyzelle. Maeterlinck, M. 5428
Juan Moreira. Gutierrez, E. and J. J. Podesta 3791
Juan Palmieri Tupamaro. Larreta, A. 4822
Juarez the Just. Baker, N. B. 521
Jubilee. Chekhov, A. 1770
Jubilee. Heijermans, H. 4031
Judas. Pagnol, M. 6930
Judas the Maccabee and Me. Samuels, G. 7899
Judge Douglas Presides. Nolan, J. C. 6626

743

Judge Lynch. Rogers, J. W., Jr. 7652
Judge Monkey. Colbert, M. 1925
Judge of the Divorce Court. Cervantes Saavedra, M. 1694
Judge's Diary, The. Miller, H. L. 5922
Judgment. Burr, A. J. 1444
Judgment Day. Pawley, T. D. 7020
Judgment of Paris, The. Lucian 5079
Judgment of Paris. Marcus, J. 5545
Judith. Giraudoux, J. 3571
Judith's Father. Widdemer, M. 9345
Juggler of Our Lady, The. France, A. 3243
Jules. Breal, P.-A. 1279
Jules, Juliette et Julien. Bernard, T. 841
Julie. Strindberg, A. 8569
Julius Cesar. Shakespeare, W. 8179, 8180
Jump for George. Miller, H. L. 5923
Jump for Joy. Schaaf, A. 8012
Junction Santa Claus. McQueen, M. H. and N. McQueen 5344
Junior Partisans, The. Longstreth, T. M. 5026
Junior Prom. Wilde, C. F. 9357
Juno and the Paycock. O'Casey, S. 6755
Jupiter Laughs. Cronin, A. J. 2119
Jury Duty. Martens, A. C. 5602
Jusqu'a Minuit. Santelli, C. 7918
Just and Lasting Peace, A. DuBois, G. 2638
Just in Time. Ziegler, E. E. 9649
Just Like Shaw. MacDonagh, J. 5165
Just Neighborly. Dean, A. 2213
Just Relax, Mother. McQueen, M. H. and N. McQueen 5345
Just Visiting? Boiko, C. 1083
Just What the Doctor Ordered. Miller, H. L. 5924
Justice Box, The. David, M. R. 2194
Justice du Corregidor, La. Casona, A. 1640

Jute. Witherspoon, L. 9510

K

Kachoo! Newman, D. 6503
Kaddish. Lerner, W. Z. 4933
Kafka. Shein, B. 8234
Kaltouma. Bebnone, P. 692
Kalypso. Csokor, F. T. 2132
Kanawa, A Crown of Iron Spikes. Motokiyo, Z. 6270
Kanjincho, A Kabuki Play. 4545
Karl et Anna. Frank, L. 3264
Karl Marx: A Prolet-Play. Wilson, E. 9460
Karma. Dell, J. 2300
Karma. Mew, T. 5799
Kartoteka. Rozewicz, T. 7776
Kasimir und Karoline. Horvath, O. von 4176
Kaspar. Handke, P. 3883
Kataki. Wincelberg, S. 9472
Kate Larsen. Sifton, C. G. and P. Sifton 8273
Kathleen Listens In. O'Casey, S. 6756
Katy Did. Crothers, R. 2121
Keep It Under Cover. McCoy, P. S. 5148
Keep Tightly Closed in a Cool Dry Place. Terry, M. 8768
Keeper of the Gate. Hagedorn, H. 3816
Keeping Christmas. Peacock, M. 7025
Kempy. Nugent, J. C. and E. Nugent 6705
Kennedy's Children. Patrick, R. 7002
Kessa Gozène. Gillois, A. 3536
Ketchup. Edson, R. 2818
Kettle of Brains, A. Williams, G. M. 9414
Key. Sender, R. J. 8150
Key to Understanding, The. Biggs, L. 923
Keys to Peace, The. Newman, D. 6504
Keystone (The Last Mile). Wexley, J. 9313
Kid Avalanche. Murray, J. 6357
Kidnapped. Stevenson, R. L. 8516
Kidnapped by the Indians. Perlmutter, R. 7070
Kidnapping of David Balfour, The. Stevenson, R. L. 8517
Kill Viet Cong. Hed 4021

744

Killer Crusade. Scott, A. 8105
Killer on the Prowl. Combs, R. 1960
Killing Frost. Ostertag, D. E. 6910
Killing of Sister George, The. Marcus, F. 5541
Killing Them All. Palmer, F. 6942
Kills-With-Her-Man. Alexander, H. B. 128
Kim. Kipling, R. 4639
Kindly Little Tailor, The. Rawe, M. 7441
King Alfred and the Cakes. Thane, A. 8805
King and the Bee, The. Whitworth, V. P. 9340
King and the Vowels, The. 4633
King Argimenes and the Unknown Warrior. Dunsany, E. J. M. D. P. 2717
King Arthur and His Knights. Morley, O. J. 6229
King Arthur and His Sword. Schwartz, L. S. 8096
King Cole's Blues. Spamer, C. N. 8414
King Glumpus. Thackeray, W. M. 8780
King Henry. Wildenbruch, E. von 9388
King Horn. Hall, M. C. 3849
King-Hunger. Andreyev, L. N. 233
King in the Kitchen, The. Slattery, M. E. 8314
King Is Born, A. Olfson, L. 6802
King Lear. Shakespeare, W. 8181
King Midas. Gardner, M. and J. S. Smith 3388
King of Hearts. Kerr, J. and E. Brooke 4604
King of Spain's Daughter. Deevy, T. 2245, 2246
King of the Dark Chamber, The. Tagore, R. 8686
King of the Golden River, The. Ruskin, J. 7800, 7801
King of the Great Clock Tower, The. Yeats, W. B. 9598
King of the Jews, The. Browne, M. 1375
King of the Jews, The. Harris, F. 3922, 3923
King, the Greatest Alcalde. Vega, L. de 9055
King Thrushbeard. Thane, A. 8806

King to Be. Leech, M. T. 4888
King Tutankhamon's Ruin. Perry, L. 7083
King Who Couldn't Be Fooled, The. Elfenbein, J. A. 2841
King Who Hated Birthdays, The. Thornton, J. F. 8850
King Who Scoffed, The. Williams, O. and J. Brady 9416
King Who Was Bored, The. Thane, A. 8807
Kingdom of Oceanus, The. Moran, I. 6212
King-Hunger. Andreyev, L. N. 126
King's Bean Soup, The. Werner, S. 9295
King's Calendar, The. Oser, J. A. 6900
King's Creampuffs, The. Swintz, M. 8650
King's Dreams, The. Blumenfeld, L. 1022
King's Holiday, The. Bennett, R. 783
King's Jester, The. Leuser, E. 4948
King's Son, The. Oliver, M. S. 6820
King's Valentine Tarts, The. Watts, F. B. 9233
King's Weather, The. Oser, J. A. 6901
Kiri No Meijiyama. Damon, S. F. 2171
Kiss, The. Clarke, A. 1852
Kiss for Madeline, A. Jackson, D. 4417
Kiss Me, Kate. Spewack, S. and Spewack, B. 8448
Kiss the Book. Daley, G. A. 2163
Kisses. Kaufman, S. J. 4562
Kissing Goes by Favor. Brown, L. N. 1368
Kitchen Absurd, The. Saphier, W. and M. Bodenheim 7923
Kitchenette. Tavel, R. 8717
Kitsch. Siro, C. 8308
Kitten. Gilbert, M. H. 3510
Kitten Capers. Boiko, C. 1084
Kitty Hawk-1903. Ickler, L. M. 4366
Knack, The. Jellicoe, A. 4453
Knights of the Square Table, The. Dias, E. J. 2427
Knights, Prologue. Aristophanes 333
Knock on the Door, The. Gay, C. M. 3430

Knock on the Door, The. Parrella, I. 6986
Knock, ou, Le Triomphe de la Medecine. Romains, J. 7669
Known But to God. DuBois, G. 2639
Komateekay. Cook, A. C. 1996
Kommen und Gehen. Beckett, S. 387
Konig Stirbt, Der. Ionesco, E. 4394
Kontraption. Owens, R. 6925
Korane. Borie, G. 1199
Koyoi Komachi; The Nightly Courting of Komachi. Motokiyo, Z. 6271
Krafte. Stramm, A. 8547
Krapp's Last Tape. Beckett, S. 706, 707
Kreslo N. 16. Ugrjumov, D. 8965
Kreutzer Sonata, The. Tolstoy, L. 8877
Kuckuck, Der. Grass, G. 3689

L

Laboremus. Bjørnson, B. 976
Lacey's Last Garland. Miller, H. L. 5925
Lache, Un. Gilles, A. 3528
Lacreme e le stelle, Le. Chiarelli, L. 1798
Ladies at Twelve. O'Neil, G. 6833
Ladies Go to the Festival, The. Theocritus 8817
Ladri. Duse, E. 2767
Ladro in paradiso, Un. Marotta, G. 5567
Ladro sono io! Cenzato, G. 1681
Lady Amaranth, The. Woodmeald, J. E. 9548
Lady Cathleen. Yeats, W. B. 9599
Lady Compassionate, The. Kirker, K. 4643
Lady from the Sea, The. Ibsen, H. 4362
Lady Godiva. Canolle, J. 1572
Lady Griselda's Dream. Morris, M. 6236
Lady Jane's Highwayman. Mathews, F. A. 5654
Lady Lawyer, The. Kinney, F. L., Jr. 4597

Lady Loses Her Hoop, The. Wilson, L. G. 9463
Lady Macbeth. Balachova, T. 525
Lady Moon and the Thief. Boiko, C. 1085
Lady of Eternal Springtime. Sabath, B. 7833
Lady of Larkspur Lotion, The. Williams, T. 9430
Lady of the Hair-Pins, The. Fenollosa, M. M. 2983
Lady of the Lake, The. Scott, Sir W. 8113
Lady of the Weeping Willow Tree. Walker, S. 9189
Lady or the Tiger, The. Stockton, F. R. 8526
Lady per la morte, Una. Bellussi, G. 740
Lady Wildcat. Kleibacker, F. 4657
Lady Windermere's Fan. Wilde, O. 9371
Lady with the Dagger. Schnitzler, A. 8068, 8069
Lady with the Mirror, The. Wellman, R. 9283
Ladybug Ladybug. Mitchell, W. O. 6087
Lady's Not for Burning, The. Fry, C. 3331
Laitier, Le. Klein, J. 4659
Lake Darby Monster, The. Dias, E. J. 2428
Lambs, The. Grant, R. 3687
Lamentable Comedy of Willow Wood. Kipling, R. 4640
Lamento e rabbia per i gatti. Castelli, C. 1649
Lamma's Eve. Randolph, E. 7403
Lamp in the Forest. MacLellan, E. and C. V. Schroll 5253
Lampada dell'orco, La. Pompei, M. 7239
Lampe de Gallé, La. Barillet, P. and J.-P. Gredy 592
Lamplighter, The. Dickens, C. 2474
Lancio riuscito, Un. Simonetta, U. 8296
Land Ho! Lamb, E. H. 4774
Land of Heart's Desire. Yeats, W. B. 9600, 9601
Land of Make-Believe. Williams, B. G. 9409
Land of Nobody. Chin-Yang, L. 1805
Land of the Aiouwas, The. Piper, E. F. 7180

Land of the Free. Block, B. 1006
Landscape. Pinter, H. 7177
Landslide for Shakespeare. Dias, E. J. 2429
Langrevin Pere et Fils. Bernard, T. 842
Language Shop, The. Hall, M. 3862
Lansky Soliloquies, The. Weitz, E. R. 9276
Lanzichenecca, La. Di Mattia, V. 2503
Laodice and Danaë. Bottomley, G. 1202
Larbins, Les. Menthon, H. de 5755
Lares. Rimanelli, G. 7586
Lark, The. Anouilh, J. 266
Larry Park's Day in Court. Bentley, E. 808
Lascio alle mie donne. Fabbri, D. 2897
Last Boat, The. Johnson, D. H. 4482
Last Capitalist, The. Jasudowicz, D. 4451
Last Eligible Man, The. Smith, R. P. 8351
Last Frontier, The. Rowell, A. C. 7767
Last Laugh, The. DuBois, G. 2640
Last Man, The. Arlett, V. I. 338
Last Mrs. Blakeley, The. Saffold, V. 7847
Last of Mr. Weekney, The. Willoughby, E. E. 9453
Last of Mrs. Cheney, The. Lonsdale, F. 5030
Last of the Ghastleys. Huff, B. T. 4285
Last of the Order, The. Benner, R. V. 767
Last Party, The. Gordon, C. 3638
Last Rising, The. Macphail, A. 5282
Last Snake in Ireland, The. Malone, M. 5480
Last Stop. Cable, H. 781
Last Time I Saw Paris, The. Olfson, L. 6803
Last Woman, The. Soule, G. 8392
Last Word, The. Broughton, J. 1352

Lastrico d'inferno. Levi, P. 4957
Late Mr. Scarface, The. McQueen, M. H. and N. McQueen 5346
Late Spring, A. Bobb, R. 1033
Late Spring. Petersen, R. J. 7088
Latent Heterosexual, The. Chayefsky, P. 1745
Laughing Gas. Dreiser, T. 2595
Laughing Princess, The. Nicholson, M. A. 6571
Laughter. Bindamin, M. 941
Laughter of the Gods, The. Dunsany, E. J. M. D. P. 2718, 2719
Launcelot and Elaine. 4827
Laure et les Jacques. Aroutcheff, G. 366
Lavinia fra i dannati. Terron, C. 8757
Law. Luther, L. 5094
Law Takes Its Toll, The. Blake, R. 990, 991
Lawyer's Mistake, A. Burghlie, J. 1421
Lay By. Brenton, H., B. Clark, T. Griffiths, D. Hare, S. Poliakoff, H. Stoddart, and S. Wilson 1320
Lay Confessional, A. 4863
Lazy Fox, The. Howard, V. 4224
Lazy Little Raindrop, The. Barr, J. 616
Lazzaroni, I. Palmieri, F. 6946
Leading Lady, The. Gordon, R. 3641
Leaguers and Peelers. Mitchell, S. L. 6086
Leak in the Dike, A. Nolan, P. T. 6654
Lear. Bond, E. 1170
Learning the Ropes. Kitaif, T. 4650
Least Gift, The. Thane, A. 8788
Leave Us Blow. Schumann, D. 8091
Leaves, The. Young, S. 9620
Lebbra. Böll, H. 1153
Leben des Galilei. Brecht, B. 1301
Leçon, La. Ionesco, E. 4395, 4396, 4397
Leçon de Français, La. Bernard, J.-J. 825
'Lection. Conkle, E. P. 1973
Leela Means to Play. Simons, B. 8300

Left-Over Reindeer, The. Miller, H. L. 5926
Legacy, The. Richmond, S. S. 7562
Legacy, The. Schnitzler, A. 8070
Legacy of Cain: Favela, The. Beck, J. and J. Malina 693
Legend of Saint Nicholas, The. Dix, B. M. 2508
Legend of Sleepy Hollow. Irving, W. 4404
Legend of the Christmas Rose, The. Leuser, E. 4949
Leghorn Hat, The. Labiche, E. and M. Michel 4754
Lei e il suo ritratto. Michelotti, G. 5808
Leibeskonzil, Das. Panizza, O. 6951
Leocadia. Anouilh, J. 267
Léon, ou la Bonne Formule. Magnier, C. 5440
Leonard de Vinci. Aguila, C. 80
Leonarda. Bjørnson, B. 977
Leone della piazza, Il. Eremburg, I. 2870
Leonida non è qui. Monicelli, F. 6171
Leonzio e Lena. Büchner, G. 1401
Leprechaun Shoemaker, The. Watts, F. B. 9234
Leprechaun's Pot of Gold, The. Watts, F. B. 9235
Lesson, The. Ionesco, E. 2260
Lesson in Acting, A. Aide, C. H. 87
Lesson in Acting, The. Parsons, Mrs. C. 6989
Lesson in History, A. Farrell, J. T. 2935
Let George Do It. McQueen, M. H. and N. McQueen 5347
Let It Snow. Blaine, B. G. 986
Let Sleeping Beauties Lie. Fontaine, R. 3204
Let the Law Take Its Course. Torcross, J. 8890
"Let the Next Generation Be My Client." Craven, E. 2097
Let's End It All. Seiler, C. 8140
Let's Go Formal. McQueen, M. H. and N. McQueen 5348, 5349
Let's Speak Vietnamese. Clark, M. 1850

Letter, The. Maugham, W. S. 5672
Letter for Charlotte, A. Malone, M. 5481
Letter of Introduction, A. Howells, W. D. 4247
Letter to Lincoln, A. Barbee, L. 568
Letter to Private Smith. Reines, B. J. 7474
Lettera, La. Zimmer, B. 9652
Lettera raccomandata, La. Moineaux, G. 6105
Lettera smarrita, La. Franzero, C. M. 3271
Letteratura. Natanson, J. 6447
Letteratura. Schnitzler, A. 8071
Letters. Ryerson, F. 7826
Letters from the South. Sha Seh, Fu To, Ma Yung, and Li Chi-huang. 8163
Lettiga deserta, La. 4942
Lettre Perdue, Un. Caragiale, I. L. 1592
Lettres de la Religieuse Portugaise. 4943
Lettura del copione, La. Munoz-Seca, P. 6297
Levate li occhi e resguardate. 4955
Lezione di inglese. Mauri, R. 5686
Li-Ma-Tong, Nuvoletta Rosa. Vergani, O. 9079
Liar, The. Foote, S. 3212
Libere stanze. Lerici, R. 4930
Libertà, La. Terron, C. 8758
Libertà provvisoria. Antòn E. 290
Liberté Provisoire. Durand, M. 2734
Liberty Comes to Krahwinkel. Nestroy, J. 6467
Library Circus, The. Miller, H. L. 5927
Library Come to Life, The. Trowbridge, W. R. H. 8941
Library Operetta, A. Sagoff, M. 7849
Libreria del sole, La. Fabbri, D. 2898
Licenza di matrimonio. Bigiaretti, L. 924
Licha's Birthday Serenade. Nolan, P. T. 6655
Lick. Boyajian, A. 1250
Lidia o l'infinito. Giovaninetti, S. 3557

Lie, The. Lewisohn, L. 4975
Liebelei. Schnitzler, A. 8072
Liebeskonzil, Das. Panizza, O. 6951
Lien de Sang. Valle Inclan, R. de 8999
Lies. Molnar, F. 6147
Lieto fine. Falconi, D. 2914
Lieutenant Pays His Respects, The. McCoy, P. S. 5149
Lieutenant Tenant. Gripari, P. 3757
Life and Deaths of St. George of Lydda. Herring, R. 4081
Life and Times of J. Walter Smintheus, The. White, E. 9324
Life for Mother, The. McQueen, M. H. and N. McQueen 5350
Life Is a Bowl of Eugene O'Neills. Sullivan, F. 8615
Life Is a Dream. Clements, C. C. 1894
Life Is Always the Same. Cann, L. G. 1563
Life of Confucius. Brecht, B. 1302
"Life on Broadway." Van Campen, H. G. 9013
Life Price. O'Neill, M. and J. Seabrook 6869
Life with Father. Lindsay, H. and R. Crouse 4988
Lifeguards. Lehan, R. R. 4895
Lifting of the Dark, The. Swinley, E. I. 8649
Light, The. Duhamel, G. 2681
Light Along the Rails. MacDonald, Z. K. 5170
Light in Darkness, A. DuBois, G. 2641
Light of Other Days, The. Porter, L. S. 7255
Light Up the Sky. Hart, M. 3941
Light-Bearer. Chatterji, T. 1741
Lighthouse Keepers. Colquemin, P. 1905
Lighting of the Torch, The. Buchanan, F. R. 1399
Light-o'-Love. Schnitzler, A. 8073
Lights. Marinetti, F. T. 5549
Lights! Camera! Action! Murray, J. 6358
Lights of Bohemia. Valle-Inclan, R. M. del 9000
Lights with Us. Newton, D. 6535

Ligne de Coeur. Puget, C. -A. 7326
Like Father, Like Son. Wilson, L. G. 9464
Like Mother Used to Make. Murray, J. 6359
Likely Lad, A. Boiko, C. 1086
Likely Story, A. Howells, W. D. 4248
Likeness of the Night. Clifford, L. L. 1899
Liliom. Molnar, F. 6148, 6149
Lilith. Gourmont, R. de 3670
Lilly in Little India, A. Howarth, D. 4232
Lily of the Label Department. Huff, B. T. 4286
Limpid River. De Burea, S. 2234
Lincoln Coat, The. Sealock, T. W. 8118
Lincoln Cupboard, The. McGowan, J. 5197
Lincoln Heart, The. Miller, H. L. 5928
Lincoln: Hero Unlimited. Hollingsworth, L. 4144
Lincoln Lady, The. Seymour, J. 8162
Lincoln Meseum, A. Miller, H. L. 5929
Lincoln Reminders. McQueen, M. H. and N. McQueen 5351
Lincoln Umbrella, The. McQueen, M. H. and N. McQueen 5352
Lincoln's Buckskin Breeches. York, M. A. 9613
Lincoln's Library Fine. Miller, H. L. 5930
Linden Tree, The. Priestley, J. B. 7297
Line. Horovitz, I. 4174
Line-up for Victory. Burack, A. S. 1418
Link with Lincoln, A. Miller, H. L. 5931
Links. Heijermans, H. 4032
Linnaun Shee, The. Fitzmaurice, G. 3141
Lion, The. Kenan, A. 4589
Lion and the Mouse, The. Barr, J. 619
Lion and the Mouse. Bennett, R. 784
Lion and the Mouse, The. Christmas, J. S. 1827
Lion in Love, The. Delaney, S. 2289
Lion to Lamb. Boiko, C. 1087

749

Liquore dell'amore, Il. Pakots, G. 6936
Liseron, ou Le Destin de la Fille. Chose, R. 1820
Listen to the Hokja. Winther, B. 9484
Listen to the People. Benet, S. V. 759
Listening. Froome, J. R., Jr. 3324
Literati. Garrison, T. 3400
Little Bird in the Tree. Leuser, E. 4950
Little Blue Guienea-Hen, The. Martel de Janville, Comtesse de 5585
Little Cake, The. McCarty, E. C. 5125
Little Chip's Christmas Tree. Duvall, L. M. 2778
Little Christmas Guest. Asbrand, K. 402
Little Cosette and Father Christmas. Hugo, V. 4316
Little Decameron. John, G. 4475
Little Devil Dought. Weblowe, B. 9249
Little Dream, The. Galsworthy, J. 3355
Little Evergreen Tree, The. Jennings, A. 4457
Little Eyolf. Ibsen, H. 4363
Little Face. Oliver, R. 6822
Little Father of the Wilderness. Strong, A. and L. Osbourne. 8584
Little February. Spamer, C. 8415
Little Fir Tree, The. Very, A. 9117
Little Fish. Gamble, H. V. 3361
Little Fool, The. Meyer, A. E. 5800
Little Forget-me-not. Spamer, C. 8416
Little Foxes. Hellman, L. 4047
Little Friend. Peacock, M. 7026
Little Glimpses of Great People. Bradford, G. 1262
Little Hero of Holland. Asbrand, K. 403
Little Hut, The. Roussin, A. 7747
Little Ida and the Flowers. Ormandy, E. 6881
Little Jackie and the Beanstalk. Cable, H. 1476

Little Johnny. Drinkwater, J. 2603
Little Ki and the Serpent. Melchior, H. K. 5738
Little King, The. Bynner, W. 1463
Little Known Louisa. Wefer, M. 9261
Little Lambs Eat Ivy. Langley, N. 4797
Little Lion, The. Longstreth, T. M. 5027
Little Malcolm and His Struggle Against the Eunuchs. Halliwell, D. 3866, 3867
Little Man Who Wasn't There, The. Dias, E. J. 2430
Little Mary Sunshine. Besoyan, R. 884
Little Men. Gould, E. L. 3662
Little Minister, The. Barrie, Sir J. M. 625
Little Miracle, The. Akins, Z. 90
Little Moral Child. Evans, G. 2882
Little Mouse-Deer. Winther, B. 9485
Little Nut Tree, The. Miller, H. L. 5932
Little Pilgrim's Progress, A. Mackay, C. D. 5223
Little Polka Dot. Asbrand, K. 404
Little Princess, The. Burnett, F. H. 1439, 1440
Little Princess, The. Thane, A. 8808
Little Prop Boy, The. Spamer, C. 8417
Little Rebellion, A. Wortis, A. 9567
Little Red Hen, The. Barker, C. and J. Medina. 600
Little Red Hen, The. Boiko, C. 1088
Little Saint, The. Bracco, R. 1255
Little Snow White. King, W. 4632
Little Tailor, The. Arnold, P. 354
Little Theatre of Love, The. Marinetti, F. T. 5549
Little White Cloud. Cooper, E. 2002
Little Witch Who Forgot, The. Spamer, C. 8418
Little Witch Who Tried, The. Leuser, E. 4951
Little Women. Alcott, L. M. 110, 111

Little Women. Gould, E. L. 3363
Littlest Artist, The. Bennett, R. 785
Littlest Elf, The. Watts, F. B. 9236
Littlest Month, The. Faux, D. 2948
Living Dead, The. Tolstoy, L. N. 8878
Living Hours. Schnitzler, A. 8074
Living Room, The. Greene, G. 3715
Living Room with 6 Oppressions. Mandel, O. 5492
Living Up to Lincoln. McQueen, M. H. and N. McQueen 5353
Living Water. Oost, R. 6870
Livree de M. Le Comte. Croisset, F. de 2111
Llareggub. Thomas, D. 8824
Local Board Makes Good. Fine, S. and M. Liebman. 3025
Locataire, Le. Orton, J. 6884
Lock, Stock, and Barrel. Murray, J. 6360
Locker Room, The. Fodor, J. 3174
Loft's Wish. Sigurjonsson, J. 8274
Lofty Motives. Weinberg, A. 9267
Log in the Bog, The. Watts, F. B. 9237
Logense, La. Audiberti, J. 445
Logical Extreme, The. Soule, G. 8391
Lohengrin. De Benedetti, A. 2226
Loin de la Mer ... Loin de L'Eté. Eliraz, I. 2855
Lointain. Keskin, Y. 4605
Loki's Flyting. 5021
London Bridge. Swortzell, L. 8656
Lonely Fir Tree, The. Roberts, H. M. 7611
Lonely Little Old Lady, The. King, P. C. 4631
Lonesome Train, The. Lampell, M. 4778
Long Ago in Bethlehem. Newman, D. 6505
Long Box, The. MacDonald, Z. K. 5171
Long Christmas Dinner, The. Wilder, T. 9395
Long Day's Journey into Night. O'Neill, E. 6854

Long Duel. Clifford, L. L. 1900
Long Leather Bag, The. Feather, J. 2963
Long Live Christmas. Benson, I. 806
Long Live Father! Fisher, A. 3053
Long Mirror, The. Priestley, J. B. 7298
Long Table, The. Boiko, C. 1089
Long Time Ago. Dell, F. 2298
Long Voyage Home, The. O'Neill, E. 6855, 6856
Long-Haired Warriors, The. Marsh, J. 5580
Lontana parente, La. Possenti, E. 7258
Look Back on Today! Wolas, E. 9524
Look to a New Day. Fisher, A. 3054
Looking for Lincoln. Newman, D. 6506
Looking-Glass, The. Firkins, O. W. 3029
Looking Glass Murder, The. Murray, J. 6361
Loose Ends. Treen, D. A. 8926
Loot. Orton, J. 6885
Lope de Vega. Santelli, C. 7919
Lord Byron's Love Letter. Williams, T. 9431
Lord Malapert of Moonshine Castle. Brooks, E. S. 1346
Lord Westbury and Bishop Wilberforce. Traill, H. D. 8916
Lord's Will, The. Green, P. 3703
Lorna Doone. Blackmore, R. D. 982
Lorsque L'Enfant Parait. Roussin, A. 7748
Loser, The. Eldridge, P. 2838
Loss of Roses, A. Inge, W. 4376
Lost Cherub, The. Thane, A. 8789
Lost Christmas Cards, The. Miller, H. L. 5933
Lost Feed, The. Koch, K. 4676
Lost in the Stars. Anderson, M. and K. Weill. 213
Lost Light. O'Farachain, R. 6776
Lost Note, The. Oser, J. A. 6902
Lost Princess, The. Totheroh, D. 8897
Lost Saint, The. Hyde, D. 4350
Lost Sheep. Forrest, B. 3225
Lost Silk Hat, The. Dunsany, E. J. M. D. P. 2720

Lotta con l'angelo. Pinelli, T. 7161
Lotta fino all'alba. Betti, U. 895
Loud Speaker, The. Schwartz, M. K. 8099
Louis Quinze Salon, The. Glaenzer, R. B. 3580
Louisa Alcott's Wish. Goldsmith, S. L. 3613
Louve, Le. Thomas, R. 8837
Love. Schisgal, M. 8031
Love and Death. Alma-Tadema, Sir, L. 151
Love and How to Cure It. Wilder, T. 9396
Love Child, The. Fenn, F. and R. Pryce. 2982
Love Feast, The. Benner, R. 768
Love from Bud. McQueen, M. H. and N. McQueen 5354
Love from the Madhouse. Nass, E. 6442
Love in a French Kitchen. 5060
Love in the West. Emory, W. C. 2864
Love in Three Acts. Burckhardt, R. 1419
Love Is Stronger Than Walls. Sardeson, C. T. 7928
Love Letter, The. Woolf, D. 9552
Love Magic. Martinez Sierra, G. 5628
Love Me, Love My Dog. Speyer, Lady. 8450
Love of Four Colonels. Ustinov, P. 8982, 8983
Love of One's Neighbour. Andreyev, L. N. 234, 235
Love of the Poor, The. MacDonald, L. 5167
Love of Women, The. Kummer, F. A. 4737
Love, Poetry, and Civic Service. Blok, A. 1009
Love Test, The. 5061
Loveliest Things, The. Pertwee, R. 7085
Lover, The. Pinter, H. 7178
Lover of the Queen of Sheba. Symons, A. 8664
Lovers, The. Bernard, K. 832
Lover's Knot, A. Merington, M. 5777
Love's Comedy. Ibsen, H. 4364

Love's in Fashion. Murray, J. 6362
Love's Young Dream. Garland, R. 3393
Loving Cup, The. Brown, A. 1355
Loyalties. Galsworthy, J. 3356
Luce. Lopez, S. 5037
Luce di Santa Agnese, La. Bracco, R. 1256
Luce sul letto matrimoniale. Di Mattia, V. 2504
Luces de Bohemia. Valle Inclan, R. M. del 9001
Lucian, The Mark Twain of Antiquity. Ylirnusi, T. 9609
Luciella Catena. Russo, F. 7805
Lucienne et le Boucher. Ayme, M. 471
Lucilla's Proposal. Reed, D. 7458
Luck Takes a Holiday. Fisher, A. 3055
Luckiest Man, The. Springer, T. G. and E. Gage. 8455
Lucrece Borgis. Hugo, V. 4317
Lucy Crown. Shaw, I. and J.-P. Aumont. 8227
Luigi Steps Aside. Hackett, W. 3802
Lulu. Wedekind, F. 9256
Lumière, La. Duhamel, G. 2682
Lumière, La. Provins, M. 7320
Lumière dans le Tombeau. Berton, R. 879
Luna di Miele. Gabirondo, V. and E. Enderiz. 3343
Luna di Miele. Grella, E. 3735
Luncheon for Three. McCoy, P. S. 5150
Lunchtime Concert. Wymark, O. 9580
Lune ou L'Autre. Schreiber, I. 8085
Lunga notte di Medea. Alvaro, C. 175
Luogo che vuol chiamassi Roma, Un. Osborne, J. 6894
Lupi, I. Giovaninetti, S. 3558
Lupo mannara, Il. Lothar, R. 5057
Luther. Osborne, J. J. 6895
Luv. Schisgal, M. 8032
Lysistrata. Aristophanes. 334
Lysistrata Takes Command. Aristophanes. 335

M

M. T. Di Benedetti, A. 2227

Ma Chance et Ma Chanson. Neveux, G. 6475
Ma Liberté! Amiel, D. 186
Ma non la siamo un poco tutti? Lonsdale, F. 5031
Ma Soeur de Luxe. Birabeau, A. 952
Maastricht Play. 5111
Macaire. Stevenson, R. L. and W. E. Henley. 8521, 8522
Macbeth. Shakespeare, W. 8182, 8183
Macbeth: Murder at the Gate-Keeper's House. Brecht, B. 1303
Macbett. Ionesco, E. 4348
Macbird. Garson, B. 3402
McDonough's Wife. Gregory, Lady A. 3725
Machine a ecrire, La. Cocteau, J. 1914
Macrune's Guevara. Spurling, J. 8456
Mad About Art. Murray, J. 6363
Mad Dog. Kedrov, V. 4572
Mad Dutchman's Magic Eye, The. Williams, R. E. 9417
Mad Musician, The. Eberhart, R. 2805
Mad Piper, The. Cheney, J. V. 1788
Madam Takes a Bath. Bellido, J. M. 735
Madame Bovary. Baty, G. 674
Madame C. I. A. Gibson, M. 3496
Madame Filoume. Filippo, E. de 3018
Madame Major. Shpazhinsky, I. V. 8263
Madame Marguerite. Athayde, R. 427
Madame Quinze. Sarment, J. 7936
Madame USA. Woock, C. C. 9541
Madame, Will You Walk. Howard, S. 4218a
Maddalena, occhi di menta. Duse, E. 2768
Madelon, A Little Shepherdess at Bethlehem. Hazeltine, A. I. 3996
Mademoiselle. Boularan, J. 1222, 1223
"Mlle. Mystic." Richardson, A. S. 7528
Mademoiselle Plato. Dunham, C. 2704
Madge. Conkle, E. P. 1974
Madhouse at Cairo, The. McClure, J. 5133
Madison Avenue Merry-Go-Round. Dias, E. J. 2431
Madman and the Nun, The. Witkiewicz, S. I. 9515
Madman Divine, The. Echegaray, J. 2810
Madman or Saint. Echegaray, J. 2811
Madonna and the Scarecrow. Kaplan, Y. D. 4547
Madre Allegria. Sevilla, L. F. de and R. Sepulveda 8159
Madre natura. Birabeau, A. 953
Madwoman of Chaillot, The. Giraudoux, J. 3572
Maestro, Il. Antonelli, L. 302
Maestro e il discepolo, Il. Hyakuzo, K. 4348
Maeterlinckian Moving Day, A. Swain, C. R. 8643
Mafiosi, I. Sciascia, L. 8102
Magic. Chesterton, G. K. 1790
Magic Bookshelf, The. Clapp, P. 1841
Magic Box, The. Moore, W. H. 6207
Magic Box, The. Peterson, M. N. 7105
Magic Bread, The. Brinker, E. 1332
Magic Broom, The. Cooper, E. 2003
Magic Carpet Sweeper, The. Miller, H. L. 5934
Magic Cloak, The. Whitworth, V. P. 9341
Magic Cookie Jar, The. Miller, H. L. 5935
Magic Egg, The. McQueen, M. H. and N. McQueen 5355
Magic Fishbone, The. Dickens, C. 2475
Magic Goose, The. Newman, D. 6507
Magic Grapes, The. Leuser, E. 4952
Magic Hat, The. Martens, A. C. 5603
Magic in the Deep Woods. DeBra, E. 2232
Magic Jack-O-Lantern, The. Howard, H. L. 4207
Magic Mirror, The. Very, A. 9118

Magic Mushrooms, The. Jones, D. C. 4500
Magic Nutmeg-Grater, The. Thane, A. 8790
Magic of Flowers, The. Asbrand, K. 405
Magic of Salamanca, The. Nolan, P. T. 6656
Magic Pencils, The. Miller, H. L. 5936
Magic Pumpkin Patch, The. Thomas, E. M. 8828
Magic Sea Shell, The. Farrar, J. C. 2934
Magic Shoes, The. Jones, D. C. 4502
Magic Shoes, The. Turnbull, L. 8955
Magic Smile, The. Roam, P. 7601
Magic Spear, The. Thane, A. 8809
Magic Spell, The. Cooper, E. 2004
Magic Sword, The. Pyle, K. 7350
Magic Telephone, The. Miller, H. L. 5937
Magic Theatre. Fahnstock, E. and F. D. White 2910
Magic Touchstone, The. Watts, F. B. 9238
Magic Weaver, The. Bennett, R. 786
Magic Well, The. Leuser, E. 4953
Magic Wishing Ring, The. Chaloner, G. 1708
Magical City, The. Akins, Z. 91
Magnolia Tree, The. Manson, H. W. D. 5505
Magnus and Morna. Mulock-Craik, D. 6294
Magnus the Magnificent. Robbins, J. 7602
Mago moderno, Il. Folgore, L. 3193
Maharajah Is Bored, The. Winther, B. 9497
Maid Who Wouldn't Be Proper, The. Mick, H. L. 5813
Maiden Over the Wall. Bloch, B. 1003
Maids of Athens. Bottomley, G. 1203
Maid's Prologue, The. Ketchum, A. 4609

Maie. Purnal, R. 1793
Mail Call. Nelson, R. 6460
Mail Goes Through, The. Fisher, A. 3056
Mais qu-est-ce Que Fait Courir les Femmes, la Nuit a Madrid. Ceccaldi, C. 1677
Maison Clarette. Minervini, R. 6070
Maison de la Nuit. Talagrand, J. 8694, 8695
Maison du Crime. Bernard, T. 853
Maison Monestier. Amiel, D. 187
Maître de Santiago, Le. Montherlant, H. de 6190
Maître François est Mort. Brune, J. 1385
Major Barbara. Shaw, G. B. 8209
Majority of One. Spigelgass, L. 8451
Make a Million. Barasch, N. and C. Moore 552
Make Him Smile! Arnold, E. W. 351
Making Room for the Little King. Higgins, H. B. 4099
Mal amies, Les. Mauriac, F. 5689
Mal Court, La. Audiberti, J. 446
Malentendu, Le. Camus, A. 1553
Mall, The. Inge, W. 4377
Malle de Berlingue, La. Duranty, L. 2735
Mama com'e, La. Siciliano, E. 8267
Maman Colibri'. Bataille, H. 662
Mamma, La. Roussin, A. 7749
Mamma del diavolo, La. Pizzinelli, C. 7209
Mamme, Le. Terron, C. 8759
Mamouret. Sarment, J. 7937
Man and a Computer Machine. Kish, J. 4644
Man and His Wife. Clements, C. C. 1894
Man and Superman. Shaw, G. B. 8210
Man and the Satyr. Bennett, R. 787
Man and the Turtle, The. Barr, M. 622
Man and Wife. Arnold, S. J. 356
Man Born to Be Hanged, The. Hughes, R. 4308
Man for All Seasons, A. Bolt, R. 1157
Man from Cemetery Ridge, The. Johnson, D. H. 4483

Man from Kiriot, The. Davidson, G. 2196
Man Hunt, The. Thompson, H. 8843
Man in the Bowler Hat, The. Milne, A. A. 6061
Man in the Glass Booth, The. Shaw, R. 8229
Man in the Moon, The. Spamer, C. 8419
Man in the Red Suit. Messenger, B. 5793
Man in the Tree, The. La Guma, A. 4767
Man Like Lincoln, A. Miller, H. L. 5938
Man of Honour, A. Maugham, W. S. 5673
Man of Science, A. Payne, G. H. 7021
Man of the World, A. Ebner-Eschenbach, M. 2808
Man That Corrupted Hadleyburg, The. Clemens, S. L. 1881
Man to Order, A. Masterson, K. 5653
Man Who Came to Dinner, The. Hart, M. and G. S. Kaufman 3943
Man Who Couldn't Talk, The. Kotzebue, A. von 4695
Man Who Didn't Believe in Christmas, The. Austin, M. H. 461
Man Who Discovered the Sun, The. Schmitt, G. 8045
Man Who Married a Dumb Wife, The. France, A. 3244, 3245
Man Who Set Fire to a Lady, The. Labiche, E. 4747
Man Who Stayed at Home, The. DuBois, G. 2642
Man Who Walked in a Beam of Sunlight, The. Char, R. 1722
Man Who Walked in a Ray of Sunshine, The. Char, R. 1723
Man with the Flower in His Mouth, The. Pirandello, L. 7194, 7195
Man with the Four Legs. O'Brien, F. 6746
Man with the Green Necktie. Averchenko, A. 464
Man with the Heart in the Highlands. Saroyan, W. 7951
Man with the Oboe, The. Smalley, W. 8324
Man Without a Country, The. Hale, E. E. 3834, 3835
Man Without a Face, The. Weisenborn, G. 9272
Mancia compentente. Aladar, L. 95
Mandarin Coat, The. Riley, A. C. D. 7582
Mandoline. Silvain, J. 8278
Manège Conjugal. Parise, G. 6971
Mango Tree, The. Gargi, B. 3389
Mani, Le. Marinetti, F. T. 5554
Mani in alto. Giannini, G. 3486
Maniera forte, La. Cenzato, G. 1682
Maniere Forte, La. Boularan, J. 1224
Manitoba. Gauthier, G. 3424a
Manivelle, La. Pinget, R. 7168
Manny. Vail, W. J. 8990
Man's a Man for a 'That, A. Schmitt, G. 8046
Man's Man. Kearney, P. 4567
Mantello, Il. Buzzati, D. 1455
Mantle, The. Dias, E. J. 2432
Mantle of the Virgin. Sutton, V. R. 8637
Many. Adam, A. R. 48
Many a Slip. Fisher, A. 3057
Many Loves. Williams, W. C. 9446
Many Thanks. McQueen, M. H. and N. McQueen 5356
Marchand d'Estampes. Porto-Riche, G. de 7253
Marchesa! Sardou, V. 7930
Marcia di Radetzky, La. Castellaneta, C. 1647
Mare e whisky. Rocca, G. 7633
Margherita di Navarra. Fodor, L. 3183
Margot. Bourdet, E. 1235
Mari, la Femme et la Mort, Le. Roussin, A. 7750, 7751
Mari Singulier. Durtain, L. 2762
Mari sur Mesure. Lery, M. and G. D'Abzac 4935
Maria. Babel, I. 255
Maria. Obey, A. 6738
Maria del Carmen. Feliu y Condina, J. 2980
Maria et les Isles. Gonthie, M. H. 3621
Maria Maddalena. Hebbel, C. F. 4017
Maria Stuarda. Schiller, J. C. F. von 8026
Mariage de M. Mississippi. Durrenmatt, F. 2744

Mariage Forcé, Le. Molière.
6121
Mariana Pineda. Garcia Lorca,
F. 3382, 5045, 5046
Marie. Babel, I. 477, 478
Marie Stuart. Schiller, J. C. F.
von 8027
Maries de la Tour Eiffel, Les.
Cocteau, J. 1915, 1916, 1917
Marinaio Flip, Il. Luciani, M.
5080
Marine for Mother, A. Miller,
H. L. 5939
Mario in the Land of the Green
Queen. Tagliabue, J. 8683
Mario in the Land of the Unicorn.
Tagliobue, J. 8684
Marius. Pagnol, M. 6931
Marjorie Daw. Aldrich, T. B.
121
Mark Twain. Hollingsworth, L.
4145
Mark Twain Digs for Gold.
Schmitt, G. 8047, 8048
Market, The. Cahoon, H. Three
Verse Plays. 1489
Marko's. Bernard, K. 833
Marla the Mechanic. Garver, J.
3412
Marmalade Overture, The. Boiko,
C. 1090
Marquise and Woman. Askew,
C. 422
Marraine de Musset. Blanc-
Peridier, A. 992
Marriage, The. Hyde, D. 4351,
4352
Marriage Has Been Arranged, A.
Sutro, A. 8635
Marriage Is so Difficult. Harris,
L. 3926
Marriage Lease, The. Lee, H.
4877
Marriage of Drama and Censor-
ship, The. Garcia, J. C. 3371
Marriage of Little Eva, The.
Nicholson, K. 6565
Marriage of Olympe. Augier, E.
456
Marriage of Toto, The. Hutchins,
M. P. 4335
Married Man. Lawrence, D. H.
4853
Mart of Addenda. Dewey, K. G.
2390
Martha Has a Vision. Barbee,
L. 569
Martha Washington's Spy. Dias,
E. J. 2433
Martha's Mourning. Hoffman, P.
4127
Martin Chuzzlewit. Dickens, C.
2476
Martina the Ant. Blumenfeld, L.
1025
Martin's Lie. Menotti, G. C.
5752
Martyrs. De Mille, W. C. 2315
Martyrs' Idyl, The. Guiney, L.
I. 3778
Marvelous Romance of Wen Chun-
Chin, The. Hsiung, C. C. 4264
Marvelous Time Machine, The.
Boiko, C. 1091
Marvels of Science, The. Hibbard,
G. A. 4092
Mary Elizabeth's Wonderful Dream.
Mason, M. E. 5642
Mary Jane. Bernard, K. 834
Mary Play. Hutchins, M. P. 4336
Mary Rose. Barrie, Sir J. M.
626
Mary Stuart. Hildesheimer, W.
4104
Mary's Cake. Spamer, C. 8420
Mary's Garden. Spamer, C. 8421
Mary's Invitation. Miller, H. L.
5940
Marziani, I. Zardi, F. 9635
Marziano, Il. Fayad, S. 2954
Masaniello. Porta, E. and A.
Pugliese. 7248
Mascarin. Lacour, J. 4760
Maschera, La. Traversi, C. A.
8921
Mascherata di San Silvestro. Dello
Siesto, A. 2309
Maschere scandalizzate. Rietmann,
C. M. 7578
Maschio. Bassano, E. 650
Masked Choir, The. McClure, M.
5138
Maskerman. Woodcock, G. 9544
Masks. Corneau, P. B. 2021
Masks of Various Colors. Nolan,
P. T. 6657
Masque for Democrats, A. Mae-
vius. 5434
Masque of Dead Florentines. Hew-
lett, M. H. 4090
Masque of Mercy, A. Frost, R.
3326
Masque of the Red Death, The.
Poe, E. A. 7221
Masque of Tomes. Binkley, F.
W. 943

Masquerade. Hillyer, R. 4109
Masseur, Il. Kranz, H. B. 4708
Mastello, Il. 5649
Master, The. Hale, W. G. 3840
Master in the House, The. Fitzgerald, B. 3132
Master of All Masters. Whitworth, V. P. 9342
Master of Palmyra. Wilbrandt, A. von 9350
Master of the Strait, The. Waite, H. E. and E. M. Hoppenstedt 9187
Master Patelin, The Lawyer. 5649a
Master Salesman, The. Upson, W. H. 8971
Master Zacharius. Verne, J. 9091
Masterpiece of Diplomacy, A. Howells, W. D. 4249
Mastro Don Gesualdo. Verga, G. 9077
Match a la une. Novak, A. 6699
Matchmaker, The. Wilder, T. 9397
Matchmakers. O'Kelly, S. 6786
Matinee de Soleil. Alvarez Quintero, S. and J. Alvarez Quintero 165
Matinee d'un Homme de Lettres, La. Balachova, T. 526
Matrimonio probabile, Un. Di Salle, G. 2507
Matriomonio, Il. Donnay, M. 2539
Matron of Ephesus. Cunningham, W. J. 2142
Matter of Business, A. Wilkes, E. 9405
Matter of Conscience, A. Coyle, R. W. 2087
Matter of Health, A. McGowan, J. 5198
Matter of Honour, A. Dunsany, E. J. M. D. P. 2721
Matter of Opinion, A. Hibbard, G. A. 4093
Matters of Taste. Parsons, F. M. 6990
Mattina di sole. Alvarez Quintero, S. and J. Alvarez Quintero 166
Mattinata a Kurosawa. 5661
Mattinate d'Aprile. De Stefani, A. 2371
Mattutino. Minervini, R. 6071

Mattutino. Pinelli, T. 7162
Matty and the Moron and Madonna. Lieberman, H. H. 4978
Maurice. Bolt, C. 1156
Mauvais Jour, Un. Peneau, Y. 7059
Mauvaise Semence. Vandenberghe, P. and T. Mihalakeas. 9022
May Basket Fantasia. Boiko, C. 1092
May Baskets New. Larson, E. M. 4825
May Day for Mother. Miller, H. L. 5941
May-Day Indoors. Diaz, A. M. 2461
May Witch. Brydon, M. W. and E. Ziegler. 1395
Mayday! Beach, M. M. 684
Mayflies, The. Blackwood, T. 983
Mayflower, The. Very, A. 9119
Mayflower Compact, The. Andersson, D. and S. Dimond 223
Mayflower Passengers, The. Hamby, R. 3875
Mayor of Burgville, The. Spamer, C. 8422
Meanest Witch, The. McBride, D. 5116
Meaning of Christmas, The. Swanson, B. 8644
Measure for Measure. Shakespeare, W. 8184
Meat Rack, The. Kimball, K. 4626
Mechanical Maid, The. Whitworth, V. P. 9343
Mechanical Man, The. Murray, J. 6364
Mechanical-Drawing Broadcast, A. Herr, L. A. 4080
Medea. Euripides 2880, 2881
Medecin de Cucugnan, Le. Rouquette, M. 7731
Medico della signora malata, Il. Bonelli, L. 1182
Medico Volante, Il. Molière 6122
Meet Miss Stone-Age! Olfson, L. 6804
Meet Mr. Muffin. Miller, H. L. 5942
Meet Mr. Murchinson. Huff, B. T. 4287
Meet the Pilgrims. Boiko, C. 1093
Meet the Wife. Nicholson, K. 6566

Meeting, The. Brown, L. 1370
Meeting, The. Linebarger, J. M. 4992
Meeting at the Well, Three Chinese Folk-Dramas.... 8855
Meeting in the Woods, A. Godsey, T. 3591
Megere Apprivoisee, La. Audiberti, J. 447
Mein Maultien Meine Frau und Meine Ziege. Renn, L. 7491
Meisterschaft. Clemens, S. L. 1882
Melilotte. Stevens, D. 8509
Melinda's Incredible Birthday. Boiko, C. 1094
Melisenda per me. Meano, C. 5723
Melissa's Muffins. Barbee, L. 570
Melodrama. Milne, J. R. 6065
Melody for Lincoln. Miller, H. L. 5943
Melon Thief, The. Noguchi, Y. 6617
Melon Thief, The. Obata, S. 6735
Membres de la Famille. Garnung, F. 3396
Meme Heure l'Annee Prochaine. Slade, B. 8310
Mementos of Our Ancestors. McQueen, M. H. and N. McQueen 5357
Memorial Day for the Blue and Gray. Newman, D. 6508
Memorie del sottosuolo. Dostoevski, F. 2565
Men and No. Pedrolo, M. de 7037
Mensonge, Le. Sarraute, N. 7960
Menteur, Le. Goldoni, C. 3607
Mentons bleus. Moineaux, G. 6106
Mephiboseth. Milosz, A. W. 6067
Mercedes. Aldrich, T. B. 122
Merchant of Venice, The. Shakespeare, W. 8185
Merciful Soul. Alma-Tadema, Sir L. 152
Merluse. Pagnol, M. 6932
Mermaid Club, The. Deming, D. 2325
Merry Christmas, Crawfords! McQueen, M. H. and N. McQueen 5358

Merry Christmas Customs. McQueen, M. H. and N. McQueen 5359
Merry Christmas Elf, The. Fisher, A. 3058
Merry Christmas from Little Women, A. Alcott, L. M. 112
Merry, Merry Cuckoo, The. Marks, J. 5561
Merry Mix-Up, The. Watts, F. B. 9239
Merry Mount. Bates, W. O. 672
Merry Tyll and the Three Rogues. Thane, A. 8810
Merry-Go-Round, The. Lawrence, D. H. 4854
Merry-Go-Round for Mother. Miller, H. L. 5944
Message from Garcia. Drexler, F. 2600
Message from Robin Hood, A. Colson, J. G. 1948
Message of Lazarus. Lawrence, C. E. 4850
Message of the Hearts, The. Newman, D. 6509
Messengers. Housman, L. 4190
Mestiere di padre. Viviani, R. 9163
Metafisica di un vitello a due teste, La. Witkiewicz, S. I. 9516
Metamorfosi di Pulcinella, Le. 5795
Metamorfosi di un suonatore ambulante, Le. De Filippo, P. 2273
Metempsychosis. MacDonagh, T. 5166
Meteor, Der. Durrenmatt, F. 2745
Metier d'Amant. See, E. 8129
Metodo per diventar celbri, Il. Lavedan, H. 4839
Metropoli. De Stefani, A. 2372
Mettiamoci d'accordo. Fraschetti, V. 3274
Meunier de Delft, Le. Peyrou, P. 7115
Meurtres en fa Diese. Valmain, F. 9007
Mexico City. Koch, K. 4676
Mezze maniche. Mor, E. and Borhesio 6210
"Mezzo gaudio." Rocca, G. 7636
Mi amerai sempre? Halàsz, A. 3832
Mia famiglia. De Filippo, E. 2256
Mia moglie. Delaquis, G. 2293
Michael Angelo. Longfellow, H. W. 5024

Michal, the Daughter of Saul. Ashman, A. 419
Michel. Natanson, J. 6448
Michi's Blood. Kroetz, F. X. 4727
Michu. Grumberg, J.-C. 3769
Mick and Mick. Leonard, H. 4924
Midge Rings the Bell. Paradis, M. B. 6958
Midnight Burial. Hill, K. 4107
Midnight Crossing. Murray, J. 6365
Midsummer Night's Dream, A. Shakespeare, W. 8186
Midwinter-Eve Fire. Osgood, P. E. 6907
Miettes. See, E. 8130
Mi-Figue, Mi-Raisin. Tardieu, J. 8704
Mighty Reservoy, The. Terson, P. 8772
Miguel Manara. Milosz, O. W. 6068
Mikado, The. Gilbert, W. S. and Sir A. S. Sullivan 3517
Mila Whendle. Musselman, N. H. 6417
Milano del 1848 e Milano nel 1859 5827
Milioni dello zio Peteroff, I. Garcia-Alvarez, E. and P. Munoz-Seca 3373
Milky Way Conference, The. Gray, M. 3695
Mille et Quatre. Gantillon, S. 3368
Mille Francs de Récompense. Hugo, V. 4318
Millesima seconda. Meano, C. 5724
Million Pound Bank Note, The. Clemens, S. L. 1883
Million-Dollar Quiz Show, The. Janey, S. E. 4443
Mime I (The Matchmaker). Herondas. 4079
Mind Over Matter. Nicholson, J. 6555
Mind Your P's and Q's. McQueen, M. H. and N. McQueen 5360
Minding the Store. Nichols, R. 6546
Ming-Y. Collaci, M. 1936
Minister's Dream, The. Lord, K. 5051
Minister's First "At Home," The. Bangs, J. K. 545
Ministers of Grace. Manners, J. H. 5499
Minor Characters. Bell, R. 731
Minority of Millions. McQueen, M. H. and N. McQueen 5361
Minuet. Parker, L. N. 6972
Minuet. Verlaine, P. 9085
Minuit en Plein Jour. Arnaud, M. 348
Minute's Wait. McHugh, M. J. 5214
Minyana's Daughters, The. Treitel, R. 8927
Mio cliente ricciolo, Il. Corwin, N. 2048
Mio cuore e' nel sud, Il. Griffi, G. P. 3744
Mio dente e il tuo cuore, Il. Giachetti, C. 3474
Mio figlio ecco il guaio. Antonelli, L. 303
Mio figlio ha un grande avvenire. Casella, A. 1630
Mio miglior nemico, Il. Franciosa, M. 3247
Mio padre aveva ragione. Guitry, S. 3781
Miquette's First Dinner Party. 6075
Miracle Flower, The. DeBra, E. 2233
Miracle in Louisiana. Schmitt, G. 8049
Miracle Merchant, The. Munro, H. H. 6299
Miracle of Paper, The. Harkins, P. J. 3912
Miracle of Spring, The. Hanna, H. 3893
Miracle of the Corn, The. Colum, P. 1956
Miracle Worker, The. Gibson, W. 3502
Miracolo. Manzari, N. 5511
Miracolo d'amore. Lakatos, L. 4770
Miraculous Eclipse, The. Clemens, S. L. 1884
Miraculous Tea Party, The. McGowan, J. 5199
Miranda. Blackmore, P. 981
Miroir, Le. Higuera, P. de la 4101
Miroir, Le. Salacrou, A. 7876
Mirror Children, The. Spamer, C. 8423
Mirror of Matsuyama, The. Blumenfeld, L. 1023

Mirthful Marionettes. Totheroh, D. 8898
Misalliance. Shaw, G. B. 8211
Miserabili sono due, I. Doletti, M. 2522
Miserables, Les. Achard, P. 42
Misere et Noblesse. Scarpetta 8010
Miseria bella. De Filippo, P. 2274
Mish-Mash Bird, The. Murray, J. 6366
Miss Barton Is Needed. Nolan, J. C. 6627
Miss Cast. Heinzen, B. B. 4037
Miss Fix-It. McCoy, P. S. 5151
Miss Forsythe Is Missing. Murray, J. 6367
Miss France. Berr, G. and L. Verneuil. 867
Miss Frankenstein. Miller, H. L. 5945
Miss Gloom's Dream. Greene, A. M. and F. Dixon. 3714
Miss Hepplewhite Takes Over. Murray, J. 6368
Miss Liberty Goes to Town. Rosten, N. 7723
Miss Lonelyheart. Miller, H. L. 5946
Miss Louisa and the Outlaws. Watts, F. B. 9240
Miss Manda. Taber, G. B. 8681
Miss Marlow at Play. Milne, A. A. 6062
Miss Robin's School. Spamer, C. 8424
Missing Gift, The. Ronan, R. 7678
Missing Guest, The. Young R. K. 9615
Missing "Linc," The. Miller, H. L. 5947
Missing Link, The. Miller, H. L. 5948
Missing Missionary, The. Willment, F. 9449
Missing Person. Taylor, P. Three Ghost Plays. 8729
Mission of the Vega. Durrenmatt, F. 2746
Mission to Athens. Max, A. 5697
Mississippi ... Father of Waters. Jennings, G. 4461
Mister A. Lincoln. Paradis, M. B. 6959

Mr. and Mrs. P. Roe. Johnson, M. 4487
Mister Antonio. Tarkington, B. 8709
Mr. Bates Goes to the Polls. Reay, N. B. 7451
Mister Bosphorus and the Muses. Ford, F. M. 3215
Mister Catchy Cold. Deming, D. 2326
Mr. Efficiency. Huff, B. T. 4288
Mr. Elliot's Crazy Notion. Schmitt, G. L. 8050
Mr. Enright Entertains. Abbott, A. 3
Mr. Filbert's Claim to Fame. Murray, J. 6369
Mr. Icky. Fitzgerald, F. S. 3134
Mr. Jardyne. John, G. 4476
Mr. Jay Does Some Thinking. Alexander, L. E. 131
Mr. Kilt and the Great I Am. Ross, K. 7707
Mr. Lazy Man's Family. Ward, M. 9208
Mr. Leonida Face to Face with the Reaction. Caragliale, I. L. 1593
Mr. Lincoln's Beard. Newman, D. 6510
Mr. Lincoln's Grave. O'Connell, T. E. 6762
Mr. Longfellow Observes Book Week. Moore, E. G. 6199
Mr. Lorelei. Armstrong, P. 346
Mr. Luck and Little Chance. Nolan, P. T. 6658
Mr. Man. Miller, L. 6054
Mr. Mergenthwirker's Lobblies. Bond, M. and D. Kent 1177
Mr. Moore and Mr. Chew. Chew, S. C. 1792
Mister Owl. Spamer, C. 8425
Mr. Owl's Advice. McQueen, M. H. and N. McQueen 5362
Mister Roberts. Heggen, T. and J. Logan 4025
Mr. S. Claus's Predicament. Whitney, J. D. 9335
Mr. Scrooge Finds Christmas. Dickens, C. 2477
Mr. Scrooge Finds Christmas. Fisher, A. 3102
Mr. Shakespeare at School. Duer, C. 2673
Mr. Smooch's Trap. Werner, S. 9296
Mr. Snow White's Thanksgiving. Miller, H. L. 5949

Mr. Thanks Has His Day.
   Kingman, L. 4634
Mr. Togo and His Friends.
   Maltz, A. 5485
Mister Twister. Murray, J.
   6370
Mistletoe Mystery, The. Miller,
   H. L. 5950
Mrs. Belfiore. Meehan, B.
   5729
Mrs. Claus' Christmas Present.
   Urban, C. 8973
Mrs. Dolly. Hanley, W. 3889
Mrs. Gibbs Advertises. Pyle,
   M. T. 7353
Mrs. Mack's Example. Dodge,
   F. B. 2514
Mrs. Malvolio. Bakeless, J.
   512
Mrs. Margaret Calhoun. Bodenheim, M. and B. Hecht. 1041
Mrs. Middleman's Descent. Halpern, M. 3870
Mrs. Molly. Crothers, R. 2122
Mrs. Mouse, Are You Within?
   Marcus, F. 5542
Mrs. Pipp's Waterloo. Jones,
   E. O. 4504
Mrs. Potiphar Pays a Call. McCoy, S. D. 5160
Mrs. Santa's Christmas Gift.
   Newman, D. 6511
Mistress Shakespeare. Seiler,
   C. 8141
Mrs. Sniffit's Christmas. Brown,
   A. V. 1357
Mrs. Tubbs's Telegram. Rice,
   K. M. 7521
Misunderstanding in the LadyChapel. Masterman, M. 5650
M'Lord of Massachusetts. Jagendorf, M. 4429
Mobile. Rivemale, A. 7598
Mobius Strip, The. Boiko, C.
   1095
Models for Health. Gordon, C.
   3635
Modern Autocrat, The. Collins,
   L. 1940
Modern Child, A. Chance, J.
   G. 1710
Modern Cinderella, A. Hollingsworth, L. 4146
Modern Daughter, A. Chance, J.
   G. 1711
Modern Dialogue, A. Herford, O.
   4072
Modern Harlequinade in Three Plays,
   A. Clements, C. C. 1893

Modern Mother, A. Chance, J.
   G. 1712
Modern No Play, A. Mishima, Y.
   6080
Moglie di entrambi, A. Donaudy,
   A. 2531
Moglie innamorata, La. Cenzato,
   G. 1683
Moglie preziosa, Una. Donnay, M.
   2540
Moi, Napoleon! Dieudonne, A.
   2492
Moise a Mao, De 6109
Moisson Verte. Sorbets, G. 8384
Moj bednyj Marat. Arbuzov, A.
   315
Molinera de Arcos, La. Casona,
   A. 1641
Mollusk or Suffragette? Cuppy, E.
   O. 2145
Molly Meets the General. Hall, M.
   3856
Moment After, The. Hayes, J. J.
   3992
Moment due, Il. Pistilli, G. 7208
Mom's a Grandma Now. McQueen,
   M. H. and N. McQueen 5363
Mom's Perfect Day. Pendleton, E.
   7050
Mon Ami le Cambrioleur. Haguet,
   A. 3818
Mon bèguin piazzato e vincente.
   Conty, J. and G. de Vissant
   1992
Mon Crime! Berr, G. and L.
   Verneuil. 868
Mon Cure Chez les Pauvres. Lorde,
   A. de and P. Chaine 5053
Mon Cure Chez les Riches. Lorde,
   A. de and P. Chaine. 5054
Mon Fils. Didier, P. 2489
Mon Mari et Toi. Ferdinand, R.
   2987
Mon Mari S'Endort. Gevel, C.
   3452
Monday, A Lame Minuet. Kreymborg, A. 4715
Mondo d'acqua, Il. Nicolai, A.
   6583
Mondo e' quello che e', Il. Pincherle, A. 7155, 7156
Mondo mai visto, Un. Lanza, G.
   4807
Money Tree, The. Garver, J.
   3413
Money Tower, The. Living Theatre
   Collective 5005
Money-Question, The. Dumas, A.
   2689

Mongrel, The. Bahr, H. 498
Monk Who Wouldn't, The. Mandel, O. 5493
Monkey Business. Boiko, C. 1096
Monkey Without a Tail, The. Winther, B. 9498
Monkey's Paw, The. Parker, L. N. 6973
Monna Vanna. Maeterlinck, M. 5429
Monnaie des ses Reves. Ransan, A. 7407
Monnaie du Pape, A La. Velle, L. 9061
Monologo alla radio. Roedel, R. 7646
Monsieur Alexandre. Cosmos, J. 2053
Monsieur Amilcar. Jamiaque, Y. 4440
Monsieur Barnett. Anouilh, J. 268
Monsieur Beaucaire. Tarkington, B. 8710
Monsieur Bob'le. Schehade, G. 8021
Monsieur Corbillon veut Rompre en Beaute. Santelli, C. 7915
Monsieur et Madame Molière. Chabannes, J. 1700
Monsieur et Mesdames Kluck. Lefrancq, G. 4894
Monsieur Galespard and Mademoiselle Jeanne. Craven, J. V., Jr. 2098
Monsieur Klebs et Rozalie. Obaldia, R. de 6731
Monsieur Masure. Magnier, C. 5441, 5442
Monsieur Prudhomme. Monnier, H. and G. Vaez 6174
Monsieur Santa Claus. Miller, H. L. 5951
Monsieur Teste. Franck, P. 3255
Monsieur Vautrin. Charpak, A. 1730
Monsieur Vernet. Renard, J. 7481
Montagna di carta, Una. Rocco, G. 7634
Montagne, Le. Romualdi, G. 7674
Montecarlo. D'Ambra, L. 2168
Montemor, ou La Couronue et le Sang. Bailac, G. 501
Month in the Country, A. Turgenev, I. 8950, 8951
Montreur, Deux Périodes, Le. Chedid, A. 1762
Montserrat. Roblès, E. 7630
Monzu. D'Ambra, L. and A. Donaudy 2170
Moon for the Misbegotten, A. O'Neill, E. 6857
Moon Is Blue, The. Herbert, H. F. 4063, 4064
Moon Is Down, The. Steinbeck, J. 8492
Moon Keeps Shining, The. McQueen, M. H. and N. McQueen 5364
Moon Miracle. Carpenter, M. H. 1612
Moon of the Caribbees, The. O'Neill, E. 6858, 6859
Moon on a Rainbow Shawl. John, E. 4472
Moonbeam Dares. Lee, S. 4884
Moonlight Is When. Arthur, K. 385
Moonlight Sonata. Petit, V. P. 7106
Moon's Up There, The. Nolan, P. T. 6659
Moonshine. Hopkins, A. 4162, 4163
Moonstone, The. Collins, W. 1941
Moon-Struck. Steele, J. 8483
Moosical Comedy, The. Harrold, W. 3935
Morale et le Hasard. Bernard, T. 853
Morality Play for the Leisure Class, A. Balderston, J. L. 528
Morals and Circumstances. Bloch, B. 1004
Morder, Hoffnung der Frauen. Kokoschka, O. 4682
More About Apples. Phipps, A. H. 7142
More Than a Million. Kelly, M. 4581
More Than Courage. MacLellan, E. and C. V. Schroll 5254
More the Merrier, The. Kauffmann, S. 4558
Morituri: Teias. Sudermann, H. 8603
Morning Maker, The. Campbell, C. 1538
Morning's Work, A. Maxwell, G. 5698
Morraca. Parkhurst, W. 6980
Mort de Maximilien d'Autriche, La. Perret, J. 7076

Mort d'un Rat. Hartog, J. de 3953
Mortal Coils. Huxley, A. 4346
Morte de Lord Chatterley, La. Frank, C. 3259
Morte degli amanti, La. Chiarelli, L. 1799
Morte del dottor Faust, La. Ghelderode, M. de 3459
Morte di Flavia e delle sue bambole. Cappelli, S. 1586
Morte di Ulisse, La. Meano, C. 5725
Morte di un bengalino. Antòn, E. 291
Morte in vacanza, La. Casella, A. 1631
Morte lieta, La. Evreinov, N. N. 2888
Morti non fanno paura, I. De Filippo, E. 2257
Morts. Aub, M. 434
Morts Sans Sépulture. Sartre, J.-P. 7963
Morts Vivent le Dimanche, Les. Matsas, N. 5657
Morwynion. Green, R. L. 3713
Moscow Is Burning. Mayakovsky, V. 5702
Moskovsky Charatkter. Sofronov, A. V. 8362
Most Happy Fella. Loesser, F. 5016
Most Important Guests, The. DuBois, G. 2643
Most Memorable Voyage. Bakeless, K. L. 514
Most Special Dragon, A. Ferguson, D. 2993
Most Unusual Ghost, The. Haugh, G. L. 3964
Mother, The. Ford, F. M. 3216
Mother. Howells, W. D. 4250
Mother Beats the Band. Miller, H. L. 5952
Mother Courage. Brecht, B. 1304
Mother Earth's New Dress. McQueen, M. H. and N. McQueen 5365
Mother for Mayor. Miller, H. L. 5953
Mother Goes Modern. Arthur, K. 386
Mother Goose and Her Family. Eggleston, E. 2823
Mother Goose Bakeshop, The. Miller, H. L. 5954

Mother Goose Christmas, A. Smith, S. D., Jr. 8353
Mother Goose Gives a Dinner. Vandevere, J. L. 9023
Mother Goose's Children. Nothnagle, C. 6697
Mother Goose's Christmas Surprise. Boiko, C. 1097
Mother Goose's Magic Cookies. Blaine, B. G. 987
Mother Goose's Party. Fisher, A. 3059
Mother Goose's Sleeping Cap. McMeekin, I. M. 5274
Mother Makes a Choice. Whittaker, H. 9339
Mother-love. Buck, G. 1406
Mother's Admirers. McQueen, M. H. and N. McQueen 5366
Mother's Apron Strings. Miller, H. L. 5955
Mother's Big Day. Miller, H. L. 5956
Mother's Burden, A. Robinson, M. 7629
Mother's Choice. McQueen, M. H. 5285
Mother's Day Treasure Hunt, A. Miller, H. L. 5957
Mother's Day--2005 A.D. Block, B. 1007
Mother's Fairy Godmother. Miller, H. L. 5958
Mother's Gift. Howard, H. L. 4208
Mother's V.I.P.'s. McQueen, M. H. and N. McQueen 5367
Motor Show, The. Ionesco, E. 4399
Mouches, Les. Sartre, J.-P. 7964
Mouette, La. Chekhov, A. P. 1771
Mougnou-Mougnou, ou Un Coeur de Mère. Worms, J. 9563
Moulin de la Galette, Le. Achard, M. 32, 33
Mount Vernon Cricket, The. Miller, H. L. 5959
Mountain Madness. Dias, E. J. 2434
Mountain She-Devil, The. Noguchi, Y. 6618
Mourning Becomes Electra. O'Neill, E. 6860
Mouse and the Country Mouse, The. Bennett, R. 788
Mouse That Soared, The. Miller, H. L. 5960
Mouse-Trap, The. Howells, W. D. 4251
Mousetrap, The. Christie, A. 1823

763

Moving Day. Klein, E. 4658
Moving on Tomorrow. Phillips, M. K. 7133
Mozart and Salieri. Pushkin, A. 7345
Mozart and the Gray Steward. Wilder, T. 9392, 9398, 9399
Mozartement votre. Westphal, E. 9310
Much Ado About Ants. Heath, A. L. 4010
Much Ado About Nothing. Shakespeare, W. 8187
Mud. McKinney, I. 5233
Mud Pack Madness. French, D. and M. French. 3295
Mulan. Taketomo, T. 8689
Mulatto. Hughes, L. 4304
Mulini a vento. Antòn, E. 292
Muller von sans souci, Der. Hacks, P. 3812
Mulvaney's First Case. Murray, J. 6371
Mummers' Play, The. Smith, J. K. 8336
Murder at Mother Goose's Place. Majeski, B. 5462
Murder in the Cathedral. Eliot, T. S. 2853
Murder in the Kitchen. Fisher, A. 3060
Murder of Marat. Kearney, P. 4568
Murder Pattern. Voaden, H. 9167
Murderer. Ross, C. 5150
Murderer, The Women's Hope. Kokoschka, O. 4683
Muro di silenzio, Il. Messina, P. 5794
Muse, Le. Baldini, G. 530
Music at Night. Priestley, J. B. 7299
Music Far Away. FitzGibbon, C. 3138
Music Hath Charms. McQueen, M. H. and N. McQueen 5368
Music of the Toilette. Marinetti, F. T. and G. Calderone 5549
Musicians of Bremen Town. Roberts, W. 7613
Mussolini at Breakfast. Thomas, D. 8825
Mutatis Mutandis. Campton, D. 1549
Mutcrogpro. Rieder, R. 7575
Mutilated, The. Williams, T. 9432

My Chosen People. Nidess, D. A. 6591
My Cousin from Tycho. Boiko, C. 1098
My Darlin' Aida. Friedman, C. 3303
My Darling Clementine. Thornton, J. F. 8851
My Dear! O'Connor, P. 6766
My Fair Linda. Garver, J. 3414
My Fair Monster. Dias, E. J. 2435
My Foot My Tutor. Handke, P. 3884
My Heart's in the Highlands. Saroyan, W. 7952
My Host--the Ghost. Murray, J. 6372
My Kinsman, Major Molineux. Lowell, R. 5070
My Own Self. Brown, A. V. 1358
My Patriot Mother. Bakeless, K. L. 515
My Sister, My Spouse. Sutherland, D. 8627
My Son, the Prince. Olfson, L. 6805
My Swinging Swain. Martens, A. C. 5604
My Taylor. Capus, A. 1591
My 3 Angels. Spewack, S. and B. Spewack 8449
My Unfinished Portrait. Voteur, F. 9173
Myrrha. Petrova, O. 7112
Mystere des Trois Rois. Cammaerts, E. 1523
Mystere Sans Importance. Bernard, T. 853
Mysteres de Paris, Les. Vidalie, A. 9142
Mysterious Mix-Up, The. Gilbreath, A. 3522
Mysterious Portrait, The. Gogol, N. 3602
Mysterious Stranger, The. Nicholson, J. 6556
Mystery at Knob Creek Farm. Miller, H. L. 5961
Mystery at Tumble Inn, The. Lello, E. 4906
Mystery in the Lab. Murray, J. 6373
Mystery Liner. Murray, J. 6374
Mystery Manor. Murray, J. 6375
Mystery of Patriot Inn, The. Nicholson, J. 6557
Mystery of the Gumdrop Dragon, The. Burtle, G. L. 1445

Mystery of the Missing Money, The. Martens, A. C. 5605
Mystery of the Seventh Witch, The. Huff, B. T. 4289
Mystery of Turkey-Lurkey, The. Miller, H. L. 5962
Mystery Ring, The. Gross, N. F. 3763

N

"N" for Nuisance. Miller, H. L. 5963
Nabuchodonosor. Faramond, M. de 2931
Nacht de Mörder, Die. Triana, J. 2154
Naissance de Tristan. Delaquys, G. 2294
Naked Lady Is Bare, A. Litvack, B. 5002
Names to Remember. Ramsey, H. 7400
Naming of the Flowers, The. York, M. A. 9614
Naming the Novel. Hunt, L. 4324
Napoleon. Bouhelier, St.-G. de 1213
Napoleon Crossing the Rockies. Mackaye, P. 5229
Napoleon IV. Rostand, M. 7722
Napoleon III a la Barre de l'Histoire. Castelot, A. 1650
Napoleon Unique. Raynal, P. 7447
Napoleon's Samovar. Murnik, R. 6308
Narciso. Dursi, M. 2756
Narcissus. Lourson, L. 5059
Narcotique. Bernard, T. 853
Narrow Man, The. Bailey, A. H. 504
Narrow Road to the Deep North. Bond, E. 1171, 1172
Narrow Squeak, A. Deming, D. 2327
Narrowest Street. Morse, R. M. 6243
Natale. Aurio, A. 457
Natale in casa Cupiello. De Filippo, E. 2258
Natale nel mondo. 6443
Nathan Hale. Hughes, R. 4312
Nathaniel Hawthorne and the Curse of the Pyncheons. Taylor, M. A. 8723

National Everything, The. Murray, J. 6376
Nationale 6. Bernard, J.-J. 826
Nation's Song Is Born, A. Bakeless, K. L. 516
Native Son. Wright, R. and P. Green 9575
Natives Are Restless Tonight, The. Dias, E. J. 2436
Nativity, The. 6451
Nativity, The. Morse, K. D. 6242
Naufrage ou Miss Ann Saunders, Le. Dubreuilh, S. 2667
Nausicaa du Mackensie. Balachova, T. and G. Arest 527
Nautical Sheep, The. Nicholson, J. 6558
Navel Engagement. Goering, R. 3592
Navette, La. Becque, H. 713
Ne Dites Pas: Fontaine. Villiers, M.-L. 9150
Ne Faisons pas un Reve. Noe, Y. 6612
Ne Reveillez Pas Madame! Anouilh, J. 269
Near Nature's Heart. Woodmeald, J. E. 9549
Nebbie. Ronfani, U. 7692
Neck and Neck. O'Donnell, M. Three Short Plays 6775
Necklace, The. Maupassant, G. de 5679, 5680, 5681
Need for Polygamy, The. Sampaio, S. 7897
Needle Fights for Freedom, A. MacLellan, E. and C. V. Schroll 5255
Neger, Die. Genet, J. 3438
Negerinde! Swanson, W. S. J. 8645
Neige Etait Sale, La. Simenon, G. 8282
Neighbors. Gorostiza, C. 3654
Neighbors to the North. McQueen, M. H. and N. McQueen 5369
Neighbours. Saunders, J. 7981, 7982
Nel quartiere dei piaceri. 6458
Nelle migliori famiglie. Hart, A. and M. Braddel. 3936
Nellie's Fishy Fate. 6459
Nemesis. Thomas, A. 8822
Nemici dell'amore. Duse, E. 2769
Nemico, Il. Giannini, G. 3487
Nemico del teatro, Il. Molnar, F. 6150
Nero come un canarino. Nicolai, A. 6584

Nerve of Napoleon, The. Garver, J. 3415
Nervi esistono, I. Sorescu, M. 8386
Nervous Prostration. Manning, M. 5501
Nessuno. Dursi, M. 2757
Neurotic Lion, A. Bolotowsky, I. 1155
Never Say Diet. Savelli, A. 7993
Never Stretch Your Legs in a Taxi. Behrman, S. N. 729
Never the Time and the Place. Robinson, L. 7625
Never the Twain. Deseo, L. G. 2359
Neveu de Rameau. Diderot, D. 2487
New Angle on Christmas, A. Albert, R. 107
New Cinderella, A. Albert, R. 108
New Compass, A. Hall, M. E. 3860
New Deliverance, The. Witkiewicz, S. I. 9517
New Hearts for Old. Fisher, A. 3061
New Home for Mice, A. Werner, S. 9297
New Look at American History, A. Robinson, M. 7627
New New Year. Skinner, A. M. 8309
New Pages for Our History Textbooks. McBrown, G. P. 5120
New Pygmalion, The. Lang, A. 4792
New Red Riding-Hood, The. Brooks, E. S. 1347
New Shoes. Miller, H. L. 5964
New Song, A. Yates, E. 9584
New Washington, The. Newman, D. 6512
New Way to Pay Old Debts. Massinger, P. 5646
New Wing at Elsinore, A. Hankin, St. J. 3888
New Worlds. Gould, J. 3665
New Year's Day. Palmer, H. M. 4944
"Newa" Kommt! Wolf, F. 9526
New-Fangled Thanksgiving. McQueen, M. H. and N. McQueen 5370
New-Old Christmas, The. Edwards, D. L. 2819

Next Stop--Spring! Boiko, C. 1099
Nice People. Crothers, R. 2123
Nicolas Flamel. Nerval, G. de 6465
Niederlage, Die. Grieg, N. 3743
Niente. Rocca, G. 7637
Niggerlovers. Tabori, G. 8682
Night at an Inn, A. Dunsany, E. J. M. D. P. 2722
Night Before Christmas. Howells, W. D. 4252
Night Brings a Counselor. Saunders, L. 7984
Night Freight. Yates, J. M. 9585
Night of Decision. DuBois, G. 2644
Night of "Mr. H," The. Brighouse, H. 1327
Night of the Iguana, The. Williams, T. 9433
Night of the Trolls. Rahn, S. 7392
Night of the Wedding, The. Duffy, R. 2676
Night Stick. Gerould, D. Tripstych 3445
Night the Angels Sang, The. Bryant, P. 1394
Night Train. Reinecker, H. 7470
Nightcap of the Prophet Elias, The. Kotzebue, A. von 4696
Nightingale. Ernst, A. H. 2871
Night's Lodging, A. Gorky, M. 3647
Nikluk and the Loon. Winther, B. 9499
Nina. Roussin, A. 7752, 7753
Nine Cheers for Christmas. Fisher, A. 3062
Nine Times Christmas. Jokai, M. 4492
9 to 5 to 0. Wunderlich, L. 9577
Ninety and Nine, The. Paul, E. 7011
Ninfa immortale, La. Sterling, G. 8503
Ninotchka. Lengyel, M. 4913
Ninth Night. Dyk, V. 2797
No a tutti. Conti, A. 1986
No Braver Soldier. Bierling, J. C. E. 920
No c'e un cane. Cangiullo, F. 1558
No Christmas Here. McCallum, P. 5121
No 'Count Boy, The. Green, P. 3704, 3705

No de Saint-Denis, Le. Gripari, P. 3758
No Garden This Year. McCoy, P. S. 5152
No Hats, No Banquets. Brodsky, R. 1335
No Medals. Knight, R. A. 4669
No More War. Kreymborg, A. 4716
No One's Safe. Kennedy, L. 4593
No Room at the Inn. Patterson, E. L. 7005
No Room in the Hotel. Wilson, D. C. 9459
No Sale. Richmond, S. S. 7563
No Smoking. Benavente y Martinez, J. 745
No Strings Attached. Moss, H. 6264
No Treat for Gilbert. McCoy, P. S. 5153
No Why. Whiting, J. 9331
Noah's Ark. Seiffert, M. A. 8136
Nobel Prize, The. Bergman, H. 813
"Noblesse Oblige." De Mille, W. C. and J. Erskine 2317
Nobody Believes in Witches. Watkins, M. S. 9219
Noces d'Argent. Gilles, A. 3529
Noche de les Asesinos, La. Triana, J. 8932, 8933
Nodo nel fazzoletto, Il. Bernard, T. 843
Noè. Obey, A. 6739
Noel. Lewis, W. 4974
Noël sur la Place, Le. Ghéon, H. 3463
Noi che restiamo. Cenzato, G. 1684
Noi due. Biancoli, O. 913
Noi tre. Martinez Sierra, G. 5629
Nommé Juda, Un. Puget, C.-A. and P. Bost 7329
Non c'e pace per l'antico fauno. Terron, C. 8760
Non c'e regola, ahime! Saitta, A. 7866
Non cerco un amante. Renard, J. 7482
Non mi sposate! Lauwick, H. 4834
Non si dorme a Kirkwall. Perrini, A. 7080
Non si sa Come. Pirandello, L. 7196

Non ti conosco piú. De Benedetti, A. 2228
Non tradire. Tieri, V. 8862
Non voglio sposare Minnie. Bonelli, L. 1183
None but the Fair. Paradis, M. B. 6960
None So Blind. DuBois, G. 2645
Non-Fiction Party. Dean, R. 2214
Nonnes, Les. Manet, E. 5497
Noon Hour. Scott, W. T. 8115
Noose, The. Mygatt, T. D. 6427
Nor Long Remember. Martens, A. C. 5606
Nora Seconda. Viola, C. G. 9152
North Pole Confidential. Jensen, S. C. 4463
Northern Night, A. Sharp, W. 8199
Nose, The. Stone, J. A. 8532
Nosebag, The. MacNeice, L. 5280
Nostos. Bacchelli, R. 480
Nostra fortuna, La. Possenti, E. 7259
Nostri cari bambini, I. Manzari, N. 5512
Nostro viaggio, Il. Gherardi, G. 3468
Not at Home. Lavedan, H. 4838
Not Counting the Savages. Johnson, B. S. 4480
Not Enough Rope. May, E. 5700
Not Fit for Man or Beast. McQueen, M. H. and N. McQueen 5371
Not for Girls. Miller, H. L. 5965
Not for Ladies. Schmitt, G. 8051
Not for Publication. Dias, E. J. 2437
Not Only the Strong. Waite, H. E. and E. M. Hoppenstedt 9188
Not So Simple Simon. Spamer, C. 8426
Not Worth a Continental. Miller, M. L. 6056
Notes on a Love Affair. Marcus, F. 5543
Nothing. Benjamin, J. 765
Nothing But the Truth. Montgomery, J. 6185
Nothing to Be Thankful For. McQueen, M. H. and N. McQueen 5372
Nothing to Be Thankful For. Pendleton, E. 7051
Nothing to Wear. Miller, H. L. 5966
Nothing Very Much Thank You. O'Connor, P. 6767

Notice to Quit. Rutherford, E. 7814
Noticia, La. Olmo, L. 6826
Notre Déesse. DuBois, A. 2615
Notre Peau. Lacour, J. -A. 4763
Notre-Dame d'En Haut. Bernard, J. -J. 827
Notte, Una. Romualdi, G. 7675
Notte a Barcellona, Una. De Stefani, A. 2379
Notte alla reggia. Chiusano, I. A. 1810
Notte d'avventure. Càglieri, E. 1487
Notte degli uomini. Boudousse, J. 1211
Notte del 16 Gennaio, La. Rand, A. 7402
Notte di un nevras tenico, La. Bacchelli, R. 481
Notte è bella, La. Bevilacqua, G. 907
Notte fatidica, La. Folgore, L. 3194
Notte Italiana. Horvath, O. von 4177
Notti a Milano. Terron, C. 8761
Notturni. Bertolini, A. 878
Notturno. Pratella, F. B. 7272
Notturno del tempo nostro. Bevilacqua, G. 908
Nous Avons Tous Fait la Même Chose. Letraz, J. de 4941
Nous Irons à Valparaiso. Achard, M. 34
Nous N'Avons Plus de Souvenirs. Blondel, J. 1013
Nouveaux maîtres, Les. Nivoix, P. 6607
Nouvelle, Amusette. Lebesque, M. 4869
Now Barabbas. Home, W. D. 4152
Now I Lay Me Down to Sleep. Ryan, E. 7818
Nowadays Call, A. De Vere, M. A. 2388
Nozze di Giovanna Phile, Le. Magnoni, B. 5445
Nozze di Quinita, Le. Alvarez Quintero, S. and J. Alvarez Quintero 167
Nuda. Borg, W. 1197
Nuit Blanche de Monsieur de Musset, La. Marais, C. and C. d'Aguila 5525
Nuit Close, La. Limbour, G. 4981

Nuit d'Augerge. Nigond, G. 6601
Nuit d'avril, La. Roussin, A. 7754
Nuit de Feu. Marcelle-Maurette 5533
Nuit de Gel. Camp, A. 1529
Nuits Blanches, Les. Dostoevsky, F. 2566
Nuits de la colere, Les. Salacrou, A. 7877
Number of Absurd and Poetic Events in the Life of the Great American Goof. Saroyan, W. Three Entertainments. 7958
Number One Apple Tree Lane. Boiko, C. 1100
Number sbagliato, Il. De Angelis, R. M. 2219
"No. 6." Phillips, S. 7140
Numero, Le. Roudy, P. 7727
Nun Singen Sie Wieder. Frisch, M. 3317, 3318
Nuova isola, La. Balducci, A. 533
Nuova liberazione, La. Witkiewicz, S. I. 9518
Nurnberg Stove, The. Ramée, L. de la 7394
Nursery Rhyme Diet. McQueen, M. H. and N. McQueen 5373
Nursery Tale Trio. Barker, C. and J. Medina 600
Nuvola. Surchi, S. 8624
N'y a Pas d'Automne sans Eté, Il. Ruth, L. 7807
N'y a Pas Que l'Amour. See, E. 8131
Nyanysa. A Zulu Play. 6712

O

O Come, Let Us Adore Him. Jones, E. S. 4505
O Little Town of Bethlehem. Morley, O. J. 6230
O marinheiro. Pessoa, F. 7086
O Mistress Mine. Rattigan, T. 7424
O, That Way Madness Lies. F., H. B. 2894
Oberosterreich. Kroetz, F. X. 4728
Object, L'. Des Presles, C. 2360
Oblomov. Cuvelier, M. 2152
Obsequies, The. Morgan, J. L. 6218
Obstacle, ou Alexandre le Petit. Brainville, Y. 1268

Obyknovenny Celovik. Leonov, L. M. 4928
Occhio del re, L'. Cenzato, G. 1685
Ocenao, L'. Mensio, C. 5754
Ode to a Scenic Northwest. Rappapport, D. 7416
Ode to Spring, An. McQueen, M. H. and N. McQueen 5374
Odio balcanico. Roda, R. 7643
Odissea di Runyon Jones, L'. Corwin, N. 2049
Ododrama. Braibanti, A. 1266
Odore del sud, L'. Paolieri, F. 6952
Odysseus and Calypso. Arthur, R. 388
Odyssey, The. Homer 4156
Oedipe, ou Le Silence des Dieux. Kihm, J.-J. 4620
Oedipus. Perreault, J. 7074
Oedipus. Seneca 8153
Oeil Anonyme. Shaffer, P. 8170
Oeil du Maître. Magnan, J.-M. 5437
Oeuf. Carette, L. 1602, 1603
Oeufs a la Moutarde, Les. Roudy, P. 7728
Oeufs de l'Autruche, Les. Roussin, A. 7755
Of Mice and Men. Steinbeck, J. 8493, 8494
Of You and Me. Soper, M. J. 8379
O'Fallon's Cup. Marz, R. 5636
Off the Shelf. McQueen, M. H. and N. McQueen 5375
Office, The, or Derision. Aron, J.-P. 357
Office de l'Etoile, L'. 6777
O'Flaherty. Shaw, G. B. 8212
Ognuno la sua croce. Fulchignoni, E. 3338
Ogre Who Built a Bridge, The. Mapp, F. 5521
Oh Starlings! Eveling, S. 2884
Oh, These Ghosts! Filippo, E. de 3019
Oh What a Lovely War. Littlewood, J. 5001
Oiseaux de Lune, Les. Ayme, M. 472
Ol-Dopt. Dozer, D. 2583
Old Baba Yaga. Winther, B. 9486
Old Four-Legs. Peterson, M. N. 7100

Old Ghosts at Home. Murray, J. 6377
Old Glory Grows Up. Miller, H. L. 5967
Old History Book, The. Armstrong, L. V. V. 345
Old King, The. Gourmont, R. de 3671
Old King Cole's Christmas. Atherton, M. 429
Old Man Minds His Wife, The. Heshmati, L. B. 4088
Old Mother Hubbard. Barr, J. 620
Old Ones, The. Wesker, A. 9303, 9304
Old Order. Emig, E. 2862
Old Order, The. Neumann, S. 6472
Old Pipes and the Dryad. Stockton, F. R. 8527
Old Stuff. Dangerfield, T. 2180
Old Times. Pinter, H. 7179
Old Tune. Pinget, R. 7169
Old Walnut. Harris, A. 3915
Old Wash Lucas. Green, P. 3706
Old Woman, The. Seiffert, M. A. 8137
Old Woman and Her Pig, The. Very, A. 9120
Old Year and the New, The. Chubb, P. 1830
Oldest Trick in the World. Thompson, J. 5774
Olimpia o del mestiere. Pallavicini, R. 6939
Olimpia, o gli occhi azzurri dell' imperatore. Molnar, F. 6151
Olimpiadi. De Stefani, A. 2373
Olive Jar, The. McFarlan, E. 5177
Oliver Bean. Meredith, B. 5767
Oliver Twist. Dickens, C. 2478, 2479, 2480
Olives, The. Rueda, L. de 7785
Ollanlay. Mossi, P. 6267
Oltre l'oceano. Gordin, G. 3633
Olympus, Farewell. Bayley, J. 683
Ombra dietro la porta, L'. De Stefani, A. 2374
Ombra, la moglie bella. Gotta, S. 3658
Ombrages. Raylambert, J. 7445
Ombre, Le. Sbragia, A. 8006
Ombre Cinesi. Gherardi, G. 3469
Ombre du Cavalier. Husson, A. 4331

769

Ombrellino verde, L'. Brunelli, B. 1386
Ombres. Praga, A. 7270
Omega's Ninth. Delgado, R. 2297
Omphale and the Hero. Herbert, J. 4065
Omphalos Hotel. Ribes, J.-M. 7509
On a Theme by Thoreau. Francis, R. 3249
On Bail. Middleton, G. 5817
On Borrowed Time. Osborn, P. 6888
On Camera, Noah Webster! Boiko, C. 1101
On Finit Quelquefois Par. Turpin, F. 8959
On Loge la Nuit-Cafe a L'Eau. Ribes, J.-M. 7510
On Ne Sait Jamais. Roussin, A. 7756
On Probation. Dreyer, M. 2601
On Strike. Fisher, A. 3063
On Such a Night. Fisher, A. 3064
On the Air. Hollingsworth, L. 4147
On the Border. Nikl, P. 6602a
On the Docks. 6832
On the Eve of Publication. Mercer, D. 5759
On the Fence. Beach, M. M. 685
On the High Road. Chekhov, A. 1772
On the Highway. Chekhov, A. 1773
On the Hill. O'Byrne, D. 6752
On the Hire System. Lang, L. L. 4794
On the Lot. Ryerson, F. and C. Clements 7828
On the Racecourse. Gregory, Lady A. 3726
On the Terrace. Vojnovich, I. 9169
On the Trail of Injun Joe. Clemens, S. L. 1885
On the Veldt. Patterson, F. C. 7007
On Trial. Richmond, S. S. 7564
On Tue Toujours Celle Qu'on Aime. Menestrel, M. 5750
On with the New. Goddard, F. 3589
Once a Giant. Bush, S. 1448

Once and Future Frog, The. Olfson, L. 6806
Once Around the Block. Saroyan, W. 7953
Once I Chased a Butterfly. Olfson, L. 6807
Once in a Lifetime. Kaufman, G. S. and M. Hart 4561
Once Upon a Mattress. Thompson, J., M. Barer, and D. Fuller. 8847
Once Upon a Midnight Dreary. Murray, J. 6378
Once Upon a Time. Fisher, A. 3065
Once Upon a Tinderbox. Andersen, H. C. 197
Oncle, L'. Presles, C. de 7284
Ondine. Giraudoux, J. 3573, 3574
One Big Family. Wang Fa and Chu Ya-nan 9201
One by One. Thompson, H. 8844
One Day Awake. Monro, H. 6175
One Day in the Life of a Fairy Tale Princess. Levin, C. 4962
One Day More. Conrad, J. 1980, 1981
One Evening Gleam. Fitzmaurice, G. 3142
One Flew Over the Cuckoo's Nest. Wasserman, D. 9215
One for the Grave. MacNeice, L. 5281
100 donne nude. Ridenti, L. and D. Falconi. 7574
145 Wall Street. Curie, E. 2149
One Hundred Pounds Reward. Brennan, M. M. 1316
120 all'ora. Szecsen, S. 8679
120 giornate di sodoma, Le. Vasilico, G. 9046
One Hundred Words. Boiko, C. 1102
One in a Million. Murray, J. 6379
One Leg Over the Wrong Wall. Bermel, A. 821
One Life to Lose. Martens, A. C. 5607
"One Man Escapes." Davidson, G. and J. Auslander 2197
One Man in His Time. Mayr, G. A. 5705
One May Spin a Thread Too Finely. Turgenev, I. 8952
One Night in Bethlehem. Newman, D. 6513
One the Two of Us. Stevenson, W. A., III 8523

One to Grow On. Miller, H. L. 5968
1, 2, 3. Molnar, F. 6152
One Wish Too Many. Feather, J. 2964
Only a Man in Black. Castro, J. A. 1658
Only Jealousy of Emer, The. Yeats, W. B. 9602
Ontological Proof of My Existence. Oates, J. C. 6713
Onze Degres d'Aptitude. Charras, C. 1733
Open Door, The. Harris, M. 3928
Open House. Martens, A. C. 5608
Open House for Shakespeare. Miller, H. L. 5969
Open Letter on Race Hatred. Robson, W. N. 7631
Open Mind, The. Walter, O. M. 9200
Open Twenty-Four Hours. Cornish, R. N. 2024
Opening of the Indian Era. Hacks, P. 3813
Opera, Opera. Saroyan, W. Three Entertainments 7958
Operation, The. Dennison, G. 2338
Operation Litterbug. Boiko, C. 1103
Operation Magistrale. Bernard, T. 853
Operation Sidewinder. Shepard, S. 8238
Operette. Gombrowicz, W. 3617
Or et la Paille, L'. Barillet, P. and J.-P. Gredy. 590
Ora azzurra, L'. Gàbor, A. 3344
Ora blu, L'. Salsa, C. 7886
Ora d'amore, Un. Topol, J. 8889
Ora di religione, L'. Mazzetti, L. 5711
Ora precisa, L'. Cangiullo, F. 1559
Oracle a Parle. Durtain, L. 2763
Orange Soufflé. Bellow, S. 737
Oratorio scenico alla memoria di Bob Kennedy. Santucci, L. 7922
Orchestre. Anouilh, J. 270
Orchids for Margaret. Allred, P. and T. Allred 150

Ordeal by Battle. Wilder, P. 9380
Order, The. Hochwalder, F. 4123
Order of Release. Housman, L. 4191
Orecchio di Dionisio, L'. Cassieri, G. 1645
Orfeo. Poliziano, A. A. 7229
Orgy Bureau, The. Benedikt, M. 756
Orlando Furioso. Sanguineti, E. 7912
Ornifle, ou Le Courant d'Air. Anouilh, J. 271
Orologeria Taus, L'. Naum, G. 6452
Orologia a cuccù, L'. Donini, A. 2533
Orphans, The. Murphy, T. 6310
Orpheus and Eurydice. Moore, T. S. 6206
Orpheus Below. Honig, E. 4158
Orpheus Descending. Williams, T. 9434, 9435, 9436
Orrendo delitto di Penaranda del Campo, L'. Baroja, P. 612
Orthodoxy. Putnam, N. W. 7347
Osbern and Ursyne. Craigie, P. M. T. 2091
Oscar. Magnier, C. 5443
Ospite inatteso, L'. Tonelli, G. 8884
Ospizio "La Pace." Nicolosi, V. M. 6590
Ossido di Carbonio. Malerba, L. 5470
Osteria degli immortali, L'. Massa, M. 5644
Otage. Claudel, P. 1865
Other, The. Unamuno y Jugo, M. de 8968
Other Danger, The. Donnay, C. M. 2541
Other Room, The. Paull, H. M. 7013
Other Room, The. Witherspoon, F. 9509
Other Side of the Swamp, The. Ryton, R. 7832
Other Side of the Wall, The. Clapp, P. 1842
Other Woman, The. Hale, L. C. 3838
Ou Vivrez-Vous Demain? Fellows, M. S. 2981
"Oui" des Jeunes Filles, Le. Ruth, L. 7808
"Ounce of Safety, An." Moss, L. Q. 6266

Our Betters. Maugham, W. S. 5674
Our Famous Ancestors. McQueen, M. H. and N. McQueen 5376
Our 49th State. Fisher, A. 3066
Our Great Declaration. Fisher, A. 3113
Our Kind. Saunders, L. 7986
Our Learned Philhellenes. Traill, H. D. 8917, 8918
Our Library. Gilmore, A. F. 3538
Our Man in Madras. Hofmann, G. 4128
Our Own Four Walls. McQueen, M. H. and N. McQueen 5377
Our Sister, Sitya. Nolan, P. T. 6660
Out of the Clock. Bennett, R. 789
Out of the Darkness. O'Neill, M. D. 6867
Out of the Midst of Hatred. Troubetzkoy, A. R. 8938
Out of the Question. Howells, W. D. 4253
Out of This World. Dias, E. J. 2438
Outcast. Strindberg, A. 8570
Outclassed. Glick, C. 3583
Outgoing Tide, The. Hackett, W. 3803
Outline for a Pageant. Kramme, W. 4707
Outport. Braid, A. 1267
Outrageous Saint, The. Vega, L. de 9056
Outside the Gate. Clark, I. K. 1849
Outside the Gate. McChesney, D. G. 5129
Outward Bound. Vane, S. 9034
Over Gardens Out. Gill, P. 3524
Over the Garden Wall. Vance, D. M. 9014
Over the Hills. Palmer, J. 6945
Over the Hills and Far Away. Frank, F. K. 3261
Over the River. Martens, A. C. 5609
Over the Toast. Strong, L. A. G. 8585
Over the Wire. Cocteau, J. 1918
Overruled. Shaw, G. B. 8213, 8214

Ovvero, il commendatore. Federici, M. 2970
Owl Answers. Kennedy, A. 4591
Owl's Answer, The. Hagy, J. 3820
Owners. Churchill, C. 1835
Oxtiern. Sade, D.-A.-F. de 7845
Oyster and the Pearl, The. Saroyan, W. 7954

P

PTA Triumphs Again. Cheatham, V. R. 1755
Package for Ponsonby. Smith, B. and R. Finch 8330
Padrona, La. Betti, U. 896
Pagare i debiti. Bernard, T. 844
Pageant of Boston. Copeland, J. F. 2013
Pageant of Spring, A. Thurston, A. 8857
Pageant of the Shearmen and Tailors, The. Brown, J. M. 1365
Pageant of Women, A. Driscoll, L. 2608
Paging John Harvard. Kelley, E. 4577
Pagoda Slave, A. Keeler, C. 4573
Paid on Both Sides. Auden, W. H. 438
Pain Blanc, Le. Spaak, C. 8398
Pain dur, Le. Claudel, P. 1866
Paint Your Wagon. Lerner, A. J. 4932
Painter, The. Vitrac, R. 9159
Painter and the Millionaire, The. Paull, H. M. 7014
Pair of Drawers, A. Sternheim, C. 8506
Pair of Them, A. Lampton, W. J. 4780
Pajama Game, The. Abbott, G. and R. Bissell 4
Palace at 4 A. M., The. Moss, H. 6265
Pamela diviorziata. Solari, P. 8363
Pamperers. Loy, M. 5072
Pamplemousse. Birabeau, A. 954
Pan Passes Northward. Hanlon, J. 3890
Pandora. 6949
Pandora's Box. Asbrand, K. 406
Pandora's Box. Wedekind, F. 9257
Pandora's Perilous Predicament. Boiko, C. 1104

Pane amaro, Il. Gorky, M. 3648
Pane di casa, Il. Renard, J. 7483
Panic in a Desk Drawer. Woster, A. C. 9570
Panic in the Palace. Swintz, M. 8651
Panne, Die. Dürrenmatt, F. 2747
Pantagleize. Ghelderode, M. de 3460
Pants and the Man. Thompson, H. 8845
Paola Travasa. Adami, G. 54
Paolino ha disegnato un cavallo. Storm, L. 8540
Papa and Mama. Barrios, E. 636
Papa Bon Dieu. Sapin, L. 7924
Papa Juan, or The Centenarian. Alvarez Quintero, S. and J. Alvarez Quintero 168
Papa Pepper--Patriot. Miller, H. L. 5970
Papa Pepper's Bombshell. Miller, H. L. 5971
Paparino. Falconi, D. 2915
Paper Bag Mystery, The. Miller, H. L. 5972
Paper Princess, The. Draper, C. C. 2589
Papiers, Les. Avermaete, R. 465
Par, Le. Catteau, F. 1666
Par Dela les Marronniers. Ribes, J. -M. 7511
Parabolic Quartet, A. Wagner, A. 9182
Paracelsus and the Hero. Ryga, G. 7830
Parachutistes, Les. Cau, J. 1667
Parcel Pick-Up. Schwartz, P. 8101
Pardon, Madame. Weill, R. and A. Rivoire 9265
Parentesi chiusa. Casella, A. 1632
Pari. Pirandello, L. 7197, 7198
Paria, La. Strindberg, A. 8571
Paris and Helen. Schwartz, D. 8092
Paris and Oenone. Binyon, L. 944
Paris and Oenone. Hale, W. G. 3841
Paris Impromptu. Giraudoux, J. 3575
Paris Interlude. Brenman, M. 1315
Park, The. Ursell, G. 8979
Parla Kellermann. Bauer, J. M. 675
Parlor Car, The. Howells, W. D. 4258
Parnell and Butt. Traill, H. D. 8919
Parole. Chiti, R. 1809
Parrot and the Pirates, The. Miller, H. L. 5973
Parrot Who Would Not Talk, The. Steingold, R. W. 8498
Partage de midi. Claudel, P. 1867
Parte di Amleto, La. De Filippo, E. 2259
Parte difficile, Una. Roma, E. 7666
Partie de Bridge. Bernard, T. 845
Parting Friends. Howells, W. D. 4255
Partita in quattro. Varaldo, A. 9042
Partita vinta. Philips, F. C. 7119
Partners in Velvet. Hazam, L. 3995
Party Dress. Paradis, M. B. 6961
Party Line. Miller, H. L. 5974
Party of the Third Part, The. Stow, C. 8542
Pas d'Histoires ... Deutsch, L. 2385
Pas de deux. Mainardi, R. 5458
Pascolo dell'alpino, Il. Caballo, E. 1466
Pascualas, The. Aguirre, I. 81
Pascualina. Souza, A. 8394
Pask. Strindberg, J. A. 8572
Passage to India, A. Rau, S. R. 7432
Passaggio dell'equatore. Morucchio, U. 6251
Passagio. Milhaud, D. 5830
Passatismo. Corra, B. 2035
Passe-porc, ou Le Confessionnal. Pech, C. -H. 7030
Passer. Nutting, H. C. 6710
Passer-By, The. Coppee, F. 2015
Passe-Temps. Mithois, M. 6095
Passing. Sarr, K. 7959
Passing of Dana's People. Craig, A. T. 2088
Passing of Muhammad. Arnold, Sir E. 350

773

Passing to the Third Floor Back. Jerome, J. K. 4466
Passion. Bond, E. 1173
Passion d'Anna Karenine, La. Arout, G. 367
Passion du General Franco. Gatti, A. 3421
Passion Play, A. Barnes, D. 605
Passion Play, A. Soloman, N. 8369
Passions Contraires. Soria, G. 8388
Passy 08-45. Savoir, A. 8000
Paste Cut Paste. Hale, L. C. 3839
Pasticceria Kiss. Molnar, F. 6153
Pastiche. Hall, N. 3864
Pasto dell'attore, Il. Raggio, E. 7386
Pastor Hall. Toller, E. 8875
Pastorale. Turpin, F. 8958
Pastrybaker. Vega, L. de 9057
Patate. Achard, M. 35, 36
Patchwork Princess, The. Slattery, M. E. 8315
Path of Flowers. Kataev, V. 4552
Pathetic Prologue. Sastre, A. 7975
Paths. Khaytov, N. 4617
Patrick Pearse Motel, The. Leonard, H. 4925
Patriota per me, Un. Osborne, J. 6896
Paul Bunyan and His Blue Ox. Cone, M. 1968
Paul Revere of Boston. Kane, E. B. 4540
Paul Revere Rides Again. Miller, H. L. 5975
Paul Revere Rides to Lexington. Mayr, G. A. 5706
Paul Revere's Cloak. Robinson, G. 7619
Paul Thompson Forever. Gorelik, M. 3642
Pauline Pavlovna. Aldrich, T. B. 123
Paura, La. Binazzi, M. 940
Paura, La. Tieri, V. 8863
Paura numbero uno, La. De Filippo, E. 2260
Pauvre Bougre et le Bon Genie, Le. Allais, A. 136
Pavillon des Enfants, Le. Sarment, J. 7938

Pazzi sulla montagna, I. De Stefani, A. 2375
Peace at Home. Moineaux, G. 6107
Peace at Home--At Any Price. Maupassant, G. de 5682
Peace, Good Tickle-Brain. Gay, R. M. 3431
Peace on Earth. Hostetter, V. V. 4180
Peace on Earth. Mixon, A. 6098
Peace, Pilgrim. Cable, H. 1477
Peach Marmalade. Craven, J. V., Jr. 2099
Peach Tree Kingdom, The. Musil, R. G. 6416
Pear Tree, The. McFarlan, E. 5178
Pearl, The. Lavedan, H. 4840
Pearls. Totheroh, D. 8899
Peau d'Espagne. Sarment, J. 7939
Peau de Vache. Barillet, P. and J.-P. Gredy. 591
Peccato, Il. Lanza, G. 4808
Peccatuccio. Birabeau, A. 955
Pecos Bill Meets the Trickster. Magnuson, J. 5447
Pedro and the Burro. Peterson, M. N. 7101
Pegaso. Pinelli, T. 7163
Peggy. Crothers, R. 2124
Peinture sur Bois. Bergman, I. 816
Pelele, El. Deza, S. de 2395, 2396
Pelican. Strindberg, A. 8573
Pelisse. Sonnier, G. 8378
Pelleas and Melisande. Maeterlinck, M. 5430
Pellicano ribelle, Il. Bassano, E. 652
Pelliccia di Martora, La. Grismondi, G. A.-T. 3759
Pellicola de Re del Siam, La. D'Amora, F. 2176
Pendolo, Il. Nicolai, A. 6585
Penelope. Maugham, W. S. 5675
Penelope, Pride of the Pickle Factory. Huff, B. T. 4290
Pennsylvania Parakeet, The. Miller, H. L. 5976
Penny a Flower. Kester, K. 4607
Penny That Beauty Spent, The. Wilder, T. 9392
Penny Wise. Boiko, C. 1105
Pensée. Andreyev, L. N. 236
Penultimate Test, The. Peacocke, L. T. 7027

People Show, The. Nuttall, J. 6707
People with Light Coming Out of Them, The. Saroyan, W. 7955
Pepe and the Cornfield Bandit. Boiko, C. 1106
Peppermint Easter Egg, The. Slattery, M. E. 8316
Per non morire. Mainardi, R. 5459
Per una giovanetta che nessuno piange. Mainardi, R. 5460
Per uso di memoria. Castri, M. 1656
Peralopez Ranjel. 7062
Perambulating Pie, The. Pyle, M. T. 7354
Perbene, Il. Vulpescu, R. 9176
Père Damien, Le. Silvain, J. 8279
Père Humilie, Le. Claudel, P. 1868
Perela' uomo di fumo. Palazzeschi, A. and R. Guicciardini 6938
Pères Ennemis, Les. Messager, C. 5789
Perfect Analysis Given by a Parrot, A. Williams, T. 9437
Perfect Couple, The. Murray, J. 6380
Perfect Gift, The. DuBois, G. 2646
Perfect Jewel Maiden, The. Noguchi, Y. 6619
Perfect Machine, The. Craven, A. S. and J. D. Beresford. 2096
Perfection in Black. Clark, C. 1848
Peril Bleu, Le. Lanoux, V. 4803
Perils of Prophecy, The. Nolan, P. T. 6661
Period of Adjustment, A. Williams, T. 9438
Permanent Anaesthesia. Seiler, C. 8142
Permutations Among the Nightingales. Huxley, A. L. 4347
Perplexing Pirandello, The. Palm, C. L. 6940
Persephone in Eden. Damon, S. F. 2172
Perseus and Andromeda. Owen, P. 6921
Persimmon Thief, The. Nakazawa, K. 6432
Person in the Chair, The. Shaw, F. 8201
Persona fidata, Una. De Filippo, P. 2275
Personaggi al caffè. Sarazani, F. 7927
Personnage, Le. Chedid, A. 1763
Pertinent and Impertinent. Hatteras, O. 3961
Pescaballo. Child, F. J. 1802
Pescatore di Balene, Il. Veneziani, C. 9069
Peter and the Wolf. Chermak, S. 1789
Peter Gink. Nethercot, A. H. 6470
Peter, Peter, Peter! Boiko, C. 1107
Peter Rabbit. Simonds, N. 8294
Peter Rabbit Volunteers. Miller, H. L. 5977
Peter Salem, Minuteman. Keats, M. 4571
Peter Tomorrow. Hirshberg, B. 4113
Peter's Easter Basket Company. Blaine, B. G. 988
Petit Drame, Un. Shaw, G. B. 8215
Petit Retable de Don Cristobal. Garcia Lorca, F. 3383
Petite Bête, La. Roncoroni, J.-L. 7684
Petite Cuiller, La. Louki, P. 5058
Petite Datcha. Chkvarkine, V. 1812
Petite Hutte, La. Roussin, A. 7757
Petite Molière, La. Anouilh, J. and R. Laudenbach 282
Petite Suite Poetique Resolument Optimiste. Obaldia, R. de 6732
Petites Têtes, Les. Regnier, M. 7466
Petits Bourgeois, Les. Gorky, M. 3649
Petr Vok Rozmberk. Subert, F. A. 8599
Petrescu Is My Name. Naghiu, I. 6431
Petrified Forest, The. Sherwood, R. 8257
Petrified Prince, The. Miller, H. L. 5978
Petrus. Achard, M. 37

Petticoat Brigade, The. Schmitt, G. 8057
Petticoat Revolution, The. Boiko, C. 1108
Peu de Tendresse, Un. Novac, A. 6700
Pezzenti in paradiso. Martens, G. M. and A. Obey 5623
Phaedra. Rexroth, K. 7499
Phantasms. Bracco, R. 1257
Phantoms. Waddel, S. 9179
Pharaoh's Daughter. Kotzebue, A. von 4697
Phedre. Racine, J. 7378
Philanthropist, The. Hampton, C. 3881
Phillip Hotz's Fury. Frisch, M. 3319, 3320
Philoktet. Müller, H. 6191
Philosopher, The. Ashbery, J. 417
Philosopher in Grain: Michael Faraday. Hughes, R. 4313
Philosopher of Butterbiggins, The. Chapin, H. 1719
Philosophers. Colman, M. 1943
Philosopher's Stone, The. Artaud, A. 382
Phi-Phi. Willemetz, A. and F. Sollar 9406
Phoenices. Cahoon, H. 1488
Phoenix Too Frequent, A. Fry, C. 3332, 3333
Phryne. Ransan, A. 7408
Physiker, Die. Durrenmatt, F. 2748
Piacere di dirsi addio, Il. Rènard, J. 7484, 7485
Piacevole menzogna, La. Molnar, F. 6154
Pianissimo. Kreymborg, A. 4717
Pianista sentimentale, Il. Mencken, H. L. 5744
Piatto d'argento, Il. Ronco, M. 7681
Piazza Parleys. Loomis, C. B. 5033
Piccola. Bennett, R. 803
Piccola felicità, La. Adami, G. 55
Piccole commedie, Le. Testoni, A. 8777
Pick-Up Girl. Shelley, E. 8235
Pickwick Papers, The. Dickens, C. 2481
Picnic. Inge, W. 4378, 4379
Picnic on the Battlefield. Arrabal, F. 374
Pied Piper. Towles, L. R. 8907
Pied Piper of Hamelin. Browning, R. 1376, 1377, 1378
Pied Piper of Hamelin. Kennedy, L. 4594
Pied Piper's Land. Norcross, E. B. 6688
Piege Pour un Homme Seul. Thomas, R. 8838
Pierre ou Jack...? Croisset, F. de 2112
Pierre Patelin. Koon, H. 4685
Pierrot by the Light of the Moon. Church, V. 1832
Pieta de novembre, La. Brusati, F. 1391
Pig Prince. Garnett, L. A. 3395
Pigeon. McKnight, R. W. 5236
Piggy Bank Helps Uncle Sam, The. Vosatka, H. 9172
Pigrizia. Lopez, S. and E. Possenti 5039
Pile et Face. Costine, J. 2054
Pile ou Face. Verneuil, L. 9098
Pilgrim. Messager, C. 5790
Pilgrim Painting, The. Rawls, J. 7444
Pilgrim Parting. Miller, H. L. 5979
Pilgrim Rebel, The. Hall, M. 3857
Pilgrim Spirit, The. MacLellan, E. and C. V. Schroll 5256
Pilgrim Who Didn't Care, The. Miller, H. L. 5980
Pilgrims and Pebbles. MacLellan, E. and C. V. Schroll 5257
Pilot Lights of the Apocalypse. Ridenour, L. N. 7572
Pinata. MacLellan, E. and C. V. Schroll 5258
Pinch-Hitter, The. Paradis, M. B. 6962
Pinedus Affair, The. Levi, P. 4958
Ping-Pong, Le. Adamov, A. 65
Pink Parasol, The. Miller, H. L. 5982
Pink Roses for Christmas. Campbell, J. E. 1543
Pinkie and the Robins. Lehman, J. F. 4898
Pinocchio. Lorenzini, C. 5055
Pinocchio and Friends. Cheatham, V. R. 1756
Pinocchio Goes to School. Lorenzini, C. 5056

Pinocchio Strikes It Rich. Crichton, M. 2105
Pinter's Main Course. Clark, A. 1846
Pin-Up Pals. Miller, H. L. 5981
Pioggia, stato d'animo. Fersen, A. 3002
Piove sulla libertà. Mazzucco, R. 5720
Pip Visits Miss Havisham. Thane, A. 8811
Pipe in the Fields, The. Murray, T. C. 6409
Pique-Nique en Ville. Tervagne, C. de 8775
Pirates of Penzance, The. Gilbert, W. S. and A. S. Sullivan. 3518
Pistol of the Beg, The. Capek, K. M. 1577
Pistola a tamburo, La. Jona, A. 4497
Pit, The. Hartweg, N. L. 3955
Pittore di ventagli, Il. Alvarez Quintero, S. and J. Alvarez Quintero 169
Pittore esigente, Il. Bernard, T. 846
Pittura su legno. Bergmen, I. 817
Pity on the Wapentake. Nelson, R. 6461
Piu bella avventura, La. Faraci, G. 2929
Piu cari affetti, I. Buridan, G. 1423
Pixie in a Trap. Bennett, R. 790
Pixy Jester's Joke, The. Howard, H. L. 4209
Place in the Family, A. Thane, A. 8791
Place in the Sun. Hansberry, L. 3899, 3900
Placing a Play. Mawson, H. P. 5696
Plagiarized. Parlakian, N. 6981
Plague, The. Hansenclever, W. 3958
Plain and Fancy. Stein, J. and W. Glickman 8490
Plainte Contre Inconnu. Neveux, G. 6476, 6477
Plan C. Iannelli, R. A. 4358
Plancher des Vaches. Sarment, J. 7940
Planet Parade. Thornton, J. F. 8852

Plant in the Sun. Bengal, B. 764
Planting Time. Very, A. 9121
Play. Beckett, S. 708, 709
Play, A. Marlowe, A. 5563
Play About Somebody Who Just Wanted Something to Happen to Him, A. Litvack, B. 5003
Play for Christmas Eve, A. Duff, A. 2674
Play, Life, Illusion. Schawinsky, X. 8019
Play Without a Name, A. Fisher, A. 3067
Playboy of the Western World. Synge, J. M. 8671, 8672, 8673
Player Queen. Yeats, W. B. 9603, 9604
Players' Dressing-Room, The. Dukes, A. 2683
Playground. Broughton, J. 1353
Play's the Thing, The. Molnar, F. 6155
"Play's the Thing, The." Reyher, F. 7501
Playwright and the Public. Saroyan, W. 7949
Pleasant Dreams. McQueen, M. H. and N. McQueen 5378
Please, No Flowers. Ensana, J. A. 2868
Pleasure of His Company, The. Taylor, S. and C. O. Skinner 8734, 8735
Pleasures of Poverty, The. Blouet, P. 1017
Pleut Bergère, Il. Musso, L. 6421
Plight of Farmer Jones, The. Tennen, S. 8743
Plot in the Palace, The. Watson, R. 9221
Plot Thickens, The. Fisher, A. 3068
Plot to Overthrow Christmas, The. Corwin, N. 2050
Plouft, Le Petit Fantome. Machado, M. C. 5211
Plough and the Stars, The. O'Casey, S. 6757, 6758
Plugged In. McGrath, J. 5208
Plugged in to History. McGrath, J. 5208
Plum Blossom and the Dragon. Newman, D. 6414
Plumes. Johnson, G. D. 4485
Plus Heureux des Trois, Le. Labiche, E. 4748
Plus Saisi des Trois, Le. Richter, C. de 7570

Po' d'amore, Un. Saviotti, G. 7997
Po' di bufera.... Artu', Galar, E. 390
Poacher, The. Francis, J. O. 3248
Poco per bene. Sturges, P. 8592
Podivne odpoledne dr. Zvonka Burkeho. Smocek, L. 8357
Poet and the Emperor. Aspenstrom, W. 424
Poeti servono a qualche cosa, I. Manzari, N. 5513
Poetic Licenses. 7223
Poetic Situation in America Since Alexandre Dumas and Several Others, The. Saroyan, W. Three Entertainments. 7958
Poetry Recital, The. Abel, L. 9
Poet's Day, A. Ribemont-Dessaignes, G. 7506
Poet's Heart. Bodenheim, M. 1038
Poet's Nightmare. Hoppenstedt, E. M. 4166
Poet's Wife, A. Harris, M. 3929
Poichè io l'amo. Junichiro, T. 4527
Point H. Jamiaque, Y. 4441
Point of No Return. Osborn, P. 6889
Pointed Stick, The. Devin, L. 2389
Poison. Ruth, L. 7809
Poison. Vitrac, R. 9160
Poison Ivy. DuBois, G. 2647
Poisons. Parnac, J.-M. 6983
Poissons d'Or, Les. Aubert, R. 437
Poissons Rouges, ou Mon Père ce Héros, Les. Anouilh, J. 272
Policjy. Mrozek, S. 6285
Politics of Passion. Callaghan, B. 1507
Polka Dot Pup, The. Miller, H. L. 5983
Pollution. Tholy, R. 8820
Poltrona di teatro, La. Ridenti, L. 7573
Polydora. Gillois, A. 3537
Pomegranate Seed. Wharton, E. 9314
Pommes Pour Eve, Des. Aroutcheff, G. 368

Pomo di paride, Il. Pettinato, C. 7114
Pompadour's Protege, The. Vermilye, K. J. 9086
Pom-Pom. Munro, H. W. 6300
Poof. Salacrou, A. 7878
Poof. Saluron, A. 7894
Poof! Schoenewolf, G. 8078
Pool of Bethesda, The. Hagedorn, H. 3817
Poor Fool. Bahr, H. 499
Poor General Prescott. Hackett, W. 3804
Poor House, The. Driscoll, L. 2609
Poor John. Martinez Sierra, G. 5630
Poor Man's Clever Daughter, The. Feather, J. 2959
Poor Oliver. Rulkotter, F. 7794
Poor Relation, The. Barlach, E. 604
Poor Wives, Lazy Husbands. Blumenfeld, L. 1026
Poorhouse, The. Hyde, D. 4353
Pope's Right Knee, The. Bagg, R. 490
Popopeeka. Vail, L. 8988
Pop-Up Books, The. Spamer, C. 8427
Porcelain and Pink. Fitzgerald, F. S. 3135
Porgy. Heyward, D. and D. Heyward 4091a
Port Royal. De Montherlant, H. 6191
Porta della fortuna, La. Mor, E. 6208
Portal, The. Mierow, H. E. 5825
Porte des Lilas. Chomette, R. 1815
Porte di giada, Le. Franzero, C. M. 3272
Portes Claquent, Les. Fermaud, M. 2996
Portrait, The. Wormser, F. R. 9566
Portrait de Famille. Gilson, P. and N. Frank 3548
Portrait of a Pioneer. Lamb, A. C. 4773
Portrait of an American. McQueen, M. H. and N. McQueen 5379
Portrait of the Artist's Wife. Hartley, R. E. 3948
Portrait of Tiero, The. Akins, Z. 92
Portrait Sur les Bras, Un. Dominquez, F. 2526

Posies for the Potentate. Swintz, M. 8652
Posing of Vivette, The. Taylor, J. R. 8720
Position, The. Ballesteros, A. M. 537
Post Office, The. Tagore, R. 8687
Posteri, I. Dursi, M. 2758
Posterite, La. Ransan, A. 7409
Posticino molto tranquillo, Un. Reinach, M. 7469
Post-Mortem. Matilla, L. 5655
Pot Luck. Arthur, K. 384
Pot Maker, The. Bonner, M. 1189
Pot of Broth, The. Yeats, W. B. 9605
Pot of Gold, The. Spamer, C. 8428
Pot of Gold for Mother. Asbrand, K. 407
Pot pourri. Freeman, B. 3290
Pottery Lane. Asbrand, K. 408
Potting Shed, The. Greene, G. 3715a
Pour Etre Joue. Wissant, G. de 9508
Pour Finalie. Billetdoux, F. 933
Pourquoi la Rob d'Anna ne vent pas Redescendre. Eyen, T. 2893
Pourquoi Pas Moi? Salacrou, A. 7879
Poveri davanti a Dio. Viola, C. G. 9153
Povero Piero. Campanile, A. 1533
Povero ragazzo, Un. De Filippo, P. 2276
Power and the Glory, The. Greene, G. 3716
Power of Flattery, The. Clarke, V. 1860
Power of Love. Ilf, I. and E. Petrov 4368
Power Without Glory. Hutton, M. C. 4341
Pozzo die miracoli, Il. Corradini, B. and G. Achille 2031
Pragmatisti, I. Witkiewicz, S. I. 9519
Pragmatists, The. Witkiewicz, S. I. 9520
Pranziamo assieme. De Filippo, P. 2277
Prayer-Meeting, The. Green, P. 3707
Prearranged Accident, A. Lee, A. 4875
Precedent in Pastries, A. Rowland, E. 7771
Preda, La. Havas, N. 3979
Prelimbo. Priest, P. 7288
Prelude. Oppenheim, J. 6872
Preludio per una vita galante. Minervini, R. 6072
Premier Amour. Josset, A. 4521
Premier Jeudi. Marniere, J. 5566
Premier Jour, Le. Lem, A. 4907
"Première," Una. Fischer, M. and A. Fischer. 3034
Prenez Garde a la Peinture. Fauchois, R. 2942
Pré-Papa. Gomez-Arcos, A. 3619
Pre-Paradise Sorrow Now. Fassbinder, R. W. 2938
Preparation, The. Dow, H. 2570
Prepare the Way of the Lord. Corneilson, E. N. 2022
Presa al laccio! Madis, A. 5423
Presca notturna. Grella, E. 3736
Prescription for Success. Richmond, S. S. 7565
Present from Abe, A. Newman, D. 6515
Present Laughter. Coward, N. 2071, 2072
Preservatives. Blake, G. 989a
President Houdecoeur, Le. Roger-Ferdinand. 7649
President Lincoln's Children. Very, A. 9122
President Lincoln's Shawl Pin. Robinson, G. 7620
President of the Holding Company, The. Niedecker, L. 6593
President's Bride, The. Malone, A. 5482
Presidents on Parade. Boiko, C. 1109
Presso i cani. Savoir, A. 8001
Prestige Male, Le. Costine, J. 2055
Prestigiazione. Cami. 1521
Pretendento. Bernard, T. 847
Pretez-moi Votre Fils. Dumas, R.-L. 2692
Pretore di minimis, Il. Giannini, G. 3488
Pretties (All Her Life). Calhoun, D. D. 1506
Pretty Sabine Women, The. Andreyev, L. N. 237

Preuve par Quatre, La. Carette, L. 1604, 1605
Previous Engagement. Howells, W. D. 4256
Price of Eggs, The. Nicholson, M. A. 6572
Price of Love, The. Rouveyrol, A. 7764
Price of Orchids, The. Hawkridge, W. 3986
Price We Pay, The. 7287
Pride and Prejudice. Austen, J. 458, 459
Prigioniera, La. Bourdet, E. 1236
Prima comunion. Arrabal, F. 375
Prima pagare, e poi.... Donnay, M. 2542
Primary Day. Oliver, V. 6824
Primavera. Pedder, D. C. 7034
Primavera di San Martino. Coward, N. 2073
Primavera sulla neve. Romualdi, G. 7676
Primitif, Le. Rosselson, L. 7711
Primo amante, Il. Amiel, D. 188
Primo amore. Josset, A. 4522
Primo amore, Il. Vergani, O. 9080
Primo peccato, Il. Gotta, S. 3659
Primo premio all'amore. Di Luca, D. 2500
Primrose Lane. Meigs, C. L. 5734
Prince and the Pauper, The. Clemens, S. L. 1886, 1887, 1888, 1889
Prince and the Peddlers, The. Bennett, R. 791
Prince Charmant. Bernard, T. 848
Prince Charming's Fate. Lovell, C. C. 5062
Prince d'Egypte, Le. Fry, C. 3334
Prince Ilan. Burke, K. 1424
Prince Is Where You Find Him, A. Chisholm, J. R. 1806
Prince of Semberia, The. Nooshich, B. 6687
Prince Rama. Wither, B. 9500
Prince, the Wolf, and the Firebird, The. Lacey, J. 4757
Prince Who Learned Everything

Out of Books, The. Benavente y Martinez 746
Princely Fortune, Three Chinese Folk-Dramas.... 8855
Princess Aline, The. Smith, S. D., Jr. 8354
Princess and the Crystal Pipe, The. Folmsbee, B. 3196
Princess and the Dragon, The. Wolfys, N. 9536
Princess and the Greenies, The. Kane, E. B. 4541
Princess and the Herd Boy, The. Boiko, C. 1110
Princess and the Pea, The. Andersen, H. C. 198, 199
Princess and the Rose-Colored Glasses, The. McQueen, M. H. and N. McQueen 5380
Princess' Choice, The. Rabe, M. 7373
Princess from Norway, The. MacLellan, E. and C. V. Schroll 5259
Princess Lonely Heart. Miller, H. L. 5984
Princess Nimble-Wit. Nicholson, M. A. 6573
Princess of Hearts. McQueen, M. H. and N. McQueen 5381
Princess Pampelishka, The. Kvapil, J. 4742
Princess Too Little, A. Nicholson, M. A. 6574
Princess Weaver of the Skies. Kaplan, Y. D. 4548
Princess Who Was Hidden from the World. Winther, B. African Trio 9478
Princess with the Broken Heart, The. Keenan, M. 4574
Princesse Lointaine. Rostand, E. 7718
Princesse Turandot, La. Sates, C. and A. Lion. 7977
Printemps. Marcelle-Maurette 5534
Printemps Perdus. Vandenberghe, P. 9019
Printer in Queen Street, The. Mayr, G. A. 5707
Printer's Devil. Dias, E. J. 2439
Prisma, Il. Raggio, E. 7387
Prison, La. Golea, A. 3615
Prisoner. Ross, C. 7702
Prisoner, The. Woodford, B. P. 9545
Prisoner of Zenda, The. Hope, A. 4161

Prisoners. Atkins, C. L. 430
Private Jim Crow. Hughes, L. 4305
Private Life of Helen of Troy, The. Roussin, A. and M. Gray 7763
Private Lives. Coward, N. 2074
Privilege and Privation. Kreymborg, A. 4718
Privilegio dell'amicizio, Il. Ferdinand, R. 2988
Prize Shamrock, The. Newman, D. 6516
Problema del quarto atto, Il. Conti, A. 1987
Procès à Jesus. Fabbri, D. 2899
Procès et L'Execution de Ravaillac. Arnaud, R. 170
Processo, Il. Gide, A. and J. -L. Barrault 3506
Processo a Gesú. Fabbri, D. 2900
Processo a Giovanna. Pandolfi, V. 4648
Processo agli innocenti. Terron, C. 8762
Processo crainquebille, Il. France, A. 3246
Processo di famiglia. Fabbri, D. 2901
Prodigal, The. Feldhaus-Weber, M. 2978
Prodigal Doll. Rusinol y Prats, S. 7799
Prodigal Son, The. Holck, T. M. 4139
Prodigal Son, The. Kemp, H. 4586
Prodigies, The. Vauthier, J. 9049
Profanateur, Le. Talagrand, J. 8696
Professeur. Duvernois, H. 2789
Professional Attitude, The. Males, U. H. 5471
Professor Countdown Takes Off. Bradley, P. L. 1264
Professor Hobo. Huff, B. T. 4291
Professor Mamlock. Wolf, F. 9527
Professor Snaffle's Polypon. Mandel, O. 5494
Professor Taranne. Adamov, A. 66
Professor Willy's Wisher-Switcher.

Oser, J. A. 6903
Profumo delle magnolie, Il. Lanza, G. 4809
Profumo di mia moglie, Il. Lenz, L. 4919
Progress of Mrs. Alexander. Stanwood, L. R. 8473
Projectionist, The. Guyan, A. 3793
Prologue. Glick, C. 3584
Prologue. Hofmannsthal, H. von 4135
Prologue, A. Waddell, S. 9180
Prologue to Balloon. Colum, P. 1957
Prologue to Brecht's Baal. Hofmannsthal, H. von 4136
Promesse, La. Ryner, H. 7831
Prometheus. Talarico, E. 8699
Prometheus Bound. Aeschylus. 78, 79
Prometheus Found. Hitchcock, G. 4116, 4117
Prometheus Rebound. Wunderlich, L. 9578
Promise, The. Arbusov, A. N. 316
Propos de la Champmesle, A. Gaillard, R. 3345
Proposal, The. Chekhov, A. 1774
Proposal, A. Duncan, G. 2700
Proposal of Marriage, A. Chekhov, A. 1775, 1776
Proposal Under Difficulties, A. Bangs, J. K. 546
Protagonist. Kaiser, G. 4533
Proteo. Claudel, P. 1869
Proteus. Claudel, P. 1870
Proverbs in Porcelain. Dobson, H. A. 2512
Provetta, La. Birabeau, A. 956
Provincia. Adami, G. 56
Prozess der Jeanne D'Arc zu Rouen, Der. Brecht, B. 1305
Prozess um des Esels Schatten, Der. Dürrenmatt, F. 2749
Prune et la Prunelle. Marcel, G. 5531
Psychiatrie. Sabatier, P. 7837
P'tit Tailleur, Le. Arnold, P. 355
Public Eye. Shaffer, P. 8171
Public Gardens. Marinetti, F. T. and F. Cangiullo. 5549
Publicity. Harris, L. 3927
Publisher's Choice. Murray, J. 6381
Puce a l'Oreille, La. Feydeau, G. 3009

Pucelle. Audiberti, J. 448
Puck's Pranks. Clarke, M. C. 1858
Pudore. Manzari, N. 5514
Pulce, La. Zamjatin, E. I. 9632
Pumpkin, The. Dunsany, E. J. M. D. P. 2723
Pumpkin Giant, The. Freeman, M. E. W. 3293
Pumpkineaters' Pumpkin, The. Newman, D. 6517
Punch and Judy. Leech, M. T. 4889
Punctuation Proclamation, The. Boiko, C. 1111
Puppenspiel. Jung, F. 4526
Puppets, The. Solorzano, C. 8371
Puppy Love. Miller, H. L. 5985
Purloined. Casper, L. 1643
Purloined Portrait, The. Dias, E. J. 2440
Purple Cobwebs. Crane, F. D. 2094
Purple Path to the Poppy Field Meldon, M. 5740
Puss-in-Boots. 7346
Puss-in-Boots. Elfenbein, J. A. 2842
Puss in Boots. Perrault, C. 7071, 7072
Pussy Pleases. Spamer, C. 8429
Putain Respectueuse, La. Sartre, J.-P. 7965
Putting Pop in His Place. McQueen, M. H. and N. McQueen 5382
Putty Club, The. Molnar, F. 6156
Pygmalion. Shaw, G. B. 8216
Pygmalion Tries Again. Nolan, P. T. 6662
Pyrrhic Victory. 7356

Q

Quadrature du Cercle, La. Kataiev, V. 4553
Quadretto di Don Cristobal. Garcia Lorca, F. 3384
Quadrille. Coward, N. 2075
Qualcosa comunque. Martini, D. G. 5634
Qualcuno. Molnar, F. 6157
Qualcuno al cancello. D'Errico, E. 2353

Quale onore! De Filippo, P. 2278
Quality of Mercy 7358
Quality Street. Barrie, Sir J. M. 627
Qualm, The. Henderson, K. and G. Whitworth 4055
Quando l'amore brucia. Alvarez Quintero, S. and J. Alvarez Quintero 170
Quare Fellow, The. Behan, B. 727
Quarreling Pair, A. Bowles, J. 1244
Quarta parete, La. Bonelli, L. 1184
Quartetto per corni. Salsa, C. 7887
Quarto arriva, Il. Luzi, G. F. 5099
4 Pieces sur Jardin. Barillet, P. and J.-P. Gredy 592
Quatre Saisons, Les. Wesker, A. 9305
Quatre Verites, Les. Ayme, M. 473, 474
Quatres Petites Filles, Les. Picasso, P. 7145
Quatrieme. Piechaud, M. 7148
Quattr'occhi, A. Lakatos, L. 4771
Quattro di cuori. Vanni, A. 9039
Quattro donne. Mouloudji, M. 6275
Quattro Giovani sonore. Cajoli, V. 1498
Quay of Magic Things, The. Mosher, J. C. 6262
Que Ferez-Vous en Novembre? Ehni, R. 2826, 2827
Queen Jezebel. Squires, E. L. 8465
Queen of Sew-and-Sew, The. Morse, C. 6240
Queen of Sheba, The. Young, S. 9621
Queen with the Broken Heart, The. Urban, C. 8974
Queenes Majesties Entertainment. 7361
Queen's Christmas Cake, The. Watts, F. B. 9241
Queen's Crags, The. Gibson, W. W. 3501
Queen's Enemies, The. Dunsany, E. J. M. D. P. 2724, 2725
Queen's Hour, The. McCauley, C. V. 5128
Queen's Mirror, The. Slattery, M. E. 8317

Queens of France. Wilder, T. 9400, 9401
Quell'angelo azzurro che si chiama TV. Simongini, Fr. and M. Costanzo. 8297
Quella che attendevo. Bernard, T. 849
Quella che passa. Chabannes, J. 1701
Quella vecchia canaglia.... Nozière, F. 6704
Quelle che prendiamo tra le braccia. De Montherlant, H. 6192
Quelle oneste signore. Duse, E. 2770
Quello che ci voleva. Della Pura, E. 2305
Quentin Durward. Scott, Sir W. 8114
Quest for an Ancester, The. Chalmers, R. M. 1704
Questa o quella. Lopez, S. 5038
Questa sera o mai. Hatvany, L. 3962
Questa sera si recita a soggetto. Pirandello, L. 7199
Questi fantasmi. De Filippo, E. 2261
Questi nostri figli. Crivelli, F. M. 2108
Questi poveri amanti. Tieri, V. 8864
Questi ragazzi. Gherardi, G. 3470
Question of Morality, A. Wilde, P. 9381
Question of Understanding, A. O'Connell, T. E. 6763
Questione Russa, La. Simonov, K. 8299
Questions. Sax, C. and M. Christie 8003
Questo Danaro. Massa, M. 5645
Questo non è l'amore. Cantini, G. 1574
Qui si insegna a rubare. Pirandello, L. 7200
Quick-Witted Jack. Feather, J. 2965
Quiet Christmas, A. McQueen, M. H. and N. McQueen 5383
Quiet Evening, A. Torcross, J. 8891
Quinte dell'anima, Le. Evreinov, N. N. 2889
Quintila. Jolly, A. 4495
Quite Private. Goodale, Mrs. D. H. R. 3624
Quits. Jenks, T. 4454
Quitting Business. Larra, M. J. de 4821
Quiz Biz. Murray, J. 6382
Quoat-Quoat. Audiberti, J. 449, 450, 451

R

R. U. R. Capek, K. M. 1578
Rabbia nel cuore, La. Vandenberghe, P. 9020
Rabbit Who Refused to Run, The. Miller, H. L. 5986
Rabbit-Hutch, The. Sterling, G. 8504
Rabbit's Foot. Miller, H. L. 5987
Rabbits, Rabbits, Rabbits. Newman, D. 6518
Rabbits Who Changed Their Minds, The. Miller, H. L. 5988
Rabouilleuse. Fabre, E. 2907
Race Errante. Porche, F. 7245
Races. Bruckner, F. 1382
Racketty-Packetty House. Burnett, F. H. 1441
Radiance and Death of Joaquin Murieta. Neruda, P. 6464
Radio Felicity. Kimmel, H. B. 4628
Radio-Intermezzo per Microfono. Solari, P. 8364
Raduz and Mahulena. Zeyer, J. 9646
Raffaele. Brancati, V. 1271
Raft of the Medusa, The. Kaiser, G. 4534
Rag Doll, A. Lent, E. M. 4918
Ragazza al balcone, La. Anton, E. 293
Ragazza del porto, La. Molnar, F. 6158
Ragazza di stoccolma, La. Leto, A. 4939
Ragazza e i soldanti, La. Pugnetti, G. 7335
Ragazze bruciateverdi, Le. Callegari, G. P. 1511
Ragazze Tunderlak, Le. Heltai, E. 4050
Ragazzi mangiano i fiori, I. Bassano, E. 653
Ragazzi miei. Conti, A. 1988
Ragazzi se ne vanno, I. Manzari, N. 5515
Raid on the White Tiger Regiment. 7393

Railway Tragedy--Perhaps. Hubert, P. G., Jr. 4268
Rain. Burnett, D. 1438
Rain and Rebellion. DuBois, G. 2648
Rainbow. Jackson, P. M. 4418
Rainbow Colors. McQueen, M. H. and N. McQueen 5384
Rainbow Palace. Slattery, M. E. 8318
Rainbow Walkers, The. Collins, E. F. 1939
Rainmaker, The. Nash, N. R. 6437, 6438
Raisin in the Sun, A. Hansberry, L. 3899, 3900
Raison des Autres, La. Pirandello, L. 7201
Ramon and the Artist. Raborg, F. A., Jr. 7377
Ramoscello d'olivo, Il. De Filippo, P. 2279
Rancore. Fabbri, D. 2902
Ransom, The. Radford, D. 7379
Rapaci, I. Giannini, G. 3489
Rape of the Belt, The. Levy, B. W. 4970
Raphael ... Fais Tourner le Monde. Jaquine, J. 4446
Rapport Dont Vous Etes l'Object, Le. Havel, V. 3981
Rapunzel. Barr, J. 621
Rapunzel. Brody, A. 1336
Rapunzel. Thane, A. 8812
Rastifarian, The. White, E. 9325
Rats. Fruchter, M. J. 3328
Rattenfänger bei den Schildbürgen, Der. Stübs, A. 8590
Raven's First Flight, The. Schmitt, G. L. 8052
Ravissement de Scapin, Le. Claudel, P. 1871, 1872
Re jazz, Il. Elton, R. 2858
Reaching for the Moon. 7448
Real April Fool's Day, A. Phillips, M. K. 7134
Real Old English Christmas, A. Boiko, C. 1112
Real Princess, The. Anderson, H. C. 200
Real "Q," The. Terrell, M. and H. O. Stechhan. 8748
Real Thing, The. Bangs, J. K. 547
Really, My Dear. Morley, C. 6226
Really Rural. Murray, J. 6383

Reason, The. Middleton, G. 5818
Reason. Wilson, S. 9468
Rebecca. Du Maurier, D. 2693
Rebellion of Women, The. McClure, J. 5134
Rebellious Robots, The. Newman, D. 6519
Rebezahl, Scenes de Don Juan. Lubicz-Milosz, O. V. de 5073
Rebirth in Barrows Inlet. Liss, J. 4999
Rebrousse-Poil. Roncoroni, J.-L. 7685
Rechtsfindung 1934. Brecht, B. 1306
Recipe for Rain. Huff, B. T. 4292
Reclining Figure. Kurnitz, H. 4739
Reconciliation, The. Hauptmann, G. 3974
Reconsiderations: The Murderer; The Derelict. Ross, C. 7703
Records Show, The. Schmitt, G. L. 8053
Red Carpet Christmas. Miller, H. L. 5989
Red Flannel Suit, The. Miller, H. L. 5990
Red Lantern, The. Wong Ou-hung and Ah Chia. 9540
Red Man's Call. MacArdle, D. 5112
Red Riding Hood and Friends. Cheatham, V. R. 1757
Red Riding Hood and the Wolf. Nutter, C. F. 6708
Red, the Pink, and the True Blue, The. Miller, P. V. 6057
Red Velvet Goat. Niggli, J. 6594
Red, White and Blue. Cain, J. M. 1494
Redentin Easter Play. 7455
Reel Life, Inc. Boiko, C. 1113
Reference, The. Firkins, O. W. 3030
Reflexions. Lawson, W. 4862
Reform of Sterling Silverheart, The. Cable, H. 1478
Refrigeration, The. Fratti, M. 3281
Refrigerator, The. Quiles, E. 7366
Refuge. Petrova, O. 7113
Regali a Nelly. Gavi, V. 3426
Regardant Tomber les Murs. Foissy, G. 3188
Reggie the Ghost. Hall, M. 3850

Regina e gli insorti, La. Betti, U. 897
Regina morta, La. de Montherlant, H. 6193
Regina pomaré, La. Falena, U. 2924
Register. Howells, W. D. 4257
Registered Letter. Moineaux, G. 6108
Règlement de Comptes. Petresco, J. 7111
Regola del 3, La. Salsa, C. 7888
Rehearsal, The. Baring, M. 599
Rehearsal, The. Maltz, A. 5486
Reicen. Schnitzler, A. 8076
Reindeer on the Roof. McQueen, M. H. and N. McQueen 5385
Reine Blanche, La. Barillet, P. and J.-P. Gredy 593
Reine de Cesaree, La. Brasillach, R. 1272
Reine et le Sorcier. Gaillard, R. 3346
Reine Faustine, La. François, R. 3257
Reine sans Repos, La. Arauz, A. 312
Rejected. Warren, R. 9214
Relative Values. Coward, N. 2076
Relatively Speaking. Ayckbourn, A. 467
Release. Hull, H. R. 4321
Relief. Seiler, C. 8143
Reliques, Les. De Richaud, A. 2343
Reluctant Columbus, The. Cable, H. 1479
Reluctant Debutante, The. Home, W. D. 4152a
Reluctant Dragon, The. Grahame, K. 3682, 3683
Reluctant Ghost, The. Brydon, M. W. and E. Zeigler 1397
Remarkable Mr. Pennypacker, The. O'Brien, L. 6748, 6749
Remède de Cheval, Un! Sands, L. 7907
Removal of the Academy, The. Cahoon, H. Three Verse Plays. 1489
Renaissance. Drachmann, H. H. H. 2584
Renaissance, The. Gobineau, J. A., Count de 3588
Rencontre, La. Rit, G. 7590
Rent in the Universe, A. States, B. D. 8475
Reparto scandali. Molnar, F. 6159
Repetition Generale, Une. Vandenberghe, P. 9021
Repetition, ou L'Amour Puni, La. Anouilh, J. 273
Replacement, The. Elliott, W. D. 2856
Representation of the Holy Ghost, The. 7495
Reprise. Wheatcroft, J. 9315
Reprouvee. Ransan, A. 7410
Requiem for a Nun. Faulkner, W. 2943, 2944
Requiem for Five Runs, with One Eye on William Faulkner's Latest Novel and the Other on the World Series. Gwynn, F. L. 3794
Resa di Titi, La. De Benedetti, A. and G. Zorzi 2231
Resemblance, The. Pollock, A. L. and A. W. Brantzell 7231
Reservations. Halpern, M. 3871
Resident of Nowhere. Curnow, A. 2150
Resolution of Mossie Wax. Foreman, S. H. 3221
Respectful Prostitute, The. Sartre, J.-P. 7966
Respective Virtues of Héloise and Maggie, The. Bartlett, R. 642
Responsabilité Limitée. Hosseinoff, R. 4179
Rest for Mr. Winkle, A. Howard, V. 4225
Restaurant, Au. Barrier, M. 634
Restituitemi mio marito. Molnar, F. 6160
Restoration of Arnold Middleton, The. Story, D. 8539
Resurrection. Corkery, D. 2019
Resurrection Ezra. Mitchell, R. E. 6085
Resurrezione di Cristo. 7496
Retable des Merveilles, Le. Cervantes Saavedra, M. de 1695, 1696
Reticent Convict, The. Firkins, O. W. 3031
Retour de Jerusalem, Le. Donnay, C. M. 2543
Retour de l'Ille d'Elbe. Arnaud, R. 170
Retour de Lumière, Le. Didier, P. 2490
Retours Imprevus, Les. See, E. 8132
Return, The. Morgan, E. J. 6217

Return of Bobby Shafto, The. Miller, H. L. 5991
Return of Columbus. Very, A. 9123
Return of Harlequin. Clements, C. C. 977
Return of Proserpine, The. Frank, F. K. 3262
Return of the Nina. MacLellan, E. and C. V. Schroll 5260
Return Trip, The. Douglas, F. 2568
Returning to the Capital. Howard, R. Three Short Plays 4218
Reuccio malinconico, Il. Veneziani, C. 9070
Reunion in Vienna. Sherwood, R. E. 8258
"Revanche"--A Mystery. Rubinstein, H. F. 7779
Reve de L'Infante, Le. Mercier, M. 5762
Revelation. Bernard, T. 853
Revelation, La. Clot, R. -J. 1906
Revellers. Housman, L. 4192
Revizor, Le. Gogol, N. 3603
Revolt of Santa Claus, The. Clarke, E. P. 1856
Revolt of the Vegetables, The. Crichton, M. C. 2107
Revolte, La. Adam, V. de L'i 51
Revolte Dans les Asturies. Camus, A. 1554
"Revolutionary/Birth" Play, The. Allen, H. 138
Rex Helvetiorum. Lawler, L. B. 4845
Rhapsody in Blue 7504
Rhapsody in Blue. Hackett, W. 3805
Rheingold, Das. Wagner, R. 9183
Rhetoric and Rhymes. Heath, A. L. 4011
Rhinoceros. Ionesco, E. 4400
Rhubarb. Boiko, C. 1114
Rhyme in Times Saves Nine, A. Garrison, C. B. 3397
Riabilitazione, La. Arpino, G. 370
Ricatto a teatro, Il. Maraini, D. 5524
Ricevimento di gala. Rocca, G. 7638
Richard III. Shakespeare, W. 8188

Richard's Cork Leg. Behan, B. 728
Richiamo, Il. Giordana, G. P. 3553
Ricky and the Eggs. Ritchie, E. 7592
Ricordi. Heltai, J. 4052
Ride Across Lake Constance, The. Handke, P. 3885
Ride the Gooberville Stage! Huff, B. T. 4293
Ride Your Hobby. Fontaine, R. 3205
Riders to the Sea. Synge, J. M. 8674, 8675, 8676, 8677, 8678
Ridicolo, Il. Ferrari, P. 2998
Riding to Lithend. Bottomley, G. 1204
Rifiuto, Il. Fratti, M. 3282
Riflessi di conoscenza. Augias, C. 454
Right of Adoption. Miller, H. L. 5992
Rightful Heir, The. Lytton, E. B. 5106
Rimailho. Gilles, A. 3530
Ring on Her Finger. Hoffman, C. H. 4126
Ring Once for Central. Allensworth, C. 146
Rip Van Winkle. Irving, W. 4405, 4406, 4407
Rip's Wrinkle. Greth, R. 3739
Rising of the Moon, The. Gregory, Lady A. 3727
Riso verde. Terron, C. 8763
Rites. Duffy, M. 2675
Ritiro del divino amore. Minervini, R. 6073
Ritornero. Cangiullo, F. 1560
Ritorno, Il. Fratti, M. 3283
Ritorno, Il. Ribulsi, E. 7513
Ritorno del re. Giannini, G. 3490
Ritorno di Gorgia, Il. Lo Presti, C. 5041
Ritorno di solitudine. Bonora, A. L. 1190
Ritorno di Ulisse, Il. Lauwick, H. 4835
Ritorno di Ulisse. Solari, P. 8365
Ritratto d'attore. Williams, E. 9411
Ritual, The. Ibbitson, J. 4359
Rival for Dad, A. McQueen, M. H. and N. McQueen 5386
Rival of His Master. Lesage, A. -R. 4936
Rivals, The. Sheridan, R. B. 8245
Rivelazione, La. Bernard, T. 850
River in Spate. Rowley, R. 7773

Rivincita delle mogli, La. Valori, G. 9012
Rixe. Grumberg, J.-C. 3770
Rizal of the Philippines. Reines, B. L. 7475
Road, The. Soyinka, W. 8397
Road Ahead, The. Martens, A. C. 5610
Road Blocks to the Gospel. Lindquist, J. 4985
Road of Dreams. Harris, P. 3931
Road to Bethlehem, The. DuBois, G. 2649
Road to Connaught, The. Lord, D. A. 5050
Road to London, The. Elder, J. 2836
Road to Valley Forge. DuBois, G. 2650
Roamin' Jo and Juli, or How the West Was Lost. Boiko, C. 1115
Roaring All Day Long. Bentley, E. 809
Roaring March Lion, The. Streacker, L. 8559
Roaring Twenties in Whippoorwill Falls, The. Boiko, C. 1116
Robe de Soie. Charasson, H. 1725
Robe Mauve de Valentine. Quoirez, F. 7369
Robert Guiscard, Duke of the Normans. Kleist, H. von 4663
Robert Macaire. Neveux, G. 6478
Robin Hood and Friends. Cheatham, V. R. 1758
Robin Hood and the Gentle Knight. Morley, O. 6231
Robin Hood and the Match at Nottingham. Nolan, P. T. 6663
Robin Hood in Sherwood Forest. Colson, J. G. 1949
Robin Hood Outwits the Sheriff. Baher, C. W. 495
Robin Hood Tricks the Sheriff. Jacob, E. 4420
Robina in Search of a Husband. Jerome, J. K. 4467
Robinson, ou l'Amour Vient de Loin. Supervielle, J. 8620
Robinson, Venderdi e Domenica. Donati, P. L. 2530
Robots for Sale. Miller, J. V. 6053
Rock, The. Simon, S. 8287

Rock Garden, The. Shepard, S. 8239
Rocket to Freedom. Fisher, A. and O. Rabe 3114
Roddy's Candy Bar. Barr, J. 617
Roguish Tricks of Coviello, The 7655
Roi, Le. Caillavet, G.-A. de, R. de Flers and E. Arene 1490
Roi Borgne, Le. Spriaux, A. 8453
Roi de la fete, Le. Puget, C.-A. 7327
Roi des Cons, Le. Wolinski 9537
Roi, Deux Dames et un Valet. Porche, F. 7246
Roi Est Mort, Le. Ducreux, L. 2669, 2670
Roi Sans Couronne, Le. Bouhelier, S.-G. de 1214
Rollo il grande. Falconi, D. 2916
Roly-Poly Freckle-Face. McCarty, S. S. 5126
Roma. Palazzeschi, A. 6937
Romagnola. Squarzina, L. 8460
Roman Romance, A. Boiko, C. 1117
Romance for Jo March. Alcott, L. M. 113
Romancers. Rostand, E. 7719
Romanoff and Juliet. Ustinov, P. 8984, 8985
Romantic Ladies, The. Molière 6123
Romeo and Juliet. Shakespeare, W. 8189
Romeo and Juliet. Speare, D. 8438
Romeo and Juliet: The Servants. Brecht, B. 1307
Romulus. Durrenmatt, F. 2750, 2751
Romulus der Grosse. Durrenmatt, F. 2752
Ronny, Donny, and Susy. Howard, H. L. 4210
Room, The. Pedrolo, M. de 7038
Room for a King, A. DuBois, G. 2651
Room 226. Fagin, M. 2909
Room Without a Number, The. Davis, R. H. 2206
Rootabaga Processional. Sayers, F. C. 8004
Rope, The. O'Neill, E. 6861
Rope Dancers, The. Wishengrad, M. 9506
Ropes. Steele, W. D. 8485
Rosa dei venti, La. Antonelli, L. 304

Rosa di carta, La. Valle-Inclan, R. 9002
Rosa di Gerico, La. Bisson, A. 971
Rosa di zolfo, La. Aniante, A. 244
Rosa e il nero, Il. Bene, C. 753
Rosa e Rosina. Alvarez Quintero, S. and J. Alvarez Quintero 171
Rosalind. Barrie, Sir J. M. 628
Rosario. De Roberto, F. 2344
Roscoe the Robot. Martens, A. C. 5611
Rose and the Ring, The. Thackeray, W. M. 8781
Rose au Petit Dejeuner, Une. Barillet, P. and J.-P. Gredy 594
Rose de Jericho. Bisson, A. 972
Rose des Vents, La. Spaak, C. 8399
Rose Leaves and Asparagus Tips. Cowan, F. 2063
Rose of Persia, The. Howeis, L. 4234
Rose Tattoo, The. Williams, T. 9439
Rose Windows. Young, S. 9622
Rosemary for Remembrance. Martens, A. C. 5612
Rosenberg ne Doivent pas Mourir, Les. Decaux, A. 2236
Rosenhagens, The. Halbe, M. 3833
Roses for Johnny Johnson. Green, P. 3708
Roses for Mother. Newman, D. 6520
Ross. Rattigan, T. 7425
Rosso e nero. Marcellini, G. 5535
Rosso malpelo. Renard, J. 7486
Rosy-cheeked Ghost, The. Blaine, B. G. 989
Roti de Veau, Le. Kerautem, L. de 4601
Rouge! Duvernois, H. 2790
Roulette. Fodor, L. 3184
Rounding the Triangle. Quarella, D. 7359
Rowdy Kate. Boiko, C. 1118
Roxy. Conners, B. 1978
Royal Cloth of China, The. Adcock, I. F. 74

Royal Dog, The. Lynch, M. 5101
Royal Gambit. Gressieker, H. 3738
Royal Hunt of the Sun, The. Shaffer, P. 8172
Royal Magic. Slattery, M. E. 8319
Rozeno, Le. Traversi, C. A. 8922
Rubber. Burlingame, C. 1431
Rubber Heart, The. Malanga, G. 5467
Rubber Won't Stretch. 7778
Ruby Red. Stratton, C. 8557
Ruddigore. Gilbert, W. S. and Sir A. S. Sullivan. 3519
Rude Awakening. Sarment, J. 7941
Rudimentar. Stramm, A. 8548, 8549
Rue de Richelieu. Diez, B. 2495
Rufus Robin's Day in Court. Rybak, R. K. 7825
Rule Is a Rule, A. Moineaux, G. 6108
Rules of the Game, The. Pirandello, L. 7202
Ruling Class, The. Barnes, P. 609, 610
Ruling Class, The. Winter, M. 9477
Ruling Powers. Housman, L. 4193
Rummage for Victory. Miller, H. L. 5993
Rumpelstiltskin. Bennett, H. C. 774, 7795
Rumpelstiltskin. Mahlmann, L. 5450
Rumpelstiltskin. Thane, A. 8813
Rumpelstiltskin Revisited. Dewey, P. B. 2392
Runaway. Martens, A. C. 5613
Runaway Balloon, The. McMeekin, I. M. 5275
Runaway Bookmobile, The. Boiko, C. 1119
Runaway Genie, The. Watts, F. B. 9242
Runaway Pirate, The. Bennett, R. 792
Runaway Toys, The. Miller, H. L. 5994
Runaway Unicorn, The. Miller, H. L. 5995
Running the Country. Oser, J. A. 6904
Ruota. Lodovici, C. V. 5014

Rupture. Roussin, A. 7758
Rural Justice of the Peace, A.
    Pena, M. 7042
Rushlight, The. O'Shea, M. B.
    6908
Ruth and Boaz. Lutz, G. M.
    5095
Ruy Blas. Hugo, V. 4319

S

S. M. la Primattrice. Bodet,
    R. 1043
S. O. S. from Santa. Miller, H.
    L. 5996
S. O. S. isola felice. Chiarelli,
    U. and V. Curti 1801
Sabato, domenica e lunedi. De
    Filippo, E. 2262
Sabbie mobili. Conti, A. 1989
Sabotage. Hellem, C., W. Valcros, P. d'Estor. 4042
Sabotage. Thayer, J. A. 8816
Sabrina Fair. Taylor, S. 8733
Sacra rappresentazione, La.
    Pinelli, T. 7164
Sacramental melodrama. Jodorowsky, A. 4470
Sacred Cup, The. Daugherty, S.
    2190
Sacred Flame. Maugham, W. S.
    5676
Sacrifice. MacQueen, L. I. 5283
Sacrifice. Noblston, A. 6610
Sacrifice of Helen, The. Hildesheimer, W. 4105
Sacro esperimento. Hochwaelder, F. 4124
Sad Mistake, A. Masson, T.
    5648
Sadco. Pumphrey, B. 7340
Safe for Today. Wainwright, F.
    9184
Safety First. Bartlett, R. 643
Safety First, Safety Last, Safety
    Always. Larson, E. 4823
Safety Parade, The. Fisher, A.
    3069
Safety Pup, The. Pink, C. 7170
Saga, Une. Bergman, H. 814, 815
Saga of Davey Rocket, The.
    Tausheck, R. M. 8715
Saga of John Trueheart, The.
    Olfson, L. 6808
Sage of Monticello, The. Faier,
    J. S. 2911

Sail On! Sail On! Olfson, L.
    6809
Sailor's Wife. Vicente, G. 9138
Saint Euloge de Cordone. Clavel,
    B. 1875
Saint Joan. Shaw, G. B. 8217, 8218
Saint John and the Orphan. De
    Selincourt, H. 2358
Saint John's Fire. Sudermann, H.
    8604
St. Nicholas. Oldmeadow, K. L.
    6787
St. Patrick and the Last Snake in
    Ireland. Davis, L. R. 2204
St. Patrick Saves the Day. DuBois, G. 2652
St. Patrick's Day. Sheridan, R.
    B. 8246
St. Patrick's Eve. Campbell, J.
    E. 1544
Saint's Day. Whiting, J. 9332
Sait-on Jamais! Turpin, F. 8960
Sale Egoiste, Un. Dorin, F. 2553
Salesman, The. Richardson, P.
    7532
Salesman Ruptured by a Streetcar,
    The. Ashburn, W. D. 418
Salesmanship. Deming, D. 2328
Salle d'Attente. Praga, A. 7271
Sally Ann Remembers. Nothnagle,
    C. 6698
Salome. Wilde, O. 9372, 9373, 9374
Salome and the Head. Lutz, G.
    M. 5095
Salome's Head. Montellano, B. O.
    de 6180
Salotto della signora Bihàr, Il.
    Manzari, N. 5516
Salt for Savor. Wilde, P. 9382
Salt in the Sea, The. Colbert, M.
    1926
Salted Almonds. Guthrie, T. A.
    3790
Saltimbank. Heijermans, H. 4033
Salto mortale, Il. Cassieri, G.
    1646
Saltuzza, Il. Calmo, A. 1512
Salud. Manzari, N. 5517
Salute Mr. Washington. Brink, C.
    R. 1331
Salute to the Flag, A. Trudell, B.
    8943
Salvage. Thompson, D. K. and J.
    Assur 8840
Salvation's Story. Isherwood, C.
    4410

Sam Clemens of Hannibal. Rutherford, M. C. 7816
Sam, Sam. Griffiths, T. 3747
Sam Tucker. Green, P. 3709
Samaritan, The. Terson, P. 8773
Same Old Thing, The. Megrue, R. C. 5733
Sammy. Quentin, P. 7362
Samson. Corwin, N. 2051
Sancho Panza Dans Son Ile. Casona, A. 1642
Sancta Susanna, the Song of a May Night. Stramm, A. 8550, 8551, 8552, 8553
Sancticity. Head, R. 4002
Sanctuary. MacKaye, P. 5230
Sand Dune Hillbillies, The. Dias, E. J. 2441
Sand Is My Uniform. Mauroc, D. 5691
Sandokan. Trionfo, A. and T. Conte 8935
Sands of Fate: Berlin. Barclay, Sir T. 583
Sands of Time, The. Dias, E. J. 2442
Sandy Scarecrow's Halloween. Miller, H. L. 5997
Sang de Danton. Bouhelier, S. 1215
Sangue del padrone delle ferriere, Il. Jona, A. 4498
Sangue verde, Il. Giovaninetti, S. 3559
Sans Temoin. Renard, M. -C. and A. Dubeux 7490
Santa and Priorities. Urban, C. 8975
Santa and the Efficiency Expert. Watts, F. B. 9243
Santa and the Spacemen. Urban, C. 8976
Santa Calls a Conference. Miller, H. L. 5998
Santa Changes His Mind. Sroda, A. 8470
Santa Claus. Cummings, E. E. 2137
Santa Claus and the Three Polar Bears. Bennett, R. 793
Santa Claus for President. Miller, H. L. 5999
Santa Claus Is Twins. Martens, A. C. 5614
Santa Claus Parade, The. Pendleton, E. 7052
Santa Goes to Town. Paradis, M. B. 6963
Santa's Lost Sack. James, B. B. 4433
Santa's Magic Hat. Thornton, J. F. 8853
Sargasses, Les. Mouloudji, M. 6276
Sassi ne le Scarpe, I. Mandich, F. 5496
Satire en Trois Temps. Mallet, R. 5476
Satisfaction of Vietnam, The. Bly, R. 1027
Saturday Night. Benavente y Martinez, J. 747
Saturday Night, A. Green, P. 3710, 3711
Satyre de la Villette. Obaldia, R. de 6733
Sauce for the Emperor. Mosher, J. C. 6263
Saucy Scarecrow, The. Thane, A. 8792
"Saujud," Der. Dolf, B. 2523
Saul's Jealousy 7980
Saut du Lit, Le. Cooney, R. and J. R. Chapman 2001
Sauvage, Bernard, T. 851
Savant, Le. Church, H. 1831
Save the Wild Flowers. Duncan, F. and E. D. Yale 2699
Saved. Bond, E. 1174, 1175
Saved! Wilde, P. L. 9383
Saving the Old Homestead. Fay, M. 2951
Savonarola. Beerholm, M. 718, 719
Savonarole, ou Le Plaisir de Dieu Seul. Suffran, M. 8610
Say It with Flowers. Miller, H. L. 6000
Scabs, The. Mulet, P. 6289
Scales of Justice. Moineaux, G. 6108
Scarecrow and the Witch, The. Bennett, R. 794
Scarecrow Party, The. Howard, V. 4226
Scarecrow's Hat, The. Urban, C. 8977
Scaredy Cat. Boiko, C. 1120
Scaredy Cat. Murray, J. 6384
Scarlet Pimpernel, The. Orczy, Baroness E. 6874
Scars of Zalagai. Potter, R. S. 7263
Scatola, La. Codignola, L. 1920

Scatola dei gioielli, La. Roda,
  R. 7644
Scena in Montagna. Cesco, B.
  de 1697
Scène à Quatre. Ionesco, E.
  4401
Sceneggiatura, Una. Patti, E.
  7009
Scenes from Domestic Life. Russ,
  J. 7802
Scheherazade. Lynch, M. 5102
Schiavo impazzito, Lo. Giannini,
  G. 3491
Schlagwetter. Altendorf, W. 156
Schnitzleresque. Palm, C. L.
  6941
Scholarship Shenanigans. Heinzen,
  B. 4038
School. Craig, G. 2090
School for Jesters. Whitman, C.
  9333
School for Mothers-In-Law, The.
  Brieux, E. 1325
School for Scamperers. Bennett,
  R. 795
School for Scandal. Sheridan, R.
  B. 8247
School for Scaring, A. Miller,
  H. L. 6001
School for Wifes, The. Molière
  6124
School's Done. Robinson, G.
  7621
Schwarmer, Die. Musil, R. 6414
Schwaze Schwan, Der. Walser,
  M. 9196
Schweyk. Brecht, B. 1308
Sciangai. Colton, J. 1951
Science in a Democracy. Jaffe,
  B. 4427
Scientific Mother, The. Meyer,
  A. N. 5801
Scienza dell'amore, La. Valabrègue, A. 8992
Scintillante, La. Romains, J.
  7670
Scontri generali. Scabia, G. 8008
Scoperta dell'Europa, La. De
  Stefani, A. 2376
Scorpion, The. Bellido, J.-M.
  736
Screen, The. Brown, C. 1362
Screen Test. Meredith, B. 5768
Scribe to George Washington.
  Robinson, G. 7622
Scuffletown Outlaws, The. Cox,
  W. N. 2083, 2084
Sculpteur de Masques, Le.

Crommelynck, F. 2116
Scuola degli amanti, La. Wolff,
  P. 9532
Scylla and Charybdis. Feuillet, O.
  3005
Se tu non m'ami.... Riccora, P.
  7517
Se vincessi.... Pompei, M. 7240
Sea, The. Bond, E. 1176
Sea Battle at Night 8117
Sea People, The. Huff, B. T.
  4294
Sea-Gull, The. Chekhov, A. 1777
Seaman's Pipe, The 8119
Search for the Sky-Blue Princess,
  The. Boiko, C. 1121
Search Me! Morgan, C. D. 6216
Searching Wind, The. Hellman, L.
  4048
Search-Light, The. Clifford, L.
  1901
Season in the Sun. Gibbs, W.
  3494
Season's Greetings. Miller, H. L.
  6002
Sebastien. Troyat, H. 8942
Second Chance. Olfson, L. 6810
Second Door Left. Popovic, A.
  7243
Second Kiss, The. Clarke, A.
  1853
Second Mortgage. Shaw, I. 8226
Second Shepherd's Play, The. Head,
  F. E. 4001
Second Sunday in May. Downing,
  R. 2575
Second Threshold. Barry, P. 639
Secondo tempo, Il. Biancoli, O.
  914
Secret, A. Copani, P. 2009
Secret. Roof, K. M. 7695
Secret. Sender, R. 8151
Secret Hiding Place, The. Wein,
  S. B. 9266
Secret Island, The. McFarlan, E.
  5179
Secret Life of Dan Ingram, The.
  Roberts, E. G. 7605
Secret of Freedom, The. MacLeish,
  A. 5243
Secret of Pinchpenny Manor, The.
  Ravetch, H. 7436
Secret of the Church Mouse, The.
  Asbrand, K. 409
Secret of the Princess, The. MacLellan, E. and C. V. Schroll
  5261
Secret of the Roman Stairs. Heshmati, L. B. 4089

791

Secret of the Windmill, The. MacLellan, E. and C. V. Schroll 5262
Secret the Bell Told Boston, The. Cochran, B. H. 1908
Secret Weapon, The. Schmitt, G. L. 8054
Secretary Bird, The. Home, W. D. 4153
Secretissimo. Camoletti, M. 1526
Secrets de la Comedie, Les. Carette, L. 1606
Secrets of the Citizens Correction Committee. Tavel, R. 8718
Secular Trilogy. Lutz, G. M. 5095
Sedia a Dondolo, La. D'Errico, E. 2354
Sedicesima notte, La. Mortari, C. 6244
Seducteur, Le. Fabbri, D. 2903
See the Jaguar. Nash, N. R. 6439
See You in the Funnies. Dias, E. J. 2443
See Wee the Octopus. Burleson, C. 1427
Seeing the Pictures. Chalmers, R. M. 1705
Seeker of a Secret, The. Hanlon, J. 3891
See-Saw. Oliver, T. 6823
Seggiola, La. Mogherini, I. 6102
Sei atti unici senza parole. Wilcock, R. J. 9355
Segreto d'Arvers, Il. Bernard, J. -J. 828
Segreto di famiglia, Il. Herczeg, F. 4067
Sei tu l'amore? Mazzolotti, P. 5714
Seize on Tragic Time. Sherry, R. F. 8253
Sekala Ka'ajma. Austin, M. H. 462
Sekhet: A Dream. Galsworthy, J. 3357
Selfish Giant, The. Brown, C. 1363
Self-Respect. Healy, C. 4005
Self-Sacrifice. Howells, W. D. 4258
Semiramis. Camoletti, M. 1527
"Send Me In, Coach." Fitzgerald, F. S. 3136
Send Me No Flowers. Barasch,
N. and C. Moore 553
Senora Ama, La. Benavente y Martinez, J. 748
Sens Interdit. Salacrou, A. 7881
Sensualita meccanica. Fillia. 3021
Sentiero degli scalori, Il. Birabeau, A. 957
Sentimental Journey, 1902, A. Livingston, F. M. 5008
Sentimental Materialist, The. Fodor, J. 3175
Sentimentali, I. Gianesi, R. 3479
Sentimentalists, The. Meredith, G. 5769
Senza parole. Alvarez Quintero, S. and J. Alvarez Quintero 172
Sepang Loca. Lapena, A. 4812
Separate Tables. Rattigan, T. 7426, 7427
Separation. Charasson, H. 1726
Seppia, La. Rangoni, R. 7405
September Lemonade. Denney, R. 2333
September Tide. Du Maurier, D. 2694
Sequel, The. Colvin, I. 1959
Sera del sabato, La. Giannini, G. 3492
Sera di notivà. Raggio, E. 7388
Sera d'inverno. Geyer, S. 3455
Sera di pioggia. Prosperi, C. 7309
Sera di pioggia. Riccora, P. 7518
Serata di gala. Zardi, F. 9636
Serata in famiglia, Una. Soffici, A. 8361
Serenade. Vicente, G. 9138
Serenissime, La. Wise, C. 9505
Serenissimo Principe de Castilla.... Montemayor, G. de 6181
Sergeant Santa Claus. Miller, H. L. 6003
Serin Muet, Le. Ribemont-Dessaignes, G. 7507
Serjeant Musgrave's Dance. Arden, J. 322, 323
Serments Indiscrets, Les. Marivaux, P. 5557
Serpente a sonagli, Il. Anton, E. 294
Servant in the House, The. Kennedy, C. R. 4592
Servant of Two Masters, The. Goldoni, C. 3608
Servante Sans Gages. Yole, J. 9611
Servants of the People. Cain, J. M. 1495

Servants of the People. Ferlinghetti, L. 2994
Service for Hubert. Richmond, S. S. 7566
Service for Joseph Axminster. Dennison, G. 2339
Servizio sanitario nazionale. Nichols, P. 6545
Sesto piano. Gehri, A. 3433
Set It Down with Gold on Lasting Pillars. Bailey, F. 506
Set Up, The. Weiger, E. 9264
Sette scalini azzurri. Vergani, O., C. Silva, and I. Terzoli 9083
Settembre 1920: Occupazione delle fabbriche. Sani, M. 7909
Settimo: ruba un po' meno. Fo, D. 3171
Setting Santa Straight. Fisher, A. 3070
Seuil du Jardin. Suffran, M. 8611
Seven Ages of Man, The. Slater, M. 8311
Seven Deadly Sins of the Lower Middle Class. Brecht, B. 1309
Seven Little Dwarfs, The. Beaumont, A. 691
Seven Little Seeds, The. Gould, J. 3666
Seven Plays. Koch, K. 4676
Seven Plays of Old Japan. Clements, C. C. 1894
Seven Princesses. Maeterlinck, M. 5431
Seven Year Itch. Axelrod, G. 466
1789--La Revolution Doit s'Arreter a la Perfection du Bonheur (Saint Just) 8157
1789/1793. 8158
1789. The French Revolution, Year One. Lemasson, S. and J.-C. Penchenat 4909
Seventy-three Voted Yes. Mygatt, T. D. 6428
Severed Head, The. Murdoch, I. 6304
Sexe Fort. Bernard, T. 852
Shachiapang 8164
Shade. Udoff, Y. M. 8963
Shades of Ransom. Chisholm, J. R. 1807
Shades of Shakespeare. Dias, E. J. 2444
Shadow. Johns, O. 4479

Shadow in the White House. Oppenheim, J. 6873
Shadow of a Woman, The. Gourmont, R. de 3672
Shadow-of-Death. Murray, J. 6385
Shadowy Waters, The. Yeats, W. B. 9606, 9607
Shady Shadows, The. Miller, H. L. 6004
Shakespeare Dringend Gesucht. Kipphardt, H. 4642
Shakespeare 1564-1616. Sherman, L. A. 8250
Shakespearean Touch, The. Miller, H. L. 6005
Shakespeare's Funeral. 8193
Shakespeares, The. Boiko, C. 1122
Shall We Join the Ladies? Barrie, Sir. J. M. 629
Shambles, a Sketch of the Present War. Schnittkind, H. T. 8059
Shame of It, The. Cronin, A. 2120
Shared Thing, A. Clinton, C. 1904
Sharing the Circus. Campbell, C. 1537
Shatter the Day. Abbe, G. 1
She Also Serves. Paradis, M. B. 6964
She Laughs Last. Paradis, M. B. 6965
She Stoops to Conquer. Goldsmith, O. 3610, 3611, 3612
She Tells Her Daughter. Barnes, D. 606
She Was No Lady. Ervine, St. J. 2875
She Who Returned to Life. Monterde, F. 6183
She Who Was Fished. 8230
Shearwater. Hauptman, W. 3966
Sheep Skin Po. Wimsatt, G. 9471
Shelley. De Ford, M. A. 2283
Shelter for the Night. DuBois, G. 2653
Shenandoah, or The Naming of the Child. Schwartz, D. 8093, 8094
Sherlock Holmes and the Gorgon's Head. Paulus, M. 7017
Sherlock Holmes and the Red-Headed League. Doyle, Sir A. C. 2578
Sherlock Holmes and "The Second Stain." Doyle, Sir A. C. 2579
Sherlock Holmes and the Stockbroker's Clerk. Doyle, Sir A. C. 2580

She's Dead Now. Chisolm, E. 1808
She's not Talking. McCoy, P. S. 5154
Shine On, Pecos Bill. Winther, B. 9487
Shining Hour, The. Winter, K. 9476
Ship, The. Jornet, J. B. I. 4517
Ship Forever Sailing. Young, S. 9616
Ship's Boy to the Indies. MacLellan, E. and C. V. Schroll 5263
Ships on the Sand. Myall, C. A. 6423
Shipwrecked King, The. Slattery, M. E. 8320
Shirley Holmes and the FBI. Miller, H. L. 6006
Shirt of Rain. Owens, P. 6922
Shivaree. Odea, M. L. H. 6769
Shiver My Timbers. Murray, J. 6386
Shoemaker and the Elves, The. Bennett, R. 796
Shoemaker's Guest, The. Krum, C. 4734
Shoes and Stockings and Solomon. Fisher, A. 3071
Shoes for Washington. Arnold, D. and E. W. Williams 353
Shoo Fly Pudding. Hoppenstedt, E. M. 4167
Shop Girl's Revenge, The. Downing, R. 2576
Shopping. Fisk, M. I. 3129
Shore Leave. Osborne, H. 6891
Short Cut, The. Wilde, P. 9384
Short Play About Joseph Smith, Jr., A. Hutchins, M. P. 4338
Short Plays. Marinetti, F. T. 5549
Shortest Play in the World, The. Squire, J. C. 8464
Shot Through the Head. Hale, E. E. 3836
Shouting Head of Prophet John, The. Burleson, B. 1425
Show Booth, The. Blok, A. 1010
Show-Off, The. Kelly, G. 4580
Shower of Hearts, The. Miller, H. L. 6007
Shower, The: The Moon. Noguchi, Y. 6620
Shrimp! Knight, E. L. 4667

Shsh! He's Becoming a Republic. Bland, P. 997
Shy Prince, The. Spamer, C. N. 8430
Si accorciano le distanze. Carpi, A. 1613
Si Camille me Voyait.... Dubillard, R. 2614
Si delle fanciulle, Il. De Moratin, L. F. 2329
Si deve dire? Labiche, E. 4749
Si dira della misere donne. Sarzano, L. 7967
Si la Foule Nous Voit Ensemble. Bal, C. 524
Si Madame me Permet. Bacon, J. 485
Si recita come si può. Chlumberg, H. von 1813
Sibylle de la Rue de Tournon. Gaillard, R. 3347
Sic Passim. Galahad, J. A. 3348
Sicilian Idyl, A. Ledoux, L. V. 4871
Sicilian Limes. Pirandello, L. 7203
Sick Doctor, The. Vibert, J. G. 9137
Sidhe of Ben-Mor. Sawyer, R. 8002
Siecle des Lumieres, Le. Brule, C. 1383
Sigaro, Il. Duvernois, H. 2791
Sightless. Maeterlinck, M. 5432
Signal Service. Gleason, E. and A. Gleason 3582
Signe de Kikota. Ferdinand, R. 2989
Signe du Feu. Fabbri, D. 2904
Signor Bracoli. Boularan, J. 1225
Signor Leonida e la reazione, Il. Caragiale, I. L. 1594
Signor Pigmalione, Il. Grau, G. 3694
Signor Vernet, Il. Renard, J. 7487, 7488
Signora che rubava i cuori, La. Pompei, M. 7241
Signora che vuol divorziare, Una. Vajda, E. 8991
Signora dalle camelie. De Stefani, A. 2377
Signora e da buttare, La. Fo, D. 3172
Signora è partita, La. Cataldo, G. 1661
Signora è servita, La. Birabeau, A. 958

794

Signora vestita di bianco, La. Achard, M. 38
Signora, vi ho già vista in qualche luogo! Fodor, L. 3185
Signore che passava, Un. Johnson, L. E. 4486
Signore dalle gardenie, Il. Biancoli, O. 915
"Signore di Tebe," Il. Dello Siesto, A. 2310
Signore è servito, Il. Veneziani, C. 9071
Signore in poltrona, Un. Gavi, V. 3427
Signore le Trouhadec si lascia traviare, Il. Romains, J. 7671
Signorina, La. Boularan, J. 1226
Signorina bionda, La. Gunther, O. 3784
Signorina Chimera, La. Mazzolotti, P. 5715
Signorina senza dote. Ostrovsky, A. 6915
Signorina, vi voglio sposare. Verneuil, L. 9099
Signpost, The. Clapp, P. 1843
Silences. Klein, J. 4660
Silent. Ritter, M. L. 7595
Silent Night. Crichton, M. 2106
Silent Night. Diers, T. 2491
Silent Night. Hollingsworth, L. 4148, 4149
Silent Night, Lonely Night. Anderson, R. 215
Silent Prince, The. Slattery, M. E. 8321
Silent Voice, The. Alma-Tadema, Sir L. 153
Silly Ass, The. Rowell, A. C. 7768
Silly Citizens of Happy Valley, The. Scott, G. G. 8107
Silly Princesses, The. Slattery, M. E. 8322
Silver Whistle, The. McEnroe, R. E. 5174
Silverheels. Lovett, H. M. 5064
Simili a Dio. Galeazzi, A. G. 3352
Simon Game, The. Maloon, J. 5484
Simon Sez. Major, M. 5465
Simon Simon. Freund, P. 3297
Simona è fatta così. Mirande, Y. and A. Madis 6079
Simoom. Strindberg, A. 8574, 8575, 8576
Simple Sam. Peterson, M. N. 7102
Simple Simon's Reward. Miller, H. L. 6008
Simpleton Peter. Hall, M. 3854
Simultaneita. Marinetti, F. T. 5550
Simultaneity. Marinetti, F. T. 5549
Sin Secreto no ay Amor. Vega, L. de 9058
Sindaco del rione, Il. De Filippo, E. 2263
Sing a Song of Holidays. Olfson, L. 6811
Sing, America, Sing. Fisher, A. and O. Rabe 3115
Sing the Songs of Christmas. Fisher, A. 3072
Sing the Songs of Cowboys. Fisher, A. 3073
Sing the Songs of Freedom. Fisher, A. 3074
Sing the Songs of Lincoln. Fisher, A. 3075
Sing the Songs of Pioneers. Fisher, A. 3076
Sing the Songs of Springtime. Fisher, A. 3077
Sing the Songs of Thanksgiving. Fisher, A. 3078
Sing the Songs of Travel. Fisher, A. 3079
Singing Girl of Copan. Alexander, H. B. 129
Singing Lesson, The. Diller, M. E. T. 2499
Singing Piedmont. Buttitta, A. 1453
Singing Pool. Mobert, H. L. 6100
Singing Shark, The. Howard, V. 4227
Sinn des Lebens und die Reichstagswahl, Der. Hiller, K. 4108
Sir David Wears a Crown. Walker, S. 9190
Sir Osbert and Lester. McGregor, D. 5209
Sir Peter Harpdon's End. Morris, W. 6239
Sir Rat. Herford, O. 4073
Sir Robin of Locksley. Gibson, P. 3497
Sire de Maletroit's Door, The. Stevenson, R. L. 8518
Sister, The. Joyce, J. 4525
Sister Beatrice. Maeterlinck, M. 5433

Sister Eucharia. Clarke, A. 1854
Situalae. Nutting, H. C. 6711
Six Characters in Search of an Author. Pirandello, L. 7204, 7205
Six Dialogues with Lenco. Pavese, C. 7018
Six Heures, Chaussee d'Antin. Ferdinand, R. 2990
Sixteen. Daly, M. 2166
16th Century Christmas, A. Murdock, C. A. 6307
Sixth Juror, The. Murray, J. 6387
Sizwe Bansi Is Dead. Fugard, A., J. Kani, and W. Ntshona 3336
Skeleton. Dunster, M. 2730
Skeletons and Assegais. Wilson, A. 9456
Sketches Radiophoniques.... Bernard, T. 853
Skill of Pericles, The. Nolan, P. T. 6664
Skin Deep. Asbrand, K. 410
Skipper Next to God. Hartog, J. de 3954
Sky's the Limit, The. Olfson, L. 6812
Slag. Hare, D. 3911
Slaughter of the Innocents. Saroyan, W. 7956
Sleepers Den, The. Gill, P. 3525
Sleeping Beauty. Bennett, H. C. 775
Sleeping Beauty, The. Perrault, C. 7073
Sleeping Beauty, The. Verhoeff, C. 9084
Sleeping Chinese Beauty, The. Locke, K. 5010
Sleeping Mountains, The. Winther, B. 9501
Sleeping Prince, The. Rattigan, T. 7428
Sleeping Princess, The. Sears, J. V. 8121
Sleepy Little Elf, The. Robertson, O. J. 7615
Slight Misunderstanding, A. M., A. A. 5109
Slippers. MacFarlane, A. 5183
Slippers That Broke of Themselves, The. Drennan, M. 2597
Slow Blue. Kreymborg, A. 4719

Slow But Sure. Smith, M. S. 8345
Slow Night on Spring Street. Hart, J. Sonata for Mott Street 3938
Slumming. Jasudowicz, D. 4452
Small Change. Gill, P. 3526
Small Craft Warning. Williams, T. 9440
Small Crimson Parasol. Boiko, C. 1123
Small Shoes and Small Tulips. MacLellan, E. and C. V. Schroll 5264
Small War on Murray Hill. Sherwood, R. E. 8259
Small World, A. Oser, J. A. 6905
Smell of New Bread, The. Simon, S. 8288
Smithfield Preserv'd. Brown, I. 1364
Smokey Wins His Star. McGowan, J. 5200
Smug Citizen, The. Gorky, M. 3650
Snake, The. Langford, E. 4796
Snake Chief. Brown, B. S. 1360
Snaring the Lion. Ehrlich, I. 2828
Snickering Horses. Basshe, E. 658
Snipe Hunt. Williams, G. L. 9413
Snoop's Scoop. Miller, H. L. 6009
Snow Birds. Tipe, D. 8869
Snow Girl, The. Very, A. 9124
Snow Goose, The. Gallico, P. 3353
Snow Queen, The. Anderson, H. C. 201
Snow Steals Down, The. Mauroc, D. 5692
Snow White. Crowell, A. 2127
Snow White. Jacob, E. 4421
Snow White and Friends. Cheatham, V. 1759
Snow-White and Rose-Red. Bennett, R. 804
Snow White and Rose Red. Creegan, G. R. 2104
Snow White and the Seven Dwarfs. Grimm, J. and W. Grimm 3754
Snow White or The Modern School Girl. Ryan, R. M. 7819
Snow White's Rescue. Creegan, G. R. 2103
Snow Witch, The. MacKay, C. D. 5224

Snowed Up. Woodmeald, J. E. 9550
Snowflake. Boiko, C. 1151
Snowman Who Overstayed, The. Boiko, C. 1124
So Gracious Is the Time. Smith, B. 8328
So Long at the Fair. Miller, H. L. 6010
So Long, Miss Jones. Caplan, L. 1579
So Much of Light. Plimpton, H. 7219
So Precious a Gift. Reines, B. J. 7476
So Proud to Serve. Barbee, L. 571
So Shines a Good Deed. DuBois, G. 2654
So This Is China. Asbrand, K. 411
Soap Opera. Wolas, E. 9525
Sob Sister. Saunders, L. 7985
Social Service for All Creatures Great and Small. Cotterell, A. F. 2058
Social Success, A. Beerbohm, M. 720
Social Worker and the Alcoholic, The. Kauffman, G. 4557
Society Page. Allred, J. and P. Allred 149
Socrates Saves the Day. Paradis, M. B. 6966
Socrates Up to Date. Myers, I. H. 6425
Sodom and Gomorrah. Kazantzakis, N. 4565
Soeurs Guedonec. Bernard, J.-J. 829
Soft Hearted Ghost, The. Miller, H. L. 6011
Softy the Snow Man. Miller, H. L. 6012
Sognare! Tonelli, G. 8885
Sognare insieme. Di Luca, D. 2501
Sogni di minorenni. Lakatos, L. 4772
Sogno, Un. Serretta, E. 8156
Sogno delle mille e una notte. Vanni, A. 9040
Sogno di una notte d'inverno. Musatescu, T. 6412
Soif, La. Bernstein, H. 864
Soir des Diplomates, Le. Bouteille, R. 1240
Soir du Conquérant, Le. Talagrand, J. 8697
Soiree on the Neva, The. Lengyel, M. 4914
Sojourner Truth. Dunster, M. 2731
Sojourners. Harnwell, A. J. and I. Meeker. 3913
Sola su questo mare. Perrini, A. 7081
Solange. Barbeau, J. 555
Solar Spectrum. Wedekind, F. 9258
Soldat et la Sorciere, Le. Salacrou, A. 7882
Soldato piccicó, Il. Nicolai, A. 6588
Soldiers on the Home Front. McQueen, M. H. and N. McQueen 5387
Sole. Nicolosi, V. M. 1609
Sole di Austerlitz, Il. Salsa, C. 7889
Sole e la luna, Il. Biraghi, G. 961
Sole negli occhi, Il. Cenzato, G. 1686
Sole per due. Bassano, E. 654
Soleil et les Parapluies, Le. Deutsch, L. 2386
Solemn Communion. Arrabal, F. 376, 377
Solid Gold Cadillac, The. Teichmann, H. and G. S. Kaufman. 8738
Solid House. Garro, E. 3401
Solitaire. Soler, A. 8368
Solitudine. D'Ambra, L. 2169
Solo. Duvernois, H. 2792
Solo Recital. Taikeff, S. 8688
Soltanto il rogo. Borgese, E. M. 1198
Soluna. Asturias, M. A. 425
Solution Is the Window to the Soul, The. Kalos, P. 4536
Some of My Best Friends Are Spies. Dias, E. J. 2445
Some One Waiting. Williams, E. 9412
Some Tricks Are Treats. Schroll, F. L. 8087
Somebodies, The. Osborn, C. 6887
Somebody-Nothing. 8373
Somebody's Valentine. Lawrence, J. 4859
Somebody's Valentine. Newman, D. 6521
Something New for Halloween. Newman, D. 6522

Somewhat Forgetful. Schwartz, M. K. 8100
Sommossa, La. Mosca, G. 6257
Son Image, A. Lescure, P. 4937
Son Left in the Plantation of Mulberry Trees. Chin Lin Chen 1804
Son of a Tanner, The. Burlingame C. 1432
Son of Learning, The. Clarke, A. 1855
Son of Liberty. Lipnick, E. 4995
Son of William Tell, The. Nolan, P. T. 6665
Sonata for Mott Street. Hart, J. 3938
Sonata in do minore, La. Carpi, A. 1614
Song at Twilight, A. Coward, N. 2077
Song for All Saints, A. Lineberger, J. 4993
Song for American Union. McHugh, V. 5215
Song Goes Forth, A. Boiko, C. 1125
Song in the Night, A. DuBois, G. 2655
Song of Fate, The. Blok, A. 1011
Song of Solomon, The. Odea, M. L. H. 6770
Song of Songs. Giraudoux, J. 3576
Song of Songs of Solomon, The. 8375
Song of the Dragon River. 8376
Song of the Forest. Howard, V. 4228
Songbook of the Baby Jesus. Moock, A. 6196
Songe, Le. Strindberg, A. 8577
Songe d'un Soir d'Amour, Le. Bataille, H. 663
Songe de la Nuit d'un Couple, Le. Magnan, J.-M. 5438
Songe du Critique. Anouilh, J. 274
Songs of America Growing. Fisher, A. 3080
Sonnambuli, I. Grassi, E. 3692
Sonno dei carnefici, Il. Celli, G. 1678
Sophia the Seamstress. Dias, E. J. 2446
Sorcerer's Apprentices, The. Olson, E. 6829
Sorelle di Segovia, Le. Ribeiro, G. D. 7505
Sorry, No Answer. Schaaf, A. K. 8013
Sospiro no. 3. Benedetti, B. 754
Sotoba Komachi. Mishima, Y. 6080
Sotoba Komachi. Motokiyo, Z. 6272
Sotto il sicomoro. Spewack, S. 8446
Sottoscala, Il. Dyer, C. 2795
Soul Gone Home. Hughes, L. 4306
Souls Exchanged. Scholz, W. von 8082
Sound of Christmas, The. Elness, W. P. 2857
Sound of Night, The. Kitani, S. 4652
Sound on the Goose. Biel, N. 917
Sounding Brass. Haymon, D. 3994
Soup Stone, The. Peterson, M. N. 7103
Soup Stone, The. Stigler, W. A. 8524
Souper. Molnar, F. 6161
Souper de Venise, Le. Sabatier, P. 7838
Souper Intime. Chatelain, Y. 1740
Soupiere, La. Lamoureux, R. 4777
Sourdough Sally. Miller, H. L. 6013
Sourire de la Joconde, Le. Benavente y Martinez, J. 749
Sourires Inutiles, Les. Achard, M. 39
South American Hero. Jose San Martin 4518
South Kensington Hellenism. Traill, H. D. 8920
Souviens Toi Mon Amour. Birabeau, A. 959
Spacca il centesimo. De Filippo, P. 2280
Space Suit with Roses. Garver, J. 3416
Spaceship Santa Maria. Boiko, C. 1126
[Spanish Farce of the 16th Century] 8436
Spark, The. Pailleron, E. 6934
Sparrow Family, The. McQueen, M. H. and N. McQueen 5388

Spartan Dorothy and Her Fox.
Teeple, L. R. 8737
Spatial Episode, A. Hyman, M.
4357
Speakers, The. Gaskill, W. and
M. Stafford-Clark 3419
Specchio, Lo. Stevenson, R. L.
8519
Special Delivery. Sutphen, W.
G. van T. 8632
Special Edition. Fisher, A.
3081
Spelling Match, The. Sickels, E.
R. 8271
Spettacolo fuori programma.
Meano, C. 5726
Spiel vom Herrn und vom Jockel,
Das. Zweig, A. 9661
Spies and Dolls. Murray, J.
6388
Spindle, the Shuttle, and the
Needle, The. Grimm, J. and
W. Grimm 3755
Spineless Drudge, The. Harris,
R. W. 3932
Spinning a Spider's Tale. Ross,
S. 7709
Spirit of Christmas, The. Fisher,
A. 3082
Spirit of Christmas, The. St.
Clair, R. 7857
Spirit of Christmas Joy, The.
MacKay, C. D. 5225
Spirit of Negro History, The.
Eubanks, T. 2878
Spiritismo. Franzero, C. M.
3273
Spiritismo nell' antica casa.
Betti, U. 898
Spiropanosome. Perks, A. E.
7069
Spitting Image. Spencer, C.
8443
Spitzel, Der. Brecht, B.
1310
Splendid Offering, A. King, G.
E. 4630
Spooks in Books. Miller, H. L.
6014
Spokesong. Parker, S. 6975
Spooky Spectacles. Miller, H.
L. 6015
Sposa molto ricca, Una. Szenes,
B. 8680
Sposami! Conty, J. and E.
Codey 1991
Spot in the Sun, A. Murray,
T. C. 6410

Spot on the Porch, The. Gilbert,
H. 3509
Spouse for Susie Mouse, A. Head,
F. E. 4000
Spreading the News. Gregory,
Lady A. 3728, 3729
Spring Daze. McQueen, M. H.
and N. McQueen 5389
Spring Fever. McQueen, M. H.
and N. McQueen 5390
Spring Harvest. Wade, I. W.
9181
Spring Is Coming. Rabenhorst, L.
C. 7375
Spring Is Here! Duvall, L. M.
2779
Spring Neighbors. Newman, D.
6523
Spring, 1943. McGaughan, G. E.
5186
Spring Recital, The. Dreiser, T.
2596
Spring Secrets. Lee, S. 4885
Spring Sluicing. Ernst, A. H.
2872
Spring to the Rescue. Newman, D.
6524
Spring Tonic. McQueen, M. H.
and N. McQueen 5391
Spring Will Come. DuBois, G.
2656
Spring-Heeled Jack. Terson, P.
8774
Springtime for Dan. Martens, A.
C. 5616
Spudorata verita. Muller, P. 6292
Spunky Punky. Miller, H. L. 6016
Spunti per commedie. Molnar, F.
6162
Spurt of Blood. Artaud, A. 383
Spy, The. Cooper, J. F. 2008
Spy for a Day. Huff, B. T. 4295
Spying High. Olfson, L. 6813
Squabbles of Chioggia. Goldoni, C.
3609
Squander Bug's Christmas Carol,
The. Fisher, A. 3083
Squarciagola, Lo. Squarzina, L.
and L. Pavoni 8461
Square Box, The. Hall, M. 3863
Square Peg. Hosain, K. S. 4178
Square X. Bihan, M. le 926
Squaring the Family Circle. Mac-
Campbell, D. 5122
Squawk of a Distant Gull. Major,
M. 5466
Squaw-man, The. Royle, E. M.
7774

Squeaknibble's Christmas. Mc-
Gowan, J. 5201
Stage Bore. Dias, E. J.
2447
Stage Set for Murder. Murray,
J. 6389
Stage Struck. Perkins, E. B.
7068
Stagione sulle baracche. Silori,
L. 8276
Staircase. Dyer, C. 2796
Stalag 17. Bevan, D. and E.
Trzcinski 901
Stand in the Mountains, A. Tay-
lor, P. 8727
Standing on a Streetcorner. Corso,
G. 2039
Standing Up for Santa. Fisher,
A. 3084
Stanislaw and the Wolf. Nolan,
P. T. 6666
Stanzone, Lo. Kezich, T.
4615
Star Bright. Boiko, C. 1127
Star Dust. Asbrand, K. 412
Star Dust Path. Clements, C.
C. 1894
Star Fever. Boiko, C. 1128
Star for Old Glory, A. Fisher,
A. and O. Rabe 3116
Star in the Window, The. Mc-
Queen, M. H. and N. McQueen
5392
Star in the Window, The. Pendle-
ton, E. 7053
Star of Bethlehem. Martens, A.
C. 5616
Star Over Bethlehem. DuBois,
G. 2657
Star-Spangled Time Machine, The.
Boiko, C. 1129
Stars and Stripes, The. Newman,
D. 6525
Starveling. De Mille, W. C.
2316
Stasera arsenico ovvero. Terron,
C. 8764
State Supreme, The. Bowhay, B.
L. 1243
State Versus Joe Miller, The.
Schmitt, G. L. 8055
Station Champbaudet, La. La-
biche, E. and Marc-Michel
4755
Station YYYY. Tarkington, B.
8711
Statue for Joey, A. Volzer, M.
9171

Statue's Daughter, The. O'Connor,
F. 6765
Steamer Tenacity. Messager, C.
5791
Steed in the Senate, A. Andreyev,
L. N. 238
Stefano Pelloni Called the Ferryman.
Dursi, M. 2759
Steinway Grand. Karinthy, F.
4550
Stephen D. Leonard, H. 4926
Sterling Silver Tree, The. Fisher,
A. and O. Rabe 3117
Stevie Guy. Orlovitz, G. 6880
Stick Up. Gerould, D. Tripstych.
3445
Sticks and Stones. Downing, R.
2577
Sticks and Stones. Reaney, J.
7449
Stilita, Lo. Pinelli, T. 7165
Still Fires. Quackenbush, J. 7357
"Still It Is Spring." Basudeb, S.
660
Stiopic et Mania. Evreinov, N. N.
2890
Stolen Cook, The. Slattery, M.
E. 8323
Stolen Heart, The. Newman, D.
6526
Stolen Prince, The. Topelius, Z.
8900, 8901
Stolen Prince, The. Totheroh, D.
W. 8887
Stolen Pumpkin, The. Arnold, E.
W. 352
Stone Soup. Buechler, J. 1412
Stop the Presses! Dias, E. J.
2448
Storia d'amore, Una. Lefevre-
Geraldry, P. 4893
Storia di Giovanna. Cuomo, F.
2144
Storienko. Bonelli, L. 1185
Storm, The. Drinkwater, J. 2604,
2605
Storm Warning. Kao Hung 4546
Stormbird, The. Roelvink, H. C.
J. 7647
Stormy Passage. Donahue, P. M.
2529
Stornelli vocali. Cangiullo, F. 1562
Story Machine, The. Asimov, I.
421
Story of a Kidnapping. Diament,
M. 2397
Story of Benjamin Banneker, The.
Johnson, T. H. 4489

800

Story of Christmas, The. Petrea, R. A. 7108
Story of Gilbert and Sullivan, The. Leech, M. T. 4890
Story of Samuel Slater, The. Hackett, W. 3806
Story Told in Indiana. Smith, B. 8329
Storybook Revolt, The. Watts, F. B. 9244
Strada, La. Falconi, D. 2917
Strada morta, La. Dursi, M. 2760
Straight from the Heart. Whitman, C. 9334
Strained Relation, A. Bierce, A. 919
Strana quiete, Una. Mainardi, R. 5461
Strange and Wonderful Object, The. Plescia, G. L. 7214
Strange Birth. Deevy, T. 2247, 2248
Strange Inheritance. Murray, J. 6390
Strange Interlude. O'Neill, E. 6862
Strange Morning. Pech, C. -H. 7031
Strange Passenger, The. Karpowicz, T. 4551
Strange Rider, A. Ghelderode, M. de 3461
Stranger, The. De La Mare, W. 2287
Stranger, The. Zacks, R. 9628
Strangers and Neighbors. Nolan, P. T. 6667
Stranger's Choice, The. Howard, H. L. 4211
Strano tè in casa Halden, Uno. Koselka, F. 4692
Straw Boy, The. Nolan, P. T. 6668
Straw in the Wind. Brill, B. 1329
Straw Men, The. Ballesteros, A. M. 538
Straw Patriot. Moreno, V. R. 6215
Strawberry Cottage. Cooper, E. 2005
Street and Number. Molnar, F. 6163
Street Attends a Funeral. Kozlenko, W. 2416
Street in Samarkand, A. Huff, B. T. 4296

Street Singer, The. Echegaray, J. 2812, 2813
Streetcar Named Desire, A. Williams, T. 9441
Stretch a Point. McQueen, M. H. and N. McQueen 5393
Strictly for Relatives. Phillips, M. K. 7135
Strictly Puritan. Miller, H. L. 6017
String of Pearls, The. Flynn, C. W. 3163
Strip-Tease of Jealousy. Arrabal, F. 378
Stripwell. Barker, H. 603
Strong and Silent. Dias, E. J. 2449
Stronger, The. Giacosa, G. 3477
Stronger, The. Strindberg, A. 8578, 8579, 8580
Stronger Woman, The. Strindberg, A. 8581
Struggle for an Unknown Cause. Blank, F. 998
Study in the Nude, A. Downey, J. E. 2573
Stuff a Writer Is Made Out Of, The. Jasudowicz, D. 4451
Stuff of Heroes, The. Pendleton, E. 7054
Stupid Lady. Vega, L. de 9059
Sua Breve ora Felice, La. Mauro, G. 5690
Subject to Fits. Montgomery, R. 6186
Subject Was Roses, The. Gilroy, F. D. 3546
Substitute, The. Weston, E. 9309
Substitute Bride, The. Stedman, A. 8480
Substitute Government. Bahr, H. 500
Such a Charming Young Man. Akins, Z. 93
Such Things Only Happen in Books. Wilder, T. 9402
Sud. Green, J. 3699
Sud. Paluel-Marmont, A. 6947
Sugar and Spice. Nicholson, J. 6559
Sugar Cain. Wilson, F. H. 9461
Suggeritore nudo, Il. Marinetti, F. T. 5551
Suicide, The. Campbell, A. 1535
Suisses, Les. Breal, P. -A. 1280
Sulla porta. Bruck, E. 1379
Sulle soglie della storia. Bonacci, A. 1167

Sulle strade di notte. Lelli, R. 4905
Summer in the Country. Chekhov, A. 1778
Summer of the Seventeenth Doll. Lawler, R. 4846, 4847
Summer Soldier. Smith, J. V. 8337
Summer Stock a la Carte. Dias, E. J. 2450
Summer-folk. Gorky, M. 3651
Sun. Galsworthy, J. 3358
Sun Bride. St. Clair, R. 7858
Sun Is a Red Dwarf, The. Levoy, M. 4969
Sun Machine, The. Morley, C. 6227
Sun Trampled Beneath the Horses' Hooves, The. Adoum, J. E. 77
Sun Up! Boiko, C. 1130
Sun Yat-Sen. Buck, P. S. 1410
Sunbeam. Mariani, F. 5546
Sunday Breakfast. Rubio, E. and M. Balf 7780
Sunday Costs Five Pesos. Niggli, J. 6595
Sunday on Sunday Goes By. Lavedan, H. 4841
Sundial, The. Jones, H. M. 4507
Sundial, The. Molinaro, U. 6130
Sunken Bell, The. Hauptmann, G. 3975
Sunrise at Campobello. Schary, D. 8018
Sunshine and Smiles. Nolan, P. T. 6669
Super-Duper Market, The. Murray, J. 6391
Super-Sleuths, Inc. Paradis, M. B. 6967
Superintendent, The. Haavikko, P. 3795
Supermarket Blues, The. Fontaine, R. 3206
Supreme Moment, A. Clifford, L. 1902
Sur Mon Beau Navire. Sarment, J. 7942
Sur un Banc. Mahieu, C. 5449
Sur une Plage de L'Ouest. Larra, C. 4820
Surface and Shadows. Chandler, D. 1714
Surprise for Mother, A. Miller, H. L. 6018
Surprise Guests. McQueen, M. H. and N. McQueen 5394

Surprise-Partie. Sabatier, P. 7839
Surprise Party, A. Dias, A. M. 2462
Surprise Party. Dorand, J. 2546
Survivre. Philippot, M. 7118
Susan and Aladdin's Lamp. Clapp, P. 1844
Susan Goes Hollywood. Wilde, C. F. 9358
Suspected Truth, The. Mendoza, J. R. de A. y 5747
Sutter's San Francisco. Hamby, R. 3876
Suzanne. Morin, E. C. 6220
Sveca Na Vetru. Solzhenitsyn, A. I. 8372
Swamp, The. MacKaye, R. K. 5231
Swan, The. Molnar, F. 6164
Swap-Shop Special. Mayr, C. A. 5708
Sweeps of Ninety-Eight. Masefield, J. 5640
Sweet Alice. Eveling, S. 2885
Sweet Bird of Youth. Williams, T. 9442
Sweet Confessions. Arnaud, G. 347
Sweet Liberty. Malkind, M. 5472
Sweet Sixteen. McQueen, M. H. and N. McQueen 5395
Sweet Talk. Abbensetts, M. 2
Sweethearts. Gilbert, W. S. 3512
Swift's Pastoral. Colum, P. 1958
Swifty. Willment, F. 9450
Swineherd, The. Anderson, H. C. 202
Swings. DeGrazia, E. 2284
Swiss Chalet Mystery, The. Murray, J. 6392
Swiss Family Robinson, The. Wyss, J. R. 9581
Swiss Mystery. MacLellan, E. and C. V. Schroll 5265
Switch-About Shopkeepers, The. Sagoff, S. E. 7851
Sword and Crozier. Einarsson, I. 2834
Sword in Hand. Barbee, L. 572
Sword of Damocles. 8654
Symphony in O Flat. O'Grady, M. 6782
System of Doctor Goudron and Professor Plume. Lorde, A. de 5052
Systeme Deux, Le. Neveux, G. 6479, 6480

Système Fabrizzi. Husson, A. 4332

T

"T" Party, The. Boiko, C. 1131
Tabaccheria della generalessa, La. Bush-Fekete, L. 1451
Tabernaria, La. Della Porta, G. B. 2304
Tabique Taboque, Le. Capron, M. 1588
Table Set for Himself, The. Wilbur, E. 9351
Tables Turned, The. Brown, J. 1366
Tabloid, A. Eckersley, A. 2815
Tacchino, Il. Feydeau, G. 3010
Tactile Quartet, The. Marinetti, F. T. 5549
Taffy and Sylvie. Simon, S. 8289
Tagliatori di teste, I. Caleffi, F. 1505
Take a Deep Breath. van Itallie, J. -C. 9033
Take Care, Anne! McCoy, P. S. 5155
Take, Eat: This Is My Body. Estrin, M. Four Infiltration Pieces 2877
Take Her, She's Mine. Ephron, P. and H. Ephron 2869
Take It from the Beginning. Nolan, P. T. 6670
Take Me to Your Marshall. Boiko, C. 1132
Take My Advice. Murray, J. 6393
Taken. Davis, J. 2200
Taking Goods to the Countryside. Chao Shu-jen 1717
Taking the Bandit's Stronghold. 8690
Taking Tiger Mountain by Strategy. 8691
Tale of Two Cities, A. Dickens, C. 2482, 2483
Tale of Two Drummers, A. Boiko, C. 1133
Tale That Wagged the Dog, A. Kelly, T. 4583
Talent Tree, The. Brown, T. L. 1373
Taliesin. Hovey, R. 4199
Talisman, The. Brotherton, A. W. 1351
Talismano, Il. Wachthausen, R. 9177

Talk in a Taxi. 8700
Talk Their Language. Lampell, M. 4779
Talking Christmas Tree, The. Fawcett, M. G. 2950
Talking Flag, The. McGowann, J. 5202
Tall Silk Hat, The. Boiko, C. 1134
Tall Stranger, The. Dias, E. J. 2451
Tall Tale Tournament, The. Boiko, C. 1135
Tamburo di panno, Il. 8701
Tamburo di panno, Il. Motokiyo, K. 6268
Tamburo e sonaglio. Alvarez Quintero, S. and J. Alvarez Quintero 173
Taming of the Screw, The. Sankey, T. 7911
Taming of the Shrew, The. Shakespeare, W. 8190
Tango. Mrozek, S. 6286, 6287
Tanjka macht die Augen Auf. Hay, J. 3991
Tant Belle Fille, Une. Boularan, J. 1227
Tapage Nocturne. Sauvajon, M. G. 7989
Taper and the Torch. The. Stuart, D. M. 8587
Tappeto verde, Il. Varaldo, A. 9043
Taps Is Not Enough. Carmer, C. 1608
Tarot Terrors, The. Murray, J. 6394
Tarts for the King. Morse, C. 6241
Tartuffe--Act VI. Marie, A. 5547
Tartuffe, ou L'Imposteur. Molière 6125
Tartuffe Repenti. Diez, B. 2496
Taste of Honey, A. Delaney, S. 2290, 2291, 2292
Tata, ou de l'Education. Borel, J. 1195
Tatters. Burton, R. 1446
Tattica sbagliata. Abony, A. 13
Tatyana Riepin. Chekhov, A. 1779
Tausk. Harris, A. B. 3916
Tavern Meeting. Jones, R. C. 4511
Tavola dei pover, La. Viviani, R. 9164
Taxi. Riley, A. C. D. 7583
Tazza, La. Siciliano, E. 8268

Tchao! Sauvajon, M. G. 7990
Tchin-Tchin. Billetdoux, F. 934
Tcinderella. 8736
Te' in casa Picasso. Rimanelli, G. 7587
Tea and Sympathy. Anderson, R. 216, 217, 218
Tea for Six. Butterfield, W. 1452
Teache Comes, The. Uhler, J. E. 8966
Teahouse of the August Moon. Patrick, J. 7000, 7001
Teapot Trouble. Nicholson, J. 6560
Tears of Dawn. Vilas, F. V. V. 9146
Tears of the Birds, The. Noguchi, Y. 6621
Teatrino dell'amore, Il. Marinetti, F. T. 5552
Teddy and Partner. Noe, Y. 6614
Teddy Bear Hero, The. McGowan, J. 5203
Teddy Bears, The. Burleson, C. 1428
Teddy e il suo partner. Noè, Y. 6613
Teen and Twenty. Dorand, J. 2547
Teen Tycoon. Heinzen, B. B. 4039
Teja. Sudermann, H. 8605
Telegram, The. Lohman, F. 5019
Telemachus. Norman, C. 6692
Telephonitis. Martens, A. C. 5617
Television-itis. McQueen, M. H. and N. McQueen 5396
Temoin. Germoz, A. 3442
Temoins. Soria, G. 8389
Temperament. Terrell, M. 8746
Tempest, The. Shakespeare, W. 8191
Tempest in a Teapot. McQueen, M. H. and N. McQueen 5397
Tempo addosso, Il. Terron, C. 8765
Tempo di cavallete. D'Errico, E. 2355
Tempo di mezzo. Miroglia, G. N. 6076
Tempo e la signorina Angoscia, Il. Nulli, E. 6706
Temporary Job. Nolan, P. T. 6671

Temps des Cerises. Roncoroni, J.-L. 7686
Temps Difficiles. Bourdet, E. 1237
Ten'. Svartz, E. L. 8640
Ten Days Later. Glick, C. 3585
Ten Dollars. Thorne, O. 8848
Ten Fingers of François. Oglesbee, D. H. 6780
Ten Little Indians. Christie, A. 1824
Ten P. M. Aldis, M. 120
Ten Pennies for Lincoln. Miller, H. L. 6019
Ten Years After. Hutten, Baroness von 4340
Tender Edge. Brower, B. 1354
Tender Trap, The. Shulman, M. and R. P. Smith 8265
Ten-Penny Tragedy, The. Elfenbein, J. A. 2843
10-10 Till We Read You Again, Good Buddy. Shoemaker, C. 8260
Ten-Year-Old Detective. Olfson, L. 6814
Tennessee Day in St. Louis. Taylor, P. 8728
Tenor, The. Wedekind, F. 9259
Tenth Circle, The. Michaelson, L. W. 5804
Tenth Man, The. Chayefsky, P. 1746, 1747, 1748
Tenth Man, The. Levinger, E. E. 4964
Tents of the Arabs, The. Dunsany, E. J. M. D. P. 2726, 2727, 2728
Terakoya. Isumo, T. 4415
Teresa. Ginzburg, N. 3550
Teresa Desqueyroux. Fabbri, D. 2905
Teresa-Angelica. Bompiani, V. 1164
Teresina. Nicolai, A. 6589
Terminal. Open Theater, The. 6871
Teropia. Pratella, F. B. 7273
Terra sconosciuta. Capriolo, G. 1587
Terre est Basse, La. Adam, A. R. 49
Terrible Baisht, The. Fitzmaurice, G. 3143
Terrible Gypsy Mala, The. Winther, B. 9502
Terrible Terry's Surprise. Boiko, C. 1136

Terrible Turkey, The. Merow, E. L. 5779
Terrible Woman. Steele, W. D. 8486
Terror on the Island. Murray, J. 6395
Terrore di Roma, Il. Marotta, G. 5571
Tessie, the Tea Bag Maker. Huff, B. T. 4297
Test, The. Marivaux, P. 5558
Test, The. Nolan, P. T. 6672
Test, The. Rabenhorst, L. C. 7376
Test for a Witch. MacLellan, E. and C. V. Schroll 5266
Testament, The. Moza, J. L. 6283
Tête des Autres, La. Ayme, M. 476, 476
Thankful Elf, The. Chaloner, G. 1709
Thankful Indeed. Howard, H. L. 4212
Thankful's Pumpkin. Asbrand, K. 413
Thankful's Red Beads. Miller, H. L. 6020
Thankless Tate. Draper, C. C. 2590
Thanks for Thanksgiving. Newman, D. 6527
Thanks to Billy. McQueen, M. H. and N. McQueen 5398
Thanks to Butter-Fingers. Miller, H. L. 6021
Thanks to George Washington. McQueen, M. H. and N. McQueen 5399
Thanks to George Washington. Pendleton, E. 7055
Thanks to Sammy Scarecrow. Howard, H. L. 4213
Thanks to the Indians. Newman, D. 6528
Thanksgiving à la Carte. Miller, H. L. 6022
Thanksgiving Before Detroit. Pomerance, B. 7237
Thanksgiving Dinner. Jenks, T. 4455
Thanksgiving Dream, A. Marshall, S. L. 5582
Thanksgiving Farm. Newman, D. 6529
Thanksgiving Feast. Fisher, A. 3085
Thanksgiving for Frieda. Miller, H. L. 6023
Thanksgiving Is for Everybody. Gould, J. 3667
Thanksgiving Night. Very, A. 9125
Thanksgiving Postscript. McQueen, M. H. and N. McQueen 5400
Thanksgiving Riddle, A. Miller, H. L. 6024
Thanksgiving Wishbone. McQueen, M. H. and N. McQueen 5401
Thar She Blows. Dias, E. J. 2452
That Boy, Call Him Back. Hendry, T. 4056
That Christmas Feeling. McQueen, M. H. and N. McQueen 5402
That Franklin Boy. Martens, A. C. 5618
That Lady. O'Brien, K. 6747
That Time of Year. Cable, H. 1480
That's the Spirit. Murray, J. 6396
Theatre. Maugham, W. S. 5677
Theatre Dans une Bouteille. Neveux, G. 6481
Theatre pare. Rittner, T. 7596
Their Anniversary. Riley, A. C. D. 7584
Their Heart. Lavedan, H. 4842
Their Very Own and Golden City. Wesker, A. 9306
Then Came the Good Harvest. Scott, C. E. 8106
Theodat. Gourmont, R. de 3673
Théodat. Verdot, G. 9075
Theory of the Pathetic. Goodman, P. 3630
Theory of Tragedy. Goodman, P. 3630
There Are Tragedies and Tragedies. Fitzmaurice, G. 3144
There Goes the West End. Gilbert, W. S. 3511
There Is a Tide. Rawe, M. 7442
There Is Room. Noble, C. C. 6609
There Was an Old Woman. Meili, J. 5735
There's a Girl in My Soup. Frisby, T. 3306, 3307
There's a Nation. Kreymborg, A. 4720
There's Some Milk in the Icebox. Henderson, B. J. 4053
There's Something I Got to Tell You. Saroyan, W. 7957

Thérèse, ou L'Ecole des Vocations. Courant, P. 2059
Thersites. Trevelyan, R. C. 8930
Thesmophoriazusae. Aristophanes. 336
They Banish Our Anger. DuBois, G. 2658
They Burned the Books. Benet, S. V. 760
They Dared to Teach. Fishburn, E. 3035
They're Knocking Down the Pie-Shop. McGrath, J. 5208
Thing of Beauty, A. Arthur, K. 387
Third Daughter, The. Fratti, M. 3284
Third Fourth of July. Cullen, C. and O. Dodson 2136
Third Lamb, The. Hershey, M. B. 4083
Third Richest Man in the World, The. Murray, J. 6397
Thirteen. Martens, A. C. 5619
13 a tavola. Eger, R. and J. De Letraz 2821
Thirteen and Hallowe'en. Barbee, L. 573
Thirteenth Christmas, The. Molinaro, U. 6131
31 Flavors and Law'n' Order. Estrin, M. Four Infiltration Pieces 2877
This Earth Is Ours. Kozlenko, W. 2417
This I Believe. Saroyan, W. 7949
This Is Only Wednesday. Sanderson T. 7905
This Is the Heir. Housman, L. 4194
This Is the Worst News. Nettleford, W. T. and W. A. Rathkey 6471
This Is Villa! Niggli, J. 6596
This Isn't Exactly How I Expected It. Steelsmith, M. 8487
This Little Pig Went to Market. Howard, H. L. 4214
This Might Happen to You. Spain, L. 8401
This Moment. Anshutz, H. L. 283
This Music Crept by Me on the Wafer. MacLeish, A. 5244
This Property Is Condemned. Williams, T. 9443

This Story of Yours. Hopkins, J. 4165
This Train. Mitchell, K. 6082
This Younger Generation. Nolan, P. T. 6673
Thomas Chatterton. Jahnn, H.-H. 4430
Thomas More. Bolt, R. 1158
Thou Shalt Not Steal. Tupper, E. S. 8949
Thousand Clowns, A. Gardner, H. 3387
Thracian Horses, The. Valency, M. J. 2165
3, A Play. Boyajian, A. 1251
Three Against Death. Henderson, J. 4054
Three and the Dragon. Fisher, A. 3086
Three Aunts, The. Rowland, E. 7772
Three Billy Goats Gruff. Barker, C. and J. Medina 600
Three Cheers for Mother. Miller, H. L. 6025
Three Chinese Folk-Dramas. 8855
Three Couples. Kielland, A. L. 4618
Three Entertainments. Saroyan, W. 7958
Three Eschatologists and a Bassoon. Benesch, W. 757
Three Fables from a Broken Fortune Cookie. Olfson, L. 6815
Three Friends, The. Morton, F. M. 6250
Three From the Earth. Barnes, D. 607
Three Ghost Plays. Taylor, P. 8729
Three Ghosts Walk. Coxe, C. 2085
Three Golden Hairs. Houston, S. 4197
Three Heron's Feathers. Suderman, H. 8606
Three Kisses. Scott, M. 8110
Three Little Kittens. Miller, H. L. 6026
Three Little Kittens' Christmas. Christmas, J. S. 1826
Three Little Pigs, The. Jones, D. C. 4503
Three Months Gone. Howarth, D. 4233
Three Musketeers, The. Dumas, A. 2686
Three Princes of Salerno, The. 8856

Three Royal R's, The. Pyle, M. T. 7355
Three Short Plays. Howard, R. 4218
Three Short Plays. O'Donnell, M. 6775
Three Short Sketches. Ordway, S. 6875
Three Sillies, The. Very, A. 9126
Three Sisters, The. Chekhov, A. 1780
Three Souls in Search of a Dramatist. Schwartz, E. D. 8095
Three Spinners, The. Frank, F. K. 3263
Three Sundays in a Week. Poe, E. A. 7222
Three Swine of Most Small Stature, The. Olfson, L. 6816
Three Travelers Watch a Sunrise. Stevens, W. 8512
Three Verse Plays. Cahoon, H. 1489
Three Visitors, The. Irwin, M. 4408
Three Wars. Cahoon, H. Three Verse Plays 1489
Three Wise Men. Vicente, G. 9138
Three Wishes, The. Burlingame, C. 1433
Three Wishes, The. Phillips, E. 7122
Three Wishes, The. Thane, A. 8814
Three Wishes for Mother. McQueen, M. H. and N. McQueen 5403
Three Wishing Bags, The. Swintz, M. 8653
Three-sided Question, A. Herford, O. 4074
Thrice Promised Bride, The. Hsiung, C. C. 4265, 4266
Thrift. Berridge, W. L. 870
Thrift, Chinese Style. Blumenfeld, L. 1024
Throne, The. Norse, J. 6695
Through the Looking-Glass. Carroll, L. 2518
Through You I Live. McQueen, M. H. and N. McQueen 5404
Thumbscrew, The. Lyttelton, E. S. 5104
Thump-ity Bump-ity Box, The. Leitner, I. A. 4903
Th(us). Beye, H. 911

Thy Kingdom Come. Converse, F. 1993
Ti voglio tanto bene. Giannini, G. 3493
Tic-Tac. Rody, A. 7645
Tick Tock. Asbrand, K. 414
Ticket, The. Hitchcock, G. 4118
Tickets Please! Fair, F. 2912
Ties of Blood. Pelee, L. S. 7040
Tiger. Bynner, W. 1464
Tiger. Schisgal, M. 8033, 8034
Tiger and the Brahman, The. Simon, S. 8290
Tiger Catcher, The. McFarlan, E. 5182
Tiger in the Rockery, The. Drain, R. 2587
Tiger, the Brahman, and the Jackal, The. Smith, G. V. 8334
Tiger Who Wanted a Boy, The. Hall, M. G. 3851
Tiger's Promise, The. McHale, E. K. 5212
Time and the Conways. Priestley, J. B. 7300
Time for Mom. Fisher, A. 3087
Time for Purpose, A. Rawe, M. 7443
Time for Now, A. Kingman, L. 4635
Time Limit! Denker, H. and R. Berkey 2332
Time of Innocence. Lenz, S. 4920
Time of the Cuckoo. Laurents, A. 4831
Time Out for Ginger. Alexander, R. 132
Time Remembered. Anouilh, J. 275
Time to Kill. Houston, J. D. 4195
Time to Reap, A. Benet, S. V. 761
Time Tunnel to Christmas. Sauer, K. 7978
Time's Abstract and Brief Chronicle. Chesterton, G. K. 1791
Timid Little Witch, The. Urban, C. 8978
Timothy the Tailor's Christmas. Potter, B. 7262
Timpani della verità, I. Tanzi, G. 8702
Tin to Win. Hughes, R. 4314
Tinderbox, The. Andersen, H. C. 203
Tiniest Heart, The. Watts, F. B. 9245

Tinker's Christmas, The. St. Clair, R. 7859
Tir Clara, Le. Roncoroni, J.-L. 7687
Tiroler Passionsspiel. 8870
'Tis Pity She's a Whore. Ford, J. 3217, 3218
To Be or Not to Be. McQueen M. H. and N. McQueen 5405
To Be Perfectly Frank. Meyer, J. A. 5802
To Bethlehem. Porter, L. S. 7256
To Damascus. Strindberg, A. 8582
To Kill a Man. Timmory, G. 8867
To Live in Peace. Forzano, G. 3235
To Mother, with Love. Pendleton, E. 7056
To Test the Truth. Grinins, T. A. 3756
To the Moon. Fontaine, R. 3207
To the Rescue. Rabe, O. 7374
To the Stars. Andreyev, L. N. 239
To You the Torch. Marcus, I. H. 5544
To You This Day. Schroeder, C. 8086
Toa. Guitrz, S. 3782
Tobacco Evil, The. Chekhov, A. 1781
Tobacco Road. Caldwell, E. and J. Kirkland 1504
Tod Julius des Zweiten, Der. Mund, W. M. 6295
Today? Strange, J. G. 8554
Together Tonight. Vilalta, M. 9144
Togetherness. Merritt, R. 5783
Toi et Tes Nuages. Westphal, E. 9311
Toinette and the Elves. Woolsey, S. C. 9554
Told in a Chinese Garden. Wilcox, C. G. 9356
Tom and the Leprechaun, The. Feather, J. 2966
Tom Paine. Kennedy, L. 4595
Tom Sawyer and Injun Joe. Clemens, S. L. 1890
Tom Sawyer, Pirate. Clemens, S. L. 1891
Tom Tit Tot. Very, A. 9127
Tom Tyler and His Wife. 8881
Tomboy and the Dragon, The.

Miller, H. L. 6027
Tomboy Princess, The. Roberts, H. M. 7612
Tommaso d'Amalfi. De Filippo, E. 2264
Tommy Allen Show, The. Terry, M. 8769
Tomorrow Will Be Ours. Fast, H. 2939, 2940
Tongues of Fire. Kearney, P. 4569
Tonsillitis. Vogel, J. 9168
Tony Kytes, the Arch Deceiver. Hardy, T. 3907
Too Many Angels. Miller, H. L. 6028
Too Many Cooks. Huff, B. T. 4298
Too Many Kittens. McQueen, M. H. and N. McQueen 5406
Tooth of Crime, The. Shepard, S. 8240
Top of the Bill. Colson, J. G. 1950
Topaze. Pagnol, M. 6933
Topo, Il. Bonelli, L. 1186
Topsy-Turvy Foodland. Steiner, B. A. 8497
Topsy-Turvy Weather. Spamer, C. 8431
Toreádor. Barillet, P. and J.-P. Gredy 592
Torn Transfer. Moineaux, G. 6108
Torotumbo. Asturias, M. A. 426
Torre sul pollaio, La. Calvino, V. 1519
Tortoise and the Hare, The. Cote, C. K. 2057
Tortoise, the Hare, and Friends, The. Cheatham, V. R. 1760
Totek. Orkeny, I. 6878
Toto. Frank B. 3258
Touch of Brightness, A. Sharma, P. 8195
Touch of Genius, The. Dias, E. J. 2453
Touch of the Poet, A. O'Neill, E. 6863
Touch the Blue Bird's Song. Catron, L. E. 1664
Touch Too Much, A. Schaaf, A. K. 8014
Touchstone. Runnette, H. V. 7797
Tour d'Ivoire, La. Ardrey, R. 329
Tour Eiffel Qui Tue, La. Hanoteau, G. 3898

Tournant, Le. Dorin, F. 2554
Tourniquet, Le. Lanoux, V. 4804
Tourniquet, The. Molinaro, U. 6132
Tous Contre Tous. Adamov, C. 67
Tout a l'Heure. Worms, J. 9564, 9565
Tout Contre un Petit Bois. Ribes, J.-M. 7512
Tout un Dimanche Ensemble. Bouchet, P. 1206
Tovaritch. Boularan, J. 1228
Tower, The. Post, E. 7261
Tower of Babel, The. Goodman, P. 3631
Tower of Marl. Campbell, J. 1540
Town, The. Anagnostaki, L. 192
Town Mouse and His Country Cousin, The. Muse, V. 6413
Town That Learned, The. Simon, S. 8291
Toy Scout Jamboree, The. Miller, H. L. 6029
Toys for Santa. Robertson, O. J. 7616
Toys in the Attic. Hellman, L. 4049
Toys on Strike, The. Adams, P. L. 73
Tra due signori per bene. Gavi, V. 3428
Tra un mese tra un anno. Quoirez, F. 7370
Tracian Horses, The. Valency, M. J. 8994
Trafic. Calaferte, L. 1500
Tragedia d'amore. Heiberg, G. E. R. 4027
Tragedia de los Amores de Eneas de la Reyna Dido 8912
Tragedia senza eroe. Rocca, G. 7639
Tragedian in Spite of Himself, The. Chekhov, A. 1782
Tragedie d'Alexandre. Demasy, P. 2313
Tragedie de l'Absence. Dalbray, M. 2162
Tragedie in due battute. Campanile, A. 1534
Tragedie Optimiste, La. Vichnevski, V. 9139
Tragedy, The. Scott, M. 8111
Tragedy of True Love, The. 8913
Tragic Spark, The. Duffy, R. 2677

Tragical Comedy, or Comical Tragedy of Punch and Judy. 8914
Tragico affare die sonnambuli, Il. Cami 1522
Tragicomedy of Don Cristabita and Dona Rosita. Lorca, F. G. 5047
Train to H. Cormenzana, J. M. B. 2020
Traitor's Wife, The. Buck, D. P. 1405
Trajet, Le. Kattan, N. 4555
Trampoli. Pugliese, S. 7333
Transcontinental. Sullivan, A. M. 8614
Transferred Ghost, The. Stockton, F. R. 8528, 8529
Transit. Stevenson, P. 8515
Transit of Fire. Odio, E. 6774
Transparency. Stuart, D. M. 8588
Trap, The. Salerno, H. F. 7885
Trap Door. Kreymborg, A. 4721, 4722
Trappola per vecchia letteratura. Rosso di San Secondo, P. 7716
Trash and Treasure. Nolan, P. T. 6674
Trattato scomparso, Il. Artu', G. E. 391
Travel Game, A. Miller, H. L. 6030
Travelers, The. Tarkington, B. 8712
Traveling Man, The. Gregory, Lady A. 3730, 3731
Traveller and Peasant. Tolstoy, L. N. 8879
Travels of Marco Polo, The. Thane, A. 8793
Travels of Yi Yuk-Sa to the Caves of Yenan, The. Howard, R. Three Short Plays 4218
Traversata nera. Corradini, B. and G. Achille 2032
Traversee, La. Ransan, A. 7411
Tre figliole di Pinco Pallino, Le. Pompei, M. 7242
Tre Marie, Le. Caramello, M. 1595
Tre Maurizi, I. Falconi, D. 2918
Tre "No" giapponesi. 8925
Tre "No" giapponesi dei XV secolo. 8924
Tre, Rosso, Dispari. Amiel, D. 189
Tre signori Chantrel, I. Verneuil, L. 9100

Tre vie, Le. Raggio, E. 7389
Trealberi. Pea, E. 7022
Treasure! Hunt, S. 4325
Treasure. Shea, G. F. 8231
Treasure at Bentley Inn. Dias, E. J. 2454
Treasure Chest, The. Bond, V. 1178
Treasure Hunt. Fisher, A. 3088
Treasure in the Smith House. Barnett, G. T. 611
Treasure Island. Stevenson, R. L. 8520
Tredicesima sedia, La. Bajard and Vailler. 510
Tredici a tavola. Fayard, J. 2956
Tredici a tavola. Sauvajon, M. G. 7991
Tree Friends, The. McCarty, S. S. 5127
Tree of Hearts, The. McGowan, J. 5204
Tree on the Plains, A. Horgan, P. 4170
Tree to the Sky. Nolan, P. T. 6675
Tree to Trim, A. Fisher, A. 3089
Trees at School, The. Very, A. 9128
Trees Go to School, The. Brown, A. V. 1359
Treizième Arbre, Le. Gide, A. 3505
Trencavel. Collon, R. 1942
Trent' anni di servizio. Salvatore, A. 7896
Trenta secondi d'amore. De Benedetti, A. 2229
Tres Pasos de la Pasion. 8929
Trial by Fury. Bingham, J. 942
Trial by Jury. Cain, J. M. 1496
Trial by Jury. Gilbert, W. S. 3513, 3520
Trial Horse No. 1. Williams, W. C. 9447
Trial of a Heart, The. Wilson, J. R. 9462
Trial of Manfred the Magician, The. Baher, C. W. 496
Trial of Mary Dugan. Veiller, B. 9060
Trial of Mother Goose, The. Miller, H. L. 6031
Trial of Peter Zenger, The. Nolan, P. T. 6676

Triangle Inmortel, Le. Evreinoff, N. 2891
Triangolo magico. De Stefani, A. 2378
Trick or Treat for UNICEF. Boiko, C. 1137
Trickery. Hicks, W. 4095
Tricycle, The. Arrabal, F. 379
Trigamo, Il. Chiara, P. 1794
Trilogy of Dubrovnik, A. Vojnovich, I. 9169
Trio en Sol Majeur. Ruth, L. 7810
Trio fulgor. Viviani, V. 9165
Triomphe de la Science. Bernard, T. 853
Trionfo del diritto, Il. Manzari, N. 5518
Tripe. Micallef, L. 5803
Tripes d'Or. Crommelynck, F. 2117
Triple Saut. Delavaux, R. 2295
Triplepatte. Bernard, T. and A. Godfernaux 856
Tripstych. Gerould, D. 3445
Triptych. Eberhart, R. 2806
Tristram the Jester. Hardt, E. 3904
Triumph for Trimbly, A. Murray, J. 6398
Triumph for Two. Corson, H. W. 2040
Triumph of Death. Teternikov, F. K. 8778
Triumph of Instinct, The. Learsi, R. 4865
Trois Cents Mètres d'Elévation. Charras, C. 1734
Trois Chapeaux Claque. Mihura, M. 5826
Trois Coups de Minuit, Les. Obey, A. 6740
Trois Couverts. Oulmont, C. 6919
Trois et Une.... Amiel, D. 190
Trois Fois le Jour. Spaak, C. 8400
Trois garçons et une fille. Ferdinand, R. 2991
Trois Henry. Lang, A. 4791
Trois Hommes sur un Cheval. Moussy, M. 6280
Trois Mois de Prison. Messager, C. 5792
Trois Musiciens. Higuera, P. de la 4102
Trois Pages d'Histoire.... Arnaud, R. 349
Trois Pretendants, un Mari. Oyono, G. 6926

Trois Valses. Marchand, L. and Willemetz, A. 5538
Troisième Agnes. Mithois, M. 6096
Troll King's Breakfast, The. Topelius, Z. 8887
Trolls' Christmas, The. Thorne-Thomsen, G. 8849
Trolls of Glittertop Mountain, The. Winther, B. 9488
Tromboni, I. Zardi, F. 9637
Tropics. Montague, C. M. 6177
Troppo equali. Rocca, G. 7640
Troppo tardi. Chiarelli, L. 1800
Troubadour's Dream. Clements, C. E. 1892
Trouble in Dental City. Plescia, G. L. 7211
Trouble in Outer Space. Anderson, R. A. 221
Trouble in the Air. Fisher, A. and O. Rabe 3118
Trouble in Tick Tock Town. Miller, H. L. 6032
Trouble in Tree-Land. Boiko, C. 1138
Trouble with Christmas, The. Nolan, P. T. 6677
Troupe du Roy. Deiber, P. E. 2285
Trovar marito. Herczeg, F. 4068
Trovata dell'avvocato Max. Corradini, B. 2028
Troy Was Never Like This. Dias, E. J. 2455
Truccature. Gherardi, G. 3471
Truce. Lindsay, D. 4986
True Gift of Christmas, The. Nissen, P. J. 6605
True Hero. Howells, W. D. 4259
True History of Squire Jonathan and His Unfortunate Treasure, The. Arden, J. 324
True Legend, A. Sos, G. 8390
Trumpets of Wrath. Kozlenko, W. 4705
Truth, The. McCourt, E. W. 5140
Truth About Blayds, The. Milne, A. A. 6063
Truth About Croesus, The. Nightingale, E. M. 6600
Truth About Liars. Mullins, H. 6293
Truth About Russian Dancers, The. Barrie, Sir J. M. 630

Truth Suspected, The. Alarcon y Mendoza, J. R. de 96
Try Data-Date! Olfson, L. 6817
Trying a Dramatist. Gilbert, W. S. 3514
Trysting Place, The. Tarkington, B. 8713
Tu Etais si Gentil Quand tu Etais Petit! Anouilh, J. 276
Tua carne, La. Bassano, E. 655
Tub. Nichol, J. W. 6539
Tube, Le. Dorin, F. 2555
Tudor Touch, The. Coghill, N. 1922
Tueur sans Gages. Ionesco, E. 4402
Tuez-Moi. Gevel, C. 3453
Tug-of-War. Nolan, P. T. 6678
Tugging. Cox, N. B. 2081
Tulips and Two Lips. DuBois, G. 2659
Tumulto dei ciompi, Il. Dursi, M. 2761
Tune of a Tune. Totheroh, D. W. 8902
Tunnel, Il. Lagerkvist, P. 4766
Turista, La. Shepard, S. 8241
Turkey, Anyone? Garver, J. 3417
Turkey Gobblers. McQueen, M. H. and N. McQueen 5407
Turkey Turns the Tables. Miller, H. L. 6033
Turlututu. Achard, M. 40
Turnabout. Edwards, M. B. 2820
Turnabout in Time. Martens, A. C. 5620
Turning the Tables. Fisher, A. and O. Rabe 3119
Turning the Tables. Miller, H. L. 6034
Turn-Out, The. Campbell, J. 1541
Turns. Wildman, E. 9403
Turtle, a Flute and the General's Birthday. Davis, L. R. 2205
Tutti i colori, Di. Cangiullo, F. 1561
Tutto. Rocca, G. 7641
Tutto il male vien di lì. Tolstoy, L. N. 8880
Tutto per Bene. Pirandello, L. 7206
Tutto per la donna. Manzari, N. 5519
Tuzmadar. Zilahy, L. 9650
'Twas the Night After Christmas--1776. Dawson, E. W. 2207
'Twas the Night Before Christmas.

McQueen, M. H. and N. Mc-
Queen 5408
Twelfth Night. Shakespeare, W.
8192
Twelfth Night at Fisher's Cross-
ing. Frederick, J. T. 3289
Twelve Angry Men. Rose, R.
7699
Twelve Dancing Princesses, The.
Thane, A. 8815
Twelve Days of Christmas, The.
Wright, D. 9574
Twelve Months, The. Very, A.
9129
Twenty Thousand Leagues Under
the Sea. Verne, J. 9092
29 gradi all'ombra. Labiche, E.
4750
29 luglio di 1900; vita e morte
di Gaetano Bresci, Il. Libero-
vici, S. and E. Jona 4977
Twenty-One Episodes for the
Aquarian Theater. Higgins,
D. 4097
27 Wagons Full of Cotton. Wil-
liams, T. 9444
Twice One. Hastings, B. M.
3959
Twice-told Tale, A. Laws, A.
C. 4860
Twilight. Bernstein, E. P. 861
Twilight. Vojnovich, I. 9169
Twilight Bar. Koestler, A. 4679
Twilight of the Gods. Bacon, J.
D. D. 487
Twinkle. Spamer, C. 8432
Twins of Bergamo, The. Florian,
J.-P. C. de 3161
Twisting of the Rope, The. Hyde,
D. 4354, 4355
'Twixt the Giltinans and the Car-
modys. Fitzmaurice, G. 3145
Two Against Napoleon. Kane, E.
B. 4542
Two Barrels, The. Douglas, F.
2569
Two Black Sheep. White, A. C.
9321
Two Blind Men and a Donkey.
Dondo, M. M. 2532
Two Blind Mice. Spewack, S.
8447
Two Curtain Raisers. McClure,
J. 5135
Two Dialogues. Koenig, E. C.
4678
Two Dilemma Tales. Winther,
B. 9489

Two Doctors at Akragas. Peterson,
F. 7093
Two Ears. Blossom, R. 1015
Two Faces of Liberty, The. Hop-
penstedt, E. M. 4168
Two for the Money. Murray, J.
6399
Two for the Show. McCoy, P. S.
5156
Two Gentlemen of Soho. Herbert,
A. P. 4060, 4061
Two Gods. Price, D. 7286
Two Husbands. Lavedan, H. L. E.
4843
Two Images. Taylor, P. Three
Ghost Plays 8729
Two Masks. Greth, R. 3740
Two Men. Bernard, J.-J. 830
Two Milords, or The Blow of Thun-
der. Leacock, S. 4864
Two Minds in the Matter. Sutphen,
W. G. Van T. 8633
Two Nights Before Christmas. Mc-
Meekin, I. M. 5276
Two of a Kind. Dunne, D. 2705
Two of Them, The. Hartley, R.
E. and C. M. Power 3950
Two Oranges. Gorsh, C. 3656
Two Passengers for Chelsea. Fir-
kins, O. W. 3032
2 + 2 non fa piu 4. Wertmuller,
L. 9299
Two Slaps in the Face. Molnar,
F. 6165
Two Strangers from Nazareth. Du-
Bois, G. 2660
Two Temptations, The. Bloch, J.
-R. 1005
Two-Penny Show. Lehman, J. F.
4899
Tyl Ulenspiegel, or The Song of
Drums. Dukes, A. 2684
Tyll's Clever Pranks. Winther, B.
9503
Typists. Schisgal, M. 8035, 8036
Tyrone and the Robbers. Alston,
T. 154

U

U.S.A. Dos Passos, J. and P.
Shyre 2560, 2561
"U.S. # 6" Play, The. Allen, H.
F. 139
Ubu Bound. Jarry, A. 4449
Ubu Cocu. Jarry, A. 4450
Uccelliera, L'. Landi, S. 4786

Uccidere un uomo. London, J. 5023
Ufficio della stella, L. 8964
Uguale ma diverso. Artu', G. E. 392
Uhr, Die. Langer, F. 4795
Ultima carta, L'. Romualdi, G. 7677
Ultima Letra. Vilalta, M. 9145
Ultima notte dell'uomo. Kraus, K. 4710
Ultima notte di Marlowe, L'. Ninchi, A. 6604
Ultima stazione, L'. Jappolo, B. 4445
Ultima visita, L'. Renard, J. 7489
Ultimatum. Chiusano, I. A. 1811
Ultimo fiore, L'. Grella, E. 3737
Ultimo romanzo di Domenico Barnaba, L'. De Stefani, A. and M. Doletti 2383
Ultimo sogno della signora Catri, L'. Pugnetti, G. 7336
Umbrella Magic. MacLellan, E. and C. V. Schroll 5267
Un Bel Di. Patrick, R. 7003
Unaccustomed As I Am. McQueen, M. H. and N. McQueen 5409, 5410
Unbestechliche, Der. Hofmannstahl, H. von 4137
Unbidden Guest, The. Firkins, O. W. 3033
Uncle Jimmy. Gale, Z. 3350
Uncle Tertius on the Home Front. Lambeck, F. 4775
Uncle Tom's Cabin. Fisher, A. and O. Rabe 3120
Uncle Vanya. Chekhov, A. 1783, 1784, 1785
Uncolored Easter Egg, The. Spamer, C. 8433
Unconjugable Lives. Tucci, N. 8946
Under Conviction. Dorey, J. M. 2548
Under Milk Wood. Thomas, D. 8826, 8827
Under the Arch. Campbell, P. 1548
Under the Harvest Moon. McQueen, M. H. and N. McQueen 5411
Under the Mango Tree. Winther, B. 9504
Under the Skin. Ross, K. 7708

"Under Their Skins." England, G. A. 2867
Undercurrent. Ehlert, F. 2825
Underground. Newman, B. W. 6487
Undine. Courtney, W. L. 2061
Une Heure Pour Dejeuner. Mortimer, J. 6248
Uneasy Street. Kreymborg, A. 4723
Unequal Triangle, An. Sutphen, W. G. V. T. 8634
Unexpected Guests. Howells, W. D. 4260
Unfinished Masterpiece. Phillips, S. 7141
Unforeseen. Jimenez Rueda, J. 4468
Unhappy Santa, The. Simonds, N. 8295
Unhoodwinkable. Wolff, P. 9533
Unhoppy Bunny, The. Haugh, G. L. 3965
Unica scusa, L'. Antona-Traversi, G. 295
Unicorn from the Stars, The. Yeats, W. B. 9608
Unimagined Heaven. Bodenheim, M. 1039
Uninvited, The. MacCarthy, E. 5123
Uninvited Guests, The. Miller, H. L. 6035
Unique Jour de l'Annee. Seymour, A. 8161
United Animals, The. Gronowicz, A. 3761
United Spies. Fontaine, R. 3208
Unknown Star, The. Paull, H. M. and L. Housman 7016
Unknown Woman, The. Blok, A. 1012
Uno dopo l'alteo. Aceto, G. 16
Uno qualunque. Rossato, A. 7710
Unpublished Story. Levi, P. 4959
Unquiet Warriors, The. Hall, K. D. 3845
Unseen Hand, The. Shepard, S. 8242
Unsinkable Molly Brown, The. Willson, M. and R. Morris 9454
Unsought Land, The. Zeller, W. 9640
Unsuspected Fruit. Dias, E. J. 2456
Until She Screams. Orton, J. 6886

Untitled. Corwin, N. 2052
Unto the Least of These. Rowell, A. C. 7769
Unusual Flower, The. Graham, M. S. 3678
Uomini e no. Crovi, R. 2126
Uomo amore, L'. Alessio, G. 126
Uomo arrivato, Un. Della Seta, F. 2306
Uomo cattivo, Un. Edmonds, R. 2816
Uomo che andra' in America, L'. Buzzati, D. 1456
Uomo che incontrò se stesso, L'. Antonelli, L. 305
Uomo che sorride, L'. Bonelli, L. and A. De Benedetti 1187
Uomo da niente, Un. Conti, A. 1990
Uomo di Birzulàh, L'. Falconi, D. and O. Biancoli 2919
Uomo di cenere, L'. Obey, A. 6741
Uomo di Dio, L'. Ghéon, H. 3464
Uomo d'oro, Un. Ferdinand, R. 2992
Uomo e una donna, Un. Di Carpenetto, D. 2465
Uomo in maschera, L'. Capo, G. 1580
Uomo malato, L'. Benco, S. 752
Uomo onesto, Un. Besnard, L. 883
Uomo-corno, L'. Molnar, F. 6166
Uova della struzzo, Le. Roussin, A. 7759
Uova di Struzzo, Le. Roussin, A. 7760
Up. Sassoon, R. L. and D. H. Elliott 7969
Up a Christmas Tree. Fisher, A. 3090
Up in the Air. Paradis, M. B. 6968
Up-and-Doing Day, An. Fisher, A. 3091
Upon the Waters. Hanna, T. M. 3896
Upward, Upward. Hitchcock, G. 4119
Uriel Acosta. Gutzkow, K. 3792
Urlo, L'. De Stefani, A. and F. F. Cerio 2382
Useful Scarecrow, The. Spamer, C. 8434

Uva, L'. Tozzi, F. 8909

V

Va Donc Chez Torpe. Billetdoux, F. 935
Va Faire un Tour au Bois. Dornes, R. 2559
Vacances Revées, Les. Mithois, M. 6097
Vacation: Limited. Hackett, W. 3807
Vado per vedove. Marotta, G. and B. Randone 5572
Vagabond Vampires, The. Murray, J. 6400
Vagabonda, La. Colette, S. G. C. and L. Marchand 1935
Vagues Etaient Trop Fortes, Les. Deutsch, L. 2387
Valentine Antics. Very, A. 9130
Valentine for Kate, A. Miller, H. L. 6036
Valentine for Mary, A. Bennett, R. 797
Valentine Stardust. Nicholson, J. 6561
Valentine Tree, The. Barrows, M. 637
Valentine's Dance, A. Barbee, L. 574
Valentine's Day. Duvall, L. M. 2780
Valerie's Valentine. Asbrand, K. 415
Valiant, The. Porter, H. E. and R. Middlemass 7251, 7252
Valiant Villain, The. Combs, R. 1961
Valley of Gloom, The. Drennan, M. 2598
Valley of Lost Men. Ernst, A. H. 2873
Valore dell'intervista, Il. Molnar, F. 6167
Valse des Toreadors, La. Anouilh, J. 277
Valzer del defunto signor Giobatta, Il. Carsana, E. 1627
Vampire. Wilson, S. 9469
Vampire, Le. Youri 9623
Vampire Cat of Nabeshima, The. Fuji-Ku 3337
Vampire de Bougival. Neveux, G. 6482
Vanessa. Menotti, G. C. 5753
Vanessa and the Blue Dragon. Baher, C. W. 497

Vangelo seconda Borges. Porzio, D. 7257
Vanishing Easter Egg, The. Miller, H. L. 6037
Vanity Fair. Thackeray, W. M. 8782
Variation on the Theme of Jonah. Petersen, S. 7090
Varnishing Day. Pohl, F. J. 7225
Vasco. Schehade, G. 8022
Vase Etrusque. Gevel, C. 3454
Vast Domain, The. Schnitzler, A. 8077
Vautours. Prins, P. de 7304
Vedova nera, La. Terron, C. 8766
Vegetable, The. Fitzgerald, F. S. 3137
Vegetable Salad. Howard, V. 4229
Veglia d'armi. Fabbri, D. 2906
Veglie inutili, Le. Sbragia, G. 8007
Veils. Cone, T. 1969
Veine d'Or. Zorzi, G. 9657
Veldt, The. Bradbury, R. 1258
Velo bianco, Il. Bertuetti, E. and S. Pugliese 880
Velo impigliato, Il. Rocca, G. 7642
Velo strappato, Il. Wolff, P. 9534
Vendetta. Suzuki, S. 8639
Vendetta del pescatore, La. 9062
Venditore di fumo, Il. Napolitano, G. G. 6433
Venerdi' santo. Viola, C. G. 9154
Vengeance in Leka. McCracken, W. 5161
Vengeance of Catullus. Frida, E. B. 3300
Vengeur de son Pere, Le. 9072
Vengono. Marinetti, F. T. 5553
Venoni. Lewis, M. G. 4972
Vent dans les Branches des Sassafras. Obaldia, R. de 6723
Ventiquattr'ore di un uomo qualunque. Grassi, E. 3693
Vento d'agosto. Bassano, E. and D. G. Martini 657
Vento notturno, Il. Betti, U. 899
Vento sotto la porta, Il. Rietmann, C. M. 7579
Ventose. Boularan, J. 1229
Ventriloquist, The. Frankel, M. 3267
Venus de Milo, La. Boularan, J. 1230
Ver Kundigung. Claudel, P. 1873
Vera Mirzewa. Niccodemi, D. 6537
Vera verk. Tomizza, F. 8883
Vera vita di Jacob Ceherda, La. Brecht, B. 1311
Verbo amare, Il. Mortier, P. 6245
Verfolgung und Ermordung Jean Paul Marats Dargestellt Durch die Schauspielgruppe des Hospizer zu Charenton unter Anleitung des Herren de Sade. Weiss, P. 9275
Vergonzoso en Palacio. Tellez, G. 8741
Veridique Proces de Barbe-Bleue, Le. Pelland, L. 7041
Verme al ministero, Un. Buzzati, D. 1457
Vero corraggio, Il. Bernard, T. 854
Veronica e gli ospiti. Marotta, G. and B. Randone 5573
Verre d'ean, Le. Scribe, E. 8116
Verre de Vin Blanc. Wachthausen, R. 9178
Verspätung, Die. Hildesheimer, W. 4106
Very Crude Oil. Whipkey, S. D. 9320
Very Nearest Room. Whiton, H. E. 9336
Very Social Service. Church, V. 1833
Vestire gli ignudi. Pirandello, L. 7207
Vestiti della donna amata, I. Raggio, E. 7390
Vestiti su misura. Minnucci, V. 6074
Vestito di Gisella, Il. Raggio, E. 7391
Vetri appannati, I. Printzlau, O. 7305
Veuf, ou Il n'y a pas d'Eternelles Douleurs. Carmontelle, L. 1610
Veuves, Les. Billetdoux, F. 936
Via delle Indie, La. Harwood, H. M. 3957
Via lattea, La. Bevilacqua, G. 909
Viaggio de signor Perrichon, Il. Labiche, E. 4751

Viaggio di astolfo, Il. Cenzato, G. 1687
Viaggio in paradiso. Guitry, S. 3783
Vicar Saves the Day, The. Schmitt, G. 8056
Vicky Gets the Vote. Miller, H. L. 6038
Vicolo senza sole. Zerboni, R. 9644
Victime, La. Fortuno, C. 3233
Victime, La. Praxy, R. 7275
Victims. Lindenberger, H. 4984
Victor, ou Les Enfants au Pouvoir. Vitrac, R. 9161
Victorious Surrender of Lady Sybil, The. Peacocke, L. T. 7028
Victory for Liberty. Very, A. 9131
Victory Garden, The. Day, B. 2208
Victory Gardens. Very, A. 9132
Victory Over the Sun. Kruchenykh, A. 4733
Video Christmas. Dias, E. J. 2457
Vie a l'envers, La. Delprat, S. 2311
Vie de Polichinelle, Le. Jonquille, N. 4513
Vie est un Songe. Calderon de la Barca, P. 1503
Vie Imaginaire de l'Eboueur Auguste Geai. Gatti, A. 3422, 3423
Vieil Ulysse, Le. Verdot, G. 9076
Viens chez Moi J'Habite chez un Copine. Rego, L. and D. Kaminka 7467
"Vient de Paraitre." Bourdet, E. 1238
Viet Hut. Wildman, E. 9404
Vieux Roi, Le. Gourmont, R. de 3674
Vieux Soleil. Ducreux, L. 2671
View from the Bridge. Miller, A. 5849, 5850
View of the Sea, A. Nolan, P. T. 6679
Vigliacco, Un. Vergani, O. 9082
Vilains, Les. Ruzzante 7817
Villain and the Toy Shop, The. Winther, B. 9490
Ville Dont le Prince est un Enfant, La. Montherlant, H.
M. J. M. de 6194
Villetta alla periferia. Possenti, E. 7260
Vincitori, I. Bettini, P. and E. Albini 900
Violent Wedding. Lowry, R. 5071
Violenza no. Guidotti, M. 3776
Violet Under the Snow, The. Cleugh, D. 1898
Violets. Schehade, G. 8024
Violets for Christmas. Phillips, M. K. 7136
Violettes, Les. Schehade, G. 8023
Violons Parfois. Quoirez, F. 7371
Virage Dangereux. Priestley, J. B. 3934
Virgin and the Unicorn, The. Mandel, O. 5495
Virgin, the Lizard, and the Lamb, The. Feldhous-Weber, M. 2979
Virginie. Andre, M. 225
Virtue Is Her Own Reward. Hervey, M. 4084
Virtuoso, The. Mencken, H. L. 5745
Vision, The. Paull, H. M. 7015
Vision of the Silver Bell. Weathers, W. 9248
Vision of Youth, A. Colby, E. 1927
Visionary Farms. Eberhart, R. 2807
Visions of Sugar Plums. Martens, A. C. 5621
Visions of Sugar Plums. Pritchard, B. 7307
Visit, The. Castro, J. A. 1659
Visit, The. Durrenmatt, F. 2753
Visit from St. Nicholas, A. Moore, C. C. 6198
Visit of Mother Cloud, The. Jennings, A. 4458
Visit of the Tomter, The. Goodlander, M. R. 3626
Visit to a Small Planet. Vidal, G. 9141
Visit to Goldilocks, A. McGowan, J. 5205
Visit to the Library. Searcy, K., J. T. McNeel and C. Oliver 8120
Visit to the Planets. Melchior, H. K. 5739
Visit to the White House, A. McQueen, M. H. and N. McQueen 5412
Visite, La. Haim, V. 3825
Visite. Negis, A. 6455

Visite de la Vieille Dame. Durrenmatt, F. 2754
Visite de Noces, Une. Dumas, A. 2690
Visiteur, Le. Dubeux, A. 2613
Visiteur de Minuit, Le. Schlumberger, J. 8039
Visiting Mamma. Emmons, M. 2863
Visiting Uncles. Steele, J. 8484
Visitor from Outer Space. Murray, J. 6401
Visitor to Gettysburg. Dias, E. J. 2458
Visitors for Nancy Hanks. Bennett, R. 798
Vita di William Shakespeare. Dallagiacoma, A. 2164
Vita e morte di cola di Rienzo. Siciliano, E. 8269
Vita in due, La. Cenzato, G. 1688
Vita privata di un uomo celebre. Bratt, H. 1274
Vitamin "U." 9157
Vitraux. Sommer, L. 8374
Vittoria. Sherwood, M. 8256
Vivata di Bordo. Filippo, T. de 2281
Vive le Roi! Verneuil, L. 9101
Viveur e il cocchiere, Il. Molnar, F. 6168
Vladimir Mayakovsky. Mayakovsky, V. 5703
Vocazione, La. Brunori, A. 1388
Voce dell'amore, La. Lang, A. 4793
Voce nella tempesta, La. Brönte, E. 1339
Voci di dentro, Le. De Filippo, E. 2265
Voice Behind the Curtain, The. Benn, G. 766
Voice of Liberty, The. Fisher, A. 3092
Voices. Flexner, H. 3158
Voices of America. McQueen, M. H. and N. McQueen 5413
Voile du Bonheur. Clemenceau, G. 1876
Voisins, Les. Saunders, J. 7981
Voix Dans la Ville, Des. Teyssandier, E. 8779
Vol Nuptial. Croisset, F. 2113
Voleur d'Enfants, Le. Supervielle, J. 8621
Voleuse de Londres. Neveux, G. 6483

Volksbuch vorn Herzog Ernst, Das. Hacks, P. 3814
Volodia. Mai, F. 5453
Volpe azzurra, La. Herczeg, F. 4069
Volta nuovo, Il. Sée, E. 8133
Vote for Miss Checkout. Murray, J. 6402
Vote for Uncle Sam. McQueen, M. H. and N. McQueen 5414
Vote for Your Hero. Pendleton, E. 7057
Votre Silence, Cooper? Halet, P. 3842
Voyage, Le. Sussmann, C. J. 8626
Voyage à Biarritz. Sarment, J. 7943
Voyage autour de ma Marmite. Labiche, E. 4752
Voyage Round My Father, A. Mortimer, J. 6249
Voyageur et l'Amour. Morand, P. 6213
Voyageur sans Bagage. Anouilh, J. 278, 279
Voyageurs de l'Espoir, Les. Masson, A. 5647
Voyante. Roussin, A. 7761
Vraie Carmen. Laparcerie-Richepin, C. 4811
Vrais Dieux. Porto-Riche, G. 7254
Vsegda v Prodaze. Aksjonov, V. 94
Vyrozumeni. Havel, V. 3982

W

Wages of War, The. Wiegand, J. and W. Scharrelmann 9346
Wait and See. Smith, M. F. 8341
Waiting. Fratti, M. 3285
Waiting for Godot. Beckett, S. 710
Waiting for Lefty. Odets, C. 6773
Waiting for Santa. Parsons, C. 6988
Waiting for Santa Claus. Bumstead, E. S. 1416
Waiting for the Ring. Jenks, T. 4456
Waiting in the Wings. Coward, N. 2078
Waiting Room, The. Baird, G. M. P. 509
Waiting Room, The. Weinstein, S. 9271

Wake Up, Aurora! Thornton, J. F. 8854
Wake Up! Santa Claus! Miller, H. L. 6039
Waking the Daffodil. Bennett, R. 799
Walk Proudly Here--Americans. Ickler, L. M. 4367
Walking Berg. Dennis, R. 2337
Wall, The. Caldwell, B. 1503a
Wall Street. Curie, E. 1097
Wallenstein. Schiller, F. 8028
Walpole, or, Every Man Has His Place. Lytton, E. B. 5107
Walt. Morley, C. 6228
Walt Whitman: Poet of Democracy. Cote, C. K. 2056
Waltz of the Toreadors. Anouilh, J. 280
Wanderer. Bodenheim, M. 1040
Wanderer, The. Roof, K. M. 7696
Wanderers, The. Bacon, J. D. D. 488
Wanderers, The. Ferber, M. 2984
Wandering Jew, The. Hutchins, M. P. 4337
Wanted: A House to Haunt. Corson, H. W. 2041
Wanted--A Stenographer. Richmond, S. S. 7567
Wanze, Die. Maiakowski, W. 5456
War. Artsybashev, M. P. 389
War--A Te Deum. Hauptmann, C. 3969
War Brides. Wentworth, M. C. 9293
War Drums on the Equator. Li Huang, Chang Feng-yi, Lin Yin-wu and Chu Tsu-yi. 4976
War Indemnities, The. Shaw, G. B. 8219
War Woman, The. Lovell, C. C. 5063
Was Her Face Red! Paradis, M. B. 6969
Washington at Home. Shenk, E. 8237
Washington Shilling, The. Miller, H. L. 6040
Washington Square. James, H. 4436
Washington's Gold Button. Newman, D. 6530
Washington's Leading Lady. Miller, H. L. 6041

Washington's Lucky Star. Miller, H. L. 6042
Washington's Paper Army. Nicholson, M. A. 6575
Washingtons Slept Here, The. Miller, H. L. 6043
Waste Disposal Unit, The. Brophy, B. 1348
Watch Out for Aunt Hattie. Shore, M. 8262
Watchers, The. Kildare, G. 4621
Watching for Santa Claus. Varney, H. 9045
Water Hen, The. Witkiewicz, S. I. 9521
Waters of the Moon. Hunter, N. C. 4326
Wax Engine, The. Nichols, R. 6547
Way, The. Runnette, H. V. 7798
Way of an Eagle, The. Daugherty, S. 2191
Way Out, A. Frost, R. 3327
Way Out, A. Kilaif, T. 4651
Way the Noise Began, The. Knowlton, D. and B. Knowlton 4672
Way to the Inn, The. Gordon, C. 3636
Way to the Inn, The. Newman, D. 6531
Way, Way Down East. Dias, E. J. 2459
Way, Way Down South. Cable, H. 1481
Way, Way Off Broadway. Huff, B. T. 4299
Way-Out Cinderella, The. Cable, H. 1482
Wayward Witch, The. Boiko, C. 1139
We Are Besieged. Acheson, S. 43
We Are God. Canton, W. 1575
We Are the History of the U. S. Wheatcroft, J. 9316
We Are the Rising Wing. Leichlitner, R. 4870
We Are There--At Christmas. 9247
We Are Three. Fife, E. H. 3016
We But Teach. Richmond, S. S. 7568
We Choose a Name. Batchelder, F. R. 664
We Have Ceased to Live. Carroll, P. V. 1622
We Interrupt This Program. Boiko, C. 1140

We Need Another Man. Press, S. 7285
We Pledge Ourselves. Rugg, M. M. 7786
We Speak for Ourselves. Riggs, L. 7580
We, the People. Toles, M. 8872
We, the Tools. Halman, D. F. 3869
We Three, You and I. Greenland, B. 3718
We Want Mother. McQueen, M. H. and N. McQueen 5415
We Write a Play. Stone, W. 8533
Weatherman on Trial, The. Miller, H. L. 6044
Weaver's Son, The. Fisher, A. 3093
Wedded. Langner, L. 4798
Wedded Husband. Hung, S. 4323
Wedding Anniversary, The. Smith, M. S. 8346
Wedding Dress, The. O'Brien, E. 6743
Wedding Finger. Purdy, J. 7343
Wedding Guest, The. Barrie, Sir J. M. 631
Wedding Guest, The. Kerley, R. 4602
Week Before Christmas, The. Fisher, A. 3094
Week End. Coward, N. 2079
Welcome, Baby Bear. Franklin, J. 3269
Welcome, Parents. Cole, E. 1929
Welcome to Our City. Wolfe, T. 9528
Welded. O'Neill, E. 6864
Well of Hazels, The. Craig, A. T. 2089
Welsh Honeymoon, A. Marks, J. 5562
West from the Panhandle. Smith, B. and C. White 8331
West Point Regulation. Andrews, M. R. S. 229
West Side Story. Laurents, A. 4832
West to the Indies. Fisher, A. and O. Rabe 3121
Westward Ho! Ho! Ho! Lee, J. 4880
Westward People. Rogers, J. W., Jr. 7653
Wet Saturday. Anderson, L. 205
What a Man! Liese, E. F. 4979
What Are You Thinking About?

Villaurrutia, X. 9148
What Can I Do? Wilson, C. 9458
What D'You Call It? Conkle, E. P. 1975
What Did You Learn in School Today? Johnson, W. 4491
What Did You Say "What" For? Dey, J. 2394
What Does Greta Garbo Mean to You? Parlakian, N. 6982
What Dreams May Come. Willenberg, C. H. 9407
What Happened in Toyland. Fisher, A. 3095
What Happened on Center Street. Murray, J. 6403
What Happened on Clutter Street. Fisher, A. 3096
What Happened to the Cakes. Very, A. 9133
What Happened to the Tarts. Smith, N. A. 8348
What Ho! Dias, E. J. 2460
What Is a Patriot? Fisher, A. and O. Rabe 3122
What Makes It Tick? Miller, H. L. 6045
What Makes Thanksgiving. Fisher, A. 3097
What Men Live By. Church, V. 1834
What Never Dies. Wilde, P. 9385
What, No Santa Claus? McQueen, M. H. and N. McQueen 5416
What, No Venison? McQueen, M. H. and N. McQueen 5417
What Now, Planet Earth? Fisher, A. 3098
What Society Is Coming To. Goddard, F. 3590
What the Animals Say at Christmas. Moore, H. L. 6203
What the Public Wants. Bennett, A. 771, 772, 773
What They Think. Crothers R. 2125
What Will the Toys Say? Bennett, R. 800
Whatever Happened to Good Old Ebenezer Scrooge? Majeski, B. 5463
Whatever Happened to Mother Nature? Boiko, C. 1141
What's Cooking? Miller, H. L. 6046
What's in a Name? DuBois, G. 2661
What's Right. Hartley, R. E. 3949
What's Zymurgy with You? Nolan, P. T. 6680
Wheels! A Ballad of the Highway. Boiko, C. 1142
Wheels Within Wheels. Fisher, A. and O. Rabe 3123

When a Man Wanders. Harris, H. H. 3924
When Angry, Count a Hundred. Cavazza, E. 1675
When Do We Eat? McQueen, M. H. and N. McQueen 5418
When Greek Meets Greek. Terrell, M. 8747
When Mozart Was Sixteen. James, P. 4437
When Shakespeare's Ladies Meet. George, C. 3439
When the Bugle Blows. Paschall, A. 6995
When the Cat's Away. McFarlan, E. 5180
When the Hare Brought the Sun. Winther, B. African Trio 9478
When the Hurlyburly's Done. Murray, J. 6404
When the New Wine Blooms. Bjørnson, B. 978
When the Sandman Went to Sleep. Asbrand, K. 416
When the Sap's a 'Runnin.' Baker, V. L. 522
When the Ship Goes Down. McGuire, H. 5210
When the Willow Nods. Kreymborg, A. 4724
When We Dead Awaken. Ibsen, H. 4365
When You're Twenty-One. Thoma, L. 8821
Where Banking Is a Pleasure. Fontaine, R. 3209
Where But In America. Wolff, O. M. 9531
Where Have All the Lightning Bugs Gone? Catron, L. E. 1665
Where Is Phronsie Pepper? Kimball, R. P. 4627
Where Shall We Go? Lavedan, H. 4838
Where the Cross Is Made. O'Neill, E. 6865
Where You Are. Nolan, P. T. 6681
Where's the Baby? Bence, B. 750
Which Is Witch? Martens, A. C. 5622
Which of the Nine? Jokai, M. 4493
Which, Three R's or Three R's Plus Industrial Arts and Domestic Science? Feuerstein, A. 3004

Which Way to Halloween? Miller, H. L. 6047
Which Witch Is Which? Hoppenstedt, E. M. 4169
While the Mushrooms Bubble. Totheroh, D. W. 8903
While You Wait. Hood, C. N. 4160
Whirlwind Comes, The. Lee, S. 4886
Whisper in God's Ear, A. Birnkraut, S. 964
Whistle Blows, The. Ketchum, P. L. 4611
Whistler, The. Langston, L. E. 4800
Whistler, The. Taylor, P. 8730
Whistler's Mother. MacKay, E. T. 5227
White Devil, The. Webster, J. 9250, 9251
White Dresses. Green, P. E. 3712
White Elephant. Winther, B. 9491
White Elephants. Nicholson, K. 6567
White Fan, The. Hoffmannsthal, H. von 4138
White House Rabbit, The. Miller, H. L. 6048
White Liars, The. Shaffer, P. 8173
White Steed, The. Carroll, P. V. 1623
White Whale, The. Taylor, M. A. 8724
White-Negro. Blossom, R. 1016
Whites of Their Eyes, The. Willment, F. 9451
Whither. Griffith, A. M. M. 3745
Whitman Portrait, A. Shyre, P. 8266
"Who Fears to Speak?" MacNamara, G. 5278
Who Goes Home? Maxwell, G. 5699
Who Is Strongest? Feather, J. 2967
Who Scared Whom? Chapin, M. 1720
Who Will Bell the Cat? Boiko, C. 1143
Whole City's Down Below, The. Nolan, P. T. 6682
Who'll Save the Plowboy? Gilroy, F. D. 3547
"Whom God Hath Joined." Heard, J. 4006

820

(W)hor(e)s Opera, A. Bledsoe, T. 1001
Who's Afraid of the Big Pumpkin? Boiko, C. 1144
Who's Afraid of Virginia Woolf? Albee, E. 100, 101
Who's Compatible? Nolan, P. T. 6683
Who's Got the Button? Willment, F. 9452
Who's How. Waterhouse, K. and W. Hall 9218
Who's Necessary? Porter, E. W. 7250
Who's Old-Fashioned? McQueen, M. H. and N. McQueen 5419
Who's Sylvia? Rattigan, T. 7429
Who's the President? McQueen, M. H. 5286
Who's Who at the Zoo. Miller, H. L. 6049
Whose Birthday Is It? Thompson, D. F. 8841
Why I Am a Bachelor. Seiler, C. 8144
Why Marry? Williams, J. L. 9415
Why She Would Not. Shaw, G. B. 8220, 8221, 8222
Why the Butterfly Reminds Us of Easter. Weidlich, A. W. 9262
Why the Indians Wear Moccasins. Lackmann, R. 4759
Why the Peacock Is Proud. Swortzell, L. 8657
Why the Sea Is Salt. Mahlmann, L. and D. C. Jones 5452
Why the Sleepy Dormouse. Fisher, A. 3099
Widdy's Mite, The. Totheroh, D. W. 8904
Widow, The. Honig, E. 4159
Widow of Ephesus, The. Owen, P. 6923
Widower's Comedy. Vicente, G. 9138
Widowing of Mrs. Holroyd, The. Lawrence, D. H. 4855
Widows' Eyes. Alvarez Quintero, S. and J. Alvarez Quintero 174
Wife of Flanders. Buchan, S. 1398
Wife of Usher's Well. Martin, J. J. 5625

Wild Boar, The. O'Brien, S. 6751
Wild Indian and the Gentleman's Gentleman, The. Boiko, C. 1145
Wild Oats. O'Keef, J. 6784
Wild Rabbit Chase, The. Boiko, C. 1146
Wild Swans, The. Crowell, A. 2128
Will. Cannon, M. 1569
Will o' the Wisp. Kvapil, J. 4743
Will of the People, The. Cain, J. M. 1497
Will Somebody Please Say Something? Baxter, D. 680
Will This Earth Hold? Buck, P. S. 1411
William Conrad. Boulle, P. 1231
William Rob Attacks a Problem. Simon, S. 8292
William Smith, Editor. M., A. A. 5110
Willie Bignigga. Gordon, C. 3639
Will-o'-Wisp. Murray, J. 6405
Willow Tree, The. Noguchi, Y. 6622
Wind, The. Peterson, A. E. 7092
Wind, The. Sender, R. 8152
Wind and the Lady Moon, The. Sheridan, E. 8244
Wind Blows. Allen, J. M. 141
Wind in the Branches of the Sassafras. Obaldia, R. de 6734
Wind Wand, The. Dennis, A. 2334
Windblown. Harris, E. M. 3919
Windfalls and Grand Designs. Oglesbee, F. W. 6781
Window Dressing. Russ, J. 7803
Windows. Schisgal, M. 8037
Windows of Heaven, The. Wincelberg, S. 9473
Windy Shot, The. Conway, E. H. 1994
Wings. Peabody, J. P. 7023, 7024
Wings for the King. Sroda, A. 8471
Wings in the Mesh. Levick, M. 4961
Wings of It Cast Wide Dark Shadows, The. Fox, H. 3238
Winning Combination. Snelling, D. 8358
Winslow Boy, The. Rattigan, T. 7430, 7431
Winter Garden, The. McFarlan, E. 5181

Winter of Our Discontent, The. DuBois, G. 2662
Winter Thaw, A. Barr, J. 618
Winter Wizards, The. Bennett, R. 801
Winterset. Anderson, M. 212
Wireless. Pollock, A. I. 7230
Wise Man and the Hodja, The. Kelsey, A. G. 4584
Wise People of Gotham, The. Leuser, E. 4954
Wise Wife, The. Nicholson, M. A. 6576
Wishing Stream, The. Miller, H. L. 6050
Wishing Well or Ill. Nolan, P. T. 6684
Wishing-Well, The. Hall, M. E. 3861
Wispy. Spamer, C. 8435
Witch in the Golden Hat, The. Watts, F. B. 9246
Witch with the Golden Hair, The. McKinney, J. B. 5235
Witches' Delight. MacLellan, E. and C. V. Schroll 5268
Witches' Sabbath. Granick, H. 3686
Witch's Pattern, The. Lehman, J. F. 4900
Witch's Pumpkin, The. Cooper, E. 2006
With Chains of Gold. Vazquez, J. A. 9051
With Malice Toward None. DuBois, G. 2663
Within the Gates. Ward, E. S. 9205
Within Two Shadows. Haire, W. J. 3826, 3827
Witness. Frida, E. B. 3301
Witness for the Prosecution. Christie, A. 1825
Wizard of Oz, The. Baum, L. F. 676, 677, 678
Wizard of the Wireless, The. Burlingame, C. 1434
Wolfe at the Door. Schaaf, A. K. 8015
Wolves, The. Rolland, R. 7662
Wolves and Sheep. Ostrovsky, A. 6916
Wolves and the Lamb, The. Thackeray, W. M. 8783
Woman Alone, A. Clifford, L. 1903
Woman Courageous. Reines, B. 7477

Woman Intervenes, The. Manners, J. H. 5500
Woman of No Importance, A. Wilde, O. 9375
Woman, of No One. Lodovici, C. 5015
Woman Who Never Gets Any Sympathy, The. Fisher, D. C. 3124
Woman Who Owned the West, The. Murray, J. 6406
Woman-Song 8855
Woman's Choice, A. Dazey, L. H. and C. T. Dazey 2211
Woman's Luncheon, A 9539
Woman's Place, A. Yliruusi, T. 9610
Women. Luce, C. B. 5075
Women as Advocates. Litchfield, G. D. 5000
Women in Parliament. Mallock, W. H. 5477
Women of Alexandria, The. Mitchell, L. B. 6083
Women of Trachis. Sophocles 8381
Wonderful, Beautiful Day, The. Peterson, M. N. 7104
Wonderful Circus of Words, The. Boiko, C. 1147
Wonderful Halloween Cape, The. Newman, D. 6532
Wonderful Woman, A. Wilde, P. L. 9386
Wonderful Witchware Store, The. Alderman, E. R. 117
Wonderful Wizard of Oz, The. Baum, L. F. 371
Wonderful World of Hans Christian Andersen, The. Newman, D. 6533
Wonders of Storybook Land. D'Arcy, A. 2186
Wondership. Cunningham, L. 2140
Wondrous Gift, The. Jones, E. S. 4506
Wood Demon, The. Chekhov, A. P. 1786
Wood Painting. Bergman, I. 818
Wooden Box, The. O'Connor, P. 6768
Wooden Dish, The. Morris, E. 6235
Woods of Ida, The. Dragan, O. T. 2585
"Woof" for the Red, White and Blue. Marra, D. B. 5577
Wooing of Penelope, The. Field, E. D. 3012
Word of Honor. McCoy, P. S. 5157

Word with Sir Francis Drake During His Last Night in London. A. Masefield, J. 5641
Words and Music. Beckett, S. 711
Words We Live By. Ravetch, H. 7437
Workhouse Ward, The. Gregory, Lady A. 3732
Working the Dolls. Guinness, B. 3779
Work-Out, The. Bremel, A. 822
World Is in Your Hands, The. Sampson, E. 7898
World Resounds, The. Sukosky, D. G. 8612
World Without Words, A. Cornish, R. 2025
World's My Village, The. Lengyel, C. A. 4911
Worm, The. Salt, J. 7891
Worm Turns, The. 9555
Worms. Greth, R. 3741
Worthy Guest, A. Bailey, P. 508
Would-Be Gentleman, The. Molière 6126
Would-Be Swingers, The. Greth, R. 3742
Woven Wir Leben und Woran Wir Sterben. Eisenreich, H. 2835
Woyzeck. Buchner, G. 1402, 1403, 1404
Wraiths of Destiny. 9572
Wrecked Blackship, The. Winther, J. 9475
Wrecker, The. Bellow, S. 739
Wrong Time, The. Howard, V. 4230
Wuthering Heights. Brontë, E. 1340

X

Xanthippe on Woman Suffrage. Osborne, D. 6890

Y

Y'Avait un Prisonnier. Anouilh, J. 281
Yankee Doodle Came to Cranetown. Clapp, P. 1845
Yankee Doodle Dandy. Fisher, A. 3100
Yankee Doodle Kitten, The. Newman, D. 6534
Yankee vs. Redcoats. Boiko, C. 1148
Yashima. Zeami, M. 9639
Year Lacertis, The. Eich, G. 2832
Yellow Fever. Burlingame, C. 1435
Yellow Season, The. Menken, J. 5751
Yerma. Lorca, F. G. 5048, 5049
Yes, I'm Going Away. Brecht, B. 1312
Yes, M'Lord. Home, W. D. 4154
Yes, Virginia, There Is a South Pole Santa Claus. Beatty, J., Jr. 688
Yes, Yes, A Thousand Times Yes! Boiko, C. 1149
Yet Not as One. Lutz, G. M. 5096
Yet They Endure...! Irvine, C. 4403
Yoemen of the Guard, The. Gilbert, W. S. and Sir A. Sullivan 3521
Yorktown Lass, The. Gordon, C. 3637
You. Clements, C. C. 1895
You Are the Only Wasp I Know. Richardson, G. 7529
You Can't Run Away from It. Ravetch, H. 7438
You Don't Belong to Me! McCoy, P. S. 5158
You Know I Can't Hear You When the Water's Running. Anderson, R. 219
You Never Can Tell About a Woman. Terrell, M. and H. O. Stechhan 8749
You'd Never Think It! McCoy, P. S. 5159
You'll Come to Love Your Sperm Test. Antrobus, J. 306
Young Abe Lincoln. Fisher, A. 3101
Young Abe's Destiny. Boiko, C. 1150
Young and Fair, The. Nash, N. R. 6440
Young D'Arcy. Dresser, J. S. van 2599
Young Forever. Cable, H. 1483
Young Franklin Takes Over. Reines, B. J. 7478
Young Irving. Phillips, M. K. 7137

Young Man of Considerable Value, A. Nolan, P. T. 6685
Young Michael Angelo. Mackay, C. D'A. 5226
Young Mr. Santa Claus. Harris, C. L. 3918
Young Wonder, The. Pillot, E. 7152
Youngest Witch, The. Miller, H. L. 6051
Your Money Cheerfully Refunded. Schaaf, A. K. 8016
Your Neck o' the Woods. Carmer, C. 1609
Your Opportunity. Parsons, G. L. 6991
You're Human Like the Rest of Them. Johnson, B. S. 4481
You're Such a Respectable Person, Miss Morrison. Earle, D. K. 2798
Youth, Bolivar, The. Ullman, S. S. 8967
Youth Day at the U. N. Hackett, W. 3808
Youth of Don Juan, The. Gorman, A. J. 3652
Yu T'Ang Ch'un 9624
Yutzy Brown. Puggioni, P. 7330

Z

Zahradni Slavnost. Havel, V. 3983
Zakouskis, Les. Saint-Martin, A. 7861
Zamore. Neveux, G. 6484, 6485
Zapatera prodigiosa, La. Garcia Lorca, F. 3385
Zaragueta. Carrion, M. R. and V. Aza 1617
Zdotnaja Kareta. Leonov, L. M. 4929
Zeit der Schuldlosen. Lenz, S. 4921
Zemlja. Virta, N. 9155
Zerbrochene Krug. Kleist, H. von 4664
Zero a Vingt, De. Dabril, L. and L. Dietrich 2156
Zeugen, Die. Rozewicz, T. 7777
Zikaden, Die. Bachmann, I. 483
Zimmerschlacht, Die. Walser, M. 9197
Zio Paperone. Boal, A. 1028
Zio prete, Lo. Tonelli, G. 8886
Zombi. Scott, N. V. 8112
Zoo. Bruller, J. 1384
Zoo Story, The. Albee, E. 102, 103
Ztizena Moznost Soustredeni. Havel, V. 3984
Zuda. Lanza, G. 4810
Zutik il processo di Burgos. Maffei, M. 5435
Zwiebel, Die. Nicolai, A. 6586
Zwischenspiel im Himmel. Balk, T. 534